Identification and Inference for Econometric Models

This volume contains the papers presented in honor of the lifelong achievements of Thomas J. Rothenberg on the occasion of his retirement. The authors of the chapters include many of the leading econometricians of our day, and the chapters address topics of current research significance in econometric theory. The chapters cover four themes: identification and efficient estimation in econometrics, asymptotic approximations to the distributions of econometric estimators and tests, inference involving potentially nonstationarity in time series, such as processes that might have a unit autoregressive root, and nonparametric and semiparametric inference. Several of the chapters provide overviews and treatments of basic conceptual issues, while others advance our understanding of the properties of existing econometric procedures and/or propose new ones. Specific topics include identification in nonlinear models, inference with weak instruments, test for nonstationarity in time series and panel data, generalized empirical likelihood estimation, and the bootstrap.

Donald W. K. Andrews is the William K. Lanman Jr., Professor of Economics in the Department of Economics at Yale University. The author of more than 70 professional publications, Professor Andrews is a Fellow of the Econometric Society, former coeditor of the journal *Econometric Theory*, and a Fellow of the *Journal of Econometrics*. He did his graduate work at the University of California, Berkeley, where he obtained an M.A. in statistics and a Ph.D. from the Economics Department under the supervision of Peter J. Bickel and Thomas J. Rothenberg.

James H. Stock is Professor of Economics in the Department of Economics at Harvard University. Previously he was the Roy E. Larson Professor of Political Economy at the Kennedy School of Government, Harvard, and Professor of Economics at the University of California, Berkeley. He has authored more than 90 professional publications, including a popular undergraduate econometrics textbook (coauthored by Mark Watson). He is a Fellow of the Econometric Society, the former chair of the Board of Editors of *The Review of Economics and Statistics*, and a research associate of the National Bureau of Economic Research. Stock did his graduate work at the University of California, Berkeley, where he obtained an M.A. in statistics and a Ph.D. from the Economics Department under the supervision of Thomas J. Rothenberg.

Identification and Inference for Econometric Models

Essays in Honor of Thomas Rothenberg

Edited by

Donald W. K. Andrews

Yale University

James H. Stock

Harvard University

CAMBRIDGE
UNIVERSITY PRESS

CAMBRIDGE UNIVERSITY PRESS
Cambridge, New York, Melbourne, Madrid, Cape Town,
Singapore, São Paulo, Delhi, Tokyo, Mexico City

Cambridge University Press
The Edinburgh Building, Cambridge CB2 8RU, UK

Published in the United States of America by Cambridge University Press, New York

www.cambridge.org
Information on this title: www.cambridge.org/9780521844413

First published 2005
First paperback printing 2010

A catalogue record for this publication is available from the British Library

Library of Congress Cataloguing in Publication Data

Identification and inference for econometric models / edited by Donald W. K.
Andrews, James H. Stock.
p. cm.
"A Festschrift in Honor of Thomas J. Rothenberg."
Includes bibliographical references.
ISBN 0-521-84441-X (hardback)
1. Econometric models. I. Andrews, Donald W. K. II. Stock, James H.
III. Rothenberg, Thomas J. IV. Title.
HB141.I143 2005
330'.01'5195 – dc22 2004025817

ISBN 978-0-521-84441-3 Hardback
ISBN 978-0-521-15474-1 Paperback

Contents

List of Contributors

Donald W. K. Andrews
Yale University

Jushan Bai
New York University and Tsinghua University, Beijing

Ole E. Barndorff-Nielsen
University of Aarhus

Peter J. Bickel
University of California, Berkeley

David A. Freedman
University of California, Berkeley

Arthur S. Goldberger
University of Wisconsin, Madison

Brownwyn H. Hall
University of California, Berkeley

Andrew C. Harvey
University of Cambridge

David F. Hendry
University of Oxford

Bo E. Honoré
Princeton University

Hidehiko Ichimura
University College, London

Guido W. Imbens
University of California, Berkeley

Michael Jansson
University of California, Berkeley

George G. Judge
University of California, Berkeley

Oliver Linton
London School of Economics

Jacques Mairesse
CREST-INSEE and EHESS

Ron C. Mittelhammer
Washington State University

Grayham E. Mizon
University of Southampton

Whitney K. Newey
Massachusetts Institute of Technology

Serena Ng
University of Michigan

James L. Powell
University of California, Berkeley

Joaquim J. S. Ramalho
University of Evora

Ya'acov Ritov
The Hebrew University of Jerusalem

Thomas J. Rothenberg
University of California, Berkeley

Paul A. Ruud
University of California, Berkeley

N. E. Savin
University of Iowa

Ron Schoenberg
Aptech Systems

Neil Shephard
Nuffield College, Oxford

Richard J. Smith
University of Warwick

Richard H. Spady
Northwestern University and Nuffield College, Oxford

Douglas G. Steigerwald
University of California, Santa Barbara

James H. Stock
Harvard University

Thomas M. Stoker
Massachusetts Institute of Technology

Samuel B. Thompson
Harvard University

Richard J. Vagnoni
University of California, Santa Barbara

Jeffrey M. Wooldridge
Michigan State University

Allan H. Würtz
University of Aarhus

Motohiro Yogo
University of Pennsylvania

Preface

Donald W. K. Andrews and James H. Stock

The chapters in this volume are dedicated to Thomas Rothenberg in honor of his retirement from the Economics Department at the University of California, Berkeley. Tom Rothenberg has made fundamental contributions to econometric theory and has been an inspiring teacher, advisor, and colleague. Rothenberg's early work focused on efficient estimation and identification in simultaneous equations models. In a paper (written with C. T. Leenders) published in *Econometrica* while he was still a graduate student, Rothenberg established the asymptotic efficiency of the linearized maximum likelihood estimator for simultaneous equations models and thus the asymptotic efficiency of three-stage least squares. This line of research was summarized in his monograph *Efficient Estimation with A Priori Information*, where he laid out a unified theory of efficient estimation in simultaneous equations systems.

Because exact optimality results for estimators and tests in simultaneous equations models are generally unavailable, the notion of efficiency in Rothenberg's initial work typically is first-order asymptotic efficiency. Often, however, there are a number of estimators that are asymptotically equivalent to first order; k-class estimators in a single equation with multiple endogenous regressors is a leading example. In finite samples, these estimators have different behavior, but their finite-sample distributions can be either unavailable or so complicated that they fail to provide useful comparisons between the estimators. Thus, Rothenberg undertook to examine the differences between first-order equivalent estimators and tests by studying their higher-order properties using Edgeworth expansions. Much of this work is summarized in his masterful chapter in the 1984 *Handbook of Econometrics*, which remains a key reference for researchers interested in the deviations of the distributions of instrumental variables estimators from their first-order asymptotic distributions. More recently, Rothenberg's interest in efficient inference led him to consider efficient testing in time series with a possible unit root.

Both of the editors of this Festschrift had the privilege of being students of Tom Rothenberg. Like his other students, we benefited from traits that are hallmarks of his research: an insistence on working on problems that are important to econometrics, bringing common sense to both the economics and the econometric theory at hand, an appreciation for the statistical foundations of econometric theory, and a realization that careful analysis of simple models can yield deeper insights about econometric procedures applied in the more complicated settings found in practice.

Most of the papers in this volume fall into one of the three main areas of Rothenberg's research: identification and efficient estimation; analysis of asymptotic approximations, for example, via higher-order asymptotic analysis; and inference involving potentially nonstationary time series. In addition, several papers are in the area of nonparametric and semiparametric inference.

The majority of the papers in this volume were presented at a National Science Foundation conference in honor of Tom Rothenberg held in Berkeley, California, in August 2001. This conference was organized by James Powell and Paul Ruud.

Identification and Efficient Estimation (Part I)

At the request of the editors, this Festschrift starts with a classic unpublished paper in which Rothenberg explores the subtle role of modeling assumptions for causal inferences. By illustrating how seemingly innocuous assumptions can lead to incredible inferential conclusions, the chapter emphasizes the importance of thoughtful consideration of the assumptions underlying a statistical analysis and of focusing on results that are robust to untestable modeling assumptions.

The chapter by Arthur Goldberger continues this theme. Goldberger considers studies of twins in behavioral genetics. He illustrates how modeling assumptions that seem plausible on their face can lead to implausibly strong conclusions that are not robust to questionable assumptions on unobservables – specifically, assumptions about correlations between genetic characteristics and the environment.

Jeffrey Wooldridge's chapter addresses the identification and estimation of causal effects in nonlinear models and examines how certain estimands are more robust than others to violation of assumptions on unmodeled heterogeneity. In particular, he shows that, under certain conditional independence assumptions, it is possible to estimate average partial effects in nonlinear models consistently, even with unobserved heterogeneity and even though this heterogeneity can lead to inconsistency of estimated parameters (such as probit slope coefficients) of standard nonlinear models.

David Freedman's chapter also considers what assumptions are needed to provide a causal interpretation to regression coefficients estimated using nonexperimental data and emphasizes the importance of having prior information about causal mechanisms – that is, a model in which one believes – if one is to draw causal inferences. Freedman makes these arguments using graphical causal models, a framework more commonly encountered outside rather than inside the field of econometrics. His conclusions reinforce those in the chapters by Rothenberg and Goldberger about the key role played in identification by subsidiary modeling assumptions.

James Stock and Motohiro Yogo consider a different aspect of identification in econometrics: instrumental variables regression when the coefficient of interest is identified but, for the sample size at hand, the marginal explanatory power of the instruments is small, that is, the instruments are weak. As Rothenberg and others have shown, in this case the distributions of IV estimators are poorly approximated by their first-order asymptotic distributions, and Stock and Yogo propose tests of the hypothesis that the instruments are weak against the alternative that they are strong. In a companion chapter, they also derive alternative asymptotic distributions for k-class IV estimators when there are many weak instruments.

The chapter by Douglas Steigerwald and Richard Vagnoni examines the role of modeling assumptions in achieving identification in the context of a dynamic financial model of stock and stock option prices. The model captures salient stylized empirical facts, including serial correlation in stock trades, serial correlation in stock price changes, and more persistent serial correlation in stock trades than in squared stock price changes. Steigerwald and Vagnoni use this model to illustrate how subsidiary modeling assumptions (in this case, assumptions about the process of trader arrival) play an important role in the identification of the model parameters.

Asymptotic Approximations (Part II)

Rothenberg's teaching and research have emphasized the virtues of using alternative asymptotic frameworks, beyond conventional $\sqrt{n}$-normal asymptotics, to understand and compare the performance of estimators and test statistics. For example, Rothenberg's work on higher-order expansions is well known. The chapters by Hidehiko Ichimura and Oliver Linton, by Donald Andrews, by Guido Imbens and Richard Spady, and by Whitney Newey, Joaquim Ramalho, and Richard Smith all follow this approach and employ higher-order expansions to analyze and improve methods based on first-order asymptotics.

Ichimura and Linton calculate higher-order expansions for semiparametric estimators of treatment effects. They use these expansions to define a method for bandwidth selection and to specify a degrees of freedom–like bias correction.

Andrews uses Edgeworth expansions to compare competing bootstrap methods for parametric time series models. In particular, he shows that a parametric bootstrap based on the maximum likelihood estimator achieves greater improvements in coverage probabilities than the nonparametric block bootstrap. Moreover, he shows that these improvements can be achieved using a linearized k-step version of the estimator, resulting in substantial computational savings.

Imbens and Spady calculate higher-order biases and mean-squared errors of generalized method of moments (GMM) and generalized empirical likelihood (GEL) estimators in a simple model with a sequence of moment conditions. Their analysis suggests that GEL estimators outperform feasible GMM estimators. In addition, they find that the relative performances of different GEL estimators depend on the magnitudes of third moments of the moment conditions.

Newey, Ramalho, and Smith establish stochastic expansions for GMM and GEL estimators that may depend on preliminary nuisance parameters. Examples considered include estimators of models with sample selection corrections and estimators of covariance structures. Their results also cover two-step GMM estimators with sample splitting employed to estimate the weight matrix. The stochastic expansions are used to analytically bias-correct the GMM and GEL estimators. Simulation experiments are used to show that this method works well in the case of covariance structure models.

The chapter by Ron Mittelhammer, George Judge, and Ron Schoenberg uses Monte Carlo simulation methods to analyze the finite-sample properties of GEL, GMM, and two-stage least-squares estimators in a linear structural model. They also provide an algorithm for computation of GEL estimators.

The chapter by Ole Barndorff-Nielsen and Neil Shephard considers asymptotic approximations in time series models. The authors numerically compare different first-order equivalent approximations to the distribution of the local sum of squared financial returns (the so-called realized variance).

The chapter by Gene Savin and Allan Würtz considers tests concerning the transformation parameter in Box–Cox regression models with unknown error distributions. Using Monte Carlo simulations, they find that Wald tests based on first-order asymptotics have poor size properties. In contrast, they find that GMM residual-based bootstrap tests have only small discrepancies between nominal and true null rejection probabilities.

Inference Involving Potentially Nonstationary Time Series (Part III)
The chapters by Michael Jansson, by Samuel Thompson, and by Andrew Harvey consider inference about the degree of persistence in time series. Jansson considers tests of the null hypothesis that a vector time series is cointegrated. Specifically, he applies the theory of point optimal tests for a unit moving average root to the residual from a cointegrating regression to develop a new family of tests of the null hypothesis of cointegration. Thompson focuses on the problem of constructing confidence intervals for autoregressive coefficients when the true value is nearly one. Thompson shows that intervals based on inverting robust tests can result in substantial improvements over procedures using only second moments when the errors are heavy-tailed. In his chapter, Harvey proposes a unified framework for testing for stationarity and unit roots in both univariate and multivariate time series. The unifying concept is that the tests have generalized Cramér–von Mises distributions, and Harvey shows how to derive such tests via the Lagrange multiplier principle.

The chapters by Jushan Bai and Serena Ng and by Brownwyn Hall and Jacques Mairesse examine inference in potentially persistent panel data. Bai and Ng consider a common components model and study tests for the stationarity of the common components against the alternative that one or more common components have a unit root. In their chapter, Hall and Mairesse use Monte Carlo simulations to compare the performance of various unit root tests that have been proposed for panel data, focusing on the common case in which there are few time series observations on a large number of individuals or firms. They find that many existing tests have substantial size distortions, especially when there is firm-level heteroskedasticity.

David Hendry and Grayham Mizon consider forecasting in the presence of a different sort of nonstationarity: structural breaks and policy regime shifts. They develop a framework in which structural shifts in causal structural models lead those causal models to produce poor forecasts, whereas nonstructural models can produce reliable forecasts; one of their conclusions is that forecast failure of an econometric model need not rule out its usefulness for forecasting.

Nonparametric and Semiparametric Inference (Part IV)

The chapter by Peter Bickel, Ya'acov Ritov, and Tom Stoker examines the fundamental question of the choice of regressors in a regression model. In contrast to much of the literature on this problem, they analyze a nonparametric regression model rather than a linear model. They develop tests for exclusion restrictions in the nonparametric regression context.

Bo Honoré and James Powell exploit the pairwise differencing approach commonly used to eliminate a fixed effect in a linear panel data model to estimate various semiparametric nonlinear models, including the partially linear logit model. They establish $\sqrt{n}$-consistency and asymptotic normality of estimators that are minimizers of kernel-weighted U-statistics.

The chapter by Whitney Newey and Paul Ruud considers semiparametric estimation of single-index models. The authors establish $\sqrt{n}$-consistency and asymptotic normality of the inverse-density-weighted quasi–maximum likelihood estimator introduced by Ruud in 1986. This estimator has an advantage over alternative estimators in that it allows for discontinuities in the unknown transformation function.

PART I

IDENTIFICATION AND EFFICIENT ESTIMATION

CHAPTER 1

Incredible Structural Inference

Thomas J. Rothenberg

1. INTRODUCTION

In the course of their everyday work, economists routinely employ statistical techniques to analyze data. Typically, these techniques are based on probability models for the observations and justified by an appeal to the theory of statistical inference. An important example is the estimation of structural equations relating economic variables. Such equations are interpreted as representing causal mechanisms and are widely used for forecasting and policy analysis. This econometric approach is arguably the dominant research methodology today among applied economists both in and out of academia.

The econometric approach is not without its critics. Scholars from other disciplines often seem puzzled by the emphasis that economists place on regression analysis. Statisticians express surprise that their techniques should be applicable to so many situations. Recently, a number of leading econometricians have added to the critique. In his paper "Let's Take the Con Out of Econometrics," Ed Leamer (1983) chides economists for ignoring the fragility of their estimates. The title of this paper comes from Christopher Sims's (1980) paper "Macroeconomics and Reality," which argues that the economic and statistical assumptions underlying most macromodels are not believable. They are, he asserts, literally "incredible."

Although my purpose is similar to that of Leamer and Sims, my approach will be rather different. In any area of application there will always be differences of opinion on what constitutes a reasonable set of assumptions on which to base the statistical analysis. Particularly in macroeconomics, where one is trying to summarize in a manageable aggregate model the behavior of millions of decision makers with regard to thousands of products, the disagreements are bound to be enormous. Therefore, instead of discussing typical economic examples

Presented at the International Symposium on Foundations of Statistical Inference, December 1985, Tel Aviv, Israel. This paper evolved from a series of lectures given in June 1985 at the University of Canterbury, Christchurch, New Zealand. I am grateful to Yoel Haitovsky and Richard Manning for providing me with the opportunity to discuss these ideas in such marvelous settings.

where assumptions are always controversial, I shall go to the other extreme and discuss two very simple, almost trivial, examples of statistical inference where the assumptions are quite conventional yet the inferences could naturally be called incredible. Although the examples have nothing to do with economics, I hope to persuade the reader that the key problems with econometric inference are illuminated by their analysis.

2. EXAMPLE ONE: A MEASUREMENT PROBLEM

In order to learn the dimensions of a rectangular table, I ask my research assistant to measure its length and width a number of times. The measuring device is imperfect, so the measurements do not yield the exact length and width. I believe, however, that the measurement errors behave like unpredictable random noise, with any particular error having equal probability of being positive or negative. Therefore, I decide to treat the measurement errors as independent, identically distributed random variables, each with median zero. In addition, I assume that the common error distribution is symmetric and possesses finite fourth moment. For example, the normal probability curve (truncated to insure the measurements are positive) might serve as an approximate model for the error distribution.

These assumptions would not usually be called incredible. They might not be valid for every measurement situation, but they could be reasonable for many such situations. (One might worry about my ruling out thick-tailed distributions that could capture the effects of gross measurement errors. I do that to simplify my story; the analysis could be conducted using medians rather than means, but only with harder distribution theory.) Now I shall make one further assumption. My research assistant mistakenly thinks I care only about the *area* of the table and hence multiplies the length and width measurements. Instead of receiving n length measurements $L_1, L_2, \ldots, L_n$ and n width measurements $W_1, W_2, \ldots, W_n$, I get only n area measurements $A_1 = L_1W_1, A_2 = L_2W_2, \ldots, A_n = L_nW_n$. Worse yet, my research assistant throws away the original data so they are lost forever.

Can I get reasonable estimates of the true length and width of the table using only these area measurements? Can I salvage anything from this badly reported experiment? If there were no measurement error, the answer is clearly no; I will learn the true area of the table, but there are an infinity of length and width pairs that are consistent with any given area. Length and width are simply not identifiable in this experiment. In the presence of measurement error, the answer is quite different. Both length and width are identifiable and can be well estimated from a moderately large sample. In this case credible assumptions seem to lead us to incredible inference!

To demonstrate that inference about length and width is possible, some notation will prove useful. Suppose α is the true length of the table and β is the true width. Let u_i be the error in the ith length measurement, let v_i be the error in the ith width measurement, and let σ^2 be the common error variance. Then we can write

$$A_i = \alpha\beta + \alpha v_i + \beta u_i + u_i v_i. \tag{1.1}$$

Given the assumption that u_i and v_i are independent random variables distributed symmetrically about zero and possessing third moments, we find:

$$E[A_i] = \alpha\beta, \quad \text{Var}\,[A_i] = \sigma^2(\alpha^2 + \beta^2 + \sigma^2)$$
$$E(A_i - \alpha\beta)^3 = 6\alpha\beta\sigma^4.$$

By convention, $\alpha \geq \beta > 0$. Simple algebra demonstrates that the three population moments uniquely determine the three parameters α, β, and σ^2. Furthermore, under our assumptions, the sample moments converge in probability to the population moments as n tends to infinity. Denoting the sample mean of the area measurements by M_1, the sample variance by M_2, and the sample third central moment by M_3, a natural method of moments estimator of σ^4 is $M_3/6M_1$. Assuming this is positive and denoting its square root by S, we can estimate $(\alpha + \beta)^2$ by the equation

$$(\alpha + \beta)^2 = \frac{M_2}{S} - S + 2M_1. \tag{1.2}$$

If $\sigma^2 > 0$, the probability that both estimates are positive goes to 1 as n tends to infinity. Define A to be the square root of expression (1.2) if real, and zero otherwise. Then A is a consistent estimate of $\alpha + \beta$. A natural estimate of $(\alpha - \beta)^2$ is

$$(\alpha - \beta)^2 = \frac{M_2}{S} - S - 2M_1. \tag{1.3}$$

If this expression is positive, its square root is a consistent estimate of $\alpha - \beta$. However, if the table is almost square, a negative value for (1.3) is quite likely. Define B to be the square root of expression (1.3) if real, and zero otherwise. Then $(A + B)/2$ and $(A - B)/2$ should be reasonable estimates of α and β.

These method of moments estimates will converge in probability to the true values as long as there is some measurement error. Central limit theory can be employed to develop large sample approximations of their sampling distributions. These approximate distributions are typically normal, although things get slightly more complicated when the table is square (because then the length and width estimates are confounded). To avoid this technical problem in the asymptotic distribution theory, I shall continue the discussion using $\alpha + \beta$ as the parameter of interest and A as my estimate. The essential feature of my example – that the parameter is estimable in the presence of measurement error but not otherwise – is unchanged.

If $\sigma > 0$ and the errors possess finite sixth moments, then the standardized estimator $\sqrt{n}(A - \alpha - \beta)$ converges in distribution to a zero-mean normal

Table 1.1. *Asymptotic relative standard errors for estimates of* $\alpha + \beta$

		Relative standard error[a]		
σ/α	β/α	σ unknown	σ known	Original data
0.01	1.0	14.44	0.35	0.01
0.05	1.0	2.91	0.36	0.04
0.10	1.0	1.50	0.37	0.07
0.20	1.0	0.84	0.41	0.14
0.30	1.0	0.69	0.47	0.21
0.40	1.0	0.68	0.54	0.28
0.50	1.0	0.73	0.62	0.35
0.60	1.0	0.82	0.71	0.42
1.00	1.0	1.53	1.15	0.71
2.00	1.0	7.87	2.67	1.41
0.01	0.5	15.86	0.39	0.01
0.05	0.5	3.23	0.40	0.05
0.10	0.5	1.70	0.42	0.09
0.20	0.5	1.05	0.48	0.19
0.30	0.5	0.96	0.67	0.28
0.40	0.5	1.03	0.68	0.38
0.50	0.5	1.20	0.81	0.47
0.60	0.5	1.44	0.94	0.57
1.00	0.5	3.39	1.60	0.94
2.00	0.5	22.91	4.12	1.89
0.01	0.2	39.13	0.51	0.01
0.05	0.2	8.04	0.52	0.05
0.10	0.2	4.35	0.54	0.12
0.20	0.2	2.86	0.62	0.24
0.30	0.2	2.74	0.74	0.35
0.40	0.2	3.05	0.89	0.47
0.50	0.2	3.65	1.05	0.59
0.60	0.2	4.53	1.25	0.71
1.00	0.2	11.67	2.19	1.18
2.00	0.2	84.67	5.98	2.34

[a] Standard deviation of the limiting distribution of $\sqrt{n}(A - \alpha - \beta)/(\alpha + \beta)$ for alternative estimates A. Approximate relative standard errors for any given sample size n are obtained by dividing by $\sqrt{n}$.

random variable as the sample size n tends to infinity. The asymptotic variance is a complicated function of α, β, σ^2, and the higher moments of the error distribution. Table 1.1 gives the asymptotic relative standard error for the estimate of $\alpha + \beta$ [i.e., the standard deviation of the limiting distribution of $\sqrt{n}(A - \alpha - \beta)/(\alpha + \beta)$] for the special case where the fourth and sixth moments are equal to those of a normal random variable. Also given in the table are the asymptotic relative standard errors for the estimate using the true variance

σ^2 in place of the estimate S in (1.2) and for the estimate using the sample means of the original length and width data. (Note that the tabulated values must be divided by $\sqrt{n}$ to get approximate standard errors for sample size n.)

The table suggests the following conclusions. Depending on the values of α, β, and σ, the efficiency loss from having only the area data ranges from very large to quite modest. If one knows σ^2, the best results are obtained by measuring the table as carefully as possible (but not perfectly!). If one does not know σ^2, the best results are obtained by measuring the table rather badly; for a table that is nearly square, σ/α should be approximately 0.5. In this latter case, there is a simple moral to the story: if one cannot have a smart research assistant, at least have a sloppy one. Truly, an incredible result! Needless to say, I do not seriously propose estimating the length and width of a table from area measurements. My point is quite different. No sensible person would ever use the estimation method derived here. Yet many sensible people would use the sample means of the original observations – if they were available. The assumptions made are not incredible. But they are also not credible enough to justify the inference procedure described. I shall return to this point in a moment, but let me first develop another example.

3. EXAMPLE TWO: A REGRESSION PROBLEM

In order to estimate the gravitational constant I ask another of my research assistants to drop a coin from various heights and to report how long it takes before the coin hits the ground. On the basis of my study of physics, I believe that the true time ought to be proportional to the square root of the distance the coin travels and that the constant of proportionality is related in a simple way to the gravitational constant. This particular research assistant is very good at measuring lengths, but not so good at stopping the stopwatch at the right moment. I therefore propose the regression model

$$y_i = \alpha + \beta x_i + u_i \qquad (i = 1, \ldots, n), \tag{1.4}$$

where y_i is interpreted as the measured time on the ith trial, x_i is the (correctly measured) square root of distance, and u_i is the error in measuring the time. (Of course, here I know α is zero, but I shall not use that fact). I am tempted to estimate β by the least-squares slope coefficient $b = \sum(x_i - \bar{x})y_i / \sum(x_i - \bar{x})^2$ and to form a confidence interval using the statistic

$$T = (b - \beta)\left[\sum \frac{(x_i - \bar{x})^2}{s^2}\right]^{1/2}, \tag{1.5}$$

where s^2 is the sum of squared residuals divided by $n - 2$.

If the errors are independent, identically distributed random variables with mean zero and finite variance, the least-squares estimates are unbiased and have small variance as long as the sample is reasonably large and there is sufficient variation in x_i. Furthermore, if the errors are normal, these estimates are best unbiased and the statistic T is distributed exactly as Student's t with $n-2$ degrees of freedom.

It would be nice to assume that the measurement errors behave like zero-mean random noise. But what if my research assistant is not so regular in making errors? Maybe he sometimes forgets to stop the stopwatch when he goes out for coffee. Maybe he forgets to reset the watch at zero when he starts a new trial. Given my previous experience with research assistants, anything is possible! I would not like to assume any more than that his errors are a sequence of unobserved numbers. It would be more attractive if the analysis could be conducted on the basis of assumptions on observables, like the regressors, rather than on these mysterious unobserved errors. In fact, as R. A. Fisher (1939) showed many years ago, this can easily be done. Least-squares regression can be justified with almost no assumptions on the errors if we are willing to make some assumptions about the process generating the regressors. The following is a special case of a general result on linear models with multivariate normal regressors:[1]

Theorem 1.1. *In the regression model (1.4), suppose the x_i are i.i.d. normal random variables with variance σ^2 and are distributed independently of the errors. Then the least-squares slope estimate b is distributed symmetrically about β and the statistic T is distributed exactly as Student's t with $n-2$ degrees of freedom,* no matter how the errors are generated. *If the errors have second moments, the mean and variance of b are given by*

$$E(b) = \beta, \quad Var(b) = E\sum \frac{(u_i - \bar{u})^2}{\sigma^2(n-3)(n-1)}.$$

When the Eu_i^2 are uniformly bounded, the variance is $O(n^{-1})$ as n tends to infinity and b is a consistent estimate of β.

Thus, I have a simple solution to my problem of coping with a research assistant whose errors cannot be easily modeled. Before the experiment begins, I randomly draw n numbers from a normal distribution with large mean and unit variance. (I truncate to avoid negative outcomes, but with a large mean the results will look almost normal.) I then instruct my research assistant to use the square of these numbers as the heights (in meters) in the coin-dropping experiment. If the sample is large enough, I can rely on Theorem 1.1 to convince myself that I will get good estimates of the gravitational constant no matter how badly my assistant botches the time measurements. Statistical theory triumphs over a flawed experiment. Once again, credible assumptions lead to incredible inference.

[1] Although this result is not new, I have not found a good reference. A multivariate version is derived in the mimeographed paper by C. Cavanagh and T. Rothenberg (1984). See also Box and Watson (1962). For asymptotic results, the normality assumption can be dropped; symmetry of the x distribution is all that really matters.

Of course, I do not really believe that I can get good estimates of the gravitational constant without making any assumptions about the errors. Indeed, the point of the example is to emphasize that the key assumption in the linear model is that the errors are independent of the regressors. The other assumptions about the errors are easily dispensed with. Moreover, if I am really unhappy about modeling the error process, I should be just as unhappy about trying to model the relation between the errors and the regressors. Independence between regressors and errors is a powerful assumption and cannot be taken lightly.

4. IMPLICATIONS FOR ECONOMETRICS

What has any of this to do with econometrics? Measuring the length of a table and the time it takes a coin to drop seem totally unrelated to the activities that occupy economists. Nevertheless, these examples are, I believe, relevant. Actual econometric models are much more complicated than the ones I have presented and concern more important phenomena. But, deep down, they possess the same key features that drive the examples.

Economists are usually interested in parameters that have a structural or causal interpretation. If, other things equal, the price of coffee doubles, by how much would price-taking consumers decrease their purchases? Such numbers are treated by economists in much the same way as the length of the table and the gravitational constant in my examples. They are parameters of interest that could in principle be determined by very carefully conducted experiments. Unfortunately, these experiments are much too difficult, so we have to rely on different ones. Usually, the actual data we have available were generated by someone else using methods very far from the ones we would have used in our ideal experiment. Instead of actually changing the price of coffee, we simply observe the historical variation that has taken place over time. Just as in the artificial examples given earlier, structural inference in economics involves the analysis of data from flawed experiments.

The error terms in econometric equations represent misspecifications of functional form, omitted variables, and pure measurement error. It is not hard to make assumptions about these errors that are moderately plausible. Unfortunately, their converses are often also moderately plausible. Most econometric models are reasonable, but they are not compelling. There always exist alternative models that are just as reasonable. Yet, as in the examples, the results are often very sensitive to the assumptions. If we are suspicious of estimating the length of a table from area measurements and if we are suspicious of estimating the gravitational constant from an experiment where the measurement errors may take on arbitrary values, then we should be even more suspicious of structural econometric inference in models where the number of unknown parameters and the number of unverified assumptions are much larger. The estimation of separate supply and demand curves from equilibrium market data is considerably more difficult than the estimation of the length of a table.

Using cross-sectional variation in the crime rate to determine the effect of longer jail sentences on the level of crime is certainly just as difficult as using flawed experimental data to determine the gravitational constant. Relevant research is not easier than trivial research.

Not all econometrics involves structural inference. Sometimes we collect economic data just to describe the current state of affairs or to indicate trends. Sometimes we run regressions simply to summarize the pattern of correlations in a data set or to take advantage of stable relations for use in forecasting. Many of the most successful applications of statistics in economics have nothing to do with the estimation of structural relations. Nevertheless, the temptation to interpret empirical regularities as representing causal mechanisms is overwhelming. For better or worse, econometrics is generally viewed as a method for learning about the underlying structure of the economy.

Structural inference in econometrics, like the structural inference in my simple examples, is indeed incredible. Surprisingly strong conclusions about causal mechanisms can be drawn from seemingly weak assumptions. Unfortunately, the conclusions are often not very robust to changes in these assumptions. In those cases, it is difficult to put much credence in the results. More emphasis by applied econometricians on presenting alternative estimates based on alternative models might help make econometrics less incredible.

References

Box, G., and G. Watson (1962), "Robustness to Non-normality of Regression Tests," *Biometrika*, 49, 93–106.

Cavanagh, C., and T. Rothenberg (1984), Linear Regression with Non-normal Errors, mimeo.

Fisher, R. A. (1939), "The Sampling Distributions of Some Statistics Obtained from Nonlinear Equations," *Annals of Eugenics*, 9, 238–49.

Leamer, E. (1983), "Let's Take the Con Out of Econometrics," *American Economic Review*, 73, 31–43.

Sims, C. (1980), "Macroeconomics and Reality," *Econometrica*, 48, 1–48.

CHAPTER 2

Structural Equation Models in Human Behavior Genetics

Arthur S. Goldberger

1. INTRODUCTION

That IQ is a highly heritable trait has been widely reported. Rather less well known are recent reports in major scientific journals such as those announcing that the heritability of controllable life events is 53 percent among women and 14 percent among men (Saudino et al. 1997), while the heritabilities of inhibition of aggression, openness to experience, and right-wing authoritarianism are respectively 12, 40, and 50 percent (Pedersen et al. 1989; Bergeman et al. 1993; McCourt et al. 1999). It seems that milk and soda intake are in part heritable, but not the intake of fruit juice or diet soda (de Castro 1993).

These reported heritabilities are parameter estimates obtained in structural modeling of measures taken on pairs of siblings – prototypically, identical (monozygotic) twins and fraternal (dizygotic) twins, some reared together and others reared apart. The models are of the linear random effects type, in which an observed trait – a phenotype – is expressed in terms of latent factors – genetic and environmental – whose prespecified cross-twin correlations differ by zygosity and rearing status. Estimation is by maximum likelihood applied to the phenotypic variances and covariances. Heritability, the key parameter of interest, refers to the proportion of the variance of the phenotype that is attributable to the variance of the genetic factors.

Regarding these studies, various issues arise. Those that I will touch on here include identification, nonnegativity constraints, alternative estimators, pretest estimation, conditioning of the design matrix, multivariate analyses, and the objectives of structural modeling. Some of these issues were featured in Thomas Rothenberg's dissertation (1972), a remarkable book that led me to appreciate the generality of the minimum chi-square principle in estimation, and the contrast between equality and inequality constraints in efficient estimation.

In the present chapter, I will focus on the SATSA project – the Swedish Adoption/Twin Study of Aging – which, from the early 1980s on, has assembled a sample of adult twin pairs: approximately 200 MZT (identical twins reared together), 200 DZT (fraternal twins reared together), 100 MZA (identical twins reared apart), and 150 DZA (fraternal twins reared apart). The fraternal twins are all same-sex pairs. The twins have been assessed in person and via mail questionnaires on several occasions, on a wide range of traits, some cognitive and others relating to personality, temperament, and recollections of childhood upbringing. Concerns about the representativeness of the samples and the reliability and validity of the measures were raised in Goldberger and Kamin (1998) and Kamin and Goldberger (2002). I suppress those concerns here in order to focus on the modeling.

2. PRIMARY MODEL

The specification of the main SATSA model is captured as follows. Consider a typical individual, whose phenotype (observable trait value) Y is determined by unobservable factors as

$$Y = \alpha_1 G + \alpha_2 D + \alpha_3 S + \alpha_0 U. \tag{2.1}$$

Here G is the additive genetic factor, D the nonadditive genetic factor, S the shared environment factor, and U the nonshared environment factor. (The distinction between the two genetic factors will be exposited later). Assume that the factors are uncorrelated and standardize all variables to have zero means and unit variances, so that the phenotypic variance is

$$V(Y) = \alpha_1^2 + \alpha_2^2 + \alpha_3^2 + \alpha_0^2 = 1. \tag{2.2}$$

The individual is paired with his or her sibling, whose phenotype is determined as

$$Y' = \alpha_1 G' + \alpha_2 D' + \alpha_3 S' + \alpha_0 U'. \tag{2.3}$$

Across the sibling pair, all factor correlations are assumed to be zero except perhaps for those that link one sibling's additive genetic, nonadditive genetic, and shared environment factors with the corresponding factors of the other sibling. So the phenotypic sibling covariance is

$$C(Y, Y') = C(G, G')\alpha_1^2 + C(D, D')\alpha_2^2 + C(S, S')\alpha_3^2. \tag{2.4}$$

Referring to identical and fraternal twins (MZs and DZs), reared together and apart (Ts and As), those factor covariances are assumed to be

$$\begin{aligned} C(G, G') &= 1 \text{ for MZs, } 1/2 \text{ for DZs} \\ C(D, D') &= 1 \text{ for MZs, } 1/4 \text{ for DZs} \\ C(S, S') &= 1 \text{ for Ts, } 0 \text{ for As.} \end{aligned} \tag{2.5}$$

With all variables standardized, covariances are also correlations. The consequence is that in the population, the phenotypic correlations for the four twin types are

$$\begin{array}{ll} \text{MZT} & \rho_1 = \alpha_1^2 + \alpha_2^2 + \alpha_3^2 \\ \text{DZT} & \rho_2 = \alpha_1^2/2 + \alpha_2^2/4 + \alpha_3^2 \\ \text{MZA} & \rho_3 = \alpha_1^2 + \alpha_2^2 \\ \text{DZA} & \rho_4 = \alpha_1^2/2 + \alpha_2^2/4. \end{array} \tag{2.6}$$

Let $\beta_1 = \alpha_1^2$, $\beta_2 = \alpha_2^2$, and $\beta_3 = \alpha_3^2$, and define the vectors

$$\boldsymbol{\rho} = \begin{bmatrix} \rho_1 \\ \rho_2 \\ \rho_3 \\ \rho_4 \end{bmatrix}, \quad \mathbf{x}_1 = \begin{bmatrix} 1 \\ 0.5 \\ 1 \\ 0.5 \end{bmatrix}, \quad \mathbf{x}_2 = \begin{bmatrix} 1 \\ 0.25 \\ 1 \\ 0.25 \end{bmatrix}, \quad \mathbf{x}_3 = \begin{bmatrix} 1 \\ 1 \\ 0 \\ 0 \end{bmatrix}. \tag{2.7}$$

Then SATSA's primary model has this linear specification for the population phenotypic correlations:

$$\boldsymbol{\rho} = \mathbf{x}_1\, \beta_1 + \mathbf{x}_2\, \beta_2 + \mathbf{x}_3\, \beta_3. \tag{2.8}$$

These βs are components of phenotypic variance, as is the implied nonshared environment component, $\beta_0 = \alpha_0^2 = 1 - (\beta_1 + \beta_2 + \beta_3)$. The parameter β_1 is called narrow heritability, while the sum $\beta_1 + \beta_2$ is called broad heritability.

With four correlations expressed in terms of three parameters, there is one equality restriction, namely

$$\rho_1 - \rho_3 = \rho_2 - \rho_4,$$

which says that the difference between MZ and DZ correlations is the same whether the twins are reared together or apart. Further, with all four βs assumed to be nonnegative, there is an inequality restriction, namely

$$\rho_3/4 \le \rho_4 \le \rho_3/2,$$

which says that the DZA correlation should lie between one-fourth and one-half of the MZA correlation.

Given random samples from each of the four twin groups, one might take observed phenotypic correlations r_1, r_2, r_3, r_4, interpret them as estimates of the population correlations, and estimate $\boldsymbol{\beta} = (\beta_1\ \beta_2\ \beta_3)'$ by running the least-squares linear regression of the 4×1 vector $\mathbf{r} = (r_1\ r_2\ r_3\ r_4)'$ on the 4×3 matrix $\mathbf{X} = (\mathbf{x}_1\ \mathbf{x}_2\ \mathbf{x}_3)$, thus minimizing

$$\sum_{i=1}^{4} (r_i - \rho_i)^2.$$

A more appropriate procedure would take into account the fact that the variance of a sample correlation coefficient depends on the population correlation coefficient as well as the sample size, and choose values for the β estimates to minimize

$$\sum_{i=1}^{4} w_i (r_i - \rho_i)^2,$$

where $w_i = n_i/(1 - r_i^2)^2$, with n_i being the number of observations in the ith twin group.

However, it is most convenient to work with Fisher's z transforms of correlation coefficients, namely

$$z = (1/2)\log[(1 + r)/(1 - r)],$$
$$\zeta = (1/2)\log[(1 + \rho)/(1 - \rho)],$$

relying on the presumption that in random sampling, sample size n, the variable z is distributed approximately $N(\zeta, 1/n)$; see Wilks (1962, p. 276). So a particular application of the minimum chi-square principle, which I label FZLS, chooses values for the β-estimates to minimize

$$\sum_{i=1}^{4} n_i (z_i - \zeta_i)^2,$$

which amounts to a straightforward, albeit nonlinear, regression problem. With four observations and three parameters, the minimized criterion provides an asymptotic χ^2 (1) statistic of model fit that can serve to test the equality restriction $\rho_1 - \rho_3 = \rho_2 - \rho_4$.

I have oversimplified the procedure of the SATSA group in several respects. They do not standardize the observed variables, but rather work with variances and covariances, taking β_0 as a free parameter. (They then rescale parameter estimates ex post to obtain the proportional components of variance.) They do not use FZLS, but rather Gaussian ML, following Neale and Cardon (1992, Chapters 6 and 7). Often, they take as data eight phenotypic variances: for each twin group, the between-family and within-family components. That gives them three additional degrees of freedom for model fit, which are implicitly allocated to the hypothesis that the four phenotypic variances are the same. This may be an interesting hypothesis, but has little to do with behavior-genetic theory. Sometimes they work with twelve observed phenotypic variances and covariances: for each twin group, a variance for twin A, a variance for twin B, and a covariance. This gives four additional degrees of freedom for model fit, which are implicitly allocated to equating the phenotypic variances for twins A and B in each twin group. The labeling of the twins was arbitrary, so those four additional degrees of freedom are in effect allocated to the hypothesis that SATSA's own assignment of the labels was in fact random. This is hardly an interesting hypothesis, and has nothing to do with behavior-genetic theory. (The economists Ashenfelter and Krueger [1994], working with twins, albeit not with behavior genetics, also treat an arbitrary labeling of twin A and twin B as meaningful.)

Typically, the SATSA group residualize the observed traits on age and gender before beginning the modeling exercise, but occasionally they introduce age into the model itself as a covariate. This adds two parameters (a population age variance and a population trait-on-age slope), and adds twelve observed moments: for each twin group, the covariance of twin A's trait with age, the covariance to twin B's trait with age, and the variance of age. (Twins in Sweden, as elsewhere, have the same age.) In this manner, Lichtenstein, Pedersen, and McClearn (1992) were able to report a total of 18 degrees of freedom for model fit, while the core of the model in correlation terms had just 1.

3. GENETIC THEORY

The genetic basis for this line of research is minimal. The biological content of the model, after all, consists of the ratios 1/2 and 1/4 for DZ twins relative to MZ twins. (It is true that the theory does extend to cover kinships other than twins.) The formal distinction between the two genetic factors should be familiar to econometricians: it lies in the distinction between the conditional expectation function and the best linear predictor. Consider a gene with two variants (alleles), $-$ and $+$. At this locus, an individual may be $--$, $-+$, $+-$, or $++$. Score these as $Z = 0, 1, 1, 2$, and consider the distribution of phenotypes Y for persons of each score Z. If $E(Y \mid Z)$ is linear, that is if the expected observable trait for heterozygotes ($Z = 1$) is halfway between those for homozygotes ($Z = 0$ and $Z = 2$), then only an additive genetic factor is present. If $E(Y \mid Z)$ is nonlinear, for example if the expected observed trait for $Z = 2$ is the same as for $Z = 0$, then a nonadditive genetic factor is present. In that case, the BLP($Y \mid Z$) gives the additive factor, and the deviations $E(Y \mid Z) -$ BLP ($Y \mid Z$) give the nonadditive factor. So the two genetic factors are uncorrelated by construction. The Appendix sketches why, under certain assumptions, MZs and DZs correlate 1/2 and 1/4 on those two factors. Remarkably, the argument for a single locus extends directly to multiple loci. On all this, see Falconer and Mackay (1996, Chapters 7–9).

In SATSA's primary model, identification is obtained by ruling out many possibilities a priori. Covariance between an individual's genetic factors and shared environment factor is not allowed, conventional wisdom on the role of parents to the contrary notwithstanding. Nor is there any allowance for the possibility that the separated twins were placed into similar environments. Nor is there any allowance for MZTs to have more similar environments than DZTs, that is, for $C(S, S')$ to differ by zygosity; any excess phenotypic similarity of MZTs over DZTs is attributed to their excess genetic similarity. Joseph (1998) provides a critical assessment of the evidence in favor of this "equal environment assumption." Even the specified ratios 1/2 and 1/4 are not sacred; those values are valid under random mating, but would be different if there is assortative mating for the trait.

It is quite ironic that the assumptions of the behavior-genetic model refer so directly to social behavior, rather than biological processes.

4. SECONDARY MODEL

On occasion, the SATSA group adopts an alternative model that makes allowance for some environmental similarity for twins reared apart, thus addressing the objection that the separated twins may not have been reared in randomly different environments. This is accomplished by replacing the nonadditive genetic factor with a "selective placement" or "correlated environment" factor that correlates perfectly across twins of all types. In terms of the display in (2.7) replace $\mathbf{x}_2$ with a new variable whose value is 1 for all four twin groups. Then $\mathbf{x}_4 = (1, 1, 1, 1)'$ and the secondary model has

$$\rho = \mathbf{x}_1\gamma_1 + \mathbf{x}_4\gamma_2 + \mathbf{x}_3\gamma_3. \tag{4.1}$$

As the SATSA group recognizes, it is not feasible to include both genetic factors along with the new environmental factor because exact collinearity would result: $\mathbf{x}_4 = 3\mathbf{x}_1 - 2\mathbf{x}_2$.

The design columns in (4.1) span the same space as those in (2.8) so the secondary model implies the same equality constraint, namely $\rho_1 - \rho_3 = \rho_2 - \rho_4$. However, with all its γs assumed to be nonnegative, the implied inequality constraint is now

$$\rho_3/2 \leq \rho_4 \leq \rho_3,$$

which says that the DZA correlation should lie between 1/2 and 1 times the MZA correlation. So SATSA researchers are either attracted to this model immediately when the observed DZ correlations run high relative to the MZ correlations, or else choose it retroactively after observing that the nonnegativity constraint binds when fitting the primary model.

5. AGNOSTIC MODEL

The need to choose between the primary and secondary models may be avoided by freeing up the relation between ρ_4 and ρ_3. This can be accomplished by allowing two distinct genetic factors, one for MZs and one for DZs. If we let $\mathbf{x}_5 = (1\ 0\ 1\ 0)'$ and $\mathbf{x}_6 = (0\ 1\ 0\ 1)'$, we can write the agnostic model as

$$\rho = \mathbf{x}_5\delta_1 + \mathbf{x}_6\delta_2 + \mathbf{x}_3\delta_3. \tag{5.1}$$

Observe that $\mathbf{x}_5 = -\mathbf{x}_1 + 2\mathbf{x}_2$ and $\mathbf{x}_6 = 4\mathbf{x}_1 - 4\mathbf{x}_2$, so the columns of this design span the same space as the previous ones did, and this model implies the same equality constraint, $\rho_1 - \rho_3 = \rho_2 - \rho_4$. One may suppose that all three δs are nonnegative, and also $\delta_1 > \delta_2$ (genetic similarity greater for MZs than for DZs). But even with all δs assumed to be nonnegative, it allows ρ_4 to range from 0 up to ρ_3. (A similar idea was employed by Lykken et al., 1988). Adopting the agnostic model would reduce the need to follow SATSA's model selection strategy and would also dispel some of the mystique of a rigorous biological foundation for the SATSA analyses.

6. SKEPTICAL MODEL

A crucial feature of SATSA's models is that they make no allowance for environmental resemblance to differ between MZTs and DZTs, as a result, say, of more similar treatment by parents and peers. A simple alternative three-parameter specification would include the additive genetic factor $\mathbf{x}_1$, an MZT shared environment factor $\mathbf{x}_7 = (1\,0\,0\,0)'$, and a DZT shared environment factor $\mathbf{x}_8 = (0\;1\;0\;0)'$. This skeptical model can be written as

$$\rho = \mathbf{x}_1\theta_1 + \mathbf{x}_7\theta_2 + \mathbf{x}_8\theta_3. \tag{6.1}$$

These design columns span a different space, and the single equality restriction is now

$$\rho_4 = \rho_3/2.$$

One may suppose that all three θs are nonnegative, and also $\theta_2 > \theta_3$ (environmental similarity greater for MZTs than DZTs). This model has, as far as I know, not been used by the SATSA researchers, and only rarely by other behavior geneticists, for example, Loehlin (1987, pp. 122–6).

7. IDENTIFICATION AND CONSTRAINTS

In practice it is rare for SATSA to publish estimates of a full three-factor version of either their primary or secondary model. Almost invariably, one or another of the three factors will be dropped and a reduced model fitted and reported. That happens either when one of the estimated parameters is "nonsignificant," or when their algorithm (which apparently precludes negative estimates) finds a nonnegativity constraint to be binding and sets the offending parameter at zero. As a consequence of this general-to-specific strategy, almost always the only model published is a reduced two-factor, or one-factor, model.

In particular, throughout the SATSA publications, one rarely – perhaps 5 percent of the time – finds traits for which both additive and nonadditive genetic variance components are estimated to be nonzero. It is not hard to see why. Consider the primary model. If only MZT and DZT data were available, it would be impossible to distinguish between the additive and nonadditive genetic components. The availability of separated twins formally identifies β_1, β_2, and β_3, but the identification is tenuous. Treating the 4×3 design matrix $\mathbf{X} = (\mathbf{x}_1\,\mathbf{x}_2\,\mathbf{x}_3)$ as if it simply had four observations, the "correlation" (about zero) between $\mathbf{x}_1$ and $\mathbf{x}_2$ is 0.97. That high degree of collinearity carries over to FZLS and ML estimation, producing unreliable and negatively correlated estimates of β_1 and β_2. Pedersen et al. (1992) cast their lot with the additive side; Plomin et al. (1994), analyzing the same cognitive traits, cast their lot with the nonadditive side. Similar considerations apply to the secondary model.

Had the agnostic model been used, in many cases the SATSA group could have maintained a full three-factor model for the correlation coefficients. For example, the condition $\delta_1 > \delta_2 > 0$ is equivalent to $\beta_1 + \beta_2 > 0.5\beta_1 + 0.25\beta_2 > 0$, implying $0.5\beta_1 + 0.75\beta_2 > 0$, and even when unconstrained estimates of one of those βs was negative, the corresponding estimates of the δs might be admissible.

8. EMPIRICAL IMPLEMENTATION

To illustrate the applications, for three traits selected from SATSA publications, I give estimates of the various models. In Pedersen et al. (1988), extraversion and neuroticism were each measured as the sum of yes–no responses (coded 1–0) to nine items drawn from a short form of the Eysenck Personality Inventory, residualized on age and gender. In Lichtenstein et al. (1992), occupation was measured by four nonfarm occupational categories (coded 1, 2, 3, 4, then logged), gender-specific and residualized on age; I use only the results for men.

Table 2.1 refers to those three traits. First, the observed correlations are given along with sample sizes. Then come model-fitting results, with Roman letters denoting estimates of the corresponding Greek-letter parameters, and standard errors where available in parentheses. SATSA's ML estimates for the particular reduced primary model that they published are given, followed by my FZLS estimates for that model. (Reassuringly, our numbers are generally close; the exception, b_3 for occupation, I take to be a misprint. For neuroticism, Pedersen et al. (1988) also report and prefer the full secondary model, with parameter estimates $b_1 = .13, b_4 = .16, b_3 = .07$.)

Then follow results of my fitting the full primary, secondary, agnostic, and skeptical models by FZLS. Readers may, for each model, readily calculate the fitted correlations from the parameter estimates. And they may also estimate reduced versions of these models: the FZLS method requires only the r_is and n_is, which are often what is available in SATSA publications.

Throughout the table, the chi-square statistic is the minimized value of the FZLS criterion. Degrees of freedom for model fit are the number of correlations, 4, minus the number of parameters estimated, 3 for full models and 2 for the reduced models. For their reduced models, the χ^2s for model-fit approach or exceed significance by conventional standards. As is to be expected, chi-square values coincide when design matrices span the same space.

A curiosity of the SATSA analyses, one that is not inherent in the behavior-genetic approach, is that they typically formulate the model in terms of path coefficients (such as our αs) rather than the variance components (such as our βs, the squared αs). As a result, they report ML standard errors for estimated path coefficients, which do not translate into standard errors for the parameters of theoretical interest, namely the contributions to variance. For our FZLS estimates, standard errors are routinely calculated.

In the table, we observe that the total genetic component, $\beta_1 + \beta_2$, is estimated to be virtually the same whether the full or reduced primary model is used, and is the same (apart from rounding) as the estimate of δ_1 in the agnostic model. So it might be argued that broad heritability of each trait is clearly discernible in the data. On the other hand, we also observe that the agnostic and skeptical models appear as plausible competitors for SATSA's preferred models,

Table 2.1. *Alternative models for three traits*

	Extraversion				Neuroticism				Occupation			
Observed												
Correlations	r_1	r_2	r_3	r_4	r_1	r_2	r_3	r_4	r_1	r_2	r_3	r_4
	.54	.06	.30	.04	.41	.24	.25	.28	.82	.36	.44	.44
Sample sizes	n_1	n_2	n_3	n_4	n_1	n_2	n_3	n_4	n_1	n_2	n_3	n_4
	150	204	95	220	151	204	202	201	38	42	24	36
Model-Fitting												
Reduced Primary Model												
	b_1	b_2	b_3	χ^2	b_1	b_2	b_3	χ^2	b_1	b_2	b_3	χ^2
SATSA ML	0	.41	.07		.31	0	.10		.60	0	.09	
FZLS	0	.40	.06	5.84	.35	0	.06	3.83	.59	0	.20	3.46
		(.07)	(.06)		(.07)		(.06)		(.11)		(.11)	
Full models												
Primary	b_1	b_2	b_3		b_1	b_2	b_3		b_1	b_2	b_3	
	−.41	.80	.12	2.29	.64	−.31	.04	1.83	.49	.10	.20	3.40
	(.22)	(.22)	(.07)		(.21)	(.22)	(.07)		(.43)	(.49)	(.12)	
Secondary	c_1	c_2	c_3		c_1	c_2	c_3		c_1	c_2	c_3	
	.78	−.40	.12	2.29	.17	.16	.04	1.83	.64	−.05	.20	3.40
	(.14)	(.11)	(.07)		(.15)	(.11)	(.07)		(.22)	(.20)	(.12)	
Agnostic	d_1	d_2	d_3		d_1	d_2	d_3		d_1	d_2	d_3	
	.38	−.01	.12	2.29	.33	.24	.04	1.83	.59	.27	.20	3.40
	(.07)	(.06)	(.07)		(.07)	(.06)	(.07)		(.11)	(.12)	(.12)	
Skeptical	t_1	t_2	t_3		t_1	t_2	t_3		t_1	t_2	t_3	
	.22	.37	−.05	1.79	.35	−.01	.06	3.83	.53	.29	.10	1.78
	(.08)	(.10)	(.08)		(.07)	(.10)	(.08)		(.13)	(.14)	(.15)	

while providing alternative interpretations of the data. For example, the skeptical model attributes only 22 percent of the variance in extraversion to genetic factors, rather than 40 percent or so.

The FZLS method does not constrain the parameter estimates to be nonnegative, and indeed for many of the SATSA data sets, FZLS produces negative estimates where SATSA would reduce the model and effectively report zeros. One could test the nonnegativity constraints, a task never undertaken by the SATSA researchers. For example, in the primary model for extraversion, forcing $b_1 = 0$ increases χ^2 by 3.55 (= 5.84 − 2.29), approaching significance by conventional standards for a single constraint. To be sure, the appropriate test procedure is that for inequality constraints, which is more tolerant of departures; see Kodde and Palm (1986) and Wolak (1987). Recently, some behavior geneticists have reported confidence intervals using the profile likelihood. The source article is Neale and Miller (1997), which recommends discarding any negative portion of the interval, that is, left-truncating the interval at zero.

If the SATSA group insist on the requirement that all βs be nonnegative, it is because of their insistence on interpreting them as components of variance. Perhaps the frequent occurrence of binding constraints should serve as an indication that their general behavior-genetic approach is not valid. On the other hand, there is nothing in principle that precludes factors that contribute to dissimilarity rather than similarity of twins. Perhaps negative parameter estimates should not serve to reject a particular full model out of hand.

9. PRETESTING ISSUES

SATSA's empirical implementation of the behavior-genetic approach is not a routine exercise, but involves a sequence of choices and stopping rules. Nothing about the track that leads to their final variant is accounted for when they engage in statistical inference. So the standard errors and confidence intervals that they do report are merely nominal. The pretesting issues associated with such model selection are not mentioned in the behavior-genetic reports or in the standard textbook of Neale and Cardon (1992). My impression from the econometric and statistical literature is that, under pretesting, nominal standard errors are misleadingly low, so that actual precision is overstated.

To investigate this, Monte Carlo runs may be useful. I report on one here. Adopt the primary model with parameter values $\beta_1 = 0.4$, $\beta_2 = 0.1$, $\beta_3 = 0.3$, implying $\rho_1 = 0.800$, $\rho_2 = 0.525$, $\rho_3 = 0.500$, $\rho_4 = 0.225$. Take the sample sizes to be $n_1 = 100$, $n_2 = 100$, $n_3 = 50$, $n_4 = 100$. Generate sample correlations $r_i (i = 1, \ldots, 4)$, or rather the z transforms thereof z_i, by random sampling from $z_i \sim N(\zeta_i, 1/n_i)$. Estimate parameters by FZLS, reducing the model and reestimating when a parameter estimate is negative.

Table 2.2 summarizes results of a 1000-replication run. Column 1 gives, for estimation of the full model, the average parameter estimates, their average standard errors, and their actual standard deviations. The next three columns

Table 2.2. *Monte Carlo results*

	Unrestricted		Pretest estimator: Conditional			Pretest estimator: Unconditional
	(1)		(2)	(3)	(4)	(5)
Mean b_1	.389	Mean b_1^*	–	.499	.291	.343
Mean b_2	.109	Mean b_2^*	.463	–	.208	.154
Mean b_3	.298	Mean b_3^*	.343	.293	.302	.302
Mean $s(b_1)$	.268	Mean $s(b_1^*)$	–	.079	.272	.185
Mean $s(b_2)$	.248	Mean $s(b_2^*)$	.077	–	.252	.151
Mean $s(b_3)$	.081	Mean $s(b_3^*)$	.075	.076	.082	.079
SD (b_1)	.264	SD (b_1^*)	–	.079	.146	.179
SD (b_2)	.247	SD (b_2^*)	.079	–	.131	.164
SD (b_3)	.079	SD (b_3^*)	.078	.078	.077	.078

give that information conditionally for the three branches of the pretest estimator: column 2 refers to the 71 samples in which the additive genetic factor was dropped because its unrestricted coefficient estimate was negative, column 3 refers to the 349 samples in which the nonadditive factor was dropped because its unrestricted coefficient estimate was negative, and column 4 refers to the 580 samples in which all factors were retained because none of the unrestricted estimates were negative. In the rightmost column, the information is given unconditionally for the pretest estimator, blanks in columns 2 and 3 being treated as zeroes. We observe some bias in the pretest estimators of β_1 and β_2, and more variability in them than would be indicated by the standard errors for the reduced models. On the other hand, we observe that the sum $\beta_1 + \beta_2$ is virtually unbiasedly estimated by $b_1^* + b_2^*$.

10. MULTIVARIATE MODELS

Having analyzed dozens of observed traits individually in the same manner, the SATSA group has moved on to multivariate analyses, in which several phenotypes are modeled jointly in terms of latent factors. So now the concern is with accounting for covariances, as well as variances, of observed traits. For example, Lichtenstein and Pedersen (1995) analyze five phenotypes jointly: life events, loneliness, preceived support, quantity of relationships, and health.

Their structure may be captured as follows. For an individual,

$$\mathbf{y} = \mathbf{A}_1\mathbf{g} + \mathbf{A}_3\mathbf{s} + \mathbf{A}_0\mathbf{u}, \tag{10.1}$$

where the observed vector $\mathbf{y}$ is 5×1, and the uncorrelated latent factors $\mathbf{g}$, $\mathbf{s}$, and $\mathbf{u}$ are 5×1 with identity variance matrices, while the parameter matrices $\mathbf{A}_1$, $\mathbf{A}_3$, and $\mathbf{A}_0$ are at most lower triangular. (Nonadditive genetic factors are dropped a priori, so $\mathbf{A}_2$ is absent.) An individual is paired with his or her twin, for whom

$$\mathbf{y}' = \mathbf{A}_1\mathbf{g}' + \mathbf{A}_3\mathbf{s}' + \mathbf{A}_0\mathbf{u}'. \tag{10.2}$$

The now familiar assumptions are made about cross-twin correlations among the latent factors. Gaussian maximum-likelihood estimation of the parameter matrices yields a decomposition of the 5×5 variance matrix of $\mathbf{y}$ into its genetic and environmental constituents. This leads Lichtenstein and Pedersen to conclude, for example, that of the 0.17 correlation between perceived support and health among women, 0.15 is due to genetic factors, and 0.02 to nonshared environment.

Following Neale and Cardon (1992, Chapter 12), they refer to their specification as a Cholesky model. Indeed, the recursive structure will be familiar to macroeconomists, but here the ordering of the elements of $\mathbf{y}$ is to some extent arbitrary. Behavior geneticists credit Martin and Eaves (1977) for introducing the idea of multivariate twin modeling. In the same year the economists Behrman, Taubman, and Wales (1977) empirically implemented such a twin model, one with a natural recursive ordering running from education to initial occupation to current occupation to earnings.

11. OBJECTIVES

The stream of human behavior-genetic research tapped here represents structural modeling in several senses: the equations depict causal links rather than mere empirical associations, the regressions among observable variables are derived in terms of more fundamental parameters, and the parameters of interest are not those of the conditional expectation of one observed variable given others. However, the requirement that one of the structural parameters may change while others remain unchanged has not been invoked by the behavior geneticists.

It is fair to ask what the objectives of the behavior-genetic exercises are. Should one be reassured by a finding that broad heritability $\beta_1 + \beta_2$ is estimated robustly? What indeed does one learn from a report that genetic factors account for, say, 50 percent of the variance of a certain trait? It might be argued that to the extent that a trait is heritable, it is not malleable, that is, not subject to change by policy intervention. That argument is incorrect. The geneticist Newton Morton (1974) wrote:

> [O]ne would be quite unjustified in claiming that heritability is relevant to educational strategy. The teacher confronted with a neighborhood in which a substantial fraction of the children appear uneducable by either academic or vocational criteria seems to me like a physical therapist treating a case of poliomelitis: neither need be concerned with the extent to which susceptibility to the observed disorder is genetic.

The geneticist Richard Lewontin (1974) wrote:

> The fallacy is that a knowledge of the heritability of some trait in a population provides an index of the efficacy of environmental or clinical intervention in altering the trait either in individuals or in the population as a whole.

In a review article that does recognize some contributions of the behavior-genetic approach, the developmental psychologist Maccoby (2000) wrote:

> ... high heritability of a trait does not imply that it is not also subject to the influence of environmental factors, or that it cannot be changed by alterations in environmental conditions.

But economists need not go that far afield. After all, the behavior-genetic parameters are effectively R^2s: they measure the proportion of the variation in an observed trait that is accounted for by variation in this or that latent factor. As Cain and Watts (1970) explained years ago, such measures of "importance" are simply not indicators of policy effectiveness. Their argument was applied to the heritability context by Goldberger (1979).

ACKNOWLEDGMENTS

The research reported here derives from joint work with Leon J. Kamin. I am grateful also to Donald Hester and Molly Martin for instructive advice.

APPENDIX

Consider a single locus at which there are two possible alleles $-$ and $+$, so that individuals are either $--$, $-+$, $+-$, or $++$. Let $Z =$ "the score" denote the number of $+$'s an individual has at that locus, so $Z = 0, 1, 2$. For simplicity, suppose that the two alleles are equally prevalent, and that in equilibrium, Prob($Z = 0$) $= 1/4$, Prob($Z = 1$) $= 1/2$, Prob($Z = 2$) $= 1/4$. Assuming that all phenotypic variance is genetic, for each Z there is a phenotype $Y = Y(Z)$, which we can code as

$$Y(0) = -a, \quad Y(1) = b, \quad Y(2) = a.$$

Then $E(Y) = b/2$ and $V(Y) = a^2/2 + b^2/4$. The two terms in V(Y) are the additive and nonadditive genetic variances, respectively. If $b = 0$, Y is linear in Z, the heterozygote's phenotype is halfway between those of the homozygotes: all genetic variance is additive. If $a = 0$, there is no linear component in $Y(Z)$, the two homozygotes' phenotypes are the same: all genetic variance is nonadditive.

Denote the scores of husband, wife, and child by H, W, and S, respectively. It is easy to verify the tabulations of Pr($S \mid H, W$) below, and then $E(Y \mid H, W)$ for the two extreme cases. The final column gives the probabilities for each H–W combination under the assumption of random-mating equilibrium.

H	W	Conditional probabilities $S=0$	$S=1$	$S=2$	Expected phenotypes If $b=0$	If $a=0$	$\Pr(H, W)$
0	0	1	0	0	$-a$	0	1/16
0	1	1/2	1/2	0	$-a/2$	$b/2$	2/16
0	2	0	1	0	0	b	1/16
1	0	1/2	1/2	0	$-a/2$	$b/2$	2/16
1	1	1/4	1/2	1/4	0	$b/2$	4/16
1	2	0	1/2	1/2	$a/2$	$b/2$	2/16
2	0	0	1	0	0	b	1/16
2	1	0	1/2	1/2	$a/2$	$b/2$	2/16
2	2	0	0	1	a	0	1/16

Conditional on H, W, any two (non-MZ) siblings are drawn independently, so across all families, $C(Y, Y')$, the covariance of their phenotypes, is the same as the variance of the subship means.

For the $b = 0$ case, where $E(Y) = 0$ and $V(Y) = a^2/2$, we calculate

$$V[E(Y \mid H, W)] = (a^2/16)(1 + 4/2 + 1) = a^2/4,$$

which is one-half of the additive variance. For the $a = 0$ case, where $E(Y) = b/2$ and $V(Y) = b^2/4$, we calculate

$$E[E^2(Y \mid H, W)] = (b^2/16)(1 + 4/2 + 1 + 1) = b^2(5/16),$$

so

$$V[E(Y \mid H, W)] = b^2(5/16) - (b/2)^2 = b^2/16,$$

which is one-fourth of the nonadditive variance. (A similar calculation will show that parent and child share one-half of the additive variance, and none of the nonadditive variance.)

The same conclusions follow when $Y(Z)$ has both additive and nonadditive components, when allele probabilities are unequal, when there is random variation in Y for given Z, and when multiple loci are introduced; see Falconer and Mackay (1996, Chapter 9). When $Y(Z)$ is not deterministic, then one extreme case has $E(Y \mid Z)$ linear so $\text{BLP}(Y \mid Z) = E(Y \mid Z)$, and the other has $\text{BLP}(Y \mid Z)$ horizontal with $E(Y \mid Z)$ not constant.

References

Ashenfelter, O., and A. Krueger (1994), "Estimates of the Economic Return to Schooling from a New Sample of Twins," *American Economic Review*, 84, 1157–73.

Behrman, J., P. Taubman, and T. Wales (1977), "Controlling for and Measuring the Effects of Genetics and Family Environment in Equations for Schooling and Labor

Market Success," in *Kinometrics: The Determinants of Socio-economic Success Within and Between Families* (ed. by P. Taubman), Amsterdam: North-Holland, 35–96.

Bergeman, C. S., H. M. Chipuer, R. Plomin, N. L. Pedersen, G. E. McClearn, J. R. Nesselroade, P. T. Costa, and R. R. McCrae (1993), "Genetic and Environmental Effects on Openness to Experience, Agreeableness, and Conscientiousness: An Adoption/Twin Study," *Journal of Personality*, 61, 159–79.

Cain, G. G., and H. W. Watts (1970), "Problems in Making Inferences from the Coleman Report," *American Sociological Review*, 35, 228–42.

de Castro, J. M. (1993), "A Twin Study of Genetic and Environmental Influences on Medical and Psychological Traits," *Physiology and Behavior* 54, 677–87.

Falconer, D. S., and T. F. C. Mackay (1996), *Introduction to Quantitative Genetics*, fourth edition, Harlow, Essex: Longman.

Goldberger, A. S. (1979), "Heritability," *Economica*, 46, 327–47.

Goldberger, A. S., and L. J. Kamin (1998), "Behavior-Genetic Modeling of Twins: A Deconstruction," Working Paper 9824, Social Systems Research Institute, University of Wisconsin.

Joseph, J. (1998), "The Equal Environment Assumption of the Classical Twin Method: A Critical Analysis," *Journal of Mind and Behavior*, 19, 325–58.

Kamin, L. J., and A. S. Goldberger (2002), "Twin Studies in Behavioral Research: A Skeptical View," *Theoretical Population Biology*, 61, 83–95.

Kodde, D. A., and F. C. Palm (1986), "Wald Criteria for Jointly Testing Equality and Inequality Restrictions," *Econometrica*, 54, 1243–8.

Lewontin, R. C. (1974), "The Analysis of Variance and the Analysis of Causes," *American Journal of Human Genetics*, 26, 400–11.

Lichtenstein, P., N. L. Pedersen, and G. E. McClearn (1992), "The Origins of Individual Differences in Occupational Status and Educational Level," *Acta Sociologica*, 35, 13–31.

Lichtenstein, P., and N. L. Pedersen (1995), "Social Relationships, Stressful Life Events, and Self-reported Physical Health: Genetic and Environmental Influences," *Psychology and Health*, 10, 295–319.

Loehlin, J. C. (1987), *Latent Variable Models*, Hilldale, NJ: Erlbaum.

Lykken, D. T., W. G. Iacono, K. Haroian, M. McGue, and T. J. Bouchard (1988), "Habituation of the Skin Conductance Response to Strong Stimuli: A Twin Study," *Psychophysiology*, 25, 4–15.

Maccoby, E. E. (2000), "Parenting and Its Effects on Children: On Reading and Misreading Behavior Genetics," *Annual Review of Psychology*, 51, 1–27.

Martin, N. G., and L. J. Eaves (1977), "The Genetical Analysis of Covariance Structure," *Heredity*, 38, 79–95.

Morton, N. E. (1974), "Analysis of Family Resemblance I. Introduction," *American Journal of Human Genetics*, 26, 318–330.

McCourt, K., T. J. Bouchard, D. T. Lykken, A. Tellegen, and M. Keyes (1999), "Authoritarianism Revisited: Genetic and Environmental Influences Examined in Twins Reared Apart and Together," *Personality and Individual Differences*, 27, 985–1014.

Neale, M. C., and L. R. Cardon (1992), *Methodology for Genetic Studies of Twins and Families*, Dordrecht: Kluwer Academic.

Neale, M. C., and M. B. Miller (1997), "The Use of Likelihood-Based Confidence Intervals in Genetic Models," *Behavior Genetics*, 27, 113–20.

Pedersen, N. L., P. Lichtenstein, R. Plomin, U. DeFaire, G. E. McClearn, and K. A. Matthews (1989), "Genetic and Environmental Influences for Type A-Like Measures and Related Traits: A Study of Twins Reared Apart and Twins Reared Together," *Psychosomatic Medicine*, 51, 428–440.

Pedersen, N. L., R. Plomin, G. E. McClearn, and L. Friberg (1988), "Neuroticism, Extraversion, and Related Traits in Adult Twins Reared Apart and Reared Together," *Journal of Personality and Social Psychology*, 55, 950–7.

Pedersen, N. L., R. Plomin, J. T. Nesselroade, and G. E. McClearn (1992), "A Quantitative Genetic Analysis of Cognitive Abilities During the Second Half of the Life Span," *Psychological Science*, 3, 346–53.

Plomin, R., N. L. Pedersen, P. Lichtenstein, and G. E. McClearn (1994), "Variability and Stability in Cognitive Abilities are Largely Genetic Later in Life," *Behavior Genetics*, 24, 207–15.

Rothenberg, T. J. (1972), *Efficient Estimation with A Priori Information*, New Haven, CT: Yale University Press.

Saudino, K. J., N. L. Pedersen, P. Lichtenstein, G. E. McClearn, and R. Plomin (1997), "Can Personality Explain Genetic Influences on Life Events?," *Journal of Personality and Social Psychology*, 72, 196–206.

Wilks, S. S. (1962), Mathematical Statistics, New York: John Wiley and Sons.

Wolak, F. A. (1987), "An Exact Test for Multiple Inequality and Equality Constraints in the Linear Regression Model," *Journal of the American Statistical Association*, 82, 782–93.

CHAPTER 3

Unobserved Heterogeneity and Estimation of Average Partial Effects

Jeffrey M. Wooldridge

ABSTRACT

I study the problem of identifying average partial effects (APEs), which are partial effects averaged across the population distribution of unobserved heterogeneity, under different assumptions. One possibility is that the unobserved heterogeneity is conditionally independent of the observed covariates. When the unobserved heterogeneity is independent of the original covariates, or conditional mean independent but heteroskedastic, the derivations of APEs provide a new view of traditional specification problems in widely used models such as probit and Tobit. In addition, the focus on average partial effects resolves scaling issues that arise in estimating the parameters of probit and Tobit models with endogenous explanatory variables.

1. INTRODUCTION

Econometric models, especially at the individual, family, or firm level, are often specified to depend on unobserved heterogeneity in addition to observable covariates. Models with unobserved heterogeneity are sometimes derived from economic theory; at other times they are based on introspection.

In nonlinear models, much has been made about the deleterious effects that ignoring heterogeneity can have on the estimation of parameters, even when the heterogeneity is assumed to be independent of the observed covariates. A leading case is the probit model with an omitted variable. Yatchew and Griliches (1985) show that when the omitted variable is independent of the explanatory variables and normally distributed, the probit estimators suffer from (asymptotic) attenuation bias. This result is sometimes cited to illustrate how a misspecification that is innocuous in linear models leads to problems in nonlinear models (see, for example, Greene [2000, p. 828]). Discussions of bias caused by omitted heterogeneity in nonlinear models tend to focus on the problems with estimating parameters. In this paper I argue that the focus on parameters is often misguided. Instead, I consider estimating partial effects that are averaged across the distribution of the unobserved heterogeneity.

Rather than the assumption that the unobserved heterogeneity is independent of the observed covariates in the structural conditional expectation, a weaker assumption is that the heterogeneity and covariates are independent conditional on a set of additional controls. In many cases, the additional controls can be viewed as proxy variables for the unobserved heterogeneity. (Sometimes the additional controls are referred to as "control functions," as in Heckman and Robb [1985] and Blundell and Powell [2002].) Conditional independence between unobserved heterogeneity and covariates is often implicit in regression analyses that include many explanatory variables in addition to the key theoretical or policy variables of interest. Conditional independence assumptions have also been used in the treatment effect literature, where they are called "ignorability" assumptions.

Under ignorability assumptions, I show that the quantities of primary interest for empirical analysis – partial effects averaged across the population distribution of any unobserved heterogeneity – are identified by the conditional expectation of the observed response given all observed conditioning variables. While this result is a rather simple application of the law of iterated expectations, it has important practical implications. One special case is where the unobserved heterogeneity is assumed to be independent of the structural covariates – a common assumption in random coefficient and mixture models. In such cases I show that we have tended to focus too much on identification of parameters and not enough on identification of partial effects. The same is true when proxy variables are brought into the analysis.

The basic insights of this paper have been used by others. Chamberlain (1984) shows how to estimate average partial effects in the context of his random effects probit model. Angrist (1991) derives the average treatment effect in a probit model with a single binary, endogenous explanatory variable. Blundell and Powell (2002) study semiparametric estimation of a class of nonlinear models with endogenous explanatory variables. I routinely use the basic results in Wooldridge (2002) for analyzing nonlinear models. Here, I hope to give a systematic treatment that helps to unify the discussion of estimating partial effects for cross-sectional applications. I also provide some new, fairly complicated examples of where average partial effects can be identified and estimated.

The rest of the paper is organized as follows. Section 2 gives some basic results that are applications of the law of iterated expectations. Section 3 shows how the basic results apply to some commonly used parametric models for cross-sectional data, including some interesting extensions. Section 4 considers models with endogenous explanatory variables, of the kind studied by Smith and Blundell (1986), Rivers and Vuong (1988), and Blundell and Powell (2002), among others. I derive scale adjustments that turn estimates from simple two-step procedures into estimates of the parameters indexing the average partial effects, and I show how heteroskedasticity in the conditional heterogeneity distribution is easily handled. Section 5 contains some caveats and concluding thoughts.

2. THE FRAMEWORK AND SOME BASIC RESULTS

It is useful to have a framework for unifying the discussion of partial effects in models with unobserved heterogeneity. Let y be an observed scalar response, let $\mathbf{x}$ be a K-vector of observed explanatory variables taking values in $\mathcal{X}$, and let $\mathbf{q}$ denote a J-vector of unobserved heterogeneity taking values in $\mathcal{Q}$. The random vector $(y, \mathbf{x}, \mathbf{q})$ represents the underlying population. (In many examples, $\mathbf{q}$ is a scalar, but the general setup is no easier in that case.)

The structural expectation of interest is

$$E(y|\mathbf{x}, \mathbf{q}) \equiv \mu_1(\mathbf{x}, \mathbf{q}), \tag{2.1}$$

where $\mu_1(\mathbf{x}, \mathbf{q})$ is the conditional mean function. Because $\mathbf{x}$ is the vector of observed covariates in (2.1), as a shorthand we call $\mathbf{x}$ the "structural covariates." Often, we would model μ_1, parametrically, but that is not required at this level. We are interested in how the x_j affect $E(y|\mathbf{x}, \mathbf{q})$. When x_j is continuous the partial effect is

$$\partial E(y|\mathbf{x}, \mathbf{q})/\partial x_j, \tag{2.2}$$

which, for small changes in x_j, can be multiplied by Δx_j to obtain the approximate change in $E(y|\mathbf{x}, \mathbf{q})$, holding the other elements in $\mathbf{x}$ and $\mathbf{q}$ fixed. If x_j is discrete, we can instead look at the difference in $E(y|\mathbf{x}, \mathbf{q})$ for two different x_j values – such as 1 and 0 when x_j is binary – holding $\mathbf{q}$ and the other elements of $\mathbf{x}$ fixed. We focus on (2.2) for concreteness, but all of the following discussion applies to partial effects based on differences in $E(y|\mathbf{x}, \mathbf{q})$.

Heckman (2001) discusses the notion of a "Marshallian structural function," and (2.1) is in the same spirit. The idea is that economic theory postulates that a response variable depends on observed and unobserved individual factors. In the current notation, Heckman (2001) would write y as a deterministic function of $(\mathbf{x}, \mathbf{q})$, say $y = m(\mathbf{x}, \mathbf{q})$, whereas (2.1) allows for randomness in y even after conditioning on $(\mathbf{x}, \mathbf{q})$. Blundell and Powell (2002) use essentially the same setup as Heckman (2001). Whether one prefers (2.1) or $y = m(\mathbf{x}, \mathbf{q})$ is mostly a matter of taste, as each formulation can be expressed in the other form. Nevertheless, as we will see in Section 3, (2.1) allows us to make direct connections between the notion of average partial effects and more traditional treatments that focus on parameter estimation.

Unless $E(y|\mathbf{x}, \mathbf{q})$ is separable in $\mathbf{x}$ and $\mathbf{q}$, the partial effect in (2.2) depends on $\mathbf{q}$ as well as $\mathbf{x}$. While we can plug in interesting values for the x_j – such as sample averages, medians, quartiles, minimums, maximums, and values representing policy changes – it is less clear what to do about the dependence of (2.2) on $\mathbf{q}$. In parametric models, usually the heterogeneity can be normalized to have a zero mean without loss of generality. Sometimes a different normalization is more convenient, but for concreteness suppose $E(\mathbf{q}) = \mathbf{0}$. Then, we might estimate the effect of x_j by evaluating (2.2) at $\mathbf{q} = \mathbf{0}$.

If $\mathbf{q}$ has a continuous distribution, setting $\mathbf{q} = \mathbf{0}$ may be representative of only a small fraction of the population, a point made by Chamberlain (1984,

p. 1273) in the context of unobserved effects panel data models. [Technically, $P(\mathbf{q} = \mathbf{0}) = 0$ when $\mathbf{q}$ is continuous.] An alternative is to average the partial effect over the distribution of $\mathbf{q}$; that is, we "integrate out" $\mathbf{q}$ in (2.2). This leads to the *average partial effect* (APE) of x_j. To define the APE, let $\boldsymbol{\theta}_j(\mathbf{x}, \mathbf{q})$ be the partial derivative in (2.2) or, for discrete changes, define $\boldsymbol{\theta}_j(\mathbf{x}, \mathbf{q})$ as the difference in $E(y|\mathbf{x}, \mathbf{q})$ at two different values of x_j, holding $\mathbf{q}$ and the other elements of $\mathbf{x}$ fixed. The APE of x_j, evaluated at $\mathbf{x}^\circ$, is

$$\delta_j(\mathbf{x}^\circ) \equiv \int_{\mathcal{Q}} \boldsymbol{\theta}_j(\mathbf{x}^\circ, \mathfrak{q}) f(\mathfrak{q}) \eta(d\mathfrak{q}) \equiv E_{\mathbf{q}}[\boldsymbol{\theta}_j(\mathbf{x}^\circ, \mathbf{q})], \tag{2.3}$$

where $f(\cdot)$ is the density of $\mathbf{q}$, which we take to be absolutely continuous with respect to the σ-finite measure $\eta(\cdot)$. If $\mathbf{q}$ is continuous, $\eta(\cdot)$ can be taken to be Lebesgue measure; if $\mathbf{q}$ is discrete, $\eta(\cdot)$ is counting measure, in which case the integral is a weighted average. These are the leading cases, but heterogeneity distributions with $\mathbf{q}$ neither continuous nor discrete are allowed. We use script variables as dummy arguments in the integration, and $E_{\mathbf{q}}[\cdot]$ denotes expectation with respect to the distribution of $\mathbf{q}$. Given $\mu_1(\cdot, \cdot)$, $f(\cdot)$, and, in the case of (2.2), the assumption that the derivative and integral can be interchanged, $\delta_j(\mathbf{x}^\circ)$ can be computed as a function of $\mathbf{x}^\circ$.

The definition of an average partial effect is implicit in Chamberlain's (1984) treatment of unobserved effects probit panel data models. In the current notation, Blundell and Powell (2002) would write $y = \mu_1(\mathbf{x}, \mathbf{q})$ and then call $E_{\mathbf{q}}[\mu_1(\mathbf{x}^\circ, \mathbf{q})]$ the *average structural function* (ASF). By taking differences of the ASF or derivatives with respect to the elements of $\mathbf{x}$, and assuming the derivative and expectation can be interchanged, we arrive at the APEs. For the remainder of the paper, I assume that partial derivatives and expectations can be interchanged without saying so explicitly. The assumptions under which this interchange is allowed are quite weak; see, for example, Bartle (1966, Corollary 5.9).

In some cases we may want to estimate partial effects averaged over only a subset of the original population. For example, we may specify a wage equation for the population of all working-age adults, but we might want the average partial effect of schooling for those growing up in poverty. Let z denote an observed variable that appropriately stratifies the population. Then the average partial effect for subpopulation z° is

$$\delta_j(\mathbf{x}^\circ, z^\circ) \equiv \int_{\mathcal{Q}} \theta_j(\mathbf{x}^\circ, \mathfrak{q}) f(\mathfrak{q}|z^\circ) \eta(d\mathfrak{q}) \equiv E_{(\mathbf{q}|z=z^\circ)}[\theta_j(\mathbf{x}^\circ, \mathbf{q})], \tag{2.4}$$

where $f(\mathfrak{q}|z^\circ)$ is the density of $\mathbf{q}$ given $z = z^\circ$. For simplicity, we will focus on (2.3).

Heckman (2001) seems to imply that, for policy analysis, we should be interested in estimating $\mu_1(\mathbf{x}, \mathbf{q})$. Unfortunately, $\mu_1(\mathbf{x}, \mathbf{q})$ is often unidentified, and so we could not estimate the structural function even if we had interesting values to plug in for $\mathbf{q}$. We will see examples of how $\mu_1(\mathbf{x}, \mathbf{q})$ is unidentified in the probit and Tobit examples of Section 3. Unless we assume that the unobserved heterogeneity is additively separable in $\mu_1(\mathbf{x}, \mathbf{q})$, we need to confront the twin issues of lack of identification of $\mu_1(\mathbf{x}, \mathbf{q})$ and interesting values to plug in for $\mathbf{q}$. As I show in this paper, the focus on average partial effects often resolves both problems.

Of course, nothing guarantees that the APEs are identified, even if $\mu_1(\mathbf{x}, \mathbf{q})$ is specified parametrically, for two reasons: (1) the relevant parameters in $\mu_1(\mathbf{x}, \mathbf{q})$ may not be identified; and (2) the density of $\mathbf{q}$ might not be known. Often, the APEs are identified if we specify a conditional distribution of $\mathbf{q}$ given some observed covariates, $\mathbf{w}$. The following simple lemma follows by the law of iterated expectations.

Lemma 2.1. *For an L-vector* $\mathbf{w}$ *taking values in* $\mathcal{W}$, *let* $g(\cdot|\mathbf{w})$ *be the conditional density of* $\mathbf{q}$ *given* $\mathbf{w}$ *with respect to a* σ*-finite measure,* $\eta(\cdot)$. *For any* $\mathbf{x}^\circ \in \mathcal{X}$, $\mathbf{w}^\circ \in \mathcal{W}$, *define*

$$\mu_2(\mathbf{x}^\circ, \mathbf{w}^\circ) \equiv \int_{\mathcal{Q}} \mu_1(\mathbf{x}^\circ, \mathfrak{q}) g(\mathfrak{q}|\mathbf{w}^\circ)\eta(d\mathfrak{q}). \tag{2.5}$$

Then

$$E_{\mathbf{q}}[\mu_1(\mathbf{x}^\circ, \mathbf{q})] \equiv E_{\mathbf{w}}[\mu_2(\mathbf{x}^\circ, \mathbf{w})], \tag{2.6}$$

and so APEs can be obtained by taking derivates or changes of $E_{\mathbf{w}}[\mu_2(\mathbf{x}, \mathbf{w})]$ *with respect to the elements of* $\mathbf{x}$, *and inserting* $\mathbf{x}^\circ$ *for* $\mathbf{x}$. *If instead we are interested in the APE for a subpopulation described by* $z = r(\mathbf{w})$ *for some function* $r(\cdot)$, *then we have*

$$E_{(\mathbf{q}|z=z^\circ)}[\mu_1(\mathbf{x}^\circ, \mathbf{q})] = E_{(\mathbf{w}|z=z^\circ)}[\mu_2(\mathbf{x}^\circ, \mathbf{w})]. \tag{2.7}$$

Because the right-hand side of (2.5) is $E[\mu_1(\mathbf{x}^\circ, \mathbf{q})|\mathbf{w} = \mathbf{w}^\circ]$, (2.6) follows directly by iterated expectations, and similarly for (2.7) because $z = r(\mathbf{w})$. At this point, $\mu_2(\mathbf{x}^\circ, \mathbf{w}^\circ)$ is not necessarily the same as $E(y|\mathbf{x} = \mathbf{x}^\circ, \mathbf{w} = \mathbf{w}^\circ)$.

Whether Lemma 2.1 is useful hinges on whether $\mu_2(\cdot, \cdot)$ is identified, and this depends, loosely, on whether enough features of $\mu_1(\cdot, \cdot)$ and $g(\cdot|\cdot)$ are identified. If $\mu_2(\cdot, \cdot)$ is identified, then the right hand side of (2.6) can be consistently estimated by averaging $\hat{\mu}_2(\mathbf{x}^\circ, \mathbf{w}_i)$ across the random sample $i = 1, \ldots, N$, where $\hat{\mu}_2$ is a consistent estimator of $\mu_2(\cdot, \cdot)$. In particular, a consistent estimator of $\hat{\delta}_j(\mathbf{x}^\circ)$ when x_j is continuous is simply

$$\hat{\delta}_j(\mathbf{x}^\circ) = N^{-1} \sum_{i=1}^{N} \partial\hat{\mu}_2(\mathbf{x}^\circ, \mathbf{w}_i)/\partial x_j. \tag{2.8}$$

[Estimation of (2.7) follows by restricting the average to those i with $z_i = z^\circ$. Consistency is straightforward provided $P(z = z^\circ) > 0$.] When x_j is discrete, or we simply want to estimate the discrete difference at two different values, say $x_j^{(1)}$ and $x_j^{(0)}$, we use

$$\hat{\delta}_j(\mathbf{x}^\circ) = N^{-1} \sum_{i=1}^{N} \left[\hat{\mu}_2 \left(x_j^{(1)}, \mathbf{x}_{(j)}^\circ, \mathbf{w}_i \right) - \hat{\mu}_2 \left(x_j^{(0)}, \mathbf{x}_{(j)}^\circ, \mathbf{w}_i \right) \right], \qquad (2.9)$$

where $\mathbf{x}_{(j)}^\circ$ denotes fixed values of the other elements of $\mathbf{x}$.

Nothing prevents us from choosing $\mathbf{w} = \mathbf{x}$ in stating Lemma 2.1. However, with $\mathbf{w} = \mathbf{x}$ and $\mathbf{q}$ and $\mathbf{x}$ dependent, we will not be able to identify APEs unless the dependence is restricted in some way. (Section 3 covers probit and Tobit models when the scalar heterogeneity, q, has zero mean conditional on $\mathbf{x}$ but a conditional variance that depends on $\mathbf{x}$. In this case, the APEs are shown to be identified.) Wooldridge (2004) effectively uses Lemma 2.1 to identify APEs in nonlinear, dynamic unobserved effects panel data models once a distribution for the unobserved heterogeneity, given the initial condition and a set of strictly exogenous covariates, has been specified. Wooldridge (2002, Chapters 15, 16) uses Lemma 2.1 to estimate APEs in unobserved effects probit and Tobit panel data models.

In many cases, we want to apply Lemma 2.1 when $\mathbf{w}$ and $\mathbf{x}$ can vary freely. Provided we make ignorability assumptions about the structural expectation and the conditional distribution of heterogeneity, we can identify the APEs by identifying $E(y|\mathbf{x}, \mathbf{w})$. The first assumption is that $\mathbf{w}$ is appropriately excluded from the structural mean.

Assumption A.1. *The L-vector* $\mathbf{w}$ *is redundant, or ignorable, in* (2.1):

$$E(y|\mathbf{x}, \mathbf{q}, \mathbf{w}) = E(y|\mathbf{x}, \mathbf{q}). \qquad (2.10)$$

In cross-sectional settings, Assumption A.1 is not especially controversial because any element in $\mathbf{w}$ that we think belongs in the structural expectation should be included in $\mathbf{x}$ as well. Assumption A.1 simply allows for the fact that we have observed variables that are properly omitted from a structural equation that contains unobserved heterogeneity. For example, suppose that y is earnings, $\mathbf{x}$ is schooling, and $\mathbf{q}$ is innate ability. Suppose that $\mathbf{w}$ contains outcomes on cognitive tests. Then (2.10) simply means that *if* we could control for "ability," the test scores (such as IQ) would not be helpful in explaining average earnings. This exclusion restriction essentially holds by the definition of "ability."

The second assumption is ignorability of $\mathbf{x}$ in the distribution of $\mathbf{q}$ given $(\mathbf{x}, \mathbf{w})$:

Assumption A.2. *Conditional on* $\mathbf{w}$, $\mathbf{q}$ *and* $\mathbf{x}$ *are independent:* $D(\mathbf{q}|\mathbf{x}, \mathbf{w}) = D(\mathbf{q}|\mathbf{w})$, *where* $D(\cdot|\cdot)$ *denotes conditional distribution.*

Assumption A.2 is typically much more restrictive than Assumption A.1. If $\mathbf{w}$ is closely related to $\mathbf{q}$, Assumption A.2 is often reasonable. As we will see in Section 4, Assumption A.2 can apply to models where we need instrumental variables for one or more endogenous explanatory variables. Then, $\mathbf{w}$ is a set of reduced-form errors and $\mathbf{x}$ contains endogenous explanatory variables correlated with $\mathbf{q}$.

Assumption A.2 has been called "selection on observables" in the econometrics literature because $\mathbf{q}$ is not dependent on $\mathbf{x}$ once we control for $\mathbf{w}$. (See, for example, Heckman and Robb [1985].) In the treatment effect literature, Assumption A.2 is the "igorability of treatment" assumption, where $\mathbf{x}$ is the vector of treatments, $\mathbf{q}$ contains the counterfactual outcomes on y, and $\mathbf{w}$ is a set of observed controls.

For special forms of $\mu_1(\mathbf{x}, \mathbf{q})$, Assumption A.2 can be relaxed; sometimes a conditional mean independence assumption suffices. But to handle general nonlinear models we need full conditional independence. The following lemma is simple but fundamental.

Lemma 2.2. *Define $\mu_2(\mathbf{x}^\circ, \mathbf{w}^\circ)$ as in Equation* (2.5). *Then, under Assumptions* A.1 *and* A.2,

$$\mu_2(\mathbf{x}^\circ, \mathbf{w}^\circ) = E(y|\mathbf{x} = \mathbf{x}^\circ, \mathbf{w} = \mathbf{w}^\circ) \tag{2.11}$$

for $\mathbf{x}^\circ \in \mathcal{X}, \mathbf{w}^\circ \in \mathcal{W}$. Therefore, if $E(y|\mathbf{x}, \mathbf{w})$ is identified, so are the average partial effects with respect to $\mathbf{x}$.

Proof. The law of iterated expectations implies that

$$\begin{aligned} E(y|\mathbf{x}, \mathbf{w}) &= E[E(y|\mathbf{x}, \mathbf{q}, \mathbf{w})|\mathbf{x}, \mathbf{w}] \\ &= E[\mu_1(\mathbf{x}, \mathbf{q})|\mathbf{x}, \mathbf{w}] &\quad (2.12) \\ &= \int_{\mathcal{Q}} \mu_1(\mathbf{x}, \mathfrak{q}) g(\mathfrak{q}|\mathbf{w}) \eta(d\mathfrak{q}) &\quad (2.13) \end{aligned}$$

where (2.12) follows from Assumption A.1 [$E(y|\mathbf{x}, \mathbf{q}, \mathbf{w})$ does not depend on $\mathbf{w}$] and (2.13) follows from A.2 [$D(\mathbf{q}|\mathbf{x}, \mathbf{w})$ does not depend on $\mathbf{x}$]. But (2.13) with $\mathbf{x} = \mathbf{x}^\circ$ and $\mathbf{w} = \mathbf{w}^\circ$ is simply (2.5). ■

If $E(y|\mathbf{x}, \mathbf{w})$ is identified, usually it can be consistently estimated given a random sample on $(y, \mathbf{x}, \mathbf{w})$ from the population, which means that we have a consistent estimator $\hat{\mu}_2(\mathbf{x}, \mathbf{w})$ of $\mu_2(\mathbf{x}, \mathbf{w})$ for all $\mathbf{x}$ and $\mathbf{w}$. Then we can estimate $\delta_j(\mathbf{x}^\circ)$ generally as in (2.8) or (2.9). In some of the examples we cover in Sections 3 and 4, we will have a parametric distribution for $\mathbf{w}$, and so we can compute $E_{\mathbf{w}}[\mu_2(\mathbf{x}^\circ, \mathbf{w})]$ as a function of parameters and then take derivatives or changes with respect to the elements in $\mathbf{x}^\circ$.

One way to view Lemma 2.2 is that it says, under the ignorability Assumptions A.1 and A.2, we should simply estimate $E(y|\mathbf{x}, \mathbf{w})$, compute the partial derivative or discrete change of interest with respect to elements of $\mathbf{x}$, and either average across the population distribution of $\mathbf{w}$ or average $E(y|\mathbf{x}, \mathbf{w} = \mathbf{w}_i)$ across the sample. For estimating (2.7), we just average $E(y|\mathbf{x}, \mathbf{w} = \mathbf{w}_i)$ across the subsample with $z_i = z^\circ$. We need never explicitly account for unobserved heterogeneity: all quantities of interest are obtained from $E(y|\mathbf{x}, \mathbf{w})$.

In light of Lemma 2.2, one might wonder what all the fuss about unobserved heterogeneity is, if one is willing to make the ignorability assumptions A.1 and A.2. Indeed, one branch of the treatment effect literature is based on estimating expectations of the form $E(y|x, \mathbf{w})$, where x is a binary treatment and $\mathbf{w}$ is a set of controls that might be needed to control for self-selection into treatment. The conclusion of Lemma 2.2 is that, regardless of an underlying "structural" response model that contains unobserved heterogeneity, we should simply estimate $E(y|x, \mathbf{w})$ for $x = 1$ and $x = 0$, and then average the difference, $[\hat{E}(y|1, \mathbf{w}_i) - \hat{E}(y|0, \mathbf{w}_i)]$, across the sample. The resulting estimator is a well-known estimate of the average treatment effect. (See, for example, Heckman, Ichimura, and Todd [1997], Hahn [1998], and Wooldridge [2002, Section 18.3].)

The claim that it is sufficient to focus on $E(y|\mathbf{x}, \mathbf{w})$, without any reference to $E(y|\mathbf{x}, \mathbf{q})$, can be questioned when the focus is on "structural" parameters that are needed for general policy analysis; see, for example, Heckman (2001). Still, as I mentioned above, there is a general issue of identifiabilty of $E(y|\mathbf{x}, \mathbf{q})$ along with the distribution of $\mathbf{q}$, whether or not these features change when applied to a new population. In the next section I show how Lemmas 2.1 and 2.2 can be applied to several common parametric models with unobserved effects. The basic message is that if we insist on specifying models of $E(y|\mathbf{x}, \mathbf{q})$, we still must be careful in interpreting the parameters, and in making claims about "biases" caused by neglected heterogeneity.

As a corollary to Lemma 2.2, we have the case when $\mathbf{q}$ is independent of $\mathbf{x}$, which is a common assumption in nonlinear models with unobserved heterogeneity. We replace Assumption A.2 with

Assumption A.2′. $\mathbf{q}$ *is independent of* $\mathbf{x}$.

Corollary 2.1. *Under Assumption* A.2′,

$$E_{\mathbf{q}}[\mu_1(\mathbf{x}^\circ, \mathbf{q})] = E(y|\mathbf{x} = \mathbf{x}^\circ).$$

Therefore, average partial effects are obtained directly from $E(y|\mathbf{x})$.

Corollary 2.1 follows from Lemma 2.2 by taking $\mathbf{w}$ to be empty. Note that Assumption A.1 has no content when $\mathbf{q}$ and $\mathbf{x}$ are independent because then A.1 simply defines $\mu_1(\mathbf{x}, \mathbf{q}) \equiv E(y|\mathbf{x}, \mathbf{q})$.

Many cross-sectional models, and panel data models, assume that unobserved heterogeneity is independent of the observed covariates. A large class of mixture models for all kinds of responses typically assume that the heterogeneity is independent of the covariates. One way to interpret Corollary 2.1 is that complicated ways of modeling unobserved heterogeneity is largely a waste of time: if we are just going to assume that the heterogeneity is independent of the covariates, and if we are interested in average partial effects of the observed covariates on mean responses, it suffices to focus on flexible ways of modeling $E(y|\mathbf{x})$ and forget about $\mathbf{q}$.

The conclusions of Lemmas 2.1 and 2.2, and Corollary 2.1, clearly hold if we replace $E(y|\mathbf{x}, \mathbf{q})$ with $E[g(y)|\mathbf{x}, \mathbf{q}]$ for any known function $g(\cdot)$. Sometimes we are interested in higher moments of y, or conditional probabilities of the form $P(y \in A|\mathbf{x}, \mathbf{q})$. The latter can be written as $E[g(y)|\mathbf{x}, \mathbf{q}]$ by taking $g(y) = 1[y \in A]$, where $1[\cdot]$ is the indicator function.

3. APPLICATION TO SOME POPULAR CROSS-SECTIONAL PARAMETRIC MODELS

I now provide several examples that illustrate the usefulness of the simple results from Section 2. Throughout this section the unobserved heterogeneity, q, is a scalar.

3.1. Random Coefficient Model

Let x be a scalar and let $\mathbf{w}$ be a $1 \times L$ vector. Consider a structural model linear in parameters, but where the structural covariate of interest, x, interacts with unobserved heterogeneity:

$$E(y|x, q, \mathbf{w}) = \eta + \beta x + q + \gamma x \cdot q. \tag{3.1}$$

We can think of x as a variable whose effect is predicted by an economic theory, or as a key policy variable. Without loss of generality, the coefficient on q is normalized at unity and $E(q) = 0$. The partial effect of x on $E(y|x, q)$ is $\partial E(y|x, q)/\partial x = \beta + \gamma q$. Therefore, the APE of x is $\beta + \gamma E(q) = \beta$. Importantly, β is the APE with respect to x regardless of any correlation between q and x.

To identify β, we assume that

$$E(q|x, \mathbf{w}) = E(q|\mathbf{w}), \tag{3.2}$$

which is a conditional mean independence version of Assumption A.2. Assumption (3.2) is the so-called "selection on observables" assumption in the random coefficient context, and it is implicit in studies that put many controls in $\mathbf{w}$ in order to estimate the causal effect of x. Under (3.1) and (3.2),

$$\begin{aligned} E(y|x, \mathbf{w}) &= \alpha + \beta x + E(q|\mathbf{w}) + \gamma x \cdot E(q|\mathbf{w}) \\ &= \alpha + \beta x + \psi(\mathbf{w}) + \gamma x \cdot \psi(\mathbf{w}), \end{aligned} \tag{3.3}$$

where $\psi(\mathbf{w}) \equiv E(q|\mathbf{w})$. If we knew $\psi(\cdot)$ we could estimate β from a regression that includes x, $\psi(\mathbf{w})$, and the interaction between x and $\psi(\mathbf{w})$. In the linear case, $\psi(\mathbf{w}) = (\mathbf{w} - \boldsymbol{\xi})\delta$ where $\boldsymbol{\xi} = E(\mathbf{w})$. [Demeaning $\mathbf{w}$ ensures that $E[\psi(\mathbf{w})] = 0$, which must hold because $E(q) = 0$.] In practice, we would replace $\boldsymbol{\xi}$ with $\bar{\mathbf{w}}$, the sample mean, and run the OLS regression

$$y_i \text{ on } 1, x_i, \mathbf{w}_i, x_i(\mathbf{w}_i - \bar{\mathbf{w}}), \qquad i = 1, \ldots, N; \tag{3.4}$$

the coefficient on x_i, say $\hat{\beta}$, is a consistent, asymptotically normal estimator of β. The focus on the APE implies that we should demean the extra covariates, $\mathbf{w}_i$, before interacting them with x_i.

Equation (3.3) suggests the possibility that β can be estimated using a semiparametric method, that is, without imposing a parametric form on $\psi(\cdot)$. Certainly, we can always approximate $\psi(\mathbf{w})$ using various series expansions, being sure to demean each term so that the coefficient on x_i keeps its APE interpretation. Robinson (1988) considers the case without the interaction term and shows how to use kernel methods to estimate the relevant conditional expectations. It would be useful to extend Robinson's method to (3.3), using the interactive nature of the additional term $x \cdot \psi(\mathbf{w})$ and the restriction $E[\psi(\mathbf{w})] = 0$.

When x is a binary variable and we explicitly consider the counterfactual framework in Rosenbaum and Rubin (1983), we are led immediately to a standard estimator of the average treatment effect. First, we estimate $E(y|x = 1, \mathbf{w})$ and $E(y|x = 0, \mathbf{w})$ by flexible methods, which could be nonparametric or parametric with good approximating properties. If $\hat{m}_1(\mathbf{w})$ and $\hat{m}_0(\mathbf{w})$ denote such estimates, then the average treatment effect is estimated as $\hat{\beta} \equiv N^{-1} \sum_{i=1}^{N} [\hat{m}_1(\mathbf{w}_i) - \hat{m}_0(\mathbf{w}_i)]$.

3.2. Probit Model

We now consider the structural probit model

$$P(y = 1|\mathbf{x}, q, \mathbf{w}) = \Phi(\alpha + \mathbf{x}\beta + q) = E(y|\mathbf{x}, q), \tag{3.5}$$

where Φ is the standard normal cumulative distribution function and the coefficient on q is normalized at unity without loss of generality. The vector $\mathbf{x}$ is $1 \times K$ and $\mathbf{w}$ is $1 \times L$; by assumption, $\mathbf{w}$ is redundant in (3.5) once $\mathbf{x}$ and q have been included. Yatchew and Griliches (1985) assume that q and $\mathbf{x}$ are independent, where q has a normal distributed with zero mean. We allow for a weaker ignorability assumption:

$$q|\mathbf{x}, \mathbf{w} \sim \text{Normal}\,(\eta + \mathbf{w}\boldsymbol{\delta}, \tau^2). \tag{3.6}$$

Because Assumptions A.1 and A.2 are satisfied, we can use Lemma 2.2 to compute the APE of each x_j. First, we need to find $E(y|\mathbf{x}, \mathbf{w}) = P(y = 1|\mathbf{x}, \mathbf{w})$. We can show that this follows a probit model by writing $y = 1[\lambda + \mathbf{x}\beta + \mathbf{w}\delta + a + u \geq 0]$, where $\lambda = \alpha + \eta$, $a = q - (\eta + \mathbf{w}\boldsymbol{\delta})$, and $u|(\mathbf{x}, \mathbf{w}, a) \sim \text{Normal}\,(0, 1)$. Because $a|(\mathbf{x}, \mathbf{w}) \sim \text{Normal}(0, \tau^2)$, it follows that $a + u$ is independent of $(\mathbf{x}, \mathbf{w})$ and distributed as Normal $(0, \tau^2 + 1)$. Therefore,

$$P(y = 1|\mathbf{x}, \mathbf{w}) = \Phi\left[(\lambda + \mathbf{x}\beta + \mathbf{w}\boldsymbol{\delta})/(1 + \tau^2)^{1/2}\right], \tag{3.7}$$

and the partial derivative with respect to x_j is

$$\left[\beta_j/(1 + \tau^2)^{1/2}\right]\phi(\mathbf{z}\boldsymbol{\theta}), \tag{3.8}$$

where $\phi(\cdot)$ is the standard normal density function, $\mathbf{z} = (1, \mathbf{x}, \mathbf{w})$, and $\boldsymbol{\theta} = (\lambda, \boldsymbol{\beta}', \boldsymbol{\delta}')'/(1 + \tau^2)^{1/2}$. From Lemma 2.2 it follows immediately that the APE of x_j is the average of (3.8) across the distribution of $\mathbf{w}$.

From (3.7) we can also read off the plims from a probit of y on 1, $\mathbf{x}$, $\mathbf{w}$. In particular, if $\hat{\theta}_j$ is the coefficient on x_j, then

$$\text{plim}\, \hat{\theta}_j = \beta_j/(1 + \tau^2)^{1/2} = \theta_j. \tag{3.9}$$

Equation (3.9) implies an attenuation bias in estimating the β_j. This bias is also present when we drop $\mathbf{w}$ and assume that q and $\mathbf{x}$ are independent, a fact that has been cited as a serious problem in omitting unobserved heterogeneity in probit models. But why are the β_j of interest? Rarely do the magnitudes of the parameters in the underlying latent variable model have meaning; only the effects of the x_j on the response probability have quantitative meaning. For obtaining the directions and relative magnitudes of the effects, the scaled parameters $\beta_j/(1 + \tau^2)^{1/2}$ are just as informative as the β_j.

One reason to be interested in the β_j is that they appear directly in the structural partial effects evaluated at $q = 0$:

$$\partial P(y = 1|\mathbf{x}, q = 0)/\partial x_j = \beta_j \phi(\alpha + \mathbf{x}\boldsymbol{\beta}). \tag{3.10}$$

However, as we discussed in Section 2, (3.10) applies only to a small part of the population, and plugging in any other value of q is arbitrary, as q rarely has known units of measurement. But there is another subtle point about attenuation bias that seems to have gone unnoticed. Even if we claim we are interested in (3.10), it is not obvious for what values of $\mathbf{x}$ unobserved heterogeneity causes an attenuation bias. To see this, drop $\mathbf{w}$ and assume that q and $\mathbf{x}$ are independent. The average partial effect, which we consistently estimate from probit of y on $(1, \mathbf{x})$, is

$$\left[\beta_j/(1 + \tau^2)^{1/2}\right] \phi\left[(\alpha + \mathbf{x}\boldsymbol{\beta})/(1 + \tau^2)^{1/2}\right]. \tag{3.11}$$

Now, while $\theta_j = \beta_j/(1 + \tau^2)^{1/2}$ is attenuated toward zero compared with β_j, the bias works in the opposite direction in the second term because $\phi[\cdot]$ is symmetric about zero and reaches its maximum at zero, and $|(\alpha + \mathbf{x}\boldsymbol{\beta})/(1 + \tau^2)^{1/2}| < |\alpha + \mathbf{x}\boldsymbol{\beta}|$. Without knowing α, $\boldsymbol{\beta}$, τ^2, and a particular value of $\mathbf{x}$, we cannot know which is greater in magnitude, (3.10) or (3.11). (And remember, α, $\boldsymbol{\beta}$, and τ^2 are not separately identified.)

A related point involves comparing estimated coefficients on the covariates of interest, $\mathbf{x}$, across studies that use different control variables. It is quite common to see several studies address the same policy question using different sets of controls. Let $\mathbf{w}_1$ and $\mathbf{w}_2$ denote different proxy variables such that (3.5) and (3.6) are both assumed when $\mathbf{w}$ is replaced with $\mathbf{w}_1$ or $\mathbf{w}_2$ [with appropriate subscripts in (3.6)]. Then, for the coefficient on x_j, the probability limits of the MLEs in the two cases are $\beta_j/(1 + \tau_1^2)^{1/2}$ and $\beta_j/(1 + \tau_2^2)^{1/2}$, respectively. While it makes sense to compare signs and relative effects, it makes no sense to use the magnitudes of the estimates to argue that controlling for $\mathbf{w}_1$ versus

$\mathbf{w}_2$ makes the effect of x_j more or less important. One should compute average partial effects by averaging out $\mathbf{w}_1$ and $\mathbf{w}_2$.

My view is that the so-called attenuation bias from neglected heterogeneity is a *good* thing: we want to estimate $\boldsymbol{\beta}/(1+\tau^2)^{1/2}$ because this is exactly the parameter vector that appears in the APEs. In particular, for a continuous x_j, the APE evaluated at $\mathbf{x}^\circ$ is estimated as

$$\hat{\theta}_j \left(N^{-1} \sum_{i=1}^{N} \phi(\hat{\theta}_0 + \mathbf{x}^\circ \hat{\boldsymbol{\theta}}_1 + \mathbf{w}_i \hat{\boldsymbol{\theta}}_2) \right), \tag{3.12}$$

where the estimates are from probit of y_i on $(1, \mathbf{x}_i, \mathbf{w}_i)$. A similar expression holds for discrete changes in x_j.

What if we claim to be interested in $(\alpha, \boldsymbol{\beta})$ in the structural equation (3.5) because we want to evaluate the effects of a policy on a new population, as described in Heckman (2001)? Assume that (3.5) holds for the new population as well as the old. Then, because $(\alpha, \boldsymbol{\beta})$ is not identified, we cannot estimate the partial effects on $P(y = 1|\mathbf{x}, q)$; this has nothing to do with whether the distribution of q is the same in the new population. (However, we would still face the issue of interesting values to plug in for q in the new population.) At least we can consistently estimate the average partial effects under the assumption that the distribution of q has not changed. Unfortunately, if, say, the variance of q is different in the new population – say, ψ^2 – then we cannot estimate the APEs for the new population because we only have estimates of $\boldsymbol{\beta}/(1+\tau^2)^{1/2}$, not $\boldsymbol{\beta}/(1+\psi^2)^{1/2}$.

In cases where the magnitudes of the β_j are clearly of interest – in particular, where the probit model arises from data censoring – it turns out that ignoring the heterogeneity *still* does not have any harmful effects. A leading case is estimating willingness-to-pay functions using survey data. Suppose we assume an underlying classical linear model,

$$y^* = \alpha + \mathbf{x}\boldsymbol{\beta} + q + u$$
$$u|\mathbf{x}, q, \mathbf{w} \sim \text{Normal}\,(0, \sigma^2),$$

where y^* is unobserved willingness to pay. Now we are interested in $E(y^*|\mathbf{x}, q)$. We also assume (3.6). Then

$$y^* = \lambda + \mathbf{x}\boldsymbol{\beta} + \mathbf{w}\boldsymbol{\delta} + a + u \equiv \mathbf{z}\boldsymbol{\gamma} + v,$$

where $\mathbf{z} = (1, \mathbf{x}, \mathbf{w})$ and $v = a + u$. Let i denote a random draw from the population. Each individual i is presented with a cost, c_i, of the project or good. Usually, c_i is generated to be independent of all other factors, or, at least, of a_i and u_i. Individual i approves of the project if $y_1^* \geq c_i$. Let $y_i = 1[y_i^* \geq c_i]$ denote the observed binary response (accept or reject). Then

$$\begin{aligned} P(y_i = 1|\mathbf{x}_i, \mathbf{w}_i, c_i) &= P(\mathbf{z}_i\boldsymbol{\gamma} + v_i \geq c_i|\mathbf{z}_i, c_i) \\ &= P[v_i/\omega \geq -\mathbf{z}_i(\boldsymbol{\gamma}/\omega) + (1/\omega)c_i] \\ &= \Phi[\mathbf{z}_i(\boldsymbol{\gamma}/\omega) - (1/\omega)c_i], \end{aligned} \tag{3.13}$$

where $\omega^2 = \tau^2 + \sigma^2 = \text{Var}(v_i)$. Equation (3.13) shows that γ and ω are identified and can be consistently estimated by maximum likelihood. In particular, the β_j are identified. While τ^2 and σ^2 are not separately identified, this is irrelevant for estimating the partial effects of interest, the β_j.

The derivations in this example lead me to one conclusion: there is no reason to fret about the effects of unobserved heterogeneity in probit models when the heterogeneity and structural covariates satisfy a conditional independence assumption, and the heterogeneity is conditionally normally distributed. A corollary is that if q and $\mathbf{x}$ are independent, we should not worry about the effects of unobserved heterogeneity.

Of course, the previous discussion presupposes that assumptions (3.5) and (3.6) hold. If either assumption fails, $P(y = 1|\mathbf{x}, \mathbf{w})$ does not have the probit form in (3.7). For example, if we keep (3.6) but start with a logit model in (3.5), α, $\boldsymbol{\beta}$, and τ^2 would be identified, and we could estimate $\partial P(y = 1|\mathbf{x}, q)$ at different values of q. Or, if we keep (3.5) but change (3.6), α and $\boldsymbol{\beta}$, and the parameters in the distribution of q, could be identified. But this means we would be getting identification of α and $\boldsymbol{\beta}$ by excluding the leading case in (3.5) and (3.6). By contrast, if we focus on APEs, all we have to do is estimate $P(y = 1|\mathbf{x}, \mathbf{w})$. So why not model this probability directly? It is not very difficult to specify and estimate models that are more flexible than probit and logit models without being wedded to a particular form of unobserved heterogeneity.

If q and $\mathbf{x}$ cannot be made conditionally independent, identification of APEs is much more tenuous. Still, under assumptions that restrict the dependence between q and $\mathbf{x}$, the APEs can be identified by applying Lemma 2.1. To illustrate this point, we assume

$$E(y|\mathbf{x}, q) = \Phi(\alpha + \mathbf{x}\boldsymbol{\beta} + q), \tag{3.14}$$

where q has zero mean and variance τ^2. If q is independent of $\mathbf{x}$ and normally distributed, we just saw that probit of y on $(1, \mathbf{x})$ consistently estimates the average partial effects. Whether or not q and $\mathbf{x}$ are independent, if x_j is continuous, the APE of x_j at $\mathbf{x}^\circ$ in (3.14) is

$$\beta_j E_q[\phi(\alpha + \mathbf{x}^\circ\beta + q)], \tag{3.15}$$

which can be estimated only if we have consistent estimators of α, $\boldsymbol{\beta}$, and the distribution of q. Even though we cannot estimate (3.15) in general, Equation (3.15) has an important implication: if we can estimate the β_j consistently up to a common, nonzero scale factor, then the relative effects of the continuous variables on the APEs can be found. [In fact, we can replace $\Phi(\cdot)$ in (3.14) with an unknown function.] Manski (1975, 1985) and Horowitz (1992) show how to estimate coefficients up to a common scale under a zero conditional median assumption, which would apply to the composite error underlying (3.14). In particular, q and $\mathbf{x}$ need not be independent. Estimation of even the relative APEs for discrete x_j does not seem possible unless we know more, although the signs of the APEs can be estimated using Manski's approach.

Under what additional assumptions can we estimate the APEs when q and $\mathbf{x}$ are dependent? Certainly, we cannot allow general dependence. For example, if we assume that q given $\mathbf{x}$ has a conditional normal distribution, say $q|\mathbf{x} \sim$ Normal $(\eta + \mathbf{x}\boldsymbol{\delta}, \omega^2)$, then only $(\boldsymbol{\beta} + \boldsymbol{\delta})/(1 + \omega^2)^{1/2}$ is identified without additional information. This is an example of the usual kind of endogeneity problem encountered in econometric models, linear or nonlinear. We study estimation of these models in Section 4. But suppose we assume that the dependence between q and $\mathbf{x}$ is only in the conditional variance, and not the conditional mean:

$$q|\mathbf{x} \sim \text{Normal}\,[0, \exp(\mathbf{x}\boldsymbol{\delta})]. \tag{3.16}$$

Interestingly, Assumption (3.16), along with (3.14), is enough to identify the APEs. To see why, we apply Lemma 2.1 with $\mathbf{w} = \mathbf{x}$. For fixed $\mathbf{x}^\circ$, we first need to find $E[\Phi(\alpha + \mathbf{x}^\circ\boldsymbol{\beta} + q)|\mathbf{x}]$. If we let u denote the standard normal random variable underlying (3.14), which is independent of $(q, \mathbf{x})$, then $\Phi(\alpha + \mathbf{x}^\circ\boldsymbol{\beta} + q) = E[1(\alpha + \mathbf{x}^\circ\boldsymbol{\beta} + q + u \geq 0)|q, \mathbf{x}]$, where $1(\cdot)$ is the indicator function. By iterated expectations, $E[\Phi(\alpha + \mathbf{x}^\circ\boldsymbol{\beta} + q)|\mathbf{x}] = E[1(\alpha + \mathbf{x}^\circ\boldsymbol{\beta} + q + u \geq 0)|\mathbf{x}] = P\{(q + u)/[1 + \exp(\mathbf{x}\boldsymbol{\delta})]^{1/2} \geq -(\alpha + \mathbf{x}^\circ\boldsymbol{\beta})/[1 + \exp(\mathbf{x}\boldsymbol{\delta})]^{1/2}\}$. Therefore,

$$E[\Phi(\alpha + \mathbf{x}^\circ\boldsymbol{\beta} + q)|\mathbf{x}] = \Phi\left\{(\alpha + \mathbf{x}^\circ\boldsymbol{\beta})/[1 + \exp(\mathbf{x}\boldsymbol{\delta})]^{1/2}\right\} \tag{3.17}$$

Provided α, $\boldsymbol{\beta}$, and $\boldsymbol{\delta}$ can be consistently estimated – they can be, as we show below – the APEs are consistently estimated by taking derivatives, or changes, with respect to $\mathbf{x}^\circ$ in

$$N^{-1}\sum_{i=1}^{N}\Phi\left\{(\hat{\alpha} + \mathbf{x}^\circ\hat{\boldsymbol{\beta}})/[1 + \exp(\mathbf{x}_i\hat{\boldsymbol{\delta}})]^{1/2}\right\}. \tag{3.18}$$

Notice the different roles played by $\mathbf{x}^\circ$ and $\mathbf{x}_i$. The vector $\mathbf{x}^\circ$ multiplies $\hat{\boldsymbol{\beta}}$, whereas $\mathbf{x}_i$ appears in the variance function. The $\mathbf{x}_i$ are averaged out, whereas we compute changes or derivatives with respect to $\mathbf{x}^\circ$. Letting $h(\mathbf{x}, \boldsymbol{\delta}) \equiv 1 + \exp(\mathbf{x}\boldsymbol{\delta})$ and taking the derivative with respect to x_j° shows that the APE for a continuous variable, evaluated at $\mathbf{x}^\circ$, is estimated as

$$\hat{\beta}_j\left(N^{-1}\sum_{i=1}^{N}[1/h(\mathbf{x}_i\hat{\boldsymbol{\delta}})]\phi[(\hat{\alpha} + \mathbf{x}^\circ\hat{\boldsymbol{\beta}})/h(\mathbf{x}_i\hat{\boldsymbol{\delta}})]\right). \tag{3.19}$$

The scale factor needed to turn $\hat{\beta}_j$ into an APE can be easily estimated in this context. APEs defined as discrete changes are also easy to estimate.

Why are the parameters in (3.17) identified? The reason is simple. Under (3.14) and (3.16),

$$P(y = 1|\mathbf{x}) = \Phi[(\alpha + \mathbf{x}\boldsymbol{\beta})/h(\mathbf{x}\boldsymbol{\delta})], \tag{3.20}$$

and, given the form of the variance function, α, $\boldsymbol{\beta}$, and $\boldsymbol{\delta}$ are identified and can be consistently estimated by maximum likelihood.

Equations (3.17) and (3.20) reveal something curious about this example. While the response probability, conditional only on $\mathbf{x}$, has the same form as

Equation (3.17), the average partial effects are *not* obtained by differentiating (3.20) with respect to $\mathbf{x}$.

The peculiar feature that the APEs are not obtained by differentiating (3.20) with respect to $\mathbf{x}$ hinges on the specification of $E(y|\mathbf{x}, q)$ and, just as importantly, on the special way that q and $\mathbf{x}$ are allowed to be dependent. If, instead, $q|\mathbf{x} \sim$ Normal $(\eta + \mathbf{x}\delta, \omega^2)$ – so that the conditional mean of q depends on $\mathbf{x}$, rather than just the conditional variance – then the APEs are not identified, let alone obtainable from estimating the model for $P(y = 1|\mathbf{x})$.

A linear example may help. Suppose that, for a scalar, continuous variable x, $E(y|x, q) = \alpha + \beta x + q$, so that the APE with respect to x is simply β. If $E(q|\mathbf{x}) = \eta + \delta x$, then β is not identified; only $\beta + \delta$ is. But suppose $E(q|\mathbf{x}) = \eta + \delta x^2$. Then $E(y|x) = (\alpha + \eta) + \beta x + \delta x^2$, and so β is identified from the population regression $E(y|x)$. But the APE of x is not obtained by taking the derivative of $E(y|x)$.

It is difficult to envision a researcher running a regression of y on 1, x, and x^2, but then reporting the coefficient on x as the relevant partial effect. This simple example is a reminder that one cannot distinguish omitted heterogeneity from a misspecified functional form in the observable covariates. The same is true in the probit example. While (3.19) is the appropriate APE under (3.14) and (3.16), the response probability in (3.20) is indistinguishable from $P(y = 1|\mathbf{x})$ obtained from the model

$$P(y = 1|\mathbf{x}, q) = \Phi[\alpha + \mathbf{x}\beta + \exp(\mathbf{x}\delta/2)q] \tag{3.21}$$

$$q|\mathbf{x} \sim \text{Normal } (0, 1). \tag{3.22}$$

Since q is independent of $\mathbf{x}$, under (3.21) and (3.22) it follows from Lemma 2.2 that the APEs are computed by taking derivatives of, or changes in, (3.20), which is the common way of obtaining partial effects in heteroskedastic probit models. We might claim to prefer (3.19) because (3.14) seems more appealing than (3.21) as a way of introducing unobserved heterogeneity. [In addition, (3.19) has the simplifying feature that the signs of the APEs are the same as the signs of the $\hat{\beta}_j$.] Still, (3.21) is a way to allow observed and unobserved heterogeneity to have an interaction effect inside $\Phi(\cdot)$, a feature that can hardly be labeled bizarre. Unfortunately, we cannot settle the issue statistically because both models lead to the same form of $P(y = 1|\mathbf{x})$: fundamentally, we lack the identification of the APEs. Rather, we must take a stand on how the observed covariates and unobserved heterogeneity enter the probit function, as well as on whether we think unobserved heterogeneity should be assumed to be independent of the observed covariates. This is not a promising state of affairs, especially given that the average partial effects computed in the two different ways can differ in sign as well as magnitude. [Notice that this is not just an issue with the APEs; the same is true of the unaveraged partial effects based on $P(y = 1|\mathbf{x}, q)$.]

A few more comments are in order before we leave this example. First, the same conclusions follow if we start with the more standard binary response formulation $y = 1[\alpha + \mathbf{x}\beta + q \geq 0]$, so that all unobservables are lumped into q. Then, if q satisfies (3.16), we obtain a probit model with standard exponential heteroskedasticity. The APEs are computed as in (3.19) but with $h(\mathbf{x}_i\hat{\delta}) = \exp(\mathbf{x}_i\hat{\delta})$. Second, if we specify a different distribution for $q|\mathbf{x}$, given by a density $g(\cdot|\mathbf{x})$, we would still obtain the APEs by integrating $\Phi(\alpha + \mathbf{x}^{\circ}\beta + q)$ against $g(q|\mathbf{x})$. Provided the parameters are identified, the APEs are identified, and are easily estimated by generalizing (3.18). A third point is that the formulation in (3.14) applies to more than just binary responses. In particular, y could be a fractional response taking any value in [0, 1]. The estimation method, maximizing the Bernoulli log-likelihood with the probit response function, is a consistent and $\sqrt{N}$-asymptotically normal estimator. [See, for example, Gourieroux, Monfort and Trognon (1984), Papke and Wooldridge (1996).]

3.3. Tobit Model

For the basic Tobit model, the literature appears to be silent on the consequences of unobserved heterogeneity that satisfies an assumption like (3.6). I think this is partly a case of getting the right answer for the wrong reason. Recall that Tobit models are applied to two conceptually different problems. One application is to data censoring, where an underlying response variable satisfies the classical linear model but is censored because of data collection methods or institutional constraints. As in the willingness-to-pay probit example, interest centers unambiguously on the coefficients β_j in $E(y^*|\mathbf{x})$. It is easy to see that unobserved heterogeneity satisfying (3.6) causes no problems in estimating β. But here my interest is in a more common application of Tobit models: the response we are interested in, y, has a population distribution that piles up at zero, but is roughly continuously distributed over strictly positive values. [In Wooldridge (2000, 2002) I call such responses *corner solution outcomes*.] Then, we are interested in conditional means involving y, and these are nonlinear functions of $E(y^*|\mathbf{x}) = \alpha + \mathbf{x}\beta$ and $\text{Var}(y^*|\mathbf{x}) = \sigma^2$. So how does the presence of unobserved heterogeneity affect estimation of the quantities of interest in corner solution applications? While the argument is a little more subtle, the conclusions are very similar to the probit case: we cannot identify the partial effects evaluated at the average heterogeneity, but we can identify the partial effects averaged across the distribution of heterogeneity.

Write the Tobit model with unobserved heterogeneity as

$$y = \max(0, \alpha + \mathbf{x}\beta + q + u) \tag{3.23}$$

$$u|\mathbf{x}, q, \mathbf{w} \sim \text{Normal}\ (0, \sigma^2). \tag{3.24}$$

Here we have in mind cases where y is not a censored variable but, rather, a corner solution outcome. Often, we are interested in $E(y|\mathbf{x}, q)$, which depends on the parameters α, β, and σ^2. (See, for example, Wooldridge [2000a, Section 17.2].) Since $E(q) = 0$, we might evaluate the expectations at $q = 0$. But even if we assume (3.6) – as we now do – σ^2 is not identified, and therefore, nor is $E(y|\mathbf{x}, q)$ for any value of q. But the average partial effects are identified, as we now show.

Under (3.23), (3.24), and (3.6), we have

$$\begin{aligned} y &= \max(0, \lambda + \mathbf{x}\boldsymbol{\beta} + \mathbf{w}\boldsymbol{\delta} + a + u) \\ &\equiv \max(0, \lambda + \mathbf{x}\boldsymbol{\beta} + \mathbf{w}\boldsymbol{\delta} + v), \end{aligned} \tag{3.25}$$

where λ, a, and v are defined as in the probit case. Under the assumptions made, $v|(\mathbf{x}, \mathbf{w}) \sim$ Normal $(0, \omega^2)$, where $\omega^2 = \tau^2 + \sigma^2$. It follows immediately that Tobit of y on $(1, \mathbf{x}, \mathbf{w})$ consistently estimates λ, $\boldsymbol{\beta}$, $\boldsymbol{\delta}$, and ω^2. For data censoring, this is fine, as $\boldsymbol{\beta}$ is the vector of interest, and we can compute the appropriate asymptotic variance by estimating ω^2. But for corner solution outcomes, we might initially worry about our inability to estimate σ^2 and, therefore, $\partial E(y|\mathbf{x}, q)/\partial x_j$. Nevertheless, Lemma 2.2 implies that $\partial E(y|\mathbf{x}, q)/\partial x_j$, averaged across the distribution of $q|\mathbf{w}$, is exactly the conditional mean function we estimate from Tobit of y on $(1, \mathbf{x}, \mathbf{w})$. To get the APEs, we estimate λ, $\boldsymbol{\beta}$, $\boldsymbol{\delta}$, and ω^2, apply the usual formula for the partial effects in a Tobit model, and then average across $\mathbf{w}_i$. More precisely, for $z \in \mathbb{R}$ and $s > 0$, define

$$m(z, s) \equiv \Phi(z/s)z + s\phi(z/s). \tag{3.26}$$

Then the APEs are estimated from

$$N^{-1} \sum_{i=1}^{N} m(\hat{\lambda} + \mathbf{x}^{\circ}\hat{\boldsymbol{\beta}} + \mathbf{w}_i\hat{\boldsymbol{\delta}}, \hat{\omega}), \tag{3.27}$$

where all estimates are the Tobit MLEs. Therefore, our initial reaction that we may safely ignore the heterogeneity is correct, but for the wrong reason: we are not only interested in $\boldsymbol{\beta}$, but we obtain consistent estimators of the APEs by ignoring the heterogeneity.

If we drop $\mathbf{w}$ but introduce heteroskedasticity into Var($q|\mathbf{x}$), as in the probit example, the conclusions are very similar. In particular, the parameters indexing the APEs are generally identified from the distribution of y given $\mathbf{x}$, and can be consistently estimated by conditional maximum likelihood. However, the APEs are not obtained from differentiating or differencing $E(y|\mathbf{x})$. Instead, they would be obtained from

$$N^{-1} \sum_{i=1}^{N} m\left\{\hat{\alpha} + \mathbf{x}^{\circ}\hat{\boldsymbol{\beta}}, [h(\mathbf{x}_i, \hat{\boldsymbol{\theta}})]^{1/2}\right\}, \tag{3.28}$$

where $h(\mathbf{x}, \boldsymbol{\theta})$ is the model for Var($q + u|\mathbf{x}$), for example, $h(\mathbf{x}_i, \boldsymbol{\theta}) = \sigma^2[1 + \exp(\mathbf{x}\boldsymbol{\delta})]$.

4. APPLICATION TO MODELS WITH ENDOGENOUS EXPLANATORY VARIABLES

I now turn to some examples of models where instrumental variables assumptions are needed to identify the average partial effects. Blundell and Powell

(2002) cover semiparametric and nonparametric approaches, and so some of the results in this section are subsumed by their work. Here, I focus on flexible parametric models and the adjustments needed to turn parameter estimates from common two-step procedures, and some interesting extensions, into estimates of the APEs. Lemmas 2.1 and 2.2 still apply once we properly define the vectors $\mathbf{x}$ and $\mathbf{w}$.

4.1. Random Coefficient Model

I now consider the random coefficient model but where instrumental variables are needed for at least one covariate. A general model is

$$E(y_1|\mathbf{z}, y_2, q_1) = \alpha_1 + \mathbf{x}_1\boldsymbol{\beta}_1 + a_1 + b_1\mathbf{x}_1\boldsymbol{\gamma}_1, \tag{4.1}$$

where a_1 and b_1 are the unobserved heterogeneity and $\mathbf{x}_1$ is a $1 \times K_1$ vector function of exogenous variables, $\mathbf{z}_1$, and endogenous variable, y_2: $\mathbf{x}_1 = \mathbf{f}_1(\mathbf{z}_1, y_2)$. The leading case is $\mathbf{x}_1 = (\mathbf{z}_1, y_2)$, but general nonlinear functions are allowed. The parameters are α_1, $\boldsymbol{\beta}_1$, and $\boldsymbol{\gamma}_1$. We assume, without loss of generality, that $E(a_1) = E(b_1) = 0$, so that $\boldsymbol{\beta}_1$ indexes the average partial effects. Notice that (4.1) assumes that some elements of $\mathbf{z}$, those in $\mathbf{z}_2$, are excluded from (4.1). If $\mathbf{z}_1$ is $1 \times M_1$ and $\mathbf{z}$ is $1 \times M$, then we should have, at a minimum, the order condition for identification: $M > M_1$.

For a strictly monotonic function $h(y_2)$ defined on the support of y_2, we assume a linear reduced form for $h(y_2)$ in the conditional expectations sense:

$$h(y_2) = \mathbf{z}\boldsymbol{\delta}_2 + v_2 \tag{4.2}$$

$$E(v_2|\mathbf{z}) = 0. \tag{4.3}$$

These assumptions imply that $E[h(y_2)|\mathbf{z}] = \mathbf{z}\boldsymbol{\delta}_2$, which is not a trivial restriction because it means that we can transform the endogenous explanatory variable so that it has a linear conditional mean given the exogenous variables. The idea is that we might want y_2 to appear linearly, or perhaps as a quadratic, in the structural equation, but we think a priori that linearity of $E(y_2|\mathbf{z})$ might not be a reasonable assumption. If y_2 is a continuous variable with large support, we might just take $h(y_2) = y_2$. But if y_2 is a fraction in the open unit interval, we might take h to be $h(y_2) = \log[y_2/(1 - y_2)]$; this can transform a fractional variable into one that takes on unbounded positive and negative values, and therefore might roughly have a conditional expectation linear in parameters. For a strictly positive, unbounded endogenous explanatory variable, we might use the logarithmic transformation. Because $h(\cdot)$ is an invertible function, we can write $y_2 = h^{-1}(\mathbf{z}\boldsymbol{\delta}_2 + v_2)$, which means that y_2 is a well-defined function of $(\mathbf{z}, v_2)$. If y_2 has discrete characteristics, (4.2) and (4.3) rule out common models, such as logit, probit, Tobit, and count data models.

To estimate the parameters, we need to make further assumptions about the distribution of (a_1, b_1, v_2) conditional on $\mathbf{z}$. We extend an approach due to Garen (1984), who assumes that (a_1, b_1, v_2) is multivariate normal and independent of $\mathbf{z}$. A weaker set of assumptions is

$$E(a_1|v_2, \mathbf{z}) = (\eta_1 + \mathbf{z}\boldsymbol{\lambda}_1)v_2 \tag{4.4}$$

$$E(b_1|v_2, \mathbf{z}) = (\xi_1 + \mathbf{z}\psi_1)v_2. \tag{4.5}$$

Assumptions (4.4) and (4.5) assume that, given $\mathbf{z}$, the expectations of a_1 and b_1, given v_2, are linear in v_2. [Assumptions (4.3), (4.4), and (4.5) imply that $E(a_1|\mathbf{z}) = E(b_1|\mathbf{z}) = 0$ by iterated expectations.] Relaxing these assumptions to allow for polynomials or higher powers in v_2 is, as we will see, straightforward. In Garen (1984), Wooldridge (1997a), and Heckman and Vytlacil (1998), $\boldsymbol{\lambda}_1 = \mathbf{0}$ and $\psi_1 = \mathbf{0}$. Allowing the exogenous variables to interact with v_2 may be important in practice. For example, Card (2001) discusses why this generality might be necessary in a wage function where y_2 is years of schooling and z is a binary variable that shifts the schooling supply function. While it may be reasonable to assume $E(a_1|z) = E(b_1|z) = 0$ along with $E(v_2|z) = 0$, Card (2001) shows, in an economic model of education choice, that the joint distribution of (a_1, b_1, v_2) given z can depend on z because of heteroskedasticity in the 3×3 conditional variance–covariance matrix $\text{Var}(a_1, b_1, v_2|z)$. Generally, assumptions (4.3), (4.4), and (4.5) can hold when $\text{Var}(a_1, b_1, v_2|\mathbf{z})$ depends on $\mathbf{z}$. With a change in notation, one can replace the linear functions in $\mathbf{z}$ with general functions that are linear in parameters.

To obtain an estimating equation, we take the expectation of Equation (4.1) with respect to $(\mathbf{z}, v_2)$, use the fact that y_2 is a deterministic function of $(\mathbf{z}, v_2)$, and use (4.4) and (4.5):

$$E(y_1|\mathbf{z}, v_2) = \alpha_1 + \mathbf{x}_1\beta_1 + (\eta_1 + \mathbf{z}\boldsymbol{\lambda}_1)v_2 + (\xi_1 + \mathbf{z}\psi_1)v_2\mathbf{x}_1\gamma_1. \tag{4.6}$$

If we multiply all of the interaction terms, we see that the expectation involves linear functions in $(\mathbf{x}_1, v_2)$, interactions in $\mathbf{z}$ and v_2, interactions in $\mathbf{x}_1$ and v_2, and interactions between $\mathbf{z}$ and $\mathbf{x}_1 v_2$. (The last set of interactions contains $M \cdot K_1$ terms.) Importantly, the elements of $\mathbf{z}_2$ – the instrumental variables excluded from the structural model (4.1) – neither show up in linear form nor interact with just the elements of $\mathbf{x}_1$. If we allowed either of these, we would lose identification unless we made tenuous functional form assumptions. The exclusion of $\mathbf{z}_2$ along with the interactions $z_{2j}\mathbf{x}_1$ is implied by the exclusion restriction in (4.1) *and* the way in which $\mathbf{z}$ is allowed to appear in (4.4) and (4.5).

A two-step method that consistently estimates all of the parameters in (4.6) is fairly clear:

1. Run the OLS regression of
$$h(y_{i2}) \text{ on } \mathbf{z}_i, \qquad i = 1, \ldots, N \tag{4.7}$$
and save the residuals, $\hat{v}_{i2}, i = 1, \ldots, N$.
2. Run the OLS regression
$$y_{i1} \text{ on } 1, \mathbf{x}_{i1}, \hat{v}_{i2}, \mathbf{z}_i\hat{v}_{i2}, \mathbf{x}_{i1}\hat{v}_{i2}, \text{vec}[(\mathbf{z}_i \otimes \mathbf{x}_{i1})]'\hat{v}_{i2}, \qquad i = 1, \ldots, N. \tag{4.8}$$

to obtain $\hat{\alpha}_1$, $\hat{\beta}_1$, and the other parameter estimates. The term $\text{vec}[(\mathbf{z}_i \otimes \mathbf{x}_{i1})]'$ simply denotes all possible interactions between $\mathbf{z}_i$ and $\mathbf{x}_{i1}$. With large M and K_1, one might be selective about which to include.

In step 2, we are interested in the coefficient estimates on $\mathbf{x}_{i1}$, $\hat{\beta}_1$, particularly those involving y_2. In the case of a model with just an additive, linear term in y_2, we simply want the coefficient on y_2. But we might have a quadratic in y_2, or we might have y_2 interacted with the elements of $\mathbf{z}_1$. In any case, the estimation procedure is unchanged.

A practical problem with (4.8) is that the standard errors, and joint test statistics, should be adjusted for the first-stage estimation of $\boldsymbol{\delta}_2$ in the reduced form of $h(y_2)$. Newey and McFadden (1994) contains a general discussion about how these adjustments can be made. The simplest approach might be to stack the first-order conditions for the two estimation problems and use the formulas for generalized method of moments.

Adding polynomials in $\hat{v}_2$, interacted with the elements in $\mathbf{z}$ and $\mathbf{x}_1$, poses no difficulties, except that it further complicates standard errors and reduces degrees of freedom. If we replace y_2 with $\mathbf{y}_2$, a $1 \times G_1$ vector, then v_2 is replaced with the $1 \times G_1$ vector $\mathbf{v}_2$. (We would assume, at a minimum, that $M - M_1 \geq G_1$.) Then, we must run G_1 reduced form regressions, $h_j(y_{i2j})$ on $\mathbf{z}_1, i = 1, \ldots, N$, and collect these in the residuals $\hat{\mathbf{v}}_{i2}$. (Each h_j should be a strictly monotonic transformation of the corresponding endogenous explanatory variable.) Regression (4.8) would become

$$\begin{aligned} &y_{i1} \text{ on } 1, \mathbf{x}_{i1}, \hat{\mathbf{v}}_{i2}, \ \text{vec}[(\mathbf{z}_1 \otimes \hat{\mathbf{v}}_{i2})]', \\ &\text{vec}\ [(\mathbf{x}_{i1} \otimes \hat{\mathbf{v}}_{i2})]', \ \text{vec}\{\text{vec}[(\mathbf{z}_i \otimes \mathbf{x}_{i1})]' \otimes \hat{\mathbf{v}}_{i2}\}', \qquad i = 1, \ldots, N. \end{aligned}$$

The notation is a bit daunting and the mechanics are tedious, but the idea is conceptually straightforward. We simply include $\mathbf{x}_{i1}$, the G_1 reduced form residuals $\hat{\mathbf{v}}_{i2}$, and each reduced form residual interacted with all elements of $\{\mathbf{z}_i, \mathbf{x}_{i1}, \text{vec}[(\mathbf{z}_i \otimes \mathbf{x}_{i1})]'\}$. Even for moderate M and G_1, a large sample size might be needed to make this approach practical.

4.2. Probit Response Function

We consider a model where y_1 has a conditional expectation that follows a probit model. This is applicable to the binary response case, but, as mentioned at the end of Section 3.2, it can also be applied when y_1 is a fractional response that may take on the extreme values of 0 and 1. (Examples include cases when y_1 is the fraction of pension assets invested in the stock market and the fraction of students in a class passing a standardized exam.) The probit conditional mean function keeps all predicted values in the unit interval, and, as in Section 3.2, is very convenient for identifying APEs. Wooldridge (2002) covers the standard model where the index is linear in the single endogenous explanatory variable. Here we allow for a vector of endogenous explanatory variables that may need to be transformed to satisfy a conditional normality assumption.

The structural expectation is

$$E(y_1|\mathbf{z}, \mathbf{y}_2, q_1) = E(y_1|\mathbf{z}_1, \mathbf{y}_2, q_1) = \Phi(\alpha_1 + \mathbf{x}_1\boldsymbol{\beta}_1 + q_1), \tag{4.9}$$

where $\mathbf{x}_1 \equiv \mathbf{f}_1(\mathbf{z}_1, \mathbf{y}_2)$, $\mathbf{y}_2$ is the vector of G_1 endogenous explanatory variables, $\mathbf{z}$ is the $1 \times M$ vector of all exogenous variables, and q_1 is the unobserved heterogeneity. As in Section 4.1, the function $\mathbf{f}_1(\cdot)$ is assumed to be known, with the leading case $\mathbf{f}_1(\mathbf{z}_1, \mathbf{y}_2) = (\mathbf{z}_1, \mathbf{y}_2)$. Because of the intercept inside the probit function, we can assume that $E(q_1) = 0$ without loss of generality. In fact, we make the strong assumption that $q_1 \sim \text{Normal}(0, \sigma_1^2)$. While q_1 is assumed to be independent of $\mathbf{z}$, it is allowed to be correlated with all elements of $\mathbf{y}_2$. Unless $\mathbf{f}_1$ depends on $\mathbf{y}_2$ in a restrictive fashion, we need at least G_1 elements in $\mathbf{z}$ that are not also in $\mathbf{z}_1$.

Under the normality assumption for q_1, the average partial effects in (4.9) with respect to the elements of $(\mathbf{z}_1, \mathbf{y}_2)$ are indexed by the vector $\boldsymbol{\beta}_1/(1 + \sigma_1^2)^{1/2}$, something that follows directly from Section 3.2. Without further assumptions, the APEs are not identified. We add the assumption that monotonic transformations of each y_{2j} can be found so that a linear reduced form with additive, normal disturbances can be found. (This is more restrictive than in Section 4.1, where we simply required a linear conditional expectation.) Let $h_j(\cdot)$, $j = 1, \ldots, G_1$, denote strictly monotonic transformations, and define $\mathbf{h}(\mathbf{y}_2) \equiv [h_1(y_{21}), \ldots, h_{G_1}(y_{2G_1})]$. Then we assume

$$\mathbf{h}(\mathbf{y}_2) = \mathbf{z}\Delta_2 + \mathbf{v}_2, \quad \mathbf{v}_2|\mathbf{z} \sim \text{Normal}(0, \Sigma_2), \tag{4.10}$$

where $\boldsymbol{\Delta}_2$ is an $M \times G_1$ matrix and Σ_2 is a $G_1 \times G_1$ positive definite matrix. [In (4.10) we assume that $\mathbf{z}$ includes an intercept.]

Under joint normality of $(q_1, \mathbf{v}_2)$, with independence from $\mathbf{z}$, we can write

$$q_1 = \mathbf{v}_2\gamma_1 + e_1 \tag{4.11}$$

where $\gamma_1 = \Sigma_2^{-1}E(\mathbf{v}_2'q_1)$, so that e_1 is independent of $(\mathbf{z}, \mathbf{v}_2)$ with a Normal $(0, \sigma_1^2 - \gamma_1'\Sigma_2\gamma_1)$ distribution. (The vector $\mathbf{y}_2$ is exogenous if and only if $\gamma_1 = \mathbf{0}$.) A simple two-step estimation approach follows Smith and Blundell (1986) and Rivers and Vuong (1988), with the extension that we are generally applying a conditional quasi-MLE unless y_1 is binary. Using the assumptions we have made,

$$E(y_1|\mathbf{z}, \mathbf{y}_2, \mathbf{v}_2) = \Phi\left[(\mathbf{x}_1\boldsymbol{\beta}_1 + \mathbf{v}_2\gamma_1)/(1 + \eta_1^2)^{1/2}\right], \tag{4.12}$$

where $\eta_1^2 = \text{Var}(e_1) = \sigma_1^2 - \gamma_1'\Sigma_2\gamma_1 \leq \sigma_1^2$. [That $\mathbf{h}(\cdot)$ in (4.10) is invertible ensures that $\text{D}(e_1|\mathbf{z}, \mathbf{y}_2, \mathbf{v}_2) = \text{D}(e_1|\mathbf{z}, \mathbf{v}_2)$ because $\mathbf{y}_2$ is a function of $(\mathbf{z}, \mathbf{v}_2)$.] The parameters that are identified from (4.12) (assuming, for the moment, that we know $\mathbf{v}_2$), are $\boldsymbol{\beta}_{\eta 1} \equiv \boldsymbol{\beta}_1/(1 + \eta_1^2)^{1/2}$ and $\gamma_{\eta 1} \equiv \gamma_1/(1 + \eta_1^2)^{1/2}$. The following two-step procedure is justified by standard two-step estimation results and the fact that the Bernoulli log-likelihood is in the linear exponential family (see Gourieroux et al. [1984]; Papke and Wooldridge [1996]):

1. For $j = 1, \ldots, G_1$, run the OLS regression

$$h_j(y_{i2j}) \text{ on } \mathbf{z}_i, \qquad i = 1, \ldots, N \tag{4.13}$$

and save the residuals, $\hat{v}_{i2j}, i = 1, \ldots, N$. Put these into $1 \times G_1$ vectors $\hat{\mathbf{v}}_{i2}, i = 1, \ldots, N$. [Alternatively, use SUR estimation on the system (4.10), which is algebraically identical to OLS equation by equation.]

2. Use the Bernoulli quasi–log-likelihood function and do "probit" of

$$y_{i1} \text{ on } \mathbf{x}_{i1}, \hat{\mathbf{v}}_{i2}, \qquad i = 1, \ldots, N \tag{4.14}$$

to obtain $\hat{\beta}_{\eta 1}$ and $\hat{\gamma}_{\eta 1}$.

If $\gamma_1 \neq \mathbf{0}$, the asymptotic variance matrix from step 2 needs to be adjusted for the first-stage estimation of $\boldsymbol{\delta}_2$ (see, for example, Newey and McFadden [1994].) If $\gamma_1 = \mathbf{0}$ – as occurs under the null hypothesis that $\mathbf{y}_2$ is exogenous – first-stage estimation of Δ_2 can be ignored, but the variance matrix estimator should have the Huber–White "sandwich" form unless y_1 is a binary response. See, for example, Papke and Wooldridge (1996) for the specific formulas for the Bernoulli case.

The main question is: How can we turn the estimates from the second-stage estimation into parameter estimates that index the APEs? This is potentially important because, when $\gamma_1 \neq \mathbf{0}$, $\boldsymbol{\eta}_1^2 < \boldsymbol{\sigma}_1^2$. Focusing on the parameter estimates from the second-stage probit can lead us to overestimate the importance of the explanatory variables (although, of course, the relative effects are unaffected). It is somewhat common to compare the parameter estimates from a probit that assumes exogeneity of $\mathbf{y}_2$ with those from a two-step procedure. But the magnitudes are not directly comparable because of the rescaling that occurs when adding $\hat{\mathbf{v}}_{i2}$ to the probit. (Evidently, whether we underestimate or overestimate the partial effects depends on the values of $(\mathbf{z}_1, \mathbf{y}_2)$ that we plug in.) Moreover, in order to compare the nonlinear probit model that accounts for endogeneity with those from a linear probability model estimated by two-stage least squares, we need to estimate the APEs.

Fortunately, it is very easy to adjust $\hat{\beta}_{\eta 1}$ to obtain estimates of $\beta_{\sigma 1} = \beta/(1 + \sigma_1^2)^{1/2}$. One possibility is to simply apply Lemma 2.2 with $\mathbf{x} \equiv (\mathbf{z}_1, \mathbf{y}_2)$, $q \equiv q_1$, and $\mathbf{w} \equiv \mathbf{v}_2$. First, Assumption A.1 holds because $\mathbf{v}_2$ is a function of $(\mathbf{z}, \mathbf{y}_2)$, and so $E(y_1|\mathbf{z}, \mathbf{y}_2, q_1, \mathbf{v}_2) = E(y_1|\mathbf{z}, \mathbf{y}_2, q_1)$. Second, Assumption A.2 holds because $\mathbf{y}_2$ is a function of $(\mathbf{z}, \mathbf{v}_2)$ and $(q_1, \mathbf{v}_2)$ is independent of $\mathbf{z}$: $E(q_1|\mathbf{z}, \mathbf{y}_2, \mathbf{v}_2) = E(q_1|\mathbf{z}, \mathbf{v}_2) = E(q_1|\mathbf{v}_2)$. It now follows from Lemma 2.2 that the APEs with respect to $(\mathbf{z}_1, \mathbf{y}_2)$ are obtained from

$$E_{\mathbf{v}_2}[\Phi(\mathbf{x}_1^\circ \beta_{\eta 1} + \mathbf{v}_2 \gamma_{\eta 1})], \tag{4.15}$$

where $\mathbf{x}_1^\circ$ is nonrandom and the expectation is over the distribution of $\mathbf{v}_2$. Write the function inside the expectation as $\mathrm{r}(\mathbf{v}_2)$. Then $\mathrm{r}(\mathbf{v}_2) = E[\mathrm{s}(\mathbf{v}_2, a_1)|\mathbf{v}_2]$, where $\mathrm{s}(\mathbf{v}_2, a_1) = 1(\mathbf{x}_1^\circ \beta_{\eta 1} + \mathbf{v}_2 \gamma_{\eta 1} + a_1 \geq 0)$ and a_1 is independent of $\mathbf{v}_2$, with a standard normal distribution. By iterated expectations, $E[\mathrm{r}(\mathbf{v}_2)] = E[\mathrm{s}(\mathbf{v}_2, a_1)]$, where the latter expectation is over the distribution of $(\mathbf{v}_2, a_1)$. But $\mathbf{v}_2\gamma_{\eta 1} + a_1 \sim \text{Normal}(0, 1 + \gamma'_{\eta 1}\Sigma_2\gamma_{\eta 1})$, and so $E[1(\mathbf{x}_1^\circ\beta_{\eta 1} + \mathbf{v}_2\gamma_{\eta 1} + a_1 \geq 0)] = \Phi[(\mathbf{x}_1\beta_{\eta 1}/(1 + \gamma'_{\eta 1}\Sigma_2\gamma_{\eta 1})^{1/2}]$. Therefore, we have shown that (4.15) equals

$$\Phi\left[(\mathbf{x}_1^\circ\beta_{\eta 1}/(1 + \gamma'_{\eta 1}\Sigma_2\gamma_{\eta 1})^{1/2}\right] \qquad (4.16)$$

We already have obtained $\hat{\beta}_{\eta 1}$ and $\hat{\gamma}_{\eta 1}$ from (4.14). We estimate Σ_2 from the G_1 sets of reduced form residuals: $\hat{\Sigma}_2 = N^{-1}\sum_{i=1}^{N}\hat{\mathbf{v}}'_{i2}\hat{\mathbf{v}}_{i2}$. A SUR routine would report $\hat{\Sigma}_2$ routinely. Then, we simply divide each element of $\hat{\beta}_{\eta 1}$ by $(1 + \hat{\gamma}'_{\eta 1}\hat{\Sigma}_2\hat{\gamma}_{\eta 1})^{1/2}$ to obtain the parameter estimates used in obtaining estimated APEs.

An alternative approach, which does not exploit the normality of $\mathbf{v}_2$, is to directly use the sample analog of (4.15):

$$N^{-1}\sum_{i=1}^{N}\Phi(\mathbf{x}_1^\circ\hat{\beta}_{\eta 1} + \hat{\mathbf{v}}_{i2}\hat{\gamma}_{\eta 1}). \qquad (4.17)$$

This kind of estimate is used by Blundell and Powell (2002) in semiparametric contexts. If all of the assumptions are correct, (4.16) and (4.17) should yield similar estimates of the APEs.

As in Section 3.2, the derivations here have implications for comparing estimates across studies that use different sets of IVs. Different IVs imply different error variances for $\mathbf{v}_2$, which means that different scale factors are implicit in the IV estimation. Once we focus on APEs, the effects obtained from different IV estimates are comparable.

As exploited by Blundell and Powell (2002), the focus on APEs is liberating in the sense that much more flexible methods for estimating $E(y_1|\mathbf{x}_1, \mathbf{v}_2)$ are possible. A simple parametric extension would be to allow q_1 given $\mathbf{v}_2$ to have normal distribution with a mean that is polynomial in $\mathbf{v}_2$ and possibly heteroskedastic, too. (Then, unconditional normality of q_1 would be unrealistic, but that might be tolerable since we often specify conditional, rather than unconditional, normal distributions.) If we also specify an exponential function for the heteroskedasticity, we would add a low-order polynomial in $\hat{\mathbf{v}}_2$ to the quasi-probit in Equation (4.14) and also allow exponential heteroskedasticity in $\hat{\mathbf{v}}_2$ (or a polynomial in $\hat{\mathbf{v}}_2$). The APEs would be estimated from the analog of (4.17). For example, with scalar y_2, we might put a quadratic in $\hat{v}_2$ in the mean and allow $\text{Var}(q_1|v_2) = \exp(\theta_2 v_2)$. The estimated APEs would come from

$$N^{-1}\sum_{i=1}^{N}\Phi\left\{\left(\mathbf{x}_1^\circ\hat{\beta}_1 + \hat{\gamma}_1\hat{v}_{i2} + \hat{\rho}_1\left(\hat{v}_{i2}^2 - \hat{\sigma}_2^2\right)\right)/[1 + \exp(\hat{\theta}_2\hat{v}_{i2})]^{1/2}\right\},$$

where the estimates denote the quasi-MLEs from the two-step heteroskedastic probit and the scaling is now implicit. While analytical standard errors would be cumbersome to compute, simulation methods should be tractable.

The possibility of allowing heteroskedasticity in $\text{Var}(q_1|\mathbf{v}_2)$ suggests a simple extension that allows a test of the assumption that q_1 and $\mathbf{x}_1$ are independent, conditional on $\mathbf{v}_2$. For example, we could specify a variance function $\text{Var}(q_1|\mathbf{v}_2, \mathbf{x}_1) = \exp(\mathbf{v}_2\boldsymbol{\theta}_{21} + \mathbf{x}_1\boldsymbol{\theta}_{22})$ in the probit model and test $\boldsymbol{\theta}_{22} = \mathbf{0}$. This produces a test of conditional independence even if we do not have overidentification in the usual sense.

4.3. Tobit Model

Obtaining APEs after two-step estimation of a Tobit model with an endogenous explanatory variable is also simple. Along with (4.10), write

$$y_1 = \max[0, \mathbf{f}_1(\mathbf{z}_1, \mathbf{y}_2)\boldsymbol{\beta}_1 + q_1], \tag{4.18}$$

where $(q_1, \mathbf{v}_2)$ is independent of $\mathbf{z}$ with a zero mean normal distribution. Define e_1 as in (4.9), where $\sigma_1^2 = \text{Var}(q_1)$, $\Sigma_2 = \text{Var}(\mathbf{v}_2)$, and $\boldsymbol{\gamma}_1 = \Sigma_2^{-1}E(\mathbf{v}_2'q_1)$.

For estimating APEs, we need the function $m(\mathbf{x}_1^\circ\boldsymbol{\beta}_1, \sigma_1)$, where the function $m(\cdot,\cdot)$ is defined in Equation (3.26). The Smith–Blundell (1986) approach is to write

$$y_1 = \max(0, \mathbf{x}_1\boldsymbol{\beta}_1 + \mathbf{v}_2\boldsymbol{\gamma}_1 + e_1), \tag{4.19}$$

where $e_1|\mathbf{z}, \mathbf{v}_2 \sim \text{Normal}(0, \eta_1^2)$ and $\mathbf{x}_1 = \mathbf{f}_1(\mathbf{z}_1, \mathbf{y}_2)$. The Smith–Blundell procedure for estimating $\boldsymbol{\beta}_1, \gamma_1$, and η_1^2 is the same as for the probit, except that in step 2 we do Tobit of y_{i1} on $\mathbf{x}_{i1}, \hat{\mathbf{v}}_{i2}, i = 1, \ldots, N$.

Since $\sigma_1^2 = \gamma_1'\Sigma_2\gamma_1 + \eta_1^2$, and $\hat{\eta}_1^2$, and $\hat{\Sigma}_2$ are immediately available, the APEs are easy to obtain. The same sorts of embellishments possible for probit – namely, adding polynomials in $\mathbf{v}_2$ to $E(q_1|\mathbf{v}_2)$ and allowing Var $(q_1|\mathbf{v}_2)$ to be heteroskedastic – apply to Tobit, too.

5. CONCLUSIONS, CAVEATS, AND FURTHER CONSIDERATIONS

There are two main points I have tried to make in this paper. The first is that average partial effects can be estimated rather easily in commonly used nonlinear models, even when some explanatory variables are endogenous and require instrumental variables. Further, the general approach applies easily to useful extensions of the basic models. Several of the models in Sections 3 and 4, along with the simple two-step estimation methods and estimation of average partial effects, have not previously appeared in the literature.

A second, and more controversial, point concerns how we should view the problem of unobserved heterogeneity when it is assumed to be independent, or conditionally independent, of observed covariates, at least when we are interested in expectations of the form $E[g(y)|\mathbf{x}, \mathbf{q}]$ for some known function $g(\cdot)$. The focus on average partial effects suggests that, under independence, we should ignore unobserved heterogeneity and model, or estimate in a flexible manner, $E(y|\mathbf{x})$ or $D(y|\mathbf{x})$. The same conclusion holds if we have some proxy or control variables that deliver conditional independence between $\mathbf{q}$ and $\mathbf{x}$. Discussions of bias in parameter estimators in nonlinear models that contain unobserved heterogeneity are largely off the mark if the heterogeneity and covariates satisfy an independence, or a conditional independence, assumption.

The conclusions of the previous paragraph rely entirely on population considerations, and have nothing to do with the sampling environment. But the case where the data might be censored because of data collection – such as in top coding or duration censoring – deserves some comment. Estimating $E(y|\mathbf{x})$ or $E(y|\mathbf{x}, \mathbf{w})$ with a nonrandom sample generally requires additional distributional assumptions. If we are wedded to explicitly including unobserved heterogeneity in a "structural" model, data censoring typically requires us to model the entire distribution of y given $(\mathbf{x}, q)$ along with the distribution of q given $\mathbf{w}$. For example, in the random coefficient model (3.1), suppose for each i we observe only $\min(y_i, c_i)$, where c_i is a censoring variable independent of $(\mathbf{x}_i, q_i)$. Because of the censoring, estimating $E(y|\mathbf{x}, \mathbf{w})$ requires more than just assumptions (3.1) and (3.2). But since the APEs are eventually obtained from $E(y|\mathbf{x}, \mathbf{w})$, why not focus our efforts there? It is not as if we have widely agreed upon distributions for unobserved heterogeneity. Instead, we can use flexible densities to model $D(y|\mathbf{x}, \mathbf{w})$, and then account for the censoring by using standard maximum likelihood methods.

There is a stronger case for explicitly introducing unobserved heterogeneity when features of a distribution other than $E[g(y)|\mathbf{x}, \mathbf{q}]$ are of interest, although there is room for skepticism about what can be learned. One case is testing assumptions about variances conditional on unobserved heterogeneity. Lemma 2.2 does not apply because $\text{Var}(y|\mathbf{x}, \mathbf{q}) = E(y^2|\mathbf{x}, \mathbf{q}) - [E(y|\mathbf{x}, \mathbf{q})]^2$ is not in the form $E[g(y)|\mathbf{x}, \mathbf{q}]$. That is, even if $\mathbf{q}$ and $\mathbf{x}$ are independent, we cannot obtain $\partial \text{Var}(y|\mathbf{x}, \mathbf{q})/\partial x_j$, averaged across the distribution of $\mathbf{q}$, as $\partial \text{Var}(y|\mathbf{x})/\partial x_j$. Therefore, in order to learn interesting things about $\text{Var}(y|\mathbf{x}, \mathbf{q})$, we must model it directly and place restrictions on how the covariates and unobserved heterogeneity appear in the conditional moments.

As an illustration, consider testing for overdispersion after controlling for unobserved heterogeneity. Specifically, let y be a count variable, let $\mathbf{x}$ be observed covariates, and let q be the scalar unobserved heterogeneity. The hypothesis of interest is

$$H_0\colon \text{Var}(y|\mathbf{x}, q) = E(y|\mathbf{x}, q), \tag{5.1}$$

as would occur if y given $(\mathbf{x}, \text{q})$ has a Poisson distribution. Evidently, without more structure, it is impossible to test (5.1). A common approach is to assume that heterogeneity affects the conditional mean multiplicatively:

$$E(y|\mathbf{x}, q) = q \cdot m(\mathbf{x}), \tag{5.2}$$

where $q > 0$ is independent of $\mathbf{x}$ and $E(q) = 1$ is a normalization. The function $m(\cdot) > 0$ is usually modeled parametrically, say $m(\mathbf{x}) = \exp(\alpha + \mathbf{x}\beta)$, but the point of this example is best made by allowing $m(\cdot)$ to be a general function.

A common model that allows for under- or overdispersion in the variance, after conditioning on $(\mathbf{x}, q)$, is

$$\text{Var}(y|\mathbf{x}, q) = \delta E(y|\mathbf{x}, q) = \delta q \cdot m(\mathbf{x}), \tag{5.3}$$

where $\delta > 0$ is the variance–mean ratio. In the context of assumptions (5.2) and (5.3), the null of variance–mean equality (after controlling for $\mathbf{x}$ and q) is $H_0 : \delta = 1$. This is a testable hypothesis because

$$E(y|\mathbf{x}) = m(\mathbf{x}), \tag{5.4}$$

which means that $m(\cdot)$ is (nonparametrically) identified, and

$$\begin{aligned} \text{Var}(y|x) &= E[\text{Var}(y|\mathbf{x}, q)|\mathbf{x}] + \text{Var}[E(y|\mathbf{x}, q)|\mathbf{x}] \\ &= \delta \cdot E(y|\mathbf{x}) + \tau^2[E(y|\mathbf{x})]^2 = \delta \cdot m(\mathbf{x}) + \tau^2[m(\mathbf{x})]^2, \end{aligned} \tag{5.5}$$

where $\tau^2 = \text{Var}(q)$. Since $m(\cdot)$ is identified, Equation (5.5) implies that δ and τ^2 are generally identified provided $m(\mathbf{x})$ actually depends on $\mathbf{x}$.

The above derivations show that, under (5.2) and (5.3), we can test hypothesis (5.1). But our ability to do so hinges crucially on assumption (5.2), which limits the way in which unobserved heterogeneity can interact with the observed covariates in the conditional mean. In particular, under (5.2), $\log[E(y|\mathbf{x}, q)] = \log(q) + \log[m(\mathbf{x})]$, and so all semielasticities of $E(y|\mathbf{x}, q)$ with respect to $\mathbf{x}$ do not depend on q. If we want to allow more generality – for example, an exponential random coefficient model would have $E(y|\mathbf{x}, \mathbf{q}) = \exp(a + \mathbf{x}\mathbf{b})$, where $\mathbf{q} \equiv (a, \mathbf{b})$ is the vector of unobserved heterogeneity – then we cannot test (5.1) without a full distributional assumption for $\mathbf{q}$. (And this is still assuming $\mathbf{q}$ is independent of $\mathbf{x}$.)

Should we care about being able to test (5.1)? Not if we are interested in estimating average partial effects on the mean response. As is well known, the Poisson quasi-MLE consistently estimates the conditional mean parameters for any variance function $\text{Var}(y|\mathbf{x})$, and robust inference is very simple (see, for example, Wooldridge [1997b]). Further, a method of moments procedure, or a weighted least-squares procedure with a flexible variance function for $\text{Var}(y|\mathbf{x})$, could be used to improve asymptotic efficiency over the Poisson quasi-MLE without sacrificing robustness. There is no need to introduce unobserved heterogeneity to arrive at variance models such as (5.5), or even more general models.

One argument in favor of testing $H_0 : \delta = 1$ in (5.3) is to determine whether the Poisson distribution is sensible for $D(y|\mathbf{x}, q)$, because we may want to estimate partial effects on probabilities such as $P(y = j|\mathbf{x}, q)$, rather than partial effects on the mean. But, since $P(y = j|\mathbf{x}, q) = E\{1[y = j]|\mathbf{x}, q\}$, we obtain the average partial effects on $P(y = j|\mathbf{x}, q)$ by differentiating or differencing $P(y = j|\mathbf{x})$. We can model the distribution $D(y|\mathbf{x})$ in a flexible manner without introducing unobserved heterogeneity.

A similar analysis applies to duration models, where it is very common to add unobserved heterogeneity to a hazard function. A question of considerable interest is whether duration dependence is present conditional on observed covariates *and* unobserved heterogeneity. This hypothesis makes the most sense when the hazard function has the proportional hazard form

$$\lambda(t, \mathbf{x}, q) = \kappa(\mathbf{x}, q)\lambda_0(t), \tag{5.6}$$

where $\kappa(\mathbf{x}, q) > 0$ is a function of observed covariates and unobserved heterogeneity, and $\lambda_0(t)$ is the baseline hazard. The null hypothesis is that $\lambda_0(t)$ is constant. Unfortunately, even when we assume that q and $\mathbf{x}$ are independent, $\lambda(t, \mathbf{x}, q)$ is fundamentally unidentified without further assumptions.

A very common assumption is that $\kappa(\mathbf{x}, q) = q \cdot h(\mathbf{x})$, so that the hazard is multiplicative in the unobserved heterogeneity

$$\lambda(t, \mathbf{x}, q) = q \cdot h(\mathbf{x})\lambda_0(t), \tag{5.7}$$

in which case $\lambda_0(\cdot)$, $h(\cdot)$, and the distribution of q are all identified under fairly weak assumptions; see, for example, Lancaster (1990, Section 7.3) and Van den Berg (2001, Section 5). An important finding in the duration literature – see, for example, Lancaster (1990, Chapter 10) and Van den Berg (2001, Section 5.1) – is that under (5.7) and independence between q and $\mathbf{x}$, failure to account for heterogeneity can easily lead one to find duration dependence when none exists conditional on $(\mathbf{x}, q)$. From the perspective of the current paper, the problem is that the analog of Lemma 2.2 does not hold: averaging the hazard $\lambda(t, \mathbf{x}, q)$ across the distribution of q is not the same as computing the hazard of y (now a duration) conditional only on $\mathbf{x}$. In other words, if we normalize $E(q) = 1$, it is not true that $h(\mathbf{x})\lambda_0(t)$ is the hazard of y given $\mathbf{x}$. (Lemma 2.2 does not apply because the hazard function is obtained by conditioning on an event involving y, namely, $y > t$, for a fixed length of time t.)

Testing for duration dependence shares the same weakness as testing for overdispersion: in order to test the hypothesis of interest, one must either restrict the way in which the unobserved heterogeneity appears – multiplicatively, in both examples – or specify parametric functions of $(\mathbf{x}, \mathbf{q})$ along with a parametric distribution for $\mathbf{q}$. While (5.7) may seem natural for testing for duration dependence, it is not especially general. When $h(\mathbf{x}) = \exp(\alpha + \mathbf{x}\boldsymbol{\beta})$, Lancaster (1990, Section 2.3) justifies (5.7) by appealing to omitted variables among the original covariates. Unfortunately, the argument assumes no interactions among covariates within the exponential function in the "structural" model. Extensions that allow for interaction effects lead to serious difficulties in identifying duration dependence. For example, a random coefficient extension of the standard model $\kappa(\mathbf{x}, q) = q \cdot \exp(\alpha + \mathbf{x}\boldsymbol{\beta})$ is $\kappa(\mathbf{x}, \mathbf{q}) = \exp(a + \mathbf{x}\mathbf{b})$, where $\mathbf{q} = (a, \mathbf{b})$ is the vector of random coefficients with $E(\mathbf{q}) = (\alpha, \boldsymbol{\beta})$. Even for this parametric function of $(\mathbf{x}, \mathbf{q})$, identification results for $\lambda_0(\cdot)$ seem to be unavailable unless $\mathbf{q}$ follows a known parametric distribution. If we want average partial effects on the expected duration, or on probabilities of the form $P(y \in A|\mathbf{x}, \mathbf{q})$, then these are fully identified from $E(y|\mathbf{x})$ and $D(y|\mathbf{x})$, respectively.

ACKNOWLEDGMENTS

I would like to thank an anonymous referee, Jim Stock, and the participants of the NSF Symposium on Identification and Inference for Econometric Models, Berkeley, August 2–7, 2001, for reactions and comments on an earlier draft.

References

Angrist, J. D. (1991), "Instrumental Variables Estimation of Average Treatment Effects in Econometrics and Epidemiology," National Bureau of Economic Research, Technical Working Paper 115.

Bartle, R. G. (1966), *The Elements of Integration*. New York: John Wiley & Sons.

Blundell, R. and J. L. Powell (2003), "Endogeneity in Nonparametric and Semiparametric Regression Models," in *Advances in Economics and Econometrics: Theory and Applications, Eighth World Congress* (ed. by M. Dewatripont, L. P. Hansen and S. J. Turnovsky), Cambridge: Cambridge University Press.

Card, D. (2001), "Estimating the Return to Schooling: Progress on Some Persistent Econometric Problems," *Econometrica*, 69, 1127–60.

Chamberlain, G. (1984), "Panel Data," in *Handbook of Econometrics*, Vol. 2 (ed. by Z. Griliches and M. Intriligator), Amsterdam: North-Holland, 1247–318.

Garen, J. (1984), "The Returns to Schooling: A Selectivity Bias Approach with a Continuous Choice Variable," *Econometrica*, 52, 1199–218.

Gourieroux, C., A. Monfort, and A. Trognon (1984), "Pseudo-Maximum Likelihood Methods: Theory," *Econometrica*, 52, 681–700.

Greene, W. H. (2000), *Econometric Analysis*, fourth edition. New York: Macmillan.

Hahn, J. (1998), "On the Role of the Propensity Score in Efficient Semiparametic Estimation of Average Treatment Effects," *Econometrica*, 66, 315–31.

Heckman, J. J. (2001), "Micro Data, Heterogeneity, and the Evaluation of Public Policy: Nobel Lecture," *Journal of Political Economy*, 109, 673–748.

Heckman, J. J., H. Ichimura, and P. Todd (1997), "Matching as an Econometric Evaluation Estimator," *Review of Economic Studies*, 65, 261–94.

Heckman, J., and R. Robb (1985), "Alternative Methods for Evaluating the Impact of Interventions," in *Longitudinal Analysis of Labor Market Data* (ed. by J. Heckman and B. Singer), New York: Wiley, 156–245.

Heckman, J. J., and E. Vytlacil (1998), "Instrumental Variables Methods for the Correlated Random Coefficient Model," *Journal of Human Resources*, 33, 974–87.

Horowitz, J. L. (1992), "A Smoothed Maximum Score Estimator for the Binary Response Model," *Econometrica*, 60, 505–31.

Lancaster, T. (1990), *The Econometric Analysis of Transition Data*. Cambridge: Cambridge University Press.

Manski, C. F. (1975), "Maximum Score Estimation of the Stochastic Utility Model of Choice," *Journal of Econometrics*, 3, 205–8.

Manski, C. F. (1985), "Semiparametric Analysis of Discrete Response: Asymptotic Properties of the Maximum Score Estimator," *Journal of Econometrics*, 27, 313–33.

Mundlak, Y. (1978), "On the Pooling of Time Series and Cross Section Data," *Econometrica*, 46, 69–85.

Newey, W. K., and D. McFadden (1994), "Large Sample Estimation and Hypothesis Testing," in *Handbook of Econometrics*, Vol. 4 (ed. by R. F. Engle and D. McFadden), Amsterdam: North-Holland, 2111–45.

Papke, L. E., and J. M. Wooldridge (1996), "Econometric Methods for Fractional Response Variables with an Application to 401(k) Plan Participation Rates," *Journal of Applied Econometrics*, 11, 619–32.

Rivers, D., and Q. H. Vuong (1988), "Limited Information Estimators and Exogeneity Tests for Simultaneous Probit Models," *Journal of Econometrics*, 39, 347–66.

Robinson, P. M. (1988), "Root-N-Consistent Semiparametric Regression," *Econometrica*, 56, 931–54.

Rosenbaum, P. R., and D. B. Rubin (1983), "The Central Role of the Propensity Score in Observational Studies for Causal Effects," *Biometrika*, 70, 41–55.

Smith, R., and R. Blundell (1986), "An Exogeneity Test for a Simultaneous Equation Tobit Model with an Application to Labor Supply," *Econometrica*, 54, 679–85.

Van den Berg, G. J. (2001), "Duration Models: Specification, Identification, and Multiple Durations," in *Handbook of Econometrics*, Vol. 5 (ed. by J. J. Heckman and E. Leamer), Amsterdam: North-Holland, 3381–460.

Wooldridge, J. M. (1997a), "On Two Stage Least Squares Estimation of the Average Treatment Effect in a Random Coefficient Model," *Economics Letters*, 56, 129–133.

Wooldridge, J. M. (1997b), "Quasi-Likelihood Methods for Count Data," in *Handbook of Applied Econometrics*, Vol. 2 (ed. by M. H. Pesaran and P. Schmidt), Oxford: Blackwell, 352–406.

Wooldridge, J. M. (2000), *Introductory Econometrics: A Modern Approach.* Cincinnati, OH: South-Western.

Wooldridge, J. M. (2000b), "The Initial Conditions Problem for Dynamic, Nonlinear Panel Data Models with Unobserved heterogeneity," Working Paper 00/496, Department of Economics, University of Bristol.

Wooldridge, J. M. (2002), *Econometric Analysis of Cross Section and Panel Data.* Cambridge: MIT Press.

Yatchew, A., and Z. Griliches (1985), "Specification Error in Probit Models" *Review of Economics and Statistics*, 67, 134–39.

CHAPTER 4

On Specifying Graphical Models for Causation and the Identification Problem

David A. Freedman

ABSTRACT

This paper (which is mainly expository) sets up graphical models for causation, having a bit less than the usual complement of hypothetical counterfactuals. Assuming the invariance of error distributions may be essential for causal inference, but the errors themselves need not be invariant. Graphs can be interpreted using conditional distributions, so that we can better address connections between the mathematical framework and causality in the world. The identification problem is posed in terms of conditionals. As will be seen, causal relationships cannot be inferred from a data set by running regressions unless there is substantial prior knowledge about the mechanisms that generated the data. The idea can be made more precise in several ways. There are few successful applications of graphical models, mainly because few causal pathways can be excluded on a priori grounds. The invariance conditions themselves remain to be assessed.

1. INTRODUCTION

In this paper, I review the logical basis for inferring causation from regression equations, proceeding by example. The starting point is a simple regression; next is a path model, and then simultaneous equations (for supply and demand). After that come nonlinear graphical models. The key to making a causal inference from nonexperimental data by regression is some kind of invariance, exogeneity being a subsidiary problem. Parameters need to be invariant to interventions: this well-known condition will be stated here with a little more precision than is customary. Invariance is also needed for (i) errors or (ii) error distributions, a topic that has attracted less attention. Invariance for distributions is a weaker assumption than invariance for errors. I will focus on invariance of error distributions in stochastic models for individual behavior, eliminating the need to assume sampling from an ill-defined superpopulation.

With graphical models, the essential mathematical features can be formulated in terms of conditional distributions ("Markov kernels"). To make causal inferences from nonexperimental data using such techniques, the kernels need to be invariant to intervention. The number of plausible examples is at best quite limited, in part because of sampling error, and in part because of measurement error, but more fundamentally because few causal pathways can be excluded on a priori grounds. The invariance condition itself remains to be assessed.

$X \longrightarrow Y$

Figure 4.1. Linear regression.

Many readers will "know" that causal mechanisms can be inferred from nonexperimental data by running regressions. I ask from such readers an unusual boon – the suspension of belief. (Suspension of disbelief is all too readily at hand, but that is another topic.) There is a complex chain of assumptions and reasoning that leads from the data via regression to causation. One objective in the present essay is to explicate this logic. Please bear with me: what seems obvious at first may become less obvious on closer consideration, and properly so.

2. A FIRST EXAMPLE: SIMPLE REGRESSION

Figure 4.1 is the easiest place to start. In order to make causal inferences from simple regression, it is now conventional (at least for a small group of mathematical modelers) to assume something like the setup in Equation (2.1) below. I will try to explain the key features in the formalism, and then offer an alternative. As will become clearer, the equation makes very strong invariance assumptions, which cannot be tested from the data on X and Y.

$$Y_{i,x} = a + bx + \delta_i. \tag{2.1}$$

The subscript i indexes the individuals in a study, or the occasions in a repeated-measures design, and so forth. A treatment may be applied at various levels x. The expected response $a + bx$ is by assumption linear in x, with intercept a and slope b; these parameters are the same for all subjects and all levels of treatment. When treatment at level x is applied to subject i, the actual response $Y_{i,x}$ deviates from the expected by a "random error" or "disturbance" δ_i. This presumably reflects the impact of chance. For some readers, it may be more natural to think of $a + \delta_i$ in (2.1) as a random intercept.

In this paper, as is commonplace in statistics, random variables like δ_i are functions on a probability space Ω. Informally, chance comes in when Nature chooses a point at random from Ω, which fixes the value of δ_i. The choice is made once and once only: Nature does not re-randomize if x is changed in (2.1). More technically, $Y_{i,x}$ is a function of x and δ_i, but δ_i does not vary with x. (The formalism is compact, which has certain advantages; on the other hand, it is easy to lose track of the ideas.)

The δ_i are assumed to be independent and identically distributed. The common "error distribution" $\mathcal{D}$ is unknown, but its mean is assumed to be 0. Nothing in the equation is observable. To generate the data, Nature is assumed to choose $\{X_i : i = 1, \ldots, n\}$ independently of $\{\delta_i : i = 1, \ldots, n\}$, showing us

$$(X_i, Y_i),$$

where

$$Y_i = Y_{i,X_i} = a + bX_i + \delta_i$$

for $i = 1, \ldots, n$.

Notice that x could have been anything: the model features multiple parallel universes, all of which remain counterfactual hypotheticals – because, of course, we did no intervening at all. Instead, we passively observed X_i and Y_i. (If we had done the experiment, none of these interesting issues would be worth discussing.) Nature obligingly randomizes for us. She chooses X_i at random from some distribution, independently of δ_i, and sets $Y_i = a + bX_i + \delta_i$ as required by (2.1).

"Exogeneity" is the assumed independence between the X_i and the errors δ_i. Almost as a bookkeeping matter, your response Y_i is computed from your X_i and error term δ_i: nobody else's X and δ get into the act, precluding interactions across subjects. According to the model, δ_i exists – incorruptible and unchanging – in all the multiple unrealized counterfactual hypothetical universes, as well as in the one real factual observed universe. This is a remarkably strong assumption: all is flux, except a, b and δ_i.

An alternative setup will be presented next – more like standard regression – to weaken the invariance assumption. We start with parameters a, b and an error distribution $\mathcal{D}$. The last is unknown, but has mean 0. Nature chooses $\{X_i : i = 1, \ldots, n\}$ at random from some n-dimensional distribution. Given the X's, the Y's are assumed to be conditionally independent, and the random errors

$$Y_i - a - bX_i$$

are assumed have a common distribution $\mathcal{D}$. In other words, the Y's are built up from the X's as follows: Nature computes the linear function $a + bX_i$, then adds some noise drawn at random from $\mathcal{D}$ to get Y_i. We get to see the pairs (X_i, Y_i) for $i = 1, \ldots, n$.

In this alternative formulation, there is a fixed error distribution $\mathcal{D}$, but there are no context-free random errors: the latter may be functions of the treatment levels among other things. The alternative has both a causal and an associational interpretation. (i) Assuming invariance of error distributions to interventions leads to the causal interpretation. (ii) Mere insensitivity to x when we condition on $X_i = x$ gives the associational interpetation – the probability distribution of $Y_i - a - bX_i$ given $X_i = x$ is the same for all x. This can at least in principle be tested against the data; invariance to interventions cannot, unless interventions were part of the design.

The key difference between Equation (2.1) and the alternative is this: in (2.1), the errors themselves are invariant, whereas in the alternative, only the error distribution is invariant. In (2.1), inference is to the *numerical value* that Y_i would have had, if X_i had been set to x. In the alternative formulation, causal inference can only be to the *probability distribution* that Y_i would have had. With either setup, the inference is about specific individuals, indexed by i; inference at the level of individuals is possible because, by assumption, b is constant across individuals. The two formulations of invariance, with the restrictions on the Xs, express different ideas of exogeneity. The second set of assumptions is weaker than the first and seems generally more plausible.

An example to consider is Hooke's law. The stretch of a spring is proportional to the load: a is length under no load and b is stretchiness. The disturbance term would represent measurement error. We could run an experiment to determine a and b, or we could passively observe the behavior of springs and weights. If heavier weights are attracted to bigger errors, there are problems. Otherwise, passive observation might give the right answer. Moreover, we can with more or less power test the hypothesis that the random errors $Y_i - a - bX_i$ are independent and identically distributed. By contrast, consider the hypothesis that $Y_i - a - bX_i$ itself would have been the same if X_i had been 7 rather than 3. Even in an experiment, testing that seems distinctly unpromising.

What happens without invariance? The answer will be obvious. If intervention changes the intercept a, the slope b, or the mean of the error distribution, the impact of the intervention becomes difficult to determine. If the variance of the error term is changed, the usual confidence intervals lose their meaning. How would any of this be possible? Suppose, for instance, that – unbeknownst to the statistician – both X and Y are the effects of a common cause operating through linear statistical laws like (2.1), errors are independent and normal, and Nature has randomized the common cause to have a normal distribution. The scatter diagram will look lovely, a regression line is easily fitted, and the straightforward causal interpretation will be wrong.

3. CONDITIONALS

Let us assume (informally) that the regression in Figure 4.1 is causal. What the Y_i's would have been if we had intervened and set X_i to x_i – this too isn't quite mathematics, but does correspond to either of two formal objects. One object is generated by equation (2.1): the random variables $Y_i = a + bx_i + \delta_i$ for $i = 1, \ldots, n$. The second object is this: n independent Ys, the ith being distributed as $a + bx_i$ plus a random draw from the error distribution $\mathcal{D}$. One object is defined in terms of random variables; the other, in terms of conditional distributions. There is a similar choice for the examples presented below.

So far, I have been discussing linear statistical laws. In Figure 4.1, for example, if we set $X = x$, then the conditional distribution of Y is $a + bx$, plus some random noise with distribution $\mathcal{D}$. Call this conditional distribution $K_x(dy)$. On the one hand, K_x may just represent the conditional distribution of Y given $X = x$, a rather dry statistical idea. On the other hand, K_x may represent the result of a hypothetical intervention: the distribution that Y would have had, if only we had intervened and set X to x. This is the more exciting causal interpretation. Data analysis on X and Y cannot decide whether the causal interpretation is viable. Instead, to make causal inferences from a system of regression equations, causation is assumed from the beginning. As Cartwright

(1989) says, "No causes in, no causes out." This view contrasts rather sharply with rhetoric that one finds elsewhere.

Of course, solid arguments for causation have been made from observational data, but fitting regressions is only one aspect of the activity (Freedman 1999). Replication seems to be critical, with good study designs and many different kinds of evidence. Also see Freedman (1997, pp. 120–21), noting the difference between conditional probabilities that arise from selection of subjects with $X = x$, and conditional probabilities arising from an intervention that sets X to x. The data structures may look the same, but the implications can be worlds apart.

4. A SECOND EXAMPLE: TWO LINEAR REGRESSIONS

The discussion can now be extended to path diagrams, with similar conclusions. Figure 4.2 involves three variables and is a cameo version of applied statistics. If we are interested in the effect of Y on Z, then X confounds the relationship. Some adjustment is needed to avoid biased estimates, and regression is often used. The diagram unpacks into two response schedules:

$$Y_{i,x} = a + bx + \delta_i \tag{4.1a}$$

$$Z_{i,x,y} = c + dx + ey + \epsilon_i. \tag{4.1b}$$

We assume that $\delta_1, \ldots, \delta_n, \epsilon_1, \ldots, \epsilon_n$ are all independent. The δ's have a common distribution $\mathcal{D}$. The ϵ's have another common distribution $\mathcal{F}$. These two distributions are unknown, but are assumed to have mean 0. Again, nothing in (4.1) is observable.

To generate the data, Nature chooses $\{X_i : i = 1, \ldots, n\}$ independently of $\{\delta_i, \epsilon_i : i = 1, \ldots, n\}$. We observe

$$(X_i, Y_i, Z_i)$$

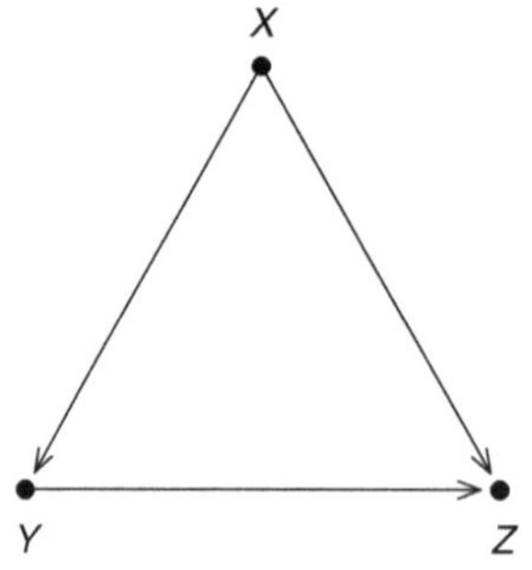

Figure 4.2. A linear path model.

for $i = 1, \ldots, n$, where

$$Y_i = Y_{i,X_i} = a + bX_i + \delta_i$$
$$Z_i = Z_{i,X_i,Y_i} = c + dX_i + eY_i + \epsilon_i.$$

Basically, this is a recursive system with two equations. The X's are "exogenous," that is, independent of the δ's and ϵ's. According to the model, Nature plugs the X's into (4.1a) to compute the Y's. In turn, those very X's and Y's get plugged into (4.1b) to generate the Z's. That is the recursive step. In other words, Y_i is computed as a linear function of X_i, with intercept a and slope b, plus the error term δ_i. Then Z_i is computed as a linear function of X_i and Y_i. The intercept is c, the coefficient on X_i is d, the coefficient on Y_i is e; at the end, the error ϵ_i is tagged on. Again, the δ's and ϵ's remain the same no matter what x's and y's go into (4.1); so do the parameters a, b, c, d, e. (Interactions across subjects are precluded because, for instance, subject i's response Y_i is computed from X_i and δ_i rather than X_j and δ_j.)

The proposed alternative involves not random errors but their distributions $\mathcal{D}$ and $\mathcal{F}$. These distributions are unknown but have mean 0. We still have the parameters a, b, c, d, e. To generate the data, we assume that Nature chooses $X_1, \ldots, X_n$ at random from some n-dimensional distribution. Given the X's, the Y's are assumed to be conditionally independent: Y_i is generated by computing $a + bX_i$, then adding some independent noise distributed according to $\mathcal{D}$. Given the X's and Y's, the Z's are assumed to be conditionally independent: Z_i is generated as $c + dX_i + eY_i$, with independent additive noise distributed according to $\mathcal{F}$. The exogeneity assumption is the independence between the X's and the errors.

As before, the second setup assumes less invariance than the first: it is error distributions that are invariant, not error terms; the inference is to distributions rather than specific numerical values. Either way, there are unbiased estimates for the parameters a, b, c, d, e; the error distributions $\mathcal{D}$ and $\mathcal{F}$ are identifiable: parameters and error distributions are constant in both formulations. As before, the second setup may be used to describe conditional distributions of random variables. If those conditional distributions admit a causal interpretation, then causal inferences can be made from observational data. In other words, regression succeeds in determining the effect of Y on Z if we know that (i) X is the confounder and (ii) the statistical relationships are linear and causal.

What can go wrong? Omitted variables are a problem, as discussed before. Assuming the wrong causal order is another issue. For example, suppose Equation (4.1) is correct; the errors are independent and normally distributed; moreover, the exogenous variable X has been randomized to have a normal distribution. However, the unfortunate statistician regresses (i) Y on Z, then (ii) X on Y and Z. Diagnostics will indicate success: the distribution of residuals will not depend on the explanatory variables. But causal inferences will be all wrong. The list of problem areas can easily be extended beyond omitted variables and causal orderings to include functional form, stochastic specification, measurement, and so forth.

The issue boils down to this. Does the conditional distribution of Y given X represent mere association, or does it represent the distribution Y would have had if we had intervened and set the values of X? There is a similar question for the distribution of Z given X and Y. These questions cannot be answered just by fitting the equations and doing data analysis on X, Y, and Z; additional information is needed. From this perspective, the equations are "structural" if the conditional distributions inferred from the equations tell us the likely impact of interventions, thereby allowing a causal rather than an associational interpretation. The take-home message is clear: you cannot infer a causal relationship from a data set by running regressions – unless there is substantial prior knowledge about the mechanisms that generated the data.

5. SIMULTANEOUS EQUATIONS

Similar considerations apply to models with simultaneous equations. The invariance assumptions will be familiar to many readers. Changing pace, I will discuss hypothetical supply and demand equations for butter in the state of Wisconsin. The endogenous variables are Q and P, the quantity and price of butter. The exogenous variables in the supply equation are the agricultural wage rate W and the price H of hay. The exogenous variables in the demand equation are the prices M of margarine and B of bread (substitutes and complements). For the moment, "exogeneity" just means "externally determined." Annual data for the previous twenty years are available on the exogeneous variables, and on the quantity of Wisconsin butter sold each year as well as its price. Linearity is assumed, with the usual stochastics.

The model can be set up formally with two linear equations in two unknowns, Q and P:

$$\text{Supply} \quad Q = a_0 + a_1 P + a_2 W + a_3 H + \delta_t, \tag{5.1a}$$

$$\text{Demand} \quad Q = b_0 + b_1 P + b_2 M + b_3 B + \epsilon_t. \tag{5.1b}$$

On the right-hand side, there are parameters (the as and bs). There are also error terms (δ_t, ϵ_t), which are assumed to be independent and identically distributed for $t = 1, \ldots, 20$. The common two-dimensional "error distribution" C for (δ_t, ϵ_t) is unknown, but is assumed to have mean 0.

Each equation describes a thought experiment. In the first, we set P, W, H, M, B and observe how much butter comes to market: by assumption, M and B have no effect on supply, while P, W, H have additive linear effects. In the second we set P, W, H, M, B and observe how much butter is sold: W and H have no effect on demand, while P, M, B have additive linear effects. In short, we have linear supply and demand schedules. Again, the error terms themselves are invariant to all interventions, as are the parameters. Since this is a hypothetical, there is no need to worry about the EEC, NAFTA, or the economics.

A third gedanken experiment is described by taking Equations (5.1a) and (5.1b) together. Any values of the exogenous variables W, H, M, B – perhaps within certain ranges – can be substituted in on the right, and the two equations solved together for the two unknowns Q and P, giving us the transacted quantity and price in a free market, denoted

$$Q_{W,H,M,B} \quad \text{and} \quad P_{W,H,M,B}. \tag{5.2}$$

Since δ and ϵ turn up in the formulas for both Q and P, the random variables in (5.2) are correlated – barring some rare parameter combinations – with the error terms. The correlation is "simultaneity."

So far, we have three thought experiments expressing various assumptions, but no data: nothing so far is observable. We assume that Nature generates data for us by choosing W_t, H_t, M_t, B_t for $t = 1, \ldots, 20$, at random from some high-dimensional distribution, independently of the δ's and ϵ's. This independence is the exogeneity assumption, which gives the concept a more technical shape. For each t, we get to see the values of the exogenous variables

$$W_t, H_t, M_t, B_t,$$

and the corresponding endogenous variables computed by solving (5.1a) and (5.1b) together, namely,

$$Q_t = Q_{W_t,H_t,M_t,B_t} \quad \text{and} \quad P_t = P_{W_t,H_t,M_t,B_t}.$$

Of course, we do not get to see the parameters or the disturbance terms. A regression of Q_t on P_t and the exogenous variables leads to "simultaneity bias," because P_t is correlated with the error term; hence two-stage least squares and related techniques. With such estimators, enough data, and the assumptions detailed above, we can (almost) recover the supply and demand schedules (5.1a) and (5.1b) from the free market data – using the exogenous variables supplied by Nature.

The other approach, sketched above for Figures 4.2 and 4.3, suggests that we start from the parameters and the error distribution $\mathcal{C}$. If we were to set P, W, H, M, B, then Nature would be assumed to choose the errors in (5.1) from $\mathcal{C}$: farmers would respond according to the supply equation (5.1a), and consumers according to the demand equation (5.1b). If we were to set only W, H, M, B and allow the free market to operate, then quantity and price would in this parable be computed by solving the pair of equations (5.1a) and (5.1b).

The notation for the error terms in (5.1) is a bit simplistic now, since these terms may be functions of W, H, M, B. Allowing the errors to be functions of P may make sense if (5.1a) and (5.1b) are considered in isolation; but if the two equations are considered together, this extra generality would lead to a morass. To generate data, we assume that Nature chooses the exogenous variables at random from some multidimensional distribution. The market quantities and prices are still computed by solving the pair of equations (5.1a) and (5.1b) for

Q and P, with independent additive errors for each period drawn from C; the usual statistical computations can still be carried out.

In this setup, it is not the error terms that are invariant, but their distribution. Of course, parameters are taken to be invariant. The exogeneity assumption is the independence of $\{W_t, H_t, M_t, B_t : t = 1, 2 \ldots\}$ and the error terms. The inference is for instance to the probability distribution of butter supply, if we were to intervene in the market by setting price as well as the exogenous variables. By contrast, with assumed invariance for the error terms themselves, the inference is to the numerical quantity of butter that would be supplied.

I have presented the second approach with a causal interpretation; an associational interpretation is also possible, although less interesting. The exposition may seem heavy-handed, because I have tried to underline the critical invariance assumptions that need to be made in order to draw causal conclusions from nonexperimental data: parameters are invariant to interventions, and so are errors or their distributions. Exogeneity is another concern. In a real example, as opposed to a butter hypothetical, real questions would have to be asked about these assumptions. Why are the equations "structural," in the sense that the required invariance assumptions hold true?

Obviously, there is some tension here. We want to use regression to draw causal inferences from nonexperimental data. To do that, we need to know that certain parameters and certain distributions would remain invariant if we were to intervene. That invariance can seldom, if ever, be demonstrated by intervention. What then is the source of the knowledge? "Economic theory" seems like a natural answer, but an incomplete one. Theory has to be anchored in reality. Sooner or later, invariance needs empirical demonstration, which is easier said than done.

6. NONLINEAR MODELS: FIGURE 4.1 REVISITED

Graphical models can be set up with nonlinear versions of Equation (2.1), as in Pearl (1995, 2000). The specification would be something like $Y_{i,x} = f(x, \delta_i)$, where f is a fairly general (unknown) function. The interpretation is this: if the treatment level were set to x, the response by subject i would be $Y_{i,x}$. The same questions about interventions and counterfactual hypotheticals would then have to be considered. Instead of rehashing such isues, I will indicate how to formulate the models using conditional distributions ("Markov kernels"), so that the graphs can be interpreted either distributionally or causally. In the nonlinear case, K_x – the conditional distribution of Y given that $X = x$ – depends on x in some fashion more complicated than linearity with additive noise. For example, if X, Y are discrete, then K can be visualized as the matrix of conditional probabilities $P(Y = y|X = x)$. For any particular x, K_x is a row in this matrix.

Inferences will be to conditional distributions, rather than specific numerical values. There will be some interesting new questions about identifiability. And the plausibility of causal interpretations can be assessed separately, as will be shown later. I will organize most of the discussion around two examples used by Pearl (1995); also see Pearl (2000, pp. 66–8 and 83–5). But first, consider Figure 4.1. In the nonlinear case, the exogenous variables have to be assumed independent and identically distributed in order to make sense out of the mathematics; otherwise, there are substantial extra complications, or we have to impose additional smoothness conditions on the kernel.

Now assume that (X_i, Y_i) are independent and distributed like (X, Y) for $i = 1, \dots, n$; the conditional distribution of Y_i given $X_i = x$ is K_x, where K is an unknown Markov kernel. With a large-enough sample, the joint distribution of (X, Y) can be estimated reasonably well; so can K_x, at least for xs that are likely to turn up in the data. If K is only a conditional probability, that is what we obtain from data analysis. If K admits a causal interpretation – by prior knowledge or assumption, not by data analysis on the Xs and Ys – then we can make a causal inference: What would the distribution of Y_i have been if we had intervened and set X_i to x? (Answer: K_x.)

7. TECHNICAL NOTES

The conditional distribution of Y given X tells you the conditional probability that Y is in one set C or another, given that $X = x$. A Markov kernel K assigns a number $K_x(C)$ to pairs (x, C); the first element x of the pair is a point; the second, C, is a set. With x fixed, K_x is a probability. With C fixed, the function that sends x to $K_x(C)$ should satisfy some minimal regularity condition. Below, I will write $K_x(dy)$ as shorthand for the kernel whose value at (x, C) is $K_x(C)$, where C is any reasonable set of values for Y. Matters will be arranged so that $K_x(C)$ is the conditional probability that $Y \in C$ given $X = x$, and perhaps some other information: $K_x(C) = P(Y \in C | X = x \dots)$.

Without further restrictions, graphical models are nonparametric, because kernels are infinite-dimensional "parameters." Our ability to estimate such things depends on the degree of regularity that is assumed. With minimal assumptions, you may get minimal performance – but that is a topic for another day. Even in the linear case, some of the fine points about estimation have been glossed over. To estimate the model in Figure 4.1, we would need some variation in X and δ. To get standard errors, we would assume finite variances for the error terms. Conditions for identifiability in the simultaneous-equations setup do not need to be rehearsed here, and I have assumed a unique solution for (5.1). Two-stage least squares will have surprising behavior unless variances are assumed for the errors; some degree of correlation between the exogenous and endogenous variables would also be needed.

More general specifications can be assumed for the errors. For example, in (2.1), the δ_i may be assumed to be independent, with common variances and uniformly bounded fourth moments; then the hypothesis of a common distribution can be dropped. In (5.1), an ARIMA model may be assumed. And so forth. The big picture does not change, because (i) questions about invariance remain, and (ii) even an ARIMA model requires some justification.

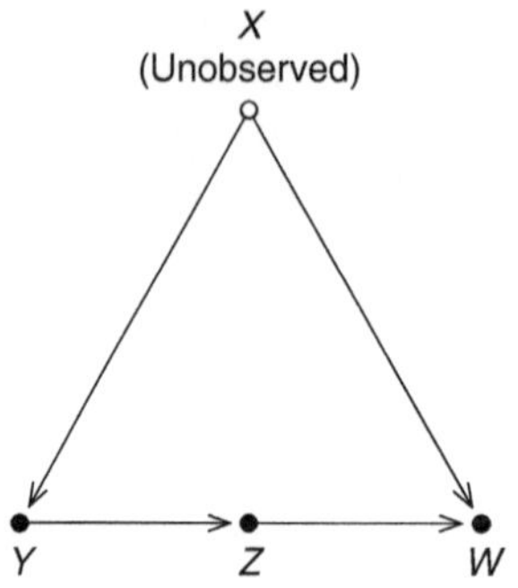

Figure 4.3. A graphical model.

8. MORE COMPLICATED EXAMPLES

The story behind Figure 4.3 will be explained below. For the moment, it is an abstract piece of mathematical art. The diagram corresponds to three kernels, $K_x(dy)$, $L_y(dz)$, and $M_{x,z}(dw)$. These kernels describe the joint distribution of the random variables shown in the diagram (X, Y, Z, W). The conditional distribution of Y given $X = x$ is K_x. The conditional distribution of Z given $X = x$ and $Y = y$ is L_y: there is no subscript x on L because, by assumption, there is no arrow from X to Z in the diagram. The conditional distribution of W given $X = x$, $Y = y$, $Z = z$ is $M_{x,z}$: there is no subscript y on M because, again by assumption, there is no arrow leading directly from Y to W in the diagram.

You can think of building up the variables X, Y, Z, W from the kernels and a base distribution μ for X, in a series of steps:

(i) Choose X at random according to $\mu(dx)$.
(ii) Given the value of X from step (i), say $X = x$, choose Y at random from $K_x(dy)$.
(iii) Given $X = x$ and $Y = y$, choose Z at random from $L_y(dz)$.
(iv) Given $X = x, Y = y$, and $Z = z$, choose W at random from $M_{x,z}(dw)$.

The recipe is equivalent to the graph.

By assumption, the variables (X_i, Y_i, Z_i, W_i) are independent and distributed like (X, Y, Z, W) for $i = 1, \ldots, n$. There is one more wrinkle: the circle marked "X" in the diagram is open, meaning that X is not observed. In other words, Nature hides $X_1, \ldots, X_n$ but shows us

$$Y_1, \ldots, Y_n, \quad Z_1, \ldots, Z_n, \quad W_1, \ldots, W_n.$$

That is our data set.

The base distribution μ and the kernels K, L, M are unknown. However, with many observations on independent and identically distributed triplets (Y_i, Z_i, W_i), we can estimate their joint distribution reasonably well.

Moreover – and this should be a little surprising – we can compute L_y from that joint distribution, as well as

$$\mathcal{M}_z(dw) = \int M_{x,z}(dw)\,\mu(dx), \tag{8.1a}$$

where μ is the distribution of the unobserved confounder X. Hence we can also compute

$$\mathcal{L}_y(dw) = \int \mathcal{M}_z(dw)\,L_y(dz). \tag{8.1b}$$

Here is the idea: L is computable because the relationship between Y and Z is not confounded by X. Conditional on Y, the relationship between Z and W is not confounded, so $\mathcal{M}_z$ in (8.1a) is computable. Then (8.1b) follows.

More specifically, with "P" for probability, the identity

$$P(Z \in C|Y = y) = P(Z \in C|X = x, Y = y) = L_y(C)$$

can be used to recover L from the joint distribution of Y, Z. Likewise, we can recover $\mathcal{M}$ in (8.1a) from the joint distribution of Y, Z, W, although the calculation is a little more intricate. Let $P_{x,y,z} = P(\bullet|X = x, Y = y, Z = z)$ be a regular conditional probability given X, Y, Z. Then

$$\begin{aligned} P(W \in D|Y = y, Z = z) &= \int P_{x,y,z}(W \in D)\,P(X \in dx|Y = y, Z = z) \\ &= \int M_{x,z}(D)\,P(X \in dx|Y = y), \end{aligned}$$

because

$$P_{x,y,z}(W \in D) = M_{x,z}(D)$$

by construction, and X is independent of Z given Y by a side calculation. We have recovered $\int M_{x,z}(D)\,P(X \in dx|Y = y)$ from the joint distribution of Y, Z, W. Hence we can recover

$$\begin{aligned} \int\int M_{x,z}(D)\,P(X \in dx|Y = y)P(Y \in dy) &= \int M_{x,z}(D)\,\mu(dx) \\ &= \mathcal{M}_z(D), \end{aligned}$$

although the distribution μ of X remains unknown, and so does the kernel M.

These may all just be facts about conditional distributions, in which case (8.1) is little more than a curiosity. On the other hand, if K, L, M have causal interpretations, then $\mathcal{M}_z$ in (8.1a) tells you the effect of setting $Z = z$ on W, averaged over the possible X's in the population. Similarly, $\mathcal{L}_y$ in (8.1b) tells you the effect of Y on W: if you intervene and set Y to y, then the distribution of W will be $\mathcal{L}_y$, on the average over all X and Z in the population. (There may be exceptional null sets, which are being ignored.) How to estimate $\mathcal{M}$ and $\mathcal{L}$ in a finite sample is another question, not discussed here.

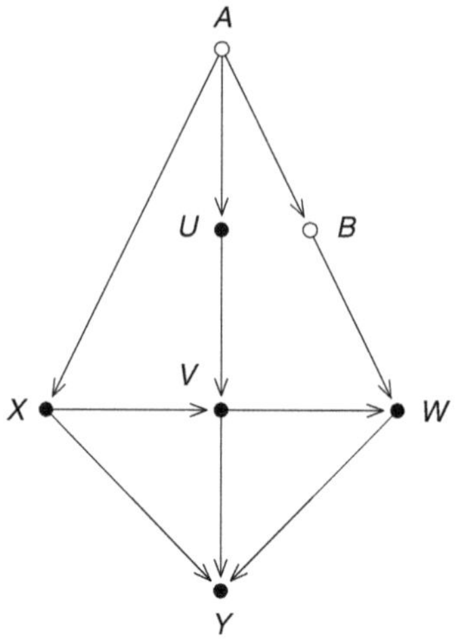

Figure 4.4. A graphical model: seven variables, of which five are observed.

The next example (Figure 4.4) is a little more complicated; again, the story behind the figure is deferred. There are two unobserved variables, A and B. The setup involves six kernels, which characterize the joint distribution of the random variables (A, B, U, X, V, W, Y) in the diagram:

$$\begin{aligned}
K_a(db) &= P(B \in db | A = a), \\
L_a(du) &= P(U \in du | A = a), \\
M_a(dx) &= P(X \in dx | A = a), \\
N_{u,x}(dv) &= P(V \in dv | A = a, B = b, U = u, X = x), \\
Q_{b,v}(dw) &= P(W \in dw | A = a, B = b, U = u, X = x, V = v), \\
R_{x,v,w}(dy) &= P(Y \in dy | A = a, B = b, U = u, X = x, V = v, W = w).
\end{aligned}$$

Here, P represents "probability"; it seemed more tasteful not to have kernels labeled O or P. There is no a, b, u among the subscripts on R because there are no arrows going directly from A, B, U to Y in the diagram; similarly for the other kernels. The issue is to determine the effect of X on Y, integrating over the unobserved confounders A, B. This is feasible, because conditional on the observed U, V, W, the relationship between X and Y is not confounded. (If the kernels have causal interpretations, "effect" is meant literally; if not, figuratively.)

To fix ideas, we can go through the construction of the random variables. There is a base probability μ for A. First, choose A at random from μ. Given A, choose B, U, X independently at random from K_A, L_A, M_A, respectively. Given A, B, U, X, choose V at random from $N_{U,X}$. Given A, B, U, X, V, choose W at random from $Q_{B,V}$. Finally, given A, B, U, X, V, W, choose Y at random from $R_{X,V,W}$. The data set consists of n independent septuples $A_i, B_i, U_i, X_i, V_i, W_i, Y_i$, distributed as A, B, U, X, V, W, Y – except that the

A's and B's are hidden. The "parameters" are μ and the six kernels. Calculations proceed as for Figure 4.3. Again, the graph and the description in terms of kernels are equivalent. Details are (mercifully?) omitted.

9. PARAMETRIC NONLINEAR MODELS

Similar considerations apply to parametric nonlinear models. Take the logit specification, for example. Let X_i be a p-dimensional random vector, with typical values x; the random variable Y_i is 0 or 1. Let β be a p-dimensional vector of parameters. Let K_x assign mass

$$\frac{e^{\beta x}}{1+e^{\beta x}}$$

to 1, and the remaining mass to 0. Given $X_1, \ldots, X_n$, suppose the Y_i are conditionally independent, and

$$P(Y_i = 1 | X_1 = x_1, \ldots, X_n = x_n) = K_{x_i}. \tag{9.1}$$

On the right-hand side of (9.1), the subscript on K is x_i: the conditional distribution of Y for a subject depends only on that subject's x. If the $x_1, \ldots, x_n$ are reasonably spread out, we can estimate β by maximum likelihood. (With a smooth, finite-dimensional parametrization, we do not need the X_i to be independent and identically distributed.)

Of course, this model could be set up in a more strongly invariant form, like (2.1). Let U_i be independent (unobservable) random variables with a common logistic distribution $P(U_i < u) = e^u/(1+e^u)$. Then

$$Y_{i,x} = 1 \Longleftrightarrow U_i < \beta x. \tag{9.2}$$

The exogeneity assumption would make the Xs independent of the Us, and the observable Y_i would be Y_{i,X_i}. That is, $Y_i = 1$ if $U_i < \beta X_i$, else $Y_i = 0$.

This is all familiar territory, except perhaps for (9.2), so familiar that the critical question may get lost. Does K_x merely represent the conditional probability $P(Y_i = 1 | X_i = x)$, as in (9.1)? Or does K_x tell us what the law of Y_i would have been if we had intervened and set X_i to x? Where would the U_i come from, and why would they be invariant if we manipulated x? Nothing in the mysteries of Euclidean geometry and likelihood statistics can possibly answer this sort of question: other kinds of information are needed.

10. CONCOMITANTS

Some variables are potentially manipulable; others ("concomitants") are not. For example, education and income may be manipulable; age, sex, race, personality, etc., are concomitants. So far, we have ignored this distinction, which is less problematic for kernels, but a difficulty for the kind of strong invariance in

Equation (2.1). However, if Y depends on a manipulable X and a concomitant W through a linear causal law with additive error, we can rewrite (2.1) as

$$Y_{i,x} = a + bx + cW_i + \delta_i. \tag{10.1}$$

In addition to the usual assumptions on the δ's, we would have to assume independence between the δs and the Ws. In applications, defining and isolating the intervention may not be so easy, but that is a topic for another day. Also see Robins (1986, 1987).

11. THE STORY BEHIND FIGURES 4.3 AND 4.4

When some variables are unobserved, Pearl (1995) develops an interesting calculus to define confounding and decide which kernels or composites – see (8.1) for example – can be recovered from the joint distribution of the observed variables. That is a solution to the identification problem for such diagrams. He uses Figure 4.3 to illustrate his "backdoor criterion." The unobserved variable X is genotype; the observed variables Y, Z, W represent smoking, tar deposits in the lung, and lung cancer, respectively (Figure 4.5). The objective is to determine the effect of smoking on lung cancer, via (8.1).

Data in this example would consist of a long series of independent triplets (Y_i, Z_i, W_i), each distributed like (Y, Z, W). Pearl interprets the graph causally. The timeworn idea that subjects in a study form a random sample from some hypothetical superpopulation still deserves a moment of respectful silence. Moreover, there are three special assumptions in Figure 4.5:

(i) Genotype has no direct effect on tar deposits.
(ii) Smoking has no direct effect on lung cancer.
(iii) Tar deposits can be measured with reasonable accuracy.

There is no support for these ideas in the literature. (i) The lung has a mechanism – "the mucociliary escalator" – for eliminating foreign matter,

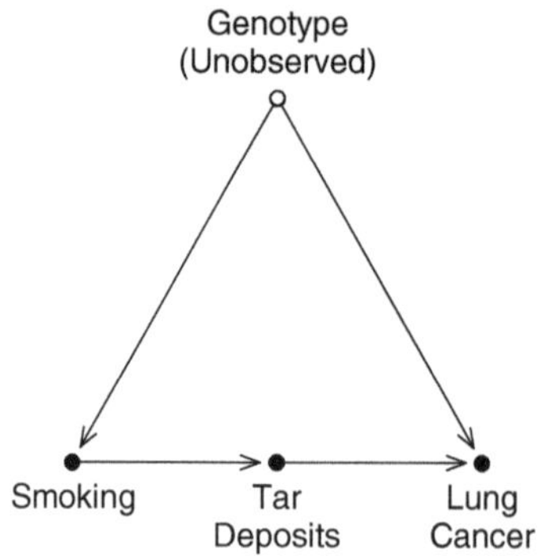

Figure 4.5. A graphical model for smoking and lung cancer.

including tar. This mechanism seems to be under genetic control. (Of course, clearance mechanisms can be overwhelmed by smoking.) The forbidden arrow from genotype to tar deposits may have a more solid empirical basis than the permitted arrows from genotype to smoking and lung cancer. Assumption (ii) is just that – an assumption. And (iii) is clearly wrong. The consequences are severe: if arrows are permitted from genotype to tar deposits or from smoking to lung cancer, or if measurements of tar are subject to error, then formula (8.1) does not apply. Graphical models cannot solve the problem created by an unmeasured confounder without introducing strong and artificial assumptions.

The intellectual history is worth mentioning. Fisher's "constitutional hypothesis" explained the association between smoking and disease on the basis of a gene that caused both. This idea is refuted not by making assumptions but by doing some empirical work. For example, Kaprio and Koskenvuo (1989) present data from their twin study. The idea is to find pairs of identical twins where one smokes and one does not. That sets up a race: who will die first, the smoker or the nonsmoker? The smokers win hands down for total mortality or death from heart disease. The genetic hypothesis is incompatible with these data.

For lung cancer, the smokers win two out of the two races that have been run. (Why only two? Smoking-discordant twin pairs are unusual, lung cancer is a rare disease, and the population of Scandinavia is small.) Carmelli and Page (1996) have a similar analysis with a larger cohort of twins. Do not bet on Fisher. The International Agency for Research on Cancer (1986) reviews the health effects of smoking and indicates the difficulties in measuring tar deposits (pp. 179–98). Nakachi et al. (1993) and Shields et al. (1993) illustrate conflicts on the genetics of smoking and lung cancer. The lesson: finding the mathematical consequences of assumptions matters, but connecting assumptions to reality matters even more.

Pearl uses Figure 4.4 to illustrate his "front-door criterion," calling the figure a "classical example due to Cochran," with a citation to Wainer (1989). Pearl's vision is that soil fumigants X are used to kill eelworms and improve crop yields Y for oats. The decision to apply fumigants is affected by the worm population A before the study begins – hence the arrow from A to X. The worm population is measured at base line, after fumigation, and later in the season: the three measurements are U, V, W. The unobserved B represents "birds and other predators."

This vision is whimsical. The example originates with Cochran (1957, p. 266), who had several fumigants applied under experimental control, with measurements of worm cysts and crop yield. Pearl converts this to an observational study with birds, bees, and so forth – entertaining, a teaching tool, but unreal. It might be rude to ask too many questions about Figure 4.4, but surely crops attract predators. Don't birds eat oat seeds? If early birds get the worms, what stops them from eating worms at baseline? In short, where have all the arrows gone?

12. MODELS AND KERNELS REVISITED

Graphical models may lead to some interesting mathematical developments. The number of successful applications, however, is at best quite limited. Figures 4.4 and 4.5 are not atypical (there are citations to the literature below). And it is all too tempting to forget the limitations of such methods. Given that the arrows and kernels represent causation, while variables are independent and identically distributed, we can use Pearl's framework to determine from the diagram which effects are estimable. This is a step forward. However, we cannot use the framework to answer the more basic question: Does the diagram represent the causal structure? As everyone knows, there are no formal algorithmic procedures for inferring causation from association; everyone is right.

Pearl (1995) considers only models with a causal interpretation, the latter being partly formalized; and there is new terminology that some readers may find discouraging. On the other hand, he draws a clear distinction between averaging Y's when the corresponding X is

- set to x, and
- observed to be x in the data.

That is a great advantage of his formalism.

The approach sketched here would divide the identification problem into two: (i) reconstructing kernels – viewed as ordinary conditional distributions – from partial information about joint distributions, and (ii) deciding whether these kernels bear a causal interpretation. Problem (i) can be handled entirely within the conventional probability calculus. Problem (ii) is one of the basic problems in applied statistics. Of course, kernels – especially mixtures like (8.1) – may not be interesting without a causal interpretation.

In sum, graphical models can be formulated using conditional distributions ("Markov kernels"), without invariance assumptions. Thus, the graphs can be interpreted either distributionally or causally. The theory governing recovery of kernels and their mixtures can be pushed through with just the distributional interpretation. That frees us to consider whether or not the kernels admit a causal interpretation. So far, however, the graphical modelers have few if any examples where the causal interpretation can be defended.

Pearl generally agrees with analysis presented here; he says,

> Causal analysis with graphical models does not deal with defending modeling assumptions, in much the same way that differential calculus does not deal with defending the physical validity of a differential equation that a physicist chooses to use. In fact no analysis void of experimental data can possibly defend modeling assumptions. Instead, causal analysis deals with the conclusions that logically follow from the combination of data and a given set of assumptions, just in case one is prepared to accept the latter. Thus, all causal inferences are necessarily *conditional*. These limitations are not unique to graphical models. In complex fields like the social sciences and epidemiology,

> there are only few (if any) real life situations where we can make enough compelling assumptions that would lead to identification of causal effects. [private communication]

13. LITERATURE REVIEW

The model in (4.1) was proposed by Neyman (1923). It has been rediscovered many times since; see, for instance, Hodges and Lehmann (1964, Section 9.4). The setup is often called "Rubin's model," but this simply mistakes the history: see Speed (1990), with a comment by Rubin; also see Rubin (1974) and Holland (1986). Holland (1986, 1988) explains the setup with a superpopulation model to account for the randomness, rather than individualized error terms. These error terms are often described as the overall effects of factors omitted from the equation. But this description introduces difficulties of its own, as shown by Pratt and Schlaifer (1984, 1988). Stone (1993) presents a clear superpopulation model with some observed covariates and some unobserved.

Dawid (2000) objects to counterfactual inference. Counterfactual distributions may be essential to any account of causal inference by regression methods. On the other hand, as the present paper tries to show, invariant counterfactual random variables – such as δ_i in Equation (2.1) – are dispensable. In particular, with kernels, there is no need to specify the joint distribution of random variables across inconsistent hypotheticals.

There is by now an extended critical literature on linear statistical models for causation, starting perhaps with the exchange between Keynes (1939, 1940) and Tinbergen (1940). Other familiar citations in the economics literature include Liu (1960), Lucas (1976), Leamer (1978), Sims (1980), Hendry (1993), Manski (1993), Angrist, Imbens, and Rubin (1996). Heckman (2000) traces the development of econometric thought from Haavelmo and Frisch onwards, stressing the role of "structural" or "invariant" parameters. According to Heckman, the enduring contributions of the field are the following insights:

> ... that causality is a property of a model, that many models may explain the same data and that assumptions must be made to identify causal or structural models... recognizing the possibility of interrelationships among causes... [clarifying] the conditional nature of causal knowledge and the impossibility of a purely empirical approach to analyzing causal questions.... The information in any body of data is usually too weak to eliminate competing causal explanations of the same phenomenon. There is no mechanical algorithm for producing a set of "assumption free" facts or causal estimates based on those facts. [pp. 89–91]

For other accounts of causal models from an econometric perspective, see Angrist (2001) or Heckman and Vytlacil (2001). Angrist and Krueger (2001) provide a nice introduction to instrumental variables; an early application of the technique was to fit supply and demand curves for butter (Wright 1928, p. 316).

Engle, Hendry, and Richard (1983) distinguish several kinds of exogeneity, with different implications for causal inference.

Any discussion of empirical foundations must take into account a remarkable series of papers, initiated by Kahneman and Tversky (1974), that explores the limits of rational choice theory. These papers are collected in Kahneman, Slovic, and Tversky (1982), and in Kahneman and Tversky (2000). The heuristics and biases program has attracted its own critics (Gigerenzer 1996). That critique is interesting and has some merit; but in the end, the experimental evidence demonstrates severe limits to the descriptive power of choice theory (Kahneman and Tversky 1996). If people are trying to maximize expected utility, they don't do it very well. Errors are large and repetitive, go in predictable directions, and fall into recognizable categories: these are biases, not random errors. Rather than making decisions by optimization – or bounded rationality, or satisficing – people seem to use plausible heuristics that can at least in part be identified.

Recently, modeling issues have been much canvased in sociology. Abbott (1997) finds that variables (like income and education) are too abstract to have much explanatory power. Clogg and Haritou (1997) review various difficulties with regression, noting in particular that you can all too easily include endogenous variables as regressors. Hedström and Swedberg (1998) edited a lively collection of essays by a number of sociologists, who turn out to be quite skeptical about regression models; rational choice theory also takes its share of criticism. Goldthorpe (1998, 2001) describes several ideas of causation and corresponding methods of statistical proof, with different strengths and weaknesses. Ní Bhrolcháin (2001) has some particularly forceful examples to illustrate the limits of regression. There is an influential book by Lieberson (1985), with a followup by Lieberson and Lynn (2002); the latest in a series of papers is Sobel (2000). Meehl (1978) reports the views of an empirical psychologist; also see Meehl (1954), with data showing the advantage of using regression to make predictions – rather than experts. In political science, Brady and Collier (2004) compare regression methods with case studies; invariance is discussed under the rubric of causal homogeneity. Citations from other perspectives include Freedman, Rothenberg, and Sutch (1985), as well as Freedman (1985, 1987, 1991, 1995, 1999).

There is an extended literature on graphical models for causation. Greenland, Pearl, and Robins (1999) give a clear account in the context of epidemiology. Lauritzen (1996, 2001) has a careful treatment of the mathematics. These authors do not recognize the difficulties in applying the methods to real problems. Equation (8.1) is a special case of the "g-computation algorithm" due to Robins (1986, 1987); also see Gill and Robins (2001), Pearl (1995, 2000), or Spirtes, Glymour, and Scheines (1993). If charitably read, the last-named text offers a formulation in terms of kernels. Robins (1995) explains – all too briefly – how to state Pearl's results as theorems about conditionals. For critical reviews of graphical models (with responses and further citations) see Freedman (1997), Humphreys (1997), Humphreys and Freedman (1996, 1999): among other things, these papers discuss various applications proposed by the modelers. Woodward (1997, 1999) stresses the role of invariance. Freedman and Stark (1999) show that different models for the correlation of outcomes across counterfactual scenarios can have markedly different consequences in the legal context. Scharfstein, Rotnitzky, and Robins (1999) demonstrate a large range of uncertainty in estimates, due to incomplete specifications; also see Robins (1999).

ACKNOWLEDGMENTS

Over the years, I learned a great deal about statistics from Tom Rothenberg; it is a pleasure to acknowledge the debt. I would also like to thank some other friends for many helpful conversations on the topics of this paper: Dick Berk, Paul Holland, Paul Humphreys, Máire Ní Bhrolcháin, Judea Pearl, and Jamie Robins. At the risk of the obvious, thanking people does not imply they agree with my opinions, nor does this caveat imply disagreement.

References

Abbott, A. (1997), "Of Time and Space: The Contemporary Relevance of the Chicago School," *Social Forces*, 75, 1149–82.

Angrist, J. D. (2001), "Estimation of Limited Dependent Variable Models with Binary Endogenous Regressors: Simple Strategies for Empirical Practice. *Journal of Business and Economic Statistics*, 19, 2–16.

Angrist, J. D., G. W. Imbens, and D. B. Rubin (1996), "Identification of Causal Effects using Instrumental Variables," *Journal of the American Statistical Association*, 91, 444–72.

Angrist, J. D., and A. K. Krueger (2001), "Instrumental Variables and the Search for Identification: From Supply and Demand to Natural Experiments," *Journal of Business and Economic Statistics*, 19, 2–16.

Brady, H., and D. Collier (eds.) (2004), *Rethinking Social Inquiry: Diverse Tools, Shared Standards*. Rowman & Littlefield.

Carmelli, D., and W. F. Page (1996), "24-year Mortality in Smoking-Discordant World War II U. S. Male Veteran Twins," *International Journal of Epidemiology*, 25, 554–59.

Cartwright, N. (1989), *Nature's Capacities and their Measurement*. Oxford: Clarendon Press.

Clogg, C. C., and A. Haritou (1997), "The Regression Method of Causal Inference and a Dilemma Confronting this Method," in *Causality in Crisis* (ed. by V. McKim and S. Turner), South Bend, IN: University of Notre Dame Press, pp. 83–112.

Cochran, W. G. (1957), "Analysis of Covariance: Its Nature and Uses," *Biometrics*, 13, 261–81.

Dawid, A. P. (2000), "Causal Inference Without Counterfactuals," *Journal of the American Statistical Association*, 95, 407–48.

Engle, R. F., D. F. Hendry, and J. F. Richard (1983), "Exogeneity," *Econometrica*, 51, 277–304.

Freedman, D. A. (1985), "Statistics and the Scientific Method," in *Cohort Analysis in Social Research: Beyond the Identification Problem* (ed. by W. M. Mason and S. E. Fienberg), New York: Springer-Verlag, 343–90 (with discussion).

Freedman, D. A. (1987), "As Others See Us: A Case Study in Path Analysis," *Journal of Educational Statistics*, 12, 101–223 (with discussion). Reprinted in *The Role of Models in Nonexperimental Social Science* (ed. by J. Shaffer), Washington, DC: AERA/ASA, 1992, 3–125.

Freedman, D. A. (1991), "Statistical Models and Shoe Leather," Chapter 10 in *Sociological Methodology 1991* (ed. by Peter Marsden), Washington, DC: American Sociological Association (with discussion).

Freedman, D. A. (1995), "Some Issues in the Foundation of Statistics," *Foundations of Science*, 1, 19–83 (with discussion). Reprinted in *Some Issues in the Foundation of Statistics* (ed. by B. van Fraasen), Dordrecht: Kluwer, 19–83 (with discussion).

Freedman, D. A. (1997), "From Association to Causation via Regression," in *Causality in Crisis?* (ed. by V. McKim and S. Turner), South Bend, IN: University of Notre Dame Press, 113–82 (with discussion).

Freedman, D. A. (1999), "From Association to Causation: Some Remarks on the History of Statistics," *Statistical Science*, 14, 243–58.

Freedman, D., T. Rothenberg, and R. Sutch (1983), "On Energy Policy Models," *Journal of Business and Economic Statistics*, 1, 24–36 (with discussion).

Freedman, D. A., and P. B. Stark (1999), "The Swine Flu Vaccine and Guillain-Barré Syndrome: A Case Study in Relative Risk and Specific Causation," *Evaluation Review*, 23, 619–47.

Gigerenzer, G. (1996), "On Narrow Norms and Vague Heuristics," *Psychological Review*, 103, 592–96.

Gill, R. D., and J. M. Robins (2001), "Causal Inference for Complex Longitudinal Data: The Continuous Case," *Annals of Statistics*, in press.

Goldthorpe, J. H. (1998), *Causation, Statistics and Sociology*. Twenty-ninth Geary Lecture, Nuffield College, Oxford. Published by the Economic and Social Research Institute, Dublin, Ireland.

Goldthorpe, J. H. (2001), "Causation, Statistics, and Sociology," *European Sociological Review*, 17, 1–20.

Greenland, S., J. Pearl, and J. Robins (1999), "Causal Diagrams for Epidemiologic Research," *Epidemiology*, 10, 37–48.

Heckman, J. J. (2000), "Causal Parameters and Policy Analysis in Economics: A Twentieth Century Retrospective," *The Quarterly Journal of Economics*, 115, 45–97.

Heckman, J. J., and E. Vytlacil (2001), "Causal Parameters, Structural Equations, Treatment Effects and Randomized Evaluations of Social Programs." Technical Report, Economics Department, Stanford.

Hedström, P., and R. Swedberg, eds. (1998), *Social Mechanisms*. Cambridge: Cambridge University Press.

Hendry, D. F. (1993), *Econometrics – Alchemy or Science?* Oxford: Blackwell.

Hodges, J. L., Jr., and E. Lehmann (1964), *Basic Concepts of Probability and Statistics*. San Francisco: Holden-Day.

Holland, P. (1988), "Causal Inference, Path Analysis, and Recursive Structural Equation Models," Chapter 13 in *Sociological Methodology 1988* (ed. by C. Clogg), Washington, DC: American Sociological Association.

Holland, P. (1986), "Statistics and Causal Inference," *Journal of the American Statistical Association*, 8, 945–60.

Humphreys, P. (1997), "A Critical Appraisal of Causal Discovery Algorithms, in *Causality in Crisis?* (ed. by V. McKim and S. Turner), South Bend, IN: University of Notre Dame Press, 249–63 (with discussion).
Humphreys, P., and D. A. Freedman (1996), "The Grand Leap," *British Journal for the Philosophy of Science*, 47, 113–23.
Humphreys, P., and D. A. Freedman (1999), "Are There Algorithms That Discover Causal Structure?" *Synthese*, 121, 29–54.
International Agency for Research on Cancer (1986), *Tobacco Smoking*. Lyon, France: IARC, Monograph 38.
Kahneman, D., P. Slovic, and A. Tversky, (Eds.) (1982), *Judgment under Uncertainty: Heuristics and Biases*. Cambridge: Cambridge University Press.
Kahneman, D., and A. Tversky (1996), "On the Reality of Cognitive Illusions," *Psychological Review*, 103, 582–91.
Kahneman, D., and A. Tversky, (Eds.) (2000), *Choices, Values, and Frames*. Cambridge: Cambridge University Press.
Kahneman, D., and A. Tversky (1974), "Judgment under Uncertainty: Heuristics and Bias," *Science*, 185, 1124–31.
Kaprio, J., and M. Koskenvuo, (1989), "Twins, Smoking and Mortality: A 12-Year Prospective Study of Smoking-Discordant Twin Pairs," *Social Science and Medicine*, 29, 1083–9.
Keynes, J. M. (1939), "Professor Tinbergen's Method," *The Economic Journal*, 49, 558–70.
Keynes, J. M. (1940), "Comment on Tinbergen's Response," *The Economic Journal*, 50, 154–56.
Lauritzen, S. (1996), *Graphical Models*. Oxford: Clarendon Press.
Lauritzen, S. (2001), "Causal Inference in Graphical Models," in *Complex Stochastic Systems* (ed. by O. E. Barndorff-Nielsen, D. R. Cox, and C. Klüppelberg), Boca Raton, FL: Chapman & Hall, 63–108.
Leamer, E. (1978), *Specification Searches*. New York: Wiley.
Lieberson, S. (1985), *Making it Count*. Berkeley: University of California Press.
Lieberson, S., and F. B. Lynn (2002), "Barking Up the Wrong Branch: Alternative to the Current Model of Sociological Science." *Annual Review of Sociology*, 28, 1–19.
Liu, T. C. (1960), "Under-identification, Structural Estimation, and Forecasting," *Econometrica*, 28, 855–65.
Lucas, R. E., Jr. (1976), "Econometric Policy Evaluation: A Critique and Labor Markets," in *The Phillips Curve and Labor Markets* (ed. by K. Brunner and A. Meltzer, with discussion), Amsterdam: North-Holland, 19–64. Vol. 1 of the *Carnegie-Rochester Conferences on Public Policy*, supplementary series to the *Journal of Monetary Economics*.
Manski, C. F. (1995), *Identification Problems in the Social Sciences*, Harvard University Press.
Meehl, P. E. (1978), "Theoretical Risks and Tabular Asterisks: Sir Karl, Sir Ronald, and the Slow Progress of Soft Psychology," *Journal of Consulting and Clinical Psychology*, 46, 806–34.
Meehl, P. E. (1954), *Clinical Versus Statistical Prediction: A Theoretical Analysis and a Review of the Evidence*. Minneapolis: University of Minnesota Press.
Nakachi, K., K. Ima, S.-I. Hayashi, and K. Kawajiri (1993), "Polymorphisms of the CYP1A1 and Glutathione S-Transferase Genes Associated with Susceptibility to Lung

Cancer in Relation to Cigarette Dose in a Japanese Population," *Cancer Research*, 53, 2994–99.

Neyman, J. (1923), "Sur les applications de la théorie des probabilités aux experiences agricoles: Essai des principes," *Roczniki Nauk Rolniczki* 10: 1–51, in Polish. English translation by D. Dabrowska and T. Speed (1990), *Statistical Science*, 5, 463–80 (with discussion).

Ní Bhrolcháin, M. (2001), "Divorce Effects and Causality in the Social Sciences," *European Sociological Review*, 17, 33–57.

Oakes, M. (1986), *Statistical Inference*. Chestnut Hill, MA: Epidemiology Resources Inc.

Pearl, J. (1995), "Causal Diagrams for Empirical Research," *Biometrika*, 82, 669–710 (with discussion).

Pearl, J. (2000): *Causality: Models, Reasoning, and Inference*. Cambridge: Cambridge University Press.

Pratt, J., and R. Schlaifer (1984), "On the Nature and Discovery of Structure," *Journal of the American Statistical Association*, 79, 9–21.

Pratt, J., and R. Schlaifer (1988), "On the Interpretation and Observation of Laws, "*Journal of Econometrics*, 39, 23–52.

Robins, J. M. (1999), "Association, Causation, and Marginal Structural Models," *Synthese*, 121, 151–79.

Robins, J. M. (1995), "Discussion," *Biometrika*, 82, 695–8.

Robins, J. M. (1987), "A Graphical Approach to the Identification and Estimation of Causal Parameters in Mortality Studies with Sustained Exposure Periods," *Journal of Chronic Diseases* 40, Supplement 2, 139S–161S.

Robins, J. M. (1986), "A New Approach to Causal Inference in Mortality Studies with a Sustained Exposure Period – Application to Control of the Healthy Worker Survivor Effect, *Mathematical Modelling*, 7, 1393–512.

Rubin, D. (1974), "Estimating Causal Effects of Treatments in Randomized and Non-randomized studies," *Journal of Educational Psychology*, 66, 688–701.

Scharfstein, D. O., A. Rotnitzky, and J. M. Robins (1999), "Adjusting for Non-Ignorable Drop-Out using Semiparametric Non-Response Models, *Journal of the American Statistical Association*, 94, 1096–1146 (with discussion).

Shields, P. G., N. E. Caporaso, K. T. Falk, H. Sugimura, G. E. Trivers, B. P. Trump, R. N. Hoover, A. Weston, and C. C. Harris (1993), "Lung Cancer, Race and a CYP1A1 Genetic Polymorphism," *Cancer Epidemiology, Biomarkers and Prevention*, 2, 481–5.

Sims, C. A. (1980), "Macroeconomics and Reality," *Econometrica*, 48, 1–47.

Sobel, M. E. (2000), "Causal Inference in the Social Sciences," *Journal of the American Statistical Association*, 95, 647–51.

Speed, T. P. (1990), "Introductory Remarks on Neyman (1923)," *Statistical Science*, 463–80.

Spirtes, P., C. Glymour, and R. Scheines (1993), *Causation, Prediction, and Search*. Springer Lecture Notes in Statistics, No. 81, New York: Springer-Verlag.

Stone, R. (1993), "The Assumptions on Which Causal Inferences Rest," *Journal of the Royal Statistical Society*, Series B, 55, 455–66.

Tinbergen, J. (1940), "Reply to Keynes," *The Economic Journal*, 50, 141–54.

Wainer, H. (1989), "Eelworms, Bullet Holes, and Geraldine Ferraro: Some Problems with Statistical Adjustment and Some Solutions." *Journal of Educational Statistics*, 14, 121–40 (with discussion). Reprinted in *The Role of Models in*

Nonexperimental Social Science (ed. by J. Shaffer), Washington, DC: AERA/ASA, 1992, pp. 129–207.
Woodward, J. (1997), "Causal Models, Probabilities, and Invariance," in *Causality in Crisis?* (ed. by In V. McKim and S. Turner), South Bend, IN: University of Notre Dame Press, 265–315 (with discussion).
Woodward, J. (1999), "Causal Interpretation in Systems of Equations," *Synthese*, 121, 199–247.
Wright, P. G. (1928), *The Tariff on Animal and Vegetable Oils*. New York: MacMillan.

CHAPTER 5

Testing for Weak Instruments in Linear IV Regression

James H. Stock and Motohiro Yogo

ABSTRACT

Weak instruments can produce biased IV estimators and hypothesis tests with large size distortions. But what, precisely, are weak instruments, and how does one detect them in practice? This paper proposes quantitative definitions of weak instruments based on the maximum IV estimator bias, or the maximum Wald test size distortion, when there are multiple endogenous regressors. We tabulate critical values that enable using the first-stage F-statistic (or, when there are multiple endogenous regressors, the Cragg–Donald [1993] statistic) to test whether the given instruments are weak.

1. INTRODUCTION

Standard treatments of instrumental variables (IV) regression stress that for instruments to be valid they must be exogenous. It is also important, however, that the second condition for a valid instrument, instrument relevance, holds, for if the instruments are only marginally relevant, or "weak," then first-order asymptotics can be a poor guide to the actual sampling distributions of conventional IV regression statistics.

At a formal level, the strength of the instruments matters because the natural measure of this strength – the so-called concentration parameter – plays a role formally akin to the sample size in IV regression statistics. Rothenberg (1984) makes this point in his survey of approximations to the distributions of estimators and test statistics. He considers the single equation IV regression model

$$\mathbf{y} = \mathbf{Y}\beta + \mathbf{u}, \tag{1.1}$$

where $\mathbf{y}$ and $\mathbf{Y}$ are $T \times 1$ vectors of observations on the dependent variable and endogenous regressor, respectively, and $\mathbf{u}$ is a $T \times 1$ vector of i.i.d. $N(0, \sigma_{uu})$ errors. The reduced form equation for $\mathbf{Y}$ is

$$\mathbf{Y} = \mathbf{Z}\boldsymbol{\Pi} + \mathbf{V}, \tag{1.2}$$

where $\mathbf{Z}$ is a $T \times K_2$ matrix of fixed, exogenous instrumental variables, $\boldsymbol{\Pi}$ is a $K_2 \times 1$ coefficient vector, and $\mathbf{V}$ is a $T \times 1$ vector of i.i.d. $N(0, \sigma_{VV})$ errors, where $\text{corr}(u_t, V_t) = \rho$.

The two-stage least-squares (TSLS) estimator of β is $\hat{\beta}^{\text{TSLS}} = (\mathbf{Y}'\mathbf{P_Z y})/(\mathbf{Y}'\mathbf{P_Z Y})$, where $\mathbf{P_Z} = \mathbf{Z}(\mathbf{Z}'\mathbf{Z})^{-1}\mathbf{Z}'$. Rothenberg (1984) expresses $\hat{\beta}^{\text{TSLS}}$ as

$$\mu(\hat{\beta}^{\text{TSLS}} - \beta) = \left(\frac{\sigma_{uu}}{\sigma_{VV}}\right)^{1/2} \frac{\zeta_u + (S_{Vu}/\mu)}{1 + (2\zeta_V/\mu) + (S_{VV}/\mu^2)}, \tag{1.3}$$

where $\zeta_u = \mathbf{\Pi}'\mathbf{Z}'\mathbf{u}/(\sigma_{uu}\mathbf{\Pi}'\mathbf{Z}'\mathbf{Z}\mathbf{\Pi})^{1/2}$, $\zeta_V = \mathbf{\Pi}'\mathbf{Z}'\mathbf{V}/(\sigma_{VV}\mathbf{\Pi}'\mathbf{Z}'\mathbf{Z}\mathbf{\Pi})^{1/2}$, $S_{Vu} = \mathbf{V}'\mathbf{P_Z u}/(\sigma_{uu}\sigma_{VV})^{1/2}$, $S_{VV} = \mathbf{V}'\mathbf{P_Z V}/\sigma_{VV}$, and μ is the square root of the concentration parameter $\mu^2 = \mathbf{\Pi}'\mathbf{Z}'\mathbf{Z}\mathbf{\Pi}/\sigma_{VV}$.

Under the assumptions of fixed instruments and normal errors, ζ_u and ζ_V are standard normal variables with correlation ρ, and S_{Vu} and S_{VV} are elements of a matrix with a central Wishart distribution. Because the distributions of ζ_u, ζ_V, S_{Vu}, and S_{VV} do not depend on the sample size, the sample size enters the distribution of the TSLS estimator only through the concentration parameter. In fact, the form of (1.3) makes it clear that μ^2 can be thought of as an effective sample size, in the sense that μ formally plays the role usually associated with $\sqrt{T}$. Rothenberg (1984) proceeds to discuss expansions of the distribution of the TSLS estimator in orders of μ, and he emphasizes that the quality of these approximations can be poor when μ^2 is small. This has been underscored by the dramatic numerical results of Nelson and Startz (1990a, 1990b) and Bound, Jaeger, and Baker (1995).

If μ^2 is so small that inference based on some IV estimators and their conventional standard errors are potentially unreliable, then the instruments are said to be weak. But this raises two practical questions. First, precisely how small must μ^2 be for instruments to be weak? Second, because $\mathbf{\Pi}$, and thus μ^2, is unknown, how is an applied researcher to know whether μ^2 is in fact sufficiently small and that his or her instruments are weak?

This paper provides answers to these two questions. First, we develop precise, quantitative definitions of weak instruments for the general case of n endogenous regressors. In our view, the matter of whether a group of instrumental variables is weak cannot be resolved in the abstract; rather, it depends on the inferential task to which the instruments are applied and how that inference is conducted. We therefore offer two alternative definitions of weak instruments. The first definition is that a group of instruments is weak if the bias of the IV estimator, relative to the bias of ordinary least squares (OLS), could exceed a certain threshold b, for example 10%. The second is that the instruments are weak if the conventional α-level Wald test based on IV statistics has an actual size that could exceed a certain threshold r, for example $r = 10\%$ when $\alpha = 5\%$. Each of these definitions yields a set of population parameters that defines weak instruments, that is, a "weak instrument set." Because different estimators (e.g., TSLS or LIML) have different properties when instruments are weak, the resulting weak instrument set depends on the estimator being used. For TSLS and other k-class estimators, we argue that these weak instrument sets can be characterized in terms of the minimum eigenvalue of the matrix version of μ^2/K_2.

Second, given this quantitative definition of weak instrument sets, we show how to test the null hypothesis that a given group of instruments is weak against the alternative that it is strong. Our test is based on the Cragg–Donald (1993) statistic; when there is a single endogenous regressor, this statistic is simply the "first-stage F-statistic," the F-statistic for testing the hypothesis that the instruments do not enter the first stage regression of TSLS. The critical values for the test statistic, however, are *not* Cragg and Donald's (1993): our null hypothesis is that the instruments are weak, even though the parameters might be identified, whereas Cragg and Donald (1993) test the null hypothesis of underidentification. We therefore provide tables of critical values that depend on the estimator being used, whether the researcher is concerned about bias or size distortion, and the numbers of instruments and endogenous regressors. These critical values are obtained using weak instrument asymptotic distributions (Staiger and Stock 1997), which are more accurate than Edgeworth approximations when the concentration parameter is small.[1]

This paper is part of a growing literature on detecting weak instruments, surveyed in Stock, Wright, and Yogo (2002) and Hahn and Hausman (2003). Cragg and Donald (1993) proposed a test of underidentification, which (as discussed earlier) is different from a test for weak instruments. Hall, Rudebusch, and Wilcox (1996), following the work by Bowden and Turkington (1984), suggested testing for underidentification using the minimum canonical correlation between the endogenous regressors and the instruments. Shea (1997) considered multiple included regressors and suggested looking at a partial R^2. Neither Hall et al. (1996) nor Shea (1997) provide a formal characterization of weak instrument sets or a formal test for weak instruments, with controlled type I error, based on their respective statistics. For the case of a single endogenous regressor, Staiger and Stock (1997) suggested declaring instruments to be weak if the first-stage F-statistic is less than 10. Recently, Hahn and Hausman (2002) suggested comparing the forward and reverse TSLS estimators and concluding that instruments are strong if the null hypothesis that these are the same cannot be rejected. Relative to this literature, the contribution of this paper is twofold. First, we provide a formal characterization of the weak instrument set for a general number of endogenous regressors. Second, we provide a test of whether the given instruments fall in this set, that is, whether they are weak, where the size of the test is controlled asymptotically under the null of weak instruments.

The rest of the paper is organized as follows. The IV regression model and the proposed test statistic are presented in Section 2. The weak instrument sets are developed in Section 3. Section 4 presents the test for weak instruments and provides critical values for tests based on TSLS bias and size, Fuller-k bias, and LIML size. Section 5 examines the power of the test, and conclusions are presented in Section 6.

[1] See Rothenberg (1984, p. 921) for a discussion of the quality of the Edgeworth approximation as a function of μ^2 and K_2.

2. THE IV REGRESSION MODEL, THE PROPOSED TEST STATISTIC, AND WEAK INSTRUMENT ASYMPTOTICS

2.1. The IV Regression Model

We consider the linear IV regression model (1.1) and (1.2), generalized to have n included endogenous regressors $\mathbf{Y}$ and K_1 included exogenous regressors $\mathbf{X}$:

$$\mathbf{y} = \mathbf{Y}\beta + \mathbf{X}\gamma + \mathbf{u}, \tag{2.1}$$
$$\mathbf{Y} = \mathbf{Z}\Pi + \mathbf{X}\Phi + \mathbf{V}, \tag{2.2}$$

where $\mathbf{Y}$ is now a $T \times n$ matrix of included endogenous variables, $\mathbf{X}$ is a $T \times K_1$ matrix of included exogenous variables (one column of which is 1's if (2.1) includes an intercept), $\mathbf{Z}$ is a $T \times K_2$ matrix of excluded exogenous variables to be used as instruments, and the error matrix $\mathbf{V}$ is a $T \times n$ matrix. It is assumed throughout that $K_2 \geq n$. Let $\underline{\mathbf{Y}} = [\mathbf{y}\,\mathbf{Y}]$ and $\underline{\mathbf{Z}} = [\mathbf{X}\,\mathbf{Z}]$ respectively denote the matrices of all the endogenous and exogenous variables. The conformable vectors β and γ and the matrices Π and Φ are unknown parameters. Throughout this paper, we exclusively consider inference about β.

Let $\mathbf{X}_t = (X_{1t} \cdots X_{K_1t})'$, $\mathbf{Z}_t = (Z_{1t} \cdots Z_{K_2t})'$, $\mathbf{V}_t = (V_{1t} \cdots V_{nt})'$, and $\underline{\mathbf{Z}}_t = (\mathbf{X}_t'\,\mathbf{Z}_t')'$ denote the vectors of the tth observations on these variables. Also let Σ and $\mathbf{Q}$ denote the population second moment matrices,

$$E\left[\begin{pmatrix} u_t \\ V_t \end{pmatrix}\begin{pmatrix} u_1 & \mathbf{V}_t' \end{pmatrix}\right] = \begin{bmatrix} \sigma_{uu} & \Sigma_{u\mathbf{V}} \\ \Sigma_{\mathbf{V}u} & \Sigma_{\mathbf{VV}} \end{bmatrix} = \Sigma \quad \text{and}$$
$$E(\underline{\mathbf{Z}}_t\underline{\mathbf{Z}}_t') = \begin{bmatrix} \mathbf{Q}_{\mathbf{XX}} & \mathbf{Q}_{\mathbf{XZ}} \\ \mathbf{Q}_{\mathbf{Z}X} & \mathbf{Q}_{\mathbf{ZZ}} \end{bmatrix} = \mathbf{Q}. \tag{2.3}$$

2.2. k-Class Estimators and Wald Statistics

Let the superscript "$\perp$" denote the residuals from the projection on $\mathbf{X}$, so for example $\mathbf{Y}^{\perp} = \mathbf{M_X Y}$, where $\mathbf{M_X} = \mathbf{I} - \mathbf{X}(\mathbf{X}'\mathbf{X})^{-1}\mathbf{X}'$. In this notation, the OLS estimator of β is $\hat{\beta} = (\mathbf{Y}^{\perp\prime}\mathbf{Y}^{\perp})^{-1}(\mathbf{Y}^{\perp\prime}\mathbf{y})$. The k-class estimator of β is

$$\hat{\beta}(k) = [\mathbf{Y}^{\perp\prime}(\mathbf{I} - kM_{\mathbf{Z}^{\perp}})\mathbf{Y}^{\perp}]^{-1}[\mathbf{Y}^{\perp\prime}(\mathbf{I} - kM_{\mathbf{Z}^{\perp}})\mathbf{y}^{\perp}]. \tag{2.4}$$

The Wald statistic, based on the k-class estimator, testing the null hypothesis that $\beta = \beta_0$, is

$$W(k) = \frac{[\hat{\beta}(k) - \beta_0]'[\mathbf{Y}^{\perp\prime}(I - k\mathbf{M}_{\mathbf{Z}^{\perp}})\mathbf{Y}^{\perp}][\hat{\beta}(k) - \beta_0]}{n\hat{\sigma}_{uu}(k)}, \tag{2.5}$$

where $\hat{\sigma}_{uu}(k) = \hat{\mathbf{u}}^{\perp}(k)'\hat{\mathbf{u}}^{\perp}(k)/(T - K_1 - n)$, where $\hat{\mathbf{u}}^{\perp}(k) = \mathbf{y}^{\perp} - \mathbf{Y}^{\perp}\hat{\beta}(k)$.

This paper considers four specific k-class estimators: TSLS, the limited information maximum likelihood estimator (LIML), the family of modified LIML estimators proposed by Fuller (1977) ("Fuller-k estimators"), and bias-adjusted TSLS (BTSLS) (Nagar 1959; Rothenberg 1984). The values of k for these estimators are (cf. Donald and Newey 2001):

$$\text{TSLS:} \quad k = 1, \tag{2.6}$$

$$\text{LIML:} \quad k = \hat{k}_{\text{LIML}} \text{ is the smallest root of det } (\underline{\mathbf{Y}}'\mathbf{M_X}\underline{\mathbf{Y}} - k\underline{\mathbf{Y}}'\mathbf{M_Z}\underline{\mathbf{Y}}) = 0, \tag{2.7}$$

$$\text{Fuller-}k\text{:} \quad k = \hat{k}_{\text{LIML}} - c/(T - K_1 - K_2), \text{ where } c \text{ is a positive constant,} \tag{2.8}$$

$$\text{BTSLS:} \quad k = T/(T - K_2 + 2), \tag{2.9}$$

where det($\mathbf{A}$) is the determinant of the matrix $\mathbf{A}$. If the errors are symmetrically distributed and the exogenous variables are fixed, LIML is median unbiased to second order (Rothenberg 1983). In our numerical work, we examine the Fuller-k estimator with $c = 1$, which is the best unbiased estimator to second order among estimators with $k = 1 + a(\hat{k}_{\text{LIML}} - 1) - c/(T - K_1 - K_2)$ for some constants a and c (Rothenberg 1984). For further discussion, see Donald and Newey (2001) and Stock et al. (2002, Section 6.1).

2.3. The Cragg–Donald Statistic

The proposed test for weak instruments is based on the eigenvalue of the matrix analog of the F-statistic from the first-stage regression of TSLS,

$$\mathbf{G}_T = \hat{\mathbf{\Sigma}}_{\mathbf{VV}}^{-1/2\prime} \mathbf{Y}^{\perp\prime} \boldsymbol{P}_{\mathbf{Z}^{\perp}} \mathbf{Y}^{\perp} \hat{\mathbf{\Sigma}}_{\mathbf{VV}}^{-1/2} / K_2, \tag{2.10}$$

where $\hat{\mathbf{\Sigma}}_{\mathbf{VV}} = (\mathbf{Y}'\mathbf{M}_{\underline{\mathbf{Z}}}\mathbf{Y})/(T - K_1 - K_2)$.[2] The test statistic is the minimum eigenvalue of $\mathbf{G}_T$:

$$g_{\min} = \text{mineval}(\mathbf{G}_T). \tag{2.11}$$

This statistic was proposed by Cragg and Donald (1993) to test the null hypothesis of underidentification, which occurs when the concentration matrix is singular. Instead, we are interested in the case that the concentration matrix is nonsingular but its eigenvalues are sufficiently small that the instruments are weak. To obtain the limiting null distribution of the Cragg–Donald statistic (2.11) under weak instruments, we rely on weak instrument asymptotics.

2.4. Weak Instrument Asymptotics: Assumptions and Notation

We start by summarizing the elements of weak instrument asymptotics from Staiger and Stock (1997). The essential idea of weak instruments is that $\mathbf{Z}$ is only weakly related to $\mathbf{Y}$, given $\mathbf{X}$. Specifically, weak instrument asymptotics are developed by modeling $\mathbf{\Pi}$ as local to zero:

[2] The definition of $\mathbf{G}_T$ in (2.10) is $\mathbf{G}_T$ in Staiger and Stock (1997, Equation (3.4)), divided by K_2 to put it in F-statistic form.

Assumption L_Π. $\mathbf{\Pi} = \mathbf{\Pi}_T = \mathbf{C}/\sqrt{T}$, *where* $\mathbf{C}$ *is a fixed* $K_2 \times n$ *matrix.*

Following Staiger and Stock (1997), we make the following assumption on the moments:

Assumption M. *The following limits hold jointly for fixed* K_2*:*

(a) $(T^{-1}\mathbf{u}'\mathbf{u}, T^{-1}\mathbf{V}'\mathbf{u}, T^{-1}\mathbf{V}'\mathbf{V}) \xrightarrow{p} (\sigma_{uu}, \mathbf{\Sigma}_{\mathbf{V}u}, \mathbf{\Sigma}_{\mathbf{VV}})$;

(b) $T^{-1}\underline{\mathbf{Z}}'\underline{\mathbf{Z}} \xrightarrow{p} \mathbf{Q}$;

(c) $(T^{-1/2}\mathbf{X}'\mathbf{u}, T^{-1/2}\mathbf{Z}'\mathbf{u}, T^{-1/2}\mathbf{X}'\mathbf{V}, T^{-1/2}\mathbf{Z}'\mathbf{V}) \xrightarrow{d} (\mathbf{\Psi}_{\mathbf{X}u}, \mathbf{\Psi}_{\mathbf{Z}u}, \mathbf{\Psi}_{\mathbf{XV}}, \mathbf{\Psi}_{\mathbf{ZV}})$, *where* $\mathbf{\Psi} \equiv [\mathbf{\Psi}_{\mathbf{X}u}', \mathbf{\Psi}_{\mathbf{Z}u}', \mathrm{vec}(\mathbf{\Psi}_{\mathbf{XV}})', \mathrm{vec}(\mathbf{\Psi}_{\mathbf{ZV}})']'$ *is distributed* $N(0, \mathbf{\Sigma} \otimes \mathbf{Q})$.

Assumption M can hold for time series or cross-sectional data. Part (c) assumes that the errors are homoskedastic.

Notation and Definitions. The following notation in effect transforms the variables and parameters and simplifies the asymptotic expressions. Let $\boldsymbol{\rho} = \mathbf{\Sigma}_{\mathbf{VV}}^{-1/2\prime}\mathbf{\Sigma}_{\mathbf{V}u}\sigma_{uu}^{-1/2}$, $\boldsymbol{\theta} = \mathbf{\Sigma}_{\mathbf{VV}}^{-1}\mathbf{\Sigma}_{\mathbf{V}u} = \sigma_{uu}^{1/2}\mathbf{\Sigma}_{\mathbf{VV}}^{-1/2}\boldsymbol{\rho}$, $\boldsymbol{\lambda} = \mathbf{\Omega}^{1/2}\mathbf{C}\mathbf{\Sigma}_{\mathbf{VV}}^{-1/2}$, $\mathbf{\Lambda} = \boldsymbol{\lambda}'\boldsymbol{\lambda}/K_2$, and $\mathbf{\Omega} = \mathbf{Q}_{\mathbf{ZZ}} - \mathbf{Q}_{\mathbf{ZX}}\mathbf{Q}_{\mathbf{XX}}^{-1}\mathbf{Q}_{\mathbf{XZ}}$. Note that $\boldsymbol{\rho}'\boldsymbol{\rho} \le 1$. Define the $K_2\times 1$ and $K_2 \times n$ random variables $\mathbf{z}_u = \mathbf{\Omega}^{-1/2\prime}(\mathbf{\Psi}_{\mathbf{Z}u} - \mathbf{Q}_{\mathbf{ZX}}\mathbf{Q}_{\mathbf{XX}}^{-1}\mathbf{\Psi}_{\mathbf{X}u})\sigma_{uu}^{-1/2}$ and $\mathbf{z}_\mathbf{V} = \mathbf{\Omega}^{-1/2\prime}(\mathbf{\Psi}_{\mathbf{ZV}} - \mathbf{Q}_{\mathbf{ZX}}\mathbf{Q}_{\mathbf{XX}}^{-1}\mathbf{\Psi}_{\mathbf{XV}})\mathbf{\Sigma}_{\mathbf{VV}}^{-1/2}$, so

$$\begin{pmatrix} \mathbf{z}_\mathbf{u} \\ \mathrm{vec}(\mathbf{z}_\mathbf{V}) \end{pmatrix} \sim N(\mathbf{0}, \overline{\mathbf{\Sigma}} \otimes \mathbf{I}_{K_2}), \quad \text{where } \overline{\mathbf{\Sigma}} = \begin{bmatrix} 1 & \boldsymbol{\rho}' \\ \boldsymbol{\rho} & \mathbf{I}_n \end{bmatrix}. \tag{2.12}$$

Also let

$$\boldsymbol{\nu}_1 = (\boldsymbol{\lambda} + \mathbf{z}_\mathbf{V})'(\boldsymbol{\lambda} + \mathbf{z}_\mathbf{V}) \quad \text{and} \tag{2.13}$$

$$\boldsymbol{\nu}_2 = (\boldsymbol{\lambda} + \mathbf{z}_\mathbf{V})'\mathbf{z}_\mathbf{u}. \tag{2.14}$$

2.5. Selected Weak Instrument Asymptotic Representations

We first summarize some results from Staiger and Stock (1997).

OLS Estimator. Under assumptions L_Π and M, the probability limit of the OLS estimator is $\hat{\boldsymbol{\beta}} \xrightarrow{p} \boldsymbol{\beta} + \boldsymbol{\theta}$.

k-class Estimators. Suppose that $T(k-1) \xrightarrow{d} \kappa$. Then under assumptions L_Π and M,

$$\hat{\boldsymbol{\beta}}(k) - \boldsymbol{\beta} \xrightarrow{d} \sigma_{uu}^{1/2}\mathbf{\Sigma}_{\mathbf{VV}}^{-1/2}(\boldsymbol{\nu}_1 - \kappa\mathbf{I}_n)^{-1}(\boldsymbol{\nu}_2 - \kappa\boldsymbol{\rho}) \quad \text{and} \tag{2.15}$$

$$W(k) \xrightarrow{d} \frac{(\boldsymbol{\nu}_2 - \kappa\boldsymbol{\rho})'(\boldsymbol{\nu}_1 - \kappa\mathbf{I}_n)^{-1}(\boldsymbol{\nu}_2 - \kappa\boldsymbol{\rho})}{n[1 - 2\boldsymbol{\rho}'(\boldsymbol{\nu}_1 - \kappa\mathbf{I}_n)^{-1}(\boldsymbol{\nu}_2 - \kappa\boldsymbol{\rho}) + (\boldsymbol{\nu}_2 - \kappa\boldsymbol{\rho})'(\boldsymbol{\nu}_1 - \kappa\mathbf{I}_n)^{-2}(\boldsymbol{\nu}_2 - \kappa\boldsymbol{\rho})]}, \tag{2.16}$$

where (2.16) holds under the null hypothesis $\boldsymbol{\beta} = \boldsymbol{\beta}_0$.

For LIML and the Fuller-k estimators, κ is a random variable, while for TSLS and BTSLS κ is nonrandom. Let Ξ be the $(n+1) \times (n+1)$ matrix, $\Xi = [z_u(\boldsymbol{\lambda} + \mathbf{z_V})]'[z_u(\boldsymbol{\lambda} + \mathbf{z_V})]$. Then the limits in (2.15) and (2.16) hold with

$$\text{TSLS:} \quad \kappa = 0, \tag{2.17}$$

$$\text{LIML:} \quad \kappa = \kappa^*, \text{ where } \kappa^* \text{ is the smallest root of } \det(\Xi - \kappa\bar{\Sigma}) = 0, \tag{2.18}$$

$$\text{Fuller-}k\text{:} \quad \kappa = \kappa^* - c, \text{ where } c \text{ is the constant in (2.8), and} \tag{2.19}$$

$$\text{BTSLS:} \quad \kappa = K_2 - 2. \tag{2.20}$$

Note that the convergence in distribution of $T(\hat{k}_{\text{LIML}} - 1) \xrightarrow{d} \kappa^*$ is joint with the convergence in (2.15) and (2.16). For TSLS, the expressions in (2.15) and (2.16) simplify to

$$\hat{\beta}^{\text{TSLS}} - \beta \xrightarrow{d} \sigma_{uu}^{1/2} \Sigma_{\mathbf{VV}}^{-1/2} \nu_1^{-1} \nu_2 \quad \text{and} \tag{2.21}$$

$$W^{\text{TSLS}} \xrightarrow{d} \frac{\nu_2' \nu_1^{-1} \nu_2}{n\left(1 - 2\rho' \nu_1^{-1} \nu_2 + \nu_2' \nu_1^{-2} \nu_2\right)}. \tag{2.22}$$

Weak Instrument Asymptotic Representations: The Cragg–Donald Statistic. Under the weak instrument asymptotic assumptions, the matrix $\mathbf{G}_T$ in (2.10) and the Cragg–Donald statistic (2.11) have the limiting distributions

$$\mathbf{G}_T \xrightarrow{d} \nu_1 / K_2 \quad \text{and} \tag{2.23}$$

$$g_{\min} \xrightarrow{d} \text{mineval}(\nu_1 / K_2). \tag{2.24}$$

Inspection of (2.13) reveals that ν_1 has a noncentral Wishart distribution with noncentrality matrix $\boldsymbol{\lambda}'\boldsymbol{\lambda} = K_2 \boldsymbol{\Lambda}$. This noncentrality matrix is the weak instrument limit of the concentration matrix

$$\boldsymbol{\Sigma}_{\mathbf{VV}}^{-1/2} \boldsymbol{\Pi}' \mathbf{Z}' \mathbf{Z} \boldsymbol{\Pi} \boldsymbol{\Sigma}_{\mathbf{VV}}^{-1/2\prime} \xrightarrow{p} K_2 \boldsymbol{\Lambda}. \tag{2.25}$$

Thus the weak instrument asymptotic distribution of the Cragg–Donald statistic $g_{\min}$ is that of the minimum eigenvalue of a noncentral Wishart, divided by K_2, where the noncentrality parameter is $K_2 \boldsymbol{\Lambda}$. To obtain critical values for the weak instrument test based on $g_{\min}$, we characterize the weak instrument set in terms of the eigenvalues of $\boldsymbol{\Lambda}$, the task taken up in the next section.

3. WEAK INSTRUMENT SETS

This section provides two general definitions of a weak instrument set, the first based on the bias of the estimator and the second based on size distortions of the associated Wald statistic. These two definitions are then specialized to TSLS,

LIML, the Fuller-k estimator, and BTSLS, and the resulting weak instrument sets are characterized in terms of the minimum eigenvalues of the concentration matrix.

3.1. First Characterization of a Weak Instrument Set: Bias

One consequence of weak instruments is that IV estimators are in general biased, so our first definition of a weak instrument set is in terms of its maximum bias.

When there is a single endogenous regressor, it is natural to discuss bias in the units of β, but for $n > 1$, a bias measure must scale β so that the bias is comparable across elements of β. A natural way to do this is to standardize the regressors $\mathbf{Y}^{\perp}$ so that they have unit standard deviation and are orthogonal or, equivalently, to rotate β by $\mathbf{\Sigma}_{\mathbf{Y}^{\perp}\mathbf{Y}^{\perp}}^{1/2}$, where $\mathbf{\Sigma}_{\mathbf{Y}^{\perp}\mathbf{Y}^{\perp}} = \text{plim}(\mathbf{Y}^{\perp\prime}\mathbf{Y}^{\perp}/T)$. In these standardized units, the squared bias of an IV estimator, which we generically denote by $\hat{\beta}^{\text{IV}}$, is $(E\hat{\beta}^{\text{IV}} - \beta)'\mathbf{\Sigma}_{\mathbf{Y}^{\perp}\mathbf{Y}^{\perp}}(E\hat{\beta}^{\text{IV}} - \beta)$. As our measure of bias, we therefore consider the relative squared bias of the candidate IV estimator $\hat{\beta}^{\text{IV}}$, relative to the squared bias of the OLS estimator

$$B_T^2 = \frac{(E\hat{\beta}^{\text{IV}} - \beta)'\mathbf{\Sigma}_{Y^{\perp}Y^{\perp}}(E\hat{\beta}^{\text{IV}} - \beta)}{(E\hat{\beta} - \beta)'\mathbf{\Sigma}_{Y^{\perp}Y^{\perp}}(E\hat{\beta} - \beta)}. \tag{3.1}$$

If $n = 1$, then the scaling matrix in (3.1) drops out and the expression simplifies to $B_T = |E\hat{\beta}^{\text{IV}} - \beta|/|E\hat{\beta} - \beta|$. The measure (3.1) was proposed, but not pursued, in Staiger and Stock (1997).

The asymptotic relative bias, computed under weak instrument asymptotics, is denoted by $B = \lim_{T\to\infty} B_T$. Under weak instrument asymptotics, $E(\hat{\beta} - \beta) \to \boldsymbol{\theta} = \sigma_{uu}^{1/2}\mathbf{\Sigma}_{\mathbf{VV}}^{-1/2}\rho$ and $\mathbf{\Sigma}_{\mathbf{Y}^{\perp}\mathbf{Y}^{\perp}} \to \mathbf{\Sigma}_{\mathbf{VV}}$, so that the denominator in (3.1) has the limit $(E\hat{\beta} - \beta)'\mathbf{\Sigma}_{Y^{\perp}Y^{\perp}}(E\hat{\beta} - \beta) \to \sigma_{uu}\rho'\rho$. Thus for $\rho'\rho > 0$, the square of the asymptotic relative bias is

$$B^2 = \sigma_{uu}^{-1}\lim_{T\to\infty}\frac{(E\hat{\beta}^{\text{IV}} - \beta)'\mathbf{\Sigma}_{Y^{\perp}Y^{\perp}}(E\hat{\beta}^{\text{IV}} - \beta)}{\rho'\rho}. \tag{3.2}$$

We deem instruments to be strong if they lead to reliable inferences for all possible degrees of simultaneity ρ; otherwise they are weak. Applied to the relative bias measure, this leads us to consider the worst-case asymptotic relative bias

$$B^{\max} = \max_{\rho:0<\rho'\rho\leq 1} |B|. \tag{3.3}$$

The first definition of a weak instrument set is based on this worst-case bias. We define the weak instrument set, based on relative bias, to consist of those instruments that have the potential of leading to asymptotic relative bias greater than some value b. In population, the strength of an instrument is determined by the parameters of the reduced form Equation (2.2). Accordingly, let $\mathcal{Z} = \{\mathbf{\Pi}, \mathbf{\Sigma_{VV}}, \mathbf{\Omega}\}$. The relative bias definition of weak instruments is

$$\mathcal{W}_{\text{bias}} = \{\mathcal{Z}: B^{\max} \geq b\}. \tag{3.4}$$

Relative Bias vs. Absolute Bias. Our motivation for normalizing the squared bias measure by the bias of the OLS estimator is that it helps to separate the two problems of endogeneity (OLS bias) and weak instrument (IV bias). For example, in an application to estimating the returns to education, based on a reading of the literature the researcher might believe that the maximum OLS bias is ten percentage points; if the relative bias measure in (3.1) is 0.1, then the maximum bias of the IV estimator is one percentage point. Thus formulating the bias measure in (3.1) as a relative bias measure allows the researcher to return to the natural units of the application using expert judgment about the possible magnitude of the OLS bias.

This said, we will show that the maximal TSLS relative bias is also its maximal absolute bias in standardized units, so that for TSLS the maximal relative and absolute bias can be treated interchangeably. We return to this point in Section 3.3.

3.2. Second Characterization of a Weak Instrument Set: Size

Our second definition of a weak instrument set is based on the maximal size of the Wald test of all the elements of $\boldsymbol{\beta}$. In parallel to the approach for the bias measure, we consider an instrument strong from the perspective of the Wald test if the size of the test is close to its level for all possible configurations of the IV regression model. Let W^{IV} denote the Wald test statistic based on the candidate IV estimator $\hat{\boldsymbol{\beta}}^{\text{IV}}$. For the estimators considered here, under conventional first-order asymptotics, W^{IV} has a chi-squared null distribution with n degrees of freedom, divided by n. The actual rejection rate R_T under the null hypothesis is

$$R_T = \Pr_{\beta_0}\left[W^{\text{IV}} > \chi^2_{n;\alpha}/n\right], \tag{3.5}$$

where $\chi^2_{n;\alpha}$ is the α-level critical value of the chi-squared distribution with n degrees of freedom and α is the nominal level of the test.

In general, the rejection rate in (3.5) depends on $\boldsymbol{\rho}$. As in the definitions of the bias-based weak instrument set, we consider the worst-case limiting rejection rate

$$R^{\max} = \max_{\rho:\rho'\rho \leq 1} R, \quad \text{where } R = \lim_{T\to\infty} R_T. \tag{3.6}$$

The size-based weak instrument set $\mathcal{W}_{\text{size}}$ consists of instruments that can lead to a size of at least $r > \alpha$:

$$\mathcal{W}_{\text{size}} = \{\mathcal{Z}: R^{\max} \geq r\}. \tag{3.7}$$

For example, if $\alpha = .05$ then a researcher might consider it acceptable if the worst-case size is $r = 0.10$.

3.3. Weak Instrument Sets for TSLS

We now apply these general definitions of weak instrument sets to TSLS and argue that the sets can be characterized in terms of the minimum eigenvalue of $\mathbf{\Lambda}$.

3.3.1. *Weak Instrument Set Based on TSLS bias*

Under weak instrument asymptotics,

$$\left(B_T^{\text{TSLS}}\right)^2 \to \frac{\rho'\mathbf{h}'\mathbf{h}\rho}{\rho'\rho} \equiv \left(B^{\text{TSLS}}\right)^2 \quad \text{and} \tag{3.8}$$

$$(B^{\max,\text{TSLS}})^2 = \max_{\rho:0<\rho'\rho\leq 1} \frac{\rho'\mathbf{h}'\mathbf{h}\rho}{\rho'\rho}, \tag{3.9}$$

where $\mathbf{h} = E[\nu_1^{-1}(\boldsymbol{\lambda} + \mathbf{z_V})'\mathbf{z_V}]$. The asymptotic relative bias B^{TSLS} depends on ρ and $\boldsymbol{\lambda}$, which are unknown, as well as on K_2 and n.

Because $\mathbf{h}$ depends on $\boldsymbol{\lambda}$ but not on ρ, by (3.8) we have $B^{\max,\text{TSLS}} = [\text{maxeval}(\mathbf{h}'\mathbf{h})]^{1/2}$, where maxeval($\mathbf{A}$) denotes the maximum eigenvalue of the matrix $\mathbf{A}$. By applying the singular value decomposition to $\boldsymbol{\lambda}$, it is further possible to show that the maximum eigenvalue of $\mathbf{h}'\mathbf{h}$ depends only on K_2, n, and the eigenvalues of $\boldsymbol{\lambda}'\boldsymbol{\lambda}/K_2 = \mathbf{\Lambda}$. It follows that, for a given K_2 and n, the maximum TSLS asymptotic bias is a function only of the eigenvalues of $\mathbf{\Lambda}$.

When the number of instruments is large, it is possible to show further that the maximum TSLS asymptotic bias is a decreasing function of the minimum eigenvalue of $\mathbf{\Lambda}$. Specifically, consider sequences of K_2 and T such that $K_2 \to \infty$ and $T \to \infty$ jointly, subject to $K_2^4/T \to 0$, where $\mathbf{\Lambda}$ (which in general depends on K_2) is held constant as $K_2 \to \infty$.[3] We write this joint limit as $(K_2, T \to \infty)$ and, following Stock and Yogo (2005), we refer to it as representing "many weak instruments." It follows from (3.9) and Theorem 4.1(a) of Stock and Yogo (2003) that the many weak instrument limit of B_T^{TSLS} is

$$\lim_{(K_2,T\to\infty)} \left(B_T^{\text{TSLS}}\right)^2 = \frac{\rho'(\mathbf{\Lambda}+\mathbf{I})^{-2}\rho}{\rho'\rho}. \tag{3.10}$$

By solving the maximization problem (3.9), we obtain the many weak instrument limit, $B^{\max,\text{TSLS}} = [1 + \text{mineval}(\mathbf{\Lambda})]^{-1}$. It follows that, for many instruments, the set $\mathcal{W}_{\text{bias,TSLS}}$ can be characterized by the minimum eigenvalue of $\mathbf{\Lambda}$, and the TSLS weak instrument set $\mathcal{W}_{\text{bias,TSLS}}$ can be written as

$$\mathcal{W}_{\text{bias,TSLS}} = \{\mathcal{Z}\text{: mineval}(\mathbf{\Lambda}) \leq \ell_{\text{bias,TSLS}}(b; K_2, n)\}, \tag{3.11}$$

where $\ell_{\text{bias,TSLS}}(b; K_2, n)$ is a decreasing function of the maximum allowable bias b.

Our formal justification for the simplification that $\mathcal{W}_{\text{bias,TSLS}}$ depends only on the smallest eigenvalue of $\mathbf{\Lambda}$, rather than on all its eigenvalues, rests on

[3] In Stock and Yogo (2005), the assumption that $\mathbf{\Lambda}$ is constant is generalized to consider sequences of $\mathbf{\Lambda}$, indexed by K_2, that have a finite limit $\mathbf{\Lambda}_\infty$ as $K_2 \to \infty$.

the many weak instrument asymptotic result (3.10). Numerical analysis for $n = 2$ suggests, however, that $B^{\max,\text{TSLS}}$ is decreasing in each eigenvalue of $\boldsymbol{\Lambda}$ for all values of K_2. These numerical results suggest that the simplification in (3.11), relying only on the minimum eigenvalue, is valid for all K_2 under weak instrument asymptotics, even though we currently cannot provide a formal proof.[4]

3.3.2. *Reinterpretation in Terms of Absolute Bias*

Although $B^{\max}$ was defined as maximal bias relative to OLS, for TSLS $B^{\max}$ is also the maximal absolute bias in standardized units. The numerator of (3.9) is evidently maximized when $\rho'\rho = 1$. Thus, for TSLS, (3.2) can be restated as $(B^{\max})^2 = \sigma_{uu}^{-1} \max_{\rho:\rho'\rho=1} \lim_{T\to\infty}(E\hat{\beta}^{\text{TSLS}} - \beta)'\Sigma_{Y^\perp Y^\perp}(E\hat{\beta}^{\text{TSLS}} - \beta)$. But $(E\hat{\beta}^{\text{TSLS}} - \beta)'\Sigma_{Y^\perp Y^\perp}(E\hat{\beta}^{\text{TSLS}} - \beta)$ is the squared bias of $\hat{\beta}^{\text{TSLS}}$, not relative to the bias of the OLS estimator. For TSLS, then, the relative bias measure can alternatively be reinterpreted as the maximal bias of the candidate IV estimator, in the standardized units of $\sigma_{uu}^{-1/2}\boldsymbol{\Sigma}_{\mathbf{Y}^\perp\mathbf{Y}^\perp}^{1/2}$.

3.3.3. *Weak Instrument Set Based on TSLS Size*

For TSLS, it follows from (2.22) that the worst-case asymptotic size is

$$R^{\max,\text{TSLS}} = \max_{\rho:\rho'\rho\le 1} \Pr\left[\frac{\nu_2'\nu_1^{-1}\nu_2}{1 - 2\rho'\nu_1^{-1}\nu_2 + \nu_2'\nu_1^{-2}\nu_2} > \chi^2_{n;\alpha}\right]. \tag{3.12}$$

$R^{\max,\text{TSLS}}$, and consequently $\mathcal{W}_{\text{size,TSLS}}$, depends only on the eigenvalues of $\boldsymbol{\Lambda}$ as well as n and K_2 (the reason is the same as for the similar assertion for $B^{\max,\text{TSLS}}$).

When the number of instruments is large, the Wald statistic is maximized when $\rho'\rho = 1$ and is an increasing function of the eigenvalues of $\boldsymbol{\Lambda}$. Specifically, it is shown in Stock and Yogo (2005), Theorem 4.1(a), that the many weak instrument limit of the TSLS Wald statistic, divided by K_2, is

$$W^{\text{TSLS}}/K_2 \xrightarrow{p} \frac{\rho'(\boldsymbol{\Lambda} + \mathbf{I}_n)^{-1}\rho}{n[1 - 2\rho'(\boldsymbol{\Lambda} + \mathbf{I}_n)^{-1}\rho + \rho'(\boldsymbol{\Lambda} + \mathbf{I}_n)^{-2}\rho]}. \tag{3.13}$$

The right-hand side of (3.13) is maximized when $\rho'\rho = 1$, in which case this expression can be written as $\rho'(\boldsymbol{\Lambda} + \mathbf{I}_n)^{-1}\rho/n^{-1}\rho'[\mathbf{I}_n - (\boldsymbol{\Lambda} + \mathbf{I}_n)^{-1}]^2\rho$. In turn, the maximum of this ratio over ρ depends only on the eigenvalues of $\boldsymbol{\Lambda}$ and is decreasing in those eigenvalues.

[4] Because in general the maximal bias depends on all the eigenvalues, the maximal bias when all the eigenvalues are equal to some value ℓ_0 might be greater than the maximal bias when one eigenvalue is slightly less than ℓ_0 but the others are large. For this reason the set $\mathcal{W}_{\text{bias}}$ is potentially conservative when K_2 is small. This comment applies to size-based sets as well.

The many weak instrument limit of $R^{\max,\text{TSLS}}$ is

$$R^{\max,\text{TSLS}} = \max_{\rho:\rho'\rho\leq 1} \lim_{(K_2,T\to\infty)} \Pr\left[W^{\text{TSLS}}/K_2 > \chi^2_{n;\alpha}/nK_2\right] = 1, \tag{3.14}$$

where the limit follows from (3.13) and from $\chi^2_{n;\alpha}/(nK_2) \to 0$. With many weak instruments, the TSLS Wald statistic W^{TSLS} is $O_p(K_2)$, so that the boundary of the weak instrument set, in terms of the eigenvalues of $\mathbf{\Lambda}$, increases as a function of K_2 without bound.

For small values of K_2, numerical analysis suggests that $R^{\max,\text{TSLS}}$ is a nonincreasing function of all the eigenvalues of $\mathbf{\Lambda}$, which (if so) implies that the boundary of the weak instrument set can, for small K_2, be characterized in terms of this minimum eigenvalue. The argument leading to (3.11) therefore applies here and leads to the characterization

$$\mathcal{W}_{\text{size,TSLS}} = \{\mathcal{Z}: \text{mineval}(\mathbf{\Lambda}) \leq \ell_{\text{size,TSLS}}(r; K_2, n, \alpha)\}, \tag{3.15}$$

where $\ell_{\text{size,TSLS}}(r; K_2, n, \alpha)$ is decreasing in the maximal allowable size r.

3.4. Weak Instrument Sets for Other k-Class Estimators

The general definitions of weak instrument sets given in Sections 3.1 and 3.2 can also be applied to other IV estimators. The weak instrument asymptotic distribution for general k-class estimators is given in Section 2.2. What remains to be shown is that the weak instrument sets, defined for specific estimators and test statistics, can be characterized in terms of the minimum eigenvalue of $\mathbf{\Lambda}$. As in the case of TSLS, the argument for the estimators considered here has two parts, for small K_2 and for large K_2.

For small K_2, the argument applied for the TSLS bias can be used generally for k-class statistics to show that, given K_2 and n, the k-class maximal relative bias and maximal size depend only on the eigenvalues of $\mathbf{\Lambda}$. In general, this dependence is complicated and we do not have theoretical results characterizing this dependence. Numerical work for $n = 1$ and $n = 2$, however, indicates that the maximal bias and maximal size measures are decreasing in each of the eigenvalues of $\mathbf{\Lambda}$ in the relevant range of those eigenvalues.[5] This in turn means that the boundary of the weak instrument set can be written in terms of the minimum eigenvalue of $\mathbf{\Lambda}$, although this characterization could be conservative (see Footnote 4).

For large K_2, we can provide theoretical results, based on many weak instrument limits, showing that the boundary of the weak instrument set depends only on mineval($\mathbf{\Lambda}$). These results are summarized here.

[5] It appears that there is some nonmonotonicity in the dependence on the eigenvalues for Fuller-k bias when the minimum eigenvalue is very small, but for such small eigenvalues the bias is sufficiently large so that this nonmonotonicity does not affect the boundary eigenvalues.

3.4.1. LIML and Fuller-k

As shown in Stock and Yogo (2003), Theorem 2(c), the LIML and Fuller-k estimators and their Wald statistics have the many weak instrument asymptotic distributions

$$\sqrt{K_2}(\hat{\beta}^{\text{LIML}} - \beta) \xrightarrow{d} N\left(0, \sigma_{uu}\boldsymbol{\Sigma}_{\mathbf{VV}}^{-1/2}\boldsymbol{\Lambda}^{-1}(\boldsymbol{\Lambda} + \mathbf{I}_n - \rho\rho')\boldsymbol{\Lambda}^{-1}\boldsymbol{\Sigma}_{\mathbf{VV}}^{-1/2\prime}\right), \tag{3.16}$$

$$W^{\text{LIML}} \xrightarrow{d} \mathbf{x}'(\boldsymbol{\Lambda} + \mathbf{I}_n - \rho\rho')^{1/2}\boldsymbol{\Lambda}^{-1}(\boldsymbol{\Lambda} + \mathbf{I}_n - \rho\rho')^{1/2\prime}\mathbf{x}/n, \quad \text{where} \quad x \sim N(0, \mathbf{I}_n), \tag{3.17}$$

where these distributions are written for LIML but also apply to Fuller-k.

An implication of (3.16) is that the LIML and Fuller-k estimators are consistent under the sequence $(K_2, T) \to \infty$, a result shown by Chao and Swanson (2002) for LIML. Thus the many weak instrument maximal relative bias for these estimators is zero.

An implication of (3.17) is that the Wald statistic is distributed as a weighted sum of n independent chi-squared random variables. When $n = 1$, it follows from (3.17) that the many weak instrument size has the simple form

$$\begin{aligned} R^{\max,\text{LIML}} &= \max_{\rho:\rho'\rho \le 1} \lim_{(K_2,T\to\infty)} \Pr\left[W^{\text{LIML}} > \chi^2_{1;\alpha}\right] \\ &= Pr\left[\chi^2_1 > \frac{\boldsymbol{\Lambda}}{\boldsymbol{\Lambda}+1}\chi^2_{1;\alpha}\right], \end{aligned} \tag{3.18}$$

that is, the maximal size is the tail probability that a chi-squared distribution with one degree of freedom exceeds $[\boldsymbol{\Lambda}/(\boldsymbol{\Lambda}+1)]\chi^2_{1;\alpha}$. Evidently, this is decreasing in $\boldsymbol{\Lambda}$ and depends only on $\boldsymbol{\Lambda}$ (which, trivially, here is its minimum eigenvalue).

3.4.2. BTSLS

The many weak instrument asymptotic distributions of the BTSLS estimator and Wald statistic are (Stock and Yogo 2003, Theorem 2(b))

$$\sqrt{K_2}(\hat{\beta}^{\text{BTSLS}} - \beta) \xrightarrow{d} N\left[0, \sigma_{uu}\boldsymbol{\Sigma}_{\mathbf{VV}}^{-1/2}\boldsymbol{\Lambda}^{-1}(\boldsymbol{\Lambda} + \mathbf{I}_n + \rho\rho')\boldsymbol{\Lambda}^{-1}\boldsymbol{\Sigma}_{\mathbf{VV}}^{-1/2\prime}\right], \tag{3.19}$$

$$W^{\text{BTSLS}} \xrightarrow{d} \mathbf{x}'(\boldsymbol{\Lambda} + \mathbf{I}_n + \rho\rho')^{1/2}\boldsymbol{\Lambda}^{-1}(\boldsymbol{\Lambda} + \mathbf{I}_n + \rho\rho')^{1/2\prime}\mathbf{x}/n, \quad \text{where} \quad x \sim N(0, \mathbf{I}_n). \tag{3.20}$$

It follows from (3.19) that the BTSLS estimator is consistent and that its maximal relative bias tends to zero under many weak instrument asymptotics.

For $n = 1$, the argument leading to (3.18) applies to BTSLS, except that the factor is different: the many weak instrument limit of the maximal size is

$$R^{\max,\text{BTSLS}} = \Pr\left[\chi^2_1 > \frac{\boldsymbol{\Lambda}}{\boldsymbol{\Lambda}+2}\chi^2_{1;\alpha}\right], \tag{3.21}$$

which is a decreasing function of $\boldsymbol{\Lambda}$.

It is interesting to note that, according to (3.18) and (3.21), for a given value of $\boldsymbol{\Lambda}$ the maximal size distortion of LIML and Fuller-k tests is less than that of BTSLS when there are many weak instruments.

3.5. Numerical Results for TSLS, LIML, and Fuller-k

We have computed weak instrument sets based on maximum bias and size for several k-class statistics. Here, we focus on TSLS bias and size, Fuller-k (with $c = 1$ in (2.8)) bias, and LIML size. Additional results are reported in Stock et al. (2002). Because LIML does not have moments in finite samples, LIML bias is not well defined so we do not analyze it here.

The TSLS maximal relative bias was computed by Monte Carlo simulation for a grid of minimal eigenvalue of $\boldsymbol{\Lambda}$ from 0 to 30 for $K_2 = n + 2, \ldots, 100$, using 20,000 Monte Carlo draws. Computing the maximum TSLS bias entails computing $\mathbf{h}$, defined following (3.8), by Monte Carlo simulation, given n, K_2, and then computing the maximum bias $[\text{maxeval}(\mathbf{h}'\mathbf{h})]^{1/2}$. Computing the maximum bias of Fuller-k and the maximum size distortions of TSLS and LIML is more involved than computing the maximal TSLS bias because there is no simple analytic solution to the maximum problem (3.6). Numerical analysis indicates that R^{TSLS} is maximized when $\rho'\rho = 1$, and so the maximization for $n = 2$ was done by transforming to polar coordinates and performing a grid search over the half unit circle (half because of symmetry in (2.22)). For Fuller-k bias and LIML size, maximization was performed over this half circle and over $0 \leq \rho'\rho \leq 1$. Because the bias and size measures appear to be decreasing functions of all the eigenvalues, at least in the relevant range, we set $\boldsymbol{\Lambda} = \ell \mathbf{I}_n$. The TSLS size calculations were performed using a grid of ℓ with $0 \leq \ell \leq 75$ (100,000 Monte Carlo draws); for Fuller-k bias, $0 \leq \ell \leq 12$ (50,000 Monte Carlo draws); and for LIML size, $0 \leq \ell \leq 10$ (100,000 Monte Carlo draws).

The minimal eigenvalues of $\boldsymbol{\Lambda}$ that constitute the boundaries of $\mathcal{W}_{\text{bias,TSLS}}$, $\mathcal{W}_{\text{size,TSLS}}$, $\mathcal{W}_{\text{bias,Fuller-k}}$, and $\mathcal{W}_{\text{size,LIML}}$ are plotted, respectively, in the top panels of Figures 5.1–5.4 for various cutoff values b and r. The figures show the boundary eigenvalues for $n = 1$; the corresponding plots of boundary eigenvalues for $n = 2$ are qualitatively, and in many cases quantitatively, similar. First consider the regions based on bias. The boundary of $\mathcal{W}_{\text{bias,TSLS}}$ is essentially flat in K_2 for K_2 sufficiently large. The boundary of the relative bias region for $b = 0.1$ (10% bias) asymptotes to approximately 8. In contrast, the boundary of the bias region for Fuller-k tends to zero as the number of instruments increases, which agrees with the consistency of the Fuller-k estimator under many weak instrument asymptotics.

Turning to the regions based on size, the boundary of $\mathcal{W}_{\text{size,TSLS}}$ depends strongly on K_2; as suggested by (3.14), the boundary is approximately linear in K_2 for K_2 sufficiently large. The boundary eigenvalues are very large when the degree of overidentification is large. For example, if one is willing to tolerate a maximal size of 15%, so the size distortion is 10% for the 5% level test, then

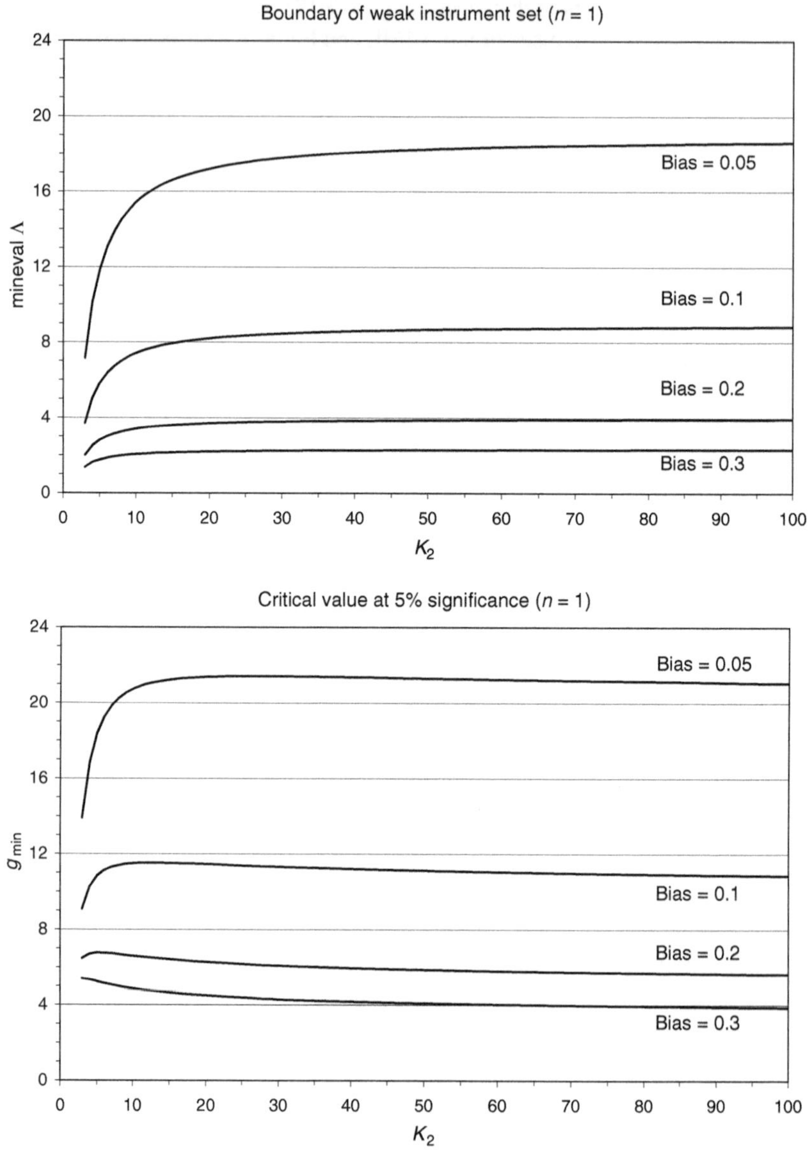

Figure 5.1. Weak instrument sets and critical values based on bias of TSLS relative to OLS.

with 10 instruments the minimum eigenvalue boundary is approximately 20 for $n = 1$ (it is approximately 16 for $n = 2$). In contrast, the boundary of $\mathcal{W}_{\text{size,LIML}}$ decreases with K_2 for both $n = 1$ and $n = 2$. Comparing these two plots shows that tests based on LIML are far more robust to weak instruments than tests based on TSLS.

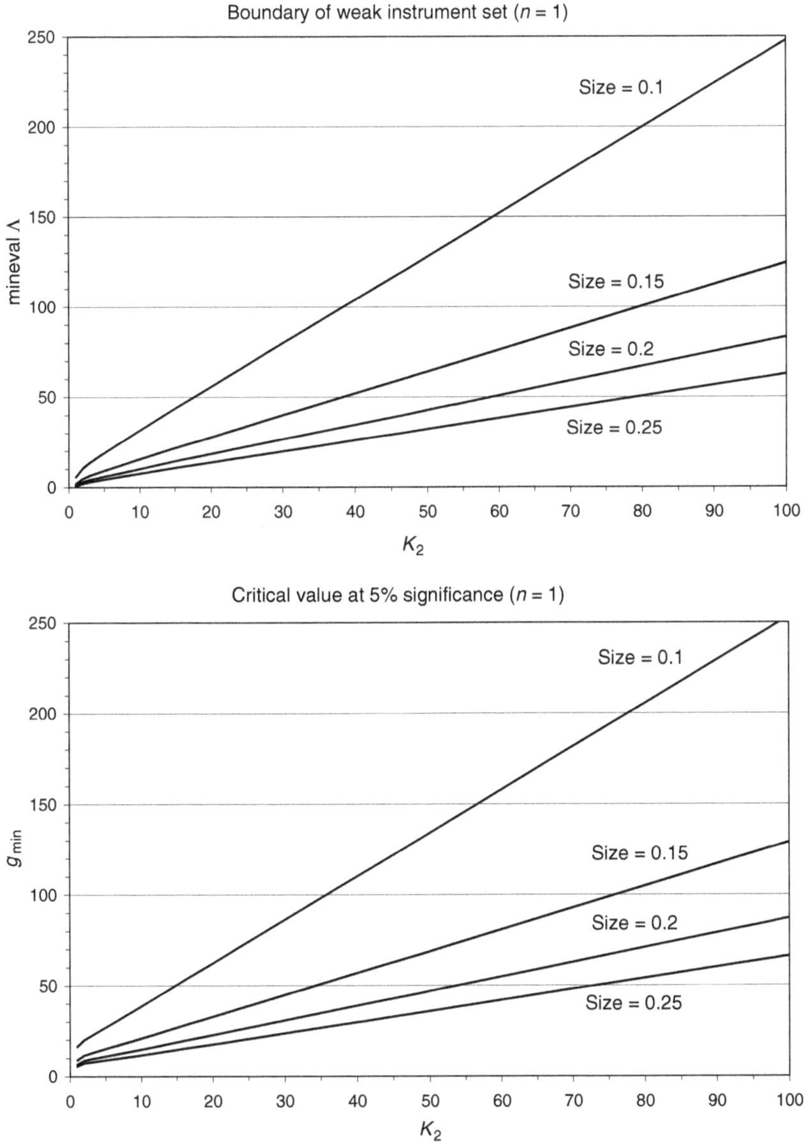

Figure 5.2. Weak instrument sets and critical values based on size of TSLS Wald test.

4. TEST FOR WEAK INSTRUMENTS

This section provides critical values for the weak instrument test based on the Cragg–Donald (1993) statistic $g_{\min}$. These critical values are based on the boundaries of the weak instrument sets obtained in Section 3 and on a bound on the asymptotic distribution of $g_{\min}$.

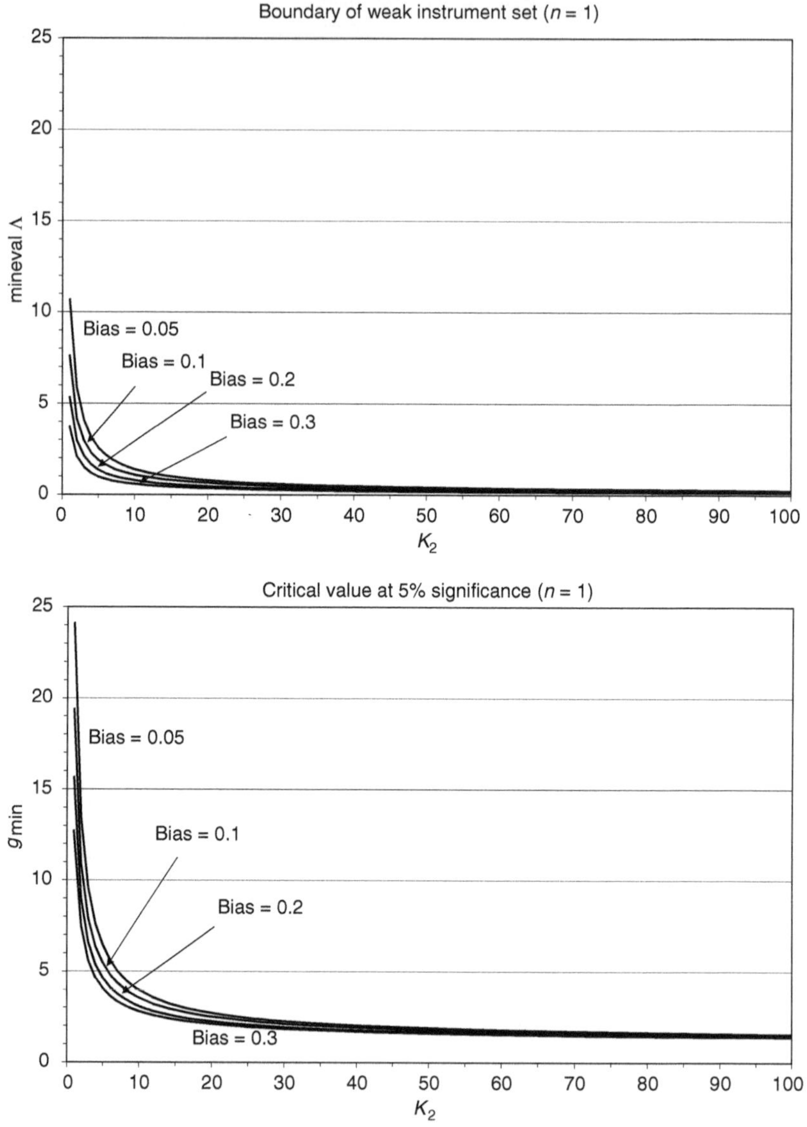

Figure 5.3. Weak instrument sets and critical values based on bias of Fuller-k relative to OLS.

4.1. A Bound on the Asymptotic Distribution of $g_{\min}$

Recall that the Cragg–Donald statistic $g_{\min}$ is the minimum eigenvalue of $\mathbf{G}_T$, where $\mathbf{G}_T$ is given by (2.10). As stated in (2.23), under weak instrument asymptotics, $K_2\mathbf{G}_T$ is asymptotically distributed as a noncentral Wishart with dimension n, degrees of freedom K_2, identity covariance matrix,

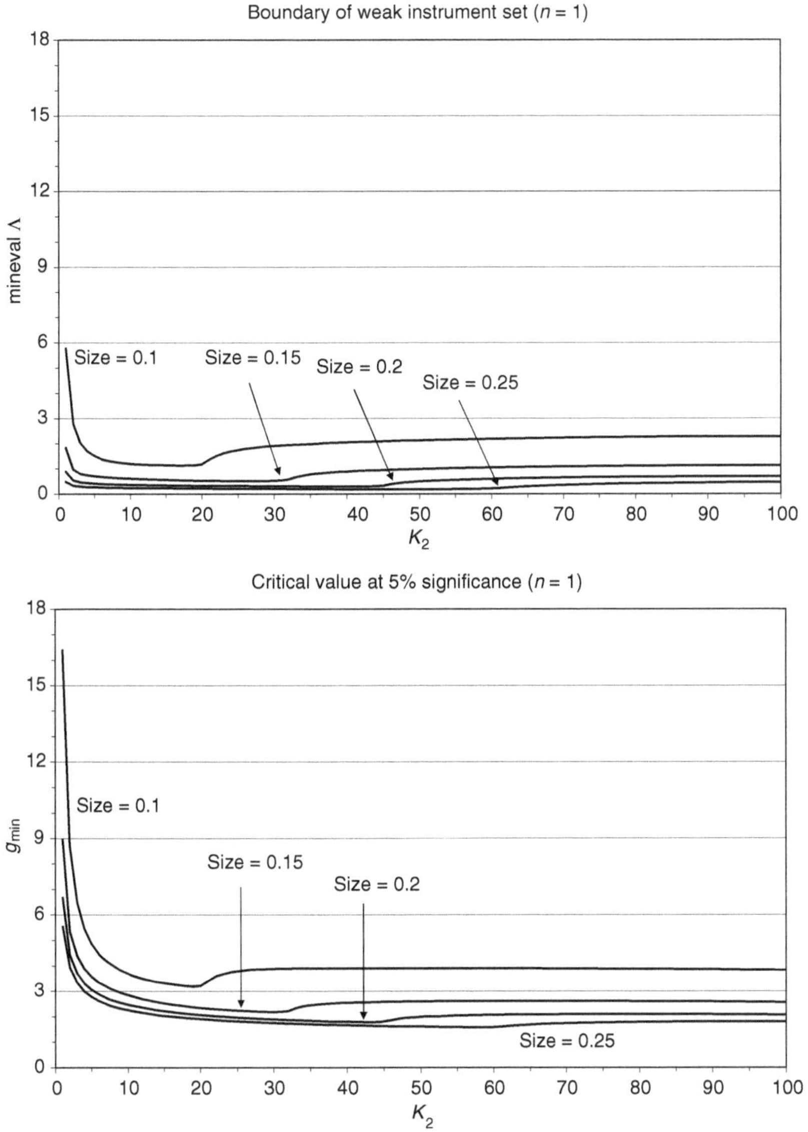

Figure 5.4. Weak instrument sets and critical values based on size of LIML Wald test.

and noncentrality matrix $K_2\mathbf{\Lambda}$; that is,

$$\mathbf{G}_T \xrightarrow{d} \boldsymbol{\nu}_1/K_2 \sim \mathrm{W}_n(K_2, \mathbf{I}_n, K_2\mathbf{\Lambda})/K_2. \tag{4.1}$$

The joint pdf for the n eigenvalues of a noncentral Wishart has an infinite series expansion in terms of zonal polynomials (Muirhead 1978). This joint pdf depends on all the eigenvalues of $\mathbf{\Lambda}$, as well as n and K_2. In principle the pdf for the minimum eigenvalue can be determined from this joint pdf for all the eigenvalues. It appears that this pdf (the "exact asymptotic" pdf of $g_{\min}$) depends on all the eigenvalues of $\mathbf{\Lambda}$.

This exact asymptotic distribution of $g_{\min}$ is not very useful for applications both because of the computational difficulties it poses and because of its dependence on all the eigenvalues of $\mathbf{\Lambda}$. This latter consideration is especially important because in practice these eigenvalues are unknown nuisance parameters, and so critical values that depend on multiple eigenvalues would produce an infeasible test.

We circumvent these two problems by proposing conservative critical values based on the following bounding distribution.

Proposition 4.1. $\Pr[mineval(\mathrm{W}_n(k, \mathbf{I}_n, \mathbf{A})) \geq x] \leq \Pr[\chi_k^2(mineval(\mathbf{A})) \geq x]$, *where* $\chi_k^2(a)$ *denotes a noncentral chi-squared random variable with noncentrality parameter* a.

Proof. Let $\boldsymbol{\alpha}$ be the eigenvector of $\mathbf{A}$ corresponding to its minimum eigenvalue. Then $\boldsymbol{\alpha}'\mathbf{W}\boldsymbol{\alpha}$ is distributed $\chi_k^2(\text{mineval}(\mathbf{A}))$ (Muirhead 1982, Theorem 10.3.6). But $\boldsymbol{\alpha}'\mathbf{W}\boldsymbol{\alpha} \geq \text{mineval}(\mathbf{W})$, and the result follows. ■

Applying (4.1), the continuous mapping theorem, and Proposition 4.1, we have

$$\begin{aligned} \Pr[g_{\min} \geq x] &\to \Pr[\text{mineval}(\boldsymbol{\nu}_1/K_2) \geq x] \\ &\leq \Pr\left[\frac{\chi_{K_2}^2(\text{mineval}(K_2\mathbf{\Lambda}))}{K_2} \geq x\right]. \end{aligned} \tag{4.2}$$

Note that this inequality holds as an equality in the special case $n = 1$.

Conservative critical values for the test based on $g_{\min}$ are obtained as follows. First, select the desired minimal eigenvalue of $\mathbf{\Lambda}$. Next, obtain the desired percentile, say the 95% point, of the noncentral chi-squared distribution with noncentrality parameter equal to K_2 times this selected minimum eigenvalue, and divide this percentile by K_2.[6]

[6] The critical values based on Proposition 4.1 can be quite conservative when all the eigenvalues of $\mathbf{\Lambda}$ are small. For example, the boundary of the TSLS bias-based weak instrument set with $b = 0.1$, $n = 2$, and $K_2 = 4$ is mineval($\mathbf{\Lambda}$) = 3.08, and the critical value for a 5% test with $b = 0.1$ based on Proposition 1 is 7.56. If the second eigenvalue in fact equals the first, the correct critical value should be 4.63, and the rejection probability under the null is only 0.1%. (Of course, it is infeasible to use this critical value because the second eigenvalue of $\mathbf{\Lambda}$ is unknown.) If the second eigenvalue is 10, then the rejection rate is approximately 2%. On the other hand, if the second eigenvalue is large, the Proposition 1 bound is tighter. For example, for values of K_2 from 4 to 34 and $n = 2$, if the second eigenvalue exceeds 20 the rejection probability under the null ranges from 3.3% to 4.1% for the nominal 5% weak instrument test based on TSLS bias with $b = 0.1$.

4.2. The Weak Instruments Test

The bound (4.2) yields the following testing procedure to detect weak instruments. To be concrete, this is stated for a test based on the TSLS bias measure with significance level $100\delta\%$. The null hypothesis is that the instruments are weak, and the alternative is that they are not:

$$H_0\colon \mathcal{Z} \in \mathcal{W}_{\text{bias,TSLS}} \quad \text{vs.} \quad H_1\colon \mathcal{Z} \notin \mathcal{W}_{\text{bias,TSLS}}. \tag{4.3}$$

The test procedure is

$$\text{Reject } H_0 \text{ if } g_{\min} \geq d_{\text{bias,TSLS}}(b; K_2, n, \delta), \tag{4.4}$$

where $d_{\text{bias,TSLS}}(b; K_2, n, \delta) = K_2^{-1}\chi^2_{K_2,1-\delta}(K_2\ell_{\text{bias,TSLS}}(b; K_2, n))$, where $\chi^2_{K_2,1-\delta}(m)$ is the $100(1-\delta)\%$ percentile of the noncentral chi-squared distribution with K_2 degrees of freedom and noncentrality parameter m, and the function $\ell_{\text{bias,TSLS}}$ is the weak instrument boundary minimum eigenvalue of $\mathbf{\Lambda}$ in (3.11).

The results of Section 3 and the bound resulting from Proposition 1 imply that, asymptotically, the test (4.4) has the desired asymptotic level:

$$\lim_{T\to\infty} \Pr[g_{\min} \geq d_{\text{bias,TSLS}}(b; K_2, n, \delta) \mid \mathcal{Z} \in \mathcal{W}_{\text{bias,TSLS}}] \leq \delta. \tag{4.5}$$

The procedure for testing whether the instruments are weak from the perspective of the size of the TSLS (or LIML) is the same, except that the critical value in (4.4) is obtained using the size-based boundary eigenvalue function, $\ell_{\text{size,TSLS}}(r; K_2, n, \alpha)$ (or, for LIML, $\ell_{\text{size,LIML}}(r; K_2, n, \alpha)$).

4.3. Critical Values

Given a minimum eigenvalue ℓ, conservative critical values for the test are percentiles of the scaled noncentral chi-squared distribution $\chi^2_{K_2,1-\delta}(K_2\ell)/K_2$. The minimum eigenvalue ℓ is obtained from the boundary eigenvalue functions in Section 3.5.

Critical values are tabulated in Tables 5.1–5.4 for the weak instrument tests based on TSLS bias,TSLS size, Fuller-k bias, and LIML size, respectively, for one and two included endogenous variables (and three for TSLS bias) and up to 30 instruments. These critical values are plotted in the panel below the corresponding boundaries of the weak instrument sets in Figures 5.1–5.4. The critical value plots are qualitatively similar to the corresponding boundary eigenvalue plots, except of course that the critical values exceed the boundary eigenvalues to take into account the sampling distribution of the test statistic.

These critical value plots provide a basis for comparing the robustness to weak instruments of various procedures: the lower the critical value curve, the

Table 5.1. *Critical values for the weak instrument test based on TSLS bias* (Significance level is 5%)

	$n = 1, b =$				$n = 2, b =$				$n = 3, b =$			
K_2	0.05	0.10	0.20	0.30	0.05	0.10	0.20	0.30	0.05	0.10	0.20	0.30
3	13.91	9.08	6.46	5.39								
4	16.85	10.27	6.71	5.34	11.04	7.56	5.57	4.73				
5	18.37	10.83	6.77	5.25	13.97	8.78	5.91	4.79	9.53	6.61	4.99	4.30
6	19.28	11.12	6.76	5.15	15.72	9.48	6.08	4.78	12.20	7.77	5.35	4.40
7	19.86	11.29	6.73	5.07	16.88	9.92	6.16	4.76	13.95	8.50	5.56	4.44
8	20.25	11.39	6.69	4.99	17.70	10.22	6.20	4.73	15.18	9.01	5.69	4.46
9	20.53	11.46	6.65	4.92	18.30	10.43	6.22	4.69	16.10	9.37	5.78	4.46
10	20.74	11.49	6.61	4.86	18.76	10.58	6.23	4.66	16.80	9.64	5.83	4.45
11	20.90	11.51	6.56	4.80	19.12	10.69	6.23	4.62	17.35	9.85	5.87	4.44
12	21.01	11.52	6.53	4.75	19.40	10.78	6.22	4.59	17.80	10.01	5.90	4.42
13	21.10	11.52	6.49	4.71	19.64	10.84	6.21	4.56	18.17	10.14	5.92	4.41
14	21.18	11.52	6.45	4.67	19.83	10.89	6.20	4.53	18.47	10.25	5.93	4.39
15	21.23	11.51	6.42	4.63	19.98	10.93	6.19	4.50	18.73	10.33	5.94	4.37
16	21.28	11.50	6.39	4.59	20.12	10.96	6.17	4.48	18.94	10.41	5.94	4.36
17	21.31	11.49	6.36	4.56	20.23	10.99	6.16	4.45	19.13	10.47	5.94	4.34
18	21.34	11.48	6.33	4.53	20.33	11.00	6.14	4.43	19.29	10.52	5.94	4.32
19	21.36	11.46	6.31	4.51	20.41	11.02	6.13	4.41	19.44	10.56	5.94	4.31
20	21.38	11.45	6.28	4.48	20.48	11.03	6.11	4.39	19.56	10.60	5.93	4.29
21	21.39	11.44	6.26	4.46	20.54	11.04	6.10	4.37	19.67	10.63	5.93	4.28
22	21.40	11.42	6.24	4.43	20.60	11.05	6.08	4.35	19.77	10.65	5.92	4.27
23	21.41	11.41	6.22	4.41	20.65	11.05	6.07	4.33	19.86	10.68	5.92	4.25
24	21.41	11.40	6.20	4.39	20.69	11.05	6.06	4.32	19.94	10.70	5.91	4.24
25	21.42	11.38	6.18	4.37	20.73	11.06	6.05	4.30	20.01	10.71	5.90	4.23
26	21.42	11.37	6.16	4.35	20.76	11.06	6.03	4.29	20.07	10.73	5.90	4.21
27	21.42	11.36	6.14	4.34	20.79	11.06	6.02	4.27	20.13	10.74	5.89	4.20
28	21.42	11.34	6.13	4.32	20.82	11.05	6.01	4.26	20.18	10.75	5.88	4.19
29	21.42	11.33	6.11	4.31	20.84	11.05	6.00	4.24	20.23	10.76	5.88	4.18
30	21.42	11.32	6.09	4.29	20.86	11.05	5.99	4.23	20.27	10.77	5.87	4.17

Notes. The test rejects if $g_{\min}$ exceeds the critical value. The critical value is a function of the number of included endogenous regressors (n), the number of instrumental variables (K_2), and the desired maximal bias of the IV estimator relative to OLS (b).

Table 5.2. *Critical values for the weak instrument test based on TSLS size* (Significance level is 5%)

	$n = 1, r =$				$n = 2, r =$			
K_2	0.10	0.15	0.20	0.25	0.10	0.15	0.20	0.25
1	16.38	8.96	6.66	5.53				
2	19.93	11.59	8.75	7.25	7.03	4.58	3.95	3.63
3	22.30	12.83	9.54	7.80	13.43	8.18	6.40	5.45
4	24.58	13.96	10.26	8.31	16.87	9.93	7.54	6.28
5	26.87	15.09	10.98	8.84	19.45	11.22	8.38	6.89
6	29.18	16.23	11.72	9.38	21.68	12.33	9.10	7.42
7	31.50	17.38	12.48	9.93	23.72	13.34	9.77	7.91
8	33.84	18.54	13.24	10.50	25.64	14.31	10.41	8.39
9	36.19	19.71	14.01	11.07	27.51	15.24	11.03	8.85
10	38.54	20.88	14.78	11.65	29.32	16.16	11.65	9.31
11	40.90	22.06	15.56	12.23	31.11	17.06	12.25	9.77
12	43.27	23.24	16.35	12.82	32.88	17.95	12.86	10.22
13	45.64	24.42	17.14	13.41	34.62	18.84	13.45	10.68
14	48.01	25.61	17.93	14.00	36.36	19.72	14.05	11.13
15	50.39	26.80	18.72	14.60	38.08	20.60	14.65	11.58
16	52.77	27.99	19.51	15.19	39.80	21.48	15.24	12.03
17	55.15	29.19	20.31	15.79	41.51	22.35	15.83	12.49
18	57.53	30.38	21.10	16.39	43.22	23.22	16.42	12.94
19	59.92	31.58	21.90	16.99	44.92	24.09	17.02	13.39
20	62.30	32.77	22.70	17.60	46.62	24.96	17.61	13.84
21	64.69	33.97	23.50	18.20	48.31	25.82	18.20	14.29
22	67.07	35.17	24.30	18.80	50.01	26.69	18.79	14.74
23	69.46	36.37	25.10	19.41	51.70	27.56	19.38	15.19
24	71.85	37.57	25.90	20.01	53.39	28.42	19.97	15.64
25	74.24	38.77	26.71	20.61	55.07	29.29	20.56	16.10
26	76.62	39.97	27.51	21.22	56.76	30.15	21.15	16.55
27	79.01	41.17	28.31	21.83	58.45	31.02	21.74	17.00
28	81.40	42.37	29.12	22.43	60.13	31.88	22.33	17.45
29	83.79	43.57	29.92	23.04	61.82	32.74	22.92	17.90
30	86.17	44.78	30.72	23.65	63.51	33.61	23.51	18.35

Notes. The test rejects if $g_{\min}$ exceeds the critical value. The critical value is a function of the number of included endogenous regressors (n), the number of instrumental variables (K_2), and the desired maximal size (r) of a 5% Wald test of $\beta = \beta_0$.

more robust is the procedure. For discussion and comparisons of TSLS, BTSLS, Fuller-k, JIVE, and LIML, see Stock et al. (2002, Section 6).

4.3.1. *Comparison to the Staiger–Stock Rule of Thumb*

Staiger and Stock (1997) suggested the rule of thumb that, in the $n = 1$ case, instruments be deemed weak if the first-stage F is less than 10. They motivated

Table 5.3. *Critical values for the weak instrument test based on Fuller-k bias* (Significance level is 5%)

	$n = 1, b =$				$n = 1, b =$			
K_2	0.05	0.10	0.20	0.30	0.05	0.10	0.20	0.30
1	24.09	19.36	15.64	12.71				
2	13.46	10.89	9.00	7.49	15.50	12.55	9.72	8.03
3	9.61	7.90	6.61	5.60	10.83	8.96	7.18	6.15
4	7.63	6.37	5.38	4.63	8.53	7.15	5.85	5.10
5	6.42	5.44	4.62	4.03	7.16	6.07	5.04	4.44
6	5.61	4.81	4.11	3.63	6.24	5.34	4.48	3.98
7	5.02	4.35	3.75	3.33	5.59	4.82	4.08	3.65
8	4.58	4.01	3.47	3.11	5.10	4.43	3.77	3.39
9	4.23	3.74	3.25	2.93	4.71	4.12	3.53	3.19
10	3.96	3.52	3.07	2.79	4.41	3.87	3.33	3.02
11	3.73	3.34	2.92	2.67	4.15	3.67	3.17	2.88
12	3.54	3.19	2.80	2.57	3.94	3.49	3.04	2.77
13	3.38	3.06	2.70	2.48	3.76	3.35	2.92	2.67
14	3.24	2.95	2.61	2.41	3.60	3.22	2.82	2.58
15	3.12	2.85	2.53	2.34	3.47	3.11	2.73	2.51
16	3.01	2.76	2.46	2.28	3.35	3.01	2.65	2.44
17	2.92	2.69	2.39	2.23	3.24	2.92	2.58	2.38
18	2.84	2.62	2.34	2.18	3.15	2.84	2.52	2.33
19	2.76	2.56	2.29	2.14	3.06	2.77	2.46	2.28
20	2.69	2.50	2.24	2.10	2.98	2.71	2.41	2.23
21	2.63	2.45	2.20	2.07	2.91	2.65	2.36	2.19
22	2.58	2.40	2.16	2.04	2.85	2.60	2.32	2.16
23	2.52	2.36	2.13	2.01	2.79	2.55	2.28	2.12
24	2.48	2.32	2.10	1.98	2.73	2.50	2.24	2.09
25	2.43	2.28	2.06	1.95	2.68	2.46	2.21	2.06
26	2.39	2.24	2.04	1.93	2.63	2.42	2.18	2.03
27	2.36	2.21	2.01	1.90	2.59	2.38	2.15	2.01
28	2.32	2.18	1.99	1.88	2.55	2.35	2.12	1.98
29	2.29	2.15	1.96	1.86	2.51	2.31	2.09	1.96
30	2.26	2.12	1.94	1.84	2.47	2.28	2.07	1.94

Notes. The test rejects if g_{min} exceeds the critical value. The critical value is a function of the number of included endogenous regressors (n), the number of instrumental variables (K_2), and the desired maximal bias of the IV estimator relative to OLS (b).

this suggestion based on the relative bias of TSLS. Because the 5% critical value for the relative bias weak instrument test with $b = 0.1$ is approximately 11 for all values of K_2, the Staiger–Stock rule of thumb is approximately a 5% test that the worst-case relative bias is approximately 10% or less. This provides a formal, and not unreasonable, testing interpretation of the Staiger–Stock rule of thumb.

Table 5.4. *Critical values for the weak instrument test based on LIML size* (Significance level is 5%)

	$n = 1, r =$				$n = 1, r =$			
K_2	0.10	0.15	0.20	0.25	0.10	0.15	0.20	0.25
1	16.38	8.96	6.66	5.53				
2	8.68	5.33	4.42	3.92	7.03	4.58	3.95	3.63
3	6.46	4.36	3.69	3.32	5.44	3.81	3.32	3.09
4	5.44	3.87	3.30	2.98	4.72	3.39	2.99	2.79
5	4.84	3.56	3.05	2.77	4.32	3.13	2.78	2.60
6	4.45	3.34	2.87	2.61	4.06	2.95	2.63	2.46
7	4.18	3.18	2.73	2.49	3.90	2.83	2.52	2.35
8	3.97	3.04	2.63	2.39	3.78	2.73	2.43	2.27
9	3.81	2.93	2.54	2.32	3.70	2.66	2.36	2.20
10	3.68	2.84	2.46	2.25	3.64	2.60	2.30	2.14
11	3.58	2.76	2.40	2.19	3.60	2.55	2.25	2.09
12	3.50	2.69	2.34	2.14	3.58	2.52	2.21	2.05
13	3.42	2.63	2.29	2.10	3.56	2.48	2.17	2.02
14	3.36	2.57	2.25	2.06	3.55	2.46	2.14	1.99
15	3.31	2.52	2.21	2.03	3.54	2.44	2.11	1.96
16	3.27	2.48	2.18	2.00	3.55	2.42	2.09	1.93
17	3.24	2.44	2.14	1.97	3.55	2.41	2.07	1.91
18	3.20	2.41	2.11	1.94	3.56	2.40	2.05	1.89
19	3.18	2.37	2.09	1.92	3.57	2.39	2.03	1.87
20	3.21	2.34	2.06	1.90	3.58	2.38	2.02	1.86
21	3.39	2.32	2.04	1.88	3.59	2.38	2.01	1.84
22	3.57	2.29	2.02	1.86	3.60	2.37	1.99	1.83
23	3.68	2.27	2.00	1.84	3.62	2.37	1.98	1.81
24	3.75	2.25	1.98	1.83	3.64	2.37	1.98	1.80
25	3.79	2.24	1.96	1.81	3.65	2.37	1.97	1.79
26	3.82	2.22	1.95	1.80	3.67	2.38	1.96	1.78
27	3.85	2.21	1.93	1.78	3.74	2.38	1.96	1.77
28	3.86	2.20	1.92	1.77	3.87	2.38	1.95	1.77
29	3.87	2.19	1.90	1.76	4.02	2.39	1.95	1.76
30	3.88	2.18	1.89	1.75	4.12	2.39	1.95	1.75

Notes. The test rejects if $g_{\min}$ exceeds the critical value. The critical value is a function of the number of included endogenous regressors (n), the number of instrumental variables (K_2), and the desired maximal size (r) of a 5% Wald test of $\beta = \beta_0$.

The rule of thumb fares less well from the perspective of size distortion. When the number of instruments is one or two, the Staiger–Stock rule of thumb corresponds to a 5% level test that the maximum size is no more than 15% (so that the maximum TSLS size distortion is no more than 10%). However, when the number of instruments is moderate or large, the critical value is much larger and the rule of thumb does not provide substantial assurance that the size distortion is controlled.

5. ASYMPTOTIC PROPERTIES OF THE TEST AS A DECISION RULE

This section examines the asymptotic rejection rate of the weak instrument test as a function of the smallest eigenvalue of $\mathbf{\Lambda}$. When this eigenvalue exceeds the boundary minimum eigenvalue for the weak instrument set, the asymptotic rejection rate is the asymptotic power function.

The exact asymptotic distribution of $g_{\min}$ depends on all the eigenvalues of $\mathbf{\Lambda}$. It is bounded above by (4.2). On the basis of numerical analysis, we conjecture that this distribution is bounded below by the distribution of the minimum eigenvalue of a random matrix with the noncentral Wishart distribution $\mathrm{W}_n(K_2, \mathbf{I}_n, \text{mineval}(K_2\mathbf{\Lambda})\mathbf{I}_n)/K_2$. These two bounding distributions are used to bound the distribution of $g_{\min}$ as a function of mineval($\mathbf{\Lambda}$).

The bounds on the asymptotic rejection rate of the test (4.4) (based on TSLS maximum relative bias) are plotted in Figure 5.5 for $b = 0.1$ and $n = 2$. The value of the horizontal axis (the minimum eigenvalue) at which the upper rejection rate curve equals 5% is $\ell_{\text{bias}}(.1; K_2, 2)$. Evidently, as the minimum eigenvalue increases, so does the rejection rate. The rejection curve becomes steeper as K_2 increases. The bounding distributions give a fairly tight range for the actual power function, which depends on all the eigenvalues of $\mathbf{\Lambda}$.

The analogous curves for the test based on Fuller-k bias,TSLS size, or LIML size are centered differently because the tests have different critical values but otherwise are qualitatively similar to those in Figure 5.5 and thus are omitted.

Interpretation as a Decision Rule

It is useful to think of the weak instrument test as a decision rule: if $g_{\min}$ is less than the critical value, conclude that the instruments are weak, otherwise conclude that they are strong.

Under this interpretation, the asymptotic rejection rates in Figure 5.5 bound the asymptotic probability of deciding that the instruments are strong. Evidently, for values of mineval($\mathbf{\Lambda}$) much below the weak instrument region boundary, the probability of correctly concluding that the instruments are weak is effectively equal to 1. Thus, if in fact the researcher is confronted by instruments that are quite weak, this will be detected by the weak instruments test with probability essentially equal to 1. Similarly, if the researcher has instruments with a minimum eigenvalue of $\mathbf{\Lambda}$ substantially above the threshold for the weak instruments set, then the probability of correctly concluding that they are strong also is essentially equal to 1.

The range of ambiguity of the decision procedure is given by the values of the minimum eigenvalue for which the asymptotic rejection rates effectively fall between 0 and 1. When K_2 is small this range can be 10 or more, but for K_2 large this range of potential ambiguity of the decision rule is quite narrow.

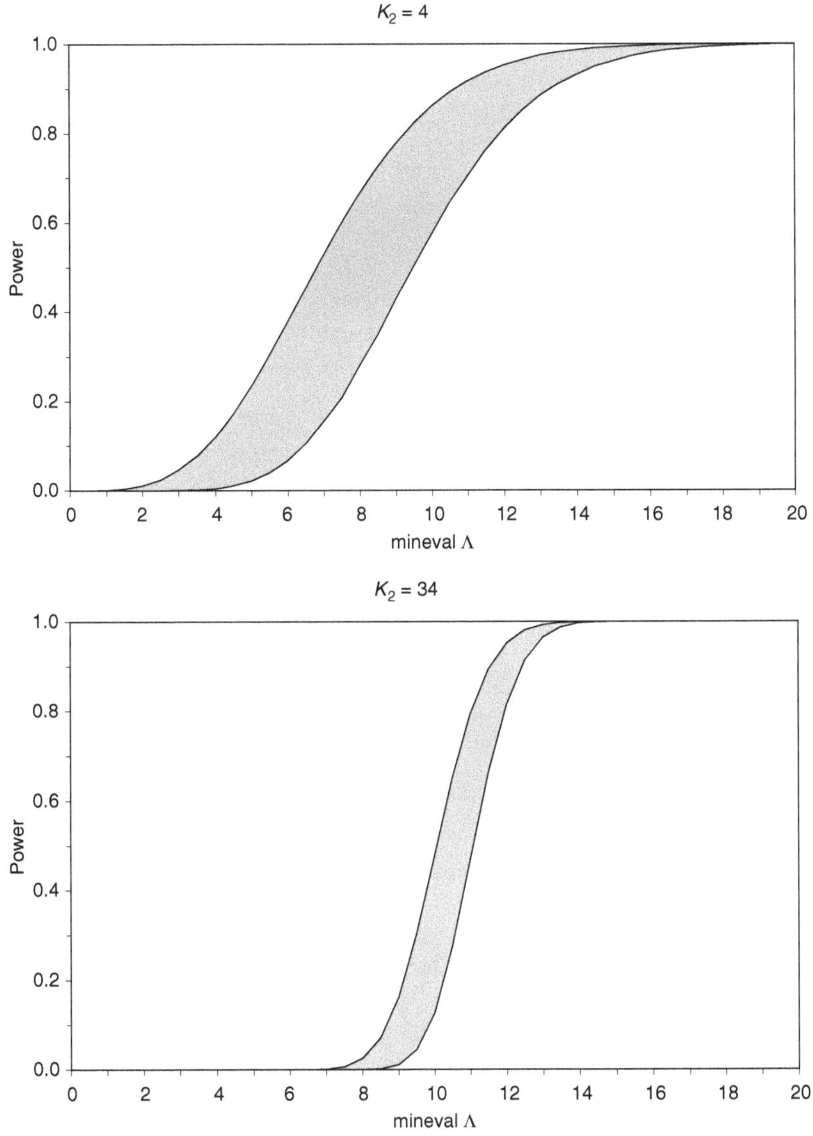

Figure 5.5. Power function for TSLS bias test (Relative bias $= 0.1$, $n = 2$).

6. CONCLUSIONS

The procedure proposed here is simple: compare the minimum eigenvalue of $\mathbf{G}_T$, the first-stage F-statistic matrix, to a critical value. The critical value is determined by the IV estimator the researcher is using, the number of instruments K_2, the number of included endogenous regressors n, and how much bias or size distortion the researcher is willing to tolerate. The test statistic is the same whether one focuses on the bias of TSLS or Fuller-k or on the size of TSLS or LIML; all that differs is the critical value.

Viewed as a test, the procedure has good power, especially when the number of instruments is large. Viewed as a decision rule, the procedure effectively discriminates between weak and strong instruments, and the region of ambiguity decreases as the number of instruments increases.

Our findings support the view that LIML is far superior to TSLS when the researcher has weak instruments, at least from the perspective of coverage rates. Actual LIML coverage rates are close to their nominal rates even for quite small values of the concentration parameter, especially for moderately many instruments. Similarly, the Fuller-k estimator is more robust to weak instruments than TSLS when viewed from the perspective of bias. Additional comparisons are made in Stock et al. (2002).

When there is a single included endogenous variable, this procedure provides a refinement and improvement to the Staiger–Stock (1997) rule of thumb that instruments be deemed "weak" if the first-stage F is less than 10. The difference between that rule of thumb and the procedure of this paper is that, instead of comparing the first-stage F to 10, it should be compared to the appropriate entry in Table 5.1 (TSLS bias), Table 5.2 (TSLS size), Table 5.3 (Fuller-k bias), or Table 5.4 (LIML size). Those critical values indicate that their rule of thumb can be interpreted as a test, with approximately a 5% significance level, of the hypothesis that the maximum relative bias is at least 10%. The Staiger–Stock rule of thumb is too conservative if LIML or Fuller-k are used unless the number of instruments is very small, but it is insufficiently conservative to ensure that the TSLS Wald test has good size.

This paper has two loose ends. First, the characterization of the set of weak instruments is based on the premise that the maximum relative bias and the maximum size distortion are nonincreasing in each eigenvalue of $\mathbf{\Lambda}$, for values of those eigenvalues in the relevant range. This was justified formally using the many weak instrument asymptotics of Stock and Yogo (2003); although numerical analysis suggests it is true for all K_2, this remains to be proven. Second, the lower bound of the power function in Section 5 is based on the assumption that the cdf of the minimum eigenvalue of a noncentral Wishart random variable is nondecreasing in each of the eigenvalues of its noncentrality matrix. This too appears to be true on the basis of numerical analysis, but we do not have a proof, nor does this result seem to be available in the literature.

Beyond this, several avenues of research remain open. First, the tests proposed here are conservative when $n > 1$ because they use critical values computed using the noncentral chi-squared bound in Proposition 4.1. Although the tests appear to have good power despite this, tightening the Proposition 4.1 bound (or constructing tests based on all the eigenvalues) could produce more powerful tests. Second, we have considered inference based on TSLS, Fuller-k, and LIML, but there are other estimators to explore as well. Third, the analysis here is predicated upon homoskedasticity, and it remains to extend these tests to GMM estimation of the linear IV regression model under heteroskedasticity.

ACKNOWLEDGMENTS

We thank Alastair Hall, Jerry Hausman, Takesi Hayakawa, George Judge, Whitney Newey, and Jonathan Wright for helpful comments and/or suggestions. This research was supported by NSF grants SBR-9730489 and SBR-0214131.

References

Bound, J., D. A. Jaeger, and R. M. Baker (1995), "Problems with Instrumental Variables Estimation when the Correlation Between the Instruments and the Endogenous Explanatory Variable is Weak," *Journal of the American Statistical Association*, 90, 443–50.

Bowden, R., and D. Turkington (1984), *Instrumental Variables*. Cambridge: Cambridge University Press.

Chao, J. C., and N. R. Swanson (2002), "Consistent Estimation with a Large Number of Weak Instruments," unpublished manuscript, University of Maryland.

Cragg, J. G., and S. G. Donald (1993), "Testing Identifiability and Specification in Instrumental Variable Models," *Econometric Theory*, 9, 222–40.

Donald, S. G., and W. K. Newey (2001), "Choosing the Number of Instruments," *Econometrica*, 69, 1161–91.

Fuller, W. A. (1977): "Some Properties of a Modification of the Limited Information Estimator," *Econometrica*, 45, 939–53.

Hall, A., G. D. Rudebusch, and D. Wilcox (1996), "Judging Instrument Relevance in Instrumental Variables Estimation," *International Economic Review*, 37, 283–98.

Hahn, J., and J. Hausman (2002), "A New Specification Test for the Validity of Instrumental Variables," *Econometrica*, 70, 163–89.

Hahn, J., and J. Hausman (2003), "Weak Instruments: Diagnosis and Cures in Empirical Econometrics," *American Economic Review, Papers and Proceedings*, 93, 118–25.

Muirhead, R. J. (1978), "Latent Roots and Matrix Variates: A Review of Some Asymptotic Results," *Annals of Statistics*, 6, 5–33.

Muirhead, R. J. (1982), *Aspects of Multivariate Statistical Theory*. New York: Wiley.

Nagar, A. L. (1959), "The Bias and Moment Matrix of the General k-Class Estimators of the Parameters in Simultaneous Equations," *Econometrica*, 27, 575–95.

Nelson, C. R., and R. Startz (1990a), "Some Further Results on the Exact Small Sample Properties of the Instrumental Variables Estimator," *Econometrica*, 58, 967–76.

Nelson, C. R., and R. Startz (1990b), "The Distribution of the Instrumental Variables Estimator and Its t-Ratio when the Instrument is a Poor One," *Journal of Business*, 63, 5125–40.

Rothenberg, T. J. (1983), "Asymptotic Properties of Some Estimators in Structural Models," in (ed. by S. Karlin, T. Amemiya, and L. Goodman), *Studies in Econometrics, Time Series, and Multivariate Statistics*. Orlando: Academic Press.

Rothenberg, T. J. (1984), "Approximating the Distributions of Econometric Estimators and Test Statistics," Chapter 15 in *Handbook of Econometrics*, Vol. II (ed. by Z. Griliches and M. D. Intriligator), Amsterdam: North Holland, 881–935.

Shea, J. (1997), "Instrument Relevance in Multivariate Linear Models: A Simple Measure," *Review of Economics and Statistics*, 79, 348–52.

Staiger, D., and J. H. Stock (1997): "Instrumental Variables Regression with Weak Instruments," *Econometrica*, 65, 557–86.

Stock, J. H., J. H. Wright, and M. Yogo (2002), "A Survey of Weak Instruments and Weak Identification in Generalized Method of Moments," *Journal of Business and Economic Statistics*, 20, 518–29.

Stock, J. H., and M. Yogo (2005), "Asymptotic Distributions of Instrumental Variables Statistics with Many Weak Instruments," Chapter 6 in this volume.

CHAPTER 6

Asymptotic Distributions of Instrumental Variables Statistics with Many Instruments

James H. Stock and Motohiro Yogo

ABSTRACT

This paper extends Staiger and Stock's (1997) weak instrument asymptotic approximations to the case of many weak instruments by modeling the number of instruments as increasing slowly with the number of observations. It is shown that the resulting "many weak instrument" approximations can be calculated sequentially by letting first the sample size, and then the number of instruments, tend to infinity. The resulting distributions are given for k-class estimators and test statistics.

1. INTRODUCTION

Most of the literature on the distribution of statistics in instrumental variables (IV) regression assumes, either implicitly or explicitly, that the number of instruments (K_2) is small relative to the number of observations (T); see Rothenberg's (1984) survey of Edgeworth approximations to the distributions of IV statistics. In some applications, however, the number of instruments can be large; for example, Angrist and Krueger (1991) had 178 instruments in one of their specifications. Sargan (1975), Kunitomo (1980), and Morimune (1983) provided early asymptotic treatments of many instruments. More recently, Bekker (1994) obtained first-order distributions of various IV estimators under the assumptions that $K_2 \to \infty$, $T \to \infty$, and $K_2/T \to c$, $0 \leq c < 1$, when the so-called concentration parameter (μ^2) is proportional to the sample size and the errors are Gaussian. Chao and Swanson (2002) have explored the consistency of IV estimators with weak instruments when the number of instruments is large, in the sense that K_2 is also modeled as increasing to infinity, but more slowly than T.

This paper continues this line of research on the asymptotic distribution of IV estimators when there are many instruments. Our focus is on the case of many weak instruments, that is, when there are many instruments that are, on average, only weakly correlated with the included endogenous regressors. Specifically, we extend the weak instrument asymptotics developed in Staiger and Stock (1997) to the case of many instruments. The key technical device of the Staiger–Stock (1997) weak instrument asymptotics is fixing the expected value of the concentration parameter, along with the number of instruments, as the sample size increases. Here, we extend this to the case that the expected value of the concentration parameter is proportional to the number of instruments, and the number of instruments is allowed to increase slowly with the sample size, specifically, as $T \to \infty$, $K_2 \to \infty$, $E(\mu^2)/K_2 \to \Lambda_\infty$ (a fixed matrix), and $K_2^4/T \to 0$. We refer to asymptotic limits taken under sequences satisfying these conditions as *many weak instrument limits*. (The term "many" should not be overinterpreted because while the number of instruments is allowed to tend to infinity, the condition $K_2^4/T \to 0$ requires it to do so very slowly relative to the sample size.) Under these conditions, and some additional technical conditions stated in Section 2 (including i.i.d. sampling and existence of fourth moments), it is shown that the limits of k-class IV statistics as K_2 and T jointly tend to infinity can in general be computed using sequential asymptotic limits. Under sequential asymptotics, the fixed-K_2 weak instrument limit is obtained first, then the limit of that distribution is taken as $K_2 \to \infty$. The advantage of this "first T then K_2" approach is that the sequential calculations are simpler than the calculations that arise along the joint sequence of (K_2, T). A potential disadvantage of this approach is that this simplicity comes at the cost of a stronger rate condition than might be obtained along the joint sequence.

We begin in Section 2 by specifying the model, the k-class IV statistics of interest, and our assumptions. Section 3 justifies the sequential asymptotics by showing that, under these assumptions, a key uniform convergence condition holds. In Section 4, we derive the many weak instrument limits of k-class estimators and test statistics using sequential asymptotics. These many weak instrument limits are used in Stock and Yogo (2004) to develop tests for weak instruments when the number of instruments is moderate. Some of these results might be of more general interest, however; for example, Chao and Swanson (2002) show that LIML is consistent under these conditions, and in this paper we provide its $\sqrt{K_2}$-limiting distribution. Section 5 provides some concluding remarks.

2. THE MODEL, STATISTICS, AND ASSUMPTIONS

2.1. Model and Notation

We consider the IV regression model with n included endogenous regressors:

$$\mathbf{y} = \mathbf{Y}\beta + \mathbf{u}, \tag{2.1}$$

$$\mathbf{Y} = \mathbf{Z}\Pi + \mathbf{V}, \tag{2.2}$$

where $\mathbf{y}$ is the $T \times 1$ vector of T observations on the dependent variable, $\mathbf{Y}$ is the $T \times n$ matrix of n included endogenous variables, $\mathbf{Z}$ is the $T \times K_2$ matrix of K_2 excluded exogenous variables to be used as instruments, and $\mathbf{u}$ and $\mathbf{V}$ are a $T \times 1$ vector and $T \times n$ matrix of disturbances, respectively. The $n \times 1$

vector $\boldsymbol{\beta}$ and $K_2 \times n$ matrix $\boldsymbol{\Pi}$ are unknown parameters. Throughout this paper we exclusively consider inference about $\boldsymbol{\beta}$.

It is useful to introduce some additional notation. Let $\mathbf{Z}_t = (Z_{1t} \cdots Z_{K_2t})'$, $\mathbf{V}_t = (V_{1t} \cdots V_{nt})'$, $\underline{\mathbf{Y}} = [\mathbf{y}\,\mathbf{Y}]$, $\mathbf{Q}_{ZZ} = E(\mathbf{Z}_t\mathbf{Z}_t')$,

$$\boldsymbol{\Sigma} = E\left[\begin{pmatrix} u_t \\ \mathbf{V}_t \end{pmatrix}\begin{pmatrix} u_t & \mathbf{V}_t' \end{pmatrix}\right] = \begin{bmatrix} \sigma_{uu} & \boldsymbol{\Sigma}_{u\mathbf{V}} \\ \boldsymbol{\Sigma}_{\mathbf{V}u} & \boldsymbol{\Sigma}_{\mathbf{VV}} \end{bmatrix}, \tag{2.3}$$

$$\boldsymbol{\rho} = \boldsymbol{\Sigma}_{\mathbf{VV}}^{-1/2\prime}\boldsymbol{\Sigma}_{\mathbf{V}u}\sigma_{uu}^{-1/2}, \tag{2.4}$$

$$\mathbf{C} = \sqrt{T}\boldsymbol{\Pi}, \quad \text{and} \tag{2.5}$$

$$\boldsymbol{\Lambda}_{K_2} = T\boldsymbol{\Sigma}_{\mathbf{VV}}^{-1/2}\boldsymbol{\Pi}'\mathbf{Q}_{ZZ}\boldsymbol{\Pi}\boldsymbol{\Sigma}_{\mathbf{VV}}^{-1/2\prime}/K_2 = \boldsymbol{\Sigma}_{\mathbf{VV}}^{-1/2}\mathbf{C}'\mathbf{Q}_{ZZ}\mathbf{C}\boldsymbol{\Sigma}_{\mathbf{VV}}^{-1/2\prime}/K_2. \tag{2.6}$$

The $n \times n$ matrix $\boldsymbol{\Lambda}_{K_2}$ is the expected value of the concentration parameter, divided by the number of instruments, K_2. Note that $\boldsymbol{\rho}'\boldsymbol{\rho} \leq 1$.

2.2. *k*-Class Statistics

The k-class estimator of $\boldsymbol{\beta}$ is

$$\hat{\boldsymbol{\beta}}(k) = [\mathbf{Y}'(\mathbf{I} - k\mathbf{M}_{\mathbf{Z}})\mathbf{Y}]^{-1}[\mathbf{Y}'(\mathbf{I} - k\mathbf{M}_{\mathbf{Z}})\mathbf{y}], \tag{2.7}$$

where $\mathbf{M}_Z = \mathbf{I} - \mathbf{Z}(\mathbf{Z}'\mathbf{Z})^{-1}\mathbf{Z}'$ and k is a scalar. The Wald statistic, based on the k-class estimator, testing the null hypothesis $\boldsymbol{\beta} = \boldsymbol{\beta}_0$ is

$$W(k) = \frac{[\hat{\boldsymbol{\beta}}(k) - \boldsymbol{\beta}_0]'[\mathbf{Y}'(I - k\mathbf{M}_{\mathbf{Z}})\mathbf{Y}][\hat{\boldsymbol{\beta}}(k) - \boldsymbol{\beta}_0]}{n\hat{\sigma}_{uu}(k)}, \tag{2.8}$$

where $\hat{\sigma}_{uu}(k) = \hat{\mathbf{u}}(k)'\hat{\mathbf{u}}(k)/(T - n)$ and $\hat{\mathbf{u}}(k) = \mathbf{y} - \mathbf{Y}\hat{\boldsymbol{\beta}}(k)$.

Specific k-class estimators of interest include two-stage least squares (TSLS), the limited information maximum likelihood (LIML) estimator, Fuller's (1977) k-class estimator, and bias-adjusted TSLS (BTSLS; Nagar 1959; Rothenberg 1984). The values of k for these estimators are (cf. Donald and Newey 2001):

TSLS: $k = 1,$ (2.9)

LIML: $k = \hat{k}_{\text{LIML}}$ is the smallest root of $\det(\underline{\mathbf{Y}}'\underline{\mathbf{Y}} - k\underline{\mathbf{Y}}'\mathbf{M}_Z\underline{\mathbf{Y}}) = 0,$ (2.10)

Fuller-k: $k = \hat{k}_{\text{LIML}} - c/(T - K_2)$, where c is a positive constant, (2.11)

BTSLS: $k = T/(T - K_2 + 2),$ (2.12)

where $\det(\mathbf{A})$ is the determinant of matrix $\mathbf{A}$.

2.3. Assumptions

We assume that the random variables are i.i.d. with four moments, the instruments are not multicollinear, and the errors are homoskedastic; that is, we assume:

Assumption A

(a) There exists a constant $D_1 > 0$ *such that mineval*$(\mathbf{Z}'\mathbf{Z}/T) \geq D_1$ *a.s. for all* K_2 *and for all* T *greater than some* T_0.

(b) $\mathbf{Z}_t$ *is i.i.d. with* $E\mathbf{Z}_t\mathbf{Z}_t' = \mathbf{Q}_{\mathbf{ZZ}}$, *where* $\mathbf{Q}_{\mathbf{ZZ}}$ *is positive definite, and* $EZ_{it}^4 \leq D_2 < \infty$, *where* $i = 1, \ldots, K_2$.

(c) $\boldsymbol{\eta}_t = [u_t \mathbf{V}_t']'$ *is i.i.d. with* $E(\boldsymbol{\eta}_t | \mathbf{Z}_t) = 0$, $E(\boldsymbol{\eta}_t\boldsymbol{\eta}_t' | \mathbf{Z}_t) = \boldsymbol{\Sigma}$, *which is positive definite, and* $E(|\eta_{it}\eta_{jt}\eta_{kt}\eta_{lt}| \mid \mathbf{Z}_t) = E(|\eta_{it}\eta_{jt}\eta_{kt}\eta_{lt}|) \leq D_3 < \infty$, *where* $i, j, k, l = 1, \ldots, n+1$.

The next assumption is that the instruments are weak in the sense that the amount of information per instrument does not increase with the sample size, that is, the concentration parameter is proportional to the number of instruments. For fixed K_2, this assumption is achieved by considering the sequence of models in which $\mathbf{C} = \boldsymbol{\Pi}/\sqrt{T}$ is fixed, so that $\boldsymbol{\Pi}$ is modeled as local to zero (Staiger and Stock 1997). We adopt this nesting here, specifically:

Assumption B. $max_{i,j}|\mathbf{C}_{i,j}| \leq D_4 < \infty$, *where* D_4 *does not depend on* T *or* K_2, *and* $\mathbf{C}'\mathbf{C}/K_2 \to \mathbf{H}$ *as* $T \to \infty$, *where* $\mathbf{H}$ *is a fixed* $n \times n$ *matrix.*

Assumption B implies that $\boldsymbol{\Lambda}_{K_2} \to \boldsymbol{\Lambda}_\infty$ as $T \to \infty$, where $\boldsymbol{\Lambda}_\infty$ is a fixed matrix with maxeval$(\boldsymbol{\Lambda}_\infty) < \infty$. When the number of instruments is fixed, this assumption is equivalent to the weak-instrument Assumption L_Π in Staiger and Stock (1997).

Our analysis focuses on sequences of K_2 that, if they increase, do so slower than $\sqrt{T}$. Specifically, we assume:

Assumption C. $K_2^4/T \to 0$ *as* $T \to \infty$.

Note that Assumption C does not require K_2 to increase, but it limits the rate at which it can increase.

3. UNIFORM CONVERGENCE RESULT

This section provides the uniform convergence result (Theorem 3.1) that justifies the use of sequential asymptotics to compute the many weak instrument limiting representations. We adopt Phillips and Moon's (1999) notation in which $(T, K_2 \to \infty)_{\text{seq}}$ denotes the sequential limit in which first $T \to \infty$, then $K_2 \to \infty$; the notation $(K_2, T \to \infty)$ denotes the joint limit in which K_2 is implicitly indexed by T.

Lemma 6 of Phillips and Moon (1999) provides general conditions under which sequential convergence implies joint convergence.

Phillips and Moon (1999), Lemma 6

(a) Suppose there exist random vectors X_K and X on the same probability space as $X_{K,T}$ satisfying, for all K, $X_{K,T} \xrightarrow{p} X_K$ as $T \to \infty$ and $X_K \xrightarrow{p} X$ as $K \to \infty$. Then $X_{K,T} \xrightarrow{p} X$ as $(K, T \to \infty)$ if and only if

$$\limsup_{K,T} \Pr\left[\|X_{K,T} - X_K\| > \varepsilon\right] = 0 \text{ for all } \varepsilon > 0. \tag{3.1}$$

(b) Suppose there exist random vectors X_K such that, for any fixed K, $X_{K,T} \xrightarrow{d} X_K$ as $T \to \infty$ and $X_K \xrightarrow{d} X$ as $K \to \infty$. Then $X_{K,T} \xrightarrow{d} X$ as $(K, T \to \infty)$ if and only if, for all bounded continuous functions f,

$$\limsup_{K,T} |E[f(X_{K,T})] - E[f(X_K)]| = 0. \tag{3.2}$$

Note that condition (3.2) is equivalent to the requirement

$$\limsup_{K,T} \sup_x |F_{X_{K,T}}(x) - F_{X_K}(x)| = 0, \tag{3.3}$$

where $F_{X_{K,T}}$ is the c.d.f. of $X_{K,T}$ and F_{X_K} is the c.d.f. of X_K.

The rest of this section is devoted to showing that the conditions of this lemma, that is, (3.1) and (3.3), hold under assumptions A, B, and C for the statistics that enter the k-class estimators and test statistics. To do so, we use the following Berry–Esseen bound proven by Bertkus (1986):

Berry–Esseen Bound (Bertkus 1986). Let $\{X_1, \ldots, X_T\}$ be an i.i.d. sequence in $\mathbb{R}^K$ with zero means, a nonsingular second moment matrix, and finite absolute third moments. Let P_T be the probability measure associated with $T^{-1/2}\sum_{t=1}^{T} X_t$, and let P be the limiting Gaussian measure. Then for each T,

$$\begin{aligned} \sup_{A \in C^K} |P_T(A) - P(A)| &\le \text{const} \times (K/T)^{1/2} E\|X\|^3 \\ &= O\left(\left[K_2^4/T\right]^{1/2}\right) \end{aligned} \tag{3.4}$$

where C^K is the class of all measurable convex sets in $\mathbb{R}^K$.

We now turn to k-class statistics. First note that, for fixed K_2, under Assumptions A and B, the weak law of large numbers and the central limit theorem imply that the following limits hold jointly for fixed K_2:

$$(T^{-1}\mathbf{u}'\mathbf{u}, T^{-1}\mathbf{V}'\mathbf{u}, T^{-1}\mathbf{V}'\mathbf{V}) \xrightarrow{p} (\sigma_{uu}, \mathbf{\Sigma}_{\mathbf{V}u}, \mathbf{\Sigma}_{\mathbf{VV}}), \tag{3.5}$$

$$\mathbf{\Pi}'\mathbf{Z}'\mathbf{Z}\mathbf{\Pi} \xrightarrow{p} \mathbf{C}'\mathbf{Q}_{\mathbf{ZZ}}\mathbf{C}, \tag{3.6}$$

$$(\mathbf{\Pi}'\mathbf{Z}'\mathbf{u}, \mathbf{\Pi}'\mathbf{Z}'\mathbf{V}) \xrightarrow{d} (\mathbf{C}'\mathbf{\Psi}_{\mathbf{Z}u}, \mathbf{C}'\mathbf{\Psi}_{\mathbf{ZV}}), \tag{3.7}$$

$$\begin{aligned} (\mathbf{u}'\mathbf{P_Z}\mathbf{u}, \mathbf{V}'\mathbf{P_Z}\mathbf{u}, \mathbf{V}'\mathbf{P_Z}\mathbf{V}) \xrightarrow{d} \big(&\Psi_{\mathbf{Z}u}' Q_{\mathbf{ZZ}}^{-1}\Psi_{\mathbf{Z}u}, \Psi_{\mathbf{ZV}}' Q_{\mathbf{ZZ}}^{-1}\Psi_{\mathbf{Z}u}, \\ &\Psi_{\mathbf{ZV}}' Q_{\mathbf{ZZ}}^{-1}\Psi_{\mathbf{ZV}}\big), \end{aligned} \tag{3.8}$$

where Ψ_{Zu} and Ψ_{ZV} are, respectively, $K_2 \times 1$ and $K_2 \times n$ random variables and $\Psi \equiv [\Psi'_{Zu}, \text{vec}(\Psi_{ZV})']'$ is distributed $N(0, \Sigma \otimes \mathbf{Q}_{ZZ})$.

The following theorem shows that the limits in (3.5)–(3.8) and related limits hold uniformly in K_2 under the sampling assumption (Assumption A), the weak instrument assumption (Assumption B), and the rate condition (Assumption C). Let $\|\mathbf{A}\| = [\text{tr}(\mathbf{A}'\mathbf{A})]^{1/2}$ denote the norm of the matrix $\mathbf{A}$ and, as in (3.3), let F_X denote the c.d.f. of the random variable X (etc.).

Theorem 3.1. *Under Assumptions A, B, and C,*

(a) $\lim\sup_{K_2,T} \Pr[\|(\mathbf{u}'\mathbf{u}/T, \mathbf{V}'\mathbf{u}/T, \mathbf{V}'\mathbf{V}/T) - (\sigma_{uu}, \Sigma_{\mathbf{V}u}, \Sigma_{\mathbf{VV}})\| > \varepsilon] = 0 \;\forall\, \varepsilon > 0,$

(b) $\lim\sup_{K_2,T} \Pr[\|\mathbf{\Pi}'\mathbf{Z}'\mathbf{Z}\mathbf{\Pi}\|/K_2 - \mathbf{C}'\mathbf{Q}_{ZZ}\mathbf{C}/K_2\| > \varepsilon] = 0 \;\forall\, \varepsilon > 0,$

(c) $\lim\sup_{K_2,T}\sup_x |F_{\mathbf{\Pi}'\mathbf{Z}'\mathbf{u}}(\mathbf{x}) - F_{\mathbf{C}'\Psi_{Zu}}(\mathbf{x})| = 0,$

(d) $\lim\sup_{K_2,T}\sup_x |F_{\mathbf{\Pi}'\mathbf{Z}'\mathbf{V}}(\mathbf{x}) - F_{\mathbf{C}'\Psi_{\mathbf{ZV}}}(x)| = 0,$

(e) $\lim\sup_{K_2,T}\sup_x |F_{\mathbf{u}'P_Z\mathbf{u}}(x) - F_{\Psi'_{Zu}\mathbf{Q}_{ZZ}^{-1}\Psi_{Zu}}(x)| = 0,$

(f) $\lim\sup_{K_2,T}\sup_x |F_{\mathbf{V}'P_Z\mathbf{u}}(\mathbf{x}) - F_{\Psi'_{\mathbf{ZV}}\mathbf{Q}_{ZZ}^{-1}\Psi_{Zu}}(\mathbf{x})| = 0,$

(g) $\lim\sup_{K_2,T}\sup_x |F_{\mathbf{V}'P_Z\mathbf{V}}(\mathbf{x}) - F_{\Psi'_{\mathbf{ZV}}\mathbf{Q}_{ZZ}^{-1}\Psi_{\mathbf{ZV}}}(\mathbf{x})| = 0.$

The proof of Theorem 3.1 is contained in the Appendix.

Theorem 3.1 verifies the conditions (3.1) and (3.3) of Phillips and Moon's (1999) Lemma 6 for statistics that enter the k-class estimator and Wald statistic. Some of these objects converge in probability uniformly under the stated assumptions (parts (a) and (b)), while others converge in distribution uniformly (parts (c)–(g)). It follows from the continuous mapping theorem that continuous functions of these objects also converge in probability (and/or distribution) uniformly under the stated assumptions. Because the k-class estimator $\hat{\beta}(k)$ and Wald statistic $W(k)$ are continuous functions of these statistics (after centering and scaling as needed), it follows that the $(K_2, T \to \infty)$ joint limit of these k-class statistics can be computed as the sequential limit $(T, K_2 \to \infty)_{\text{seq}}$.

4. MANY WEAK INSTRUMENT ASYMPTOTIC LIMITS

This section collects calculations of the many weak instrument asymptotic limits of k-class estimators and Wald statistics. These calculations are done using sequential asymptotics (justified by Theorem 3.1), in which the fixed-K_2 weak instrument asymptotic limits of Staiger and Stock (1997, Theorem 1) are analyzed as $K_2 \to \infty$. The limiting distributions differ depending on the limiting behavior of k. The main results are collected in Theorem 4.1, which is proven in the Appendix.

Theorem 4.1. *Suppose that Assumptions A, B, and C hold, and that $K_2 \to \infty$. Let* $\mathbf{x}$ *be an n-dimensional standard normal random variable. Then the following* *limits hold as* $(K_2, T \to \infty)$*:*

(*a*) *TSLS: If* $T(k-1)/K_2 \to 0$, *then*

$$\hat{\beta}(k) - \beta \xrightarrow{p} \sigma_{uu}^{1/2} \boldsymbol{\Sigma}_{\mathbf{VV}}^{-1/2} (\Lambda_\infty + \mathbf{I}_n)^{-1} \rho \text{ and} \tag{4.1}$$

$$W(k)/K_2 \xrightarrow{p} \frac{\rho'(\boldsymbol{\Lambda}_\infty + \mathbf{I}_n)^{-1}\rho}{n[1 - 2\rho'(\boldsymbol{\Lambda}_\infty + \mathbf{I}_n)^{-1}\rho + \rho'(\boldsymbol{\Lambda}_\infty + \mathbf{I}_n)^{-2}\rho]}. \tag{4.2}$$

(*b*) *BTSLS: If* $\sqrt{K_2}[T(k-1)/K_2 - 1] \to 0$ *and mineval* $(\boldsymbol{\Lambda}_\infty) > 0$, *then*

$$\sqrt{K_2}(\hat{\beta}(k) - \beta) \xrightarrow{d} N(0, \sigma_{uu} \Sigma_{\mathbf{VV}}^{-1/2} \boldsymbol{\Lambda}_\infty^{-1} (\boldsymbol{\Lambda}_\infty + \mathbf{I}_n + \rho\rho') \boldsymbol{\Lambda}_\infty^{-1} \Sigma_{\mathbf{VV}}^{-1/2\prime}) \quad \text{and} \tag{4.3}$$

$$W(k) \xrightarrow{d} \mathbf{x}'(\boldsymbol{\Lambda}_\infty + \mathbf{I}_n + \rho\rho')^{1/2} \boldsymbol{\Lambda}_\infty^{-1} (\boldsymbol{\Lambda}_\infty + \mathbf{I}_n + \rho\rho')^{1/2\prime} \mathbf{x}/n. \tag{4.4}$$

(*b*) *LIML, Fuller-k: If* $T(k - k_{\text{LIML}})/\sqrt{K_2} \to 0$ *and* mineval$(\boldsymbol{\Lambda}_\infty) > 0$, *then*

$$\sqrt{K_2}[T(k-1)/K_2 - 1] \xrightarrow{d} N(0, 2), \tag{4.5}$$

$$\sqrt{K_2}(\hat{\beta}(k) - \beta) \xrightarrow{d} N(0, \sigma_{uu} \Sigma_{\mathbf{VV}}^{-1/2} \boldsymbol{\Lambda}_\infty^{-1} (\boldsymbol{\Lambda}_\infty + \mathbf{I}_n - \rho\rho') \boldsymbol{\Lambda}_\infty^{-1} \Sigma_{\mathbf{VV}}^{-1/2\prime}) \text{ and} \tag{4.6}$$

$$W(k) \xrightarrow{d} \mathbf{x}'(\boldsymbol{\Lambda}_\infty + \mathbf{I}_n - \rho\rho')^{1/2} \Lambda_\infty^{-1} (\boldsymbol{\Lambda}_\infty + \mathbf{I}_n - \rho\rho')^{1/2\prime} \mathbf{x}/n. \tag{4.7}$$

5. DISCUSSION

To simplify the proofs we have assumed i.i.d. sampling. Götze (1991) provides a Berry–Esseen bound for i.n.i.d. sampling. The bound in the i.n.i.d. case is const $\times\ (K_1^2/T)E\|X\|^3 = O([K_2^5/T]^{1/2})$, so the rate in Assumption C would be slower, $K_2^5/T \to 0$. With this slower rate, the results in Section 3 would extend to the case where the errors and instruments are independently but not necessarily identically distributed.

The many weak instrument representations in Theorem 4.1 for BTSLS, LIML, and the Fuller-k estimator rule out the partially identified and unidentified cases, for which mineval$(\boldsymbol{\Lambda}_\infty) = 0$. This suggests that the approximations in Theorem 4.1, parts (b) and (c), might become inaccurate as $\boldsymbol{\Lambda}_{K_2}$ becomes nearly singular. The behavior of the many weak instrument approximations in partially identified and unidentified cases remain to be explored.

ACKNOWLEDGMENTS

We thank an anonymous referee for helpful suggestions that spurred this research, and Whitney Newey for pointing out an error in an earlier draft. This work was supported by NSF grant SBR-0214131.

APPENDIX

This appendix contains the proofs of Theorems 3.1 and 4.1. The proof of Theorem 3.1 uses the following lemma.

Lemma A.1. *Let* $\Delta_T = (\mathbf{Z}'\mathbf{Z}/T)^{-1} - \mathbf{Q}_{\mathbf{ZZ}}^{-1}$. *Under Assumptions A and C,*

(a) $\limsup_{K_2,T} \Pr[|T^{-1}\mathbf{u}'\mathbf{Z}\Delta_T\mathbf{Z}'\mathbf{u}| > \varepsilon] = 0\ \forall\, \varepsilon > 0,$
(b) $\limsup_{K_2,T} \Pr[\|T^{-1}\mathbf{V}'\mathbf{Z}\Delta_T\mathbf{Z}'\mathbf{u}\| > \varepsilon] = 0\ \forall\, \varepsilon > 0,$
(c) $\limsup_{K_2,T} \Pr[\|T^{-1}\mathbf{V}'\mathbf{Z}\Delta_T\mathbf{Z}'\mathbf{V}\| > \varepsilon] = 0\ \forall\, \varepsilon > 0.$

Proof of Lemma A.1. The strategy for proving each part is first to show that the relevant quadratic form (for example, in (a), the quadratic form $T^{-1}\mathbf{u}'\mathbf{Z}\Delta_T\mathbf{Z}'\mathbf{u}$) has expected mean square that is bounded by const $\times$ (K_2^2/T), and then to apply Chebychev's inequality and the condition in Assumption C that $K_2^2/T \to 0$. The details of these calculations are tedious and are omitted; they can be found in an earlier working paper (Stock and Yogo 2002, Lemma A.2).

Proof of Theorem 3.1. (a) This follows from the weak law of large numbers because $(\mathbf{u}'\mathbf{u}/T, \mathbf{V}'\mathbf{u}/T, \mathbf{V}'\mathbf{V}/T)$ do not depend on K_2.

(b) Note that $E[\mathbf{\Pi}'\mathbf{Z}'\mathbf{Z}\mathbf{\Pi}/K_2 - \mathbf{C}'\mathbf{Q}_{\mathbf{ZZ}}\mathbf{C}/K_2] = 0$. The (1,1) element of this matrix is

$$(\mathbf{\Pi}'\mathbf{Z}'\mathbf{Z}\mathbf{\Pi} - \mathbf{C}'\mathbf{Q}_{\mathbf{ZZ}}\mathbf{C})_{1,1}/K_2$$
$$= (TK_2)^{-1}\sum_{t=1}^{T}\sum_{i=1}^{K_2}\sum_{j=1}^{K_2} C_{i1}C_{j1}(Z_{it}Z_{jt} - q_{ij}),$$

where q_{ij} is the (i, j) element of $\mathbf{Q}_{\mathbf{ZZ}}$. Because $\mathbf{Z}_t$ is i.i.d. (Assumption A(b)) and the elements of $\mathbf{C}$ are bounded (Assumption B), the expected value of the square of this element is

$$E\{[(\Pi'\mathbf{Z}'\mathbf{Z}\Pi - \mathbf{C}'\mathbf{Q}_{\mathbf{ZZ}}\mathbf{C})_{1,1}/K_2]^2\}$$
$$= E\left[\frac{1}{TK_2}\sum_{t=1}^{T}\sum_{i=1}^{K_2}\sum_{j=1}^{K_2} C_{i1}C_{j1}(Z_{it}Z_{jt} - q_{ij})\right]^2$$
$$= \frac{1}{TK_2^2}\sum_{i=1}^{K_2}\sum_{j=1}^{K_2}\sum_{k=1}^{K_2}\sum_{l=1}^{K_2} C_{i1}C_{j1}C_{k1}C_{l1}E[(Z_{it}Z_{jt} - q_{ij})(Z_{kt}Z_{lt} - q_{kl})]$$
$$\le \text{const} \times \frac{K_2^2}{T} \times \left(\frac{1}{K_2}\sum_{i=1}^{K_2}|C_{i1}|\right)^4 \le \text{const} \times \frac{K_2^2}{T}.$$

By the same argument applied to the (1,1) element, the remaining elements of $\Pi'\mathbf{Z}'\mathbf{Z}\Pi/K_2 - \mathbf{C}'\mathbf{Q}_{\mathbf{ZZ}}\mathbf{C}/K_2$ are also bounded in mean square by const $\times$ (K_2^2/T). The matrix $\mathbf{\Pi}'\mathbf{Z}'\mathbf{Z}\mathbf{\Pi}/K_2$ is $n \times n$ and so the number of elements does not depend on K_2, and the result (b) follows by Chebychev's inequality and noting that, under Assumption C, $K_2^2/T \to 0$.

(c) Under Assumption B, $\mathbf{\Pi}'\mathbf{Z}'\mathbf{u} = T^{-1/2}\mathbf{C}'\mathbf{Z}'\mathbf{u} = \mathbf{C}'(T^{-1/2}\sum_{t=1}^{T}\mathbf{Z}_t u_t)$. Let P_T denote the probability measure associated with $T^{-1/2}\mathbf{Z}'\mathbf{u}$ and let P denote the limiting probability measure associated with $\mathbf{\Psi}_{\mathbf{Z}u}$. Define the convex set $A(\mathbf{x}) = \{\mathbf{y} \in \mathbb{R}^{K_2}\colon \mathbf{C}'\mathbf{y} \le \mathbf{x}\}$, so that $P_T(A(\mathbf{x})) = F_{\Pi'Z'u}(\mathbf{x})$ and $P(A(\mathbf{x})) = F_{C'\Psi_{Zu}}(\boldsymbol{x})$. By Assumption A, $\mathbf{Z}_t u_t$ is an i.i.d., mean zero K_2-dimensional random variable with finite third moments, so the Berry–Esseen bound (3.4) applies and $\sup_x |F_{\Pi'Z'u}(\mathbf{x}) - F_{\mathbf{C}'\Psi_{\mathbf{Z}u}}(\boldsymbol{x})| \le \text{const} \times \sqrt{K_2^4/T}$. The result (c) follows from Assumption C. We note that this line of argument is used in Jensen and Mayer (1975).

(d) The proof is the same as for (c).

(e) Write $\mathbf{u}'\mathbf{P}_{\mathbf{Z}}\mathbf{u} = (T^{-1/2}\mathbf{u}'\mathbf{Z})(T^{-1}\mathbf{Z}'\mathbf{Z})(T^{-1/2}\mathbf{Z}'\mathbf{u}) = \xi_1 + \xi_2$, where $\xi_1 = (T^{-1/2}\mathbf{u}'\mathbf{Z})\mathbf{Q}_{\mathbf{ZZ}}^{-1}(T^{-1/2}\mathbf{Z}'\mathbf{u})$ and $\xi_2 = (T^{-1/2}\mathbf{u}'\mathbf{Z})\Delta_T(T^{-1/2}\mathbf{Z}'\mathbf{u})$. As in the proof of (c), let P_T denote the probability measure associated with $T^{-1/2}\mathbf{Z}'\mathbf{u}$ and let P denote the limiting probability measure of $\mathbf{\Psi}_{\mathbf{Z}u}$. Let $B(x)$ be the convex set, $B(x) = \{\mathbf{y} \in \mathbb{R}^{K_2}\colon \mathbf{y}'Q_{\mathbf{ZZ}}^{-1}\mathbf{y} \le x\}$, so that $P_T(B(x)) = F_{\xi_1}(x)$ and $P(B(x)) = F_{\Psi_{Zu}'Q_{ZZ}^{-1}\Psi_{Zu}}(x)$. It follows from (3.4) that $\sup_x |F_{\xi_1}(x) - F_{\Psi_{Zu}'Q_{ZZ}^{-1}\Psi_{Zu}}(x)| \le \text{const} \times \sqrt{K_2^4/T}$. By Lemma A.1(a), $\xi_2 \xrightarrow{p} 0$ uniformly as $(K_2, T \to \infty)$, and the result (e) follows.

(f) and (g). The dimensions of $\mathbf{V}'\mathbf{P}_{\mathbf{Z}}\mathbf{u}$ and $\mathbf{V}'\mathbf{P}_{\mathbf{Z}}\mathbf{V}$ do not depend on K_2, and the proofs of (f) and (g) are similar to that of (e).

Proof of Theorem 4.1. We first state the fixed-K_2 weak instrument asymptotic representations of the k-class estimators. Define the $K_2 \times 1$ and $K_2 \times n$ random variables $\mathbf{z}_u = \mathbf{Q}_{\mathbf{ZZ}}^{-1/2\prime}\Psi_{\mathbf{Z}u}\sigma_{\mathbf{uu}}^{-1/2}$ and $\mathbf{z}_{\mathbf{V}} = \mathbf{Q}_{\mathbf{ZZ}}^{-1/2\prime}\Psi_{\mathbf{ZV}}\Sigma_{\mathbf{VV}}^{-1/2}$ ($\Psi_{\mathbf{Z}u}$ and $\Psi_{\mathbf{Z}V}$ are defined following (3.8)), so that

$$\begin{pmatrix} \mathbf{z}_u \\ \text{vec}(\mathbf{z}_{\mathbf{V}}) \end{pmatrix} \sim N(\mathbf{0}, \bar{\Sigma} \otimes \mathbf{I}_{K_2}), \text{ where } \bar{\Sigma} = \begin{bmatrix} 1 & \rho' \\ \rho & \mathbf{I}_n \end{bmatrix}. \tag{A.1}$$

Also let

$$\nu_1 = (\boldsymbol{\lambda} + \mathbf{z}_{\mathbf{V}})'(\boldsymbol{\lambda} + \mathbf{z}_{\mathbf{V}}) \text{ and} \tag{A.2}$$

$$\nu_2 = (\boldsymbol{\lambda} + \mathbf{z}_{\mathbf{V}})'\mathbf{z}_u, \tag{A.3}$$

where $\lambda = \mathbf{Q}_{\mathbf{ZZ}}^{1/2}\mathbf{C}\Sigma_{\mathbf{VV}}^{-1/2}$. Then under Assumptions A and B, with fixed K_2,

$$\hat{\beta}(k) - \beta \xrightarrow{d} \sigma_{uu}^{1/2}\Sigma_{\mathbf{VV}}^{-1/2}(\nu_1 - \kappa\mathbf{I}_n)^{-1}(\nu_2 - \kappa\rho) \text{ and} \tag{A.4}$$

$$W(k) \xrightarrow{d} \frac{(\nu_2 - \kappa\rho)'(\nu_1 - \kappa\mathbf{I}_n)^{-1}(\nu_2 - \kappa\rho)}{n[1 - 2\rho'(\nu_1 - \kappa\mathbf{I}_n)^{-1}(\nu_2 - \kappa\rho) + (\nu_2 - \kappa\rho)'(\nu_1 - \kappa\mathbf{I}_n)^{-2}(\nu_2 - \kappa\rho)]}, \tag{A.5}$$

where (A.5) holds under the null hypothesis $\beta = \beta_0$. The representations (A.4) and (A.5) follow from Staiger and Stock (1997, Theorem 1) because Assumptions A and B imply Staiger and Stock's Assumptions M and L_Π when K_2 is fixed.

The following limits hold jointly as $K_2 \to \infty$:

$$\nu_1/K_2 \xrightarrow{p} \mathbf{\Lambda}_\infty + \mathbf{I}_n, \tag{A.6}$$

$$\nu_2/K_2 \xrightarrow{p} \rho, \tag{A.7}$$

$$\begin{pmatrix} \dfrac{\mathbf{z}_u'\mathbf{z}_u - K_2}{\sqrt{K_2}} \\ \dfrac{\lambda'\mathbf{z}_u}{\sqrt{K_2}} \\ \dfrac{\mathbf{z}_\mathbf{V}'\mathbf{z}_u - K_2\rho}{\sqrt{K_2}} \end{pmatrix} \xrightarrow{d} N(0, B), \quad \text{where} B = \begin{bmatrix} 2 & 0 & 2\rho' \\ 0 & \mathbf{\Lambda}_\infty & 0 \\ 2\rho & 0 & \mathbf{I}_n + \rho\rho' \end{bmatrix}, \tag{A.8}$$

$$(\nu_2 - K_2\rho)/\sqrt{K_2} \to N(0, \mathbf{\Lambda}_\infty + \mathbf{I}_n + \rho\rho'). \tag{A.9}$$

The results (A.6)–(A.9) follow by straightforward calculations using the central limit theorem, the weak law of large numbers, and the joint normal distribution of $\mathbf{z}_u$ and $\mathbf{z}_\mathbf{V}$ in (A.1).

We now turn to the proof of Theorem 4.1.

(a) From (A.4), the fixed-K_2 weak instrument approximation to the distribution of the TSLS estimator is $\hat{\beta}^{\text{TSLS}} - \beta \sim \sigma_{uu}^{1/2}\Sigma_{VV}^{-1/2}\nu_1^{-1}\nu_2 = \sigma_{uu}^{1/2}\Sigma_{\mathbf{VV}}^{-1/2}$ $(\nu_1/K_2)^{-1}(\nu_2/K_2)$. The limit stated in the theorem for the estimator follows by substituting (A.6) and (A.7) into this expression. The many weak instrument limit for the TSLS Wald statistic follows by rewriting (A.5) as

$$W^{\text{TSLS}}/K_2 \sim \frac{(\nu_2/K_2)'(\nu_1/K_2)^{-1}(\nu_2/K_2)}{n[1 - 2\rho'(\nu_1/K_2)^{-1}(\nu_2/K_2) + (\nu_2/K_2)'(\nu_1/K_2)^{-2}(\nu_2/K_2)]}$$

and applying (A.6) and (A.7).

(b) The fixed-K_2 weak instrument approximation to the distribution of a k-class estimator, given in (A.4), in general can be written as

$$\sqrt{K_2}[\hat{\beta}(k) - \beta] \sim \sigma_{uu}^{1/2}\mathbf{\Sigma}_{\mathbf{VV}}^{-1/2}\left[\frac{\nu_1 - K_2\mathbf{I}_n}{K_2} - \frac{1}{\sqrt{K_2}}\left(\frac{\kappa - K_2}{\sqrt{K_2}}\right)\mathbf{I}_n\right]^{-1}$$
$$\times \left[\frac{\nu_2 - K_2\rho}{\sqrt{K_2}} - \left(\frac{\kappa - K_2}{\sqrt{K_2}}\right)\rho\right], \tag{A.10}$$

where $T(k-1) \xrightarrow{d} \kappa$ for fixed K_2. The assumption $\sqrt{K_2}[T(k-1)/K_2 - 1] \to 0$ implies that $(\kappa - K_2)/\sqrt{K_2} \to 0$, so by (A.6) and (A.9) we have, as $K_2 \to \infty$,

$$\frac{\nu_1 - K_2\mathbf{I}_n}{K_2} - \frac{1}{\sqrt{K_2}}\left(\frac{\kappa - K_2}{\sqrt{K_2}}\right)\mathbf{I}_n \xrightarrow{p} \mathbf{\Lambda}_\infty \text{ and}$$

$$\frac{\nu_2 - K_2\rho}{\sqrt{K_2}} - \left(\frac{\kappa - K_2}{\sqrt{K_2}}\right)\rho \xrightarrow{d} N(0, \mathbf{\Lambda}_\infty + \mathbf{I}_n + \rho\rho'),$$

and the result (4.3) follows. The assumption mineval$(\Lambda_\infty) > 0$ is used to ensure the invertibility of $\mathbf{\Lambda}_\infty$. The distribution of the Wald statistic follows.

(c) For fixed K_2, $T(k_{\text{LIML}} - 1) \xrightarrow{d} \kappa^*$. We show below that, as $K_2 \to \infty$,

$$\frac{\kappa^* - K_2}{\sqrt{K_2}} = \frac{\mathbf{z}_u'\mathbf{z}_u - K_2}{\sqrt{K_2}} + o_p(1). \tag{A.11}$$

The result (4.5) follows from (A.11) and (A.8). Moreover, applying (A.6), (A.8), (A.9), and (A.11) yields

$$\frac{\boldsymbol{\nu}_1 - K_2\mathbf{I}_n}{K_2} - \frac{1}{\sqrt{K_2}}\left(\frac{\kappa^* - K_2}{\sqrt{K_2}}\right)\mathbf{I}_n \xrightarrow{p} \boldsymbol{\Lambda}_\infty \text{ and}$$

$$\begin{aligned}\frac{\boldsymbol{\nu}_2 - K_2\boldsymbol{\rho}}{\sqrt{K_2}} - \left(\frac{\kappa^* - K_2}{\sqrt{K_2}}\right)\boldsymbol{\rho} &= \frac{\lambda'\mathbf{z}_u}{\sqrt{K_2}} + \frac{\mathbf{z}_V'\mathbf{z}_u - K_2\boldsymbol{\rho}}{\sqrt{K_2}} \\ &\quad - \left(\frac{\mathbf{z}_u'\mathbf{z}_u - K_2}{\sqrt{K_2}}\right)\boldsymbol{\rho} + o_p(1) \xrightarrow{d} N(0, \Lambda_\infty + \mathbf{I}_n - \boldsymbol{\rho}\boldsymbol{\rho}'),\end{aligned}$$

where Λ_∞ is invertible by the assumption mineval($\boldsymbol{\Lambda}_\infty$) > 0. The result (4.6) follows, as does the distribution of the Wald statistic.

It remains to show (A.11). From (2.11), κ^* is the smallest root of

$$0 = \det\left[\begin{pmatrix} \mathbf{z}_u'\mathbf{z}_u & \boldsymbol{\nu}_2' \\ \boldsymbol{\nu}_2 & \boldsymbol{\nu}_1 \end{pmatrix} - \kappa^* \begin{pmatrix} 1 & \boldsymbol{\rho}' \\ \boldsymbol{\rho} & \mathbf{I}_n \end{pmatrix}\right]. \tag{A.12}$$

Let $\phi = (\kappa^* - K_2)/\sqrt{K_2}$, $a = (\mathbf{z}_u'\mathbf{z}_u - K_2)/\sqrt{K_2}$, $\mathbf{b} = (\boldsymbol{\nu}_2 - K_2\boldsymbol{\rho})/\sqrt{K_2}$, and $\mathbf{L} = (\boldsymbol{\nu}_1 - K_2\mathbf{I}_n)/K_2$. Then (A.12) can be rewritten so that ϕ is the smallest root of

$$0 = \det\begin{bmatrix} a - \phi & (\mathbf{b} - \phi\boldsymbol{\rho})' \\ \mathbf{b} - \phi\boldsymbol{\rho} & \sqrt{K_2}\mathbf{L} - \phi\mathbf{I}_n \end{bmatrix}. \tag{A.13}$$

We first show that $K_2^{-1/4}\phi \xrightarrow{p} 0$. Let $\tilde{\phi} = K_2^{-1/4}\phi$. By (A.6), (A.8), and (A.9), $K_2^{-1/4}a \xrightarrow{p} 0$, $K_2^{-1/4}\mathbf{b} \xrightarrow{p} 0$, and $\mathbf{L} \xrightarrow{p} \boldsymbol{\Lambda}_\infty$. By the continuity of the determinant, it follows that in the limit $K_2 \to \infty$, $\tilde{\phi}$ is the smallest root of the equation

$$0 = \det\begin{bmatrix} \tilde{\phi} & \tilde{\phi}\boldsymbol{\rho}' \\ \tilde{\phi}\boldsymbol{\rho} & \tilde{\phi}\mathbf{I}_n + O_p(K_2^{1/4}) \end{bmatrix}, \tag{A.14}$$

from which it follows that $\tilde{\phi} = K_2^{-1/4}\phi \xrightarrow{p} 0$.

To obtain (A.11), write the determinantal equation (A.13) as

$$\begin{aligned} 0 &= [(a - \phi) - (\mathbf{b} - \phi\boldsymbol{\rho})'(K_2^{1/2}\mathbf{L} - \phi\mathbf{I}_n)^{-1}(\mathbf{b} - \phi\boldsymbol{\rho})]\det(K_2^{1/2}\mathbf{L} - \phi\mathbf{I}_n) \\ &= K_2^{n/2}\{(a - \phi) - [K_2^{-1/4}(\mathbf{b} - \phi\boldsymbol{\rho})]'(\mathbf{L} - K_2^{-1/2}\phi\mathbf{I}_n)^{-1} \\ &\quad \times [K_2^{-1/4}(\mathbf{b} - \phi\boldsymbol{\rho})]\det(\mathbf{L} - K_2^{-1/2}\phi\mathbf{I}_n) \\ &= K_2^{n/2}\{[(a - \phi)]\det(\boldsymbol{\Lambda}_\infty) + o_p(1)\}, \end{aligned} \tag{A.15}$$

where the final equality follows from $K_2^{-1/4}\mathbf{b} \xrightarrow{p} 0$, $\mathbf{L} \xrightarrow{p} \boldsymbol{\Lambda}_\infty$, $K_2^{-1/4}\phi \xrightarrow{p} 0$, and $\det(\boldsymbol{\Lambda}_\infty) > 0$. By the continuity of the solution to (A.13), it follows that $\phi = a + o_p(1)$, which, in the original notation, is (A.11).

References

Angrist, J. D., and A. B. Krueger (1991), "Does Compulsory School Attendance Affect Schooling and Earnings," *Quarterly Journal of Economics*, 106, 979–1014.

Bekker, P. A. (1994), "Alternative Approximations to the Distributions of Instrumental Variables Estimators," *Econometrica*, 62, 657–81.

Bertkus, V. Y. (1986), "Dependence of the Berry–Esseen Estimate on the Dimension," *Litovsk. Mat. Sb.*, 26, 205–10.

Chao, J. C., and N. R. Swanson (2002), "Consistent Estimation with a Large Number of Weak Instruments," unpublished manuscript, University of Maryland.

Donald, S. G., and W. K. Newey (2001), "Choosing the Number of Instruments," *Econometrica*, 69, 1161–91.

Fuller, W. A. (1977), "Some Properties of a Modification of the Limited Information Estimator," *Econometrica*, 45, 939–53.

Götze, F. (1991), "On the Rate of Convergence in the Multivariate CLT," *Annals of Probability*, 19, 724–39.

Jensen, D. R., and L. S. Mayer (1975), "Normal-Theory Approximations to Tests of Linear Hypotheses," *Annals of Statistics*, 3, 429–44.

Kunitomo, N. (1980), "Asymptotic Expansions of the Distributions of Estimators in a Linear Functional Relationship and Simultaneous Equations," *Journal of the American Statistical Association*, 75, 693–700.

Morimune, K. (1983), "Approximate Distributions of k-Class Estimators when the Degree of Overidentifiability is Large Compared with the Sample Size," *Econometrica*, 51, 821–41.

Nagar, A. L. (1959), "The Bias and Moment Matrix of the General k-Class Estimators of the Parameters in Simultaneous Equations," *Econometrica*, 27, 575–95.

Phillips, P. C. B., and H. R. Moon (1999), "Linear Regression Limit Theory for Nonstationary Panel Data," *Econometrica*, 67, 1057–111.

Rothenberg, T. J. (1984), "Approximating the Distributions of Econometric Estimators and Test Statistics," Chapter 15 in *Handbook of Econometrics*, Vol. II (ed. by Z. Griliches and M. D. Intriligator), Amsterdam: North Holland, pp. 881–935.

Sargan, D. (1975), "Asymptotic Theory and Large Models," *International Economic Review*, 16, 75–91.

Staiger, D., and J. H. Stock (1997), "Instrumental Variables Regression with Weak Instruments," *Econometrica*, 65, 557–86.

Stock, J. H., and M. Yogo (2002), "Testing for Weak Instruments in Linear IV Regression," NBER Technical Working Paper 284.

Stock, J. H., and M. Yogo (2004), "Testing for Weak Instruments in Linear IV Regression," Chapter 5 in this volume.

CHAPTER 7

Identifying a Source of Financial Volatility

Douglas G. Steigerwald and Richard J. Vagnoni

ABSTRACT

Our primary goal is to develop and analyze a dynamic economic model that takes into account several sources of information-based trade – the markets for a stock and options on that stock. We study identification within the model, paying particular attention to assumptions about the latent trader arrival process. We also derive the stochastic properties of trade-by-trade decisions and prices. Finally, we aggregate trade-by-trade quantities and to show that data generated by the model is consistent with empirical benchmarks from exchange data.

1. INTRODUCTION

Much of Tom Rothenberg's long and insightful career has focused on identification in econometrics. The theme is perhaps most evident in Rothenberg (1973), which has long been the standard for identification in simultaneous equation models. We analyze a market microstructure model, paying particular attention to issues of identification. (The term *micro*structure refers to study of asset markets at the highly disaggregated level corresponding to the arrival of individual traders.) Working from the asymmetric information model in Easley, O'Hara, and Srinivas (1998), we first detail the assumptions needed to identify the parameters. We then derive the stochastic properties of trades and squared price changes for each market and the dynamic pattern of trade across markets. Finally, we use the methods in Kelly and Steigerwald (2004) to construct aggregate trades and squared price changes and compare these to empirical benchmarks. Together, these results provide a theory-based link between asymmetric information, the behavior of market participants, and stochastic volatility.

In Section 2 we first present a model of informed trade in stock and options markets and the resultant likelihood function needed to estimate the parameters. Parameter identification requires specification of the frequency at which traders arrive. We show how misspecification of the arrival frequency imparts bias. In particular, we find that arrival frequency misspecification leads to downward bias of informed trade frequencies. Even with correct specification of the arrival frequency, the likelihood function is sensitive to aggregation and we pinpoint the difficulty. Empirical identification requires a further assumption, by which trades are assigned to a quote. Estimates of the accuracy of the assignment rules typically find an error rate of 15 percent. We determine the bias that arises from such an error rate and again find that informed trade frequencies are biased downward.

In Section 3 we focus on the dynamic pattern of trade within and across markets. We derive (in Theorem 3.1) how frequently, in equilibrium, the informed trade in the options market. Our results nest those of Easley et al. (1998) who implicitly derive conditions under which the informed trade with constant frequency in the options market. We next derive the properties of trade-by-trade price changes. Because informed traders may choose to trade in the options market, option trades can convey information about the stock price (Black 1975; Back 1993; Biais and Hillion 1994). As a result, options are *not* redundant assets as assumed by the Black–Scholes pricing model (Black and Scholes 1973). We detail these linkages and, in Theorem 3.3, we show that the (conditional) variance of price changes in a market is bounded by the squared bid–ask spread for that market. As trade reveals information the bid–ask spread shrinks, thereby reducing the conditional variance. The evolution of the bid–ask spread leads to autocorrelation in the conditional variance, although not specifically of the form modeled in a GARCH process.

In Section 4, we aggregate the trade-by-trade quantities of Section 3 to study the behavior of trades and prices over calendar periods. Three empirical features of stock market data form natural benchmarks for testing the model. There is strong evidence of serial correlation in calendar period squared price changes and in the number of trades across calendar periods, and the serial correlation in the number of trades tends to be larger and to diminish more slowly than serial correlation in squared price changes (Andersen 1996; Harris 1987; Steigerwald 1997). We first show that both trades (or trading volume) and squared price changes are positively correlated. Because the conditional variance of trade-by-trade price changes shrinks as information is revealed through trading, while trade decisions are unaffected, the serial correlation in trades is larger and tends to diminish more slowly than does the serial correlation in squared price changes.

2. IDENTIFICATION IN A MICROSTRUCTURE MODEL WITH OPTIONS MARKETS

We consider a model with markets for a stock and for call and put options on the stock. We base our dual-market, sequential-trade, asymmetric information model on the market microstructure models of Easley and O'Hara (1992); Easley et al. (1998). Full details of the model and the derivations that follow are contained in Steigerwald and Vagnoni (2001).

Trade in the stock and options markets occurs over a sequence of trading days, indexed by m. On trading day m, the stock realizes some per share dollar value, given by the random variable $V_m \in \{v_{L_m}, v_{H_m}\}$, with $v_{L_m} < v_{H_m}$. The stock takes the lower value, v_{L_m}, with positive probability δ. Prior to the commencement of trading on day m, informed traders receive a randomly determined signal, S_m, about the value of the stock on m. This signal takes one of three values, $S_m \in \{s_L, s_H, s_O\}$. The informative signals, s_L and s_H, reveal the true value of the stock. The uninformative signal, s_O, provides no information regarding the true value of the stock. Informed traders learn the true value of the stock with probability $\theta > 0$. Proportion α of the traders receives the signal, characterizing the universe of informed traders. The proportion of traders that does not receive the signal characterizes the universe of uninformed traders. Neither market maker is privy to the signal. At the end of each trading day, the signal is revealed to the market makers and uninformed traders and, hence, all agree on the value of a share of the stock.[1]

The market makers set an ask and a bid, collectively termed the quotes, for either one share of stock or an option contract that controls $\lambda \geq 1$ shares of the stock. Each option is of the European type – precluding the possibility of exercise prior to the end of the trading day – and expires upon revelation of the signal. Consider the call option, which provides the owner with the right to buy one share of the stock for a specified strike price, κ_{C_m}, with $\kappa_{C_m} \in \left[v_{L_m}, v_{H_m}\right]$, from the call option writer at the end of the trading day. The value of the call option, V_{C_m}, is $\max\left(V_m - \kappa_{C_m}, 0\right)$.

As all traders are risk neutral, informed traders will trade only if they receive an informative signal. For example, if $S_m = s_L$, then an informed trader implements one of three possible "bearish" strategies, selling short one share of the stock with probability ϵ_{IB}, writing λ call options with probability ϵ_{IBC}, or buying λ put options with probability $\epsilon_{IAP} = 1 - \epsilon_{IB} - \epsilon_{IBC}$. Conditional on receiving an informative signal, the informed trader employs the strategy that provides the largest net gain. Uninformed traders are assumed to trade for liquidity reasons and not speculation. The uninformed trade with positive frequency in each market. For example, proportion ϵ_{UB} potentially sells the stock short and proportion ϵ_{UAC} potentially buys λ call options. The sum of the positive frequencies in each market is ϵ, thus $1 - \epsilon$ is the proportion of the uninformed traders that never trade.

Traders randomly arrive to the markets one at a time, so we index them by their order of arrival, i. The ith trader arrives, observes the quotes, and makes a trade decision, D_i. The random variable, D_i, takes one of seven values. For example, if trader i buys the stock at the ask, A_i, then $D_i = d_A$. If trader i writes λ call options at the bid, B_{C_i}, then $D_i = d_{BC}$. If trader i elects not to trade, then $D_i = d_N$. We define the sequence of trading decisions on m as $\{D_k\}_{k=1}^{i}$. Given all publicly available information prior to the commencement of trade on m, Z_0, we specify the publicly available information set prior to the arrival of trader $i+1$ on m as Z_i, with $Z_i = \{Z_0, D_k\}_{k=1}^{i}$.

The information set, Z_i, is shared by the market makers and all traders. The market makers (and uninformed traders) perform Bayesian updating, by which

[1] A trading day captures the interval over which asymmetric information due to a particular signal persists in the markets and is not necessarily coincident with a calendar day.

they learn the signal received by the informed. After witnessing the ith trading decision, the market makers' beliefs regarding the signal that the informed traders received are

$$P(S_m = s_L|Z_i) = x_i \quad \text{and} \quad P(S_m = s_H|Z_i) = y_i.$$

Each trading decision – even if the decision is not to trade – conveys information about the signal received by the informed traders.

Quotes are determined by two equilibrium conditions. The first condition is that a market maker earns zero expected profit from each trade. From the zero expected profit condition it follows that the quotes are equal to the expected value of the asset conditional on the trade. The second condition is that the informed will trade the asset that offers the highest net gain. From the second condition it follows that the quotes are set so that an informed trader earns an equal net gain from each possible trade.

The microstructure model yields the likelihood of each trade decision D_i as a function of the parameters $\Phi = (\alpha, \delta, \bar{\epsilon}, \theta)$, where $\bar{\epsilon}$ is the vector of trade probabilities (for both the informed and uninformed) for each trade decision. As trader arrivals are independent, the likelihood for a sequence of n arrivals is

$$L(\Phi|D_1 = d_1, \ldots, D_n = d_n) = \Pi_{i=1}^n P(D_i = d_i|\Phi).$$

From the structure of the model, the probability of each trade decision is straightforward. For example, the probability of a trade at the ask in the stock market is

$$\begin{aligned} P(D_i = d_A|\Phi) = {} & \theta(1-\delta)[\alpha\epsilon_{IA} + (1-\alpha)\epsilon_{UA}] + \theta\delta(1-\alpha)\epsilon_{UA} \\ & + (1-\theta)(1-\alpha)\epsilon_{UA}. \end{aligned}$$

If $n = (n_A, n_B, \ldots, n_N)$ is the vector of trade counts that correspond to each trade decision, then the corresponding value of the likelihood function is

$$\begin{aligned} L(\Phi) = {} & \theta\,(1-\delta)\, p_{1A}^{n_A} \cdot p_{0B}^{n_B} \cdot p_{1AC}^{n_{AC}} \cdot p_{0BC}^{n_{BC}} \cdot p_{1BP}^{n_{BP}} \cdot p_{0AP}^{n_{AP}}\, [(1-\alpha)\,(1-\epsilon)]^{n_N} \\ & + \theta\delta\, p_{0A}^{n_A} \cdot p_{1B}^{n_B} \cdot p_{0AC}^{n_{AC}} \cdot p_{1BC}^{n_{BC}} \cdot p_{0BP}^{n_{BP}} \cdot p_{1AP}^{n_{AP}}\, [(1-\alpha)\,(1-\epsilon)]^{n_N} \\ & + (1-\theta)\, p_{0A}^{n_A} \cdot p_{0B}^{n_B} \cdot p_{0AC}^{n_{AC}} \cdot p_{0BC}^{n_{BC}} \cdot p_{0BP}^{n_{BP}} \cdot p_{0AP}^{n_{AP}}\, [\alpha + (1-\alpha)\,(1-\epsilon)]^{n_N} \end{aligned}$$

where $p_{1j} = \alpha\epsilon_{Ij} + (1-\alpha)\,\epsilon_{Uj}$ and $p_{0j} = (1-\alpha)\,\epsilon_{Uj}$ with j indexing trade decisions.

Two assumptions are needed to construct the sequence of trade decisions that identify the parameters. The first assumption identifies the length of time that corresponds to a decision not to trade.[2] As the no-trade decision is designed to isolate periods in which information is not present, the assumption is needed to identify α and ϵ. We first investigate how misspecification of the no-trade interval affects estimation. Let c correspond to the true length of the interval and let $\hat{c}$ correspond to the assumed length of the interval. Because all trades

[2] Specifying the no-trade interval is equivalent to specifying the frequency of trader arrivals.

are observed, only n_N – the number of no-trade decisions, is affected by the misspecification. If $c > \hat{c}$, then the number of no trades is biased upward, while if $c < \hat{c}$ the number of no trades is biased downward (as a sequence of actual no-trade decisions are required to record an observed no trade). Given the structure of the likelihood function, it is not straightforward to analytically determine the bias on individual parameters. To measure the bias, we simulate data under c and construct estimators under $\hat{c}$. We use the equal payoff condition (derived later), under which the uninformed trade frequency in each market is $\frac{\epsilon}{6}$ while the informed trade frequency in each market is $\frac{1}{3}$. For the population model we use parameter values that correspond to estimates in Easley, Kiefer, and O'Hara (1997); news arrives on half of the trading days ($\theta = .5$), bad news is slightly more prevelant than good news ($\delta = .6$), 20 percent of traders are informed ($\alpha = .2$), and the overall frequency of trade by uninformed traders is 80 percent ($\epsilon = .8$). The population model assumes a trader arrives every minute during a six-hour-trading day, for thirty trading days. The estimates are constructed under each of the alternative assumptions that a trader arrives every two, three, four, or five minutes.

As revealed in Panel A of Table 7.1, incorrectly specifying the no-trade interval underestimates the impact of informed traders (α is biased downward and ϵ is biased upward). The parameters governing behavior at the daily level, θ and δ, are largely invariant to misspecification of the no-trade interval. For the case in which the specified no-trade interval is too long, the number of recorded no trades declines and days with and without news become more similar. To account for the greater relative frequency of trades on all days, ϵ must increase. To account for the infrequency of no-trade decisions on days without news, α must decline. If the specified no-trade interval is too short, the number of

Table 7.1. *Impact of misspecification on parameter estimates*

	Panel A			
No-trade interval length	α	ϵ	θ	δ
1 minute	.2017	.7982	.4667	.5714
	(.0082)	(.0059)	(.0913)	(.1433)
2 minutes	.1633	.8360	.4667	.5714
	(.0095)	(.0064)	(.1173)	(.1409)
3 minutes	.1428	.8583	.4666	.5714
	(.0108)	(.0064)	(.1588)	(.1421)
4 minutes	.1238	.8767	.4667	.5714
	(.0117)	(.0067)	(.2045)	(.1426)
5 minutes	.1114	.8899	.4672	.5712
	(.0104)	(.0063)	(.2011)	(.1405)
	Panel B			
15% Trade misclassification	.1862	.7954	.4667	.5714
	(.0093)	(.0063)	(.1021)	(.1435)

recorded no trades increases and, again, days with news become more similar to days without news. Because the relative frequency of trades has declined on all days, ϵ decreases. To account for the infrequency of trade decisions on days with news, α declines. Incorrect specification of the no-trade interval, in either direction, biases the estimator of α downward and makes the presence of informed traders more difficult to detect.

Even if the no-trade interval is correctly specified, empirical identification may be problematic. The analysis of a related likelihood in Easley et al. (1997) is confined to a stock that is not heavily traded. For more heavily traded stocks, numerical difficulties prevent analysis. Rewriting the likelihood makes investigation of the numerical difficulties quite straightforward. Under the equal payoff condition, for which p_{0j} equals $p_0 = (1-\alpha)\frac{\epsilon}{6}$ for all j, the likelihood is

$$p_0^{n-n_N}\left[(1-\alpha)(1-\epsilon)\right]^{n_N}\cdot\left\{\theta(1-\delta)\left(\frac{\alpha}{3p_0}+1\right)^{n_A+n_{AC}+n_{BP}}\right.$$
$$\left.+\,\theta\delta\left(\frac{\alpha}{3p_0}+1\right)^{n_B+n_{BC}+n_{AP}}+(1-\theta)\left(\frac{\alpha}{c}+1\right)^{n_N}\right\}.$$

The issue concerns the three terms $(\frac{\alpha}{3p_0}+1)^{n_A+n_{AC}+n_{BP}}$, $(\frac{\alpha}{3p_0}+1)^{n_B+n_{BC}+n_{AP}}$, and $(\frac{\alpha}{c}+1)^{n_N}$. For frequently traded stocks, the observed value of trade decisions is quite large. As all three terms are greater than one, these terms dominate the likelihood function when raised to a large power and render the likelihood numerically unstable. (The most common difficulty is simply overflow, the calculated value exceeds the largest number the computer is able to store.) Figures 7.1 and 7.2 reveal the issue. In Figure 7.1, a trader arrives every minute and with 360 trader arrivals in one day no numerical problems are encountered. In Figure 7.2, a trader arrives every twenty seconds, with 1,080 trader arrivals numerical difficulties are prevelant.[3] Because the three terms are increasing functions of α and decreasing functions of ϵ, the likelihood function is correctly computed only for smaller values of α and larger values of ϵ. For the population values $\alpha = .2$ and $\epsilon = .8$ the likelihood function cannot be evaluated with an arrival frequency of twenty seconds.

The second assumption regards the classification of trades. Within the model, all trades occur at a quote. In practice, many trades are recorded at prices between the quotes. To empirically identify the model, all trades must be assigned to a quote. While there are several assignment rules popular in the literature, each of the rules has an estimated error rate of 15 percent. To understand the impact of the misclassification of trades, we randomly misclassify 15 percent of trades. Panel B of Table 7.1 contains the results. Estimation of θ and δ is again largely unaffected. As misclassification of trades does not alter the relative frequency of trades, estimation of ϵ is also unaffected. Yet random misclassification of trades

[3] For ease of viewing, we set the numerically unstable values to an arbitrarily small value, to emphasize that the empirical likelihood is essentially flat.

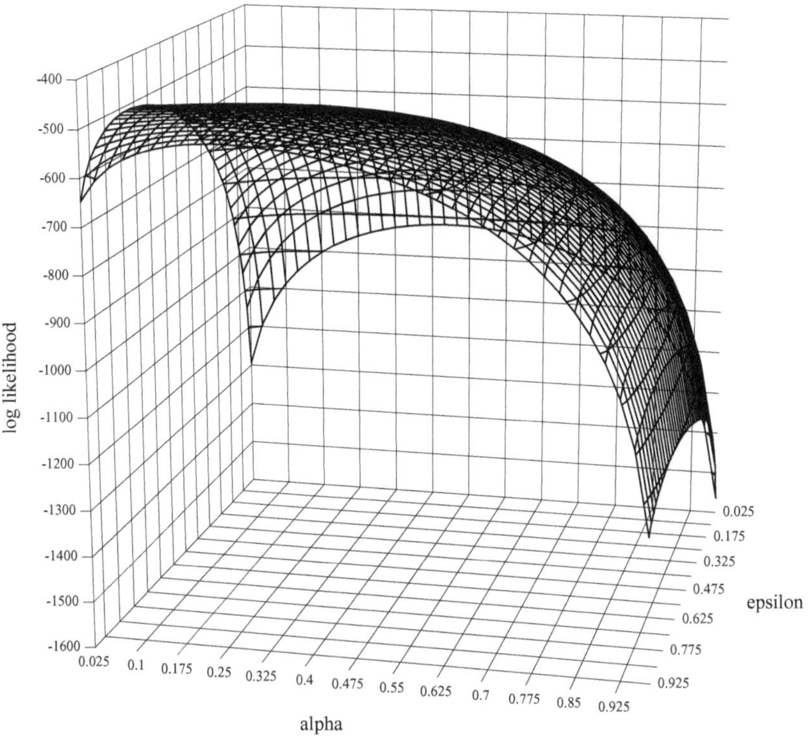

Figure 7.1. Log-likelihood function for 360 arrivals in a trading day.

does impact estimation of α. On days without news, random misclassification is equally likely to affect trades at either set of quotes. Yet on days with good news, for which there are more trades at the ask, misclassification is more likely to affect trades at the ask quotes. Similarly, on days with bad news, misclassification is more likely to affect trades at the bid quotes. As a result, the imbalance of trades (the number of ask trades minus bid trades) on news days is reduced and the presence of informed traders are again hidden.

3. INTRA-TRADING DAY DYNAMICS

The evolution of the quotes over the course of the trading day reflects the information revealed through trading. We show that at each point in the trading day the quotes have bounds that reflect the information asymmetry facing the market makers. We then study the frequency with which the informed trade in each market. We show that informed trade frequency in the options market generally declines over the course of the trading day and we derive the effect of the underlying parameters on this frequency. In doing so, we demonstrate that the separating equilibrium derived in Easley et al. (1998), in which the informed trade only in the options market, will not generally prevail over an entire trading

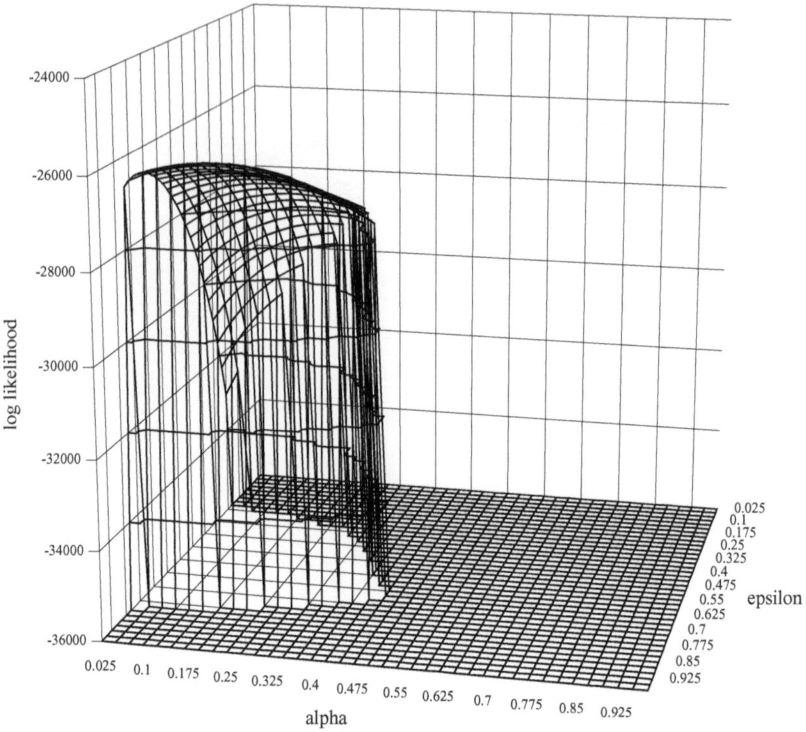

Figure 7.2. log-likelihood function for 1080 trader arrivals.

day. We also show how the bid–ask spread changes as the informed trade frequencies change. The spread in the options market declines more rapidly than does the spread in the stock market, reflecting the flow of informed traders into the stock market. Finally, we derive a condition under which the informed trade with constant frequency in the options market over the course of the trading day; constant informed trade frequencies greatly simplify the analysis of calendar period aggregates in Section 3.

In parallel to the opening quotes for the call, the ith-trade quotes for each asset are obtained as the solution to the zero profit condition with the relevant informed trade frequency. For example, the ith-trade quotes for one share of the stock are

$$A_i = v_{H_m} - \frac{(1-\alpha)\left[v_{H_m} - E\left(V_m|Z_{i-1}\right)\right]\left(\varphi_S\epsilon_{UA} + \lambda\varphi_C\epsilon_{UAC} + \lambda\varphi_P\epsilon_{UBP}\right)}{\left[\alpha y_{i-1} + (1-\alpha)\left(\epsilon_{UA} + \epsilon_{UAC} + \epsilon_{UBP}\right)\right]\varphi_S}$$

and

$$B_i = v_{L_m} + \frac{(1-\alpha)\left[E\left(V_m|Z_{i-1}\right) - v_{L_m}\right]\left(\varphi_S\epsilon_{UB} + \lambda\varphi_C\epsilon_{UBC} + \lambda\varphi_P\epsilon_{UAP}\right)}{\left[\alpha x_{i-1} + (1-\alpha)\left(\epsilon_{UB} + \epsilon_{UBC} + \epsilon_{UAP}\right)\right]\varphi_S}.$$

From these equations it is easy to see that each set of quotes is bounded by the respective limit values of the asset, with strict inequality unless the market maker is certain the informed learn the true value of V_m (no adverse selection). We also find that the quotes for the stock and the options bound the respective expected values of the assets, which illustrates the spread generated by the market makers in an effort to offset expected losses to traders with superior information.

The quotes process is driven by x_i and y_i, which are the market makers' beliefs about the signal received by the informed traders. The beliefs evolve according to Bayes' Rule and are determined in large part by the equilibrium informed trade frequencies. In general, informed trade frequencies vary throughout the trading day. The dynamic behavior of the options market trade frequency is intuitive; as private information is revealed through trading, the advantage gained by the informed through trade in the options market declines. To make the analysis of variable informed trade frequencies concise, we focus on an empirically relevant case in which options offer leverage and the option payoffs are symmetric, $(\lambda(\kappa_{P_m} - \upsilon_{L_m}) = \lambda(\upsilon_{H_m} - \kappa_{C_m}) \equiv \lambda\beta)$.

Theorem 3.1. *If the options offer greater leverage and have symmetric payoffs, then the informed trade frequencies behave in the following ways:*

- *(a) As λ increases, the informed are less likely to trade in the stock market. As α increases, the informed are more likely to trade in the stock market.*
- *(b) As learning evolves, the informed flow from the options market to the stock market. The rate of flow declines over the course of a trading day. The rate of flow also declines as α increases.*
- *(c) Informed trade frequencies in the option market are always positive. If the uninformed trade each asset with equal frequency, then $\epsilon_{IAC_i} = \epsilon_{IBP_i} > \epsilon_{IA_i}$ and $\epsilon_{IBC_i} = \epsilon_{IAP_i} > \epsilon_{IB_i}$.*
- *(d) The ith informed trade frequencies in the stock market are positive if, for $j = H, L$,*

$$\lambda < \frac{(\upsilon_{H_m} - \upsilon_{L_m})}{\beta}\left(1 + \frac{\alpha}{1-\alpha}\frac{1}{\epsilon_j}b_{j,i-1}\right),$$

with $\epsilon_H = \epsilon_{UAC} + \epsilon_{UBP}$, $\epsilon_L = \epsilon_{UBC} + \epsilon_{UAP}$, $b_{H,i-1} = y_{i-1}$, and $b_{L,i-1} = x_{i-1}$.

Proof. See Appendix. ■

An increase in the proportion of informed traders reduces the depth (the ratio of uninformed traders to informed traders) of the options market, which in turn makes the stock market more attractive to informed traders, as detailed in (*a*). To understand the dynamic pattern revealed in (*b*), consider a day on which

$S_m = s_H$. As the informed trade and reveal their information, y_i increases. As y_i increases, the gains to trade on information shrink, as does the advantage from trading in the options market. Hence, over the course of a trading day the informed flow from the options market to the stock market. As the updating of y_i slows over the course of a trading day to reflect the reduced information content of trades, so too does the rate of flow of informed traders. In similar fashion, as α increases, the information gain from each trader increases, so higher values of α lead to faster learning and greater attenuation of the rate of flow of informed between markets over the course of a trading day. While the informed flow from the options market to the stock market over the course of a trading day, if the uninformed are equally likely to trade in each market then the informed trade frequency is higher in the options market uniformly over the trading day, as stated in (c).

Leverage attracts informed traders to the options market. If λ exceeds the separating bound in (d), then the frequency of informed trade in the stock market is zero and the equilibrium separates the markets in which the informed trade. As either α decreases or ϵ_j increases, the informed are able to hide more easily in the options market, so the separating bound in (d) decreases and informed trade is more likely to occur only in the options market. Because λ is fixed over the course of a trading day while b_i evolves with the trade flow, it will generally not be the case that a separating equilibrium exists in all periods.

The bid–ask spread reflects the dynamic pattern of informed trade frequencies. To illustrate the dynamic pattern of the spread, we simulate the arrival of traders over the course of 1,000 trading days on which $S_m = s_H$. We set the information advantage of the informed at 5 percent of the initial value of the asset, so $v_{H_m} = 105$, $v_{L_m} = 95$, and $\delta = .5$. (We ensure that option payoffs are symmetric and set $\kappa_{C_m} = v_{L_m}$ and $\kappa_{P_m} = v_{H_m}$. The greater leverage afforded by options is then captured by $\lambda > 1$.[4]) We further suppose that the uninformed are equally likely to trade each asset, so that the informed trade frequencies, and hence the spreads, are identical for the two options. Finally, we suppose that $\alpha = .2$ and $\epsilon = .75$, noting that the essential features we report hold as α and ϵ vary over $[0, 1]$. In Figure 7.3 we present the average bid–ask spread over the course of a trading day. First, as λ increases the adverse selection problem in the options is exacerbated and forces the market maker to widen the bid–ask spreads for the call and put options, while the adverse selection problem in the stock is mitigated and allows the market maker to reduce the spread for the stock. As the trading day evolves the options spread declines more rapidly than the stock spread, reflecting the movement of informed traders into the stock market.

If the payoff from all three assets is equal, then the informed trade with *constant* frequency throughout the trading day. Because constant informed trade

[4] For the given parameter values, the separating bound is 1.2.

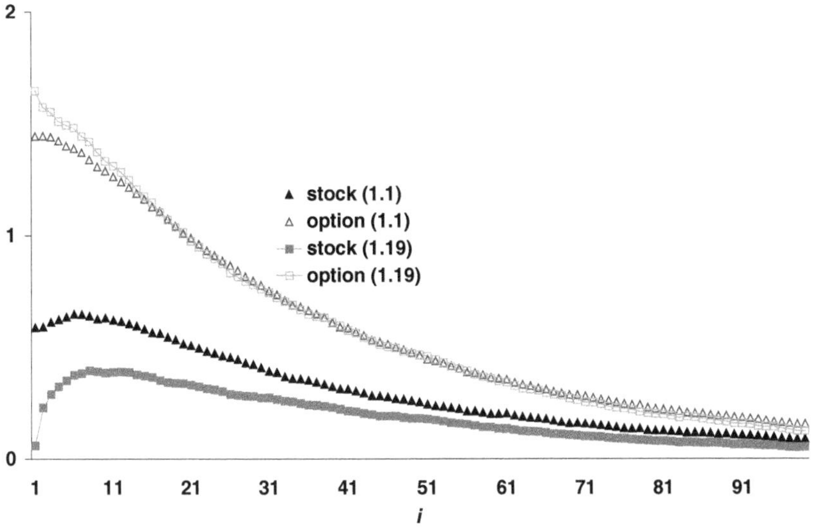

Figure 7.3. Bid–ask spreads with (λ) for $\alpha = .2$ and $\epsilon = .75$.

frequencies greatly simplify analysis when trade-by-trade variables are aggregated into calendar periods, we make note of the condition.

Equal Payoff Condition. The options leverage and strike prices satisfy

$$v_{H_m} - v_{L_m} = \lambda(v_{H_m} - \kappa_{C_m}) = \lambda(\kappa_{P_m} - v_{L_m}).$$

The constant informed trade frequencies mirror the behavior of uninformed traders in that the informed and uninformed trade with identical relative frequency in each market

$$\epsilon_{IA_i} = \frac{\epsilon_{UA}}{\epsilon_{UA} + \epsilon_{UAC} + \epsilon_{UBP}}, \quad \epsilon_{IAC_i} = \frac{\epsilon_{UAC}}{\epsilon_{UA} + \epsilon_{UAC} + \epsilon_{UBP}},$$

and

$$\epsilon_{IBP_i} = \frac{\epsilon_{UBP}}{\epsilon_{UA} + \epsilon_{UAC} + \epsilon_{UBP}}.$$

If the informed trade frequencies are constant, then ratios of x_i and y_i are recursive. (If the informed trade frequencies are variable, then it is difficult to obtain a recursive structure.) With constant informed trade frequencies we establish that if there were an infinite number of trader arrivals on m, then market makers would learn the signal, S_m. As a result, the quotes for each asset converge to the strong-form efficient value of that asset, reflecting both public and private information. As transaction prices are determined by the quotes, these prices also converge to the respective strong-form efficient values of the assets.

Theorem 3.2. *If the equal payoff condition is satisfied, then the sequence of quotes and, hence, the sequence of transaction prices for each asset converge almost surely to the strong-form efficient value of that asset at an exponential rate. Specifically, the following results obtain as* $i \longrightarrow \infty$.

If $S_m = s_L$ then $x_i \xrightarrow{as} 1,\ y_i \xrightarrow{as} 0$, so $A_i \xrightarrow{as} v_{L_m},\ B_i \xrightarrow{as} v_{L_m},\ A_{C_i} \xrightarrow{as} 0,$
$B_{C_i} \xrightarrow{as} 0,\ A_{P_i} \xrightarrow{as} \kappa_{P_m} - v_{L_m}$ and $B_{P_i} \xrightarrow{as} \kappa_{P_m} - v_{L_m}$.
If $S_m = s_H$ then $x_i \xrightarrow{as} 0,\ y_i \xrightarrow{as} 1$, so $A_i \xrightarrow{as} v_{H_m},\ B_i \xrightarrow{as} v_{H_m},\ A_{C_i} \xrightarrow{as}$
$v_{H_m} - \kappa_{C_m},\ B_{C_i} \xrightarrow{as} v_{H_m} - \kappa_{C_m},\ A_{P_i} \xrightarrow{as} 0$ and $B_{P_i} \xrightarrow{as} 0$.
If $S_m = s_O$ then $x_i \xrightarrow{as} 0,\ y_i \xrightarrow{as} 0$, so $A_i \xrightarrow{as} EV_m,\ B_i \xrightarrow{as} EV_m,\ A_{C_i} \xrightarrow{as}$
$EV_{C_m},\ B_{C_i} \xrightarrow{as} EV_{C_m},\ A_{P_i} \xrightarrow{as} EV_{P_m}$ and $B_{P_i} \xrightarrow{as} EV_{P_m}$.

Proof. See Appendix. ■

Convergence of the beliefs $\{x_i\}_{i\geq 0}$ and $\{y_i\}_{i\geq 0}$ immediately implies that $U_i \xrightarrow{as} 0$, so that individual trader price volatility converges to zero.

Careful analysis of individual trader price changes reveals three interesting features. First, option trades affect stock prices. Many standard option pricing models assume that the option price is derived from the stock price. Such models are misspecified when informed trade occurs in option markets. Second, price changes are predictable with respect to private information (in contrast to public information). Third, price changes are dependent and heterogenous, and the conditional variance of each price change is bounded by the squared bid–ask spread.

Price changes reflect public information after the decision of trader i but before the arrival of trader $i+1$. The stock price change associated with a specific trade decision for trader i is $U_i(D_i = d_j) = E(V_m|Z_{i-1}, D_i = d_j) - E(V_m|Z_{i-1})$. Consider a trade at the ask in the stock. Because $E(V_m|Z_i) = x_i v_{L_m} + y_i v_{H_m} + (1 - x_i - y_i)EV_m$, the stock price change is

$$U_i(D_i = d_A) = [v_{H_m} - E(V_m|Z_{i-1})]\frac{\alpha\epsilon_{IA_i} y_{i-1}}{P(D_i = d_A|Z_{i-1})}.$$

The price change reflects expected learning from the informed; if the market maker knows that the trader is uninformed, there is no learning from the trade and the price change is zero.

Because informed trade occurs in the options market, options are not redundant assets. If trader i elects to buy the call option contract, then

$$U_i(D_i = d_{AC}) = [v_{H_m} - E(V_m|Z_{i-1})]\frac{\alpha\epsilon_{IAC_i} y_{i-1}}{P(D_i = d_{AC}|Z_{i-1})}.$$

Trade in an option affects the price of the stock.

Prices are predictable with respect to private information. Consider the stock price change expected by an informed trader with $S_m = s_H$. The informed trader's expectation differs from that of the market maker because the market maker is unsure of the signal. The stock price change expected by an informed trader is

$$E(U_i|Z_{i-1}) + \alpha(1 + y_{i-1})[v_{H_m} - E(V_m|Z_{i-1})] + \alpha x_{i-1}[EV_m - v_{L_m}] > 0.$$

A direct implication is that price changes are serially correlated with respect to private information. If $S_m = s_H$, then the serial correlation expected by an informed trader is

$$E(U_h U_i|Z_{i-1}, S_m = s_H) = U_h E(U_i|Z_{i-1}, S_m = s_H) \neq 0.$$

Price changes are conditionally heteroskedastic with

$$E\left(U_i^2|Z_{i-1}\right) = \sum_{j=A,B,AC,BC,AP,BP,N} P(D_i = d_j|Z_{i-1})U_i^2(D_i = d_j).$$

As the conditional heteroskedasticity is path dependent, we construct analytic bounds. To do so, we use the effective bid–ask spread, $\hat{A}_i - \hat{B}_i$, which is the maximum revision in price resulting from a trade. In almost all cases, $\hat{A}_i - \hat{B}_i$ is simply the bid–ask spread. If, however, a decision not to trade is quite rare and generally made by informed traders (when ϵ is very large and α is very small) then a decision not to trade can yield a larger price change than a decision to trade. Hence,

$$\hat{A}_i - \hat{B}_i = \max_{j\in\{AC,BP,N\}} \left[A_i, E\left(V_m|Z_{i-1}, D_i = d_j\right)\right] - \min_{j\in\{BC,AP,N\}} \left[B_i, E\left(V_m|Z_{i-1}, D_i = d_j\right)\right].$$

(The effective bid–ask spreads for the call option and the put option, $\hat{A}_{C_i} - \hat{B}_{C_i}$ and $\hat{A}_{P_i} - \hat{B}_{P_i}$, are defined in the same way.)

We find that price changes conditional on public information are *dependent and not identically distributed*, although they are mean zero and serially uncorrelated. An asset's bid–ask spread drives the conditional variance of its price changes, introducing autoregressive heteroskedasticity.

Theorem 3.3. *Price changes in economic time for each asset are mean zero and serially uncorrelated with respect to the public information set. In addition*

$$E\left(U_i^2 \mid Z_{i-1}\right) \leq \left(\hat{A}_i - \hat{B}_i\right)^2, \quad and \quad E\left(U_{j_i}^2 \mid Z_{i-1}\right) \leq \left(\hat{A}_{j_i} - \hat{B}_{j_i}\right)^2$$

for $j = C, P$.

Proof. See Appendix. ■

The fact that the price change variance is bounded by the effective bid–ask spread is an important component of the model. (This was shown in Kelly and Steigerwald (2004) in the context of a single asset market.) Because the

Table 7.2. $E_H(U_i^2|Z_{i-1}) - E_O(U_i^2|Z_{i-1})$

Trader	1	2	3	4	5	6	7	8	9	10
$\epsilon = 0.9$	14.40	1.12	1.80	0.25	0.23	0.05	0.04	0.01	0.01	0.00
$\epsilon = 0.8$	15.06	1.21	1.81	0.20	0.20	0.04	0.03	0.01	0.00	0.00
$\epsilon = 0.7$	15.77	1.24	1.78	0.21	0.18	0.04	0.02	0.01	0.00	0.00
$\epsilon = 0.6$	16.53	1.22	1.65	0.23	0.15	0.04	0.02	0.00	0.00	0.00
$\epsilon = 0.5$	17.34	1.17	1.43	0.24	0.10	0.03	0.01	0.00	0.00	0.00
$\epsilon = 0.4$	18.23	1.11	1.15	0.27	0.06	0.04	0.01	0.00	0.00	0.00
$\epsilon = 0.3$	19.17	1.10	0.82	0.30	0.05	0.03	0.01	0.00	0.00	0.00
$\epsilon = 0.2$	20.19	1.20	0.52	0.31	0.04	0.01	0.01	0.00	0.00	0.00
$\epsilon = 0.1$	21.30	1.52	0.29	0.22	0.05	0.00	0.00	0.00	0.00	0.00

price uncertainty associated with informed trading widens the effective bid–ask spread, Theorem 3.3 suggests that price change behavior is systematically different on days for which the signal is informative.

To show that the price uncertainty is greater on days with an informative signal, we examine the market maker's price uncertainty on a trading day with $S_m = s_H$, $E_H(U_i^2|Z_{i-1})$, relative to the price uncertainty on a trading day with $S_m = s_O$, $E_O(U_i^2|Z_{i-1})$. Straightforward calculations reveal that for the first trader $E_H(U_1^2|Z_{i-1})$ is larger than $E_O(U_1^2|Z_{i-1})$. To determine the sign of $E_H(U_i^2|Z_{i-1}) - E_O(U_i^2|Z_{i-1})$ for $i > 1$, we study the behavior of U_i^2.[5] If α is large, then learning is rapid and largely occurs with the first ten traders. For illustration, in Table 7.2 we calculate $E_H(U_i^2|Z_{i-1}) - E_O(U_i^2|Z_{i-1})$ for $\alpha = .9$, from the exact distributions for U_i^2. We first note that as traders arrive to the market, the market maker learns and the relative price uncertainty decreases. The speed of learning increases as the proportion of uninformed traders who trade, ϵ, decreases. Most importantly, the price uncertainty during a day with an informative signal is always at least as large as the price uncertainty during a day with an uninformative signal.

For smaller values of α, learning is slowed and reduction of an asset's bid–ask spread to zero requires many more trader arrivals. For trader i, there are 7^i possible values for U_i, so calculation of the distribution of U_i^2 is cumbersome for large i. In Figure 7.4 we approximate $E_H(U_i^2|Z_{i-1}) - E_O(U_i^2|Z_{i-1})$ for $\alpha = .2$, with 1,000 simulations. We confirm the results of Table 7.2. Again, learning is more rapid if the uninformed trade with less frequency. Also, we again find that the variance of U_i is higher, uniformly, on a day with an informative signal than it is on a day with an uninformative signal.

4. CALENDAR PERIOD IMPLICATIONS

Aggregation of trader arrivals into calendar periods allows us to compare the model with three empirical benchmarks. For constant informed trade frequencies, we prove that the number of trades has positive serial correlation in each

[5] We assume that the equal payoff condition is satisfied, with $\lambda = 1$.

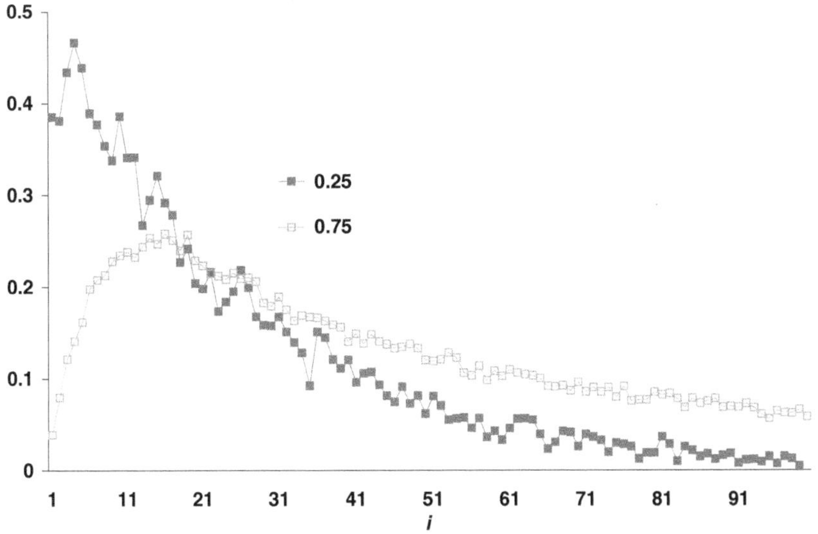

Figure 7.4. $E_H(U_i^2|Z_{i-1}) - E_O(U_i^2|Z_{i-1})$ with $\epsilon = .25$ and $\epsilon = .75$.

market in accord with the first benchmark. We are also able to compare the serial correlation for different levels of aggregation and find that, generally, serial correlation is higher for data gathered at five minute intervals than for data gathered at hourly intervals. For variable informed trade frequencies, we derive the formula for trade correlation and a sufficient condition for the correlation to be positive. We then demonstrate that squared price changes are positively serially correlated, in accord with the second benchmark. Last, we verify that the model is able to satisfy the third benchmark and produce serial correlation in trades that is larger and diminishes more slowly than the serial correlation in squared price changes.

To determine the serial correlation properties for calendar periods, such as thirty-minute intervals, we divide each trading day into k calendar periods. We let t index, calendar periods. To understand how t maps into k and m, suppose that $t = 1, \ldots, n$ in which $t = 1$ corresponds to the first calendar period on a trading day. The sample would then consist of the vectors of k calendar periods drawn from $\frac{n}{k}$ consecutive trading days. Each calendar period contains η trader arrivals (each trader arrival can be thought of as a unit of economic time). For a given trading day, we have $\tau = k\eta$ trader arrivals.

We first derive the serial correlation in trades (per calendar period). Under the assumption of constant informed trade frequencies, we show that trades are positively correlated. We also find that correlation in trades in an individual market is less than the correlation in total trades, as segmenting trades into three markets is not a scale transformation. (Our result for total trades corresponds to the result reported in Kelley and Steigerwald (2004), in which only one market is analyzed and so informed trade frequencies are constant.) The formula for serial correlation directly links the parameters of the market microstructure model to the serial correlation pattern in trades. We analyze the more complex case, in which the informed trade frequency is not constant, in Proposition 4.6. The proposition contains both a formula for trade correlation and a condition that ensures the correlation is positive. The intuition is straightforward: Positive trade correlation arises from the entry and exit of informed traders in response to the arrival of private information.

For correlation in trades in a specific asset, we focus on trades in the call option I_{C_t}. (Analogous results hold for the stock and the put option.) Given η trader arrivals in t, I_{C_t} takes integer values between 0 and η and so is a binomial random variable for which the number of trades in t corresponds to the number of successes in η trials. For each period on trading day m we have

$$E\left(I_{C_t}|S_m \neq s_O\right) = \eta(1-\alpha)\epsilon_{UC} + \sum_{i=\eta(t-1)+1}^{\eta t} \alpha\left[\delta\epsilon_{IBC_i} + (1-\delta)\epsilon_{IAC_i}\right] = \mu_{C1}$$

and

$$E\left(I_{C_t}|S_m = s_O\right) = \eta(1-\alpha)\epsilon_{UC} = \mu_{C0}.$$

In general, derivation of calendar period trades is quite complicated, as the informed trade frequencies are not constant. To begin, we assume that equal payoff condition holds so that the informed trade frequencies are constant throughout the trading day. For simplicity, we assume that the uninformed trade frequencies are equal across assets, so that each informed trade frequency is $\frac{1}{3}$. We then arrive at the following theorem and corollary in which $r > 0$.

Theorem 4.4. *Let the equal payoff condition hold. If $r < k$, then $I_{C_{t-r}}$ and I_{C_t} are positively serially correlated. If $r \geq k$, then $I_{C_{t-r}}$ and I_{C_t} are uncorrelated. For all r, we have*

$$\text{Cor}\left(I_{C_{t-r}}, I_{C_t}\right) = \frac{\theta(1-\theta)\left(\frac{\alpha}{3}\eta\right)^2}{\text{Var}\left(I_{C_t}\right)}\left[\frac{k-\min(k,r)}{k}\right].$$

Proof. Straightforward, but tedious, calculations yield the formula. ∎

The correlation in trades for each market is less than the correlation in total trades, which as derived in Kelley and Steigerwald (2004) is

$$\text{Cor}(I_{t-r}, I_t) = \frac{\theta(1-\theta)(\alpha\eta)^2}{\sigma^2}\left(\frac{k-r}{k}\right).$$

The correlations differ because the probability of success for a binomial random variable is not the scale of the random variable, so the variance of trades in a specific asset is not a scale transformation of the variance of total trades.

Corollary 4.5: *Let $r < k$. The positive correlation between $I_{C_{t-r}}$ and I_{C_t} is increasing in α, η, and k. The correlation is decreasing in r. The effects of changing the market parameters, ϵ and θ, and of altering calendar period aggregation through $\tau = k\eta$, on the positive correlation between $I_{C_{t-r}}$ and I_{C_t} are ambiguous.*

Proof. The comparative static results follow from differentiation. ■

As either the frequency of informed trade, α, the number of trader arrivals, η; or the number of calendar periods, k, increases, the trade serial correlation increases through the heightened impact of the entry and exit of informed traders. In general, increasing the frequency of uninformed trade reduces serial correlation, but if ϵ is close to one, then further increases in ϵ can amplify the impact of the informed trader flows and increase serial correlation. Increasing the probability of an informative signal, θ, leads to higher serial correlation if informative signals are rare. Perhaps most importantly for empirical work, we can compare the serial correlation in hourly observations with the serial correlation in five-minute observations. We find that serial correlation is generally higher in five-minute intervals, but that the impact is not constant across r. For longer lags, $r \geq \frac{k}{2}$, the serial correlation in five-minute data is unambiguously higher than the serial correlation in hourly data.

For the case in which the informed trade frequencies vary over the course of the day, we focus on trades in the stock market, I_{S_t}. From the results of Section 3, we deduce that the frequency of informed trade in the stock market rises as the trading day evolves. We capture this evolution with a simple structure in which (because informed trading frequencies are zero if $S_m = s_O$)

$$E\left(I_{S_j} | S_m = s_O\right) = \mu_{S0} \text{ for } j = 1, \ldots, k,$$

and

$$E\left(I_{S_j} | S_m \neq s_O\right) = \mu_{Sj} \text{ for } j = 1, \ldots, k,$$

with $0 < \mu_{S0} < \mu_{S1} < \mu_{S2} < \cdots < \mu_{Sk}$.

As any one calendar period is drawn at random from the periods of a trading day, the unconditional mean of stock trades in a calendar period is

$$EI_{S_t} = \theta \overline{\mu_{Sk}} + (1 - \theta)\,\mu_{S0} \text{ with } \overline{\mu_{Sk}} = \frac{1}{k}\sum_{j=1}^{k} \mu_{Sj}.$$

In deriving the serial correlation properties of $\left\{I_{S_t}\right\}_{t \geq 1}$, an important condition emerges that ensures the correlation is positive.

Positive Trade Covariance Condition. *The positive trade covariance condition is said to hold for period $\underline{j}$, with $1 \leq \underline{j} \leq k$, if $\underline{j}$ is the smallest value of j for which*

$$\mu_{Sj} > \theta \overline{\mu_{Sk}} + (1 - \theta)\,\mu_{S0}.$$

The positive trade covariance condition is most intuitive for the case $k = 2$. From the structure for the expectation of calendar period trades it follows that μ_{SO} lies below the unconditional mean and μ_{S2} lies above the unconditional mean. Suppose that $t - 1$ corresponds to the first calendar interval – the morning – of the trading day. For days without private news, we have $E\left(I_{S_{t-1}} | S_m = s_O\right) = \mu_{SO}$ and $E\left(I_{S_t} | S_m = s_O\right) = \mu_{SO}$. Thus, for days on which the morning observation tends to be below the unconditional mean, the afternoon observation also tends to be below the unconditional mean. For days with private news, we have $E\left(I_{S_{t-1}} | S_m \neq s_O\right) = \mu_{S1}$ and $E\left(I_{S_t} | S_m \neq s_O\right) = \mu_{S2}$. While it is clear that the afternoon observation tends to be above the unconditional mean, it is not clear whether $E I_{S_t} < \mu_{S1}$. If the positive trade covariance condition holds (for period 1), then $E I_{S_t} < \mu_{S1}$. As a result, on days with private news both the morning and afternoon observations tend to lie above the unconditional mean and positive serial correlation is assured.

Proposition 4.6. *Let $r > 0$. The covariance of calendar period stock trades is*

$$\left[\frac{k - \min(k, r)}{k}\right]\left[\begin{array}{c}\theta(1-\theta)\sum_{j=1}^{k-r}\left(\mu_{Sj} - \mu_{SO}\right)\left(\mu_{Sj+r} - \mu_{SO}\right) \\ +\theta^2 \sum_{j=1}^{k}\left(\overline{\mu_{Sk}} - \mu_{Sj}\right)\left(\overline{\mu_{Sk}} - \mu_{Sj+r}\right)\end{array}\right],$$

where the addition is wrapped at k. That is, if $j + r > k$, then replace $j + r$ with $j + r - k$.

If $r < k = 2$ and the positive trade covariance condition holds for period one, then

$$\operatorname{Cov}(I_{S_{t-r}}, I_{S_t}) = \left[\frac{2-r}{2}\right]\left[\begin{array}{c}\theta(1-\theta)\left(\mu_{S1} - \mu_{SO}\right)\left(\mu_{S2} - \mu_{SO}\right) \\ +\theta^2\left(\overline{\mu_{S2}} - \mu_{S1}\right)\left(\overline{\mu_{S2}} - \mu_{S2}\right)\end{array}\right] \geq 0.$$

Proof. See Appendix. ■

Serial correlation in squared price changes follows directly from serial correlation in trades if trade-by-trade price changes are i.i.d. As trade-by-trade price changes are not i.i.d, serial correlation in squared price changes is more complex than serial correlation in trades. As a result, formulae linking the parameters of the market microstructure model to the serial correlation are intractable. Positive serial correlation in squared price changes will obtain if squared price changes are higher in periods with higher trading (due to trade by informed traders). We numerically construct the distribution of squared price changes and show that expected squared price changes are higher in periods in which the informed are trading. We then verify that squared price changes are serially correlated, satisfying the second benchmark.

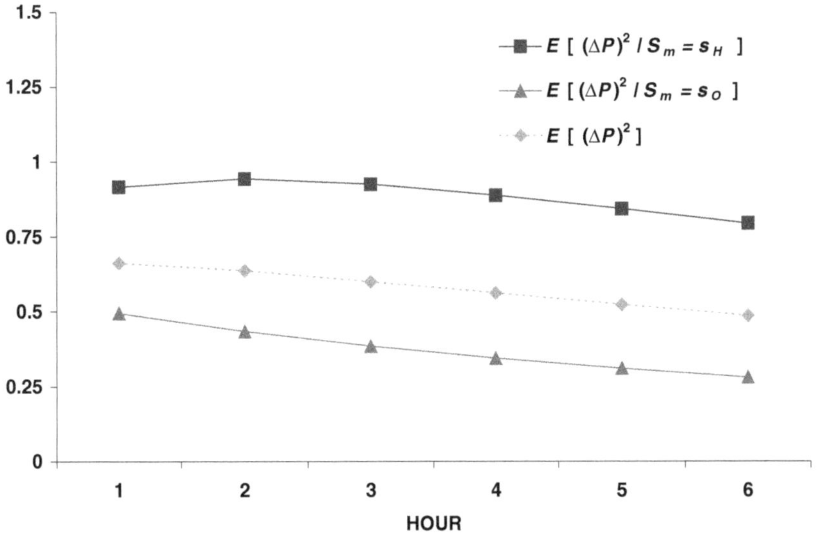

Figure 7.5. Behavior of expected squared price changes.

Serial correlation in an asset's squared price changes stems from the information content of trades, which in turn depends on the history of trades. Trade decisions in early economic time contain more information than later trade decisions. We define the (stock) price change over calendar period t on day m as

$$\Delta P_t = \sum_{i=(t-1)\eta+1}^{t\eta} U_i = E\left(V_m | Z_{t\eta}\right) - E\left(V_m | Z_{(t-1)\eta}\right).$$

A closed-form expression for the population moments of squared price changes as a function of all of the underlying parameters is, in general, intractable. To show that squared price changes have positive serial correlation, we compare price change volatility on days with and without news. If price change volatility is systematically higher on news days, then the random arrival of information leads to positive serial correlation in squared price changes. To illustrate, in Figure 7.5 we present expected squared price changes on trading days with and without news. A trading day is assumed to consists of six calendar periods, with two trader arrivals per period. (In detail, we consider only the stock market and we set $\alpha = .2$ and $\epsilon = .5$.[6]) Expected squared price changes are uniformly higher on news days, which implies that squared price changes are positively serially correlated.

To show that squared price changes are positively serially correlated, we consider a sequence of trading days in which $\theta = .4$ have news (with good and

[6] Estimates of $\alpha = .17$ and $\epsilon = .33$ are obtained in Easley et al. (1997) for an actively traded stock.

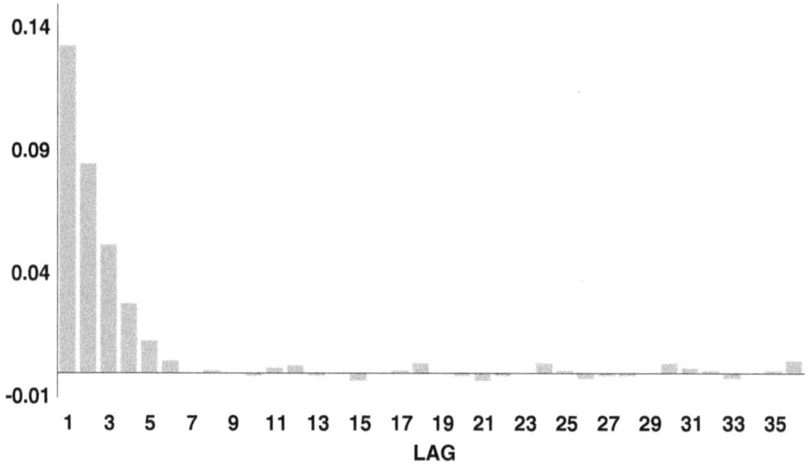

Figure 7.6. Autocorrelation in squared price changes.

bad news equally likely). As is evident in Figure 7.6, the interplay between sequences of squared price changes that lie above the unconditional mean (from news days) with sequences of squared price changes that lie below the unconditional mean (from days without news) leads to positive serial correlation in prices. Further, the serial correlation declines as we move from lag 1 to lag 5, as it is less likely that observations separated by five periods occur on the same trading day. Because the news arrival process is independent across trading days, it would seem that squared price changes are uncorrelated after lag 5. Yet the nonstationarity of the process due to the signal arrival at the start of each trading day leads to correlation in squared price changes at longer lags, which is more pronounced as θ moves away from .5. The first hour of each trading day is noisier than other hours, which leads to serial correlation at lag 6 (and at integer multiples of lag 6) that mirrors the cyclical effects in asset market data.

To verify the third benchmark, we must show that positive serial correlation in trades declines more slowly than does the positive serial correlation in squared price changes. We alter the setting slightly to more closely approximate behavior in a liquid stock traded on the NYSE. We define a trading day to be 32.5 hours, which corresponds to a normal trading week on the NYSE. We measure price and trades at thirty-minute intervals, so there are sixty-five calendar periods in a trading day. A trader arrives every five minutes, so there are six trader arrivals in each calendar period and 390 trader arrivals in a trading day. We simulate 195,000 trader arrivals over the course of 500 trading days.

The strike prices of the options are at their respective limits, $\kappa_{C_m} = v_{L_m} = 95$ and $\kappa_{P_m} = v_{H_m} = 105$, so that $\lambda = 1.15$ captures the greater leverage of an option. In Figure 7.7, we find the positive serial correlation in the total number of trades declines more slowly than does the positive serial correlation in the

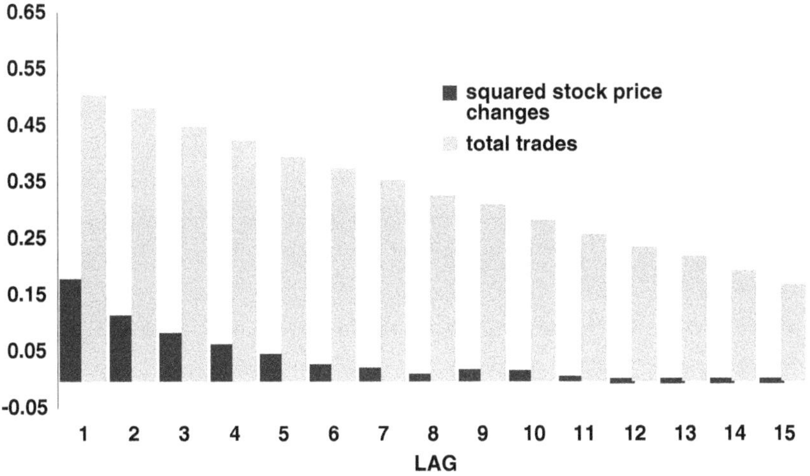

Figure 7.7. Thirty minute autocorrelations ($\lambda = 1.15$).

squared (stock) price changes. A similar picture emerges if we consider stock trades, rather than total trades, although the level of the trade correlation is reduced.

5. CONCLUSIONS

We focus on the role of private information in the formation of securities prices. The model captures the link between asset prices and informational asymmetries among traders, given a stylized arrival process for private information. But in actual markets the arrival and existence of private information is not easily captured, and the theoretical construct of a defined period over which asymmetric information persists is elusive. Moreover, the possibility of the occurrence of multiple, overlapping information events introduces significant complexity. It is not surprising, therefore, that without knowledge of the existence of private information it may be difficult to accurately detect such a pattern in actual data. Further, there is widespread consensus that adverse selection problems faced by market makers are not solely responsible for bid–ask spreads; rather, they are the result of multiple additional factors, including market maker inventory considerations and market power. Nonetheless, our simple economic model provides a theory-based explanation for observed empirical phenomena and, in so doing, establishes an economic foundation for the use of statistical models employed to capture stochastic volatility in asset prices.

6. ACKNOWLEDGMENTS

We thank Steve LeRoy and John Owens for helpful comments.

APPENDIX

Proof of Theorem 3.1. We present the analysis for ϵ_{IAC_i} and ϵ_{IA_i}. Identical logic holds for the remaining informed trade frequencies in the options and stock markets, respectively.

(a) Calculation reveals that $\frac{\partial \epsilon_{Ij_i}}{\partial \lambda} > 0$ for j indexing an option trade and $\frac{\partial \epsilon_{Ij_i}}{\partial \lambda} > 0$ for j indexing a stock trade. The sign of $\frac{\partial \epsilon_{IAC_i}}{\partial \alpha}$ is the sign of

$$\epsilon_{UA}\left[\left(v_{H_m} - v_{L_m}\right) - \lambda\beta\right],$$

which is negative by the greater leverage of options. The sign of $\frac{\partial \epsilon_{IA_i}}{\partial \alpha}$ is the sign of

$$\left(\epsilon_{UAC} + \epsilon_{UBP}\right)\left[\lambda\beta - \left(v_{H_m} - v_{L_m}\right)\right],$$

which is positive by the greater leverage of options.

(b) The sign of $\frac{\partial \epsilon_{IAC_i}}{\partial y_{i-1}}$ is the sign of the first displayed equation in (a) while the signs of $\frac{\partial^2 \epsilon_{IAC_i}}{\partial y_{i-1}^2}$ and $\frac{\partial^2 \epsilon_{IAC_i}}{\partial y_{i-1}\partial \alpha}$ are opposite to the sign of $\frac{\partial \epsilon_{IAC_i}}{\partial \alpha}$. The sign of $\frac{\partial \epsilon_{IA_i}}{\partial y_{i-1}}$ is the sign of the second displayed equation in (a) while the signs of $\frac{\partial^2 \epsilon_{IA_i}}{\partial y_{i-1}^2}$ and $\frac{\partial^2 \epsilon_{IA_i}}{\partial y_{i-1}\partial \alpha}$ are opposite to the sign of $\frac{\partial \epsilon_{IAC_i}}{\partial \alpha}$.

(c) Consider ϵ_{IAC_i}. This informed trade frequency is positive if

$$\begin{aligned}&\epsilon_{UA}\left[\lambda\left(v_{H_m} - \kappa_{C_m}\right) - \left(v_{H_m} - v_{L_m}\right)\right]\\ &+ \epsilon_{UBP}\left[\lambda\left(v_{H_m} - \kappa_{C_m}\right) - \lambda\left(\kappa_{P_m} - v_{L_m}\right)\right] > 0.\end{aligned}$$

The first term on the left side is positive because of the greater leverage of options. The second term on the left side is zero because of equal option payoffs. If the uninformed trade each asset with equal frequency, then the remaining inequalities are deduced by inspection of the informed trade frequencies.

(d) For informed trade in the stock market, symmetric option payoffs imply that ϵ_{IA_i} is positive if

$$\alpha y_{i-1}\left(v_{H_m} - v_{L_m}\right) + (1-\alpha)\left(\epsilon_{UAC} + \epsilon_{UBP}\right)\left[\left(v_{H_m} - v_{L_m}\right) - \lambda\beta\right] > 0.$$

Because options offer greater leverage, the second term on the left is negative and the inequality becomes

$$\alpha y_{i-1}\left(v_{H_m} - v_{L_m}\right) > (1-\alpha)\left(\epsilon_{UAC} + \epsilon_{UBP}\right)\left[\lambda\beta - \left(v_{H_m} - v_{L_m}\right)\right],$$

from which the bound in the text is easily deduced. ■

Proof of Theorem 3.2. The proof follows from calculations similar to those in Kelley and Steigerwald (2004) [**Theorem 3.1**].

Proof of Theorem 3.3. For the proof of Theorem 3.3, let D_j represent $D_i = d_j$. We verify the theorem for U_i; identical logic holds for U_{C_i} and U_{P_i}. Proof that $E\left(U_i|Z_{i-1}\right) = 0$ and $E(U_h U_i|Z_{i-1}) = 0$ is straightforward. The upper bound for the conditional variance is

$$
\begin{aligned}
E\left(U_i^2|Z_{i-1}\right) &\le \sum_{j=A,AC,BP} P\left(D_j\right)\left[\hat{A}_i - E\left(V_m|Z_{i-1}\right)\right]^2 \\
&\quad + \sum_{j=B,BC,AP} P\left(D_j\right)\left[\hat{B}_i - E\left(V_m|Z_{i-1}\right)\right]^2 \\
&\quad + P(D_N)\left[E\left(V_m|Z_{i-1}, D_N\right) - E\left(V_m|Z_{i-1}\right)\right]^2 \\
&\le \sum_{j=A,AC,BP,N} P\left(D_j\right)\left[\hat{A}_i - E\left(V_m|Z_{i-1}\right)\right]^2 \\
&\quad + \sum_{j=B,BC,AP,N} P\left(D_j\right)\left[\hat{B}_i - E\left(V_m|Z_{i-1}\right)\right]^2 \\
&\le \left[\hat{A}_i - E\left(V_m|Z_{i-1}\right)\right]^2 + \left[\hat{B}_i - E\left(V_m|Z_{i-1}\right)\right]^2 \\
&\le \left[\left(\hat{A}_i - E\left(V_m|Z_{i-1}\right)\right) - \left(\hat{B}_i - E\left(V_m|Z_{i-1}\right)\right)\right]^2 \\
&= \left(\hat{A}_i - \hat{B}_i\right)^2,
\end{aligned}
$$

where the first inequality follows from the definition of $\hat{A}_i$ and $\hat{B}_i$ and the fourth inequality follows from $B_i \le E\left(V_m|Z_i\right) \le A_i$. ■

Proof of Proposition 4.6. We derive $\mathrm{Cov}(I_{S_{t-r}}, I_{S_t})$ for $k = 2$. Derivation of the general covariance expression follows similar logic. Let $N = 1$ if $t - 1$ is the first calendar period in a trading day and $N = 2$ if $t - 1$ is the second calendar period. First note that

$$
\mathrm{Cov}\left(I_{S_{t-r}}, I_{S_t}\right) = E\left\{\begin{array}{l}\left[E\left(I_{S_{t-r}} I_{S_t}|N\right) - E\left(I_{S_{t-r}}|N\right)E\left(I_{S_t}|N\right)\right] \\ +\left[E I_{S_{t-r}} - E\left(I_{S_{t-r}}|N\right)\right]\left[E I_{S_t} - E\left(I_{S_t}|N\right)\right]\end{array}\right\},
$$

or the sum of the conditional covariance and the covariance of the conditional means. Given that

$$
E\left(I_{S_{t-1}}|N=1\right) = \theta\mu_{S1} + (1-\theta)\mu_{S0} = E\left(I_{S_t}|N=2\right)
$$

and

$$
E\left(I_{S_{t-1}}|N=2\right) = \theta\mu_{S2} + (1-\theta)\mu_{S0} = E\left(I_{S_t}|N=1\right).
$$

Because $P(N=1) = P(N=2) = \frac{1}{2}$, the conditional covariance is

$$
\begin{aligned}
&P(N=1)\cdot\mathrm{Cov}\left(I_{S_{t-1}}, I_{S_t}|N=1\right) + P(N=2)\cdot\mathrm{Cov}(I_{S_{t-1}}, I_{S_t}|N=2) \\
&\quad = \tfrac{1}{2}\left[E(I_{S_{t-1}} I_{S_t}|N=1) - E(I_{S_{t-1}}|N=1)E(I_{S_t}|N=1)\right] \\
&\quad\quad + \tfrac{1}{2}\left[E(I_{S_{t-1}} I_{S_t}|N=2) - E(I_{S_{t-1}}|N=2)E(I_{S_t}|N=2)\right]
\end{aligned}
$$

which simplifies to

$$
\tfrac{1}{2}\theta(1-\theta)\left(\mu_{S1} - \mu_{S0}\right)\left(\mu_{S2} - \mu_{S0}\right).
$$

As $\mu_{S0} < \mu_{S1} < \mu_{S2}$, the conditional covariance is unequivocally positive. The covariance of the conditional means,

$$P(N=1)\cdot\left[EI_{S_{t-1}} - E(I_{S_{t-1}}|N=1)\right]\left[EI_{S_t} - E(I_{S_t}|N=1)\right] \\ + P(N=2)\cdot\left[EI_{S_{t-1}} - E(I_{S_{t-1}}|N=2)\right]\left[EI_{S_t} - E\left(I_{S_t}|N=2\right)\right]$$

simplifies to

$$\theta^2\left(\frac{\mu_{S1}-\mu_{S2}}{2}\right)\left(\frac{\mu_{S2}-\mu_{S1}}{2}\right).$$

As $\mu_{S1} < \mu_{S2}$, the covariance of the conditional means is negative. We have $\mathrm{Cov}\left(I_{S_{t-1}}, I_{S_t}\right) > 0$ if $(1-\theta)\left(\mu_{S1}-\mu_{S0}\right)\left(\mu_{S2}-\mu_{S0}\right) > \frac{\theta}{2}\left(\mu_{S2}-\mu_{S1}\right)^2$. By inspection, $\mu_{S2}-\mu_{S0} > \mu_{S2}-\mu_{S1}$, so it is enough to show that

$$(1-\theta)\left(\mu_{S1}-\mu_{S0}\right) > \frac{\theta}{2}\left(\mu_{S2}-\mu_{S1}\right).$$

Now, as $\frac{\theta}{2}\left(\mu_{S2}-\mu_{S1}\right) = \theta\left(\overline{\mu_{S2}}-\mu_{S1}\right)$, this is equivalent to showing that

$$(1-\theta)\left(\mu_{S1}-\mu_{S0}\right) > \frac{\theta}{2}\left(\overline{\mu_{S2}}-\mu_{S1}\right).$$

From the positive trade correlation condition,

$$(1-\theta)\left(\mu_{S1}-\mu_{S0}\right) > \theta(1-\theta)\left(\overline{\mu_{S2}}-\mu_{S0}\right).$$

Then

$$(1-\theta)\left(\mu_{S1}-\mu_{S0}\right) - \theta\left(\overline{\mu_{S2}}-\mu_{S1}\right) \\ > \theta(1-\theta)\left(\overline{\mu_{S2}}-\mu_{S0}\right) - \theta\left(\overline{\mu_{S2}}-\mu_{S1}\right).$$

The right side of the preceding inequality equals

$$\theta\left[\left(\mu_{S1}-\mu_{S0}\right) - \theta\left(\overline{\mu_{S2}}-\mu_{S0}\right)\right],$$

which is positive by the positive trade correlation condition. ■

References

Andersen, T. (1996), "Return Volatility and Trading Volume: An Information Flow Interpretation of Stochastic Volatility," *Journal of Finance*, 51, 169–204.

Back, K. (1993), "Asymmetric Information and Options," *Review of Financial Studies*, 6, 435–72.

Biais, B., and P. Hillion (1994), "Insider and Liquidity Trading in Stock and Options Markets," *Review of Financial Studies*, 7, 743–80.

Black, F. (1975), "Fact and Fantasy in the Use of Options," *Financial Analysts Journal*, 31, 36–41, 61–72.

Black, F., and M. Scholes (1973), "The Pricing of Options and Corporate Liabilities," *Journal of Political Economy*, 81, 637–54.

Easley, D., N. Kiefer, and M. O'Hara (1997), "One Day in the Life of a Very Common Stock," *The Review of Financial Studies*, 10, 805–35.

Easley, D., and M. O'Hara (1992), "Time and the Process of Security Price Adjustment," *Journal of Finance*, 47, 577–605.

Easley, D., M. O'Hara, and P. Srinivas (1998), "Option Volume and Stock Prices: Evidence on Where Informed Traders Trade," *Journal of Finance*, 53, 431–65.

Harris, L. (1987), "Transaction Data Tests of the Mixture of Distributions Hypothesis," *Journal of Financial and Quantitative Analysis*, 22, 127–41.

Kelly, D., and D. Steigerwald (2004), "Private Information and High-Frequency Stochastic Volatility," *Studies in Nonlinear Dynamics and Economitrics*, 8, 1–30.

Rothenberg, T. (1973), *Efficient Estimation with A Priori Information*. Cowles Foundation Monograph 23, New Haven: Yale University.

Steigerwald, D. (1997), "Mixture Models and Conditional Heteroskedasticity," manuscript, University of California, Santa Barbara.

Steigerwald, D., and R. Vagnoni (2001), "Option Market Microstructure and Stochastic Volatility," web manuscript, University of California, Santa Barbara.

PART II

ASYMPTOTIC APPROXIMATIONS

CHAPTER 8

Asymptotic Expansions for Some Semiparametric Program Evaluation Estimators

Hidehiko Ichimura and Oliver Linton

ABSTRACT

We investigate the performance of a class of semiparametric estimators of the treatment effect via asymptotic expansions. We derive approximations to the first two moments of the estimator that are valid to "second order." We use these approximations to define a method of bandwidth selection. We also propose a degrees of freedom–like bias correction that improves the second-order properties of the estimator but without requiring estimation of higher-order derivatives of the unknown propensity score. We provide some numerical calibrations of the results.

1. INTRODUCTION

In a series of classic papers Tom (Rothenberg 1984a,b,c, 1988) introduced Edgeworth expansions to a broad audience. His treatment of the generalized least-squares estimator (1984b) in particular was immensely influential because it dealt with an estimator of central importance and the analysis was both deep and precise, but comprehensible. This is in contrast with some of the more frenzied publications about Edgeworth expansions that had hitherto appeared in econometrics journals. The use of Basu's theorem in that paper to establish the independence of the correction terms from the leading term is a well-known example of his elegant work. The review paper (1984a) was also very influential and highly cited.

It is our purpose here to present asymptotic expansions for a class of semiparametric estimators used in the program evaluation literature. We have argued elsewhere (Linton 1991, 1995; Heckman et al. 1998) that the first-order asymptotics of semiparametric procedures can be misleading and unhelpful. The limiting variance matrix of the semiparametric procedure Σ does not depend on the specific details of how the nonparametric function estimator $\widehat{g}$ is constructed, and thus sheds no light on how to implement this important part of the procedure. Specifically, bandwidth choice cannot be addressed by using the first-order theory alone. Also, the relative merits of alternative first-order equivalent implementations, for example, one-step procedures, cannot be determined by the first-order theory alone. Finally, to show when bootstrap methods can provide asymptotic refinements for asymptotically pivotal statistics requires some knowledge of higher-order properties. This motivates the study of higher-order expansions. Carroll and Härdle (1989) was to our knowledge the first published paper that developed second-order mean squared error expansions for a semiparametric, that is, smoothing-based but root-n consistent, procedure, in the context of a heteroskedastic linear regression. Härdle et al. (1992) developed expansions for scalar average derivatives, which were extended to the multivariate case, actually only the simpler situation of density-weighted average derivatives, by Härdle and Tsybakov (1993); these papers used the expansions to develop automatic bandwidth selection routines. This work was extended to the slightly more general case of density-weighted averages by Powell and Stoker (1996). In his Ph.D. thesis (Linton 1991), written under Tom's supervision, the second author developed expansions for a variety of semiparametric regression models including the partially linear model and the heteroskedastic linear regression model; some of this work was later published in Linton (1995, 1996a). The Linton (1995) paper also provided some results on the optimality of the bandwidth selection procedures proposed therein. Xiao and Phillips (1996) worked out the same approximations for a time series regression model with serial correlation of unknown form; Xiao and Linton (2001) give the analysis for Bickel's (1982) adaptive estimator in the linear regression model. Nishiyama and Robinson (2000) proved the validity of an Edgeworth approximation to the distribution of the density-weighted average derivative estimator. Linton (2001a) derived an Edgeworth approximation to the distribution of the standardized estimator and a Wald statistic in a semiparametric instrumental variables model.

In this paper, we develop asymptotic expansions for an estimator of the treatment effect recently proposed in Hirano, Imbens, and Ridder (2000), henceforth HIR. Propensity score matching is a nonexperimental method for estimating the average effect of social programs.[1] The method compares average outcomes of participants and nonparticipants conditioning on the propensity score value. When averaged over the propensity score, the average measures the average impact of a program if the conditioning on the observable variables makes the choice of the program conditionally mean-independent of the potential outcomes. This methodology has received much attention recently in econometrics. While the method often in practice uses the nearest match in either regressors or estimated propensity score to compare the treatment and the comparison groups, the asymptotic distribution theory for these methods have not been developed. The asymptotic distribution theory has been developed by Heckman, Ichimura, and Todd (1998) for the kernel-based matching method. HIR consider reweighting the estimator that estimates the treatment effect as well. Both methods require choosing smoothing parameters, but optimal methods to choosing the smoothing parameter have not been discussed. In this paper we consider optimal bandwidth selection for the reweighting estimator.

[1] See Cochran (1968), Rosenbaum and Rubin (1983), and Heckman, Ichimura, and Todd (1998).

2. THE MODEL AND ESTIMATOR

We investigate a class of estimators for the treatment effect, studied by HIR. Let Y_1 and Y_0 denote potential outcome for an individual with and without "the treatment," respectively. Define

$$Y = Y_1 \cdot T + Y_0 \cdot (1 - T),$$

where T is an indicator variable denoting the presence of treatment, that is,

$$T = \begin{cases} 1 & \text{if treated} \\ 0 & \text{if untreated.} \end{cases}$$

Let X be a vector of covariates or pretreatment variables. Actually, for convenience we will take X to be a scalar and to have a continuous density f bounded away from zero on its compact support. We will also assume that Y possesses many finite moments. We are interested in the average treatment effect parameter

$$\tau_0 = E(Y_1) - E(Y_0).$$

We shall assume the following identifying conditions:

$$\begin{aligned} &E[Y_1|X, T = 1] = E[Y_1|X, T = 0] \\ &E[Y_0|X, T = 1] = E[Y_0|X, T = 0] \\ &0 < p(X) < 1 \end{aligned}$$

with probability 1 in X, where

$$p(x) = \Pr[T = 1|X = x] = E(T|X = x)$$

is the propensity score. The first two assumptions are that treatment and potential outcome are mean independent given covariates; the final assumption is that there are at least some unobserved influences on the probability of receiving the treatment. See Rosenbaum and Rubin (1983) and Heckman et al. (1998). Clearly, under these assumptions, $E[Y_1|X = x, T = 1] = E[Y_1|X = x] = m_1(x)$ and $E[Y_0|X, T = 0] = E[Y_0|X = x] = m_0(x)$. Furthermore, the following observable regressions are related to the unobservable regressions:

$$\begin{aligned} g_1(x) &\equiv E[Y \cdot T|X = x] = m_1(x) \cdot p(x), \quad \text{and} \\ g_0(x) &\equiv E[Y \cdot (1 - T)|X = x] = m_0(x) \cdot (1 - p(x)). \end{aligned}$$

It now follows that the average treatment effect parameter τ_0 satisfies

$$\begin{aligned} \tau_0 &= E(Y_1) - E(Y_0) = E[m_1(X)] - E[m_0(X)] \\ &= E\left[\frac{g_1(X)}{p(X)}\right] - E\left[\frac{g_0(X)}{1 - p(X)}\right] \\ &= E\left[\frac{E(Y \cdot T|X)}{p(X)}\right] - E\left[\frac{E(Y \cdot (1 - T)|X)}{1 - p(X)}\right] \\ &= E\left[\frac{Y \cdot T}{p(X)}\right] - E\left[\frac{Y \cdot (1 - T)}{1 - p(X)}\right], \end{aligned}$$

where the last line follows from the law of iterated expectations. The last line is the relation that HIR use to suggest an estimator. Suppose now that we observe a sample $\{Z_i, i = 1, \ldots, n\}$, where $Z_i = (Y_i, T_i, X_i)$. The HIR estimator is

$$\widehat{\tau} = \frac{1}{n} \sum_{i=1}^{n} \left[\frac{Y_i \cdot T_i}{\widehat{p}(X_i)} - \frac{Y_i \cdot (1 - T_i)}{1 - \widehat{p}(X_i)} \right],$$

where $\widehat{p}(X_i)$ was a nonparametric estimate of $p(X_i)$ – in fact, they chose series estimates.

We allow a slightly greater degree of generality; in particular, we consider the estimator $\widehat{\tau}$ of τ_0 to be any sequence that solves

$$\frac{1}{\sqrt{n}} \sum_{i=1}^{n} \Psi(Z_i, \tau, \widehat{p}(X_i)) = o_p\left(n^{-5/4}\right), \tag{2.1}$$

where

$$\Psi(Z_i, \tau, \widehat{p}(X_i)) = \frac{Y_i \cdot T_i}{\widehat{p}(X_i)} - \frac{Y_i \cdot (1 - T_i)}{1 - \widehat{p}(X_i)} - \tau \tag{2.2}$$

and

$$\widehat{p}(X_i) = \sum_{j=1}^{n} w_{ij} T_j,$$

where w_{ij} are smoothing weights that only depend on the covariates $X_1, \ldots, X_n$.[2] As we mentioned earlier, HIR used series estimates. The bias correction method we propose below can also be applied to series estimates and indeed to any linear smoother, but detailed discussion of smoothing bias terms requires that we use kernel or local polynomial estimators. We will also adopt the leave-one-out paradigm that is used in many semiparametric estimates. To be specific we let the parameter vector $(\widehat{\alpha}_0(X_i), \widehat{\alpha}_1(X_i))$ minimize the criterion function

$$\sum_{j \neq i} K\left(\frac{X_j - X_i}{h}\right) \{T_j - \alpha_0 + \alpha_1(X_j - X_i)\}^2, \tag{2.3}$$

with respect to (α_0, α_1), where K is a differentiable probability density function symmetric about zero with support $[-1, 1]$, while $h = h(n)$ is a positive bandwidth sequence. Then let $\widehat{p}(X_i) = \widehat{\alpha}_0(X_i)$ and let w_{ij} be the corresponding smoothing weights. We have taken the fixed bandwidth leave-one-out local linear kernel smoother as our estimator of the regression function. This estimator is preferable to the local constant kernel estimator because of its superior bias properties both at interior and boundary regions (see Fan and Gijbels 1996).

[2] The precise magnitude of the error of (2.1) is sufficient for both of our higher order expansions in Theorems 3.1 and 3.2 below. It is certainly much smaller than is needed for root-n consistency.

3. MAIN RESULTS

HIR showed that the standardized estimator $\mathcal{T} = \sqrt{n}(\widehat{\tau} - \tau_0)$ satisfies

$$\mathcal{T} = \frac{1}{\sqrt{n}} \sum_{i=1}^{n} \rho_i + o_p(1) = \mathcal{T}_0 + o_p(1), \tag{3.1}$$

where $\rho_i = \Psi(Z_i; \tau_0, p(X_i)) + s_p(X_i)\varepsilon_i$, where $\varepsilon_j = T_j - p(X_j)$ and

$$s_p(x) = E[\Psi_p(Z_i; \tau_0, p(X_i))|X_i = x] = -\left[\frac{m_1(x)}{p(x)} + \frac{m_0(x)}{1 - p(x)}\right].$$

Here, the derivatives of Ψ with respect to p are denoted by Ψ_p, Ψ_{pp}, and so forth. Therefore, $\mathcal{T}$ is asymptotically normal with finite variance

$$v_0 = E\left[\left(\Psi(Z_i; \tau_0, p(X_i)) + s_p(X_i)\varepsilon_i\right)^2\right]. \tag{3.2}$$

In fact, they rewrote the asymptotic variance in the more interpretable form

$$v_0 = \text{var}\left[E(Y_1 - Y_0|X)\right] + E\left[\frac{\text{var}(Y_1|X)}{p(X)}\right] + E\left[\frac{\text{var}(Y_0|X)}{1 - p(X)}\right].$$

They also established that this estimator is semiparametrically efficient, that is, it has the smallest asymptotic variance amongst the class of all feasible estimators.

We are interested in the higher-order properties of their estimator. We derive a stochastic expansion for $\mathcal{T}$ by Taylor-expanding $\Psi(Z_i, \tau, \widehat{p}(X_i))$ around $\Psi(Z_i, \tau, p(X_i))$, thereby obtaining the representation

$$\mathcal{T} = \mathcal{T}_0 + \mathcal{T}_1 + R = \mathcal{T}^* + R, \tag{3.3}$$

where the leading term $\mathcal{T}_0$ is as defined in (3.1), $\mathcal{T}_1$ contains the second-order terms, while R is a remainder term that is of smaller order in probability. To be specific, we show that $R = o_p(n^{-\alpha})$ in probability for some $\alpha > 0$, where α is determined by the order of magnitude of the bandwidth and of course by the number of terms in the Taylor expansion we retain. The magnitude $o_p(n^{-\alpha})$ is determined to ensure that our results in Theorems 3.1 and 3.2 below are sensible. The random variable $\mathcal{T}^*$ has finite moments to various orders and indeed it is a linear combination of certain U-statistics. We shall calculate the moments of $\mathcal{T}^*$ and interpret them as if they were the moments of $\mathcal{T}$. This methodology has a long tradition of application in econometrics following Nagar (1959).[3] The two largest (in probability) second-order terms in $\mathcal{T}_1$ are both

[3] When $\sup_n E[\mathcal{T}^2] < \infty$, we might reasonably expect that $E[\mathcal{T}^2] = E[\mathcal{T}^{*2}] + o(n^{-\alpha})$, but see Srinavasan (1970) for a cautionary tale in this regard. In any case, our $\mathcal{T}$ does not necessarily have uniformly bounded moments. Therefore, some additional justification for examining the moments of the truncated statistic must be given. With some additional work and regularity conditions, it is possible to establish the stronger regularity that $\mathcal{T}$ and $\mathcal{T}^*$ have the same distribution to order $n^{-\alpha}$, which requires some restrictions on the tails of R; see the discussion in Rothenberg (1984a). In this case our moment approximations can be interpreted as the moments of the approximating distribution.

nonzero mean and are

$$O_p(h^2\sqrt{n}) + O_p(n^{-1/2}h^{-1}). \tag{3.4}$$

In $\mathcal{T}_1$ there are also mean zero random variables of order h^2 and order $n^{-1/2}h^{-1/2}$. However, according to the criterion of mean squared error, these stochastic terms are dominated by the bias terms, and the optimal thing to do is to minimize the size of (3.4) by choosing h appropriately. The optimal bandwidth is therefore of order $h \asymp n^{-1/3}$, in which case both terms in (3.4) are of the same magnitude, and indeed are both of order $n^{-1/6}$. Thus, the second-order terms are very large and are mostly bias related. This suggests that the usual (first-order) asymptotic approximation may not be very well located. We shall now assume that a bandwidth of the optimal order $h \asymp n^{-1/3}$ has been chosen so as to simplify the discussion of the results. Define the functions

$$\beta(x) = p''(x)$$

$$s_{pp}(x) = E[\Psi_{pp}(Z_i; \tau_0, p(X_i))|X_i = x] = 2\left[\frac{m_1(x)}{p(x)^2} - \frac{m_0(x)}{(1-p(x))^2}\right]$$

$$\mu_2(K) = \int \frac{u^2K(u)}{2}\,du, \qquad \|K\|^2 = \int K(u)^2\,du.$$

Theorem 3.1. *Under some regularity conditions, as $n \to \infty$, $R = o_p(n^{-1/3})$ in* (3.3) *and*

$$E(\mathcal{T}^*) \simeq \sqrt{n}h^2 b_{n1} + \frac{1}{\sqrt{n}h} b_2 + o(n^{-1/3})$$

$$\operatorname{var}(\mathcal{T}^*) \simeq v_0 + o(n^{-1/3}),$$

where b_{n1} is deterministic and satisfies $b_{n1} \to b_1$ with

$$b_1 = \mu_2(K)E\left[s_p(X_i)\beta(X_i)\right],$$

$$b_2 = \|K\|^2\, E\left[s_{pp}(X_i)\frac{p(X_i)(1-p(X_i))}{2f(X_i)}\right].$$

The leading smoothing bias term b_1 can take either sign, since it depends on the covariance between the smoothing bias quantity $\beta(X)$ and on the conditional expectation $s_p(X)$. When p is a standard normal c.d.f., $p''(x) < 0$ for all x and the smoothing bias function is always negative; in this case the direction of the bias is effectively determined by the sign of the treatment effect. The term b_2 can also take either sign depending on the sign of $s_{pp}(x)$. Suppose there is a constant treatment effect τ independent of X, that $p(x) = 1/2$ for all x, and that f is uniform with range 1. Then $b_2 = \|K\|^2 \times \tau$, and the sign of b_2 is determined by the direction of the treatment effect. The correction term in the variance is clearly of smaller order than the squared bias no matter what bandwidth is chosen.

Define the asymptotic mean squared error of the estimator to be (apart from a factor of order n^{-1})

$$\text{AMSE}(\widehat{\tau}) = E(\mathcal{T}^{*2}) = \text{var}(\mathcal{T}^{*}) + E^{2}(\mathcal{T}^{*}), \tag{3.5}$$

and define an optimal bandwidth h_{opt} to be a sequence that minimizes AMSE($\widehat{\tau}$). By Theorem 3.1,

$$\text{AMSE}(\widehat{\tau}) = v_0 + \left(\sqrt{n}h^2 b_1 + \frac{1}{\sqrt{n}h} b_2\right)^2 + o(n^{-1/3})$$

and it suffices to minimize the size of the term inside the brackets. If the biases have opposite signs, then the optimal bandwidth is going to set

$$\sqrt{n}h^2 b_1 + \frac{1}{\sqrt{n}h} b_2 = 0,$$

and this second-order bias will then be of smaller order. Otherwise, the optimal bandwidth will minimize this second-order bias and there will be an interior solution to the optimization problem that can be found by calculus. To summarize, we have

$$h_{\text{opt}} = \begin{cases} \left(\frac{-b_2}{b_1}\right)^{1/3} n^{-1/3} & \text{if } \text{sign}(b_2) \neq \text{sign}(b_1) \\ \left(\frac{b_2}{2b_1}\right)^{1/3} n^{-1/3} & \text{if } \text{sign}(b_2) = \text{sign}(b_1). \end{cases}$$

A feasible bandwidth selection method can be defined on the basis of estimates of the quantities b_j, $j = 1, 2$, either nonparametric estimates or parametric estimates suggested from some sort of Silverman's rule-of-thumb idea.[4]

In some semiparametric estimators it has been shown that by using leave-one-out estimators and other devices, one can eliminate the degrees of freedom bias terms of order $n^{-1/2}h^{-1}$; see, for example, Hall and Marron (1987) and Linton (1995). Indeed, we have used a leave-one-out estimator here. Unfortunately, it has not completely eliminated the degrees of freedom bias. Instead, we define an explicit bias correction method and show that it does indeed "knock" this term out and therefore permits a smaller bandwidth and a better AMSE. Specifically, we define the bias-corrected estimator

$$\widehat{\tau}^{\text{bc}} = \widehat{\tau} - \widehat{b}_{n2}, \tag{3.6}$$

where

$$\widehat{b}_{n2} = \frac{1}{n}\sum_{i=1}^{n}\sum_{\substack{j=1 \\ j\neq i}}^{n}\left[\frac{Y_i \cdot T_i}{\widehat{p}(X_i)^3} - \frac{Y_i \cdot (1 - T_i)}{[1 - \widehat{p}(X_i)]^3}\right] w_{ij}^2 \widehat{\varepsilon}_j^2,$$

where $\widehat{\varepsilon}_j = T_j - \widehat{p}(X_j)$. Note that the way we have defined the bias correction can be applied to any linear smoother with weights w_{ij}. Conceptually, this bias

[4] This would require a model for m_j, p, and f. See Fan and Gijbels (1996, p. 111) for the solution to a similar problem.

correction is similar to using $n-1$ instead of n in estimating a population variance; significantly, in this context we do not need to estimate higher derivatives of the unknown functions, and it follows that the sampling properties of this bias estimator should be relatively good.[5]

The stochastic expansion for $\widehat{\tau}^{\text{bc}}$ is the same as that for $\widehat{\tau}$ except for the additional bias-correcting term $\widehat{b}$. On computing the moments of the leading terms of this expansion, however, we find that the bias term b_2 has been eliminated; we therefore end up with a better trade-off in the mean squared error of this estimator. The largest terms are a squared bias of order $h^4 n$ and a variance of order $n^{-1}h^{-1}$. This trade-off leads to an optimal bandwidth $h \propto n^{-2/5}$ and mean squared error of $n^{-3/5}$. Let

$$\zeta_i = \Psi_p(Z_i;\tau_0, p(X_i)) - E[\Psi_p(Z_i;\tau_0, p(X_i))|X_i]$$

$$(K * K)(t) = \int K(t)K(t-u)\,du$$

$$\langle f, g\rangle = \int f(t)g(t)\,dt.$$

Now let $\mathcal{T} = \sqrt{n}(\widehat{\tau}^{\text{bc}} - \tau_0)$ and obtain the stochastic expansion $\mathcal{T} = \mathcal{T}^* + R$ as in (3.3).

Theorem 3.2. *Under some regularity conditions, as $n \to \infty$, $R = o_p(n^{-3/5})$ in* (3.3) *and*

$$E(\mathcal{T}^*) \simeq \sqrt{n}h^2 b_1 + o(n^{-3/5})$$

$$\text{var}(\mathcal{T}^*) \simeq v_0 + \frac{1}{nh}v_1 + o(n^{-3/5}),$$

where

$$v_1 = \|K\|^2 \times \left\{E\left[\frac{E(\varepsilon_j^2|X_j)E(\zeta_j^2|X_j)}{f(X_j)}\right] + 2E\left[\frac{E^2(\varepsilon_j\zeta_j|X_j)}{f(X_j)}\right]\right\}$$
$$+ \|K * K\|^2 \times E\left[\frac{3s_{pp}^2(X_j)E^2(\varepsilon_j^2|X_j)}{4f(X_j)}\right]$$
$$+ \langle K, K * K\rangle \times E\left[\frac{3s_{pp}(X_j)E(\varepsilon_j^2|X_j)E(\varepsilon_j\zeta_j|X_j)}{f(X_j)}\right].$$

[5] Effectively, we are estimating the quantity b_2/nh. We could alternatively estimate b_2 itself by

$$\widehat{b}_2 = \|K\|^2 \frac{1}{n}\sum_{i=1}^{n} \widehat{s}_{pp}(X_i)\frac{\widehat{p}(X_i)(1-\widehat{p}(X_i))}{2\widehat{f}(X_i)}.$$

This is just a sample average of nonparametric estimators, and is similar in this respect to a weighted average derivative (in our case second derivatives) estimator. Therefore, under some regularity conditions we can expect it to satisfy $\sqrt{n}(\widehat{b}_2 - b_2) = O_p(1)$.

This shows that the bias correction can lead to improved mean squared error properties.[6] In this case,

$$\text{AMSE}(\widehat{\tau}^{\text{bc}}) = v_0 + nh^4 b_1^2 + \frac{1}{nh} v_1 + o(n^{-3/5}),$$

and the optimal bandwidth is

$$h_{\text{opt}} = \left(\frac{v_1}{4b_1^2}\right)^{1/5} n^{-2/5},$$

since b_1^2, v_1 are both nonnegative. This bandwidth is smaller in magnitude than is optimal for the raw estimator $\widehat{\tau}$. A feasible bandwidth selection method can be defined on the basis of estimates of the quantities b_1, v_1, either nonparametric estimates or parametric estimates suggested from some sort of Silverman's rule-of-thumb idea.

The degrees of freedom bias correction has been analyzed before in other contexts. For example, Jones and Sheather (1991) investigated squared density derivatives, the situation of Hall and Marron (1987). They argued against doing the degrees of freedom bias correction by itself in this case. Their reasoning was that the leading smoothing bias term was always negative, while the degrees of freedom bias term was always positive. Therefore, by a judicious choice of bandwidth one could cancel these terms out. If we applied their method successfully to our problem, we would end up with (assuming that $h \asymp n^{-1/3}$)

$$\text{AMSE}(\widehat{\tau}^{\text{JS}}) \simeq v_0 + \left(\sqrt{n} h^4 b_{11}\right)^2 + \frac{1}{nh} v_1,$$

say, where b_{11} is a higher-order smoothing bias term (assuming that the underlying functions are smooth enough). In this case, the correction term is of order $n^{-2/3}$, which is even smaller than the order $n^{-3/5}$ obtained with our degrees of freedom bias correction. The catch is that in our more complicated model, the signs of the two bias terms are not necessarily opposite and so the Jones and Sheather method is not guaranteed to work, and the resulting correction term is then larger than ours. In any case, the Jones and Sheather method requires estimation of higher-order derivatives of the regression function and is (a) unlikely to work well in practice, and (b) against the spirit of our approach.

We have just presented results concerning the moments of the estimators, but this can also be extended to distributional approximations. In fact, to the relevant order $\widehat{\tau}$ is normally distributed, that is,

$$\Pr\left[\sqrt{n}(\widehat{\tau} - \tau_0) \leq x\right] = \Phi\left(\frac{x - \sqrt{n}h^2 b_1 + \frac{1}{\sqrt{nh}} b_2}{\sqrt{v_0}}\right) + o(n^{-1/3}).$$

[6] We are happy to report that this finding is partly in agreement with Rothenberg (1984a, p. 909), who says, "This suggests that correction for bias may be more important than second order efficiency consideration when choosing among estimators."

In our case, correction for bias improves mean squared error.

Table 8.1. *Rates of convergence for bandwidth and mean squared error correction*

Model	Optimal bandwidth	Optimal MSE correction
1. Average derivative	$n^{-2/7}$	$n^{-1/7}$
2. Variance estimation	$n^{-1/5}$	$n^{-3/5}$
3. Partially linear model	$n^{-2/9}$	$n^{-7/9}$
4. Heteroskedastic linear regression	$n^{-1/5}$	$n^{-4/5}$
5. Variance, a function of mean	$n^{-2/11}$	$n^{-5/11}$
6. Symmetric location	$n^{-1/7}$	$n^{-4/7}$
7. HIR	$n^{-1/3}$	$n^{-1/3}$
8. HIR with bias correction	$n^{-2/5}$	$n^{-3/5}$

Notes. Models 2–6 are given in Linton (1991, Chapter 3). The result for model 1 is taken from Härdle et al. (1992).

The approximation for $\sqrt{n}(\widehat{\tau}^{\text{bc}} - \tau_0)$ is more complicated because if we require an error rate consistent with our mean squared error (i.e., of order $n^{-3/5}$), then we will have to include the skewness terms of order $n^{-1/2}$.[7] In this case the approximate distribution is not normal in general but can be expressed in terms of the Edgeworth signed measures and the first three cumulant approximations. See Linton (2001a) for a computation of this type.

Finally, we remark that the standard errors of $\widehat{\tau}$ also depend on the nonparametric estimator $\widehat{p}(\cdot)$, and there are similar concerns about the small sample properties of these quantities. These standard errors also suffer from a degrees of freedom bias problem, which can be corrected in the same way as we have done for the estimator of τ.

4. SOME NUMERICAL RESULTS

For comparison we present the optimal rates associated with a variety of semiparametric models that have been studied before. These are all for the univariate case with second-order kernels or a similar method.

The optimal bandwidth for nonparametric regression is of order $n^{-1/5}$ and has a consequent MSE of order $n^{-4/5}$. Table 8.1 shows that there is quite a variety of magnitudes for the optimal bandwidth in semiparametric estimation problems; sometimes the optimal bandwidth is bigger, but usually it is smaller than the optimal rates for nonparametric estimation. These different rates reflect different magnitudes for bias and variance in these semiparametric functionals.

[7] In both cases,

$$E[\{T^* - E(T^*)\}^3] \simeq O(n^{-1/2}),$$

which is the same magnitude as in parametric models.

We investigate the magnitudes of the second-order effects in Theorems 3.1 and 3.2 and the optimal bandwidth size. We theoretically compute the optimal bandwidths and mean squared errors for the following model.

Design 4.1.

$$
\begin{aligned}
X &\sim U[-0.5, 0.5]; T = 1(\beta X + \delta > 0) \\
m_0(x) &= x; m_1(x) = \tau + m_0(x) \\
Y_0 &= m_0(X) + \eta; Y_1 = y_0 + \tau,
\end{aligned}
$$

where $\eta, \delta \sim N(0, 1)$ and are mutually independent. We vary the parameters τ and β with $\tau \in \{-2, -1, 0, 1, 2\}$ and $\beta \in \{1, 2, 3\}$.[8]

We compute the quantities in Theorem 3.1 and 3.2 by simulation methods. Note that v_0 changes substantially with β and less so with τ. For example, when $(\beta, \tau) = (1, -2)$, $v_0 = 4.28$, while when $(\beta, \tau) = (1, +2)$, $v_0 = 4.31$. However, when $(\beta, \tau) = (3, -2)$, $v_0 = 29.57$, and when $(\beta, \tau) = (3, +2)$, $v_0 = 42.86$. By contrast, b_1 and b_2 are quite small in absolute terms. For $(\beta, \tau) = (1, 2)$, $(b_1, b_2) = (0.031, 0.484)$, while for $(\beta, \tau) = (3, -2)$, $(b_1, b_2) = (12.88, -3.59)$. In most cases b_1 and b_2 have opposite signs. The constant v_1 is very large when $\beta = 3$. When $(\beta, \tau) = (1, 0)$, $v_1 = 0.5$, while when $(\beta, \tau) = (3, -2)$, $v_1 = 110.36$.

We report the relative root mean squared error against bandwidth ($\text{RRMSE} = \sqrt{\text{AMSE}/v_0}$) in Figures 8.1 and 8.2 for a sample size of $n = 100$ and $n = 1000$, respectively. The solid line is for the raw estimator and the dashed line is for the bias corrected estimator. The effects of bandwidth on performance are quite clear from these pictures. As discussed earlier, there is a bandwidth in this case for which the RRMSE of $\widehat{\tau}$ is exactly equal to 1, but this never happens for $\widehat{\tau}^{\text{bc}}$. This gives the misleading impression that the uncorrected estimator is better. But of course the error in the expansion for $\widehat{\tau}^{\text{bc}}$ is of much smaller order than in $\widehat{\tau}$ – for a meaningful comparison, we should include more terms in expansion of $\widehat{\tau}$. It is clear from the pictures that $\widehat{\tau}^{\text{bc}}$ has better RRMSE when h is small, but that the estimators have similar RRMSE when h is large.

Note that the Silverman's rule-of-thumb bandwidth (for Gaussian kernels) $h_{\text{rot}} = 1.06\sigma n^{-1/5}$ is for $n = 100$, $h_{\text{rot}} = 0.35$, $n = 200$, $h_{\text{rot}} = 0.30$, $n = 500$, $h_{\text{rot}} = 0.25$, $n = 1000$, $h_{\text{rot}} = 0.22$, and $n = 10,000$, $h_{\text{rot}} = 0.14$. Another common bandwidth choice is just $0.2\times$*range*, which in this case would result in $h = 0.2$. For the small sample size, these bandwidths rarely do dreadfully, but such large bandwidths can have disastrous effects in the larger samples.

[8] The regression R^2 of $\beta X + \delta$ on X is $R^2 = 2\beta^2/(2\beta^2 + 3)$ and of Y_j on X is given by the same formula with $\beta = 1$, that is, $R^2 = 0.4$.

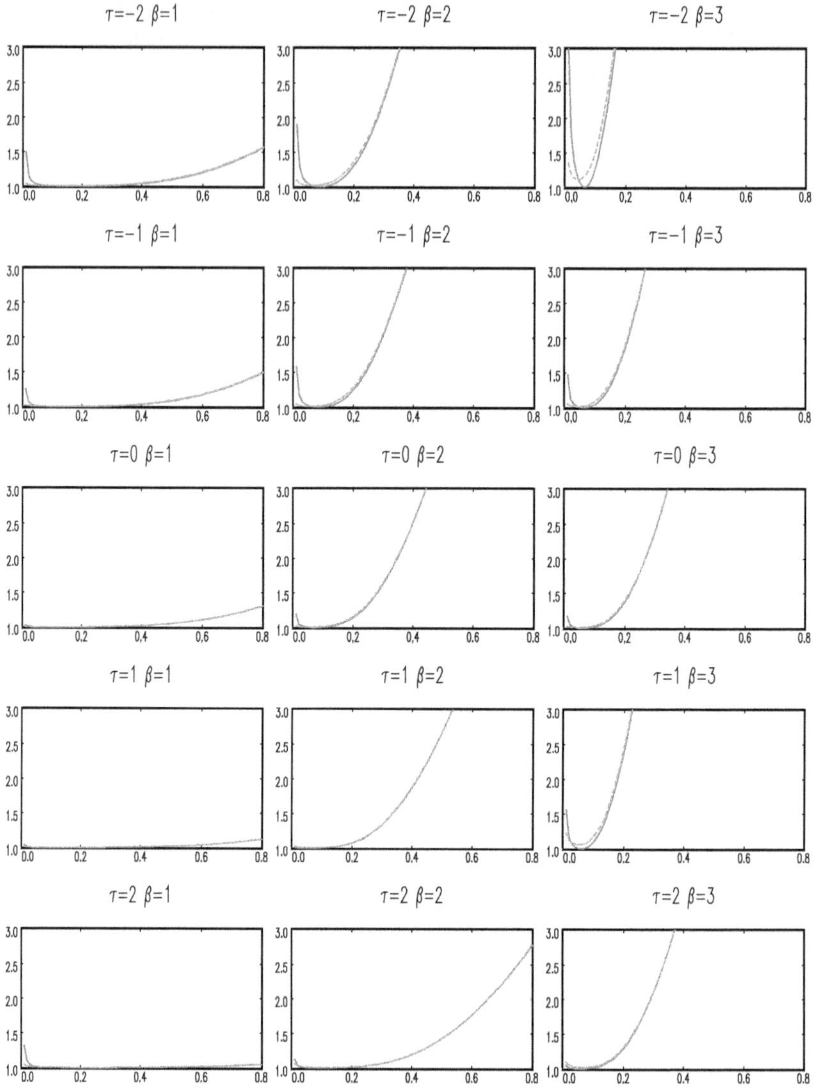

Figure 8.1. Relative root mean squared error against bandwidth [RRMSE = $\sqrt{\text{AMSE}/v_0}$] for $n = 100$. The solid line is for the raw estimator and the dashed line is for the bias corrected estimator. The figure shows RRMSE against bandwidth h.

5. CONCLUSIONS

Our asymptotic expansions revealed some facts about the HIR estimator. The main thing is that its properties are dominated by bias: one bias term is related to the curvature of the function p and the covariate density f, and would naturally be called a smoothing bias; the second bias term is what we have called a

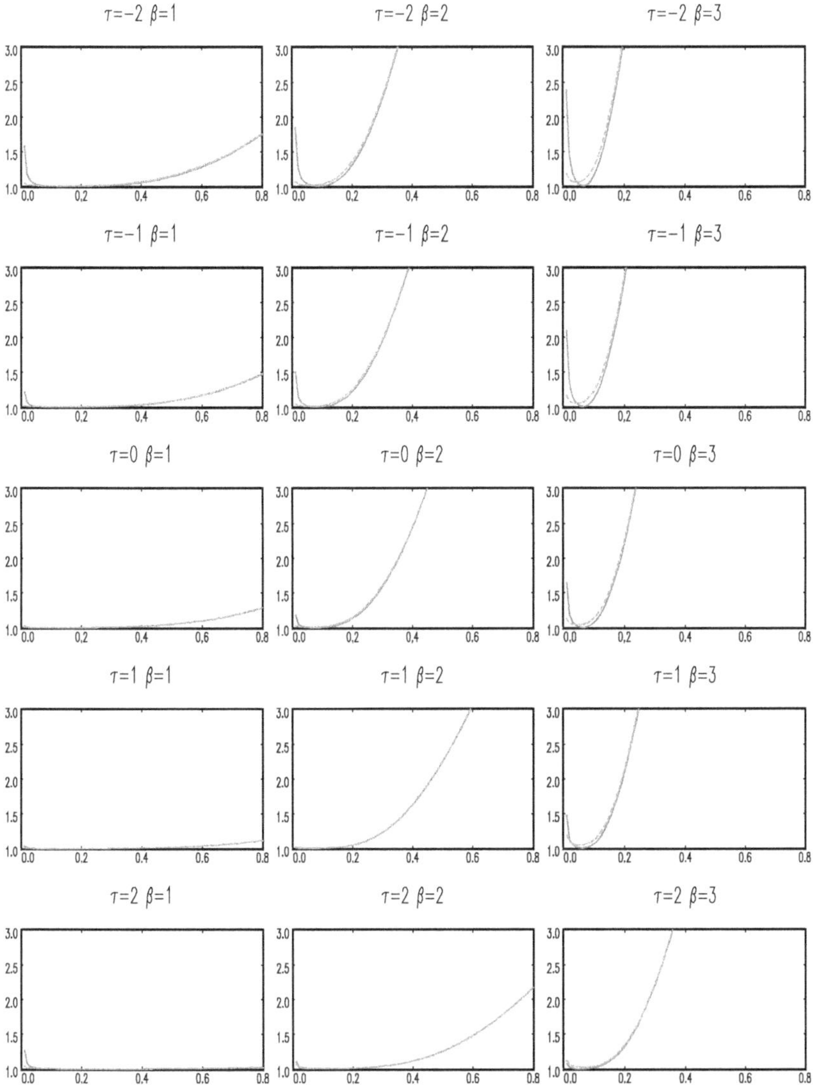

Figure 8.2. Relative root mean squared error against bandwidth [RRMSE $= \sqrt{\text{AMSE}/v_0}$] for $n = 1,000$. The solid line is for the raw estimator and the dashed line is for the bias corrected estimator. The figure shows RRMSE against bandwidth h.

degrees of freedom bias. The magnitude of the bias terms can be quite large, and their signs are unknown in general. We proposed a simple bias correction that eliminates the degrees of freedom bias term, thereby permitting a smaller bandwidth and consequently better mean squared error.

ACKNOWLEDGMENTS

We would like to thank Tom Rothenberg, two referees, and seminar participants for helpful comments, and David Jacho-Chavez for research assistance. We are grateful to the National Science Foundation, to CEMMAP, and to the Economic and Social Science Research Council for financial support.

APPENDIX

Sufficient conditions for consistency and asymptotic normality of semiparametric estimators can be found in numerous places for a variety of nonparametric estimators and estimation criteria. See, for example, Andrews (1994), Newey and McFadden (1994), Bickel et al. (1993), and so forth. Linton (1996b) develops higher-order asymptotic expansions for a general class of semiparametric estimators. We will clearly require smoothness conditions on p, f. We require that both p and f be bounded away from zero on the compact support of X. We also need some moment conditions on Y_{ji}. The conditions should at least imply that

$$\sup_{x \in C} |\widehat{p}(x) - p(x)| = o_p(n^{-1/4}), \tag{A.1}$$

where C is the support of X. Sufficient conditions for this can be found in Masry (1996a,b), who actually shows that

$$\sup_{x \in C} |\widehat{p}(x) - p(x)| = O_p(h^2) + O_p\left(\sqrt{\frac{\log n}{nh}}\right), \tag{A.2}$$

which is $O_p(n^{-1/3}\sqrt{\log n})$ when $h \asymp n^{-1/3}$ and $O_p(n^{-3/10}\sqrt{\log n})$ when $h \asymp n^{-2/5}$; in either case this magnitude is $o_p(n^{-1/4})$, as required. We also use the decomposition

$$\widehat{p}(X_i) - p(X_i) = \sum_{j \neq i} w_{ij}\varepsilon_j + \beta_n(X_i), \tag{A.3}$$

where w_{ij} are the smoothing weights that just depend on the covariates $X_1, \ldots, X_n$, while $\beta_n(X_i) = E[\widehat{p}(X_i)|X_1, \ldots, X_n] - p(X_i)$ is the conditional smoothing bias that also just depends on the covariates $X_1, \ldots, X_n$. It can be shown that $h^{-2}\beta_n(x) \to^p \beta(x)$ and that this convergence is uniform; see, for example, Masry (1996a,b). In fact,

$$E[(\widehat{p}(X_i) - p(X_i))^2|X_1, \ldots, X_n]$$
$$\simeq \frac{1}{nh}||K||^2 \frac{p(X_i)(1 - p(X_i))}{f(X_i)} + \frac{h^4}{4}\mu_2^2(K)\beta^2(X_i) \equiv M_n(X_i).$$

See Fan and Gijbels (1996) for more discussion.

Proof of Theorem 3.1. By a geometric series expansion,

$$\sqrt{n}(\widehat{\tau} - \tau_0) = \frac{1}{\sqrt{n}}\sum_{i=1}^{n} \Psi(Z_i; \tau_0, p(X_i))$$
$$+ \frac{1}{\sqrt{n}}\sum_{i=1}^{n} \Psi_p(Z_i; \tau_0, p(X_i))(\widehat{p}(X_i) - p(X_i))$$

$$+\frac{1}{2\sqrt{n}}\sum_{i=1}^{n}\Psi_{pp}(Z_i;\tau_0,p(X_i))(\widehat{p}(X_i)-p(X_i))^2$$
$$+\frac{1}{6\sqrt{n}}\sum_{i=1}^{n}\Psi_{ppp}(Z_i;\tau_0,p(X_i))(\widehat{p}(X_i)-p(X_i))^3$$
$$+\frac{1}{24\sqrt{n}}\sum_{i=1}^{n}\Psi_{pppp}(Z_i;\tau_0,p(X_i))(\widehat{p}(X_i)$$
$$-p(X_i))^4+o_p(n^{-3/4}). \qquad \text{(A.4)}$$

The magnitude of the remainder in (A.4) follows from (A.1) and because the derivatives of Ψ with respect to p are dominated by a function with finite moment (since p is bounded away from zero).

When $h \asymp n^{-1/3}$ and we only require expansion to order $n^{-1/3}$, we can further drop the cubic and quartic terms to obtain

$$\begin{aligned}\sqrt{n}(\widehat{\tau}-\tau_0) &= \frac{1}{\sqrt{n}}\sum_{i=1}^{n}\Psi(Z_i;\tau_0,p(X_i))\\ &\quad+\frac{1}{\sqrt{n}}\sum_{i=1}^{n}s_p(X_i)(\widehat{p}(X_i)-p(X_i))\\ &\quad+\frac{1}{\sqrt{n}}\sum_{i=1}^{n}\zeta_i\cdot(\widehat{p}(X_i)-p(X_i))\\ &\quad+\frac{1}{2\sqrt{n}}\sum_{i=1}^{n}s_{pp}(X_i)(\widehat{p}(X_i)-p(X_i))^2\\ &\quad+\frac{1}{2\sqrt{n}}\sum_{i=1}^{n}\xi_i\cdot(\widehat{p}(X_i)-p(X_i))^2+o_p(n^{-1/3})\\ &\equiv J_1+J_2+J_3+J_4+o_p(n^{-1/3}),\end{aligned}$$

where the random variables $\zeta_i=\Psi_p(Z_i;\tau_0,p(X_i))-E[\Psi_p(Z_i;\tau_0,p(X_i))|X_i]$ and $\xi_i=\Psi_{pp}(Z_i;\tau_0,p(X_i))-E[\Psi_{pp}(Z_i;\tau_0,p(X_i))|X_i]$ are both i.i.d. and conditional mean zero given X_j.

We then write

$$\begin{aligned}J_1 &= \frac{1}{\sqrt{n}}\sum_{i=1}^{n}s_p(X_i)(\widehat{p}(X_i)-p(X_i))\\ &= \frac{1}{\sqrt{n}}\sum_{j=1}^{n}s_p(X_j)\varepsilon_j+\frac{1}{\sqrt{n}}\sum_{j=1}^{n}\varepsilon_j\left[\sum_{i\neq j}w_{ij}s_p(X_i)-s_p(X_j)\right]\\ &\quad+\frac{1}{\sqrt{n}}\sum_{i=1}^{n}s_p(X_i)\beta_n(X_i)\\ &\equiv J_{11}+J_{12}+J_{13}, \qquad \text{(A.5)}\end{aligned}$$

where $J_{11} = O_p(1)$ and is asymptotically normal (also jointly asymptotically normal with the leading term in our expansion, $n^{-1/2}\sum_{i=1}^n \Psi(Z_i; \tau_0, p(X_i))$), and the term J_{12} is mean zero and has variance of the same magnitude as $E[\sum_{i\neq j} w_{ij}s_p(X_i) - s_p(X_j)]^2$, which we expect to be $O(h^4)$. The reason is that w_{ij} are approximately symmetric (see Linton 2001b), and so $\sum_{i\neq j} w_{ij}s_p(X_i) - s_p(X_j)$ is rather like $\sum_{i\neq j} w_{ji}s_p(X_i) - s_p(X_j)$ in terms of its magnitude, and this latter quantity is just the bias function from smoothing $s_p(X_i)$ against X_i. Therefore, $J_{12} = O_p(h^2)$. The term J_{13} is a bias term with magnitude $h^2\sqrt{n}$ and variance also h^4. This term contributes to the second approximation of Theorem 3.1, specifically,

$$h^{-2}\frac{1}{n}\sum_{i=1}^n s_p(X_i)\beta_n(X_i) \to^p b_1,$$

as stated.

We next turn to the term

$$\begin{aligned} J_2 &= \frac{1}{\sqrt{n}}\sum_{i=1}^n \zeta_i \cdot (\widehat{p}(X_i) - p(X_i)) \\ &= \frac{1}{\sqrt{n}}\sum_{i=1}^n \zeta_i \sum_{j\neq i} w_{ij}\varepsilon_j + \frac{1}{\sqrt{n}}\sum_{i=1}^n \zeta_i\beta_n(X_i) \equiv J_{21} + J_{22}, \qquad \text{(A.6)} \end{aligned}$$

where J_{21} is a second-order degenerate U-statistic that has mean zero and variance of order $n^{-1}h^{-1}$; it is also uncorrelated with the leading terms. The second term, J_{22}, is mean zero and $O_p(h^2)$, and hence of smaller order.

We next turn our attention to the term J_3. First,

$$\begin{aligned} J_3 &= \frac{1}{\sqrt{n}}\sum_{i=1}^n s_{pp}(X_i)(\widehat{p}(X_i) - p(X_i))^2 \\ &= \frac{1}{\sqrt{n}}\sum_{i=1}^n s_{pp}(X_i)E[(\widehat{p}(X_i) - p(X_i))^2|X_1, \ldots, X_n] \\ &\quad + O_p(n^{-1/2}h^{-1/2}) \\ &= \frac{1}{h\sqrt{n}}||K||^2\frac{1}{n}\sum_{i=1}^n s_{pp}(X_i)\frac{p(X_i)(1-p(X_i))}{f(X_i)} \\ &\quad + O_p(h^4\sqrt{n}) + O_p(n^{-1/2}h^{-1/2}), \qquad \text{(A.7)} \end{aligned}$$

where we have substituted in the expression for $E[(\widehat{p}(X_i) - p(X_i))^2|X_1, \ldots, X_n]$. Finally, taking probability limits,

$$h\sqrt{n}J_3 = b_2 + o_p(1),$$

using the fact that $h^5n \to 0$. The omitted term in (A.7) is mean zero and uncorrelated with the lead, so that only its variance, which is of order $n^{-1}h^{-1}$, contributes to the mean squared error; with the bandwidth magnitude of Theorem 3.1, it is of smaller order. To make clearer the claim in (A.7), and in anticipation of the proof of Theorem 3.2 where this term is important, we give another argument here. Using (A.3), we can write

$$
\begin{aligned}
J_3 &= \frac{1}{\sqrt{n}} \sum_{i=1}^{n} s_{pp}(X_i) \left[\sum_{j \neq i} w_{ij} \varepsilon_j + O_p(h^2) \right]^2 \\
&= \frac{1}{\sqrt{n}} \sum_{i=1}^{n} s_{pp}(X_i) \left[\sum_{j \neq i} w_{ij} \varepsilon_j \right]^2 + O_p(h^4 \sqrt{n}) \\
&\simeq \frac{1}{\sqrt{n}} \sum_{i=1}^{n} s_{pp}(X_i) \sum_{j \neq i} w_{ij}^2 E\left(\varepsilon_j^2 | X_j\right) \\
&\quad + \frac{1}{\sqrt{n}} \sum_{i=1}^{n} s_{pp}(X_i) \sum_{j \neq i} w_{ij}^2 \left[\varepsilon_j^2 - E\left(\varepsilon_j^2 | X_j\right)\right] \\
&\quad + \frac{1}{\sqrt{n}} \sum_{i=1}^{n} s_{pp}(X_i) \sum_{\substack{j \neq 1 \\ j \neq i}} \sum_{l \neq 1} w_{ij} w_{il} \varepsilon_j \varepsilon_l \equiv J_{31} + J_{32} + J_{33}.
\end{aligned}
$$

The first term, J_{31}, is the leading bias term of order $h^{-1}n^{-1/2}$, analyzed above. The second term, J_{32}, is mean zero and is of order $n^{-1}h^{-1}$ in probability, and so is insignificant in both Theorems 3.1 and 3.2. The third term, J_{33}, is mean zero and $O_p(n^{-1/2}h^{-1/2})$. We can rewrite this term as

$$
\begin{aligned}
&\frac{1}{\sqrt{n}} \sum_{i=1}^{n} s_{pp}(X_i) \sum_{\substack{j \neq 1 \\ j \neq i}} \sum_{l \neq 1} w_{ij} w_{il} \varepsilon_j \varepsilon_l \\
&= \sum_{j \neq i} \sum \left(\frac{1}{\sqrt{n}} \sum_{i=1}^{n} s_{pp}(X_i) w_{ij} w_{il} \right) \varepsilon_j \varepsilon_l \\
&\simeq \frac{1}{n\sqrt{nh}} \sum_{j \neq i} \sum (K * K) \left(\frac{X_j - X_l}{h} \right) \frac{s_{pp}(X_j)}{f(X_j)} \varepsilon_j \varepsilon_l,
\end{aligned}
$$

where $K * K(u) = \int K(t-u)K(t)\,dt$. See Linton (1995) for a similar calculation. This term does not feature in the expansion of Theorem 3.1 (but does contribute in Theorem 3.2, as will be seen).

Finally, it is easy to see that

$$
J_4 = \frac{1}{2\sqrt{n}} \sum_{i=1}^{n} \xi_i \cdot (\widehat{p}(X_i) - p(X_i))^2 = O_p(h^4 + n^{-1}h^{-1}).
$$

Specifically, because we are using a leave-one-out estimator, ξ_i is independent of $\widehat{p}(X_i) - p(X_i)$ conditional on X_i. Therefore, this term is mean zero and its order in probability is the same as $EM_n(X_i)$.

In conclusion, we have

$$\begin{aligned}\sqrt{n}(\widehat{\tau}-\tau_0) &\simeq \frac{1}{\sqrt{n}}\sum_{i=1}^{n}\Psi(Z_i;\tau_0,p(X_i))+s_p(X_i)\varepsilon_i \quad [=O_p(1)]\\ &+\frac{1}{\sqrt{n}}\sum_{j=1}^{n}\varepsilon_j\left[\sum_{i\neq j}w_{ij}s_p(X_i)-s_p(X_j)\right] \quad [=O_p(h^2)]\\ &+\sum\sum_{j\neq i}\varphi_n(Z_i,Z_j) \quad [=O_p(n^{-1/2}h^{-1/2})]\\ &+\frac{1}{\sqrt{n}}\sum_{i=1}^{n}s_p(X_i)\beta_n(X_i) \quad [=O_p(h^2\sqrt{n})]\\ &+\frac{1}{2\sqrt{n}}\sum_{i=1}^{n}s_{pp}(X_i)M_n(X_i) \quad [=O_p(h^4\sqrt{n})+O_p(n^{-1/2}h^{-1})],\end{aligned} \tag{A.8}$$

where

$$\begin{aligned}\varphi_n(Z_i,Z_j) = \frac{1}{nh\sqrt{n}}\frac{1}{f(X_i)}\bigg[&K\left(\frac{X_i-X_j}{h}\right)\zeta_i\varepsilon_j\\ &+\frac{1}{2}(K*K)\left(\frac{X_i-X_j}{h}\right)s_{pp}(X_i)\varepsilon_i\varepsilon_j\bigg].\end{aligned}$$

Clearly, $E[\varphi_n(Z_i,Z_j)|Z_i]=E[\varphi_n(Z_i,Z_j)|Z_j]=0$ and $\sum\sum_{j\neq i}\varphi_n(Z_i,Z_j)$ is a degenerate weighted U-statistic of the stated order in probability. Because this term is uncorrelated with the leading term, it does not contribute to the mean squared error expansion of Theorem 3.1. Likewise, the $O_p(h^2)$ term does not contribute because it is mean zero. Therefore, the leading terms in the mean squared error expansion come from

$$\begin{aligned}\sqrt{n}(\widehat{\tau}-\tau_0) &\simeq \frac{1}{\sqrt{n}}\sum_{i=1}^{n}[\Psi(Z_i;\tau_0,p(X_i))+s_p(X_i)\varepsilon_i]\\ &+\frac{1}{\sqrt{n}}\sum_{i=1}^{n}s_p(X_i)\beta_n(X_i)+\frac{1}{2\sqrt{n}}\sum_{i=1}^{n}s_{pp}(X_i)M_n(X_i).\end{aligned}$$

■

Proof of Theorem 3.2. In this case we have $h\propto n^{-2/5}$ and require a mean squared error expansion up to order $n^{-3/5}$.

Write $\widehat{b_2}=h\sqrt{n}\,\widehat{b}_{n2}$, where (recall the target quantity)

$$b_2=||K||^2E\left[s_{pp}(X_i)\frac{p(X_i)(1-p(X_i))}{2f(X_i)}\right].$$

First of all, we suppose that

$$\sqrt{n}(\widehat{b}_2 - b_2) = \frac{1}{\sqrt{n}} \sum_{i=1}^{n} \psi(X_i) + o_p(1), \tag{A.9}$$

where $E\psi(X_i) = 0$ and $\mathrm{var}(\psi(X_i)) < \infty$. This can be justified by a lengthy argument using standard techniques of semiparametric estimation; see, for example, Andrews (1994), Newey and McFadden (1994), and so forth. The consequence of (A.9) is

$$\begin{aligned}\sqrt{n}(\widehat{\tau}^{\mathrm{bc}} - \tau_0) &= \sqrt{n}(\widehat{\tau} - \tau_0) - \frac{b_2}{h\sqrt{n}}(1 + O_p(n^{-1/2})) \\ &= \sqrt{n}(\widehat{\tau} - \tau_0) - \frac{b_2}{h\sqrt{n}} + O_p(n^{-3/5}),\end{aligned}$$

where the $O_p(n^{-3/5})$ term is mean zero. Furthermore, this remainder term is uncorrelated with the leading term because $E[\Psi(Z_i; \tau_0, p(X_i)) + s_p(X_i)\varepsilon_i | X_i] = 0$, and therefore this term does not contribute to the mean squared error expansion.

We must examine (A.4) again because the bandwidth magnitude is different from that in Theorem 3.1. The term

$$\frac{1}{6\sqrt{n}} \sum_{i=1}^{n} \Psi_{ppp}(Z_i; \tau_0, p(X_i))(\widehat{p}(X_i) - p(X_i))^3 = O_p(n^{-2/5}(\log n)^{3/2})$$

in principle must be analyzed in this case. It can be shown that it does not contribute to the mean squared error because essentially the correlations with leading terms are of smaller order (the square of this term is obviously $n^{-3/5}$).

In conclusion,

$$\begin{aligned}\sqrt{n}(\widehat{\tau}^{\mathrm{bc}} - \tau_0) \simeq{}& \frac{1}{\sqrt{n}} \sum_{i=1}^{n} \Psi(Z_i; \tau_0, p(X_i)) + s_p(X_i)\varepsilon_i \\ &+ \sum\sum_{j \neq i} \varphi_n(Z_i, Z_j) + \frac{1}{\sqrt{n}} \sum_{i=1}^{n} s_p(X_i)\beta_n(X_i),\end{aligned}$$

where omitted terms do not contribute to the mean squared error to order $n^{-3/5}$. Finally,

$$\begin{aligned}&\mathrm{var}\left[\sum\sum_{j \neq i} \varphi_n(Z_i, Z_j)\right] \\ &\quad = n(n-1)E\left[\varphi_n^2(Z_i, Z_j)\right] + 2n(n-1)E[\varphi_n(Z_i, Z_j)\varphi_n(Z_j, Z_i)],\end{aligned}$$

where, by the law of iterated expectations,

$$
\begin{aligned}
&E\left[\varphi_n^2(Z_i, Z_j)\right] \\
&\quad = \frac{1}{n^3h^2} E\left[\frac{1}{f^2(X_i)} K^2\left(\frac{X_i - X_j}{h}\right) E\left[\zeta_i^2|X_i\right] E\left[\varepsilon_j^2|X_j\right]\right] \\
&\quad + \frac{1}{4n^3h^2} E\left[\frac{1}{f^2(X_i)} (K * K)^2\left(\frac{X_i - X_j}{h}\right) s_{pp}^2(X_i) E\left[\varepsilon_i^2|X_i\right] E\left[\varepsilon_j^2|X_j\right]\right] \\
&\quad + \frac{1}{n^3h^2} E\left[\frac{1}{f^2(X_i)} (K{*}K) \times K\left(\frac{X_i - X_j}{h}\right) s_{pp}(X_i) E\left[\zeta_i\varepsilon_i|X_i\right] E\left[\varepsilon_j^2|X_j\right]\right]
\end{aligned}
$$

$$
\begin{aligned}
&E[\varphi_n(Z_i, Z_j)\varphi_n(Z_j, Z_i)] \\
&\quad = \frac{1}{n^3h^2} E\left[\frac{1}{f(X_i)f(X_j)} K^2\left(\frac{X_i - X_j}{h}\right) E[\zeta_i\varepsilon_i|X_i] E[\zeta_j\varepsilon_j|X_j]\right] \\
&\quad + \frac{1}{4n^3h^2} E\left[\frac{s_{pp}(X_i)s_{pp}(X_j)}{f(X_i)f(X_j)} (K * K)^2\left(\frac{X_i - X_j}{h}\right) E\left[\varepsilon_i^2|X_i\right] E\left[\varepsilon_j^2|X_j\right]\right] \\
&\quad \times \frac{1}{n^3h^2} E\left[\frac{s_{pp}(X_i)}{f(X_i)f(X_j)} (K \times (K{*}K))\left(\frac{X_i - X_j}{h}\right) E[\zeta_i\varepsilon_i|X_i] E\left[\varepsilon_j^2|X_j\right]\right].
\end{aligned}
$$

We use the fact that $K * K$ is symmetric, then take expectations with respect to X_j and use the localizing operation of K and $K * K$ to see that

$$
\begin{aligned}
n(n-1)E\left[\varphi_n^2(Z_i, Z_j)\right] \simeq{}& \frac{1}{nh}\|K\|^2 E\left[\frac{E\left[\zeta_i^2|X_i\right] E\left[\varepsilon_i^2|X_i\right]}{f(X_i)}\right] \\
&+ \frac{1}{4nh}\|K * K\|^2 E\left[\frac{s_{pp}^2(X_i) E^2\left[\varepsilon_i^2|X_i\right]}{f(X_i)}\right] \\
&+ \frac{1}{nh}\langle K, K * K\rangle E\left[\frac{s_{pp}(X_i) E[\zeta_i\varepsilon_i|X_i] E\left[\varepsilon_i^2|X_i\right]}{f(X_i)}\right]
\end{aligned}
$$

$$
\begin{aligned}
&2n(n-1)E[\varphi_n(Z_i, Z_j)\varphi_n(Z_j, Z_i)] \\
&\quad = \frac{2}{nh}\|K\|^2 E\left[\frac{E^2[\zeta_i\varepsilon_i|X_i]}{f(X_i)}\right] \\
&\quad + \frac{1}{2nh}\|K * K\|^2 E\left[\frac{s_{pp}^2(X_i) E^2\left[\varepsilon_i^2|X_i\right]}{f(X_i)}\right] \\
&\quad \times \frac{2}{nh}\langle K, K * K\rangle E\left[\frac{s_{pp}(X_i) E[\zeta_i\varepsilon_i|X_i] E\left[\varepsilon_i^2|X_i\right]}{f(X_i)}\right].
\end{aligned}
$$

Therefore, the result is as stated. ■

References

Andrews, D. W. K. (1994), "Asymptotics for Semiparametric Econometric Models via Stochastic Equicontinuity," *Econometrica*, 62, 43–72.

Bickel, P. J. (1982), "On Adaptive Estimation," *Annals of Statistics*, 10, 647–71.

Bickel, P. J., C. A. J. Klaassen, Y. Ritov, and J. A. Wellner (1993), *Efficient and Adaptive Estimation for Semiparametric Models*. Baltimore, MD: John Hopkins University Press.

Carroll, R. J., and W. Härdle (1989), "Second Order Effects in Semiparametric Weighted Least Squares Regression," *Statistics*, 2, 179–86.

Cochran, W. G. (1968), "The Effectiveness of Adjustment by Subclassification in Removing Bias in Observational Studies," *Biometrics*, 24, 295–313.

Fan, J., and I. Gijbels (1996), *Local Polynomial Modelling and Its Applications*. London: Chapman & Hall.

Hall, P., and J. S. Marron (1987), "Estimation of Integrated Squared Density Derivatives," *Statistics and Probability Letters*, 6, 109–15.

Härdle, W., J. Hart, J. S. Marron, and A. B. Tsybakov (1992), "Bandwidth Choice for Average Derivative Estimation," *Journal of the American Statistical Association*, 87, 218–26.

Härdle, W., and A. B. Tsybakov (1993), "How Sensitive are Average Derivatives," *Journal of Econometrics*, 58, 31–48.

Heckman, J., H. Ichimura, J. Smith, and P. Todd (1998), "Characterization of Selection Bias Using Experimental Data," *Econometrica*, 66, 1017–1098.

Heckman, J., H. Ichimura, and P. Todd (1998), "Matching as an Econometric Estimator," *Review of Economic Studies*, 65, 261–294.

Hirano, K., G. Imbens, and G. Ridder (2000), "Efficient Estimation of Average Treatment Effects using the Estimated Propensity Score," NBER Technical Working Paper 251.

Jones, M. C., and S. J. Sheather (1991), "Using Non-Stochastic Terms to Advantage in Kernel-Based Estimation of Integrated Squared Density Derivatives," *Statistics and Probability Letters*, 11, 511–514.

Linton, O. B. (1991), "Edgeworth Approximation in Semiparametric Regression Models," Ph.D. Thesis, Department of Economics, University of California at Berkeley.

Linton, O. B. (1995), "Second Order Approximation in the Partially Linear Regression Model," *Econometrica*, 63, 1079–1112.

Linton, O. B. (1996a), "Second Order Approximation in a Linear Regression with Heteroskedasticity of Unknown Form," *Econometric Reviews*, 15, 1–32.

Linton, O. B. (1996b), "Edgeworth Approximation for MINPIN Estimators in Semiparametric Regression Models," *Econometric Theory*, 12, 30–60.

Linton, O. B. (2001a), "Edgeworth Approximations for Semiparametric Instrumental Variable Estimator and Test Statistics," *Journal of Econometrics*, 106, 325–368.

Linton, O. B. (2001b), "Symmetrizing and Unitizing Transformations for Linear Smoothing Weights," *Computational Statistics*, 16, 153–164.

Masry, E. (1996a), "Multivariate Local Polynomial Regression for Time Series: Uniform Strong Consistency and Rates," *Journal of Time Series Analysis*, 17, 571–599.

Masry, E. (1996b), "Multivariate Regression Estimation Local Polynomial Fitting for Time Series," *Stochastic Processes and Their Applications*, 65, 81–101.

Nagar, A. L. (1959), "The Bias and Moment Matrix of the General k-Class Estimator of the Parameters in Simultaneous Equations," *Econometrica*, 27, 575–595.

Newey, W. K., and D. F. McFadden (1994), "Large Sample Estimation and Hypothesis Testing," in *Handbook of Econometrics,* Vol. IV (ed. by D. F. McFadden and R. F. Engle III), Amsterdam: North Holland.

Nishiyama, Y., and Robinson, P. M. (2000), "Edgeworth Expansions for Semiparametric Averaged Derivatives," *Econometrica*, 68, 931–980.

Powell, J. L., and T. M. Stoker (1996), "Optimal Bandwidth Choice for Density-Weighted Averages," *Journal of Econometrics*, 75, 291–316.

Rosenbaum, P., and D. B. Rubin (1983), "The Central Role of the Propensity Score in Observational Studies for Causal Effects," *Biometrika*, 70, 41–55.

Rothenberg, T. (1984a), "Approximating the Distributions of Econometric Estimators and Test Statistics," in *Handbook of Econometrics*, Vol. 2 (ed. by Z. Griliches and M. Intriligator), Amsterdam: North-Holland, 881–935.

Rothenberg, T. (1984b), "Approximate Normality of Generalized Least Squares Estimates," *Econometrica*, 52, 811–825.

Rothenberg, T. (1984c), "Hypothesis Testing in Linear Models When the Error Covariance Matrix is Nonscalar," *Econometrica*, 52, 827–842.

Rothenberg, T. (1988), "Approximate Power Functions for Some Robust Tests of Regression Coefficients," *Econometrica*, 56, 997–1019.

Srinavasan, T. N. (1970), "Approximations to Finite Sample Moments of Estimators Whose Exact Sampling Distributions are Unknown," *Econometrica*, 38, 533–541.

Xiao, Z., and O. B. Linton (2001), "Second Order Approximation for an Adaptive Estimator in a Linear Regression," *Econometric Theory*, 17, 984–1024.

Xiao, Z., and P. C. B. Phillips (1996), "Higher Order Approximation for a Frequency Domain Regression Estimator," *Journal of Econometrics*, 86, 297–336.

CHAPTER 9

Higher-order Improvements of the Parametric Bootstrap for Markov Processes

Donald W. K. Andrews

ABSTRACT

This paper provides bounds on the errors in coverage probabilities of maximum likelihood-based, percentile-t, parametric bootstrap confidence intervals for Markov time series processes. Analogous results are given for delta method confidence intervals (which are based on first-order asymptotics). The bounds show that the parametric bootstrap for Markov time series provides higher-order improvements over delta method confidence intervals that are comparable to those obtained by the parametric and nonparametric bootstrap for i.i.d. data and are better than those obtained by the block bootstrap for time series. Additional results are given for Wald-based confidence regions.

The paper also shows that k-step parametric bootstrap confidence intervals achieve the same higher-order improvements as the standard parametric bootstrap for Markov processes. The k-step bootstrap confidence intervals are computationally attractive. They circumvent the need to compute a nonlinear optimization for each simulated bootstrap sample. The latter is necessary to implement the standard parametric bootstrap when the maximum likelihood estimator solves a nonlinear optimization problem.

1. INTRODUCTION

A line of research to which Tom Rothenberg has made significant contributions is that of Edgeworth expansions for parametric models. His *Econometrica* papers on Edgeworth expansions for estimators and tests statistics in the normal linear model, (Rothenberg 1984a,b) are paradigms of elegance. The current paper is in the same line of research, though it is not so elegant. We develop Edgeworth expansions in parametric time series models and utilize these Edgeworth expansions to explore the properties of the parametric bootstrap.

Specifically, this paper analyzes the higher-order properties of the parametric bootstrap for maximum likelihood (ML)–based confidence intervals (CIs) for κth order Markov processes, possibly with exogenous variables. It is shown that under correct model specification the parametric bootstrap obtains essentially the same higher-order improvements in coverage probabilities relative to standard delta method CIs in the time series context as do the parametric and nonparametric bootstraps for independent and identically distributed (i.i.d.) observations. This contrasts with the (nonparametric) block bootstrap for time series, which does not obtain as large improvements; see, for example, Andrews (2002b), Zvingelis (2003), and Inoue and Shintani (2005).

In particular, the paper shows that symmetric two-sided percentile t CIs constructed using the parametric bootstrap have errors in coverage probability of order $O(N^{-2})$, where N is the sample size. Two-sided percentile t CIs constructed using the delta method, which utilizes the asymptotic normal distribution, are shown to have coverage probability errors of magnitude $O(N^{-1})$. Hence, the use of the parametric bootstrap reduces the errors in coverage probability by $O(N^{-1})$.

For one-sided percentile t CIs, the use of the parametric bootstrap is shown to yield errors in coverage probabilities of order $o(N^{-1} \ln N)$, whereas those of the delta method are shown to be $O(N^{-1/2})$. (Here the $\ln N$ factor is a product of the method of proof. The sharp result for the parametric bootstrap is probably $O(N^{-1})$, as in the i.i.d. case.) Hence, for one-sided CIs, the parametric bootstrap reduces the errors in coverage probability by $o(N^{-1/2} \ln(N))$.

In contrast, the improvements established in Andrews (2002b) for the block bootstrap are only of magnitude $O(N^{-1/4})$ for both two- and one-sided CIs. This is due to the effect of the independence across blocks, which does not mimic the dependence in the time series of interest, and to the fact that the number of blocks employed must be of smaller order than $O(N)$.

This paper also analyzes the higher-order properties of a k-step parametric bootstrap procedure for ML estimators. We show that for suitable choice of k, the k-step parametric bootstrap CIs yield the same higher-order improvements over delta method CIs as does the standard parametric bootstrap. The k-step bootstrap has computational advantages over the standard bootstrap. It was first proposed by Davidson and MacKinnon (1999a). For the case of the (nonparametric) block bootstrap, its properties are analyzed in Andrews (2002b). The k-step bootstrap is related to the one-step and k-step estimators considered by Fisher (1925), LeCam (1956), Rothenberg and Leenders (1964), Pfanzagl (1974), Janssen, Jureckova, and Veraverbeke (1985), and Robinson (1988), among others.

The standard bootstrap for an ML estimator requires that one solve B nonlinear optimization problems to obtain B bootstrap estimators, where B denotes the number of bootstrap repetitions. These estimators are then used to construct bootstrap CIs, test statistics, and so on. On the other hand, the k-step bootstrap involves calculation of a closed-form expression for each of the B bootstrap repetitions. The k-step bootstrap estimator is obtained by taking k-steps of a Newton–Raphson (NR), default NR, line-search NR, or Gauss–Newton (GN) iterative procedure initiated at the estimate based on the original sample. For the NR, default NR, and line-search NR k-step bootstraps, it is often sufficient to take $k \geq 2$ for $a = 1$ and $k \geq 3$ for $a = 2$. For the GN k-step bootstrap, it is often sufficient to take $k \geq 3$ for $a = 1$ and $k \geq 5$ for $a = 2$.

The method of proof of the results outlined above is as follows. First, we establish Edgeworth expansions for the ML estimator and the t statistic based on the ML estimator that hold uniformly over a compact set in the parameter space. The method of doing so is similar to that of Bhattacharya and Ghosh (1978). This method is also used by Hall and Horowitz (1996) and Andrews (2002b), among others. We utilize an Edgeworth expansion for the normalized sum of strong mixing random variables due to Lahiri (1993), which is an extension of a result of Götze and Hipp (1983), whereas Bhattacharya and Ghosh (1978) consider i.i.d. random variables and use a standard Edgeworth expansion for i.i.d. random variables. These Edgeworth expansions yield the bounds on the coverage probability errors of delta-method CIs.

Second, we convert the (uniform) Edgeworth expansions for the ML estimator and t statisitc into Edgeworth expansions for the bootstrap ML estimator and bootstrap t statistic using the fact that the ML estimator lies in a neighborhood of the true value with probability that goes to 1 at a sufficiently fast rate. This gives the bounds on coverage probabilities of one-sided parametric bootstrap CIs. For symmetric percentile t bootstrap CIs, we use the argument of Hall (1988) to obtain the errors in coverage probability using the Edgeworth expansions for the t statistics and bootstrap t statistics.

Third, to prove the results for the k-step parametric bootstrap, we use the method in Andrews (2002a,b). In particular, we show that the distribution function of a k-step bootstrap statistic differs from that of a standard bootstrap statistic by at most N^{-a} with probability $1 - o(N^{-a})$ for any $a > 0$, provided k is sufficiently large and sufficient smoothness and moment conditions hold. The method is related to that used in the numerical analysis literature to establish the quadratic convergence of the Newton–Raphson algorithm. It is also similar to that used in the statistics and econometrics literature to determine the distributional and stochastic differences between statistics; see, for example, Pfanzagl (1974) and Robinson (1988).

The results of the paper are for parametric time series models in which the likelihood is a smooth function of the parameter and the observations are weakly asymptotically dependent. Thus, the type of models covered include ARCH/GARCH-type models, threshold autoregressive models, regime switching models, and so forth (although the results do not cover nonstandard testing problems in such models, such as testing for the existence of thresholds or regimes). The results do not cover long-memory models. Results for the parametric bootstrap for long-memory models are given in Andrews and Lieberman (2005).

The results of the paper apply to a correctly specified model. In a misspecified model, the parametric bootstrap typically does not provide higher-order improvements over the delta method for CIs and tests regarding the pseudo–true value (although it is still valid for first order). The reason is that the bootstrap generates samples according to the parametric model evaluated (approximately) at the pseudo–true value for n large. In contrast, the original sample is generated by some distribution not in the parametric family. In consequence, the coefficients of the Edgeworth expansions of original sample statistics and corresponding bootstrap statistics typically are different, even in the limit. Since the Edgeworth expansions of the bootstrap statistics do not mimic those of the original sample statistics, the bootstrap does not yield higher-order improvements.

This paper provides some Monte Carlo results to illustrate the performance of the parametric bootstrap compared to the delta method in the second-order autoregressive (AR(2)) model with Gaussian errors. This model is convenient for Monte Carlo experiments because the ML estimator is the LS estimator, which is available in closed form and, hence, computation is quick. We consider CIs for a nonlinear function of the AR parameters, namely, the cumulative impulse response (CIR), as well as for the AR parameters themselves. We consider sample sizes of 50 and 100 and a variety of different parameter combinations. To see how robust the (Gaussian) parametric bootstrap is to nonnormal errors, we also consider errors with t distribution with five degrees of freedom, which exhibits fat tails, and χ^2 distribution with one degree of freedom, which exhibits skewness.

The performances of the delta method and the parametric bootstrap CIs are found to depend on how close the sum of the AR coefficients is to 1. When the sum is close to 1, both types of CIs perform much more poorly than otherwise. In virtually all parameter combinations, the parametric bootstrap outperforms the delta method in terms of coverage probability. The difference is most pronounced when the sum of AR coefficients is close to 1. For example, when the AR parameters are .90 and 0.0, the sample size is 100, the errors are normal, and the nominal coverage probabilities of the CIs are .95; the actual coverage probabilities of the delta method, symmetric parametric bootstrap, and equal-tailed parametric bootstrap CIs for the CIR are .714, .876, and .847, respectively. As a second example, when the AR parameters are .50 and 0.0 and everything else is the same as above, the analogous coverage probabilities are .880, .929, and .915. The results change very little when t_5 or χ_1^2 errors are used. Overall, the simulation results indicate that in one Markov model of interest the parametric bootstrap outperforms the delta method.

An alternative bootstrap procedure that can be used in the AR(2) model is the residual-based (RB) bootstrap; see Bose (1988). We compare the (Gaussian) parametric bootstrap to the RB bootstrap when the errors are normal, t_5, and χ_1^2. For normal and t_5 errors, there is very little difference in the coverage probabilities of the parametric and RB bootstraps. For χ_1^2 errors, the differences are larger. The coverage probabilities of the parametric bootstrap CIs are almost always higher than those of the RB bootstrap CIs. For about half of the parameter combinations considered, the parametric bootstrap coverage probabilities are closer to the nominal value .95 than the RB bootstrap coverage probabilities, and vice versa. Hence, the overall performance of the parametric and RB bootstraps are quite similar in the AR(2) model.

Note that Bose (1988) shows that the RB bootstrap estimates the distribution function of the LS estimator with known covariance matrix up to $o(n^{-1/2})$, whereas the delta method does so up to $O(n^{-1/2})$. Bose's results do not apply to the RB bootstrap considered in the Monte Carlo section because the covariance matrix of the LS estimator is taken to be unknown, as would be the case in practice.

No other papers in the literature that we are aware of consider higher-order improvements of the parametric bootstrap for time series processes. In fact, there are few papers that consider higher-order improvements of the parametric bootstrap even for i.i.d. observations. Two papers that do are Davidson and MacKinnon (1999b) and Kim (2002). On the other hand, numerous papers in the literature consider different types of bootstrap procedures for time series observations. Rajarshi (1990), Datta and McCormick (1995), and Horowitz (2003) consider a nonparametric bootstrap for Markov processes that utilizes a nonparametric estimator of the transition densities of the process. Bose (1988) and Inoue and Kilian (2002) consider an RB bootstrap for AR processes that relies on transforming the data to obtain approximately i.i.d. residuals. Paparoditis (1996), Bühlmann (1998), Choi and Hall (2000), Park (2001), and Chang and Park (2003), consider sieve bootstraps for linear time series processes. Hansen (1999) considers a grid bootstrap. Many other papers consider the block bootstrap. These include Carlstein (1986), Künsch (1989), Lahiri (1992, 1993, 1996), Hall and Horowitz (1996), Götze and Künsch (1996), Andrews (2002b), Zvingelis (2003), Gonçalves and White (2004), and Inoue and Shintani (2005).

The results of the present paper differ from those of Andrews (2002b) in the following ways. First, the parametric bootstrap is considered rather than the block bootstrap. In consequence, the form of the Edgeworth expansions for the bootstraps differ and, in consequence, different higher-order improvements result. Second, in the present paper, we establish the Edgeworth expansions for the parametric bootstrap by establishing Edgeworth expansions for the original sample that hold uniformly over certain subsets of the parameter space. This differs from the approach taken in Andrews (2002b). Third, the results of the present paper apply with fixed exogenous variables and, hence, the observations are neither identically distributed nor stationary. We consider fixed exogenous variables because it is preferable to take the exogenous variables to be the same in each bootstrap sample. In contrast, the results for the block bootstrap of Andrews (2002b) are for stationary random variables, because one cannot take exogenous variables to be the same in each block bootstrap sample and, hence, one typically does not condition on exogenous variables when using the block bootstrap. Fourth, we impose much weaker moment conditions and smoothness conditions here than in Andrews (2002b). This is possible because the parametric bootstrap is simpler than the block bootstrap.

The remainder of the paper is organized as follows. Section 2 introduces the parametric Markov model that is considered in the paper and defines the ML estimator, the t and Wald statistics, the delta method CIs, and the delta method confidence regions (CRs). Section 3 defines the parametric bootstrap CIs and CRs. Section 4 states the assumptions. Section 5 provides bounds on the coverage probability errors of the delta method CIs and CRs. Section 6 does likewise for the parametric bootstrap CIs and CRs. Section 7 introduces k-step parametric bootstrap CIs and CRs and shows that the same bounds on the coverage probability errors apply as for the standard parametric bootstrap, provided k is taken to be large enough. Section 8 presents some Monte Carlo simulation results for the parametric bootstrap for an AR(2) model. The Appendix contains proofs of the results.

2. MARKOV MODEL AND MAXIMUM LIKELIHOOD ESTIMATOR

In this section, we provide results for likelihood-based methods using the *parametric* bootstrap. The parametric bootstrap utilizes the ML estimator to generate bootstrap samples. It can be used for both bootstrap confidence intervals and tests.

We obtain higher-order improvements of the parametric bootstrap that are the same whether or not the data are dependent.

We consider a correctly specified parametric model for a time series $\{W_i : i = 1, \ldots, n\}$, where $W_i \in R^{L_w}$. Let $W_i = (Y_i', X_i')'$, where Y_i is a vector of dependent (or response) variables and X_i is a vector of "regressor" variables. The dependent random variables $\{Y_i : i = 1, \ldots, n\}$ form a κth order Markov process. The regressor variables $\{X_i : i = 1, \ldots, n\}$ are strictly exogenous and, hence, are taken to be fixed (i.e., nonrandom). All probabilities are based on the randomness in $\{Y_i : i = 1, \ldots, n\}$ alone.

Assumption 2.1. *(a) The parametric model specifies the density of Y_i given $(X_i, W_{i-1}, W_{i-2}, \ldots, W_1)$ (with respect to some σ-finite measure μ) to be $d(\cdot|X_i, W_{i-1}, W_{i-2}, \ldots, W_{i-\kappa}; \theta)$ for $i = \kappa + 1, \ldots, n$, for some integer $\kappa \geq 0$, where θ is a parameter in the parameter space $\Theta \subset R^{L_\theta}$. (b) For any $\theta_0 \in \Theta$, when $\{Y_i : i \geq 1\}$ is distributed with true parameter θ_0, then $\{Y_i : i \geq 1\}$ is a strong mixing sequence of random variables with strong mixing numbers $\{\alpha(\theta_0, m) : m \geq 1\}$ that satisfy $\sup_{\theta_0 \in \Theta} \alpha(\theta_0, m) \leq C_1 \exp(-C_2 m)$ for some constants $0 < C_1, C_2 < \infty$.*

Let E_{θ_0} and P_{θ_0} denote expectation and probability, respectively, when the distribution of the observations is given by the parametric model with true parameter θ_0.

It is convenient notationally to define overlapping observations $\widetilde{W}_i = (W_i', \ldots, W_{i+\kappa}')'$ for $i = 1, \ldots, N$, where $N = n - \kappa$. The sample in terms of the overlapping variables is denoted by χ_N:

$$\chi_N = \{\widetilde{W}_i : i = 1, \ldots, N\}. \tag{2.1}$$

The normalized negative of the log likelihood function is

$$\rho_N(\theta) = N^{-1} \sum_{i=1}^{N} \rho(\widetilde{W}_i, \theta), \quad \text{where}$$
$$\rho(\widetilde{W}_i, \theta) = -\log d(Y_{i+\kappa}|X_{i+\kappa}, W_{i+\kappa-1}, W_{i+\kappa-2}, \ldots, W_i; \theta).^1 \tag{2.2}$$

By definition, the ML estimator $\widehat{\theta}_N$ solves

$$\min_{\theta \in \Theta} \rho_N(\theta). \tag{2.3}$$

The ML estimator also satisfies the first-order conditions

$$N^{-1} \sum_{i=1}^{N} g(\widetilde{W}_i, \widehat{\theta}_N) = 0, \quad \text{where}$$
$$g(\widetilde{W}_i, \theta) = (\partial/\partial\theta)\rho(\widetilde{W}_i, \theta). \tag{2.4}$$

The asymptotic covariance matrix, $\Sigma(\theta_0)$, of the ML estimator $\widehat{\theta}_N$ when the true parameter is θ_0 is

$$\Sigma(\theta_0) = D(\theta_0)^{-1} V(\theta_0) D(\theta_0)^{-1}, \quad \text{where}$$
$$V(\theta) = \lim_{N\to\infty} N^{-1} \sum_{i=1}^{N} E_\theta g(\widetilde{W}_i, \theta) g(\widetilde{W}_i, \theta)' \quad \text{and}$$
$$D(\theta) = \lim_{N\to\infty} N^{-1} \sum_{i=1}^{N} E_\theta \frac{\partial}{\partial\theta'} g(\widetilde{W}_i, \theta). \tag{2.5}$$

A consistent variance matrix estimator Σ_N for $\widehat{\theta}_N$ can be defined in several ways because $D(\theta_0)$ and $V(\theta_0)$ are square matrices and the information matrix equality implies that $D(\theta_0)$ and $V(\theta_0)$ are equal. In particular, one can use

$$\Sigma_N = \Sigma_N(\widehat{\theta}_N) \quad \text{for}$$
$$\Sigma_N(\theta) = D_N^{-1}(\theta) V_N(\theta) D_N^{-1}(\theta), \quad \Sigma_N(\theta) = D_N^{-1}(\theta), \quad \text{or}$$
$$\Sigma_N(\theta) = V_N^{-1}(\theta), \quad \text{where}$$
$$V_N(\theta) = N^{-1} \sum_{i=1}^{N} g(\widetilde{W}_i, \theta) g(\widetilde{W}_i, \theta)', \quad \text{and}$$
$$D_N(\theta) = N^{-1} \sum_{i=1}^{N} \frac{\partial}{\partial\theta'} g(\widetilde{W}_i, \theta). \tag{2.6}$$

Let θ_r, $\theta_{0,r}$, and $\widehat{\theta}_{N,r}$ denote the rth elements of θ, θ_0, and $\widehat{\theta}_N$, respectively. Let $(\Sigma_N)_{rr}$ denote the (r, r)-th element of Σ_N. The t statistic for testing the null hypothesis $H_0 : \theta_r = \theta_{0,r}$ is

$$T_N(\theta_{0,r}) = N^{1/2}(\widehat{\theta}_{N,r} - \theta_{0,r})/(\Sigma_N)_{rr}^{1/2}. \tag{2.7}$$

Two-sided and upper one-sided delta method CIs for $\theta_{0,r}$ of confidence level $100(1-\alpha)\%$ are given by

$$\Delta_{2S} = [\widehat{\theta}_{N,r} - z_{\alpha/2}(\Sigma_N)_{rr}^{1/2}/N^{1/2},\ \widehat{\theta}_{N,r} + z_{\alpha/2}(\Sigma_N)_{rr}^{1/2}/N^{1/2}] \quad \text{and}$$
$$\Delta_{UP} = [\widehat{\theta}_{N,r} - z_\alpha(\Sigma_N)_{rr}^{1/2}/N^{1/2},\ \infty), \tag{2.8}$$

[1] This specification of the log likelihood does not utilize the first κ observations, except as conditioning variables. It should be possible to extend the results of the paper without much difficulty to the case where the likelihood for the first κ observations is included in the likelihood function.

respectively, where z_α denotes the $1-\alpha$ quantile of the standard normal distribution.

Suppose $\beta \in R^{L_\beta}$ is a sub-vector of θ, say, $\theta = (\beta', \delta')'$. The Wald statistic for testing $H_0 : \beta = \beta_0$ versus $H_1 : \beta \neq \beta_0$ is

$$\mathcal{W}_N(\beta_0) = H_N(\widehat{\theta}_N, \beta_0)' H_N(\widehat{\theta}_N, \beta_0), \quad \text{where}$$
$$H_N(\theta, \beta_0) = ([I_{L_\beta} \vdots 0]\Sigma_N(\theta)[I_{L_\beta} \vdots 0]')^{-1/2} N^{1/2}(\beta - \beta_0). \tag{2.9}$$

The delta method confidence region (CR) for β_0 of confidence level $100(1-\alpha)\%$ is

$$\begin{aligned}\Delta_{\text{REG}} = \{\beta \in R^{L_\beta} : N(\widehat{\beta}_N - \beta)'([I_{L_\beta} \vdots 0]\Sigma_N[I_{L_\beta} \vdots 0]')^{-1} \\ \times (\widehat{\beta}_N - \beta) \leq z_{L_\beta, \alpha}\},\end{aligned} \tag{2.10}$$

where $z_{L_\beta, \alpha}$ is the $1-\alpha$ quantile of the chi-square distribution with L_β degrees of freedom.

3. PARAMETRIC BOOTSTRAP

The parametric bootstrap sample $\{W_i^* : i = 1, \ldots, n\}$ is defined as follows. The bootstrap regressors are the same fixed regressors as in the original sample and the bootstrap dependent variables are generated recursively for $i = 1, \ldots, n$ using the parametric density evaluated at the unrestricted ML estimator $\widehat{\theta}_N$. That is, one takes $W_i^* = (Y_i^{*\prime}, X_i')'$, where Y_i^* has density $d(\cdot | X_i, W_{i-1}^*, W_{i-2}^*, \ldots, W_{i-\kappa_i}^*; \widehat{\theta}_N)$ for $i = 1, \ldots, n$, where $\kappa_i = \min\{\kappa, i+1\}$. The bootstrap observations $\widetilde{W}_i^*$ are defined to be $\widetilde{W}_i^* = (W_i^{*\prime}, \ldots, W_{i+\kappa}^{*\prime})'$ for $i = 1, \ldots, N$. Under Assumption 2.1, the conditional distribution of the bootstrap sample given $\widehat{\theta}_N$ is the same as the distribution of the original sample, except that the true parameter is $\widehat{\theta}_N$ rather than θ_0.

The bootstrap estimator θ_N^* is defined exactly as the original estimator $\widehat{\theta}_N$ is defined, but with the original sample $\{\widetilde{W}_i : i = 1, \ldots, N\}$ replaced by the bootstrap sample $\{\widetilde{W}_i^* : i = 1, \ldots, N\}$. That is, θ_N^* solves

$$\min_{\theta \in \Theta} \rho_N^*(\theta), \quad \text{where } \rho_N^*(\theta) = N^{-1} \sum_{i=1}^{N} \rho(\widetilde{W}_i^*, \theta). \tag{3.1}$$

The bootstrap covariance matrix estimator, Σ_N^*, is defined to be $\Sigma_N^*(\theta_N^*)$, where $\Sigma_N^*(\theta)$ has the same definition as $\Sigma_N(\theta)$ (see (2.6)), but with the bootstrap sample in place of the original sample. (For example, $V_N^*(\theta)$ equals $V_N(\theta)$ with $\widetilde{W}_i$ replaced by $\widetilde{W}_i^*$.)

The bootstrap t and Wald statistics need to be defined such that their distributions mimic the null nonbootstrap distribution even when the sample is generated by a parameter in the alternative hypothesis. This is done by centering the statistics at $\widehat{\theta}_{N,r}$ and $\widehat{\beta}_N$, respectively, rather than at the values specified under the null hypotheses. We define

$$\begin{aligned} T_N^*(\widehat{\theta}_{N,r}) &= N^{1/2}((\theta_N^*)_r - \widehat{\theta}_{N,r})/(\Sigma_N^*)_{rr}^{1/2} \quad \text{and} \\ \mathcal{W}_N^*(\widehat{\beta}_N) &= H_N^*(\theta_N^*, \widehat{\beta}_N)' H_N^*(\theta_N^*, \widehat{\beta}_N), \quad \text{where} \\ H_N^*(\theta, \widehat{\beta}_N) &= \left([I_{L_\beta} \vdots 0] \Sigma_N^*(\theta) [I_{L_\beta} \vdots 0]' \right)^{-1/2} N^{1/2}(\beta - \widehat{\beta}_N), \end{aligned} \tag{3.2}$$

$(\theta_N^*)_r$ denotes the rth element of θ_N^*,[2] and $(\Sigma_N^*)_{rr}$ denotes the (r, r)-th element of Σ_N^*.

Let $z_{|T|,\alpha}^*$, $z_{T,\alpha}^*$, and $z_{\mathcal{W},\alpha}^*$ denote the $1 - \alpha$ quantiles of $|T_N^*(\widehat{\theta}_{N,r})|$, $T_N^*(\widehat{\theta}_{N,r})$, and $\mathcal{W}_N^*(\widehat{\beta}_N)$, respectively. To be precise, we define $z_{|T|,\alpha}^*$ to be a value that minimizes $|P^*(|T_N^*(\widehat{\theta}_{N,r})| \leq z) - (1 - \alpha)|$ over $z \in R$. (This definition allows for discreteness in the distribution of $|T_N^*(\widehat{\theta}_{N,r})|$.) The precise definitions of $z_{T,\alpha}^*$ and $z_{\mathcal{W},\alpha}^*$ are analogous.

The symmetric two-sided bootstrap CI for the rth element of θ_0, $\theta_{0,r}$, of confidence level $100(1 - \alpha)\%$ is

$$\text{CI}_{\text{SYM}} = \left[\widehat{\theta}_{N,r} - z_{|T|,\alpha}^* (\Sigma_N)_{rr}^{1/2} / N^{1/2}, \; \widehat{\theta}_{N,r} + z_{|T|,\alpha}^* (\Sigma_N)_{rr}^{1/2} / N^{1/2}\right]. \tag{3.3}$$

The equal-tailed two-sided bootstrap CI for $\theta_{0,r}$ of confidence level $100(1 - \alpha)\%$ is

$$\text{CI}_{\text{ET}} = \left[\widehat{\theta}_{N,r} - z_{T,\alpha/2}^* (\Sigma_N)_{rr}^{1/2} / N^{1/2}, \; \widehat{\theta}_{N,r} + z_{T,1-\alpha/2}^* (\Sigma_N)_{rr}^{1/2} / N^{1/2}\right]. \tag{3.4}$$

The upper one-sided bootstrap CI for $\theta_{0,r}$ of confidence level $100(1 - \alpha)\%$ is

$$\text{CI}_{\text{UP}} = [\widehat{\theta}_{N,r} - z_{T,\alpha}^* (\Sigma_N)_{rr}^{1/2} / N^{1/2}, \; \infty). \tag{3.5}$$

The bootstrap confidence region (CR) for β_0 of confidence level $100(1 - \alpha)\%$ is

$$\begin{aligned} \text{CR} = \{\beta \in R^{L_\beta} : \; & N(\widehat{\beta}_N - \beta)'([I_{L_\beta} \vdots 0] \Sigma_N [I_{L_\beta} \vdots 0]')^{-1} \\ & \times (\widehat{\beta}_N - \beta) \leq z_{\mathcal{W},\alpha}^* \}. \end{aligned} \tag{3.6}$$

Correspondingly, the symmetric two-sided bootstrap t test of $H_0 : \theta_r = \theta_{0,r}$ versus $H_1 : \theta_r \neq \theta_{0,r}$ of significance level α rejects H_0 if $|T_N(\theta_{0,r})| > z_{|T|,\alpha}^*$. The equal-tailed two-sided bootstrap t test of significance level α for the same hypotheses rejects H_0 if $T_N(\theta_{0,r}) < z_{T,1-\alpha/2}^*$ or $T_N(\theta_{0,r}) > z_{T,\alpha/2}^*$. The one-sided bootstrap t test of $H_0 : \theta_r \leq \theta_{0,r}$ versus $H_1 : \theta_r > \theta_{0,r}$ of significance level α rejects H_0 if $T_N(\theta_{0,r}) > z_{T,\alpha}^*$.

To carry out tests of the above sort, an alternative parametric bootstrap procedure can be used that employs the restricted ML estimator of θ. Results of Davidson and MacKinnon (1999b) and Kim (2002) indicate that the error in test rejection probability for one-sided tests may be smaller using such a procedure than using a bootstrap based on the unrestricted ML estimator. For

[2] The rth element of θ_N^* is denoted by $(\theta_N^*)_r$, rather than $\theta_{N,r}^*$, to distinguish it from the k-step bootstrap estimator $\theta_{N,k}^*$, defined in Section 7.

this reason, the results of this paper for one-sided procedures are more useful for CIs than for tests.

Note that while there are two types of two-sided bootstrap CIs – symmetric and equal-tailed – there is only one type of two-sided delta method CI. This is because two-sided delta method CIs are necessarily both symmetric and equal-tailed by the symmetry of the standard normal distribution.

4. ASSUMPTIONS

In this section, we state assumptions that are used in conjunction with Assumption 2.1 to obtain the results of the paper.

Let a be a nonnegative constant such that $2a$ is an integer. The following assumptions depend on a – the larger a is, the stronger are the assumptions. To obtain higher-order improvements of the parametric bootstrap CIs, we require the assumptions to hold with a equal to $1/2$, 1, $3/2$, or 2, depending upon the CI.

Let $f(\widetilde{W}_i, \theta) \in R^{L_f}$ denote the vector containing the unique components of $g(\widetilde{W}_i, \theta)$ and $g(\widetilde{W}_i, \theta)g(\widetilde{W}_i, \theta)'$ and their partial derivatives with respect to θ through order $d = \max\{2a + 2, 3\}$. Let $(\partial^j/\partial\theta^j)g(\widetilde{W}_i, \theta)$ denote the vector of partial derivatives with respect to θ of order j of $g(\widetilde{W}_i, \theta)$. Let $\lambda_{\min}(A)$ denote the smallest eigenvalue of a matrix A. Let $d(\theta, B)$ denote the usual distance between a point θ and a set B (i.e., $d(\theta, B) = \inf\{||\theta - \theta_1|| : \theta_1 \in B\}$).

We establish asymptotic refinements that hold uniformly for the true parameter lying in a subset Θ_0 of Θ. For some $\delta > 0$, let $\Theta_1 = \{\theta \in \Theta : d(\theta, \Theta_0) < \delta/2\}$ be a slightly larger set than Θ_0. To obtain the asymptotic refinements, we need to establish Edgeworth expansions that hold uniformly for the true parameter lying in Θ_1. The reason is that the parametric bootstrap uses $\widehat{\theta}_N$ as the true parameter and Θ_1 contains $\widehat{\theta}_N$ with probability that goes to 1 (at a sufficiently fast rate) when the true parameter is in Θ_0. In turn, to establish the Edgeworth expansions for all true parameters θ_0 in Θ_1, we need some assumptions to hold uniformly over the slightly larger set $\Theta_2 = \{\theta \in \Theta : d(\theta, \Theta_0) < \delta\}$.

We use the following assumptions.

Assumption 4.1. *(a) Θ is compact and Θ_1 is an open set. (b) $\widehat{\theta}_N$ minimizes $N^{-1}\sum_{i=1}^N \rho(\widetilde{W}_i, \theta)$ over $\theta \in \Theta$. (c) $\rho(\theta, \theta_0) = \lim_{N\to\infty} N^{-1}\sum_{i=1}^N E_{\theta_0}\rho(\widetilde{W}_i, \theta)$ exists and satisfies $\lim_{N\to\infty}\sup_{\theta\in\Theta,\theta_0\in\Theta_1}|N^{-1}\sum_{i=1}^N E_{\theta_0}\rho(\widetilde{W}_i, \theta) - \rho(\theta, \theta_0)| = 0$. (d) For all $\theta_0 \in \Theta_1$, $\rho(\theta, \theta_0)$ is uniquely minimized over $\theta \in \Theta$ by $\theta = \theta_0$. Furthermore, given any $\varepsilon > 0$, there exists $\eta > 0$ such that $||\theta - \theta_0|| > \varepsilon$ implies that $\rho(\theta, \theta_0) - \rho(\theta_0, \theta_0) > \eta$ for all $\theta \in \Theta$ and $\theta_0 \in \Theta_1$. (e) $\sup_{\theta_0\in\Theta_1, i\geq 1} E_{\theta_0}\sup_{\theta\in\Theta}||g(\widetilde{W}_i, \theta)||^{q_0} < \infty$ and $\sup_{\theta_0\in\Theta_1, i\geq 1} E_{\theta_0}|\rho(\widetilde{W}_i, \theta)|^{q_0} < \infty$ for all $\theta \in \Theta$ for $q_0 = \max\{2a + 1, 2\}$.*

Assumption 4.2. *(a) $g(\widetilde{w}, \theta)$ is $d = \max\{2a + 2, 3\}$ times partially differentiable with respect to θ on Θ_2 for all $\widetilde{w}$ in the support of $\widetilde{W}_i$ for all $i \geq 1$. (b) $\sup_{\theta_0\in\Theta_1, i\geq 1} E_{\theta_0}||f(\widetilde{W}_i, \theta_0)||^{q_1} < \infty$ for some $q_1 > 2a + 2$. (c) $V(\theta_0)$*

and $D(\theta_0)$ *satisfy:* $\inf_{\theta_0 \in \Theta_1} \lambda_{\min}(V(\theta_0)) > 0$, $\inf_{\theta_0 \in \Theta_1} \lambda_{\min}(D(\theta_0)) > 0$, $\lim_{N\to\infty} \sup_{\theta_0 \in \Theta_1} |E_{\theta_0} V_N(\theta_0) - V(\theta_0)| = 0$ *and* $\lim_{N\to\infty} \sup_{\theta_0 \in \Theta_1} |E_{\theta_0} D_N (\theta_0) - D(\theta_0)| = 0$. *(d) There is a function* $C_f(\widetilde{W}_i)$ *such that* $||f(\widetilde{W}_i, \theta) - f(\widetilde{W}_i, \theta_0)|| \leq C_f(\widetilde{W}_i)||\theta - \theta_0||$ *for all* $\theta \in \Theta_2$ *and* $\theta_0 \in \Theta_1$ *such that* $||\theta - \theta_0|| < \delta$ *and all* $i \geq 1$ *and* $\sup_{\theta_0 \in \Theta_1, i \geq 1} E_{\theta_0} C_f^{q_1}(\widetilde{W}_i) < \infty$ *for some* $q_1 > 2a + 2$.

Assumption 4.1 imposes some fairly standard conditions used to establish consistency of the ML estimator, as well as some moment conditions. Assumption 4.2 imposes smoothness and moment conditions on the parametric densities and their derivatives, as well as full rank conditions on the information matrix.

The next assumption comes from Lahiri (1993), which extends results of Götze and Hipp (1983). The assumption guarantees that an Edgeworth expansion holds for $N^{-1/2} \sum_{i=1}^{N} (f(\widetilde{W}_i, \theta_0) - E_{\theta_0} f(\widetilde{W}_i, \theta_0))$ with remainder $o(N^{-a})$ uniformly over $\theta_0 \in \Theta_1$, given the moment condition in Assumption 4.2b. The assumption is rather complicated and is not easy to verify in general. Nevertheless, Götze and Hipp (1983, 1994) provide a number of examples in which this condition is verified. For a fixed value θ_0, the assumption is weaker than the corresponding assumptions employed in Hall and Horowitz (1996) and Andrews (2002b), which are based on sufficient conditions for the assumption given below.

The following assumption can be replaced by any set of sufficient conditions for an Edgeworth expansion for $N^{-1/2} \sum_{i=1}^{N} (f(\widetilde{W}_i, \theta_0) - E_{\theta_0} f(\widetilde{W}_i, \theta_0))$ when the true parameter is θ_0, whose remainder is $o(N^{-a})$ uniformly over $\theta_0 \in \Theta_1$. For example, there are several Edgeworth expansions in the literature designed specifically for Markov processes. These include Malinovskii (1987, Theorem 1) and Jensen (1989, Theorem 2).[3]

Let $(\Omega, \mathcal{A}, P_{\theta_0})$ for $\theta_0 \in \Theta$ be the probability space on which the random vectors $\{W_i : i \geq 1\}$ are defined. Let $\mathcal{D}_0, \mathcal{D}_{\pm 1}, \mathcal{D}_{\pm 2}, \ldots$ be a sequence of sub-σ-fields of $\mathcal{A}$. Let $\mathcal{D}_p^q$ denote the σ-field generated by $\mathcal{D}_j$ for $p \leq j \leq q$.

Assumption 4.3. *(a) There exists a constant* $d_1 > 0$*, such that for all* $m, i = 1, 2, \ldots$ *with* $m > d_1^{-1}$*, there exist* $\mathcal{D}_{i-m}^{i+m}$*-measurable random vectors* $Z_{i,m}(\theta_0)$ *for which* $E_{\theta_0} ||f(\widetilde{W}_i, \theta_0) - Z_{i,m}(\theta_0)|| < d_1^{-1} \exp(-d_1 m)$ *for all* $\theta_0 \in \Theta_1$. *(b) There exists a constant* $d_2 > 0$*, such that for all* $m, i = 1, 2, \ldots$, $A \in \mathcal{D}_{-\infty}^{i}$*, and* $B \in \mathcal{D}_{i+m}^{\infty}$, $|P_{\theta_0}(A \cap B) - P_{\theta_0}(A)P_{\theta_0}(B)| \leq d_2^{-1} \exp(-d_2 m)$ *for all* $\theta_0 \in \Theta_1$. *(c) There exists a constant* $d_3 > 0$*, such that for all* $m, i = 1, 2, \ldots$ *with* $d_3^{-1} < m < i$ *and all* $t \in R^{L_f}$ *with* $||t|| \geq$

[3] The latter results only require strong mixing coefficients that decline polynomially fast. In this case, it is useful to weaken the conditions on the mixing numbers in Assumption 1.2b to $\sum_{m=1}^{\infty} (m+1)^{\lambda/2-1} \alpha^{\delta/(\lambda+\delta)}(m) < \infty$ for some $\lambda > \max\{2a, 2\}$ and some $\delta > 0$, where $\alpha(m) = \sup_{\theta 0 \in \Theta 1} \alpha(m, \theta_0)$. This weakening is possible because one can establish the results of Lemmas A.2a and A.2b in the Appendix using the given condition and results of Yokoyama (1980) and Doukhan (1995, Theorem 2 and Remark 2, pp. 25–30).

d_3, $E_{\theta_0}|E_{\theta_0}(\exp(\sqrt{-1}t'(\sum_{j=i-m}^{i+m} f(\widetilde{W}_j, \theta_0)))|\mathcal{D}_j : j \neq i)| \leq \exp(-d_3)$ *for all* $\theta_0 \in \Theta_1$. *(d) There exist a constant* $d_4 > 0$, *such that for all* $m, i, p = 1, 2, \ldots$ *and* $A \in \mathcal{D}_{i-p}^{i+p}$, $E_{\theta_0}|P_{\theta_0}(A|\mathcal{D}_j : j \neq i) - P_{\theta_0}(A|\mathcal{D}_j : 0 < |i - j| \leq i + p)| \leq d_4^{-1} \exp(-d_4 m)$ *for all* $\theta_0 \in \Theta_1$. *(e) There exist matrices* $\Omega(\theta_0) \in R^{L_f \times L_f}$ *for* $\theta_0 \in \Theta_1$, *such that* $\lim_{N\to\infty} \sup_{\theta_0 \in \Theta_1} ||\text{Var}_{\theta_0}(N^{-1/2} \sum_{i=1}^N f(\widetilde{W}_i, \theta_0)) - \Omega(\theta_0)|| = 0$ *and* $\Omega(\theta_0)$ *has smallest eigenvalue bounded away from* 0 *over* $\theta_0 \in \Theta_1$. *(f) There exists a constant* $d_5 > 0$, *such that for all* $i > d_5^{-1}$ *and* $m > d_5^{-1}$, $\inf\{t'\text{Var}_{\theta_0}(\sum_{j=i}^{i+m} f(\widetilde{W}_j, \theta_0))t : ||t|| = 1, \theta_0 \in \Theta_1\} > d_5 m$.

Assumption 4.3 is a conditional Cramér condition. In the case of an i.i.d. sequence of random variables, Assumption 4.3 reduces to the standard Cramér condition.

5. COVERAGE PROBABILITY ERRORS OF DELTA METHOD CONFIDENCE INTERVALS

In this section, we consider delta method CIs and CRs.

Theorem 5.1. *Suppose Assumptions 2.1 and 4.1–4.3 hold with the constant a in Assumptions 4.1 and 4.2 as specified below. Then,*

(a) $\sup_{\theta_0 \in \Theta_0} |P_{\theta_0}(\theta_0 \in \Delta_{2S}) - (1 - \alpha)| = O(N^{-1})$ *for* $a = 1$,
(b) $\sup_{\theta_0 \in \Theta_0} |P_{\theta_0}(\theta_0 \in \Delta_{UP}) - (1 - \alpha)| = O(N^{-1/2})$ *for* $a = 1/2$, *and*
(c) $\sup_{\theta_0 \in \Theta_0} |P_{\theta_0}(\theta_0 \in \Delta_{REG}) - (1 - \alpha)| = O(N^{-1})$ *for* $a = 1$.

Comments. 1. The results of Theorem 5.1 are sharp.

2. The conditions on d, q_0, and q_1 in Assumptions 4.1 and 4.2 are as follows. For $a = 1$, the assumptions require $d \geq 4$, $q_0 \geq 3$, and $q_1 > 4$. For $a = 1/2$, the assumptions require $d \geq 3$, $q_0 \geq 2$, and $q_1 > 3$.

6. HIGHER-ORDER IMPROVEMENTS OF THE PARAMETRIC BOOTSTRAP

A main result of this paper is the following theorem.

Theorem 6.1. *Suppose Assumptions 2.1 and 4.1–4.3 hold with the constant a in Assumptions 4.1 and 4.2 as specified below. Then,*

(a) $\sup_{\theta_0 \in \Theta_0} |P_{\theta_0}(\theta_0 \in \text{CI}_{SYM}) - (1 - \alpha)| = O(N^{-2})$ *for* $a = 2$,
(b) $\sup_{\theta_0 \in \Theta_0} |P_{\theta_0}(\theta_0 \in \text{CI}_{ET}) - (1 - \alpha)| = o(N^{-1} \ln(N))$ *for* $a = 1$,
(c) $\sup_{\theta_0 \in \Theta_0} |P_{\theta_0}(\theta_0 \in \text{CI}_{UP}) - (1 - \alpha)| = o(N^{-1} \ln(N))$ *for* $a = 1$, *and*
(d) $\sup_{\theta_0 \in \Theta_0} |P_{\theta_0}(\theta_0 \in \text{CR}) - (1 - \alpha)| = o(N^{-3/2} \ln(N))$ *for* $a = 3/2$.

Comments. 1. The result of Theorem 6.1a is sharp and the results of Theorem 6.1b and 6.1c are very nearly sharp. (On the basis of results available for population means in i.i.d. scenarios, sharp results would be errors of magnitude $O(N^{-1})$ in parts (b) and (c).) But, the result of part (d) for the CR probably is not sharp or nearly sharp. One may be able to obtain an error in part (d) of $O(N^{-2})$ via an argument somewhat similar to that of Hall (1988) for symmetric t CIs.

2. Theorems 5.1 and 6.1 show that two-sided symmetric parametric bootstrap CIs reduce the coverage probability errors of two-sided delta method CIs by the multiplicative factor $O(N^{-1})$.

For one-sided CIs and Wald-based CRs, the corresponding reductions are shown to be at least $o(N^{-1/2}\ln(N))$. For one-sided CIs, these higher-order improvements are almost the same as the improvements that have been established for parametric and nonparametric one-sided bootstrap CIs for a population mean (based on the sample mean) in i.i.d. scenarios, which are $O(N^{-1/2})$; see, for example, Hall (1988, 1992). (The difference is probably only due to our method of proof.) For Wald-based CRs, the improvements established by Theorems 5.1 and 6.1 probably are not sharp.

For equal-tailed two-sided parametric bootstrap CIs, the parametric bootstrap does not provide any improvement over the two-sided delta method CI in terms of overall coverage probability, as in the i.i.d. case. But, there are improvements of $o(N^{-1/2}\ln(N))$ for the probability of the equal-tailed bootstrap CI missing to the left, and similarly for its probability of missing to the right, just as in the i.i.d. case.

In sum, in contrast to the block bootstrap (e.g., see the higher-order improvement results in Andrews 2002b), the parametric bootstrap for time series observations performs essentially as well asymptotically as for independent observations. The only exception is for Wald-based CRs, and this is probably because the results in Theorem 6.2d are not sharp.

3. The conditions on d, q_0, and q_1 in Assumptions 4.1 and 4.2 are as follows. For $a = 1$, the assumptions require $d \geq 4$, $q_0 \geq 3$, and $q_1 > 4$. For $a = 3/2$, the assumptions require $d \geq 5$, $q_0 \geq 5$, and $q_1 > 6$. For $a = 2$, the assumptions require $d \geq 6$, $q_0 \geq 5$, and $q_1 > 6$.

7. k-STEP PARAMETRIC BOOTSTRAP

In this section, we define the k-step bootstrap estimator, t statistic, and Wald statistic and corresponding CIs and CRs. Then we establish bounds on the coverage probability errors of these CIs and CRs. Provided k is taken to be large enough, the bounds are of the same magnitude as those obtained for the standard parametric bootstrap.

The k-step bootstrap estimator is denoted as $\theta^*_{N,k}$. The starting value for the k-step estimator is $\widehat{\theta}_N$, the estimator based on the original sample. We recursively define

$$\theta^*_{N,j} = \theta^*_{N,j-1} - (Q^*_{N,j-1})^{-1} N^{-1} \sum_{i=1}^{N} g(\widetilde{W}^*_i, \theta^*_{N,j-1}) \quad \text{for } 1 \leq j \leq k, \tag{7.1}$$

where $\theta^*_{N,0} = \widehat{\theta}_N$.

The $L_\theta \times L_\theta$ random matrix $Q^*_{N,j-1}$ depends on $\theta^*_{N,j-1}$. It determines whether the k-step bootstrap estimator is a NR, default NR, line-search NR, GN, or some other k-step bootstrap estimator. The NR, default NR, and line-search NR choices of $Q^*_{N,j-1}$ yield k-step bootstrap estimators that have the same higher-order asymptotic behavior. The results below show that they require fewer steps, k, to approximate the ML bootstrap estimator θ^*_N to a specified accuracy than does the GN k-step estimator. The NR choice of $Q^*_{N,j-1}$ is

$$Q^{*,\mathrm{NR}}_{N,j-1} = D^*_N(\theta^*_{N,j-1}), \quad \text{where}$$

$$D^*_N(\theta) = N^{-1} \sum_{i=1}^{N} \frac{\partial}{\partial \theta'} g(\widetilde{W}^*_i, \theta). \tag{7.2}$$

The *default* NR choice of $Q^*_{N,j-1}$, denoted as $Q^{*,\mathrm{D}}_{N,j-1}$, equals $Q^{*,\mathrm{NR}}_{N,j-1}$ if $Q^{*,\mathrm{NR}}_{N,j-1}$ leads to an estimator $\theta^*_{N,j}$ via (7.1) for which $\rho^*_N(\theta^*_{N,j}) \leq \rho^*_N(\theta^*_{N,j-1})$, but equals some other matrix otherwise. In practice, one wants this other matrix to be such that $\rho^*_N(\theta^*_{N,j}) < \rho^*_N(\theta^*_{N,j-1})$ (but the theoretical results do not require this). For example, one might use the matrix $(1/\varepsilon) I_{L_\theta}$ for some small $\varepsilon > 0$. (See Ortega and Rheinboldt 1970, Theorem 8.2.1, for a result that indicates that such a choice will decrease the criterion function.)

The *line-search* NR choice of $Q^*_{N,j-1}$, denoted as $Q^{*,\mathrm{LS}}_{N,j-1}$, uses a scaled version of the NR matrix $Q^{*,\mathrm{NR}}_{N,j-1}$ that optimizes the step length. Specifically, let A be a finite subset of $(0, 1]$ of step lengths that includes 1. One computes $\theta^*_{N,j} = \theta^{*,\alpha}_{N,j}$ via (7.1) for $Q^*_{N,j-1} = (1/\alpha) Q^{*,\mathrm{NR}}_{N,j-1}$ for each $\alpha \in A$. One takes $Q^{*,\mathrm{LS}}_{N,j-1}$ to be the matrix $(1/\alpha) Q^{*,\mathrm{NR}}_{N,j-1}$ for the value of α that minimizes $\rho^*_N(\theta^{*\alpha}_{N,j})$ over all $\alpha \in A$. (If the minimizing value of α is not unique, one takes the largest minimizing value of α in A.)

The GN choice of $Q^*_{N,j-1}$, denoted as $Q^{*,\mathrm{GN}}_{N,j-1}$, uses a matrix that differs from, but is a close approximation to, the NR matrix $Q^{*,\mathrm{NR}}_{N,j-1}$. In particular,

$$Q^{*,\mathrm{GN}}_{N,j-1} = D^*_{N,j-1}, \tag{7.3}$$

where $D^*_{N,j-1}$ is determined by some function $\Delta(\cdot, \cdot)$ as follows:

$$D^*_{N,j-1} = N^{-1} \sum_{i=1}^{N} \Delta(\widetilde{W}^*_i, \theta^*_{N,j-1}) \in R^{L_g \times L_\theta} \quad \text{and}$$

$$E^*_{\theta_0} \Delta(\widetilde{W}^*_i, \theta_0) = E^*_{\theta_0} \frac{\partial}{\partial \theta'} g(\widetilde{W}^*_i, \theta_0) \quad \text{for all } i \geq 1 \quad \text{and all } \theta_0 \in \Theta_1. \tag{7.4}$$

The latter condition is responsible for $D^*_{N,j-1}$ being a close approximation to $D^*_N(\theta^*_{N,j-1}) = Q^{*,\text{NR}}_{N,j-1}$.

An example of a GN matrix $Q^{*,\text{GN}}_{N,j-1}$ is the sample outer-product estimator of the bootstrap information matrix. By the information matrix equality,

$$E^*_{\theta_0}\frac{\partial}{\partial\theta'}g(\widetilde{W}^*_i,\theta_0) = E^*_{\theta_0}g(\widetilde{W}^*_i,\theta_0)g(\widetilde{W}^*_i,\theta_0)' \quad \text{for all } i \geq 1 \text{ and all } \theta_0 \in \Theta_1. \tag{7.5}$$

In this case, the NR matrix $Q^{*,\text{NR}}_{N,j-1}$ is the sample analogue of the expectation on the left-hand side of (7.5): $Q^{*,\text{NR}}_{N,j-1} = N^{-1}\sum_{i=1}^N(\partial/\partial\theta')g(\widetilde{W}^*_i,\theta^*_{N,j-1})$. The GN matrix $Q^{*,\text{GN}}_{N,j-1}$ is the sample analogue of the expectation on the right-hand side of (7.5). Thus, $Q^{*,\text{GN}}_{N,j-1}$ is as in (7.3) and (7.4) with

$$\Delta(\widetilde{W}^*_i,\theta) = g(\widetilde{W}^*_i,\theta)g(\widetilde{W}^*_i,\theta)'. \tag{7.6}$$

The GN matrix does not require calculation of the second derivative of the log likelihood function.

Alternatively, one can use a GN matrix $Q^*_{N,j-1}$ based on the *expected* bootstrap information matrix:

$$Q^{*,\text{GN2}}_{N,j-1} = N^{-1}\sum_{i=1}^N E^*_\theta\frac{\partial}{\partial\theta'}g(\widetilde{W}^*_i,\theta)\bigg|_{\theta=\theta^*_{N,j-1}}. \tag{7.7}$$

In this case, the function $\Delta(\widetilde{W}^*_i,\theta)$ of (7.4) is $E^*_\theta(\partial/\partial\theta')g(\widetilde{W}^*_i,\theta)$, which is nonrandom. The expected information matrix is often used in the statistical literature on one-step and k-step estimators; see, for example, Pfanzagl (1974).

The bootstrap covariance matrix estimator $\Sigma^*_{N,k}$ is defined as Σ_N in (2.6), but with the bootstrap sample in place of the original sample and $\theta^*_{N,k}$ in place of $\widehat{\theta}_N$.

The k-step bootstrap t and Wald statistics, $T^*_{N,k}(\widehat{\theta}_{N,r})$ and $\mathcal{W}^*_{N,k}(\widehat{\beta}_N)$, are defined as in (3.2), but with θ^*_N and Σ^*_N replaced by $\theta^*_{N,k}$ and $\Sigma^*_{N,k}$, respectively. Let $z^*_{|T|,k,\alpha}$, $z^*_{T,k,\alpha}$, and $z^*_{\mathcal{W},k,\alpha}$ denote the $1-\alpha$ quantiles of $|T^*_{N,k}(\widehat{\theta}_{N,r})|$, $T^*_{N,k}(\widehat{\theta}_{N,r})$, and $\mathcal{W}^*_{N,k}(\widehat{\beta}_N)$, respectively (whose precise definitions are analogous to that of $z^*_{|T|,\alpha}$ given earlier.)

The k-step bootstrap CIs and confidence regions, denoted as $\text{CI}_{\text{SYM},k}$, $\text{CI}_{\text{ET},k}$, $\text{CI}_{\text{UP},k}$, and CR_k, are defined as in (3.3)–(3.6), but with $z^*_{|T|,\alpha}$, $z^*_{T,\alpha}$, and $z^*_{\mathcal{W},\alpha}$ replaced by $z^*_{|T|,k,\alpha}$, $z^*_{T,k,\alpha}$, and $z^*_{\mathcal{W},k,\alpha}$ respectively.

The matrices $\{Q^*_{N,j-1} : j = 1, \ldots, k\}$ are assumed to satisfy the following assumption.

Assumption 7.1. *The matrices* $\{Q^*_{N,j-1} : j = 1, \ldots, k\}$ *satisfy the following condition: for some sequence of nonnegative constants* $\{\psi_N : N \geq 1\}$ *with*

$\lim_{N\to\infty}\psi_N = 0$ *and for all* $\varepsilon > 0$,

$$\sup_{\theta_0\in\Theta_1} P^*_{\theta_0}(||Q^*_{N,j-1} - D^*_N(\theta^*_{N,j-1})|| > \psi_N) = o(N^{-a}) \quad \textit{for } j = 1, \ldots, k,$$

where $P^*_{\theta_0}$ *denotes the probability when the bootstrap sample is generated using the parameter* θ_0 *rather than* $\widehat{\theta}_N$, *and the initial estimator* $\theta^*_{N,0}$ *is* θ_0 *rather than* $\widehat{\theta}_N$.

We now give sufficient conditions for Assumption 7.1 for the NR, default NR, line-search NR, and GN choices of $Q^*_{N,j-1}$.

Lemma 7.1. *Suppose Assumptions* 2.1 *and* 4.1–4.3 *hold for some* $a \geq 0$ *with* $2a$ *an integer. Then Assumption* 7.1 *holds with* $\psi_N = 0$ *for all* N *for the* NR, *default* NR, *and line-search* NR *choices of* $Q^*_{N,j-1}$ *for* $j = 1, \ldots, k$. *In addition, Assumption* 7.1 *holds with* $\psi_N = N^{-1/2}\ln(N)$ *for the* GN *choice of* $Q^*_{N,j-1}$ *for* $j = 1, \ldots, k$ *provided Assumptions* 2.1 *and* 4.3 *hold with the elements of* $\Delta(\widetilde{W}_i, \theta)$ *(defined in* (7.4)*) added to* $f(\widetilde{W}_i, \theta)$ *and the function* $\Delta(\cdot, \cdot)$ *satisfies:* (i) $E_{\theta_0}(\Delta(\widetilde{W}_i, \theta_0) - (\partial/\partial\theta')g(\widetilde{W}_i, \theta_0)) = 0$ *for all* $i \geq 1$ *and all* $\theta_0 \in \Theta_1$, (ii) $\Delta(\widetilde{W}_i, \theta)$ *is continuously differentiable with respect to* θ *on* Θ_2, (iii) $\sup_{\theta_0\in\Theta_1, i\geq 1} E_{\theta_0}||\Delta(\widetilde{W}_i, \theta_0) - (\partial/\partial\theta')g(\widetilde{W}_i, \theta_0)||^{2a+3} < \infty$, *and* (iv) $\sup_{\theta_0\in\Theta_1, i\geq 1} E_{\theta_0}\sup_{\theta\in B(\theta_0,\varepsilon)} ||(\partial/\partial\theta_u)(\Delta(\widetilde{W}_i, \theta) - (\partial/\partial\theta')g(\widetilde{W}_i, \theta))||^{q_2} < \infty$ *for all* $u = 1, \ldots, L_\theta$, *for some* $\varepsilon > 0$, *and for* $q_2 = \max\{2a+1, 2\}$, *where* $B(\theta_0, \varepsilon)$ *denotes an open ball at* θ_0 *of radius* ε.

Comment. Conditions (ii)–(iv) of Lemma 7.1 hold for the outer-product GN matrix of (7.6) by Assumption 4.2.

The higher-order asymptotic equivalence of the k-step and standard bootstrap statistics is established in parts (a) and (b) of Theorem 7.1. Part (b) gives conditions under which the Kolmogorov distances (i.e., the sup norms of the differences between the distribution functions) between $N^{1/2}(\theta^*_{N,k} - \widehat{\theta}_N)$ and $N^{1/2}(\theta^*_N - \widehat{\theta}_N)$, $T^*_{N,k}(\widehat{\theta}_{N,r})$ and $T^*_N(\widehat{\theta}_{N,r})$, and $\mathcal{W}^*_{N,k}(\widehat{\beta}_N)$ and $\mathcal{W}^*_N(\widehat{\beta}_N)$, respectively, are $o(N^{-a})$ for some $a \geq 0$.

In part (a) of the theorem, the difference between the k-step bootstrap estimator and the standard ML bootstrap estimator is shown to be of greater magnitude than $\mu_{N,k}$ with bootstrap probability $o(N^{-a})$, except, on a set with probability $o(N^{-a})$, where

$$\mu_{N,k} = \begin{cases} N^{-2^{k-1}}\ln^{2^k}(N) & \text{for NR, default NR,} \\ & \text{and line-search NR matrices} \\ N^{-(k+1)/2}\ln^{k+1}(N) & \text{for GN matrices.} \end{cases} \tag{7.8}$$

Thus, for the NR procedures the difference decreases very quickly as k increases, and for the GN procedure the difference decreases more slowly as k increases.

More generally, for ψ_N as in Assumption 7.1, $\mu_{N,k}$ is defined by

$$\mu_{N,k} = \max_{j=0,\ldots,k} N^{-2^{k-j-1}} \ln^{2^{k-j}}(N)\psi_N^j. \tag{7.9}$$

The key condition in part (b) of Theorem 7.1 is

$$\mu_{N,k} = o\left(N^{-(a+1/2)}\right), \tag{7.10}$$

where $2a$ is a nonnegative integer. Given this condition, the Kolmogorov distances between the k-step and bootstrap statistics are $o(N^{-a})$, except on a set with probability $o(N^{-a})$.

If Assumption 7.1 holds with $\psi_N = 0$, as it does for the NR, default NR, and line-search NR procedures, then (7.10) holds if

$$2^k \geq 2a + 2, \tag{7.11}$$

where $2a$ is an integer. Thus, for $k = 1$, we have $a = 0$; for $k = 2$, we have $a = 1$; for $k = 3$, we have $a = 3$; for $k = 4$, we have $a = 7$; and so forth.

If Assumption 7.1 holds with $\psi_N = N^{-1/2}\ln(N)$, as it does for the GN procedure under the conditions in Lemma 7.1, then (7.10) holds if

$$k \geq 2a + 1, \tag{7.12}$$

where $2a$ is an integer. Thus, for $k = 1$, we have $a = 0$; for $k = 2$, we have $a = 1/2$; for $k = 3$, we have $a = 1$; for $k = 4$, we have $a = 3/2$; etc.

The aforementioned Theorem is as follows:

Theorem 7.1. *Suppose Assumptions* 2.1, 4.1–4.3, *and* 7.1 *hold for some* $a \geq 0$ *with* $2a$ *an integer in parts* (a) *and* (b).
(a) *Then, for all* $\varepsilon > 0$,

$$\sup_{\theta_0\in\Theta_0} P_{\theta_0}\left(P^*_{\widehat{\theta}_N}\left(\| \theta^*_{N,k} - \theta^*_N \| > \mu_{N,k}\right) > N^{-a}\varepsilon\right) = o(N^{-a}),$$

$$\sup_{\theta_0\in\Theta_0} P_{\theta_0}\left(P^*_{\widehat{\theta}_N}(|T^*_{N,k}(\widehat{\theta}_{N,r}) - T^*_N(\widehat{\theta}_{N,r})| > N^{1/2}\mu_{N,k}) > N^{-a}\varepsilon\right) = o(N^{-a}),$$

and

$$\sup_{\theta_0\in\Theta_0} P_{\theta_0}\left(P^*_{\widehat{\theta}_N}(|\mathcal{W}^*_{N,k}(\widehat{\beta}_N) - \mathcal{W}^*_N(\widehat{\beta}_N)| > N^{1/2}\mu_{N,k}) > N^{-a}\varepsilon\right) = o(N^{-a}).$$

(b) *Suppose* $\mu_{N,k} = o(N^{-(a+1/2)})$. *Then, for all* $\varepsilon > 0$,

$$\sup_{\theta_0\in\Theta_0} P_{\theta_0}\Bigg(\sup_{z\in R^{L_\theta}} \Big| P^*_{\widehat{\theta}_N}(N^{1/2}(\theta^*_{N,k} - \widehat{\theta}_N) \leq z)$$
$$- P^*_{\widehat{\theta}_N}(N^{1/2}(\theta^*_N - \widehat{\theta}_N) \leq z)\Big| > N^{-a}\varepsilon\Bigg) = o(N^{-a}),$$

$$\sup_{\theta_0\in\Theta_0} P_{\theta_0}\left(\sup_{z\in R}\left|P^*_{\widehat{\theta}_N}(T^*_{N,k}(\widehat{\theta}_{N,r}) \leq z) - P^*_{\widehat{\theta}_N}(T^*_N(\widehat{\theta}_{N,r}) \leq z)\right| > N^{-a}\varepsilon\right)$$
$$= o(N^{-a}), \quad \textit{and}$$

$$\sup_{\theta_0 \in \Theta_0} P_{\theta_0}\left(\sup_{z \in R} \left| P^*_{\widehat{\theta}_N}(\mathcal{W}^*_{N,k}(\widehat{\beta}_N) \leq z) - P^*_{\widehat{\theta}_N}(\mathcal{W}^*_N(\widehat{\beta}_N) \leq z) \right| > N^{-a}\varepsilon \right)$$
$$= o(N^{-a}).$$

We use the results of Theorem 7.1 to show that the errors in coverage probability of the k-step bootstrap CIs are the same as those of the standard bootstrap CIs given in Theorem 6.1. In consequence, one can obtain higher-order improvements using the bootstrap without doing the nonlinear optimization necessary to compute the standard bootstrap ML estimator.

Theorem 7.2. (a) *Suppose Assumptions* 2.1, 4.1–4.3, *and* 7.1 *hold with* $a = 2$ *and* $\mu_{N,k} = o(N^{-5/2})$. *Then* $\sup_{\theta_0 \in \Theta_0} |P_{\theta_0}(\theta_0 \in CI_{SYM,k}) - (1-\alpha)| = O(N^{-2})$.
(b) *Suppose Assumptions* 2.1, 4.1–4.3, *and* 7.1 *hold with* $a = 1$ *and* $\mu_{N,k} = o(N^{-3/2})$. *Then* $\sup_{\theta_0 \in \Theta_0} |P_{\theta_0}(\theta_0 \in \mathrm{CI}_{\mathrm{ET},k}) - (1-\alpha)| = o(N^{-1}\ln(N))$ *and* $\sup_{\theta_0 \in \Theta_0} |P_{\theta_0}(\theta_0 \in \mathrm{CI}_{\mathrm{UP},k}) - (1-\alpha)| = o(N^{-1}\ln(N))$.
(c) *Suppose Assumptions* 2.1, 4.1–4.3, *and* 7.1 *hold with* $a = 3/2$ *and* $\mu_{N,k} = o(N^{-2})$. *Then,* $\sup_{\theta_0 \in \Theta_0} |P_{\theta_0}(\theta_0 \in \mathrm{CR}_k) - (1-\alpha)| = o(N^{-3/2}\ln(N))$.

Comment. For the NR, default NR, and line-search NR procedures, the condition $\mu_{N,k} = o(N^{-5/2})$ in part (a) is satisfied if $k \geq 3$; the condition $\mu_{N,k} = o(N^{-3/2})$ in part (b) is satisfied if $k \geq 2$; and the condition $\mu_{N,k} = o(N^{-5/2})$ in part (c) is satisfied if $k \geq 3$. For the GN procedure, the condition $\mu_{N,k} = o(N^{-5/2})$ in part (a) is satisfied if $k \geq 5$; the condition $\mu_{N,k} = o(N^{-3/2})$ in part (b) is satisfied if $k \geq 3$; and the condition $\mu_{N,k} = o(N^{-5/2})$ in part (c) is satisfied if $k \geq 4$. Hence, the k-step NR bootstrap procedures require fewer steps than the k-step GN bootstrap procedure to achieve the same higher-order improvements as obtained by the standard parametric bootstrap. But, with NR or GN k-step bootstrap procedures, the number of steps does not need to be very large.

8. MONTE CARLO SIMULATIONS

In this section, we compare the performance of standard delta method CIs, symmetric percentile t parametric bootstrap CIs, and equal-tailed percentile t parametric bootstrap CIs using Monte Carlo simulation. We consider a stationary Gaussian AR(2) model because it is a well-known model, the standard delta method is known to perform poorly when the sum of the AR coefficients is close to 1, and the parameter estimates are available in closed form, which greatly speeds computation.

Other methods of constructing CIs for the model considered here are given in Stock (1991), Andrews and Chen (1994), Hansen (1999), and Romano and Wolf (2001). We do not provide results for these methods.

8.1. Experimental Design

The model we consider is given by

$$
\begin{aligned}
Y_i &= \mu + \rho_1 Y_{i-1} + \rho_2 Y_{i-2} + \sigma U_i \qquad \text{for } i = 3, \ldots, n,\\
Y_1 &= \left(\frac{1}{1-\rho_1^2-\rho_2^2-2\rho_1^2\rho_2/(1-\rho_2)}\right)^{1/2} U_1,\\
Y_2 &= \frac{\rho_1}{1-\rho_2} Y_1 + \left(\frac{1-\rho_1^2/(1-\rho_2)^2}{1-\rho_1^2-\rho_2^2-2\rho_1^2\rho_2/(1-\rho_2)}\right)^{1/2} U_2, \quad \text{and}\\
U_i &= \text{i.i.d. } N(0,1) \qquad \text{for } i = 1, \ldots, n.
\end{aligned}
\tag{8.1}
$$

As defined, this model is a stationary Gaussian AR(2) model. The model can also be defined in augmented Dickey–Fuller form as

$$
\begin{aligned}
Y_i &= \mu + \alpha Y_{i-1} - \rho_2 \Delta Y_{i-1} + \sigma U_i \quad \text{for } i = 3, \ldots, n, \quad \text{where}\\
\alpha &= \rho_1 + \rho_2,\\
\Delta Y_{i-1} &= Y_{i-1} - Y_{i-2},
\end{aligned}
\tag{8.2}
$$

and (Y_1, Y_2, U_i) are as in (8.1).

In terms of the notation of Section 3, $\kappa = 2$, $N = n - 2$, $W_i = Y_i$ for $i = 1, \ldots, n$, $\widetilde{W}_i = (Y_{i+2}, Y_{i+1}, Y_i)'$ for $i = 1, \ldots, N$, and $\theta = (\mu, \rho_1, \rho_2, \sigma^2)'$. The normalized negative log-likelihood of $\{\widetilde{W}_i : 1 \le i \le N\}$ (conditional on Y_1 and Y_2) is

$$
\rho_N(\theta) = \frac{1}{2}\log(2\pi) + \frac{1}{2}\log(\sigma^2) + \frac{1}{2}\sum_{i=1}^{N}(Y_{i+2} - \mu - \rho_1 Y_{i+1} - \rho_2 Y_i)^2.
\tag{8.3}
$$

The parameter space for θ is $R^3 \times R^+$. In consequence, the ML estimators of μ, ρ_1, and ρ_2, denoted by $\widehat{\mu}$, $\widehat{\rho}_1$, and $\widehat{\rho}_2$, respectively, are the least-squares estimators from the regression of Y_{i+2} on 1, Y_{i+1}, and Y_i for $i = 1, \ldots, N$. The ML estimator, $\widehat{\alpha}$, of α is $\widehat{\rho}_1 + \widehat{\rho}_2$. The ML estimator of σ^2 is

$$
\widehat{\sigma}^2 = \frac{1}{N}\sum_{i=1}^{N}(Y_{i+2} - \widehat{\mu} - \widehat{\rho}_1 Y_{i+1} - \widehat{\rho}_2 Y_i)^2.
\tag{8.4}
$$

Researchers are often interested in the persistence of a time series. This can be measured by the impulse response function (IRF). The IRF traces out the effect of an increase in the innovation σU_i by a unit quantity on the values Y_{i+h}, denoted by IRF(h), for $h = 0, 1, \ldots$ and $i \ge 3$. The cumulative impulse response (CIR), defined by CIR $= \sum_{h=0}^{\infty} \text{IRF}(h)$, provides a convenient scalar summary measure of the persistence of the time series. In the model of (8.1), the CIR equals $1/(1-\alpha)$. The ML estimator of CIR is $\widehat{\text{CIR}} = 1/(1-\widehat{\alpha})$. (For further discussion of CIR, see Andrews and Chen 1994).

In the simulation experiment, we consider CIs for the CIR, as well as for the parameters α, ρ_1, and ρ_2. Note that the CIR only depends on the parameter

α, so α also is a useful measure of persistence. (The spectrum of $\{Y_i : i \geq 1\}$ at zero equals $\sigma^2/(1-\alpha)^2$ and, hence, is another measure of persistence that depends on the regression coefficients only through α.)

The standard delta method CI for CIR with nominal coverage probability $100(1-\tau)\%$ is given by

$$\mathrm{CI}_{\mathrm{CIR}} = \left[\widehat{\mathrm{CIR}} - \frac{\widehat{\sigma}_{\mathrm{CIR}} z_{1-\tau/2}}{\sqrt{N}}, \ \widehat{\mathrm{CIR}} + \frac{\widehat{\sigma}_{\mathrm{CIR}} z_{1-\tau/2}}{\sqrt{N}}\right], \quad \text{where}$$
$$\widehat{\sigma}^2_{\mathrm{CIR}} = \widehat{\sigma}^2_{\alpha}/(1-\widehat{\alpha})^4, \tag{8.5}$$

and $\widehat{\sigma}^2_{\alpha}$ equals $\widehat{\sigma}^2$ times the $(2,2)$ element of the inverse of $N^{-1}\sum_{i=1}^{N}(1, Y_{i-1}, \Delta Y_{i-1}) \times (1, Y_{i-1}, \Delta Y_{i-1})'$. The delta method CIs for α, ρ_1, and ρ_2, denoted by CI_{α}, CI_{ρ_1}, and CI_{ρ_2}, respectively, are defined analogously with $\widehat{\sigma}_{\mathrm{CIR}}$ replaced by $\widehat{\sigma}_{\alpha}$, $\widehat{\sigma}_{\rho_1}$, and $\widehat{\sigma}_{\rho_2}$, where $\widehat{\sigma}^2_{\rho_1}$ and $\widehat{\sigma}^2_{\rho_2}$ equal $\widehat{\sigma}^2$ times the $(2,2)$ and $(3,3)$ elements, respectively, of the inverse of $N^{-1}\sum_{i=1}^{N}(1, Y_{i-1}, Y_{i-2})(1, Y_{i-1}, Y_{i-2})'$.

The symmetric and equal-tailed parametric bootstrap CIs for CIR, α, ρ_1, and ρ_2 are as defined in (3.3) and (3.4) of Section 3.[4]

Because the ML estimators of CIR, α, ρ_1, and ρ_2 are available in closed form, we do not consider k-step bootstrap CIs.

An alternative to the parametric bootstrap that can be applied in the AR(2) model above is the residual-based (RB) bootstrap. The RB bootstrap is the same as the parametric bootstrap except that the distribution of the bootstrap errors is given by the empirical distribution of the residuals from the original sample, rather than by the normal distribution. Symmetric and equal-tailed RB bootstrap CIs for CIR, α, ρ_1, and ρ_2 are defined just as with the parametric bootstrap but with the bootstrap errors being i.i.d. with distribution given by the empirical distribution of the residuals. We compute RB bootstrap CIs and compare them to the parametric bootstrap CIs. We do not consider subsampling confidence intervals. These confidence intervals do not provide higher-order improvements.

We report coverage probabilities for 95% CIs for each of the three types of CI, namely, delta method, symmetric bootstrap, and equal-tailed bootstrap, for each of the four parameters, namely, CIR, α, ρ_1, and ρ_2. In addition, for the CIs for CIR, we report the probabilities that the CIs miss the true value to the left

[4] Stationarity of an AR(2) process with AR parameters (ρ_1, ρ_2) requires that (i) $-1 < \rho_2 < 1$, (ii) $\rho_1 + \rho_2 < 1$, and (iii) $\rho_2 - \rho_1 < 1$. To ensure that the parametric bootstrap distribution of the AR(2) process is stationary, we adjust the LS estimators $(\widehat{\rho}_1, \widehat{\rho}_2)$ (only when generating bootstrap samples and not in the expressions for the CIs given in (3.3) and (3.4)), so that they necessarily satisfy the stationarity conditions. In particular, the parametric bootstrap distribution is based on the estimators $(\widetilde{\rho}_1, \widetilde{\rho}_2)$, where $\widetilde{\rho}_2 = sgn(\widehat{\rho}_2)\min\{|\widehat{\rho}_2|, .98\}$ and $\widetilde{\rho}_1 = 1(\widehat{\rho}_1 \geq 0)\min\{\widehat{\rho}_1, .98 - \widetilde{\rho}_2\} + 1(\widehat{\rho}_1 < 0)\min\{\widehat{\rho}_1, \widetilde{\rho}_2 - .98\}$. These alterations have no effect on the asymptotic properties of the bootstrap CIs (for the true parameter values that we consider) because $\widetilde{\rho}_1 = \widehat{\rho}_1$ and $\widetilde{\rho}_2 = \widehat{\rho}_2$ with probability that approaches 1 at a sufficiently fast rate as $N \to \infty$. In fact, these adjustments very rarely come into play in the simulations and, hence, have no noticeable impact on the results.

Table 9.1. *Coverage probabilities of nominal 95% confidence intervals for the cumulative impulse response,* $1/(1-\alpha)$, *for AR(2) processes, N(0, 1) Errors, and* $N = 100$

(ρ_1, ρ_2)	α	Type of confidence interval	Coverage probability	Probability CI misses left	Probability CI misses right	Average length of CI
(1.4, −.5)	.9	Delta	.802	.198	.000	11.4
		Sym boot	.909	.091	.000	24.5
		ET boot	.886	.058	.056	18.1
(.9, 0)	.9	Delta	.714	.286	.000	15.0
		Sym boot	.876	.124	.000	50.3
		ET boot	.847	.087	.067	34.8
(0, .9)	.9	Delta	.591	.409	.000	218
		Sym boot	.822	.178	.000	4018
		ET boot	.794	.131	.074	2599
(1.0, −.5)	.5	Delta	.920	.080	.001	1.11
		Sym boot	.945	.055	.000	1.35
		ET boot	.930	.033	.038	1.21
(.5, 0)	.5	Delta	.880	.121	.000	1.52
		Sym boot	.929	.071	.000	2.19
		ET boot	.915	.041	.045	1.81
(0, .5)	.5	Delta	.855	.145	.000	1.82
		Sym boot	.921	.079	.000	2.99
		ET boot	.905	.048	.046	2.36
(0, −.5)	−.5	Delta	.941	.053	.007	.215
		Sym boot	.947	.050	.003	.223
		ET boot	.937	.033	.030	.220
(−.5, 0)	−.5	Delta	.931	.067	.002	.301
		Sym boot	.944	.057	.000	.336
		ET boot	.933	.035	.033	.316
(−1.0, −.5)	−1.5	Delta	.947	.042	.011	.101
		Sym boot	.949	.043	.008	.101
		ET boot	.938	.031	.031	.101

and to the right and the average length of the CIs. We report results for sample size $N = 100$, as well as some results for $N = 50$.

We consider nine different parameter combinations for ρ_1 and ρ_2, which correspond to four different values of α, namely, .9, .5, −.5, and −1.5; see Table 9.1. These parameter combinations have been chosen because they cover a broad spectrum of different performances of the CIs considered. All results reported are invariant to the values of μ and σ^2, and so we set $\mu = 0$ and $\sigma^2 = 1$ without loss of generality.

To assess the robustness of the parametric bootstrap CIs to the distribution of the innovation U_i, we also consider the case where U_i has a t distribution with five degrees of freedom, which has fat tails, and when it has a chi-squared distribution with one degree of freedom (shifted to have mean zero), which has considerable skewness.

All results are based on $R = 10{,}000$ Monte Carlo repetitions and $B = 5199$ bootstrap repetitions. With this number of Monte Carlo repetitions, the standard deviation of the reported coverage probabilities is .0022.

8.2. Simulation Results

Table 9.1 reports results for CIs for CIR for all nine (ρ_1, ρ_2) parameter combinations and $N = 100$. Several features of the results are immediately apparent. First, all three types of CIs perform most poorly when $\alpha = .9$. They perform better when $\alpha = .5$ and best when $\alpha = -.5$ or -1.5.

Second, the error that the CIs make in almost all cases is undercoverage, not overcoverage.

Third, both bootstrap CIs perform better than the delta method CIs in terms of coverage probability whenever $\alpha = .9, .5$, or $-.5$, and are comparable when $\alpha = -1.5$. This is consistent with the asymptotic results of Section 6, which show that the error in coverage probability of the bootstrap CIs converges to zero at a faster rate than for the delta method CIs. When $\alpha = .9$ or $.5$, the bootstrap CIs perform substantially better than the delta method CIs. For example, when $(\rho_1, \rho_2) = (.9, 0)$, the coverage probabilities of nominal 95% delta, symmetric bootstrap, and equal-tailed bootstrap CIs are .71, .88, and .85, respectively. In this case and others in which the delta method performs quite poorly, the bootstrap CIs perform much better. But, they do not eliminate undercoverage.

Fourth, the symmetric bootstrap CIs perform better in terms of coverage probability than the equal-tailed bootstrap CIs in almost all cases. Especially when $\alpha = .9$, the difference is noticeable. This also is consistent with the asymptotic results of Section 6, which show that the error in coverage probability of the symmetric bootstrap CIs converges to zero at a faster rate than for the equal-tailed bootstrap CIs.

Fifth, the center of the delta method and symmetric bootstrap CIs is significantly smaller than the true value in all cases. This is reflected in the fact that the probability that these CIs miss to the right is essentially zero in all cases. On the other hand, the equal-tailed bootstrap CIs are fairly well centered around the true parameter values. The probability that these CIs miss to the left is roughly the same as the probability that they miss to the right, in most cases.

Sixth, the average length of the CIs mirrors their coverage probabilities. The delta method CIs are shorter than the bootstrap CIs in all cases except when $\alpha = -1.5$. In these cases, they are too short, which causes their coverage probabilities to be too low. Similarly, the equal-tailed bootstrap CIs are shorter than the symmetric bootstrap CIs in those cases in which the former exhibit undercoverage, which occurs in all cases except when $\alpha = -1.5$.

Overall, it is clear that both bootstrap CIs outperform the delta method CI. The comparison between the two bootstrap CIs is not as clear-cut. The

Table 9.2. *Coverage probabilities of nominal 95% Confidence intervals for α, ρ_1, and ρ_2 for AR(2) processes, N(0, 1) errors, and* $N = 100$

(ρ_1, ρ_2)	α	Type of confidence interval	Coverage probability of confidence interval for α	ρ_1	ρ_2
(1.4, −.5)	.9	Delta	.926	.933	.945
		Sym boot	.943	.947	.946
		ET boot	.930	.946	.939
(.9, 0)	.9	Delta	.907	.930	.939
		Sym boot	.934	.946	.944
		ET boot	.920	.947	.936
(0, .9)	.9	Delta	.880	.908	.853
		Sym boot	.918	.933	.916
		ET boot	.907	.932	.912
(1.0, −.5)	.5	Delta	.943	.939	.950
		Sym boot	.951	.946	.952
		ET boot	.943	.946	.945
(.5, 0)	.5	Delta	.937	.937	.943
		Sym boot	.948	.946	.948
		ET boot	.938	.945	.943
(0, .5)	.5	Delta	.933	.934	.927
		Sym boot	.944	.945	.944
		ET boot	.934	.942	.937
(0, −.5)	−.5	Delta	.945	.942	.949
		Sym boot	.948	.946	.951
		ET boot	.945	.944	.945
(−.5, 0)	−.5	Delta	.942	.942	.944
		Sym boot	.947	.947	.948
		ET boot	.942	.944	.943
(−1.0, −.5)	−1.5	Delta	.945	.942	.949
		Sym boot	.948	.947	.951
		ET boot	.943	.944	.945

symmetric bootstrap CIs outperform the equal-tailed bootstrap CIs in terms of coverage probability. But the equal-tailed bootstrap CIs are much better centered. Depending upon how one weights these two characteristics of the CIs, one might prefer one bootstrap CI or the other.

Table 9.2 reports coverage probabilities for CIs for α, ρ_1, and ρ_2 for the same cases as in Table 9.1. The results for α are quite similar to those for CIR in a qualitative sense. In particular, the delta method CIs undercover by more than the bootstrap CIs and the equal-tailed bootstrap CIs undercover by more than the symmetric bootstrap CIs. The main difference is that all three types of CIs perform much better in terms of the amount of undercoverage. For example, the coverage probabilities for $(\rho_1, \rho_2) = (.9, 0)$ are .91, .93, and .92 for the delta, symmetric bootstrap, and equal-tailed bootstrap CIs, respectively. These probabilities are much closer to .95 than the probabilities listed above for the CIR CIs.

Note that one could construct a CI for CIR by transforming the CI for α, because CIR is a monotone transform of α. (That is, the lower endpoint of such a CI for CIR is given by $1/(1 - \text{LE}_\alpha)$, where LE_α is the lower endpoint of the CI for α, and the upper endpoint is defined analogously.) The resulting CI for CIR has the same coverage probability as the CI for α.

The results of Table 9.2 for ρ_1 and ρ_2 are better than those for α for all three types of CIs. That is, the magnitudes of undercoverage are smaller. In fact, in a few cases there is a small amount of overcoverage. In the cases where the delta method CIs undercover, the bootstrap CIs undercover by a smaller amount or by none at all. Hence, the bootstrap CIs for ρ_1 and ρ_2 provide an improvement over those of the delta method.

Tables 9.1 and 9.2 do not report results for RB bootstrap CIs because they differ very little from the parametric bootstrap results. In most cases, the differences in coverage probabilities are .001 or less. In a few cases, the differences are .002.

Tables 9.3 and 9.4 report coverage probability results for the cases of t_5 errors, and χ_1^2 errors, respectively. These results show that the Gaussian parametric bootstrap CIs still outperform the delta method CIs even when the errors are not Gaussian. In fact, the most salient feature of the results in Tables 9.3 and 9.4 is how similar they are to the results when the errors are Gaussian.

Table 9.3 does not report results for RB bootstrap CIs because, as in the normal error case, the results are quite similar to those for the parametric bootstrap. The differences between the two for t_5 errors are slightly larger than for $N(0, 1)$ errors, but are still small in most cases. There are a few cases where the differences are as large as .004, but in most cases the differences are .002 or less. The coverage probabilities of the parametric bootstrap CIs are almost always the same as, or closer to, the nominal value .95 than those of the RB bootstrap CIs. This holds because it is almost always the case that the parametric bootstrap CIs have coverage probabilities that are as high or higher than those of the RB bootstrap CIs, and both bootstrap CIs usually exhibit undercoverage. These results indicate that the parametric bootstrap CIs are fairly robust to the existence of fat-tailed t_5 errors.

Table 9.4 lists the coverage probabilities of the RB bootstrap CIs for the case of χ_1^2 errors, which are skewed. The differences in coverage probabilities between the parametric and RB bootstrap CIs are noticeably larger than in the $N(0, 1)$ and the t_5 error cases. The differences are as large as .021 but, usually, are smaller. In almost all cases, the coverage probabilities of the parametric bootstrap CIs exceed those of the RB bootstrap CIs. Thus, the parametric bootstrap CIs are more conservative. In roughly half the cases, the parametric bootstrap coverage probabilities are closer to .95 than the RB bootstrap coverage probabilities. Hence, in an overall sense, the parametric bootstrap performs at

Table 9.3. *Coverage probabilities of nominal 95% confidence intervals for* $1/(1-\alpha)$, α, ρ_1, *and* ρ_2 *for AR(2) processes,* t_5 *errors, and* $N = 100$

(ρ_1, ρ_2)	α	Type of confidence interval	Coverage probabilities of confidence intervals for $1/(1-\alpha)$	α	ρ_1	ρ_2	Average length of CI for $1/(1-\alpha)$
(1.4, −.5)	.9	Delta	.805	.917	.941	.950	11.3
		Sym boot	.910	.943	.951	.953	24.1
		ET boot	.890	.932	.951	.945	17.8
(.9, 0)	.9	Delta	.713	.908	.934	.947	14.9
		Sym boot	.874	.931	.950	.952	50.4
		ET boot	.848	.920	.952	.946	34.9
(0, .9)	.9	Delta	.592	.879	.908	.850	328
		Sym boot	.824	.916	.932	.913	6120
		ET boot	.794	.906	.934	.917	3916
(1.0, −.5)	.5	Delta	.914	.943	.943	.953	1.10
		Sym boot	.938	.950	.950	.954	1.34
		ET boot	.934	.948	.948	.949	1.20
(.5, 0)	.5	Delta	.883	.939	.942	.948	1.51
		Sym boot	.929	.947	.949	.954	2.17
		ET boot	.920	.940	.948	.946	1.80
(0, .5)	.5	Delta	.854	.932	.941	.934	1.81
		Sym boot	.922	.945	.949	.948	2.96
		ET boot	.906	.936	.946	.943	2.34
(0, −.5)	−.5	Delta	.941	.948	.947	.954	.215
		Sym boot	.946	.952	.951	.955	.223
		ET boot	.940	.947	.950	.949	.219
(−.5, 0)	−.5	Delta	.932	.945	.944	.944	.300
		Sym boot	.944	.949	.950	.950	.334
		ET boot	.935	.946	.947	.947	.315
(−1.0, −.5)	−1.5	Delta	.949	.948	.948	.950	.100
		Sym boot	.951	.951	.951	.952	.101
		ET boot	.941	.946	.948	.946	.101

least as well as the RB bootstrap in the case of (skewed) χ^2_1 errors (at least for sample size 100).

Table 9.5 presents results for the case of sample size $N = 50$ and N(0, 1) errors. Comparing the results to those of Tables 9.1 and 9.2 for $N = 100$, it is found that the results are what one would expect. The magnitudes of undercoverage of the CIs and the average lengths of the CIs are larger when $N = 50$ than when $N = 100$. The comparative performances of the delta, symmetric parametric bootstrap, and equal-tailed parametric bootstrap CIs for $N = 50$ are quite similar to those for $N = 100$. The symmetric parametric bootstrap CIs outperform the delta method CIs in terms of coverage probabilities in all cases. The equal-tailed parametric bootstrap CIs outperform the delta method CIs in terms of coverage probabilities in most cases.

Table 9.4. *Coverage probabilities of nominal 95% confidence intervals for* $1/(1-\alpha)$, α, ρ_1, *and* ρ_2 *for AR(2) processes,* χ_1^2 *errors, and* $N = 100$

(ρ_1, ρ_2)	α	Type of confidence interval	Coverage probabilities of confidence intervals for $1/(1-\alpha)$	α	ρ_1	ρ_2	Average length of CI for $1/(1-\alpha)$
(1.4, −.5)	.9	Delta	.814	.939	.952	.960	11.5
		Sym boot	.925	.954	.962	.962	24.8
		ET boot	.900	.941	.960	.957	18.3
		Sym RB boot	.912	.945	.953	.955	23.1
		ET RB boot	.889	.928	.949	.942	17.0
(.9, 0)	.9	Delta	.714	.918	.950	.949	53.8
		Sym boot	.887	.944	.963	.955	522
		ET boot	.862	.929	.958	.953	342
		Sym RB boot	.870	.930	.954	.950	539
		ET RB boot	.844	.916	.954	.948	344
(0, .9)	.9	Delta	.587	.884	.915	.860	205
		Sym boot	.826	.923	.938	.924	3760
		ET boot	.806	.917	.937	.923	2422
		Sym RB boot	.812	.906	.929	.908	3619
		ET RB boot	.788	.900	.928	.908	2340
(1.0, −.5)	.5	Delta	.933	.954	.956	.958	1.10
		Sym boot	.954	.960	.963	.960	1.34
		ET boot	.942	.954	.961	.955	1.20
		Sym RB boot	.943	.951	.954	.956	1.23
		ET RB boot	.934	.947	.951	.947	1.12
(.5, 0)	.5	Delta	.900	.953	.954	.951	1.51
		Sym boot	.952	.961	.961	.957	2.18
		ET boot	.936	.953	.957	.947	1.81
		Sym RB boot	.932	.949	.952	.952	1.96
		ET RB boot	.922	.940	.951	.944	1.65
(0, .5)	.5	Delta	.866	.951	.947	.949	1.81
		Sym boot	.941	.961	.957	.964	2.98
		ET boot	.925	.948	.951	.950	2.35
		Sym RB boot	.920	.951	.949	.953	2.69
		ET RB boot	.910	.936	.947	.941	2.14
(0, −.5)	−.5	Delta	.952	.956	.953	.952	.215
		Sym boot	.959	.958	.957	.953	.224
		ET boot	.947	.954	.956	.946	.220
		Sym RB boot	.952	.953	.952	.949	.214
		ET RB boot	.945	.952	.951	.948	.211
(−.5, 0)	−.5	Delta	.949	.955	.956	.957	.300
		Sym boot	.961	.960	.960	.962	.334
		ET boot	.946	.954	.957	.954	.315
		Sym RB boot	.952	.950	.954	.953	.305
		ET RB boot	.938	.946	.951	.948	.294
(−1.0, −.5)	−1.5	Delta	.955	.954	.952	.957	.100
		Sym boot	.959	.956	.955	.959	.101
		ET boot	.946	.951	.954	.954	.101
		Sym RB boot	.951	.951	.951	.953	.098
		ET RB boot	.944	.949	.953	.948	.097

Table 9.5. *Coverage probabilities for nominal 95% confidence intervals for* $1/(1-\alpha)$, α, ρ_1, *and* ρ_2 *for AR(2) processes with* $N = 50$

(ρ_1, ρ_2)	α	Type of confidence interval	Coverage probabilities of confidence intervals for $1/(1-\alpha)$	α	ρ_1	ρ_2	Average length of CI for $1/(1-\alpha)$
(1.4, −.5)	.9	Delta	.702	.902	.919	.941	17.7
		Sym boot	.874	.930	.947	.947	93.1
		ET boot	.839	.917	.946	.933	63.3
(.9, 0)	.9	Delta	.576	.870	.913	.935	84.0
		Sym boot	.811	.912	.943	.947	1647
		ET boot	.783	.909	.943	.930	1089
(0, .9)	.9	Delta	.429	.827	.874	.790	13,355
		Sym boot	.726	.889	.914	.890	495,905
		ET boot	.714	.897	.918	.902	322,854
(1.0, −.5)	.5	Delta	.883	.937	.927	.941	1.55
		Sym boot	.928	.948	.945	.946	2.28
		ET boot	.908	.934	.944	.932	1.88
(.5, 0)	.5	Delta	.830	.930	.928	.937	2.08
		Sym boot	.913	.947	.944	.948	3.87
		ET boot	.892	.931	.945	.935	2.94
(0, .5)	.5	Delta	.787	.919	.924	.912	2.44
		Sym boot	.898	.940	.944	.935	5.50
		ET boot	.871	.924	.940	.926	4.01
(0, −.5)	−.5	Delta	.932	.942	.936	.945	.307
		Sym boot	.938	.948	.946	.948	.340
		ET boot	.925	.940	.944	.937	.322
(−.5, 0)	−.5	Delta	.907	.936	.935	.936	.422
		Sym boot	.929	.945	.946	.946	.533
		ET boot	.917	.938	.941	.936	.468
(−1.0, −.5)	−1.5	Delta	.943	.939	.942	.942	.144
		Sym boot	.946	.944	.949	.946	.148
		ET boot	.924	.936	.946	.934	.146

ACKNOWLEDGMENTS

The author thanks Jong Kim, Jim Stock, and two referees for helpful comments and Carol Copeland for proofreading the manuscript. The author gratefully acknowledges the research support of the National Science Foundation via grant number SBR-9730277.

APPENDIX OF PROOFS

In the first subsection of this Appendix, we state Lemmas A.1–A.8 that are used in the proofs of Theorems 5.1, 6.1, 7.1, and 7.2 and Lemma 7.1. In the second subsection, we prove Theorems 5.1, 6.1, 7.1, and 7.2. In the third subsection, we prove Lemmas 7.1 and A.1–A.8.

Throughout the Appendix, a denotes a constant that satisfies $a \geq 0$ and $2a$ is an integer, C denotes a generic constant that may change from one equality or inequality to another, and $B(\theta, \varepsilon)$ denotes an open ball of radius $\varepsilon > 0$ centered at θ.

Lemmas

Lemma A.1. *Suppose* $\sup_{\theta_0 \in \Theta_0} P_{\theta_0}(\widehat{\theta}_N \notin B(\theta_0, \delta/2)) = o(N^{-a})$ *(for δ as in the definitions of Θ_1 and Θ_2 given in Section 4) and $\{\lambda_N(\theta) : N \geq 1\}$ is a sequence of (nonrandom) real functions on Θ_1 that satisfies* $\sup_{\theta \in \Theta_1} |\lambda_N(\theta)| = o(N^{-a})$. *Then, for all $\varepsilon > 0$,*

$$\sup_{\theta_0 \in \Theta_0} P_{\theta_0}(|\lambda_N(\widehat{\theta}_N)| > N^{-a}\varepsilon) = o(N^{-a}).$$

Comments. 1. This is a simple, but key, result that is used to obtain bootstrap results from results that hold for statistics based on the original sample uniformly over $\theta_0 \in \Theta_0$. For example, suppose we take $\lambda_N(\theta) = P^*_\theta(||V^*_N(\theta^*_N) - V(\theta)|| > \varepsilon)$ and we show that $\sup_{\theta_0 \in \Theta_1} P_{\theta_0}(||V_N(\widehat{\theta}_N) - V(\theta_0)|| > \varepsilon) = o(N^{-a})$ and $\sup_{\theta_0 \in \Theta_0} P_{\theta_0}(\widehat{\theta}_N \notin B(\theta_0, \delta/2)) = 1 - o(N^{-a})$. Note that $\lambda_N(\theta) = P_\theta(||V_N(\widehat{\theta}_N) - V(\theta)|| > \varepsilon)$ because the bootstrap distribution of $V^*_N(\theta^*_N)$ when the true parameter is θ is the same as the original sample distribution of $V_N(\widehat{\theta}_N)$ when the true parameter is θ. Hence, we know that $\sup_{\theta \in \Theta_1} |\lambda_N(\theta)| = o(N^{-a})$ and, by Lemma A.1, we conclude that $\sup_{\theta_0 \in \Theta_0} P_{\theta_0}(P^*_{\widehat{\theta}_N}(||V^*_N(\theta^*_N) - V(\widehat{\theta}_N)|| > \varepsilon) > N^{-a}\varepsilon) = o(N^{-a})$.

2. The condition of Lemma A.1 on $\widehat{\theta}_N$ is an implication of Lemma A.4.

Lemma A.2. *Suppose Assumption* 2.1 *holds.*
(a) *Let $m(\cdot, \theta_0)$ be a matrix-valued function that satisfies $E_{\theta_0} m(\widetilde{W}_i, \theta_0) = 0$ for all $i \geq 1$ and all $\theta_0 \in \Theta_1$ and* $\sup_{\theta_0 \in \Theta_1, i \geq 1} E_{\theta_0} ||m(\widetilde{W}_i, \theta_0)||^p < \infty$ *for $p > 2a$ and $p \geq 2$. Then, for all $\varepsilon > 0$,*

$$\sup_{\theta_0 \in \Theta_1} P_{\theta_0}\left(\left\|N^{-1}\sum_{i=1}^{N} m(\widetilde{W}_i, \theta_0)\right\| > \varepsilon\right) = o(N^{-a}).$$

(b) *Let $m(\cdot, \theta_0)$ be a matrix-valued function that satisfies* $\sup_{\theta_0 \in \Theta_1, i \geq 1} E_{\theta_0} ||m(\widetilde{W}_i, \theta_0)||^p < \infty$ *for $p > 2a$ and $p \geq 2$. Then, there exists $K < \infty$ such that*

$$\sup_{\theta_0 \in \Theta_1} P_{\theta_0}\left(\left\|N^{-1}\sum_{i=1}^{N} m(\widetilde{W}_i, \theta_0)\right\| > K\right) = o(N^{-a}).$$

(c) *Suppose Assumptions* 4.2b *and* 4.3 *also hold. Then, for all $\varepsilon > 0$,*

$$\sup_{\theta_0 \in \Theta_1} P_{\theta_0}\left(\left\|N^{-1/2}\sum_{i=1}^{N}(f(\widetilde{W}_i, \theta_0) - E_{\theta_0} f(\widetilde{W}_i, \theta_0))\right\| > \ln(N)\varepsilon\right) = o(N^{-a}).$$

Lemma A.3. *Suppose Assumptions* 2.1, 4.1, *and* 4.2 *hold. Let* $\overline{\theta}_N$ *denote an estimator that satisfies: For all* $\varepsilon > 0$, $\sup_{\theta_0 \in \Theta_1} P_{\theta_0}(||\overline{\theta}_N - \theta_0|| > \varepsilon) = o(N^{-a})$. *Then, for all* $\varepsilon > 0$ *and some* $K < \infty$,

$$\sup_{\theta_0 \in \Theta_1} P_{\theta_0}(||V_N(\overline{\theta}_N) - V(\theta_0)|| > \varepsilon) = o(N^{-a}),$$

$$\sup_{\theta_0 \in \Theta_1} P_{\theta_0}(||D_N(\overline{\theta}_N) - D(\theta_0)|| > \varepsilon) = o(N^{-a}),$$

$$\sup_{\theta_0 \in \Theta_1} P_{\theta_0}\left(\left\|\frac{\partial^3}{\partial\theta^3}\rho_N(\overline{\theta}_N)\right\| > K\right) = o(N^{-a}), \quad \textit{and}$$

$$\sup_{\theta_0 \in \Theta_1} P_{\theta_0}\left(\left\|N^{-1}\sum_{i=1}^{N} g(\widetilde{W}_i, \overline{\theta}_N)\right\| > \varepsilon\right) = o(N^{-a}).$$

Lemma A.4. *Suppose Assumptions* 2.1 *and* 4.1–4.3 *hold. Then, for all* $\varepsilon > 0$,

$$\sup_{\theta_0 \in \Theta_1} P_{\theta_0}\left(N^{1/2}||\widehat{\theta}_N - \theta_0|| > \ln(N)\varepsilon\right) = o(N^{-a}).$$

Lemma A.5. *Suppose Assumption 2.1 holds. Let* $\{A_N(\theta_0) : N \geq 1\}$ *be a sequence of* $L_A \times 1$ *random vectors with Edgeworth expansions for each* $\theta_0 \in \Theta_1$ *with coefficients of order* $O(1)$ *and remainders of order* $o(N^{-a})$ *both uniformly over* $\theta_0 \in \Theta_1$. *(That is, there exist polynomials* $\{\pi_{N,i}(z, \theta_0) : i = 1, \ldots, 2a\}$ *in* z *whose coefficients are* $O(1)$ *uniformly over* $\theta_0 \in \Theta_1$, *such that* $\sup_{\theta_0 \in \Theta_1} \sup_{B \in \mathcal{B}_{L_A}} |P_{\theta_0}(A_N(\theta_0) \in B) - \int_B (1 + \sum_{i=1}^{2a} N^{-i/2}\pi_{N,i}(z, \theta_0))\phi_{\Omega_N(\theta_0)}(z)\, dz| = o(N^{-a})$, *where* $\phi_{\Omega_N(\theta_0)}(z)$ *is the density function of a* $N(0, \Omega_N(\theta_0))$ *random variable,* $\Omega_N(\theta_0)$ *has eigenvalues that are bounded away from zero and infinity as* $N \to \infty$ *uniformly over* $\theta \in \Theta_1$, *and* $\mathcal{B}_{L_A}$ *denotes the class of all convex sets in* R^{L_A}.*) Let* $\{\xi_N(\theta_0) : N \geq 1\}$ *be a sequence of random vectors with* $\sup_{\theta_0 \in \Theta_1} P_{\theta_0}(||\xi_N(\theta_0)|| > \omega_N) = o(N^{-a})$ *for some constants* $\omega_N = o(N^{-a})$, *where* $\xi_N(\theta_0) \in R^{L_A}$. *Then,*

$$\sup_{\theta_0 \in \Theta_1} \sup_{B \in \mathcal{B}_{L_A}} |P_{\theta_0}(A_N(\theta_0) + \xi_N(\theta_0) \in B) - P_{\theta_0}(A_N(\theta_0) \in B)| = o(N^{-a}).$$

Let $S_N(\theta) = N^{-1}\sum_{i=1}^{N} f(\widetilde{W}_i, \theta)$ and $S_N^*(\theta) = N^{-1}\sum_{i=1}^{N} f(\widetilde{W}_i^*, \theta)$.

Lemma A.6. *Suppose Assumptions 2.1 and 4.1–4.3 hold. Let* $\Delta_N(\theta_0)$ *denote* $N^{1/2}(\widehat{\theta}_N - \theta_0)$, $T_N(\theta_{0,r})$, *or* $H_N(\widehat{\theta}_N, \beta_0)$, *where* $\theta_0 = (\beta_0', \delta_0')'$. *Let* L *denote the dimension of* $\Delta_N(\theta_0)$. *For each definition of* $\Delta_N(\theta_0)$, *there is an infinitely differentiable function* $G(\cdot)$ *that does not depend on* θ_0 *and that satisfies* $G(E_{\theta_0} S_N(\theta_0)) = 0$ *for all* N *large and all* $\theta_0 \in \Theta_1$, *and*

$$\sup_{\theta_0 \in \Theta_1} \sup_{B \in \mathcal{B}_L} |P_{\theta_0}(\Delta_N(\theta_0) \in B) - P_{\theta_0}(N^{1/2}G(S_N(\theta_0)) \in B)| = o(N^{-a}).$$

We now define the components of the Edgeworth expansions of $T_N(\theta_{0,r})$ and $\mathcal{W}_N(\beta_0)$, as well as their bootstrap analogs $T_N^*(\widehat{\theta}_{N,r})$ and $\mathcal{W}_N^*(\widehat{\beta}_N)$. Let $\Psi_N(\theta_0) = N^{1/2}(S_N(\theta_0) - E_{\theta_0} S_N(\theta_0))$. Let $\Psi_{N,j}(\theta_0)$ denote the jth element of $\Psi_N(\theta_0)$. Let $\nu_{N,a}(\theta_0)$ denote a vector of moments of the form $N^{\alpha(m)} E_{\theta_0} \prod_{\mu=1}^{m} \Psi_{N,j_\mu}(\theta_0)$, where $2 \leq m \leq 2a+2$, $\alpha(m) = 0$ if m is even, and $\alpha(m) = 1/2$ if m is odd. Let $\pi_{Ti}(\delta, \nu_{N,a}(\theta_0))$ be a polynomial in $\delta = \partial/\partial z$ whose coefficients are polynomial functions of the elements of $\nu_{N,a}(\theta_0)$ and for which $\pi_{Ti}(\delta, \nu_{N,a}(\theta_0))\Phi(z)$ is an even function of z when i is odd and is an odd function of z when i is even for $i = 1, \ldots, 2a$. The Edgeworth expansion of $T_N(\theta_{0,r})$ depends on $\pi_{Ti}(\delta, \nu_{N,a}(\theta_0))$. In contrast, the Edgeworth expansion of $\mathcal{W}_N(\beta_0)$ depends on $\pi_{\mathcal{W}i}(y, \nu_{N,a}(\theta_0))$, where $\pi_{\mathcal{W}i}(y, \nu_{N,a}(\theta_0))$ denotes a polynomial function of y whose coefficients are polynomial functions of the elements of $\nu_{N,a}(\theta_0)$ for $i = 1, \ldots, [a]$. The Edgeworth expansions of $T_N^*(\widehat{\theta}_{N,r})$ and $\mathcal{W}_N^*(\widehat{\beta}_N)$ depend on $\pi_{Ti}(\delta, \nu_{N,a}(\widehat{\theta}_N))$ and $\pi_{\mathcal{W}i}(y, \nu_{\mathcal{W},N,a}(\widehat{\theta}_N))$, respectively.

Let $\Phi(\cdot)$ denote the distribution function of a standard normal random variable. Let χ^2_λ denote a chi-square random variable with λ degrees of freedom. Let $\theta_{0,r}$ denote the rth element of θ_0.

Lemma A.7. *Suppose Assumptions* 2.1 *and* 4.1–4.3 *hold. Then, for all* $\varepsilon > 0$,

$$\sup_{\theta_0 \in \Theta_1} P_{\theta_0}(N^{1/2}||\nu_{N,a}(\widehat{\theta}_N) - \nu_{N,a}(\theta_0)|| > \ln(N)\varepsilon) = o(N^{-a}).$$

Lemma A.8. *Suppose Assumptions* 2.1 *and* 4.1–4.3 *hold.*
(a) *Then,*

$$\sup_{\theta_0 \in \Theta_1} \sup_{z \in R} \Big| P_{\theta_0}(T_N(\theta_{0,r}) \leq z) - \left[1 + \sum_{i=1}^{2a} N^{-i/2} \pi_{Ti}(\delta, \nu_{N,a}(\theta_0))\right] \Phi(z) \Big| = o(N^{-a}) \quad \textit{and}$$

$$\sup_{\theta_0 \in \Theta_1} \sup_{z \in R} \Big| P_{\theta_0}(\mathcal{W}_N(\beta_0) \leq z) - \int_{-\infty}^{z} d\left[1 + \sum_{i=1}^{[a]} N^{-i} \pi_{\mathcal{W}i}(y, \nu_{N,a}(\theta_0))\right] P(\chi^2_{L_H} \leq y) \Big| = o(N^{-a}).$$

(b) *Then, for all* $\varepsilon > 0$,

$$\sup_{\theta_0 \in \Theta_0} P_{\theta_0}\left(\sup_{z \in R} \Big| P^*_{\widehat{\theta}_N}(T_N^*(\widehat{\theta}_{N,r}) \leq z) - \left[1 + \sum_{i=1}^{2a} N^{-i/2} \pi_{Ti}(\delta, \nu_{N,a}(\widehat{\theta}_N))\right] \Phi(z) \Big| > N^{-a}\varepsilon \right) = o(N^{-a}) \quad \textit{and}$$

$$\sup_{\theta_0 \in \Theta_0} P_{\theta_0}\left(\sup_{z \in R} \Big| P^*_{\widehat{\theta}_N}(\mathcal{W}_N^*(\widehat{\beta}_N) \leq z) - \int_{-\infty}^{z} d\left[1 + \sum_{i=1}^{[a]} N^{-i} \pi_{\mathcal{W}i}(y, \nu_{N,a}(\widehat{\theta}_N))\right] P(\chi^2_{L_H} \leq y) \Big| > N^{-a}\varepsilon \right) = o(N^{-a}).$$

Comments. 1. The terms in the Edgeworth expansions for the Wald statistic involve only integer powers of N^{-1}, not powers $N^{-1/2}$, $N^{-3/2}$, and so forth, as in the Edgeworth expansions for the t statistic, because of a symmetry property of the expansions.

2. The conditions on q_1 and d in Assumption 4.2 are not needed in all of the Lemmas A.1–A.8. In particular, Lemmas A.3 and A.4 only use $q_1 \geq \max\{2a+1, 2\}$ and $d = 3$.

Proofs of Theorems

Proof of Theorem 5.1.

The results of parts (a)–(c) hold by Lemma A.8a. In the proof of part (a), the N^{-1} term in the Edgeworth expansion of Lemma A.8(a) drops out by the evenness of $\pi_{Ti}(\delta, \nu_{N,a}(\theta_0))$ when considering the probability $P_{\theta_0}(T_N(\theta_{0,r}) \leq z_{\alpha/2}) - P_{\theta_0}(T_N(\theta_{0,r}) \leq -z_{\alpha/2})$. ■

Proof of Theorem 6.1.

We establish part (c) first. Note that $P_{\theta_0}(\theta_{0,r} \in CI_{UP}) = P_{\theta_0}(T_N(\theta_{0,r}) \leq z^*_{T,\alpha})$. We show that the latter equals $1 - \alpha + o(N^{-1}\ln(N))$ uniformly over $\theta_0 \in \Theta_0$. By Lemma A.8b, Lemma A.7, and Lemma A.8a, respectively, each with $a = 1$, we have, for all $\varepsilon > 0$,

$$\sup_{\theta_0 \in \Theta_0} P_{\theta_0}\Bigg(\sup_{z \in R} \Big| P^*_{\widehat{\theta}_N}(T^*_N(\widehat{\theta}_{N,r}) \leq z) - \left[1 + \sum_{i=1}^{2} N^{-i/2}\pi_{Ti}(\delta, \nu_{N,1}(\widehat{\theta}_N))\right]\Phi(z)\Big| > N^{-1}\Bigg) = o(N^{-1}),$$

$$\sup_{\theta_0 \in \Theta_0} P_{\theta_0}\Big(\sup_{z \in R} |[\pi_{Ti}(\delta, \nu_{N,1}(\widehat{\theta}_N)) - \pi_{Ti}(\delta, \nu_{N,1}(\theta_0))]\Phi(z)| > N^{-1/2}\ln(N)\varepsilon\Big) = o(N^{-1}) \text{ for } i = 1, 2, \text{ and}$$

$$\sup_{\theta_0 \in \Theta_0} \sup_{z \in R} \left| P_{\theta_0}(T_N(\theta_{0,r}) \leq z) - \left[1 + \sum_{i=1}^{2} N^{-i/2}\pi_{Ti}(\delta, \nu_{N,1}(\theta_0))\right]\Phi(z)\right| = o(N^{-1}). \quad \text{(A.1)}$$

The results of (A.1) combine to give

$$\sup_{\theta_0 \in \Theta_0} P_{\theta_0}\Big(\sup_{z \in R} |P^*_{\widehat{\theta}_N}(T^*_N(\widehat{\theta}_{N,r}) \leq z) - P_{\theta_0}(T_N(\theta_{0,r}) \leq z)| > N^{-1}\ln(N)\varepsilon\Big) = o(N^{-1}). \quad \text{(A.2)}$$

If $T^*_N(\widehat{\theta}_{N,r})$ is absolutely continuous, then $P^*_{\widehat{\theta}_N}(T^*_N(\widehat{\theta}_{N,r}) \leq z^*_{T,\alpha}) = 1 - \alpha$. Whether or not $T^*_N(\widehat{\theta}_{N,r})$ is absolutely continuous, the Edgeworth expansion of

Lemma A.8b with $a = 1$ implies that

$$\sup_{\theta_0 \in \Theta_0} P_{\theta_0}(|P^*_{\widehat{\theta}_N}(T^*_N(\widehat{\theta}_{N,r}) \leq z^*_{T,\alpha}) - (1-\alpha)| > N^{-1}\varepsilon) = o(N^{-1}) \qquad \text{(A.3)}$$

for all $\varepsilon > 0$. This holds because the continuity in z of the Edgeworth expansion in Lemma A.8b implies that there exists a value $z^{**}_{T,\alpha}$ for which the Edgeworth expansion at $z = z^{**}_{T,\alpha}$ equals $1 - \alpha$ and, by definition of $z^*_{T,\alpha}$, $|P^*_{\widehat{\theta}_N}(T^*_N(\widehat{\theta}_{N,r}) \leq z^*_{T,\alpha}) - (1-\alpha)| \leq |P^*_{\widehat{\theta}_N}(T^*_N(\widehat{\theta}_{N,r}) \leq z^{**}_{T,\alpha}) - (1-\alpha)|$.

Taking $z = z^*_{T,\alpha}$ in (A.2) and combining it with (A.3) gives

$$\sup_{\theta_0 \in \Theta_0} P_{\theta_0}(|1 - \alpha - P_{\theta_0}(T_N(\theta_{0,r}) \leq z^*_{T,\alpha})| > N^{-1}\ln(N)\varepsilon) = o(N^{-1}). \qquad \text{(A.4)}$$

The expression inside the absolute value sign is nonrandom. Hence, for N large, $|1 - \alpha - P_{\theta_0}(T_N(\theta_{0,r}) \leq z^*_{T,\alpha})| \leq N^{-1}\ln(N)\varepsilon$, which establishes part (c) of Theorem 6.1.

The proof of part (b) is analogous to that of part (c). The proof of part (d) is also analogous to that of part (c), but using the Wald statistic results of Lemmas A.7 and A.8, rather than the t statistic results, and with these lemmas applied with $a = 3/2$ rather than $a = 1$. In part (d), the coverage probability error is $o(N^{-3/2}\ln(N))$, rather than $o(N^{-1}\ln(N))$, which is the error in part (c), because the first terms in the Edgeworth expansions for the Wald statistic in Lemma A.8 are $O(N^{-1})$, whereas those for the t statistic are $O(N^{-1/2})$.

Next, we prove part (a). Note that $P_{\theta_0}(\theta_0 \in CI_{SYM}) = P_{\theta_0}(|T_N(\theta_{0,r})| \leq z^*_{|T|,\alpha})$. We show that the latter is $O(N^{-2})$ uniformly over $\theta_0 \in \Theta_0$.

By Lemma A.6 with $a = 2$, it suffices to establish the result with $T_N(\theta_{0,r})$ and $T^*_N(\widehat{\theta}_{N,r})$ replaced by $N^{1/2}G(S_N(\theta_0))$ and $N^{1/2}G(S^*_N(\widehat{\theta}_N))$, respectively. Part (a) now can be established using methods developed for "smooth functions of sample averages," as in Hall (1988, 1992). Define $z_{|G|,\alpha}$ by $P_{\theta_0}(|N^{1/2}G(S_N(\theta_0))| \leq z_{|G|,\alpha}) = 1 - \alpha$ and let $\Delta = z_{|G|,\alpha} - z^*_{|T|,\alpha}$. The idea of the proof is to show that

$$\begin{aligned}
&P_{\theta_0}(N^{1/2}G(S_N(\theta_0)) + \Delta \leq z_{|G|,\alpha}) \\
&\quad = 1 - \alpha/2 + N^{-3/2}r_1(z_{|G|,\alpha})\phi(z_{|G|,\alpha}) + O(N^{-2}) \quad \text{and} \\
&P_{\theta_0}(N^{1/2}G(S_N(\theta_0)) - \Delta \leq -z_{|G|,\alpha}) \\
&\quad = \alpha/2 - N^{-3/2}r_1(-z_{|G|,\alpha})\phi(-z_{|G|,\alpha}) + O(N^{-2}),
\end{aligned} \qquad \text{(A.5)}$$

uniformly over $\theta_0 \in \Theta_0$, where $r_1(x)$ is a constant times x and $\phi(\cdot)$ denotes the standard normal density function, as in of Hall (1988). Then,

$$\begin{aligned}
P_{\theta_0}(|T_N(\theta_{0,r})| \leq z^*_{|T|,\alpha}) &= P_{\theta_0}(|N^{1/2}G(S_N(\theta_0))| \leq z^*_{|T|,\alpha}) + O(N^{-2}) \\
&= 1 - \alpha + N^{-3/2}r_1(z_{|G|,\alpha})\phi(z_{|G|,\alpha}) \\
&\quad + N^{-3/2}r_1(-z_{|G|,\alpha})\phi(-z_{|G|,\alpha}) + O(N^{-2}) \\
&= 1 - \alpha + O(N^{-2}),
\end{aligned} \qquad \text{(A.6)}$$

uniformly over $\theta_0 \in \Theta_0$, using the fact that $r_1(x)$ is an odd function and $\phi(\cdot)$ is an even function. The results of (A.5) are established by the same argument as used to prove (3.2) of Hall (1988), where his T corresponds to our $N^{1/2}G(S_N(\theta_0))$. (More details of this argument can be found in Hall (1992, Proof of Theorem 5.3), which considers one-sided confidence intervals but can be extended to symmetric two-sided confidence intervals.) This argument relies on Edgeworth expansions of $N^{1/2}G(S_N(\theta_0))$ and $N^{1/2}G(S_N^*(\widehat{\theta}_N))$:

$$\begin{aligned}
&\sup_{\theta_0\in\Theta_0}\sup_{z\in R}\big|P_{\theta_0}(|N^{1/2}G(S_N(\theta_0))| \le z)\\
&\quad -[1+N^{-1}\pi_2(\delta,\nu_{N,2}(\theta_0))+N^{-2}\pi_4(\delta,\nu_{N,2}(\theta_0))](\Phi(z)-\Phi(-z))\big|\\
&\quad = o(N^{-2}) \quad \text{and}\\
&\sup_{\theta_0\in\Theta_0} P_{\theta_0}\Bigg(\sup_{z\in R}\Big|P^*_{\widehat{\theta}_N}(|N^{1/2}G(S_N^*(\widehat{\theta}_N))| \le z) - [1+N^{-1}\pi_2(\delta,\nu_{N,2}(\widehat{\theta}_N))\\
&\qquad + N^{-2}\pi_4(\delta,\nu_{N,2}(\widehat{\theta}_N))](\Phi(z)-\Phi(-z))\Big| > N^{-2}\Bigg)\\
&\qquad = o(N^{-2}),
\end{aligned} \tag{A.7}$$

which hold by Lemma A.8 with $a = 2$ and with $T_N(\theta_{0,r})$ and $T_N^*(\widehat{\theta}_{N,r})$ replaced by $N^{1/2}G(S_N(\theta_0))$ and $N^{1/2}G(S_N^*(\widehat{\theta}_N))$, respectively. The former replacements are valid by the proof of Lemma A.8. ■

Proof of Theorem 7.1

Define $\widehat{\theta}_{N,k}$, $\mathcal{Q}_{N,j-1}$, $T_{N,k}(\theta_{0,r})$, and $\mathcal{W}_{N,k}(\beta_0)$ just as $\theta^*_{N,k}$, $\mathcal{Q}^*_{N,j-1}$, $T^*_{N,k}(\widehat{\theta}_{N,r})$, and $\mathcal{W}^*_{N,k}(\widehat{\beta}_N)$ are defined but with the bootstrap sample $\{W_i^* : i = 1, 2, \ldots, N\}$ replaced by the original sample $\{\widetilde{W}_i : i = 1, 2, \ldots, N\}$ and with the initial estimator $\widehat{\theta}_{N,0}$ used to generate $\widehat{\theta}_{N,k}$ given by the true parameter θ_0. To establish part (a) of the theorem, we apply Lemma A.1 three times with

$$\begin{aligned}
\lambda_N(\theta_0) &= P^*_{\theta_0}(\|\theta^*_{N,k}-\theta^*_N\| > \mu_{N,k}) = P_{\theta_0}(\|\widehat{\theta}_{N,k}-\widehat{\theta}_N\| > \mu_{N,k}),\\
\lambda_N(\theta_0) &= P^*_{\theta_0}(|T^*_{N,k}(\theta_{0,r}) - T^*_N(\theta_{0,r})| > N^{1/2}\mu_{N,k})\\
&= P_{\theta_0}(|T_{N,k}(\theta_{0,r}) - T_N(\theta_{0,r})| > N^{1/2}\mu_{N,k}), \quad \text{and}\\
\lambda_N(\theta_0) &= P^*_{\theta_0}(|\mathcal{W}^*_{N,k}(\beta_0) - \mathcal{W}^*_N(\beta_0)| > N^{1/2}\mu_{N,k})\\
&= P_{\theta_0}(|\mathcal{W}_{N,k}(\beta_0) - \mathcal{W}_N(\beta_0)| > N^{1/2}\mu_{N,k}).
\end{aligned} \tag{A.8}$$

The condition of Lemma A.1 on $\widehat{\theta}_N$ is established in Lemma A.4. In consequence, to establish part (a) of the theorem, it suffices to show that

$$\begin{aligned}
&\sup_{\theta_0\in\Theta_1} P_{\theta_0}(\|\widehat{\theta}_{N,k}-\widehat{\theta}_N\| > \mu_{N,k}) = o(N^{-a}),\\
&\sup_{\theta_0\in\Theta_1} P_{\theta_0}(|T_{N,k}(\theta_{0,r}) - T_N(\theta_{0,r})| > N^{1/2}\mu_{N,k}) = o(N^{-a}), \quad \text{and}\\
&\sup_{\theta_0\in\Theta_1} P_{\theta_0}(|\mathcal{W}_{N,k}(\beta_0) - \mathcal{W}_N(\beta_0)| > N^{1/2}\mu_{N,k}) = o(N^{-a}).
\end{aligned} \tag{A.9}$$

We establish the first result of (A.9) first. A Taylor expansion about $\widehat{\theta}_{N,k-1}$ gives

$$\begin{aligned}
0 &= \frac{\partial}{\partial\theta}\rho_N(\widehat{\theta}_N) \\
&= \frac{\partial}{\partial\theta}\rho_N(\widehat{\theta}_{N,k-1}) + \frac{\partial^2}{\partial\theta\partial\theta'}\rho_N(\widehat{\theta}_{N,k-1})(\widehat{\theta}_N - \widehat{\theta}_{N,k-1}) + R_{N,k} \\
&= \frac{\partial}{\partial\theta}\rho_N(\widehat{\theta}_{N,k-1}) + Q_{N,k-1}(\widehat{\theta}_{N,k} - \widehat{\theta}_{N,k-1}) + Q_{N,k-1}(\widehat{\theta}_N - \widehat{\theta}_{N,k}) \\
&\quad + \left(\frac{\partial^2}{\partial\theta\partial\theta'}\rho_N(\widehat{\theta}_{N,k-1}) - Q_{N,k-1}\right)(\widehat{\theta}_N - \widehat{\theta}_{N,k-1}) + R_{N,k} \\
&= Q_{N,k-1}(\widehat{\theta}_N - \widehat{\theta}_{N,k}) + \left(\frac{\partial^2}{\partial\theta\partial\theta'}\rho_N(\widehat{\theta}_{N,k-1}) - Q_{N,k-1}\right) \\
&\quad \times (\widehat{\theta}_N - \widehat{\theta}_{N,k-1}) + R_{N,k}, \quad \text{where} \\
R_{N,k} &= \left[(\widehat{\theta}_N - \widehat{\theta}_{N,k-1})'\frac{\partial^3}{\partial\theta_u\partial\theta\partial\theta'}\rho_N(\theta^+_{N,k-1,u})(\widehat{\theta}_N - \widehat{\theta}_{N,k-1})/2\right]_{L_\theta}. \qquad \text{(A.10)}
\end{aligned}$$

$[\xi_u]_{L_\theta}$ denotes an L_θ vector whose uth element is ξ_r, $\theta^+_{N,k-1,u}$ lies between $\widehat{\theta}_N$ and $\widehat{\theta}_{N,k-1}$, the first equality holds except with supremum P_{θ_0} probability over $\theta_0 \in \Theta_1$ equal to $o(N^{-a})$ by Lemma A.4, and the fourth equality holds because $(\partial/\partial\theta)\rho_N(\widehat{\theta}_{N,k-1}) + Q_{N,k-1}\,(\widehat{\theta}_{N,k} - \widehat{\theta}_{N,k-1}) = 0$ by the definition of $\widehat{\theta}_{N,k}$. Rearranging (A.10) yields

$$\begin{aligned}
&||\widehat{\theta}_{N,k} - \widehat{\theta}_N|| \\
&\quad \le ||(Q_{N,k-1})^{-1}R_{N,k}|| + ||(Q_{N,k-1})^{-1}\left(\frac{\partial^2}{\partial\theta\partial\theta'}\rho_N(\widehat{\theta}_{N,k-1}) - Q_{N,k-1}\right) \\
&\qquad \times (\widehat{\theta}_{N,k-1} - \widehat{\theta}_N)|| \\
&\quad \le \zeta_N(||\widehat{\theta}_{N,k-1} - \widehat{\theta}_N||^2 + \psi_N||\widehat{\theta}_{N,k-1} - \widehat{\theta}_N||), \quad \text{where} \\
\zeta_N &= \max_{j=1,\dots,k}\Bigg\{||(Q_{N,j-1})^{-1})|| \cdot \sum_{u=1}^{L_\theta}||\frac{\partial^3}{\partial\theta_u\partial\theta\partial\theta'}\rho_N(\theta^+_{N,j-1,u})/2|| \\
&\qquad + ||(Q_{N,j-1})^{-1})|| \cdot \widetilde{\psi}_N||\frac{\partial^2}{\partial\theta\partial\theta'}\rho_N(\widehat{\theta}_{N,j-1}) - Q_{N,j-1}|| + 1\Bigg\}, \qquad \text{(A.11)}
\end{aligned}$$

$\widetilde{\psi}_N = \psi_N^{-1}$ if $\psi_N > 0$ and $\widetilde{\psi}_N = 0$ if $\psi_N = 0$. Repeated substitution into the right-hand side of the inequality gives an upper bound that is a finite sum of terms with dominant terms of the form

$$C\zeta_N^{\phi}||\widehat{\theta}_{N,0} - \widehat{\theta}_N||^{2^{k-j}}\psi_N^j \quad \text{for } j = 0, \dots, k, \qquad \text{(A.12)}$$

where ϕ is a positive integer and $\widehat{\theta}_{N,0} = \theta_0$ when the true parameter is θ_0. To see this, consider the solution in terms of x_0 of the equation $x_k = x_{k-1}^2 + \lambda x_{k-1}$.

Collect all terms in powers of λ that are multiplied by the smallest number of x_0 terms.

An upper bound on the right-hand side of the inequality in (A.11) is

$$C\zeta_N^{\phi} \max_{j=0,\ldots,k} (\gamma_N)^{2^{k-j}} N^{-2^{k-j-1}} \ln^{2^{k-j}}(N)\psi_N^{j}, \quad \text{where}$$
$$\gamma_N = N^{1/2}||\widehat{\theta}_{N,0} - \widehat{\theta}_N|| \ln^{-1}(N). \tag{A.13}$$

For all $\varepsilon > 0$, $\sup_{\theta_0\in\Theta_1} P_{\theta_0}(\gamma_N > \varepsilon) = o(N^{-a})$ by Lemma A.4, because $\widehat{\theta}_{N,0} = \theta_0$. In addition, by Lemma A.3 and Assumptions 4.2a and 7.1, there exists a finite constant K such that $\sup_{\theta_0\in\Theta_1} P_{\theta_0}(\zeta_N > K) = o(N^{-a})$. Assumption 7.1 applies here because $P^*_{\theta_0}(||Q^*_{N,j-1} - D^*_N(\theta^*_{N,j-1})|| > \psi_N) = P_{\theta_0}(||Q_{N,j-1} - (\partial^2/\partial\theta\partial\theta')\rho_N(\widehat{\theta}_{N,j-1})|| > \psi_N)$. Combining these results with (A.11) and (A.13) gives

$$\begin{aligned}
&\sup_{\theta_0\in\Theta_1} P_{\theta_0}\left(||\widehat{\theta}_{N,k} - \widehat{\theta}_N|| > \max_{j=0,\ldots,k} N^{-2^{k-j-1}} \ln^{2^{k-j}}(N)\psi_N^{j}\right)\\
&\quad\le \sup_{\theta_0\in\Theta_1} P_{\theta_0}(C\zeta_N^{\phi}\lambda_N > 1)\\
&\quad= \sup_{\theta_0\in\Theta_1} P_{\theta_0}(CK^{\phi}\varepsilon > 1) + o(N^{-a})\\
&\quad= o(N^{-a}),
\end{aligned} \tag{A.14}$$

where the last equality holds for $\varepsilon > 0$ sufficiently small. Hence, the first result of part (a) of the theorem holds.

Next, we establish the second result of part (a) of the theorem. Let Σ_r denote $(\Sigma_N)_{rr}$. Let $\Sigma_{k,r}$ denote Σ_r with $\widehat{\theta}_N$ replaced by $\widehat{\theta}_{N,k}$ in all parts of its definition in (2.6). We use the following:

$$\begin{aligned}
|T_{N,k}(\theta_{0,r}) - T_N(\theta_{0,r})| &\le N^{1/2}||\widehat{\theta}_{N,k} - \widehat{\theta}_N||/\Sigma_{k,r}^{1/2}\\
&\quad + N^{1/2}||\widehat{\theta}_N - \theta_0|| \cdot |\Sigma_{k,r}^{1/2} - \Sigma_r^{1/2}|/(\Sigma_{k,r}\Sigma_r)^{1/2}.
\end{aligned} \tag{A.15}$$

By (A.13), the second result of part (a) is implied by the first result plus the following. There exists a $K < \infty$ and a $\delta > 0$ such that

$$\sup_{\theta_0\in\Theta_1} P_{\theta_0}(|\Sigma_{k,r}^{1/2} - \Sigma_r^{1/2}| > \mu_{N,k}) = o(N^{-a}), \tag{A.16}$$

$$\sup_{\theta_0\in\Theta_1} P_{\theta_0}(||\widehat{\theta}_N - \theta_0|| > K) = o(N^{-a}), \tag{A.17}$$

$$\sup_{\theta_0\in\Theta_1} P_{\theta_0}(\Sigma_{k,r} < \delta) = o(N^{-a}), \quad \text{and} \tag{A.18}$$

$$\sup_{\theta_0\in\Theta_1} P_{\theta_0}(\Sigma_r < \delta) = o(N^{-a}). \tag{A.19}$$

Equation (A.17) holds by Lemma A.4. Equations (A.18) and (A.19) hold by Lemma A.4, the first result (A.9), and the first and/or second results of Lemma A.3.

Equation (A.16) is implied by (A.18), (A.19), and

$$\sup_{\theta_0 \in \Theta_1} P_{\theta_0}(|\Sigma_{k,r} - \Sigma_r| > \mu_{N,k}) = o(N^{-a}) \quad \text{(A.20)}$$

by a mean value expansion. Equation (A.20) is implied by

$$\sup_{\theta_0 \in \Theta_1} P_{\theta_0}(||D_N(\widehat{\theta}_{N,k}) - D_N(\widehat{\theta}_N)|| > \mu_{n,k}) = o(N^{-a}) \quad \text{and/or}$$
$$\sup_{\theta_0 \in \Theta_1} P_{\theta_0}(||V_N(\widehat{\theta}_{N,k}) - V_N(\widehat{\theta}_N)|| > \mu_{n,k}) = o(N^{-a}). \quad \text{(A.21)}$$

These results hold by mean value expansions, Lemma A.2b with $m(\widetilde{W}_i, \theta_0) = \sup_{\theta \in \Theta_2} ||(\partial^2/\partial\theta_u \partial\theta')g(\widetilde{W}_i, \theta)||$ and $m(\widetilde{W}_i, \theta_0) = \sup_{\theta \in \Theta_2} ||(\partial/\partial\theta_u)(g(\widetilde{W}_i, \theta)g(\widetilde{W}_i, \theta)')||$ for $u = 1, \ldots, L_\theta$, Lemma A.4, the first result of (A.9), and Assumption 4.2.

We now prove the third result of part (a). Let $H_N = H_N(\widehat{\theta}_N)$ and $H_{N,k} = H_N(\widehat{\theta}_{N,k})$. We have

$$\begin{aligned}|\mathcal{W}_{N,k}(\beta_0) - \mathcal{W}_N(\beta_0)| &= |(H_{N,k} - H_N)' H_{N,k} + H_N'(H_{N,k} - H_N)| \\ &\leq ||H_{N,k} - H_N||(||H_{N,k}|| + ||H_N||). \quad \text{(A.22)}\end{aligned}$$

Hence, it suffices to show that

$$\sup_{\theta_0 \in \Theta_1} P_{\theta_0}(||H_{N,k} - H_N|| > N^{1/2}\mu_{N,k}) = o(N^{-a}) \quad \text{and}$$
$$\sup_{\theta_0 \in \Theta_1} P_{\theta_0}(||H_N|| > M) = o(N^{-a}) \quad \text{for some } M < \infty. \quad \text{(A.23)}$$

The second result of (A.23) holds by Lemma 9(a) because $||H_N||^2 = \mathcal{W}_N(\beta_0)$. The first result of (A.23) is implied by the matrix version of (A.20) and the first result of (A.9).

To establish part (b) of the theorem, we apply Lemma A.1 three times with

$$\begin{aligned}&\lambda_N(\theta_0) \\ &= \sup_{z \in R^{L_\theta}} \left| P_{\theta_0}^*(N^{1/2}(\theta_{N,k}^* - \theta_0) \leq z) - P_{\theta_0}^*(N^{1/2}(\theta_N^* - \theta_0) \leq z) \right| \\ &= \sup_{z \in R^{L_\theta}} \left| P_{\theta_0}(N^{1/2}(\widehat{\theta}_{N,k} - \theta_0) \leq z) - P_{\theta_0}(N^{1/2}(\widehat{\theta}_N - \theta_0) \leq z) \right|,\end{aligned} \quad \text{(A.24)}$$

and so forth. In consequence, it suffices to show that

$$\sup_{\theta_0 \in \Theta_1} \sup_{z \in R^{L_\theta}} \left| P_{\theta_0}(N^{1/2}(\widehat{\theta}_{N,k} - \theta_0) \leq z) - P_{\theta_0}(N^{1/2}(\widehat{\theta}_N - \theta_0) \leq z) \right|$$
$$= o(N^{-a}),$$
$$\sup_{\theta_0 \in \Theta_1} \sup_{z \in R} \left| P_{\theta_0}(T_{N,k}(\theta_{0,r}) \leq z) - P_{\theta_0}(T_N(\theta_{0,r}) \leq z) \right| = o(N^{-a}), \quad \text{and}$$
$$\sup_{\theta_0 \in \Theta_1} \sup_{z \in R} \left| P_{\theta_0}(\mathcal{W}_{N,k}(\beta_0) \leq z) - P_{\theta_0}(\mathcal{W}_N(\beta_0) \leq z) \right| = o(N^{-a}). \quad \text{(A.25)}$$

We apply Lemma A.5 three times with $\omega_N = N^{1/2}\mu_{N,k}$ and with $(A_N(\theta_0), \xi_N(\theta_0))$ equal to $(N^{1/2}(\widehat{\theta}_N - \theta_0),\ N^{1/2}(\widehat{\theta}_{N,k} - \widehat{\theta}_N))$, $(T_N(\theta_{0,r}),\ T_{N,k}(\theta_{0,r}) - T_N(\theta_{0,r}))$, and $(H_N(\widehat{\theta}_N),\ H_N(\widehat{\theta}_{N,k}) - H_N(\widehat{\theta}_N))$. In the third application, we consider the convex sets $B_z = \{x \in R^{L_\beta} : x'x \leq z\}$ and use the fact that $\mathcal{W}_{N,k} = H_N(\widehat{\theta}_{N,k})'H_N(\widehat{\theta}_{N,k})$. By the assumption that $\mu_{N,k} = o(N^{-(a+1/2)})$, we have $\omega_N = o(N^{-a})$, as required by Lemma A.5. The condition of Lemma A.5 on $\xi_N(\theta_0)$ holds by (A.9). As required by Lemma A.5, the random vector $T_N(\theta_{0,r})$ has an Edgeworth expansion with remainder $o(N^{-a})$ by Lemma A.8a. The same is true for $\Sigma^{-1/2}N^{-1/2}(\widehat{\theta}_N - \theta_0)$ and $H_N(\widehat{\theta}_N)$ by an argument analogous to that used to prove Lemma A.8a. ■

Proof of Theorem 7.2

The proof of Theorem 7.2 is the same as that of Theorem 6.1, except that the results of Theorem 7.1b allow one to replace $T_N^*(\widehat{\theta}_{N,r})$, $z^*_{T,\alpha}$, and $z^*_{|T|,\alpha}$ by $T^*_{N,k}(\widehat{\theta}_{N,r})$, $z^*_{T,k,\alpha}$, and $z^*_{|T|,k,\alpha}$, respectively, throughout. In particular, the results of Theorem 7.1b allow one to replace $T_N^*(\widehat{\theta}_{N,r})$ by $T^*_{N,k}(\widehat{\theta}_{N,r})$ in the first line of (A.1), and the replacements elsewhere all follow. ■

Proofs of Lemmas

Proof of Lemma 7.1

The NR result of Lemma 7.1 holds by definition of $Q^{NR,*}_{N,j-1}$. For brevity, the proof of the other results is given in Andrews (2001). It is similar to the proof of Lemma 17 in Andrews (2002). ■

Proof of Lemma A.1

We have

$$
\begin{aligned}
&\sup_{\theta_0\in\Theta_0} P_{\theta_0}(|\lambda_N(\widehat{\theta}_N)| > N^{-a}\varepsilon) \\
&\quad \leq \sup_{\theta_0\in\Theta_0} P_{\theta_0}(|\lambda_N(\widehat{\theta}_N)| > N^{-a}\varepsilon, \widehat{\theta}_N \in B(\theta_0, \delta/2)) \\
&\qquad + \sup_{\theta_0\in\Theta_0} P_{\theta_0}(\widehat{\theta}_N \notin B(\theta_0, \delta/2)) \\
&\quad \leq \sup_{\theta_0\in\Theta_0} P_{\theta_0}(\sup_{\theta\in\Theta_1} |\lambda_N(\theta)| > N^{-a}\varepsilon) + o(N^{-a}) \\
&\quad = 1(o(N^{-a}) > N^{-a}\varepsilon) + o(N^{-a}) \\
&\quad = o(N^{-a}),
\end{aligned}
\tag{A.26}
$$

where the second inequality uses the fact that when $\widehat{\theta}_N \in B(\theta_0, \delta/2)$ and $\theta_0 \in \Theta_0$, one has $\widehat{\theta}_N \in \Theta_1$. ■

Proof of Lemma A.2

A strong mixing moment inequality of Yokoyama (1980) and Doukhan (1995, Theorem 2 and Remark 2, pp. 25–30) gives $\sup_{\theta_0\in\Theta_1} E_{\theta_0}||\sum_{i=1}^N m(\widetilde{W}_i,\theta_0)||^p < CN^{p/2}$ provided $p \geq 2$. Application of Markov's inequality and the Yokoyama–Doukhan inequality yields the left-hand side in part (a) of the lemma to be less than or equal to

$$\varepsilon^{-p}N^{-p}\sup_{\theta_0\in\Theta_1} E_{\theta_0}\left\|\sum_{i=1}^N m(\widetilde{W}_i,\theta_0)\right\|^p \leq \varepsilon^{-p}CN^{-p/2} = o(N^{-a}). \tag{A.27}$$

Part (b) follows from part (a) applied to $m(\widetilde{W}_i,\theta_0) - E_{\theta_0}m(\widetilde{W}_i,\theta_0)$ and the triangle inequality.

To establish part (c), we use the Edgeworth expansion given in Theorem 2.1 or 2.3 of Lahiri (1993) (also see Corollary 2.9 of Götze and Hipp 1983) with their $s = 2a + 2$. Conditions 1 and 3–6 of Lahiri (1993) hold uniformly over $\theta_0 \in \Theta_1$ by Assumption 4.3. Their condition 2 holds uniformly over $\theta_0 \in \Theta_1$ by Assumption 4.2b. Because the result of the lemma can be proved element by element, we consider an arbitrary element $f_v(\cdot,\theta_0)$ of $f(\cdot,\theta_0)$. Let $\Phi(\cdot)$ denote the standard normal distribution function. By the Edgeworth expansion, for each $\theta_0 \in \Theta_1$, there are homogeneous polynomials $\pi_i(\delta,\theta_0)$ in $\delta = \partial/\partial z$ for $i = 1,\ldots,2a$ such that

$$\begin{aligned}\sup_{z\in R}&\left|P_{\theta_0}\left(N^{-1/2}\sum_{i=1}^N(f_v(\widetilde{W}_i,\theta_0) - E_{\theta_0}f_v(\widetilde{W}_i,\theta_0)) \leq z\right)\right.\\ &\left.-\left(1+\sum_{i=1}^{2a}N^{-i/2}\pi_i(\delta,\theta_0)\right)\Phi(z)\right|\\ &= o(N^{-a}).\end{aligned} \tag{A.28}$$

The error $o(N^{-a})$ holds uniformly over $\theta_0 \in \Theta_1$ because Assumptions 4.2b and 4.3 hold uniformly over $\theta_0 \in \Theta_1$. Equation (A.28) implies that for any constant z_N

$$\begin{aligned}&P_{\theta_0}\left(|N^{-1/2}\sum_{i=1}^N\left(f_v(\widetilde{W}_i,\theta_0) - E_{\theta_0}f_v(\widetilde{W}_i,\theta_0)\right)| > z_N\right)\\ &= 1-\left(1+\sum_{i=1}^{2a}N^{-i/2}\pi_i(\delta,\theta_0)\right)(\Phi(z_N)-\Phi(-z_N)) + o(N^{-a})\\ &= 2\Phi(-z_N) - \left(\sum_{i=1}^{2a}N^{-i/2}\pi_i(\delta,\theta_0)\right)(\Phi(z_N)-\Phi(-z_N)) + o(N^{-a}),\end{aligned} \tag{A.29}$$

where the error holds uniformly over $\theta_0 \in \Theta_1$. Let $z_N = \varepsilon \ln(N)$. Using $\Phi(-z) \leq C \exp(-z^2/2)$ for $z > 1$, we have

$$\begin{aligned}\Phi(-z_N) &\leq C \exp(-\varepsilon^2 \ln^2(N)/2) \leq C \exp(-(a+1)\ln(N)) \\ &= CN^{-(a+1)} = o(N^{-a}),\end{aligned} \tag{A.30}$$

where the second inequality holds for any given $a \geq 0$ and $\varepsilon > 0$ for N sufficiently large. The expression $\pi_i(\delta, \theta_0)\Phi(z_N)$ is a finite sum of terms of the form $b(\theta_0) z_N^j \phi(z_N)$ for some integer j and some function $b(\theta_0)$ that satisfies $\sup_{\theta_0 \in \Theta_1} |b(\theta_0)| < \infty$ (which holds by the uniform moment bound over $\theta_0 \in \Theta_1$ given in Assumption 4.2b), where $\phi(\cdot)$ denotes the standard normal density. By a calculation analogous to that in (A.30), $z_N^j \phi(z_N) = \varepsilon^j \ln^j(N)(2\pi)^{-1/2} \exp(-\varepsilon^2 \ln^2(N)/2) = o(N^{-a})$. This completes the proof. ■

Proof of Lemma A.3

The first result of the lemma follows from

$$\sup_{\theta_0 \in \Theta_1} P_{\theta_0}(||V_N(\overline{\theta}_N) - V_N(\theta_0)|| > \varepsilon) = o(N^{-a}), \tag{A.31}$$

$$\sup_{\theta_0 \in \Theta_1} P_{\theta_0}(||V_N(\theta_0) - E_{\theta_0} V_N(\theta_0)|| > \varepsilon) = o(N^{-a}), \quad \text{and} \tag{A.32}$$

$$\sup_{\theta_0 \in \Theta_1} |E_{\theta_0} V_N(\theta_0) - V(\theta_0)| = o(1). \tag{A.33}$$

To establish (A.31), we take mean value expansions about θ_0, apply Lemma A.2b with $m(\widetilde{W}_i, \theta_0) = \sup_{\theta \in \Theta_2} ||g(\widetilde{W}_i, \theta)|| \cdot ||(\partial/\partial\theta')g(\widetilde{W}_i, \theta)||$ and $p = q_1$, where the sup is over $\theta \in \Theta_2$ because $\sup_{\theta_0 \in \Theta_1} P_{\theta_0}(\overline{\theta}_N \notin \Theta_2) = o(N^{-a})$, and use the assumption on $\overline{\theta}_N$. To establish (A.32), we use Lemma A.2a with $m(\widetilde{W}_i, \theta_0) = g(\widetilde{W}_i, \theta_0) g(\widetilde{W}_i, \theta_0)' - E_{\theta_0} g(\widetilde{W}_i, \theta_0) g(\widetilde{W}_i, \theta_0)'$ and $p = q_1$. Equation (A.33) holds by Assumption 4.2c.

The remaining results of the lemma hold by mean value expansions about θ_0, multiple applications of Lemma A.2b with $m(\widetilde{W}_i, \theta_0) = (\partial^j/\partial\theta^j) g(\widetilde{W}_i, \theta_0)$ for $j = 0, \ldots, 3$, multiple applications of Lemma A.2a with $m(\widetilde{W}_i, \theta_0) = (\partial^j/\partial\theta^j)\, g(\widetilde{W}_i, \theta_0) - E_{\theta_0}(\partial^j/\partial\theta^j)\, g(\widetilde{W}_i, \theta_0)$ for $j = 0, 1$ and $p = q_1$, the assumption on $\overline{\theta}_N$, and Assumption 4.2c. ■

Proof of Lemma A.4

For brevity, the proof is given in Andrews (2001). It is similar to the proof of Lemma 3 in Andrews (2002). ■

Proof of Lemma A.5

For brevity, the proof is given in Andrews (2001). It is similar to the proof of Lemma 5 in Andrews (2002). ■

Proof of Lemma A.6

Suppose $\Delta_N(\theta_0) = N^{1/2}(\widehat{\theta}_N - \theta_0)$. By Lemma A.4 and Assumption 4.1a, we have $\inf_{\theta_0 \in \Theta_1} P_{\theta_0}(\widehat{\theta}_N$ is in the interior of $\Theta) = 1 - o(N^{-a})$ and $\inf_{\theta_0 \in \Theta_1} P_{\theta_0}((\partial/\partial\theta)\rho_N(\widehat{\theta}_N) = 0) = 1 - o(N^{-a})$. Element-by-element Taylor expansions of $(\partial/\partial\theta)\rho_N(\widehat{\theta}_N)$ about θ_0 of order $d-1$ give

$$0 = \frac{\partial}{\partial\theta}\rho_N(\widehat{\theta}_N) = \frac{\partial}{\partial\theta}\rho_N(\theta_0) + \sum_{j=1}^{d-1}\frac{1}{j!}D^j\frac{\partial}{\partial\theta}\rho_N(\theta_0)$$
$$\times\left(\widehat{\theta}_N - \theta_0, \ldots, \widehat{\theta}_N - \theta_0\right) + \zeta_N(\theta_0),$$

where

$$\zeta_N(\theta_0) = \frac{1}{j!}\left(D^{d-1}\frac{\partial}{\partial\theta}\rho_N(\theta_N^+) - D^{d-1}\frac{\partial}{\partial\theta}\rho_N(\theta_0)\right)$$
$$\times\left(\widehat{\theta}_N - \theta_0, \ldots, \widehat{\theta}_N - \theta_0\right), \tag{A.34}$$

θ_N^+ lies between $\widehat{\theta}_N$ and θ_0, and $D^j(\partial/\partial\theta)\rho_N(\theta_0)(\widehat{\theta}_N - \theta_0, \ldots, \widehat{\theta}_N - \theta_0)$ denotes $D^j(\partial/\partial\theta)\rho_N(\theta_0)$ as a j-linear map, whose coefficients are partial derivatives of $(\partial/\partial\theta)\rho_N(\theta_0)$ of order j, applied to the j-tuple $(\widehat{\theta}_N - \theta_0, \ldots, \widehat{\theta}_N - \theta_0)$. Let $R_N(\theta_0)$ denote the column vector whose elements are the unique components of $(\partial/\partial\theta)\rho_N(\theta_0)$, $D^1(\partial/\partial\theta)\rho_N(\theta_0), \ldots,$ $D^{d-1}(\partial/\partial\theta)\rho_N(\theta_0)$. Each element of $R_N(\theta_0)$ is an element of $S_N(\theta_0)$. Let $e_N(\theta_0) = (\zeta_N(\theta_0)', 0, \ldots, 0)'$ be conformable to $R_N(\theta_0)$. The first equation in (A.34) can be written as $\nu(R_N(\theta_0) + e_N(\theta_0), \widehat{\theta}_N - \theta_0) = 0$, where $\nu(\cdot,\cdot)$ is an infinitely differentiable function, $\nu(E_{\theta_0}R_N(\theta_0), 0) = 0$ for all $N \geq 1$, and $(\partial/\partial x)\nu(E_{\theta_0}R_N(\theta_0), x)|_{x=0} = N^{-1}\sum_{i=1}^N E_{\theta_0}g(\widetilde{W}_i, \theta_0)g(\widetilde{W}_i, \theta_0)'$ is positive definite for N large by Assumption 4.2c. Hence, the implicit function theorem can be applied to $\nu(\cdot,\cdot)$ at the point $(E_{\theta_0}R_N(\theta_0), 0)$ to obtain

$$\inf_{\theta_0 \in \Theta_1} P_{\theta_0}(\widehat{\theta}_N - \theta_0 = \Lambda(R_N(\theta_0) + e_N(\theta_0))) = 1 - o(N^{-a}), \tag{A.35}$$

where Λ is a function that does not depend on N or θ_0, is infinitely differentiable in a neighborhood of $E_{\theta_0}R_N(\theta_0)$ for all N large, and satisfies $\Lambda(E_{\theta_0}R_N(\theta_0)) = 0$.

We apply Lemma A.5 with $A_N(\theta_0) = N^{1/2}\Lambda(R_N(\theta_0))$ and $\xi_N(\theta_0) = N^{1/2}(\Lambda(R_N(\theta_0) + e_N(\theta_0)) - \Lambda(R_N(\theta_0)))$ to obtain

$$\sup_{\theta_0 \in \Theta_1, B \in \mathcal{B}_{L_\theta}} |P_{\theta_0}(N^{1/2}\Lambda(R_N(\theta_0) + e_N(\theta_0)) \in B)$$
$$- P_{\theta_0}(N^{1/2}\Lambda(R_N(\theta_0)) \in B)| = o(N^{-a}). \tag{A.36}$$

Lemma A.5 applies because (i) $P_{\theta_0}(||\xi_N(\theta_0)|| > \omega_N) \leq P_{\theta_0}(CN^{1/2}||e_N(\theta_0)|| > \omega_N)$ by a mean value expansion; (ii) $||e_N(\theta_0)|| = ||\zeta_N(\theta_0)||$; (iii) $\zeta_N(\theta_0)$ satisfies $\inf_{\theta_0 \in \Theta_1} P_{\theta_0}(||\zeta_N(\theta_0)|| \leq C||\widehat{\theta}_N - \theta_0||^d) = 1 - o(N^{-a})$; (iv) ω_N, which is defined to equal $N^{1/2-d/2}\ln^d(N)$, is $o(N^{-a})$ because $d \geq 2a + 2$ by Assumption 4.2a; (v) $\sup_{\theta_0 \in \Theta_1} P_{\theta_0}(N^{1/2}||e_N(\theta_0)|| > \omega_N) \leq$

$\sup_{\theta_0\in\Theta_1} P_{\theta_0}(CN^{1/2}||\widehat{\theta}_N - \theta_0||^d > \omega_N) + o(N^{-a}) = o(N^{-a})$ by Lemma A.4; (vi) $\Lambda(R_N(\theta_0))$ can be written as $G(S_N(\theta_0))$, where $G(\cdot)$ is infinitely differentiable and $G(E_{\theta_0}S_N(\theta_0)) = 0$ for all N large; and (vii) $A_N(\theta_0) = N^{1/2}\Lambda(R_N(\theta_0)) = N^{1/2}G(S_N(\theta_0))$ has an Edgeworth expansion (with remainder $o(N^{-a})$ uniformly over $\theta_0 \in \Theta_1$) by the proof of Lemma A.8.

Equations (A.35) and (A.36) and $\Lambda(R_N(\theta_0)) = G(S_N(\theta_0))$ yield the result of Lemma A.8.

Each of the remaining forms of $\Delta_N(\theta_0)$ (viz., $T_N(\theta_{0,r})$ and $H_N(\widehat{\theta}_N, \beta_0)$) is a function of $\widehat{\theta}_N$. We take a Taylor expansion of $\Delta_N(\theta_0)/N^{1/2}$ about $\widehat{\theta}_N = \theta_0$ to order $d-1$ to obtain

$$\Delta_N(\theta_0) = N^{1/2}(\Lambda^{**}(S_N(\theta_0), \widehat{\theta}_N - \theta_0) + \zeta_N^{**}(\theta_0)), \tag{A.37}$$

where Λ^{**} is an infinitely differentiable function that does not depend on θ_0, $\Lambda^{**}(E_{\theta_0}S_N(\theta_0), 0) = 0$ for N large, $\zeta_N^{**}(\theta_0)$ is the remainder term in the Taylor expansion, and $||\zeta_N^{**}(\theta_0)|| = O(||\widehat{\theta}_N - \theta_0||^d)$. Combining (A.35) with (A.37) gives $\Delta_N(\theta_0) = N^{1/2}(\Lambda^{**}(S_N(\theta_0),\ \Lambda(R_N(\theta_0) + e_N(\theta_0)))\ + \zeta_N^{**}(\theta_0))$. We apply Lemma A.5 again, using the earlier result for $||\zeta_N^{**}(\theta_0)||$, to obtain an analog of (A.36) with $A_N(\theta_0) = N^{1/2}\Lambda^{**}(S_N(\theta_0), \Lambda(R_N(\theta_0)))$. We can write $G(S_N(\theta_0)) = \Lambda^{**}(S_N(\theta_0),\ \Lambda(R_N(\theta_0)))$, where $G(\cdot)$ is infinitely differentiable and $G(E_{\theta_0}S_N(\theta_0)) = \Lambda^{**}(E_{\theta_0}S_N(\theta_0), \Lambda(E_{\theta_0}R_N(\theta_0))) = \Lambda^{**}(E_{\theta_0}S_N(\theta_0), 0) = 0$ for all N large. Combining this, the analog of (A.36), and (A.37) gives the result of the lemma for $\Delta_N(\theta_0)$ equal to $T_N(\theta_{0,r})$ and $H_N(\widehat{\theta}_N, \beta_0)$. ■

Proof of Lemma A.7

We show below that for all $\theta_0 \in \Theta_1$ and all $\theta \in \Theta_2$ such that $||\theta - \theta_0|| < \delta$ (where δ is as in the definition of Θ_1),

$$\left| N^{\alpha(m)}E_\theta \prod_{\mu=1}^{m} \Psi_{N,j_\mu} - N^{\alpha(m)}E_{\theta_0} \prod_{\mu=1}^{m} \Psi_{N,j_\mu} \right| \le B_N||\theta - \theta_0||, \tag{A.38}$$

where $\limsup_{N\to\infty} B_N < \infty$. Let $\eta > 0$ satisfy $\eta < \varepsilon/(L_\nu^{1/2} \limsup_{N\to\infty} B_N)$, where L_ν denotes the dimension of $\nu_{N,a}(\theta_0)$. Then,

$$\begin{aligned}
&\sup_{\theta_0\in\Theta_1} P_{\theta_0}(N^{1/2}||\nu_{N,a}(\widehat{\theta}_N) - \nu_{N,a}(\theta_0)|| > \ln(N)\varepsilon) \\
&\quad \le \sup_{\theta_0\in\Theta_1} P_{\theta_0}(N^{1/2}||\nu_{N,a}(\widehat{\theta}_N) - \nu_{N,a}(\theta_0)|| > \ln(N)\varepsilon, \\
&\qquad N^{1/2}||\widehat{\theta}_N - \theta_0|| \le \ln(N)\eta) \\
&\qquad + \sup_{\theta_0\in\Theta_1} P_{\theta_0}(N^{1/2}||\widehat{\theta}_N - \theta_0|| > \ln(N)\eta) \\
&\quad \le \sup_{\theta_0\in\Theta_1} P_{\theta_0}(L_\nu^{1/2}B_N N^{1/2}||\widehat{\theta}_N - \theta_0|| > \ln(N)\varepsilon,\ N^{1/2}||\widehat{\theta}_N - \theta_0|| \le \ln(N)\eta) \\
&\qquad + o(N^{-a}) \\
&\quad = o(N^{-a}),
\end{aligned} \tag{A.39}$$

where the second inequality uses (A.38) and Lemma A.4.

Under the assumptions, (A.38) holds provided, for all $\theta_0 \in \Theta_1$ and all $\theta \in \Theta_2$ such that $||\theta - \theta_0|| < \delta$,

$$|E_\theta \prod_{\mu=1}^{m} f_{j_\mu}(\widetilde{W}_i, \theta) - E_{\theta_0} \prod_{\mu=1}^{m} f_{j_\mu}(\widetilde{W}_i, \theta_0)| \leq B_{1,N}||\theta - \theta_0||, \quad \text{(A.40)}$$

for all $m \leq 2a + 2$, all $i \geq 1$, and all $j_\mu \leq L_f$, where $f_{j_\mu}(\widetilde{W}_i, \theta)$ denotes the j_μth element of $f(\widetilde{W}_i, \theta)$ and $\lim\sup_{N\to\infty} B_{1,N} < \infty$. The triangle inequality, a mean value expansion, and some calculations show that (A.40) holds if

$$\sup_{\theta_0 \in \Theta_1, i \geq 1} E_{\theta_0}||C_f^j(\widetilde{W}_i) f_{j_\mu}^{2a+3-j}(\widetilde{W}_i, \theta_0)|| < \infty \quad \text{(A.41)}$$

for all $j = 0, \ldots, 2a + 2$ and for all elements j_μ of $f(\widetilde{W}_i, \theta_0)$. This holds if $q_1 \geq 2a + 3$, as is assumed. ■

Proof of Lemma A.8

We establish the first result of part (a) first. By Lemma A.6, it suffices to show that the random variable $N^{1/2}G(S_N(\theta_0))$ of Lemma A.6 possesses an Edgeworth expansion with remainder $o(N^{-a})$ uniformly over $\theta_0 \in \Theta_1$. We obtain an Edgeworth expansion for $N^{1/2}(S_N(\theta_0) - E_{\theta_0} S_N(\theta_0))$ for each $\theta_0 \in \Theta_1$ via Theorem 2.1 of Lahiri (1993) (also see Corollary 2.9 of Götze and Hipp, 1983), as in the proof of Lemma A.2c. The remainder is uniform in $\theta_0 \in \Theta_1$ because the conditions in Assumptions 4.2b, 4.2c, and 4.3 hold uniformly over $\theta_0 \in \Theta_1$. Edgeworth expansions for $N^{1/2}G(S_N(\theta_0))$ are now obtained from those of $N^{1/2}(S_N(\theta_0) - E_{\theta_0} S_N(\theta_0))$ by the argument in Bhattacharya (1985, Proof of Theorem 1) or Bhattacharya and Ghosh (1978, Proof of Theorem 2) using the smoothness of $G(\cdot)$, $G(E_{\theta_0} S_N(\theta_0)) = 0$ for all $N \geq 1$ and all $\theta_0 \in \Theta_1$, and Assumption 4.2c.

To establish the second result of part (a), we consider the convex sets $B_z = \{x \in R^{L_\beta} : x'x \leq z\}$ for $z \in R$. By Lemma A.6a, with $\Delta_N(\theta_0) = H_N(\widehat{\theta}_N, \beta_0)$, we have

$$\begin{aligned} o(N^{-a}) &= \sup_{\theta_0 \in \Theta_1} \sup_{z \in R} |P_{\theta_0}(H_N(\widehat{\theta}_N, \beta_0) \in B_z) \\ &\quad - P_{\theta_0}(N^{1/2}G(S_N(\theta_0)) \in B_z)| \\ &= \sup_{\theta_0 \in \Theta_1} \sup_{z \in R} |P_{\theta_0}(\mathcal{W}_N(\beta_0) \leq z) \\ &\quad - P_{\theta_0}(NG(S_N(\theta_0))'G(S_N(\theta_0)) \leq z)|. \end{aligned} \quad \text{(A.42)}$$

Hence, it suffices to show that the second result of part (a) holds with $\mathcal{W}_N(\beta_0)$ replaced by $NG(S_N(\theta_0))'G(S_N(\theta_0))$. By the same argument as in the previous paragraph, $N^{1/2}G(S_N(\theta_0))$ has a multivariate Edgeworth expansion with remainder $o(N^{-a})$ uniform in $\theta_0 \in \Theta_1$, when $N^{1/2}G(S_N(\theta_0))$ corresponds to $H_N(\widehat{\theta}_N, \beta_0)$. This Edgeworth expansion, coupled with Theorem 1 and Remark 2.2 of Chandra and Ghosh (1979), yields an Edgeworth expansion for $NG(S_N(\theta_0))'G(S_N(\theta_0))$ equal to that given for $\mathcal{W}_N(\beta_0)$ in Lemma A.8.

The first result of part (b) follows from Lemma A.1 with

$$\begin{aligned}\lambda_N(\theta_0) &= \sup_{z\in R} \Big| P^*_{\theta_0}(T^*_N(\theta_{0,r}) \leq z) \\ &\quad - \left[1 + \sum_{i=1}^{2a} N^{-i/2}\pi_{Ti}(\delta, \nu_{N,a}(\theta_0))\right]\Phi(z)\Big| \\ &= \sup_{z\in R} \Big| P_{\theta_0}(T_N(\theta_{0,r}) \leq z) \\ &\quad - \left[1 + \sum_{i=1}^{2a} N^{-i/2}\pi_{Ti}(\delta, \nu_{N,a}(\theta_0))\right]\Phi(z)\Big|. \end{aligned} \tag{A.43}$$

The first condition of Lemma A.1 holds by Lemma A.4, and the second condition of Lemma A.1 holds by part (a) of the present lemma. The proof of the second result of part (b) is analogous. ■

References

Andrews, D. W. K. (2001), "Higher-order Improvements of the Parametric Bootstrap for Markov Processes," Cowles Foundation Discussion Paper No. 1334. Available at http://cowles.econ.yale.edu.

Andrews, D. W. K. (2002a), "Equivalence of the Higher-order Asymptotic Efficiency of k-Step and Extremum Statistics," *Econometric Theory,* 18, 2002, 1040–85.

Andrews, D. W. K. (2002b), "Higher-order Improvements of a Computationally Attractive k-Step Bootstrap," *Econometrica,* 70, 119–62.

Andrews, D. W. K., and H.-Y. Chen (1994), "Approximately Median-unbiased Estimation of Autoregressive Models," *Journal of Business and Economic Statistics,* 12, 187–204.

Andrews, D. W. K., and O. Lieberman, "Higher-order Improvements of the Parametric Bootstrap for Long-memory Gaussian Processes," *Journal of Econometrics*, in press.

Bhattacharya, R. N. (1985), "Some Recent Results on Cramér–Edgeworth Expansions with Applications," in *Multivariate Analysis*, vol. 6 (ed. by P. R. Krishnaiah), Elsevier: New York, 57–75.

Bhattacharya, R. N., and J. K. Ghosh (1978), "On the Validity of the Formal Edgeworth Expansion," *Annals of Statistics*, 6, 434–51.

Bose, A. (1988), "Edgeworth Correction by Bootstrap in Autoregression," *Annals of Statistics,* 16, 1709–22.

Bühlmann, P. (1997), "Sieve Bootstrap for Time Series," *Bernoulli,* 3, 123–48.

Bühlmann, P. (1998), "Sieve Bootstrap for Smoothing in Nonstationary Time Series," *Annals of Statistics,* 26, 48–83.

Carlstein, E. (1986), "The Use of Subseries Methods for Estimating the Variance of a General Statistic from a Stationary Time Series," *Annals of Statistics,* 14, 1171–9.

Chandra, T. K., and J. K. Ghosh (1979), "Valid Asymptotic Expansions for the Likelihood Ratio Statistic and Other Perturbed Chi-square Variables," *Sankhya*, Series A, 41, 22–47.

Chang, Y., and J. Y. Park (2003), "A Sieve Bootstrap for the Test of a Unit Root," *Journal of Time Series Analysis*, 24, 379–400.

Choi, E., and P. Hall (2000), "Bootstrap Confidence Regions Computed from Autoregressions of Arbitrary Order," *Journal of the Royal Statistical Society,* Series B, 62, 461–77.

Datta, S., and W. P. McCormick (1995), "Some Continuous Edgeworth Expansions for Markov Chains with Applications to Bootstrap," *Journal of Multivariate Analysis,* 52, 83–106.

Davidson, R., and J. G. MacKinnon (1999a), "Bootstrap Testing in Nonlinear Models," *International Economic Review,* 40, 487–508.

Davidson, R., and J. G. MacKinnon (1999b), "The Size Distortion of Bootstrap Tests," *Econometric Theory,* 15, 361–76.

Doukhan, P. (1995), *Mixing: Properties and Examples*. New York: Springer-Verlag.

Fisher, R. A. (1925), "Theory of Statistical Estimation," *Proceedings of the Cambridge Philosophical Society,* 22, 700–725.

Gonçalves, S., and H. White (2004), "Maximum Likelihood and the Bootstrap for Nonlinear Dynamic Models," *Journal of Econometrics*, 119, 199–220.

Götze, F., and C. Hipp (1983), "Asymptotic Expansions for Sums of Weakly Dependent Random Vectors," *Z. Wahrscheinlichkeitstheorie verw. Gebiete*, 64, 211–39.

Götze, F., and C. Hipp (1994), "Asymptotic Distribution of Statistics in Time Series," *Annals of Statistics*, 22, 2062–88.

Götze, F., and H. R. Künsch (1996), "Second-order Correctness of the Blockwise Bootstrap for Stationary Observations," *Annals of Statistics,* 24, 1914–33.

Hall, P. (1988), "On Symmetric Bootstrap Confidence Intervals," *Journal of the Royal Statistical Society,* Series B, 50, 35–45.

Hall, P. (1992), *The Bootstrap and Edgeworth Expansion.* New York: Springer–Verlag.

Hall, P., and J. L. Horowitz (1996), "Bootstrap Critical Values for Tests Based on Generalized-Method-of-Moment Estimators," *Econometrica*, 64, 891–916.

Hansen, B. E. (1999), "The Grid Bootstrap and the Autoregressive Model," *Review of Economics and Statistics,* 81, 594–607.

Horowitz, J. L. (2003), "Bootstrap Methods for Markov Processes," *Econometrica*, 71, 1049–1082.

Inoue, A., and L. Kilian (2002), "Bootstrapping Autoregressive Processes with Possible Unit Roots," *Econometrica*, 70, 377–391.

Inoue, A., and M. Shintani (2005), "Bootstrapping GMM Estimators for Time Series," *Journal of Econometrics*, forthcoming.

Janssen, P., J. Jureckova, and N. Veraverbeke (1985), "Rate of Convergence of One- and Two-step M-estimators with Applications to Maximum Likelihood and Pitman Estimators," *Annals of Statistics,* 13, 1222–9.

Jensen, J. L. (1989), "Asymptotic Refinements for Strongly Mixing Harris Recurrent Markov Chains," *Scandinavian Journal of Statistics,* 16, 47–63.

Kim, Jong H. (2002), "Higher-order Improvements of the Restricted Parametric Bootstrap for Tests," unpublished manuscript, Department of Economics, Yale University.

Künsch, H. R. (1989), "The Jackknife and the Bootstrap for General Stationary Observations," *Annals of Statistics*, 17, 1217–41.

Lahiri, S. N. (1992), "Edgeworth Correction by 'Moving Block' Bootstrap for Stationary and Nonstationary Data," in *Exploring the Limits of the Bootstrap* (ed. by R. Lepage and L. Billard), New York: Wiley, 182–214.

Lahiri, S. N. (1993), "Refinements in Asymptotic Expansions for Sums of Weakly Dependent Random Vectors," *Annals of Probability,* 21, 791–9.

Lahiri, S. N. (1996), "On Edgeworth Expansion and Moving Block Bootstrap for Studentized M-estimators in Multiple Linear Regression Models," *Journal of Multivariate Analysis,* 56, 42–59.

Lahiri, S. N. (1999), "Theoretical Comparisons of Block Bootstrap Methods," *Annals of Statistics,* 27, 386–404.

LeCam, L. (1956), "On the Asymptotic Theory of Estimation and Testing Hypotheses," *Proceedings of the Third Berkeley Symposium on Mathematical Statistics and Probability,* 1, 129–56.

Malinovskii, V. K. (1987), "Limit Theorems for Harris Markov Chains, I" *Theory of Probability and Its Applications,* 31, 269–85.

Ortega, J. M., and W. C. Reinbuldt (1970), *Iterative Solution of Nonlinear Equations in Several Variables*. New York: Academic Press.

Paparoditis, E. (1996), "Bootstrapping Autoregressive and Moving Average Parameter Estimates of Infinite Order Vector Autoregressive Processes," *Journal of Multivariate Analysis,* 57, 277–96.

Park, J. Y. (2001), "Bootstrap Unit Root Tests," unpublished manuscript, School of Economics, Seoul National University, Seoul, Korea.

Pfanzagl, J. (1974), "Asymptotic Optimum Estimation and Test Procedures," in *Proceedings of the Prague Symposium on Asymptotic Statistics, 3–6 September 1973,* Vol. I (ed. by J. Hájek), Charles University: Prague.

Rajarshi, M. B. (1995), "Bootstrap in Markov Sequences Based on Estimates of Transition Density," *Annals of the Institute of Statistical Mathematics,* 42, 253–68.

Robinson, P. M. (1988), "The Stochastic Difference Between Econometric Statistics," *Econometrica*, 56, 531–48.

Romano, J. P., and M. Wolf (2001), "Subsampling Intervals in Autoregressive Models with Linear Time Trend," *Econometrica,* 69, 1283–314.

Rothenberg, T. J. (1984a), "Approximate Normality of Generalized Least Squares Estimates," *Econometrica,* 52, 811–825.

Rothenberg, T. J. (1984b), "Hypothesis Testing in Linear Models When the Error Covariance Matrix Is Nonscalar," *Econometrica,* 52, 827–42.

Rothenberg, T. J., and C. T. Leenders (1964), "Efficient Estimation of Simultaneous Equation Systems," *Econometrica,* 32, 57–76.

Stock, J. H. (1991), "Confidence Intervals for the Largest Autoregressive Root in U.S. Macroeconomic Time Series," *Journal of Monetary Economics,* 28, 435–60.

Yokoyama, R. (1980), "Moment Bounds for Stationary Mixing Sequences," *Z. Wahrscheinlichkeitstheorie verw. Gebiete*, 52, 45–57.

Zvingelis, J. J. (2003), "On Bootstrap Coverage Probability with Dependent Data," in *Computer-aided Econometrics* (ed. by D. E. A. Giles), New York: Marcel Dekker.

CHAPTER 10

The Performance of Empirical Likelihood and its Generalizations

Guido W. Imbens and Richard H. Spady

ABSTRACT

We calculate higher-order asymptotic biases and mean squared errors (MSE) for a simple model with a sequence of moment conditions. In this setup, generalized empirical likelihood (GEL) and infeasible optimal GMM (OGMM) have the same higher-order biases, with GEL apparently having an MSE that exceeds OGMM's by an additional term of order $(M-1)/N$, i.e., the degree of overidentification divided by sample size. In contrast, any two-step GMM estimator has an additional bias relative to OGMM of order $(M-1)/N$ and an additional MSE of order $(M-1)^2/N$. Consequently, GEL must be expected to dominate two-step GMM. In our simple model all GEL's have equivalent next higher order behavior because generalized third moments of moment conditions are assumed to be zero; we explore, in further analysis and simulations, the implications of dropping this assumption.

1. INTRODUCTION

This paper has two parts. In the first part, we calculate higher-order asymptotic biases and mean squared errors (MSE) for a simple model with a sequence of moment conditions. In this setup, generalized empirical likelihood (GEL) and infeasible optimal GMM (OGMM) have the same higher-order biases, with GEL having an MSE that *apparently* exceeds OGMM's by an additional term of order $(M-1)/N$, i.e., the degree of overidentification divided by sample size. In contrast, any two-step GMM estimator has an additional bias relative to OGMM of order $(M-1)/N$ and an additional MSE of order $(M-1)^2/N$. Although these features do depend on the simple framework we have adopted (and on the force of "apparently," cf. the discussion of Lemma 9) we cannot see how a more complicated framework will rescue two-step GMM (generalized method of moments) from these fundamental difficulties. Consequently, we conclude that GEL must be expected to dominate two-step GMM, and our interest shifts to distinguishing between variants of GEL and the closely related, (if not dual) empirical discrepancy (ED) estimators.

In our simple model all GEL's have equivalent next higher-order behavior because third moments of moment conditions (i.e., products of the form $\psi_j\psi_k\psi_\ell$, where any or all of j, k, and ℓ may be equal) are assumed to be zero. We explore, in further analysis and simulations, the implications of dropping this assumption. Our analysis indicates that one variant of GEL/ED, which can be identified with continuously updated GMM, ignores third and higher-order cumulants of the moment conditions used in GMM estimation, effectively treating these cumulants as zero. Whether this is advantageous depends, heuristically, on whether higher-order cumulants of moment conditions can be usefully estimated to deviate from zero, which of course depends on sample size and the data generating process. We find that when third moments are unimportant, all variants of GEL/ED provide virtually identical performance in our simple experiments. However, in cases where there is substantial skew, continuously updated GMM is usually inferior to other variants, including exponential tilting (ET) and empirical likelihood (EL), at small and moderate sample sizes. In some of these cases, ET is superior to EL; and in no case is there substantial loss in applying ET/EL in preference to the continuously updated estimator (CUE).

In their recent unpublished work Newey and Smith (2002) have demonstrated that bias-corrected EL is second-order efficient within the class of bias-corrected GEL estimators. The line of argument in some ways parallels the argument that bias corrected parametric ML is second-order efficient in the parametric case. As such, it does not explicitly calculate the higher order approximations to the mean squared error that are computed here, albeit for special cases. These calculations help us frame and examine cases where we conjecture (correctly) that ET outperforms EL in small and moderately sized samples. The practical relevance of the analogy of empirical likelihood to parametric likelihood in higher-order asymptotic behavior is problematic: for example, although the EL likelihood ratio test (ELRT) is Bartlett correctable in the absence of nuisance parameters, the behaviors of the ELRT and its Bartlett correction do not resemble their parametric counterparts (cf. Corcoran, Davison, and Spady, 1995; Imbens, Spady, and Johnson, 1998). Consequently, we feel that caution is warranted in choosing between members of the GEL class when moment conditions have nonzero third and higher order cumulants.

2. FRAMEWORK

Consider a sequence of independent and identically distributed pairs of random vectors $\{(v_i, w_i)\}_{i=1}^N$. The dimension of v_i and w_i is $M \geq 1$. We are interested in a scalar parameter θ, satisfying

$$E[\psi(v_i, w_i, \theta)] = 0,$$

for $i = 1, \ldots, N$, where

$$\psi(v_i, w_i, \theta) = (v_i + e_1) \cdot \theta - w_i = \begin{pmatrix} (v_{i1} + 1) \cdot \theta - w_{i1} \\ v_{i2} \cdot \theta - w_{i2} \\ \vdots \\ v_{iM} \cdot \theta - w_{iM} \end{pmatrix},$$

and e_1 is an M–vector with the first element equal to one and the other elements equal to zero.

We are interested in the properties of various estimators for θ as the degree of overidentification $(M-1)$, increases. Following Donald and Newey (2004) who look at the behavior of various instrumental variables estimators as the number of instruments increases, and Newey and Smith (2001) who look at bias of GEL and GMM estimators, we look at the leading terms in the asymptotic expansion of the estimators and consider the rate at which the moments of these terms increase with M.

We make the following simplifying assumptions. The pairs (v_{im}, w_{im}) and (v_{jn}, w_{jn}) are independent if either $i \neq j$ or $n \neq m$ (or both), and have the same distribution. Let $\mu_{rp} = E[v_{im}^r \cdot w_{im}^p]$ denote the moments of this distribution. Moments up to order $p + r \leq 6$ are assumed to be finite. Without essential loss of generality, let $\mu_{10} = \mu_{01} = 0$, implying the true value of θ is $\theta^* = 0$, let $\mu_{20} = \mu_{02} = 1$, and let $\mu_{11} = \rho$ be the correlation coefficient of v_{im} and w_{im}.

With these assumptions the system of moment conditions, in fact, contains no identifying information after the first moment, although this would not be known to an investigator. Since in general a system of M moment conditions being used to estimate a scalar parameter can be renormalized to a system with one efficient moment condition that depends on the parameter of interest and $(M-1)$ moment conditions that are uncorrelated with it, the above system models the situation in which successive moment conditions are increasingly less informative. One purpose of our analytical investigation is to demonstrate that some estimators are better able to resist the deterioration of efficiency caused by the addition of irrelevant moment conditions.

Let

$$\overline{v} = \frac{1}{N}\sum_{i=1}^{N} v_i,$$

$$\overline{w} = \frac{1}{N}\sum_{i=1}^{N} w_i,$$

$$\overline{ww'} = \frac{1}{N}\sum_{i=1}^{N} w_i w_i',$$

denote sample averages, let $\overline{v}_j$ and $\overline{w}_j$ denote the jth element of $\overline{v}$ and $\overline{w}$, respectively, and let $\overline{ww'}_{ij}$ denote the (i, j)th element of $\overline{ww'}$.

Denote the optimal, infeasible, GMM estimator by

$$\hat{\theta}_{\text{opt}} = \overline{w}_1/(1+\overline{v}_1).$$

This is the estimator based on using the optimal linear combination of the moments. Since only the first moment is informative, this implies using only the first moment, thus estimating θ by solving

$$\sum_{i=1}^{N}(v_{i1}+1)\cdot\theta - w_{i1}.$$

This estimator is not feasible because the researcher does not know the optimal linear combination of the moments, but it provides a useful benchmark against which to judge feasible estimators. Note that increasing M does not affect this estimator as all the additional moments are ignored.

First we expand this estimator up to terms of order $O_p(N^{-3/2})$.

Lemma 2.1. (EXPANSION OPTIMAL GMM ESTIMATOR)

$$\hat{\theta}_{\text{opt}} = \overline{w}_1 - \overline{w}_1\overline{v}_1 + \overline{w}_1\overline{v}_1^2 + o_p\left(N^{-3/2}\right).$$

Proof. See Appendix.

Define

$$\begin{aligned} &\text{(i) } R^{\text{opt}} = \overline{w}_1 = O_p(N^{-1/2}),\\ &\text{(ii) } S^{\text{opt}} = -\overline{w}_1\overline{v}_1 = O_p(N^{-1}),\\ &\text{(iii) } T^{\text{opt}} = \overline{w}_1\overline{v}_1^2 = O_p(N^{-3/2}), \end{aligned}$$

so that $\hat{\theta}_{\text{opt}} = R^{\text{opt}} + S^{\text{opt}} + T^{\text{opt}} + o_p\left(N^{-3/2}\right)$.

Lemma 2.2. (BIAS OF $\hat{\theta}_{\text{opt}}$)
The bias of the leading terms is

$$E[R^{\text{opt}} + S^{\text{opt}} + T^{\text{opt}} - \theta^*] = -\rho/N + \mu_{21}/N^2.$$

Proof. See Appendix.

Lemma 2.3. (MEAN SQUARED ERROR OF $\hat{\theta}_{\text{opt}}$)
The mean squared error of the leading terms is

$$E[(R^{\text{opt}} + S^{\text{opt}} + T^{\text{opt}} - \theta^*)^2] = 1/N - 2\mu_{12}/N^2 + 3(2\rho^2+1)/N^2 + o(1/N^2).$$

Proof. See Appendix.

3. TWO-STEP GMM ESTIMATOR

The first estimator we consider is the standard two-step generalized method of moments (GMM) estimator, due to Hansen (1982). Consider a generic GMM estimator, defined as the minimand of

$$\left(\frac{1}{N}\sum_{i=1}^{N}\psi(v_i, w_i, \theta)\right)' \cdot C \cdot \left(\frac{1}{N}\sum_{i=1}^{N}\psi(v_i, w_i, \theta)\right).$$

We focus here on the efficient GMM estimator, with the choice for the weight matrix C equal to

$$\left(\frac{1}{N}\sum_{i=1}^{N}\psi(v_i, w_i, \theta^*) \cdot \psi(v_i, w_i, \theta^*)'\right)^{-1} = (\overline{ww'})^{-1},$$

so that the GMM "weight" matrix is estimated at the true value of θ. Thus, the GMM objective function is

$$\left(\frac{1}{N}\sum_{i=1}^{N}\psi(v_i, w_i, \theta)\right)' \cdot (\overline{ww'})^{-1} \cdot \left(\frac{1}{N}\sum_{i=1}^{N}\psi(v_i, w_i, \theta)\right)$$
$$= ((\overline{v} + e_1) \cdot \theta - \overline{w})' \cdot (\overline{ww'})^{-1} \cdot ((\overline{v} + e_1) \cdot \theta - \overline{w}).$$

The first order condition for the GMM estimator is

$$0 = 2(\overline{v} + e_1)' \cdot (\overline{ww'})^{-1} \cdot ((\overline{v} + e_1) \cdot \theta - \overline{w}),$$

with the solution for the GMM estimator equal to

$$\hat{\theta}_{\text{gmm}} = \left((\overline{v} + e_1)' \cdot (\overline{ww'})^{-1} \cdot (\overline{v} + e_1)\right)^{-1} \cdot \left((\overline{v} + e_1)' \cdot (\overline{ww'})^{-1} \cdot \overline{w}\right).$$

The goal is to approximate this estimator up to terms of order $O_p(1/N)$ and evaluate the mean squared error of this approximation. In particular, the terms whose moments depend on M are of interest, and specifically how fast the mean squared error increases with the number of excess moments.

Lemma 3.4. (EXPANSION OF $\hat{\theta}_{\text{gmm}}$)

$$\begin{aligned}\hat{\theta}_{\text{gmm}} = {} & \overline{w}_1 - 2\overline{v}_1\overline{w}_1 + (\overline{ww'}_{11} - 1) \cdot \overline{w}_1 - e_1'(\overline{ww'} - \mathcal{I}_M)\overline{w} + \overline{v}'\overline{w} \\ & - \overline{v}(\overline{ww'} - \mathcal{I}_M)\overline{w} + e_1(\overline{ww'} - \mathcal{I}_M)(\overline{ww'} - \mathcal{I}_M)\overline{w} - 2\overline{v}_1\overline{v}'\overline{w} \\ & + 2\overline{v}_1 e_1'(\overline{ww'} - \mathcal{I}_M)\overline{w} + 2\overline{w}_1 e_1(\overline{ww'} - \mathcal{I}_M)\overline{v} \\ & - \overline{w}_1 e_1'(\overline{ww'} - \mathcal{I}_M)(\overline{ww'} - \mathcal{I}_M)e_1 + 4\overline{v}_1^2\overline{w}_1 \\ & + \overline{w}_1(\overline{ww'}_{11} - 1)(\overline{ww'}_{11} - 1) - 4\overline{v}_1\overline{w}_1(\overline{ww'}_{11} - 1) \\ & + (\overline{ww'}_{11} - 1)\overline{v}'\overline{w} - (\overline{ww'}_{11} - 1)e_1'(\overline{ww'} - \mathcal{I}_M)\overline{w} \\ & - \overline{w}_1\overline{v}'\overline{v} + o_p\left(N^{-3/2}\right).\end{aligned}$$

Proof. See Appendix.

Now define

(i) $R^{\text{gmm}} = \overline{w}_1 = O_p(N^{-1/2})$,
(ii) $S^{\text{gmm}} = -2\overline{v}_1\overline{w}_1 + (\overline{ww'}_{11} - 1) \cdot \overline{w}_1 - e_1' \left(\overline{ww'} - \mathcal{I}_M\right)\overline{w} + \overline{v}'\overline{w} = O_p(N^{-1})$,
(iii) $T^{\text{gmm}} = -\overline{v}(\overline{ww'} - \mathcal{I}_M)\overline{w} + e_1(\overline{ww'} - \mathcal{I}_M)(\overline{ww'} - \mathcal{I}_M)\overline{w} - 2\overline{v}_1\overline{v}'\overline{w} + 2\overline{v}_1 e_1'(\overline{ww'} - \mathcal{I}_M)\overline{w} + 2\overline{w}_1 e_1(\overline{ww'} - \mathcal{I}_M)\overline{v} - \overline{w}_1 e_1'(\overline{ww'} - \mathcal{I}_M)(\overline{ww'} - \mathcal{I}_M)e_1 + 4\overline{v}_1^2\overline{w}_1 + \overline{w}_1(\overline{ww'}_{11} - 1) \times (\overline{ww'}_{11} - 1) - 4\overline{v}_1\overline{w}_1(\overline{ww'}_{11} - 1) + (\overline{ww'}_{11} - 1)\overline{v}'\overline{w} - (\overline{ww'}_{11} - 1)\, e_1'(\overline{ww'} - \mathcal{I}_M)\overline{w} - \overline{w}_1\overline{v}'\overline{v} = O_p(N^{-3/2})$. so that

$$\hat{\theta}_{\text{gmm}} = R^{\text{gmm}} + S^{\text{gmm}} + T^{\text{gmm}} + o_p\left(N^{-3/2}\right).$$

For the bias of the GMM estimator we therefore investigate the moments of $R^{\text{gmm}} + S^{\text{gmm}} - \theta^*$.

Lemma 3.5. (Bias of $\hat{\theta}_{\text{gmm}}$)
The expectation of the leading terms is

$$E[R^{\text{gmm}} + S^{\text{gmm}} - \theta^*] = -\rho/N + \rho(M-1)/N + o(N^{-1}).$$

Proof. See Appendix.

Lemma 3.6. (Mean Squared Error of $\hat{\theta}_{\text{gmm}}$)
The mean squared error of the leading terms is

$$\begin{aligned} &E\left[(R^{\text{gmm}} + S^{\text{gmm}} + T^{\text{gmm}} - \theta^*)^2\right] \\ &= 1/N - 2\mu_{12}/N^2 + 3(2\rho^2+1)/N^2 + \rho^2(M-1)^2/N^2 \\ &\quad + (M-1)(3\rho^2 + 1 + 2\rho\mu_{03})/N^2 + o(1/N^2). \end{aligned}$$

Proof. See Appendix.

Note that the difference between the MSE for $\hat{\theta}_{\text{gmm}}$ and $\hat{\theta}_{\text{opt}}$ is in the last two terms. The first of these is proportional to $(M-1)^2$ and is the reason for the poor performance of the two-step GMM estimator when the degree of overidentification is high. If $M = 1$, the two extra terms vanish as the optimal GMM estimator and feasible GMM estimator coincide.

4. GENERALIZED EMPIRICAL LIKELIHOOD ESTIMATORS

In this section we consider alternatives to the standard two-step GMM estimators. The estimators considered include empirical likelihood (Qin and Lawless, 1994; Imbens, 1997), exponential tilting (Imbens et al., 1998;

Kitamura and Stutzer, 1997; Rothenberg, 1999), and the continuously updating estimator (Hansen, Heaton, and Yaron, 1996). The specific class of estimators we consider is related to that of the Cressie–Read family (cf. Baggerly, 1998; Corcoran, 1995), as well to the generalized empirical likelihood estimators, introduced by Smith (1997). For a given function $g(a)$, normalized to satisfy $g(0) = 1$, $g'(0) = 1$, and $g''(0) = \lambda$, the estimator for θ is defined through the system of equations

$$0 = \sum_{i=1}^{N} \psi(v_i, w_i, \theta) \cdot g(t'\psi(v_i, w_i, \theta)),$$

$$0 = \sum_{i=1}^{N} t' \frac{\partial \psi}{\partial \theta'}(v_i, w_i, \theta) \cdot g(t'\psi(v_i, w_i, \theta)),$$

solved as a function of θ and t. The leading choices for $g(a)$ are $g(a) = 1/(1-a)$ (empirical likelihood), $g(a) = \exp(a)$ (exponential tilting), and $g(a) = 1 + a$ (continuously updating).

Under standard conditions, the solution for t, denoted by $\hat{t}_g$ converges to a vector of zeros; $\hat{\theta}_g$, the solution for θ, converges to θ^*, and

$$\hat{t}_g = O_p(1/\sqrt{N}),$$

$$\hat{\theta}_g = O_p(1/\sqrt{N}).$$

The choice of $g(a)$ does not matter for the standard large sample distribution, and

$$\hat{t}_{g_1} - \hat{t}_{g_2} = o_p(1/\sqrt{N}),$$

$$\hat{\theta}_g - \hat{\theta}_{\text{opt}} = o_p(1/\sqrt{N}).$$

Lemma 4.7. (EXPANSION FOR $\hat{\theta}_g$)

$$\hat{\theta}_g = \overline{w}_1 + (\overline{ww'}_{11} - 1)\overline{w}_1 - e_1'(\overline{ww'} - \mathcal{I}_M)\overline{w}$$
$$+ \overline{w}'\overline{v} - 2\overline{w}_1\overline{v}_1 - \rho\overline{w}'\overline{w} + \rho\overline{w}_1^2 + o_p(1/N).$$

Proof. See Appendix.

Note that the choice of g in the family of generalized empirical likelihood estimators does not matter for the $O(1/N^2)$ term. This is special to our case. It relies on the fact that the first and other moments are independent. In general, with a scalar parameter one can always renormalize the moments in such a way that only the derivative of the first moment depends on the parameter of interest, and that in addition the other moments are uncorrelated with the first one. This, however, does not make the first and other moments independent and the equivalence result here depends on the cross moments of the type $E[\psi_1 \psi_2^2]$ being equal to zero.

Now define

(i) $T_1 = \overline{w}_1$,
(ii) $R_1 = -2\overline{v}_1\overline{w}_1$,
(iii) $R_2 = \overline{w}_1(\overline{ww'}_{11} - 1)$,
(iv) $R_3 = -\overline{w}'(\overline{ww'} - \mathcal{I}_M)e_1$,
(v) $R_4 = \overline{w}'\overline{v}$,
(vi) $R_5 = \rho\overline{w}_1^2$,
(vii) $R_6 = -\rho\overline{w}'\overline{w}$.

Lemma 4.8. (BIAS OF $\hat{\theta}_g$)
The expectation of the leading terms is

$$E[T_1 + R_1 + R_2 + R_3 + R_4 + R_5 + R_6 - \theta^*] = -\rho/N + o_p(1/N).$$

Proof. See Appendix.

Lemma 4.9. (MEAN SQUARED ERROR OF $\hat{\theta}_g$)
The mean squared error due to terms of magnitude $O_p(N^{-1})$ and greater (i.e., those given explicitly in Lemma 4.7) are:

$$E\left[(T_1 + R_1 + R_2 + R_3 + R_4 + r_5 + R_6 - \theta^*)^2\right]$$
$$= 1/N - 2\mu_{12}/N^2 + (1 + 2\rho^2)/N^2$$
$$+ \rho^2(M-1)/N^2 + 2(M-1)/N^2 + o_p(1/N^2).$$

Proof. See Appendix.

Lemmas 2.3 and 3.6 show that the MSE of feasible GMM exceeds that of OGMM by a term that is of order $(M-1)^2/N^2$. This term is due to an order $(M-1)/N$ bias in feasible GMM that is not in OGMM. This term is not present in the bias of GEL either. Lemma 4.9 differs from Lemmas 2.3 and 3.6 by not considering $O_p(N^{-3/2}) \cdot O_p(N^{-1/2}) = O_p(N^{-2})$ terms as they arise from the expansion of the estimator; but these terms do not give rise to the key $(M-1)^2/N^2$ order term in Lemma 3.6, which is the product of two $O_p(N^{-1})$ terms that are fully reflected in Lemma 4.9.

Consequently, we conclude that feasible GMM acquires MSE at rate $(M-1)^2/N^2$. This is basically due to the fact that the bias of feasible GMM grows at rate $(M-1)/N$, GEL's bias does not. This is not an artifact of our special situation and is consistent with the more general bias argument in Newey and Smith (2000).

5. EMPIRICAL DISCREPANCY THEORY

Having argued that generalized empirical likelihood offers "asymptotic resistance" to the deterioration of estimation efficiency as moment conditions are added, we turn to analyzing *differences* between members of this class. To do this, we interpret these estimators from the point of view of empirical discrepancy (ED, also sometimes called minimum discrepancy) theory, as found in the statistics literature in Corcoran (1995, 1998) and Baggerly (1998). In this section we show that the probabilities or reweighting implicit in GEL estimators can be expressed as functions of dot or inner products of Lagrange multipliers with moment conditions. In the following section we show that leading GEL estimators can be explicitly characterized as having reweighting functions that are polynomials in these dot products. Consequently, different GEL estimators weigh the higher-order moments of moment conditions differently, affecting their stability and ability to incorporate such higher-order information into estimation and inference.

We modify and extend some of the previous notation in order to deal with this more general context. A random variable z is i.i.d. according to $F(\cdot)$ and we have a sample $z_1, z_2, \ldots, z_n$. In addition, for unknown θ of dimension k there is a (known) function $\psi(z, \theta)$ such that $\operatorname{E}_F \psi(z, \theta) = 0$. $\psi(z, \theta)$ is of dimension $m \geq k$. Empirical discrepancy theory considers choosing θ and probabilities $p_1, \ldots, p_n$ on each of the data points such that

$$\sum_{i=1}^{n} h\left(p_i, \frac{1}{n}\right) \text{ is minimized subject to } \operatorname*{E}_{p} \psi(z, \theta) = 0 \text{ and}$$

$$\sum p_i = 1$$

where $h(\cdot, \cdot)$ is a measure of the discrepancy between two discrete measures, with the property that $h(\frac{1}{n}, \frac{1}{n}) = 0$; there are also some technical conditions on $h(\cdot, \cdot)$'s partial derivative with respect to its first argument.

Thus, empirical discrepancy theory chooses θ and a reweighting of the data so that the moment conditions hold and a discrepancy measure is minimized.

$$Q(\theta, p) = \sum_{i=1}^{n} h\left(p_i, \frac{1}{n}\right) + \alpha\left(\sum p_i - 1\right) + t \sum_{i=1}^{n} p_i \psi_i(\theta). \tag{5.1}$$

Consider the determination of p first:

$$\frac{\partial Q(\theta, p)}{\partial p_i} = \frac{\partial h}{\partial p_i} + \alpha + t\psi_i(\theta) = 0 \tag{5.2}$$

$$\begin{aligned}\sum_{i=1}^{n}\left\{\frac{\partial Q(\theta, p)}{\partial p_i} p_i\right\} &= \sum \frac{\partial h}{\partial p_i} p_i + \alpha \sum p_i + t \sum_{i=1}^{n} p_i \psi_i(\theta) \\ &= \sum \frac{\partial h}{\partial p_i} p_i + \alpha \qquad + 0\end{aligned}$$

So $\alpha = -\sum \frac{\partial h}{\partial p_i} p_i$; substituting into (5.2):

$$\frac{\partial Q(\theta, p)}{\partial p_i} = \frac{\partial h}{\partial p_i} - \sum \frac{\partial h}{\partial p_i} p_i + t\psi_i(\theta) = 0.$$

Note:

$$\frac{\partial h}{\partial p_i} = -t\psi_i(\theta) \text{ is a solution.}$$

Note that t is an m-dimensional Lagrange multiplier of the original problem.

Remaining with the problem of constructing p for given θ, there are three common choices for $h(\cdot, \cdot)$:

- $h(p_i, \frac{1}{n}) = p_i(p_i - \frac{1}{n})$, or effectively $\sum h(p_i, \frac{1}{n}) = \sum p_i^2$, in which case $p_i = k(1 + t\psi_i(\theta))$ and $t = -(\sum \psi_i \psi_i')^{-1}(\sum \psi_i)$; this is often called Euclidean likelihood.
- $h(p_i, \frac{1}{n}) = \frac{1}{n}\{\log(\frac{1}{n}) - \log p_i\}$, or effectively $-\sum h(p_i, \frac{1}{n}) = \sum \log p_i$; $p_i = k\frac{1}{1+t\psi_i(\theta)}$; this is Owen's (1988) empirical likelihood (EL).
- $h(p_i, \frac{1}{n}) = p_i\{\log(\frac{1}{n}) - \log p_i\}$, or effectively $-\sum h(p_i, \frac{1}{n}) = \sum p_i \log p_i$; $p_i = ke^{t \cdot \psi_i(\theta)}$; this is called exponential tilting (ET).

Empirical likelihood and exponential tilting exchange the role of the empirical measure and the measure p that is under construction: ET finds the p to which the empirical measure is "KLIC-closest," while EL finds the p that is KLIC-closest to the empirical measure. Thus, ET "imagines" that the data generating process is p, (which obeys $E(\psi) = 0$) while EL imagines the DGP as a repetition of the observed data, which does not obey the specified moment conditions. To us, this suggests ET should be superior to EL. But EL has some higher-order asymptotic properties that mimic those of parametric likelihood, such as Bartlett correctability of its likelihood ratio test (but only when there are no nuisance parameters) and higher-order efficiency (when bias corrected) within the bias-corrected GEL class.

The preceding three cases are all members of the Cressie–Read (Cressie and Read, 1984) family, with

$$h\left(p_i, \frac{1}{n}\right) = \left(\frac{p_i}{1/n}\right)^{-\lambda} - 1$$

$$p_i = k\left(\frac{1}{1 + t\psi_i(\theta)}\right)^{1/(\lambda+1)}$$

for $\lambda \in [-2, 1]$ so that $\lambda = -2$ is Euclidean likelihood, $\lambda = -1$ is ET, and $\lambda = 0$ is EL.

Turning now to the problem of estimating θ, the minimum discrepancy estimate is obtained by differentiating (5.1) with respect to θ to obtain:

$$\frac{\partial Q(\theta, p)}{\partial \theta} = t \sum_{i=1}^{n} p_i \frac{\partial \psi_i(\theta)}{\partial \theta} = 0,$$

a system of equations in k elements of θ. Thus, the entire system of $(m+k)$ equations can be written simply as:

$$\operatorname*{E}_{p} \psi(\theta) = 0 \qquad (m \text{ equations}) \tag{5.3a}$$

$$t \cdot \operatorname*{E}_{p} \frac{\partial \psi(\theta)}{\partial \theta} = 0 \qquad (k \text{ equations}). \tag{5.3b}$$

One way to think of these equations is that, having fixed θ and a formula for p (by choice of $h(\cdot, \cdot)$), the first m equations determine t. Similarly, for a fixed t and p, the remaining k equations determine θ.[1]

The duality of GEL and ED is examined in two papers of Newey and Smith (2000, 2001). Writing the GEL estimator as:

$$\hat{\theta}_{\text{GEL}} = \arg \min_{\theta \in \Theta} \sup_{t \in T} n^{-1} g(t \cdot \psi_i(\theta))$$

the GEL estimator's estimating equations coincide with (5.3a) in cases where the derivative of $g(\cdot)$, denoted g', can be interpreted as being proportional to a probability. This can be done for the three cases under consideration here, as well as for all members of the Cressie–Read family. Newey and Smith (2000, 2001) show that for Euclidean likelihood, $g(t\psi_i) = -t\psi_i - (t\psi_i)^2/2$ and the resulting GEL estimator coincides with the continuously updated GMM estimator of Hansen et al. (1996). Consequently, we will denote the three estimators as $\hat{\theta}_{\text{CUE}}$, $\hat{\theta}_{\text{ET}}$, and $\hat{\theta}_{\text{EL}}$.

6. A FURTHER CHARACTERIZATION OF ED/GEL ESTIMATORS

Rewriting the first equation of system (5.3a) as

$$\sum_{i=1}^{n} p(t \cdot \psi_i(\theta))\psi_i(\theta) = 0 \tag{6.4}$$

[1] This schema cannot be used to define a simple iterative procedure to compute θ, for in fact the saddlepoint nature of these equations makes the naive iterative procedure of (1) fix θ; (2) calculate t; (3) calculate new θ; unstable in a neighborhood of the solution θ_* of $\theta_* - \theta(t(\theta_*)) = 0$.

we can express the probabilities associated with CUE, ET, and EL (after absorbing some sign changes into k) as

$$\begin{aligned} p_i[\mathrm{CUE}] &= k_{\mathrm{CUE}}(1 + t\psi_i(\theta)) \\ p_i[\mathrm{ET}] &= k_{\mathrm{ET}}(e^{t\psi_i(\theta)}) \\ p_i[\mathrm{EL}] &= k_{\mathrm{EL}}\left(\frac{1}{1 - t\psi_i(\theta)}\right). \end{aligned}$$

Taking a Taylor series expansion of $p_i[ET]$ we can define a sequence of p functions:

$$\begin{aligned} p_i[\mathrm{ET}, 1] &= k_{\mathrm{ET},1}(1 + t\psi_i(\theta)) = p_i[\mathrm{CUE}] \\ p_i[\mathrm{ET}, 2] &= k_{\mathrm{ET},2}\left(1 + t\psi_i(\theta) + \frac{(t\psi_i(\theta))^2}{2}\right) \\ p_i[\mathrm{ET}, 3] &= k_{\mathrm{ET},3}\left(1 + t\psi_i(\theta) + \frac{(t\psi_i(\theta))^2}{2} + \frac{(t\psi_i(\theta))^3}{6}\right) \\ &\vdots \\ p_i[\mathrm{ET}, \infty] &= k_{\mathrm{ET},\infty}\left(1 + t\psi_i(\theta) + \frac{(t\psi_i(\theta))^2}{2} + \frac{(t\psi_i(\theta))^3}{6} + \ldots\right) \\ &\quad k_{\infty}e^{t\cdot\psi_i(\theta)} = p_i[\mathrm{ET}]. \end{aligned}$$

And similarly for $p_i[\mathrm{EL}]$ we have

$$\begin{aligned} p_i[\mathrm{EL}, 1] &= k_{\mathrm{EL},1}(1 + t\psi_i(\theta)) = p_i[\mathrm{CUE}] \\ p_i[\mathrm{EL}, 2] &= k_{\mathrm{EL},2}(1 + t\psi_i(\theta) + (t\psi_i(\theta))^2) \\ p_i[\mathrm{EL}, 3] &= k_{\mathrm{EL},3}(1 + t\psi_i(\theta) + (t\psi_i(\theta))^2 + (t\psi_i(\theta))^3) \\ &\vdots \\ p_i[\mathrm{EL}, \infty] &= k_{\mathrm{EL},\infty}(1 + t\psi_i(\theta) + (t\psi_i(\theta))^2 + (t\psi_i(\theta))^3 + \ldots) \\ &= k_{\mathrm{EL},\infty}\left(\tfrac{1}{1-t\psi_i(\theta)}\right) = p_i[\mathrm{EL}]. \end{aligned}$$

Thus, all three p functions have the same first-order Taylor series expansion, coinciding exactly with p[CUE]. Then p[ET] and p[EL] include higher powers of $(t \cdot \psi_i)$, the former having factorially declining weights or coefficients and the latter the coefficients $\{1, 1, \ldots 1\}$. Since t is an $O_p(n^{-1/2})$ object, the difference in the treatment of t^2 terms induces differences of $O_p(n^{-1})$ in $\hat{\theta}_{\mathrm{CUE}}$, $\hat{\theta}_{\mathrm{ET}}$, and $\hat{\theta}_{\mathrm{EL}}$ and consequently their MSE behavior differs at $O_p(n^{-2})$. (This will be true for all members of the Cressie–Read family.[2])

[2] The Cressie–Read expansion is $p[\mathrm{CR}] = 1 + (\mathrm{t}\cdot\psi_{\mathrm{i}})/(1+\lambda) + (2+\lambda)(\mathrm{t}\cdot\psi_{\mathrm{i}})^2/2(1+\lambda)^2 + (2+\lambda)(3+2\lambda)(\mathrm{t}\cdot\psi_{\mathrm{i}})^3/6(1+\lambda)^3 + \cdots$

To see the effect of these differences, let us consider the difference between the first two elements of the sequence of ET functions for the equation setting the expectation of the jth component of ψ:

$$\sum_{i=1}^{n} p(t \cdot \psi_i(\theta))\psi_{ij}(\theta) = 0 \tag{6.5}$$

$$\sum_{i=1}^{n} k_{\mathrm{ET},1}(1 + t\psi_i(\theta))\psi_{ij}(\theta) = 0 \tag{6.6}$$

$$\sum_{i=1}^{n} k_{\mathrm{ET},2}\left(1 + t\psi_i(\theta) + \frac{(t\psi_i(\theta))^2}{2}\right)\psi_{ij}(\theta) = 0 \tag{6.7}$$

Supressing the i subscript momentarily, the extra terms in (6.7) (relative to (6.6)) are of the form:

$$.5 * (t_1\psi_1 + t_2\psi_2 + \cdots t_m\psi_m)^2\psi_j,$$

so that sums of these involve third moments of ψ. Consequently, in problems where third moments are zero, notably those in which ψ is symmetric, these terms will be converging rapidly to zero and thus have no effect even at $O_p(n^{-2})$.

7. A DETAILED ANALYSIS OF SOME SIMPLE EXAMPLES

To examine further the relation between the choice of a GEL/ED and the higher order moments of the underlying data, consider the estimation of the scalar parameter θ from a scalar random variable x where it is known that x has mean θ and variance 2θ. Thus $\psi(x, \theta)$ is given by:

$$\begin{aligned} x - \theta &= 0 \\ x^2 - \theta^2 - 2\theta &= 0 \end{aligned} \tag{7.8}$$

Writing the second moment condition in the way indicated (rather than $(x - \theta)^2 - 2\theta = 0$) does not change the numerical values of the resulting estimates of θ, but it does simplify $\frac{\partial\psi}{\partial\theta}$ to:

$$\frac{\partial\psi}{\partial\theta} = \begin{cases} -1 \\ -2\theta - 2 \end{cases}$$

Consequently, $\frac{\partial\psi}{\partial\theta}$ does not depend on the data so $\mathrm{E}_p \frac{\partial\psi}{\partial\theta}$ does not depend on p. Using (5.3b) this means $\hat{\theta}$ can be determined from

$$\begin{aligned} t \cdot \mathop{\mathrm{E}}_{p} \frac{\partial\psi}{\partial\theta} &= 0 \\ t_1(-1) + t_2(-2\theta - 2) &= 0 \\ \theta &= \frac{-t_1}{2t_2} - 1. \end{aligned}$$

Table 10.1. *Symmetric distributions with* $E(x) = 1$ *and* $V(x) = 2$ *used in the Monte Carlo experiments*

Case	Distribution	First four cumulants
1	$N(1, 2)$	$\{1, 2, 0, 0\}$
2	Symmetric mixture of normals: $.5N(0, 1)^{\frown}.5N(2, 1)$	$\{1, 2, 0, -2\}$
3	$t(df = 4)$	$\{1, 2, 0, \infty\}$
4	Uniform (on $1 - \sqrt{6}, 1 + \sqrt{6}$)	$\{1, 2, 0, -4.8\}$

It is apparent that our three estimators will differ, in this special case, only in their choice of t. For the CUE estimator, $t = (\psi'\psi)^{-1}\overline{\psi}$, that is, the coefficients of the regression of a column of 1's on ψ, and so θ is determined by the fixed point of a function of five moment functions of ψ: the means of the two moment functions (expressed as functions of θ) and the corresponding three variances and covariances. CUE is thus committed to local (to θ) sufficiency of five statistics and will ignore, for example, differences in skew between elements of the sample space. In cases where skew is zero, we can expect the difference between CUE and ET or EL to be negligible, whereas for nonzero skew, we might expect ET and/or EL to prove superior to CUE, but only at sample sizes at which $O_p(n^{-2})$ effects are operative.

To demonstrate these effects, we construct several data-generating processes which satisfy the moment conditions in (7.8) but have different properties for their higher-order moments. For each case we compute MSE and bias, and do this for CUE, ET, and EL. In addition, for ET and EL we compute p according to successive terms in the relevant Taylor series expansion, so that $p_i[\text{EL}, 1] = k_{\text{EL},1}(1 + t\psi_i(\theta)) = p_i[\text{CUE}]$, $p_i[\text{EL}, 3] = k_{\text{EL},3}(1 + t\psi_i(\theta) + (t\psi_i(\theta))^2 + (t\psi_i(\theta))^3)$, and so forth.

In this way we can see whether the advantages, if any, of ET and EL over CUE set in after taking into account only a relatively small number of additional higher moments, and similarly if differences between EL and ET require the full limiting case of including some information about all higher-order moments.

We consider eight data generating processes: the first four of these are symmetric distributions with mean 1 and variance 2; the second four are asymmetric, also with mean 1 and variance 2. A short description of these, together with the first four cumulants of the distributions, is given in the following two tables (Tables 10.1 and 10.2).

Appendices B and C (not included here, but available at http://www.faculty.econ.northwestern.edu/spady/imbens-spady) contain tables for all eight cases, tabulating the MSE and the bias, respectively, of the parameter θ (which in all cases is 1) for a variety of sample sizes and 6,000 replications. In each of the tables, we report the value of the MSE (Appendix B) or bias (Appendix C) in 6,000 replications for CUE, ET, and EL, together with the MSE's or bias of

Table 10.2. *Asymmetric distributions with $E(x) = 1$ and $V(x) = 2$ used in the Monte Carlo experiments*

Case	Distribution	First four cumulants
5	$\chi^2(1)$	$\{1, 2, 8, 48\}$
6	Asymmetric mixture of normals: $.25N(-1, 2/3)\tilde{}.75N(5/3, 2/3)$	$\{1, 2, -1.777, -1.185\}$
7	Lognormal: $\theta = 0, \sigma^2 = \log(3)$	$\{1, 2, 20, 624\}$
8	Inverse gaussian: $\mu = 1, \lambda = .5$	$\{1, 2, 24, 84.85\}$

Table 10.3. *Estimates of MSE of $\hat{\theta}$ and jackknifed standard error estimates from 6,000 simulations of system (7.8) with normal errors*

			Case 1: $N(1, 2)$ $n = 50$			
Taylor degree	1 = CUE	3	5	7	ET(Infinity)	Sample mean
MSE	0.020821	0.020702	0.020691	0.020688	0.020687	0.039753
s.e.	0.000366	0.000365	0.000365	0.000365	0.000365	0.000705
Taylor degree	1 = CUE	3	5	7	EL(Infinity)	Sample mean
MSE	0.020821	0.020675	0.020671	0.020656	0.020586	0.039753
s.e.	0.000366	0.000365	0.000366	0.000367	0.000367	0.000705
			Case 1: $N(1, 2)$ $n = 100$			
Taylor degree	1 = CUE	3	5	7	ET(Infinity)	Sample mean
MSE	0.010304	0.010256	0.010255	0.010254	0.010254	0.019945
s.e.	0.000189	0.000188	0.000188	0.000188	0.000188	0.000353
Taylor degree	1 = CUE	3	5	7	EL(Infinity)	Sample mean
MSE	0.010304	0.010235	0.010226	0.010224	0.010218	0.019945
s.e.	0.000189	0.000188	0.000188	0.000188	0.000188	0.000353

the estimators based on the Taylor series expansion of degrees 3, 5, and 7, and the simple mean. (CUE corresponds to a Taylor series expansion of degree 1, ET and EL to degree ∞). For each entry we report a jackknife estimate of the standard error, this is given in the row labeled 's.e.'.

The results from cases 1 through 4 are easily summarized; specimen results for MSE in case 1 at $n = 50$ and 100 are given in Table 10.3.

The main points are (1) there is no important difference in the MSE performance of any of the estimators; (2) the apparent asymptotic efficiency gain from exploiting the second moment condition (as measured by the ratio of the MSE of any of the GEL estimators to the MSE of the sample mean) is achieved by $n = 50$ in case 1 and within the sample sizes presented in Appendix B in other cases. EL and ET typically offer a (very) small improvement over CUE and there is no case where employing EL or ET presents any real cost relative to CUE. Thus, taking the higher-order moments into account, as do ET and EL, does not generate an unstable estimator in these cases. This is true even in case 3 (t with $df = 4$) where the fourth cumulant of the first moment condition is infinite.

Table 10.4. *Estimates of MSE of $\hat{\theta}$ from 6,000 simulations of system (7.8) with $\chi^2(1)$ errors*

			Case 5: $\chi^2(1)$ $n = 50$			
Taylor degreee	1 = CUE	3	5	7	ET(Infinity)	Sample mean
MSE	0.047774	0.041204	0.039950	0.039545	0.037596	0.040168
s.e.	0.001024	0.000918	0.000886	0.000870	0.000740	0.000752
Taylor degree	1 = CUE	3	5	7	EL(Infinity)	Sample mean
MSE	0.047774	0.041705	0.040883	0.040684	0.033915	0.040168
s.e.	0.001024	0.000948	0.000941	0.000941	0.000679	0.000752
			Case 5: $\chi^2(1)$ $n = 100$			
Taylor degree	1 = CUE	3	5	7	ET(Infinity)	Sample mean
MSE	0.018503	0.015828	0.015564	0.015521	0.015508	0.020042
s.e.	0.000400	0.000333	0.000321	0.000317	0.000315	0.000365
Taylor degree	1 = CUE	3	5	7	EL(Infinity)	Sample mean
MSE	0.018503	0.015656	0.015386	0.015327	0.014741	0.020042
s.e.	0.000400	0.000339	0.000332	0.000330	0.000294	0.000365
			Case 5: $\chi^2(1)$ $n = 800$			
Taylor degree	1 = CUE	3	5	7	ET(Infinity)	Sample mean
MSE	0.001827	0.001832	0.001832	0.001832	0.001833	0.002444
s.e.	0.000033	0.000033	0.000033	0.000033	0.000033	0.000045
Taylor degree	1 = CUE	3	5	7	EL(Infinity)	Sample mean
MSE	0.001827	0.001843	0.001845	0.001846	0.001848	0.002444
s.e.	0.000033	0.000033	0.000033	0.000033	0.000033	0.000045

More interesting and varied results are obtained in the presence of skew. For case 5 (Table 10.4), in which x is $\chi^2(1)$, we see for CUE at $n = 50$ that the effect of adding an additional moment is to produce an estimator that is worse than the sample mean; the MSE's of the estimators at Taylor degrees 3, 5, and 7 are about the same as the sample mean; and that ET and EL are better than their corresponding degree 7 estimators and also the sample mean; both of these effects are greater for EL than ET. The superiority of EL and ET to CUE (and of EL to ET) continues through some of the larger sample sizes, but by $n = 800$ this ranking has reversed itself, though the differences are now no longer greater than estimated standard errors.

Thus, in this example with skew, we find results in accord with our earlier conjecture that EL and ET can be expected to outperform CUE because the former reflect skew and higher moments in the construction of t (and thus in general in the distribution estimates embodied in p) in a way that CUE does not. These effects must eventually disappear as the sample size grows, because all the estimators in question reach the same GMM efficiency bound.

Case 6 (an asymmetric normal mixture) is unremarkable except for the fact that the second moment condition is extremely informative in this case: adding it reduces MSE for all the estimators to the (apparent) asymptotic relative bound of 0.25 times the sample mean's MSE.

Table 10.5. *Estimates of MSE of $\hat{\theta}$ from 6,000 simulations of system (7.8) with lognormal errors*

			Case 7: lognormal $n = 50$			
Taylor degree	1 = CUE	3	5	7	ET(Infinity)	Sample mean
MSE	0.068870	0.061752	0.058380	0.056165	0.033665	0.039825
s.e.	0.001650	0.001567	0.001517	0.001481	0.000601	0.001013
Taylor degree	1 = CUE	3	5	7	EL(Infinity)	Sample mean
MSE	0.068870	0.069696	0.072404	0.073894	0.041134	0.039825
s.e.	0.001650	0.001672	0.001699	0.001719	0.000668	0.001013
			Case 7: lognormal $n = 100$			
Taylor degree	1 = CUE	3	5	7	ET(Infinity)	Sample mean
MSE	0.022288	0.018707	0.017705	0.017130	0.015554	0.020098
s.e.	0.000623	0.000508	0.000470	0.000446	0.000310	0.000578
Taylor degree	1 = CUE	3	5	7	EL(Infinity)	Sample mean
MSE	0.022288	0.022046	0.023572	0.024439	0.022448	0.020098
s.e.	0.000623	0.000569	0.000574	0.000583	0.000378	0.000578
			Case 7: lognormal $n = 400$			
Taylor degree	1 = CUE	3	5	7	ET(Infinity)	Sample mean
MSE	0.003789	0.004283	0.004310	0.004309	0.004307	0.005090
s.e.	0.000071	0.000077	0.000077	0.000077	0.000077	0.000099
Taylor degree	1 = CUE	3	5	7	EL(Infinity)	Sample mean
MSE	0.003789	0.004713	0.004858	0.004904	0.004943	0.005090
s.e.	0.000071	0.000085	0.000089	0.000091	0.000093	0.000099

Cases 7 and 8, lognormality and the inverse Gaussian distribution, have greater skew and kurtosis than case 5, the $\chi^2(1)$ example. Results for MSE in these cases for $n = 50$, 100, and 400 are shown in Tables 10.5 and 10.6. As with case 5, at small sample sizes CUE does worse than the sample mean; ET does better than the sample mean for the lognormal case, as do both ET and EL in the inverse Gaussian case. Unlike the $\chi^2(1)$ case, at small and moderate sample sizes, ET outperforms EL. In addition, as the Taylor degree is expanded from CUE to ET, ET shows continuous improvement (at those small and moderate sample sizes in which ET outperforms CUE); this is not the case for EL in these two examples.

In Appendix C, we present biases for the cases considered here and in Appendix B. Quite notably, bias does not generally make a substantial difference to the MSE. This could perhaps be expected from the fact that the correlation between ψ and $\frac{\partial \psi}{\partial \theta}$ is zero in this example, because the latter does not depend on x. This suggests that the (sometimes erratic) effects typically seen in Appendix C are $O(n^{-2})$ or higher.

The cases where bias is most evident and potentially important to the MSE ranking of the estimators, given in Tables 10.7 and 10.8, occur when x is lognormal or inverse Gaussian; the biases tend to be largest for EL. In view of

Table 10.6. *Estimates of MSE of $\hat{\theta}$ from 6,000 simulations of system (7.8) with inverse Gaussian errors*

			Case 8: inverse Gaussian $n = 50$			
Taylor degree	1 = CUE	3	5	7	ET(Infinity)	Sample mean
MSE	0.049724	0.043575	0.041270	0.039837	0.027857	0.038833
s.e.	0.001349	0.001271	0.001228	0.001197	0.000551	0.000821
Taylor degree	1 = CUE	3	5	7	EL(Infinity)	Sample mean
MSE	0.049724	0.048685	0.050107	0.051142	0.032708	0.038833
s.e.	0.001349	0.001361	0.001382	0.001399	0.000599	0.000821
			Case 8: inverse Gaussian $n = 100$			
Taylor degree	1 = CUE	3	5	7	ET(Infinity)	Sample mean
MSE	0.016042	0.013755	0.013263	0.013023	0.012420	0.019573
s.e.	0.000434	0.000356	0.000334	0.000321	0.000246	0.000387
Taylor degree	1 = CUE	3	5	7	EL(Infinity)	Sample mean
MSE	0.016042	0.015417	0.016079	0.016453	0.015510	0.019573
s.e.	0.000434	0.000392	0.000394	0.000398	0.000281	0.000387
			Case 8: inverse Gaussian $n = 400$			
Taylor degree	1 = CUE	3	5	7	ET(Infinity)	Sample mean
MSE	0.003160	0.003246	0.003247	0.003246	0.003243	0.004931
s.e.	0.000059	0.000059	0.000059	0.000059	0.000059	0.000092
Taylor degree	1 = CUE	3	5	7	EL(Infinity)	Sample mean
MSE	0.003160	0.003381	0.003419	0.003432	0.003428	0.004931
s.e.	0.000059	0.000062	0.000062	0.000063	0.000063	0.000092

the result of Newey and Smith (2000) demonstrating the higher-order efficiency of bias-corrected EL, (and EL alone among the GEL class), it is interesting to note that even after bias-correction, EL continues to have a larger MSE than ET in these particular examples.

8. SUMMARY

Higher-order asymptotic arguments suggest that GEL/ED/ "one-step efficient" estimates of overidentified moment models will prove superior to two-step GMM, since the MSE of two-step GMM grows at rate $O((M-1)^2/N^2)$ where $(M-1)$ is the degree of overidentification, whereas the GEL class apparently has (in the special case considered) an MSE that grows at rate $O((M-1)/N^2)$. Consequently, interest shifts to distinguishing between elements of the GEL family on the basis of estimation performance. With a simple argument and example, it appears that the simplest GEL variant, the continuously updated or Euclidean likelihood estimator, is dominated by the more elaborate ET and EL estimators. The difference between these two variants can be seen to lie in their treatment of third and higher-order moments of moment conditions, with EL weighing these more heavily than ET.

Table 10.7. *Estimates of bias of $\hat{\theta}$ from 6,000 simulations of system (7.8) with lognormal errors*

			Case 7: lognormal $n = 50$			
Taylor degree	1 = CUE	3	5	7	ET(Infinity)	Sample mean
Bias	−0.073549	−0.028002	−0.018381	−0.014462	0.011123	−0.000712
s.e.	0.003252	0.003188	0.003111	0.003054	0.002365	0.002577
Taylor degree	1 = CUE	3	5	7	EL(Infinity)	Sample mean
Bias	−0.073549	−0.023550	−0.012970	−0.009200	0.051964	−0.000712
s.e.	0.003252	0.003395	0.003470	0.003508	0.002531	0.002577
			Case 7: lognormal $n = 100$			
Taylor degree	1 = CUE	3	5	7	ET(Infinity)	Sample mean
Bias	−0.004507	0.034959	0.040531	0.041955	0.043940	0.002031
s.e.	0.001927	0.001707	0.001636	0.001601	0.001507	0.001830
Taylor degree	1 = CUE	3	5	7	EL(Infinity)	Sample mean
Bias	−0.004507	0.045751	0.057451	0.061930	0.080875	0.002031
s.e.	0.001927	0.001824	0.001838	0.001853	0.001628	0.001830
			Case 7: lognormal $n = 400$			
Taylor degree	1 = CUE	3	5	7	ET(Infinity)	Sample mean
Bias	0.023147	0.030086	0.030184	0.030119	0.030000	0.000490
s.e.	0.000736	0.000750	0.000753	0.000753	0.000754	0.000921
Taylor degree	1 = CUE	3	5	7	EL(Infinity)	Sample mean
Bias	0.023147	0.033090	0.033761	0.033928	0.032701	0.000490
s.e.	0.000736	0.000777	0.000787	0.000791	0.000804	0.000921

Table 10.8. *Estimates of bias of $\hat{\theta}$ from 6,000 simulations of system (7.8) with inverse Gaussian errors*

			Case 8: inverse Gaussian $n = 50$			
Taylor degree	1 = CUE	3	5	7	ET(Infinity)	Sample mean
Bias	−0.049814	−0.012106	−0.005470	−0.002999	0.009935	0.000036
s.e.	0.002806	0.002691	0.002622	0.002577	0.002151	0.002544
Taylor degree	1 = CUE	3	5	7	EL(Infinity)	Sample mean
Bias	−0.049814	−0.005333	0.004693	0.007965	0.046092	0.000036
s.e.	0.002806	0.002848	0.002889	0.002918	0.002258	0.002544
			Case 8: inverse Gaussian $n = 100$			
Taylor degree	1 = CUE	3	5	7	ET(Infinity)	Sample mean
Bias	−0.002652	0.022747	0.025227	0.025676	0.026322	−0.000678
s.e.	0.001635	0.001485	0.001451	0.001436	0.001398	0.001806
Taylor degree	1 = CUE	3	5	7	EL(Infinity)	Sample mean
Bias	−0.002652	0.032346	0.039543	0.042147	0.049622	−0.000678
s.e.	0.001635	0.001548	0.001556	0.001564	0.001475	0.001806
			Case 8: inverse Gaussian $n = 400$			
Taylor degree	1 = CUE	3	5	7	ET(Infinity)	Sample mean
Bias	0.009872	0.012438	0.012302	0.012226	0.012154	0.000467
s.e.	0.000714	0.000718	0.000718	0.000718	0.000718	0.000907
Taylor degree	1 = CUE	3	5	7	EL(Infinity)	Sample mean
Bias	0.009872	0.014237	0.014430	0.014455	0.013003	0.000467
s.e.	0.000714	0.000728	0.000732	0.000733	0.000737	0.000907

While EL has an array of higher-order theoretical properties that are in some ways similar to those of parametric likelihood, our analysis shows that it weighs higher-order moments of moment conditions much more heavily than does ET. Consequently, in contexts where these higher-order moments are likely both to be important and poorly defined in the sample sizes of interest, EL may prove to have a more erratic behavior than ET. This is borne out rather clearly in a few examples considered in this paper; this in turn suggests that no member of the GEL class will dominate the field unambiguously.

APPENDIX A

Complete details of the more mechanical aspects of the proofs can be found on http://www.nuff.ox.ac.uk/users/spady/imbens-spady.pdf.

Lemma A.10. (EXPANSION OF MATRIX INVERSION)
Let A, B, and C be $M \times M$ symmetric matrices of order $O_p(1)$, with A invertible. Then

(i) $(A + B/\sqrt{N})^{-1} = A^{-1} + o_p(1)$,
(ii) $(A + B/\sqrt{N})^{-1} = A^{-1} - A^{-1}BA^{-1}/\sqrt{N} + o_p(1/\sqrt{N})$,
(iii) $(A + B/\sqrt{N})^{-1} = A^{-1} - A^{-1}BA^{-1}/\sqrt{N} + A^{-1}BA^{-1}BA^{-1}/N + o_p(1/N)$,
(iv) $(A + B/\sqrt{N} + C/N)^{-1} = A^{-1} - A^{-1}BA^{-1}/\sqrt{N} - A^{-1}CA^{-1}/N + A^{-1}BA^{-1}BA^{-1}/N + o_p(1/N)$.

Proof of Lemma A.10. See the web page.

Proof of Lemma 2.2
We show the following three results, which then imply the main result:

(i) $E[R^{\text{opt}}] = E[\overline{w}_1] = \theta^*$,
(ii) $E[S^{\text{opt}}] = -E[\overline{v}_1\overline{w}_1] = -\rho/N$,
(iii) $E[T^{\text{opt}}] = E[\overline{w}_1\overline{v}_1\overline{v}_1] = \mu_{21}/N^2$.

(i) This is immediate.
(ii) $E[S^{\text{opt}}] = -E[\overline{v}_1\overline{w}_1] = -E\left[\frac{1}{N^2}\sum_{i=1}^N\sum_{j=1}^N v_{i1}w_{i1}\right] = -E\left[\frac{1}{N^2}\sum_{i=1}^N v_{i1}w_{i1}\right] = -\rho/N$.
(iii) $E[T^{\text{opt}}] = E[\overline{w}_1\overline{v}_1\overline{v}_1] = E\left[\frac{1}{N^3}\sum_{i=1}^N\sum_{j=1}^N\sum_{k=1}^N w_{i1}v_{j1}v_{k1}\right] = E\left[\frac{1}{N^3}\sum_{i=1}^N w_{i1}v_{i1}v_{i1}\right] = \mu_{21}/N^2$.

Proof of Lemma 2.3. We first show the following results:

(i) $E[R^{\text{opt}}R^{\text{opt}}] = E[\overline{w}_1\overline{w}_1] = 1/N$,
(ii) $E[R^{\text{opt}}S^{\text{opt}}] = -E[\overline{w}_1\overline{v}_w\overline{w}_1] = -\mu_{12}/N^2$,
(iii) $E[S^{\text{opt}}S^{\text{opt}}] = E[\overline{v}_1\overline{w}_1\overline{v}_1\overline{w}_1] = (1 + 2\rho^2)/N^2 + o(1/N^2)$
(iv) $E[R^{\text{opt}}T^{\text{opt}}] = E[\overline{w}_1\overline{w}_1\overline{v}_1\overline{v}_1] = (2\rho^2 + 1)/N^2$.

In the following, let $\delta_{mn} = 1$ if $m = n$ and zero otherwise.

(i) $E[R^{\text{opt}} R^{\text{opt}}] = E[\overline{w}_1 \overline{w}_1] = E[\sum_{i=1}^N \sum_{j=1}^N w_{i1} w_{j1}] =$
$E[\sum_{i=1}^N w_{i1}^2] = 1/N$.

(ii) $E[R^{\text{opt}} S^{\text{opt}} \cdot R_1] = -E[\overline{w}_1 \overline{w}_1 \overline{v}_1] =$
$-E[\frac{1}{N^3} \sum_{i=1}^N \sum_{j=1}^N \sum_{k=1}^N w_{i1} w_{j1} v_{k1}] =$
$-E[\frac{1}{N^3} \sum_{i=1}^N w_{i1}^2 v_{i1}] = -\mu_{12}/N^2$.

(iii) $E[S^{\text{opt}} S^{\text{opt}}] = E[(\overline{v}_1 \overline{w}_1)^2] = E[(\frac{1}{N^2} \sum_{i=1}^N \sum_{j=1}^N v_{i1} w_{j1})^2] =$
$E[\frac{1}{N^4} \sum_{i=1}^N \sum_{j=1}^N \sum_{k=1}^N \sum_{l=1}^N v_{i1} w_{j1} v_{k1} w_{l1}]$.

Because the (v_{im}, w_{im}) is independent of (v_{jn}, w_{jn}) if either $i \neq j$ or $m \neq n$, we can ignore all terms where one of the four indices i, j, k, and l, does not match up with at least one of the others. Ignoring also the N terms with all four indices matching up because they are of lower order, we only consider terms with $(i = j, k = l, i \neq k)$, $(i = l, j = k, i \neq j)$, or $(i = k, j = l, i \neq j)$, leading to

$$E[S^{\text{opt}} S^{\text{opt}}] = \frac{1}{N^4} E\left[\sum_{i=1}^N \sum_{k \neq i} v_{i1} w_{i1} v_{k1} w_{k1} \right.$$
$$\left. + \sum_{i=1}^N \sum_{j \neq i} v_{i1} w_{j1} v_{j1} w_{i1} + \sum_{i=1}^N \sum_{j \neq i} v_{i1} w_{j1} v_{i1} w_{j1} \right] + o(1/N^2)$$
$$= \frac{1}{N^2} \left(\rho^2 + \rho^2 + 1\right) + o(1/N^2) = (2\rho^2 + 1)/N^2 + o(1/N^2).$$

(iv)

$$\begin{aligned} E[R^{\text{opt}} T^{\text{opt}}] &= E[\overline{w}_1 \overline{w}_1 \overline{v}_1 \overline{v}_1] \\ &= E\left[\frac{1}{N^4} \sum_{i=1}^N \sum_{j=1}^N \sum_{k=1}^N \sum_{l=1}^N w_{i1} w_{j1} v_{i1} v_{k1}\right] \\ &= (2\rho^2 + 1)/N^2 + o(1/N^2), \end{aligned}$$

by the same argument as in Lemma 2.2(iii).

Then, adding up the three components

$$\begin{aligned} &E[(R^{\text{opt}} + S^{\text{opt}} + T^{\text{opt}} - \theta^*)^2)] \\ &= E[R^{\text{opt}} R^{\text{opt}} + 2R^{\text{opt}} S^{\text{opt}} + S^{\text{opt}} S^{\text{opt}} + 2R^{\text{opt}} T^{\text{opt}}] + o(N^{-2}) \\ &= 1/N - 2\mu_{12}/N^2 + 3(1 + 2\rho^2)/N^2 + o(N^{-2}). \end{aligned}$$

Proof of Lemma 3.4. First we expand $\overline{ww'}^{-1}$ using Lemma A.10:

$$\overline{ww'}^{-1} = \mathcal{I}_M - (\overline{ww'} - \mathcal{I}_M) + (\overline{ww'} - \mathcal{I}_M)(\overline{ww'} - \mathcal{I}_M) + o_p(N^{-1}).$$

Second, we expand $(\overline{v}+e_1)'\overline{ww'}^{-1}(\overline{v}+e_1)$:

$$
\begin{aligned}
&(\overline{v}+e_1)'\overline{ww'}^{-1}(\overline{v}+e_1)\\
&\quad=(\overline{v}+e_1)'\left(\mathcal{I}_M-(\overline{ww'}-\mathcal{I}_M)+(\overline{ww'}-\mathcal{I}_M)(\overline{ww'}-\mathcal{I}_M)\right)\\
&\qquad\times(\overline{v}+e_1)+o_p(N^{-1})\\
&\quad=1+2\overline{v}_1-(\overline{ww'}_{11}-1)+\overline{v}'\overline{v}-2e_1'(\overline{ww'}-\mathcal{I}_M)\overline{v}\\
&\qquad+e_1(\overline{ww'}-\mathcal{I}_M)(\overline{ww'}-\mathcal{I}_M)e_1+o_p(N^{-1}).
\end{aligned}
$$

Next, we invert this expression, again using Lemma A.10:

$$
\begin{aligned}
&\left((\overline{v}+e_1)'\overline{ww'}^{-1}(\overline{v}+e_1)\right)^{-1}\\
&\quad=1-2\overline{v}_1+(\overline{ww'}_{11}-1)+2e_1(\overline{ww'}-\mathcal{I}_M)\overline{v}\\
&\qquad-e_1(\overline{ww'}-\mathcal{I}_M)(\overline{ww'}-\mathcal{I}_M)e_1-\overline{v}'\overline{v}+4\overline{v}_1^2\\
&\qquad+(\overline{ww'}_{11}-1)^2-4\overline{v}_1(\overline{ww'}_{11}-1)+o_p(N^{-1}).
\end{aligned}
$$

Fourth, we expand $(\overline{v}+e_1)'\overline{ww'}^{-1}\overline{w}$:

$$
\begin{aligned}
&(\overline{v}+e_1)'\overline{ww'}^{-1}\overline{w}\\
&\quad=(\overline{v}+e_1)'\left(\mathcal{I}_M-(\overline{ww'}-\mathcal{I}_M)+(\overline{ww'}-\mathcal{I}_M)(\overline{ww'}-\mathcal{I}_M)\right)\overline{w}\\
&\qquad+o_p(N^{-3/2})\\
&\quad=\overline{w}_1+\overline{v}'\overline{w}-e_1'(\overline{ww'}-\mathcal{I}_M)\overline{w}-\overline{v}'(\overline{ww'}-\mathcal{I}_M)\overline{w}\\
&\qquad+e_1'(\overline{ww'}-\mathcal{I}_M)(\overline{ww'}-\mathcal{I}_M)\overline{w}+o_p(N^{-3/2}).
\end{aligned}
$$

Finally, we consider the product:

$$
\begin{aligned}
&\left((\overline{v}+e_1)'\overline{ww'}^{-1}(\overline{v}+e_1)\right)^{-1}(\overline{v}+e_1)'\overline{ww'}^{-1}\overline{w}\\
&\quad=\overline{w}_1+\overline{v}'\overline{w}-e_1'(\overline{ww'}-\mathcal{I}_M)\overline{w}-2\overline{v}_1\overline{w}_1+(\overline{ww'}_{11}-1)\overline{w}_1\\
&\qquad-\overline{v}(\overline{ww'}-\mathcal{I}_M)\overline{w}+e_1(\overline{ww'}-\mathcal{I}_M)(\overline{ww'}-\mathcal{I}_M)\overline{w}\\
&\qquad-2\overline{v}_1\overline{v}'\overline{w}+2\overline{v}_1e_1'(\overline{ww'}-\mathcal{I}_M)\overline{w}\\
&\qquad+2\overline{w}_1e_1(\overline{ww'}-\mathcal{I}_M)\overline{v}-\overline{w}_1e_1'(\overline{ww'}-\mathcal{I}_M)(\overline{ww'}-\mathcal{I}_M)e_1\\
&\qquad+4\overline{v}_1^2\overline{w}_1+\overline{w}_1(\overline{ww'}_{11}-1)(\overline{ww'}_{11}-1)\\
&\qquad-4\,\overline{v}_1\overline{w}_1(\overline{ww'}_{11}-1)+(\overline{ww'}_{11}-1)\overline{v}'\overline{w}\\
&\qquad-(\overline{ww'}_{11}-1)e_1'(\overline{ww'}-\mathcal{I}_M)\overline{w}-\overline{w}_1\overline{v}'\overline{v}+o_p(N^{-3/2}).
\end{aligned}
$$

Proof of Lemma 3.5. Define:

(i) $S_1^{\text{gmm}}=-2\overline{v}_1\overline{w}_1$,
(ii) $S_2^{\text{gmm}}=(\overline{ww'}_{11}-1)\cdot\overline{w}_1$,
(iii) $S_3^{\text{gmm}}=-e_1'\left(\overline{ww'}-\mathcal{I}_M\right)\overline{w}$,
(iv) $S_4^{\text{gmm}}=\overline{v}'\overline{w}$.

We show the following results:

(i) $E[R^{\text{gmm}}] = E[\overline{w}_1] = \theta^*$,
(ii) $E[S_1^{\text{gmm}}] = E[-2\overline{v}_1\overline{w}_1] = -2\rho/N$,
(iii) $E[S_2^{\text{gmm}}] = E[(\overline{ww'}_{11} - 1) \cdot \overline{w}_1] = \mu_{03}/N$,
(iv) $E[S_3^{\text{gmm}} = -e_1' \left(\overline{ww'} - \mathcal{I}_M\right) \overline{w}] = -\mu_{03}/N$,
(v) $E[S_4^{\text{gmm}}] = E[\overline{v}'\overline{w}] = M\rho/N$,

which then by adding up imply the result in Lemma 3.5. The details of the calculation are shown on the web page.

Proof of Lemma 3.6.
The proof proceeds by computing the expectations of eighteen separate terms, using methods similar to those of Lemma 3.5.The details are on the web page.

Before proving Lemma 4.7, it is useful to consider the solution for t given θ. Define $\hat{t}(\theta)$ implicitly through the first equation:

$$0 = \sum_{i=1}^{N} \psi(v_i, w_i, \theta) \cdot g(t(\theta)'\psi(v_i, w_i, \theta)).$$

Lemma A.11. (Expansion for $\hat{t}(\theta)$)
If $\theta = \hat{\theta}_{\text{opt}} + o_p(1/\sqrt{N})$, then

$$\begin{aligned}\hat{t}(\theta) = &-e_1\theta + \overline{w} - \overline{vw}_1 - \overline{ww'(\overline{w} - e_1\overline{w}_1)w'(\overline{w} - e_1\overline{w}_1)\lambda/2} \\ &+ (\overline{ww'} - \mathcal{I}_M)e_1\overline{w}_1 \\ &- (\overline{ww'} - \mathcal{I}_M)\overline{w} - 2\rho\overline{w}_1^2 e_1 + 2\rho\overline{w}_1\overline{w} + o_p(1/N).\end{aligned}$$

Proof of Lemma A.11: Use a Taylor series expansion around zero for $g(a)$, $g(a) = g(0) + g'(0)a + g''(\tilde{a})a^2/2 = 1 + a + g''(\tilde{a})a^2/2$, to write the equation characterizing $\hat{t}(\theta)$ as

$$0 = \sum_{i=1}^{N} \psi(v_i, w_i, \theta) \cdot \left(1 + t(\theta)'\psi(v_i, w_i, \theta) + g''(a)\left(t(\theta)'\psi(v_i, w_i, \theta)\right)/2\right),$$

for some a between zero and $t(\theta)'\psi(v_i, w_i, \theta)$. Hence,

$$\begin{aligned}\hat{t}(\theta) = &-\left(\frac{1}{N}\sum_{i=1}^{N} \psi(v_i, w_i, \theta)\psi(v_i, w_i, \theta)'\right)^{-1} \\ &\times \left(\sum_{i=1}^{N} \psi(v_i, w_i, \theta) + \psi(v_i, w_i, \theta)g''(a)\left(t(\theta)'\psi(v_i, w_i, \theta)\right)^2/2\right).\end{aligned}$$

The second step is to show that

$$\frac{1}{N}\sum_{i=1}^{N}\psi(v_i, w_i, \theta)g''(a)\left(t(\theta)'\psi(v_i, w_i, \theta)\right)^2/2$$
$$= \overline{ww'(\overline{w} - e_1\overline{w}_1)w'(\overline{w} - e_1\overline{w}_1)}\lambda/2 + o_p(1/N), \tag{A.9}$$

To see this, first note that because $\theta = \overline{w}_1 + o_p(1/\sqrt{N})$, we have $\hat{t}(\theta) = \overline{w} - e_1\overline{w}_1 + o_p(1/\sqrt{N})$. Hence,

$$\frac{1}{N}\sum_{i=1}^{N}\psi(v_i, w_i, \theta)\left(t(\theta)'\psi(v_i, w_i, \theta)\right)^2$$
$$= \frac{1}{N}\sum_{i=1}^{N}\psi(v_i, w_i, \theta^*)\left(t(\theta)'\psi(v_i, w_i, \theta^*)\right)^2 + o_p(1/N)$$
$$= \frac{1}{N}\sum_{i=1}^{N}w_i\left(t(\theta)'w_i\right)^2 + o_p(1/N)$$
$$= \frac{1}{N}\sum_{i=1}^{N}w_i\left((\overline{w} - e_1\overline{w}_1)'w_i\right)^2 + o_p(1/N)$$
$$= \overline{ww'(\overline{w} - e_1\overline{w}_1)w'(\overline{w} - e_1\overline{w}_1)} + o_p(1/N).$$

Since $t = o_p(1)$, $a = o_p(1)$, and $g''(a) = \lambda + o_p(1)$, so that the result in Equation (A.9) follows.

The third step is to show that, with $\theta = \overline{w}_1 + o_p(1/\sqrt{N})$, we have

$$\left[\frac{1}{N}\sum_{i=1}^{N}\psi(v_i, w_i, \theta)\psi(v_i, w_i, \theta)'\right]^{-1}$$
$$= \mathcal{I}_M + (\overline{ww'} - \mathcal{I}_M) + 2\rho\overline{w}_1\mathcal{I}_M + o_p(1/\sqrt{N}). \tag{A.10}$$

To see this, first write

$$\frac{1}{N}\sum_{i=1}^{N}\psi(v_i, w_i, \theta)\psi(v_i, w_i, \theta)'$$
$$= \overline{ww'} - 2\overline{vw'}\theta - 2e_1\overline{w}'\theta + \theta^2\overline{(v + e_1)(v + e_1)'}$$
$$= \mathcal{I}_M + (\overline{ww'} - \mathcal{I}_M) - 2\rho\mathcal{I}_M\theta + o_p(1/\sqrt{N})$$
$$= \mathcal{I}_M + (\overline{ww'} - \mathcal{I}_M) - 2\rho\mathcal{I}_M\overline{w}_1 + o_p(1/\sqrt{N}).$$

Hence, using Lemma A.10,

$$\left[\frac{1}{N}\sum_{i=1}^{N}\psi(v_i, w_i, \theta)\psi(v_i, w_i, \theta)'\right]^{-1}$$
$$= \mathcal{I}_M - (\overline{ww'} - \mathcal{I}_M) + 2\rho\mathcal{I}_M\overline{w}_1 + o_p(1/\sqrt{N}),$$

which proves the equality in Equation (A.10).

Then, using the fact that $\overline{\psi(v, w, \theta)} = (\overline{v} + e_1)\theta - \overline{w}$, we can approximate the expression for $\hat{t}(\theta)$ as

$$\begin{aligned}
\hat{t}(\theta) &= -\left(\mathcal{I}_M - (\overline{ww'} - \mathcal{I}_M) + 2\rho\mathcal{I}_M\overline{w}_1\right) \\
&\quad \times \left((\overline{v} + e_1)\theta - \overline{w} + \overline{ww'(\overline{w} - e_1\overline{w}_1)w'}(\overline{w} - e_1\overline{w}_1)\lambda/2\right) \\
&= -(\overline{v} + e_1)\theta + \overline{w} - \overline{ww'(\overline{w} - e_1\overline{w}_1)w'}(\overline{w} - e_1\overline{w}_1)\lambda/2 \\
&\quad + (\overline{ww'} - \mathcal{I}_M)e_1\overline{w}_1 - (\overline{ww'} - \mathcal{I}_M)\overline{w} - 2\rho\overline{w}_1^2 e_1 \\
&\quad + 2\rho\overline{w}_1\overline{w} + o_p(1/N). \\
&= -e_1\theta + \overline{w} - \overline{w}_1\overline{v} - \overline{ww'(\overline{w} - e_1\overline{w}_1)w'}(\overline{w} - e_1\overline{w}_1)\lambda/2 \\
&\quad + (\overline{ww'} - \mathcal{I}_M)e_1\overline{w}_1 - (\overline{ww'} - \mathcal{I}_M)\overline{w} - 2\rho\overline{w}_1^2 e_1 \\
&\quad + 2\rho\overline{w}_1\overline{w} + o_p(1/N).
\end{aligned}$$

Proof of Lemma 4.7. The solution for $\hat{\theta}_g$ is characterized by the equation

$$0 = \hat{t}(\theta)' \frac{1}{N} \sum_{i=1}^{N} \frac{\partial \psi}{\partial \theta'}(v_i, w_i, \theta) \cdot g(\hat{t}(\theta)'\psi(v_i, w_i, \theta)).$$

We can write this as

$$\begin{aligned}
0 = &\Big(\big[-e_1\theta + \overline{w} - \overline{w}_1\overline{v} - \overline{ww'(\overline{w} - e_1\overline{w}_1)w'}(\overline{w} - e_1\overline{w}_1)\lambda/2 \\
&+ (\overline{ww'} - \mathcal{I}_M)e_1\overline{w}_1 - (\overline{ww'} - \mathcal{I}_M)\overline{w} - 2\rho\overline{w}_1^2 e_1 + 2\rho\overline{w}_1\overline{w}\big] \\
&+ \hat{t}(\theta) - \big[e_1\theta + \overline{w} - \overline{w}_1\overline{v} - \overline{ww'(\overline{w} - e_1\overline{w}_1)w'}(\overline{w} - e_1\overline{w}_1)\lambda/2 \\
&+ (\overline{ww'} - \mathcal{I}_M)e_1\overline{w}_1 - (\overline{ww'} - \mathcal{I}_M)\overline{w} - 2\rho\overline{w}_1^2 e_1 + 2\rho\overline{w}_1\overline{w}\big]\Big)' \\
&\frac{1}{N}\sum_{i=1}^{N} \frac{\partial \psi}{\partial \theta'}(v_i, w_i, \theta) \cdot g(\hat{t}(\theta)'\psi(v_i, w_i, \theta)).
\end{aligned}$$

Hence,

$$\begin{aligned}
\hat{\theta}_g = &\left(e_1' \frac{1}{N}\sum_{i=1}^{N} \frac{\partial \psi}{\partial \theta'}(v_i, w_i, \theta) \cdot g(\hat{t}(\theta)'\psi(v_i, w_i, \theta))\right)^{-1} \\
&\times \Big(\big[\overline{w} - \overline{w}_1\overline{v} - \overline{ww'(\overline{w} - e_1\overline{w}_1)w'}(\overline{w} - e_1\overline{w}_1)\lambda/2 \\
&+ (\overline{ww'} - \mathcal{I}_M)e_1\overline{w}_1 - (\overline{ww'} - \mathcal{I}_M)\overline{w} - 2\rho\overline{w}_1^2 e_1 + 2\rho\overline{w}_1\overline{w}\big] \\
&+ \hat{t}(\theta) - \big[e_1\theta + \overline{w} - \overline{w}_1\overline{v} - \overline{ww'(\overline{w} - e_1\overline{w}_1)w'}(\overline{w} - e_1\overline{w}_1)\lambda/2 \\
&+ (\overline{ww'} - \mathcal{I}_M)e_1\overline{w}_1 - (\overline{ww'} - \mathcal{I}_M)\overline{w} - 2\rho\overline{w}_1^2 e_1 + 2\rho\overline{w}_1\overline{w}\big]\Big)' \\
&\frac{1}{N}\sum_{i=1}^{N} \frac{\partial \psi}{\partial \theta'}(v_i, w_i, \theta) \cdot g(\hat{t}(\theta)'\psi(v_i, w_i, \theta)).
\end{aligned}$$

We break this up in a couple of parts. First we show that

$$\frac{1}{N}\sum_{i=1}^{N}\frac{\partial\psi}{\partial\theta'}(v_i,w_i,\theta)\cdot g(\hat{t}(\theta)'\psi(v_i,w_i,\theta))$$
$$= e_1 + \overline{v} - \rho\overline{w} + \rho e_1\overline{w}_1 + o_p(1/\sqrt{N}). \qquad \text{(A.11)}$$

To see this, write out $\psi(v_i, w_i, \theta) = (v_i + e_1)\theta - w_i$ to get

$$\frac{1}{N}\sum_{i=1}^{N}(v_i + e_1)\cdot g(\hat{t}(\theta)'(v_i\theta + e_1\theta - w_i))$$
$$= \frac{1}{N}\sum_{i=1}^{N}(v_i + e_1)\cdot(1 + t(\theta)'(v_i\theta + e_1\theta - w_i)) + o_p(1/\sqrt{N})$$
$$= e_1 + \overline{v} - \frac{1}{N}\sum_{i=1}^{N} v_i\overline{w}'w_i + o_p(1/\sqrt{N})$$
$$= e_1 + \overline{v} - \rho\overline{w} + \rho e_1\overline{w}_1 + o_p(1/\sqrt{N}),$$

which proves the equality in Equation (A.11). A direct implication is that

$$\left(e_1'\frac{1}{N}\sum_{i=1}^{N}\frac{\partial\psi}{\partial\theta'}(v_i,w_i,\theta)\cdot g(\hat{t}(\theta)'\psi(v_i,w_i,\theta))\right)^{-1}$$
$$= 1 - \overline{v}_1 + o_p(1/\sqrt{N}). \qquad \text{(A.12)}$$

Second, we show that

$$\left(\hat{t}(\theta) - \left[e_1\theta + \overline{w} - \overline{w}_1\overline{v} - \overline{ww'(\overline{w} - e_1\overline{w}_1)w'(\overline{w} - e_1\overline{w}_1)}\lambda/2\right.\right.$$
$$\left.\left. + (\overline{ww'} - \mathcal{I}_M)e_1\overline{w}_1 - (\overline{ww'} - \mathcal{I}_M)\overline{w} - 2\rho\overline{w}_1^2 e_1 + 2\rho\overline{w}_1\overline{w}\right]\right)'$$
$$\frac{1}{N}\sum_{i=1}^{N}\frac{\partial\psi}{\partial\theta'}(v_i,w_i,\theta)\cdot g(\hat{t}(\theta)'\psi(v_i,w_i,\theta)) = o_p(1/N).$$

This follows from Lemma 4.7, which implies that the first factor is $o_p(1/N)$, combined with the fact that the left-hand side of Equation (A.11) is $O_p(1)$. Third, we show that

$$\left(\overline{w} - \overline{w}_1\overline{v} - \overline{ww'(\overline{w} - e_1\overline{w}_1)w'(\overline{w} - e_1\overline{w}_1)}\lambda/2 + (\overline{ww'}\right.$$
$$\left. - \mathcal{I}_M)e_1\overline{w}_1 - (\overline{ww'} - \mathcal{I}_M)\overline{w} - 2\rho\overline{w}_1^2 e_1 + 2\rho\overline{w}_1\overline{w}\right)'$$
$$\frac{1}{N}\sum_{i=1}^{N}\frac{\partial\psi}{\partial\theta'}(v_i,w_i,\theta)\cdot g(\hat{t}(\theta)'\psi(v_i,w_i,\theta))$$
$$= \overline{w}_1 - e_1'\overline{w}_1\overline{v} - e_1'\overline{ww'(\overline{w} - e_1\overline{w}_1)w'(\overline{w} - e_1\overline{w}_1)}\lambda/2$$
$$+ e_1'(\overline{ww'} - \mathcal{I}_M)e_1\overline{w}_1 - e_1'(\overline{ww'} - \mathcal{I}_M)\overline{w} - 2\rho\overline{w}_1^2$$
$$+ 2\rho\overline{w}_1^2 + \overline{w}'\overline{v} - \rho\overline{w}'\overline{w} + \rho\overline{w}_1^2 + o_p(1/N).$$

$$= \overline{w}_1 - \overline{w}_1\overline{v}_1 - e_1'\overline{ww'(\overline{w} - e_1\overline{w}_1)w'(\overline{w} - e_1\overline{w}_1)}\lambda/2$$
$$+ e_1'(\overline{ww'} - \mathcal{I}_M)e_1\overline{w}_1 - e_1'(\overline{ww'} - \mathcal{I}_M)\overline{w}$$
$$+ \overline{w}'\overline{v} - \rho\overline{w}'\overline{w} + \rho\overline{w}_1^2 + o_p(1/N).$$

Now note that although $\overline{ww'(\overline{w} - e_1\overline{w}_1)w'(\overline{w} - e_1\overline{w}_1)} = O_p(1/N)$, $e_1'\overline{ww'(\overline{w} - e_1\overline{w}_1)w'(\overline{w} - e_1\overline{w}_1)} = o_p(1/N)$, because the subtraction of $e_1\overline{w}_1$ from $\overline{w}$ makes $(\overline{w} - e_1\overline{w}_1)$ independent of $e_1 w$. This relies on the full independence assumption we are using in the sequence of the moments. Because of this the term $e_1'\overline{ww'(\overline{w} - e_1\overline{w}_1)w'(\overline{w} - e_1\overline{w}_1)}$ is of lower order, and the above expression reduces to

$$\overline{w}_1 - \overline{w}_1\overline{v}_1 + e_1'(\overline{ww'} - \mathcal{I}_M)e_1\overline{w}_1 - e_1'(\overline{ww'} - \mathcal{I}_M)\overline{w}$$
$$+ \overline{w}'\overline{v} - \rho\overline{w}'\overline{w} + \rho\overline{w}_1^2 + o_p(1/N).$$

Finally bringing all the terms together, we get

$$\hat{\theta}_g = \overline{w}_1 + e_1'(\overline{ww'} - \mathcal{I}_M)e_1\overline{w}_1 - e_1'(\overline{ww'} - \mathcal{I}_M)\overline{w}$$
$$+ \overline{w}'\overline{v} - \rho\overline{w}'\overline{w} - 2\overline{w}_1\overline{v}_1 + \rho\overline{w}_1^2 + o_p(1/N).$$

Proof of Lemma 4.8. The proof proceeds by calculating:

(i) $E[T_1] = \theta^*$,
(ii) $E[R_3] = -\mu_{03}/N$,
(iii) $E[R_5] = \rho/N$,
(iv) $E[R_4] = \rho M/N$,
(v) $E[R_6] = -\rho M/N$,
(vi) $E[R_1] = -\rho/N$,
(vii) $E[R_2] = \mu_{03}/N$,
(viii) $E[R_7] = o_p(1/N)$.

The result then follows from adding up the expectations; details are on the web page.

Proof of Lemma 4.9. The expectations of twenty-eight component terms are defined and calculated; the result then follows from summing these components. The explicit calculation is given on the web page.

References

Baggerly, K. (1998), "Empirical Likelihood As a Goodness-of-Fit Measure," *Biometrika,* 85, 535–47.

Corcoran, S. A. (1995), "Empirical Discrepancy Theory," manuscript, Department of Statistics, University of Oxford.

Corcoran, S. A., A. C. Davison, and R. Spady (1995), "Reliable Inference From Empirical Likelihoods," Technical Report, Department of Statistics, Oxford University.

Corcoran, S. A. (1998), "Bartlett Adjustment of Empirical Discrepancy Statistics," *Biometrika,* 85, 967–72.

Cressie, N., and T. Read (1984), "Multinomial Goodness-of-Fit Tests," *Journal of the Royal Statistical Society, Series B,* 46, 440–64.

Donald, S., and W. K. Newey (2004), "Choosing the Number of Instruments," *Econometrica,* 69, 1161–91.

Hansen, L.-P. (1982), "Large Sample Properties of Generalized Method of Moments Estimators," *Econometrica,* 50, 1029–54.

Hansen, L.-P., J. Heaton, and A. Yaron (1996), "Finite Sample Properties of Some Alternative GMM Estimators," *Journal of Business and Economic Statistics,* 14, 262–280.

Imbens, G. W. (1997), "One Step Estimators for Over-identified Generalized Method of Moments Models," *Review of Economic Studies,* 64, 359–83.

Imbens, G. W., R. H. Spady, and P. Johnson (1998), "Information Theoretic Approaches to Inference in Moment Condition Models," *Econometrica,* 66, 333–57.

Kitamura, Y., and M. Stutzer (1997), "An Information Theoretic Alternative to Generalized Method of Moments Estimation," *Econometrica,* 65, 861–74.

Owen, A. (1988), "Empirical Likelihood Ratio Confidence Intervals for a Single Functional," *Biometrika,* 75, 237–49.

Newey, W. K., and R. J. Smith, (2000), "Asymptotic Bias and Equivalence of GMM and GEL," mimeo, MIT and University of Bristol.

Newey, W. K., and R. J. Smith, (2001), "Higher Order Properties of GMM and Generalized Empirical Likelihood Estimators," mimeo, MIT and University of Bristol.

Qin, J., and J. Lawless (1994), "Empirical Likelihood and General Estimating Equations," *Annals of Statistics,* 22, 300–25.

Rothenberg, T. (1999), "Higher Order Properties of Empirical Likelihood for Simultaneous Equations," seminar notes, Harvard/MIT Econometrics Seminar, University of Bristol.

Smith, R. J. (1997), "Alternative Semi-Parametric Approaches to Generalized Method of Moments Estimation," *Economic Journal,* 107, 503–19.

CHAPTER 11

Asymptotic Bias for GMM and GEL Estimators with Estimated Nuisance Parameters

Whitney K. Newey, Joaquim J. S. Ramalho, and Richard J. Smith

ABSTRACT

This chapter studies and compares the asymptotic bias of GMM and generalized empirical likelihood (GEL) estimators in the presence of estimated nuisance parameters. We consider cases in which the nuisance parameter is estimated from independent and identical samples. A simulation experiment is conducted for covariance structure models. Empirical likelihood offers much reduced mean and median bias, root mean squared error and mean absolute error, as compared with two-step GMM and other GEL methods. Both analytical and bootstrap bias-adjusted two-step GMM estimators are compared. Analytical bias-adjustment appears to be a serious competitor to bootstrap methods in terms of finite sample bias, root mean squared error, and mean absolute error. Finite sample variance seems to be little affected.

1. INTRODUCTION

It is now widely recognized that the most commonly used efficient two-step GMM (Hansen, 1982) estimator may have large biases for the sample sizes typically encountered in applications. (See, for example, the Special Section, July 1996, of the *Journal of Business and Economic Statistics*). To improve the small sample properties of GMM, a number of alternative estimators have been suggested, which include empirical likelihood (EL) (Owen 1988, Qin and Lawless 1994, Imbens 1997), continuous updating (CUE) (Hansen, Heaton, and Yaron 1996), and exponential tilting (ET) (Kitamura and Stutzer 1997, Imbens, Spady, and Johnson 1998). As shown by Smith (1997), EL and ET share a common structure, being members of a class of generalized empirical likelihood (GEL) estimators. Newey and Smith (2004) showed that CUE and members of the Cressie–Read power family (Cressie and Read 1984) are members of the GEL class (see also Smith 2001). All of these estimators and GMM have the same asymptotic distribution but different higher-order asymptotic properties. In a random sampling setting, Newey and Smith (2004) used the GEL structure, which helps simplify calculations and comparisons, to analyze higher-order properties using methods like those of Nagar (1959). Newey and Smith (2004) derived and compared the (higher order) asymptotic bias for all of these estimators. They also derived bias-corrected GMM and GEL estimators and considered their higher-order efficiency.

Newey and Smith (2004) found that EL has two theoretical advantages. First, the asymptotic bias does not grow with the number of moment restrictions, whereas the bias of the others often does. Consequently, for large numbers of moment conditions the bias of EL will be less than the bias of the other estimators. The relatively low asymptotic bias of EL indicates that it is an important alternative to GMM in applications. Furthermore, under a symmetry condition, which may be satisfied in some instrumental variable settings, all the GEL estimators inherit the small bias property of EL. The second theoretical advantage of EL is that after it is bias-corrected, using probabilities obtained from EL, it is higher-order efficient relative to the other estimators. This result generalizes the conclusions of Rothenberg (1996) who showed that for a single equation from a Gaussian, homoskedastic linear simultaneous equations model the asymptotic bias of EL is the same as the limited information maximum likelihood estimator and that bias-corrected EL is higher-order efficient relative to a bias-corrected GMM estimator.

This chapter reconsiders Newey and Smith's results for scenarios in which GMM and GEL estimation criteria involve a preliminary nuisance parameter estimator (Newey and Smith 2004). This type of situation arises in a number of familiar cases. Firstly, generated regressors employed in a regression model context require a preliminary estimator of a nuisance parameter (see Pagan 1984). Heckman's sample selectivity correction (Heckman 1979) is a special case with the nuisance parameter estimator obtained from a selectivity equation. Secondly, covariance structure models typically require an initial estimator of the mean of the data, which itself may not be of primary interest. Thirdly, but trivially, the use of a preliminary consistent GMM estimator to estimate the efficient GMM metric may be regarded as a nuisance parameter estimator and is thus a special case also. Consequently, the sample-splitting method for efficient two-step GMM metric estimation proposed to ameliorate the bias of efficient GMM estimators also falls within our analysis, the preliminary estimator being obtained from one subsample with the other subsample then used to implement efficient GMM (see also Altonji and Segal 1996). The presence of the nuisance parameter estimator typically affects the first-order asymptotic distribution of the estimator for the parameters of interest in the first and third examples, with sample splitting inducing asymptotic inefficiency because of the reduction in sample size. There is no loss in efficiency in the second example because the Jacobian with respect to the nuisance parameter is null. However, the presence of the nuisance parameter estimator alters the higher-order asymptotic bias in all of these examples as compared to the nuisance parameter – free situation.

To provide sufficient generality to deal with these various setups we define a sampling structure that permits the nuisance parameter estimator to be obtained from either an identical or an independent sample. Sample selectivity and covariance structure models together with the standard method for estimation of the efficient GMM metric are examples of the first type, whereas the sample-splitting example fits the latter category. We provide general stochastic expansions for GMM and GEL estimators. These expansions are then specialized for identical and independent samples and for the case when no nuisance parameters are present. The analytical expressions for asymptotic bias obtained from these expansions may be consistently estimated as in Newey and Smith (2004) to bias-correct GMM or GEL estimators. Some simulation experiments for covariance structure models show that these analytical methods for bias adjustment of the efficient two-step GMM estimator may be efficacious as compared with bootstrap methods, which are computationally more complex.

The outline of this chapter is as follows. Section 2 describes the setup and GMM and GEL estimators. Section 3 details the asymptotic biases for situations that involve either an independent or an identical sample. A simulation experiment in Section 4 for covariance structures with a single nuisance parameter estimated from the same sample considers the finite sample properties of GMM, CUE, ET, and EL estimators and compares some bootstrap and analytical bias-adjusted versions of the efficient two-step GMM estimator. Appendix A contains general stochastic expansions for GMM and GEL estimators together with proofs of the results in the chapter. For ease of reference, some notation used extensively in the paper is given in Appendix B.

2. THE ESTIMATORS AND OTHER PRELIMINARIES

2.1. Moment Conditions

Consider the moment indicator $g^{\beta}(z, \alpha, \beta)$, an m_{β}-vector of functions of a data observation z, and the p_{β}-vector β of unknown parameters, which are the object of inferential interest, where $m_{\beta} \geq p_{\beta}$. The moment indicator $g^{\beta}(z, \alpha, \beta)$ also depends on α, a p_{α}-vector of nuisance parameters. It is assumed that the true parameter vector β_0 uniquely satisfies the moment condition

$$E[g^{\beta}(z, \alpha_0, \beta_0)] = 0,$$

where $E[\cdot]$ denotes expectation.

Estimation of the nuisance parameter vector α_0 is based on the additional moment indicator $g^{\alpha}(x, \alpha)$, an m_{α}-vector of functions of a data observation x and α, where $m_{\alpha} \geq p_{\alpha}$. The true value α_0 of the nuisance parameter vector is assumed to uniquely satisfy the moment condition

$$E[g^{\alpha}(x, \alpha_0)] = 0.$$

2.2. Sample Structure

Let z_i, $(i = 1, \ldots, n_{\beta})$, and x_j, $(j = 1, \ldots, n_{\alpha})$, denote samples of i.i.d. observations on the data vectors z and x, respectively. An additional i.i.d. sample of observations on z, z_k, $(k = 1, \ldots, n)$, is also assumed to be available. This second sample of observations on z is used to obtain the preliminary consistent estimator for β required to estimate the efficient GMM metric. We identify the indices i, j, and k uniquely with these respective samples throughout this chapter.

This sampling structure is sufficiently general to permit consideration of a number of scenarios of interest, including the various examples outlined in the introduction. Firstly, sample-splitting schemes are allowed by defining the samples z_i, $(i = 1, \ldots, n_\beta)$, and z_k, $(k = 1, \ldots, n)$, to be independent. Secondly, situations in which these samples are identical may be addressed by setting $k = i$, $(i = 1, \ldots, n_\beta)$, which allows generated regressors, such as a sample selectivity correction, to be considered in our analysis. Our framework also allows for the possibility that the nuisance parameter estimator for α is obtained from a sample that is either independent of or identical to the sample of observations z_i, $(i = 1, \ldots, n_\beta)$, the latter case obtained by setting $x = z$ and $j = i$, $(i = 1, \ldots, n_\beta)$.

2.3. GMM and GEL Estimation of α_0

Initially, we describe a two-step GMM estimator of the nuisance parameter α following Hansen (1982). Let

$$g_j^\alpha(\alpha) \equiv g^\alpha(x_j, \alpha), \qquad \hat{g}^\alpha(\alpha) \equiv \sum_{j=1}^{n_\alpha} g_j^\alpha(\alpha)/n_\alpha.$$

A preliminary estimator for α_0 is given by $\tilde{\alpha} = \arg\min_{\alpha \in \mathcal{A}} \hat{g}^\alpha(\alpha)' (\hat{W}^{\alpha\alpha})^{-1} \hat{g}^\alpha(\alpha)$, where $\mathcal{A}$ denotes the parameter space and $\hat{W}^{\alpha\alpha} = W^{\alpha\alpha} + \sum_{j=1}^{n_\alpha} \xi^\alpha(x_j)/n_\alpha + O_p(n_\alpha^{-1})$ with $W^{\alpha\alpha}$ positive definite and $E[\xi^\alpha(x)] = 0$. The two-step GMM estimator is one that satisfies

$$\hat{\alpha}_{2S} = \arg\min_{\alpha \in \mathcal{A}} \hat{g}^\alpha(\alpha)'[\hat{\Omega}^{\alpha\alpha}(\tilde{\alpha})]^{-1} \hat{g}^\alpha(\alpha), \tag{2.1}$$

where $\hat{\Omega}^{\alpha\alpha}(\alpha) \equiv \sum_{j=1}^{n_\alpha} g_j^\alpha(\alpha) g_j^\alpha(\alpha)'/n_\alpha$.

We also examine as alternatives to GMM generalized empirical likelihood (GEL) estimators, as in Smith (1997, 2001) (see also Newey and Smith 2004). Let $\varphi = (\alpha', \mu')'$, where μ is a m_α-vector of auxiliary parameters; $\rho^\varphi(\cdot)$ be a function that is concave on its domain, which is an open interval $\mathcal{V}_\alpha$ containing zero; and $\rho_v^\varphi(\cdot)$, $\rho_{vv}^\varphi(\cdot)$, and $\rho_{vvv}^\varphi(\cdot)$ denote first, second, and third derivatives of $\rho^\varphi(\cdot)$, respectively. Without loss of generality we normalize the first- and second-order derivatives of $\rho_v^\varphi(\cdot)$ at 0 as $\rho_v^\varphi(0) = \rho_{vv}^\varphi(0) = -1$. Let $\hat{\Lambda}_{n_\alpha}^\alpha(\alpha) = \{\mu : \mu' g_j^\alpha(\alpha) \in \mathcal{V}_\alpha, j = 1, \ldots, n_\alpha\}$.

The GEL estimation criterion is

$$\hat{P}^\varphi(\varphi) = \sum_{j=1}^{n_\alpha} \rho^\varphi(\mu' g_j^\alpha(\alpha))/n_\alpha. \tag{2.2}$$

Then a GEL estimator for α_0 is obtained as the solution to the saddle point problem

$$\hat{\alpha}_{\text{GEL}} = \arg\min_{\alpha \in \mathcal{A}} \sup_{\mu \in \hat{\Lambda}^{\alpha}_{n\alpha}(\alpha)} \hat{P}^{\varphi}(\varphi). \tag{2.3}$$

The GEL criterion (2.2) admits a number of estimators as special cases: empirical likelihood (EL) with $\rho^{\varphi}(v) = \log(1 - v)$ (Imbens 1997, Qin and Lawless 1994), exponential tilting (ET) with $\rho^{\varphi}(v) = -\exp(v)$ (Imbens, Spady, and Johnson 1998, Kitamura and Stutzer 1997), continuous updating (CUE) with $\rho^{\varphi}(v)$ quadratic and $\rho^{\varphi}_{v}(0) \neq 0$ and $\rho^{\varphi}_{vv}(0) < 0$ (Hansen, Heaton, and Yaron 1996), and the Cressie–Read power family $\rho^{\varphi}(v) = -(1 + \gamma v)^{(\gamma+1)/\gamma}/(\gamma + 1)$ for some scalar γ (Cressie and Read 1984). See Newey and Smith (2004) for further discussion.

Let $\hat{\alpha}$ denote a consistent estimator for α_0 obtained as described in (2.1) or (2.3).

2.4. GMM and GEL Estimation of β_0

Let

$$g_i^{\beta}(\alpha, \beta) \equiv g^{\beta}(z_i, \alpha, \beta), \qquad \hat{g}^{\beta}(\alpha, \beta) \equiv \sum_{i=1}^{n_\beta} g_i^{\beta}(\alpha, \beta)/n_\beta.$$

A two-step GMM estimator of β is obtained using $\hat{\alpha}$ as a plug-in estimator of α in $\hat{g}^{\beta}(\alpha, \beta)$. The second sample of observations on z, z_k, $(k = 1, \ldots, n)$, is used to obtain a preliminary consistent estimator $\tilde{\beta}$ for β_0 defined by $\tilde{\beta} = \arg\min_{\beta \in \mathcal{B}} \sum_{k=1}^{n} g_k^{\beta}(\hat{\alpha}, \beta)'(\hat{W}^{\beta\beta})^{-1} \sum_{k=1}^{n} g_k^{\beta}(\hat{\alpha}, \beta)$, where $\mathcal{B}$ denotes the parameter space $g_k^{\beta}(\alpha, \beta) = g^{\beta}(z_k, \alpha, \beta)$, $(k = 1, \ldots, n)$. As earlier it is assumed that $\hat{W}^{\beta\beta} = W^{\beta\beta} + \sum_{i=1}^{n_\beta} \xi^{\beta}(z_i)/n_\beta + O_p(n_\beta^{-1})$ with $W^{\beta\beta}$ positive definite and $E[\xi^{\beta}(z)] = 0$. This second sample is also used to estimate a GMM metric, which has generic form

$$\hat{\Omega}^{\beta\beta}(\alpha, \beta) \equiv \sum_{k=1}^{n} g_k^{\beta}(\alpha, \beta) g_k^{\beta}(\alpha, \beta)'/n.$$

This structure for the GMM metric allows a number of important special cases. Sample-splitting schemes are included by specifying the samples z_i, $(i = 1, \ldots, n_\beta)$, and z_k, $(k = 1, \ldots, n)$, to be mutually independent. A setup in which these samples are identical is permitted. Hence, generated regressors are a special case of our analysis. Our framework also allows the nuisance parameter estimator $\hat{\alpha}$ to be obtained from either an independent or the same sample of observations; in the latter case, we define $x = z$ and $k = i$, $(i = 1, \ldots, n_\beta)$. See Section 3 for further details of these particular specializations.

The two-step GMM estimator for β_0 is one that satisfies

$$\hat{\beta}_{2S} = \arg\min_{\beta \in \mathcal{B}} \hat{g}^{\beta}(\hat{\alpha}, \beta)'[\hat{\Omega}^{\beta\beta}(\hat{\alpha}, \tilde{\beta})]^{-1} \hat{g}^{\beta}(\hat{\alpha}, \beta). \tag{2.4}$$

For GEL estimators of β_0, let $\theta = (\beta', \lambda')'$, where λ is a m_β-vector of auxiliary parameters; $\rho^\theta(\cdot)$ be a function that is concave on its domain, which is an open interval $\mathcal{V}_\beta$ containing zero; and $\rho_v^\theta(\cdot)$, $\rho_{vv}^\theta(\cdot)$, and $\rho_{vvv}^\theta(\cdot)$ denote first, second, and third derivatives of $\rho^\theta(\cdot)$, respectively. Again without loss of generality we normalize $\rho_v^\theta(0) = \rho_{vv}^\theta(0) = -1$. Let $\hat{\Lambda}_{n_\beta}^\beta(\beta) = \{\lambda : \lambda' g_i^\beta(\hat{\alpha}, \beta) \in \mathcal{V}_\beta, i = 1, \ldots, n_\beta\}$.

When the samples z_i, $(i = 1, \ldots, n_\beta)$, and z_k, $(k = 1, \ldots, n)$, are mutually independent we assume that they are pooled for GEL estimation. Let $N = n_\beta + n$ and define $n_* = n_\beta$ if the samples z_i, $(i = 1, \ldots, n_\beta)$, and z_k, $(k = 1, \ldots, n)$, are identical and $n_* = N$ if they are independent. The GEL estimation criterion is then

$$\hat{P}^\theta(\hat{\alpha}, \theta) = \sum_{i=1}^{n_*} \rho^\theta(\lambda' g_i^\beta(\hat{\alpha}, \beta)) / n_*. \tag{2.5}$$

A GEL estimator for β_0 is obtained as the solution to the saddle point problem

$$\hat{\beta}_{\mathrm{GEL}} = \arg\min_{\beta \in \mathcal{B}} \sup_{\lambda \in \hat{\Lambda}_{n_\beta}^\beta(\beta)} \hat{P}^\theta(\hat{\alpha}, \theta). \tag{2.6}$$

Let $\hat{\lambda}_{\mathrm{GEL}} = \sup_{\lambda \in \hat{\Lambda}_{n_\beta}^\beta(\hat{\beta}_{\mathrm{GEL}})} \hat{P}^\theta(\hat{\alpha}, \hat{\beta}_{\mathrm{GEL}}, \lambda)$.

3. HIGHER-ORDER ASYMPTOTIC PROPERTIES

Before detailing the various cases delineated in Section 2, we discuss the asymptotic bias of estimators $\hat{\alpha}_{2S}$ or $\hat{\alpha}_{\mathrm{GEL}}$ for the nuisance parameter α. We use the generic notation $\hat{\alpha}$ for $\hat{\alpha}_{2S}$ or $\hat{\alpha}_{\mathrm{GEL}}$ where there is no possibility of confusion.

3.1. The Asymptotic Bias of the Nuisance Parameter Estimator

Let $g_j^\alpha = g_j^\alpha(\alpha_0)$, $G_j^\alpha(\alpha) = \partial g_j^\alpha(\alpha)/\partial\alpha'$, $G_j^\alpha = G_j^\alpha(\alpha_0)$ and

$$G^\alpha = E[G_j^\alpha], \quad \Omega^{\alpha\alpha} = E[g_j^\alpha g_j^{\alpha'}], \quad \Sigma^{\alpha\alpha} = (G^{\alpha'}(\Omega^{\alpha\alpha})^{-1} G^\alpha)^{-1},$$
$$H^\alpha = \Sigma^{\alpha\alpha} G^{\alpha'}(\Omega^{\alpha\alpha})^{-1}, \quad P^\alpha = (\Omega^{\alpha\alpha})^{-1} - (\Omega^{\alpha\alpha})^{-1} G^\alpha \Sigma^{\alpha\alpha} G^{\alpha'}(\Omega^{\alpha\alpha})^{-1}.$$

Under conditions stated in Newey and Smith (2004, Theorems 3.3 and 3.4), both two-step GMM and GEL estimators for α admit stochastic expansions of the form

$$\hat{\alpha} = \alpha_0 + \tilde{\psi}^\alpha/\sqrt{n_\alpha} + (M_\alpha^\varphi)^{-1}\left[\tilde{A}^\varphi \tilde{\psi}^\varphi + \sum_{r=1}^{q_\varphi} \tilde{\psi}_r^\varphi M_r^\varphi \tilde{\psi}^\varphi/2\right] \Big/ n_\alpha + O_p(n_\alpha^{-3/2}),$$

where $\psi_j^\alpha = -H^\alpha g_j^\alpha$, $\psi_j^\varphi = -[H^{\alpha'}, P^\alpha]' g_j^\alpha$, $\tilde{\psi}^\alpha = \sum_{j=1}^{n_\alpha} \psi_j^\alpha/\sqrt{n_\alpha}$, $\tilde{\psi}^\varphi = \sum_{j=1}^{n_\alpha} \psi_j^\varphi/\sqrt{n_\alpha}$, and $\tilde{A}^\varphi = \sum_{j=1}^{n_\alpha} A_j^\varphi/\sqrt{n_\alpha}$. The matrix $(M_\alpha^\varphi)^{-1} = (\Sigma^{\alpha\alpha}, -H^\alpha)$ and the matrices M^φ and $\tilde{A}^\varphi$ are defined by analogy with $M_{\theta\theta}^\theta$ and $\tilde{A}^\theta$ given in Eqs. (A.1) and (A.2) of Appendix A.

For GMM, to $O(n_\alpha^{-3/2})$,

$$\begin{aligned}
&Bias(\hat{\alpha}_{2S})\\
&\quad = H^\alpha\big(-a_\alpha + E\big[G_j^\alpha H^\alpha g_j^\alpha\big]\big)/n_\alpha - \Sigma^{\alpha\alpha} E\big[G_j^{\alpha\prime} P^\alpha g_j^\alpha\big]/n_\alpha\\
&\qquad + H^\alpha\big[g_j^\alpha g_j^{\alpha\prime} P^\alpha g_j^\alpha\big]/n_\alpha\\
&\qquad - H^\alpha\big(E\big[G_j^\alpha H_W^\alpha \Omega^{\alpha\alpha} P^\alpha g_j^\alpha\big] + E\big[g_j^\alpha \operatorname{tr}\big(G_j^\alpha H_W^\alpha \Omega^{\alpha\alpha} P^\alpha\big)\big]\big)/n_\alpha,
\end{aligned}$$

where $H_W^\alpha = (G^{\alpha\prime} W^{-1} G^\alpha)^{-1} G^{\alpha\prime} W^{-1}$ and a_α is an m-vector such that

$$a_{\alpha s} \equiv \operatorname{tr}\left(\Sigma^{\alpha\alpha} E\big[\partial^2 g_{js}^\alpha(\alpha_0)/\partial\alpha\partial\alpha'\big]\right)/2 \quad (s = 1, \ldots, m_\alpha), \tag{3.1}$$

where $g_{js}^\alpha(\alpha)$ denotes the sth element of $g_j^\alpha(\alpha)$ (see Newey and Smith 2004, Theorem 4.1).

For GEL, to $O(n_\alpha^{-3/2})$,

$$\begin{aligned}
Bias(\hat{\alpha}_{\text{GEL}}) &= H^\alpha\big(-a_\alpha + E\big[G_j^\alpha H^\alpha g_j^\alpha\big]\big)/n_\alpha\\
&\quad + \big[1 + \big(\rho_{vvv}^\varphi(0)/2\big)\big] H^\alpha E\big[g_j^\alpha g_j^{\alpha\prime} P^\alpha g_j^\alpha\big]/n_\alpha.
\end{aligned}$$

See Newey and Smith (2004, Theorem 4.2). If $\rho_{vvv}^\varphi(0) = -2$, then the asymptotic bias of $\hat{\alpha}_{\text{GEL}}$ is identical to that of an infeasible GMM estimator with optimal linear combination of moment indicators $G^{\alpha\prime}(\Omega^{\alpha\alpha})^{-1} g_j^\alpha(\alpha)$, a condition that is satisfied by the EL estimator; (Newey and Smith 2004, Corollary 4.3). Moreover, this property is shared by any GEL estimator when third moments are zero, $E[g_{js}^\alpha g_j^\alpha g_j^{\alpha\prime}] = 0, (s = 1, \ldots, m_\alpha)$ (Newey and Smith 2004, Corollary 4.4).

To describe the results, let $g_i^\beta = g_i^\beta(\alpha_0, \beta_0)$, $G_{\beta i}^\beta(\alpha, \beta) = \partial g_i^\beta(\alpha, \beta)/\partial\beta'$, $G_{\beta i}^\beta = G_{\beta i}^\beta(\alpha_0, \beta_0)$,

$$\begin{aligned}
&\Omega^{\beta\beta} = E\big[g_i^\beta g_i^{\beta\prime}\big], \quad G_\beta^\beta = E\big[G_{\beta i}^\beta\big], \quad \Sigma^{\beta\beta} = \big(G_\beta^{\beta\prime}(\Omega^{\beta\beta})^{-1} G_\beta^\beta\big)^{-1},\\
&H^\beta = \Sigma^{\beta\beta} G_\beta^{\beta\prime}(\Omega^{\beta\beta})^{-1}, \quad P^\beta = (\Omega^{\beta\beta})^{-1} - (\Omega^{\beta\beta})^{-1} G_\beta^\beta \Sigma^{\beta\beta} G_\beta^{\beta\prime}(\Omega^{\beta\beta})^{-1}.
\end{aligned}$$

We define a_β as an m-vector such that

$$a_{\beta r} = \operatorname{tr}\big(\Sigma^{\beta\beta} E\big[\partial^2 g_{ir}^\beta/\partial\beta\partial\beta'\big]\big)/2, \quad (r = 1, \ldots, m_\beta).$$

Also let $G_{\alpha i}^\beta(\alpha, \beta) = \partial g_i^\beta(\alpha, \beta)/\partial\alpha'$, $G_{\alpha i}^\beta = G_{\alpha i}^\beta(\alpha_0, \beta_0)$, $G_\alpha^\beta = E\big[G_{\alpha i}^\beta\big]$ and

$$\Sigma_W^{\beta\beta} = \big(G_\beta^{\beta\prime}(W^{\beta\beta})^{-1} G_\beta^\beta\big)^{-1}, \qquad H_W^\beta = \Sigma_W^{\beta\beta} G_\beta^{\beta\prime}(W^{\beta\beta})^{-1}.$$

3.2. Independent Samples

In this case, $z_i, (i = 1, \ldots, n_\beta), x_j, (j = 1, \ldots, n_\alpha)$, and $z_k, (k = 1, \ldots, n)$, are independent i.i.d. samples of observations on the variables z and x. We assume that α is estimated by $\hat{\alpha}_{2S}$ or $\hat{\alpha}_{\text{GEL}}$ as described in Section 2.

The precise form of the bias requires some additional notation. Let $a^{\beta}_{\beta\beta}$, $a^{\beta}_{\beta\alpha}$, and $a^{\beta}_{\alpha\alpha}$ be m_{β}-vectors such that

$$a^{\beta}_{\beta\beta r} = \mathrm{tr}\big(H^{\beta} G^{\beta}_{\alpha} \Sigma^{\alpha\alpha} G^{\beta\prime}_{\alpha} H^{\beta\prime} E[\partial^2 g^{\beta}_{ir}/\partial\beta\partial\beta']\big)/2,$$
$$a^{\beta}_{\beta\alpha r} = -\mathrm{tr}\big(H^{\beta} G^{\beta}_{\alpha} \Sigma^{\alpha\alpha} E[\partial^2 g^{\beta}_{ir}/\partial\alpha\partial\beta']\big),$$
$$a^{\beta}_{\alpha\alpha r} = \mathrm{tr}\big(\Sigma^{\alpha\alpha} E[\partial^2 g^{\beta}_{ir}/\partial\alpha\partial\alpha']\big)/2, \quad (r = 1, \ldots, m_{\beta}).$$

and $c^{\beta}_{\beta\beta}$ and $c^{\beta}_{\beta\alpha}$ are p_{β}-vectors with elements

$$c^{\beta}_{\beta\beta r} = \mathrm{tr}\big(E[\partial^2 g^{\beta\prime}_{i}/\partial\beta\partial\beta_r] P^{\beta} G^{\beta}_{\alpha} \Sigma^{\alpha\alpha} G^{\beta\prime}_{\alpha} H^{\beta\prime}\big),$$
$$c^{\beta}_{\beta\alpha r} = -\mathrm{tr}\big(E[\partial^2 g^{\beta\prime}_{i}/\partial\alpha\partial\beta_r] P^{\beta} G^{\beta}_{\alpha} \Sigma^{\alpha\alpha}\big), \quad (r = 1, \ldots, p_{\beta}).$$

For the two-step GMM estimator $\hat{\beta}_{2S}$, let

$$Bias_{\alpha_0}(\hat{\beta}_{2S}) = H^{\beta}\big(-a_{\beta} + E[G^{\beta}_{\beta i} H^{\beta} g^{\beta}_{i}]\big)/n_{\beta}$$
$$-\Sigma^{\beta\beta} E[G^{\beta\prime}_{\beta i} P^{\beta} g^{\beta}_{i}]/n_{\beta}.$$

This asymptotic bias corresponds to that for $\hat{\beta}_{2S}$ when α_0 and $\Omega^{\beta\beta}$ are known. For GEL estimation the samples z_i, $(i = 1, \ldots, n_{\beta})$, and z_k, $(k = 1, \ldots, n)$, are pooled. Hence,

$$Bias_{\alpha_0}(\hat{\beta}_{\mathrm{GEL}}) = H^{\beta}\big(-a_{\beta} + E[G^{\beta}_{\beta i} H^{\beta} g^{\beta}_{i}]\big)/N$$
$$+\big[1 + (\rho^{\theta}_{vvv}(0)/2)\big] H^{\beta} E[g^{\beta}_{i} g^{\beta\prime}_{i} P^{\beta} g^{\beta}_{i}]/N,$$

where $N = n + n_{\beta}$, which is the asymptotic bias for $\hat{\beta}_{\mathrm{GEL}}$ after pooling when α_0 is known. See Newey and Smith (2004, Theorems 4.1 and 4.2).

The remainders in the following results are $O(\max[n^{-3/2}, n_{\alpha}^{-3/2}, n_{\beta}^{-3/2}])$ for GMM and $O(\max[N^{-3/2}, n_{\alpha}^{-3/2}])$ for GEL.

For GMM:

Theorem 3.1. *To $O(\max[n^{-3/2}, n_{\alpha}^{-3/2}, n_{\beta}^{-3/2}])$, if z_i, $(i = 1, \ldots, n_{\beta})$, x_j, $(j = 1, \ldots, n_{\alpha})$, and z_k, $(k = 1, \ldots, n)$, are independent samples, the asymptotic bias of the two-step GMM estimator is*

$$Bias(\hat{\beta}_{2S})$$
$$= Bias_{\alpha_0}(\hat{\beta}_{2S}) - H^{\beta} G^{\beta}_{\alpha} Bias(\hat{\alpha})$$
$$+ H^{\beta}\big(-a^{\beta}_{\beta\beta} - a^{\beta}_{\beta\alpha} - a^{\beta}_{\alpha\alpha}\big)/n_{\alpha} - \Sigma^{\beta\beta}\big(-c^{\beta}_{\beta\beta} - c^{\beta}_{\beta\alpha}\big)/n_{\alpha}$$
$$- H^{\beta}\big(E[G^{\beta}_{\beta i} H^{\beta}_{W} G^{\beta}_{\alpha} \Sigma^{\alpha\alpha} G^{\beta\prime}_{\alpha} P^{\beta} g^{\beta}_{i}] + E[g^{\beta}_{i} \mathrm{tr}(G^{\beta}_{\beta i} H^{\beta}_{W} G^{\beta}_{\alpha} \Sigma^{\alpha\alpha} G^{\beta\prime}_{\alpha} P^{\beta})]\big)/n$$
$$+ H^{\beta}\big(E[G^{\beta}_{\alpha i} \Sigma^{\alpha\alpha} G^{\beta\prime}_{\alpha} P^{\beta} g^{\beta}_{i}] + E[g^{\beta}_{i} \mathrm{tr}(G^{\beta}_{\alpha i} \Sigma^{\alpha\alpha} G^{\beta\prime}_{\alpha} P^{\beta})]\big)/n_{\alpha}.$$

As in Newey and Smith (2004), we may interpret the terms comprising the bias of the two step GMM estimator $\hat{\beta}_{2S}$. The first two terms of $Bias_{\alpha_0}(\hat{\beta}_{2S})$, which is the asymptotic bias for $\hat{\beta}_{2S}$ when α_0 and $\Omega^{\beta\beta}$ are known, are the bias that would arise from the (infeasible) optimal (variance minimizing; Hansen, 1982) linear combination $G_{\beta}^{\beta'}(\Omega^{\beta\beta})^{-1}g^{\beta}(z, \alpha_0, \beta)$. The third term in $Bias_{\alpha_0}(\hat{\beta}_{2S})$ arises because of inefficient estimation of the Jacobian G_{β}^{β}. The second and third terms of $Bias(\hat{\beta}_{2S})$ reflect the presence of the nuisance parameter estimator $\hat{\alpha}$ in the (infeasible) linear combination $G_{\beta}^{\beta'}(\Omega^{\beta\beta})^{-1}g^{\beta}(z, \hat{\alpha}, \beta)$, whereas the fourth term arises because of the presence of $\hat{\alpha}$ in estimation of the Jacobian G_{β}^{β}. Likewise, the remaining terms are due to the presence of the nuisance parameter estimator $\hat{\alpha}$ used in the estimation of $\Omega^{\beta\beta}$. Overall, therefore, the only role here for the preliminary two step GMM estimator $\tilde{\beta}$ in the estimation of $\Omega^{\beta\beta}$ is through $\hat{\alpha}$ (see $\hat{\alpha}_{2S}$ earlier and also Newey and Smith (2004)). That is, if $g_k^{\beta}(\alpha, \beta) = g_k^{\beta}(\beta)$, $(k = 1, \ldots, n)$, these remaining terms vanish. If the GMM estimator is iterated at least once, H_W^{β} should be replaced by H^{β}.

We now turn to the bias formula for GEL based on the pooled samples z_i, $(i = 1, \ldots, n_{\beta})$, and z_k, $(k = 1, \ldots, n)$.

Theorem 3.2. *To* $O(\max[N^{-3/2}, n_{\alpha}^{-3/2}])$, *where* $N = n_{\beta} + n$, *if* z_i, $(i = 1, \ldots, n_{\beta})$, x_j, $(j = 1, \ldots, n_{\alpha})$, *and* z_k, $(k = 1, \ldots, n)$, *are independent samples, the asymptotic bias of the GEL estimator is*

$$\begin{aligned}
&Bias(\hat{\beta}_{\mathrm{GEL}})\\
&\quad = Bias_{\alpha_0}(\hat{\beta}_{\mathrm{GEL}}) - H^{\beta}G_{\alpha}^{\beta}\,Bias(\hat{\alpha})\\
&\quad\quad + H^{\beta}\big(-a_{\beta\beta}^{\beta} - a_{\beta\alpha}^{\beta} - a_{\alpha\alpha}^{\beta}\big)/n_{\alpha} - \Sigma^{\beta\beta}\big(-c_{\beta\beta}^{\beta} - c_{\beta\alpha}^{\beta}\big)/n_{\alpha}\\
&\quad\quad + \Sigma^{\beta\beta}E\big[G_{\beta i}^{\beta'}P^{\beta}G_{\alpha}^{\beta}\Sigma^{\alpha\alpha}G_{\alpha}^{\beta'}P^{\beta}g_i^{\beta}\big]/n_{\alpha}\\
&\quad\quad + \big(\rho_{vvv}^{\theta}(0)/2\big)\,E\big[g_i^{\beta}g_i^{\beta'}P^{\beta}G_{\alpha}^{\beta}\Sigma^{\alpha\alpha}G_{\alpha}^{\beta'}P^{\beta}g_i^{\beta}\big]/n_{\alpha}\\
&\quad\quad - H^{\beta}\big(E\big[G_{\beta i}^{\beta}H^{\beta}G_{\alpha}^{\beta}\Sigma^{\alpha\alpha}G_{\alpha}^{\beta'}P^{\beta}g_i^{\beta}\big]\\
&\quad\quad + E\big[g_i^{\beta}\mathrm{tr}\big(G_{\beta i}^{\beta'}P^{\beta}G_{\alpha}^{\beta}\Sigma^{\alpha\alpha}G_{\alpha}^{\beta'}H^{\beta'}\big)\big]\big)/n_{\alpha}\\
&\quad\quad + H^{\beta}\big(E\big[G_{\alpha i}^{\beta}\Sigma^{\alpha\alpha}G_{\alpha}^{\beta'}P^{\beta}g_i^{\beta}\big] + E\big[g_i^{\beta}\mathrm{tr}\big(G_{\alpha i}^{\beta'}P^{\beta}G_{\alpha}^{\beta}\Sigma^{\alpha\alpha}\big)\big]\big)/n_{\alpha}.
\end{aligned}$$

The first four terms are similar to those for GMM. The fifth and sixth terms arise because of the presence of the nuisance parameter estimator $\hat{\alpha}$ in the implicit estimation of $\Omega^{\beta\beta}$ and its inefficient estimation (see Newey and Smith 2004, Theorem 2.3). The remaining terms are similar to those for GMM except that H_W^{β} is replaced by H^{β} and would coincide if the GMM estimator were iterated at least once. If $G_{\alpha}^{\beta} = 0$, which ensures that $\hat{\beta}_{\mathrm{GEL}}$ is first-order efficient and occurs, for example, if $g_i^{\beta}(\alpha, \beta)$ is linear in α, there is no effect due to the implicit estimation of $\Omega^{\beta\beta}$ except through $Bias_{\alpha_0}(\hat{\beta}_{\mathrm{GEL}})$ and, except for this term, $Bias(\hat{\beta}_{\mathrm{GEL}})$ and $Bias(\hat{\beta}_{2S})$ coincide.

From Theorem 3.2, all GEL estimators have the same bias when third moments are zero as $Bias_{\alpha_0}(\hat{\beta}_{\mathrm{GEL}})$ is the same for all GEL estimators in this case (see Newey and Smith 2004, Corollary 4.4).

Corollary 3.1. *To* $O(\max[N^{-3/2}, n_\alpha^{-3/2}])$, *where* $N = n_\beta + n$, *if* z_i, $(i = 1, \ldots, n_\beta)$, x_j, $(j = 1, \ldots, n_\alpha)$, *and* z_k, $(k = 1, \ldots, n)$, *are independent samples and* $E[g_{ir}^\beta g_i^\beta g_i^{\beta\prime}] = 0$, $(r = 1, \ldots, m_\beta)$, *then all GEL estimators possess identical asymptotic bias.*

We now specialize these results for a standard sample-splitting scheme. Here the nuisance parameter vector α is not present. The remainders in the following results are $O(\max[n^{-3/2}, n_\beta^{-3/2}])$ for GMM and $O(N^{-3/2})$ for GEL. The sample-split two-step GMM estimator for β is one that satisfies

$$\hat{\beta}_{2S} = \arg\min_{\beta\in\mathcal{B}} \hat{g}^\beta(\beta)'\hat{\Omega}^{\beta\beta}(\tilde{\beta})^{-1}\hat{g}^\beta(\beta),$$

where $\hat{\Omega}^{\beta\beta}(\beta) \equiv \sum_{k=1}^n g_k^\beta(\beta)g_k^\beta(\beta)'/n$.

For GMM we have the following result:

Corollary 3.2. *In the absence of nuisance parameters, to* $O(\max[n^{-3/2}, n_\beta^{-3/2}])$, *if* z_i, $(i = 1, \ldots, n_\beta)$, *and* z_k, $(k = 1, \ldots, n)$, *are independent samples, the asymptotic bias of the two-step GMM estimator is*

$$\begin{aligned} Bias(\hat{\beta}_{2S}) &= Bias_{\alpha_0}(\hat{\beta}_{2S}) \\ &= H^\beta\big(-a_\beta + E\big[G_{\beta i}^\beta H^\beta g_i^\beta\big]\big)/n_\beta - \Sigma^{\beta\beta}E\big[G_{\beta i}^{\beta\prime} P^\beta g_i^\beta\big]/n_\beta. \end{aligned}$$

This asymptotic bias result is that in Newey and Smith (2004) when $\Omega^{\beta\beta}$ is known. In particular, it is clear that because of independent sampling comprising the sample-split scheme an inefficient preliminary estimator for β_0 may be used with no effect on asymptotic bias. However, there would be implications for higher-order variance.

We now turn to the bias formula for GEL, which uses the pooled sample z_i, $(i = 1, \ldots, n_\beta)$, and z_k, $(k = 1, \ldots, n)$.

Corollary 3.3. *In the absence of nuisance parameters, to* $O(N^{-3/2})$, *where* $N = n_\beta + n$, *if* z_i, $(i = 1, \ldots, n_\beta)$, *and* z_k, $(k = 1, \ldots, n)$, *are independent samples, the asymptotic bias of the GEL estimator is*

$$\begin{aligned} Bias(\hat{\beta}_{\mathrm{GEL}}) &= Bias_{\alpha_0}(\hat{\beta}_{\mathrm{GEL}}) \\ &= H^\beta\big(-a_\beta + E\big[G_{\beta i}^\beta H^\beta g_i^\beta\big]\big)/N \\ &\quad + \big[1 + \big(\rho_{vvv}^\theta(0)/2\big)\big]H^\beta E\big[g_i^\beta g_i^{\beta\prime} P^\beta g_i^\beta\big]/N. \end{aligned}$$

In comparison with the GMM bias, we find that the Jacobian term drops out, i.e., there is no asymptotic bias from estimation of the Jacobian. As noted in Newey and Smith (2004), the absence of bias from the Jacobian is due to its efficient estimation in the first-order conditions. However, the last term reflects the implicit inefficient estimation of the variance matrix $\Omega^{\beta\beta}$ (see Newey and Smith 2004, Theorem 2.3). The deleterious effect of this term relative to GMM will be offset at least partially by the use of the expanded pooled sample size N. However, in certain circumstances this term can be eliminated altogether.

The following corollary is immediate from Newey and Smith (2004, Corollary 4.3).

Corollary 3.4. *In the absence of nuisance parameters, to $O(N^{-3/2})$, where $N = n_\beta + n$, if z_i, $(i = 1, \ldots, n_\beta)$, and z_k, $(k = 1, \ldots, n)$, are independent samples, then*

$$Bias(\hat{\beta}_{\mathrm{EL}}) = H^\beta(-a_\beta + E[G^\beta_{\beta i} H^\beta g^\beta_i])/N.$$

EL uses an efficient second moment estimator, which leads to the aforementioned result (see Newey and Smith 2004, Theorem 2.3). Thus, for EL the bias is exactly the same as that for the infeasible optimal GMM estimator with moment functions $G^{\beta'}_\beta(\Omega^{\beta\beta})^{-1}g^\beta(z, \beta)$. This same property would be shared by any GEL estimator with $\rho^\theta_{vvv}(0) = -2$. It will also be shared by any GEL estimator when third moments are zero as detailed in Corollary 3.1 above.

3.3. Identical Samples

In this case, the samples z_i, $(i = 1, \ldots, n_\beta)$, and z_k, $(k = 1, \ldots, n)$, coincide. Hence, the estimator $\hat{\Omega}^{\beta\beta}(\alpha, \beta)$ for $\Omega^{\beta\beta}$ is based on the sample z_i, $(i = 1, \ldots, n_\beta)$. That is, $k = i$, $n = n_\beta$, and now $\hat{\Omega}^{\beta\beta}(\alpha, \beta) = \sum_{i=1}^{n_\beta} g^\beta_i(\alpha, \beta) g^\beta_i(\alpha, \beta)'$. Moreover, the nuisance parameter estimator $\hat{\alpha}$ is also based on the same sample z_i, $(i = 1, \ldots, n_\beta)$. That is, the samples z_i, $(i = 1, \ldots, n_\beta)$, and x_j, $(j = 1, \ldots, n_\alpha)$, also coincide. So $x = z$, $j = i$, and $n_\alpha = n_\beta$. The remainders in the following results are thus $O(n_\beta^{-3/2})$.

Let $g^{\beta\cdot\alpha}_i = g^\beta_i - G^\beta_\alpha H^\alpha g^\alpha_i$,

$$\Omega^{\beta\beta\cdot\alpha\alpha} = E[g^{\beta\cdot\alpha}_i g^{\beta\cdot\alpha'}_i], \qquad \Omega^{\beta\beta\cdot\alpha} = E[g^\beta_i g^{\beta\cdot\alpha'}_i],$$
$$\Omega^{\alpha\beta\cdot\alpha} = E[g^\alpha_i g^{\beta\cdot\alpha'}_i].$$

Also let $a^\beta_{\beta\beta}$, $a^\beta_{\beta\alpha}$ and $a^\beta_{\alpha\alpha}$ be m_β-vectors such that

$$a^\beta_{\beta\beta r} = \mathrm{tr}(H^\beta \Omega^{\beta\beta\cdot\alpha\alpha} H^{\beta'} E[\partial^2 g^\beta_{ir}/\partial\beta\partial\beta'])/2,$$
$$a^\beta_{\beta\alpha r} = \mathrm{tr}(H^\alpha \Omega^{\alpha\beta\cdot\alpha} H^{\beta'} E[\partial^2 g^\beta_{ir}/\partial\beta\partial\alpha']),$$
$$a^\beta_{\alpha\alpha r} = \mathrm{tr}(\Sigma^{\alpha\alpha} E[\partial^2 g^\beta_{ir}/\partial\alpha\partial\alpha'])/2, \quad (r = 1, \ldots, m_\beta),$$

and $c^\beta_{\beta\beta}$ and $c^\beta_{\beta\alpha}$ are p_β-vectors with elements

$$c^\beta_{\beta\beta r} = \mathrm{tr}(H^\beta \Omega^{\beta\beta\cdot\alpha\alpha} P^\beta E[\partial^2 g^\beta_i/\partial\beta'\partial\beta_r]),$$
$$c^\beta_{\beta\alpha r} = \mathrm{tr}(H^\alpha \Omega^{\alpha\beta\cdot\alpha} P^\beta E[\partial^2 g^\beta_i/\partial\alpha'\partial\beta_r]), \quad (r = 1, \ldots, p_\beta).$$

For GMM we have the following result:

Theorem 3.3. *To $O(n_\beta^{-3/2})$, if the samples z_i, $(i = 1, \ldots, n_\beta)$, x_j, $(j = 1, \ldots, n_\alpha)$, and z_k, $(k = 1, \ldots, n)$, are identical, the asymptotic bias of the two-step GMM estimator is*

$$\begin{aligned}
Bias(\hat{\beta}_{2S}) = &- H^\beta G_\alpha^\beta Bias(\hat{\alpha}) \\
&+ H^\beta\big(-a_{\beta\beta}^\beta - a_{\beta\alpha}^\beta - a_{\alpha\alpha}^\beta + E\big[G_{\beta i}^\beta H^\beta g_i^{\beta\cdot\alpha}\big] + E\big[G_{\alpha i}^\beta H^\alpha g_i^\alpha\big]\big)/n_\beta \\
&- \Sigma^{\beta\beta}\big(-c_{\beta\beta}^\beta - c_{\beta\alpha}^\beta + E\big[G_{\beta i}^{\beta\prime} P^\beta g_i^{\beta\cdot\alpha}\big]\big)/n_\beta \\
&+ H^\beta E\big[g_i^\beta g_i^{\beta\prime} P^\beta g_i^{\beta\cdot\alpha}\big]/n_\beta \\
&- H^\beta(E\big[G_{\beta i}^\beta H_W^\beta \Omega^{\beta\beta\cdot\alpha\alpha} P^\beta g_i^\beta\big] + E\big[g_i^\beta\, \mathrm{tr}(G_{\beta i}^\beta H_W^\beta \Omega^{\beta\beta\cdot\alpha\alpha} P^\beta)\big])/n_\beta \\
&- H^\beta\big(E\big[G_{\alpha i}^\beta H^\alpha \Omega^{\alpha\beta\cdot\alpha} P^\beta g_i^\beta\big] + E\big[g_i^\beta\, \mathrm{tr}(G_{\alpha i}^\beta H^\alpha \Omega^{\alpha\beta\cdot\alpha} P^\beta)\big]\big)/n_\beta.
\end{aligned}$$

If $\tilde{\beta}$ is iterated at least once, H_W^β is replaced by H^β. The second line arises because of the presence of the nuisance parameter estimator $\hat{\alpha}$ in the (infeasible) linear combination $G_\beta^{\beta\prime}\Omega^{\beta\beta-1}g^\beta(z, \alpha, \beta)$ and the third is due to the estimation of the Jacobian G_β^β. The remaining terms reflect using $\hat{\alpha}$ and $\tilde{\beta}$. The penultimate and final lines reflect estimation of $\Omega^{\beta\beta}$ using respectively the preliminary estimator $\tilde{\beta}$ and the nuisance parameter estimator $\hat{\alpha}$.

For GEL:

Theorem 3.4. *To $O(n_\beta^{-3/2})$, if the samples z_i, $(i = 1, \ldots, n_\beta)$, x_j, $(j = 1, \ldots, n_\alpha)$, and z_k, $(k = 1, \ldots, n)$, are identical, the asymptotic bias of the GEL estimator is*

$$\begin{aligned}
&Bias(\hat{\beta}_{\mathrm{GEL}}) \\
&= - H^\beta G_\alpha^\beta Bias(\hat{\alpha}) \\
&\quad + H^\beta\big(-a_{\beta\beta}^\beta - a_{\beta\alpha}^\beta - a_{\alpha\alpha}^\beta + E\big[G_{\beta i}^\beta H^\beta g_i^{\beta\cdot\alpha}\big] + E\big[G_{\alpha i}^\beta H^\alpha g_i^\alpha\big]\big)/n_\beta \\
&\quad - \Sigma^{\beta\beta}\big(-c_{\beta\beta}^\beta - c_{\beta\alpha}^\beta + E\big[G_{\beta i}^{\beta\prime} P^\beta(\Omega^{\beta\beta} - \Omega^{\beta\beta\cdot\alpha\alpha})P^\beta g_i^{\beta\cdot\alpha}\big]\big)/n_\beta \\
&\quad + H^\beta\big(E\big[g_i^\beta g_i^{\beta\prime} P^\beta g_i^{\beta\cdot\alpha}\big] + (\rho_{vvv}^\theta(0)/2)E\big[g_i^\beta g_i^{\beta\prime} P^\beta \Omega^{\beta\beta\cdot\alpha\alpha} P^\beta g_i^\beta\big]/n_\beta \\
&\quad - H^\beta\big(E\big[G_{\beta i}^\beta H^\beta \Omega^{\beta\beta\cdot\alpha\alpha} P^\beta g_i^\beta\big] + E\big[g_i^\beta\, \mathrm{tr}(G_{\beta i}^\beta H^\beta \Omega^{\beta\beta\cdot\alpha\alpha} P^\beta)\big]\big)/n_\beta \\
&\quad - H^\beta\big(E\big[G_{\alpha i}^\beta H^\alpha \Omega^{\alpha\beta\cdot\alpha} P^\beta g_i^\beta\big] + E\big[g_i^\beta\, \mathrm{tr}(G_{\alpha i}^\beta H^\alpha \Omega^{\alpha\beta\cdot\alpha} P^\beta)\big]\big)/n_\beta.
\end{aligned}$$

The terms in $Bias(\hat{\beta}_{\mathrm{GEL}})$ are mostly identical to those for $\hat{\beta}_{2S}$. The major differences are the third line, which reflects the inefficient estimation of the Jacobian term G_β^β. This term arises solely because of the presence of the nuisance parameter estimator $\hat{\alpha}$ and vanishes if the nuisance parameter is absent (see Newey and Smith 2004, Theorem 2.3). Other differences are, firstly, H^β in place of H_W^β in the penultimate line, a difference which is eliminated if two-step GMM is iterated once, and, secondly, the additional terms $\Sigma^{\beta\beta}E[G_{\beta i}^{\beta'}P^{\beta}\Omega^{\beta\beta\cdot\alpha\alpha}P^{\beta}g_i^{\beta\cdot\alpha}]$ and $(\rho_{vvv}^{\theta}(0)/2)E[g_i^{\beta}g_i^{\beta'}P^{\beta}\Omega^{\beta\beta\cdot\alpha\alpha}P^{\beta}g_i^{\beta}]$, which arise through the implicit estimation of $\Omega^{\beta\beta}$ using both $\hat{\alpha}$ and $\hat{\beta}_{\text{GEL}}$.

From Theorem 3.4, all GEL estimators have the same bias when third moments are zero; cf. Corollary 3.1 (see also Newey and Smith 2004, Corollary 4.4).

Corollary 3.5. *To $O(n_{\beta}^{-3/2})$, if the samples z_i, $(i = 1, \ldots, n_{\beta})$, x_j, $(j = 1, \ldots, n_{\alpha})$, and z_k, $(k = 1, \ldots, n)$, coincide and $E[g_{ir}^{\beta}g_i^{\beta}g_i^{\beta'}] = 0$, $(r = 1, \ldots, m_{\beta})$, then all GEL estimators possess identical asymptotic bias.*

The above results in Theorems 3.3 and 3.4 may be specialized straightforwardly to deal with when z_i, $(i = 1, \ldots, n_{\beta})$, and x_j, $(j = 1, \ldots, n_{\alpha})$, are independent samples. In this case, $\Omega^{\beta\beta\cdot\alpha\alpha} = \Omega^{\beta\beta} + G_{\alpha}^{\beta}\Sigma^{\alpha\alpha}G_{\alpha}^{\beta'}$, $\Omega^{\beta\beta\cdot\alpha} = \Omega^{\beta\beta}$ and $\Omega^{\alpha\beta\cdot\alpha} = -\Omega^{\alpha\alpha}H^{\alpha'}G_{\alpha}^{\beta'}$. Also, let $a_{\beta\beta}^{\beta}$, $a_{\beta\alpha}^{\beta}$, $a_{\alpha\alpha}^{\beta}$, $c_{\beta\beta}^{\beta}$, and $c_{\beta\alpha}^{\beta}$ be defined as in Section 3.2; that is, $a_{\beta\beta}^{\beta}$, $a_{\beta\alpha}^{\beta}$, and $a_{\alpha\alpha}^{\beta}$ are m_{β}-vectors such that

$$\begin{aligned}
a_{\beta\beta r}^{\beta} &= \operatorname{tr}\big(H^{\beta}G_{\alpha}^{\beta}\Sigma^{\alpha\alpha}G_{\alpha}^{\beta'}H^{\beta'}E\big[\partial^2 g_{ir}^{\beta}/\partial\beta\partial\beta'\big]\big)/2,\\
a_{\beta\alpha r}^{\beta} &= -\operatorname{tr}\big(H^{\beta}G_{\alpha}^{\beta}\Sigma^{\alpha\alpha}E\big[\partial^2 g_{ir}^{\beta}/\partial\alpha\partial\beta'\big]\big),\\
a_{\alpha\alpha r}^{\beta} &= \operatorname{tr}\big(\Sigma^{\alpha\alpha}E\big[\partial^2 g_{ir}^{\beta}/\partial\alpha\partial\alpha'\big]\big)/2, \quad (r = 1, \ldots, m_{\beta}).
\end{aligned}$$

and $c_{\beta\beta}^{\beta}$ and $c_{\beta\alpha}^{\beta}$ are p_{β}-vectors with elements

$$\begin{aligned}
c_{\beta\beta r}^{\beta} &= \operatorname{tr}\big(E\big[\partial^2 g_i^{\beta'}/\partial\beta\partial\beta_r\big]P^{\beta}G_{\alpha}^{\beta}\Sigma^{\alpha\alpha}G_{\alpha}^{\beta'}H^{\beta'}\big),\\
c_{\beta\alpha r}^{\beta} &= -\operatorname{tr}\big(E\big[\partial^2 g_i^{\beta'}/\partial\alpha\partial\beta_r\big]P^{\beta}G_{\alpha}^{\beta}\Sigma^{\alpha\alpha}\big), \quad (r = 1, \ldots, p_{\beta}).
\end{aligned}$$

The remainders in the following corollaries are $O(\max[n_{\alpha}^{-3/2}, n_{\beta}^{-3/2}])$. Let

$$\begin{aligned}
&Bias_{\alpha_0}(\hat{\beta}_{2S})\\
&\quad = H^{\beta}\big(-a_{\beta} + E\big[G_{\beta i}^{\beta}H^{\beta}g_i^{\beta}\big]\big)/n_{\beta}\\
&\qquad -\Sigma^{\beta\beta}E\big[G_{\beta i}^{\beta'}P^{\beta}g_i^{\beta}\big]/n_{\beta} + H^{\beta}E\big[g_i^{\beta}g_i^{\beta'}P^{\beta}g_i^{\beta}\big]/n_{\beta}\\
&\qquad - H^{\beta}\big(E\big[G_{\beta i}^{\beta}H_W^{\beta}\Omega^{\beta\beta}P^{\beta}g_i^{\beta}\big] + E\big[g_i^{\beta'}\operatorname{tr}\big(G_{\beta i}^{\beta}H_W^{\beta}\Omega^{\beta\beta}P^{\beta}\big)\big]\big)/n_{\beta},
\end{aligned}$$

$$\begin{aligned}
Bias_{\alpha_0}(\hat{\beta}_{\text{GEL}}) = {} & H^{\beta}\big(-a_{\beta} + E\big[G_{\beta i}^{\beta}H^{\beta}g_i^{\beta}\big]\big)/n_{\beta}\\
& + \big[1 + \big(\rho_{vvv}^{\theta}(0)/2\big)\big]H^{\beta}E\big[g_i^{\beta}g_i^{\beta}P^{\beta}g_i^{\beta}\big]/n_{\beta},
\end{aligned}$$

which are the biases for $\hat{\beta}_{2S}$ and $\hat{\beta}_{\text{GEL}}$ when α_0 is known (see Newey and Smith 2004, Theorems 4.1 and 4.2).

Corollary 3.6. *To $O(\max[n_{\alpha}^{-3/2}, n_{\beta}^{-3/2}])$, if z_i, $(i = 1, \ldots, n_{\beta})$, and x_j, $(j = 1, \ldots, n_{\alpha})$, are independent samples and the samples z_i, $(i = 1, \ldots, n_{\beta})$, and*

z_k, $(k = 1, \ldots, n)$, *are identical, the asymptotic bias of the two-step GMM estimator is*

$$\begin{aligned}
&Bias(\hat{\beta}_{2S}) \\
&\quad = Bias_{\alpha_0}(\hat{\beta}_{2S}) - H^\beta G^\beta_\alpha Bias(\hat{\alpha}) \\
&\qquad + H^\beta\left(-a^\beta_{\beta\beta} - a^\beta_{\beta\alpha} - a^\beta_{\alpha\alpha}\right)/n_\alpha - \Sigma^{\beta\beta}\left(-c^\beta_{\beta\beta} - c^\beta_{\beta\alpha}\right)/n_\alpha \\
&\qquad - H^\beta\left(E\left[G^\beta_{\beta i} H^\beta_W G^\beta_\alpha \Sigma^{\alpha\alpha} G^{\beta'}_\alpha P^\beta g^\beta_i\right] + E\left[g^\beta_i \operatorname{tr}\left(G^\beta_{\beta i} H^\beta_W G^\beta_\alpha \Sigma^{\alpha\alpha} G^{\beta'}_\alpha P^\beta\right)\right]\right)/n_\alpha \\
&\qquad + H^\beta\left(E\left[G^\beta_{\alpha i} \Sigma^{\alpha\alpha} G^{\beta'}_\alpha P^\beta g^\beta_i\right] + E\left[g^\beta_i \operatorname{tr}\left(G^\beta_{\alpha i} \Sigma^{\alpha\alpha} G^{\beta'}_\alpha P^\beta\right)\right]\right)/n_\alpha.
\end{aligned}$$

Corollary 3.7. *To* $O(\max[n_\alpha^{-3/2}, n_\beta^{-3/2}])$, *if* z_i, $(i = 1, \ldots, n_\beta)$, *and* x_j, $(j = 1, \ldots, n_\alpha)$, *are independent samples and the samples* z_i, $(i = 1, \ldots, n_\beta)$, *and* z_k, $(k = 1, \ldots, n)$, *are identical, the asymptotic bias of the GEL estimator is*

$$\begin{aligned}
&Bias(\hat{\beta}_{\mathrm{GEL}}) \\
&\quad = Bias_{\alpha_0}(\hat{\beta}_{\mathrm{GEL}}) - H^\beta G^\beta_\alpha Bias(\hat{\alpha}) \\
&\qquad + H^\beta\left(-a^\beta_{\beta\beta} - a^\beta_{\beta\alpha} - a^\beta_{\alpha\alpha}\right)/n_\alpha - \Sigma^{\beta\beta}\left(-c^\beta_{\beta\beta} - c^\beta_{\beta\alpha}\right)/n_\alpha \\
&\qquad + \Sigma^{\beta\beta} E\left[G^{\beta'}_{\beta i} P^\beta G^\beta_\alpha \Sigma^{\alpha\alpha} G^{\beta'}_\alpha P^\beta g^\beta_i\right]/n_\alpha \\
&\qquad + \left(\rho^\theta_{vvv}(0)/2\right) E\left[g^\beta_i g^{\beta'}_i P^\beta G^\beta_\alpha \Sigma^{\alpha\alpha} G^{\beta'}_\alpha P^\beta g^\beta_i\right])/n_\alpha \\
&\qquad - H^\beta(E\left[G^\beta_{\beta i} H^\beta G^\beta_\alpha \Sigma^{\alpha\alpha} G^{\beta'}_\alpha P^\beta g^\beta_i\right] + E\left[g^\beta_i \operatorname{tr}\left(G^\beta_{\beta i} H^\beta G^\beta_\alpha \Sigma^{\alpha\alpha} G^{\beta'}_\alpha P^\beta\right)\right])/n_\alpha \\
&\qquad + H^\beta\left(E\left[G^\beta_{\alpha i} \Sigma^{\alpha\alpha} G^{\beta'}_\alpha P^\beta g^\beta_i\right] + E\left[g^\beta_i \operatorname{tr}\left(G^\beta_{\alpha i} \Sigma^{\alpha\alpha} G^{\beta'}_\alpha P^\beta\right)\right]\right)/n_\alpha.
\end{aligned}$$

The representations given in Corollaries 3.6 and 3.7 are identical to those of Theorems 3.1 and 3.2, respectively. The only differences are in $Bias_{\alpha_0}(\hat{\beta}_{2S})$ and $Bias_{\alpha_0}(\hat{\beta}_{\mathrm{GEL}})$. Here, because of the use of identical samples z_i, $(i = 1, \ldots, n_\beta)$, and z_k, $(k = 1, \ldots, n)$, $Bias_{\alpha_0}(\hat{\beta}_{2S})$ additionally includes terms associated with the preliminary estimator $\tilde{\beta}$ and the estimation of $\Omega^{\beta\beta}$. For GEL, the only difference is the use of single sample n_β rather than the pooled sample $N = n_\beta + n$ when the samples z_i, $(i = 1, \ldots, n_\beta)$, and z_k, $(k = 1, \ldots, n)$, are independent.

4. SIMULATION EXPERIMENTS FOR COVARIANCE STRUCTURE MODELS

Our investigation concerns models of covariance structure estimated on the same sample. Therefore, the asymptotic bias expressions in Section 3.2 and, in particular, Theorems 3.3 and 3.4 apply. Altonji and Segal (1996) carried out an extensive analysis of the finite sample properties of GMM estimators for covariance structure models and found that the efficient two-step GMM estimator is severely downward biased in small samples for most distributions and in relatively large samples for "badly behaved" distributions. They argue that this poor performance is due to the correlation between the estimated second moments used to estimate the optimal weighting matrix and the moment indicators.

Thus, as the theoretical results in Section 3 reveal, both equally weighted GMM, which uses the identity matrix as weighting matrix, and efficient GMM estimation based on a sample-split estimator for the optimal weighting matrix produce parameter estimators with significantly improved properties in finite samples (see Theorem 3.3, Corollary 3.2, and also Horowitz 1998). Horowitz also considered a bias-adjusted GMM estimator using the re-centred nonparametric bootstrap of Hall and Horowitz (1996), which is outlined later in this chapter. This estimator, although biased in some cases, performed much better than the standard two-step GMM estimator.

The particular focus of attention of this section is GMM and GEL estimators for a common variance parameter constructed from a simulated panel data set in circumstances where the mean parameter is assumed unknown and is treated as a nuisance parameter. We initially consider the finite sample bias properties of the two-step GMM estimator, CUE, ET, and EL estimators. We also examine analytical bias adjustment methods for two-step GMM based on Theorem 3.3 and compare their finite sample properties with those of various forms of bootstrap bias-adjusted two-step GMM, both of which achieve bias adjustment of the two-step GMM estimator to the order of asymptotic approximation considered in this chapter.

4.1. Bootstrap Bias Adjustment

The generic form of bootstrap bias adjustment for the two-step GMM estimator $\hat{\beta}_{2S}$ is as follows. The original data z_i, $(i = 1, \ldots, n_\beta)$, is sampled independently with replacement to yield a bootstrap sample of size n_β and a two-step GMM estimator is thereby calculated from this bootstrap sample. This process is independently replicated. The bias of the two-step GMM estimator is estimated as the difference between the mean of the resultant bootstrap two-step GMM estimator empirical distribution and the two-step GMM estimator $\hat{\beta}_{2S}$. The bootstrap bias-adjusted two-step GMM estimator is then $\hat{\beta}_{2S}$ less the bias estimator.

We consider three forms of bootstrap bias-adjusted two-step GMM estimator. The first uses the standard nonparametric (NP) bootstrap. This resampling scheme applies equal weights $1/n_\beta$ to each observation z_i, $(i = 1, \ldots, n_\beta)$. That is, resampling is based on the empirical distribution function $F_{n_\beta}(z) = \sum_{i=1}^{n_\beta} 1(z_i \leq z)/n_\beta$, where $1(\cdot)$ is an indicator function. Direct application of the NP bootstrap in the GMM framework seems to be unsatisfactory in many cases though. When the model is over-identified as in our experiments, while the population moment condition $E[g^\beta(z, \alpha_0, \beta_0)] = 0$ is satisfied, the estimated sample moments are typically nonzero, that is, there is typically no β such that $E_{F_{n_\beta}}[g^\beta(z, \hat{\alpha}, \beta)] = 0$, where $E_{F_{n_\beta}}[\cdot]$ denotes expectation taken with respect to F_{n_β}. Therefore, F_{n_β} may be a poor approximation to the underlying distribution of the data and, hence, the NP bootstrap may not yield a substantial improvement over first-order asymptotic theory in standard applications of GMM. A second resampling scheme is the recentred nonparametric (RNP) bootstrap (see Hall and Horowitz 1996). This method replaces the moment indicator $g^{\beta}(z, \hat{\alpha}, \beta)$ used in the GMM estimation criterion (2.4) by the recentred moment indicator $g^{\beta *}(z, \hat{\alpha}, \beta) = g^{\beta}(z, \hat{\alpha}, \beta) - E_{F_{n_\beta}}[g^{\beta}(z, \hat{\alpha}, \hat{\beta}_{2S})]$. As $E_{F_{n_\beta}}[g^{\beta}(z, \hat{\alpha}, \hat{\beta}_{2S})] = \hat{g}^{\beta}(\hat{\alpha}, \hat{\beta}_{2S})$, this recentring guarantees that the moment condition is satisfied with respect to F_{n_β}, that is, $E_{F_{n_\beta}}[g^{\beta *}(z, \hat{\alpha}, \hat{\beta}_{2S})] = 0$. Apart from the reformulation of the moment indicator, the RNP bootstrap is identical in execution to the NP bootstrap. The third bootstrap suggested by Brown and Newey (2002) employs an alternative empirical distribution to F_{n_β} for resampling, which also ensures that the moment condition is satisfied. That is, the observations z_i, $(i = 1, \ldots, n_\beta)$, are assigned different rather than equal weights, the moment indicator $g^{\beta}(z, \hat{\alpha}, \beta)$ remaining unaltered. Given the two-step GMM estimator $\hat{\beta}_{2S}$, let $\hat{\lambda}_{2S} = \arg\sup_{\lambda \in \hat{\Lambda}^{\beta}_{n_\beta}(\hat{\beta}_{2S})} \hat{P}^{\theta}(\hat{\alpha}, \hat{\beta}_{2S}, \lambda)$, cf. (2.6). Each observation z_i is assigned the implied probability $\hat{\pi}_i^{2S} = \rho_v^{\theta}(\hat{\lambda}_{2S}' g_i^{\beta}(\hat{\alpha}, \hat{\beta}_{2S})) / \sum_{j=1}^{n_\beta} \rho_v^{\theta}(\hat{\lambda}_{2S}' g_j^{\beta}(\hat{\alpha}, \hat{\beta}_{2S}))$ associated with the two-step GMM estimator, $(i = 1, \ldots, n_\beta)$. The implied empirical distribution function $F_{n_\beta}^{GEL}(z) = \sum_{i=1}^{n_\beta} \hat{\pi}_i^{2S} 1(z_i \leq z)$ is thus obtained from the first step of a GEL estimation procedure and is denoted as (first-step GEL) FSGEL. From the first-order conditions for GEL, the moment condition is satisfied with respect to $F_{n_\beta}^{GEL}$ as $\sum_{i=1}^{n_\beta} \hat{\pi}_i^{2S} g_i^{\beta}(\hat{\alpha}, \hat{\beta}_{2S}) = 0$ and, thus, $E_{F_{n_\beta}^{GEL}}[g^{\beta}(z, \hat{\alpha}, \hat{\beta}_{2S})] = 0$, where $E_{F_{n_\beta}}^{GEL}[\cdot]$ denotes expectation taken with respect to $F_{n_\beta}^{GEL}$. We employ the EL criterion $\hat{P}^{\theta}(\hat{\alpha}, \hat{\beta}_{2S}, \lambda) = \sum_{i=1}^{n_\beta} \log(1 - \lambda' g_j^{\beta}(\hat{\alpha}, \hat{\beta}_{2S}))/n_\beta$ in our experiments. In the absence of nuisance parameters, the FSGEL bootstrap is asymptotically efficient relative to any bootstrap based on the empirical distribution function F_{n_β}, as shown by Brown and Newey (2002).

4.2. Analytical Bias Adjustment

We also consider direct bias adjustment of $\hat{\beta}_{2S}$ by subtraction of an estimator for $Bias(\hat{\beta}_{2S})$ given in Theorem 3.3 (see also Newey and Smith 2004, Theorem 5.1). We consider four forms of bias estimator. The first estimator for $Bias(\hat{\beta}_{2S})$, BCa, uses the empirical distribution function F_{n_β} for obtaining expectation estimators, that is, functions of observation i are equally weighted by $1/n_\beta$, $(i = 1, \ldots, n_\beta)$. The second estimator, BCb, uses the FSGEL empirical distribution function $F_{n_\beta}^{GEL}$, that is, functions of observation i are weighted by $\hat{\pi}_i^{2S}$, $(i = 1, \ldots, n_\beta)$. The third, BCc, uses F_{n_β} but with the true parameter values α_0 and β_0 substituted. The final estimator, BCd, employs the simulated counterpart of the expression for the asymptotic bias of $\hat{\beta}_{2S}$ given in Theorem 3.3.

4.3. Experimental Design

We consider an experimental design analyzed by Altonji and Segal (1996) where the objective is the estimation of a common population variance β_0 for a scalar random variable z_t, $(t = 1, \ldots, T)$, from observations on a balanced panel covering $T = 10$ time periods. Thus, $z = (z_1, \ldots, z_T)'$. We assume that n_β observations are available on z and that z_{ti} is independent over t and i.i.d. over i.

We consider the case where the mean α_0 of z is unknown. Hence, the results of Section 3.2 apply. The nuisance parameter estimator is $\hat{\alpha} = (\hat{\alpha}_1, \ldots, \hat{\alpha}_T)'$, where the unbiased estimator $\hat{\alpha}_t = \sum_{i=1}^{n_\beta} z_{ti}/n_\beta$, $(t = 1, \ldots, T)$. The moment indicator vector is $g^\beta(z, \alpha, \beta) = m(z, \alpha) - \iota\beta$, where ι is a T-vector of units, $m(z, \alpha) = (m_1(z_1, \alpha_1), \ldots, m_T(z_T, \alpha_T))'$, and

$$m_t(z_t, \alpha_t) = n_\beta(z_t - \alpha_t)^2/(n_\beta - 1), \quad (t = 1, \ldots, T).$$

Thus, $\hat{m}(\hat{\alpha}) = \sum_{i=1}^{n_\beta} m(z_i, \hat{\alpha})/n_\beta$ is an unbiased estimator for $\iota\beta_0$. Here $p_\beta = 1$, $m_\beta = T$, and $p_\alpha = m_\alpha = T$.

In this study, all observations z_{ti} are i.i.d. across both t and i, although the common mean assumption is ignored in estimation. Although the elements of $\hat{m}(\hat{\alpha})$ are independent, the estimated variance matrix $\hat{\Omega}^{\beta\beta}(\hat{\alpha}, \tilde{\beta}) = \sum_{i=1}^{n_\beta} g_i^\beta(\hat{\alpha}, \tilde{\beta}) g_i^\beta(\hat{\alpha}, \tilde{\beta})'/n_\beta$ ignores this information. Seven different distributions for z_t, scaled to have mean $\alpha_0 = 0$ and variance $\beta_0 = 1$, were considered for two sample sizes $n_\beta = 100, 500$. In each experiment, 1000 replications were performed.

In this framework, the two-step GMM estimator is a weighted mean of the sample variances, $\hat{\beta}_{2S} = w'\hat{m}(\hat{\alpha}) = \sum_{i=1}^{n_\beta} w' m_i(\hat{\alpha})/n_\beta$, where $w = (\iota'\hat{\Omega}^{\beta\beta}(\hat{\alpha}, \tilde{\beta})^{-1}\iota)^{-1}\iota'\hat{\Omega}^{\beta\beta}(\hat{\alpha}, \tilde{\beta})^{-1}$. The preliminary estimator $\tilde{\beta}$ is obtained using equal weights ($w = \iota/T$). For GEL estimators, as $G_{\beta i}^\beta = -\iota$, it can be straightforwardly shown that $\hat{\beta}_{\mathrm{GEL}} = n_\beta \sum_{i=1}^{n_\beta} \hat{\pi}_i^{\mathrm{GEL}} \iota' m_i(\hat{\alpha})/T(n_\beta - 1)$ where $\hat{\pi}_i^{\mathrm{GEL}} = \rho_v(\hat{\lambda}_{\mathrm{GEL}}' g_i^\beta(\hat{\alpha}, \hat{\beta}_{\mathrm{GEL}}))/\sum_{j=1}^{n_\beta} \rho_v(\hat{\lambda}_{\mathrm{GEL}}' g_j^\beta(\hat{\alpha}, \hat{\beta}_{\mathrm{GEL}}))$, $(i = 1, \ldots, n_\beta)$. The two-step GMM estimator ascribes equal weights over i, whereas GEL applies the GEL implied probabilities $\hat{\pi}_i^{\mathrm{GEL}}$. Over t, GMM assigns distinct weights given by the vector w while for GEL each time period receives an equal weight.

A number of important implications of this structure for the results of Section 3.2 may be deduced. Firstly, as $G_{\alpha i}^\beta = -2n_\beta \operatorname{diag}(z_{i1} - \alpha_1, \ldots, z_{iT} - \alpha_T)/(n_\beta - 1)$ and, thus, $G_\alpha^\beta = 0$, GMM or GEL estimators for β_0 are first-order efficient. Secondly, as $G_{\beta i}^\beta = -\iota$ from the linearity of $g^\beta(z, \alpha, \beta)$ in β, substantial simplifications result in the asymptotic bias expressions of Theorems 3.3 and 3.4. In particular, it is evident from the asymptotic biases given in Theorems 3.3 and 3.4 that those for two-step and iterated GMM are identical and, moreover, that CUE also possesses an identical asymptotic bias.

To be more precise, for these experiments $a_{\beta\beta}^\beta = a_{\beta\alpha}^\beta = 0$ and $c_{\beta\beta}^\beta = c_{\beta\alpha}^\beta = 0$ from the linearity of $g^\beta(z, \alpha, \beta)$ in β. Also $a_{\alpha\alpha}^\beta = 2[n_\beta/(n_\beta - 1)]\iota\beta_0$. As $g_i^{\beta\cdot\alpha} = g_i^\beta$, $\Omega^{\beta\beta\cdot\alpha\alpha} = \Omega^{\beta\beta}$, $\Omega^{\beta\beta\cdot\alpha} = \Omega^{\beta\beta}$, and $\Omega^{\alpha\beta\cdot\alpha} = E[g_i^\alpha g_i^{\beta'}] = \Omega^{\alpha\beta}$. Therefore, from Theorems 3.3 and 3.4,

$$\begin{aligned}
&Bias(\hat{\beta}_{2S}) \\
&\quad = Bias_{\alpha_0}(\hat{\beta}_{2S}) + H^\beta\big(-a_{\alpha\alpha}^\beta + E\big[G_{\alpha i}^\beta H^\alpha g_i^\alpha\big]\big)/n_\beta \\
&\qquad - H^\beta\big(E\big[G_{\alpha i}^\beta H^\alpha \Omega^{\alpha\beta} P^\beta g_i^\beta\big] + E\big[g_i^\beta \operatorname{tr}\big(G_{\alpha i}^\beta H^\alpha \Omega^{\alpha\beta} P^\beta\big)\big]\big)/n_\beta,
\end{aligned}$$

and

$$
\begin{aligned}
&Bias(\hat{\beta}_{\mathrm{GEL}})\\
&\quad = Bias_{\alpha_0}(\hat{\beta}_{\mathrm{GEL}}) + H^{\beta}\left(-a^{\beta}_{\alpha\alpha} + E\left[G^{\beta}_{\alpha i} H^{\alpha} g^{\alpha}_{i}\right]\right)/n_{\beta}\\
&\quad\quad - H^{\beta}\left(E\left[G^{\beta}_{\alpha i} H^{\alpha} \Omega^{\alpha\beta} P^{\beta} g^{\beta}_{i}\right] + E\left[g^{\beta}_{i} \operatorname{tr}\left(G^{\beta}_{\alpha i} H^{\alpha} \Omega^{\alpha\beta} P^{\beta}\right)\right]\right)/n_{\beta}.
\end{aligned}
$$

Therefore, there is no role for $Bias(\hat{\alpha})$. Moreover, $Bias(\hat{\beta}_{2S})$ and $Bias(\hat{\beta}_{\mathrm{GEL}})$ differ only in $Bias_{\alpha_0}(\hat{\beta}_{2S})$ and $Bias_{\alpha_0}(\hat{\beta}_{\mathrm{GEL}})$. Because $g^{\beta}(z, \alpha, \beta) = m(z, \alpha) - \iota\beta$ is linear in β and, thus, $G^{\beta}_{\beta i} = -\iota$ is non-stochastic, the asymptotic biases for $\hat{\beta}_{2S}$ and $\hat{\beta}_{\mathrm{GEL}}$ when the nuisance parameter α_0 is known reduce to

$$
\begin{aligned}
Bias_{\alpha_0}(\hat{\beta}_{2S}) &= H^{\beta} E\left[g^{\beta}_{i} g^{\beta\prime}_{i} P^{\beta} g^{\beta}_{i}\right]/n_{\beta},\\
Bias_{\alpha_0}(\hat{\beta}_{\mathrm{GEL}}) &= \left[1 + \left(\rho^{\theta}_{vvv}(0)/2\right)\right] H^{\beta} E\left[g^{\beta}_{i} g^{\beta\prime}_{i} P^{\beta} g^{\beta}_{i}\right]/n_{\beta}.
\end{aligned}
$$

As there is no effect due to the preliminary estimator $\tilde{\beta}$, it is evident from $Bias(\hat{\beta}_{2S})$ that the asymptotic biases for the two-step GMM and iterated GMM estimators are identical. Moreover, from $Bias_{\alpha_0}(\hat{\beta}_{\mathrm{GEL}})$, they also coincide with that of CUE as $\rho^{\theta}_{vvv}(0) = 0$. Furthermore, it is only the asymmetry of g^{β}_{i} which accounts for the differences in asymptotic biases between two-step GMM and other GEL estimators. Note that, apart from $-H^{\beta} a^{\beta}_{\alpha\alpha}/n_{\beta}$, the second and third lines in $Bias(\hat{\beta}_{2S})$ and $Bias(\hat{\beta}_{\mathrm{GEL}})$ vanish if z_{ti} is symmetrically distributed; that is, $Bias(\hat{\beta}_{2S}) = Bias_{\alpha_0}(\hat{\beta}_{2S}) - H^{\beta} a^{\beta}_{\alpha\alpha}/n_{\beta}$ and $Bias(\hat{\beta}_{\mathrm{GEL}}) = Bias_{\alpha_0}(\hat{\beta}_{\mathrm{GEL}}) - H^{\beta} a^{\beta}_{\alpha\alpha}/n_{\beta}$. Furthermore, $Bias_{\alpha_0}(\hat{\beta}_{EL}) = 0$ and $Bias_{\alpha_0}(\hat{\beta}_{\mathrm{GEL}}) = 0$ if $\rho^{\theta}_{vvv}(0) = -2$.

4.4. Results

The tables report estimated mean and median bias (as a percentage), 0.05 and 0.95 quantiles, standard error (SE), root mean squared error (RMSE), and median absolute error (MAE) of four asymptotically first-order equivalent methods for estimating moment condition models, two-step GMM (2S-GMM), CUE, ET, and EL estimators.

Table 11.1 considers a sample size of $n_{\beta} = 100$. The results obtained for the two-step GMM estimator are very similar to those presented by Altonji and Segal (1996). As in their study, this estimator is clearly downward biased. This distortion is particularly marked for "badly-behaved" distributions, namely thicker-tailed symmetric (t_5) and long-tailed skewed (lognormal and exponential) distributions. As noted above, the asymptotic bias expressions for GMM and GEL involve further terms for asymmetric distributions. Note, however, that these expressions are not strictly valid for the t_5 distribution as moments of order greater than 4 do not exist. The worst case is given by the lognormal distribution, where the biases (MAE) are −0.415 and −0.430 (0.430).

Table 11.1. *Covariance structure models* ($n_\beta = 100$)

	Bias		Quantiles				
Estimator	Mean	Median	0.05	0.95	SE	RMSE	MAE
			t_5				
2S-GMM	−.111	−.116	0.789	0.998	.065	.129	.116
CUE	−.125	−.128	0.765	0.990	.069	.143	.128
ET	−.094	−.098	0.805	1.021	.067	.115	.099
EL	−.065	−.069	0.835	1.057	.067	.094	.073
			t_{10}				
2S-GMM	−.059	−.060	0.856	1.026	.053	.079	.062
CUE	−.066	−.067	0.845	1.022	.055	.086	.068
ET	−.046	−.048	0.866	1.042	.054	.071	.053
EL	−.028	−.030	0.886	1.063	.055	.062	.043
			Normal				
2S-GMM	−.036	−.034	0.889	1.041	.047	.059	.041
CUE	−.040	−.038	0.881	1.039	.049	.063	.044
ET	−.026	−.025	0.896	1.051	.048	.055	.038
EL	−.015	−.012	0.905	1.063	.048	.050	.035
			Uniform				
2S-GMM	−.007	−.008	0.946	1.043	.029	.030	.021
CUE	−.008	−.009	0.945	1.042	.030	.031	.021
ET	−.005	−.007	0.948	1.045	.030	.030	.020
EL	−.003	−.004	0.950	1.048	.030	.030	.020
			Lognormal				
2S-GMM	−.415	−.430	0.434	0.777	.111	.429	.430
CUE	−.481	−.490	0.332	0.727	.125	.497	.490
ET	−.396	−.408	0.429	0.807	.120	.414	.408
EL	−.303	−.317	0.513	0.927	.131	.331	.317
			Exponential				
2S-GMM	−.141	−.146	0.722	1.004	.087	.166	.147
CUE	−.162	−.166	0.680	0.996	.097	.189	.166
ET	−.108	−.110	0.751	1.043	.088	.140	.113
EL	−.058	−.061	0.803	1.097	.087	.105	.076
			Bimodal				
2S-GMM	−.009	−.009	0.945	1.036	.028	.029	.020
CUE	−.010	−.010	0.944	1.035	.028	.030	.021
ET	−.006	−.005	0.948	1.040	.028	.029	.020
EL	−.002	−.001	0.951	1.044	.028	.028	.019

In this case the empirical 0.95 confidence interval does not cover the true value $\beta_0 = 1$.

Although, as noted above, the biases of GMM and CUE should be similar, Table 11.1 indicates that the results for CUE are in fact worse than for the

Table 11.2. *Covariance structure models* ($n_\beta = 500$)

	Bias		Quantiles				
Estimator	Mean	Median	0.05	0.95	SE	RMSE	MAE
			t_5				
2S-GMM	−.041	−.042	0.904	1.013	.034	.053	.042
CUE	−.042	−.043	0.903	1.012	.034	.054	.043
ET	−.029	−.029	0.917	1.024	.033	.044	.031
EL	−.016	−.016	0.929	1.039	.034	.038	.026
			t_{10}				
2S-GMM	−.016	−.016	0.945	1.024	.025	.029	.021
CUE	−.016	−.016	0.945	1.024	.025	.030	.021
ET	−.010	−.010	0.952	1.030	.024	.026	.018
EL	−.004	−.005	0.957	1.036	.025	.025	.017
			Normal				
2S-GMM	−.008	−.008	0.959	1.027	.021	.022	.015
CUE	−.008	−.008	0.959	1.027	.021	.022	.015
ET	−.005	−.005	0.962	1.030	.020	.021	.014
EL	−.001	−.001	0.965	1.034	.021	.021	.014
			Uniform				
2S-GMM	−.002	−.002	0.976	1.019	.013	.013	.009
CUE	−.002	−.002	0.976	1.019	.013	.013	.009
ET	−.001	−.001	0.977	1.019	.013	.013	.009
EL	−.001	−.001	0.977	1.019	.013	.013	.009
			Lognormal				
2S-GMM	−.225	−.227	0.652	0.917	.082	.239	.227
CUE	−.231	−.233	0.634	0.912	.085	.246	.233
ET	−.178	−.182	0.705	0.965	.079	.194	.182
EL	−.118	−.124	0.757	1.034	.081	.143	.125
			Exponential				
2S-GMM	−.041	−.042	0.894	1.029	.040	.057	.044
CUE	−.042	−.043	0.892	1.028	.040	.058	.045
ET	−.024	−.025	0.914	1.043	.039	.046	.032
EL	−.006	−.007	0.929	1.059	.039	.040	.029
			Bimodal				
2S-GMM	−.002	−.001	0.977	1.018	.012	.013	.009
CUE	−.002	−.001	0.976	1.018	.012	.013	.009
ET	−.001	−.000	0.978	1.019	.012	.012	.008
EL	−.000	.001	0.979	1.020	.012	.012	.008

two-step GMM estimator. Because the bias expressions for GMM and GEL differ only according to $Bias_{\alpha_0}(\hat{\beta}_{2S})$ and $Bias_{\alpha_0}(\hat{\beta}_{\mathrm{GEL}})$, ET and EL estimators should display better finite sample properties relative to GMM and CUE. In particular, $Bias_{\alpha_0}(\hat{\beta}_{2S}) = 2Bias_{\alpha_0}(\hat{\beta}_{\mathrm{ET}})$ and $Bias_{\alpha_0}(\hat{\beta}_{\mathrm{EL}}) = 0$. While all methods have very similar standard errors (SE), the improvement for ET and EL in terms of both mean and median bias, root mean square error (RMSE), and mean absolute error (MAE) is clear. This is particularly marked for EL estimation. For ET, the improvements over GMM are rather more modest than those for EL as predicted by our theoretical results. However, although bias is not completely eliminated, especially for the skewed lognormal and exponential distributions, even for these cases, EL shows a marked improvement over two-step GMM.

Table 11.2 deals with the increased sample size $n_\beta = 500$. Overall, all estimators display less bias with reduced SE, RMSE, and MAE. The general pattern across estimators revealed for the smaller sample size $n_\beta = 100$ is still apparent. CUE is somewhat worse than two-step GMM with ET delivering rather moderate improvements, whereas EL dominates all other estimators in terms of mean and median biases, RMSE and MAE. For the skewed distributions, lognormal and exponential, EL offers substantially reduced bias, RMSE and MAE relative to other estimators including ET with very little or no increase in SE. For a number of the symmetric distributions, EL is able to eliminate bias more or less entirely.

The results reported in Table 11.3 with $n_\beta = 100$ use 100 bootstrap samples in each replication. In all cases, the bootstrap methods substantially reduce the bias of the two-step GMM estimator, although at the expense of a rather modest increase in SE. RMSE and MAE are also reduced, also quite substantially in the asymmetric cases for the RNP and FSGEL bootstrap methods. Clearly, the gain from bias reduction outweighs the increased contribution of SE to RMSE. The behavior of these methods is not uniform, however, but overall the performances of RNP and FSGEL seem quite similar. It appears that RNP and FSGEL are rather better than NP, which may be accounted for by the sample moments evaluated at the two-step GMM estimator being far from zero in these experiments. The performance of the feasible bias adjustment methods BCa and BCb is also quite encouraging leading to a substantial reduction in bias relative to $\hat{\beta}_{2S}$ in the "badly behaved" cases with BCb tending to dominate BCa. Like the bootstrap methods, SE increases somewhat for the analytical methods but again is less important compared to bias reduction for RMSE which in some cases is also reduced by a nontrivial amount. The results for BCc and BCd indicate that the theoretical expression for asymptotic bias in Theorem 3.3 accounts for the vast majority of finite sample bias. Comparing bootstrap and bias adjustment methods, BCb is rather similar to RNP and FSGEL in most cases in terms of bias reduction, RMSE, and MAE. Therefore, BCb appears to be an efficacious rival to bootstrap methods.

Similar qualitative conclusions may be drawn from Table 11.4 for $n_\beta = 500$ with two-step GMM bias being more or less eliminated for a number of symmetric distributions. Again, for the "badly behaved" cases, bias is not eliminated entirely but is reduced substantially by RNP, FSGEL bootstrap bias adjustment methods and the analytical approach BCb.

Table 11.3. *Covariance structure models for bias-corrected and bootstrap GMM estimators* ($n_\beta = 100$)

	Bias		Quantiles				
Estimator	Mean	Median	0.05	0.95	SE	RMSE	MAE
			t_5				
2S-GMM	−.111	−.116	0.789	0.998	.065	.129	.116
NP	−.073	−.079	0.808	1.061	.076	.105	.084
RNP	−.049	−.056	0.834	1.084	.077	.091	.068
FSGEL	−.044	−.050	0.845	1.089	.075	.086	.065
BCa	−.060	−.066	0.828	1.065	.072	.094	.072
BCb	−.049	−.054	0.841	1.081	.073	.088	.067
BCc	−.067	−.073	0.817	1.065	.076	.101	.079
BCd	−.016	−.021	0.884	1.093	.065	.067	.047
			t_{10}				
2S-GMM	−.059	−.060	0.856	1.026	.053	.079	.062
NP	−.026	−.028	0.881	1.072	.060	.065	.046
RNP	−.017	−.020	0.890	1.079	.059	.061	.044
FSGEL	−.011	−.013	0.899	1.084	.058	.059	.040
BCa	−.018	−.020	0.891	1.076	.057	.060	.043
BCb	−.015	−.017	0.895	1.079	.057	.059	.043
BCc	−.022	−.024	0.882	1.077	.061	.065	.045
BCd	−.002	−.003	0.914	1.083	.053	.053	.036
			Normal				
2S-GMM	−.036	−.034	0.889	1.041	.047	.059	.041
NP	−.008	−.007	0.911	1.074	.050	.051	.036
RNP	−.005	−.004	0.916	1.076	.050	.050	.035
FSGEL	−.001	.000	0.920	1.078	.049	.049	.033
BCa	−.004	−.004	0.918	1.076	.049	.049	.034
BCb	−.003	−.002	0.918	1.076	.049	.049	.034
BCc	−.007	−.007	0.910	1.079	.053	.053	.038
BCd	.002	.003	0.926	1.078	.047	.047	.033
			Uniform				
2S-GMM	−.007	−.008	0.946	1.043	.029	.030	.021
NP	.006	.004	0.958	1.055	.030	.030	.020
RNP	.005	.004	0.959	1.055	.030	.030	.020
FSGEL	.007	.006	0.961	1.057	.030	.030	.020
BCa	.005	.004	0.958	1.055	.030	.030	.020
BCb	.005	.004	0.958	1.055	.029	.030	.020
BCc	.005	.003	0.954	1.058	.032	.032	.022
BCd	.006	.005	0.959	1.055	.029	.030	.020
			Lognormal				
2S-GMM	−.415	−.430	0.434	0.777	.111	.429	.430
NP	−.380	−.403	0.429	0.887	.145	.407	.403
RNP	−.230	−.282	0.511	1.128	.453	.508	.289
FSGEL	−.264	−.290	0.531	1.024	.158	.308	.292
BCa	−.352	−.371	0.465	0.889	.135	.377	.371
BCb	−.278	−.302	0.524	0.991	.152	.317	.303
BCc	−.369	−.393	0.449	0.874	.137	.394	.393
BCd	−.096	−.111	0.753	1.096	.111	.147	.121

	Bias		Quantiles				
Estimator	Mean	Median	0.05	0.95	SE	RMSE	MAE
			Exponential				
2S-GMM	−.141	−.146	0.722	1.004	.087	.166	.147
NP	−.089	−.095	0.744	1.096	.108	.140	.107
RNP	−.060	−.066	0.771	1.125	.105	.122	.085
FSGEL	−.042	−.048	0.799	1.136	.102	.110	.077
BCa	−.080	−.086	0.764	1.092	.099	.128	097
BCb	−.059	−.065	0.788	1.115	.098	.114	.082
BCc	−.089	−.096	0.746	1.092	.104	.137	.106
BCd	−.026	−.031	0.838	1.119	.087	.091	.060
			Bimodal				
2S-GMM	−.009	−.009	0.945	1.036	.028	.029	.020
NP	.006	.006	0.958	1.051	.029	.029	.021
RNP	.006	.006	0.959	1.052	.028	.029	.020
FSGEL	.008	.008	0.963	1.053	.028	.029	.020
BCa	.007	.007	0.960	1.052	.028	.029	.021
BCb	.007	.006	0.960	1.052	.028	.029	.021
BCc	.006	.006	0.955	1.055	.031	.031	.022
BCd	.008	.008	0.962	1.052	.028	.029	.020

5. CONCLUSIONS

The context of this chapter is the estimation of moment condition models in situations where the moment indicator depends on a nuisance parameter. The particular concern is the analysis of the higher-order bias of GMM and GEL estimators when a plug-in estimator is employed for the nuisance parameter. Such an environment covers a number of cases of interest including the use of generated regressors and sample-splitting methods. Expressions for the higher-order bias of these estimators is obtained in a general framework that allows specialization to cases when the nuisance parameter is estimated from either an identical or an independent sample.

The efficacy of these asymptotic bias expressions is explored in a number of simulation experiments for covariance structure models. A rather pleasing conclusion from these experiments is that the mean and median bias, root mean squared error, and mean absolute error properties of empirical likelihood represent a substantial improvement of those of two-step GMM, CUE, and ET estimators with little or no increase in variance. Further experiments comparing various bootstrap bias adjustment methods with those based on estimated

Table 11.4. *Covariance structure models for bias-corrected and bootstrap GMM estimators:* ($n_\beta = 500$)

	Bias		Quantiles				
Estimator	Mean	Median	0.05	0.95	SE	RMSE	MAE
			t_5				
2S-GMM	−.041	−.042	0.904	1.013	.034	.053	.042
NP	−.020	−.020	0.921	1.042	.038	.042	.029
RNP	−.014	−.015	0.927	1.050	.039	.041	.028
FSGEL	−.014	−.015	0.927	1.048	.037	.040	.028
BCa	−.017	−.018	0.924	1.043	.037	.041	.028
BCb	−.015	−.016	0.926	1.045	.037	.040	.028
BCc	−.018	−.019	0.923	1.043	.037	.041	.029
BCd	−.004	−.004	0.942	1.050	.034	.034	.023
			t_{10}				
2S-GMM	−.016	−.016	0.945	1.024	.025	.029	.021
NP	−.003	−.003	0.955	1.039	.026	.026	.018
RNP	−.002	−.002	0.957	1.040	.026	.026	.018
FSGEL	−.002	−.001	0.958	1.040	.026	.026	.018
BCa	−.002	−.002	0.957	1.039	.026	.026	.018
BCb	−.002	−.002	0.958	1.039	.026	.026	.018
BCc	−.002	−.003	0.956	1.040	.026	.026	.018
BCd	−.000	−.000	0.961	1.040	.025	.025	.017
			Normal				
2S-GMM	−.008	−.008	0.959	1.027	.021	.022	.015
NP	.000	.001	0.966	1.035	.021	.021	.014
RNP	.001	.001	0.966	1.035	.021	.021	.014
FSGEL	.001	.001	0.966	1.036	.021	.021	.014
BCa	.001	.001	0.967	1.036	.021	.021	.013
BCb	.001	.001	0.967	1.036	.021	.021	.013
BCc	.001	.000	0.967	1.036	.021	.021	.014
BCd	.001	.001	0.968	1.036	.021	.021	.013
			Uniform				
2S-GMM	−.002	−.002	0.976	1.019	.013	.013	.009
NP	.001	.001	0.979	1.022	.013	.013	.009
RNP	.001	.001	0.979	1.021	.013	.013	.009
FSGEL	.001	.001	0.980	1.022	.013	.013	.009
BCa	.001	.001	0.979	1.021	.013	.013	.008
BCb	.001	.001	0.979	1.021	.013	.013	.008
BCc	.001	.001	0.979	1.022	.013	.013	.009
BCd	.001	.001	0.979	1.022	.013	.013	.008
			Lognormal				
2S-GMM	−.225	−.227	0.652	0.917	.082	.239	.227
NP	−.161	−.166	0.674	1.027	.108	.194	.168
RNP	−.107	−.118	0.724	1.109	.123	.163	.129
FSGEL	−.121	−.128	0.720	1.068	.106	.161	.131
BCa	−.161	−.166	0.691	1.007	.097	.188	.166
BCb	−.132	−.138	0.724	1.038	.097	.164	.139
BCc	−.164	−.169	0.687	1.005	.098	.191	.170
BCd	−.044	−.046	0.833	1.098	.082	.093	.067

	Bias		Quantiles				
Estimator	Mean	Median	0.05	0.95	SE	RMSE	MAE
			Exponential				
2S-GMM	−.041	−.042	0.894	1.029	.040	.057	.044
NP	−.012	−.013	0.914	1.065	.044	.046	.032
RNP	−.009	−.011	0.919	1.066	.044	.045	.031
FSGEL	−.007	−.009	0.923	1.069	.043	.044	.030
BCa	−.011	−.013	0.917	1.062	.043	.044	030
BCb	−.009	−.011	0.921	1.064	.043	.044	.030
BCc	−.012	−.013	0.916	1.062	.043	.045	.031
BCd	−.003	−.004	0.932	1.067	.040	.040	.027
			Bimodal				
2S-GMM	−.002	−.001	0.977	1.018	.012	.013	.009
NP	.002	.002	0.980	1.021	.013	.013	.008
RNP	.002	.002	0.980	1.021	.013	.013	.008
FSGEL	.002	.002	0.981	1.022	.012	.013	.008
BCa	.002	.003	0.980	1.022	.012	.013	.008
BCb	.002	.003	0.980	1.022	.012	.013	.008
BCc	.002	.003	0.980	1.022	.013	.013	.008
BCd	.002	.003	0.981	1.022	.012	.013	.008

analytical asymptotic bias expressions indicate that the less computationally intensive analytical methods are efficacious rivals to their bootstrap counterparts.

An interesting avenue for future research would be an exploration of the usefulness of the asymptotic bias expressions for bias-adjustment of GEL estimators such as CUE, ET, and EL.

APPENDIX A: PROOFS

We find the asymptotic bias using a stochastic expansion for each estimator. Regularity conditions for the results given below may be obtained by suitable adaptation of those in Newey and Smith (2004). Lemmas A.1–A.3 generalize Newey and Smith (2004, Lemmas A4–A6) to the nuisance parameter context.

Lemma A.1. *Suppose the estimators* $\hat{\theta}$ *and* $\hat{\alpha}$ *and vector of functions* $m^{\theta}(z, \theta, \alpha)$ *satisfy (a)* $\hat{\theta} = \theta_0 + O_p(\max[n^{-1/2}, n_{\alpha}^{-1/2}, n_{\beta}^{-1/2}])$, $\hat{\alpha} = \alpha_0 + \tilde{\psi}^{\alpha}/\sqrt{n_{\alpha}} + Q^{\alpha}(\tilde{A}^{\varphi}, \tilde{\psi}^{\varphi})/n_{\alpha} + O_p(n_{\alpha}^{-3/2})$, $\tilde{\psi}^{\alpha} = O_p(1)$, $Q^{\alpha}(\tilde{a}^{\varphi}, \tilde{\psi}^{\varphi}) = O_p(1)$; *(b)* $\hat{m}^{\theta}(\hat{\theta}, \hat{\alpha}) = \sum_{i=1}^{n_{\beta}} m^{\theta}(z_i, \hat{\theta}, \hat{\alpha})/n_{\beta} = 0$ *w.p.a.1 and* $\hat{m}^{\theta}(\theta_0, \alpha_0) = O_p(\max[n^{-1/2}, n_{\alpha}^{-1/2}, n_{\beta}^{-1/2}])$, $\tilde{A}^{\theta} = n_{\beta}^{1/2}[\partial \hat{m}^{\theta}(z, \theta_0, \alpha_0)/\partial \theta' - M^{\theta}] =$

$O_p(\max[n^{-1/2}, \ n_\alpha^{-1/2}, \ n_\beta^{-1/2}])$, $\tilde{A}_\alpha^\theta = n_\beta^{1/2}[\partial \hat{m}^\theta(z,\theta_0,\alpha_0)/\partial\alpha' - M_\alpha^\theta] = O_p(\max[n^{-1/2}, n_\alpha^{-1/2}, n_\beta^{-1/2}])$, *where* $M^\theta = E[\partial m^\theta(z,\theta_0,\alpha_0)/\partial\theta']$ *and* $M_\alpha^\theta = E[\partial m(z;\theta_0,\alpha_0)/\partial\alpha']$; *(c)* $m^\theta(z,\theta,\alpha)$ *is two times continuously differentiable and for some* $d(z)$ *with* $E[d(z)] < \infty$

$$\begin{aligned}&\left\|\partial^2 m(z,\theta,\alpha)/\partial(\theta,\alpha)_r\partial(\theta,\alpha)_s - \partial^2 m(z,\theta_0,\alpha_0)/\partial(\theta,\alpha)_r\partial(\theta,\alpha)_s\right\|\\ &\quad \le d(z)\|(\theta,\alpha)-(\theta_0,\alpha_0)\|\end{aligned}$$

on a neighbourhood of (θ_0,α_0); *(d)* $E[m^\theta(z,\theta_0,\alpha_0)] = 0$ *and* M^θ *exists and is nonsingular. Let*

$$\begin{aligned}M_{\theta\theta r}^\theta &= E\left[\partial^2 m(z,\theta_0,\alpha_0)/\partial\theta_r\partial\theta'\right],\\ M_{\theta\alpha s}^\theta &= E\left[\partial^2 m(z,\theta_0,\alpha_0)/\partial\alpha_s\partial\theta'\right],\\ M_{\alpha\theta r}^\theta &= E\left[\partial^2 m(z,\theta_0,\alpha_0)/\partial\theta_r\partial\alpha'\right],\\ M_{\alpha\alpha s}^\theta &= E\left[\partial^2 m(z,\theta_0,\alpha_0)/\partial\alpha_s\partial\alpha'\right],\\ \tilde{\psi}^\theta &= -n_\beta^{1/2}\left(M^\theta\right)^{-1}\hat{m}^\theta\left(\theta_0,\alpha_0\right).\end{aligned}$$

Then

$$\begin{aligned}\hat{\theta} &= \theta_0 + \tilde{\psi}^\theta/\sqrt{n_\beta} - \left(M^\theta\right)^{-1}M_\alpha^\theta\left(\tilde{\psi}^\alpha/\sqrt{n_\alpha} + Q^\alpha\left(\tilde{a}^\varphi,\tilde{\psi}^\varphi\right)/n_\alpha\right)\\ &\quad - \left(M^\theta\right)^{-1}\left[\tilde{A}^\theta\left(\tilde{\psi}^\theta/\sqrt{n_\beta} - \left(M^\theta\right)^{-1}M_\alpha^\theta\tilde{\psi}^\alpha/\sqrt{n_\alpha}\right)\sqrt{n_\beta} + \tilde{A}_\alpha^\theta\tilde{\psi}^\alpha/\sqrt{n_\alpha n_\beta}\right]\\ &\quad - (M^\theta)^{-1}\left[\sum_{r=1}^{q_\theta} e_r'\left[\tilde{\psi}^\theta/\sqrt{n_\beta} - \left(M^\theta\right)^{-1}M_\alpha^\theta\tilde{\psi}^\alpha/\sqrt{n_\alpha}\right]M_{\theta\theta r}^\theta\right.\\ &\quad \left.\times\left[\tilde{\psi}^\theta/\sqrt{n_\beta} - (M^\theta)^{-1}M_\alpha^\theta\tilde{\psi}^\alpha/\sqrt{n_\alpha}\right]\right]/2\\ &\quad - (M^\theta)^{-1}\sum_{s=1}^{p_\alpha} e_s'\tilde{\psi}^\varphi M_{\theta\alpha s}^\theta\left[\tilde{\psi}^\theta/\sqrt{n_\beta} - \left(M^\theta\right)^{-1}M_\alpha^\theta\tilde{\psi}^\alpha/\sqrt{n_\alpha}\right]/2\sqrt{n_\alpha}\\ &\quad - (M^\theta)^{-1}\left[\sum_{r=1}^{q_\theta} e_r'\left[\tilde{\psi}^\theta/\sqrt{n_\beta} - \left(M^\theta\right)^{-1}M_\alpha^\theta\tilde{\psi}^\alpha/\sqrt{n_\alpha}\right]M_{\alpha\theta r}^\theta\tilde{\psi}^\alpha/\sqrt{n_\alpha}\right]/2\\ &\quad - (M^\theta)^{-1}\left[\sum_{s=1}^{p_\alpha} e_s'\tilde{\psi}^\alpha M_{\alpha\alpha s}^\theta\tilde{\psi}^\alpha/n_\alpha\right]/2 + O_p\left(\max\left[n^{-3/2}, n_\alpha^{-3/2}, n_\beta^{-3/2}\right]\right).\end{aligned}$$

Proof. Let $\hat{m}^\theta(\theta,\alpha) = \sum_{i=1}^{n_\beta} m_i^\theta(\theta,\alpha)/n_\beta$, $\hat{M}^\theta(\theta,\alpha) = \sum_{i=1}^{n_\beta}[\partial m_i^\theta(\theta,\alpha)/\partial\theta']/n_\beta$ and $\hat{M}_\alpha^\theta(\theta,\alpha) = \sum_{i=1}^{n_\beta}[\partial m_i^\theta(\theta,\alpha)/\partial\alpha']/n_\beta$. A Taylor expansion with Lagrange remainder gives

$$\begin{aligned}0 &= \hat{m}^\theta(\theta_0,\alpha_0) + \hat{M}^\theta(\theta_0,\alpha_0)(\hat{\theta}-\theta_0) + \hat{M}_\alpha^\theta(\theta_0,\alpha_0)(\hat{\alpha}-\alpha_0)\\ &\quad + \left[\sum_{r=1}^{q_\theta}(\hat{\theta}_r - \theta_{0r})[\partial\hat{M}^\theta(\bar{\theta},\bar{\alpha})/\partial\theta_r](\hat{\theta}-\theta_0)\right.\end{aligned}$$

$$+\sum_{s=1}^{p_\alpha}(\hat{\alpha}_s-\alpha_{0s})[\partial\hat{M}^\theta(\bar{\theta},\bar{\alpha})/\partial\alpha_s](\hat{\theta}-\theta_0)$$
$$+\sum_{r=1}^{q_\theta}(\hat{\theta}_r-\theta_{0r})[\partial\hat{M}_\alpha^\theta(\bar{\theta},\bar{\alpha})/\partial\theta_r](\hat{\alpha}-\alpha_0)$$
$$\left.+\sum_{s=1}^{p_\alpha}(\hat{\alpha}_s-\alpha_{0s})[\partial\hat{M}_\alpha^\theta(\bar{\theta},\bar{\alpha})/\partial\alpha_s](\hat{\alpha}-\alpha_0)\right]/2.$$

Then adding and subtracting $M^\theta(\hat{\theta}-\theta_0)$ and solving gives

$$\begin{aligned}\hat{\theta}&=\theta_0-(M^\theta)^{-1}[\hat{m}^\theta(\theta_0,\alpha_0)+M_\alpha^\theta(\hat{\alpha}-\alpha_0)]\\&-(M^\theta)^{-1}[(\hat{M}^\theta(\theta_0,\alpha_0)-M^\theta)(\hat{\theta}-\theta_0)\\&+(\hat{M}_\alpha^\theta(\theta_0,\alpha_0)-M_\alpha^\theta)(\hat{\alpha}-\alpha_0)]\\&-(M^\theta)^{-1}\left[\sum_{r=1}^{q_\theta}(\hat{\theta}_r-\theta_{0r})[\partial\hat{M}^\theta(\bar{\theta},\bar{\alpha})/\partial\theta_r](\hat{\theta}-\theta_0)\right.\\&+\sum_{s=1}^{p_\alpha}(\hat{\alpha}_s-\alpha_{0s})[\partial\hat{M}^\theta(\bar{\theta},\bar{\alpha})/\partial\alpha_s](\hat{\theta}-\theta_0)\\&+\sum_{r=1}^{q_\theta}(\hat{\theta}_r-\theta_{0r})[\partial\hat{M}_\alpha^\theta(\bar{\theta},\bar{\alpha})/\partial\theta_r](\hat{\alpha}-\alpha_0)\\&\left.+\sum_{s=1}^{p_\alpha}(\hat{\alpha}_s-\alpha_{0s})[\partial\hat{M}_\alpha^\theta(\bar{\theta},\bar{\alpha})/\partial\alpha_s](\hat{\alpha}-\alpha)\right]/2\end{aligned}$$

so that $\hat{\theta}=\theta_0+O_p(\max[n^{-1/2},n_\alpha^{-1/2},n_\beta^{-1/2}])$ and hence $\hat{\theta}-\theta_0=-(M^\theta)^{-1}[\hat{m}^\theta(\theta_0,\alpha_0)-M_\alpha^\theta(\hat{\alpha}-\alpha_0)]+O_p(\max[n^{-1},n_\alpha^{-1},n_\beta^{-1}])$. Note that replacing $\partial\hat{M}^\theta(\bar{\theta},\bar{\alpha})/\partial\theta_r$ by $M_{\theta\theta r}^\theta$, $\partial\hat{M}^\theta(\bar{\theta},\bar{\alpha})/\partial\alpha_s$ by $M_{\theta\alpha s}^\theta$, $\partial\hat{M}_\alpha^\theta(\bar{\theta},\bar{\alpha})/\partial\theta_r$ by $M_{\alpha\theta r}^\theta$ and $\partial\hat{M}_\alpha^\theta(\bar{\theta},\bar{\alpha})/\partial\alpha_s$ by $M_{\alpha\alpha s}^\theta$ introduces an error that is $O_p(\max[n^{-3/2},n_\alpha^{-3/2},n_\beta^{-3/2}])$ by hypothesis (c). Hence,

$$\begin{aligned}\hat{\theta}&=\theta_0-(M^\theta)^{-1}[\hat{m}^\theta(\theta_0,\alpha_0)+M_\alpha^\theta(\hat{\alpha}-\alpha_0)]\\&-(M^\theta)^{-1}[(\hat{M}^\theta(\theta_0,\alpha_0)-M^\theta)(\hat{\theta}-\theta_0)+(\hat{M}_\alpha^\theta(\theta_0,\alpha_0)-M_\alpha^\theta)(\hat{\alpha}-\alpha_0)]\\&-(M^\theta)^{-1}\left[\sum_{r=1}^{q_\theta}(\hat{\theta}_r-\theta_{0r})M_{\theta\theta r}^\theta(\hat{\theta}-\theta_0)+\sum_{s=1}^{p_\alpha}(\hat{\alpha}_s-\alpha_{0s})M_{\theta\alpha s}^\theta(\hat{\theta}-\theta_0)\right.\\&\left.+\sum_{r=1}^{q_\theta}(\hat{\theta}_r-\theta_{0r})M_{\alpha\theta r}^\theta(\hat{\alpha}-\alpha_0)+\sum_{s=1}^{p_\alpha}(\hat{\alpha}_s-\alpha_{0s})M_{\alpha\alpha s}^\theta(\hat{\alpha}-\alpha)\right]/2\\&+O_p(\max[n^{-3/2},n_\alpha^{-3/2},n_\beta^{-3/2}]).\end{aligned}$$

Therefore, by recursive substitution (see Newey and Smith 2004, Lemma A4) the result is obtained. ■

Lemma A.2. *Suppose* $\hat{\alpha} = \alpha_0 + \tilde{\psi}^{\alpha}/\sqrt{n_\alpha} + Q^{\alpha}(\tilde{a}^{\varphi}, \tilde{\psi}^{\varphi})/n_\alpha + O_p(n_\alpha^{-3/2})$, *where* $\tilde{\psi}^{\alpha}$ *and* $Q^{\alpha}(\tilde{a}^{\varphi}, \tilde{\psi}^{\varphi})$ *are* $O_p(1)$. *Let* $P_W^{\beta} = (W^{\beta\beta})^{-1} - (W^{\beta\beta})^{-1} G_{\beta}^{\beta} \Sigma_W^{\beta\beta} G_{\beta}^{\beta'} (W^{\beta\beta})^{-1}$, $\tilde{\psi}^{\theta W} = -[H_W^{\beta'}, P_W^{\beta}]' \sum_{k=1}^{n} g_k^{\beta}/\sqrt{n}$, $g_k^{\beta} = g_k^{\beta}(\alpha_0, \beta_0)$,

$$M^{\theta W} = -\begin{pmatrix} 0 & G_{\beta}^{\beta'} \\ G_{\beta}^{\beta} & W^{\beta\beta} \end{pmatrix}, \qquad (M^{\theta W})^{-1} = -\begin{pmatrix} -\Sigma_W^{\beta\beta} & H_W^{\beta} \\ H_W^{\beta'} & P_W^{\beta} \end{pmatrix},$$

$$M_{\alpha}^{\theta W} = -\begin{pmatrix} 0 \\ G_{\alpha}^{\beta} \end{pmatrix}.$$

Then for $\tilde{\lambda} = -(\hat{W}^{\beta\beta})^{-1} \hat{g}^{\beta}(\hat{\alpha}, \tilde{\beta})$, $\hat{\theta} = (\tilde{\beta}', \tilde{\lambda}')'$, *we have*

$$\hat{\theta} = \theta_0 + \tilde{\psi}^{\theta W}/\sqrt{n} - (M^{\theta W})^{-1} M_{\alpha}^{\theta W} \tilde{\psi}^{\alpha}/\sqrt{n_\alpha} + O_p(\max[n^{-1}, n_\alpha^{-1}]).$$

Proof. Let $\theta = (\beta', \lambda')'$, $\lambda_0 = 0$, $m_k^{\theta}(\theta, \alpha) = -(\lambda' \partial g_k^{\beta}(\alpha, \beta)/\partial \beta', g_k^{\beta}(\alpha, \beta)' + \lambda'[W^{\beta\beta} + \xi^{\beta}(z)])'$ and $\hat{m}^{\theta}(\theta, \alpha) = \sum_{k=1}^{n} m_k^{\theta}(\theta, \alpha)/n$. The first-order conditions for $\tilde{\beta}$, the definition of $\tilde{\lambda}$ imply

$$0 = \hat{m}^{\theta}(\hat{\theta}, \hat{\alpha}) + [0, -\tilde{\lambda}'(O_p(n^{-1}))]'.$$

Hence, it follows from Lemma A.1 that $\hat{\theta} = \theta_0 + O_p(\max[n^{-1/2}, n_\alpha^{-1/2}])$. Therefore,

$$\hat{m}^{\theta}(\hat{\theta}, \hat{\alpha}) = O_p(n^{-1} \max[n^{-1/2}, n_\alpha^{-1/2}]).$$

A further application of Lemma A.1 gives the result. ■

Lemma A.3. *Suppose that* $\hat{\alpha} = \alpha_0 + \tilde{\psi}^{\alpha}/\sqrt{n_\alpha} + Q^{\alpha}(\tilde{a}^{\varphi}, \tilde{\psi}^{\varphi})/n_\alpha + O_p(n_\alpha^{-3/2})$, *where* $\tilde{\psi}^{\alpha}$ *and* $Q^{\alpha}(\tilde{a}^{\varphi}, \tilde{\psi}^{\varphi})$ *are* $O_p(1)$. *Let* $\Omega_k^{\beta\beta} = g_k^{\beta} g_k^{\beta'} - \Omega^{\beta\beta}$, $\tilde{\Omega}^{\beta\beta} = \sum_{k=1}^{n} \Omega_k^{\beta\beta}/\sqrt{n}$, $\bar{\Omega}_{\beta r} = E[\partial[g_k^{\beta} g_k^{\beta'}]/\partial \beta_r]$ *and* $\bar{\Omega}_{\alpha s} = E[\partial[g_k^{\beta} g_k^{\beta'}]/\partial \alpha_s]$. *Then*

$$\begin{aligned} \hat{\Omega}^{\beta\beta}(\hat{\alpha}, \tilde{\beta}) &= \Omega^{\beta\beta} + \tilde{\Omega}^{\beta\beta}/\sqrt{n} \\ &\quad + \sum_{r=1}^{p_\beta} \bar{\Omega}_{\beta r} e_r' \left(\tilde{\psi}^{\theta W}/\sqrt{n} - (M^{\theta W})^{-1} M_{\alpha}^{\theta W} \tilde{\psi}^{\alpha}/\sqrt{n_\alpha} \right) \\ &\quad + \sum_{s=1}^{p_\alpha} \bar{\Omega}_{\alpha s} e_s' \tilde{\psi}^{\alpha}/\sqrt{n_\alpha} + O_p(\max[n^{-1}, n_\alpha^{-1}]). \end{aligned}$$

Proof. Similarly to the proof of Lemma A.1, expanding gives

$$\begin{aligned} \hat{\Omega}^{\beta\beta}(\hat{\alpha}, \tilde{\beta}) &= \hat{\Omega}(\alpha_0, \beta_0) + \sum_{r=1}^{p_\beta} \bar{\Omega}_{\beta r}(\tilde{\beta}_r - \beta_{0r}) + \sum_{s=1}^{p_\alpha} \bar{\Omega}_{\alpha s}(\hat{\alpha}_s - \alpha_{0s}) \\ &\quad + O_p(\max[n^{-1}, n_\alpha^{-1}]). \end{aligned}$$

By Lemma A.1, $\tilde{\beta}_r - \beta_{0r} = e_r'(\tilde{\psi}^{\theta W}/\sqrt{n} - (M^{\theta W})^{-1} M_{\alpha}^{\theta W} \tilde{\psi}^{\alpha}/\sqrt{n_\alpha}) + O_p(\max[n^{-1}, n_\alpha^{-1}])$. The conclusion follows by substitution into the above equation. ■

Let $\hat{\Omega}^{\beta\beta} = \sum_{i=1}^{n_\beta} g_i^\beta g_i^{\beta'}/n_\beta$, $\hat{G}_\beta^\beta = \sum_{i=1}^{n_\beta} G_{\beta i}^\beta/n_\beta$, $\hat{G}_\alpha^\beta = \sum_{i=1}^{n_\beta} G_{\alpha i}^\beta/n_\beta$, $G_{\beta\beta i}^{\beta r} = \partial^2 g_i^\beta/\partial\beta_r\partial\beta'$, $G_{\beta\alpha i}^{\beta s} = \partial^2 g_i^\beta/\partial\alpha_s\partial\beta'$, $g_{\beta i}^{\beta r} = \partial g_i^\beta/\partial\beta_r$, and $g_{\alpha i}^{\beta s} = \partial g_i^\beta/\partial\alpha_s$.

We detail an expansion for GMM in the general case. Let $\theta = (\beta', \lambda')'$, $\theta_0 = (\beta_0', 0')'$, $\hat{\beta}$ be the two-step GMM estimator and

$$\hat{m}^\theta(\theta, \alpha) = -\begin{pmatrix} \hat{G}_\beta^\beta(\alpha, \beta)'\lambda \\ \hat{g}^\beta(\alpha, \beta) + (\Omega^{\beta\beta} + \xi^{\Omega^{\beta\beta}})\lambda \end{pmatrix},$$

where $\xi^{\Omega^{\beta\beta}} = \tilde{\Omega}^{\beta\beta}/\sqrt{n} + \sum_{r=1}^{p_\beta} \bar{\Omega}_{\beta r} e_r'(\tilde{\psi}^{\theta W}/\sqrt{n} - (M^{\theta W})^{-1} M_\alpha^{\theta W} \tilde{\psi}^\alpha/\sqrt{n_\alpha}) + \sum_{s=1}^{p_\alpha} \bar{\Omega}_{\alpha s} e_s' \tilde{\psi}^\alpha/\sqrt{n_\alpha}$. Also, let $\hat{\lambda} = -\hat{\Omega}^{\beta\beta}(\hat{\alpha}, \tilde{\beta})^{-1}\hat{g}^\beta(\hat{\alpha}, \hat{\beta})$. Then $\hat{\lambda} = O_p(\max[n_\alpha^{-1/2}, n_\beta^{-1/2}])$. The first-order conditions for GMM and Lemmas A.1–A.3 imply

$$\begin{aligned} 0 &= \hat{m}^\theta(\hat{\theta}, \hat{\alpha}) + [0, -\hat{\lambda}'(O_p(\max[n^{-1}, n_\alpha^{-1}]))]' \\ &= \hat{m}^\theta(\hat{\theta}, \hat{\alpha}) + O_p(\max[n_\alpha^{-1/2}, n_\beta^{-1/2}]\max[n^{-1}, n_\alpha^{-1}]). \end{aligned}$$

Therefore, we can solve for $\hat{\theta}_{2S} - \theta_0$ as in the conclusion of Lemma A.1 using the definitions $\hat{m}^\theta(\theta_0, \alpha_0) = -(0', \hat{g}^\beta(\alpha_0, \beta_0)')'$,

$$\begin{aligned}
M^\theta &= -\begin{pmatrix} 0 & G_\beta^{\beta'} \\ G_\beta^\beta & \Omega^{\beta\beta} \end{pmatrix}, \quad (M^\theta)^{-1} = -\begin{pmatrix} -\Sigma^{\beta\beta} & H^\beta \\ H^{\beta'} & P^\beta \end{pmatrix}, \\
M_\alpha^\theta &= -\begin{pmatrix} 0 \\ G_\alpha^\beta \end{pmatrix}, \\
\tilde{A}^\theta &= -n_\beta^{1/2}\begin{pmatrix} 0 & (\hat{G}_\beta^\beta - G_\beta^\beta)' \\ (\hat{G}_\beta^\beta - G_\beta^\beta) & \xi^{\Omega^{\beta\beta}} \end{pmatrix}, \\
\tilde{A}_\alpha^\theta &= -n_\beta^{1/2}\begin{pmatrix} 0 \\ (\hat{G}_\alpha^\beta - G_\alpha^\beta) \end{pmatrix}, \\
M_{\theta\theta r}^\theta &= -\begin{pmatrix} 0 & E[G_{\beta\beta i}^{\beta r}]' \\ E[G_{\beta\beta i}^{\beta r}] & 0 \end{pmatrix}, \quad (r \le p_\beta), \\
M_{\theta\theta, p_\beta + r}^\theta &= -\begin{pmatrix} E[\partial^2 g_{ir}^\beta/\partial\beta\partial\beta'] & 0 \\ 0 & 0 \end{pmatrix}, \quad (r \le m_\beta). \\
M_{\theta\alpha s}^\theta &= -\begin{pmatrix} 0 & E[G_{\beta\alpha i}^{\beta s}]' \\ E[G_{\beta\alpha i}^{\beta s}] & 0 \end{pmatrix}, \quad (s \le p_\alpha), \\
M_{\alpha\theta r}^\theta &= -\begin{pmatrix} 0 \\ E[\partial^2 g_i^\beta/\partial\beta_r\partial\alpha'] \end{pmatrix}, \quad (r \le p_\beta), \\
M_{\alpha\theta, p_\beta + r}^\beta &= -\begin{pmatrix} E[\partial^2 g_{ir}^\beta/\partial\beta\partial\alpha'] \\ 0 \end{pmatrix}, \quad (r \le m_\beta). \\
M_{\alpha\alpha s}^\theta &= -\begin{pmatrix} 0 \\ E[\partial^2 g_i^\beta/\partial\alpha_s\partial\alpha'] \end{pmatrix}, \quad (s \le p_\alpha). \qquad \text{(A.1)}
\end{aligned}$$

For a general expansion for GEL, we apply Lemma A.1. Let $\theta = (\beta', \lambda')'$, $\theta_0 = (\beta_0', 0')'$, $\hat{\theta}$ be the GEL estimator and

$$\hat{m}^{\theta}(\theta, \alpha) = \sum_{i=1}^{n_*} \rho_v^{\theta}(\lambda' g_i^{\beta}(\alpha, \beta)) \begin{pmatrix} G_{\beta i}^{\beta}(\alpha, \beta)'\lambda \\ g_i^{\beta}(\beta) \end{pmatrix} \Big/ n_*.$$

Therefore, using similar arguments to those in Newey and Smith (2004) we can solve for $\hat{\theta}_{\text{GEL}} - \theta_0$ as in the conclusion of Lemma A.1 by setting $n_\beta = n_*$, dropping n and with the definitions $\hat{m}^{\theta}(\theta_0, \alpha_0) = -(0', \hat{g}^{\beta}(\alpha_0, \beta_0)')'$,

$$\begin{aligned}
M^{\theta} &= -\begin{pmatrix} 0 & G_{\beta}^{\beta'} \\ G_{\beta}^{\beta} & \Omega^{\beta\beta} \end{pmatrix}, \qquad (M^{\theta})^{-1} = -\begin{pmatrix} -\Sigma^{\beta\beta} & H^{\beta} \\ H^{\beta'} & P^{\beta} \end{pmatrix}, \\
M_{\alpha}^{\theta} &= -\begin{pmatrix} 0 \\ G_{\alpha}^{\beta} \end{pmatrix} \\
\tilde{A}^{\theta} &= -n_*^{1/2} \begin{pmatrix} 0 & (\hat{G}_{\beta}^{\beta} - G_{\beta}^{\beta})' \\ (\hat{G}_{\beta}^{\beta} - G_{\beta}^{\beta}) & \hat{\Omega}^{\beta\beta} - \Omega^{\beta\beta} \end{pmatrix}, \\
\tilde{A}_{\alpha}^{\theta} &= -n_*^{1/2} \begin{pmatrix} 0 \\ (\hat{G}_{\alpha}^{\beta} - G_{\alpha}^{\beta}) \end{pmatrix} \\
M_{\theta\theta r}^{\theta} &= -\begin{pmatrix} 0 & E[G_{\beta\beta i}^{\beta r}]' \\ E[G_{\beta\beta i}^{\beta r}] & E[g_{\beta i}^{\beta r} g_i^{\beta'} + g_i^{\beta} g_{\beta i}^{\beta r'}] \end{pmatrix}, \quad (r \leq p_\beta), \\
M_{\theta\theta, p_\beta + r}^{\theta} &= -\begin{pmatrix} E[\partial^2 g_{ir}^{\beta}/\partial\beta\partial\beta'] & E[G_{\beta i}^{\beta'} e_r g_i^{\beta'} + g_{ir}^{\beta} G_{\beta i}^{\beta'}] \\ E[g_i^{\beta} e_r' G_{\beta i}^{\beta} + g_{ir}^{\beta} G_{\beta i}^{\beta}] & -\rho_{vvv}^{\theta}(0) E[g_{ir}^{\beta} g_i^{\beta} g_i^{\beta'}] \end{pmatrix}, \quad (r \leq m_\beta). \\
M_{\theta\alpha s}^{\theta} &= -\begin{pmatrix} 0 & E[G_{\beta\alpha i}^{\beta s}]' \\ E[G_{\beta\alpha i}^{\beta s}] & E[G_{\alpha i}^{\beta} e_s g_i^{\beta'} + g_i^{\beta} e_s' G_{\alpha i}^{\beta'}] \end{pmatrix}, \quad (s \leq p_\alpha), \\
M_{\alpha\theta r}^{\theta} &= -\begin{pmatrix} 0 \\ E[\partial^2 g_i^{\beta}(\beta_0, \alpha_0)/\partial\beta_r \partial\alpha'] \end{pmatrix}, \quad (r \leq p_\beta), \\
M_{\alpha\theta, p_\beta + r}^{\beta} &= -\begin{pmatrix} E[\partial^2 g_{ir}^{\beta}/\partial\beta\partial\alpha'] \\ E[g_i^{\beta} \partial g_{ir}^{\beta}/\partial\alpha'] + E[g_{ir}^{\beta} G_{\alpha i}^{\beta}] \end{pmatrix}, \quad (r \leq m_\beta). \\
M_{\alpha\alpha s}^{\theta} &= -\begin{pmatrix} 0 \\ E[\partial^2 g_i^{\beta}/\partial\alpha_s \partial\alpha'] \end{pmatrix}, \quad (s \leq p_\alpha).
\end{aligned} \tag{A.2}$$

Proof of Theorem 3.1. The matrices M^{θ} and $(M^{\theta})^{-1}$ are as defined in (A.1). Thus, $\tilde{\psi}^{\theta} = -n_{\beta}^{1/2}[H^{\beta'}, P^{\beta}]'\hat{g}^{\beta}$. For independent samples, $\xi^{\Omega^{\beta\beta}}$ is uncorrelated with $\hat{g}^{\beta}$ as is $\tilde{A}_{\alpha}^{\theta}$ with $\tilde{\psi}^{\alpha}$. Thus,

$$\begin{aligned}
Bias(\hat{\theta}_{2S}) &= \theta_0 - (M^{\theta})^{-1} M_{\alpha}^{\theta} Bias(\hat{\alpha}) \\
&\quad - (M^{\theta})^{-1} E[\tilde{A}^{\theta}(\tilde{\psi}^{\theta}/\sqrt{n_\beta} - (M^{\theta})^{-1} M_{\alpha}^{\theta} \tilde{\psi}^{\alpha}/\sqrt{n_\alpha})]/\sqrt{n_\beta}
\end{aligned}$$

$$
\begin{aligned}
&- (M^{\theta})^{-1}\sum_{r=1}^{q_\theta} e_r'[E[\tilde{\psi}^{\theta} M^{\theta}_{\theta\theta r}\tilde{\psi}^{\theta}]/n_\beta \\
&+ (M^{\theta})^{-1} M^{\theta}_{\alpha} E[\tilde{\psi}^{\alpha} M^{\theta}_{\theta\theta r}(M^{\theta})^{-1} M^{\theta}_{\alpha}\tilde{\psi}^{\alpha}]/n_\alpha]/2 \\
&+ (M^{\theta})^{-1}\sum_{s=1}^{p_\alpha} e_s' E[\tilde{\psi}^{\alpha} M^{\theta}_{\theta\alpha s}(M^{\theta})^{-1} M^{\theta}_{\alpha}\tilde{\psi}^{\alpha}]/2n_\alpha \\
&+ (M^{\theta})^{-1}\left[\sum_{r=1}^{q_\theta} e_r'(M^{\theta})^{-1} M^{\theta}_{\alpha} E[\tilde{\psi}^{\alpha} M^{\theta}_{\alpha\theta r}\tilde{\psi}^{\alpha}]\right]\Big/2n_\alpha \\
&- (M^{\theta})^{-1}\left[\sum_{s=1}^{p_\alpha} e_s' E[\tilde{\psi}^{\alpha} M^{\theta}_{\alpha\alpha s}\tilde{\psi}^{\alpha}]/n_\alpha\right]\Big/2 \\
&+ O_p(\max[n^{-3/2}, n_\alpha^{-3/2}, n_\beta^{-3/2}]).
\end{aligned}
$$

Note that the penultimate two terms are identical. Now,

$$
E[\tilde{A}^{\theta}\tilde{\psi}^{\theta}] = \begin{pmatrix} E[G^{\beta'}_{\beta i} P^{\beta} g^{\beta}_i] \\ E[G^{\beta}_{\beta i} H^{\beta} g^{\beta}_i] \end{pmatrix},
$$

$$
\begin{aligned}
&E[\tilde{A}^{\theta}(M^{\theta})^{-1} M^{\theta}_{\alpha}\tilde{\psi}^{\alpha}] \\
&= \begin{pmatrix} 0 \\ -\sum_{r=1}^{p_\beta}\bar{\Omega}_{\beta r} P^{\beta} G^{\beta}_{\alpha}\Sigma^{\alpha\alpha} G^{\beta'}_{\alpha} H^{\beta'}_{W} e_r + \sum_{s=1}^{p_\alpha}\bar{\Omega}_{\alpha s} P^{\beta} G^{\beta}_{\alpha}\Sigma^{\alpha\alpha} e_s \end{pmatrix}.
\end{aligned}
$$

Let $(M^{\theta}_{\beta})^{-1} = (-\Sigma^{\beta\beta}, H^{\beta})$. By a similar analysis to that in Newey and Smith (2004, Proof of Theorem 4.1),

$$
(M^{\theta}_{\beta})^{-1}\sum_{r=1}^{p_\beta} e_r' E[\tilde{\psi}^{\theta} M^{\theta}_{\theta\theta r}\tilde{\psi}^{\theta}] = -H^{\beta} a_\beta.
$$

$$
(M^{\theta}_{\beta})^{-1}\sum_{r=p_\beta+1}^{q_\theta} e_r' E[\tilde{\psi}^{\theta} M^{\theta}_{\theta\theta r}\tilde{\psi}^{\theta}] = 0.
$$

$$
\begin{aligned}
&(M^{\theta}_{\beta})^{-1}\sum_{r=1}^{p_\beta} e_r'(M^{\theta})^{-1} M^{\theta}_{\alpha} E[\tilde{\psi}^{\alpha} M^{\theta}_{\theta\theta r}(M^{\theta})^{-1} M^{\theta}_{\alpha}\tilde{\psi}^{\alpha}] \\
&= \Sigma^{\beta\beta} c^{\beta}_{\beta\beta} - H^{\beta} a^{\beta}_{\beta\beta}.
\end{aligned}
$$

$$
(M^{\theta}_{\beta})^{-1}\sum_{r=p_\beta+1}^{m_\beta} e_r'(M^{\theta})^{-1} M^{\theta}_{\alpha} E[\tilde{\psi}^{\alpha} M^{\theta}_{\theta\theta r}(M^{\theta})^{-1} M^{\theta}_{\alpha}\tilde{\psi}^{\alpha}] = \Sigma^{\beta\beta} c^{\beta}_{\beta\beta}.
$$

$$
-(M^{\theta}_{\beta})^{-1}\sum_{s=1}^{p_\alpha} e_s' E[\tilde{\psi}^{\alpha} M^{\theta}_{\theta\alpha s}(M^{\theta})^{-1} M^{\theta}_{\alpha}\tilde{\psi}^{\alpha}] = \Sigma^{\beta\beta} c^{\beta}_{\beta\alpha} - H^{\beta} a^{\beta}_{\beta\alpha}.
$$

$$
(M^{\theta}_{\beta})^{-1}\sum_{s=1}^{p_\alpha} e_s' E[\tilde{\psi}^{\alpha} M^{\theta}_{\alpha\alpha s}\tilde{\psi}^{\alpha}] = -H^{\beta} a^{\beta}_{\alpha\alpha}.
$$

Therefore, as

$$\bar{\Omega}_{\beta r} = E[G^{\beta}_{\beta i} e_r g_i^{\beta\cdot\alpha} + g_i^{\beta\cdot\alpha} e_r' G^{\beta'}_{\beta i}],$$
$$\bar{\Omega}_{\alpha s} = E[G^{\beta}_{\alpha i} e_s g_i^{\beta\cdot\alpha} + g_i^{\beta\cdot\alpha} e_s' G^{\beta'}_{\alpha i}],$$

and $Bias(\hat{\beta}_{2S}) = (I_{p_\beta}, 0)Bias(\hat{\theta}_{2S})$, after simplification and collecting terms the result of the theorem is obtained. ■

Proof of Theorem 3.2. From (A.2), because of independent sampling $\tilde{A}^{\theta}$ and $\tilde{A}^{\theta}_{\alpha}$ are uncorrelated with $\tilde{\psi}^{\alpha}$. Hence,

$$\begin{aligned}\hat{\theta}_{\text{GEL}} = &-(M^{\theta})^{-1}M^{\theta}_{\alpha}Bias(\hat{\alpha})\\ &-(M^{\theta})^{-1}E[\tilde{A}^{\theta}\tilde{\psi}^{\theta}]/N\\ &-(M^{\theta})^{-1}\sum_{r=1}^{q_\theta} e_r'[E[\tilde{\psi}^{\theta}M^{\theta}_{\theta\theta r}\tilde{\psi}^{\theta}] + (M^{\theta})^{-1}M^{\theta}_{\alpha}E[\tilde{\psi}^{\alpha}M^{\theta}_{\theta\theta r}\\ &\quad\times(M^{\theta})^{-1}M^{\theta}_{\alpha}\tilde{\psi}^{\alpha}]]/2N\\ &+(M^{\theta})^{-1}\sum_{s=1}^{p_\alpha} e_s' E[\tilde{\psi}^{\alpha}M^{\theta}_{\theta\alpha s}(M^{\theta})^{-1}M^{\theta}_{\alpha}\tilde{\psi}^{\alpha}]/2n_{\alpha}\\ &+(M^{\theta})^{-1}\sum_{r=1}^{q_\theta} e_r'(M^{\theta})^{-1}M^{\theta}_{\alpha}E[\tilde{\psi}^{\alpha}M^{\theta}_{\alpha\theta r}\tilde{\psi}^{\alpha}]/2n_{\alpha}\\ &-(M^{\theta})^{-1}\sum_{s=1}^{p_\alpha} e_s' E[\tilde{\psi}^{\alpha}M^{\theta}_{\alpha\alpha s}\tilde{\psi}^{\alpha}]/2n_{\alpha} + O_p(\max[n^{-3/2}, n_{\alpha}^{-3/2}, n_{\beta}^{-3/2}]).\end{aligned}$$

Note that the penultimate two terms are identical. Also, $Bias_{\alpha_0}(\hat{\theta}_{\text{GEL}}) = -(M^{\theta})^{-1}(E[\tilde{A}^{\theta}\tilde{\psi}^{\theta}] + \sum_{r=1}^{q_\theta} e_r'[E[\tilde{\psi}^{\theta}M^{\theta}_{\theta\theta r}\tilde{\psi}^{\theta}]/2)/N$ (see Newey and Smith 2004, Proof of Theorem 4.2). Let $(M^{\theta}_{\beta})^{-1} = (-\Sigma^{\beta\beta}, H^{\beta})$. By a similar analysis to that in Newey and Smith (2004, Proof of Theorem 4.2),

$$\begin{aligned}&(M^{\theta}_{\beta})^{-1}\sum_{r=1}^{p_\beta} e_r'(M^{\theta})^{-1}M^{\theta}_{\alpha}E[\tilde{\psi}^{\alpha}M^{\theta}_{\theta\theta r}(M^{\theta})^{-1}M^{\theta}_{\alpha}\tilde{\psi}^{\alpha}]\\ &\quad= \Sigma^{\beta\beta}c^{\beta}_{\beta\beta} - H^{\beta}a^{\beta}_{\beta\beta} - H^{\beta}(E[G^{\beta}_{\beta i}H^{\beta}G^{\beta}_{\alpha}\Sigma^{\alpha\alpha}G^{\beta'}_{\alpha}P^{\beta}g_i^{\beta}])\\ &\qquad+ E[g_i^{\beta}\operatorname{tr}(G^{\beta'}_{\beta i}P^{\beta}G^{\beta}_{\alpha}\Sigma^{\alpha\alpha}G^{\beta'}_{\alpha}H^{\beta})]).\\ &(M^{\theta}_{\beta})^{-1}\sum_{r=p_\beta+1}^{q_\theta} e_r'(M^{\theta})^{-1}M^{\theta}_{\alpha}E[\tilde{\psi}^{\alpha}M^{\theta}_{\theta\theta r}(M^{\theta})^{-1}M^{\theta}_{\alpha}\tilde{\psi}^{\alpha}]\\ &\quad= \Sigma^{\beta\beta}c^{\beta}_{\beta\beta} + 2\Sigma^{\beta\beta}E[G^{\beta'}_{\beta i}P^{\beta}G^{\beta}_{\alpha}\Sigma^{\alpha\alpha}G^{\beta'}_{\alpha}P^{\beta}g_i^{\beta}]\\ &\qquad- H^{\beta}(E[G^{\beta}_{\beta i}H^{\beta}G^{\beta}_{\alpha}\Sigma^{\alpha\alpha}G^{\beta'}_{\alpha}P^{\beta}g_i^{\beta}]\\ &\qquad+ E[g_i^{\beta}\operatorname{tr}(G^{\beta'}_{\beta i}P^{\beta}G^{\beta}_{\alpha}\Sigma^{\alpha\alpha}G^{\beta'}_{\alpha}H^{\beta'})])\end{aligned}$$

$$+ \rho_{vvv}^{\theta}(0)H^{\beta}E[g_i^{\beta}g_i^{\beta'}P^{\beta}G_{\alpha}^{\beta}\Sigma^{\alpha\alpha}G_{\alpha}^{\beta'}P^{\beta}g_i^{\beta}].$$

$$(M_{\beta}^{\theta})^{-1}\sum_{s=1}^{p_{\alpha}} e_s' E[\tilde{\psi}^{\alpha}M_{\theta\alpha s}^{\theta}(M^{\theta})^{-1}M_{\alpha}^{\theta}\tilde{\psi}^{\alpha}]$$
$$= \Sigma^{\beta\beta}c_{\beta\alpha}^{\beta} - H^{\beta}a_{\beta\alpha}^{\beta}$$
$$- H^{\beta}(E[G_{\alpha i}^{\beta}\Sigma^{\alpha\alpha}G_{\alpha}^{\beta'}P^{\beta}g_i^{\beta}] + E[g_i^{\beta}\,\mathrm{tr}\,(G_{\alpha i}^{\beta'}P^{\beta}G_{\alpha}^{\beta}\Sigma^{\alpha\alpha})]).$$

$$(M_{\beta}^{\theta})^{-1}\sum_{s=1}^{p_{\alpha}} e_s' E[\tilde{\psi}^{\alpha}M_{\alpha\alpha s}^{\theta}\tilde{\psi}^{\alpha}] = -H^{\beta}a_{\alpha\alpha}^{\beta}.$$

Therefore, simpifying and collecting terms gives the result of the theorem. ■

Proof of Corollary 3.2. Immediate as $G_{\alpha}^{\beta} = 0$, $E[\partial^2 g_{ir}^{\beta}/\partial\beta\partial\alpha'] = 0$ and $E[\partial^2 g_{kr}^{\beta}/\partial\beta\partial\alpha'] = 0$. ■

Proof of Corollary 3.3. Follows immediately as in Proof of Corollary 3.2 and from Newey and Smith (2004, Theorem 4.2). ■

Proof of Theorem 3.3. From (A.1), as $Bias(\hat{\beta}_{2S}) = (I_{p_{\beta}}, 0)Bias(\hat{\theta}_{2S})$,

$$Bias(\hat{\beta}_{2S}) = -H^{\beta}G_{\alpha}^{\beta}Bias(\hat{\alpha})$$
$$- \Sigma^{\beta\beta}E[G_{\beta i}^{\beta'}P^{\beta}g_i^{\beta\cdot\alpha}]/n_{\beta} + H^{\beta}E[G_{\beta i}^{\beta}H^{\beta}g_i^{\beta\cdot\alpha}]/n_{\beta}$$
$$+ H^{\beta}E[g_i^{\beta}g_i^{\beta'}P^{\beta}g_i^{\beta\cdot\alpha}]/n_{\beta}$$
$$- H^{\beta}\left(\sum_{r=1}^{p_{\beta}}\bar{\Omega}_{\beta r}P^{\beta}E[g_i^{\beta\cdot\alpha}g_i^{\beta\cdot\alpha'}]H_W^{\beta'}e_r\right.$$
$$\left.+\sum_{s=1}^{p_{\alpha}}\bar{\Omega}_{\alpha s}P^{\beta}E[g_i^{\beta\cdot\alpha}g_i^{\alpha'}]H^{\alpha'}e_s\right)/n_{\beta}$$
$$+ H^{\beta}E[G_{\alpha i}^{\beta}H^{\alpha}g_i^{\alpha}]/n_{\beta}$$
$$+\sum_{r=1}^{p_{\beta}}(\Sigma^{\beta\beta}E[G_{\beta\beta i}^{\beta r}]'P^{\beta} - H^{\beta}E[G_{\beta\beta i}^{\beta r}]H^{\beta})E[g_i^{\beta\cdot\alpha}g_i^{\beta\cdot\alpha'}]H^{\beta'}e_r/2n_{\beta}$$
$$+\sum_{r=1}^{m_{\beta}}\Sigma^{\beta\beta}E[\partial^2 g_{ir}^{\beta}/\partial\beta\partial\beta']H^{\beta}E[g_i^{\beta\cdot\alpha}g_i^{\beta\cdot\alpha'}]P^{\beta}e_r/2n_{\beta}$$
$$+\sum_{s=1}^{p_{\alpha}}(\Sigma^{\beta\beta}E[G_{\beta\alpha i}^{\beta s}]'P^{\beta} - H^{\beta}E[G_{\beta\alpha i}^{\beta s}]H^{\beta})E[g_i^{\beta\cdot\alpha}g_i^{\alpha}]H^{\alpha'}e_s/2n_{\beta}$$
$$-\sum_{r=1}^{p_{\beta}}H^{\beta}E[\partial^2 g_i^{\beta}/\partial\beta_r\partial\alpha']H^{\alpha}E[g_i^{\alpha}g_i^{\beta\cdot\alpha'}]H^{\beta'}e_r/2n_{\beta}$$

$$+\sum_{r=1}^{m_\beta} \Sigma^{\beta\beta} E[\partial^2 g_{ir}^\beta/\partial\beta\partial\alpha']H^\alpha E[g_i^\alpha g_i^{\beta\cdot\alpha'}]P^\beta e_r/2n_\beta$$

$$-\sum_{s=1}^{p_\alpha} H^\beta E[\partial^2 g_i^\beta/\partial\alpha_s\partial\alpha']\Sigma^{\alpha\alpha} e_s/2n_\beta.$$

As

$$\bar{\Omega}_{\beta r} = E[G_{\beta i}^\beta e_r g_i^{\beta'} + g_i^\beta e_r' G_{\beta i}^{\beta'}], \qquad \bar{\Omega}_{\alpha s} = E[G_{\alpha i}^\beta e_s g_i^{\beta'} + g_i^\beta e_s' G_{\alpha i}^{\beta'}],$$

simplifying and collecting terms yields the result in Theorem 3.3. ■

Proof of Theorem 3.4. From (A.2), as $Bias(\hat{\beta}_{\mathrm{GEL}}) = (I_{p_\beta}, 0)Bias(\hat{\theta}_{\mathrm{GEL}})$,

$$\begin{aligned}
Bias(\hat{\beta}_{\mathrm{GEL}}) = & -H^\beta G_\alpha^\beta Bias(\hat{\alpha}) \\
& - \Sigma^{\beta\beta} E[G_{\beta i}^{\beta'} P^\beta g_i^{\beta\cdot\alpha}]/n_\beta + H^\beta (E[G_{\beta i}^\beta H^\beta g_i^{\beta\cdot\alpha}] \\
& + E[g_i^\beta g_i^{\beta'} P^\beta g_i^{\beta\cdot\alpha}])/n_\beta + H^\beta E[G_{\alpha i}^\beta H^\alpha g_i^\alpha]/n_\beta \\
& - \sum_{r=1}^{p_\beta} (-\Sigma^{\beta\beta} E[G_{\beta\beta i}^{\beta r}]' P^\beta + H^\beta (E[G_{\beta\beta i}^{\beta r}] H^\beta \\
& + E[g_{\beta i}^{\beta r} g_{\beta i}^{\beta'} + g_i^\beta g_{\beta i}^{\beta r'}] P^\beta)) E[g_i^{\beta\cdot\alpha} g_i^{\beta\cdot\alpha'}] H^{\beta'} e_r/2n_\beta \\
& + \sum_{r=1}^{m_\beta} \Sigma^{\beta\beta} (E[\partial^2 g_{ir}^\beta/\partial\beta\partial\beta'] H^\beta \\
& + E[G_{\beta i}^{\beta'} e_r g_i^{\beta'} + g_{ir}^\beta G_{\beta i}^{\beta'}] P^\beta) E[g_i^{\beta\cdot\alpha} g_i^{\beta\cdot\alpha}] P^\beta e_r/2n_\beta \\
& - \sum_{r=1}^{m_\beta} H^\beta (E[g_i^\beta e_r' G_{\beta i}^\beta + g_{ir}^\beta G_{\beta i}^\beta] H^\beta \\
& - \rho_{vvv}^\theta(0) E[g_{ir}^\beta g_i^\beta g_i^{\beta'}] P^\beta) E[g_i^{\beta\cdot\alpha} g_i^{\beta\cdot\alpha}] P^\beta e_r/2n_\beta \\
& - \sum_{s=1}^{p_\alpha} [-\Sigma^{\beta\beta} E[G_{\beta\alpha i}^{\beta s}]' P^\beta \\
& + H^\beta (E[G_{\beta\alpha i}^{\beta s}] H^\beta + E[g_{\alpha i}^{\beta s} g_i^{\beta'} + g_i^\beta g_{\alpha i}^{\beta s'}] P^\beta)] E[g_i^{\beta\cdot\alpha} g_i^{\alpha'}] H^{\alpha'} e_s/n_\beta \\
& - H^\beta \sum_{s=1}^{p_\alpha} E[\partial^2 g_i^\beta/\partial\alpha_s\partial\alpha'] \Sigma^{\alpha\alpha} e_s/2n_\beta.
\end{aligned}$$

Simplifying and collecting terms gives the result in Theorem 3.4. ■

APPENDIX B: SOME NOTATION

We use the generic notation e_r and e_s to indicate unit vectors of dimension indicated by context.

B.1. System-α

$$g_j^\alpha(\alpha) \equiv g^\alpha(x_j, \alpha), \quad (j = 1, \ldots, n_\beta), \qquad \hat{g}^\alpha(\alpha) \equiv \sum_{j=1}^{n_\alpha} g_j^\alpha(\alpha)/n_\alpha,$$

$$\hat{\Omega}^{\alpha\alpha}(\alpha) \equiv \sum_{j=1}^{n_\alpha} g_j^\alpha(\alpha) g_j^\alpha(\alpha)'/n_\alpha.$$

B.2. System-β

$$g_i^\beta(\alpha, \beta) \equiv g^\beta(z_i, \alpha, \beta), \quad (i = 1, \ldots, n_\beta),$$

$$\hat{g}^\beta(\alpha, \beta) \equiv \sum_{i=1}^{n_\beta} g_i^\beta(\alpha, \beta)/n_\beta,$$

$$g_k^\beta(\alpha, \beta) \equiv g^\beta(z_k, \alpha, \beta), \quad (k = 1, \ldots, n),$$

$$\hat{\Omega}^{\beta\beta}(\alpha, \beta) \equiv \sum_{k=1}^{n} g_k^\beta(\alpha, \beta) g_k^\beta(\alpha, \beta)'/n.$$

B.3. Asymptotic Bias System-α

$$\begin{aligned}
g_j^\alpha &= g_j^\alpha(\alpha_0), \qquad G_j^\alpha(\alpha) = \partial g_j^\alpha(\alpha)/\partial\alpha', \\
G_j^\alpha &= G_j^\alpha(\alpha_0), \quad (j = 1, \ldots, n_\alpha), \\
G^\alpha &= E[G_j^\alpha], \qquad \Omega^{\alpha\alpha} = E[g_j^\alpha g_j^{\alpha'}], \qquad \Sigma^{\alpha\alpha} = (G^{\alpha'}(\Omega^{\alpha\alpha})^{-1}G^\alpha)^{-1}, \\
H^\alpha &= \Sigma^{\alpha\alpha} G^{\alpha'}(\Omega^{\alpha\alpha})^{-1}, \\
P^\alpha &= (\Omega^{\alpha\alpha})^{-1} - (\Omega^{\alpha\alpha})^{-1} G^\alpha \Sigma^{\alpha\alpha} G^{\alpha'}(\Omega^{\alpha\alpha})^{-1}. \\
a_{\alpha s} &\equiv \mathrm{tr}(\Sigma^{\alpha\alpha} E[\partial^2 g_{js}^\alpha/\partial\alpha\partial\alpha'])/2, \quad (s = 1, \ldots, m_\alpha).
\end{aligned} \tag{B.1}$$

B.4. Asymptotic Bias System-β

$$\begin{aligned}
g_i^\beta &= g_i^\beta(\alpha_0, \beta_0), \qquad G_{\beta i}^\beta(\alpha, \beta) = \partial g_i^\beta(\alpha, \beta)/\partial\beta', \\
G_{\beta i}^\beta &= G_{\beta i}^\beta(\alpha_0, \beta_0), \quad (i = 1, \ldots, n_\beta), \\
\Omega^{\beta\beta} &= E[g_i^\beta g_i^{\beta'}], \quad G_\beta^\beta = E[G_{\beta i}^\beta], \quad \Sigma^{\beta\beta} = (G_\beta^{\beta'}(\Omega^{\beta\beta})^{-1} G_\beta^\beta)^{-1}, \\
H^\beta &= \Sigma^\beta G_\beta^{\beta'}(\Omega^{\beta\beta})^{-1}, \\
P^\beta &= (\Omega^{\beta\beta})^{-1} - (\Omega^{\beta\beta})^{-1} G_\beta^\beta \Sigma^{\beta\beta} G_\beta^{\beta'}(\Omega^{\beta\beta})^{-1}. \\
a_{\beta r} &\equiv tr(\Sigma^{\beta\beta} E[\partial^2 g_{ir}^\beta/\partial\beta\partial\beta'])/2, \quad (r = 1, \ldots, m_\beta).
\end{aligned} \tag{B.2}$$

$$G_{\alpha i}^\beta(\alpha, \beta) = \partial g_i^\beta(\alpha, \beta)/\partial\alpha', \quad G_{\alpha i}^\beta = G_{\alpha i}^\beta(\alpha_0, \beta_0), \quad G_\alpha^\beta = E[G_{\alpha i}^\beta]$$
$$\Sigma_W^{\beta\beta} = (G_\beta^{\beta'}(W^{\beta\beta})^{-1} G_\beta^\beta)^{-1}, \quad H_W^\beta = \Sigma_W^{\beta\beta} G_\beta^{\beta'}(W^{\beta\beta})^{-1}.$$

B.5. Independent Samples

$$
\begin{aligned}
a^{\beta}_{\beta\beta r} &= \operatorname{tr}(H^{\beta} G^{\beta}_{\alpha} \Sigma^{\alpha\alpha} G^{\beta'}_{\alpha} H^{\beta'} E[\partial^2 g^{\beta}_{ir}/\partial\beta\partial\beta'])/2,\\
a^{\beta}_{\beta\alpha r} &= -\operatorname{tr}(H^{\beta} G^{\beta}_{\alpha} \Sigma^{\alpha\alpha} E[\partial^2 g^{\beta}_{ir}/\partial\alpha\partial\beta']),\\
a^{\beta}_{\alpha\alpha r} &= \operatorname{tr}(\Sigma^{\alpha\alpha} E[\partial^2 g^{\beta}_{ir}/\partial\alpha\partial\alpha'])/2, \quad (r = 1, \ldots, m_{\beta}).
\end{aligned}
$$

$$
\begin{aligned}
c^{\beta}_{\beta\beta r} &= \operatorname{tr}(E[\partial^2 g^{\beta'}_{i}/\partial\beta\partial\beta_r] P^{\beta} G^{\beta}_{\alpha} \Sigma^{\alpha\alpha} G^{\beta'}_{\alpha} H^{\beta'}),\\
c^{\beta}_{\beta\alpha r} &= -\operatorname{tr}(E[\partial^2 g^{\beta'}_{i}/\partial\alpha\partial\beta_r] P^{\beta} G^{\beta}_{\alpha} \Sigma^{\alpha\alpha}), \quad (r = 1, \ldots, p_{\beta}).
\end{aligned}
$$

B.6. Identical Samples

$$
\begin{aligned}
g^{\beta\cdot\alpha}_{i} &= g^{\beta}_{i} - G^{\beta}_{\alpha} H^{\alpha} g^{\alpha}_{i}, \quad (i = 1, \ldots, n_{\beta}),\\
\Omega^{\beta\beta\cdot\alpha\alpha} &= E[g^{\beta\cdot\alpha}_{i} g^{\beta\cdot\alpha'}_{i}], \quad \Omega^{\beta\beta\cdot\alpha} = E[g^{\beta}_{i} g^{\beta\cdot\alpha'}_{i}], \quad \Omega^{\alpha\beta\cdot\alpha} = E[g^{\alpha}_{i} g^{\beta\cdot\alpha'}_{i}]\\
a^{\beta}_{\beta\beta r} &= \operatorname{tr}(H^{\beta} \Omega^{\beta\beta\cdot\alpha\alpha} H^{\beta'} E[\partial^2 g^{\beta}_{ir}/\partial\beta\partial\beta'])/2,\\
a^{\beta}_{\beta\alpha r} &= \operatorname{tr}(H^{\alpha} \Omega^{\alpha\beta\cdot\alpha} H^{\beta'} E[\partial^2 g^{\beta}_{ir}/\partial\beta\partial\alpha']),\\
a^{\beta}_{\alpha\alpha r} &= \operatorname{tr}(\Sigma^{\alpha\alpha} E[\partial^2 g^{\beta}_{ir}/\partial\alpha\partial\alpha'])/2, \quad (r = 1, \ldots, m_{\beta}),\\
c^{\beta}_{\beta\beta r} &= \operatorname{tr}(H^{\beta} \Omega^{\beta\beta\cdot\alpha\alpha} P^{\beta} E[\partial^2 g^{\beta}_{i}/\partial\beta'\partial\beta_r]),\\
c^{\beta}_{\beta\alpha r} &= \operatorname{tr}(H^{\alpha} \Omega^{\alpha\beta\cdot\alpha} P^{\beta} E[\partial^2 g^{\beta}_{i}/\partial\alpha'\partial\beta_r]), \quad (r = 1, \ldots, p_{\beta}).
\end{aligned}
$$

ACKNOWLEDGMENTS

We are grateful for helpful comments and criticisms by the editor and two anonymous referees. The third author also appreciates the hospitality of the Cowles Foundation for Research in Economics, Yale University, and C.R.D.E, Département des Sciences Économiques, Université de Montréal, when the initial version was being prepared. The third author is grateful for financial support of this research from a 2002 Leverhulme Major Research Fellowship.

References

Altonji, J., and L. M. Segal (1996), "Small Sample Bias in GMM Estimation of Covariance Structures," *Journal of Economic and Business Statistics*, 14, 353–366.

Brown, B. W., and W. K. Newey (2002), "Generalized Method of Moments, Efficient Bootstrapping, and Improved Inference," *Journal of Business and Economic Statistics*, 20, 507–517.

Cressie, N., and T. Read (1984), "Multinomial Goodness-of-Fit Tests," *Journal of the Royal Statistical Society, Series B*, 46, 440–464.

Hall, P., and J. L. Horowitz (1996), "Bootstrap Critical Values for Tests Based on Generalized-Method-of-Moments Estimators," *Econometrica*, 50, 1029–1054.

Hansen, L. P. (1982), "Large Sample Properties of Generalized Method of Moments Estimators," *Econometrica*, 64, 891–916.

Hansen, L. P., J. Heaton, and A. Yaron (1996), "Finite-Sample Properties of Some Alternative GMM Estimators," *Journal of Business and Economic Statistics*, 14, 262–280.

Heckman, J. J. (1979), "Sample Selection Bias as a Specification Error," *Econometrica*, 47, 153–162.

Horowitz, J. L. (1998), "Bootstrap Methods for Covariance Structures," *Journal of Human Resources*, 33, 38–61.

Imbens, G. W. (1997), "One-Step Estimators for Over-Identified Generalized Method of Moments Models," *Review of Economic Studies*, 64, 359–383.

Imbens, G. W., R. H. Spady, and P. Johnson (1998), "Information Theorctic Approaches to Inference in Moment Condition Models," *Econometrica*, 66, 333–357.

Kitamura, Y., and M. Stutzer (1997), "An Information-Theoretic Alternative to Generalized Method of Moments Estimation," *Econometrica*, 65, 861–874.

Nagar, A. L. (1959), "The Bias and Moment Matrix of the General *k*-Class Estimators of the Parameters in Simultaneous Equations," *Econometrica*, 27, 573–595.

Newey, W. K., and R. J. Smith (2004), "Higher Order Properties of GMM and Generalized Empirical Likelihood Estimators," *Econometrica*, 72, 219–255.

Owen, A. (1988), "Empirical Likelihood Ratio Confidence Intervals for a Single Functional," *Biometrika*, 75, 237–249.

Pagan, A. (1984), "Econometric Issues in the Analysis of Regressions with Generated Regressors," *International Economic Review*, 25, 221–247.

Qin, J., and Lawless, J. (1994), "Empirical Likelihood and General Estimating Equations," *Annals of Statistics*, 22, 300–325.

Rothenberg, T. J. (1996), "Empirical Likelihood Parameter Estimation Under Moment Restrictions," seminar notes, Harvard/M.I.T. and University of Bristol.

Smith, R. J. (1997), "Alternative Semi-Parametric Likelihood Approaches to Generalized Method of Moments Estimation," *Economic Journal*, 107, 503–519.

Smith, R. J. (2001), "GEL Criteria for Moment Condition Models," mimeo, University of Bristol. Revision of paper presented at Cowles Foundation Econometrics Conference on New Developments in Time Series Econometrics, Yale University, 1999.

CHAPTER 12

Empirical Evidence Concerning the Finite Sample Performance of EL-Type Structural Equation Estimation and Inference Methods

Ron C. Mittelhammer, George G. Judge, and Ron Schoenberg

ABSTRACT

This paper presents empirical evidence concerning the finite sample performance of conventional and generalized empirical likelihood–type estimators that utilize instruments in the context of linear structural models characterized by endogenous explanatory variables. There are suggestions in the literature that traditional and nontraditional asymptotically efficient estimators based on moment equations may, for the relatively small sample sizes usually encountered in econometric practice, have relatively large biases and/or variances and provide an inadequate basis for estimation and inference. Given this uncertainty we use a range of data sampling processes and Monte Carlo sampling procedures to accumulate finite sample empirical evidence concerning these questions for a family of generalized empirical likelihood–type estimators in comparison to conventional 2SLS and GMM estimators. Solutions to EL-type empirical moment-constrained optimization problems present formidable numerical challenges. We identify effective optimization algorithms for meeting these challenges.

1. INTRODUCTION

It is known in the literature that a number of moment-based estimators for the linear structural model are asymptotically normally distributed and mutually asymptotically equivalent. There is also a growing body of evidence (see, for example, Newey and Smith 2004 and the references therein) that traditional asymptotically efficient moment-based estimators may exhibit large biases and/or variances when applied to the relatively small samples usually encountered in applied economic research.

Econometric models that specify a set of moment-orthogonality conditions relating to the underlying data sampling process, and involving parameters, data outcomes, and model noise, lead to a corresponding set of unbiased empirical estimating functions. These estimating functions often involve instrumental variables (IV), whose number exceeds the number of unknown parameters of interest and overdetermines the model parameters. In some instances the IV may be only moderately or weakly correlated with the endogenous variables in the model. In this situation it is generally recognized that significant bias and/or variability problems may arise and that large sample normal approximations may provide a poor basis for evaluating finite sample performance (see, for example, Nelson and Startz 1990, Maddala and Jeong, 1992, Bound, Jaeger, and Baker 1995, Stock and Wright 2000).

In an effort to avoid an explicit likelihood function specification, semi-parametric empirical likelihood (EL)-type estimators have been proposed as moment-based estimation and inference alternatives to classical maximum likelihood methods (Owen 1988, 1991, Qin and Lawless 1994, Imbens, Spady, and Johnson 1998, Corcoran 2000, Mittelhammer, Judge, and Miller 2000). Given this new class of estimators, and in line with the ongoing search for efficient linear structural equation estimators having small finite sample bias, and associated inference procedures with accurate size, good power, and short confidence intervals with proper coverage, we provide some empirical evidence relating to the finite sample performance of a trio of EL-type estimators when estimating functions overdetermine the model parameters and parameters are moderately well-identified. The results are based on Monte Carlo sampling experiments applied to a range of underlying data sampling processes and to estimators that include the optimal estimating function (OptEF) and two stage least squares (2SLS) estimator, the generalized method of moments (GMM) estimator based on an identity weight matrix, as well as the EL, exponential empirical likelihood (EEL), and log Euclidean likelihood (LEL) estimators. As noted by Imbens et al. (1998), the computation of solutions to EL-type moment-constrained optimization problems can present formidable numerical challenges. From both a theoretical and a practical standpoint, reliable and efficient solution algorithms are critically needed. Toward this end, we suggest an algorithm that performs well.

In the context of finite sample situations where the IV are moderately well-correlated with the endogenous variables in question and the orthogonality condition between the IV and the structural equation noise holds, we seek information relative to the following questions:

(i) Do EL-type estimators offer reductions in either small sample bias or variance relative to traditional OptEF-2SLS and non-optimal GMM estimators?

(ii) In terms of a mean square measure of estimator performance, are any of the EL-type estimators superior to the traditional semiparametric estimators?

(iii) In terms of inference in small samples, do EL-type testing procedures have, relative to traditional testing procedures, more accurate coverage, shorter confidence intervals, and/or test sizes that are closer to nominal target size?

(iv) What is the relative small sample performance of the traditional and EL-type inference procedures relative to testing the moment restrictions?

(v) What is the basis for a reliable and efficient solution algorithm for EL-type moment-constrained estimation problems?

The format of this chapter is as follows: In Section 2 the linear structural model is defined and the competing semiparametric estimators and inference procedures are specified. In Section 3 the design of the sampling experiment is presented and the alternative data sampling processes are defined. Monte Carlo estimation results are presented and discussed in Section 4. Conclusions, implications, and speculations are presented in Section 5.

2. STATISTICAL MODELS, ESTIMATORS, AND INFERENCE PROCEDURES

Consider a single structural equation that is contained within a system of structural equations and that has the semiparametric linear statistical model form $\mathbf{Y} = \mathbf{X}\beta + \varepsilon$. We observe a vector of sample outcomes $\mathbf{y} = (y_1, y_2, \ldots, y_n)'$ associated with this linear model, where $\mathbf{X}$ is a $(n \times k)$ matrix of stochastic explanatory variables, ε is an unobservable random noise vector with mean vector $\mathbf{0}$ and covariance matrix $\sigma^2\mathbf{I}_n$, and $\beta \in \mathbf{B}$ is a $(k \times 1)$ vector of unknown parameters. If one or more of the regressors is correlated with the equation noise, then $E[n^{-1}\mathbf{X}'\varepsilon] \neq \mathbf{0}$ or $\text{plim}[n^{-1}\mathbf{X}'\varepsilon] \neq \mathbf{0}$ and traditional Gauss–Markov based procedures such as the least squares (LS) estimator, or equivalently the method of moments (MOM)-extremum estimator defined by $\hat{\beta}_{\text{mom}} = \arg_{\beta\in\mathbf{B}}[n^{-1}\mathbf{X}'(\mathbf{Y} - \mathbf{X}\beta) = \mathbf{0}]$, are biased and inconsistent, with unconditional expectation and probability limit given by $E[\hat{\beta}] \neq \beta$ and $p\text{lim}[\hat{\beta}] \neq \beta$.

2.1. Traditional Instrument-Based Estimators

Given a sampling process characterized by nonorthogonality of $\mathbf{X}$ and ε, in order to avoid the use of strong distributional assumptions it is conventional to introduce additional information in the form of a $(n \times m)$, $m \geq k$, random matrix $\mathbf{Z}$ of instrumental variables whose elements are correlated with $\mathbf{X}$ but uncorrelated with ε. This information is introduced into the statistical model by specifying the sample analog moment condition

$$\mathbf{h}(\mathbf{Y}, \mathbf{X}, \mathbf{Z}; \beta) = n^{-1}[\mathbf{Z}'(\mathbf{Y} - \mathbf{X}\beta)] \xrightarrow{p} \mathbf{0}, \tag{2.1}$$

relating to the underlying population moment condition derived from the orthogonality of instruments and model noise defined by

$$E\left[\mathbf{Z}'(\mathbf{Y} - \mathbf{X}\beta)\right] = \mathbf{0}. \tag{2.2}$$

If $m = k$, the vector of moment conditions just determine the model parameters, and the sample moments (2.1) can be solved for the basic IV estimator $\hat{\beta}_{iv} = (\mathbf{Z}'\mathbf{X})^{-1}\mathbf{Z}'\mathbf{Y}$. When the usual regularity conditions are fulfilled, this IV estimator is consistent, asymptotically normal distributed, and is an optimal estimating function (OptEF) estimator (Godambe 1960, Heyde 1989, Mittelhammer et al. 2000).

For $m > k$, the vector of moment conditions overdetermine the model parameters and other IV-like estimation procedures are available, such as the well-known two stage least squares (2SLS) estimator, $\beta_{2sls} = (\mathbf{X}'\mathbf{P_z X})^{-1}\mathbf{X}'\mathbf{P_z Y}$, where $\mathbf{P_z} = \mathbf{Z}(\mathbf{Z}'\mathbf{Z})^{-1}\mathbf{Z}'$ is the projection matrix for $\mathbf{Z}$. This estimator is equivalent to the estimator formed by applying the OptEF transformation $n(\mathbf{X}'\mathbf{Z}(\mathbf{Z}'\mathbf{Z})^{-1}\mathbf{Z}'\mathbf{X})^{-1}\mathbf{X}'\mathbf{Z}(\mathbf{Z}'\mathbf{Z})^{-1}$ to the moment conditions in (2.2) (Godambe 1960, Judge et al. 1985, Heyde and Morton 1998).

The GMM estimator (Hansen 1982) is another estimator that makes use of the information in (2.2). The GMM estimators minimize a quadratic form in the sample moment information

$$\begin{aligned}\hat{\beta}(\mathbf{W}) &= \arg \min_{\beta \in \mathrm{B}} [Q_n(\beta)] \\ &= \arg \min_{\beta \in \mathrm{B}} \left[\left(n^{-1}\mathbf{Z}'(\mathbf{Y}-\mathbf{X}\beta)\right)' \mathbf{W} \left(n^{-1}\mathbf{Z}'(\mathbf{Y}-\mathbf{X}\beta)\right)\right] \qquad (2.3)\\ &= \arg \min_{\beta \in \mathrm{B}} \left[n^{-2}(\mathbf{Y}-\mathbf{X}\beta)'\mathbf{ZWZ}'(\mathbf{Y}-\mathbf{X}\beta)\right].\end{aligned}$$

The GMM estimator can be shown to have optimal asymptotic properties if the weighting matrix $\mathbf{W}$ is appropriately defined. The optimal choice of $\mathbf{W}$ in the context of moment conditions (2.2) leads back to the definition of the 2SLS-OptEF estimator.

2.2. Empirical Likelihood–Type Estimators

In contrast to traditional instrument moment–based estimators, the EL approach (Owen 1988, 1991, 2001, Qin and Lawless 1994, Imbens et al. 1998, Corcoran 2000, Mittelhammer et al. 2000) allows the investigator to employ likelihood methods for model estimation and inference without having to choose a specific parametric family of probability densities on which to base the likelihood function. Under the EL concept, empirical likelihood weights supported on a sample of observed data outcomes are used to reduce the infinite dimensional problem of nonparametric likelihood estimation to a finite dimensional one.

2.2.1. Estimation

The constrained estimation problem underlying the EL approach is in many ways analogous to allocating probabilities in a contingency table where w_j and q_j are observed and expected probabilities. A solution is achieved by minimizing the divergence between the two sets of probabilities by optimizing a goodness-of-fit criterion subject to the moment constraints. One possible set of divergence measures is the power divergence family of statistics (Cressie and Read 1984, Read and Cressie 1988)

$$I(\mathbf{w}, \mathbf{q}, \lambda) = \frac{2}{\lambda(\lambda+1)} \sum_{i=1}^{n} w_i \left[\left(\frac{w_i}{q_i}\right)^{\lambda} - 1\right], \qquad (2.4)$$

where λ is an arbitrary unspecified parameter. In the limit as λ ranges from -1 to 1, several estimation and inference procedures emerge.

If in an instrumental variable context for the linear structural equation we use (2.4) as the goodness-of-fit criterion and (2.1) as the moment-estimating function information, the EL estimation problem can be formulated as the following extremum-type estimator:

$$\hat{\beta} = \arg\max_{\beta} \left[\ell_E(\beta) = \max_{w} \left\{ -I(\mathbf{w}, \mathbf{q}, \lambda) | \sum_{i=1}^{n} w_i \mathbf{z}'_{i.} (y_i - \mathbf{x}_{i.}\beta) = \mathbf{0}, \right.\right.$$
$$\left.\left. \sum_{i=1}^{n} w_i = 1, w_i \geq 0 \,\forall i, \beta \in \mathbf{B} \right\} \right]. \tag{2.5}$$

Three main variants of $I(\mathbf{w}, \mathbf{q}, \lambda)$ have received explicit attention in the literature. Letting $\lambda \to -1$ leads to the traditional empirical log-likelihood objective function, $n^{-1} \sum_{i=1}^{n} \ln(w_i)$ and the maximum empirical likelihood (MEL) estimate of β. When $\lambda \to 0$, the empirical exponential likelihood objective function $-\sum_{i=1}^{n} w_i \ln(w_i)$ is defined and the maximum empirical exponential likelihood (MEEL) estimate of β results. Finally, when $\lambda = 1$, the log Euclidean likelihood function $-n^{-1}\left(\sum_{i=1}^{n} (n^2 w_i^2 - 1)\right)$ is implied and leads to the maximum log euclidean likelihood (MLEL) estimate of β.

In the sense of objective function analogies, the Owen MEL approach is the closest to the classical maximum likelihood approach. The MEEL criterion of maximizing $-\sum_{i=1}^{n} w_i \ln(w_i)$ is equivalent to defining an estimator by *minimizing* the Kullback–Leibler (KL) information criterion $\sum_{i=1}^{n} w_i \ln(w_i/n^{-1})$ (Kullback 1959, Golan, Judge, and Miller 1996). Interpreted in the KL context, the MEEL estimation objective finds the feasible weights $\hat{\mathbf{w}}$ that define the minimum value of all possible expected log-likelihood ratios consistent with the structural moment constraints. The MLEL solution seeks feasible weights $\hat{\mathbf{w}}$ that minimize the Euclidean distance of $\mathbf{w}$ from the uniform probability distribution, the square of this Euclidean distance being $(\mathbf{w} - \mathbf{1}_n n^{-1})'(\mathbf{w} - 1_n n^{-1})$, where $\mathbf{1}_n$ denotes an $n \times 1$ vector of unit values. All of the preceding estimation objective functions achieve *unconstrained* (by moment constraints) optima when the empirical probability distribution is given by $\mathbf{w} = \mathbf{1}_n n^{-1}$.

If the optimization problem is cast in Lagrangian form, where α and η are Lagrange multipliers for the moment and adding up conditions, respectively, then the constrained optimal $w_i's$ for the MEL estimator can be expressed as

$$w_i(\beta, \alpha) = \left[n\left(\alpha' \mathbf{z}'_{i.}(y_i - \mathbf{x}_{i.}\beta) + 1\right)\right]^{-1}, \tag{2.6}$$

and the constrained optimal w_i's for the MEEL estimator can be expressed as

$$w_i(\beta, \alpha) = \frac{\exp\left(\alpha' \mathbf{z}'_{i.}(y_i - \mathbf{x}_{i.}\beta)\right)}{\sum_{j=1}^{n} \exp\left(\alpha' \mathbf{z}'_{j.}(y_j - \mathbf{x}_{j.}\beta)\right)}. \tag{2.7}$$

In the case of the MLEL estimator, the constrained optimal w_i's can be expressed as $w_i(\beta, \alpha, \eta) = (2n)^{-1}(\alpha' \mathbf{z}'_{i.}(y_i - \mathbf{x}_{i.}\beta) + \eta)$. The Lagrange multiplier η can be eliminated by solving the adding up condition $\mathbf{1}_n'\mathbf{w}(\boldsymbol{\beta}, \boldsymbol{\alpha}, \eta) = 1$ for η, yielding the expression $\eta(\alpha, \beta) = \left(2 - n^{-1}\sum_{i=1}^{n} \boldsymbol{\alpha}'\mathbf{z}_{i.}'(y_i - \mathbf{x}_{i.}\boldsymbol{\beta})\right)$, and then substitution into $w_i(\boldsymbol{\beta}, \boldsymbol{\alpha}, \eta)$ yields

$$w_i(\boldsymbol{\beta}, \boldsymbol{\alpha}) = (2n)^{-1}\left(\boldsymbol{\alpha}'\mathbf{z}_{i.}'(y_i - \mathbf{x}_{i.}\boldsymbol{\beta}) + 2 - n^{-1}\sum_{i=1}^{n} \boldsymbol{\alpha}'\mathbf{z}_{i.}'(y_i - \mathbf{x}_{i.}\boldsymbol{\beta})\right). \tag{2.8}$$

Under the usual regularity conditions assumed when establishing the asymptotics of traditional structural equation estimators, all of the preceding EL-type estimators of β obtained by optimizing the w_i's in (2.6), (2.7), or (2.8) with respect to β, α, and/or η are, *given the set of estimating equations under consideration,* consistent, asymptotically normally distributed, and asymptotically efficient relative to the OptEF estimator. Calculating the solution to the MEL, MEEL, or MLEL estimation problem will generally require that a computer-driven optimization algorithm be employed. When $m = k$, the solutions to all of the EL-type extremum problems lead back to the standard IV estimator $\hat{\beta}_{iv}$ with $w_i = n^{-1}$. When $m \geq k$, the estimating equations overdetermine the unknown parameter values to be recovered and a nontrivial EL solution results. The solution to the constrained optimization problem (2.5) based on any of the members of the Cressie–Read family of estimation objective functions yields an optimal estimate, $\hat{\mathbf{w}}$ and $\hat{\beta}$, that cannot, in general, be expressed in closed form and thus must be obtained using numerical methods.

2.2.2. *Inference*

EL-type inference methods, including hypothesis testing and confidence region estimation, bear a strong analogy to inference methods used in traditional ML and GMM approaches. Owen (1988, 1991) showed that an analog of Wilks' Theorem for likelihood ratios, $-2\ \ln(\mathrm{LR}) \overset{a}{\sim} \chi_j^2$, hold for the MEL approach, where j denotes the number of functionally independent restrictions on the parameter space. Baggerly (1998) demonstrated that this calibration remains applicable when the likelihood is replaced with any properly scaled member of the Cressie–Read family of power divergence statistics (2.4). In this context, the empirical likelihood ratio (LR) for testing the linear hypothesis $\mathbf{c}\beta = \mathbf{r}$, when *rank* $(\mathbf{c}) = j$, is given for the MEL case by

$$\mathrm{LR}_{\mathrm{EL}}(\mathbf{y}) = \frac{\max_\beta\left[\ell_E(\boldsymbol{\beta})\ \text{s.t.}\ \mathbf{c}\beta = \mathbf{r}\right]}{\max_\beta \ell_E(\boldsymbol{\beta})} \tag{2.9}$$

where $-2\ln(\mathrm{LR}_{\mathrm{EL}}(\mathbf{Y})) \overset{a}{\sim} \chi^2(j, 0)$ under H_0 when $m \geq k$. An analogous pseudo-LR approach can be applied, mutatis mutandis, to other members of the Cressie–Read family. One can also base tests of $\mathbf{c}\beta = \mathbf{r}$ on the Wald Criterion in the usual way by utilizing the inverse of the asymptotic covariance matrix of $\mathbf{c}\hat{\beta}_{\mathrm{EL}}$ as the weight matrix of a quadratic form in the vector $\mathbf{c}\hat{\beta}_{\mathrm{EL}} - \mathbf{r}$, or construct tests based on the Lagrange multipliers associated with the constraints $\mathbf{c}\beta = \mathbf{r}$ imposed on the EL-type optimization problem. Confidence region estimates can be obtained from hypothesis test outcomes in the usual way based on duality. The validity of the moment conditions (2.1)–(2.2) can be assessed via a variation of the preceding testing methodology. We provide further details later regarding the empirical implementation of inference methods.

2.3. Test Statistics

Two different types of inference contexts are examined in this paper: testing the validity of the moment constraints, and testing hypotheses and generating confidence intervals for parameters of the structural model.

2.3.1. *Moment Validity Tests*

Regarding the validity of the moment restrictions, Wald-type quadratic form tests, often referred to as average moment tests, are calculated for all five estimators. The Wald test statistics are specified as

$$\begin{aligned}\text{Wald} &= (\mathbf{1}_n'(\mathbf{Z} \odot (\mathbf{Y} - \mathbf{X}\hat{\beta})))'\left[(\mathbf{Z} \odot (\mathbf{Y} - \mathbf{X}\hat{\beta}))'(\mathbf{Z} \odot (\mathbf{Y} - \mathbf{X}\hat{\beta}))\right]^{-1} \\ &\quad \times (\mathbf{1}_n'(\mathbf{Z} \odot (\mathbf{Y} - \mathbf{X}\hat{\beta}))) \qquad (2.10)\end{aligned}$$

where $\hat{\beta}$ is any one of the five different estimators of the β vector and $\odot$ denotes the *generalized* Hadamard (elementwise) product operator. Under the null hypothesis of moment validity, the Wald statistic has an asymptotic chi square distribution with degrees of freedom equal to the degree of overidentification of the parameter vector, that is, $m - k$.

Pseudo-LR–type tests of moment validity, referred to as criterion function tests by Imbens et al. (1998, p. 342), are also calculated for the three EL-type procedures. The respective test statistics for the MEEL and MEL procedures are $\text{LR}_{\text{EEL}} = 2n(\mathbf{w}' \ln(\mathbf{w}) + \ln(n))$ and $\text{LR}_{\text{EL}} = -2(\mathbf{1}_n' \ln(\mathbf{w}) + n \ln(n))$.

In the case of MLEL, the pseudo-LR statistic is derived as a special case of the generalized empirical likelihood (GEL) class of procedures identified by Newey and Smith (2004, p. 8) given by

$$\begin{aligned}\text{LR}_{\text{LEL}} &= n\left(1 - n^{-1}\mathbf{1}_{\text{n}}'\left[(\mathbf{Z} \odot (\mathbf{Y} - \mathbf{X}\beta))\left(\frac{\alpha}{\eta}\right)\right]^2\right) \\ &= n\left(1 - \left(\frac{2}{\eta}\right)^2 n \sum_{i=1}^{n} w_i^2\right). \qquad (2.11)\end{aligned}$$

Since $\text{LR}_{\text{LEL}} \equiv \text{Wald}_{\text{LEL}}$, we later report on the performance of only one version of this particular test. The $\mathbf{w}$ weights, β vector, and Lagrange multipliers α and η appearing in the LR test statistics are replaced by the respective EL-type estimates. All of the pseudo-LR–type test statistics follow the same asymptotic chi square distribution as for the Wald statistics of moment validity.

The final set of moment validity tests are based on the Lagrange multipliers of the moment constraints. In the case of the EEL-type test statistic, we examine the following quadratic form in the Lagrange multiplier vector that incorporates a robust estimator of the covariance matrix of the moment constraints,

$$\begin{aligned} \mathrm{LM}_{\mathrm{EEL}} &= n\alpha' \left[(\mathbf{h}(\beta) \odot \mathbf{w})' \mathbf{h}(\beta)\right] \left[(\mathbf{h}(\beta) \odot \mathbf{w})' (\mathbf{h}(\beta) \odot \mathbf{w})\right]^{-1} \\ &\quad \times \left[(\mathbf{h}(\beta) \odot \mathbf{w})' \mathbf{h}(\beta)\right] \alpha \end{aligned} \tag{2.12}$$

where $\mathbf{h}(\beta) \equiv (\mathbf{Z} \odot (\mathbf{Y} - \mathbf{X}\beta))$ and $\mathbf{w}$, α, and β are estimated on the basis of the MEEL method. In the case of the MEL and MLEL methods, we instead utilize LM tests that are based on equivalences with GEL tests implied by the asymptotic results of Newey and Smith (2004, p. 8). Both of these LM tests are based on the statistic

$$\mathrm{LM} = n\alpha' \left(\Omega^{-1} - \Omega^{-1}\mathbf{G}'\mathbf{V}\mathbf{G}\Omega^{-1}\right)^{-} \alpha \tag{2.13}$$

where $\Omega \equiv n^{-1}(\mathbf{Z} \odot (\mathbf{Y} - \mathbf{X}\beta))'(\mathbf{Z} \odot (\mathbf{Y} - \mathbf{X}\beta))$, $\mathbf{G} \equiv n^{-1}\mathbf{X}'\mathbf{Z}$, $\mathbf{V} \equiv (\mathbf{G}\Omega^{-1}\mathbf{G}')^{-1}$, and the values of β and α are replaced by either MEEL or MLEL estimates. Under the null hypothesis, all of the LM tests are asymptotically chi square distributed with degrees of freedom equal to $m - k$.

2.3.2. *Tests of Parameter Restrictions*

A test of the significance of the parameters of the structural model is conducted based on the usual asymptotic normally distributed Z-statistic and concomitantly, by duality, the accuracy of confidence region coverage of the parameters is examined. The test statistic for all of the estimation procedures examined has the familiar form

$$Z = \frac{\hat{\beta}_i}{\widehat{\mathrm{std}}(\hat{\beta}_i)} \overset{a}{\sim} N(0, 1) \quad \text{under} \quad H_0 : \beta_i = 0, \tag{2.14}$$

and the associated confidence interval estimate is $(\hat{\beta}_i - z_\tau \widehat{\mathrm{std}}(\hat{\beta}_i), \hat{\beta}_i + z_\tau \widehat{\mathrm{std}}(\hat{\beta}_i))$ where z_τ denotes the $100\tau\%$ quantile of the standard normal distribution. In (2.14) $\hat{\beta}_i$ and $\widehat{\mathrm{std}}(\hat{\beta}_i)$ are the appropriate estimates of the parameter and the estimated standard error of the estimate based on one of the five alternative estimation procedures. The respective estimates of the standard errors used in the test and confidence interval procedures were obtained as the square roots of the appropriate diagonal elements of the asymptotic covariance matrices of the B2SLS-OptEF, GMM(I), and the EL-type estimators defined respectively as

$$AsyCov\left(\hat{\mathbf{B}}_{2\mathrm{sls}}\right) = \hat{\sigma}^2 \left(\mathbf{X}'\mathbf{Z}(\mathbf{Z}'\mathbf{Z})^{-1}\mathbf{Z}'\mathbf{X}\right)^{-1}, \tag{2.15}$$

$$AsyCov\left(\hat{\mathbf{B}}_{\mathrm{GMM(I)}}\right) = \hat{\sigma}^2(\mathbf{X}'\mathbf{Z}\mathbf{Z}'\mathbf{X})^{-1}(\mathbf{X}'\mathbf{Z}(\mathbf{Z}'\mathbf{Z})\mathbf{Z}'\mathbf{X})(\mathbf{X}'\mathbf{Z}\mathbf{Z}'\mathbf{X})^{-1}, \tag{2.16}$$

and

$$AsyCov(\hat{\mathbf{B}}_{\text{EL-type}})$$
$$= \left[(\mathbf{X}'(\mathbf{Z} \odot \hat{\mathbf{w}}))\left[((\mathbf{Z} \odot (\mathbf{Y} - \mathbf{X}\hat{\mathbf{B}})) \odot \hat{\mathbf{w}})'((\mathbf{Z} \odot (\mathbf{Y} - \mathbf{X}\hat{\mathbf{B}})) \odot \hat{\mathbf{w}})\right]^{-1}\right.$$
$$\left. \times ((\mathbf{Z} \odot \hat{\mathbf{w}})'\mathbf{X})\right]^{-1}, \tag{2.17}$$

where $\hat{\sigma}^2$ is the usual consistent estimate of the equation noise variance, and $\hat{\mathbf{w}}$ and $\hat{\mathbf{B}}$ are the appropriate estimates obtained from applications of the MEEL, MEL, or MLEL estimation procedure.

2.4. Computational Issues and Approach

As noted by Imbens et al. (1998), the computation of solutions to EL-type constrained optimization problems can present formidable numerical challenges. This results because, in the neighborhood of the solution to such problems, the gradient matrix associated with the moment constraints will approach an ill-conditioned state. This occurs by design in these types of problems because the fundamental method by which EL-type methods resolve the overdetermined nature of the empirical moment conditions, $\sum_{i=1}^{n} w_i \mathbf{z}'_{i.}(y_i - \mathbf{x}_{i.}\beta) = 0$, is to choose sample weights that ultimately transform the m moment equations into a functionally dependent, lower rank $(k < m)$ system of equations capable of being solved uniquely for the parameters. This creates instability in gradient-based constrained optimization algorithms regarding the representation of the feasible spaces and feasible directions for such problems. Moreover, attempting to solve the optimization problems in primal form is complicated by the dimensionality of the problem, where there are as many w_i sample weights as there are sample observations, and requires that explicit constrained optimization methods be used to enforce the moment conditions and the convexity properties of the sample weights.

Given these complications, Imbens et al. (1998) found it advantageous in their EEL and EL simulations to utilize a dual penalty function method for enforcing the moment constraints, whereby a penalty-augmented objective function is optimized within the context of an unconstrained optimization problem. Although their penalty-function approach appeared to perform well for the range of applications that were examined in their work, the algorithm failed (nonconvergence) too frequently when applied to the IV-based moment constrained problems examined in this chapter.

The computational approach utilized in this work for solving the EL-type problems consisted of concentrating out the Lagrange multiplier vector and scalar, α and η, from the EL-type optimization problems, expressing α and η as a function of the β vector (in the case of MEEL and MEL, the optimal η is simply the scalar 1). The actual process of concentrating out the Lagrange multipliers cannot be accomplished in closed form, requiring a numerical nonlinear equation solving procedure, but solving the system of equations proved to be quite stable and efficient. Then the resulting concentrated Lagrange representations of the EL-type estimation problems were optimized with respect to the choice of β, leading to the parameter estimates.

More specifically, in the first step of the computational procedure the Lagrange multiplier vector α was expressed as a function of β by utilizing the empirical moment conditions and the weight representation (2.6)–(2.8) for the vector $\mathbf{w}(\beta, \alpha)$ as

$$\alpha(\beta) \equiv \arg_{\alpha}\left[(\mathbf{Z} \odot (\mathbf{Y} - \mathbf{X}\beta))' \mathbf{w}(\beta, \alpha) = \mathbf{0}\right]. \tag{2.18}$$

The solution to (2.18) was determined numerically using the NLSYS nonlinear equation solver in the GAUSS mathematical programming language (Aptech Systems, Maple Valley, Washington, Version 3.6). Regarding the Lagrange multiplier η, the first-order conditions for either the MEL or MEEL estimation problems imply that $\eta(\beta) \equiv 1$. In the case of the MLEL problem, $\eta(\beta)$ can be defined by substituting the value of $\alpha(\beta)$ obtained from (2.18) into the definition of $\eta(\alpha, \beta)$ that precedes (2.8), yielding

$$\eta(\beta) \equiv \left(2 - n^{-1} \sum_{i=1}^{n} \alpha(\beta)' \mathbf{z}_{i.}' (y_i - \mathbf{x}_{i.}\beta)\right). \tag{2.19}$$

In the second step relating to optimization, the concentrated Lagrange function can be represented as

$$\begin{aligned} L_*(\beta) &\equiv L(\mathbf{w}(\beta, \alpha(\beta)), \beta, \alpha(\beta), \eta(\beta)) \\ &\equiv \phi(\mathbf{w}(\beta, \alpha(\beta))) - \alpha(\beta)' \sum_{i=1}^{n} w_i(\beta, \alpha(\beta))\, \mathbf{z}_{i.}' (y_i - \mathbf{x}_{i.}\beta) \\ &\quad - \eta(\beta)\left(\sum_{i=1}^{n} w_i(\beta, \alpha(\beta)) - 1\right). \end{aligned} \tag{2.20}$$

The value of $L_*(\beta)$ is then optimized (maximized for MEL, minimized for MEEL and MLEL) with respect to the choice of β, where $\phi(\cdot)$ can also denote any of the estimation objective functions in the Cressie–Read family. The algorithm used to accomplish the optimization step was based on a Nelder–Meade polytope-type direct search procedure written by the authors and implemented in the GAUSS programming language (Nelder and Mead 1965, Jacoby, Kowalik, and Pizzo 1972, Bertsekas 1995) using the values 0.5, 0.5, and 1.1, respectively, for the reflection, contraction, and expansion coefficients. The Nelder–Meade approach is especially well-suited for this problem because it requires that only the function itself be evaluated at trial values of the β vector, and does not require calculation of the numerical derivatives of the first or second order used by gradient-based search algorithms, which were inaccurate and unstable in the current context.

3. DESIGN OF SAMPLING EXPERIMENTS

The finite sample properties of the EL-type estimators and associated inference procedures delineated in Section 2 cannot be derived from a direct evaluation of closed functional forms applied to distributions of random variables. Moreover, the finite sample probability distributions of the traditional 2SLS and GMM estimators are also generally intractable. Consequently, we use Monte Carlo sampling experiments to examine and compare the finite sample performance of competing estimators and inference methods. Although these results are specific to the collection of particular Monte Carlo experiments analyzed, the wide ranging sampling evidence reported does provide an indication of the types of relative performance that can occur over a range of scenarios for which the unknown parameters of a model are moderately well-identified.

3.1. Experimental Sampling Design

Consider a data sampling process of the following form:

$$Y_{i1} = Z_{i1}\beta_1 + Y_{i2}\beta_2 + e_i = \mathbf{X}_{i.}\boldsymbol{\beta} + \varepsilon_i \tag{3.1}$$

$$Y_{i2} = \sum_{j=1}^{5} \pi_j Z_{ij} + v_i = \mathbf{Z}_{i.}\pi + v_i \tag{3.2}$$

where $\mathbf{X}_{i.} = (Z_{i1}, Y_{i2})$ and $i = 1, 2, \ldots, n$. In the sampling experiment, the two-dimensional vector of unknown parameters, $\boldsymbol{\beta}$, in (3.1) is arbitrarily set equal to the vector $[-1, 2]'$. The outcomes of the (6×1) random vector $[Y_{i2}, \varepsilon_i, Z_{i1}, Z_{i2}, Z_{i3}, Z_{i4}]$ are generated i.i.d. from a multivariate normal distribution with a zero mean vector and standard deviations uniformly set to 5 for the first two random variables and 2 for the remaining random variables, and $Z_{i5} \equiv 1, \forall i$. Also various other conditions relating to the correlations among the six scalar random variables were assumed. The values of the π_j's in (3.2) are determined by the regression function between Y_{i2} and $[Z_{i1}, Z_{i2}, Z_{i3}, Z_{i4}, Z_{i5}]$, which is itself a function of the covariance specification relating to the marginal normal distribution associated with the (5×1) random vector $[Y_{i2,} Z_{i1}, Z_{i2}, Z_{i3}, Z_{i4}]$. Thus the π_j's generally change as the scenario postulated for the correlation matrix of the sampling process changes. In this sampling design, the outcomes of $[Y_{i1}, V_i]$ are then calculated by applying the equations (3.1 and 3.2) to the outcomes of $[Y_{i2}, Z_{i1}, Z_{i2}, Z_{i3}, Z_{i4}, Z_{i5}]$.

3.2. Sample Characteristics and Outcome Basis

Regarding the details of the sampling scenarios simulated for these Monte Carlo experiments, sample sizes of $n = 50$, 100, and 250 were examined. The outcomes of ε_i were generated independently of the vector $[Z_{i1}, Z_{i2}, Z_{i3}, Z_{i4}]$ so that the

Table 12.1. *Monte Carlo experiment definitions, with* $\beta = [-1, 2]'$, $\sigma_{\varepsilon_i} = \sigma_{Y_{2i}} = 5$, *and* $\sigma_{Z_{ij}} = 2, \forall i$ *and* $j = 1, \ldots, 5$

Experiment number	$\rho_{y_{2i},\varepsilon_i}$	$\rho_{y_{2i},z_{i,1}}$	$\rho_{y_{2i},z_{ij}}\ ;\ j>1$	$\rho_{z_{ij},z_{ik}}$	$R^2_{Y_1,\hat{Y}_1}$	$R^2_{Y_2,\hat{Y}_2}$
1	0.25	0.25	0.25	0	0.84	0.25
2	0.25	−0.25	0.25	0.5	0.86	0.40
3	0.50	0.25	0.25	0	0.89	0.25
4	0.50	−0.25	0.25	0.5	0.90	0.40
5	0.75	0.25	0.25	0	0.95	0.25
6	0.75	−0.25	0.25	0.5	0.94	0.40
7	0.50	0.1	0.5	0.25	0.89	0.53
8	0.50	0.1	0.5	0.5	0.89	0.50
9	0.50	0.1	0.5	0.75	0.89	0.68
10	0.50	0.5	0.1	0.75	0.89	0.53

Note: $\rho_{y_{2i},\varepsilon_i}$ denotes the correlation between Y_{2i} and e_i and measures the degree of nonorthogonality; $\rho_{y_{2i},z_{ij}}$ denotes the common correlation between Y_{2i} and each of the four random instrumental variables, the Z_{ij}'s; $\rho_{z_{ij},z_{ik}}$ denotes the common correlation between the four random instrumental variables; $R^2_{Y_1,\hat{Y}_1}$ denotes the population squared correlation between $\mathbf{Y}_1$ and $\hat{\mathbf{Y}}_1 = \mathbf{X}\beta$; and $R^2_{Y_2,\hat{Y}_2}$ denotes the population squared correlation between $\mathbf{Y}_2$ and $\hat{\mathbf{Y}}_2 = \mathbf{Z}\pi$.

correlations between ε_i and the $Z'_{ij}s$ were zero, thus fulfilling a fundamental condition for $[Z_{i1}, Z_{i2}, Z_{i3}, Z_{i4}]$ to be considered a set of valid instrumental variables for estimating the unknown parameters in (3.1). Regarding the degree of nonorthogonality and identifiability in (3.1), correlations of 0.25, 0.50, and 0.75 between the random variables Y_{i2} and ε_i were utilized to simulate moderately to relatively strongly correlated nonorthogonality relationships between the explanatory variable Y_{i2} and the equation noise ε_i.

For each sample size, alternative scenarios were examined relating to both the degree of correlation existing between each of the random instruments in the matrix $\mathbf{Z}$ and the $\mathbf{Y}_2$ variable, and the levels of collinearity existing among the instrumental variables themselves. By varying the degrees of intercorrelation among the variables, the overall correlation of the instrumental variables with $\mathbf{Y}_2$ is effected and contributes to determining the overall effectiveness of the set of instruments in predicting values of the endogenous $\mathbf{Y}_2$. The joint correlation between $\mathbf{Y}_2$ and the set of instruments range from a relatively low 0.25 to a relatively strong 0.68.

The major characteristics of each sampling scenario are delineated in Table 12.1. In general, the scenarios range from relatively weak but independent instruments to stronger but more highly multicollinear instruments. All models have a relatively strong signal component in the sense that the squared correlation between the dependent variable $\mathbf{Y}_1$ and the explanatory variables $(\mathbf{Z}_{.1}, \mathbf{Y}_2)$ ranges between 0.84 and 0.95. In total there are 10 different MC experimental designs in combination with the 3 different sample sizes, resulting in 30 different sampling scenarios in which to observe estimator and inference behavior.

The sampling results, reported in Section 4, are based on 5,000 Monte Carlo repetitions, which was sufficient to produce stable estimates of the empirical mean squared error (MSE), expressed in terms of the mean of the empirical squared Euclidean distance between the true parameter vector $\boldsymbol{\beta}$ and $\hat{\boldsymbol{\beta}}$ (measuring parameter estimation risk), the MSE between $\mathbf{y}$ with $\hat{\mathbf{y}}$ (measuring predictive risk), the average estimated bias in the estimates, Bias $(\hat{\boldsymbol{\beta}}) = E[\hat{\boldsymbol{\beta}}] - \boldsymbol{\beta}$, and the average estimated variances, $\text{Var}(\hat{\beta}_i)$.

Regarding inference performance, we (i) compare the empirical size of 10 alternative tests of moment equation validity with the typical nominal target size of 0.05, (ii) examine the empirical coverage probability of confidence interval estimators based on a target coverage probability of 0.99, (iii) compare the empirical expected lengths of confidence intervals, and (iv) examine power of significance tests associated with the different estimation methods.

4. MONTE CARLO SAMPLING RESULTS

The results of the estimation and inference simulations are presented in this section. We report MSE results for the entire parameter vector β, but limit our reporting of bias, variance, hypothesis tests, and confidence region estimation performance to the structural parameter β_2 and note that the results for the remaining structural parameter were qualitatively similar. (Tables containing the detailed simulation results are available from the authors.)

4.1. Estimator MSE Performance

The simulated mean squared errors associated with estimating the β vector are presented in Figure 12.1, where results are expressed relative to the MSE of the 2SLS estimator and scenarios are numbered sequentially to repeatedly represent the 10 sampling scenarios in Table 12.1 for each of the sample sizes 50, 100, and 250. A number of general patterns are evident from the MC results. First of all, the 2SLS estimator dominates the other four estimators in terms of parameter MSE, with the exception of the smallest sample size and scenario 5, in which case the MEEL estimator is marginally superior to all others. Second, the MSEs of the GMM(I) estimator are very close to the MEEL estimator across all scenarios, but MEEL is actually MSE superior to GMM(I) in only a few cases. Third, there is a general order ranking of the MSEs of the EL-type estimators whereby generally MSE(MEEL) < MSE(MEL) < MSE(MLEL). However, differences in MSE performance among these estimators is small at $n = 100$ and practically indistinguishable at $n = 250$. Fourth, the MSE differences between *all* of the estimators dissipate as the sample size increases, with the differences being negligible at the largest sample size ($n = 250$).

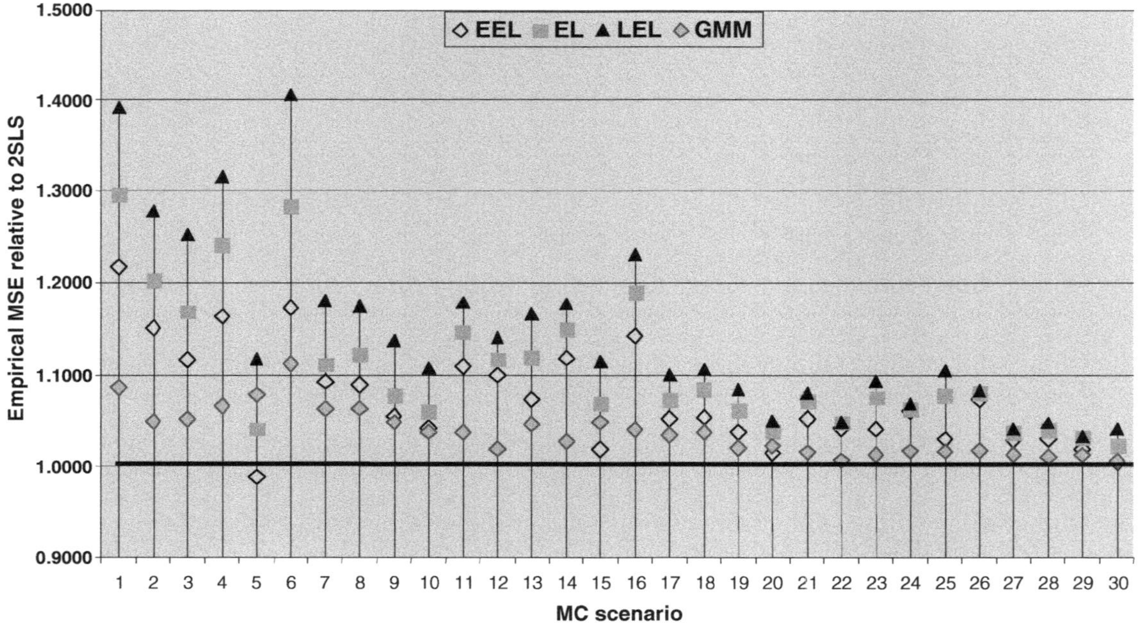

Figure 12.1. Parameter vector relative MSE.

4.2. Bias and Variance

Empirical bias and variance results for the estimators of β_2 are presented in Figures 12.2 and 12.3. Again some general estimator performance patterns emerge. First of all, the EL-type estimators, as a group, generally tend to be less biased than either the 2SLS or GMM estimators, but the EL estimators also tend to exhibit more variation than the traditional estimators. These performance patterns are especially evident for the small sample size ($n = 50$). Second, volatility in bias across MC scenarios is notably more pronounced for 2SLS and GMM than for the EL estimators, whereas just the opposite is true regarding volatility in variance measures across MC scenarios. Again this performance pattern is notably more pronounced at the smallest sample size than for the larger sample sizes. Third, regarding comparisons among EL-type estimators, the MEEL estimator tends to be the least variable among the three EL alternatives, with the ranking of variability tending to be in the order var(MEEL) < var(MEL) < var(MLEL). The ranking of relative bias performance among the EL estimators is less distinct, where, especially for the smallest sample size, each of the EL-type estimators exhibits least bias for at least one MC scenario. For larger sample sizes the MEEL estimator more often than not has the smallest bias, but again there are exceptions for some scenarios, and in any case the bias of all of the EL-type estimators tends to be small, bordering on inconsequential for most of the scenarios when sample sizes are $n = 100$ or larger. Fourth, for the largest sample size ($n = 250$), both bias and variance tend to be quite small for all of the estimators considered, although in a relative sense, the traditional estimators continued to have notably larger bias for most scenarios than any of the EL-type estimators.

4.3. Prediction MSE

In the context of generating predictions closest in expected Euclidean distance to actual dependent variable outcomes, the 2SLS and GMM estimators were notably superior to the EL-type estimators across the majority of sampling scenarios, and in any case were never worse. On the other hand, if one intended to use estimated residuals to generate an estimate of the model noise variance, the EL-type methods exhibited MSE measures that were closer in proximity to the true noise variance of $\sigma^2 = 25$. Among the EL-type methods, the general rank ordering of prediction MSE was MSE(MEEL) < MSE(MEL) < MSE(MLEL).

4.4. Size of Moment Validity Tests

Figure 12.4 presents empirical sizes of the 10 different tests of moment validity decribed in Section 2.3. The target size of the test was set to the typical 0.05 level, and when $n = 250$ all of the test are generally within ± 0.01 of this level across all MC scenarios. However, a number of the test procedures, most notably the LR tests for MEEL and MEL, the LM test for MEL, and to a lesser extent

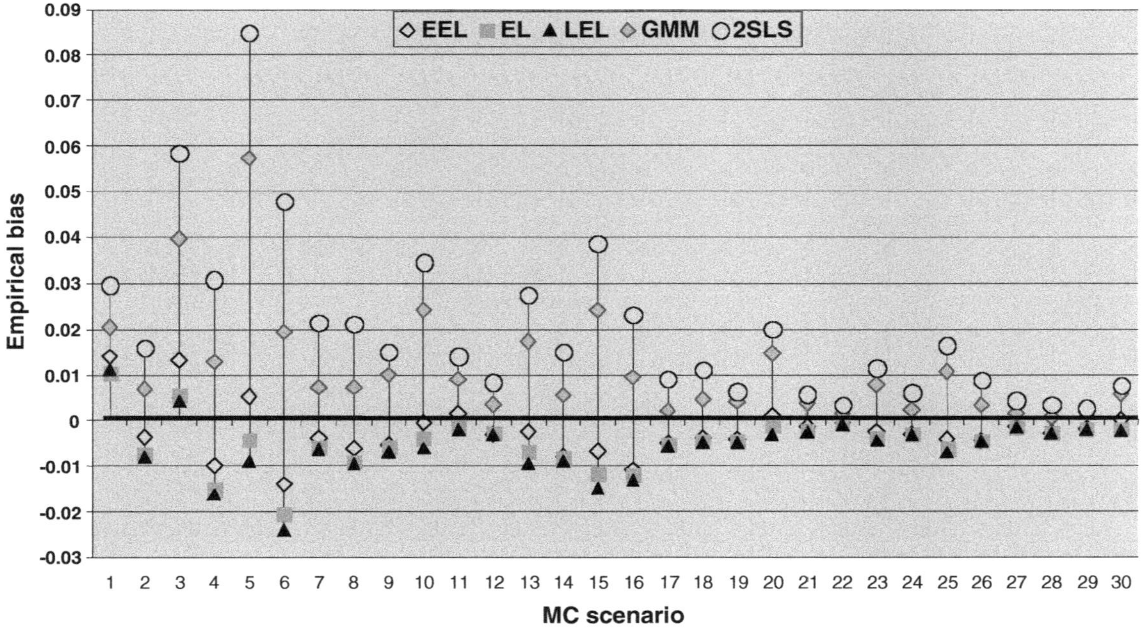

Figure 12.2. Bias in estimating B2 = 2.

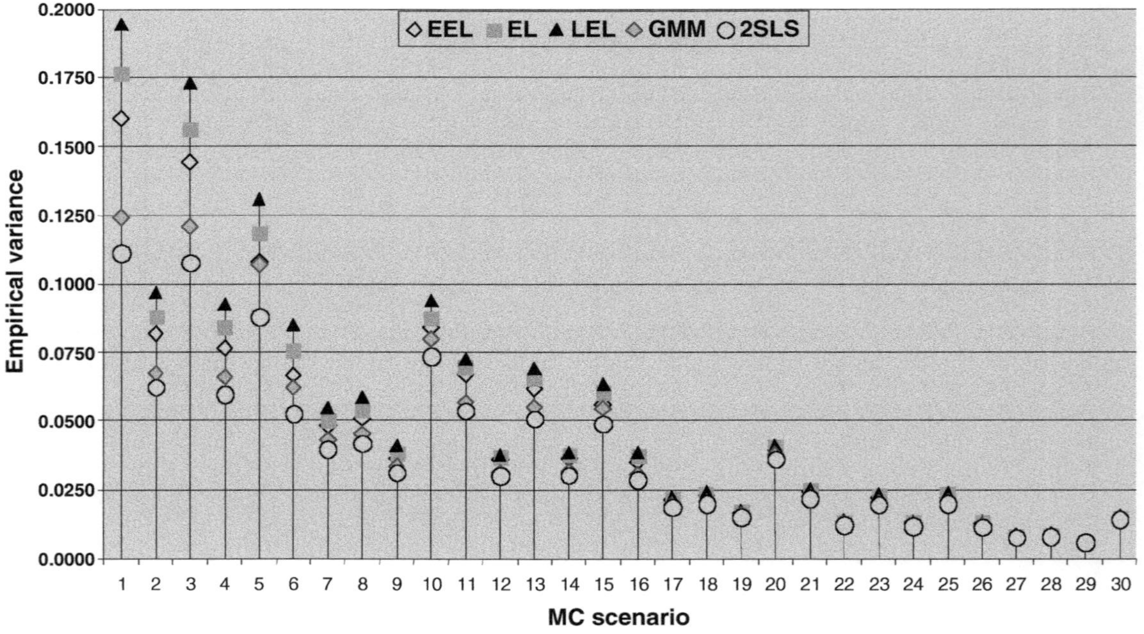

Figure 12.3. Variance in estimating B2 = 2.

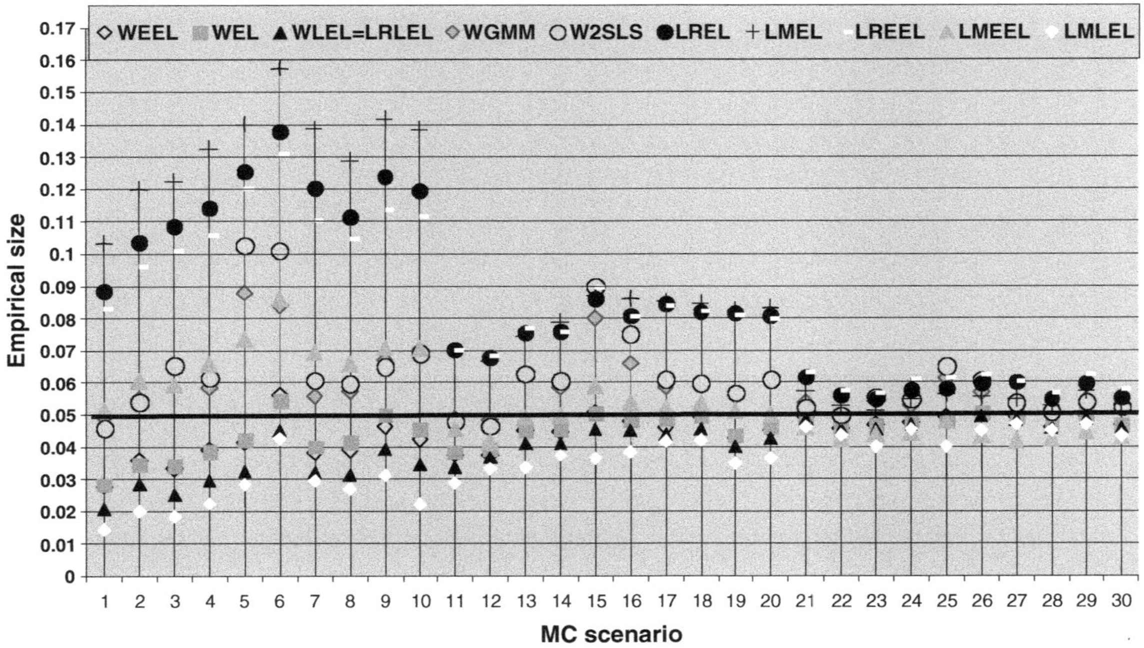

Figure 12.4. Size of moment validity test, target = 0.05.

the Wald–average moment test for 2SLS and GMM, are erratic and notably distant from the target test size when $n = 50$. The most consistent suite of tests in terms of average proximity to the true test size across MC scenarios were the Wald–average moment tests for all three of the EL-type estimators. In addition the LM tests in the case of MEEL and MLEL was reasonably accurate when $n \geq 100$. As noted in the literature, for a subset of the scenarios, the size of the tests based on the traditional 2SLS and GMM methods were substantially distant from target size.

4.5. Confidence Interval Coverage and Expected Length

Figure 12.5 displays results relating to the empirical coverage probability of confidence intervals for the β_2 parameter, where target coverage is 0.99. Except for two scenarios involving the 2SLS and GMM methods, all of the confidence intervals are generally within 0.01 of the target coverage for the large sample size of $n = 250$. Again with the preceding two exceptions noted relating to the traditional estimators, coverage is generally within 0.03 of target for the sample size of $n = 100$. Coverage degrades significantly for the small sample size $n = 50$, with the traditional estimators generally having better coverage, although they also exhibit demonstrably the worst coverage performance for two sampling scenarios. Moreover, the traditional methods exhibited more volatility across MC scenarios than EL-methods. We note that the coverage results observed for the EL-methods are consistent with other observations in the literature that the EL-type methods consistently underachieve target coverage probability under the asymptotic chi square calibration (Baggerly, 2001). In the large majority of cases, the traditional inference procedures also underachieved target coverage.

In the case of expected confidence interval (CI) length, a clearer relative performance pattern was apparent. In particular, the general relative ranking of CI length among the five alternative estimators was given by the following ordering of empirical average lengths: CI(MEEL) < CI(MEL) < CI(MLEL) < CI(2SLS) < CI(GMM). As expected, differences in length were most pronounced at the smallest sample size, in some cases exceeding 15%, but differences dissipated to effectively negligible levels when $n = 250$.

4.6. Test Power

All of the test procedures exhibited substantial power in rejecting the false null hypothesis $H_0 : \beta_2 = 0$, where all rejection probabilities were in the range of 0.92 or higher. Among the EL-type methods, the relative power performance ranking was P(MEEL) > P(MEL) > P(MLEL). When comparing power performance to traditional methods, it was generally the case that 2SLS resulted in the most test power, followed by either MEEL or GMM, depending on the scenario, although the powers of the latter two procedures were in any case always very close to each other. The differences in power dissipated substantially for the higher sample sizes, and when $n = 250$, there was effectively no difference in

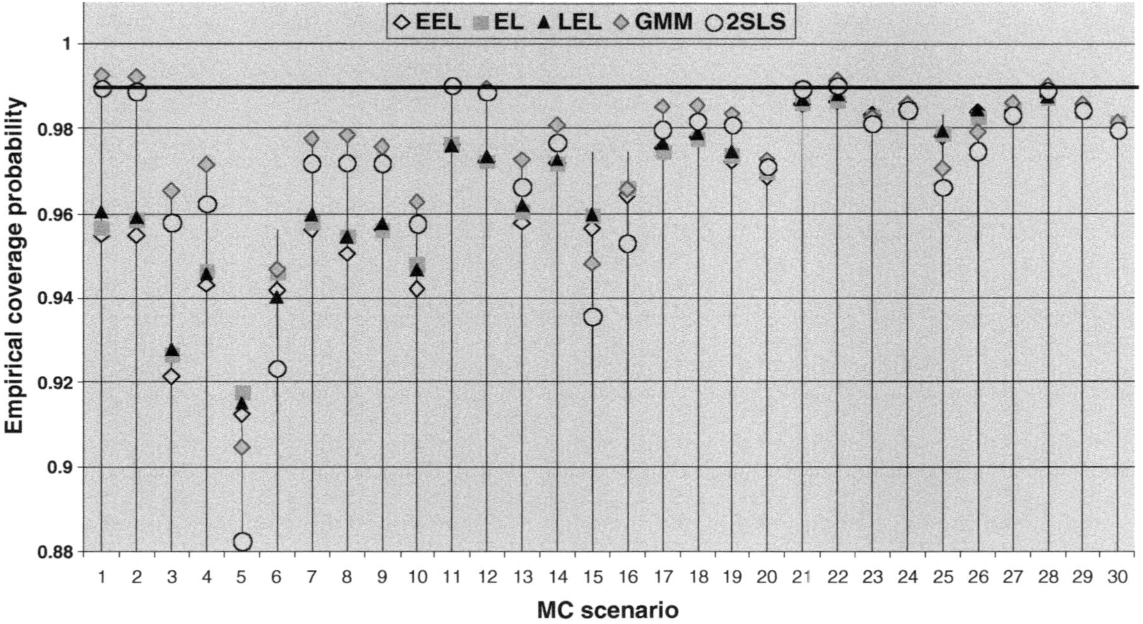

Figure 12.5. Confidence interval coverage probability for B2, target = 0.99.

power between any of the procedures, with all procedures achieving the ideal power of 1.

5. SOME FINAL REMARKS

In statistical models consisting of linear structural equations, the 2SLS and GMM estimators have long been the estimator of choice when the number of moment conditions IV variables exceeded the number of unknown response parameters in the equation in question. Both the 2SLS and GMM estimators solve the problem of overidentification by defining particular rank-k linear combinations of the moment conditions. In contrast the nontraditional EL-type estimator transforms the overdetermined moments problem into a set of equations that is solvable for the model parameters by imposing a functional dependence on the moment equations through the choice of sample observation weights. Although both the traditional and EL-type estimators perform well in terms of first-order asymptotics, questions persist as to their small sample bias and variance performance in estimation, and their coverage, interval width, and power characteristics in terms of inference.

Given these questions and corresponding conjectures that appear in the literature, in this chapter we provide some empirical evidence concerning the sampling performance of 2SLS, GMM, and EL-type methods by simulating a range of sampling processes and observing empirical sampling behavior of the estimators and associated inference procedures. While MC sampling results are never definitive, the base results presented in this paper provide insights into the relative sampling performance of different types of general moment based estimators for a range of data sampling processes. Some distinct and interesting estimation and inference properties that we observed and did not know prior to our study are as follows:

(i) The EL-type estimators tend to exhibit less bias and more variance than the traditional estimators.

(ii) In terms of MSE, the 2SLS estimator wins almost all competitions. At a sample size of 100 or more, the estimators exhibit similar performances.

(iii) In terms of accurate size of moment tests, the EL-type inference methods are superior, based on the average moment (or Wald) statistics, across all sample sizes. For sample sizes of 100 or more the LM tests also do reasonably well, especially in the case of MEEL and MLEL, and for a sample size of 250 all of the moment tests are in the neighborhood of the correct size.

(iv) On CI coverage, the traditional estimators perform somewhat erratically across differing data sampling processes until the highest sample size is reached. The EL-type methods are similar to each other in interval coverage performance, and exhibit a more orderly convergence to the correct coverage.

(v) Test power for significance tests is very high for a sample size of 100 and is essentially 1 and ideal across all significance tests for sample size 250.

(vi) A combination of concentrating out Lagrangian multipliers via numerical nonlinear equation solving algorithms and then optimizing the concentrated optimization problem based on a nongradient driven, direct search polytope (Nelder–Meade) type optimization algorithm appears to be a tractable and computationally efficient method for calculating solutions to EL-type problems in the IV-based moment constraint setting.

Many of the results appear reasonable and consistent with the limited amount of previous finite sample results (Mittelhammer and Judge, 2002, 2003a) and speculations in the literature relating to applications of EL-type estimators to structural equation estimation. The different pseudo-distance measures optimized by the trio of EL-type methods result in differing sampling performances for the varying estimator and test statistics, and those preferring a particular pseudodistance measure will no doubt still be able to rationalize why their choice was not superior for a particular estimation or inference comparison. However, it is striking that none of the EL-type methods was found to be a compelling alternative to the ubiquitous 2SLS approach for parameter estimation, and there were only limited cases where the EL-type methods exhibited competitive inference properties.

Speculating further about the observed results, both the 2SLS and EL-type methods begin with the same ill-posed, overidentified set of moment conditions but transform them in differing ways into well-posed systems of equations that are solvable for the parameters. The 2SLS approach applies an optimal (in the optimal estimating function, OptEF, sense) linear transformation to the moment conditions that has a unique solution. This OptEF transformation can be derived analytically, its functional form is completely known, and it does not depend on any of the β or σ^2 parameters to be estimated. Even though the unknown variance parameter σ^2 does appear in the explicit OptEF transformation, it is a scale factor that is redundant and can be eliminated when the optimal transform matrix is applied. On the other hand, the EL-type methods introduce n additional unknown parameters in order to resolve the overdetermined nature of the moment equations. These parameters must be estimated from the data, and act as slack variables that scale the sample observation components of the moment conditions to define a functionally dependent set of equations with rank equal to the dimension of the β parameter vector. The particular set of transformed moment conditions that is solved for β in EL-type methods is, in a sense, arbitrarily determined by an arbitrary choice of pseudodistance measure (some member of the Cressie–Read family), and an optimal choice for finite samples, if it exists at all, is a measure zero set. Thus, it is to be expected that almost all EL-type methods are suboptimal in the class of estimating function-type estimators.

Looking toward future research, there are several ways to extend the empirical evidence concerning the performance of EL-type estimators in recovering unknown response parameters in structural equations. We and others have noted that confidence regions generated by EL-type distance measures using χ^2 calibrations consistently under cover. Baggerly (2001) has suggested forming empirical regions through the use of a studentization of the moment constraints. Studentizing permits an escape from the convex hull of the moment data observations and may yield more accurate inferences in small samples.

It would be interesting to extend performance questions to data sampling processes that involve non-normal, nonsymmetric distributions. Here the EL methods may exhibit improved performance because the moment information obtained from nonsymmetric and/or improperly centered distributions may be better accommodated by the flexible data weights available within the EL framework However, the answer is not clear because EL may attain smaller levels of bias, but at the expense of increased variance.

One interesting alternative data sampling process would be a statistical model in which Y is a discrete random variable. On the basis of the preliminary work, we speculate that the use of EL-type estimators would perform well relative to semiparametric alternatives in terms of quadratic loss.

Finally, in pursuit of achieving finite sample reductions in mean squared error, it is useful to consider, in a semiparametric Stein-type of way, a mixture estimator that combines a consistent estimator having questionable finite properties, with an estimator that is inconsistent but has small finite sample variability. Such an estimator, which utilizes an EL-type moment formulation, has been proposed by Mittelhammer and Judge (2003b) and is currently under further evaluation.

References

Baggerly, K. A. (1998), "Empirical Likelihood as a Goodness of Fit Measure," *Biometrika*, 85, 535–547.

Baggerly, K. A. (2001), "Studentized Empirical Likelihood and Maximum Entropy: Empirical t," Working Paper, Department of Statistics, Rice University.

Bertsekas, D. P. (1995), *Nonlinear Programming*. Belmont: Athena Scientific.

Bound, J., D. Jaeger, and R. Baker (1995), "Problems with Instrumental Variable Estimation When the Correlation Between the Instruments and the Endogenous Variables is Weak," *Journal of the American Statistical Association*, 90, 443–450.

Corcoran, S. A. (2000), "Empirical Exponential Family Likelihood Using Several Moment Conditions," *Statistica Sinica*, 10, 545–557.

Cressie, N., and T. Read (1984), "Multinomial Goodness of Fit Tests," *Journal of Royal Statistical Society, Series B*, 46, 440–464.

Godambe, V. (1960), "An Optimum Property of Regular Maximum Likelihood Estimation," *Annals of Mathematical Statistics*, 31, 1208–1212.

Golan, A., G. G. Judge, and D. Miller (1996), *Maximum Entropy Econometrics*. New York: John Wiley and Sons.

Hansen, L. P. (1982), "Large Sample Properties of Generalized Method of Moments Estimators," *Econometrica*, 50, 1029–1054.
Heyde, C. (1989), "Quasi-Likelihood and Optimality of Estimating Functions: Some Current and Unifying Themes," *Bulletin of International Statistical Institute*, 1, 19–29.
Heyde, C., and R. Morton (1998), "Multiple Roots in General Estimating Equations," *Biometrika*, 85(4), 954–959.
Imbens, G. W., R. H., Spady, and P. Johnson (1998), "Information Theoretic Approaches to Inference in Moment Condition Models," *Econometrica*, 66, 333–357.
Jacoby, S. L. S., J. S. Kowalik, and J. T. Pizzo (1972), *Iterative Methods for Nonlinear Optimization Problems*. New York: Prentice Hall.
Judge, G., R. Hill, W. Griffiths, H. Lutkepohl, and T. Lee (1985), *The Theory and Practice of Econometrics*. New York: John Wiley and Sons.
Kullback, S. (1959), *Information Theory and Statistics*. New York: John Wiley and Sons.
Maddala, G. S., and J. Jeong (1992), "On the Exact Small Sample Distribution of the Instrumental Variable Estimator," *Econometrica*, 60, 181–183.
Mittelhammer, R., and G. Judge (2002), "Endogeneity and Moment Based Estimation under Squared Error Loss," in *Handbook of Applied Econometrics and Statistical Inference* (ed. by Alan Wan, Aman Ullah, and Anoop Chaturvedi), New York: Marcel Dekker, 347–71.
Mittelhammer, R., and G. Judge (2003a), "Finite Sample Performance of the Empirical Likelihood Estimation under Endogeneity," in *Computer Aided Econometrics* (ed. by David Giles), New York: Marcel Dekker, 149–74.
Mittelhammer, R., and G. Judge (2003b), "Robust Empirical Likelihood Estimation of Models with Non-Orthogonal Noise Components," Volume in Honor of Henri Theil, *Journal of Agricultural and Applied Economics*, 35, 91–102.
Mittelhammer, R., G. Judge, and D. Miller (2000), *Econometric Foundations*. Cambridge: Cambridge University Press.
Nelder, J. A., and R. Mead (1965), "A Simplex Method for Function Minimization," *Computer Journal*, 7, 308–313.
Nelson, C. R., and R. Startz (1990), "Some Further Results on the Exact Small Sample Properties of the Instrumental Variable Estimator," *Econometrica*, 58, 967–976.
Newey, W. K., and R. J. Smith (2004), "Asymptotic Bias and Equivalence of GMM and GEL Estimators," *Econometrica*, 72, 219–256.
Owen, A. (1988), "Empirical Likelihood Ratio Confidence Intervals for a Single Functional," *Biometrika*, 75, 237–249.
Owen, A. (1991), "Empirical Likelihood for Linear Models," *The Annals of Statistics*, 19(4), 1725–1747.
Owen, A. (2001), *Empirical Likelihood*. New York: Chapman and Hall.
Qin, J., and J. Lawless (1994), "Empirical Likelihood and General Estimating Equations," *The Annals of Statistics*, 22(1), 300–325.
Read, T. R., and N. A. Cressie (1988), *Goodness of Fit Statistics for Discrete Multivariate Data*. New York: Springer Verlag.
Stock, J. H., and J. H. Wright (2000), "GMM with Weak Identification," *Econometrica*, 68(5), 1055–1096.

CHAPTER 13

How Accurate Is the Asymptotic Approximation to the Distribution of Realised Variance?

Ole E. Barndorff-Nielsen and Neil Shephard

ABSTRACT

In this paper we study the reliability of the mixed normal asymptotic distribution of realized variance error, which we have previously derived using the theory of realized power variation. Our experiments suggest that the asymptotics is reliable when we work with the logarithmic transform of the realized variance.

1. INTRODUCTION

Tom Rothenberg's outstanding teaching and research has raised the level of understanding econometricians have of the asymptotic properties of estimators and testing procedures used in economics. His frequent trips away from the United States, and his particular kindness to research students during his academic visits, has spread his influence changing the way we carry out theoretical econometric research. This paper touches on some of Tom's research interests. It will look at the effectiveness of an asymptotic theory. His influential paper Rothenberg (1984) was devoted to issues of this type.

1.1. The Model

This paper assesses the accuracy of the mixed normal asymptotic approximation to the distribution of realized variance (that is the sum of squares of financial returns) we recently derived in Barndorff-Nielsen and Shephard (2002) and extended in Barndorff-Nielsen and Shephard (2003, 2004). This theory assumes a flexible stochastic volatility (SV) model for log prices.

In the SV model for log prices a basic Brownian motion is generalized to allow the volatility term to vary over time. Then the log price y^* follows

$$y^*(t) = \alpha(t) + \int_0^t \sigma(u)dw(u) \qquad t \geq 0, \tag{1.1}$$

where σ and α is assumed to be stochastically independent of the standard Brownian motion w. We call σ the *instantaneous* or *spot volatility*, σ^2 the corresponding *variance*, and α the *mean* process. A simple example of this is

$$\alpha(t) = \mu t + \beta\sigma^{2*}(t), \qquad \text{where } \sigma^{2*}(t) = \int_0^t \sigma^2(u)du,$$

in which case we might call β a risk premium. The process σ^{2*} is called the *integrated variance*. Throughout we will assume the following conditions hold with probability one:

(C) $\sigma^2 > 0$ is càdlàg on $[0, \infty)$ and α has the property

$$\hbar^{-3/4} \max_{1 \le j \le M} |\alpha(j\hbar) - \alpha((j-1)\hbar)| = o(1), \tag{1.2}$$

in $\hbar$.

Condition (**C**) implies that the α process is continuous and so is predictable. Hence, y^* is a rather flexible special semimartingale. See, for example, Back (1991) for a discussion of the economic implications of this type of property. Assumption (**C**) also allows the volatility to have, for example, deterministic diurnal effects, jumps, long memory, no unconditional mean, or be nonstationary. The mean process α is much more constrained (e.g., it cannot be a Lévy process). A rather flexible example of the process is

$$\alpha(t) = \int_0^t g(\sigma^2(s))ds,$$

where g is a smooth function. Note that condition (**C**) implies that σ^2 and α are bounded Riemann integrable functions on any finite interval $[0, t]$.

Over an interval of time of length $\hbar > 0$, which could represent a day or a month for example, returns are defined as

$$y_i = y^*(\hbar i) - y^*((i-1)\hbar) \qquad i = 1, 2, \ldots, T, \tag{1.3}$$

which implies that

$$y_i | \alpha_i, \sigma_i^2 \sim N(\alpha_i, \sigma_i^2), \qquad \text{where } \alpha_i = \alpha(i\hbar) - \alpha\{(i-1)\hbar\},$$

while

$$\sigma_i^2 = \sigma^{2*}(i\hbar) - \sigma^{2*}\{(i-1)\hbar\}.$$

Here σ_i^2 is called *actual variance* and α_i is the *actual mean*. Reviews of the literature on the SV topic are given in Taylor (1994), Shephard (1996), and Ghysels, Harvey, and Renault (1996), while statistical and probabilistic aspects are studied in detail in Barndorff-Nielsen and Shephard (2001).

1.2. Realized variance

Suppose one was interested in estimating actual volatility σ_i^2 using M intra-$\hbar$ observations (that is M equally spaced increments in the interval $(i-1)\hbar$ to $i\hbar$).

A natural candidate is the *realized variance*[1]

$$[y_M^*]_i = \sum_{j=1}^{M} y_{j,i}^2, \quad \text{where}$$

$$y_{j,i} = y^*\left((i-1)\hbar + \frac{\hbar j}{M}\right) - y^*\left((i-1)\hbar + \frac{\hbar(j-1)}{M}\right) \qquad (1.4)$$

and its cousin *realized volatility*

$$\sqrt{\sum_{j=1}^{M} y_{j,i}^2},$$

have been used in financial economics for many years by, for example, Poterba and Summers (1986), Schwert (1989), Taylor and Xu (1997), Christensen and Prabhala (1998), Andersen, Bollerslev, Diebold, and Labys (2001), and Andersen, Bollerslev, Diebold, and Ebens (2001). However, until recently little theory was known about realized variance outside the Brownian motion case. See the review by Andersen, Bollerslev, and Diebold (2004).

In independent and concurrent work Barndorff-Nielsen and Shephard (2001) and Andersen and Bollerslev (1998) pointed out that the theory of quadratic variation (e.g., Jacod and Shiryaev, 1987, p. 55; Protter, 1990; Back, 1991) implies $[y_M^*]_i$ is a consistent estimator of σ_i^2 as $M \to \infty$. This is an interesting result for it is semi-parametric – it does not depend upon the exact form of α or σ^2. Unfortunately, quadratic variation does not provide a theory of the magnitude of the *realized variance error*

$$u_i = [y_M^*]_i - \sigma_i^2, \qquad \text{or} \qquad e_i = [y_M^*]_i / \sigma_i^2$$

the *realized variance ratio*. This is important, for although modern econometricians routinely have transaction based data, continuous sample paths processes such as SV models are rather poorly fitting at very short time horizons. There are a number of reasons for this, mostly due to market microstructure effects. In particular assets are usually quoted and traded on fixed meshes of points (e.g., decimals or eighths), while the quoting and trading process tends to occur at irregular points in time. Bai, Russell, and Tiao (2000) discusses the impact of these type of effects on realized variance. The implication of this is that it is

[1] Sums of squared returns are often called realized volatility in econometrics, while we use the name realized variance for that term and realized volatility for the corresponding square root. The use of volatility to denote standard deviations rather than variances is standard in financial economics. See, for example, the literature on volatility and variance swaps, which are derivatives written on realized volatility or variance, which includes Demeterfi, Derman, Kamal, and Zou (1999), Howison, Rafailidis, and Rasmussen (2000) and Chriss and Morokoff (1999). We have chosen to follow this nomenclature rather than the one more familiar in econometrics. Confidence intervals for the realized volatility follow by square rooting the confidence intervals for the realized variance.

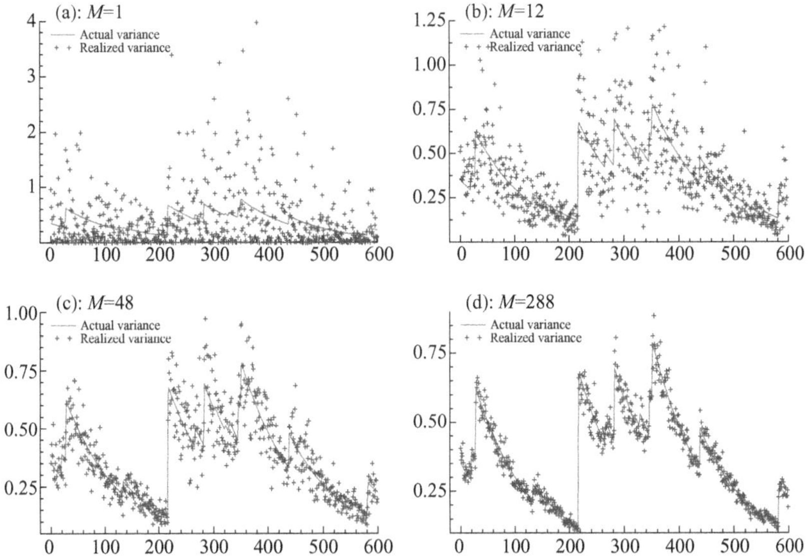

Figure 13.1. Actual σ_i^2 and realized $[y_M^*]_i$ (with M varying) variance based upon a $\Gamma(4, 8)$-OU process with $\lambda = -\log(.98)$ and $\hbar = 1$. This implies $\xi = .5$ and $\xi\omega^{-2} = 8$.

dangerous to make inference based on extremely large values of M for the effect of model misspecification can swamp the effects we are trying to measure. Instead it seems sensible to use moderate values of M and properly account for the fact that the realized variance error is not negligible.

To see that realized variance error can be substantial, we have carried out a small simulation. This could have been based on the familiar constant elasticity of variance (CEV) process, which is the solution to the SDE

$$d\sigma^2(t) = -\lambda\{\sigma^2(t) - \xi\}dt + \omega\sigma(t)^\eta db(\lambda t) \qquad \eta \in [1, 2],$$

where b is standard Brownian motion uncorrelated with w. Of course, the special cases of $\eta = 1$ delivers the square root process, while when $\eta = 2$ we have Nelson's GARCH diffusion. These models have been heavily favored by Meddahi and Renault (2002) in this context. Instead of this we will mainly work with the non-Gaussian Ornstein–Uhlenbeck, or OU type for short process, which is the solution to the

$$d\sigma^2(t) = -\lambda\sigma^2(t)dt + dz(\lambda t), \qquad (1.5)$$

where z is a subordinator (that is a Lévy process with nonnegative increments). These models have been developed in this context by Barndorff-Nielsen and Shephard (2001). In Figure 13.1 we have taken $\alpha = 0$ and drawn a curve to represent a simulated sample path of σ_i^2 from an OU process where $\sigma^2(t)$ has a $\Gamma(4, 8)$ stationary distribution, $\lambda = -\log(0.99)$ and $\hbar = 1$, along with the associated realized variance (depicted using crosses) computed using a variety of values of M. In this case z is a simple compound Poisson process whose details are given in, for example, Barndorff-Nielsen and Shephard (2001). We see that as M increases the precision of realized variance increases, while Figure 13.1(d) shows that the variance of the realized variance error increases with the actual variance. We will return to this important observation in a moment.

1.3. Mixed Normal Asymptotic Theory

In a recent paper Barndorff-Nielsen and Shephard (2002), subsequently extended in Barndorff-Nielsen and Shephard (2003, 2004), have strengthened the above consistency result $[y_M^*]_i \xrightarrow{p} \sigma_i^2$ considerably. The results have two parts. The first gives the asymptotic distribution of realized variance.

Theorem 1.1. *For the SV model in (1), for any positive $\hbar$ and $M \to \infty$*

$$\frac{\sqrt{\frac{M}{\hbar}}\left([y_M^*]_i - \sigma_i^2\right)}{\sqrt{2\sigma_i^{[4]}}} \xrightarrow{\mathcal{L}} N(0,1), \quad \textit{where } \sigma_i^{[4]} = \int_{(i-1)\hbar}^{i\hbar} \sigma^4(u)du. \tag{1.6}$$

We call σ^4 and $\sigma_i^{[4]}$ the *spot* and *actual quarticity*, respectively. This theorem implies the mixed normal limit

$$\sqrt{\frac{M}{\hbar}}\left([y_M^*]_i - \sigma_i^2\right) | \sigma_i^{[4]} \xrightarrow{\mathcal{L}} N\left(0, 2\sigma_i^{[4]}\right). \tag{1.7}$$

Of course, the problem with this theory is that $\sigma_i^{[4]}$ is unknown. This is tackled by the following theorem on realized power variation which is due to Barndorff-Nielsen and Shephard (2003).

Theorem 1.2. *Let y^* be a stochastic process of the form (1). Define the realized power variation (of order $2q$)*

$$[y_M^*]_i^{[2q]} = \sum_{j=1}^{M} y_{j,i}^{2q}.$$

Then, for $M \to \infty$,

$$(\hbar/M)^{-q+1} c_q [y_M^*]_i^{[2q]} \xrightarrow{p} \int_{\hbar(i-1)}^{\hbar i} \sigma^{2q}(u)du,$$

where q denotes a positive integer and $c_q = \{1 \cdot 3 \cdot \cdots \cdot (2q-1)\}^{-1}$.

The case of $q = 1$ is the standard quadratic variation result. When $q = 2$ we obtain

$$\frac{M}{\hbar}[y_M^*]_i^{[4]} = \frac{M}{\hbar}\sum_{j=1}^{M} y_{j,i}^4 \xrightarrow{p} 3\sigma_i^{[4]}.$$

An implication of this is that we can use the feasible limit theory

$$\frac{[y_M^*]_i - \sigma_i^2}{\sqrt{\frac{2}{3}\sum_{j=1}^{M} y_{j,i}^4}} \xrightarrow{\mathcal{L}} N(0,1). \tag{1.8}$$

Of course, in practice it may make sense to transform the above limit theorem to impose, a priori, positivity on the approximating distribution (see, for example, the discussion of transformations in Rothenberg 1984, pp. 887–889). In particular it seems natural to work with the logarithmic transformation of the realized variance ratio so that

$$\frac{\sqrt{\frac{M}{\hbar}}\left\{\log[y_M^*]_i - \log\sigma_i^2\right\}}{\sqrt{2\sigma_i^{[4]}/\left(\sigma_i^2\right)^2}} \xrightarrow{\mathcal{L}} N(0,1)$$

and so, using the realized power variation theory,

$$\frac{\log[y_M^*]_i - \log\sigma_i^2}{\sqrt{\frac{2}{3[y_M^*]_i^2}\sum_{j=1}^{M} y_{j,i}^4}} \xrightarrow{\mathcal{L}} N(0,1). \tag{1.9}$$

It is not clear, without further study, whether the log-based asymptotic theory (1.9) is more or less accurate in finite samples than the nontransformed version (1.8).

The following remarks can be made about these results:

- $\sum_{j=1}^{M} y_{j,i}^2$ converges to $\int_{\hbar(i-1)}^{\hbar i}\sigma^2(u)du$ at rate $\sqrt{M}$. This considerably strengthens the quadratic variation result, for now we know the rate of convergence, not just that it converges.
- The limit theorem is unaffected by the form of the drift process α; the smoothness assumption (**C**) is sufficient for its effect to becomes negligible. Again this considerably strengthens the quadratic variation result which says the p-lim is unaffected by the drift. Now we know this result extends to the next order term as well.
- Knowledge of the form of the volatility dynamics is not required in order to use this theory. In a sense this is a semiparametric result.
- The fourth moment of returns need not exist for the asymptotic normality to hold. In such heavy-tailed situations, the stochastic denominator $\int_{(i-1)\hbar}^{i\hbar}\sigma^4(u)du$ loses its unconditional mean. However, this property is irrelevant to the workings of the theory.
- The volatility process $\sigma^2(t)$ can be nonstationary, exhibit long memory, or include intraday effects.
- $\sum_{j=1}^{M} y_{j,i}^2 - \int_{\hbar(i-1)}^{\hbar i}\sigma^2(u)du$ has a mixed Gaussian limit implying that marginally it will have heavier tails than a normal.

- The magnitude of the error $\sum_{j=1}^{M} y_{j,i}^2 - \int_{\hbar(i-1)}^{\hbar i} \sigma^2(u)du$ is likely to be large in times of high volatility. This can been seen in the simulation results in Figure 13.1.
- Conditionally on $\int_{\hbar(i-1)}^{\hbar i} \sigma^4(u)du$ and $\int_{\hbar(k-1)}^{\hbar k} \sigma^4(u)du$, the errors

$$\sum_{j=1}^{M} y_{j,i}^2 - \int_{\hbar(i-1)}^{\hbar i} \sigma^2(u)du \quad \text{and} \quad \sum_{j=1}^{M} y_{j,k}^2 - \int_{\hbar(k-1)}^{\hbar k} \sigma^2(u)du$$

are asymptotically independent and jointly normal for $i \neq k$.
- Some of the features of (1.6) appear in the usual cross-section asymptotic theory of the estimation of σ^2 when $z_i \sim NID(0, \sigma^2)$. Then

$$\frac{\sqrt{M}\left\{\frac{1}{M}\sum_{j=1}^{M} z_i^2 - \sigma^2\right\}}{\sqrt{2\sigma^4}} \xrightarrow{L} N(0,1),$$

whose natural feasible version is

$$\frac{\sqrt{M}\left\{\frac{1}{M}\sum_{j=1}^{M} z_i^2 - \sigma^2\right\}}{\sqrt{\frac{2}{3M}\sum_{j=1}^{M} z_i^4}} \xrightarrow{L} N(0,1).$$

This has quite a few differences from (1.8). In particular the denominator divides by M rather than multiplies by M, while in the numerator $\sum_{j=1}^{M} z_i^2$ is divided by M while in the theory for realized variance it is left unscaled. Bartlett and Kendall (1946) have studied the asymptotic and finite sample behavior of $log \sum_{j=1}^{M} z_i^2$ in this case.
- These results are also quite closely related to the work of Foster and Nelson (1996) (note also the work of Geno-Catalot, Laredo, and Picard, 1992; Florens-Zmirou, 1993; Hansen, 1995). In the case where the volatility follows a scalar diffusion, they provided an asymptotic distribution theory for an estimator of $\sigma^2(t)$. Their idea was to compute a local variance from the lagged data, for example,

$$\widehat{\sigma^2}(t) = \hbar^{-1}\sum_{j=1}^{M}\left\{y^*\left(t - \hbar j M^{-1}\right) - y^*\left(t - \hbar(j-1)M^{-1}\right)\right\}^2. \tag{1.10}$$

They then studied its behavior as $M \to \infty$ and $\hbar \downarrow 0$ under some assumptions. This "double asymptotics" yields a Gaussian limit theory so long as $\hbar \downarrow 0$ and $M \to \infty$ at the right, related rates. Of course, this type of argument is familiar also in nonparametric econometrics (e.g., Pagan and Ullah, 1999). The double asymptotics makes it harder to use in practice than our own simpler analysis, which just needs $M \to \infty$. It is possible because our goal is to estimate the easier integrated variation rather than the harder spot variance.

In this paper we use simulation to study the finite sample behavior of (1.8) and (1.9). We will show that (1.9) works well even for moderately small values of M, while (1.8) will typically require too large a value of M to be empirically very reliable, although it is a helpful guide.

This paper has three other sections. In Section 2 we run Monte Carlo experiments to assess the finite sample behavior of (1.8) and (1.9). In Section 3 some new theory is introduced, which improves the small sample performance of the statistics. Section 4 draws conclusions from this paper.

2. HOW GOOD IS THE FEASIBLE ASYMPTOTIC DISTRIBUTION?

2.1. Simple Model

In this Section we will use simulation to assess the accuracy of our asymptotic approximations (1.8) and (1.9). Throughout this subsection the simulations will be based upon the type of OU-based variance process described in the introduction. In particular we will work with a process where σ^2 has a $\Gamma(4, 8)$ stationary distribution, $\lambda = -\log(0.99)$ and $\hbar = 1$.

Figure 13.2 and Table 13.1 show the results from the use of the two asymptotic results (1.8) and (1.9) in cases where $M = 12$ and $M = 48$. In the figure the dots in the left hand graphs show a short sequence of realized variance errors $[y_M^*]_i - \sigma_i^2$, together with plus and minus twice their associated standard errors $\sqrt{\frac{2}{3}\sum_{j=1}^{M} y_{j,i}^4}$. The graphs show dramatic increases and decreases in the error bands. With $M = 12$ the bands range from 0.1 to around 0.75. These fluctuations correspond to increases and decreases in the overall level of the variance process, with wide bands occurring at periods of high levels of variance. The right-hand graphs in Figure 13.2 give a corresponding normal QQ-plot for (1.8), which should lay on the 45 degree line if the asymptotics were to hold. The plot is calculated off a larger simulation run than that used to draw the plots in the middle and left-hand side of the figure. It uses $T = 1,500$. The graph suggests that the asymptotic theory provides a very poor guide to the finite sample behavior of the standardized realized variance.

The bottom graphs in Figure 13.2, which correspond to having $M = 48$, show similar effects. However, the standard error bands have sharply contracted, now ranging from 0.08 upto 0.3. The QQ plot is much better, although the asymptotic theory still only provides a rather rough guide to the finite sample behavior.

The results for the log-based asymptotic theory (1.9) are much better. The top graphs show that, even with $M = 12$, the standard error for $\log[y_M^*]_i - \log\sigma_n^2$ does not vary dramatically with n. A failing of the approximation is that there are quite a few errors which are extremely negative. This is picked up in the QQ plot which is much better than any of the ones we have so far seen, but fails in the left-hand tail to a much greater degree than in the right-hand tail. By the time M has reach 48 the asymptotics seems to give a rather better guide to

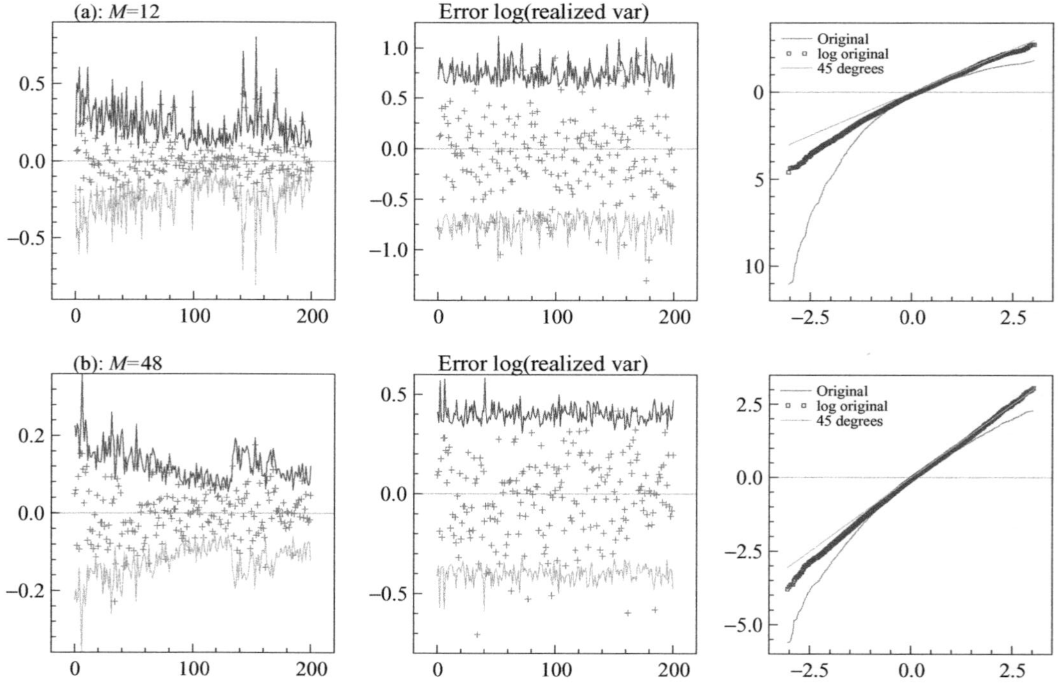

Figure 13.2. Actual $[y_M^*]_i - \sigma_i^2$ and twice asymptotic S.E.s. Middle graphs: $\log[y_M^*]_i - \log \sigma_i^2$ and twice asymptotic S.E.s. QQ plot of the standardized realized variance error (X-axis has the expected quantiles, Y-axis the observed).

Table 13.1. *Bias and standard error of the realized variance errors using the raw asymptotics and the log-based asymptotics. Simulations use a Γ-OU process variance model. Cove denotes estimated finite sample coverage using the asymptotic theory setting the nomimal level at 95.0. The table deals with the no leverage ($\rho = 0$) and strong leverage ($\rho = -1$) cases. File:* `simple.ox`

	Raw			Log		
M	Bias	S.E.	Cove	Bias	S.E.	Cove
12	−.531	1.64	86.5	−.222	1.17	91.2
48	−.226	1.14	92.4	−.110	1.05	94.1
96	−.152	1.07	93.9	−.075	1.03	94.5
288	−.091	1.02	95.0	−.049	1.00	95.0

the behavior of the distribution. Further, the standard errors have again become much smaller, reducing from around 0.8 to 0.35.

When we look at higher values of M these broad conclusions continue to hold, with the log based asymptotics substantially outperforming the nontransform version. This can be seen in Figure 13.3, which looks at the cases where $M = 96$ and $M = 288$. Overall the figure shows it is preferable to rely on the log-based theory.

Table 13.1 gives an alternative view on these simulations. It records the bias from zero of the standardized realized variances (1.8) and log realized variances (1.9), together with their standard error. The standard error should be around one if the asymptotic theory is a good description of the behavior of the statistics. Finally, the table records the coverage rate of the statistic. This is the percentage of standardized statistics, which are larger than two in absolute value.

The results again suggest that the raw statistic has poorer behavior in terms of bias, standard error and coverage compared to the log version. By the time M reaches 48 the log version of the statistic seems quite well approximated by the asymptotic theory.

2.2. Superposition

Similar results hold when we build more sophisticated models based on a superposition of OU type models. Such processes also have potential for modeling long-range dependence and self-similarity in variance. This is discussed in the OU case in Barndorff-Nielsen and Shephard (2001) and in more depth by Barndorff-Nielsen (2001), who formalizes the use of superpositions as a way of modeling long-range dependence and approximate self-similarity.

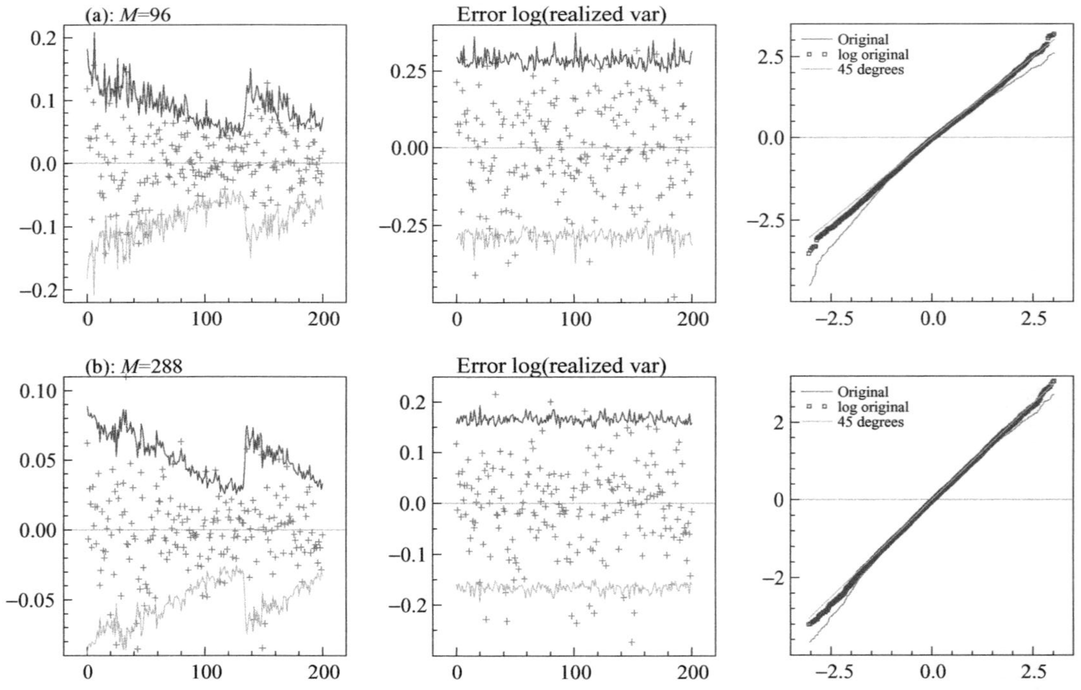

Figure 13.3. Actual $[y_M^*]_i - \sigma_i^2$ and twice asymptotic S.E.s. Middle graphs: $\log[y_M^*]_i - \log \sigma_i^2$ and twice asymptotic S.Es. QQ plot of the standardized realized variance error for $M = 96$ and 288. (X-axis has the expected quantiles, Y-axis the observed).

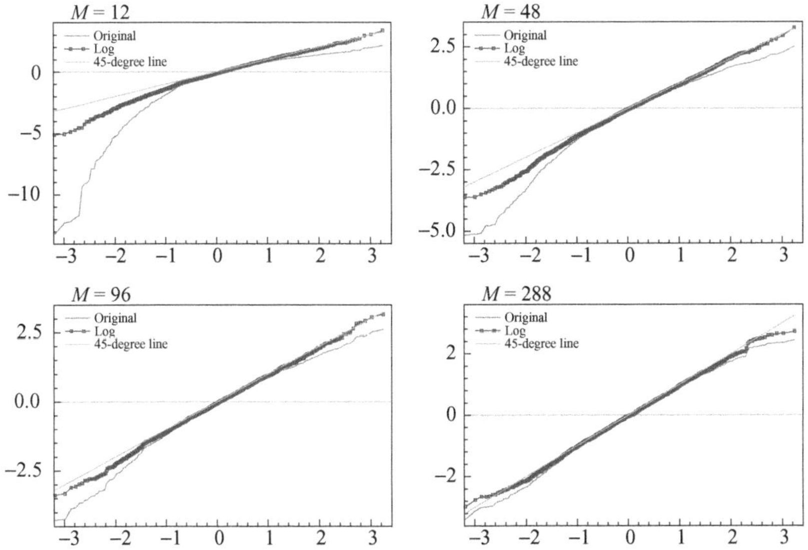

Figure 13.4. Superposition case. QQ plot for standardized $\log[y^*_M]_i - \log \sigma_i^2$. Based on $M = 12$, 48, 96, and $= 288$. (X-axis has the expected quantiles, Y-axis the observed).

This follows earlier related work by Granger (1980), Cox (1991), Ding and Granger (1996), Engle and Lee (1999), Shephard (1996, pp. 36–7), Andersen and Bollerslev (1997), Barndorff-Nielsen, Jensen, and Sørensen (1998) and, Comte and Renault (1998).

Consider variance based on the sum of J independent OU processes

$$\sigma^2(t) = \sum_{i=1}^{J} \sigma^{2(i)}(t), \qquad \text{where } d\sigma^{2(i)}(t) = -\lambda_i \sigma^{2(i)}(t)dt + dz^{(i)}(\lambda_i t)$$

where the $\sigma^{2(i)}(t)$ process has the memory parameter λ_i. We parametrize the model, in the simplest possible way in the following gamma based example, so that

$$\sigma^{2(i)}(t) \sim \Gamma(w_i \nu, \alpha), \qquad \text{where } \{w_i \geq 0\} \quad \text{and} \quad \sum_{i=1}^{J} w_i = 1.$$

Barndorff-Nielsen and Shephard (2002) showed that such extensions to the basic OU model were necessary in order to satisfactorily fit high-frequency exchange rate data. Here we repeat the above analysis with $\nu = 4$ and $\alpha = 8$, but take $J = 2$, $w_1 = 0.8$, $\lambda_1 = 4$, $\lambda_2 = 0.03$. This means that the second component in the variance has considerable memory, while the first component has very little indeed.

The normal QQ plots for the standardized asymptotic realized variance errors are given in Figure 13.4. They show the results for $M = 12$, $M = 48$, $M = 96$, and $M = 288$. We broadly repeat the results from the OU case, with the log version of the asymptotics being reasonably reliable even for moderate values of M, particularly in the right-hand tail of the distribution. On the other hand the nontransformed version again requires a high value of M to yield satisfactory results.

2.3. Diffusion Case

This section will repeat the experiments reported in the previous subsections but this time based on the Cox, Ingersoll, and Ross (1985) square root process for the volatility dynamics. In the context of SV models this is often called the Heston (1993) model. The experiment has two aims:

- To demonstrate that the results we indicated above are not sensitive to the type of volatility processes used in building the model.
- To explore the effect of leverage terms (that is, correlation between the returns and future volatility movements) on the performance of our theory. This is interesting as it is outside the assumptions that Barndorff-Nielsen and Shephard (2002, 2003, 2004) have been able to prove the asymptotics for realized variance.

We write the dynamics as

$$dy^*(t) = \sigma(t)dw(t)$$

and

$$d\sigma^2(t) = -\lambda\{\sigma^2(t) - \xi\}dt + \omega\sigma(t)db(\lambda t) \qquad \xi \geq \omega^2/2 \qquad (2.11)$$

where $b(t)$ is a standard Brownian motion process. To allow for the possibility of leverage we will assume

$$\text{Cor}\,\{b(\lambda t), w(t)\} = \rho t\sqrt{\lambda}.$$

The correlation parameter ρ indexes the leverage effect in the model and would be expected to be negative for equity data (e.g., Black, 1976; Nelson, 1991). The square root process has a marginal distribution

$$\sigma^2(t) \sim \Gamma(2\omega^{-2}\xi, 2\omega^{-2}) = \Gamma\,(\nu, a) \qquad \nu \geq 1,$$

with a mean of $\xi = \nu/a$ and a variance of $\omega^2 = \nu/a^2$. Throughout this section we again take $\hbar = 1$, $\nu = 4$, and $a = 8$.

The results, based on 10,000 replications, in the no leverage case are given in the left-hand part of Figure 13.5. It shows that moving to the diffusion based volatility model does not really change any of the conclusions from the previous subsection – the asymptotics still provide a useful guide to the finite sample behavior of these statistics. Although not surprising, since this case is covered by our theory, this is a reassuring result.

These results are reinforced by Table 13.2 which shows the mean and standard error of the normalized statistics (1.8) and (1.9). In the table the former

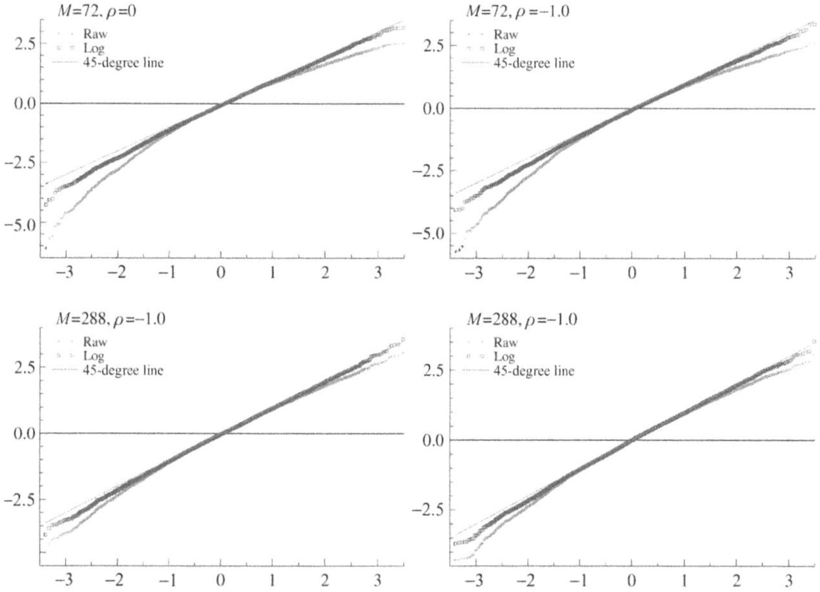

Figure 13.5. Simulation from a diffusion based SV model based on the square root volatility processes with low and high amounts of leverage. QQ plots are drawn. Top line has $M = 72$, bottom $M = 288$. Left-hand graphs show results for no leverage, right-hand graphs for high leverage. The results for the raw and log based theory is drawn.

is called the raw statistics, the latter the log version. The table shows that there is a negative bias in the raw statistic, which corresponds to the realized variance being too small and at the same time the corresponding denominator being too small. This bias is an order of magnitude smaller on the log version of the statistic. In both cases the standard error of the normalized statistic is roughly one.

Table 13.2 also gives some results on the coverage performance of the asymptotic theory. This records the percentage of times the realized variance minus the actual variance is larger, in absolute value, than twice the feasible asymptotic standard error. Thus, if the asymptotic theory was exact then we would expect the coverage percentage to be 95. The results suggest that this is not a poor approximation for moderately large values of M.

The results with strong leverage are given in the right-hand side of Figure 13.5[2]. They are very much in line with those we reported for the nonleverage case and suggest that our analysis may be robust to this effect. The right-hand column of Table 13.2 confirms these observations. Proving this conjecture turns out to be challenging mathematically even in the univariate case and is the subject of on-going research. In a stimulating piece of work Meddahi (2002) has

[2] In the simulation, common random numbers are used in the leverage and nonleverage cases.

Table 13.2. *Bias and standard error of the realized variance errors using the raw asymptotics and the log-based asymptotics. Simulations use a CIR variance model. Cove denotes estimated finite sample coverage using the asymptotic theory setting the nomimal level at 95.0. The table deals with the no leverage ($\rho = 0$) and strong leverage ($\rho = -1$) cases. File:* `simple.ox`

	No leverage						Strong leverage					
	Raw			Log			Raw			Log		
M	Bias	S.E.	Cove	Bias	S.E.	Cove	Bias	S.E.	Cove	Bias	S.E.	Cove
18	−.428	1.40	88.4	−.203	1.12	92.0	−.411	1.38	88.8	−.190	1.11	92.5
36	−.275	1.18	91.8	−.137	1.06	94.0	−.262	1.18	91.9	−.125	1.06	93.7
72	−.196	1.09	92.9	−.104	1.04	94.1	−.182	1.08	93.5	−.093	1.03	94.4
288	−.099	1.03	94.5	−.055	1.02	94.8	−.083	1.03	94.4	−.039	1.02	94.6
576	−.067	1.02	94.8	−.036	1.01	95.2	−.069	1.01	95.2	−.039	1.00	95.2
1152	−.034	1.00	95.3	−.013	1.00	95.3	−.061	1.00	95.1	−.040	1.00	95.1
2304	−.024	1.00	95.5	−.009	1.00	95.5	−.036	1.00	95.5	−.021	1.00	95.5

shown that the effect of leverage on the unconditional mean square error of the realized covariation error is asymptotically negligible in a wide class of diffusion based volatility models. This again points to the more general result of our asymptotics working in the leverage case.

2.4. Alternative Estimators of Quarticity

An important feature of the above results is the use of empirical quarticity as $M \to \infty$

$$\frac{M}{\hbar}\sum_{j=1}^{M} y_{j,i}^4 \xrightarrow{p} 3\int_{(i-1)\hbar}^{i\hbar} \sigma^4(u)du,$$

which allows us to produce a feasible limit theory for realized variance. A difficulty with estimating quarticity using the fourth powers of returns is that it is not very robust. In some recent work Barndorff-Nielsen and Shephard (2004) managed to avoid this by showing that as $M \to \infty$ so for $s > 0$ the time series estimator

$$\frac{M}{\hbar}\sum_{j=1}^{M-s} y_{j,i}^2 y_{j+s,i}^2 \xrightarrow{p} \int_{(i-1)\hbar}^{i\hbar} \sigma^4(u)du.$$

This can be used to provide an alternative to the standard feasible limit theory (1.8). In particular it implies that the standardized realized variance

$$\frac{[y_M^*]_i - \sigma_i^2}{\sqrt{2S^{-1}\sum_{s=1}^{S}\sum_{j=1}^{M-s} y_{j,i}^2 y_{j+s,i}^2}} \xrightarrow{L} N(0,1). \tag{2.12}$$

Here we study its finite sample behavior, as well as the log-transformed version

$$\frac{\log[y_M^*]_i - \log\sigma_i^2}{\sqrt{\frac{2}{[y_M^*]_i^2} S^{-1}\sum_{s=1}^{S}\sum_{j=1}^{M-s} y_{j,i}^2 y_{j+s,i}^2}} \xrightarrow{L} N(0,1). \tag{2.13}$$

Throughout this subsection we return to using simulations to investigate the finite sample behavior of these asymptotic results (2.12) and (2.13). These will again be based upon the type of OU based variance process described in the introduction. In particular we will start work with a process where σ^2 has a $\Gamma(4, 8)$ stationary distribution, $\lambda = -\log(0.99)$, and $\hbar = 1$. The time series versions of these results will be based on using (2.12) and (2.13) with $S = 4$.

Figure 13.6 gives the results for the time series based method. Thus, this figure is directly comparable with the results given in Figures 13.2 and 13.3. Throughout the results indicate that the new time series based estimator may very slightly improve the finite sample behavior of the statistics, however, the difference is very marginal compared to shifting from the raw asymptotic approximation to the one based on the logarithmic transformation.

To see how these results vary with the model, we have rerun these calculations varying the persistence parameter λ and the marginal distribution of $\Gamma(4, 8)$.

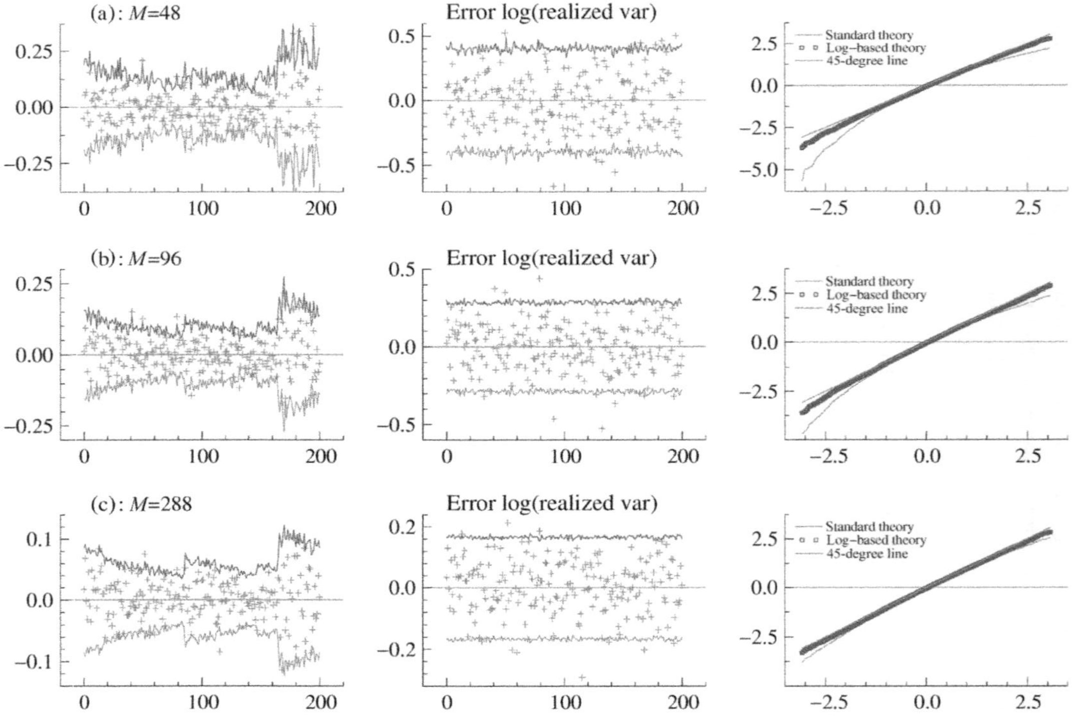

Figure 13.6. Finite sample performance based on an alternative estimator of quarticity. Here we use an average of 4 lags. Actual $[y_M^*]_i - \sigma_i^2$ and twice asymptotic S.E. Middle graphs: $\log[y_M^*]_i - \log \sigma_i^2$ and twice asymptotic S.E.s. QQ plot of the standardized realized variance error for $M = 48$, 96, and 288. (X-axis has the expected quantiles, Y-axis the observed).

Table 13.3. *Bias and standard error of the realized variance errors. First group based on an* $\Gamma(4,8)$*-OU process with* $\lambda = -\log(0.99)$*. Second group changes to an* $\Gamma(4,8)$*-OU process with* $\lambda = -\log(0.9)$*. Third to* $\Gamma(2,4)$*-OU process with* $\lambda = -\log(0.99)$ *File:* `simple.ox`

		Time series estimator				4th moment estimator			
		Raw		Log		Raw		Log	
Model	M	Bias	S.E.	Bias	S.E.	Bias	S.E.	Bias	S.E.
$e^{\lambda} = e^{-0.99}, \Gamma(4,8)$	48	−0.216	1.11	−0.104	1.03	−0.224	1.13	−0.111	1.04
	96	−0.155	1.05	−0.0809	1.01	−0.158	1.05	−0.0832	1.01
	288	−0.103	1.02	−0.0611	1.00	−0.104	1.02	−0.0614	1.01
$e^{\lambda} = e^{-0.9}, \Gamma(4,8)$	48	−0.228	1.13	−0.112	1.04	−0.238	1.15	−0.121	1.06
	96	−0.163	1.07	−0.0857	1.02	−0.165	1.07	−0.0881	1.02
	288	−0.0961	1.01	−0.0541	0.998	−0.0970	1.01	−0.0548	1.00
$e^{\lambda} = e^{-0.99}, \Gamma(2,4)$	48	−0.215	1.11	−0.101	1.04	−0.226	1.14	−0.110	1.05
	96	−0.150	1.06	−0.0734	1.02	−0.152	1.07	−0.0755	1.03
	288	−0.0902	1.01	−0.0481	1.00	−0.0913	1.02	−0.0491	1.00

Table 13.3 reinforces the same points as made by the figure using the bias and the standard errors of the standardized feasible approximations given in (2.12) and (2.13). These are shown with the corresponding results (1.8) and (1.9) based on the fourth moments reported in the previous subsections. These again show a slight improvement using the time series method compared to those obtained by using the fourth moment.

3. SOME THEORETICAL OBSERVATIONS

3.1. Asymptotic Distribution of $\log[y_M^*]_i$

The variance of $\log[y_M^*]_i - \log\sigma_i^2$ seem to only mildly fluctuate with i, with values around $\frac{2}{M}$. The conditional variance in the mixed normal asymptotic theory is

$$\frac{2}{M}\frac{\hbar^{-1}\int_{(i-1)\hbar}^{i\hbar}\sigma^4(u)du}{\left(\hbar^{-1}\int_{(i-1)\hbar}^{i\hbar}\sigma^2(u)du\right)^2} \geq \frac{2}{M},$$

by Jensen's inequality. If σ is continuous the lower bound is obtained when $\hbar \to 0$ for

$$\frac{\hbar^{-1}\int_{(i-1)\hbar}^{i\hbar}\sigma^4(u)du}{\left(\hbar^{-1}\int_{(i-1)\hbar}^{i\hbar}\sigma^2(u)du\right)^2} \overset{a.s.}{\to} 1.$$

On the other hand, for $\hbar \to \infty$ and assuming the spot variance is ergodic then

$$\frac{\hbar^{-1}\int_{(i-1)\hbar}^{i\hbar}\sigma^4(u)du}{\left(\hbar^{-1}\int_{(i-1)\hbar}^{i\hbar}\sigma^2(u)du\right)^2} \overset{a.s.}{\to} \frac{\mathrm{E}\sigma^4(t)}{\{\mathrm{E}\sigma^2(t)\}^2}.$$

In the above examples we had $\sigma^2(t) \sim \Gamma(\nu, \alpha)$, which implies

$$\frac{\mathrm{E}\sigma^4(t)}{\{\mathrm{E}\sigma^2(t)\}^2} = \frac{\nu/\alpha^2 + (\nu/\alpha)^2}{(\nu/\alpha)^2} = 1 + \frac{1}{\nu}.$$

Throughout ν took the value 4, which implies again that the lower bound of $\frac{2}{M}$ is a good rough approximation. Of course, in examples where the fourth moment of the variance process does not exist the lower bound will be wildly off.

3.2. Relationship between Integrals and Sums

In the asymptotics for $[y_M^*]_i$ we replace

$$2\hbar\sigma_i^{[4]} \qquad \text{with} \qquad \frac{2}{3}M\sum_{j=1}^{M} y_{j,i}^4,$$

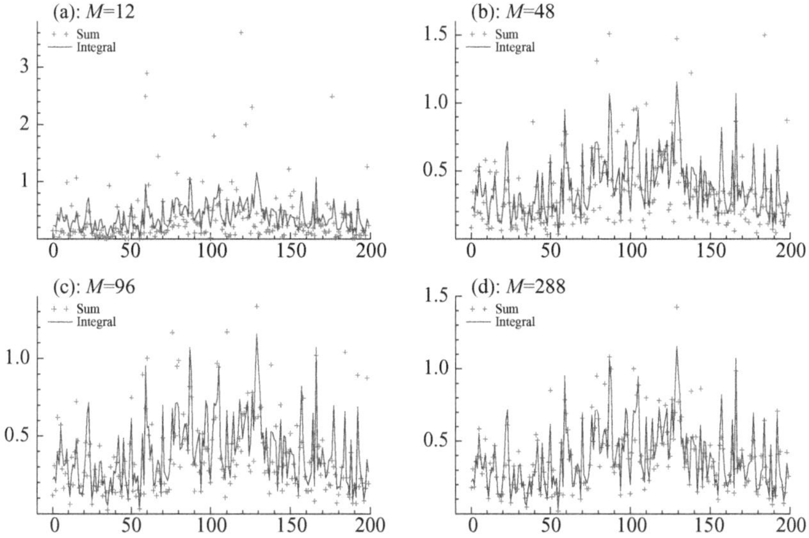

Figure 13.7. $[y_M^*]_i$ case. Plot of the integrals $2\hbar\sigma_i^{[4]}$ and the their consistent estimators $\frac{2}{3}M\sum_{j=1}^{M} y_{j,i}^4$. Based on $M = 12, 48, 96$, and 288.

while in the $\log[y_M^*]_i$ case we estimate

$$2\hbar\sigma_i^{[4]} / \left(\sigma_i^2\right)^2 \qquad \text{by} \qquad \frac{2}{3[y_M^*]_i^2} M \sum_{j=1}^{M} y_{j,i}^4.$$

Although these sums are consistent estimators of the required integrals, in practice they could be rather noisy. Here we report evidence on this issue using the same gamma based superposition model employed in the previous section.

Figure 13.7 shows a plot of $2\hbar\sigma_i^{[4]}$ and its estimator $\frac{2M}{3\sum_{j=1}^{M} y_{j,i}^4}$ against i for a variety of values of M. The key observation is that the estimator is very noisy when M is moderate, with quite large values of M needed in order to accurately estimate $2\hbar\sigma_i^{[4]}$. This is a major cause of the poor nature of the finite sample behavior in the QQ plots we recorded in Figures 13.1, 13.2, and 13.4 above.

Figure 13.8 gives the corresponding results for the asymptotics for $\log[y_M^*]_i$. It shows that $2\hbar\sigma_i^{[4]}/(\sigma_i^2)^2$ does not vary very much with n and hovers just about 2. Thus, dividing by $(\sigma_i^2)^2$ we have approximately stabilized $\sigma_i^{[4]}$. The plot of $\frac{2M}{3[y_M^*]_i^2}\sum_{j=1}^{M} y_{j,i}^4$ shows that this estimator is still quite variable, however, it is a very substantial improvement over the case of $\frac{2M}{3\sum_{j=1}^{M} y_{j,n}^4}$. An interesting feature is that the estimator sometimes goes below 2, which we have seen is the lower bound for the ratio of integrals.

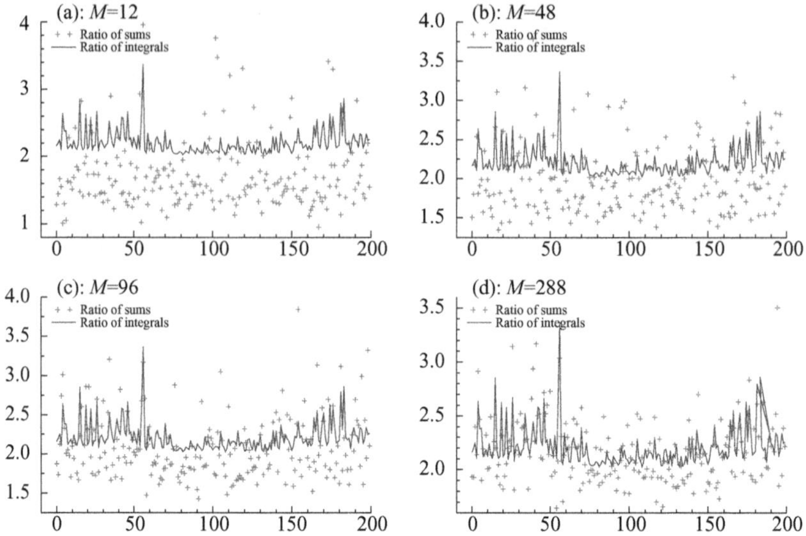

Figure 13.8. $\log[y_M^*]_i$ case. Plot of the ratio of integrals $2\hbar\sigma_i^{[4]}/(\sigma_i^2)^2$ and the their consistent estimators $\frac{2}{3[y_M^*]_i^2} M \sum_{j=1}^{M} y_{j,i}^4$. Based on $M = 12, 48, 96$, and 288.

3.3. Finite Sample Corrections

The observation that the feasible bound sometimes goes below 2 suggests imposing it directly in the standardization formula. In particular we work with

$$\frac{\log[y_M^*]_i - \log \sigma_i^2}{s_i} \xrightarrow{\mathcal{L}} N(0,1),$$

$$\text{where } s_i^2 = \max\left\{ \frac{2}{3[y_M^*]_i^2} \sum_{j=1}^{M} y_{j,i}^4, \frac{2}{M} \right\}.$$

It is also sensible to make a finite sample mean correction to this for $[y_M^*]_i$ is an unbiased estimator of σ_i^2 when $\alpha(t) = 0$, but this implies $\log[y_M^*]_i$ will only biasedly estimate $\log \sigma_i^2$. This means using approximate log normality, working with

$$\frac{\log[y_M^*]_i - \log \sigma_i^2 + \frac{1}{2}s_i^2}{s_i} \xrightarrow{\mathcal{L}} N(0,1),$$

$$\text{where } s_n^2 = \max\left\{ \frac{2}{3[y_M^*]_i^2} \sum_{j=1}^{M} y_{j,i}^4, \frac{2}{M} \right\}$$

The corresponding QQ plot given in Figure 13.9 suggests this improves the finite sample behavior of the method. Separate calculations indicate there is

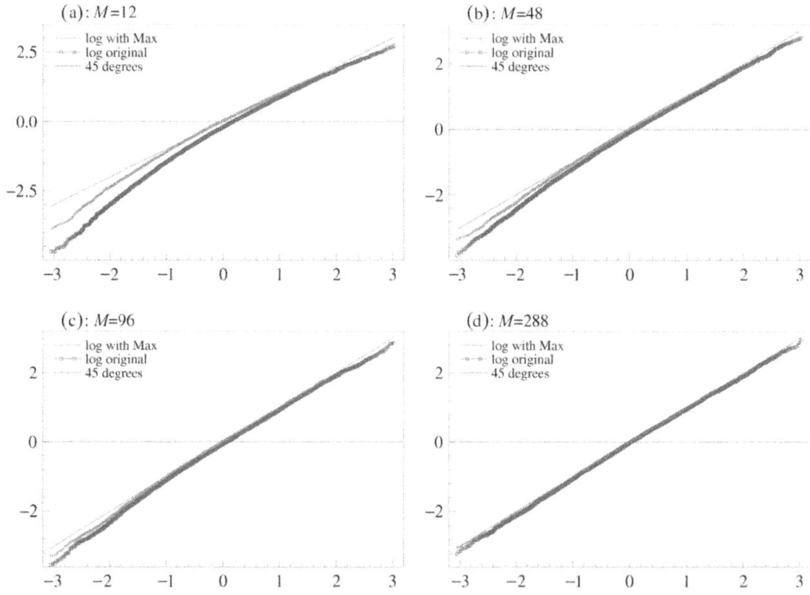

Figure 13.9. $\log[y^*_M]_i$ case. QQ plot for standardized $\log[y^*_M]_i - \log\sigma_i^2$ (denoted log original) and the finite sample version $\frac{\log[y^*_M]_i - \log\sigma_i^2 + \frac{1}{2}s_i^2}{s_i}$ (denoted log with Max in the figure). Based on $M = 12, 48, 96$, and 288.

very little difference between the performance of this statistic and the infeasible version

$$\frac{\log[y^*_M]_i - \log\sigma_i^2 + \frac{1}{2}2\hbar M^{-1}\sigma_i^{[4]}/\left(\sigma_i^2\right)^2}{\sqrt{2\hbar M^{-1}\sigma_i^{[4]}/\left(\sigma_i^2\right)^2}}.$$

3.4. Alternative Transformations

Throughout this paper we have studied the effect of using a log transformation on the realized variance. We have seen this is very beneficial. We now ask if this is the best transformation to use.

Consider a natural exponential family

$$p(x;\theta) = a(\theta)b(x)e^{\theta x},$$

where $p(x;\theta)$ is a probability density function and θ are some parameters. Let $\tau(\mu)$ be the variance function of x expressed as a function of the mean μ of x. For each $\kappa \in (0, 1)$ introduce the transformation

$$\eta_\kappa(\mu) = \int \tau(\mu)^{-\kappa} d\mu,$$

that is, $\eta_\kappa(\mu)$ is the indefinite integral of $\tau(\mu)^{-\kappa}$. Then (subject to the usual type of smoothness conditions) we have (cf. Barndorff-Nielsen, 1978, pp. 177–179) the following.

- For $\kappa = \frac{1}{3}$ the skewness of $\eta_k(x)$ is approximately 0.
- For $\kappa = \frac{1}{2}$ the variance of $\eta_k(x)$ is approximately constant.
- For $\kappa = \frac{1}{2}$ the spread of the log-likelihood function, expressed in terms of $\eta_k(\mu)$, is approximately constant.[3]
- For $\kappa = \frac{2}{3}$ the log-likelihood function, expressed in terms of $\eta_k(\mu)$, is approximately "normal".[4]

Example Barndorff-Nielsen and Shephard (2002) showed that the marginal distribution of realized variance is well approximated by the inverse Gaussian $IG(\delta, \gamma)$ family where $\delta > 0, \gamma > 0$. This has the density

$$f(x) = \frac{\delta}{\sqrt{2\pi}} e^{\delta\gamma} x^{-3/2} \exp\left\{-\tfrac{1}{2}\left(\delta^2 x^{-1} + \gamma^2 x\right)\right\} \qquad x > 0.$$

Further work on this approximation is given in Bollerslev and Forsberg (2002), while Andersen, Bollerslev, Diebold, and Labys (2001) looked at a log-normal approximation. Here δ^2 is a scale parameter and $\tau(\mu) = \delta^{-2}\mu^3$. Hence, $\log x$ is approximately normal in the sense of having an approximately symmetric distribution. And $x^{-1/2}$ has approximately constant variance. For fixed value of the mean δ/γ of x the approximation is better the larger the value of δ.

The above discussion indicates that the log transformation has particular attractive features in the context of realized variances.

4. CONCLUSION

In this note we have looked at the finite sample performance of our asymptotic approximation to the distribution of realized variance. The evidence suggests that the finite sample log version of the result:

$$\frac{\log[y_M^*]_i - \log\sigma_i^2 + \frac{1}{2}s_i^2}{s_i} \xrightarrow{\mathcal{L}} N(0,1),$$

$$\text{where } s_i^2 = \max\left\{\frac{2}{3[y_M^*]_i^2}\sum_{j=1}^{M} y_{j,i}^4, \frac{2}{M}\right\},$$

is reasonably reliable for moderate values of M, say 12 or above.

[3] The precise statement is as follows. Let $l(\eta)$ denote the log likelihood expressed as a function of $\eta = \eta_{1/2}(\mu)$. Then $l''(\hat{\eta}) = 0$.

[4] The precise statement is as follows. Let $l(\eta)$ denote the log likelihood expressed as a function of $\eta = \eta_{2/3}(\mu)$. Then $l^{(3)}(\hat{\eta}) = 0$.

ACKNOWLEDGMENTS

Ole E. Barndorff-Nielsen's work is supported by CAF (www.caf.dk), which is funded by the Danish Social Science Research Council; and by MaPhySto (www.maphysto.dk), which is funded by the Danish National Research Foundation. Neil Shephard's research is supported by UKs ESRC through the grant "High frequency financial econometrics based upon power variation." All the calculations made in this paper are based on software written by Neil Shephard using the Ox language of Doornik (2001). We would like to thank Torben Andersen, Tim Bollerslev, and Nour Meddahi for helpful conversations on this topic.

References

Andersen, T. G., and T. Bollerslev (1997), "Heterogeneous Information Arrivals and Return Volatility Dynamics: Uncovering the Long-run in High Frequency Returns," *Journal of Finance*, 52, 975–1005.

Andersen, T. G., and T. Bollerslev (1998), "Answering the Skeptics: Yes, Standard Volatility Models Do Provide Accurate Forecasts," *International Economic Review*, 39, 885–905.

Andersen, T. G., T. Bollerslev, and F. X. Diebold (2004), "Parametric and Nonparametric Measurement of Volatility," in *Handbook of Financial Econometrics*, (ed. by Y. Ait-Sahalia, and L. P. Hansen), Amsterdam: North Holland. In press.

Andersen, T. G., T. Bollerslev, F. X. Diebold, and H. Ebens (2001), "The Distribution of Realized Stock Return Volatility," *Journal of Financial Economics*, 61, 43–76.

Andersen, T. G., T. Bollerslev, F. X. Diebold, and P. Labys (2001), "The Distribution of Exchange Rate Volatility," *Journal of the American Statistical Association*, 96, 42–55. Correction published in 2003, vol. 98, p. 501.

Back, K. (1991), "Asset Pricing for General Processes," *Journal of Mathematical Economics*, 20, 371–95.

Bai, X., J. R. Russell, and G. C. Tiao (2000), "Beyond Merton's Utopia: Effects of Non-normality and Dependence on the Precision of Variance Estimates Using High-frequency Financial Data," unpublished manuscript, Graduate School of Business, University of Chicago.

Barndorff-Nielsen, O. E. (1978), *Information and Exponential Families in Statistical Theory*. Chichester, UK: John Wiley and Sons.

Barndorff-Nielsen, O. E. (2001), "Superposition of Ornstein–Uhlenbeck Type Processes," *Theory of Probability and Its Applications*, 45, 175–94.

Barndorff-Nielsen, O. E., J. L. Jensen, and M. Sørensen (1998), "Some Stationary Processes in Discrete and Continuous Time," *Advances in Applied Probability*, 30, 989–1007.

Barndorff-Nielsen, O. E., and N. Shephard (2001), "Non-Gaussian Ornstein–Uhlenbeck-based Models and Some of Their Uses in Financial Economics" (with discussion), *Journal of the Royal Statistical Society, Series B*, 63, 167–241.

Barndorff-Nielsen, O. E., and N. Shephard (2002), "Econometric Analysis of Realised Volatility and Its Use in Estimating Stochastic Volatility Models," *Journal of the Royal Statistical Society, Series B*, 64, 253–80.

Barndorff-Nielsen, O. E., and N. Shephard (2003), "Realised Power Variation and Stochastic Volatility," *Bernoulli*, 9, 243–65, 1109–11.

Barndorff-Nielsen, O. E., and N. Shephard (2004), "Econometric Analysis of Realised Covariation: High Frequency Covariance, Regression and Correlation in Financial Economics," *Econometrica*, 72, 885–925.

Bartlett, M. S., and D. G. Kendall (1946), "Statistical Analysis of Variance-heterogeneity and the Logarithmic Transformation. *Journal of the Royal Statistical Society Supplement*, 8, 128–38.

Black, F. (1976), "Studies of Stock Price Volatility Changes," *Proceedings of the Business and Economic Statistics Section, American Statistical Association*, 177–81.

Bollerslev, T., and L. Forsberg (2002), "Bridging the Gap between the Distribution of Realized (ECU) Volatility and ARCH Modeling (of the Euro): The GARCH Normal Inverse Gaussian Model," *Journal of Applied Econometrics*, 17, 535–48.

Chriss, N., and W. Morokoff (1999), "Volatility and Variance Swaps," *Risk*, 12, 55–9.

Christensen, B. J., and N. R. Prabhala (1998), "The Relation between Implied and Realized Volatility," *Journal of Financial Economics*, 37, 125–50.

Comte, F., and E. Renault (1998), "Long Memory in Continuous-time Stochastic Volatility models," *Mathematical Finance*, 8, 291–323.

Cox, D. R. (1991), "Long-range Dependence, Non-linearity and Time Irreversibility," *Journal of Time Series Analysis*, 12, 329–35.

Cox, J. C., J. E. Ingersoll, and S. A. Ross (1985), "A Theory of the Term Structure of Interest Rates. *Econometrica*, 53, 385–407.

Demeterfi, K., E. Derman, M. Kamal, and J. Zou (1999), "A Guide to Volatility and Variance Swaps," *Journal of Derivatives*, 6, 9–32.

Ding, Z., and C. W. J. Granger (1996), "Modeling Volatility Persistence of Speculative Returns: A New Approach," *Journal of Econometrics*, 73, 185–215.

Doornik, J. A. (2001), *Ox: Object Oriented Matrix Programming, 3.0*. London: Timberlake Consultants Press.

Engle, R. F., and G. G. J. Lee (1999), A Permanent and Transitory Component Model of Stock Return Volatility," in *Cointegration, Causality, and Forecasting. A Festschrift in Honour of Clive W.J. Granger*, (ed. by R. F. Engle and H. White) Oxford: Oxford University Press, pp. 475–97.

Florens-Zmirou, D. (1993), "On Estimating the Diffusion Coefficient from Discrete Observations. *Journal of Applied Probability*, 30, 790–804.

Foster, D. P., and D. B. Nelson (1996), "Continuous Record Asymptotics for Rolling Sample Variance Estimators," *Econometrica*, 64, 139–74.

Genon-Catalot, V., C. Laredo, and D. Picard (1992), "Non-parametric Estimation of the Diffusion Coefficient by Wavelet Methods," *Scandinavian Journal of Statistics*, 19, 317–35.

Ghysels, E., A. C. Harvey, and E. Renault (1996), "Stochastic Volatility," *Statistical Methods in Finance*, in (ed. by C. R. Rao and G. S. Maddala). Amsterdam: North-Holland, pp. 119–191.

Granger, C. W. J. (1980), "Long Memory Relationships and the Aggregation of Dynamic Models," *Journal of Econometrics*, 14, 227–38.

Hansen, B. E. (1995), "Regression with Non-stationary Volatility," *Econometrica*, 63, 1113–32.

Heston, S. L. (1993), "A Closed-form Solution for Options with Stochastic Volatility, with Applications to Bond and Currency Options," *Review of Financial Studies*, 6, 327–43.

Howison, S. D., A. Rafailidis, and H. O. Rasmussen (2000), "A Note on the Pricing and Hedging of Volatility Derivatives," unpublished paper: Mathematical Institute, University of Oxford.

Jacod, J., and A. N. Shiryaev (1987), *Limit Theorems for Stochastic Processes*. Berlin: Springer-Verlag.

Meddahi, N. (2002), "A theoretical Comparison between Integrated and Realized Volatilities," *Journal of Applied Econometrics*, 17, 479–508.

Meddahi, N., and E. Renault (2002), "Temporal Aggregation of Volatility Models," *Journal of Econometrics*. Forthcoming.

Nelson, D. B. (1991), "Conditional Heteroskedasticity in Asset Pricing: A New Approach," *Econometrica*, 59, 347–70.

Pagan, A. R., and A. Ullah (1999), *Nonparametric Econometrics*. Cambridge: Cambridge University Press.

Poterba, J., and L. Summers (1986), "The Persistence of Volatility and Stock Market Fluctuations," *American Economic Review*, 76, 1124–41.

Protter, P. (1990), *Stochastic Integration and Differential Equations: A New Approach*. New York: Springer-Verlag.

Rothenberg, T. J. (1984), "Approximating the Distributions of Econometric Estimators and Test Statistics," in *Handbook of Econometrics*, Vol. 2, (ed. by Z. Griliches and M. D. Intriligator), Amsterdam: Elsevier, pp. 881–935.

Schwert, G. W. (1989), "Why Does Stock Market Volatility Change Over Time?," *Journal of Finance*, 44, 1115–53.

Shephard, N. (1996), "Statistical Aspects of ARCH and Stochastic Volatility," in *Time Series Models in Econometrics, Finance and Other Fields* (ed. by D. R. Cox, D. V. Hinkley, and O. E. Barndorff-Nielsen), London: Chapman & Hall, pp. 1–67.

Taylor, S. J. (1994), "Modelling Stochastic Volatility," *Mathematical Finance*, 4, 183–204.

Taylor, S. J., and X. Xu (1997), "The Incremental Volatility Information in One Million Foreign Exchange Quotations," *Journal of Empirical Finance*, 4, 317–40.

CHAPTER 14

Testing the Semiparametric Box–Cox Model with the Bootstrap

N.E. Savin and Allan H. Würtz

ABSTRACT

This paper considers tests of the transformation parameter of the Box–Cox model when the distribution of the error is unknown. Monte Carlo experiments are carried out to investigate the rejection probabilities of the GMM-based Wald and Lagrange multiplier (LM) tests when the null hypothesis is true. The results show that the differences between empirical and nominal levels can be large when asymptotic critical values are used. In most cases, the bootstrap reduces the differences between the empirical and nominal levels, and, in many cases, essentially removes the distortions in levels that occur with asymptotic critical values. Experiments are also carried out to investigate the ability of the bootstrap to provide improved finite-sample critical values with Wald tests based on the semiparametric estimation procedure recently developed by Foster, Tian, and Wei (2001).

1. INTRODUCTION

The Box–Cox (1964) regression model is a transformation model of the form

$$T(Y, \alpha) = X'\beta + U, \tag{1.1}$$

where T is a strictly increasing function, Y is an observed positive dependent variable, X is an observed K-dimensional random column vector, β is a vector of constant parameters that is conformable with X, and U is an unobserved random variable that is independent of X. Let the cumulative distribution function of U be denoted by F. It is assumed that $E(U) = 0$, $\mathrm{V}(U) < \infty$ for all x in the support of X and that F is unknown.

The Box–Cox transformation is

$$T(y, \alpha) = \begin{cases} \frac{y^{\alpha}-1}{\alpha}, & \text{if } \alpha \neq 0,\ y \geq 0, \\ \log y, & \text{if } \alpha = 0,\ y \geq 0. \end{cases} \tag{1.2}$$

The transformation provides a flexible parameterization of the relation between Y and X. In particular, the model is a linear model if $\alpha = 1$, a power transformation model if $\alpha \neq 0$ or 1, and a log-linear model if $\alpha = 0$.

If F is known or known up to finite dimensional parameters, then α and β and any parameters of F can be estimated by maximum likelihood. A widely used procedure, which was suggested by Box and Cox (1964), is to estimate α and β by maximum likelihood (ML), assuming that U is normally distributed.

The resulting estimator of α and β is referred to as the *Box–Cox ML estimator*. The Box–Cox ML estimator is discussed in many econometric textbooks, for example, Amemiya (1985), Greene (2000), Ruud (2000), and Mittlehammer, Judge, and Miller (2000).

The assumption of normality cannot be strictly true, however. The Box–Cox transformation $T(y,\alpha)$ is bounded from below if $\alpha > 0$ (and from above if $\alpha < 0$), unless α is an odd integer or 0. Thus, the Box–Cox transformation cannot be applied to models in which the dependent variable can be negative or the distribution of U has unbounded support, and, hence, this rules out the case where U is normally distributed.

In practice, however, F is often unknown. Thus, an empirically relevant statistical problem is to obtain consistent estimators of α and β when F is unknown. A solution proposed by Amemiya and Powell (1981) is to use the nonlinear two-stage least-squares (NL2SLS) estimator of α and β. The NL2SLS estimator is a generalized method of moments (GMM) estimator (Hansen 1982), and it is the efficient GMM estimator for the choice of instruments used by Amemiya and Powell if U is independent of X. Horowitz (1998) discusses GMM estimation of α and β.

Khazzoom (1989) pointed out that the NL2SLS estimates for this model are ill-defined for data sets in which the dependent variable always exceeds (or is exceeded by) 1. The nonnegative GMM objective function has a global minimum of zero as α tends to minus infinity when $y > 1$ and infinity when $y < 1$. Powell (1996) has proposed a simple rescaling of the GMM objective function that helps ensure that the estimates are interior points of the parameter space.

The focus of this paper is on testing the transformation parameter α in the Box–Cox model when F is unknown. This null is tested using the GMM-based Wald and Lagrange multiplier (LM) tests proposed by Newey and West (1987). The test of the null is based on an estimator of the *type I critical value*. Horowitz and Savin (2000) define this critical value as one that would be obtained if the exact finite sample distribution of the test statistic under the true data generation process is known. In our setting, the true type I critical value is unknown because the null hypothesis is composite: the exact finite-sample distribution of the test statistic depends on β and F, the population parameters that are not specified by the null. Thus, an approximation to the type I critical value is required to implement the test.

An approximation to the type I critical value can be obtained by using the first-order asymptotic distribution of the test statistic to approximate its finite-sample distribution. The approximation is useful because most test statistics in econometrics are asymptotically pivotal: their asymptotic distributions do not depend on unknown population parameters when the null hypothesis being tested is true. In particular, this is true for the GMM-based Wald and LM statistics employed to test null hypotheses about the transformation parameter. Hence, an approximate type I critical value can be obtained from first-order asymptotic distribution theory without knowledge of the true data-generation process.

However, the Monte Carlo experiments discussed in this paper show that the first-order asymptotic distribution is often a poor approximation to the true, finite-sample distributions for the sample sizes available in applications. In other contexts, many investigators have found that the asymptotic approximation for GMM-based tests is poor; for example, see the 1996 special issue of the *Journal of Business and Economics*.

The bootstrap often provides a practical method for improving first-order asymptotic approximations. It is a method for estimating the distribution of a statistic or a feature of the distribution, such as a moment or a quantile. The bootstrap can be implemented for model (1.1)–(1.2) by randomly resampling (Y, X) pairs with replacement or by randomly resampling GMM residuals with replacement, provided the bootstrap takes into account that Y can only take positive values. This paper reports the numerical performance of the bootstrap for both the resampling schemes. The Monte Carlo experiments show that when bootstrap critical values obtained by resampling residuals are used, the differences between the empirical and the nominal levels of the tests are often very small.

In the context of the Box–Cox model, the linear model can be tested against models that are indexed by the transformation parameter. For example, the linear model can be tested against the log-linear model by testing the null hypothesis $\alpha = 1$ against the alternative $\alpha = 0$. The tests must be able to discriminate between alternative models in order to be useful. This paper also carries out a Monte Carlo investigation of the powers of the tests with bootstrap critical values.

Recently, Foster, Tian, and Wei (2001) proposed an alternative to GMM estimation when U and X are independent and the distribution of U is unknown. Monte Carlo experiments are conducted to investigate the performance of Wald and LM tests when the model is estimated using the Foster, Tian, and Wei (FTW) estimator. In the experiments reported here, the tests are carried out with asymptotic critical values and bootstrap critical values.

The organization of the paper is as follows. Section 2 reviews the GMM estimation of the Box–Cox model, Section 3 introduces the GMM-based Wald and LM tests, Section 4 describes the calculation of the bootstrap critical values, and Section 5 presents the design of the experiments and the methods used to calculate the empirical rejection probabilities. Section 6 reports the Monte Carlo evidence on the numerical performance of the GMM-based tests with asymptotic and bootstrap critical values, and Section 7 presents the results of the experiments using the FTW estimator. The concluding comments are contained in Section 8.

2. GMM ESTIMATORS

This section introduces the Box–Cox model employed in the Monte Carlo study, reviews GMM estimation of the parameters, and presents the rescaling procedure proposed by Powell (1996) to address the problem noted by Khazzoom (1989).

The model simulated in the Monte Carlo experiments is

$$T(Y, \alpha) = \beta_0 + \beta_1 X + U, \tag{2.1}$$

where X is a scalar random variable and X and U are independent. The instruments used are those employed by Amemiya and Powell (1981), namely, 1, X, and X^2. With this set of instruments, the number of moment conditions is equal to the number of the parameters, and hence the parameters are exactly identified. In the exactly identified case, NL2SLS is (trivially) the efficient GMM estimator.

Denote the estimation data by $\{Y_i, X_i\colon i = 1, \ldots, \text{n}\}$ and assume that they are a random sample from the joint distribution of (Y, X). Let $\theta = (\alpha, \beta')'$, $U_i(\theta) = T(Y_i, \alpha) - X_i'\beta$, and $U(\theta) = (U_1(\theta), \ldots, U_n(\theta))'$. Also let $W = [W_1, \ldots, W_n]'$ denote the matrix of instruments where W_i is a vector of functions of X_i. Finally, let $\hat{\theta}_n = (\hat{a}_n, \hat{b}_n')'$ where $\hat{a}_n$ and $\hat{b}_n$ denote the unconstrained GMM estimators of α and β, respectively.

The unconstrained GMM estimator solves

$$\min_{\theta} : \; S_n(\theta) = U(\theta)'\mathrm{W}\Omega_n\mathrm{W}'U(\theta), \tag{2.2}$$

where the weight matrix Ω_n is a positive definite, possibly stochastic, matrix. One possible choice of the weight matrix is $\Omega_n = [W'W]^{-1}$, in which case (2.2) gives the NL2SLS estimator of Amemiya (1974, 1985). This choice is asymptotically efficient if the errors U_i are homoskedastic. Amemiya and Powell (1981) and Amemiya (1985) discuss the use of NL2SLS for estimation of the Box–Cox model. The weight matrix does not matter in the exactly identified case, provided the sample moment conditions are solved by the unconstrained GMM estimator.

The change in the NL2SLS estimate of β due to a rescaling of X is the same as the change in the ordinary least-squares (OLS) estimate in the linear regression model. By contrast, the effect of rescaling Y depends on whether the parameters are exactly identified or overidentified. In the exactly identified case, rescaling Y has no effect on the NL2SLS estimate of α; only β is affected. In the overidentified case, rescaling Y changes the estimates of both α and β.

The consistency of the estimator minimizing (2.2) is established by verification of three conditions: compactness of the parameter space; convergence in probability of the objective function S_n to its expected value, uniformly in α and β; and uniqueness of the solutions satisfying the population moment condition $E\{W\{T(Y, \alpha) - X'\beta]\} = 0$. The compactness and identification conditions turn out to be demanding because of the nature of the transformation function $T(Y, \alpha)$.

As Khazzoom (1989) notes, if $y > 1$, then $T(y, \alpha) \to 0$ as $\alpha \to -\infty$, and, similarly, if $y < 1$, $T(y, \alpha) \to 0$ as $\alpha \to \infty$. This implies that compactness of the parameter space plays a crucial role in the uniqueness of the solution of the population moment condition. In particular, each residual $U_i(\theta) = T(y_i, \alpha) - x_i'\beta$ can be set equal to 0 by setting $\alpha = -\infty$ and $\beta = 0$ if each $y_i > 1$. The resulting pathology of the objective function is important in practice, since in many data sets all values of the dependent variable exceed 1.

To avoid the problem associated with the scaling of the dependent variable, Powell (1996) suggested the following rescaling of the GMM objective function:

$$Q_n(\theta) = S_n(\theta) \cdot (\dot{y})^{-2\alpha}, \tag{2.3}$$

where the GMM objective function S_n is given in (2.2) and $\dot{y}$ is the geometric mean of the absolute values of the dependent variable:

$$\dot{y} \equiv \exp\left\{\frac{1}{n}\sum_{i=1}^{n}\log(|y_i|)\right\}. \tag{2.4}$$

The rescaled GMM objective function Q_n is less likely than S_n to be minimized by values on the boundary of the parameter space. However, as Powell (1996) notes, rescaling the original GMM function by $\dot{y}^{-2\alpha}$ cannot guarantee that a unique and finite minimizing value of α will exist. Following Powell, the estimator based on the rescaled GMM objective function is denoted by RNL2SLS.

The estimation procedure for rescaled GMM simplifies to a one-dimensional grid search, and similarly for the original GMM. The objective function

$$Q_n(\theta) = [U(\theta)'\mathrm{W}/\dot{y}^{\alpha}]'\Omega[\mathrm{W}'U(\theta)/\dot{y}^{\alpha}] \tag{2.5}$$

can be concentrated as a function of α only. The reason is that for a given α, the optimal β in (2.5) is

$$\beta(\alpha) = \left[\left(\sum_{i=1}^{n} W_i X_i'\right)' \Omega \left(\sum_{i=1}^{n} W_i X_i'\right)\right]^{-1} \left(\sum_{i=1}^{n} W_i X_i'\right)' \Omega \sum_{i=1}^{n} W_i(T(Y_i, \alpha)], \tag{2.6}$$

since $\dot{y}^{-\alpha}$ cancels. The concentrated objective function is obtained by substituting (2.6) into (2.5), which gives

$$Q_n(\alpha) = Q_n(\alpha, \beta(\alpha)) = S_n(\alpha, \beta(\alpha))/\dot{y}^{2^{\alpha}}. \tag{2.7}$$

Note that if NL2SLS and RNL2SLS give the same estimate of α, then they both give the same estimate of β.

Powell (1996) argues that the original and rescaled GMM estimators have the same asymptotic distribution. Hence, the standard formulae for the first-order asymptotic distribution and asymptotic covariance matrix estimators for GMM estimators apply directly to the rescaled estimators.

3. GMM-BASED TESTS

This section introduces the null hypotheses tested in the experiments and presents the GMM-based Wald and LM test statistics proposed by Newey and West (1987).

The null hypotheses specify the value of the transformation parameter: H_0: $\alpha = \alpha_0$. Two values of α are considered, 0 and 1. The first value specifies a log-linear model and the second a linear model.

The GMM-based Wald test statistic is derived from the asymptotic distributional properties of the unconstrained GMM estimator. Hansen (1982) showed, under mild regularity conditions, that $\hat{\theta}_n = (\hat{a}_n, \hat{b}_n')'$ is a consistent estimator of θ and that $\hat{\theta}_n$ is asymptotically normally distributed:

$$n^{1/2}(\hat{\theta}_n - \theta) \to^d N(0, V) \tag{3.1}$$

where

$$V = (D'\Omega D)^{-1}, \tag{3.2}$$

with $D = E\frac{\partial}{\partial\theta} W[T(Y, \alpha) - X\beta]$ and $\Omega = p \lim_{n\to\infty} \Omega_n$. Letting $U_\theta = \partial U(\theta)/\partial\theta$ and $\hat{U}_\theta = \partial U(\hat{\theta}_n)/\partial\theta$, V can be estimated by replacing D in (3.2) by $\mathrm{W}'\hat{U}_\theta$ and Ω by Ω_n. Thus, (3.1) and (3.2) with V replaced by

$$\hat{V}_n = \hat{U}_\theta' \mathrm{W}\Omega_n \mathrm{W}' \hat{U}_\theta \tag{3.3}$$

makes it possible to carry out inference in sufficiently large samples.

The Wald test statistic for testing H_0: $\alpha = \alpha_0$ is

$$\text{Wald} = \frac{n(\hat{a}_n - \alpha_0)^2}{\hat{s}_n^2}, \tag{3.4}$$

where $\hat{s}_n^2$ is the first diagonal element in $\hat{V}_n$.The Wald statistic (3.4) is distributed asymptotically as chi-square variables with one degree of freedom when the null hypothesis is true. The GMM estimators that can be used in computing (3.4) include, as special cases, the NL2SLS and RNL2SLS estimators. The principle disadvantage of the GMM-based Wald statistic is that it is not invariant to reparametrization of the null hypothesis or rescaling of the dependent variable. Spitzer (1984) has shown a similar lack of invariance for the Wald statistic based on the Box–Cox ML estimator; see also Drucker (2000).

Newey and West (1987) have developed an LM test based on the constrained GMM estimator. This LM test is presented in Greene (2000). Suppose the constrained estimator, denoted by $\tilde{\theta}_n = (\tilde{a}_n, \tilde{b}_n')'$, solves (2.2) subject to a constraint of the form H_0: $h(\theta) = 0$. Then the GMM-based LM statistic is

$$\text{LM} = \frac{\partial S_n(\tilde{\theta}_n)}{\partial\theta'} \left[\text{Var}\left(\frac{\partial S_n(\tilde{\theta}_n)}{\partial\theta}\right)\right]^{-1} \frac{\partial S_n(\tilde{\theta}_n)}{\partial\theta}. \tag{3.5}$$

The LM statistic can also be written as

$$\text{LM} = n \cdot \tilde{U}' P_W \tilde{U}_\theta [\tilde{U}_\theta' P_W \tilde{U}_\theta]^{-1} \tilde{U}_\theta' P_W \tilde{U} / \tilde{U}'\tilde{U}, \tag{3.6}$$

where $P_W = W(W'W)^{-1}W'$, $\tilde{U} = U(\tilde{\theta}_n)$ and $\tilde{U}_\theta = \partial U(\tilde{\theta}_n)/\partial\theta$. The (3.6) version of the LM statistic is $n \cdot R^2$ from a regression of $\tilde{U}$ on $P_W \tilde{U}_\theta$. That is, the LM statistic can be obtained from regressing $\tilde{U}_\theta$ on W, calculating the predicted value, and then calculating $n \cdot R^2$ from a regression of the restricted residual on these predicted values. The constrained NL2SLS and RNL2SLS estimates of α are the same, and, hence, the constrained NL2SLS and RNL2SLS estimates of β are the same. As a result, the values of the LM statistic for NL2SLS and RNL2SLS are also the same.

Newey (personal communication, 2001) shows that the calculation of the GMM-based LM test statistic simplifies when the constraint imposed by the null hypothesis is $H_0{:}\alpha = \alpha_0$ and X is included among the instruments. Note first that by having X_i included in W_i, the constrained estimator is $\tilde{\theta}_n = (\alpha_0, \tilde{b}_n')'$, where $\tilde{\beta}$ is the OLS estimator obtained by regressing $T(Y_i, \alpha_0)$ on X_i. Therefore the constrained residual vector $\tilde{U}$ is just the residual vector from the OLS regression of $T(Y_i, \alpha_0)$ on X_i . Also $\tilde{U}_\theta = \partial U(\tilde{\theta}_n)/\partial\theta = [\tilde{T}_\alpha, -X]$, where $\tilde{T}_\alpha = (\partial T(y_1, \alpha_0)/\partial\alpha, \ldots, \partial T(y_n, \alpha_0)/\partial\alpha)'$ and $X = [X_1, \ldots, X_n]'$. Furthermore, if X_i is included in W_i, then $P_W \tilde{U}_\theta = [P_X \tilde{T}_\alpha, -X]$. Thus, the LM statistic for testing α can be obtained in three steps as follows:

1. Obtain the OLS residuals by regressing $T(Y_i, \alpha_0)$ on X_i.
2. Obtain the predicted values by regressing $T(Y_i, \alpha_0)$ on W_i.
3. Calculate the test statistic as $n \cdot R^2$ by regressing the residuals from step 1 on the predicted values from step 2 and the X_is.

The GMM-based LM statistic is invariant to reparametrization of the null hypothesis, but not always to the rescaling of the dependent variable. Invariance to rescaling depends on whether the parameters are exactly identified. The LM statistic is invariant to rescaling of the dependent variable in the exactly identified case, but not in the overidentified case.

4. BOOTSTRAP CRITICAL VALUES

This section describes the Monte Carlo procedure for computing the bootstrap critical values. The description is given for two resampling schemes, a nonparametric and a parametric scheme. In the nonparametric scheme, (Y, X) pairs are randomly sampled with replacement, and in the parametric scheme, residuals are randomly sampled with replacement. Resampling the (Y, X) pairs is used only for the GMM-based Wald test.

When resampling (Y, X) pairs, the Monte Carlo procedure for computing the bootstrap critical value for the Wald test is the following:

1. Generate a bootstrap sample of size n by random sampling (Y, X) pairs from the estimation data with replacement.

2. Compute the unconstrained GMM estimators of θ and V from the bootstrap sample. Call the results $\hat{\theta}_n{}^* = (\hat{a}_n{}^*, \hat{b}_n{}^{*\prime})'$and $\hat{V}_n{}^*$.
3. Compute the bootstrap version of the Wald statistic

$$\text{Wald}^* = \frac{n(\hat{a}_n{}^* - \hat{a}_n)^2}{\hat{s}_n^{2*}}, \tag{4.1}$$

where $\hat{s}_n^{2*}$ is the first element of $\hat{V}_n{}^*$. Note that Wald* is centered by replacing α_0 by $\hat{a}_n$.
4. Obtain the empirical distribution function (EDF) of the test statistic Wald* by repeating steps 2 and 3 many times. The bootstrap critical value is obtained from the EDF. For example, the 0.01 type I critical value is estimated by the 0.99 quantile of the EDF of Wald*. Let $z^*_{n,0.01}$ denote the bootstrap critical value for the nominal 0.01 level test. The 0.05 and 0.10 bootstrap critical values are obtained similarly.

The Monte Carlo procedure using resampled residuals is based on the functional form of the model (1.1)–(1.2). The bootstrap critical values are calculated as follows:

(a) Estimate θ_0 by constrained GMM using the estimation sample $\{Y_i, X_i$: $i = 1, \ldots, n\}$ and compute the constrained GMM residuals$\tilde{U}_1, \ldots, \tilde{U}_n$.
(b) Generate the bootstrap sample by setting $Y_i^* = [\alpha_0(\tilde{b}_{0n} + X_i^* \tilde{b}_{1n} + U_i^*) + 1]^{1/\alpha_0}$, where U_i^* is sampled randomly with replacement from the $\tilde{U}_i$. The X_i are fixed in repeated samples.
(c) Estimate θ_0 by unconstrained GMM using the bootstrap sample and compute the Wald statistic

$$\text{Wald}^{**} = \frac{n(\hat{a}_n{}^* - \alpha_0)^2}{\hat{s}_n^{2*}}. \tag{4.2}$$

(d) Obtain the EDF of Wald** by repeating steps (b) and (c) many times. The bootstrap critical values are obtained from the EDFs. The 0.01 type I critical value is estimated by the 0.99 quantile of the EDF. The 0.05 and 0.10 bootstrap critical values are obtained similarly.

The advantage of resampling residuals compared to resampling (Y, X) pairs is numerical accuracy. Monte Carlo evidence (Horowitz 1997) indicates that the numerical accuracy of the bootstrap tends to be much higher when residuals are resampled than when (Y, X) pairs are resampled. This because the functional form of the model is exploited and the null hypothesis is imposed when obtaining the parameter estimate.

In this paper, there is no need to recenter the GMM moment conditions due to overidentifying restrictions. In general, when there are overidentifying restrictions, the GMM moment conditions have to be recentered for the bootstrap to improve first-order approximations. This is because the sample analog of $E(WU) = 0$ is not satisfied in the estimation sample, and, hence, the bootstrap implements a moment condition that does not hold in the population that the bootstrap samples.

When resampling the $\tilde{U}_i$, it may happen that the value of Y_i^*cannot be calculated (the implied value is complex) because of estimation error in the $\tilde{U}_i$. In such cases, Y_i^* is chosen to be 0.0001. This procedure is valid given that the estimation error vanishes rapidly as the sample size increases.

The Monte Carlo procedure for computing the bootstrap critical value for the LM test when resampling residuals is similar to the one used for the Wald test. The main difference occurs in step (c). For the LM test, estimate θ_0 in the bootstrap sample by constrained GMM and compute the LM statistic

$$\mathrm{LM} = \frac{\partial S_n^*(\tilde{\theta}_n^*)}{\partial \theta'} \left[\mathrm{Var}\left(\frac{\partial S_n^*(\tilde{\theta}_n^*)}{\partial \theta} \right) \right]^{-1} \frac{\partial S_n^*(\tilde{\theta}_n^*)}{\partial \theta}, \tag{4.3}$$

where S_n^* is the objective function (4.4), and $\tilde{\theta}_n^*$is the constrained GMM estimator of θ.

5. DESIGN OF EXPERIMENTS AND COMPUTATIONS

This section presents the design of the Monte Carlo experiments used to investigate the ability of the bootstrap to reduce the distortions in the level of the Wald and the LM tests that occur when asymptotic critical values are used.

Two different specifications for the distribution function of U are considered for the Box–Cox model. The first specification is a truncated normal distribution suggested by Poirier (1978). Let U be $N(0, (0.5)^2)$ with left truncation point -1. The second is an exponential distribution for $U$with parameter $\lambda = 4$. In both specifications, the distribution of U is corrected to have mean 0; for example, in the exponential case, $U - 1/4$ is used instead of U. Foster et al. (2001) use the exponential distribution in their Monte Carlo experiments. The values of $X$are obtained by random-sampling the following marginal distributions of X: uniform $[-0.5, 0.5]$, lognormal based on $N(0, 1)$, and exponential with $\lambda = 1$.

The above specifications of the distribution function of U and of X are combined to produce four basic specifications of the model. The specifications are the following:

Model 1: $\beta_0 = 1$, $\beta_1 = 1$, F truncated normal, $\sigma = 0.5$, X uniform $[-0.5, 0.5]$.

Model 2: $\beta_0 = 0.1$, $\beta_1 = 1$, F truncated normal, $\sigma = 0.5$, X lognormal. ($\beta_0 = 0.1$ instead of $\beta_0 = 0$ to avoid negative values of Y.)

Model 3: $\beta_0 = 0$, $\beta_1 = 1$, F exponential, X uniform $[-0.5, 0.5]$.

Model 4: $\beta_0 = 0$, $\beta_1 = 1$, F exponential, X exponential.

Using these models, tests of the null hypothesis H_0: $\alpha = \alpha_0$, $\alpha_0 = 0$ and 1 are conducted at three nominal levels: 0.01, 0.05, and 0.10. The sample sizes investigated are $n = 25$ and $n = 50$.

The rejection probabilities of the tests when the null is true were estimated by conducting Monte Carlo experiments. The number of Monte Carlo replications in each experiment with the GMM estimators is 10,000. Each replication consists of the following steps:

(i) Generate an estimation data set of size n by random sampling from the model (1.1)–(1.2) with the null hypothesis H_0: $\alpha = \alpha_0$ imposed. Compute the value of the Wald statistic and the value of the LM statistic for testing H_0.
(ii) Generate a bootstrap sample of size n for the bootstrap-based test. Compute the bootstrap critical value for the Wald test by following steps 1–4 when the bootstrap samples are generated by resampling (Y, X) pairs, and denote the estimated 0.01 critical value by $z^*_{n,0.01}$. Compute the bootstrap critical value for the Wald test by following steps (a)–(d) when the bootstrap samples are generated by resampling residuals, and denote the estimated 0.01 critical value by $z^{**}_{n,0.01}$. In (ii) the EDF is obtained from 999 bootstrap replications.
(iii) Reject H_0 at the nominal 0.01 level with the asymptotic critical value if Wald > 6.66, with the bootstrap critical value based on resampling (Y, X) pairs if Wald* > $z^*_{n,0.01}$ and with the bootstrap critical value based on resampling residuals if Wald** > $z^{**}_{n,0.01}$. The rules are similar for the nominal 0.05 and 0.10 Wald tests and for the nominal 0.01, 0.05, and 0.10 LM tests.

The powers of the Wald and the LM tests with asymptotic and bootstrap critical values are also estimated by conducting Monte Carlo experiments. In each replication of the power experiments, the first step consists of generating the estimation data set under the alternative hypothesis instead of under the null. The remaining steps in each replication are the same as (i)–(iii).

In the experiments, the unconstrained GMM estimate is calculated by minimizing the objective function over a grid of values of the transformation parameter α. To speed up the calculations the grid search is implemented in two steps. The first step is to use a coarse grid with width δ and precision p. The precision is the distance between two neighboring points in the grid. The coarse grid is located with the true value in the middle of the grid. Suppose that the minimum of the objective function is located at a point inside the coarse grid. Denote this point by P. The second step is to construct a fine grid with a width δ' that is two times the precision of the coarse grid $\delta' = 2\,p$ and a precision p'. The fine grid is located with point P in the middle. Thus, the fine grid evaluates the objective function between two points in the coarse grid that are neighbors of point P.

In some cases, the solution using the coarse grid is a point on the boundary. If this occurs, then the coarse grid is shifted to cover the interval in the neighborhood of the boundary solution. Then a new minimum is located, and the algorithm proceeds to the fine grid. The sample is discarded if the new solution is also a boundary solution. Therefore, the estimate of the rejection probability under H_0 is computed as R/G where R is the number of rejections of H_0 in G nondeleted estimation samples.

The total precision of this algorithm is a grid with a total width 3δ and precision p'. This algorithm is faster than simply using a grid with a width 3δ and a precision p', because it is usually not necessary to shift the coarse grid to find the minimum. Also the fine grid is only evaluated around the minimum located with the coarse grid. This algorithm worked well for the objective function of the Box–Cox model.

6. EMPIRICAL REJECTION PROBABILITIES

This section reports the empirical rejection probabilities of the Wald and the LM tests based on the GMM estimators. The results illustrate the numerical performance of the tests with asymptotic critical values and those with bootstrap critical values. The empirical rejection probabilities under H_0 are reported for models 1–4 in Tables 14.1–14.4 respectively.

The following is a summary of the main features of the results.

Asymptotic Critical Values

The results are first summarized for the Wald tests with asymptotic critical values. The tables show that the model influences the differences between the empirical and nominal levels. In Table 14.1, the empirical levels are much smaller than the nominal levels for model 1. By contrast, Table 14.4 shows that the differences between the empirical and nominal levels are usually very small for model 4.

Table 14.2 shows that the empirical levels are sensitive to the estimation method and the null hypothesis. Using NL2SLS estimation, the empirical levels are much smaller than the nominal levels when testing H_0: $\alpha = 0$ and larger than the nominal levels when testing H_0: $\alpha = 1$. On the other hand, when the model is estimated by RNL2SLS, empirical levels are larger than the nominal levels.

The tables also show that the experimental evidence is mixed when comparing RNL2SLS and NL2SLS. The differences between the empirical and nominal levels of the RNL2SLS Wald tests are often, but not always, smaller than those of the NL2SLS Wald tests. Note that in Table 14.4 the empirical rejection probabilities for the NL2SLS and RNL2SLS Wald tests with asymptotic critical values are identical when testing H_0: $\alpha = 1$. The explanation here is that NL2SLS and RNL2SLS give the same estimate of α. When this occurs, both estimation methods produce the same estimate of β.

Turning to the LM tests, the differences between the empirical and nominal levels are much smaller for the LM tests than for the Wald tests, both for $n = 25$ and $n = 50$. Indeed, inspection of Tables 14.1–14.4 shows that when $n = 50$ the differences between the empirical and nominal levels are, almost without exception, essentially zero for all models.

Table 14.1. *Empirical rejection probabilities (percent) of Wald and LM tests for model 1:* $\beta_0 = 1, \beta_1 = 1$, *F truncated normal,* $\sigma = 0.5$, *X uniform* $[-0.5, 0.5]$

		Nominal Rejection Probabilities								
		1	5	10	1	5	10	1	5	10
		Wald						LM		
Critical values	Hypothesis	NL2SLS			RNL2SLS			NL2SLS		
$n = 25$										
Asymptotic	$\alpha = 0$	0.00	0.05	0.29	0.44	1.34	2.64	1.04	5.83	11.4
	$\alpha = 1$	0.00	0.17	0.78	1.21	3.26	5.62	1.04	5.83	11.4
Bootstrap (Y, X) pair	$\alpha = 0$	0.03	0.17	0.49	0.00	0.01	0.02			
	$\alpha = 1$	0.03	0.03	1.89	0.00	0.00	0.01			
Bootstrap residuals	$\alpha = 0$	0.69	3.23	7.10	0.03	3.05	6.98	1.10	5.17	9.89
	$\alpha = 1$	0.85	3.74	7.80	0.44	3.61	8.04	1.10	5.17	9.89
$n = 50$										
Asymptotic	$\alpha = 0$	0.00	0.13	0.70	0.16	0.90	2.16	1.02	5.23	10.4
	$\alpha = 1$	0.03	0.43	1.66	0.72	2.15	4.45	1.02	5.23	10.4
Bootstrap (Y, X) pair	$\alpha = 0$	0.00	0.17	0.78	0.00	0.00	0.05			
	$\alpha = 1$	0.06	0.75	3.84	0.00	0.00	0.01			
Bootstrap residuals	$\alpha = 0$	0.83	3.84	8.16	0.11	3.31	7.86	1.06	5.10	9.87
	$\alpha = 1$	0.90	4.56	9.17	0.41	3.43	8.41	1.06	5.10	9.87

Notes: The empirical rejection probabilities are computed using 10,000 Monte Carlo replications and 999 bootstrap replications. The 95% confidence intervals for the 0.01, 0.05, and 0.10 levels are (0.80, 1.12), (4.57, 5.43) and (9.41, 10.59), respectively; the 99% confidence intervals are (0.744, 1.26), (4.44, 5.56), and (9.23, 10.8), respectively.

Table 14.2. *Empirical rejection probabilities (percent) of Wald and LM tests for model 2: $\beta_0 = 0.1$, $\beta_1 = 1$, F truncated normal, $\sigma = 0.5$, X lognormal*

		Nominal rejection probabilities								
		1	5	10	1	5	10	1	5	10
		Wald						LM		
Critical values	Hypothesis	NL2SLS			RNL2SLS			NL2SLS		
$n = 25$										
Asymptotic	$\alpha = 0$	1.05	2.89	5.39	2.78	7.44	12.4	1.09	6.20	12.2
	$\alpha = 1$	2.38	6.87	11.6	2.43	7.01	11.8	1.09	6.20	12.2
Bootstrap (Y, X) Pair	$\alpha = 0$	0.69	3.05	6.49	0.35	1.94	4.45			
	$\alpha = 1$	1.20	5.51	11.7	0.97	4.72	10.5			
Bootstrap residuals	$\alpha = 0$	1.06	4.27	8.70	1.19	5.33	10.2	1.10	5.44	10.8
	$\alpha = 1$	1.19	5.45	10.2	1.16	5.41	10.2	1.10	5.44	10.8
$n = 50$										
Asymptotic	$\alpha = 0$	0.38	1.63	3.17	1.91	6.71	11.7	1.06	5.35	10.8
	$\alpha = 1$	1.46	5.66	10.9	1.50	5.78	11.1	1.06	5.35	10.8
Bootstrap (Y, X) pair	$\alpha = 0$	0.43	1.98	4.44	0.32	1.31	2.67			
	$\alpha = 1$	1.26	5.64	11.4	1.20	5.55	11.2			
Bootstrap residuals	$\alpha = 0$	0.81	3.97	8.53	1.02	4.72	9.33	1.10	5.25	10.1
	$\alpha = 1$	1.05	4.97	10.1	1.04	4.97	10.0	1.10	5.25	10.1

Notes: The empirical rejection probabilities are computed using 10,000 Monte Carlo replications and 999 bootstrap replications. The 95% confidence intervals for the 0.01, 0.05, and 0.10 levels are (0.80, 1.12), (4.57, 5.43) and (9.41, 10.59), respectively; the 99% confidence intervals are (0.744, 1.26), (4.44, 5.56), and (9.23, 10.8), respectively.

Table 14.3. *Empirical rejection probabilities (percent) of GMM Wald and LM tests for model 3:* $\beta_0 = 0, \beta_1 = 1$, *F exponential, X uniform* [−0.5, 0.5]

		Nominal rejection probabilities								
		1	5	10	1	5	10	1	5	10
		Wald						LM		
Critical values	Hypothesis	NL2SLS			RNL2SLS			NL2SLS		
$n = 25$										
Asymptotic	$\alpha = 0$	0.31	1.86	4.32	0.27	1.63	3.95	1.15	5.31	10.6
	$\alpha = 1$	0.64	2.85	6.17	0.58	2.63	5.72	1.15	5.31	10.6
Bootstrap (Y, X) pair	$\alpha = 0$	0.32	1.67	4.44	0.03	0.40	1.91			
	$\alpha = 1$	0.44	2.51	6.51	0.01	0.61	3.28			
Bootstrap residuals	$\alpha = 0$	1.25	5.24	9.83	0.76	4.49	9.00	1.22	4.79	9.44
	$\alpha = 1$	1.41	5.62	10.3	1.26	5.14	9.75	1.22	4.79	9.44
$n = 50$										
Asymptotic	$\alpha = 0$	0.34	2.91	6.39	0.31	2.67	5.95	0.73	5.04	10.6
	$\alpha = 1$	0.96	4.45	8.13	0.91	4.20	7.77	0.73	5.04	10.6
Bootstrap (Y, X) pair	$\alpha = 0$	0.35	2.52	7.35	0.00	0.57	3.27			
	$\alpha = 1$	0.71	4.62	9.22	0.02	0.98	5.81			
Bootstrap residuals	$\alpha = 0$	1.09	5.40	10.4	0.77	4.85	9.82	0.84	4.84	9.95
	$\alpha = 1$	1.11	5.57	10.4	1.02	5.38	10.2	0.84	4.84	9.95

Notes: The empirical rejection probabilities are computed using 10,000 Monte Carlo replications and 999 bootstrap replications. The 95% confidence intervals for the 0.01, 0.05, and 0.10 levels are (0.80, 1.12), (4.57, 5.43) and (9.41, 10.59), respectively; the 99% confidence intervals are (0.744, 1.26), (4.44, 5.56), and (9.23, 10.8), respectively.

Table 14.4. *Empirical rejection probabilities (percent) of Wald and LM tests for model 4: $\beta_0 = 0$, $\beta_1 = 1$, F exponential, X exponential*

		Nominal rejection probabilities								
		1	5	10	1	5	10	1	5	10
		Wald						LM		
Critical values	Hypothesis	NL2SLS			RNL2SLS			NL2SLS		
$n = 25$										
Asymptotic	$\alpha = 0$	1.89	6.41	11.3	1.95	6.65	11.7	1.58	5.89	11.2
	$\alpha = 1$	1.82	6.23	11.2	1.82	6.22	11.3	1.58	5.89	11.2
Bootstrap (Y, X) pair	$\alpha = 0$	0.75	3.61	8.39	0.73	3.53	8.24			
	$\alpha = 1$	0.55	3.50	8.12	0.48	3.21	7.77			
Bootstrap residuals	$\alpha = 0$	1.26	5.03	9.72	1.26	5.01	9.74	1.47	5.23	9.85
	$\alpha = 1$	1.32	4.91	9.70	1.30	4.90	9.68	1.47	5.23	9.85
$n = 50$										
Asymptotic	$\alpha = 0$	1.33	5.47	10.2	1.46	5.66	10.5	1.42	5.32	10.3
	$\alpha = 1$	1.39	5.48	10.2	1.39	5.48	10.2	1.42	5.32	10.3
Bootstrap (Y, X) pair	$\alpha = 0$	0.83	4.97	10.5	0.81	5.01	10.5			
	$\alpha = 1$	0.71	4.92	10.3	0.70	4.89	10.3			
Bootstrap residuals	$\alpha = 0$	1.19	4.87	9.83	1.27	4.92	9.57	1.27	4.95	10.0
	$\alpha = 1$	1.24	4.99	9.74	1.24	4.99	9.74	1.27	4.95	10.0

Notes: The empirical rejection probabilities are computed using 10,000 Monte Carlo replications and 999 bootstrap replications. The 95% confidence intervals for the 0.01, 0.05, and 0.10 levels are (0.80, 1.12), (4.57, 5.43) and (9.41, 10.59), respectively; the 99% confidence intervals are (0.744, 1.26), (4.44, 5.56), and (9.23, 10.8), respectively.

A striking feature of Tables 14.1–14.4 is that the empirical levels of the LM tests do not depend on the hypothesized value of α. In particular, the levels for the test of H_0: $\alpha = 0$ are identical to those for the test of H_0:$\alpha = 1$. The key to the explanation is provided by the Newey (personal communication, 2001) procedure for calculating the LM statistic, which is presented in Section 3. In this procedure, the LM statistic is obtained by regressing $T(Y_i, \alpha_0)$ on X_i and W_i. In the Monte Carlo experiments, when H_0: $\alpha = \alpha_0$ is true, the value of $T(Y_i, \alpha_0)$ is the same no matter what the value of α_0. This is because $T(Y_i, \alpha_0) = \beta_0 + \beta_1 X_i + U_i$ and $\beta_0 + \beta_1 X_i + U_i$is the same, independently of α_0; that is, β_0, β_1, X_i, and U_i are determined independently of α_0. Even though Y_i is different for different values of α_0, Y_i only enters in the calculation of the LM statistic through $T(Y_i, \alpha_0)$. Hence, the results of the steps 1 and 2 of the Newey procedure do not depend on the value of α_0. The same argument applies to the LM tests based on bootstrap critical values.

Bootstrap Critical Values: (Y, X) Pairs

The experiments investigated the ability of the bootstrap critical values obtained by resampling (Y, X) pairs to reduce the distortions in the levels of the Wald tests that occur when asymptotic critical values are used. The results are generally negative: the bootstrap based on resampling (Y, X) pairs does not reduce the distortions in the levels for most of the cases considered. Tables 14.1 and 14.3 show that the distortions in models 2 and 3, are often larger, not smaller, when bootstrap critical values obtained by resampling (Y, X) pairs are used. The poor numerical performance of these bootstrap critical values is disappointing, but not surprising because resampling (Y, X) pairs does not impose the null hypothesis in the population that the bootstrap samples.

Monte Carlo experiments were also carried out to investigate the rejection probabilities of the NL2SLS Wald test with bootstrap critical values obtained by resampling (Y, X) pairs when $n = 100$. At this sample size, the distortions in the levels of the tests tended to be much reduced.

Bootstrap Critical Values: Residuals

The results for the Wald tests show that bootstrap critical values obtained by resampling residuals reduce, in most cases, the differences between the empirical and nominal levels that occur when asymptotic critical values are used. In some cases, however, the bootstrap does not remove the distortions. This is shown in Table 14.1, especially for $n = 25$. In other cases, the bootstrap essentially eliminates the level distortions present with asymptotic critical values. For example, this is illustrated for model 3 by the results for the NL2SLS Wald test of H_0:$\alpha = 0$ with $n = 50$ in Table 14.3. Again, the experimental evidence is mixed when comparing RNL2SLS and NL2SLS.

As noted earlier, distortions in the levels of LM tests with asymptotic critical values occur only when $n = 25$. The tabled results show that these distortions

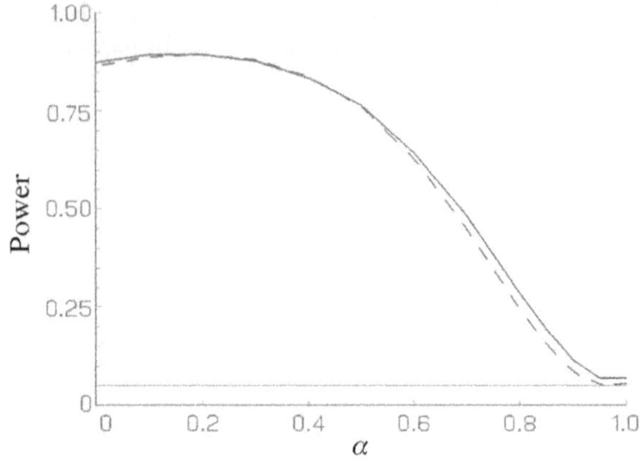

Model 2: F truncated normal, $\beta_0 = 0.1$, $\beta_1 = 1$, $\sigma = .5$, X lognormal, $n = 25$

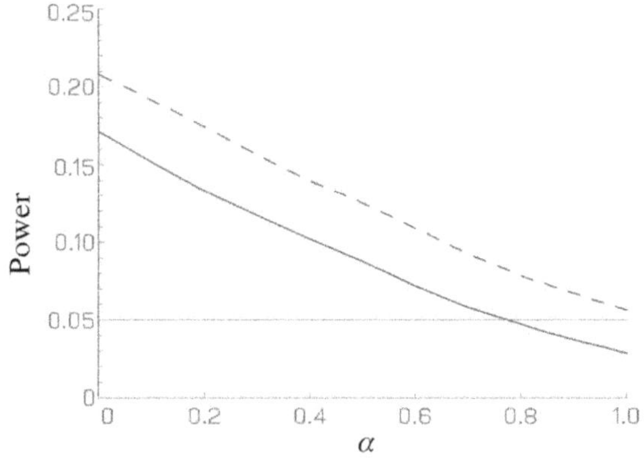

Model 3: F exponential, $\beta_0 = 0$, $\beta_1 = 1$, X uniform [−0.5, 0.5], $n = 25$

Figure 14.1. Empirical powers of nominal 0.05 level NL2SLS-based Wald tests of H_0: $\alpha = 1$ are given for α equal to 0, 0.1, 0.2, 0.3, 0.4, 0.5, 0.6, 0.7, 0.8, 0.85, 0.9, 0.95, 1.0 using asymptotic critical values (solid line) and bootstrap critical values (dashed line) obtained by randomly resampling residuals with replacement.

are essentially removed when the LM tests use bootstrap critical values obtained by resampling residuals.

Finally, Monte Carlo power experiments were performed to investigate the ability of the Wald tests to discriminate between alternative values of the transformation parameter. The powers were computed for NL2SLS Wald tests with bootstrap critical values obtained by resampling residuals. The empirical powers were calculated for a 0.05 level test of H_0: $\alpha = 1$ when the values of α are equal to 0.0, 0.1, 0.2, 0.3, 0.4, 0.5, 0.6, 0.7, 0.8, 0.85, 0.9, 0.95, and $n = 25$. Figure 14.1 illustrates the empirical powers in the case of model 2: $\beta_0 = 0.1$, $\beta_1 = 1$, F

truncated normal, $\sigma = .5$, X lognormal; and model 3: $\beta_0 = 0$, $\beta_1 = 1$, F exponential, X uniform $[-0.5, 0.5]$.

In Figure 14.1, the solid line shows the empirical powers for the tests with asymptotic critical values, and the dashed line shows the empirical powers for the tests with bootstrap critical values. For model 2, the test using asymptotic critical values appears to have a bit higher power, which is partly because the test overrejects under the null when asymptotic critical values are used. The empirical powers for model 3 are dramatically lower than those for model 2. This illustrates that the experimental design can make a substantial difference to the test's potential to discriminate among alternatives. Here, the powers are lower using asymptotic critical values, in part because the test underrejects when asymptotic critical values are used.

We conducted additional power experiments. These show that the Wald tests based on the NL2SLS and the RNL2SLS estimators have about the same power when they use bootstrap critical values. The LM tests appears to have higher power than the NL2SLS Wald test for model 2 and lower power for model 3, again when the tests are based on bootstrap critical values.

7. FTW ESTIMATOR

This section introduces the semiparametric estimator of the parameters of the Box–Cox model proposed in 2001 by Foster, Tian, and Wei (henceforth FTW) and reports the results of a Monte Carlo investigation of the Wald test based on the FTW estimator.

FTW (2001) motivate their estimation procedure by considering the case where α is known. Again let $Y_i, X_i : i = 1, \ldots, n$ be a random sample from (Y, X). Then the least-squares estimator of β is

$$b_n(a) = \left[\sum\nolimits_i X_i X_i'\right]^{-1} \sum\nolimits_i X_i' T(Y_i, \alpha). \tag{7.1}$$

To estimate α, consider the process $\{I(Y_i < t), t \geq 0\}$, where $I()$ is the indicator function. The expected value of $I(Y_i < t)$ is

$$\begin{aligned} E[I(Y_i < t)] = P(Y_i < t) = P[T(Y_i, \alpha) - X_i'\beta \\ < (T(t, \alpha) - X_i'\beta)] = F(T(t, \alpha) - X_i'\beta). \end{aligned} \tag{7.2}$$

A consistent estimate of the distribution function of U can be obtained using the empirical distribution of the residuals:

$$F_n(t) = \frac{1}{n} \sum_{i=1}^{n} [I(T(Y_i, \alpha) - X_i' b_n(\alpha)) < t]. \tag{7.3}$$

The FTW estimator of α solves

$$\min_{\alpha} S_n(\alpha) = \frac{1}{n} \sum_{i=1}^{n} \int_{0}^{\infty} [I(Y_i < t) - F_n(T(t, \alpha) - X_i' b_n(\alpha))]^2 dh(t), \qquad (7.4)$$

where $h(\ )$ is a strictly increasing deterministic weight function. The resulting estimate of α is used to obtain the estimate of β via (7.1). A limitation of this procedure is that $X_i'\beta$ cannot be degenerate; that is, β cannot be equal to 0.

FTW use the theory of U processes to show for large n that the estimator of α is the unique global minimizer of $S_n(\alpha)$ and is strongly consistent for α_0 and that the estimator of β is strongly consistent for β_0. The authors also show that the joint distribution of the estimators is asymptotically normal with a finite covariance matrix that involves the unknown density function of F, which may not be well estimated by directly using nonparametric density estimation. They propose a new resampling method that they claim provides reliable estimates of the covariance matrix.

In the Monte Carlo experiments reported here, the empirical rejection probabilities of the FTW Wald tests are investigated using the four models considered previously. The tests are carried out with asymptotic critical values and with bootstrap critical values obtained by resampling residuals. The sample size in the experiments is restricted to $n = 25$ because the simulations are very time-consuming, which is a consequence of the method used by FTW to compute an estimate of the covariance matrix. For the same reason, only 500 Monte Carlo replications are used in each experiment. The bootstrap critical values are computed using 199 bootstrap replications.

The Monte Carlo results are presented in Table 14.5. The empirical levels of the FTW Wald tests based on the asymptotic critical value are larger than the nominal levels, except for model 1. In models 2, 3, and 4, the differences between the empirical and nominal levels are especially large when testing H_0: $\alpha = 0$. The evidence from these experiments suggests that there may be no advantage in using the FTW Wald test instead of the GMM Wald test when asymptotic critical values are employed. In most cases, the bootstrap reduces the distortions in the levels of the Wald tests that occur with asymptotic critical values. In the case of models 1, 2, and 4, the bootstrap essentially removes the distortions in the levels that occur with asymptotic critical values.

The bootstrap is very time-consuming because the estimation of the covariance matrix also involves simulation. Moreover, several tuning parameters have to be chosen to implement the simulation approach. An alternative approach is to use a non-Studentized test statistic to test the hypothesis. The non-Studentized test statistic proposed here is $\sqrt{n}(\bar{a}_n - \alpha_0)$, where $\bar{a}_n$ is the FTW estimator of α. This statistic has the advantage that it does not require calculation of the covariance matrix. This approach is motivated by the fact that higher-order approximations to the distributions of statistics that are not asymptotically pivotal

Table 14.5. *Empirical rejection probabilities (percent) of FTW tests*

Form of test and critical value	Nominal rejection probabilities: 1	5	10	1	5	10
Hypothesis	$\alpha = 0$			$\alpha = 1$		
Model 1: $\beta_0 = 1, \beta_1 = 1$, F truncated normal, $\sigma = 0.5$, X uniform $[-0.5, 0.5]$						
Wald						
Asymptotic	1.00	5.20	12.4	1.80	5.20	10.2
Bootstrap	1.40	5.40	10.8	1.20	5.20	10.6
Non-Studentized						
Single bootstrap	0.80	3.40	8.20	0.40	5.62	11.4
Double bootstrap	0.40	4.00	8.40	0.80	5.20	10.6
Model 2: $\beta_0 = 0.1, \beta_1 = 1$, F truncated normal, $\sigma = 0.5$, X lognormal						
Wald						
Asymptotic	9.80	17.8	23.4	3.20	7.80	15.6
Bootstrap	1.20	4.20	8.80	0.80	4.80	11.6
Non-Studentized						
Single bootstrap	1.40	3.80	9.60	0.80	4.80	9.20
Double bootstrap	0.80	5.20	10.6	0.80	4.20	6.80
Model 3: $\beta_0 = 0, \beta_1 = 1$, F exponential, X uniform $[-0.5, 0.5]$						
Wald						
Asymptotic	3.40	10.8	17.4	2.80	8.40	15.2
Bootstrap	2.60	7.40	12.8	2.40	7.60	12.2
Non-Studentized						
Single bootstrap	1.20	5.80	10.6	0.40	2.80	7.00
Double bootstrap	0.60	4.80	8.80	0.20	3.20	6.60
Model 4: $\beta_0 = 0, \beta_1 = 1$, F exponential, X exponential						
Wald						
Asymptotic	7.20	13.6	17.6	1.80	8.0	12.4
Bootstrap	0.60	3.00	9.20	1.00	5.80	10.2
Non-Studentized						
Single bootstrap	1.40	5.00	8.40	0.80	3.60	8.80
Double bootstrap	0.20	4.00	8.60	0.40	4.20	9.20

Notes: The empirical rejection probabilities are computed using 500 Monte Carlo replications and 199 bootstrap replications in both the single and the double bootstrap. The 95% confidence intervals for the 0.01, 0.05, and 0.10 levels are (0.013, 1.87), (3.09, 6.91), and (7.37, 12.63), respectively; the 99% confidence intervals are (−0.15, 2.15), (2.49, 7.51), and (6.54, 13.5), respectively.

can be obtained through the use of bootstrap iteration (Beran 1988). The idea is to obtain the critical values of the non-Studentized test using the double bootstrap. Although the double bootstrap itself is computationally intensive, it is, nevertheless, less so than bootstrapping the FTW Wald statistic.

Table 14.5 also reports the results of Monte Carlo experiments using the non-Studentized tests with single and double bootstrap critical values obtained by resampling residuals. Again, 500 Monte Carlo replications are used in each experiment. Both the single bootstrap and double bootstrap results are based on 199 bootstrap replications.

Table 14.5 shows that the differences between the empirical and nominal levels are small when critical values based on the single bootstrap are used. There are essentially no distortions in the levels of the non-Studentized tests. The exception occurs when testing H_0: $\alpha = 0$ in design 3. The empirical levels when the critical values are based on the double bootstrap tend to be similar to the empirical levels based on the single bootstrap. This is surprising because the single bootstrap applied to statistics that are not asymptotically pivotal does not provide higher-order approximations to their distributions. This does not imply, of course, that the single bootstrap cannot be better than the asymptotical FTW Wald test. The comparison of the numerical performance of the asymptotical FTW Wald test and the bootstrap for the non-Studentized tests suggests that applying the bootstrap to the non-Studentized test is competitive with calculating the variance of the FTW estimator and using the asymptotical FTW Wald test.

Finally, in a small power experiment, the FTW Wald test appears to have a bit higher power than the GMM Wald tests when both tests use bootstrap critical values. This result also appears to carry over to the case of the non-Studentized test based on the FTW estimator.

8. CONCLUDING COMMENTS

In this section, the results are briefly reviewed and three topics are recommended for further research. The first involves the NL2SLS and RML2SLS estimators, the second the wild bootstrap with GMM-based tests, and the third is the double bootstrap with tests based on the new estimation method proposed by FTW (2001).

This study has focused on testing the transformation parameter in a Box–Cox model where U is independent of X. In a setting where U and X are independent, bootstrap critical values can be obtained by randomly resampling (Y, X) pairs with replacement or by randomly resampling residuals with replacement. The Monte Carlo experiments show that the bootstrap often essentially eliminates the level distortions that occur with asymptotic critical values when the bootstrap critical values are obtained by resampling residuals.

Two versions of the GMM estimator developed for the Box–Cox model are NL2SLS and RNL2SLS, where the latter was designed to address certain shortcomings of the former. The experiments compared Wald tests based on the NL2SLS estimator with Wald tests based on the RNL2SLS estimator. The results are somewhat mixed. The differences between the empirical and nominal levels for the RNL2SLS Wald tests are often, but not always, smaller than those for the NL2SLS Wald tests. This is true when asymptotic or bootstrap critical values are used. As a consequence, more evidence is needed to determine which estimator among the two is preferable for testing purposes.

In applications, U may have heteroskedasticity of unknown form. In particular, the variance of U may depend on the value of X. In this situation, the bootstrap can be implemented by resampling (Y, X) pairs. However, in our experiments, the Wald and the LM tests using bootstrap critical values obtained from resampling (Y, X) pairs often do not provide satisfactory control over the type I error. An alternative to resampling (Y, X) pairs is to use the wild bootstrap. Liu (1988) introduced the wild bootstrap following a suggestion by Wu (1986). Horowitz (1997) reports the performance of the wild bootstrap in experiments using a linear regression model with heteroskedasticity of unknown form. The results show that using critical values obtained from the wild bootstrap substantially reduces the error in the rejection probability under the null hypothesis. In the case of the Box–Cox model, the wild bootstrap has the drawback that it does not constrain the value of Y to be positive. Adapting the wild bootstrap to a Box–Cox model is a topic that merits further research.

FTW (2001) have recently proposed a semiparametric estimation procedure for the Box–Cox model. A small Monte Carlo experiment was carried out to investigate the Wald test based on the FTW estimator. The results show that the differences between the empirical and the nominal levels can be large when the test uses asymptotic critical values. The bootstrap reduces, and often eliminates, the distortions that occur with asymptotic critical values. But there is a complication. The bootstrap is very time-consuming because of the fact that the estimation of the covariance matrix also involves simulation. The alternative explored here is to avoid the computation of a covariance matrix estimate by using a non-Studentized test and to obtain the critical values of the non-Studentized test by using the double bootstrap. The double bootstrap approach appears to be promising and one that merits further investigation. Indeed, what is surprising is that the empirical levels are often close to the nominal levels when the non-Studentized test uses critical values based on the single bootstrap.

ACKNOWLEDGEMENTS

The authors thank Don Andrews, the editor, the referees, and Joel Horowitz, George Judge, Whitney Newey, as well as the participants of the NSF Summer Symposium 2001 on Identification and Inference for Econometric Models, University of California, Berkeley, for useful comments and suggestions. Allan Würtz acknowledges the support from the Center for Applied Microeconometrics (CAM). The activities of CAM are financed from a grant from the Danish National Research Foundation.

References

Amemiya, T. (1974), "The Nonlinear Two-stage Least-squares Estimator," *Journal of Econometrics*, 2, 105–10.

Amemiya, T. (1985), *Advanced Econometrics*, Cambridge: Harvard University Press.

Amemiya, T., and J. L. Powell (1981), "A Comparison of the Box–Cox Maximum Likelihood Estimator and the Non-linear Two-stage Least-squares Estimator," *Journal of Econometrics*, 17, 351–81.

Beran, R. (1998), "Prepivoting Test Statistics: A Bootstrap View of Asymptotic Refinements," *Journal of the American Statistical Association*, 83 (403), 687–97.

Box, G. E. P., and D. R. Cox (1964), "An Analysis of Transformations," *Journal of the Royal Statistical Society*, Series B, 26, 296–311.

Drucker, D. M. (2000), "On the Manipulability of Wald Tests in Box–Cox Regression Models (sg1301)," *Stata Technical Bulletin*, 54, 36–42.

Foster, A. M., L. Tian, and J. L. Wei (2001), "Estimation of the Box–Cox Transformation Model without Assuming Parametric Error Distribution," *Journal of the American Statistical Association*, 96, 1097–101.

Greene, W. H. (2000), *Econometric Analysis*, second edition. New York: Macmillian.

Hansen, L. P. (1982), "Large Sample Properties of Generalized Method of Moments Estimators," *Econometrica*, 50, 1029–54.

Horowitz, J. L. (1997), "Bootstrap Methods in Econometrics," in *Advances in Economics and Econometrics: Theory and Applications, Seventh World Congress*, (ed. by D. M. Kreps and K. R. Wallis), Cambridge: Cambridge University Press, 188–222.

Horowitz, J. L. (1998), *Semiparametric Methods in Econometrics*. New York: Springer-Verlag.

Horowitz, J. L., and N. E. Savin (2000), "Empirically Relevant Critical Values for Hypothesis Tests: A Bootstrap Approach," *Journal of Econometrics*, 95, 375–89.

Khazzoom, D. J. (1989), "A Note on the Application of the Non-linear Two-Stage Least-squares Estimator to a Box–Cox Transformed Model," *Journal of Econometrics*, 42, 377–9.

Liu, R. Y. (1988), "Boostrap Procedures Under Some Non-i.i.d. Models," *Annals of Statistics*, 16, 1696–708.

Mittlehammer, R. C., G. C. Judge, and D. J. Miller (2000), *Econometric Foundations*. Cambridge: Cambridge University Press.

Newey, W. K., and K. D. West (1987), "Hypothesis Testing with Efficient Method of Moments Estimation," *International Economic Review*, 28, 777–87.

Poirier, D. J. (1978), "The Use of the Box–Cox Transformation in Limited Dependent Variable Models," *Journal of American Statistical Association*, 73, 284–7.

Powell, J. L. (1996), "Rescaling Methods-of-Moments Estimation for the Box–Cox Regression Model," *Economic Letters*, 51, 259–65.

Ruud, P. (2000), *Classical Econometric Theory*. New York: Oxford University Press.

Spitzer, J. J. (1984), "Variance Estimates in Models of the Box–Cox Transformation: Implications for Estimation and Hypothesis Testing," *The Review of Economics and Statistics*, 66, 645–52.

Wu, C. F. J. (1986), "Jacknife, Bootstrap and Other Resampling Methods in Regression Analysis," *Annals of Statistics*, 14, 1261–95.

PART III

INFERENCE INVOLVING POTENTIALLY NONSTATIONARY TIME SERIES

CHAPTER 15

Tests of the Null Hypothesis of Cointegration Based on Efficient Tests for a Unit MA Root

Michael Jansson

ABSTRACT

A new family of tests of the null hypothesis of cointegration is proposed. Each member of this family is a plug-in version of a point optimal stationarity test. Appropriately selected tests dominate existing cointegration tests in terms of local asymptotic power.

1. INTRODUCTION

In recent years, several papers have studied the problem of testing the null hypothesis of cointegration against the alternative of no cointegration. A variety of testing procedures have been proposed, but very little is known about the asymptotic power properties of these tests. In an attempt to shed some light on the issue of power, this chapter makes two contributions.

First, a new test of the null hypothesis of cointegration is introduced. Similar to the tests proposed by Park (1990), Shin (1994), Choi and Ahn (1995), and Xiao and Phillips (2002), the test developed in this chapter can be viewed as an extension of an existing test of the null hypothesis of stationarity. Unlike the tests introduced in the cited studies, the test proposed herein is based on a stationarity test (derived in Rothenberg (2000)), which is known to enjoy nearly optimal local asymptotic power properties.

Second, the paper compares the power of the new test to the power of previously proposed tests by numerical evaluation of the local asymptotic power functions. It turns out that a cointegration test based on an optimal stationarity test inherits the good (relative to competing test procedures) local asymptotic power properties of the stationarity tests upon which it is based. In particular, the new test dominates existing tests in terms of local asymptotic power.

Section 2 motivates the testing procedure introduced in this paper. Section 3 presents the model and the assumptions under which the development of formal results will proceed. The new family of tests is introduced in Section 4. Section 5 investigates the asymptotic properties of the tests and two competing test

This paper draws on material in Chapter 2 of the author's Ph.D. dissertation at University of Aarhus, Denmark.

procedures. Finally, Section 6 offers a few concluding remarks, while mathematical derivations appear in three Appendices.

2. MOTIVATION

The leading special case of the testing problem considered in this chapter is the problem of testing the null hypothesis $\theta = 1$ against the alternative hypothesis $\theta < 1$ in the model

$$y_t = \beta' x_t + v_t, \quad t = 1, \ldots, T, \tag{2.1}$$

where v_t and x_t are independent zero mean Gaussian time series (of dimensions 1 and k, respectively), $\Delta x_t \sim$ i.i.d. $\mathcal{N}(0, I_k)$ with initial condition $x_0 = 0$, and v_t is generated by the model

$$\Delta v_t = u_t^y - \theta u_{t-1}^y, \quad t = 2, \ldots, T, \tag{2.2}$$

where Δ is the difference operator, $u_t^y \sim$ i.i.d. $\mathcal{N}(0, 1)$, and the initial condition is $v_1 = u_1^y$. The parameters $\beta \in \mathbb{R}^k$ and $\theta \in (-1, 1)$ are assumed to be unknown.

In the literature on stationarity testing, the model (2.2) of v_t is often referred to as the moving average model. A convenient feature of the moving average model is that the null hypothesis of stationarity can be formulated as a simple parametric restriction.[1] Indeed, v_t is stationary if and only if the moving average coefficient θ in (2.2) equals unity. (The "if" part is true because $v_t = u_t^y \sim$ i.i.d. $\mathcal{N}(0, 1)$ when $\theta = 1$, whereas the "only if" part follows from the fact v_t is an integrated process with a random walk-type nonstationarity whenever θ differs from unity.) By implication, the time series y_t and x_t are cointegrated (in the sense of Engle and Granger (1987)) if and only if $\theta = 1$.

If β was known, the null hypothesis of cointegration could be tested by applying a stationarity test to the observed series $v_t = y_t - \beta' x_t$. Studying the moving average model (2.2), Rothenberg (2000, Section 4) derived the family of point optimal (PO) tests of the null hypothesis $\theta = 1$.[2] The stationarity test derived in Rothenberg (2000) rejects for large value of

$$P_T(\bar{\lambda}) = \sum_{t=1}^{T} u_t^y(0)^2 - \sum_{t=1}^{T} u_t^y(\bar{\lambda})^2,$$

where $u_t^y(l) = \sum_{i=0}^{t-1}(1 - T^{-1}l)^i \Delta v_{t-i}$ (for $l \in \{0, \bar{\lambda}\}$ and $t \in \{1, \ldots, T\}$), $v_0 = 0$, and $\bar{\lambda} > 0$ is some prespecified constant. The test based on $P_T(\bar{\lambda})$ is the PO test of $\theta = 1$ against the point alternative $\theta = 1 - T^{-1}\bar{\lambda}$ in the model (2.2).

[1] An alternative to the moving average model, which also parameterizes stationarity as a point, is the "local-level" unobserved components model. As discussed by Stock (1994), the two models are closely related. In fact, it can be shown that the two models give rise to identical Gaussian power envelopes for tests of the null hypothesis cointegration whenever a constant term is included in the model (Jansson 2005). For this reason, only the moving average model will be studied here.

[2] See also Saikkonen and Luukkonen (1993), who derived the family of PO location invariant tests of $\theta = 1$.

By implication, the test is also the PO test of $\theta = 1$ against $\theta = 1 - T^{-1}\bar{\lambda}$ in the model (2.1)–(2.2) when β is known and $\{x_t\}$ is independent of $\{v_t\}$.[3]

It follows from Rothenberg (2000) that the test based on $P_T(\bar{\lambda})$ is "nearly" optimal (has local asymptotic power function "close" to the Gaussian power envelope) if $\bar{\lambda}$ is chosen appropriately. In particular, such PO stationarity tests have better local asymptotic power properties than the stationarity tests by Park and Choi (1988), Kwiatkowski et al. (1992), Choi and Ahn (1998), and Xiao (2001), respectively.

When β is unknown (as is assumed here), it seems natural to test the null hypothesis of cointegration by using a plug-in approach in which a stationarity test is applied to an estimate of v_t. The cointegration tests proposed by Park (1990), Shin (1994), Choi and Ahn (1995), and Xiao and Phillips (2002) are all of the plug-in variety, being based on the stationarity tests proposed by Park and Choi (1988), Kwiatkowski et al. (1992), Choi and Ahn (1998), and Xiao (2001), respectively. This chapter explores the extent to which the superiority of Rothenberg's stationarity test (Rothenberg 2000) is inherited by a plug-in cointegration test based upon it. Specifically, it is explored whether a plug-in cointegration test based on Rothenberg's stationarity test dominates the tests by Park (1990), Shin (1994), Choi and Ahn (1995), and Xiao and Phillips (2002) in terms of local asymptotic power.

3. THE MODEL AND ASSUMPTIONS

The plug-in cointegration test based on Rothenberg's stationarity test (Rothenberg 2000) will be developed under the assumption that $z_t = (y_t, x_t')'$ is an observed $(k+1)$-vector time series (partitioned into a scalar y_t and a k-vector x_t) generated by

$$z_t = \mu_t^z + z_t^0, \quad t = 1, \dots, T, \tag{3.1}$$

where μ_t^z is a deterministic component and z_t^0 is a zero mean stochastic component. Partitioning z_t^0 conformably with z_t as $z_t^0 = (y_t^0, x_t^{0\prime})'$, it is assumed that z_t^0 is generated by the potentially cointegrated system

$$y_t^0 = \beta' x_t^0 + v_t, \tag{3.2}$$
$$\Delta x_t^0 = u_t^x, \tag{3.3}$$

where v_t is an error process with initial condition $v_1 = u_1^y$ and generating mechanism

$$\Delta v_t = u_t^y - \theta u_{t-1}^y, \quad t = 2, \dots, T. \tag{3.4}$$

[3] If $\{x_t\}$ and $\{v_t\}$ are not independent, more powerful tests can often be found. Jansson (2004) has developed PO tests under the assumption that β is known and $(u_t^y, \Delta x_t')'$ is Gaussian white noise. These tests are more powerful than the test based on $P_T(\bar{\lambda})$ whenever the correlation between u_t^y and Δx_t is nonzero, but the source of these power gains is not exploitable when β is unknown (as is assumed in this chapter).

In (3.2) – (3.4), $\beta \in \mathbb{R}^k$ and $\theta \in (-1, 1]$ are unknown parameters and $u_t = (u_t^y, u_t^{x\prime})'$ is a stationary process whose long-run variance covariance matrix

$$\Omega = \lim_{T\to\infty} T^{-1} \sum_{t=1}^{T} \sum_{s=1}^{T} E\left(u_t u_s'\right)$$

is assumed to be positive definite.

For concreteness, the deterministic component μ_t^z is assumed to be a pth order polynomial time trend:

$$\mu_t^z = \alpha_z' d_t, \quad t = 1, \ldots, T, \tag{3.5}$$

where $d_t = (1, \ldots, t^p)'$ and α_z is a $(p+1) \times m$ matrix of unknown parameters. The leading special cases of (3.5) are the constant mean ($p = 0$) and linear trend ($p = 1$) cases corresponding to $d_t = 1$ and $d_t = (1, t)'$, respectively.

In the development of distributional results, it will be assumed that

$$T^{-1/2} \sum_{t=1}^{\lfloor T\cdot \rfloor} u_t \to_d \Omega^{1/2} W(\cdot), \tag{3.6}$$

and

$$T^{-1} \sum_{t=2}^{T} \left(\sum_{s=1}^{t-1} u_s \right) u_t' \to_d \Omega^{1/2} \int_0^1 W(r)\, dW(r)' \Omega^{1/2\prime} + \Gamma', \tag{3.7}$$

where $\lfloor \cdot \rfloor$ denotes the integer part of the argument, $W(\cdot)$ is a Wiener process of dimension m, and

$$\Gamma = \lim_{T\to\infty} T^{-1} \sum_{t=2}^{T} \sum_{s=1}^{t-1} E\left(u_t u_s'\right)$$

is the one-sided long-run covariance matrix of u_t.

Similar to the model of Section 2, the model (3.1)–(3.7) enjoys the property that the null hypothesis of cointegration can be formulated as a simple parametric restriction. Indeed, the problem of testing the null hypothesis of cointegration against the alternative of no cointegration can once again be formulated as the problem of testing

$$H_0 : \theta = 1 \quad \text{versus} \quad H_1 : \theta < 1.$$

The model (3.1)–(3.7) generalizes (2.1) and (2.2) in several respects. The presence of the deterministic component μ_t^z in (3.1) relaxes the zero mean assumption of (2.1) and (2.2). Moreover, the high-level assumptions (3.6) and (3.7) on the latent errors u_t accommodate quite general forms of contemporaneous and serial correlation (and do not require normality). Indeed, the convergence results (3.6) and (3.7) hold (jointly) under a variety of weak dependence conditions on u_t. For instance, the following assumption suffices:

A1. $u_t = \sum_{i=0}^{\infty} C_i \varepsilon_{t-i}$, where $\{\varepsilon_t : t \in \mathbb{Z}\}$ is i.i.d. $(0, I_m)$, $\sum_{i=0}^{\infty} C_i$ has full rank, and $\sum_{i=1}^{\infty} i \|C_i\| < \infty$, where $\| \cdot \|$ is the Euclidean norm.

Under A1, the long-run covariance matrix of u_t is $\Omega = (\sum_{i=0}^{\infty} C_i)(\sum_{i=0}^{\infty} C_i)'$, a positive definite matrix. The assumption that Ω is positive definite is a standard, but important, regularity condition. It implies that x_t^0 is a non-cointegrated integrated process and rules out multicointegration (in the sense of Granger and Lee 1990) under the null hypothesis of cointegration.

4. A FAMILY OF COINTEGRATION TESTS

Conformably with z_t, partition α_z as $\alpha_z = (\alpha_y, \alpha_x)$. Defining $\alpha = \alpha_y - \alpha_x \beta$, the following relation can be obtained by combining (3.1), (3.2), and (3.5):

$$y_t = \alpha' d_t + \beta' x_t + v_t, \quad t = 1, \ldots, T. \tag{4.1}$$

The family of cointegration tests proposed herein is obtained by applying (a suitably modified version of) Rothenberg's stationarity test (Rothenberg 2000) to an estimate of the error term v_t in (4.1).

Suppose (4.1) is estimated by OLS:

$$y_t = \hat{\alpha}' d_t + \hat{\beta}' x_t + \hat{v}_t. \tag{4.2}$$

As it turns out, tests constructed by applying stationarity tests to $\hat{v}_t$ generally have limiting distributions with complicated nuisance parameter dependencies unless x_t satisfies a certain exogeneity condition.[4] In the case of the stationarity tests proposed by Park and Choi (1988), Kwiatkowski et al. (1992), Choi and Ahn (1998), and Xiao (2001), this problem can be circumvented by employing an asymptotically efficient (under H_0) estimation procedure when constructing a plug-in cointegration tests (for details, see Park (1990), Shin (1994), Choi and Ahn (1995), and Xiao and Phillips (2002)). These properties are shared by the PO stationarity test, implying that the plug-in versions of Rothenberg's stationarity tests (Rothenberg 2000) should employ asymptotically efficient (under H_0) estimators of α and β in the construction of estimates of v_t. For concreteness, it is assumed that Park's canonical cointegrating regression (CCR) (Park 1992) estimators of α and β are used. (A brief discussion of alternative estimation strategies is provided at the end of this section.)

To construct the CCR estimators, consistent (under H_0 and local alternatives) estimators of Ω and Γ are needed. Suppose Ω and Γ are estimated by kernel estimators of the form

$$\hat{\Omega} = T^{-1} \sum_{t=1}^{T} \sum_{s=1}^{T} k\left(\frac{|t-s|}{\hat{b}_T}\right) \hat{u}_t \hat{u}_s', \tag{4.3}$$

[4] Specifically, $\lim_{T\to\infty} T^{-1} \sum_{t=1}^{T} \sum_{s=1}^{T} E(u_t^y u_s^{x\prime})$ and $\lim_{T\to\infty} T^{-1} \sum_{t=1}^{T} \sum_{s=1}^{t} E(u_t^y u_s^{x\prime})$ must be zero if these nuisance parameter dependencies are to be avoided. That is, Ω must be block diagonal and Γ must be block upper triangular, where Ω and Γ are the matrices defined in Section 3.

and

$$\hat{\Gamma} = T^{-1} \sum_{t=2}^{T} \sum_{s=1}^{t-1} k\left(\frac{|t-s|}{\hat{b}_T}\right) \hat{u}_t \hat{u}_s', \tag{4.4}$$

where $k(\cdot)$ is a (measurable) kernel function, $\hat{b}_T$ is a sequence of (possibly random) bandwidth parameters, and $\hat{u}_t = (\hat{v}_t, \Delta\hat{x}_t^{0\prime})'$, where $\hat{v}_t$ are the OLS residuals from (4.2) and $\hat{x}_t^0$ are the OLS residuals from

$$x_t = \hat{\alpha}_x' d_t + \hat{x}_t^0. \tag{4.5}$$

The consistency requirement on $\hat{\Omega}$ and $\hat{\Gamma}$ is met under the following assumption on $k(\cdot)$ and $\hat{b}_T$.

A2. (i) $k(0) = 1$, $k(\cdot)$ is continuous at zero and $\bar{k}(0) + \int_0^\infty \bar{k}(r)\,dr < \infty$, where $\bar{k}(r) = \sup_{s \geq r} |k(s)|$ (for all $r \geq 0$).
(ii) $\hat{b}_T = \hat{a}_T b_T$, where $\hat{a}_T$ and b_T are positive, $\hat{a}_T + \hat{a}_T^{-1} = O_p(1)$, and, b_T is nonrandom with $b_T^{-1} + T^{-1/2} b_T = o(1)$.

Assumption A2 (i) is adapted from Jansson (2002) and is discussed there, while A2 (ii) is adapted from Andrews (1991).

Partition $\hat{\Gamma}$ and $\hat{\Omega}$ in conformity with $u_t = (u_t^y, u_t^{x\prime})'$ and let $\hat{\Gamma}_{x\cdot} = (\hat{\gamma}_{xy}, \hat{\Gamma}_{xx})$, $\hat{\omega}_{yy\cdot x} = \hat{\kappa}'\hat{\Omega}\hat{\kappa}$, and $\hat{\gamma}_{yy\cdot x} = \hat{\kappa}'\hat{\Gamma}\hat{\kappa}$, where $\hat{\kappa} = (1, -\hat{\omega}_{xy}'\hat{\Omega}_{xx}^{-1})'$. Let $\tilde{\alpha}$ and $\tilde{\beta}$ be the OLS estimators obtained from the multiple regression

$$y_t^\dagger = \tilde{\alpha}' d_t + \tilde{\beta}' x_t^\dagger + \tilde{v}_t, \tag{4.6}$$

where $y_t^\dagger = y_t - \hat{\omega}_{xy}'\hat{\Omega}_{xx}^{-1}\Delta\hat{x}_t^0 + \hat{\beta}'\hat{\Gamma}_{x\cdot}\hat{\Sigma}^{-1}\hat{u}_t$, $x_t^\dagger = x_t + \hat{\Gamma}_{x\cdot}\hat{\Sigma}^{-1}\hat{u}_t$, $\hat{\Sigma} = T^{-1}\sum_{t=1}^{T} \hat{u}_t\hat{u}_t'$, and $\hat{\beta}$ is the OLS estimator from (4.2). The estimators $\tilde{\alpha}$ and $\tilde{\beta}$ from (4.6) are Park's CCR estimators (Park 1992) of α and β. Under H_0, these estimators are asymptotically efficient (in the sense of Saikkonen (1991)). In addition, the behavior of suitably normalized partial sums involving the residuals $\tilde{v}_t$ is such that asymptotically pivotal (under H_0) test statistics can be constructed using these residuals.

Let $\tilde{v}_0 = 0$ and define $\tilde{u}_t^y(l) = \sum_{i=0}^{t-1}(1 - T^{-1}l)^i \Delta\tilde{v}_{t-i}$ (for $l \in \{0, \bar{\lambda}\}$ and $t \in \{1, \ldots, T\}$). The proposed test rejects H_0 for large values of

$$Q_T(\bar{\lambda}) = \frac{\sum_{t=1}^{T} \tilde{u}_t^y(0)^2 - \sum_{t=1}^{T} \tilde{u}_t^y(\bar{\lambda})^2 - 2\bar{\lambda}\hat{\gamma}_{yy\cdot x}}{\hat{\omega}_{yy\cdot x}}, \tag{4.7}$$

where $\bar{\lambda} > 0$ is a prespecified constant. (Guidance on the choice of $\bar{\lambda}$ will be provided in Section 5.)

In the numerator of $Q_T(\bar{\lambda})$, the term $\sum_{t=1}^{T} \tilde{u}_t^y(0)^2 - \sum_{t=1}^{T} \tilde{u}_t^y(\bar{\lambda})^2$ is a plug-in version of the test statistic $P_T(\bar{\lambda})$ of Section 2. The statistic $Q_T(\bar{\lambda})$ is a modified version of $P_T(\bar{\lambda})$ in which two nonparametric corrections are employed in order to produce a test statistic which is asymptotically pivotal under H_0. Specifically, the term $-2\bar{\lambda}\hat{\gamma}_{yy\cdot x}$ corrects $\sum_{t=1}^{T}\tilde{u}_t^y(0)^2 - \sum_{t=1}^{T}\tilde{u}_t^y(\bar{\lambda})^2$ for "serial correlation bias," while the denominator removes scale parameter dependencies from the limiting distribution of $Q_T(\bar{\lambda})$.

Remark. Lemma A.2 in Appendix A summarizes the properties of $\tilde{v}_t$ that are used in the derivation of the distributional result reported in Theorem 5.1 of Section 5. These properties are shared by the "fully modified" (Phillips and Hansen 1990) residual process

$$\check{v}_t = y_t - \hat{\omega}_{xy}'\hat{\Omega}_{xx}^{-1}\Delta\hat{x}_t^0 - \check{\alpha}'d_t - \check{\beta}'x_t,$$

where $\check{\alpha}$ and $\check{\beta}$ are asymptotically efficient estimators of α and β. As a consequence, the test can also be based on $\check{v}_t$. Likewise, the test can be based on the DOLS (Stock and Watson 1993) residuals $\ddot{v}_t$ from the regression

$$y_t = \ddot{\alpha}'d_t + \ddot{\beta}'x_t + \ddot{\gamma}(L)\Delta x_t + \ddot{v}_t,$$

where $\ddot{\gamma}(L)$ is a two-sided lag polynomial.

5. ASYMPTOTIC THEORY

Similar to the existing cointegration tests, the test based on $Q_T(\bar{\lambda})$ has nontrivial power against local alternatives of the form $1-\theta = O(T^{-1})$. This fact motivates the reparameterization $\theta = \theta_T = 1 - T^{-1}\lambda$, where λ is a non-negative constant. Under this reparameterization, the null and alternative hypotheses are $\lambda = 0$ and $\lambda > 0$, respectively. A similar reparameterization was implicitly employed in the definition of $Q_T(\bar{\lambda})$, which is a plug-in version of the optimal test against the alternative $\theta = 1 - T^{-1}\bar{\lambda}$. Theorem 5.1 characterizes the limiting distribution of $Q_T(\bar{\lambda})$ under H_0 and local alternatives.

Theorem 5.1. *Let z_t be generated by (3.1)–(3.5) and suppose A1–A2 hold. Moreover, suppose $\theta = \theta_T = 1 - T^{-1}\lambda$ for some $\lambda \geq 0$. Then*

$$Q_T(\bar{\lambda}) \to_d 2\bar{\lambda}\int_0^1 \tilde{U}_{\bar{\lambda}}^{\lambda}(r)\,d\tilde{U}^{\lambda}(r) - \bar{\lambda}^2\int_0^1 \tilde{U}_{\bar{\lambda}}^{\lambda}(r)^2 dr,$$

where $\tilde{U}_{\bar{\lambda}}^{\lambda}(r) = \int_0^r e^{-\bar{\lambda}(r-s)}\,d\tilde{U}^{\lambda}(s)$,

$$d\tilde{U}^{\lambda}(r) = dU^{\lambda}(r) - \left(\int_0^1 X(s)\,dU^{\lambda}(s)\right)' \times \left(\int_0^1 X(s)X(s)'\,ds\right)^{-1} X(r)\,dr,$$

$U^{\lambda}(r) = U(r) + \lambda\int_0^r U(s)ds$, $X(r) = \left(V(r)', 1, \ldots, r^p\right)'$ and U and V are independent Wiener processes of dimensions 1 and k, respectively.

Table 15.1. *Percentiles of $Q_T(\bar{\lambda})$*

	$k = 1$	$k = 2$	$k = 3$	$k = 4$	$k = 5$	$k = 6$
Constant Mean						
$\bar{\lambda}$	10	12	14	16	18	20
90%	−4.19	−5.78	−7.24	−8.68	−10.14	−11.61
95%	−3.24	−4.82	−6.34	−7.74	−9.17	−10.64
97.5%	−2.33	−3.90	−5.46	−6.83	−8.23	−9.66
99%	−1.09	−2.74	−4.21	−5.62	−7.08	−8.63
Linear trend						
$\bar{\lambda}$	14	16	18	19	21	23
90%	−6.72	−8.25	−9.64	−10.74	−12.15	−13.55
95%	−5.70	−7.24	−8.57	−9.83	−11.20	−12.59
97.5%	−4.73	−6.27	−7.53	−8.84	−10.19	−11.60
99%	−3.50	−4.96	−6.26	−7.67	−8.98	−10.43

To implement the test, the analyst must specify an alternative $\theta = 1 - T^{-1}\bar{\lambda}$ against which good power is desired. The approach recommended here is to choose $\bar{\lambda}$ in such a way that the local asymptotic power against the alternative $\theta = 1 - T^{-1}\bar{\lambda}$ is approximately equal to 50% when the 5% test based on $Q_T(\bar{\lambda})$ is used. In related testing problems, a similar approach has been advocated by Elliott, Rothenberg, and Stock (1996), Stock (1994), and Rothenberg (2000). Table 15.1 tabulates the recommended values of $\bar{\lambda}$ for $k = 1, \ldots, 6$ regressors in the constant mean and linear trend) case and reports selected percentiles of the asymptotic null distributions of the corresponding $Q_T(\bar{\lambda})$ statistics.[5]

The local asymptotic power properties of the new test will be compared to those of the cointegration tests proposed by Xiao and Phillips (2002) and Shin (1994), respectively.[6] The cointegration test proposed by Xiao and Phillips (2002) rejects H_0 for large values of

$$R_T = \hat{\omega}_{yy\cdot x}^{-1/2} \max_{1\le t\le T} \left| T^{-1/2} \sum_{s=1}^{t} \tilde{u}_s^y(0) \right|, \tag{5.1}$$

whereas Shin's test (Shin 1994) rejects for large values of

$$S_T = \hat{\omega}_{yy\cdot x}^{-1} T^{-2} \sum_{t=1}^{T-1} \left[\sum_{s=1}^{t} \tilde{u}_s^y(0) \right]^2, \tag{5.2}$$

[5] The percentiles were computed by generating 20,000 draws from the discrete time approximation (based on 2,000 steps) to the limiting random variables.

[6] The local power results of Jansson and Haldrup (2002) indicate that none of the cointegration tests proposed by Park (1990) and Choi and Ahn (1995) are superior to the test by Shin (1994). Therefore, cointegration tests by Park (1990) and Choi and Ahn (1995) are not studied here.

where $\hat{\omega}_{yy\cdot x}$ and $\tilde{u}_t^y(0)$ are defined as in Section 4.[7] It is shown in Appendix B that $R_T \to_d \sup_{0 \le r \le 1} |\tilde{U}^\lambda(r)|$ and $S_T \to_d \int_0^1 \tilde{U}^\lambda(r)^2 \, dr$ under the assumptions of Theorem 5.1, where $\tilde{U}^\lambda(r) = \int_0^r d\tilde{U}^\lambda(s)$.

Figure 15.1(a) plots the local asymptotic power functions of the constant mean $Q_T(10)$, R_T, and S_T tests in the case where x_t is a scalar ($k = 1$).[8] The test based on $Q_T(10)$ dominates existing tests in terms of local asymptotic power whenever λ exceeds 5. Even for alternatives close to H_0, where S_T enjoys certain optimality properties (Harris and Inder 1994), the new test is very competitive in terms of power.

Figure 15.1(b) investigates the optimality properties of $Q_T, (10)$ by plotting its local asymptotic power function against two benchmarks. For any alternative $\lambda > 0$, the level of the quasi-envelope plotted in Figure 15.1(b) is obtained by maximizing (over $\bar{\lambda} > 0$) the power of a cointegration test based on a member of the family $\{Q_T(\bar{\lambda}) : \bar{\lambda} > 0\}$ of test statistics proposed herein. As a consequence, the optimality of the choice $\bar{\lambda} = 10$ can be evaluated by comparing the power of $Q_T(10)$ to the quasi-envelope. The power of $Q_T(10)$ is almost indistinguishable from the quasi-envelope for values of λ between 8 and 16 and is reasonably close to the quasi-envelope for values of λ outside this range. By choosing $\bar{\lambda}$ smaller (greater) than 10, the difference between the power of $Q_T(\bar{\lambda})$ and the quasi-envelope can be decreased for small (large) values of λ at the expense of a greater gap for large (small) values of λ. Therefore, although $Q_T(10)$ fails to attain the quasi-envelope, no other value of $\bar{\lambda}$ delivers a test statistic $Q_T(\bar{\lambda})$ with uniformly better power properties.

The envelope plotted in Figure 15.1(b) is an upper bound on the local asymptotic power of (a class of cointegration tests that contains all) plug-in cointegration tests. That bound, developed in a follow-up paper (Jansson 2005), can be used to investigate the optimality properties of $\{Q_T(\bar{\lambda}) : \bar{\lambda} > 0\}$ within the class of tests that are invariant under transformations of the form $y_t \to y_t + a'd_t + b'x_t$, where $a \in \mathbb{R}^{p+1}$ and $b \in \mathbb{R}^k$. The presence of a visible difference between the quasi-envelope and the power envelope suggests that an even more powerful cointegration test might exist. A confirmation of that conjecture is provided in Jansson (2005), where a cointegration test (not of the plug-in variety) with nearly optimal local asymptotic power properties is developed.

7 Strictly speaking, R_T and S_T are modifications of the test statistics proposed by Xiao and Phillips (2002) and Shin (1994). Unlike R_T and S_T, tests by Shin (1994) and Xiao and Phillips (2002) are not based on estimation procedure by Park (1992). Under the assumptions of Theorem 5.1, the difference between R_T and Xiao and Phillips's test statistic (Xiao and Phillips 2002) is asymptotically negligible, as is the difference between S_T and test statistic by Shin (1994).

8 The power functions were obtained by generating 20,000 draws from the discrete time approximation (based on 2,000 steps) to the limiting distributions of the test statistics for selected values of λ.

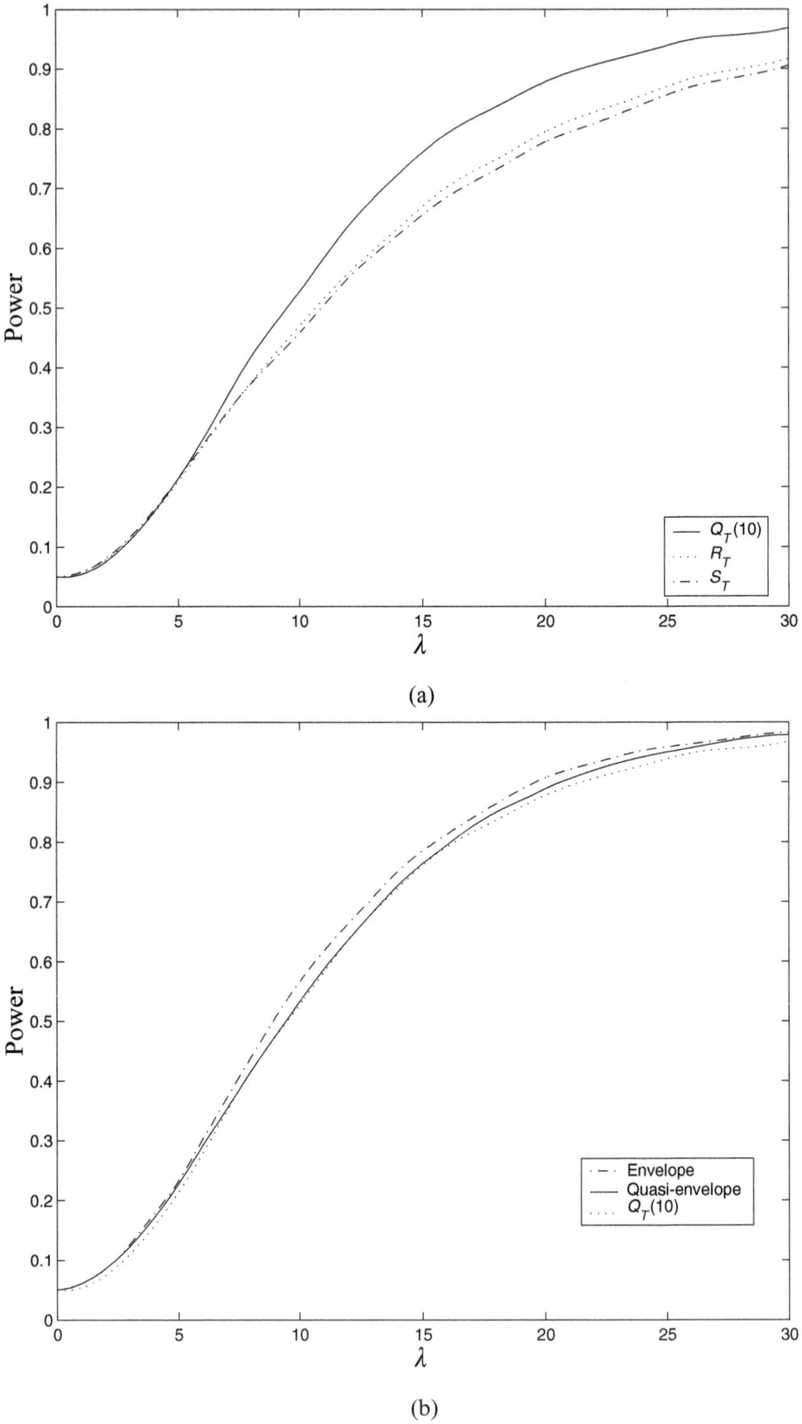

Figure 15.1. Power curves (5% level tests, constant mean, scalar x).

The result for the linear trend case are qualitatively similar to those for the constant mean case as can be seen from Figures 15.2(a) and 15.2(b).

The test statistic $Q_T(\bar{\lambda})$ has been constructed with local alternatives in mind. As the following theorem shows $Q_T(\bar{\lambda})$ can also be used to detect distant alternatives. Indeed, the test which rejects for large values of $Q_T(\bar{\lambda})$ is consistent in the sense that power against any fixed alternative $\theta = \bar{\theta} < 1$ tends to one as T increases without bound.

Theorem 5.2. *Let z_t be generated by (3.1)–(3.5) and suppose A1–A2 hold. Moreover, suppose $\theta < 1$ is fixed. Then $\lim_{T\to\infty} \Pr[Q_T(\bar{\lambda}) > c] = 1$ for any $c \in \mathbb{R}$.*

6. CONCLUSION

A new family of tests of the null hypothesis of cointegration was proposed. Each member of this family is a plug-in version of a PO stationarity test. Similar to the PO stationarity tests upon which they are based, the cointegration tests proposed in this chapter have good power properties. In particular, an appropriately selected version of the new test dominates existing cointegration tests in terms of local asymptotic power.

APPENDIX A: PROOF OF THEOREM 5.1

The proof of Theorem 5.1 utilizes the following two lemmas.

Lemma A.1. *Under the assumptions of Theorem 5.1, $\hat{\Omega} \to_p \Omega$ and $\hat{\Gamma} \to_p \Gamma$.*

Lemma A.2. *Under the assumptions of Theorem 5.1,*

$$T^{-1/2} \sum_{t=1}^{\lfloor T\cdot \rfloor} \tilde{u}_t^y(0) \to_d \omega_{yy\cdot x}^{1/2} \tilde{U}^{\lambda}(\cdot)$$

and

$$T^{-1} \sum_{t=2}^{T} \left[\sum_{s=1}^{t-1} \tilde{u}_s^y(0) \right] \tilde{u}_t^y(0) \to_d \omega_{yy\cdot x} \int_0^1 \tilde{U}^{\lambda}(r)\, d\tilde{U}^{\lambda}(r) + \gamma_{yy\cdot x}$$

jointly, where $\omega_{yy\cdot x} = \kappa'\Omega\kappa$, $\gamma_{yy\cdot x} = \kappa'\Gamma\kappa$, and $\kappa = (1, -\omega_{xy}'\Omega_{xx}^{-1})'$.

Under H_0, Lemma A.1 follows from Corollary 4 of Jansson (2002). The extension to local alternatives is straightforward, but tedious, and can be established by proceeding as in the proof of Lemma 5 of Jansson and Haldrup (2002). Lemma A.2 follows from Lemma 6(c)–(f) of Jansson and Haldrup (2002) and the fact that $\tilde{u}_t^y(0) = \tilde{v}_t$.

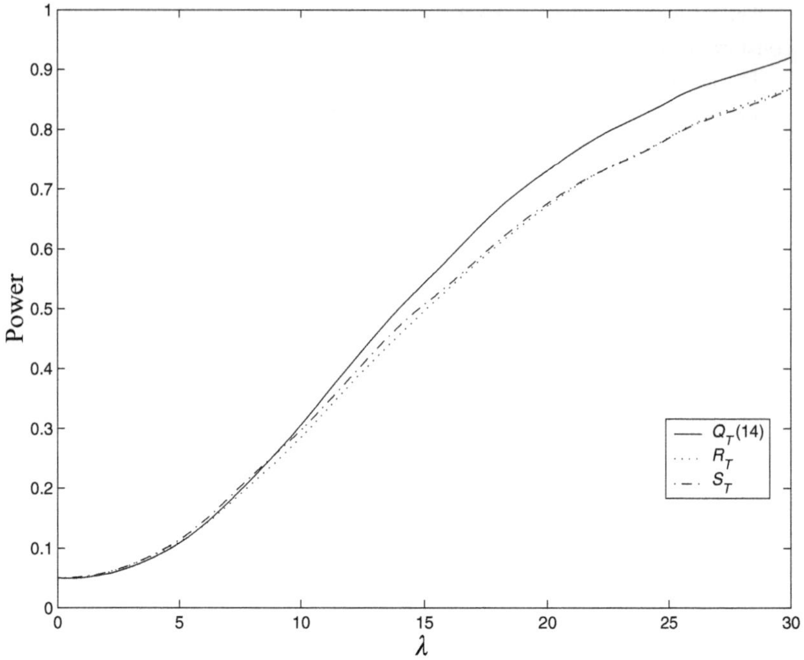

(a)

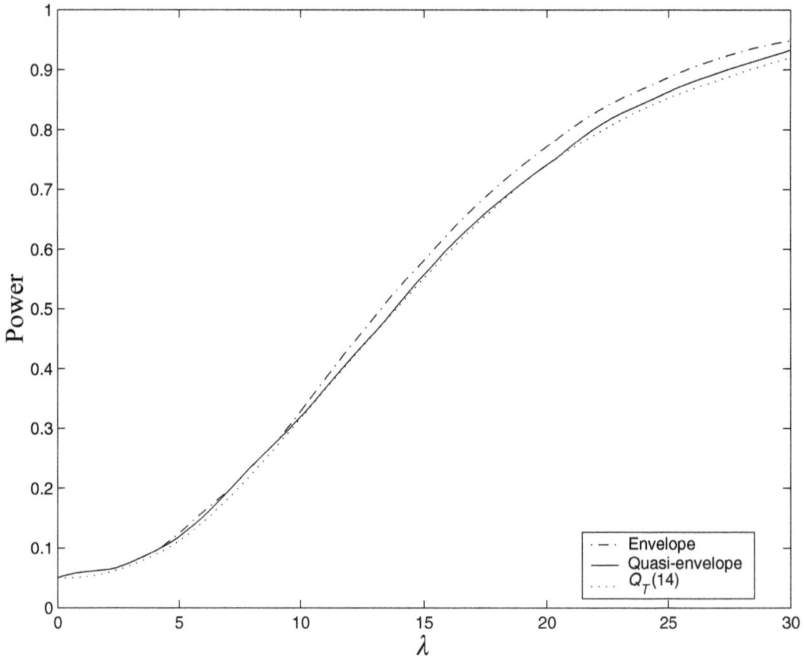

(b)

Figure 15.2. Power curves (5% level tests, linear trend, scalar x).

Proof of Theorem 5.1. By Lemma A.1, $\hat{\gamma}_{yy\cdot x} \to_p \gamma_{yy\cdot x}$ and $\hat{\omega}_{yy\cdot x} \to_p \omega_{yy\cdot x}$. Since

$$\begin{aligned}
&\sum_{t=1}^{T} \tilde{u}_t^y(0)^2 - \sum_{t=1}^{T} \tilde{u}_t^y(\bar{\lambda})^2 \\
&\quad = \sum_{t=1}^{T} \tilde{u}_t^y(0)^2 - \sum_{t=1}^{T} \left[\tilde{u}_t^y(0) + \tilde{u}_t^y(\bar{\lambda}) - \tilde{u}_t^y(0)\right]^2 \\
&\quad = -\sum_{t=1}^{T} \left[\tilde{u}_t^y(0) - \tilde{u}_t^y(\bar{\lambda})\right]^2 + 2\sum_{t=1}^{T} \left[\tilde{u}_t^y(0) - \tilde{u}_t^y(\bar{\lambda})\right] \tilde{u}_t^y(0),
\end{aligned}$$

the proof of Theorem 5.1 can therefore be completed by establishing the following convergence results:

$$\sum_{t=1}^{T} \left[\tilde{u}_t^y(0) - \tilde{u}_t^y(\bar{\lambda})\right]^2 \to_d \bar{\lambda}^2 \omega_{yy\cdot x} \int_0^1 \tilde{U}_{\bar{\lambda}}^{\lambda}(r)^2\, dr, \tag{A.1}$$

$$\sum_{t=1}^{T} \left[\tilde{u}_t^y(0) - \tilde{u}_t^y(\bar{\lambda})\right] \tilde{u}_t^y(0) \to_d \bar{\lambda} \left(\omega_{yy\cdot x} \int_0^1 \tilde{U}_{\bar{\lambda}}^{\lambda}(r)\, d\tilde{U}^{\lambda}(r) + \gamma_{yy\cdot x}\right). \tag{A.2}$$

Let $\bar{\theta}_T = 1 - T^{-1}\bar{\lambda}$. Using the relation $\tilde{u}_t^y(\bar{\lambda}) = \tilde{u}_t^y(0) - \bar{\lambda}T^{-1}\sum_{j=1}^{t-1} \bar{\theta}_T^{t-1-j}\tilde{u}_j^y(0)$ and summation by parts,

$$\tilde{u}_t^y(0) - \tilde{u}_t^y(\bar{\lambda}) = T^{-1}\bar{\lambda}\left(\tilde{U}_{t-1}^y - \bar{\lambda}\bar{\theta}_T^{t-2}T^{-1}\sum_{j=1}^{t-2}\bar{\theta}_T^{-j}\tilde{U}_j^y\right), \tag{A.3}$$

where $\tilde{U}_t^y = \sum_{j=1}^{t} \tilde{u}_j^y(0)$. Now, $T^{-1/2}\tilde{U}_{\lfloor T\cdot\rfloor}^y \to_d \omega_{yy\cdot x}^{1/2}\tilde{U}^{\lambda}(\cdot)$ by Lemma A.2. Moreover, $\lim_{T\to\infty}\sup_{0\le r\le 1}|\bar{\theta}_T^{\lfloor Tr\rfloor} - \exp(-\bar{\lambda}r)| = 0$, so

$$T^{1/2}\left[\tilde{u}_{\lfloor T\cdot\rfloor}^y(0) - \tilde{u}_{\lfloor T\cdot\rfloor}^y(\bar{\lambda})\right] \to_d \bar{\lambda}\omega_{yy\cdot x}^{1/2}\tilde{U}_{\bar{\lambda}}^{\lambda}(\cdot) \tag{A.4}$$

by the continuous mapping theorem (CMT), Theorem 13.4 of Billingsley (1999), and the fact that

$$\tilde{U}_{\bar{\lambda}}^{\lambda}(r) = \tilde{U}^{\lambda}(r) - \bar{\lambda}\int_0^r \exp\left[\bar{\lambda}(s-r)\right]\tilde{U}^{\lambda}(s)\, ds, \qquad r \in [0, 1].$$

Using (A.4) and applying CMT,

$$\begin{aligned}
\sum_{t=1}^{T} \left[\tilde{u}_t^y(0) - \tilde{u}_t^y(\bar{\lambda})\right]^2 &= \int_0^1 \left(T^{1/2}\left[\tilde{u}_{\lfloor Tr\rfloor}^y(0) - \tilde{u}_{\lfloor Tr\rfloor}^y(\bar{\lambda})\right]\right)^2 dr \\
&\quad + \left[\tilde{u}_T^y(0) - \tilde{u}_T^y(\bar{\lambda})\right]^2 \\
&\to_d \int_0^1 \left(\bar{\lambda}\omega_{yy\cdot x}^{1/2}\tilde{U}_{\bar{\lambda}}^{\lambda}(r)\right)^2 dr,
\end{aligned}$$

establishing (A.1).

By (A.3),

$$\sum_{t=1}^{T}\left(\tilde{u}_t^y(0)-\tilde{u}_t^y(\bar{\lambda})\right)\tilde{u}_t^y(0)=T^{-1}\bar{\lambda}\sum_{t=1}^{T}\tilde{U}_{t-1}^y\tilde{u}_t^y(0)+T^{-1}\bar{\lambda}\sum_{t=1}^{T}\times\left(-\bar{\lambda}\bar{\theta}_T^{t-2}T^{-1}\sum_{j=1}^{t-2}\bar{\theta}_T^{-j}\tilde{U}_j^y\right)\tilde{u}_t^y(0).$$

Now,

$$T^{-1}\sum_{t=1}^{T}\tilde{U}_{t-1}^y\tilde{u}_t^y(0)\to_d \omega_{yy\cdot x}\int_0^1\tilde{U}^\lambda(r)\,d\tilde{U}^\lambda(r)+\gamma_{yy\cdot x}$$

by Lemma A.2. Moreover,

$$\begin{aligned}T^{-1}\sum_{t=1}^{T}&\left(-\bar{\lambda}\bar{\theta}_T^{t-2}T^{-1}\sum_{j=1}^{t-2}\bar{\theta}_T^{-j}\tilde{U}_j^y\right)\tilde{u}_t^y(0)\\&=T^{-1}\sum_{t=1}^{T}\left[\tilde{u}_{t-1}^y(0)-\tilde{u}_{t-1}^y(\bar{\lambda})\right]\tilde{U}_{t-1}^y\to_d\bar{\lambda}\omega_{yy\cdot x}\int_0^1\tilde{U}_{\bar{\lambda}}^\lambda(r)\tilde{U}^\lambda(r)\,dr,\end{aligned}$$

where the equality uses summation by parts, (A.3), and $\tilde{U}_T^y=0$, while the last line uses (A.4), Lemma A.2, and CMT. Combining the preceding displays, the limiting distribution of $\sum_{t=1}^{T}(\tilde{u}_t^y(0)-\tilde{u}_t^y(\bar{\lambda}))\tilde{u}_t^y(0)$ can be represented as

$$\begin{aligned}\bar{\lambda}&\left(\omega_{yy\cdot x}\left[\int_0^1\tilde{U}^\lambda(r)\,d\tilde{U}^\lambda(r)+\bar{\lambda}\int_0^1\tilde{U}_{\bar{\lambda}}^\lambda(r)\tilde{U}^\lambda(r)\,dr\right]+\gamma_{yy\cdot x}\right)\\&=\bar{\lambda}\left(\omega_{yy\cdot x}\int_0^1\tilde{U}_{\bar{\lambda}}^\lambda(r)d\tilde{U}^\lambda(r)+\gamma_{yy\cdot x}\right),\end{aligned}$$

where the equality follows from integration by parts. Therefore, (A.2) holds and the proof is complete. ■

APPENDIX B: LIMITING DISTRIBUTIONS OF R_T AND S_T

The limiting distribution of R_T is derived as follows:

$$\begin{aligned}R_T&=\hat{\omega}_{yy\cdot x}^{-1/2}\max\nolimits_{1\le t\le T}\left|T^{-1/2}\sum_{s=1}^{t}\tilde{u}_s^y(0)\right|\\&=\left(\omega_{yy\cdot x}^{-1/2}+o_p(1)\right)\sup\nolimits_{0\le r\le 1}\left|T^{-1/2}\sum_{s=1}^{\lfloor Tr\rfloor}\tilde{u}_s^y(0)\right|\\&\to_d\sup\nolimits_{0\le r\le 1}\left|\tilde{U}^\lambda(r)\right|,\end{aligned}$$

where the second equality uses Lemma A.1, while the last line uses Lemma A.2 and CMT.

Similarly,

$$\begin{aligned} S_T &= \hat{\omega}_{yy\cdot x}^{-1} T^{-2} \sum_{t=1}^{T-1} \left(\sum_{s=1}^{t} \tilde{u}_s^y(0) \right)^2 \\ &= \left[\omega_{yy\cdot x}^{-1} + o_p(1)\right] \left[\int_0^1 \left(T^{-1/2} \sum_{s=1}^{\lfloor Tr \rfloor} \tilde{u}_s^y(0) \right)^2 dr \right] \\ &\to_d \int_0^1 \tilde{U}^{\lambda}(r)^2 dr, \end{aligned}$$

where the second equality uses Lemma A.1, while the last line uses Lemma A.2 and CMT.

APPENDIX C: PROOF OF THEOREM 5.2

Let $\hat{u}_t^y(l) = \sum_{j=0}^{t-1}(1 - T^{-1}l)^j \Delta\hat{v}_{t-j}$ for $l \in \{0, \bar{\lambda}\}$ and $t \in \{1, \ldots, T\}$, where $\hat{v}_0 = 0$ and $\{\hat{v}_t\}$ are the residuals from (4.2). The following lemmas are used in the proof of Theorem 5.2.

Lemma C.1. *Under the assumptions of Theorem 5.2,*

$$T^{-1/2}\hat{v}_{\lfloor T\cdot \rfloor} \to_d (1-\theta)\omega_{yy\cdot x}^{1/2}\hat{U}(\cdot),$$

where $\hat{U}(r) = U(r) - (\int_0^1 X(s)U(s))'(\int_0^1 X(s)X(s)'ds)^{-1}X(r)$, *while* U *and* X *are defined as in Theorem 5.1.*

Lemma C.2. *Under the assumptions of Theorem 5.2,* $T^{-3/2}\hat{\gamma}_{yy} \to_p 0$, $T^{-1}\hat{\gamma}_{xy} \to_p 0$ *and* $T^{-1}\hat{\gamma}_{yx} \to_p 0$.

Lemma C.3. *Under the assumptions of Theorem 5.2,*

$$T^{-2}\left[\sum_{t=1}^{T}\tilde{u}_t^y(0)^2 - \sum_{t=1}^{T}\tilde{u}_t^y(\bar{\lambda})^2\right] = T^{-2}\left[\sum_{t=1}^{T}\hat{u}_t^y(0)^2 - \sum_{t=1}^{T}\hat{u}_t^y(\bar{\lambda})^2\right] + o_p(1).$$

Lemma C.1 follows from standard spurious regression results. The proof of Lemma C.2 uses $T^{-1}\hat{\sigma}_{yy} = T^{-2}\sum_{t=1}^{T}\hat{v}_t^2 = O_p(1)$, $\hat{\Sigma}_{xx} = T^{-1}\sum_{t=1}^{T}\Delta\hat{x}_t^0\Delta\,\hat{x}_t^{0\prime} = O_p(1)$, and the fact that $T^{-1/2}\sum_{i=0}^{T-1}|k(i/\hat{b}_T)| \to_p 0$ under A2

(Jansson 2002). For instance,

$$\begin{aligned}\left|T^{-3/2}\hat{\gamma}_{yy}\right| &= \left|T^{-3/2}\sum_{i=0}^{T-1}k\left(\frac{i}{\hat{b}_T}\right)\left(T^{-1}\sum_{t=1}^{T-i}\hat{\upsilon}_{t+i}\hat{\upsilon}_t\right)\right| \\ &\leq T^{-1/2}\sum_{i=0}^{T-1}\left|k\left(\frac{i}{\hat{b}_T}\right)\right|\left|\left(T^{-2}\sum_{t=1}^{T-i}\hat{\upsilon}_{t+i}\hat{\upsilon}_t\right)\right| \\ &\leq T^{-1/2}\sum_{i=0}^{T-1}\left|k\left(\frac{i}{\hat{b}_T}\right)\right|\left(T^{-2}\sum_{t=1}^{T-i}\hat{\upsilon}_{t+i}^2\right)^{1/2}\left(T^{-2}\sum_{t=1}^{T-i}\hat{\upsilon}_t^2\right)^{1/2} \\ &\leq \left(T^{-2}\sum_{t=1}^{T}\hat{\upsilon}_t^2\right)\left(T^{-1/2}\sum_{i=0}^{T-1}\left|k\left(\frac{i}{\hat{b}_T}\right)\right|\right) \to_p 0,\end{aligned}$$

where the second inequality uses the Cauchy–Schwarz inequality. Finally, the proof of Lemma C.3 uses $T^{-1}\hat{\gamma}_{yx} \to_p 0$ and a considerable amount of tedious algebra. To conserve space, the details are omitted.

Proof of Theorem 5.2. For any T,

$$\begin{aligned}&Pr\left[Q_T(\bar{\lambda}) > c\right] \\ &= Pr\left[\sum_{t=1}^{T}\tilde{u}_t^y(0)^2 - \sum_{t=1}^{T}\tilde{u}_t^y(\bar{\lambda})^2 - 2\bar{\lambda}\hat{\gamma}_{yy\cdot x} - c\hat{\omega}_{yy\cdot x} > 0\right].\end{aligned}$$

By Lemmas C.2 and C.3 and using $T^{-1}\hat{\sigma}_{yy} = O_p(1)$,

$$\begin{aligned}&T^{-2}\left[\sum_{t=1}^{T}\tilde{u}_t^y(0)^2 - \sum_{t=1}^{T}\tilde{u}_t^y(\bar{\lambda})^2 - 2\bar{\lambda}\hat{\gamma}_{yy\cdot x} - c\hat{\omega}_{yy\cdot x}\right] \\ &= T^{-2}\left[\sum_{t=1}^{T}\hat{u}_t^y(0)^2 - \sum_{t=1}^{T}\hat{u}_t^y(\bar{\lambda})^2\right] + o_p(1).\end{aligned}$$

In view of the portmanteau theorem (for example, Billingsley 1999), the proof of Theorem 5.2 can therefore be completed by showing that $T^{-2}[\sum_{t=1}^{T}\hat{u}_t^y(0)^2 - \sum_{t=1}^{T}\hat{u}_t^y(\bar{\lambda})^2]$ has a limiting distribution with positive support.

Let $\bar{\theta}_T = 1 - T^{-1}\bar{\lambda}$. The relation $\hat{u}_t^y(\bar{\lambda}) = \hat{u}_t^y(0) - \bar{\lambda}T^{-1}\sum_{j=1}^{t-1}\bar{\theta}_T^{t-1-j}\hat{u}_j^y(0)$ can be restated as follows:

$$\hat{u}_{T,\lfloor Tr\rfloor}^y(l) = \hat{u}_{T,\lfloor Tr\rfloor}^y - \bar{\lambda}\bar{\theta}_T^{\lfloor Tr\rfloor-1}\int_0^{\lfloor Tr\rfloor/T}\bar{\theta}_T^{-\lfloor Ts\rfloor}\hat{u}_{T,\lfloor Ts\rfloor}^y ds, \quad 0 \leq r \leq 1.$$

Now, $\lim_{T\to\infty}\sup_{0\leq r\leq 1}|\bar{\theta}_T^{\lfloor Tr\rfloor} - \exp(-\bar{\lambda}r)| = 0$, so it follows from the preceding display, Lemma C.1, and CMT that $T^{-1/2}\hat{u}_{\lfloor T\cdot\rfloor}^y(\bar{\lambda}) \to_d (1-\theta)\omega_{yy\cdot x}^{1/2}\hat{U}_{\bar{\lambda}}(\cdot)$, where

$$\hat{U}_{\bar{\lambda}}(r) = \hat{U}(r) - \bar{\lambda}\int_0^r \exp(-\bar{\lambda}(r-s))\hat{U}(s)ds.$$

Using this result, Lemma C.1, and CMT,

$$T^{-2}\left[\sum_{t=1}^{T}\hat{u}_t^y(0)^2-\sum_{t=1}^{T}\hat{u}_t^y(\bar{\lambda})^2\right]$$
$$\rightarrow_d (1-\theta)^2\omega_{yy\cdot x}\left[\int_0^1\hat{U}(r)^2dr-\int_0^1\hat{U}_{\bar{\lambda}}(r)^2dr\right],$$

so it suffices to show that $\Pr[\int_0^1\hat{U}(r)^2dr-\int_0^1\hat{U}_{\bar{\lambda}}(r)^2dr>0]=1$.

Since $\hat{U}_{\bar{\lambda}}(r)=\hat{U}(r)-\bar{\lambda}\int_0^1 1(s\le r)\exp[-\bar{\lambda}(r-s)]\hat{U}(s)ds$, where $1(\cdot)$ is the indicator function, it follows from straightforward algebra that

$$\int_0^1\hat{U}(r)^2dr-\int_0^1\hat{U}_{\bar{\lambda}}(r)^2dr=\int_0^1\int_0^1 K_{\bar{\lambda}}(r,s)\hat{U}(r)\hat{U}(s)drds,$$

where

$$K_{\bar{\lambda}}(r,s)=\frac{\bar{\lambda}}{2}\left(\exp\left[-\bar{\lambda}(2-r-s)\right]+\exp\left[-\bar{\lambda}\,|r-s|\right]\right).$$

The desired result now follows from the fact that the function $K_{\bar{\lambda}}(\cdot,\cdot)$ is positive definite in the sense that $\int_0^1\int_0^1 K_{\bar{\lambda}}(r,s)f(r)f(s)drds>0$ for any nonzero, continuous function $f(\cdot)$. ■

ACKNOWLEDGMENTS

Helpful comments from Jim Stock, two referees, and participants at the 2001 NSF Symposium on Identification and Inference for Econometric Models are gratefully acknowledged.

References

Andrews, D. W. K. (1991), "Heteroskedasticity and Autocorrelation Consistent Covariance Matrix Estimation," *Econometrica*, 59, 817–858.

Billingsley, P. (1999), *Convergence of Probability Measures*, 2nd edn. New York: Wiley.

Choi, I., and B. C. Ahn (1995), "Testing for Cointegration in a System of Equations," *Econometric Theory*, 11, 952–983.

Choi, I., and B. C. Ahn (1998), "Testing the Null of Stationarity for Multiple Time Series," *Journal of Econometrics*, 88, 41–77.

Elliott, G., T. J. Rothenberg, and J. H. Stock (1996), "Efficient Tests for an Autoregressive Unit Root," *Econometrica*, 64, 813–836.

Engle, R. F., and C. W. J. Granger (1987), "Cointegration and Error Correction: Representation, Estimation, and Testing," *Econometrica*, 55, 251–276.

Granger, C. W. J., and T. Lee (1990), "Multicointegration," in *Advances in Econometrics: Co-integration, Spurious Regressions, and Unit Roots* (ed. by T. B. Fomby and G. F. Rhodes, Jr.), Greenwich, CT: Jai Press, pp. 71–84.

Harris, D., and B. Inder (1994), "A Test of the Null Hypothesis of Cointegration," in *Nonstationary Time Series Analysis and Cointegration* (ed. by C. Hargreaves), Oxford: Oxford University Press, 133–152.

Jansson, M. (2002), "Consistent Covariance Matrix Estimation for Linear Processes," *Econometric Theory*, 18, 1449–1459.

Jansson, M. (2005), "Point Optimal Tests of the Null Hypothesis of Cointegration," *Journal of Econometrics* 124, 187–201.

Jansson, M. (2004), "Stationarity Testing with Covariates," *Econometric Theory*, 20, 56–94.

Jansson, M., and N. Haldrup (2002), "Regression Theory for Nearly Cointegrated Time Series," *Econometric Theory*, 18, 1309–1335.

Kwiatkowski, D., P. C. B. Phillips, P. Schmidt, and Y. Shin (1992), "Testing the Null Hypothesis of Stationarity Against the Alternative of a Unit Root: How Sure are We that Economic Time Series have a Unit Root?," *Journal of Econometrics*, 54, 159–178.

Park, J. Y. (1990), "Testing for Unit Roots and Cointegration by Variable Addition," in *Advances in Econometrics: Co-integration, Spurious Regression, and Unit Roots* (ed. by T. B. Fomby and G. F. Rhodes, Jr.), Greenwich, CT: JAI Press, pp. 107–133.

Park, J. Y. (1992), "Canonical Cointegrating Regressions," *Econometrica*, 60, 119–143.

Park, J. Y., and B. Choi (1988), "A New Approach to Testing for a Unit Root," CAE Working Paper 88–23, Cornell University.

Phillips, P. C. B., and B. E. Hansen (1990), "Statistical Inference in Instrumental Variables Regression with I(1) Variables," *Review of Economic Studies*, 57, 99–125.

Rothenberg, T. J. (2000), "Testing for Unit Roots in AR and MA Models," in *Applications of Differential Geometry to Econometrics* (ed. by P. Marriott and M. Salmon), Cambridge, U.K.: Cambridge University Press, pp. 281–293.

Saikkonen, P. (1991), "Asymptotically Efficient Estimation of Cointegration Regressions," *Econometric Theory*, 7, 1–21.

Saikkonen, P., and R. Luukkonen (1993), "Point Optimal Tests for Testing the Order of Differencing in {ARIMA} Models," *Econometric Theory*, 9, 343–362.

Shin, Y. (1994), "A Residual-Based Test of the Null of Cointegration Against the Alternative of No Cointegration," *Econometric Theory*, 10, 91–115.

Stock, J. H. (1994), "Unit Roots, Structural Breaks and Trends," in *Handbook of Econometrics, Volume IV* (ed. by R. F. Engle and D. L. McFadden), New York: North Holland, pp. 2739–2841.

Stock, J. H., and M. W. Watson (1993), "A Simple Estimator of Cointegrating Vectors in Higher Order Integrated Systems," *Econometrica*, 61, 783–820.

Xiao, Z. (2001), "Testing the Null Hypothesis of Stationarity Against an Autoregressive Unit Root Alternative," *Journal of Time Series Analysis*, 22, 87–105.

Xiao, Z., and P. C. B. Phillips (2002), "A CUSUM Test for Cointegration Using Regression Residals," *Journal of Econometrics*, 108, 43–61.

CHAPTER 16

Robust Confidence Intervals for Autoregressive Coefficients Near One

Samuel B. Thompson

ABSTRACT

We construct outlier robust confidence sets for autoregressive roots near unity. There are a few difficulties in doing this – the asymptotics for robust methods generally involve several poorly estimated nuisance parameters, and robust procedures are more difficult to compute than least-squares-based methods. We propose a family of "aligned" robust procedures that eliminate the need to estimate some of the nuisance parameters. The procedures are computationally no more burdensome than least squares. In thick-tailed data the robust sets outperform those based on normality.

1. INTRODUCTION

A recurring problem in financial econometrics is how to conduct valid inference on a linear mean function estimated from monthly, weekly, or daily data. For example, most interest rate models specify the conditional mean to be linear in the previous value of the process. The data typically exhibit outliers and substantial serial dependence, and in most cases standard methods do not reject the presence of a unit root in the autoregressive representation of the series. For empirical problems such as quantifying the effect of parameter uncertainty on short-term forecasts and asset pricing formulas, reporting only the unit root test and the parameter estimates are an unsatisfying way to describe the data. For these applications it can be useful to construct confidence sets for the largest autoregressive root of the series.

Both directly and through his students, Thomas Rothenberg has made many contributions to our understanding of inference for integrated and nearly integrated data. One way to construct a confidence set is to invert a sequence of tests, where each test in the sequence evaluates a particular point null hypothesis. The confidence set contains all the point nulls that are not rejected by the sequence of tests. Elliott and Stock (2000) argued that, since a more powerful test leads to a more accurate interval, inverting the asymptotically point optimal tests in Elliott, Rothenberg, and Stock (1996) should lead to more accurate confidence sets than had been previously proposed (see Stock 1991; Andrews 1993; Hansen 1999). While it is not possible to do better than the tests in Elliott et al.

(1996) when the innovations are normal, the outliers present in financial data suggest that other methods may lead to improvements.

This paper proposes "robust" confidence sets which have good accuracy for a variety of error distributions. We create the confidence sets by inverting a sequence of robust t tests. Unlike the tests in Elliott et al. (1996), t tests do not efficiently model the deterministic trend and are not point optimal for any particular distribution. We use t tests because they are robust. Thompson (2004a) showed that point optimal tests based on nonnormal likelihoods can behave very badly when the true error density is unknown and asymmetric. Thus, there is a trade-off between Elliott and Stock's (2000) confidence sets, which efficiently handle deterministic trends, and the confidence sets described here, which are robust to outliers.

Since the robust test statistics generally have null distributions that depend on unknown nuisance parameters, finding appropriate critical values is a nontrivial problem. Furthermore, all the robust tests require estimation of more nuisance parameters than do the least-squares tests, and the cumulative effect of estimation error can be large. In some cases nonparametric estimators must be used, resulting in slow rates of convergence. An additional problem is that robust tests are somewhat more difficult to compute than least-squares-based tests.

We construct a sequence of robust tests which eliminate the need to estimate several of the unknown nuisance parameters. To compute critical values we extend a simple procedure suggested by Rothenberg and Stock (1997). Following Rothenberg and Thompson (2001) we compute "aligned" robust tests which are no more difficult to compute than least-squares-based tests.

The resulting confidence sets perform well so long as the errors are known to follow an i.i.d. process. In this case both asymptotic analysis and a Monte Carlo study show that the robust sets are useful alternatives to the sets proposed by Elliott and Stock (2000). While the sets in Elliott and Stock (2000) have accurate coverage probabilities only for integrated or nearly integrated data, the robust sets exhibit accurate coverage probabilities for integrated data and when the true data generating process is i.i.d. We also compare the areas of the various sets and conclude that with normal errors the robust sets are slightly longer than sets in Elliott and Stock (2000), and with nonnormal errors the robust sets are much shorter. However, when the errors follow an unknown serially correlated process neither the robust sets nor the Elliott and Stock (2000) sets have satisfactory small sample coverage properties.

2. INVERTING A SEQUENCE OF TESTS

The observations $\{y_t\}_{t=1}^{T}$ come from the data generating process

$$\begin{aligned} y_t &= \mu_1 + \mu_2 t + u_t \\ u_t &= (1+\gamma)\,u_{t-1} + v_t \\ \Gamma(L)\,v_t &= \varepsilon_t \end{aligned}$$

where $\{\varepsilon_t\}_{t=1}^T$ is an i.i.d. sequence with mean 0 and variance σ_ε^2. $\Gamma(L)$ is the lag polynomial $1 - \Gamma_1 L - \cdots - \Gamma_p L^p$, and I assume that the roots of $\Gamma(z) = 0$ all lie outside the unit circle. I also assume that the initial value u_0 has a finite variance. I wish to put a confidence region around γ.

Since I am interested in inference when γ is close to zero, I adopt the local-to-zero reparameterization $\gamma = c/T$ so that the parameter space is a shrinking neighborhood of zero as the sample size grows. Following Bobkoski (1983), Cavanagh (1985), Chan and Wei (1987), and Phillips (1987), I take c fixed when making limiting arguments, obtaining asymptotic representations as a function of the local alternative c. With this reparameterization, the augmented Dickey and Fuller (1979) representation of the model is

$$\Delta Y = X\alpha + Z\beta + \epsilon \tag{2.1}$$

where $\Delta Y = (y_{p+2} - y_{p+1}, \ldots, y_T - y_{T-1})'$, $X = (y_{p+1}, \ldots, y_{T-1})'/T$, and Z is the design matrix with row $t - p - 1$ equal to $(1, t, \Delta y_{t-1}, \ldots, \Delta y_{t-p})$. The parameter α is $c\Gamma(1)$, β is a $(p+2) \times 1$ parameter vector and $\epsilon = (\varepsilon_{p+2}, \ldots, \varepsilon_T)'$. For the intercept only model (e.g., $\mu_2 = 0$) the design matrix Z has rows $(1, \Delta y_{t-1}, \ldots, \Delta y_{t-p})$.

A $100\,(1 - a)\%$ confidence set $C(y)$ where y is the data has the property that $\Pr_c[c \in C(y)] \geq 1 - a$ for all c. Here $\Pr_c$ indicates that the probability is computed assuming c is the true autoregressive parameter. We construct $C(y)$ from a sequence of tests. Suppose, for each point $\bar{c}$ in the parameter space Θ, we construct a test of asymptotic size a for the hypothesis $c = \bar{c}$ versus $c \neq \bar{c}$. We define $C(y)$ as the set of all $\bar{c}$ that we fail to reject. In large samples $C(y)$ has the desired property that $\Pr_c[c \in C(y)] \geq 1 - a$ for all c.

Stock (1991) constructed confidence sets by inverting a sequence of t tests based on the ordinary least squares (OLS) estimator for α in Equation (2.1). Each null hypothesis $\alpha = \bar{\alpha}$ versus $\alpha \neq \bar{\alpha}$ is rejected when the t statistic $\left[X'MX\right]^{1/2}\widehat{\alpha}_{ls}$ is too large or too small, where $\widehat{\alpha}_{ls}$ is the OLS estimator and M is the projection matrix $I - Z\left(Z'Z\right)^{-1}Z'$. This procedure gives us a confidence region for α which, combined with a consistent estimate of $\Gamma(1)$, leads to a confidence region for c. Andrews (1993) and Hansen (1999) also proposed confidence intervals based on the OLS estimator.

Elliott and Stock (2000) attempted to improve on Stock's (1991) intervals by inverting tests that are point optimal for Gaussian errors. In a stationary autoregressive model with Gaussian errors, the least-squares t test is asymptotically uniformly most powerful against all one-sided alternatives. Elliott et al. (1996) have shown that when γ is local to zero this result does not hold, and there does not exist a uniformly most powerful test, even in large samples. Instead, for each null $c = \bar{c}$ we have a family of point optimal tests, each one most powerful only against the point alternative $c = \bar{c}$. While none of the point optimal tests dominate the others, they are generally more powerful than the t test because the point optimal tests efficiently model the trend coefficients μ_1 and μ_2.

Table 16.1. *Some robust tests*

Test	ψ or φ function	ω
Least squares	$\psi(x) = x$	1
LAD	$\psi(x) = \text{sign}(x)$	$2f(\eta)$
Huber's M	$\psi(x) = x1(\|x\| \leq k)$ $+ k\text{sign}(x)1(\|x\| > k)$	$\Pr[\|\varepsilon_1 - \eta\| \leq k]$
Student's t	$\psi(x) = \log(1 + x^2/n)$	$\text{E}\psi'(\varepsilon_1 - \eta)$
Wilcoxon ranks	$\varphi(s) = s - 1/2$	$\text{E}f(\varepsilon_1)$
Normal ranks	$\varphi(s) = \Phi^{-1}(s)$	$\text{E}f(\varepsilon_1)/\Phi'\left(\Phi^{-1}(F(\varepsilon_1))\right)$
Sign ranks	$\varphi(s) = \text{sign}(s - 1/2)$	$2f(m)$

Notes: $F(x) = \Pr[\varepsilon_1 \leq x]$ and $f(x) = F'(x)$. k is chosen by the researcher. n is the number of degrees of freedom. m is the median of the errors. η solves $\text{E}\phi(\varepsilon_1 - \eta) = 0$.

Confidence sets inherit the properties of the tests used to form them. In the present paper we prefer confidence sets that tend to cover small areas. While there is no direct link between test power and confidence set area, in Section 3.2 we will see that the point-optimal tests lead to smaller sets than the OLS t tests.

Elliott et al.'s (1996) tests are not point optimal in thick-tailed data. The present paper proposes a method for creating confidence sets from a sequence of traditional robust t tests which inefficiently handle the deterministic trend. An alternative approach would be to invert point-optimal tests for non-Gaussian likelihoods. I prefer to invert t statistics because Thompson (2004a) has shown that point-optimal robust tests can behave badly when the error density is unknown and asymmetric. Robust t tests perform well for a variety of asymmetric error distributions.

One way to "robustify" the least-squares-based t test is to replace the OLS estimate for α with a robust M estimate. M estimators may be characterized as solutions to maximization problems or, equivalently, as solutions to first order conditions. It will be convenient to adopt the notation that, for any function $h(\cdot)$ mapping $\mathfrak{R}$ into $\mathfrak{R}$ and any n-dimensional column vector x with components x_i, $h(x)$ is the n-dimensional column vector with components $h(x_i)$. The M estimators $(\widehat{\alpha}, \widehat{\beta})$ solve the equations

$$\begin{aligned} Z'\psi\left(\Delta Y - X\widehat{\alpha} - Z\widehat{\beta}\right) &= 0 \\ X'\psi\left(\Delta Y - X\widehat{\alpha} - Z\widehat{\beta}\right) &= 0 \end{aligned} \tag{2.2}$$

where $\psi(\cdot)$ is a scalar "score"-type function chosen by the researcher. The choice of ψ determines the sensitivity of $\widehat{\alpha}$ to outliers; when $\psi(x) = x, \widehat{\alpha}$ is the OLS estimator, and when $\psi(x) = \text{sign}(x)$, $\widehat{\alpha}$ is the least absolute deviations (LAD) estimator. Some common choices for ψ are given in Table 16.1. Robust t tests of the unit root hypothesis $\bar{\alpha} = 0$ have been proposed by Lucas (1995) and Herce (1996).

I propose an alternative sequence of tests based on a locally asymptotic representation of the t statistic. Under both, the null $\alpha = \bar{\alpha}$ and fixed alternatives $\alpha \neq \bar{\alpha}$, the t statistic satisfies the approximation

$$\left[X'MX\right]^{1/2}(\widehat{\alpha} - \bar{\alpha}) = \frac{1}{\omega}\frac{X'M\psi\left(\Delta Y - X\bar{\alpha} - Z\widehat{\beta}_R(\bar{\alpha})\right)}{[X'MX]^{1/2}} + o_p(1)$$

where $\widehat{\beta}_R(\bar{\alpha})$ is the restricted estimator that solves the first-order conditions with the null hypothesis $\alpha = \bar{\alpha}$ imposed:

$$Z'\psi\left(\Delta Y - X\bar{\alpha} - Z\widehat{\beta}_R(\bar{\alpha})\right) = 0.$$

ω is the nuisance parameter $\int_{\mathbb{R}} f(x)d\psi(x - \eta)$, where f denotes the density function for ε_1, and η solves $\mathrm{E}\psi(\varepsilon_1 - \eta) = 0$. Some robust tests and the corresponding ω parameters are given in Table 16.1. When $\psi(x) = x$, $\widehat{\alpha}$ is the OLS estimator and $\omega = 1$, and it is straightforward to show that the approximation holds exactly, with the $o_p(1)$ term equal to zero.

The parameter ω appears in the asymptotic null distribution of the t statistic, and it must be estimated in order to obtain critical values. In large samples the estimates will converge to their true values and the estimation error will have an asymptotically negligible effect on inference. In small samples estimation error may affect the size and power of the tests. This is especially true if ω is poorly estimated. For example, $\omega = 2f(\eta)$ for LAD estimation. The standard kernel estimate of a density at a point does not converge to the true value at root-T speed and is quite variable in small samples.

Since eliminating the $(1/\omega)$ term does not affect asymptotic power, a natural alternative is to reject the null when the ratio

$$\text{(aligned } M \text{ test) } Q(\bar{\alpha}) = \frac{X'M\psi\left(\Delta Y - X\bar{\alpha} - Z\widehat{\beta}_R(\bar{\alpha})\right)}{[X'MX]^{1/2}} \tag{2.3}$$

is too large or too small. Theorem 3.1 shows that the asymptotic null distribution of this statistic does not depend on ω.

Computing the sequence of tests requires solving for $\widehat{\beta}_R(\bar{\alpha})$ at each $\bar{\alpha}$. Depending on the choice of ψ, this can be a computationally burdensome procedure. Instead of computing $\widehat{\beta}_R(\bar{\alpha})$ using ψ, compute it using an alternative set of first-order conditions:

$$Z'\phi\left(\Delta Y - X\bar{\alpha} - Z\widehat{\beta}_R(\bar{\alpha})\right) = 0. \tag{2.4}$$

ϕ is a function chosen by the researcher. We could take $\phi = \psi$, or we could take ϕ to be a function that leads to computationally convenient solutions for $\widehat{\beta}_R(\bar{\alpha})$. For example, $\phi(x) = x$ leads to OLS estimates of $\widehat{\beta}_R(\bar{\alpha})$, and $\phi(x) = \mathrm{sign}(x)$ leads to LAD estimates. If ϕ, ψ, and the error density are all symmetric around zero, the asymptotic distribution of $Q(\bar{\alpha})$ does not depend on ϕ. When symmetry of the errors does not hold $Q(\bar{\alpha})$ will in many cases retain its robustness to outliers. I should note that choosing ϕ not equal to ψ changes the definition of

η: it solves $E\phi(\varepsilon_1 - \eta) = 0$. Following Adichie (1986) and Akritas (1991), we call the test based on $Q(\bar{\alpha})$ an "aligned" M test.

It is also possible to construct robust confidence sets based on a single statistic, like $Q(0)$. We choose instead to compute a sequence of test statistics, because under each null hypothesis $\alpha = \bar{\alpha}$ the parameter ω does not appear in the null distribution of $Q(\bar{\alpha})$. Inverting $Q(0)$ requires us to calculate its distribution under both the null and under various alternatives. The asymptotic theory in Theorem 3.1 shows that ω appears in the distribution of $Q(0)$ when $\alpha \neq 0$. Thus, computing a sequence of test statistics allows us to avoid computing the additional nuisance parameter.

Hansen's (1999) parametric bootstrap might provide an alternative method to avoid estimation of ω. Thompson (2004b) demonstrates that under the null the limiting distribution of the t statistic $[X'MX]^{1/2}(\widehat{\alpha} - \bar{\alpha})$ depends on α and several nuisance parameters that can be consistently estimated. Therefore, the test statistic fits into Hansen's (1999) framework.[1]

We can also construct $Q(\bar{\alpha})$ statistics which are asymptotically equivalent to the rank-based unit root tests described in Hasan and Koenker (1997). Consider a test of the null hypothesis $\alpha = \bar{\alpha}$ using the test statistic $[X'MX]^{-1/2}X'Mb$, where $b = \int_0^1 \widehat{a}(s)\, d\varphi(s)$ and $\widehat{a}$ solves the linear programming problem

$$\widehat{a}(\tau) = \operatorname{argmax} \left\{a'(\Delta Y - X\bar{\alpha}) \mid Z'a = (1-\tau)\, Z'1, a \in [0,1]^{T-p}\right\} \tag{2.5}$$

φ is a function chosen by the researcher. This construction for b is a way to handle the nuisance parameters β and allows the researcher to consider general functions of the ranked residuals: when Z is a vector of ones and $\varphi(\tau) = \tau$, each element of b is the rank of the corresponding element of $\Delta Y - X\bar{\alpha}$. Table 16.1 lists some common choices for φ.

Confidence regions for α may be constructed using a sequence of tests of the form $[X'MX]^{-1/2}X'Mb$. We instead use a computationally simpler family of aligned rank tests. Given a pair of functions φ and ϕ, for each null hypothesis $\alpha = \bar{\alpha}$ use the ϕ function to compute the residuals $\Delta Y - X\bar{\alpha} - Z\widehat{\beta}_R(\bar{\alpha})$ from Equation (2.4). Letting R_t denote the rank of the tth residual and $R(\bar{\alpha})$ the $(T-p-1)$-dimensional vector of the ranks, form the statistic

$$(\text{"aligned" rank test})\ Q(\bar{\alpha}) = \frac{X'M\varphi\left(\frac{R(\bar{\alpha})-.5}{T-p-1}\right)}{[X'MX]^{1/2}}.$$

[1] Here is one adaptation of Hansen's (1999) bootstrap. 1. Draw a bootstrap sample ϵ^* from the residuals $\Delta Y - X\widehat{\alpha} - Z\widehat{\beta}$. 2. For each $\bar{\alpha}$, form data vectors ΔY^*, X^*, Z^* from the model $\Delta Y^* = X^*\bar{\alpha} + Z^*\widehat{\beta} + \epsilon^*$. 3. Use Equation (2.2) to compute the estimate $\widehat{\alpha}^*$ from ΔY^*, X^*, and Z^*, and form the t statistic $[X'MX]^{1/2}(\widehat{\alpha}^* - \bar{\alpha})$. 4. Repeat this procedure many times to obtain bootstrap quantiles of the distribution of $[X'MX]^{1/2}(\widehat{\alpha} - \bar{\alpha})$ and apply Hansen's (1999) procedure for constructing confidence intervals. This procedure does not require the estimation of ω.

This test is based on the idea that under the null, functions of the ranked residuals should be approximately independent of MX. So long as $\widehat{\beta}_R(\bar{\alpha})$ is a root-T consistent estimate, any choice of ϕ leads to a $Q(\bar{\alpha})$ test with the same asymptotic null distribution and power function as the test based on $[X'MX]^{-1/2}X'Mb$.

3. ASYMPTOTIC ANALYSIS

Deriving a large sample representation for $Q(\bar{\alpha})$ requires assumptions about ψ, φ, and the error distribution.

Assumption 3.1. *The errors* $\{\varepsilon_t\}_{t=1}^T$ *are i.i.d. with* $E|\varepsilon_1|^{2+\delta}$ *finite for some* $\delta > 0$. *The density function* f *has uniformly continuous derivatives* f' *and finite Fisher Information.*

We require that the preliminary estimator $\widehat{\beta}_R(\bar{\alpha})$ is root-T consistent. Let ξ denote the $(p+2)$-dimensional vector with first element equal to one and the remaining elements equal to zero.

Assumption 3.2. *There exists a constant* η *so that* $\sqrt{T}(\widehat{\beta}_R(\bar{\alpha}) - \beta - \xi\eta)$ *has a limiting distribution.*

The assumption on $\widehat{\beta}_R(\bar{\alpha})$ is easy to verify when preliminary estimation is by least squares. Theorem 3.1 in Thompson (2004b) can be adapted to verify that the assumption also holds when ϕ is the derivative of a convex function with finitely many points of nondifferentiability. This covers preliminary LAD and Huber's M estimates.

Since many of the ψ and φ functions considered in this paper are discontinuous or nondifferentiable, continuity is not required.

Assumption 3.3. *(for M tests):* ψ *satisfies*

$$\mathrm{E} \sup_{u_1:\|u-u_1\|<\delta} (\psi(\varepsilon_t + u_1) - \psi(\varepsilon_t + u))^2 \leq C^2\delta^{2\varrho}$$

for all fixed u and all $\delta > 0$ *in a neighborhood of zero, and for some finite constants C and* ϱ. *Furthermore,* $\mathrm{E}\sup_{\|u\|<\delta}(\psi(\varepsilon_t - u))^2$ *exists for* $\delta > 0$ *in a neighborhood of zero.*

The assumption is satisfied by differentiable ψ like the least squares and Student's t functions, as well as by nondifferentiable ψ like the LAD and Huber's M functions.

Assumption 3.4. *(for rank tests):* φ *is continuous from the right and nondecreasing on the interval* $[\varphi_0, 1-\varphi_0]$ *for some* $\varphi_0 \in (0, .5)$ *and* φ *is constant on the set* $[0, \varphi_0] \cup [1-\varphi_0, 1]$.

The assumption on φ is taken from Hasan and Koenker (1997). As they point out, we can weaken the requirement that φ is constant in the tails at the cost of adding complexity to the proof.

The limiting distribution of $Q(\bar{\alpha})$ can be expressed as a functional of Brownian motion. Define $W(\cdot)$ to be standard Brownian motion and define $W_c(\cdot)$ to be the Ornstein–Uhlenbeck process $W_c(t) = \int_0^t \exp\{c(t-s)\}\, dW(s)$. Under the null that $\alpha = \bar{\alpha}$, the limiting form of the OLS-based statistic $\left[X'MX\right]^{1/2}(\widehat{\alpha}_{ls} - \bar{\alpha})$ is $\sigma_\varepsilon DF(\bar{c})$, where

$$DF(\bar{c}) \equiv \frac{\int_0^1 D_{\bar{c}}(r)\, dW(r)}{\sqrt{\int_0^1 D_{\bar{c}}^2(r)\, dr}}$$

and $\bar{c} = \Gamma^{-1}(1)\bar{\alpha}$. The process $D_c(r)$ is defined to be $W_c(r) - \int_0^1 W_c(s)\, ds$ in the intercept only model (e.g., $\mu_2 = 0$ and there is no time trend in the design matrix Z), and $D_c(r)$ equals $W_c(r) - 2\int_0^1 (2 - 3s - r(3 - 6s))W_c(s)\, ds$ in the model with a linear time trend. We have the following result, which is proven in the Appendix.

Theorem 3.1. *Under Assumptions 1–4,* $\widehat{\sigma}_q^{-1} Q(\widehat{\Gamma}(1)\bar{c})$ *converges weakly to* $\mathcal{Q}(c, \rho) + \lambda(c - \bar{c})\sqrt{\int D_c^2(r)\, dr}$, *where*

$$\mathcal{Q}(c, \rho) \equiv \rho DF(c) + \sqrt{1 - \rho^2} N(0, 1).$$

$N(0, 1)$ *denotes a standard normal variable, independent of* $DF(\bar{c})$. ρ *and* λ *are nuisance parameters.* $\widehat{\sigma}_q^{-1}$ *and* $\widehat{\Gamma}(1)$ *are consistent estimates of the nuisance parameters* σ_q *and* $\Gamma(1)$.

For the M tests $\rho = \mathrm{Corr}[\varepsilon_1, \psi(\varepsilon_1 - \eta)]$, where η solves $\mathrm{E}\phi(\varepsilon_1 - \eta) = 0$. For the rank tests $\rho = \mathrm{Corr}[\varepsilon_1, \varphi(F(\varepsilon_1))]$, where $F(x)$ is the distribution function $\Pr[\varepsilon_1 \leq x]$. σ_q^2 is $\mathrm{Var}[\psi(\varepsilon_1 - \eta)]$ for the M tests and $\mathrm{Var}[\varphi(F(\varepsilon_1))]$ for the rank tests. Notice that for the rank tests, $F(\varepsilon_1)$ has a uniform $[0, 1]$ distribution and σ_q is known. λ is defined to be $\omega\sigma_\varepsilon/\sigma_q$, where ω is $\int_{\mathbb{R}} f(x)\, d\psi(x - \eta)$ for the M tests and $\int_{\mathbb{R}} f(x)\, d\varphi(F(x))$ for the rank tests.

In large samples ρ and λ determine the null distribution and power function of each test. Under each null, $\bar{c} = c$ and λ disappears from the asymptotic representation. Thus, ρ controls the null distribution of the test, while ρ and λ together affect power.

The limiting distributions in the theorem are identical to the distributions derived by Hasan and Koenker (1997) for their rank tests. Thus, for each of Hasan and Koenker's (1997) rank tests, there is a corresponding aligned rank test with the same large sample null distribution and power function as the original, no matter what the choice for ϕ. Thompson (2004b) derived the asymptotic properties of the robust M tests; comparison of his results with the theorem reveal that the choice of ϕ affects the value of the nuisance parameters. Thompson (2004b) obtains the same limiting theory given here, except that η

Table 16.2. *Values of ρ and λ*

	ρ				λ			
	$N(0, 1)$	DE	Log norm	Mix	$N(0, 1)$	DE	Log norm	Mix
Least squares	1.00	1.00	1.00	1.00	1.00	1.00	1.00	1.00
LAD	.80	.71	.63	.47	.80	1.42	.99	1.86
Huber's M	.97	.94	.82	.78	.97	1.13	1.59	1.98
Student's $t3$	.95	.89	.72	.61	.95	1.21	1.70	2.19
Wilcoxon	.98	.92	.68	.64	.98	1.22	2.72	2.17
Normal ranks	1.00	.98	.76	.77	1.00	1.28	3.55	2.06
Sign ranks	.80	.71	.52	.47	.80	1.42	1.73	1.86

Notes: Expectations were computed as empirical averages of 1,000,000 simulated draws from the error distribution. $N(0, 1)$ indicates standard normal draws, DE indicates double exponential, log norm is log normal, and mixture is mixture normal. The random draws are normalized to have zero mean and unit variance. For each test $\phi(x) = x$.

solves $E\psi(\varepsilon_1 - \eta) = 0$. Thus, the aligned M tests are asymptotically equivalent to the traditional M tests when $\phi = \psi$, as well as when ϕ, ψ, and the error density are all symmetric (in which case $\eta = 0$ for both tests).

It is worth noting that the asymptotic representation for $Q(\bar{\alpha})$ does not depend on the trend parameteres μ_1 and μ_2. In large samples $Q(\bar{\alpha})$ is invariant to the trend parameters, and under normality will be dominated by the optimal invariant tests described by Elliott et al. (1996). A $Q(\bar{\alpha})$ test can only be more powerful than Elliott et al.'s (1996) tests in nonnormal data.

3.1. Obtaining Rejection Regions

Obtaining a rejection region for $Q(\bar{\alpha})$ requires us to calculate the quantiles of $\mathcal{Q}(\bar{c}, \rho)$ and to consistently estimate the nuisance parameters. Let $k_l(\bar{c}, \rho)$ and $k_u(\bar{c}, \rho)$ denote the quantiles of $\mathcal{Q}(\bar{c}, \rho)$ that solve $\Pr[k_l(\bar{c}, \rho) \le \mathcal{Q}(\bar{c}, \rho) \le k_u(\bar{c}, \rho)] = a$. Let $\widehat{\rho}$, $\widehat{\sigma}_q^{-1}$, and $\widehat{\Gamma}(1)$ denote consistent estimates of the nuisance parameters. The null hypothesis $c = \bar{c}$ is rejected in favor of the two-sided alternative $c \neq \bar{c}$ when $\widehat{\sigma}_q^{-1} Q(\widehat{\Gamma}^{-1}(1)\bar{c})$ is either below $k_l(\bar{c}, \widehat{\rho})$ or above $k_u(\bar{c}, \widehat{\rho})$. In large samples this test has size equal to a.

In most cases ρ depends on both the test and the error density. An exception to this is Stock's (1991) OLS-based test, where $\psi(x) = x$ and $\rho = 1$ no matter what the error density. For other tests ρ differs from 1 and the limiting null representation becomes a linear combination of the "Dickey–Fuller" term $DF(\bar{c})$ and a standard normal variable. For the M tests σ_q depends on both ψ and the error density, and for the rank tests σ_q is known and does not need to be estimated.

Table 16.2 lists values for ρ for various tests and error densities. It includes the aligned M tests based on least squares, LAD, Huber's function, and the Student's t density with three degrees of freedom (denoted $t3$).[2] It also includes

[2] Following Lucas (1995), the scale parameter k in Huber's function is set to $1.345\sigma_\varepsilon$.

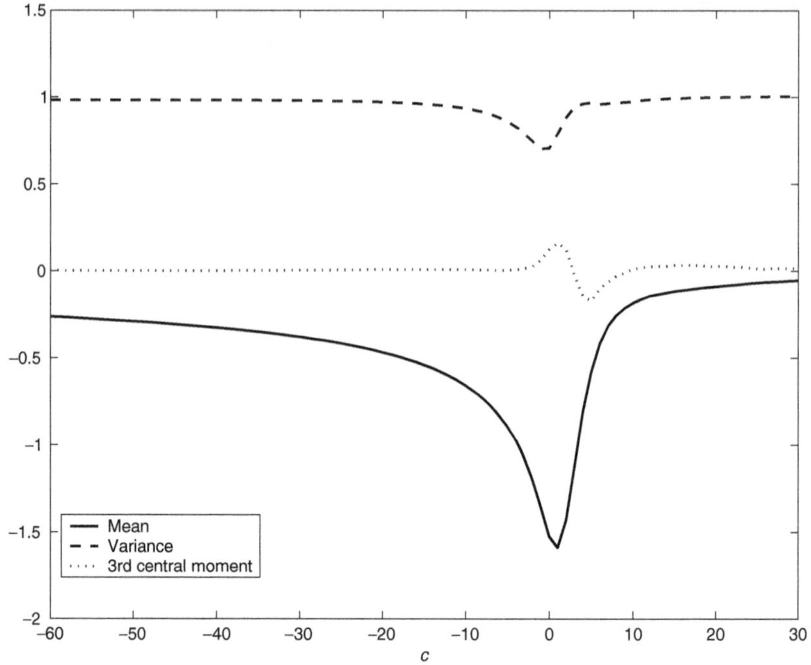

Figure 16.1. First, second, and third moments of $DF(c)$, intercept only model.

the three rank tests considered in Hasan and Koenker (1997): the tests based on Wilcoxon, Normal, and Sign ranks. The error distributions considered are the standard normal as well as the thicker-tailed double exponential, log normal, and mixture normal distributions. For the mixture distribution a standard normal variable is drawn with probability .95 and a $N(0, 100)$ variable is drawn with probability .05.

The values of ρ fall as the errors become thicker-tailed. For normal errors the parameter is close to 1, except for the LAD and Sign rank tests. Under normality the null distributions of the other tests are similar to the null for the least-squares-based tests. When the errors have thick tails the null distributions are different from the least-squares distribution and from each other.

The quantiles of $\mathcal{Q}(\bar{c}, \rho)$ are not known in closed form. A number of methods have been proposed for approximating quantiles of statistics similar to $\mathcal{Q}(\bar{c}, \rho)$. Stock (1991) calculated quantiles of $\mathcal{Q}(\bar{c}, 1)$. Lucas (1995), Herce (1996), Hasan and Koenker (1997), Seo (1999), and Thompson (2004b) all proposed methods to handle null distributions of the form $\mathcal{Q}(0, \rho)$. All of these methods could be extended to the general statistic $\mathcal{Q}(\bar{c}, \rho)$.

We adopt a method proposed by Rothenberg and Stock (1997), who encountered a statistic similar to $\mathcal{Q}(\bar{c}, \rho)$. It turns out that, no matter what the trend specification or the value for $\bar{c}$, the "Dickey–Fuller" term $DF(\bar{c})$ is approximately normally distributed. Thus, $\mathcal{Q}(\bar{c}, \rho)$ is approximately a linear combination of two normal variables and is approximately normal. The

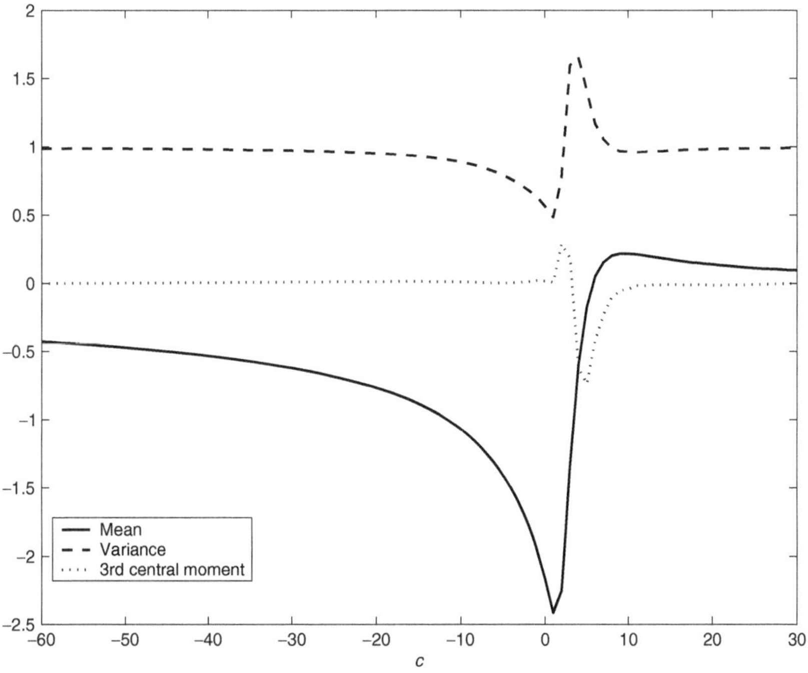

Figure 16.2. First, second, and third moments of $DF(c)$, intercept and trend case.

Cornish–Fisher expansion provides good approximations to the quantiles of distributions with approximately Gaussian shapes.

The Cornish–Fisher expansion for the a quantile of a statistic u is

$$E(u) + [\mathrm{Var}(u)]^{1/2}\left[q_a + K_3(u)\left(q_a^2 - 1\right)/6\right]$$

where $K_3(u) = E[u - Eu]^3/(\mathrm{Var}(u))^{3/2}$ and q_a is the a-percentile of the standard normal distribution. The first three moments of $\mathcal{Q}(\bar{c}, \rho)$ are[3]

$$\begin{aligned} E(\mathcal{Q}(\bar{c}, \rho)) &= \rho \mathrm{E}(DF(\bar{c})), \\ \mathrm{Var}(\mathcal{Q}(\bar{c}, \rho)) &= \rho^2 \mathrm{Var}(DF(\bar{c})) + \left(1 - \rho^2\right), \\ E(\mathcal{Q}(\bar{c}, \rho) - E\mathcal{Q}(\bar{c}, \rho))^3 &= \rho^3 E(DF(\bar{c}) - EDF(\bar{c}))^3. \end{aligned}$$

Figures 16.1 and 16.2 provide Monte Carlo estimates of the first three moments of $DF(\bar{c})$.[4] Tables 16.3 and 16.4 give numerical approximations to the moments which can be easily inputted into a computer.

[3] Rothenberg and Stock (1997) made an algebraic mistake when calculating the moments. The formulas given here correct their mistake.

[4] Unless stated otherwise, the simulations which appear in this paper were performed by computing stochastic integrals as normalized sums of 500 successive draws from a discrete time Gaussian AR(1) process with autoregressive parameter $1 + c/T$. There are 25, 000 Monte Carlo replications.

Table 16.3. *Moments of $DF(c)$, model includes an intercept only*

c	E $DF(c)$	Var($DF(c)$)	E($DF(c)$ − E $DF(c))^3$
$c < -60$	$-8.065/(c-50)$	1	0
$-60 \le c \le 1$	$-.148 - \frac{8.058}{5.7-c}$	$1.056 + \frac{.865}{1000}c - \frac{1.562}{3.3-c}$	$\frac{.380}{100} + \frac{.0311}{-.5-c}$
0	−1.524	.709	.126
1	−1.589	.794	.164
2	−1.428	.886	.123
3	−1.116	.947	−.029
4	−.808	.963	−.145
5	−.576	.969	−.169
6	−.417	.961	−.099
7	−.317	.964	−.061
8	−.253	.971	−.026
9	−.212	.972	−.009
10	−.182	.976	.014
$11 \le c \le 30$	$-2.83 + .0144c - \frac{.227}{1000}c^2$	$.950 + \frac{.390}{100}c - \frac{.701}{100^2}c^2$	$.0432 - \frac{.896}{1000}c$
$c > 30$	$1.641/c$	1	0

Table 16.4. *Moments of $DF(c)$, model includes a linear time trend*

c	E$DF(c)$	Var($DF(c)$)	E($DF(c)$ − E$DF(c))^3$
$c < -60$	$-20\,(62-c)^{-.8}$	1	0
$-60 \le c \le 1$	$-2.013 - \frac{15.809}{8.1-c}$	$1.112 + \frac{.123}{100}c - \frac{3.635}{6.7-c}$	$.0136 + \frac{.203}{1000}c$
2	−2.253	.772	.288
3	−1.348	1.594	.188
4	−.602	1.658	−.621
5	−.176	1.411	−.737
6	.051	1.169	−.417
7	.154	1.056	−.231
8	.202	.991	−.106
9	.216	.968	−.056
10	.215	.961	−.042
$11 \le c \le 30$	$.347 - .0147c + \frac{.209}{1000}c^2$	$.913 + \frac{.524}{100}c - \frac{.870}{100^2}c^2$	$-.0213 + \frac{.591}{1000}c$
$c > 30$	$400/(35+c)^2$	1	0

3.2. Asymptotic Interval Length

Asymptotic power is the probability in large samples that the test rejects the null. Simulation results suggest that power increases with λ. This may occur because λ magnifies the shift term $\lambda\,(c-\bar{c})\sqrt{\int D_c^2(r)\,dr}$ appearing in the asymptotic distribution. Power also depends on ρ, which changes the shape of the distribution. Simulation results in Thompson (2004b) suggest that for the unit root hypothesis $c = 0$, asymptotic power is much more sensitive to λ than to ρ.

Table 16.2 lists values of λ for various tests and error densities. λ increases as the errors become thicker tailed, suggesting that thicker tailed errors lead to increased power. Under normal errors the parameter for the LAD and Sign-median rank tests are far below 1, so we expect these tests to have poor power relative to the least-squares-based tests when errors are normal. For the rest of the tests λ is close to 1 with normal errors, implying that these tests have power almost as good as least squares when errors are normal and better than least squares when errors are thick tailed. In this sense they are robust to different error densities.

Thompson (2004b) showed that for a given error density, λ is maximized by choosing $-\psi$ or $-\varphi(F(x))$ equal to the log density of the errors. For the aligned rank tests this result holds for any choice of ϕ, and for the aligned M tests it is true if $\phi = \psi$. The result is not surprising, since it corresponds to testing under correct specification of the error distribution. Thus, to maximize λ with Gaussian errors use the least squares or Normal ranks tests, and with double exponential errors use the LAD or Sign ranks tests.

In Figure 16.3 we compare the large sample properties of the various confidence sets. Six data generating processes are considered: $c = 0$ with i.i.d. innovations v_t drawn from the standard normal, log normal, and mixture normal distributions, and $c = -30$ with i.i.d. innovations drawn from the same three distributions. We ignore the possibility of serially correlated innovations because they do not affect the asymptotic representations. The figure includes confidence sets based on seven t tests as well as Elliott and Stock's (2000) P_T test.[5] The P_T test efficiently handles trend coefficients and is point optimal in a Gaussian model. For the robust tests $\phi(x) = x$ so that preliminary estimation is by OLS. The model includes an intercept and time trend.

Figure 16.3 displays measures of the area covered by the simulated confidence sets. Area is a standard optimality criterion for confidence sets. Sets with smaller areas are generally considered superior. For each test and data generating process, a confidence set was constructed from the sequence of ninety-one hypothesis tests of the nulls $c = -60, -59, \ldots, 30$. The area of each confidence set was approximated by the number of null hypotheses which were not rejected. For example, if the confidence set contains only the two values -10 and -11, the area is 2. The figure displays the 25%, 50%, and 75% empirical quantiles of the areas of 25,000 simulated intervals.

In large samples the robust confidence sets are useful alternatives to the P_T-based sets. Predictably, the P_T sets perform slightly better for Gaussian errors. When $c = 0$ half of the simulated P_T-based areas fall between 11 and 20, while half of the sets based on the Wilcoxon and Normal ranks tests fall between 13 and 23. However, with thick tailed error distributions the robust sets dominate

[5] The asymptotic representation for P_T is given in Elliott and Stock (2000). We use the representation for the the "fixed initial case."

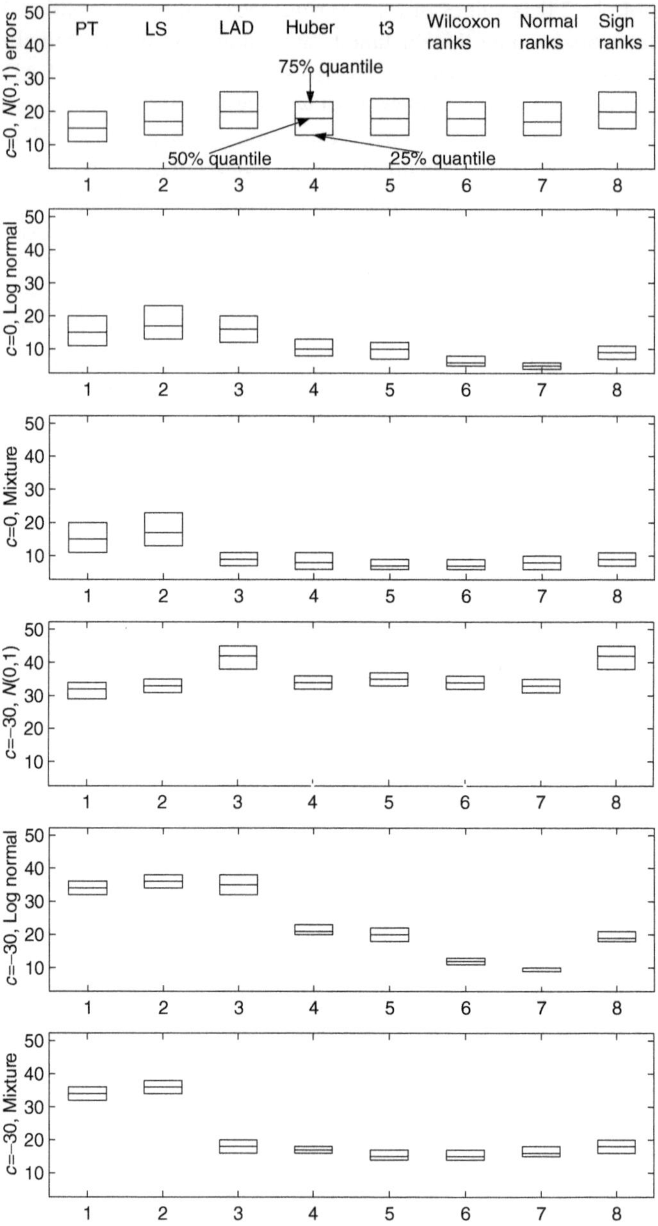

Figure 16.3. Asymptotic 25th, 50th, and 75th quantiles of the area covered by each confidence set. The model includes an intercept and time trend, with $(\mu_1, \mu_2) = (1, 1)$. (Key to tests: $1 = P_T$, $2 =$ least squares, $3 =$ LAD, $4 =$ Huber, $5 = t3$, $6 =$ Wilcoxon ranks, $7 =$ Normal ranks, $8 =$ Sign ranks.).

P_T-based sets. When $c = -30$ and the errors are log normal, half of the P_T-based areas range from 32 to 36, compared with areas from 11 to 13 for the Wilcoxon ranks test and 9 to 10 for the Normal ranks test.

The performance of the robust sets is surprising. Thompson (2004a) showed that when testing the unit root hypothesis, the efficiency loss due to using a point optimal test (thus ignoring thick-tailed errors) is often less than the loss from using a robust t test (and inefficiently modeling the trend coefficients). For example, the point-optimal Gaussian unit root test is more powerful than many traditional robust unit root tests when the errors are drawn from a Student's t distribution with five or more degrees of freedom. The results in Figure 16.3 suggest that the large power improvements translate into small improvements in confidence set area. Even the least-squares-based t test, which is everywhere dominated by the P_T test, performs only slightly worse in terms of area.

The case for using robust sets is weaker in the intercept only model. In Figure 16.4, which depicts the intercept only case, the P_T-based sets are so short at $c = 0$ that there is little room for improvement. At normal errors half of the simulated P_T-based areas fall between 6 and 11, while half of the sets based on the Wilcoxon and Normal ranks tests fall between 8 and 16. At the alternative $c = -30$ the robust sets lead to larger gains with thick-tailed distributions. While half of the P_T areas are from 29 to 34 at log normal errors, the numbers for the Wilcoxon and Normal ranks sets are 11 to 13 and 8 to 10.

Figures 16.3 and 16.4 provide a number of additional interesting results. All of the sets are larger at $c = -30$ than at $c = 0$. The Wilcoxon and Normal ranks tests have good properties for all the error distributions. In contrast to the other robust sets, the LAD-based sets perform poorly with the thick-tailed log normal distribution. The performance of the LAD-based set can be improved by choosing $\phi(x)$ equal to sign(x) instead of x. The formulas for the nuisance parameters lead immediately to the result that picking $\psi(x) = \phi(x) = \text{sign}(x)$ is asymptotically equivalent to constructing intervals from the Sign ranks test. Thus, the much improved large sample results for the LAD-based set appear in the figures.

4. MONTE CARLO EVIDENCE

We conducted a Monte Carlo study to investigate the small sample properties of the various confidence sets. In all of the simulations that follow we chose $\phi(x)$ equal to x so that estimation is by least squares. Our algorithm for constructing a confidence region for c follows:

1. Choose a finite list of points $\{\bar{c}_i\}_{i=1}^{r}$. We pick $\bar{c}_i = -60 + i$ for $i = 0, \ldots, 90$.
2. For each $\bar{c}_i$, compute the hypothesis test of the null $c = \bar{c}_i$ against the two-sided alternative $c \neq \bar{c}_i$:

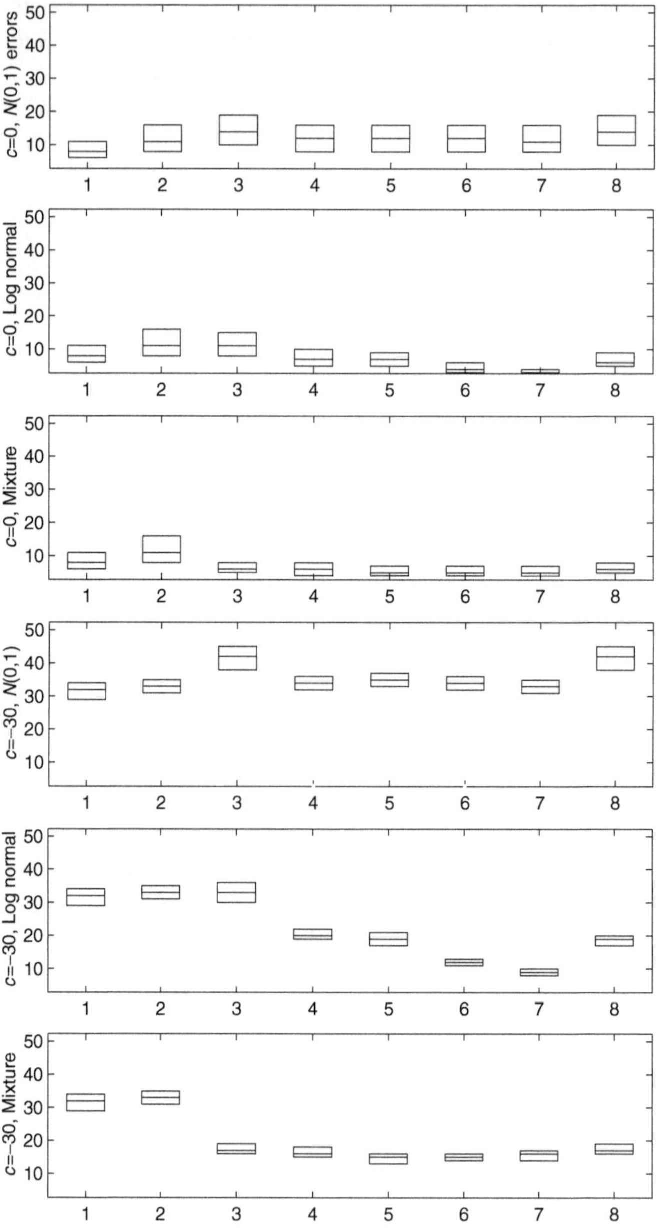

Figure 16.4. Asymptotic 25th, 50th, and 75th quantiles of the area covered by each confidence set. The model includes an intercept only, with $\mu_1 = 1$. (Key to tests: $1 = P_T$, 2 = least squares, 3 = LAD, 4 = Huber, 5 = $t3$, 6 = Wilcoxon ranks, 7 = Normal ranks, 8 = Sign ranks.).

(a) Compute the estimates $\widehat{\rho}$, $\widehat{\sigma}_q^{-1}$, and $\widehat{\Gamma}(1)$. For the P_T test, we compute the various nuisance parameters by Elliott and Stock's (2000) method of GLS detrending. For the aligned M tests, $\widehat{\sigma}_\varepsilon = \widehat{\epsilon}'\widehat{\epsilon}/T$, $\widehat{\sigma}_q = \psi(\widehat{\epsilon})'\psi(\widehat{\epsilon})/T - (1'\psi(\widehat{\epsilon})/T)^2$, and $\widehat{\rho} = \widehat{\epsilon}'\psi(\widehat{\epsilon})/(T\widehat{\sigma}_\varepsilon\widehat{\sigma}_q^{-1})$, where $\widehat{\epsilon}$ are the residuals from an ordinary least-squares regression of ΔY on $[X, Z]$. For the rank tests the same formulas hold with $\psi(\widehat{\epsilon})$ replaced by $\varphi(\widehat{R})$, where $\widehat{R}$ are the ranks of $\widehat{\epsilon}$. Taking $\widehat{\beta}_i$ to be the ith element of $\widehat{\beta}$, $\widehat{\Gamma}(1)$ is estimated by $1 - \sum_{i=1}^{p} \widehat{\beta}_{i+3}$ for the model with a time trend and $1 - \sum_{i=1}^{p} \widehat{\beta}_{i+2}$ for the model with an intercept only. The lag length p is chosen by Ng and Perron's (2001) MAIC procedure with the number of lags restricted to between 0 and 4.

(b) Calculate $\widehat{\beta}_R(\bar{c}_i\widehat{\Gamma}(1))$ by regressing $Y - \bar{c}_i\widehat{\Gamma}(1)X$ on Z. Calculate the residuals MX from a regression of X on Z.

(c) Choose a ψ or φ function and compute the test statistic $Q(\bar{c}_i\widehat{\Gamma}(1))$.

(d) Use the method in Section 3.1 to calculate the a_l-th and a_h-th quantiles of $\mathcal{Q}(\bar{c}, \rho)$. In the Monte Carlo study we use the 2.5 percent and 97.5 percent quantiles. The null is rejected when $\widehat{\sigma}_q^{-1}Q(\bar{c}_i\widehat{\Gamma}(1))$ is greater than the a_h-th quantile or less than the a_l-th quantile.

3. The $100\,(a_h - a_l)$-percent confidence region consists of all $\bar{c}_i$ which the hypothesis tests fail to reject.

Figure 16.5 provides encouraging results about the small sample coverage probabilities of the robust intervals. The four graphs depict empirical coverage probabilities from 2,000 Monte Carlo replications of sample size 100 from the model with i.i.d. errors v_t drawn from the standard normal, double exponential, log normal, and mixture normal distributions. The true value for $1 - \gamma$ ranges from 0 to 1.2. We make the unrealistic assumption that the researcher knows that the errors are i.i.d. and includes no lagged Δy_t terms in the design matrix. The model includes an intercept and time trend.

In this simple setup the small sample coverage probabilities of the robust sets are quite close to the nominal probabilities of .95. This holds for each robust test and error distribution, even for values of γ far from the integrated case $\gamma = 0$. The P_T test exhibits large size distortions with stationary data. For $1 - \gamma < .5$, the coverage probability of the P_T is zero for each error distribution. It appears that the local to zero asymptotics provide good small sample approximations for the t ratios in both integrated and stationary data. This occurs because under the null the test statistic $Q\,(\bar{\alpha})$ is stochastically bounded for both the integrated and stationary cases. In the stationary case $Q(\bar{\alpha})$ has a limiting standard normal null distribution and as c decreases the local to zero, asymptotics lead to complicated representations of standard normal variables.

The small sample coverage probabilities are much less accurate when the researcher estimates the dependence structure of the errors. Table 16.5 gives empirical coverage probabilities of the various confidence sets for several types

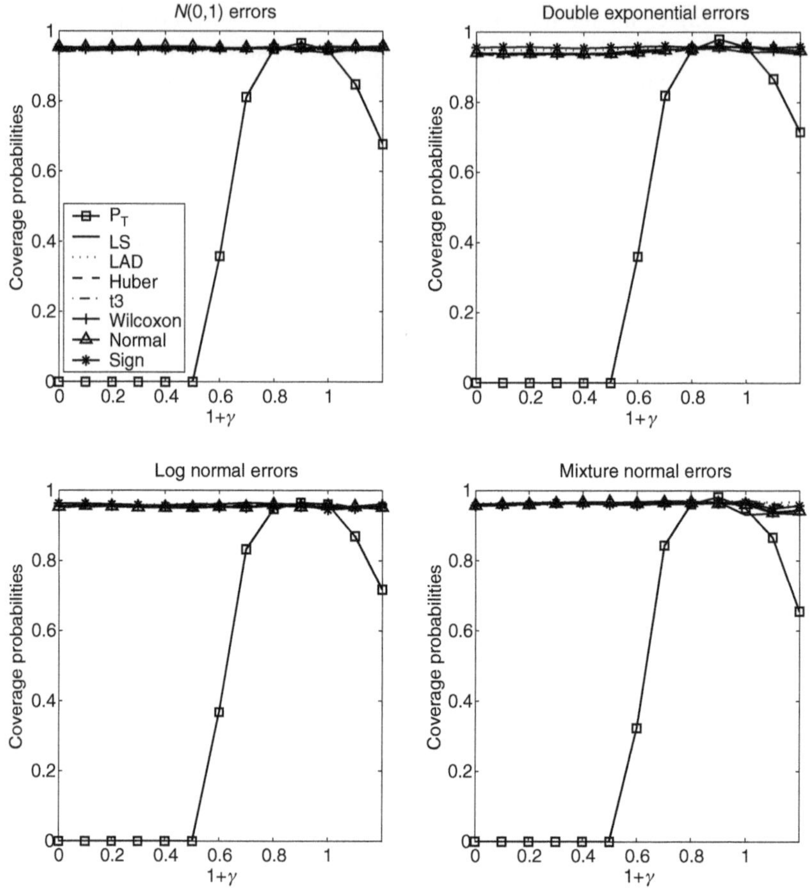

Figure 16.5. Empirical coverage probabilities when the researcher knows that v_t are i.i.d.
Notes: The model includes an intercept and time trend, with $(\mu_1, \mu_2) = (1, 1)$. There are 2,000 Monte Carlo replications. Sample size is $n = 100$.

of serial correlation:

$$\begin{aligned}
\text{IID:}\quad & v_t = \zeta_t \\
\text{AR:}\quad & v_t = .3v_{t-1} + \zeta_t \\
\text{MA:}\quad & v_t = \zeta_t - .3\zeta_{t-1} \\
\text{GARCH MA:}\quad & v_t = \vartheta_t - .3\vartheta_{t-1}, \qquad \vartheta_t = h_t^{1/2}\zeta_t \\
& h_t = 1 + .65h_{t-1} + .25\vartheta_{t-1}^2, \qquad h_0 = 0.
\end{aligned}$$

The fundamental innovations ζ_t have initial condition $\zeta_0 = 0$. The empirical coverage rates are reasonably close to the nominal rate of .95 so long as the true value of c is 0. For $c = -30$, the coverage rates are strongly biased downward.

Table 16.5. *Empirical coverage probablities*

	N(0,1) errors				Log Norm errors				Mixture errors			
Test	IID	AR	MA	GM	IID	AR	MA	GM	IID	AR	MA	GM
					True $c = 0$							
P_T	.94	.92	.93	.91	.95	.93	.94	.90	.95	.94	.95	.92
Least squares	.94	.93	.93	.93	.95	.94	.93	.91	.94	.92	.92	.91
LAD	.96	.95	.95	.95	.96	.96	.97	.95	.97	.96	.96	.95
Huber's M	.95	.94	.94	.94	.96	.96	.94	.83	.97	.95	.94	.91
Student's $t3$	.95	.93	.94	.95	.96	.95	.94	.92	.97	.96	.94	.93
Wilcoxon	.96	.95	.95	.95	.96	.95	.92	.79	.96	.95	.95	.92
Normal ranks	.96	.95	.95	.95	.96	.95	.90	.75	.96	.95	.94	.91
Sign ranks	.96	.96	.95	.95	.95	.95	.95	.90	.96	.96	.95	.94
					True $c = -30$							
P_T	.61	.31	.56	.56	.65	.26	.59	.62	.71	.28	.64	.58
Least squares	.81	.59	.69	.66	.81	.57	.69	.63	.87	.55	.76	.67
LAD	.84	.71	.77	.77	.80	.44	.73	.78	.85	.45	.69	.69
Huber's M	.81	.62	.70	.70	.77	.30	.56	.54	.83	.29	.57	.55
Student's t3	.81	.63	.71	.80	.77	.29	.58	.71	.82	.28	.56	.62
Wilcoxon	.81	.62	.71	.71	.75	.23	.50	.52	.82	.32	.57	.59
Normal ranks	.81	.61	.70	.69	.75	.23	.45	.46	.83	.32	.57	.58
Sign ranks	.84	.71	.78	.78	.78	.34	.64	.70	.85	.46	.69	.72

Notes: The model includes an intercept and time trend, with $(\mu_1, \mu_2) = (1, 1)$. There are 2,000 Monte Carlo replications. Sample size is $n = 100$. GM indicates GARCH MA errors.

This is true of all the tests and the effect is strongest for the P_T test. IID errors lead to the best coverage rates, with probabilities close to .9 in many cases. A possible explanation for these results is that the estimator for $\Gamma(1)$ performs poorly at alternatives far from $c = 0$. Another explanation is that the asymptotic approximations work only when the largest root of the autoregressive polynomial for u_t dominates the other roots. As the alternative moves from $c = 0$ to $c = -30$, the largest root shrinks relative to the other roots.

A simulation experiment suggests that an accurate estimate for $\Gamma(1)$ can dramatically improve the coverage probabilities. We simulated 2,000 draws of 100 observations from the model at $c = -30$ with Gaussian, AR(1) errors: $v_t = \rho v_{t-1} + \varepsilon_t$. We constructed confidence sets by the algorithm described earlier, except that the number of lags p was set to 1 and the estimate $\widehat{\Gamma}(1)$ was replaced by the true value $1 - \rho$. The empirical coverage rates were close to the nominal rates for ρ varying from -1 to .75. Only for ρ close to 1 did the empirical rates drop below .90 percent.

We also conducted a Monte Carlo experiment to evaluate interval area in small samples. In Figure 16.6 we plot the 25 percent, 50 percent and 75 percent quantiles of 2,000 intervals obtained from 100 observations from the model with trend. The simulation design is the same as in Figure 16.3, so Figure 16.6 provides the small sample counterpart to the asymptotic results in Figure 16.3. To obtain accurate coverage probabilities, we make the unrealistic assumption that the errors v_t are known to be i.i.d.

The Monte Carlo results weaken the case for using a robust set. As the asymptotics predicted, the robust sets are almost as short as the P_T-based sets at normal errors and are shorter with thick-tailed distributions. However, the gains from using a robust set with nonnormal errors are smaller than in the asymptotic experiment. At $c = 0$ with mixture normal errors, asymptotic median area decreases by a factor of 3 when the Wilcoxon ranks-based set replaces the P_T-based set. In small samples the median decreases by a factor of 2. At $c = -30$, the robust intervals lead to larger declines in area relative to the least-squares-based set. We do not evaluate the P_T sets at $c = -30$ because of the inaccurate coverage probabilities exhibited in Figure 16.5.

ACKNOWLEDGMENTS

I thank Graham Elliot, Andrew Harvey, Gene Savin, an anonymous referee, and seminar participants at Berkeley for useful comments. I thank Thomas Rothenberg for everything.

APPENDIX A

Here we prove Theorem 3.1 for M functions ψ and rank functions φ. We will discuss the model with a linear time trend. All of the results may be extended to the model with an intercept only (e.g., $\mu_2 = 0$). Throughout the Appendix $\|\cdot\|$ denotes the usual Euclidean norm: $\|b_{ij}\| = (\sum_{i,j} b_{ij}^2)^{1/2}$.

It will prove convenient to adopt a reparametrization. Define $a = \bar{\alpha} - \Gamma(1)c$, and define θ to be the $(p+2)$-dimensional vector with elements,

$$\theta_1 = \left[(\bar{\alpha} - c\Gamma(1))(\mu_1 - \mu_2)/T + \mu_2 \sum_{i=3}^{p}(\bar{\beta}_i - \beta_i) + (\bar{\beta}_1 - \beta_1) - \eta\right]$$

$$\theta_2 = T\left[(\bar{\alpha} - c\Gamma(1))\mu_2/T + (\bar{\beta}_2 - \beta_2)\right]$$

$$\theta_{2+i} = (\bar{\beta}_i - \beta_i)$$

for $i = 1, \ldots, p$. There is a one-to-one mapping from (a, θ) to $(\bar{\alpha}, \bar{\beta})$.

Proof of Theorem 3.1 for M Functions

A reparametrization leads to an expression for $Q(\bar{\alpha})$ which is more suitable for deriving asymptotic results. Let $z_t = (1, t, \Delta y_{t-1}, \ldots, \Delta y_{t-p})'$ and let $w_t = (1, t/T, \Delta u_{t-1}, \ldots, \Delta u_{t-p})'$. The vector of residuals $\Delta Y - X\bar{\alpha} - Z\bar{\beta}$ has elements $\Delta y_t - \bar{\alpha} y_{t-1}/T - z_t\bar{\beta}$ equal to $\varepsilon_t - \eta - a u_{t-1}/T - w_t'\theta$. The test

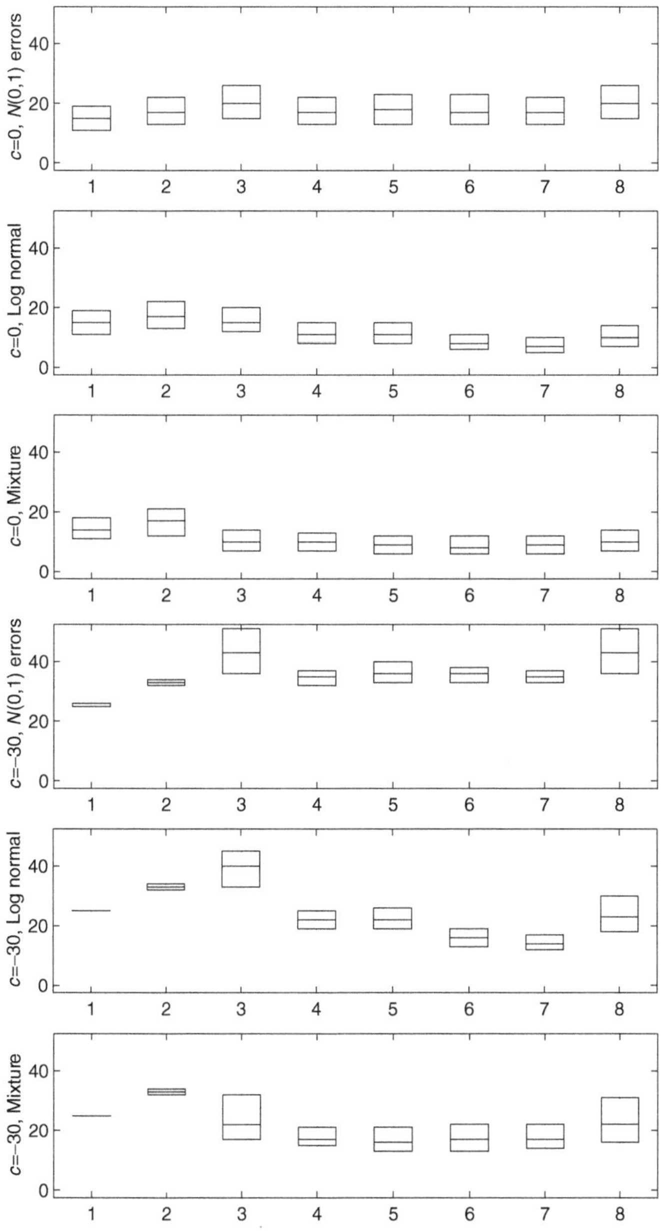

Figure 16.6. Empirical 25th, 50th, and 75th quantiles of the area covered by each confidence set. There are 2,000 Monte Carlo simulations of 100 observations from the model with an intercept and time trend, with $(\mu_1, \mu_2) = (1, 1)$. The researcher knows that the errors v_t are i.i.d. (Key to tests: $1 = P_T$, 2 = least squares, 3 = LAD, 4 = Huber, $5 = t3$, 6 = Wilcoxon ranks, 7 = Normal ranks, 8 = Sign ranks.).

statistic may be written

$$Q(\bar{\alpha}) = \left[T^{-2}\sum(y_{t-1} - \widehat{y}_{t-1})^2\right]^{-1/2} S_\psi\left(T^{-1/2}a, \widehat{\theta}_{\bar{\alpha}}\right),$$

$$S_\psi(x,\theta) = T^{-1}\sum(y_{t-1} - \widehat{y}_{t-1})\,\psi\left(\varepsilon_t - \eta - xu_{t-1}/T^{1/2} - w_t'\theta\right)$$

where $\widehat{\theta}_{\bar{\alpha}}$ is equal to θ evaluated at $\bar{\beta} = \widehat{\beta}_R(\bar{\alpha})$), and $\widehat{y}_{t-1}$ is the fitted value from a least-squares regression of y_{t-1} on z_t. Straightforward algebraic manipulations lead to the result that $T^{-1}(y_{t-1} - \widehat{y}_{t-1}) = r_t$, where r_t is the residual from a least-squares regression of u_{t-1}/T on $T^{-1/2}w_t$. So we may write

$$S_\psi(x,\theta) = \sum r_t \psi\left(\varepsilon_t - \eta - xu_{t-1}/T^{1/2} - w_t'\theta\right).$$

We will establish a limiting representation for S_ψ using the bracketing methods described in Andrews (1994). Existing bracketing proofs require weakly dependent data. I cannot use those results since y_t is a strongly dependent, nearly integrated process. The following lemma uses bracketing arguments to establish the stochastic equicontinuity of an empirical process based on S_ψ. The proof is long and is omitted. The proof is available from the author upon request. It very closely follows the proof of the theorem in Section 11.2 of Pollard (2004).

Lemma A.1. *Under Assumptions 3.1 and 3.3, the process* $S_\psi(a,\theta) - S_\psi^*(a,\theta)$ *is stochastically equicontinuous in* (x,θ), *where*

$$S_\psi^*(x,\theta) = \sum r_t E_{t-1}\psi\left(\varepsilon_t - \eta - xu_{t-1}/T^{1/2} - w_t'\theta\right).$$

The next two lemmas use this result to establish an asymptotically linear representation for S_ψ.

Lemma A.2. *Under Assumptions 3.1–3.3,* $R\left(T^{-1/2}a, \widehat{\theta}_{\bar{\alpha}}\right) \xrightarrow{p} 0$, *where*

$$R(x,\theta) = S_\psi(x,\theta) - S_\psi^*(x,\theta) - S_\psi(0,0) + S_\psi^*(0,0).$$

Since $T^{-1/2}a \to 0$ and $\widehat{\theta}_{\bar{\alpha}} \xrightarrow{p} 0$ by Assumption 3.2, this result follows immediately from the previous lemma.

Lemma A.3. *Under Assumptions 3.1–3.3,*

$$S_\psi^*\left(T^{-1/2}a, \widehat{\theta}_{\bar{\alpha}}\right) - S_\psi^*(0,0) = -\omega T^{-1}\sum r_t u_{t-1}a + o_p(1).$$

Define $I(u) = \mathrm{E}\psi(\varepsilon_t - u)$. By the change of variables $y = \varepsilon_t - u$ we obtain

$$I(u) = \int \psi(y)\, f(y+u)\, dy.$$

Assumptions 3.1 and 3.3 imply that the derivative $I'(u) = \int \psi(y) f'(y+u)dy$ exists. Integration by parts leads to the expression $I'(u) = -\int f(y+u)d\psi(y)$, which is uniformly continuous in u since f is uniformly continuous.

By the mean value theorem,

$$\begin{aligned} S_{\psi}^{*}\left(T^{-1/2}a,\widehat{\theta}_{\bar{\alpha}}\right) &= \sum r_t I\left(\eta + au_{t-1}/T + w_t'\widehat{\theta}_{\bar{\alpha}}\right) \\ &= I(\eta)\sum r_t + I(\eta)\sum r_t\left(au_{t-1}/T + w_t'\widehat{\theta}_{\bar{\alpha}}\right) + R_T, \\ \text{with } R_T &= T^{-1}\sum T^{1/2}r_t\left(I'\left(u_t^*\right) - I'(\eta)\right) \\ &\quad \times\left(au_{t-1}/T^{1/2} + w_t'\widehat{\theta}_{\bar{\alpha}}T^{1/2}\right), \end{aligned}$$

where $\left|u_t^* - \eta\right| \leq |au_{t-1}/T + w_t'\widehat{\theta}_{\bar{\alpha}}|$. By the usual asymptotic results for nearly integrated processes, $u_{[sT]}/T^{1/2}$, $w_{[sT]}$, and $T^{1/2}r_{[sT]}$ all converge weakly to Gaussian processes in s and for each process the maximum over s is a stochastically bounded random variable (see Phillips (1988) lemma 3.1). This result, combined with the uniform continuity of I', leads to the result

$$|R_T| \leq O_p(1)T^{-1}\sum\left|I'\left(u_t^*\right) - I(\eta)\right| = o_p(1),$$

so R_T is asymptotically negligible. Since r_t is the residual from regressing u_{t-1}/T on w_t, $\sum r_t = \sum r_t w_t' = 0$ and we obtain

$$S_{\psi}^{*}\left(T^{-1/2}a,\widehat{\theta}_{\bar{\alpha}}\right) = I(\eta)\,T^{-1}\sum r_t u_{t-1}a + o_p(1).$$

Since $I'(\eta) = -\omega$ and $S_{\psi}^{*}(0,0) = I(0)\sum r_t = 0$, the lemma follows.

Proof of Theorem 3.1 for M functions

By Lemmas A.2 and A.3, and since $\sum r_t = 0$,

$$\begin{aligned} S_{\psi}\left(T^{-1/2}a,\widehat{\theta}_{\bar{\alpha}}\right) &= \sum r_t\psi_{\phi}(\varepsilon_t) - \omega T^{-1} \\ &\quad \times\sum r_t u_{t-1}\left(\bar{\alpha} - \Gamma(1)c\right) + o_p(1), \end{aligned}$$

where $\psi_{\phi}(\varepsilon_t) = \psi(\varepsilon_t - \eta) - \mathrm{E}\psi(\varepsilon_t - \eta)$. By the usual asymptotic results for nearly integrated processes, r_t and $\psi_{\phi}(\varepsilon_t)$ satisfy the bivariate weak convergence result

$$\begin{aligned} &\left(\frac{u_{[sT]}}{T^{1/2}},\ \sum_{t\leq[sT]}\frac{\psi_{\phi}(\varepsilon_t)}{T^{1/2}}\right)' \\ &\quad\Rightarrow\left(\frac{\sigma_{\varepsilon}}{\Gamma(1)}W_c(s),\ \sigma_q\left[\rho W(s) + \sqrt{1-\rho^2}\widetilde{W}(s)\right]\right)', \end{aligned}$$

where $\widetilde{W}$ is standard Brownian motion, independent of W. See Phillips (1988) Lemma 3.1 for details. This implies that

$$\begin{aligned} \sum r_t\psi_{\phi}(\varepsilon_t) &\Rightarrow \sigma_q\sigma_{\varepsilon}\Gamma(1)\left[\rho\int D_c(s)\,dW(s)\right. \\ &\qquad\left. + \sigma_q\sqrt{1-\rho^2}\int D_c(s)\,d\widetilde{W}(s)\right], \end{aligned}$$

$$T^{-2}\sum\left(y_{t-1} - \widehat{y}_{t-1}\right)^2 \Rightarrow \left(\frac{\sigma_{\varepsilon}}{\Gamma(1)}\right)^2\int D_c^2(s)\,ds.$$

Since r_t is the residual from regressing u_{t-1}/T on w_t, $T^{-1}\sum r_t u_{t-1} = T^{-2}\sum(y_{t-1}-\widehat{y}_{t-1})^2$. By the continuous mapping theorem,

$$Q(\bar{\alpha}) \Rightarrow \sigma_q \rho DF(c) + \sigma_q\sqrt{1-\rho^2}\left[\int D_c^2(s)\,ds\right]^{-1/2}\left[\int D_c(s)\,d\widetilde{W}(s)\right]$$
$$+\sigma_q \lambda\omega\Gamma(1)(c-\bar{c})\left[\int D_c^2(s)\,ds\right]^{1/2}.$$

Since $\left[\int D_c^2(s)\,ds\right]^{-1/2}\left[\int D_c(s)\,d\widetilde{W}(s)\right]$ is a standard normal variable, independent of $DF(\bar{c})$, the result follows.

Proof of Theorem 3.1 for Rank Functions

It will prove convenient to reparametrize the test statistic. Let R_t denote the rank of residual e_t among $e_1,\ldots,e_N$ with $N=T-p-1$. The rank function may be expressed as an integral:

$$\varphi((R_t-.5)/N) = -\int_0^1 \psi(\tau)\,d1(\tau \le (R_t-.5)/N).$$

Since $1(\tau \le (R_t-.5)/N)$ is continuous in τ from the left and $\psi(\tau)$ is continuous from the right, this Reimann–Steiljies integral exists and through integration by parts we obtain

$$\varphi((R_t-.5)/N) = \varphi(0) + \int_0^1 1(\tau \le (R_t-.5)/N)\,d\varphi(\tau). \qquad \text{(A.6)}$$

Since the ranks of the residuals do not change when we add a constant, R_i is the rank of $e_t+\eta$ among $e_1+\eta,\ldots,e_{T-p-1}+\eta$. The indicator function can be reexpressed in terms of the inverse empirical c.d.f. of the residuals plus the constant η:

$$\begin{aligned} 1(\tau \le (R_t-.5)/N) &= 1(\tau-.5/N \le (R_t-1)/N) \\ &= 1\left(F_T^{-1}(\tau-1/N) \le e_t+\eta\right), \\ F_T^{-1}(\tau) &= \inf\{x : F_T(x) \ge \tau\}, \\ F_T(x) &= N^{-1}\sum 1(e_t+\eta \le x). \end{aligned}$$

Now return to the test statistic. Let $z_t = (1, t, \Delta y_{t-1},\ldots,\Delta y_{t-p})'$ and let $w_t = (1, t/T, \Delta u_{t-1},\ldots,\Delta u_{t-p})'$. The vector of residuals $\Delta Y - X\bar{\alpha} - Z\bar{\beta}$ has elements $\Delta y_t - \bar{\alpha} y_{t-1}/T - z_t\bar{\beta}$ equal to $\varepsilon_t - \eta - a u_{t-1}/T - w_t'\theta \equiv T^{-1/2} r_t$. Define $\widehat{b}_\tau = F_T^{-1}(\tau-1/N)$ and $b_\tau = F^{-1}(\tau)$. Since $\sum r_t = 0$, the test statistic may be written

$$\begin{aligned} Q(\bar{\alpha}) &= \left[\sum r_t^2\right]^{-1/2}\int_0^1 S\left(T^{-1/2}a, \widehat{\theta}_{\bar{\alpha}}, \widehat{b}_\tau\right)\,d\varphi(\tau), \\ S(x,\theta,b) &= \sum r_t 1\left(b \le \varepsilon_t - x u_{t-1}/T^{1/2} - w_t'\theta\right), \end{aligned}$$

where $\widehat{\theta}_{\bar{\alpha}}$ is equal to θ evaluated at $\bar{\beta} = \widehat{\beta}_R(\bar{\alpha})$). Straightforward algebraic manipulations lead to the result that r_t is the residual from a least-squares regression of u_{t-1}/T on $T^{-1/2}w_t$.

The following lemma establishes the stochastic equicontinuity of empirical processes based on S and $F_T^{-1}(\tau)$. The proof uses the bracketing methods described in Andrews (1994). The proof is long and is omitted. The proof is available from the author upon request. It very closely follows the proof of the theorem in Section 11.2 of Pollard (2004).

Lemma A.4. *Under Assumptions 3.1–3.4, $S(x, \theta, b) - S^*(x, \theta, b)$ is stochastically equicontinuous in (x, θ, b), where*

$$S^*(x, \theta, b) = \sum r_t E_{t-1} 1\left(b \le \varepsilon_t - x u_{t-1}/T^{1/2} - w_t'\theta\right).$$

Furthermore, the process $T^{1/2}\left(F_T^{-1}(\tau) - F^{-1}(\tau)\right)$ has a limiting distribution and is stochastically equicontinuous in τ for $\tau_0 \le \tau \le 1 - \tau_0$.

The next two lemmas use this result to establish an asymptotically linear representation for S.

Lemma A.5. *Under Assumptions 3.1–3.4,*

$$\sup_{\tau_0 \le \tau \le 1-\tau_0} \left| R\left(T^{-1/2}a, \widehat{\theta}_{\bar{\alpha}}, \widehat{b}_\tau\right)\right| \xrightarrow{p} 0$$

where $R(x, \theta, b) = S(x, \theta, b) - S^*(x, \theta, b) - S(0, 0, b_\tau) + S^*(0, 0, b_\tau)$.

Since $T^{-1/2}a \to 0$, $\widehat{\theta}_{\bar{\alpha}} \xrightarrow{p} 0$ by Assumption 3.2, and $\widehat{b}_\tau \xrightarrow{p} \widehat{b}_\tau$ by Lemma A.5, this result follows immediately from the previous lemma (A.5).

Lemma A.6. *Under Assumptions 3.1–3.4,*

$$\begin{aligned} &S^*\left(T^{-1/2}a, \widehat{\theta}_{\bar{\alpha}}, \widehat{b}_\tau\right) - S^*(0, 0, b_\tau) \\ &\quad = -f(b_\tau) T^{-1} \sum r_t u_{t-1} a + o_p(1). \end{aligned}$$

Define $I(u) = 1 - \Pr[\varepsilon_1 < u]$. The derivative $I'(u) = -f(u)$ exists and is uniformly continuous in u by Assumption 3.1. By the mean value theorem we obtain

$$\begin{aligned} S^*\left(T^{-1/2}a, \widehat{\theta}_{\bar{\alpha}}, \widehat{b}_\tau\right) &= \sum r_t I\left(\widehat{b}_\tau + a u_{t-1}/T + w_t'\widehat{\theta}_{\bar{\alpha}}\right) \\ &= \sum r_t I(b_\tau) - f(b_\tau) \\ &\quad \times \sum r_t\left(\widehat{b}_\tau - b_\tau + a u_{t-1}/T + w_t'\widehat{\theta}_{\bar{\alpha}}\right) + R_T, \\ \text{with } R_T &= \sum r_t\left(f(b_\tau) - f\left(u_t^*\right)\right) \\ &\quad \times \left(\widehat{b}_\tau - b_\tau + a u_{t-1}/T + w_t'\widehat{\theta}_{\bar{\alpha}}\right), \end{aligned}$$

where $\left|u_t^* - b_\tau\right| \leq |\widehat{b}_\tau - b_\tau + au_{t-1}/T + w_t'\widehat{\theta}_{\bar{\alpha}}|$. By the usual asymptotic results for nearly integrated processes, $u_{[sT]}/T^{1/2}$, $w_{[sT]}$, and $T^{1/2}r_{[sT]}$ all converge weakly to Gaussian processes in s and for each process the maximum over s is a stochastically bounded random variable (see Phillips, 1988, Lemma 3.1). This result, combined with the uniform continuity of f and Lemma A.4, leads to the result

$$|R_T| \leq O_p(1)T^{-1}\sum |f(b_\tau) - f(u_t^*)| = o_p(1),$$

so R_T is asymptotically negligible. Since r_t is the residual from regressing u_{t-1}/T on w_t, $\sum r_t = \sum r_t w_t' = 0$ and we obtain

$$S^*\left(T^{-1/2}a, \widehat{\theta}_{\bar{\alpha}}, \widehat{b}_\tau\right) = \sum r_t I\left(b_\tau\right) - f\left(b_\tau\right)T^{-1}\sum r_t u_{t-1}a + o_p(1).$$

Since $S^*\left(0, 0, b_\tau\right) = I(b_\tau)\sum r_t = 0$, the lemma follows.

Proof of Theorem 3.1 for rank functions

By Lemmas A.5 and A.6,

$$\begin{aligned} S\left(T^{-1/2}a, \widehat{\theta}_{\bar{\alpha}}, \widehat{b}_\tau\right) &= \sum r_t 1\left(F^{-1}(\tau) \leq \varepsilon_t\right) \\ &\quad - f\left(F^{-1}(\tau)\right)T^{-1}\sum r_t u_{t-1}a + o_p(1), \end{aligned}$$

Notice that, by Equation (A.6) and Assumption A.4,

$$\begin{aligned} \int_0^1 1\left(F^{-1}(\tau) \leq \varepsilon_t\right) d\varphi\left(\tau\right) &= \int_{\tau_0}^{1-\tau_0} 1\left(\tau \leq F(\varepsilon_t)\right) d\varphi\left(\tau\right) \\ &= \varphi\left(F(\varepsilon_t)\right) - \varphi\left(0\right). \end{aligned}$$

Also notice that, through integration by parts, $\int_0^1 f(F^{-1}(\tau))\,d\varphi(\tau) = \omega$. Therefore, since $\sum r_i = 0$,

$$\begin{aligned} &\int_0^1 S\left(T^{-1/2}a, \widehat{\theta}_{\bar{\alpha}}, \widehat{b}_\tau\right) d\varphi(\tau) \\ &\quad = \sum r_t \widetilde{\varphi}\left(F(\varepsilon_t)\right) - \omega T^{-1}\sum r_t u_{t-1}a + o_p(1), \end{aligned}$$

where $\widetilde{\varphi}\left(F(\varepsilon_t)\right) = \varphi\left(F(\varepsilon_t)\right) - \mathrm{E}\varphi\left(F(\varepsilon_t)\right)$.

By the usual asymptotic results for nearly integrated processes, r_t and $\varphi\left(F(\varepsilon_t)\right)$ satisfy the bivariate weak convergence result

$$\begin{aligned} &\left(\frac{u_{[sT]}}{T^{1/2}}, \sum\nolimits_{t\leq[sT]} \frac{\widetilde{\varphi}\left(F(\varepsilon_t)\right)}{T^{1/2}}\right)' \\ &\quad \Rightarrow \left(\frac{\sigma_\varepsilon}{\Gamma\left(1\right)}W_c(s),\ \sigma_q\left[\rho W\left(s\right) + \sqrt{1-\rho^2}\widetilde{W}\left(s\right)\right]\right)', \end{aligned}$$

where $\widetilde{W}$ is standard Brownian motion, independent of W. See Phillips (1988)

Lemma 3.1 for details. This implies that

$$\sum r_t \widetilde{\varphi}(F(\varepsilon_t)) \Rightarrow \sigma_q \sigma_\varepsilon \Gamma(1) \left[\rho \int D_c(s)\, dW(s) + \sigma_q \sqrt{1-\rho^2} \int D_c(s)\, d\widetilde{W}(s) \right],$$

$$T^{-2} \sum (y_{t-1} - \widehat{y}_{t-1})^2 \Rightarrow \left(\frac{\sigma_\varepsilon}{\Gamma(1)} \right)^2 \int D_c^2(s)\, ds.$$

Since r_t is the residual from regressing u_{t-1}/T on w_t, $T^{-1} \sum r_t u_{t-1} = T^{-2} \sum (y_{t-1} - \widehat{y}_{t-1})^2$. By the continuous mapping theorem,

$$Q(\bar{\alpha}) \Rightarrow \sigma_q \rho DF(c) + \sigma_q \sqrt{1-\rho^2} \left[\int D_c^2(s)\, ds \right]^{-1/2} \left[\int D_c(s)\, d\widetilde{W}(s) \right] + \sigma_q \lambda \omega \Gamma(1)(c - \bar{c}) \left[\int D_c^2(s)\, ds \right]^{1/2}.$$

Since $\left[\int D_c^2(s)\, ds\right]^{-1/2} \left[\int D_c(s)\, d\widetilde{W}(s)\right]$ is a standard normal variable, independent of $DF(\bar{c})$, the result follows.

References

Adichie, J. N. (1986), "Rank Tests in Linear Models," in *Handbook of Statistics*, Vol. 4 (ed. by P. Krishnaiah, and P. Sen), New York: Elsevier.

Akritas, M. (1991), "An Alternative Derivation of Aligned Rank Tests for Regression," *Journal of Statistical Planning and Inference*, 27, 171–86.

Andrews, D. W. K. (1993), "Exactly Median-unbiased Estimation of First Order Autoregressive/Unit Root Models," *Econometrica*, 61(1), 139–65.

Andrews, D. W. K. (1994), "Empirical Process Methods in Econometrics," in *Handbook of Econometrics*, Vol. 4 (ed. by R. Engle, and D. McFadden), New York: Elsevier.

Bobkoski, M. J. (1983), "Hypothesis testing in nonstationary time series," Unpublished Ph.D. Thesis, Department of Statistics, University of Wisconsin.

Cavanagh, C. (1985), "Roots Local to Unity," manuscript, Department of Economics, Harvard University.

Chan, N. H., and C. Z. Wei (1987), "Asymptotic Inference for Nearly Nonstationary ar(1) Processes," *The Annals of Statistics*, 15(3), 1050–63.

Dickey, D., and W. Fuller (1979), "Distribution of Estimators for Autoregressive Time Series with a Unit Root," *Journal of the American Statistical Association*, 74(366), 427–31.

Elliott, G., T. Rothenberg, and J. H. Stock (1996), "Efficient Tests for an Autoregressive Unit Root," *Econometrica*, 64(4), 813–36.

Elliott, G., and J. H. Stock (2000), "Confidence Intervals for Autoregressive Coefficients Near One," *Journal of Econometrics*, 103, 155–81.

Hansen, B. E. (1999), "The Grid Bootstrap and the Autoregressive Model," *Review of Economics and Statistics*, 81, 594–607.

Hasan, M. N., and R. W. Koenker (1997), "Robust Rank Tests of the Unit Root Hypothesis," *Econometrica*, 65(1), 133–61.

Herce, M. A. (1996), "Asymptotic Theory of Lad Estimation in a Unit Root Process with Finite Variance Errors," *Econometric Theory*, 12, 129–53.

Lucas, A. (1995), "Unit Root Tests Based on m Estimators," *Econometric Theory*, 11, 331–46.

Ng, S., and P. Perron (2001), "Lag Length Selection and the Construction of Unit Root Tests with Good Size and Power," working paper. *Econometrica*, 69, 1519–54.

Phillips, P. C. B. (1987), "Toward a Unified Asymptotic Theory for Autoregression," *Biometrika*, 74, 535–47.

Phillips, P. C. B. (1988), "Regression Theory for Near-integrated Time Series," *Econometrica*, 56, 1021–43.

Pollard, D. (2004), *Asymptopia*, Unpublished book, manuscript, Department of Statistics, Yale University.

Rothenberg, T. J., and J. H. Stock (1997), "Inference in a Nearly Integrated Autoregressive Model with Nonnormal Innovations," *Journal of Econometrics*, 80, 269–86.

Rothenberg, T. J., and S. B. Thompson (2001), "Robust Tests in the Linear Model," Working Paper.

Seo, B. (1999), "Distribution Theory for Unit Root Tests with Conditional Heteroskedasticity," *Journal of Econometrics*, 91, 113–44.

Stock, J. H. (1991), "Confidence Intervals for the Largest Autoregressive Root in u.s. Macroeconomic Time Series," *Journal of Monetary Economics*, 28, 435–59.

Thompson, S. B. (2004a), "Optimal versus Robust Inference in Nearly Integrated Non Gaussian models," *Econometric Theory*, 20, 23–55.

Thompson, S. B. (2004b), "Robust Tests of the Unit Root Hypothesis Should Not be Modified," *Econometric Theory*, 20, 360–81.

CHAPTER 17

A Unified Approach to Testing for Stationarity and Unit Roots

Andrew C. Harvey

ABSTRACT

Lagrange multiplier tests against nonstationary unobserved components such as stochastic trends and seasonals are based on statistics which, under the null hypothesis, have asymptotic distributions belonging to the class of generalized Cramér-von Mises distributions. Conversely, unit root tests can be formulated, again using the Lagrange multiplier principle, so as to yield test statistics which also have Cramér-von Mises distributions under the null hypothesis. These ideas may be extended to multivariate models and to models with structural breaks thereby providing a simple unified approach to testing in nonstationary time series.

1. INTRODUCTION

In a unit root test, the null hypothesis is that a process contains a unit root, while the alternative is that it is stationary. Stationarity tests operate in the opposite direction. The null hypothesis is that the series is stationary, while the alternative is that a nonstationary component is present; see Nyblom and Mäkeläinen (1983) and Kwiatkowski et al. (1992). Used in the context of testing the validity of a prespecified cointegrating vector, the null hypothesis is that the cointegrating relationship is true. The asymptotic distribution of the stationarity test statistic under the null hypothesis is the Cramér–von Mises distribution. When a time trend is present the distribution is different but can still be regarded as belonging to the same family. Furthermore, the test statistic against the presence of a multivariate random walk and the seasonality test of Canova and Hansen (1995) both have asymptotic distributions under the null hypothesis that belong to a class of generalised Cramér–von Mises distributions, indexed by a degree of freedom parameter.

The most widely used unit root test is the (augmented) Dickey–Fuller (ADF) test; see Fuller (1996, Chapter 10) and the references therein. However, the autoregressive formulation adopted means that the roles of the constant and time trend are different under the null and the alternative hypotheses. This problem may be avoided by working with models set up in terms of components. This is the approach taken in Elliott, Rothenberg, and Stock (1996); see also the discussion in Maddala and Kim (1998, pp. 37–9) and the papers by Bhargava

(1986), Nabeya and Tanaka (1990), and Schmidt and Phillips (1992), amongst others. As with stationarity tests, the components framework leads naturally to unit root tests, which derive from the Lagrange multiplier (LM) principle rather than being Wald tests. It is possible to formulate these "LM-type" unit root tests in such a way that under the null hypothesis the test statistics have asymptotic distributions belonging to the Cramér–von Mises family. This extends to multivariate and seasonality tests. Thus unit root and stationarity tests display an appealing symmetry, or perhaps asymmetry, in that the critical values for the unit root tests are in the lower tail of the Cramér–von Mises distributions, while those for the stationarity tests are in the upper tails.

The plan of the paper is as follows. Sections 2 defines the family of Cramér–von Mises distributions, and Section 3 follows Harvey (2001) in stressing the unification provided by these distributions in the theory of stationarity tests. The relative merits of dealing with serial correlation by parametric and nonparametric approaches are discussed, and the extensions to testing against nonstationary seasonal components and stochastic slopes are set out.

Section 4 shows how unit root tests can be set up so that the test statistics have asymptotic distributions that belong to the Cramér–von Mises family under the null hypothesis. For general unobserved components (UC) models, the test statistics can be constructed using standardized innovations – one step-ahead prediction errors – produced by the Kalman filter. We might refer to such parametric tests as "unobserved components unit root tests." Subsection 4.3 looks at seasonal unit root tests, suggesting an alternative to the procedure of Hylleberg et al. (1990). A test of the null hypothesis that there is a unit root in the slope of a trend is derived in subsection 4.4.

Section 5 extends the ideas of Section 4 to multivariate models. In particular, a multivariate unit root test based on a statistic with the Cramér–von Mises distribution is presented.

Section 6 follows Busetti and Harvey (2001) in showing how the stationarity tests are affected by the inclusion of dummy variables designed to pick up structural breaks. Although the form of the test statistics is unchanged, their asymptotic distributions are altered. However, the additive properties of the Cramér–von Mises distribution suggest a simplified test that is much easier to implement. The effect on LM type unit root tests is then examined. These remain the same unless there are breaks in the slope, in which case a modification along the lines proposed for stationarity tests leads to simplified statistics with Cramér–von Mises distributions under the null hypothesis. Similar results hold for seasonality tests when breaks in the seasonal pattern are modeled by dummy variables. All of these tests extend to multivariate models.

2. THE FAMILY OF CRAMÉR–VON MISES DISTRIBUTIONS

The unifying feature of the test statistics presented in this article is the family of Cramér–von Mises distributions. Following Harvey (2001), these distributions will be denoted as $CvM_{p+1}(k)$, where k is a degrees of freedom parameter and p denotes the order of the polynomial used in detrending. The most common cases are the first-level distribution ($p = 0$), often simply denoted as CvM, where only a constant is fitted and the second-level distribution ($p = 1$), where a time trend is fitted. The distribution when there is no deterministic component ($p = -1$) is $CvM_0(k)$. MacNeill (1978, p. 431) tabulates critical values of $CvM_{p+1}(1)$ for $p = -1, 0, 1, \ldots, 5$.

The first-level Cramér–von Mises distribution has the following representation:

$$CvM(k) = \int_0^1 B(r)'B(r)dr \tag{2.1}$$

where B(r) is an N-dimensional Brownian bridge defined as $B(r) = W(r) - rW(1)$, with $W(r)$ being a standard N-dimensional Wiener process or Brownian motion. In the $CvM_0(k)$ distribution, $W(r)$ replaces $B(r)$, while for $p = 1$ a second-level Brownian bridge is used.

The $CvM(k)$ distribution may be expanded as

$$CvM(k) = \sum_{j=1}^{\infty}(\pi j)^{-2}\chi_j^2(k). \tag{2.2}$$

There are similar series expansions for other members of the family. In particular for $CvM_0(k)$ the weights are $\pi^{-2}(j - 1/2)^{-2}$, while for $CvM_2(k)$ the weights are obtained by changing $(\pi j)^{-2}$ to λ_j^{-2}, where $\lambda_{2j-1} = 2j\pi$ and λ_{2j} is the root of $\tan(\lambda/2) = \lambda/2$ on $(2j\pi, 2(j + 1)\pi)$, $j = 1, 2, \ldots$. An important corollary is that, because of the additive property of chi-square distributions, the sum of two independent random variables with distributions $CvM(k_1)$ and $CvM(k_2)$ is $CvM(k_1 + k_2)$.

3. STATIONARITY TESTS

This section reviews the literature on testing against the presence of nonstationary unobserved components. The leading case, testing against a random walk in an otherwise stationary series, is sometimes called a stationarity test. In adopting this terminology more widely, it must be realized that the model may contain other nonstationary components, such as seasonals, which remain present under the null hypothesis.

3.1. Testing against the Presence of a Random Walk Component

Consider a univariate unobserved components model consisting of a random walk plus noise for a set of observations, y_t:

$$y_t = \mu_t + \varepsilon_t, \quad \mu_t = \mu_{t-1} + \eta_t, \qquad t = 1, \ldots, T, \tag{3.1}$$

where the η_t's and ε_t's are mutually and serially independent Gaussian disturbances with variances σ_η^2 and σ_ε^2, respectively. When $\sigma_\eta^2 = 0$ the random walk becomes a constant level. Nyblom and Mäkeläinen (1983) showed that the locally best invariant (LBI) test of the null hypothesis $\sigma_\eta^2 = 0$, against the alternative $\sigma_\eta^2 > 0$, can be formulated as

$$\eta = T^{-2} \sum_{i=1}^{T} \left[\sum_{t=1}^{i} e_t \right]^2 \Big/ s^2 > c, \tag{3.2}$$

where $e_t = y_t - \overline{y}$, $s^2 = T^{-1} \sum_{t=1}^{T} (y_t - \overline{y})^2$, and c is a critical value. In fact, one initially obtains a form of the statistic with the summations running in reverse, that is, from $t = i$ to T, but it is easily seen that the two statistics are identical. The test can also be interpreted as a one-sided LM test.

The asymptotic distribution of the η statistic under the null hypothesis is the (first-level) Cramér–von Mises distribution. The normality assumption is not necessary. It is sufficient for the observations to be martingale differences (with finite variance) to yield this asymptotic distribution; see, for example, Stock (1994, p. 2745). The result follows because the partial sum of deviations from the mean converges weakly to a standard Brownian bridge, that is,

$$\sigma^{-1} T^{-\frac{1}{2}} \sum_{s=1}^{[Tr]} e_s \Rightarrow B(r), \qquad r \in [0, 1] \tag{3.3}$$

where $[Tr]$ is the largest integer less than or equal to Tr, while $s^2 \xrightarrow{p} \sigma^2$. If a linear time trend is included in (3.1) the resulting test statistic, η_2, has a CvM_2 distribution under the null hypothesis. When there is no deterministic component, the distribution of the test statistic, η_0, is CvM_0.

An analysis of local asymptotic power of the above tests can be found in Stock and Watson (1998).

3.2. Serial Correlation

Now suppose that the model is extended so that ε_t is any indeterministic stationary process. In this case the asymptotic distribution of the η test statistic remains the same if s^2 is replaced by a consistent estimator of the long-run variance (the spectrum at frequency zero). Kwiatkowski et al. (1992) – KPSS – construct such an estimator nonparametrically as

$$\begin{aligned} s_L^2(\ell) &= T^{-1} \sum_{t=1}^{T} e_t^2 + 2T^{-1} \sum_{\tau=1}^{\ell} w(\tau, \ell) \sum_{t=\tau+1}^{T} e_t e_{t-\tau} \\ &= \hat{\gamma}(0) + 2 \sum_{\tau=1}^{\ell} w(\tau, \ell) \hat{\gamma}(\tau) \end{aligned} \tag{3.4}$$

where $w(\tau, \ell)$ is a weighting function, such as $w(\tau, \ell) = 1 - \tau/(\ell + 1)$, $\tau = 1, \ldots, \ell$, and ℓ is the lag length. A test constructed in this way will be denoted

KPSS(ℓ). Other weighting functions, such as the Parzen or Tukey windows, may also be used.

Leybourne and McCabe (1994) attack the problem of serial correlation by introducing lagged dependent variables into the model. The test statistic obtained after removing the effect of the lagged dependent variables is then of the same form as (3.2). The practical implication, as demonstrated in their Monte Carlo results, is a gain in power. However, more calculation is involved since the coefficients of the lagged dependent variables are estimated under the alternative hypothesis, and this requires numerical optimization.

Since we are testing for the presence of an unobserved component, it seems natural to work with structural time series models. If the process generating the stationary part of the model were known, the LBI test for the presence of a random walk component could be constructed. Harvey and Streibel (1997) derive such a test and show how it is formed from a set of "smoothing errors." A general algorithm for calculating these statistics is the Kalman filter and the associated smoother. The smoothing errors are, in general, serially correlated, but the form of this serial correlation may be deduced from the specification of the model. Hence a (parametric) estimator of the long-run variance may be constructed and used to form a statistic that has a Cramér–von Mises distribution, asymptotically, under the null hypothesis. An alternative possibility is to use the standardized one-step-ahead prediction errors (innovations), calculated assuming that μ_0 is fixed.[1] No correction is then needed and, although the test is not strictly LBI, its asymptotic distribution is the same and the evidence presented in Harvey and Streibel (1997) suggests that, in small samples, it is more reliable in terms of size. As in the Leybourne–McCabe test, the nuisance parameters need to be estimated, and this is best done under the alternative hypothesis. This has the compensating advantage that, since there will often be some doubt about a suitable model specification, estimation of the unrestricted model affords the opportunity to check its suitability by the usual diagnostics and goodness-of-fit tests. Once the nuisance parameters have been estimated, the test statistic is calculated from the innovations or the smoothing errors with σ_η^2 set to zero.

3.3. Testing against Nonstationary Seasonality

Consider a Gaussian model with a trigonometric seasonal component

$$y_t = \mu + \gamma_t + \varepsilon_t, \qquad t = 1, \ldots, T \tag{3.5}$$

where μ is a constant and

$$\gamma_t = \sum_{j=1}^{[s/2]} \gamma_{j,t}, \tag{3.6}$$

[1] Note that backward smoothing recursions may be avoided simply by reversing the order of the observations and calculating the innovations starting from the filtered estimator of the final state.

where s is the number of seasons and each $\gamma_{j,t}$ is generated by

$$\begin{bmatrix} \gamma_{j,t} \\ \gamma^*_{j,t} \end{bmatrix} = \begin{bmatrix} \cos\lambda_j & \sin\lambda_j \\ -\sin\lambda_j & \cos\lambda_j \end{bmatrix} \begin{bmatrix} \gamma_{j,t-1} \\ \gamma^*_{j,t-1} \end{bmatrix} + \begin{bmatrix} \omega_{j,t} \\ \omega^*_{j,t} \end{bmatrix}, \quad \begin{array}{l} j = 1, \ldots, [s/2], \\ t = 1, \ldots, T, \end{array} \tag{3.7}$$

where $\lambda_j = 2\pi j/s$ is frequency, in radians, and $\omega_{j,t}$ and $\omega^*_{j,t}$ are two mutually uncorrelated white noise disturbances with zero means and common variance σ^2_j. For s even, $[s/2] = s/2$, while for s odd, $[s/2] = (s-1)/2$. For s even, the component at $j = s/2$ collapses to

$$\gamma_{j,t} = \gamma_{j,t-1}\cos\lambda_j + \omega_{j,t} = \gamma_{j,t-1}(-1)^t + \omega_{j,t}, \qquad j = s/2. \tag{3.8}$$

If ε_t is white noise, the LBI test against the presence of a stochastic trigonometric component at any one of the seasonal frequencies, λ_j, apart from the one at π, is

$$\omega_j = 2T^{-2}s^{-2}\sum_{i=1}^{T}\left[\left(\sum_{t=1}^{i} e_t \cos\lambda_j t\right)^2 + \left(\sum_{t=1}^{i} e_t \sin\lambda_j t\right)^2\right],$$
$$j = 1, \ldots, [(s-1)/2], \tag{3.9}$$

where s^2 is the sample variance of the OLS residuals from a regression on sines and cosines. Canova and Hansen (1995) show that the asymptotic distribution of this statistic is Cramér–von Mises with two degrees of freedom,[2] that is, $CvM_1(2)$. The component at π gives rise to a test statistic

$$\omega_{s/2} = T^{-2}s^{-2}\sum_{i=1}^{T}\left(\sum_{t=1}^{i} e_t \cos\lambda_{s/2} t\right)^2, \tag{3.10}$$

which has only one degree of freedom. A joint test against the presence of stochastic trigonometric components at all seasonal frequencies is based on a statistic, ω, obtained by summing the individual test statistics.[3] This statistic has an asymptotic distribution, which is $CvM_1(s-1)$. If desired it can be combined with a test against a random walk to give a test statistic that is $CvM_1(s)$ when both level and seasonal are deterministic.

[2] Actually, Canova and Hansen derive the above statistic from a slightly different form of the stochastic cycle model in which the coefficients of a sine–cosine wave are taken to be random walks. However, it is not difficult to show that the model as defined above leads to the same test statistic.

[3] This is the LM test if $\sigma^2_j = \sigma^2_\omega$ for all j except $j = s/2$ when $\sigma^2_{s/2} = \sigma^2_\omega/2$; see Busetti and Harvey (2003).

Canova and Hansen show how the above tests can be generalized to handle serial correlation and heteroscedasticity by making a correction similar to that in KPSS. If the model contains a stochastic trend, then the test must be carried out on differenced observations. A parametric test may be carried out by fitting an unobserved components model. If there is a trend it may be a deterministic trend, a random walk, with or without drift, or a trend with a stochastic slope. Busetti and Harvey (2003) compare the two types of test.

Busetti and Harvey (2003) propose a test for any kind of seasonality, deterministic or stochastic. No seasonal dummies are fitted and the asymptotic distribution of the test statistic ω_0 is $CvM_0(s-1)$. On the other hand, if seasonal slopes are included, as in Smith and Taylor (1998), the test statistic is $CvM_2(s-1)$.

3.4. Testing against a Stochastic Slope

Generalizing the trend in (3.1) to include a stochastic slope gives

$$\begin{aligned} \mu_t &= \mu_{t-1} + \beta_{t-1} + \eta_t, & \eta_t &\sim \mathrm{NID}(0, \sigma_\eta^2), \\ \beta_t &= \beta_{t-1} + \zeta_t, & \zeta_t &\sim \mathrm{NID}(0, \sigma_\zeta^2), \end{aligned} \tag{3.11}$$

where $\mathrm{NID}(0, \sigma_\eta^2)$ denotes normally and independently distributed disturbances, and the level and slope disturbances, η_t and ζ_t, respectively, are mutually independent. If σ_η^2 is assumed to be zero, the trend μ_t is an integrated random walk, or a "smooth trend." Nyblom and Harvey (2001) derive the asymptotic distribution of the LBI test of $H_0 : \sigma_\zeta^2 = 0$ against $H_1 : \sigma_\zeta^2 > 0$. However, a Monte Carlo study of the test seems to show that it offers little gain in power over η_2.

If $\sigma_\eta^2 > 0$, then, when $\sigma_\zeta^2 = 0$, the trend reduces to a random walk plus drift. Differencing yields

$$\Delta y_t = \beta_{t-1} + \eta_t + \Delta\varepsilon_t, \qquad t = 2, \ldots, T \tag{3.12}$$

with $\eta_t + \Delta\varepsilon_t$ being invertible. The test statistic, denoted as ζ, for testing whether β_{t-1} is a random walk can be constructed as in Subsection 3.1, but its asymptotic distribution is CvM_1 rather than CvM_2.

4. UNIT ROOT TESTS

This section shows how the Lagrange multiplier principle leads to test statistics with Cramér–von Mises distributions under the null hypothesis. After discussing the treatment of serial correlation, the ideas are extended to seasonal unit root tests and tests on the slope.

4.1. Test Statistics with a Cramér–von Mises Distribution

The Dickey–Fuller test is based on the model

$$y_t = \alpha + \beta t + \phi y_{t-1} + \xi_t, \quad \xi_t \sim \text{NID}(0, \sigma^2), \qquad t = 1, \ldots, T, \tag{4.1}$$

with variations in which the trend and both the constant and the trend are omitted. The null is that ϕ is unity, and so the model is nonstationary, while the alternative is that it is less than unity, and so the model is (trend) stationary. If the model is reformulated with Δy_t as the dependent variable, the parameter associated with y_{t-1}, and denoted here as ρ, is equal to $\phi - 1$ and hence is zero under the null hypothesis. The test statistic is based on the regression coefficient of the lagged dependent variable or its "t statistic." Lagged differences can be added to the right-hand side without affecting the asymptotic distribution of the t statistic.

Formulating the unit root test in an autoregressive framework is computationally convenient. However, as Schmidt and Phillips (1992, p. 258) observe, the parameterizations of (4.1) are "not convenient" because "they handle level and trend in a clumsy and potentially confusing way." Specifically the meanings of α and β differ under the null and alternative hypotheses. These difficulties can be avoided by following Bhargava (1986), Nabeya and Tanaka (1990), Schmidt and Phillips (1992) and Elliott et al. (1996) and setting up the unit root test of $H_0 : \phi = 1$ against $H_0 : \phi < 1$ within the components framework

$$y_t = \alpha + \beta t + \mu_t, \quad \mu_t = \phi\mu_{t-1} + \eta_t, \qquad t = 1, \ldots, T, \tag{4.2}$$

with μ_0 fixed but unknown. The interpretation of α and β is now the same under both the null and alternative hypotheses.

The test with critical region

$$T^{-1}\sum_{t=1}^{T}\widetilde{\mu}_t^2 \Big/ \sum_{t=1}^{T}(\widetilde{\mu}_t - \widetilde{\mu}_{t-1})^2 = \zeta < c \tag{4.3}$$

is constructed from residuals $\widetilde{\mu}_t$, obtained by estimating α and β under the null hypothesis. Since

$$\Delta y_t = \beta + \eta_t, \qquad t = 2, \ldots, T \tag{4.4}$$

under the null hypothesis, these residuals are defined by

$$\widetilde{\mu}_t = y_t - \widetilde{\alpha}_0 - \widetilde{\beta}t, \qquad t = 1, \ldots, T,$$

where $\widetilde{\beta} = \overline{\Delta y} = \sum \Delta y_t/(T-1) = (y_T - y_1)/(T-1)$ and $\widetilde{\alpha}_0 = y_1 - \widetilde{\beta}$, where $\alpha_0 = \alpha + \mu_0$. Note that $\widetilde{\mu}_1 = 0$ as a consequence of fitting the constant, while $\widetilde{\mu}_T = 0$ provided a slope, β, is estimated; $\widetilde{\mu}_0$ is taken to be zero in all cases. The test statistic corresponds to the N_2 test suggested by Bhargava (1986), except insofar as his test statistic, being of the von Neumann ratio form, is equal to $1/T\zeta$. The test statistic in Schmidt and Lee (1991), given as T times the coefficient obtained by regressing $\Delta\widetilde{\mu}_t$ on $\widetilde{\mu}_{t-1}$ without a constant term, is equal to $-1/2\zeta$; the test is an LM test as noted[4] by Schmidt and Phillips (1992). The ζ statistic is the same as R_4 in Nabeya and Tanaka (1990), who argue that the test is locally best invariant and unbiased (LBIU). If it is written in first differences, it becomes

$$\zeta = T^{-1}\sum_{i=1}^{T}\left[\sum_{t=1}^{i}\Delta\widetilde{\mu}_t\right]^2 \Big/ \sum_{t=1}^{T}(\Delta\widetilde{\mu}_t)^2 \tag{4.5}$$

This is of the same form as the η test statistic, (3.2), except that it applies to observations in first differences. Provided the slope is estimated so that $\Delta\widetilde{\mu}_t = \Delta y_t - \overline{\Delta y}$ for $t = 2, \ldots, T$, it is immediately apparent that the statistic has a CvM_1 distribution under the null hypothesis. However, while the value of the stationarity statistic η increases under the alternative, the value of ζ decreases as it is $T\zeta$, which has a limiting distribution under the alternative. Thus the appropriate critical values are those in the lower (left-hand) tail of the CvM distribution.

If there is no time trend in the model,[5] $\widetilde{\mu}_T$ is no longer constrained to be zero, and the asymptotic distribution of the statistic is CvM_0. In this case it is useful to label the statistic ζ_1, and to denote the time trend statistic as ζ_2 when there is any ambiguity. If there is neither constant nor time trend, so that the statistic ζ_0 is constructed by setting $\widetilde{\mu}_t = y_t$ for all $t = 1, \ldots, T$, the asymptotic distribution is again CvM_0 (although a nonzero initial value can have a marked effect on the small sample distribution). The statistics ζ_0 and ζ_1 are transformations of the statistics proposed by Sargan and Bhargava (1983); indeed Stock (1994) refers to all tests based on ζ_0, ζ_1, and ζ_2 as Sargan–Bhargava tests. From Tanaka (1996, Table 9.1), the critical values at the 5% and 1% levels of significance are 0.0565 and 0.0345, respectively, if no time trend is included, and 0.0366 and 0.025, respectively, if one is included.

The statistic in which the $\widetilde{\mu}_t'$s in the numerator are in terms of deviations from their mean is a transformation of the test statistic in Schmidt and Phillips (1992) and the R_2 statistic in Bhargava (1986). It corresponds directly to R_3 in Nabeya and Tanaka (1990). Under the null, the asymptotic distribution is one in which the $B(r)$ in (2.1) is replaced by a de-meaned Brownian bridge, and so it does not belong to the CvM family. Using Monte Carlo simulations, Schmidt and Lee (1991) compare the test based on this statistic with the one based on ζ and seem to come down in its favor, though the evidence is by no means clear-cut. Nabeya and Tanaka (1990), using an analysis based on limiting powers, find that there is no dominance of one test over the other for the time trend

[4] Schmidt and Phillips (1992) formulate their test in terms of a regression analogous to the one used in the Dickey–Fuller test, with y_{t-1} replaced by $\widetilde{\mu}_{t-1}$ and a constant, but no time trend included. The tests are based on the regression coefficient of $\widetilde{\mu}_{t-1}$ or its t statistic. The variant of the test studied in Schmidt and Lee (1991) excludes the constant.

[5] The test is no longer the LM test when there is no time trend; see the discussion in Tanaka (1996, Chapter 9) and the Appendix.

model considered by Schmidt and Lee (1991). Furthermore, if a time trend is not present, then ζ is better. Further discussion can be found in Tanaka (1996, p. 348), where ζ is labeled R_2.

Figures 1, 2, and 3 in Stock (1994, p. 2774–5) and Elliott et al. (1996, p. 822–4) analyze local power and show that the ζ tests compare favorably with the Dickey–Fuller tests; see also Tanaka (1996). The same figures give some indication of the potential gain for modifications along the lines suggested by Elliott et al. (1996) or Hwang and Schmidt (1996). However, the asymptotic distributions under the null are no longer of the CvM form.

The distribution theory surrounding ζ can be generalised by letting the deterministic part of (4.2) be a pth-order polynomial. The residuals in (4.5) are then obtained by regressing Δy_t on a polynomial of order $p-1$, with the result that the test statistic ζ_{p+1} is asymptotically CvM_p under the null hypothesis.

The right-hand tail of ζ can be used to test against explosive processes, that is, $\phi > 1$; see Bhargava (1986) and Nabeya and Tanaka (1990). However, another interpretation of the alternative, which fits more nicely into the stochastic trends framework, is that the test is against a stochastic slope. In other words, it is the test motivated by (3.12); hence the ζ notation.

4.2. Serial Correlation and Unobserved Components

Nabeya and Tanaka (1990) consider methods of adjusting (4.5) so that the same asymptotic distribution is obtained under the null hypothesis when η_t is serially correlated. They suggest using a nonparametric estimator of the long-run variance, constructed in a way similar to (3.4) with $\Delta\widetilde{\mu}_t$ replacing e_t. This corresponds to the KPSS statistic computed from first differences. However, under the alternative, the spectrum of first differences is zero at the origin. Schmidt and Phillips (1992, p. 267) make a similar proposal but note that a consistent test requires the use of residuals obtained (under the alternative hypothesis) from a regression of $\widetilde{\mu}_t$ on $\widetilde{\mu}_{t-1}$; see Stock (1994, p. 2770, footnote 10) for further explanation.[6] Another option would be to base a test on the coefficient of $\widetilde{\mu}_{t-1}$ from an augmented Dickey–Fuller regression, as in Oya and Toda (1998).

If a fully parameterized UC model is set up, an LM-type test may be carried out by estimating the model under the null hypothesis and then forming a test statistic from the standardized innovations, $\widetilde{\nu}_t$. These are calculated starting with the smoothed estimator of μ_0 so they run from $t = 1$ to T. Assuming the innovations have been standardized so as to have unit variance, the unobserved components unit root test statistic is simply

$$\zeta = T^{-2}\sum_{i=1}^{T}\left[\sum_{t=1}^{i}\widetilde{\nu}_t\right]^2. \tag{4.6}$$

[6] Tanaka (1996, p. 362–7) argues that local power is not affected.

Note that backward smoothing recursions may be avoided simply by reversing the order of the observations and calculating the innovations starting from the filtered estimator of the final state.

The case for a parametric UC approach can be illustrated simply by adding white noise to (4.2) to give

$$y_t = \alpha + \beta t + \mu_t + \varepsilon_t, \qquad t = 1, \ldots, T. \tag{4.7}$$

This model is easily estimated when $\phi = 1$, and so forming the test statistic from the innovations, as in (4.6), is straightforward. (Note that if σ_ε^2 is zero, so that the model reduces to (4.2), then $\widetilde{\nu}_1 = 0$). Applying the Dickey–Fuller test when the data are best approximated by (4.7) is likely to result in too many rejections under the null hypothesis if the ratio of σ_η^2 to σ_ε^2 is low. The reduced form is an ARIMA(0,1,1) model with MA parameter close to -1, and the poor performance of the augmented Dickey–Fuller test is well documented in this situation; see, for example, Pantula (1991). Nonparametric corrections based on the estimation of the long-run variance, as in Schmidt and Phillips (1992), are also likely to be poor for this kind of model for the reasons given in Perron and Mallet (1996). Further evidence on these matters may be gleaned from Tables 1 and 2 in Stock (1994) and Tanaka (1996, p. 364–5).

There is a slight problem with LM tests for UC models such as (4.7): they are inconsistent. The reason is that under the alternative hypothesis there is a positive probability that q is estimated to be zero, and this persists as T approaches infinity; see the analysis of the ARMA(1,1) model in Saikkonen (1993). How important this is in practice is something that needs to be investigated. Note that local power is unaffected; compare Tanaka (1996, p. 363–4). Of course, a way out of the difficulty is to estimate the nuisance parameters under the alternative.

The model in (4.7) may be generalized by including other components such as seasonals and cycles. Such models are easily estimated with ϕ set to 1. The η statistic is computed from the innovations obtained from the Kalman filter by setting σ_η^2 to zero. Its aim is to determine whether a restriction should be placed on the model, while the aim of the ζ test is to find out if it should be more general.

The use of unit root tests in UC models is illustrated by the following examples.

Stochastic Volatility

The discrete time Gaussian SV model may be written as

$$r_t = \sigma_t \varepsilon_t = \sigma \varepsilon_t e^{0.5h_t}, \quad \varepsilon_t \sim \mathrm{NID}(0, 1), \qquad t = 1, \ldots, T,$$

where r_t is a return on an exchange rate or stock price, σ is a scale parameter, and h_t is a stationary first-order autoregressive process:

$$h_t = \phi h_{t-1} + \eta_t, \qquad \eta_t \sim \mathrm{NID}\left(0, \sigma_\eta^2\right). \tag{4.8}$$

Table 17.1. *Tests of stochastic volatility of daily exchange rates*

Currency	η	KPSS(9)	ζ	ADF(9)	$\tilde{\phi}$
Pound	1.319	0.853	0.228	−6.44	0.988
DM	0.423	0.256	0.371	−7.50	0.967
Yen	5.122	2.999	0.439	−7.63	0.998
Swiss Fr	0.774	0.465	0.466	−7.44	0.980

Squaring the observations and taking logarithms gives

$$y_t = \log r_t^2 = \log \sigma^2 + h_t + \log \varepsilon_t^2, \quad t = 1, \ldots, T. \tag{4.9}$$

Ignoring the time trend, the model is as in (4.7), except that $\log \varepsilon_t^2$ is far from being Gaussian, being heavily skewed with a long tail. However, this makes no difference to the asymptotic distribution of the test statistics we are about to consider.

In the application in Harvey, Ruiz, and Shephard (1994), r_t is the difference of 946 logged daily exchange rates of the dollar against another currency starting on November 1, 1981; the data are provided with the STAMP package (Koopman et al. 2000). Various tests were applied to the observations transformed with a modification made to $\log r_t^2$ to avoid distortion from inliers; see Fuller (1996, p. 496). The same transformation was used when the estimates of the ϕ parameters were obtained by quasi-ML using STAMP. The results are shown in Table 17.1. Apart from the Deutschmark, all the values of the Nyblom–Mäkeläinen statistic, η, are significant[7] at the 1% level indicating the presence of a random walk or, perhaps, a very persistent AR(1) component in volatility. Note the reduction in power if a KPSS correction is (unnecessarily) made. Higher lag length leads to even smaller statistics. For example, KPSS(25) for the pound is 0.515. The unobserved components unit root test statistics (4.6) are also shown in the table. None of these ζ statistics leads to a rejection at any conventional level of significance. Indeed their values are comfortably located near the median of the null hypothesis asymptotic distribution. The fact that the ADF t statistics (with constant included) all lie way beyond the 1% asymptotic critical value of −3.42 is a reflection of the fact that the autoregressive approximation is very poor because σ_η^2 is dominated by the variance of $\log \varepsilon_t^2$. However, if the lag length is increased to 25, the ADF statistic for the pound is −3.37, and so just fails to reject. The poor autoregressive approximation has a similar effect on the Oya–Toda version of the LM-type test.[8]

[7] The 1%, 5%, and 10% upper-tail critical values for CvM_1 are 0.743, 0.461, and 0.347, respectively.

[8] Having subtracted the first observation (and removed the constant), the ADF(9) t-statistic is found to be −6.44, while the estimate of ϕ is 0.501.

Quarterly Consumption

Harvey and Scott (1994) showed that a model consisting of a random walk with drift and a stochastic seasonal component gives a good fit to quarterly UK nondurable consumption.[9] The ς statistic calculated from the innovations from this model is 0.165. This is well away from the lower-tail 10% critical value for the CvM_1 distribution, which is 0.025, and so we cannot reject the hypothesis that the stochastic trend component is a random walk against the alternative that it is a stationary AR(1) process. The same statistic[10] can be used to test the null hypothesis that the slope β is constant against the alternative that it is a random walk; see Subsection 2.4. It is the upper tail of the CvM_1 distribution that is now relevant, but the 10% point is 0.347; so again the null is clearly not rejected.

4.3. Seasonal Unit Root Tests

The test of Hylleberg et al. (1990) – HEGY – is testing the null of a nonstationary seasonal against the alternative of a stationary seasonal. Its relationship to the Canova–Hansen (CH) test of Subsection 3.3 is analogous to that of the relationship between the (augmented) Dickey–Fuller test and KPSS.

The UC seasonal unit root test can be set up by introducing a damping factor into (3.7) so that each trigonometric term in the seasonal component is modeled by

$$\begin{bmatrix} \gamma_{j,t} \\ \gamma^*_{j,t} \end{bmatrix} = \phi_j \begin{bmatrix} \cos\lambda_j & \sin\lambda_j \\ -\sin\lambda_j & \cos\lambda_j \end{bmatrix} \begin{bmatrix} \gamma_{j,t-1} \\ \gamma^*_{j,t-1} \end{bmatrix} + \begin{bmatrix} \omega_{j,t} \\ \omega^*_{j,t} \end{bmatrix}, \quad j = 1, \ldots, [s/2], t = 1, \ldots, T. \tag{4.10}$$

with $\gamma^*_{s/2,t}$ dropping out for s even. The seasonal component, obtained by summing the $\gamma'_{j,t}s$ is then embedded in a general UC model that contains deterministic seasonal trigonometric terms. A parametric test[11] of the null hypothesis that the component at a particular frequency is nonstationary against the

[9] The data are given in the STAMP package. As in Harvey and Scott, the sample period is 57q3 to 92q2. The estimates of the level and seasonal variances, σ^2_η and σ^2_ω, are found to be 8.908×10^{-5} and 1.012×10^{-6}, respectively; these differ slightly from those reported in Harvey and Scott because of small revisions in the data. When an AR(1) component replaces the random walk, there is little change in the estimates of σ^2_η and σ^2_ω, which are now 8.817×10^{-5} and 1.010×10^{-6}, respectively. The estimate of ϕ is 0.986.

[10] The nuisance parameters are normally estimated under the alternative for a "stationarity" test. In this context it makes little difference, since the seasonal variance is not sensitive to the specification of the trend.

[11] If seasonal slopes are included, this is the LM test.

alternative that it is stationary, that is, $H_0 : \phi_j = 1$ against $H_1 : \phi_j < 1$, can be constructed from the null hypothesis innovations[12] as

$$\omega_j = 2T^{-2} \sum_{i=1}^{T} \left[\left(\sum_{t=1}^{i} \widetilde{v}_t \cos \lambda_j t \right)^2 + \left(\sum_{t=1}^{i} \widetilde{v}_t \sin \lambda_j t \right)^2 \right] < c,$$
$$j = 1, \ldots, [(s-1)/2]. \tag{4.11}$$

Under the null hypothesis the asymptotic distribution is $CvM_0(2)$, since if the nonstationary seasonal operator, $1 - 2cos\lambda_j L + L^2$, were to be applied, it would remove the corresponding deterministic seasonal. For $j = s/2$,

$$\omega_{s/2} = T^{-2} \sum_{i=1}^{T} \left(\sum_{t=1}^{i} \widetilde{v}_t \cos \pi t \right)^2 = T^{-2} \sum_{i=1}^{T} \left(\sum_{t=1}^{i} (-1)^t \widetilde{v}_t \right)^2,$$

and this has a $CvM_0(1)$ asymptotic distribution under the null. The full seasonal test statistic is formed by summing the $\omega_j's$, and its asymptotic distribution under the null is $CvM_0(s-1)$. With seasonal slopes the asymptotic distributions are $CvM_1(.)$; compare Smith and Taylor (1998).

Seasonality tests based on an autoregressive model will tend to perform poorly in situations where an unobserved components model is appropriate. The simulation evidence in Hylleberg (1995) illustrates this point by looking at the results of using the HEGY test for moving average models, which, as Harvey and Scott (1994) note, typically arise as the reduced form of unobserved components models.

A rejection of the null hypothesis in a seasonal unit root test may be an indication of a deterministic seasonal component rather than a stationary seasonal component of the form (4.10); see the evidence in Canova and Hansen (1995, p. 244). The appropriate test of the null of deterministic seasonality against the alternative of near-persistent stationary seasonality, that is, (4.10) with the ϕ_j close to 1, is, perhaps surprisingly, the same as the CH test against nonstationary seasonality; this follows from results in Harvey and Streibel (1998). This should be borne in mind when interpreting the results of seasonal stationarity and unit root tests.

4.4. Slope Unit Root Test

The stochastic trend of (3.11) may be modified so as to give what is sometimes called a damped trend, that is,

$$\mu_t = \mu_{t-1} + \beta_{t-1} + \eta_t, \qquad \eta_t \sim \text{NID}(0, \sigma_\eta^2),$$
$$\beta_t = \phi\beta_{t-1} + \zeta_t, \qquad \zeta_t \sim \text{NID}(0, \sigma_\zeta^2).$$

[12] As in the unit root test, there is the issue of consistency because there is presumably a finite probability that the variance of the seasonal disturbance is zero under the alternative.

If it is this component which appears in (4.2), a test of $H_0 : \phi = 1$ against $H_1 : \phi < 1$ is a unit root test on the slope. In the special case of the smooth trend model when $\sigma_\eta^2 = 0$, the test statistic is simply

$$\xi = T^{-1} \sum_{i=3}^{T} \left[\sum_{t=3}^{i} \Delta^2 y_t \right]^2 \Big/ \sum_{t=3}^{T} (\Delta^2 y_t)^2.$$

The asymptotic distribution of this statistic is CvM_0. If (4.2) is generalized so as to contain a deterministic pth-order polynomial trend, the residuals from a regression of $\Delta^2 y_t$ on a polynomial of order $p - 2$ are used to form the test statistic, which is then asymptotically CvM_{p-1}.

The stochastic trend component will not generally have σ_η^2 set to zero, and it will usually appear in a model of the form (4.7), possibly with other components such as stochastic cycles and seasonals. A parametric test statistic may then be constructed from the innovations from the model fitted under the null hypothesis. The test statistic is actually (4.6), but renamed ξ because what is now being tested is the null hypothesis of a second unit root.

5. MULTIVARIATE TESTS

5.1. Testing against a Multivariate Random Walk

If $\mathbf{y}_t$ is a vector containing N time series, the Gaussian multivariate local level model is

$$\begin{aligned} \mathbf{y}_t &= \boldsymbol{\mu}_t + \boldsymbol{\varepsilon}_t, & \boldsymbol{\varepsilon}_t &\sim \mathrm{NID}(\mathbf{0}, \Sigma_\varepsilon), \\ \boldsymbol{\mu}_t &= \boldsymbol{\mu}_{t-1} + \boldsymbol{\eta}_t, & \boldsymbol{\eta}_t &\sim \mathrm{NID}(\mathbf{0}, \Sigma_\eta), \quad t = 1, \ldots, T, \end{aligned} \tag{5.1}$$

where Σ_ε is an $N \times N$ positive definite (p.d.) matrix. Nyblom and Harvey (2000) show that an LBI test of the null hypothesis $\Sigma_\eta = \mathbf{0}$ can be constructed against the homogeneous alternative $\Sigma_\eta = q\Sigma_\varepsilon$. The test has the rejection region

$$\eta(N) = \mathrm{tr}\left[\mathbf{S}^{-1}\mathbf{C}\right] > c, \tag{5.2}$$

where

$$\mathbf{C} = T^{-2} \sum_{i=1}^{T} \left[\sum_{t=1}^{i} \mathbf{e}_t \right] \left[\sum_{t=1}^{i} \mathbf{e}_t \right]' \quad \text{and} \quad \mathbf{S} = T^{-1} \sum_{t=1}^{T} \mathbf{e}_t \mathbf{e}_t{}', \tag{5.3}$$

where $\mathbf{e}_t = \mathbf{y}_t - \bar{\mathbf{y}}$. Under the null hypothesis, the limiting distribution of (5.2) is Cramér–von Mises with N degrees of freedom, $CvM(N)$. The distribution is $CvM_2(N)$ if the model contains a vector of time trends. Although the test maximizes the power against homogeneous alternatives, it is consistent against all nonnull $\Sigma_\eta' s$, since $T^{-1}\eta(N)$ has a nondegenerate limiting distribution. This limiting distribution depends only on the rank of Σ_η.

The $\eta(N)$ test can be generalized along the lines of the KPSS test quite straightforwardly, as in Nyblom and Harvey (2000). Parametric adjustments can also be made by the procedure outlined for univariate models. This requires estimation under the alternative hypothesis, but is likely to lead to an increase in power. If there are no constraints across parameters, it may be more convenient to construct the test statistic (5.2) using the innovations from fitted univariate models. Kuo and Mikkola (2001) use the lagged dependent variable method of Leybourne and McCabe (1994) in their study of purchasing power parity. They conclude that dealing with serial correlation in this way leads to tests with higher power than those formed using the nonparametric correction.

5.2. Multivariate Unit Root Tests

The model in (4.2) generalizes to

$$\mathbf{y}_t = \boldsymbol{\alpha} + \boldsymbol{\beta}t + \boldsymbol{\mu}_t, \quad \boldsymbol{\mu}_t = \boldsymbol{\phi}\boldsymbol{\mu}_{t-1} + \boldsymbol{\eta}_t, \qquad t = 1, \ldots, T, \tag{5.4}$$

with $\text{Var}(\boldsymbol{\eta}_t) = \Sigma_\eta$. As in the univariate case, residuals are formed by estimating the level and the slope coefficients under the null hypothesis. Generalizing the test statistic (4.3) on the basis of detrended observations yields

$$\zeta(N) = \text{tr}\left\{\frac{1}{T}\left[\sum_{t=1}^{T} \Delta\widetilde{\boldsymbol{\mu}}_t \Delta\widetilde{\boldsymbol{\mu}}_t'\right]^{-1} \sum_{t=1}^{T} \widetilde{\boldsymbol{\mu}}_t \widetilde{\boldsymbol{\mu}}_t'\right\} \tag{5.5}$$

where $\widetilde{\boldsymbol{\mu}}_t = \mathbf{y}_t - \widetilde{\boldsymbol{\alpha}}_0 - \widetilde{\boldsymbol{\beta}}t$ for $t = 1, \ldots, T$ and $\widetilde{\boldsymbol{\mu}}_0 = \mathbf{0}$ with $\widetilde{\boldsymbol{\beta}} = (\mathbf{y}_T - \mathbf{y}_1)/(T-1)$ and $\widetilde{\boldsymbol{\alpha}}_0 = \mathbf{y}_1 - \widetilde{\boldsymbol{\beta}}$. Writing $\zeta(N)$ in a form analogous to (5.2) makes it apparent that its asymptotic distribution under the null hypothesis is $CvM_1(N)$, with the lower tail defining the critical region. If there is no time trend, the critical values are taken from the $CvM_0(N)$ distribution. The $\zeta(N)$ test is consistent but only against alternatives in which all the series are stationary. Like $\eta(N)$, the $\zeta(N)$ statistic is invariant to affine transformations of the data.

Now suppose that, as in Abuaf and Jorion (1990), $\boldsymbol{\phi} = \phi\mathbf{I}_N$, where ϕ is a scalar. The GLS estimator of $\phi - 1$, constructed from the observations detrended by setting ϕ equal to 1 and weighted by an estimator of Σ_η formed from first differences, is

$$\widetilde{\phi} - 1 = \sum_{t=2}^{T} \widetilde{\boldsymbol{\mu}}_{t-1}' \widehat{\Sigma}_\eta^{-1} \Delta\widetilde{\boldsymbol{\mu}}_t \bigg/ \sum_{t=2}^{T} \widetilde{\boldsymbol{\mu}}_{t-1}' \widehat{\Sigma}_\eta^{-1} \widetilde{\boldsymbol{\mu}}_{t-1}. \tag{5.6}$$

Provided the slope is included, a little algebraic manipulation, given in the Appendix, shows that the numerator is constant and, as a result, $\zeta(N)$ is equal to $-N/\{2T(\widetilde{\phi} - 1)\}$. The LM test of the null hypothesis $\phi = 1$ is based on the statistic

$$\text{LM} = \left(\sum_{t=1}^{T} \Delta\widetilde{\boldsymbol{\mu}}_t' \widehat{\Sigma}_\eta^{-1} \widetilde{\boldsymbol{\mu}}_{t-1}\right)^2 \bigg/ \sum_{t=1}^{T} \widetilde{\boldsymbol{\mu}}_{t-1}' \widehat{\Sigma}_\eta^{-1} \widetilde{\boldsymbol{\mu}}_{t-1},$$

and this is also a monotonic transformation of $\zeta(N)$ being equal to $N^2/4\ \zeta(N)$. As in the univariate case, a one-sided test based on the lower tail of the distribution of $\zeta(N)$ means that the alternative is $\phi < 1$.

If the model is generalized to include more components, a parametric test statistic can be constructed from the vector of standardized innovations. Corresponding to (4.6), this statistic is

$$\zeta(N) = \operatorname{tr}\left\{T^{-2}\sum_{i=1}^{T}\left[\sum_{t=1}^{i}\widetilde{\nu}_t\right]\left[\sum_{t=1}^{i}\widetilde{\nu}_t'\right]\right\}$$
$$= T^{-2}\sum_{i=1}^{T}\left[\sum_{t=1}^{i}\widetilde{\nu}_t'\right]\left[\sum_{t=1}^{i}\widetilde{\nu}_t\right]. \qquad (5.7)$$

If the innovations from fitted univariate models are used, the test statistic is of the form (5.2) so as to allow for cross-correlation.

Application to Stochastic Volatility

The multivariate stationarity and unit root test statistics for all four daily exchange rate series considered at the end of Section 3 are $\eta(4) = 8.325$ and $\zeta(4) = 0.790$. Thus the stationarity test rejects the null hypothesis that there are no random walk components in the series, while the unit root test just rejects the null that all four series have unit roots at the 10% level of significance.[13] This is not inconsistent with the conclusions in Harvey et al. (1994) and Nyblom and Harvey (2000) that the series have just two common trends.

5.3. Seasonal Unit Root Tests

The seasonality tests can be generalized to multivariate series. For example, the multivariate test against nonstationary seasonality in N series will have a $CvM_1(Ns - N)$ distribution under the null hypothesis, while the seasonal unit test will be based on $CvM_0(Ns - N)$.

6. TESTS WHEN BREAKS ARE PRESENT

Suppose there is a structural break in the trend at a known time $\tau + 1$, and let $\lambda = \tau/T$ denote the fraction of the sample before the break occurs. Consider the following models:

$$\begin{aligned}
1:&\quad y_t = \mu_t + \delta w_t + \varepsilon_t,\\
2:&\quad y_t = \mu_t + \beta t + \delta w_t + \delta_\beta(w_t t) + \varepsilon_t,\\
2a:&\quad y_t = \mu_t + \beta t + \delta w_t + \varepsilon_t,\\
2b:&\quad y_t = \mu_t + \beta t + \delta_\beta z_t + \varepsilon_t,
\end{aligned} \qquad (6.1)$$

[13] The 5% and 10% lower-tail critical values for $CvM_0(4)$ are 0.641 and 0.796, respectively.

where μ_t is a random walk, ε_t is white noise, δ and δ_β are parameters, and

$$w_t = \begin{cases} 0 & \text{for } t \le \tau \\ 1 & \text{for } t > \tau \end{cases} \quad \text{and} \quad z_t = \begin{cases} 0 & \text{for } t \le \tau \\ t - \tau & \text{for } t > \tau. \end{cases}$$

There is no slope in model 1, and so the only break is in the level. The other models all contain a time trend. In model 2, there is a structural change in both the level and the slope. Model 2a, contains a break in the level only, while model 2b, corresponds to a piecewise linear trend.

6.1. Stationarity Tests

Under Gaussianity, the LBI (and one-sided LM) test statistics for $H_0 : \sigma_\eta^2 = 0$ against $H_1 : \sigma_\eta^2 > 0$ in the models 1, 2, 2a, and 2b are of the form (3.2), but have asymptotic distributions under the null hypothesis that depend on λ. Bearing in mind the additivity property of the Cramér–von Mises distribution noted in Subsection 2.5, Busetti and Harvey (2001) propose the following simplified test statistics for models 1 and 2:

$$\eta_i^* = \frac{\sum_{t=1}^{\tau}\left(\sum_{s=1}^{t} e_s\right)^2}{\tau^2 s^2} + \frac{\sum_{t=\tau+1}^{T}\left(\sum_{s=\tau+1}^{t} e_s\right)^2}{(T-\tau)^2 s^2}, \qquad i = 1, 2, \tag{6.2}$$

where s^2 is as in (2.2). The LBI statistics differ only insofar as the two parts of (6.2) receive weights of λ^2 and $(1-\lambda)^2$, respectively. The simplified statistics still depend on the location of the break point, but their asymptotic distributions do not, since

$$\eta_i^* \Rightarrow \begin{cases} CvM_1(2) & \text{for } i = 1 \\ CvM_2(2) & \text{for } i = 2. \end{cases} \tag{6.3}$$

Not having to consult a table giving the distribution of the test statistic for all the possible values of λ is a big advantage. Furthermore, the tests immediately generalize to cases where there are several structural breaks. If there are k breaks, the distribution of the simplified statistic converges to a (second-level) generalized Cramér–von Mises distribution with $k + 1$ degrees of freedom, that is, $CvM_i(k+1)$, $i = 1, 2$. The Monte Carlo evidence presented in Busetti and Harvey (2001) indicates that the LBI test is clearly superior only in the region close to the null hypothesis and for break points near the beginning or end of the sample.

6.2. Unit Root Tests

The effects of breaks on LM-type unit root tests can be analyzed by taking first differences in (6.1). For level breaks 1 and 2a, differencing creates a single outlier at time $\tau + 1$. This may be removed by a "pulse" dummy variable that takes the value 1 at $\tau + 1$ and is zero otherwise. If the test statistics are constructed as in (4.3), their asymptotic distributions are unaffected – in terms of (4.5) all that happens is that $\Delta\widetilde{\mu}_{\tau+1}$ is zero.[14] Thus,

$$\zeta_i \Rightarrow \begin{cases} CvM_0(1) & \text{for } i = 1 \\ CvM_1(1) & \text{for } i = 2a. \end{cases} \tag{6.4}$$

The breaks in trend, on the other hand, do affect the distributions of the test statistics. Taking first differences of a piecewise linear trend, model 2b, results in a level dummy variable being fitted from $\tau + 1$ onward. In model 2, a pulse at $\tau + 1$ is also needed. However, in both cases the additivity property of the Cramér–von Mises distribution can be exploited so that statistics constructed in a similar way to those in (6.2) have $CvM_1(2)$ asymptotic distributions under the null. Thus,

$$\zeta_i^* = \frac{\sum_{t=1}^{\tau} \widetilde{\mu}_t^2}{\tau^2 s^2} + \frac{\sum_{t=\tau+1}^{T} \widetilde{\mu}_t^2}{(T-\tau)^2 s^2}, \qquad i = 2, 2b, \tag{6.5}$$

where $s^2 = \sum_{t=2}^{T} (\Delta\widetilde{\mu}_t)^2/(T-2)$, and

$$\zeta_i^* \Rightarrow CvM_1(2) \qquad \text{for } i = 2, 2b. \tag{6.6}$$

If the models are more general and parametric test statistics are constructed from innovations, estimation is carried out with the dummy variables in their original undifferenced form. The inclusion of the random walk component has the same effect as differencing.

6.3. Multivariate Series and Seasonality

Busetti and Harvey (2003) extend the Canova–Hansen test to allow for dummy variables modeling breaks in the seasonal pattern. A simplified test, constructed on the same basis as (6.2), has a $CvM_1(2s-2)$ asymptotic distribution when there is one such break. The asymptotic distributions of seasonal unit root tests, on the other hand, are not affected by the inclusion of seasonal break dummies, since these become pulse variables under the null hypothesis.

Busetti (2002) extends the multivariate tests of Subsections 4.1 and 4.2 to deal with situations where there are breaks in some or all of a set of N time series. He shows that a simplified version of the test against a multivariate random walk can be constructed by allowing for a break in all the series at the same point in time. This statistic, denoted as $\eta_i^*(N)$, generalizes (6.2) and has the $CvM(2N)$ asymptotic distribution. The modification of multivariate unit root tests follows along similar lines to yield a generalization of (6.5).

[14] Amsler and Lee (1995) give a formal proof of this result for the Schmidt–Phillips test and go on to show that an omitted or misplaced level break will have no effect on the asymptotic distribution.

7. CONCLUSIONS

Unit root tests can be set up using the LM principle so as to give statistics which, under the null hypothesis, have Cramér–von Mises distributions in large samples. Stationarity test statistics have asymptotic distributions belonging to the same family. This provides a remarkable unification and simplification of test procedures for nonstationary time series. The distributions are easily tabulated and have nice properties, such as additivity. For the simpler models, exact distributions of the test statistics can be obtained, but once the nuisance parameters are estimated, the case for just using the asymptotic distributions becomes stronger. In any case, it seems that the asymptotic critical values provide a good approximation even for relatively small sample sizes. The additivity property of the Cramér–von Mises distribution means that it is easy to set up tests with an allowance made for any intervention variables used to model structural breaks.

The tests are obtained by working within an unobserved components framework. There is a good case for estimating the nuisance parameters in such models and constructing parametric tests, since autoregressive approximations and nonparametric estimates of the long-run variance can sometimes lead to tests with unreliable size and/or low power.

Modifications could be made to the various unit root tests along the lines suggested by Elliott et al. (1996), but this would be at the cost of losing the simplicity and generality of the test statistics and their asymptotic distributions.

ACKNOWLEDGMENTS

Earlier versions of this paper were given at the universities of Birmingham, Edinburgh, and Carlos III, and at the conference on Foundations of Statistical Inference in Jerusalem in December 2000 and the conference in honor of Wayne Fuller at Iowa State University in June 2001. I would like to thank Fabio Busetti, David Dickey, Jukka Nyblom, Emmanuel Parzen, Jim Stock, Mariane Streibel, Robert Taylor, and two anonymous referees for helpful comments, and David Bates for programming assistance. I would also like to thank the ESRC for financial support as part of a project on dynamic factor analysis (grant number L138 25 1008) and the British Council for contributing toward travel expenses for the Jerusalem conference.

APPENDIX

To show the relationship between the ζ statistic in the multivariate model and $\widetilde{\phi}$ in (5.6), write the inverted matrix in (5.5) as

$$\sum_{t=1}^{T} \Delta\widetilde{\mu}_t' \Sigma_\eta^{-1} \Delta\widetilde{\mu}_t = -2 \sum_{t=1}^{T} \Delta\widetilde{\mu}_t' \Sigma_\eta^{-1} \widetilde{\mu}_{t-1} + \widetilde{\mu}_T' \Sigma_\eta^{-1} \widetilde{\mu}_T. \tag{A.1}$$

Since $\widetilde{\mu}_0 = \mathbf{0}$, the summation on the right-hand side can start at $t = 2$. With a constant, $\widetilde{\mu}_1 = \mathbf{0}$, and with a time trend, $\widetilde{\mu}_T = \mathbf{0}$ as well. If Σ_η is estimated by $T^{-1}\sum_{t=1}^{T}\Delta\widetilde{\mu}_t\Delta\widetilde{\mu}_t'$, the left-hand side of the expression (A.1) reduces to TN because $\sum_{t=1}^{T}\Delta\widetilde{\mu}_t'\widehat{\Sigma}_\eta^{-1}\Delta\widetilde{\mu}_t = \text{tr}[\widehat{\Sigma}_\eta^{-1}\sum_{t=1}^{T}\Delta\widetilde{\mu}_t\Delta\widetilde{\mu}_t']$, and so, provided the slope is estimated, it follows that $\zeta(N) = -N/\{2T(\widetilde{\phi} - 1)\}$. As regards the LM test, evaluating the first derivative of the log-likelihood function at $\phi = 1$ yields

$$\frac{\partial \log L}{\partial \phi} = \sum_{t=1}^{T}(\widetilde{\mu}_t' - \phi\widetilde{\mu}_{t-1})'\widehat{\Sigma}_\eta^{-1}\widetilde{\mu}_{t-1} = \sum_{t=1}^{T}\Delta\widetilde{\mu}_t'\widehat{\Sigma}_\eta^{-1}\widetilde{\mu}_{t-1} = -1/2NT.$$

On evaluating the second derivative, we find that $\zeta(N) = N^2/4\text{LM}$.

References

Abuaf, N., and P. Jorion (1990), "Purchasing Power Parity in the Long Run," *Journal of Finance*, 45, 157–74.

Amsler, C., and J. Lee (1995), "An LM Test for a Unit Root in the Presence of Structural Change," *Econometric Theory*, 11, 359–68.

Bhargava, A. (1986), "On the Theory of Testing for Unit Roots in Observed Time Series," *Review of Economic Studies*, 53, 36–84.

Busetti, F. (2002), "Testing for (Common) Stochastic Trends in the Presence of Structural Breaks," *Journal of Forecasting*, 21, 81–105.

Busetti, F., and A. C. Harvey (2001), "Testing for the Presence of a Random Walk in Series with Structural Breaks," *Journal of Time Series Analysis*, 22, 127–50.

Busetti, F., and A. C. Harvey (2003), "Seasonality Tests," *Journal of Business and Economic Statistics*, 21, 420–36.

Canova, F., and B. E. Hansen (1995), "Are Seasonal Patterns Constant over Time? A Test for Seasonal Stability," *Journal of Business and Economic Statistics*, 13, 237–52.

Elliot, G., T. J. Rothenberg, and J. H. Stock (1996), "Efficient Tests for an Autoregressive Unit Root," *Econometrica*, 64, 813–36.

Fuller, W. A. (1996), *Introduction to Statistical Time Series*, second edition. Wiley New York:

Harvey A. C. (2001), "Testing in Unobserved Components Models," *Journal of Forecasting*, 20, 1–19.

Harvey A. C., E. Ruiz, and N. Shephard (1994), "Multivariate Stochastic Variance Models," *Review of Economic Studies*, 61, 247–64.

Harvey, A. C., and A. Scott (1994), "Seasonality in Dynamic Regression Models," *Economic Journal*, 104, 1324–45.

Harvey, A. C., and M. Streibel (1997), "Testing for Nonstationary Unobserved Components," mimeo.

Harvey, A. C., and M. Streibel (1998), "Tests for Deterministic versus Indeterministic Cycles," *Journal of Time Series Analysis* 19: 505–29.

Hylleberg, S. (1995), "Tests for Seasonal Unit Roots: General to Specific or Specific to General?" *Journal of Econometrics*, 69, 5–25.

Hylleberg, S., R. Engle, C. W. J. Granger, and B. S. Yoo (1990), "Seasonal Integration and Co-integration," *Journal of Econometrics*, 44, 215–38.

Hwang, J., and P. Schmidt (1996), "Alternative Methods of Detrending and the Power of Unit Root Tests," *Journal of Econometrics*, 71, 227–8.

Koopman, S. J., A. C. Harvey, J. A. Doornik, and N. Shephard (2000), *STAMP 6.0 Structural Time Series Analyser, Modeller and Predictor*. London: Timberlake Consultants Ltd.

Kuo, B.-S., and A. Mikkola (2001), "How Sure are We about Purchasing Power Parity? Panel Evidence with the Null of Stationary Exchange Rates," *Journal of Money Credit and Banking,* 33, 767–89.

Kwiatkowski, D., P. C. B. Phillips, P. Schmidt, and Y. Shin (1992), "Testing the Null Hypothesis of Stationarity against the Alternative of a Unit Root: How Sure are We that Economic Time Series Have a Unit Root?" *Journal of Econometrics*, 44, 159–78.

Leybourne, S. J., and B. P. M. McCabe (1994), "A Consistent Test for a Unit Root," *Journal of Business and Economic Statistics,* 12, 157–66.

MacNeill, I. B. (1978), "Properties of Sequences of Partial Sums of Polynomial Regression Residuals with Applications to Tests for Change of Regression at Unknown Times," *The Annals of Statistics,* 6, 422–33.

Maddala, G. S., and I.-M. Kim (1998), *Unit Roots, Co-integration, and Structural Change*. Cambridge: Cambridge University Press.

Nabeya, S., and K. Tanaka (1990), "Limiting Power of Unit-Root Tests in Time-Series Regression," *Journal of Econometrics,* 46, 247–71.

Nyblom, J., and A. C. Harvey (2000), "Tests of Common Stochastic Trends," *Econometric Theory,* 16, 176–99.

Nyblom, J., and A. C. Harvey (2001), "Testing against Smooth Stochastic Trends," *Journal of Applied Econometrics,* 16, 415–29.

Nyblom, J., and T. Mäkeläinen (1983), "Comparison of Tests for the Presence of Random Walk Coefficients in a Simple Linear Model," *Journal of the American Statistical Association,* 78, 856–64.

Oya, K., and H. Y. Toda (1998), "Dickey-Fuller, Lagrange Multiplier and Combined Tests for a Unit Root in Autoregressive Time Series," *Journal of Time Series Analysis*, 19, 325–47.

Pantula, S. (1991), "Asymptotic Distributions of Unit Root Tests When the Process is Nearly Stationary," *Journal of Business and Economic Statistics*, 9, 63–71.

Perron, P., and S. Mallet (2000), "A Look at the Quality of the Approximation of the Functional Central Limit Theorem," *Economics Letters,* 68, 225–34.

Sargan, J. D., and A. Bhargava (1983), "Testing Residuals from Least Squares Regression for Being Generated by the Gaussian Random Walk," *Econometrica,* 51, 153–74.

Saikkonen, P. (1993), "A Note on a Lagrange Multiplier Test for Testing an Autoregressive Unit Root," *Econometric Theory*, 9, 494–8.

Schmidt, P., and P. C. B. Phillips (1992), "LM Tests for a Unit Root in the Presence of Deterministic Trends," *Oxford Bulletin of Economics and Statistics*, 54, 257–87.

Schmidt, P., and J. Lee (1991), "A Modification of the Schmidt–Phillips Unit Root Test," *Economics Letters,* 36, 285–89.

Smith, R. J., and A. M. R. Taylor (1998), "Additional Critical Values and Asymptotic Representations for Seasonal Unit Root Tests," *Journal of Econometrics*, 85, 269–88.

Stock, J. H. (1994), "Unit Roots, Structural Breaks and Trends," *Handbook of Econometrics*, vol. 4 (ed. by R. F. Engle and D. L. McFadden), Amsterdam: Elsevier Science, 2739–840.

Stock, J. H., and M. W. Watson (1998), "Median Unbiased Estimation of Coefficient Variance in Time-varying Parameter Model," *Journal of the American Statistical Association*, 93, 349–57.

Tanaka, K. (1996), *Time Series Analysis.* New York: Wiley.

CHAPTER 18

A New Look at Panel Testing of Stationarity and the PPP Hypothesis

Jushan Bai and Serena Ng

ABSTRACT

This paper uses a decomposition of the data into common and idiosyncratic components to develop procedures that test if these components satisfy the null hypothesis of stationarity. The decomposition also allows us to construct pooled tests that satisfy the cross-section independence assumption. In simulations, tests on the components separately generally have better properties than tests on the observed series. However, the results are less than satisfactory, especially in comparison with similar procedures developed for unit root tests. The problem can be traced to the properties of the stationarity test, and is not due to the weakness of the common-idiosyncratic decomposition. We apply both panel stationarity and unit root tests to real exchange rates. We find evidence in support of a large stationary common factor. Rejections of PPP are likely due to nonstationarity of country-specific variations.

1. INTRODUCTION

A notable result of Rothenberg (2000) and Elliott, Rothenberg and Stock (1996), is that for data with sample sizes frequently encountered, the maximal achievable power of unit root tests is rather low. There is now a growing interest in using panel data to perform unit root and stationarity analysis. One of the major motivations for using panel data for hypothesis testing is the enhanced power relative to a single time series. But most of the panel tests in the literature assume cross-sectional independence, which is difficult to satisfy for macroeconomic data. As discussed in O'Connell (1998), panel unit root tests tend to be oversized, while stationarity tests have low power. Moreover, whether or not we use panel data, testing if an observed series is stationary in finite samples can be extremely difficult if the data are driven by a mixture of I(1) and I(0) (unobserved) components. The issue was analyzed by Engel (2000) within the context of testing the PPP hypothesis, and more generally under the heading of negative moving-average errors in the unit roots literature, see, for example, Schwert (1989).

In Bai and Ng (2004), we proposed a new approach to testing the unit root hypothesis that not only alleviates the size problem arising from the mixture component problem, but is also effective in controlling for cross-section correlation in panel testing. The latter feature is attractive as it enables us to construct valid and powerful panel tests. In the present paper, the approach is extended to testing the null hypothesis of stationarity. The approach consists of three ingredients. First, the data are assumed to obey a factor structure. This allows us to model cross-section correlation and comovement of economic time series. Second, the analysis is based on a panel of data with a large number of time series observations and cross-section units. This permits us to consistently estimate the common factors and the idiosyncratic components. Third, inference is made on the common factors and the idiosyncratic components, rather than the observed series. This allows us to disentangle the I(1) and I(0) mixture and to identity the source of nonstationarity.

More specifically, the observed data $X_{it}, i = 1, 2, \ldots, N,\ t = 1, 2, \ldots, T$ are represented by

$$X_{it} = D_{it} + \lambda_i' F_t + e_{it}, \tag{1.1}$$

where D_{it} is the deterministic component, F_t is a $k \times 1$ vector of unobservable common factors, λ_i is the vector of loadings, and e_{it} is a unit-specific stochastic term. The loadings represent the exposure of cross-section i to the common factors. Some cross-sections may not be influenced by the common factors, but enough loadings must be nonzero such that F_t represents correlations that are pervasive. The specific component e_{it} can be weakly correlated cross-sectionally. Formal conditions imposed on the factor model for unit root testing are given in Bai and Ng (2004), and we will continue to use those assumptions.

The factor model makes the revealing point that stationarity of an observed series X_{it} requires stationarity of F_t and e_{it}. Nonstationarity, on the other hand, can arise because of a unit root in any one of the k factors, or in e_{it}. When one component is I(0) and the other is I(1), X_{it} becomes the sum of two components with different orders of integration. Univariate stationarity tests will have low power while unit root tests will have distorted sizes when the I(0) component is much larger than the I(1) component, even though X_{it} is fundamentally I(1). Our proposed methodology is to test F_t and e_{it} instead of the observed series, X_{it}. The hope is that more precise inference can be made by testing the components, if indeed size distortion arises because an observed series is driven by components with different orders of integration.

Panel testing of unit root and stationarity is not new. Quah (1994), Levin, Lin, and Chu (2002), Im, Pesaran, and Shin (2003), Hadri (2000), Pedroni (1995), Maddala and Wu (1999), and Choi (2001), among others, have developed panel unit root, cointegration, and stationarity tests under various assumptions about fixed effects and heterogeneous time trends. What makes our approach different is that we pool statistics that test the idiosyncratic errors, not the observed data. This distinction is important because imposing cross-section independence on the observed data is much more restrictive than imposing the assumption on the idiosyncratic errors. In cross-country and sectoral analysis, the independence assumption will rule out common shocks in the data, since such shocks will induce strong cross-section correlation that cannot be aggregated away. Cross-section correlations can also arise in a mechanical way. For example, real exchange rates are often defined using the same base country. O'Connell (1998) showed that the pooled tests will overreject the null hypothesis when the independence assumption is violated, whether the null hypothesis is unit root or stationarity. Size distortions could be misread as higher power. Banerjee, Marcellino, and Osbat (2001) argued against use of panel unit root test because of this potential problem. A factor structure provides a parsimonious way of capturing strong cross-section correlation. Once this is controlled for, the idiosyncratic errors should at most be weakly correlated. Thus, whereas the independence assumption is unlikely to be true for observed macroeconomic time series, the assumption that the idiosyncratic errors are independent across i is more likely to hold. For this reason, we consider pooled tests of the idiosyncratic errors. This has important power implications because pooled tests are, in general, more powerful than univariate tests.

As in Stock and Watson (2002), Bai and Ng (2002, 2004), we estimate λ_i and F_t by the method of principal components. The key to the present analysis lies in consistent estimation of the common and the idiosyncratic components without a priori knowledge whether they are I(1) or I(0). The trick is to apply the method of principal components to the first differenced data. The estimates are then recumulated to obtain estimates in level form, and stationarity tests are applied to these estimates. Such an analysis is possible because we work with large panels (i.e., when N and T are both large). Loosely speaking, the large N is necessary to identify variations that are common in the cross-section, while a large T is necessary to consistently estimate terms that are idiosyncratic. Section 2 proposes a suite of tests for stationarity. As will become clear, the limiting distribution of the stationarity test being considered bears relation to a specific unit root test. Accordingly, Section 3 offers results for the particular panel unit root test. Simulations are presented in Section 4, and tests are applied to real exchange rates in Section 5.

In the analysis to follow, we assume D_{it} is a polynomial in time of order p and present results for $p = 0$ (in which case $D_{it} = c_i$) and $p = 1$ (in which case $D_{it} = c_i + \beta_i t$). We assume the invariance principle holds so that for a series x_t $(t = 1, \ldots T)$ satisfying mixing conditions,

$$\frac{1}{\sqrt{T}\sigma_x}\sum_{s=1}^{[Tr]} x_s \Rightarrow B(r),$$

where $B(r)$ is a standard Brownian motion and σ_x^2 is the spectral density of x_t at frequency zero. If $\widetilde{x}_t = x_t - \bar{x}$, where $\bar{x} = \frac{1}{T}\sum_{t=1}^{T} x_t$, then

$$\frac{1}{\sqrt{T}\sigma_x}\sum_{s=1}^{[Tr]} \widetilde{x}_t \Rightarrow B(r) - rB(1) \equiv V(r)$$

is a Brownian bridge. Furthermore, if $\check{x}_t$ is the residual from a regression of x_t on a constant and a time trend,

$$\frac{1}{\sqrt{T}\sigma_x}\sum_{s=1}^{[Tr]}\check{x}_t \Rightarrow B(r) - rB(1) - 6(r^2 - r)\int_0^1\left(s - \frac{1}{2}\right)dB(s) \equiv U(r)$$

is a second level Brownian bridge.

2. PANEL STATIONARITY TESTS

Our analysis permits some, none, or all of the factors to be nonstationary. We assume

$$F_{mt} = \alpha_m F_{mt-1} + u_{mt} \quad m = 1, \dots k \tag{2.2}$$

$$e_{it} = \rho_i e_{it-1} + \varepsilon_{it} \quad i = 1, \dots N, \tag{2.3}$$

where ε_{it} and u_{mt} are i.i.d. and mutually independent. The results hold even when these errors are weakly dependent. Factor m is nonstationary if $\alpha_m = 1$. The idiosyncratic component is stationary if $\rho_i < 1$ and has a unit root if $\rho_i = 1$. We consider the KPSS test developed in Kwiatkowski, Phillips, Schmidt, and Shin (1992), the most commonly used test for stationarity. If x is the series to be tested, the KPSS test is

$$\text{KPSS}_x = \frac{\frac{1}{T}\sum_{j=1}^{T}\left(\frac{1}{\sqrt{T}}\sum_{j=1}^{t} x_j\right)^2}{\omega_x^2},$$

where ω_x^2 is a consistent estimate of σ_x^2. As our objective is not to obtain better stationarity tests, we take the properties of the univariate KPSS test as given. The proofs in the Appendix can be amended to accommodate other consistent stationarity tests of choice, such as Leybourne and McCabe (1994) and Jansson (2001).

Since the objective is to test if the level of F_t and e_{it} are stationary, it would seem natural to obtain principal component estimates of F_t and e_{it} from (1.1). These estimates would, however, be consistent only when $\rho_i < 1$. When the idiosyncratic errors are nonstationary, the principal components estimator applied to the nondifferenced data cannot guarantee consistent estimation of F_t. In consequence, the estimated common factors will be nonstationary even though the true factors are stationary. We therefore consider applying the principal components method to the data in first differenced form. As formally analyzed in Bai and Ng (2004), this guarantees consistent estimation of the common factors (upto a location shift and a scale transformation) under both the null and the alternative hypothesis.

Estimation of the differenced model yields estimates of Δe_{it} and ΔF_t. Our interest is in testing stationarity of e_{it} and F_t in level form. The construction of the test depends on whether or not there is a linear time trend.

2.1. The Intercept Only Case: $p = 0$

When $p = 0$, $X_{it} = c_i + \lambda_i' F_t + e_{it}$. The model in differenced form is:

$$\Delta X_{it} = \lambda_i' \Delta F_t + \Delta e_{it}. \tag{2.4}$$

Let ΔX be the $(T-1) \times N$ data matrix in differences such that the ith column is $(\Delta X_{i2}, \Delta X_{i3}, \ldots, \Delta X_{iT})'$ $(i = 1, 2, \ldots, N)$. Let $\Delta F = (\Delta F_2, \Delta F_3, \ldots, \Delta F_T)'$ and $\Lambda = (\lambda_1, \ldots, \lambda_N)'$. The estimated factors (in differences), $\widehat{\Delta F}_{1t}, \ldots \widehat{\Delta F}_{kt}$, are the k eigenvectors corresponding to the first k largest eigenvalues of the $(T-1) \times (T-1)$ matrix $\Delta X \cdot \Delta X'$. The estimated loading matrix, $\widehat{\Lambda}$, is equal to $\widehat{\Lambda} = \Delta X' \cdot \widehat{\Delta F}$. Finally, let $\widehat{\Delta e}_{it} = \Delta X_{it} - \hat{\lambda}_i' \widehat{\Delta F}_t$ $(t = 2, \ldots, T,\ i = 1, 2, \ldots, N)$.

The steps to test stationarity of the common factors and the idiosyncratic components can be summarized as follows:

1. Estimate ΔF_t and λ_i by the method of principal components, as described previously.
2. Given $\widehat{\Delta F}_t$, construct the following partial sum process for each $m = 1, \ldots k$,

$$\widehat{F}_{mt} = \sum_{s=2}^{t} \widehat{\Delta F}_{ms}.$$

   Test the null hypothesis that $\widehat{F}_{mt}$ is stationary for each $m = 1, \ldots k$ using the KPSS test with demeaning. Denote this test by $S_F^c(m)$.
3. For each i, construct the partial sum $\widetilde{e}_{it} = \sum_{s=2}^{t} \widehat{\Delta e}_{is}$, $t = 2, \ldots T$.
   (a) If F_{mt} is I(0) for every $m = 1, \ldots k$, for each $i = 1, \ldots N$, apply the KPSS test to $\{\widehat{e}_{it}^0\}_{t=1}^T$, where $\widehat{e}_{it}^0$ is $\widetilde{e}_{it}$ after demeaning.[1] Denote the test statistic by $S_{e0}^c(i)$.
   (b) If $\bar{k}$ of the F_ts are I(1), let $\widehat{e}_{it}^1$ be the residuals from a projection of $\widetilde{e}_{it}$ on 1 and $\widehat{F}_{1t}, \ldots \widehat{F}_{\bar{k}t}$. For each i, apply the test to $\{\widehat{e}_{it}^1\}_{t=1}^T$ to give $S_{e1}^c(i)$.

Theorem 2.1. ($p = 0$) *Suppose the KPSS statistic developed in Kwiatkowski et al. (1992) is used to test stationarity and assume that $N, T \to \infty$. Let V_{um} and $V_{\varepsilon i}$ $(i = 1, \ldots N)$, which are $N + k$ mutually independent Brownian bridges.*

1. *Under the null hypothesis that $\alpha_m < 1 (m = 1, \ldots k)$,*

$$S_F^c(m) \Rightarrow \int_0^1 V_{um}(r)^2 dr.$$

2. *Suppose F_{mt} is $I(0)$ for every m. Then under the null hypothesis that $\rho_i < 1 (i = 1, \ldots N)$,*

$$S_{e0}^c(i) \Rightarrow \int_0^1 V_{\varepsilon i}(r)^2 dr.$$

[1] That is, $\tilde{e}_{it} - \overline{\tilde{e}_i}$ with $\overline{\tilde{e}_i}$ being the sample mean of $\tilde{e}_{it}$.

3. *Suppose $\bar{k}$ of the factors are $I(1)$, then under the null hypothesis that $\rho_i < 1$, $S^c_{e1}(i)$ has the same limiting distribution as the statistic developed in Shin (1994) for testing the null hypothesis of cointegration with $\bar{k}$ integrated regressors and a constant.*

Bai and Ng (2004) showed that the average squared deviations between $\widehat{F}_t$ and F_t vanish as N and T tend to infinity. Stationarity tests can treat the estimated factors as though they were known. The S^c_F test has the same distributions as derived in Kwiatkowski et al. (1992) for the constant only case. At the 5 percent level, the critical value is 0.463.

The limiting distribution for testing $\hat{e}_{it}$ depends on whether F_t is I(1) or I(0). If all the factors are stationary, the stationarity test for $\hat{e}_{it}$ has the same limit as the KPSS test. At the 5 percent level, the critical value is also 0.463. If some $\bar{k}$ factors are I(1), stationarity of e_{it} implies cointegration between X_i and a subset of F of dimension $\bar{k}$. Then test of the estimated idiosyncratic components has the same limiting distribution as reported in Shin (1994) developed for testing the null hypothesis of cointegration. At the 5 percent level, the critical values are 0.324 and 0.225 for $\bar{k} = 1$ and 2, respectively. In each case, the null hypothesis is rejected when the test statistic exceeds the critical value.

Remarks: Step 3 can be simplified by not making the distinction as to whether F_t is I(0) or I(1) so that the statistic $S^c_{e1}(i)$ is always used. The limiting distribution of $S^c_{e1}(i)$ still depends on whether F_t is I(0) or I(1). That is, Theorem 2.1 part 2 holds by replacing $S^c_{e0}(i)$ with $S^c_{e1}(i)$.

Step 3 assumes that $\bar{k}$ is the true number of I(1) factors. Since we can only estimate the space spanned by the factors, and linear combinations of stationary and nonstationary variables are nonstationary, $\bar{k}$ may be overestimated if it is determined by testing the estimated factors one by one. The methodology developed in Bai and Ng (2004) should be used to determine the true $\bar{k}$.

2.2. The Case with a Linear Trend: $p = 1$

When $p = 1$, $X_{it} = c_i + \beta_i t + \lambda_i' F_t + e_{it}$. The model in differenced form is:

$$\Delta X_{it} = \beta_i + \lambda_i' \Delta F_t + \Delta e_{it}. \tag{2.5}$$

Let $\widetilde{\Delta X}$ be the $(T-1) \times N$ matrix such that the ith column is the ith cross-section series (in differences) with demeaning. That is, the ith column of $\widetilde{\Delta X}$ is $(\Delta X_{i2} - \overline{\Delta X}_i, \ldots, \Delta X_{iT} - \overline{\Delta X}_i)'$, where $\overline{\Delta X}_i = \frac{1}{T-1}\sum_{t=2}^{T} \Delta X_{it}$ $(i = 1, 2, \ldots, N)$. Let $\widehat{\Delta F}$ be the k eigenvectors corresponding to the k largest eigenvalues of the $(T-1) \times (T-1)$ matrix $\widetilde{\Delta X} \cdot \widetilde{\Delta X}'$ and $\widehat{\Lambda} = \widetilde{\Delta X} \cdot \widehat{\Delta F}$. Finally, define $\widehat{\Delta e}_{it} = \Delta X_{it} - \overline{\Delta X}_i - \hat{\lambda}_i' \widehat{\Delta F}_t$.

The steps to test stationarity of the common factors and the idiosyncratic components are as follows:

1. Estimate ΔF_t and λ_i by the method of principal components, as described previously.

2. Given $\widehat{\Delta F_t}$, construct the following partial sum process for each $m = 1, \ldots k$,

$$\hat{F}_{mt} = \sum_{s=2}^{t} \widehat{\Delta F_{ms}}.$$

Test the null hypothesis that $\hat{F}_{mt}$ is stationary for each $m = 1, \ldots k$ using the KPSS test with demeaning and detrending. Denote this test by $S_F^\tau(m)$.
3. For each i, construct the partial sum $\tilde{e}_{it} = \sum_{s=2}^{t} \widehat{\Delta e_{is}}$, $t = 2, \ldots T$.
   (a) If F_{jt} is I(0) for every $j = 1, \ldots k$, then for each $i = 1, \ldots N$, apply the KPSS test to $\{\hat{e}_{it}^0\}_{t=1}^T$, where $\hat{e}_{it}^0$ are the residuals from a projection of $\tilde{e}_{it}$ on a constant and a time trend. Denote the test by $S_{e0}^\tau(i)$.
   (b) If $\bar{k}$ of the $F_t s$ are I(1), let $\hat{e}_{it}^1$ be the residuals from a projection of $\tilde{e}_{it}$ on a constant, a time trend, and $\hat{F}_{1t}, \ldots \hat{F}_{\bar{k}t}$. The test statistic for the series $\{\hat{e}_{it}^1\}_{t=1}^T$ is denoted by $S_{e1}^\tau(i)$.

The remark following Theorem 2.1 is also applicable here.

Theorem 2.2. $(p = 1)$ *Suppose the KPSS statistic developed in Kwiatkowski et al. (1992) is used to test stationarity and assume that N and T both approach infinity. Let $U_{um}(m = 1, \ldots k)$ and $U_{\varepsilon i}$ be $N + k$ mutually independent second level Brownian bridges.*

1. *Under the null hypothesis that $\alpha_m < 1 (m = 1, \ldots k)$,*

$$S_F^\tau(m) \Rightarrow \int_0^1 U_{um}(r)^2 dr.$$

2. *Suppose F_{mt} is $I(0)$ for every $m = 1, \ldots r$. Then under the null hypothesis that $\rho_i < 1$ $(i = 1, \ldots N)$,*

$$S_{e0}^\tau(i) \Rightarrow \int_0^1 U_{\varepsilon i}(r)^2 dr.$$

3. *If $\bar{k}$ of the factors are $I(1)$, then $S_{e1}^\tau(i)$ has the same limiting distribution as the statistic developed in Shin (1994) for testing the null hypothesis of cointegration in an equation with $\bar{k}$ integrated regressors and a time trend.*

The limiting distribution of $S_F^\tau(m)$ coincides with that of the KPSS test derived for the linear trend case. At the 5 percent level, the critical value is 0.149. The tests are invariant to coefficients on the intercepts and the linear trends. That is, if $F_t = \mu + \pi t + \xi_t$, where μ and π are $k \times 1$ vector of coefficients, and ξ_t is a vector $(k \times 1)$ of zero mean stationary processes (under the null) or a vector of nondrifting I(1) processes (under the alternative), we can simply treat ξ_t as our F_t. This follows because the data are differenced and then demeaned. As in the case when $p = 0$, the properties of $S_e^\tau(i)$ depends on whether F_t is I(1) or I(0). Under stationarity, the limiting distribution is identical to that of $S_F^\tau(m)$ and thus also has a 5 percent critical value of 0.149. When $\bar{k}$ of the common factors are I(1), testing stationarity of e_{it} is the same as testing the null hypothesis of cointegration. As shown in Shin (1994), the limiting distribution depends on functionals of the I(1) regressors. The critical values thus depend on the rank of these regressors. For $\bar{k} = 1$ and 2, these are 0.122 and 0.100, respectively.

Pooling is valid when the limiting distribution of the test on unit i does not contain terms that are common across i. If the data admit a factor structure, tests on X_{it} will not satisfy this condition. However, Theorems 2.1 and 2.2 show that stationarity tests of the idiosyncratic components have limiting distributions that do not depend on the common innovations. Thus, if e_{it} is independent across i, statistics that test $\hat{e}^0$ are asymptotically independent over i. Using the same argument as in Maddala and Wu (1999) and Choi (2001), we have the following result:

Corollary 2.1. *Let $q(i)$ be the p-value associated with the $S_{e0}^c(i)$ test (or $S_{e0}^\tau(i)$ test). Suppose e_{it} is independent across i. Consider pooled tests defined by $Q = -2\sum_{i=1}^N \log q(i)$. If F_{mt} is $I(0)$ for every $m = 1, \ldots k$, then*

$$\frac{Q - 2N}{\sqrt{4N}} \Rightarrow N(0, 1).$$

The independence of e_{it} is sufficient for pooling to be valid, though the assumption can be relaxed so that the number of units with correlated errors is negligible as $N, T \to \infty$. Note, however, that the independence assumption is not required for the univariate tests in Theorems 2.1 and 2.2 to be valid. Note also that even if e_{it} was independent across i, pooling will not be valid if some of the factors are I(1). Integrated factors have nonvanishing effects on the projection residuals, $\hat{e}_{it}^1$. In consequence, statistics for testing $\hat{e}_{it}^1$ have limiting distributions that depend on the I(1) common factors, thus making pooling invalid.

3. A PANEL UNIT ROOT TEST

In Bai and Ng (2004), we proposed a suite of test procedures which we referred to as PANIC: panel analysis of nonstationarity of the idiosyncratic and common components. Results were derived assuming that the Dickey–Fuller test was used to test the null hypothesis of a unit root. But the key to PANIC is consistent estimation of F_t and λ_i, and applicability of the results is not limited to the Dickey–Fuller test. In this section, we present results for another unit root test. Specifically, consider testing for a unit root in the series $\{x_t\}$ using the statistic:

$$\text{MSB}_x = \frac{T^{-2}\sum_{t=1}^T x_{t-1}^2}{s_w^2}, \tag{3.6}$$

where s_w^2 is an autoregressive estimate of σ_w^2, the spectrum at frequency zero of $\{\Delta x_t\}$.[2] The MSB (modified Sargan–Bhargava) test is the square of the SB statistic developed in Sargan and Bhargava (1983) for i.i.d. errors. It is extended to the case of weakly dependent errors by Stock (1990), leading to the MSB test as defined above.

Under the null hypothesis that $\rho_i = 1$ for every i, we estimate the factor model using the first-differenced data when $p = 0$, and the demeaned first-differenced data when $p = 1$. This yields $\widehat{\Delta e_{it}}$ and $\widehat{\Delta F_t}$. Cumulating these series leads to $\tilde{e}_{it}$ and $\hat{F}_{1t} \ldots \hat{F}_{mt}$ as defined in Section 2. Now for each $i = 1, \ldots N$ and $m = 1, \ldots k$, apply the MSB test to $\tilde{e}_{it}$ and $\hat{F}_{mt}$. Denote these tests by $M_e^c(i)$ and $M_F^c(m)$ when $p = 0$, and by $M_e^\tau(i)$ and $M_F^\tau(m)$ when $p = 1$.

Theorem 3.3. *Suppose the MSB statistic is used to test the unit root null hypothesis. Let B_{um} and $B_{\varepsilon i}$ be $N + k$ mutually independent Brownian motions, and let V_{um} and $V_{\varepsilon i}$ be $N + k$ mutually independent Brownian bridges. Suppose also that $N, T \to \infty$.*

1. *When $p = 0$,*

$$M_F^c(m) \Rightarrow \int_0^1 B_{um}(r)^2 dr \tag{3.7}$$

$$M_e^c(i) \Rightarrow \int_0^1 B_{\varepsilon i}^2(r) dr. \tag{3.8}$$

2. *When $p = 1$,*

$$M_F^\tau(m) \Rightarrow \int_0^1 V_{um}(r)^2 dr \tag{3.9}$$

$$M_e^\tau(i) \Rightarrow \int_0^1 V_{\varepsilon i}^2(r) dr. \tag{3.10}$$

Examination of the results reveals that the limiting distribution of $M_e^\tau(i)$ (corresponding to $p = 1$) is the same as $S_{e0}^c(i)$ (corresponding to $p = 0$). All the distributions presented so far belong to the family of generalized Cramér-von Mises distributions. As Harvey (2001) pointed out, unit root and stationarity tests with such limiting distributions can be studied in a unified framework. Whereas inference about a unit root is based on the lower tail of a Cramér-von Mises distribution, stationarity tests are based on the upper tail.

[2] The autoregressive estimate of the spectrum is $s_w^2 = \hat{\sigma}_{wk}^2/(1 - \sum_{j=1}^k \hat{b}_j)^2$, where $\hat{b}_j$ and $\hat{\sigma}_{wk}^2$ are obtained from the regression

$$\Delta x_t = b_0 x_{t-1} + b_1 \Delta x_{t-1} + \cdots + b_k \Delta x_{t-k} + w_{tk}$$

with $\hat{\sigma}_{wk}^2 = \frac{1}{T}\sum_{t=k+1}^T \hat{w}_{tk}^2$. The estimator s_ω^2 is consistent for σ_ω^2 under the null hypothesis of a unit root and bounded under the alternative. As discussed in Perron and Ng (1998), this is required for the class of MSB to be consistent. The test is a member of a class of tests analyzed in Perron and Ng (1996).

As with the KPSS tests on the estimated idiosyncratic errors, the MSB tests can also be pooled because the limiting distributions do not depend on the common factors. Nonetheless, the KPSS and MSB tests are fundamentally different in the present context in three ways. First, stationarity tests for e_{it} depend on whether the common factors are I(1) or I(0), and in practice, pretesting of F_t will be necessary. However, a unit root test on the idiosyncratic errors is invariant to the properties of F_t and is thus immuned to inference problems that might arise in pretests. Second, the stationarity test is based on explicit detrending of $\widetilde{e}_{it}$ according to whether p is 0 or 1. In contrast, the unit root test is based on $\widetilde{e}_{it}$ detrended according to the first-differenced model. The deterministic terms will likely have a larger effect on the stationarity than the unit root test. Third, the stationarity test is based on the partial sum of the series, while the unit root test is based on the level of the series itself. Errors from estimation of the factors can be expected to have a larger impact on the stationarity test.

The results stated in (3.8) and (3.10) hold whether F_t is I(0) or I(1) and the limiting distributions are asymptotically independent of F. In contrast, consider testing the residuals from a regression of X_{it} on $\widehat{F}_t$ and the deterministic regressors. That is, consider the regression

$$X_{it} = D_{it} + \hat{F}_t'\delta_i + e_{it}^*$$

and let $\widehat{e}_{it}^*$ be the least-squares residuals. Suppose that there are $\bar{k}$ I(1) common factors. Then testing the null hypothesis that e_{it}^* has a unit root is equivalent to testing the null hypothesis of no cointegration between X_{it} and F_t. The idea is similar to the residual based cointegration tests of Phillips and Ouliaris (1990). In fact, if we were to use the Dickey–Fuller test, the limiting distribution would be the same as that of Phillips and Ouliaris (1990) with $\bar{k}$ I(1) regressors plus an intercept (if $D_{it} = c_i$) and a time trend (if $D_{it} = c_i + \beta_i t$), see Bai and Ng (2004). Even if we use the MSB, the limiting distribution is given by (3.8), but the Brownian motion in that functional is formed by projecting $B_{\varepsilon i}$ onto a vector of $\bar{k}$ Brownian motions that form the factors, F. Since F is common across i, such cointegration type tests are asymptotically dependent across i, and thus cannot be pooled. This will be the case whether we use the MSB or those developed in Phillips and Ouliaris (1990), since the limiting distribution of a residuals based cointegration test depends on the I(1) regressors.

3.1. Monte Carlo Simulations

Data are generated according to (1.1)–(2.3) with a single common factor ($k = 1$). In addition, λ_i are i.i.d. $N(1, 1)$, ε_{it} are i.i.d. $N(0, 1)$, and $u_t \sim N(0, \sigma_F^2)$. Let α be the autoregressive parameter in the common factor process F_t and let ρ be the (common) autoregressive parameter in the idiosyncratic error processes e_{it}. The following parameters are considered:

- $\sigma_F^2 = 10$, 1, and 0.5.
- $(\rho, \alpha) = \{(.5,.8),(.8,.5),(0,.9),(.9,0),(1,0),(1,.5),(1,.8),(1,.9),(1,.95),$ $(0,1),(.5,1),(.8,1),(.9,1),(.95,1)\}$.

Because the factor model is estimated with differenced data, the tests are invariant to the value of c_i in (1.1) and thus is set to zero. Similarly, when the differenced data are demeaned when $p = 1$, the tests are also invariant to β_i in (1.1) and thus also set to zero. We report results for $T = 200$ and $N = 20$.[3] Asymptotic critical values at the 5 percent significance level are used. These are obtained by first approximating the standard Brownian motion as the partial sum of 500 N(0,1) errors. The critical values for the individual tests are the percentiles from 10,000 simulations of the limiting distributions reported in Theorems 3.1 and 3.2. The pooled tests depend on the p values associated with either the stationarity or the unit root test. Approximate p-values are obtained by creating a look-up table that contains 300 percentage points of the asymptotic distributions simulated earlier. In particular, 100 points is used to approximate the upper tail, 100 to approximate the lower tail, and 100 points for the middle part of the asymptotic distributions. The p values match up very well with Table 3 of MacKinnon (1994), whenever they are available. These look-up tables are available from the authors. Tables 18.1 and 18.2 report the rejection rates of the unit root hypothesis over 1,000 replications. The column labeled $\widehat{F}$ is the rejection rate of the tests applied to the estimated common factor. The columns labeled X and $\widehat{e}$ are the average rejection rates applied to X and $\widehat{e}$, where the average is taken across N units over 1,000 trials. Results for a particular i are similar.

We first report in Table 18.1a results for the modified Sargan–Bhargava (MSB) unit root test. These rejection rates represent size in one of three cases: (i) when $\hat{F}_t$ is tested and $\alpha = 1$, (ii) when $\hat{e}_t$ is tested and $\rho = 1$, or (iii) when X is tested and either $\alpha = 1$ or $\rho = 1$. Other entries represent power.[4] The first thing to note is that the results for $p = 0$ are similar to those for $p = 1$. When both F and e are stationary, the MSB test has more power when applied to the data X directly, as indicated by the first five rows of Table 18.1a. But when F is nonstationary (implying X is nonstationary but its first difference has a negative moving average component), the MSB test on X is oversized. However, separate tests on F and e are much more accurate. As shown in rows with $\alpha = 1$, the rejection rates on F are close to the nominal size of 5 percent, while the test also has power in rejecting a unit root in F. Similarly, when only e is I(1), the test also has good size and power. The results thus show that testing the components separately is more precise than testing the sum of two series, even when the components have to be estimated from cross-sections with only twenty units.

Table 18.1b reports the rejection rates for the pooled unit root test. The entries are given size and power interpretation as described in the previous paragraph.

[3] The results change little for larger N. As expected, power is higher when T is large.

[4] The MSB test necessitates the choice of the lag length for the autoregressive spectrum. This is set to six for X and two for $\hat{e}$. This is based on analysis in Ng and Perron (2001) that a longer lag is necessary when there is a negative moving component, and a shorter lag should be used to preserve power otherwise.

Table 18.1a. *Rejection rates for the null hypothesis of a unit root*

				$\sigma^F = \sqrt{10}$			$\sigma^F = 1$			$\sigma^F = \sqrt{0.5}$		
T	N	ρ	α	X	$\widehat{F}$	$\widehat{e}^0$	X	$\widehat{F}$	$\widehat{e}^0$	X	$\widehat{F}$	$\widehat{e}^0$
						$p = 0$						
200	20	0.00	0.00	0.99	0.80	0.79	0.99	0.81	0.80	0.99	0.78	0.79
200	20	0.50	0.80	0.99	0.92	0.90	1.00	0.91	0.90	1.00	0.92	0.90
200	20	0.80	0.50	1.00	0.90	0.92	0.99	0.89	0.92	1.00	0.91	0.92
200	20	0.00	0.90	0.94	0.85	0.79	0.92	0.85	0.79	0.92	0.87	0.79
200	20	0.90	0.00	0.90	0.78	0.85	0.92	0.78	0.85	0.92	0.78	0.85
200	20	1.00	0.00	0.07	0.75	0.06	0.06	0.47	0.06	0.06	0.34	0.06
200	20	1.00	0.50	0.21	0.88	0.06	0.08	0.67	0.06	0.07	0.55	0.06
200	20	1.00	0.80	0.38	0.90	0.05	0.13	0.75	0.06	0.10	0.61	0.06
200	20	1.00	0.90	0.43	0.86	0.06	0.16	0.72	0.06	0.12	0.61	0.06
200	20	1.00	0.95	0.34	0.55	0.06	0.15	0.46	0.06	0.12	0.42	0.06
200	20	0.00	1.00	0.09	0.06	0.66	0.08	0.04	0.65	0.10	0.05	0.64
200	20	0.50	1.00	0.08	0.05	0.84	0.13	0.05	0.84	0.16	0.07	0.83
200	20	0.80	1.00	0.12	0.06	0.88	0.20	0.06	0.88	0.24	0.06	0.87
200	20	0.90	1.00	0.11	0.06	0.82	0.22	0.06	0.82	0.27	0.06	0.82
200	20	0.95	1.00	0.12	0.08	0.57	0.19	0.06	0.57	0.24	0.06	0.57
200	20	1.00	1.00	0.07	0.06	0.06	0.07	0.06	0.06	0.07	0.05	0.06
						$p = 1$						
200	20	0.00	0.00	0.96	0.74	0.74	0.95	0.76	0.74	0.96	0.73	0.75
200	20	0.50	0.80	0.95	0.85	0.90	0.96	0.85	0.90	0.97	0.86	0.89
200	20	0.80	0.50	0.98	0.90	0.85	0.96	0.89	0.85	0.96	0.90	0.85
200	20	0.00	0.90	0.77	0.61	0.73	0.73	0.60	0.73	0.73	0.62	0.73
200	20	0.90	0.00	0.70	0.77	0.61	0.72	0.71	0.61	0.74	0.69	0.62
200	20	1.00	0.00	0.03	0.69	0.06	0.02	0.49	0.06	0.03	0.34	0.06
200	20	1.00	0.50	0.12	0.87	0.06	0.03	0.74	0.06	0.03	0.62	0.06
200	20	1.00	0.80	0.26	0.84	0.06	0.06	0.75	0.06	0.05	0.65	0.06
200	20	1.00	0.90	0.28	0.63	0.06	0.08	0.55	0.06	0.05	0.51	0.06
200	20	1.00	0.95	0.18	0.27	0.06	0.07	0.26	0.06	0.06	0.26	0.06
200	20	0.00	1.00	0.03	0.06	0.64	0.04	0.06	0.63	0.06	0.06	0.63
200	20	0.50	1.00	0.04	0.06	0.85	0.08	0.06	0.86	0.10	0.06	0.85
200	20	0.80	1.00	0.05	0.05	0.83	0.13	0.05	0.83	0.16	0.06	0.82
200	20	0.90	1.00	0.05	0.05	0.60	0.14	0.06	0.60	0.17	0.06	0.60
200	20	0.95	1.00	0.06	0.06	0.29	0.10	0.07	0.29	0.13	0.05	0.28
200	20	1.00	1.00	0.03	0.07	0.06	0.03	0.05	0.06	0.03	0.06	0.06

Pooled tests based on X are invalid because of cross-sectional dependence. Only pooling on $\hat{e}$ is permitted by our theory. This is confirmed by the simulations. Consistent with the findings of O'Connell (1998), the pooled test applied to X rejects the unit root hypothesis too often. Size distortions are significantly smaller when tests based on $\hat{e}$ are pooled. Higher power is a motivation for considering pooled tests. Indeed, the power of the pooled tests on $\hat{e}$ is remarkably higher than the univariate tests reported in Table 18.1a. When a linear trend is in the model, the size of the pooled tests is somewhat inflated, but have good

Table 18.1b. *Pooled tests: rejection rates for the null hypothesis of a unit root*

				$\sigma^F = \sqrt{10}$		$\sigma^F = 1$		$\sigma^F = \sqrt{.5}$	
T	N	ρ	α	X	$\widehat{e}^0$	X	$\widehat{e}^0$	X	$\widehat{e}^0$
				$p = 0$					
200	20	0.00	0.00	1.00	1.00	1.00	1.00	1.00	1.00
200	20	0.50	0.80	1.00	1.00	1.00	1.00	1.00	1.00
200	20	0.80	0.50	1.00	1.00	1.00	1.00	1.00	1.00
200	20	0.00	0.90	1.00	1.00	1.00	1.00	1.00	1.00
200	20	0.90	0.00	1.00	1.00	1.00	1.00	1.00	1.00
200	20	1.00	0.00	0.28	0.08	0.13	0.09	0.13	0.10
200	20	1.00	0.50	0.86	0.09	0.23	0.09	0.18	0.09
200	20	1.00	0.80	0.99	0.08	0.56	0.09	0.37	0.10
200	20	1.00	0.90	0.99	0.10	0.70	0.08	0.49	0.08
200	20	1.00	0.95	0.95	0.07	0.68	0.09	0.54	0.08
200	20	0.00	1.00	0.29	1.00	0.33	1.00	0.37	1.00
200	20	0.50	1.00	0.33	1.00	0.44	1.00	0.51	1.00
200	20	0.80	1.00	0.36	1.00	0.58	1.00	0.66	1.00
200	20	0.90	1.00	0.39	1.00	0.62	1.00	0.72	1.00
200	20	0.95	1.00	0.39	1.00	0.58	1.00	0.72	1.00
200	20	1.00	1.00	0.30	0.10	0.24	0.09	0.22	0.09
				$p = 1$					
200	20	0.00	0.00	1.00	1.00	1.00	1.00	1.00	1.00
200	20	0.50	0.80	1.00	1.00	1.00	1.00	1.00	1.00
200	20	0.80	0.50	1.00	1.00	1.00	1.00	1.00	1.00
200	20	0.00	0.90	0.98	1.00	1.00	1.00	0.99	1.00
200	20	0.90	0.00	1.00	1.00	1.00	1.00	1.00	1.00
200	20	1.00	0.00	0.02	0.11	0.00	0.13	0.00	0.13
200	20	1.00	0.50	0.38	0.11	0.01	0.13	0.00	0.11
200	20	1.00	0.80	0.81	0.12	0.08	0.13	0.02	0.12
200	20	1.00	0.90	0.80	0.12	0.17	0.11	0.05	0.13
200	20	1.00	0.95	0.56	0.13	0.15	0.11	0.06	0.13
200	20	0.00	1.00	0.13	1.00	0.14	1.00	0.16	1.00
200	20	0.50	1.00	0.13	1.00	0.22	1.00	0.26	1.00
200	20	0.80	1.00	0.17	1.00	0.33	1.00	0.44	1.00
200	20	0.90	1.00	0.15	1.00	0.36	1.00	0.46	1.00
200	20	0.95	1.00	0.17	1.00	0.30	1.00	0.39	1.00
200	20	1.00	1.00	0.09	0.12	0.03	0.13	0.01	0.12

properties overall. In all, Tables 18.1a and 18.1b show that the idiosyncratic common decomposition is effective. More accurate univariate and powerful pooled tests can be obtained.

We now turn to the stationarity tests. Table 18.2a reports results for testing $\{X_{it}\}$, $\{\widehat{F}_t\}$, and $\{\hat{e}_{it}\}$ using the quadratic spectral kernel to estimate σ_x^2 with $\text{int}[12(T/100)^{1/4}]$ lags. These rejection rates represent power in one of three cases: (i) when $\widehat{F}_t$ is tested and $\alpha = 1$, (ii) when $\hat{e}_t$ is tested and $\rho = 1$, or (iii) when X is tested and either $\alpha = 1$ or $\rho = 1$. All other entries represent size. Our

Table 18.2a. *Rejection rates for the null hypothesis of stationarity, quadratic spectral kernel*

				$\sigma^F = \sqrt{10}$				$\sigma^F = 1$				$\sigma^F = \sqrt{0.5}$			
T	N	ρ	α	X	$\widehat{F}$	$\widehat{e}^0$	$\widehat{e}^1$	X	$\widehat{F}$	$\widehat{e}^0$	$\widehat{e}^1$	X	$\widehat{F}$	$\widehat{e}^0$	$\widehat{e}^1$
							$p = 0$								
200	20	0.00	0.00	0.05	0.06	0.04	0.13	0.04	0.04	0.04	0.13	0.04	0.03	0.05	0.13
200	20	0.50	0.80	0.07	0.07	0.05	0.13	0.06	0.06	0.05	0.13	0.05	0.07	0.04	0.13
200	20	0.80	0.50	0.05	0.05	0.06	0.16	0.06	0.05	0.06	0.16	0.06	0.04	0.06	0.16
200	20	0.00	0.90	0.12	0.12	0.06	0.12	0.10	0.11	0.06	0.12	0.10	0.11	0.06	0.12
200	20	0.90	0.00	0.10	0.04	0.12	0.25	0.11	0.08	0.12	0.25	0.11	0.08	0.12	0.25
200	20	1.00	0.00	0.64	0.44	0.66	0.76	0.65	0.64	0.66	0.69	0.65	0.65	0.66	0.64
200	20	1.00	0.50	0.60	0.22	0.66	0.76	0.65	0.57	0.66	0.70	0.66	0.60	0.66	0.67
200	20	1.00	0.80	0.50	0.11	0.66	0.77	0.63	0.35	0.66	0.72	0.64	0.45	0.65	0.69
200	20	1.00	0.90	0.43	0.14	0.66	0.75	0.60	0.27	0.66	0.73	0.62	0.33	0.66	0.71
200	20	1.00	0.95	0.42	0.23	0.66	0.73	0.58	0.30	0.66	0.72	0.60	0.33	0.66	0.70
200	20	0.00	1.00	0.65	0.66	0.44	0.06	0.64	0.65	0.44	0.06	0.62	0.64	0.44	0.06
200	20	0.50	1.00	0.65	0.66	0.27	0.06	0.64	0.67	0.28	0.05	0.59	0.64	0.27	0.06
200	20	0.80	1.00	0.65	0.67	0.14	0.07	0.59	0.66	0.14	0.07	0.57	0.67	0.15	0.07
200	20	0.90	1.00	0.64	0.67	0.15	0.11	0.56	0.65	0.15	0.12	0.52	0.65	0.15	0.12
200	20	0.95	1.00	0.60	0.63	0.24	0.20	0.53	0.65	0.24	0.20	0.50	0.65	0.24	0.20
200	20	1.00	1.00	0.65	0.64	0.65	0.53	0.67	0.67	0.66	0.50	0.66	0.68	0.66	0.50
							$p = 1$								
200	20	0.00	0.00	0.05	0.04	0.04	0.11	0.05	0.06	0.04	0.11	0.05	0.04	0.05	0.12
200	20	0.50	0.80	0.05	0.05	0.04	0.10	0.05	0.06	0.04	0.10	0.04	0.05	0.04	0.10
200	20	0.80	0.50	0.05	0.04	0.06	0.13	0.06	0.04	0.06	0.13	0.06	0.04	0.06	0.13
200	20	0.00	0.90	0.11	0.11	0.06	0.11	0.11	0.11	0.06	0.11	0.11	0.12	0.07	0.11
200	20	0.90	0.00	0.09	0.05	0.11	0.22	0.11	0.08	0.12	0.22	0.11	0.08	0.11	0.22
200	20	1.00	0.00	0.46	0.20	0.49	0.65	0.49	0.39	0.50	0.61	0.50	0.45	0.50	0.59
200	20	1.00	0.50	0.40	0.11	0.50	0.65	0.47	0.30	0.49	0.62	0.49	0.37	0.49	0.60
200	20	1.00	0.80	0.29	0.07	0.49	0.64	0.43	0.15	0.49	0.62	0.47	0.22	0.49	0.61
200	20	1.00	0.90	0.26	0.11	0.49	0.62	0.40	0.15	0.49	0.61	0.44	0.19	0.49	0.60
200	20	1.00	0.95	0.32	0.23	0.50	0.58	0.41	0.26	0.49	0.57	0.43	0.26	0.50	0.58
200	20	0.00	1.00	0.47	0.48	0.25	0.08	0.48	0.50	0.26	0.07	0.44	0.47	0.25	0.08
200	20	0.50	1.00	0.49	0.51	0.13	0.06	0.44	0.48	0.12	0.07	0.45	0.51	0.14	0.07
200	20	0.80	1.00	0.45	0.48	0.08	0.08	0.40	0.48	0.08	0.08	0.39	0.51	0.08	0.08
200	20	0.90	1.00	0.44	0.47	0.12	0.14	0.38	0.47	0.12	0.13	0.34	0.47	0.12	0.14
200	20	0.95	1.00	0.46	0.49	0.23	0.25	0.38	0.47	0.23	0.25	0.36	0.48	0.22	0.25
200	20	1.00	1.00	0.50	0.50	0.49	0.48	0.50	0.50	0.49	0.48	0.50	0.49	0.50	0.49

theory predicts that when $\alpha = 1$, a test on the stationarity of the idiosyncratic errors e_{it} should be based on $\hat{e}^1$, while testing $\hat{e}^0$ would be invalid. Indeed, by examining the rows of Table 18.2a with $\alpha = 1$, the tests based on $\hat{e}^1$ have less size distortion than those based on $\hat{e}^0$. Similarly, when $\alpha < 1$, theory suggests that $\hat{e}^0$ should be used. The first five rows in Table 18.2a show less size distortion when using $\hat{e}^0$ than using $\hat{e}^1$. However, when $\rho = 1$ and $\alpha < 1$, using $\hat{e}^0$ has less power than using $\hat{e}^1$. These results suggest that it would be useful in practice to pretest F, and then decide whether to use $\hat{e}^0$ or $\hat{e}^1$. It is conceivable that better size and power can be achieved.

When $(\rho, \alpha) = (0, 0.9)$, the stationarity test on $\hat{e}^0$ has a rejection rate of 0.06. When $(\rho, \alpha) = (0.9, 0)$, the rejection rate on $\hat{F}$ is 0.04. At face value,

Table 18.2b. *Pooled tests: rejection rates for the null hypothesis of stationarity, quadratic spectral kernel*

				$\sigma^F = \sqrt{10}$			$\sigma^F = 1$			$\sigma^F = \sqrt{0.5}$		
T	N	ρ	α	X	$\widehat{e}^0$	$\widehat{e}^1$	X	$\widehat{e}^0$	$\widehat{e}^1$	X	$\widehat{e}^0$	$\widehat{e}^1$
						$p = 0$						
200	20	0.00	0.00	0.28	0.09	0.83	0.20	0.07	0.84	0.17	0.08	0.83
200	20	0.50	0.80	0.34	0.09	0.81	0.28	0.10	0.79	0.26	0.07	0.78
200	20	0.80	0.50	0.24	0.19	0.92	0.21	0.21	0.92	0.20	0.20	0.93
200	20	0.00	0.90	0.43	0.25	0.78	0.43	0.24	0.80	0.44	0.25	0.79
200	20	0.90	0.00	0.53	0.68	1.00	0.67	0.69	1.00	0.66	0.69	1.00
200	20	1.00	0.00	1.00	1.00	1.00	1.00	1.00	1.00	1.00	1.00	1.00
200	20	1.00	0.50	1.00	1.00	1.00	1.00	1.00	1.00	1.00	1.00	1.00
200	20	1.00	0.80	1.00	1.00	1.00	1.00	1.00	1.00	1.00	1.00	1.00
200	20	1.00	0.90	1.00	1.00	1.00	1.00	1.00	1.00	1.00	1.00	1.00
200	20	1.00	0.95	0.99	1.00	1.00	1.00	1.00	1.00	1.00	1.00	1.00
200	20	0.00	1.00	0.90	0.85	0.33	0.90	0.84	0.32	0.88	0.84	0.32
200	20	0.50	1.00	0.90	0.72	0.30	0.89	0.73	0.30	0.88	0.71	0.31
200	20	0.80	1.00	0.90	0.58	0.38	0.89	0.57	0.39	0.90	0.59	0.39
200	20	0.90	1.00	0.90	0.80	0.57	0.88	0.80	0.58	0.90	0.81	0.59
200	20	0.95	1.00	0.91	0.99	0.77	0.96	0.99	0.79	0.97	0.98	0.80
200	20	1.00	1.00	1.00	1.00	1.00	1.00	1.00	0.99	1.00	1.00	0.99
						$p = 1$						
200	20	0.00	0.00	0.39	0.33	0.95	0.36	0.32	0.94	0.35	0.34	0.96
200	20	0.50	0.80	0.36	0.21	0.89	0.36	0.21	0.86	0.34	0.20	0.88
200	20	0.80	0.50	0.31	0.38	0.94	0.35	0.34	0.94	0.33	0.36	0.93
200	20	0.00	0.90	0.48	0.44	0.91	0.52	0.47	0.94	0.51	0.47	0.91
200	20	0.90	0.00	0.71	0.87	1.00	0.85	0.87	1.00	0.87	0.87	1.00
200	20	1.00	0.00	1.00	1.00	1.00	1.00	1.00	1.00	1.00	1.00	1.00
200	20	1.00	0.50	1.00	1.00	1.00	1.00	1.00	1.00	1.00	1.00	1.00
200	20	1.00	0.80	0.98	1.00	1.00	1.00	1.00	1.00	1.00	1.00	1.00
200	20	1.00	0.90	0.95	1.00	1.00	1.00	1.00	1.00	1.00	1.00	1.00
200	20	1.00	0.95	0.94	1.00	1.00	1.00	1.00	1.00	1.00	1.00	1.00
200	20	0.00	1.00	0.85	0.82	0.69	0.85	0.82	0.72	0.84	0.81	0.72
200	20	0.50	1.00	0.86	0.65	0.54	0.85	0.66	0.55	0.88	0.70	0.55
200	20	0.80	1.00	0.86	0.53	0.58	0.87	0.54	0.59	0.85	0.55	0.57
200	20	0.90	1.00	0.87	0.87	0.82	0.89	0.86	0.80	0.91	0.90	0.83
200	20	0.95	1.00	0.88	1.00	0.97	0.97	1.00	0.96	0.98	1.00	0.97
200	20	1.00	1.00	0.97	1.00	1.00	1.00	1.00	1.00	1.00	1.00	1.00

the stationary test has reasonably good properties. However, these results are obtained after a good deal of time was spent choosing the kernel and the bandwidth. To illustrate, Table 18.3 reports results using the Parzen kernel. Evidently, the KPSS test with the Parzen kernel is substantially oversized except in the uninteresting case when the common factors or idiosyncratic errors are very weakly serially correlated. Even though power appears high when one of the components indeed has a unit root, they are inflated by the size problem.

Table 18.3a. *Rejection rates for the null hypothesis of stationarity, Parzen kernel*

				$\sigma^F=\sqrt{10}$				$\sigma^F=1$				$\sigma^F=\sqrt{0.5}$			
T	N	ρ	α	X	$\widehat{F}$	$\widehat{e}^0$	$\widehat{e}^1$	X	$\widehat{F}$	$\widehat{e}^0$	$\widehat{e}^1$	X	$\widehat{F}$	$\widehat{e}^0$	$\widehat{e}^1$
							$p=0$								
200	20	0.00	0.00	0.05	0.06	0.05	0.12	0.05	0.05	0.04	0.12	0.04	0.03	0.05	0.12
200	20	0.50	0.80	0.12	0.13	0.06	0.14	0.10	0.11	0.06	0.13	0.09	0.12	0.05	0.13
200	20	0.80	0.50	0.08	0.06	0.11	0.23	0.10	0.06	0.11	0.23	0.10	0.06	0.11	0.23
200	20	0.00	0.90	0.22	0.23	0.08	0.11	0.20	0.22	0.08	0.11	0.20	0.23	0.09	0.11
200	20	0.90	0.00	0.18	0.05	0.23	0.38	0.22	0.14	0.24	0.39	0.23	0.15	0.23	0.38
200	20	1.00	0.00	0.76	0.51	0.79	0.89	0.79	0.75	0.79	0.84	0.79	0.77	0.79	0.81
200	20	1.00	0.50	0.71	0.26	0.79	0.89	0.78	0.65	0.79	0.85	0.79	0.71	0.79	0.83
200	20	1.00	0.80	0.61	0.18	0.80	0.89	0.75	0.47	0.79	0.86	0.77	0.57	0.79	0.84
200	20	1.00	0.90	0.57	0.28	0.79	0.88	0.74	0.41	0.79	0.87	0.76	0.48	0.79	0.85
200	20	1.00	0.95	0.58	0.42	0.80	0.86	0.72	0.47	0.79	0.85	0.75	0.52	0.79	0.84
200	20	0.00	1.00	0.79	0.80	0.51	0.05	0.77	0.80	0.52	0.05	0.76	0.80	0.52	0.05
200	20	0.50	1.00	0.78	0.79	0.33	0.06	0.76	0.81	0.33	0.06	0.72	0.78	0.32	0.06
200	20	0.80	1.00	0.79	0.81	0.22	0.10	0.72	0.81	0.22	0.11	0.69	0.80	0.23	0.11
200	20	0.90	1.00	0.77	0.80	0.28	0.20	0.68	0.78	0.27	0.21	0.66	0.79	0.28	0.21
200	20	0.95	1.00	0.74	0.77	0.41	0.35	0.69	0.78	0.41	0.35	0.66	0.78	0.41	0.36
200	20	1.00	1.00	0.78	0.79	0.79	0.72	0.80	0.80	0.79	0.70	0.80	0.79	0.80	0.70
							$p=1$								
200	20	0.00	0.00	0.04	0.04	0.04	0.10	0.05	0.06	0.04	0.10	0.04	0.04	0.04	0.10
200	20	0.50	0.80	0.13	0.14	0.05	0.11	0.10	0.11	0.05	0.10	0.08	0.11	0.05	0.10
200	20	0.80	0.50	0.08	0.05	0.13	0.23	0.11	0.06	0.13	0.22	0.11	0.06	0.13	0.22
200	20	0.00	0.90	0.27	0.28	0.08	0.09	0.26	0.29	0.09	0.09	0.25	0.29	0.09	0.09
200	20	0.90	0.00	0.21	0.05	0.28	0.43	0.27	0.13	0.29	0.43	0.28	0.17	0.29	0.43
200	20	1.00	0.00	0.70	0.25	0.77	0.85	0.76	0.61	0.77	0.83	0.76	0.69	0.77	0.82
200	20	1.00	0.50	0.61	0.14	0.77	0.85	0.74	0.46	0.77	0.84	0.75	0.55	0.76	0.82
200	20	1.00	0.80	0.48	0.16	0.77	0.85	0.68	0.30	0.76	0.83	0.72	0.39	0.77	0.83
200	20	1.00	0.90	0.49	0.28	0.76	0.83	0.66	0.35	0.76	0.82	0.70	0.41	0.77	0.82
200	20	1.00	0.95	0.60	0.53	0.77	0.81	0.69	0.53	0.76	0.79	0.72	0.55	0.77	0.80
200	20	0.00	1.00	0.73	0.75	0.35	0.06	0.72	0.77	0.36	0.05	0.69	0.75	0.36	0.06
200	20	0.50	1.00	0.75	0.77	0.18	0.06	0.68	0.76	0.18	0.06	0.69	0.79	0.19	0.06
200	20	0.80	1.00	0.72	0.76	0.16	0.14	0.66	0.78	0.17	0.15	0.61	0.78	0.17	0.14
200	20	0.90	1.00	0.71	0.76	0.29	0.29	0.63	0.77	0.29	0.29	0.58	0.76	0.30	0.30
200	20	0.95	1.00	0.72	0.76	0.50	0.49	0.66	0.75	0.50	0.48	0.64	0.77	0.50	0.49
200	20	1.00	1.00	0.76	0.75	0.77	0.73	0.77	0.78	0.77	0.73	0.77	0.76	0.76	0.74

Because of size distortion in the individual tests, the pooled tests become difficult to interpret. The prewhitening and recoloring procedure of Andrews and Monahan (1992) actually aggravates the size problem, as does use of the autoregressive spectral density estimator proposed by Berk (1974). The more persistent is the series to be tested the more severe the problem, even though in theory, these are precisely the situations when prewhitening should improve the estimates of the spectrum.

At the moment, it is somewhat of a black box why the choice of the kernel has such a significant impact on the KPSS, as in theory this should not be the case. It is possible that the errors from estimation of the factors create problems unique to our proposed methodology. But problems with the KPSS

Table 18.3b. *Pooled tests: rejection rates for the null hypothesis of stationarity, Parzen kernel*

				$\sigma^F = \sqrt{10}$			$\sigma^F = 1$			$\sigma^F = \sqrt{0.5}$		
T	N	ρ	α	X	$\widehat{e}^0$	$\widehat{e}^1$	X	$\widehat{e}^0$	$\widehat{e}^1$	X	$\widehat{e}^0$	$\widehat{e}^1$
						$p = 0$						
200	20	0.00	0.00	0.26	0.07	0.75	0.19	0.05	0.75	0.16	0.07	0.77
200	20	0.50	0.80	0.43	0.16	0.80	0.37	0.15	0.78	0.37	0.13	0.77
200	20	0.80	0.50	0.30	0.61	0.99	0.48	0.65	0.99	0.55	0.65	0.99
200	20	0.00	0.90	0.60	0.32	0.65	0.59	0.33	0.69	0.60	0.33	0.67
200	20	0.90	0.00	0.90	0.98	1.00	0.98	0.99	1.00	0.99	0.99	1.00
200	20	1.00	0.00	1.00	1.00	1.00	1.00	1.00	1.00	1.00	1.00	1.00
200	20	1.00	0.50	1.00	1.00	1.00	1.00	1.00	1.00	1.00	1.00	1.00
200	20	1.00	0.80	1.00	1.00	1.00	1.00	1.00	1.00	1.00	1.00	1.00
200	20	1.00	0.90	1.00	1.00	1.00	1.00	1.00	1.00	1.00	1.00	1.00
200	20	1.00	0.95	1.00	1.00	1.00	1.00	1.00	1.00	1.00	1.00	1.00
200	20	0.00	1.00	0.96	0.91	0.24	0.96	0.91	0.23	0.95	0.92	0.24
200	20	0.50	1.00	0.96	0.81	0.29	0.96	0.82	0.28	0.95	0.82	0.29
200	20	0.80	1.00	0.96	0.88	0.57	0.96	0.87	0.58	0.97	0.89	0.57
200	20	0.90	1.00	0.96	1.00	0.87	0.98	0.99	0.87	0.99	1.00	0.88
200	20	0.95	1.00	0.97	1.00	0.99	1.00	1.00	0.99	1.00	1.00	0.99
200	20	1.00	1.00	1.00	1.00	1.00	1.00	1.00	1.00	1.00	1.00	1.00
						$p = 1$						
200	20	0.00	0.00	0.29	0.12	0.71	0.24	0.12	0.71	0.20	0.13	0.73
200	20	0.50	0.80	0.48	0.21	0.75	0.47	0.20	0.72	0.44	0.19	0.71
200	20	0.80	0.50	0.40	0.87	0.99	0.67	0.85	1.00	0.75	0.85	1.00
200	20	0.00	0.90	0.70	0.44	0.61	0.69	0.46	0.61	0.70	0.47	0.61
200	20	0.90	0.00	0.97	1.00	1.00	1.00	1.00	1.00	1.00	1.00	1.00
200	20	1.00	0.00	1.00	1.00	1.00	1.00	1.00	1.00	1.00	1.00	1.00
200	20	1.00	0.50	1.00	1.00	1.00	1.00	1.00	1.00	1.00	1.00	1.00
200	20	1.00	0.80	1.00	1.00	1.00	1.00	1.00	1.00	1.00	1.00	1.00
200	20	1.00	0.90	1.00	1.00	1.00	1.00	1.00	1.00	1.00	1.00	1.00
200	20	1.00	0.95	1.00	1.00	1.00	1.00	1.00	1.00	1.00	1.00	1.00
200	20	0.00	1.00	0.95	0.88	0.33	0.95	0.88	0.31	0.95	0.88	0.35
200	20	0.50	1.00	0.96	0.75	0.38	0.95	0.72	0.36	0.96	0.77	0.38
200	20	0.80	1.00	0.96	0.93	0.83	0.97	0.94	0.84	0.97	0.93	0.83
200	20	0.90	1.00	0.98	1.00	1.00	0.99	1.00	0.99	1.00	1.00	1.00
200	20	0.95	1.00	0.99	1.00	1.00	1.00	1.00	1.00	1.00	1.00	1.00
200	20	1.00	1.00	1.00	1.00	1.00	1.00	1.00	1.00	1.00	1.00	1.00

test have also been reported by Caner and Kilian (2001), Hobijn, Franses, and Ooms (1998), among others.[5] The present analysis evidently provides no solution to the problems inherent in the KPSS. However, our analysis is useful in understanding size distortion arising from pooling, vis-á-vis size distortion

[5] The Leybourne and McCabe (1994) statistic is also used to test stationarity but has problems similar to the KPSS test, as pointed out by Caner and Kilian (2001).

due to the univariate test itself. As we have shown, even when the problem of cross-section dependence is solved, the panel stationarity test will still tend to overreject stationarity.

We wrap up this section by reiterating the most compelling reason for testing the idiosyncratic errors for a unit root instead of stationarity. As shown in Theorems 3.1 and 3.2, the large sample properties of stationarity tests depend on whether F_t is I(1) or I(0). This is not the case with unit root tests, a property that is appealing both in theory and in practice.

4. APPLICATION TO PPP

Under PPP, real exchange rates should be mean reverting and thus stationary. Because real exchange rates are often defined using the same base country, cross-section correlation arises almost by construction, even in the absence of global shocks. Strong cross-section correlation amounts to a common factor that cannot be aggregated away. As O'Connell (1998) found, standard panel unit root tests are biased toward the alternative hypothesis and thus also suffer from size distortions. O'Connell suggests removing the cross-section correlation by a GLS transformation of the data. This requires that the common component be stationary, which need not be the case. Also, constructing a consistent $N \times N$ covariance matrix estimator is not easy when N is allowed to go to infinity. The decomposition approach of this paper offers a useful alternative. It also allows us to discern the source of nonstationarity.

Quarterly data for nominal exchange rates and the consumer price indices are obtained from the International Finance Statistics. We use data from 1974:1–1997:4 for twenty-one countries: Canada, Australia, New Zealand, Austria, Belgium, Denmark, Finland, France, Germany, Ireland, Italy, Netherlands, Norway, Spain, Sweden, Switzerland, UK, Japan, Korea, Singapore, and Thailand. The U.S. is used as the numeraire country. Since the nominal exchange rates are expressed as the national currency per US dollar, an increase in the real currency means a real depreciation for the home country vis á vis the US dollar. To proceed with statistical analysis, we take logarithms of the data, which are then demeaned and standardized to have unit variance.

The results are reported in Table 18.4. We tag a series with a '$-$' if the KPSS test rejects stationarity. A '$+$' is used for a series that cannot reject a unit root. Thus, a series with no tagged symbol is judged stationary by both tests, and a series with a '$-$' and corresponding '$+$' are judged nonstationary by both tests. According to the column labeled X, the KPSS statistic rejects the null hypothesis of stationarity in two of the twenty-one observed series: Japan and Thailand. The MSB rejects the unit root null for all series but Ireland and Japan.

We then estimate the factors and the loadings using the method of principal components. The number of factors k is unknown. Bai and Ng (2002) proposed an information based procedure that can consistently estimate k. Using the penalty $(N+T)\log(N+T)/NT$, the criterion selects one factor. The factor associated with the largest eigenvalue explains 58 percent of the variation in

Table 18.4. *Application to real exchange rates, $p = 0$*

			KPSS		MSB	
Country	$\frac{\text{var}(\widehat{\Delta e})}{\text{var}(\Delta X)}$	$\frac{\sigma(\widehat{\lambda}_i'\widehat{F}_t)}{\sigma(\widehat{e}^0)}$	X	$\widehat{e}^0$	X	$\widehat{e}^0$
Canada	0.995	0.044	0.316	0.317	0.030	0.141^+
Australia	0.891	0.357	0.403	0.533^-	0.041	0.181^+
New Zealand	0.724	0.844	0.172	0.185	0.007	0.037
Austria	0.081	3.378	0.210	0.479^-	0.038	0.213^+
Belgium	0.093	2.330	0.105	0.411	0.033	0.131^+
Denmark	0.092	5.001	0.129	0.126	0.030	0.057
Finland	0.316	1.364	0.072	0.114	0.018	0.107^+
France	0.113	3.920	0.098	0.480^-	0.037	0.566^+
Germany	0.086	2.972	0.115	0.412	0.035	0.275^+
Ireland	0.158	1.761	0.366	0.336	0.061^+	0.119^+
Italy	0.337	1.614	0.197	0.249	0.039	0.173^+
Netherlands	0.076	2.871	0.099	0.480^-	0.029	0.054
Norway	0.173	3.438	0.083	0.340	0.047	0.015
Spain	0.385	1.264	0.201	0.335	0.031	0.165^+
Sweden	0.347	1.387	0.137	0.496^-	0.036	0.267^+
Switzerland	0.219	2.142	0.287	0.499^-	0.031	0.511^+
UK	0.415	1.312	0.177	0.187	0.024	0.029
Japan	0.560	0.594	0.548^-	0.649^-	0.089^+	0.567^+
Korea	0.988	0.187	0.083	0.074	0.001	0.000
Singapore	0.548	0.618	0.183	0.175	0.035	0.038
Thailand	0.938	0.278	0.522^-	0.580^-	0.021	0.037
5% CV			0.463	0.463	0.057	0.057
10% CV			0.343	0.343	0.076	0.076
Pooled			3.129	3.129	4.259	0.341

The stationarity tests are based on twelve lags of the quadratic spectral kernel. The unit root test is based on four lags in estimation of the autoregressive spectral density.
A '−' denotes rejection of stationarity, and a '+' indicates nonrejection of the unit root hypothesis.

the data, while the second factor explains only 14 percent of the variation. We proceed with the estimation assuming there is one common factor. The MSB test on the common factor is 0.053, very close to the critical value of 0.057 at the 5 percent level, but nonetheless rejects a unit root. The KPSS test for the common factor is 0.119. In light of the fact that the KPSS tends to overreject stationarity, this nonrejection is rather a strong evidence for a stationary common component.

We then apply the tests to the idiosyncratic errors. Since both the MSB and the KPSS suggest that the common factor is stationary, the relevant column is thus $\widehat{e}^0$. A formal test rejects stationarity for eight of the twenty-one series. The MSB test, on the other hand, cannot reject the unit root null for thirteen series. At the 5 percent level, the KPSS and MSB are in agreement with over thirteen of the idiosyncratic series. Six series (New Zealand, Denmark, Norway, UK,

Korea, and Singapore) are stationary, while seven series (Australia, Austria, Germany, Sweden, Switzerland, and Japan) are nonstationary. As the common factor is stationary, this suggests that six of the observed real exchange rate series are stationary, while seven are nonstationary because of nonstationary country specific factors. Direct testing of the data would have found eighteen series to be stationary. Pooling the stationarity tests on $\hat{e}^0_{it}$ gives a statistic of 5.897, which rejects the null hypothesis that all series are stationary. Pooling the MSB tests gives 7.591, which rejects the null hypothesis that every series has a unit root. In light of the finding from univariate tests that some series are stationary while others are not, this result is not surprising. In fact, this should be the case.

We have used a "differencing and recumulating" approach to yield consistent estimates of the factors. A by-product of this methodology is that we can analyze the relative importance of the common and idiosyncratic components. Columns 1 and 2 of Table 18.3 report the ratio of the standard deviation of the idiosyncratic component (based on one factor) to the standard deviation of the differenced data, as well as the standard deviation of the common to the idiosyncratic component. If all variations are idiosyncratic, the first statistic should be close to one and the second should be small. The Asian countries and Canada have real exchange rate variations dominated by the idiosyncratic components, as $\frac{\text{var}(\widehat{\Delta e})}{\text{var}\Delta X}$ exceeds 0.9 for all these countries. But real exchange rate variations of the fourteen European countries are apparently dominated by the common components. In light of these differences in the relative importance of the common component, a model that explains the European real exchange rate will likely not be able to explain the dynamics of non-European real exchange rates. It would be useful to develop a formal analysis in which common and specific shocks have explicit roles. Since nonstationarity seems to depend heavily on the properties of the idiosyncratic component, it would also be useful to see if the variations in this component result from differentials in productivity, fiscal, and monetary policies.

5. CONCLUSION

When a series is the sum of two components with possibly different dynamic properties, testing whether the components are I(1) or I(0) should be more accurate than testing the series itself. The motivation of this paper is to exploit the fact that common and idiosyncratic components can be consistently estimated from a factor model. We develop procedures to test if these components satisfy the null hypothesis of stationarity. The decomposition into common and idiosyncratic components also allows us to develop pooled tests that satisfy the cross-section independence assumption. In simulations, tests on the components are indeed more accurate than testing the summed series. However, the results are less than satisfactory, especially in comparison with similar procedures developed for unit root tests. The problem can be traced to the properties of the univariate stationarity test, and is not due to the weakness of the common idiosyncratic decomposition. We look forward to the development of new stationary tests with more robust properties.[6]

A primary interest in stationarity tests is the PPP hypothesis. We take our procedures to the data. Evidence from both panel unit root and stationarity tests suggest the presence of one common, stationarity factor. In view of the tendency of the KPSS test to overreject the null hypothesis, this nonrejection can be seen as strong evidence for stationarity. However, the results also find that a large number of real exchange rates have nonstationary idiosyncratic components. Understanding the structural source of this nonstationarity seems to be a promising way to understand why the evidence tends to pile up against PPP.

APPENDIX

We first explain why the estimated $\hat{F}_t$ can be treated as the true F_t process. In the literature on large dimensional factor analysis, as in Stock and Watson (1998), Bai and Ng (2002), and Bai (2003, 2004), it is shown that $\hat{F}_t$ is consistent for HF_t, where H is a $k \times k$ matrix of full rank. It is clear that F_t is stationary if and only if HF_t is stationary. That is, an invertible matrix transformation does not alter its stationarity property. Furthermore, a transformation of the regressors will not alter the regression residuals. Thus, whether one uses F_t or HF_t $(t = 1, 2, \ldots, T)$ as regressors, the same residuals will be obtained. Of course, $\hat{F}_t$ is not exactly equal to HF_t because of estimation errors. But the estimation errors are negligible if N is large. This is due to the following lemma:

Lemma A.1. *Consistency of $\hat{F}_t$ (from Bai, 2003)*

- *Suppose F_t is $I(0)$ and Assumptions A to G of Bai (2003) hold. Then $\hat{F}_t$ is $\sqrt{N}$ consistent if $\sqrt{N}/T \to 0$. If $\sqrt{N}/T \to \tau > 0$, $\hat{F}_t$ is T consistent.*
- *Suppose F_t is $I(1)$ and Assumptions A to F of Bai (2004) hold. Then $\hat{F}_t$ is $\sqrt{N}$ consistent if $N/T^3 \to 0$. If $N/T^3 \to \tau > 0$, $\hat{F}_t$ is consistent at rate $T^{3/2}$.*

It is possible to give a rigorous proof for Theorems 3.1 and 3.2 that explicitly allows for estimation errors in F_t. We provide such an analysis in Bai and Ng (2004). Here, we simply appeal to Lemma A.1 and assume F_t is known.

Proof of Theorem 3.1. When $p = 0$, the model in level and first differenced forms are

$$\begin{aligned} X_{it} &= c_i + \lambda_i' F_t + e_{it} \\ \Delta X_{it} &= \lambda_i' \Delta F_t + \Delta e_{it}. \end{aligned}$$

[6] Jansson (2001) suggests using covariates to improve the power of stationarity tests. This will not resolve the size problem.

By Lemma A.1, the method of principal components applied to ΔX_{it} will give consistent estimates of ΔF_t. For large N, ΔF_t can be treated as known. Furthermore, $\hat{\lambda}_i$ will be $\sqrt{T}$ consistent. Thus, we have

$$\Delta X_{it} = \hat{\lambda}_i \Delta F_t + \widehat{\Delta e_{it}}.$$

From $\widehat{\Delta e_{it}} = \Delta e_{it} - (\hat{\lambda}_i - \lambda_i)\Delta F_t$, the partial sum of this series is

$$\begin{aligned}\tilde{e}_{it} &= \sum_{j=2}^{t} \widehat{\Delta e_{ij}} \\ &= e_{it} - e_{i1} - (\hat{\lambda}_i - \lambda_i)'(F_t - F_1),\end{aligned}$$

which depends on e_{i1} and $(\hat{\lambda}_i - \lambda_i)'(F_t - F_1)$. Removal of these effects depend on whether F_t is I(0) or I(1). If F_t is I(0), we demean $\tilde{e}_{it}$. Let $\bar{e}_i = \frac{1}{T}\sum_{t=2}^{T} e_{it}$, $\bar{F} = \frac{1}{T}\sum_{t=2}^{T} F_t$. Then

$$\overline{\tilde{e}_i} = \frac{1}{T}\sum_{t=2}^{T} \tilde{e}_{it} = \bar{e}_i - e_{i1} - (\hat{\lambda}_i - \lambda_i)'(\bar{F} - F_1),$$

from which it follows that

$$\hat{e}_{it}^0 = \tilde{e}_{it} - \overline{\tilde{e}_{it}} = e_{it} - \bar{e}_i - (\hat{\lambda}_i - \lambda_i)'(F_t - \bar{F}).$$

Consider now the scaled partial sum of $\hat{e}_{it}^0$. We have

$$\begin{aligned}\frac{1}{\sqrt{T}}\sum_{s=1}^{t} \hat{e}_{is}^0 &= \frac{1}{\sqrt{T}}\sum_{s=1}^{t}(e_{is} - \bar{e}_i) - \sqrt{T}(\hat{\lambda}_i - \lambda_i)'\frac{1}{T}\sum_{k=1}^{t}(F_s - \bar{F}) \\ &= \frac{1}{\sqrt{T}}\sum_{s=1}^{t}(e_{is} - \bar{e}_i) + O_p\left(\frac{1}{\sqrt{T}}\right).\end{aligned}$$

Thus if F_t is I(0),

$$\frac{1}{\sqrt{T}}\sum_{k=1}^{[Tr]} \hat{e}_{ik}^0 \Rightarrow \sigma_i[B_{\varepsilon,i}(r) - rB_{\varepsilon,i}(1)] \equiv V_{\varepsilon i}(r)$$

$$\frac{1}{T^2}\sum_{t=1}^{T}\left(\sum_{k=1}^{t}\hat{e}_{it}^0\right)^2 \Rightarrow \sigma_i^2 \int_0^1 V_{\varepsilon i}(r)^2 dr,$$

where σ_i^2 is the long-run variance of e_{it}. The limiting distribution is independent across i and can thus be pooled.

If F_t is I(1), demeaning alone is not sufficient to purge the effect of $e_{i1} + (\hat{\lambda}_i - \lambda_i)'(F_t - F_1)$. We must project $\tilde{e}_{it}$ on $[1\ F_t]$ to obtain new residuals $\hat{e}_{it}^1$. Because $\tilde{e}_{it} = e_{it} - e_{i1} - (\hat{\lambda}_i - \lambda_i)'(F_t - F_1)$, $\hat{e}_{it}$ are equivalent to those obtained by projecting e_{it} on the regressors. The KPSS test on such a residual process is studied in Shin (1994), where the limiting distributions are also derived. Thus the details are omitted. Finally, because the limiting distributions across i depend on the common stochastic trends F_t, they are not independent across i. This implies that these statistics cannot be pooled. ■

Proof of Theorem 3.2. For $p = 1$, $\Delta X_{it} = \beta_i + \lambda_i' \Delta F_t + \Delta e_{it}$, and $\overline{\Delta X_i} = \frac{1}{T-1}\sum_{t=2}^{T} \Delta X_{it} = \beta_i + \lambda_i' \overline{\Delta F} + \overline{\Delta e_i}$, where $\overline{\Delta F} = \frac{1}{T-1}\sum_{t=1}^{T} \Delta F_t = \frac{F_T - F_1}{T-1}$ and $\overline{\Delta e_i} = \frac{e_{iT} - e_{i1}}{T-1}$. Thus,

$$\Delta X_{it} - \overline{\Delta X_i} = \lambda_i'(\Delta F_t - \overline{\Delta F}) + \Delta e_{it} - \overline{\Delta e_i}. \tag{A.11}$$

The principal components estimator based on the data $\Delta X_{it} - \overline{\Delta X_i}$ ($i = 1, 2, \ldots, N, t = 2, \ldots, T$) will provide estimates of λ_i and $\Delta F_t - \overline{\Delta F}$, respectively. Because $\widehat{\Delta F}_t$ is root-N consistent for $\Delta F_t - \overline{\Delta F}$, when N is large relative to T, the estimation error is negligible and we can simply assume $\widehat{\Delta F}_t = \Delta F_t - \overline{\Delta F}$. This implies that

$$\hat{F}_t = \sum_{s=2}^{t} \widehat{\Delta F}_s = \sum_{s=2}^{t} (\Delta F_s - \overline{\Delta F}) = F_t - F_1 - \frac{F_T - F_1}{T-1}(t-1).$$

The residual from projecting $\hat{F}_t$ on $[1, t]$ will remove $F_1 + \frac{F_T - F_1}{T-1}(t-1)$. This projection residual is asymptotically equivalent to the residual by projecting the true process F_t on $[1, t]$. Thus, the KPSS test based on such residuals has a second-level Brownian bridge as its limiting distribution, as shown in Kwiatkowski et al. (1992). This proves part 1 of Theorem 3.2.

By the definition of $\widehat{\Delta e}_{it}$,

$$\Delta X_{it} - \overline{\Delta X_i} = \hat{\lambda}_i' \widehat{\Delta F}_t + \widehat{\Delta e}_{it}. \tag{A.12}$$

Subtracting (A.12) from (A.11) and noting $\widehat{\Delta F}_t = \Delta F_t - \overline{\Delta F}$, we have

$$\widehat{\Delta e}_{it} = \Delta e_{it} - \overline{\Delta e_i} - (\hat{\lambda}_i - \lambda_i)(\Delta F_t - \overline{\Delta F}).$$

Then $\tilde{e}_{it} = \sum_{s=2}^{t} \Delta \hat{e}_{is}$ is given by

$$\begin{aligned}\tilde{e}_{it} &= e_{it} - e_{i1} - \frac{(e_{iT} - e_{i1})}{T}(t-1) \\ &\quad - (\hat{\lambda}_i - \lambda_i)\left[F_t - F_1 - \frac{(F_T - F_1)}{T}(t-1)\right].\end{aligned} \tag{A.13}$$

Because $\hat{\lambda}_i - \lambda_i = O_p(T^{-1/2})$, the last term of (A.13) is negligible if F_t is I(0). By projecting $\tilde{e}_{it}$ on $[1, t]$, the projection residual will further remove the effects due to $e_{i1} + \frac{(e_{iT} - e_{i1})}{T}(t-1)$. Thus, the KPSS test based on the demeaned and detrended $\hat{e}_{it}^0$ is asymptotically equivalent to the one based on the residual from a projection of e_{it} on $[1, t]$. Thus, the limiting distribution is a second-level Brownian bridge. This proves part 2 of Theorem 3.2.

If F_t is I(1), the last term of (A.13) is no longer negligible. We need to project $\tilde{e}_{it}$ on $[1,\ t; F_{1t}, \ldots F_{\bar{k}t}]$. The projection will purge the effect of F_t, the linear trends, the term e_{i1}, and $(\hat{\lambda}_i - \lambda_i)' F_1$ in (A.13). The resulting residual is asymptotically equal to the residual by projecting the true process e_{it} on $[1,\ t; F_{1t}, \ldots F_{\bar{k}t}]$. The limiting distribution of the KPSS test on such residuals is derived in Shin (1994). This proves part 3 of Theorem 3.2. ∎

Proof of Theorem 3.3. Part 1 is easier than part 2. We thus consider part 2. The MSB test is based on $\tilde{e}_{it}$ in Equation (A.13) (no further demeaning and detrending). Because $(\hat{\lambda}_i - \lambda_i) = O_p(T^{-1/2})$, the last term of (A.13) is $O_p(1)$ whether F_t is I(1) or I(0). Thus,

$$\tilde{e}_{it} = e_{it} - e_{iT}\frac{t-1}{T} + O_p(1).$$

Under the null hypothesis that e_{it} is I(1), for $t = [Tr]$,

$$\frac{\tilde{e}_{it}}{\sqrt{T}} = \frac{e_{it}}{\sqrt{T}} - \frac{e_{iT}}{\sqrt{T}}\left(\frac{t-1}{T}\right) + \frac{1}{\sqrt{T}}O_p(1) \Rightarrow \sigma_{i,\varepsilon}[B_i(r) - rB_i(1)],$$

where $\sigma^2_{i,\varepsilon}$ is the long-run variance of $\Delta e_{it} = \varepsilon_{it}$ and $B_i(r)$ is a Brownian motion process. It follows that

$$\frac{1}{T^2}\sum_{t=1}^{T}\tilde{e}^2_{it} = \frac{1}{T}\sum_{t=1}^{T}\left(\frac{\tilde{e}_{it}}{\sqrt{T}}\right)^2 \Rightarrow \sigma^2_{i,\varepsilon}\int_0^1 V_i(r)^2 dr,$$

where $V_i(r) = B_i(r) - rB_i(1)$. Dividing the preceding equation by a consistent estimator of $\sigma^2_{i,\varepsilon}$ leads to the desired result.

References

Andrews, D. W. K., and J. Monahan (1992), "An Improved Heteroskedasticity and Autocorrelation Consistent Covariance Matrix Estimator," *Econometrica*, 60, 953–66.

Bai, J. S. (2003), "Inference on Factor Models of Large Dimensions," *Econometrica*, 71(1), 135–72.

Bai, J. S. (2004), "Estimating Cross-section Common Stochastic Trends in Nonstationary Panel Data," *Journal of Econometrics*, 51, 243–73.

Bai, J., and S. Ng (2002), "Determining the Number of Factors in Approximate Factor Models," *Econometrica*, 70(1), 191–221.

Bai, J., and S. Ng (2004), "A PANIC Attack on Unit Roots and Cointegration," *Econometrica*, 72, 1127–77.

Banerjee, A., M. Marcellino, and C. Osbat (2001), "Testing for PPP: Should we Use Panel Methods?," mimeo, European University Institute.

Berk, K. N. (1974), "Consistent Autoregressive Spectral Estimates," *The Annals of Statistics*, 2, 489–502.

Caner, M., and L. Kilian (2001), "Size Distortions of Tests of Null Hypothesis of Stationarity: Evidence and Implications for the PPP Debate," *Journal of International Money and Finance*, 20(5), 639–57.

Choi, I. (2001), "Unit Root Tests for Panel Data," *Journal of International Money and Finance*, 20, 249–72.

Elliott, G., T. J. Rothenberg, and J. H. Stock (1996), "Efficient Tests for an Autoregressive Unit Root," *Econometrica*, 64, 813–36.

Engel, C. (2000), "Long Run PPP May Not Hold After All," *Journal of International Economics*, 51, 243–73.

Hadri, K. (2000), "Testing for Stationarity in Heterogeneous Panel Data," *Econometrics Journal*, 3, 148–61.

Harvey, A. C. (2001), "A Unified Approach to Testing for Stationarity and Unit Roots," mimeo, University of Cambridge.

Hobijn, B., P. Franses, and M. Ooms (1998), "Generaltions of the KPSS Test for Stationarity," Econometric Institute Report 9802, Erasmus Unversity.

Im, K., M. Pesaran, and Y. Shin (2003), "Testing for Unit Roots in Heterogeneous Panels," *Journal of Econometrics*, 115(1), 53–74.

Jansson, M. (2001), "Stationarity Testing with Covariates," mimeo, University of California Berkeley.

Kwiatkowski, D., P. Phillips, P. Schmidt, and Y. Shin (1992), "Testing the Null Hypothesis of Stationarity Against the Alternative of a Unit Root," *Journal of Econometrics*, 54, 159–78.

Levin, A., C. F. Lin, and J. Chu (2002), "Unit Root Tests in Panel Data: Asymptotic and Finite Sample Properties," *Journal of Econometrics*, 98(1), 1–24.

Leybourne, S., and P. McCabe (1994), "A Consistent Test for a Unit Root," *Journal of Business and Economic Statistics*, 12(2), 157–66.

MacKinnon, J. (1994), "Approximate Asymptotic Distribution Functions for Unit-root and Cointegration Tests," *Journal of Business and Economic Statistics*, 12, 167–77.

Maddala, G. S., and S. Wu (1999), "A Comparative Study of Unit Root Tests with Panel Data and a New Simple Test," *Oxford Bulletin of Economics and Statistics*, Special Issue, 631–52.

Ng, S., and P. Perron (2001), "Lag Length Selection and the Construction of Unit Root Tests with Good Size and Power," *Econometrica*, 69(6), 1519–54.

O'Connell, P. (1998), "The Overvaluation of Purchasing Power Parity," *Journal of International Economics*, 44, 1–19.

Pedroni, P. (1995), "Panel Cointegration: Asymptotic and Finite Sample Properties of Pooled Time Series Tests with an Application to the PPP Hypothesis: New Results," working paper, Indiana University, 95–113.

Perron, P., and S. Ng (1996), "Useful Modifications to Unit Root Tests with Dependent Errors and their Local Asymptotic Properties," *Review of Economic Studies*, 63, 435–65.

Perron, P., and S. Ng (1998), "An Autoregressive Spectral Density Estimator at Frequency Zero for Nonstationarity Tests," *Econometric Theory*, 14, 560–603.

Phillips, P. C. B., and S. Ouliaris (1990), "Asymptotic Properties of Residual Based Tests for Cointegration," *Econometrica*, 58, 165–93.

Quah, D. (1994), "Exploiting Cross-section Variations for Unit Root Inference in Dynamic Panels," *Economics Letters*, 44, 1–9.

Rothenberg, T. (2000), "Testing for Unit Roots in AR and MA Models," in *Applications of Differential Geometry to Econometrics* (ed. by P. Marriott, and M. Salmon), Cambridge, UK: Cambridge University Press, pp. 281–93.

Sargan, J. D., and A. Bhargava (1983), "Testing for Residuals from Least Squares Regression Being Generated by Gaussian Random Walk," *Econometrica*, 51, 153–74.

Schwert, G. W. (1989), "Tests for Unit Roots: A Monte Carlo Investigation," *Journal of Business and Economic Statistics*, 7, 147–60.

Shin, Y. (1994), "A Residuals Based Test for the Null of Cointegration Against the Alternative of No Cointegration," *Econometric Theory*, 10(1), 91–115.

Stock, J. H. (1990), "A Class of Tests for Integration and Cointegration," mimeo.

Stock, J. H., and M. W. Watson (2002), "Forecasting Using Principal Components from a Large Number of Predictors," *Journal of the American Statistical Association*, 97, 1167–79.

CHAPTER 19

Testing for Unit Roots in Panel Data: An Exploration Using Real and Simulated Data

Bronwyn H. Hall and Jacques Mairesse

ABSTRACT

This paper presents the results of a Monte Carlo study that compares the small sample performance of various unit root tests in short panels using simulated data that mimic the time series and cross sectional properties of commonly used firm level variables. Our conclusion is that in the presence of firm-level heteroskedasticity two methods are preferred, depending on the nature of the preferred alternative: the simplest method based on the ordinary least squares regression of the variable under consideration on its own lag and a version with a more complex alternative hypothesis suggested by Im, Pesaran, and Shin. The paper also reports the results of using these tests for sales, employment, investment, R&D, and cash-flow in three panels of large French, Japanese and US manufacturing firms. In most cases our data reject the presence of a unit root in favor of a first order autoregressive model with a very high autoregressive coefficient, so high that fixed effects are of negligible additional importance in the model.

1. INTRODUCTION

In this paper, we investigate the properties of several unit root tests in short panel data models using simulated data that look like the data typically encountered in studies on firm behavior. This investigation arose from a previous exploration of a simple question – could we find a simple parsimonious model that accounts for the time series properties of key observable variables characterizing the behavior of individual firms: sales, employment, investment, R&D, and cash flow or profits in France, Japan and the United States.[1] We started from a fairly general autoregressive model in the spirit of Holtz-Eakin, Newey, and Rosen (1988) where the heterogeneity across firms is accounted by an individual-specific intercept or firm fixed effect and a firm-specific variance of the random disturbance. We proceeded in estimation by using the GMM methodology. Our estimates, however, were both imprecise and suggestive of the presence of finite sample bias.[2] We therefore investigated the properties of our estimator using two very simple but quite different data generating processes that approximated

[1] This exploration (see Hall and Mairesse, 2001) was itself a follow up on Hall, Mairesse, Branstetter, and Crepon (1999).

[2] These estimates are documented in Hall and Mairesse (2001).

our data fairly well (random walk vs. fixed effect with no autoregression) and concluded that the first step in constructing a parsimonious univariate model for such data should probably be a test for stationarity, because the presence of a unit root will invalidate the commonly used GMM specification.[3]

Testing for stationarity in panel data models is also per se a matter of interest and it can be more directly motivated. It seems fairly intuitive that, within the general class of models where heterogeneity is restricted to an individual fixed effect, the times series behavior of an individual variable should often be well approximated either as an autoregressive process with a small positive coefficient and large fixed effects or as an autoregressive process with a near-unit root and negligible individual fixed effects. Both alternatives can be nested in a single model, in which the test of the former against the latter is a panel data unit root test. One expects, however, that such test might not perform well in a short panel, owing in particular to the problem of unobserved initial conditions and incidental parameter estimation. Trying to assess the properties of the available tests in a realistic setting is therefore of practical importance.

In recent years the econometrics literature has proposed a number of tests for unit roots in panel data. We confine our attention to the six of them that are valid when the number T of time periods (years in our case) is small and the number N of individuals (firms in our case) is large, that is those that are consistent when T is fixed and $N \to \infty$.[4] We describe these six tests in detail in Section 2 of the paper. They vary in several dimensions: (1) the degree of heterogeneity across individuals that is allowed for; (2) serial correlation, heteroskedasticity, and robustness to nonnormality; and (3) whether they follow the Wald, likelihood ratio, or Lagrange Multiplier (LM) testing principles (see Table 19.1). All of them treat the presence of a unit root, implying nonstationarity, as the null hypothesis; and the absence of unit root, or stationarity, as the alternative hypothesis.

The first test we will consider is based on CMLE (conditional maximum likelihood estimation) and is the most restrictive in terms of the assumptions necessary for validity. Then comes the HT (Harris–Tzavalis) test, which is based on bias-adjusted least-squares dummy variable (LSDV) or within estimation and therefore allows nonnormality but not heteroskedasticity.[5] We also consider a version of CMLE suggested by Kruiniger (1999b) which allows for heteroskedasticity across units and time separately and is slightly more general

[3] For a more complete discussion of the problems with GMM estimation when the data are nearly nonstationary, see Blundell and Bond (1998).

[4] We have omitted all the tests that rely on the $T \to \infty$ assumption for validity, because such tests are inappropriate for the usual data on firms. See Quah (1994) and Levin and Lin (1993) for examples of these kinds of tests. The six tests we consider are those that are appropriate for the fixed T, large N case, and were known to us as of the time of writing (2001).

[5] In fact, if we interpret the CMLE as a quasi-likelihood method, using it to construct a test is no more or less restrictive than the HT test. Both require homoskedasticity but not normality, and in principle, either one could be modified to yield a test robust to heteroskedasticity, as we do in the case of CML estimation.

Table 19.1. *Panel data unit root tests summary*

Test	Testing principle	Description	Assumptions[b]	Heterogeneity across i	Heterogeneity across t[b]
CMLE	Wald, LR	Conditional maximum likelihood (t and LR tests)	independence across i, homoskedasticity, normality[a]	means	variances
CMLE–HS	Wald, LR	Conditional maximum likelihhod (t and LR tests)	independence across i, normality[a]	means; variances	variances
HT	Wald	Bias and variance–corrected LSDV test	independence across i, homoskedasticity, no serial correlation	means	none
OLS	LM	Pooled OLS (SUR) regression with T equations	independence across i	variances	variances
IPS	Wald	Average of individual Dickey–Fuller tests without trend	independence across i	means, rho, variances	none
IPS-trend	Wald	Average of individual Dickey–Fuller tests with trend	independence across i	means, rho, trend, variances	none

[a] Could be interpreted as a quasi-maximum-likelihood estimator.
[b] The CMLE, SUR, and IPS tests can all be modified to allow for autocorrelation of the disturbances, as long as it is constant across individuals. However, the implementation in this paper assumes no serial correlation.

than HT. The next test, which we will label OLS, allows for heteroskedasticity and nonnormality, and takes a very different approach by viewing the panel data regression as a system of T year regressions. It is based on the fact that ordinary least squares is a consistent estimator for the model with a lagged dependent variable and no fixed effects.[6] The IPS (Im–Pesaran–Shin) test is the last one we consider. It also takes a different approach from the foregoing, in that it views the panel data regression as a system of N individual regressions and is based on the combination of independent Dickey–Fuller tests for these N regressions. Besides allowing heteroskedasticity, serial correlation, and nonnormality, this test also allows for heterogeneity of trends and of the lag coefficient under the alternative hypothesis of no unit root.

In the paper, we present the results of a Monte Carlo study that compares the small sample performance of these tests using simulated data mimicking the time series and cross sectional properties of the firm sales, employment, investment, R&D, and cash flow variables in three panel data samples for French, Japanese, and US manufacturing firms. The design and calibration of the simulations, which are based on the most persistent of these series, the R&D in the US, is explained in Section 3. The results of the eight different Monte Carlo experiments are presented in Section 4. Our tentative conclusion is that the simplest method, the OLS test based on the ordinary least-squares regression of the variable considered on its own lag, may actually be the best for microdata panels similar to ours. The OLS estimator is unbiased under the null of a unit root (when the fixed effect vanishes) and its estimated standard error can easily be corrected for both serial correlation and heteroskedasticity of the disturbances.

In Section 5, we also report the results of using all six tests for the five variables in our three samples. In most cases our data reject nonstationarity in favor of stationarity, but with a very high autoregressive coefficient, so high that it is not necessary to include fixed effects in the model. We very briefly conclude in Section 6.

2. TESTING FOR UNIT ROOTS IN PANEL DATA: AN OVERVIEW

The most general form of the model considered in this paper can be written as follows:

$$\begin{aligned} y_{it} &= \alpha_i + \delta t + u_{it} \quad t = 1, \ldots, T; i = 1, \ldots, N \\ u_{it} &= \rho u_{i,t-1} + \varepsilon_{it} \quad \varepsilon_{it} \sim [0, \sigma_t^2 \sigma_\varepsilon^2(i)] \\ &\Rightarrow y_{it} = (1-\rho)\alpha_i + (1-\rho)\delta t + \rho y_{i,t-1} + \varepsilon_{it} \quad |\rho| < 1 \\ \text{or } y_{it} &= y_{i,t-1} + \delta + \varepsilon_{it} \quad \varepsilon_{it} \sim [0, \sigma_t^2 \sigma_\varepsilon^2(i)] \quad \rho = 1 \end{aligned} \tag{2.1}$$

[6] This test is implicit in early work by Macurdy (1985). It was suggested to us by Steve Bond (see Bond, Nauges, and Windmeijer, 2002).

That is, we consider the possibility of either an autoregressive model with a fixed effect or a random walk with drift. In both cases, we allow for individual and time-varying heteroskedasticity of a proportional form in addition. In some cases, the various tests described below are valid only for more restrictive versions of the model in Equation (2.1).

Table 19.1 provides a schematic view of the various unit root tests we consider and the assumptions under which they are valid. All the tests assume conditional independence across the units, and all except the OLS test allow for individual-specific means in estimation. The CMLE, IPS, and OLS tests can potentially accommodate a flexible correlation structure among the disturbances, as long as it is the same for all units. However, in this paper we have assumed throughout that the disturbances are serially uncorrelated (in the presence of the lagged dependent variable) and constructed our tests accordingly. With the possible exception of the investment and cash flow series, this assumption is satisfied by our real data series.[7] In the text that follows, we indicate how to modify the tests to accommodate serial correlation.

The estimators associated with these tests allow for various degrees of heterogeneity in addition to the individual-specific means. In particular, all of them except the Harris–Tzavalis test and the homoskedastic version of the CMLE test allow the variance of the disturbances to be different for each unit.[8] The IPS tests, which are based on N individual regressions, allow both the trend and the serial correlation coefficient to vary across the units under the alternative, in addition to the mean and variance. We now describe the tests in more detail.

2.1. Maximum Likelihood Methods with Homoskedastic Errors

Lancaster and Lindenhovius (1996), Kruiniger (1999b), and Binder, Hsiao, and Pesaran (2000) have independently pointed out that the conditional maximum likelihood estimate of the linear model with individual effects and a lagged dependent variable is well-identified and consistent even when there is a unit root, that is, even when the coefficient is one, although this value is on the boundary of the parameter space. This fact can be used to construct a likelihood ratio test of $\rho = 1$ versus $\rho < 1$.[9]

7 The autocorrelograms of the level and first-differenced series are shown in Figures 19.1 and 19.2 of Appendix B. The autocorrelation of the first differences at lag one is less than 0.25 for most of the series. For our "model" series, US log R&D, the autocorrelation is −0.04.

8 The HT test could probably be modified to accommodate heteroskedasticity also, but the version we use here does not.

9 The consistency result is of considerable interest in its own right because the corresponding least-squares (LSDV) estimator is neither consistent (as $N \to \infty$, T fixed) nor unbiased when $\rho = 1$. Appendix C contains a table of results for the OLS levels, LSDV, and first-differenced OLS and IV for our simulated data. Except for level estimates of the models with no effects, the estimates are very far away from the true values.

The model to be estimated is the one given in Equation (2.1), but with homoskedastic disturbances and without the time trend:[10]

$$\begin{aligned}&y_{it} = \alpha_i + u_{it} \qquad u_{it} = \rho u_{i,t-1} + \varepsilon_{it} \quad |\rho| < 1\\ &y_{it} = y_{i,t-1} + \varepsilon_{it} \qquad\qquad\qquad\quad \rho = 1\\ &\varepsilon_{it} \sim N[0, \sigma_\varepsilon^2]\end{aligned} \tag{2.2}$$

The null hypothesis is $\rho = 1$ and therefore no fixed effects. If we denote the vector of T observations for an individual as $y_i = (y_{i1}, y_{i2}, \ldots, y_{iT})$ and similarly for u_i and $y_{i,-1}$, we can write this model in vector form as

$$\begin{aligned}&y_i = \alpha_i \iota + u_i\\ &E[u_i u_i'] = \sigma_\varepsilon^2 V_\rho = \frac{\sigma_\varepsilon^2}{1-\rho^2}\begin{bmatrix} 1 & \rho & \cdots & \rho^{T-1} \\ \rho & 1 & \cdots & . \\ . & . & \cdots & . \\ \rho^{T-1} & \rho^{T-2} & \cdots & 1 \end{bmatrix}\end{aligned} \tag{2.3}$$

or, in differenced form,

$$Dy_i = Du_i \tag{2.4}$$

Given normal disturbances, Dy_i has the joint normal distribution with mean zero and variance–covariance matrix $\Sigma = \sigma_\varepsilon^2 DV\rho D' = \sigma_\varepsilon^2 \Phi$ and the joint log likelihood for this model is the following:[11]

$$\begin{aligned}\log L(\rho, \sigma^{2\prime}\{y_{it}\}) &= -\frac{N(T-1)}{2}\log(2\pi) - \frac{N}{2}\log|\Sigma| - \frac{1}{2}\sum_{i=1}^{N}(Dy)'\Sigma^{-1}Dy_i\\ &= -\frac{N(T-1)}{2}\log(2\pi) - \frac{N(T-1)}{2}\log\sigma^2 - \frac{N}{2}\log|\Phi|\\ &\quad -\frac{1}{2\sigma^2}\sum_{i=1}^{N}(Dy_i)'\Phi^{-1}Dy_i\end{aligned} \tag{2.5}$$

Kruiniger (1999b) gives conditions under which maximizing this likelihood over the parameter space $(\rho, \sigma_\varepsilon^2) \in (-1, 1] \times (0, \infty)$ will yield consistent estimates.[12] Under those conditions, a conventional t test for $\rho = 1$ is a test for a unit root. Alternatively, one could construct a likelihood ratio test by comparing the likelihood evaluated at its unconstrained maximum with the likelihood evaluated at $\rho = 1$.[13]

[10] For simplicity of presentation, we omit the overall time trend in the presentation that follows. In practice, we removed year-specific means from the data before estimation.

[11] Higher-order serial correlation of the disturbances can be allowed for by assuming that u_{it} follows an autoregressive model with a unit root and an order $p < T$ and deriving the appropriate V_ρ matrix that corresponds to this model.

[12] Basically, he requires stationarity if $\rho < 1$ and boundedness of the initial condition if $\rho = 1$. Also note that one cannot evaluate this likelihood as written if $\rho = 1$. See Kruiniger (1999b) for details of the form of the likelihood when there is a unit root; that version collapses to the random walk model under that condition.

[13] Lancaster and Lindenhovius (1996) took a slightly different approach, using the same model and likelihood, but considering the Bayesian estimator with a flat prior on the effects (which drops

2.2. Maximum Likelihood Methods with Heteroskedastic Errors

A common feature of data on firms, even in logarithms, is that the variances of the errors vary across firms, which implies that estimation using methods assuming homoskedasticity is likely to produce wrong standard errors, at the least.[14] Consider the following variation of (2.2), which omits the trend:

$$\begin{aligned} y_{it} &= \alpha_i + u_{it} \qquad i = 1, \ldots, N; t = 1, \ldots, T \\ u_{it} &= \rho u_{i,t-1} + \varepsilon_{it} \qquad \varepsilon_{it} \sim \text{i.i.d. } N\left(0, \sigma_i^2 \sigma_t^2\right) \end{aligned} \tag{2.6}$$

At first glance, it might appear that estimation of such a model using maximum likelihood methods would lead to an incidental parameter problem due to the fact that the number of firm level parameters σ_i^2 grows with the sample size N. However, Kruiniger (1999b) shows that maximum likelihood estimation of the structural parameters $(\rho, \sigma_t^2, t = 1, \ldots, T)$ of this model is consistent. The likelihood function for this model is given by

$$\begin{aligned} \log L(\rho, \{\sigma_t^2\}; \{y_{it}\}) = &- \frac{(T-1)}{2} \log(2\pi) - \frac{(T-1)}{2} \sum_{i=1}^{N} \log(\sigma_i^2) \\ &- \frac{N}{2} \log |\Phi| - \sum_{i=1}^{N} \frac{1}{2\sigma_i^2} (Dy_i)' \Phi^{-1} Dy_i \end{aligned} \tag{2.7}$$

where

$$\Phi = DPV_pPD' \text{ and } P = \text{diag}(\sigma_t) \tag{2.8}$$

Thus, Φ depends only on the structural parameters ρ and $\{\sigma_t^2\}$. Given the values for these parameters, it is clear that the maximum likelihood estimate of the individual-specific variances has the usual form

$$\widehat{\sigma_i^2} = \frac{1}{T-1} tr(\Phi^{-1} Z_i) \qquad \text{where} \quad Z_i = Dy_i (Dy_i)' \tag{2.9}$$

We use this fact to concentrate the $\widehat{\sigma_i^2}$, $i = 1, \ldots, N$ out of the likelihood function, which greatly simplifies estimation. See Appendix A for details of the estimation procedure.

out due to the differencing) and a prior of $1/\sigma$ for σ. This yields the joint marginal posterior density

$$p(\rho, \sigma^2 | \{y_{it}\}) = -\frac{N(T-1)}{2} \log(2\pi) - \log\sigma - \frac{N}{2} \log|\Sigma| - \frac{1}{2} \sum_{i=1}^{N} (Dy_i)' \Sigma^{-1} Dy_i$$

The mode of this density is consistent for ρ and σ as $N \to \infty$. They do not consider the case $\rho = 1$. In practice, we found that evaluating the mode of this posterior gave essentially the same answer as the CMLE for samples of our size, so we do not report simulation results for this test.

[14] In fact, this is one of the several reasons why researchers often prefer methods based on the GMM methodology.

2.3. Harris–Tzavalis Test

The test for unit roots in panel data proposed by Harris and Tzavalis (1999) begins with the observation that the "Nickell" bias in the estimated coefficient of the lagged endogenous variable using LSDV (within) estimation is of known magnitude under some simple assumptions about the data generating process. Using this fact, one can compute bias adjustments to both the estimated coefficient and its standard error analytically and use the corrected estimates to construct a test of known size for a unit root.

HT consider the model in Equation (2.2) and show that under the null hypothesis that $\rho = 1$, the least-squares dummy variable estimator has a limiting normal distribution of the following form:

$$\sqrt{N}(\rho - 1 - B_2) \rightarrow N(0, C_2) \tag{2.10}$$

where $B_2 = -3/(T+1)$ and $C_2 = 3(17T^2 - 20T + 17)/[5(T-1)(T+1)^3]$. Using this fact, it is straightforward to base a t test on the estimated ρ, standardized by its mean and variance. Like the CMLE test, this test requires homoskedasticity and no serial correlation in the disturbances, although because it is based on a least-squares estimator, it does not require normality.[15]

2.4. OLS-pooled estimation under the null

Bond, Nauges, and Windmeijer (2002) suggest that a test based on the model estimated under the null of a unit root (that is, where OLS can be used because there are no "fixed effects") may have more power when the true ρ is near unity. The advantage of such a test is that it does not require bias adjustment and it is easy to allow for heteroskedasticity by using a seemingly unrelated regression framework with each year being an equation.[16] Because there are no incidental parameters under the null, asymptotics in the N dimension are straightforward and the test relies on those.

We base our OLS test on the following model:

$$\begin{aligned} &y_{it} = \delta_t + \rho y_{i,t-1} + \varepsilon_{it} \qquad i = 1, \ldots, N; t = 1, \ldots, T \\ &E[\varepsilon_i \varepsilon_i'] = \Omega \end{aligned} \tag{2.11}$$

where $\varepsilon_i = (\varepsilon_{i1}\varepsilon_{i2}, \ldots, \varepsilon_{iT})$. The method of estimation is seemingly unrelated regression with a weighting matrix based on the first stage estimate of Ω.[17]

[15] Neither normality nor homoskedasticity are required for the test based on the CMLE to be consistent either, although if these assumptions fail the conventional standard error estimates will be inconsistent and a "sandwich" estimator should be used.

[16] As in the well-known Dickey–Fuller test, if the disturbances are serially correlated, it will be necessary to include enough lagged values of the differenced y in the regression to render the disturbances uncorrelated in order to achieve consistency of the estimator.

[17] As discussed earlier, we have assumed a diagonal form for Ω. If the εs are serially correlated within individuals, lagged values of the differenced y's should be added to the model until the residuals are approximately uncorrelated, as in the augmented Dickey–Fuller test.

Although the estimation method assumes homoskedasticity, we report standard errors that are robust to heteroskedasticity across the firms.

2.5. The IPS Method

Recent work by Im, Pesaran, and Shin (1997, hereafter IPS) suggests another approach of testing for unit roots, one that allows for more heterogeneity of behavior than that allowed for by the conditional maximum likelihood or least-squares dummy variable approach. They assume a heterogeneous version of the model in Equation (2.1):

$$y_{it} = (1 - \rho_i)\alpha_i + \rho_i y_{i,t-1} + \varepsilon_{it} \qquad (2.12)$$
$$i = 1, \ldots, N; t = 1, \ldots, T$$

where initial values y_{i0} are given, and they test for the null hypothesis that ρ_i is unity for all observations versus an alternative that some of the ρ_is are less than one. Under the null there is no fixed effect, while under the alternative each fixed effect is equal to $(1 - \rho_i)\alpha_i$. They propose tests based on the average over the individual units of a Lagrange multiplier test of the hypothesis that $\rho_i = 1$ as well as tests based on the average of the augmented Dickey–Fuller statistics, which they find to have somewhat better finite sample properties than the LM test.

As in Dickey and Fuller's original work, IPS also propose tests based on a model with a deterministic trend:

$$y_{it} = (1 - \rho_i)\alpha_i + (1 - \rho_i)\delta_i t + \rho_i y_{i,t-1} + \varepsilon_{it} \qquad (2.13)$$
$$i = 1, \ldots, N; t = 1, \ldots, T$$

We will use both these tests for our data, since there is reason to believe that trends do exist in the real series. Note that an important difference between these models and the models considered in the previous sections is that both the lag coefficient and the trend coefficient are allowed to differ across firms under the alternative hypothesis of stationarity.

When we applied these tests to our simulated data, we found that allowing the data to choose the length of augmenting lag p invariably yielded a p of either 2 or 3, even though the data were in all cases generated from models where $p = 0$ was appropriate.[18] Because of this fact and the fact that the table of critical values supplied by IPS breaks down for the case where the number of observations is around ten and the length of the augmenting lag is greater than zero, we chose to focus on the tests where $p = 0$ is imposed. This makes our IPS test comparable to the others reported in this paper, which do not allow for serial correlation in the disturbances.

[18] Previous versions of this paper reported the results of tests using $p = 2$ and/or $p = 3$ on our simulated data and concluded that they had low power and were inaccurate even when we increased the number of time series observations per firm to twenty, especially when $p = 3$ was the "optimal" choice of augmenting lag.

3. DESIGN AND CALIBRATION OF SIMULATIONS

In Section 5 of the paper we apply the panel data unit root tests to five firm-level variables drawn from three countries: employment, sales, cash flow, investment, and R&D in France, Japan, and the United States. In our previous explorations using these data, we found that the process which describes each of the variables is more similar across countries than across variables, and that the variables can be clearly ranked by their long run "persistence": sales, employment, and R&D on the one hand versus cash flow and investment on the other. The behavior of the latter variables most resembled that of a stationary process.

Figures 19.1 and 19.2 in Appendix B display the autocorrelograms of the levels and first differences of our series for the three countries. These confirm the high autocorrelation in levels and the low autocorrelation in differences that characterize these data. They also show that the series most likely to exhibit the properties of a random walk is the log R&D series for all three countries, which has essentially zero autocorrelation at all lags in first differences. Therefore, we chose to investigate the performance of these tests on simulated data calibrated to match the time series and cross-sectional characteristics of the log R&D series for the United States.[19]

The general form of model or data generation process (DGP) that we use in our simulations is the model in Equation (2.1) with and without heteroskedasticity across individuals and no heteroskedasticity over time.[20] We considered eight cases: the two extreme cases of a random walk with drift ($y_{it} = y_{it-1} + \delta + \varepsilon_{it} \Rightarrow \Delta y_{it} = \delta + \varepsilon_{it}$) and a pure fixed effects process ($y_{it} = \alpha_i + \delta t + \varepsilon_{it} \Rightarrow \delta + \Delta y_{it} = \delta + \Delta\varepsilon_{it}$), and the six intermediate cases of a dynamic panel with or without fixed effects, taking $\rho = 0.3$, 0.9, and 0.99 and allowing α_i to vary across all individual units or imposing it to be the same for all of them. For each of these eight DGPs, we also consider both a homoskedastic version with $\sigma_\varepsilon^2(i)$ constant across the units, and a heteroskedastic one with $\sigma_\varepsilon^2(i)$ varying across the units.

Except for the random walk case, when constructing the DGPs we ensured that the resulting process satisfied covariance stationarity, in order to guarantee the consistency of the maximum likelihood estimators.[21] The exact calibration of the DGPs we used was derived from the first and second moments of the log R&D series and its first differences, as described here. The values of these

[19] The details of the construction of our datasets and the results of GMM estimation using these data are given in Hall et al. (1999) and Hall and Mairesse (2001).

[20] In estimation, we removed year means before performing any of the tests. For fixed T, this makes no difference to the asymptotic properties of the tests. As shown by Binder et al. (2000), when T is fixed, allowing for time-specific effects in estimation has no effect on the estimates of the other parameters so that these effects may be removed from the observed series before estimation.

[21] This stationary version of the dynamic panel model with fixed effects is denoted as Model I by Nickell (1981) and Lancaster (2002).

moments were the following:

$$\begin{array}{ll} E[y] = 2.50 & E[\Delta y] = 0.085 \\ V[y] = 4.599 & V[\Delta y] = 0.0672 \end{array} \tag{3.1}$$

The necessary parameters are δ, ρ, μ_α, σ_ε^2, and σ_α^2. Conditional on α_i (or unconditional, because it is differenced out), we have the following two equations:

$$\begin{array}{l} E(\Delta y) = \delta \\ V(\Delta y) = 2\sigma_\varepsilon^2/(1+\rho) \end{array} \tag{3.2}$$

Given a value for ρ and the moments of our data, these equations give values of δ and σ_ε^2. Once we have values for δ, ρ, and σ_ε^2, to obtain the mean and variance of the distribution of the α_is, we use the moments of the series in levels:

$$\begin{array}{l} E(y) = \mu_\alpha + \delta(T+1)/2 \\ V(y) = \sigma_\alpha^2 + \frac{\sigma_\varepsilon^2}{1-\rho^2} \end{array} \tag{3.3}$$

Values of the parameters derived from the moment estimators specified by equations (3.2) and (3.3) are used to generate the simulated data as follows:

$$\begin{array}{l} \begin{bmatrix} \alpha_i \\ y_{i0} \end{bmatrix} \sim N\left[\begin{pmatrix} \mu_\alpha \\ E(y) \end{pmatrix}, \begin{pmatrix} \sigma_\alpha^2 & \sigma_\alpha^2 \\ \sigma_\alpha^2 & V(y) \end{pmatrix} \right] \\ \varepsilon_{it} \sim N[0, \sigma_\varepsilon^2] \\ y_{it} = (1-\rho)\alpha_i + (1-\rho)\delta t + \rho y_{i,t-1} + \varepsilon_{it}, \end{array} \tag{3.4}$$

where $N(\mu,\sigma^2)$ denotes the normal distribution with mean μ and variance σ^2. It is straightforward to show that the processes generated according to these DGPs are mean and covariance stationary as long as $|\rho| < 1$.[22] The AR(1) models without individual-specific effects are generated simply by assuming that $\sigma_\alpha^2 = 0$.[23]

For the nonstationary random walk case, we used the following four equations to determine the parameters δ, σ_ε^2, μ_0, and σ_0^2:

$$\begin{array}{l} E(\Delta y) = \delta \\ V(\Delta y) = \sigma_\varepsilon^2 \\ E(y) = \mu_o + \delta(T+1)/2 \\ V(y) = \sigma_0^2 + \sigma_\varepsilon^2(T+1)/2 \end{array} \tag{3.5}$$

[22] For the "fixed effect" model, covariance stationarity is ensured by requiring the covariance of the initial condition y_{i0} and the individual-specific effect α_i to be σ_α^2.

[23] In this case it was not possible to reproduce the first two moments of the level and differenced series exactly, due to the fact that we were simulating a process that did not match our real data series that well. In all the other cases, the first two moments exactly identified the parameters needed.

and generated the process using this model:

$$\begin{aligned} y_{i0} &\sim N(\mu_0, \sigma_0^2) \quad i = 1, \ldots, N \\ \varepsilon_{it} &\sim N(0, \sigma_\varepsilon^2) \quad t = 1, \ldots, T \\ y_{it} &= \delta + y_{i,t-1} + \varepsilon_{it} \end{aligned} \tag{3.6}$$

In the heteroskedastic case, we allowed the variance of the shock ε to vary across firms. Inspection of the data revealed that a lognormal distribution of this variance was appropriate and the DGP we used was the following:

$$\begin{aligned} \sigma_\varepsilon^2(i) &= (1 - \rho^2)\sigma_\omega^2(i) \\ \log \sigma_\omega^2(i) &\sim N[-2.05, 1.33] \end{aligned} \tag{3.7}$$

4. RESULTS OF SIMULATIONS

Table 19.2(a) reports the results of simulations designed to explore the behavior of the t test and likelihood ratio test based on CML estimates.[24] The likelihood function used is given in Equation (2.5) and the null hypothesis is that $\rho = 1$. As described earlier, the data used for the simulation were generated by processes whose first and second moments were chosen to match those of the log of real R&D for the United States. The table has two panels, one for data generated with homoskedastic disturbances and one for data generated with firm-specific variances as described in Equation (3.7).

The first column of each panel gives the average value of ρ and its standard deviation that was estimated by CMLE. In both cases (homoskedastic and heteroskedastic), these are fairly close to the true value, with a hint of downward bias for very large values of ρ. The next two columns give the average t statistic for the hypothesis that $\rho = 1$, its standard deviation, and the size or power of the test as measured by the number of rejections at the 5 percent level of significance. The following two columns give the average likelihood ratio statistic for the same hypothesis and its size or power. It is clear from the table that both tests have approximately the correct size and considerable power when applied to homoskedastic data, except when the autoregressive coefficient is near unity (equal to 0.99). Note that when the true ρ is at or near unity, occasionally estimation using the simulated data will converge to the boundary of the parameter space, that is, $\rho = 1$. In this case, we consider the hypothesis to be accepted, but we record the probability that this happens in the table (about 25 percent of the time for the random walk, and about 10 percent of the time for $\rho = 0.99$).

[24] Estimating this model by maximum likelihood requires computation using the $T-1$ by $T-1$ variance–covariance matrix, which is perhaps why the CMLE method has not been used much in the literature. We implemented the estimator as an MLPROC in TSP 4.5 and found it to be fairly well-behaved, converging in five or six iterations if a good estimate of σ^2 (one based on the actual data) was used as a starting value along with a positive ρ. The TSP code is available as an example at http://www.tspintl.com.

Table 19.2a. *Testing for nonstationarity using CML estimator simulated data ($T = 12; N = 200$)*

Estimation method: DGP:	Conditional ML with homoskedastic variance Homoskedastic variance (1000 draws)					Conditional ML with homoskedastic variance Heteroskedastic variance (100 draws)				
Time series process for DGP	Estimated ρ (s.d.)	Average t statistic on ρ (s.d.)	Empirical probability of rejection $(\# = 1.0)^a$	Average likelihood ratio test	Empirical probability of rejection $(\# = 1.0)^a$	Estimated ρ (s.d.)	Average t statistic on ρ (s.d.)	Empirical probability of rejection $(\# = 1.0)^a$	Average likelihood ratio test	Empirical probability of rejection $(\# = 1.0)^a$
Random walk	0.992 (.012)	−0.53 (0.65)	0.060 (0.23)	0.53 (1.17)	0.028 (0.23)	0.984 (.023)	−0.81 (1.05)	0.14 (0.24)	1.29 (2.95)	0.10
AR(1) with $\rho = 0.3$	0.298 (.025)	−29.2 (1.0)	1.000	563.3 (33.5)	1.000	0.264 (.043)	−29.1 (1.0)	1.00	560.7 (24.2)	1.00
AR(1) with $\rho = 0.9$	0.899 (.021)	−4.82 (0.95)	0.999	22.3 (8.1)	1.000	0.900 (.022)	−4.83 (1.00)	1.00	22.5 (34.9)	1.00
AR(1) with $\rho = 0.99$	0.986 (.016)	−0.83 (0.78)	0.145 (0.12)	1.13 (1.88)	0.090 (0.12)	0.984 (.017)	−0.82 (0.86)	0.16 (0.07)	1.39 (2.50)	0.10
Fixed effect	−0.002 (.024)	−42.6 (1.2)	1.000	1031.6 (45.1)	1.000	−0.002 (.039)	−42.6 (2.0)	1.00	1031.5 (72.1)	1.00
AR(1) FE, $\rho = 0.3$	0.300 (.024)	−29.1 (1.0)	1.000	560.8 (32.5)	1.000	0.305 (.046)	−28.9 (2.0)	1.00	554.0 (63.4)	1.00
AR(1) FE, $\rho = 0.9$	0.900 (.021)	−4.79 (0.94)	1.000	22.6 (8.2)	1.000	0.890 (.039)	−5.24 (1.69)	0.96	27.0 (14.8)	0.96
AR(1) FE, $\rho = 0.99$	0.986 (.014)	−0.78 (0.72)	0.123 (0.11)	1.00 (1.57)	0.063 (0.11)	0.979 (.025)	−1.29 (1.26)	0.28 (0.18)	2.57 (4.38)	0.23

Notes: In the first row, the column labeled size or power is the size of a one-tailed t test for $\rho < 1$ with nominal size 0.05.
In the other rows, it is the empirical probability of rejection by such a test.
The model estimated is $y(i,t) = a(i) + a(t) + \rho\, y(i, t-1) + e(i,t)$.
The method of estimation is conditional maximum likelihood (fixed effects conditioned out).
[a] The fraction that converged to exactly $\rho = 1.00$ is given in parentheses, when it is nonzero.

The final four columns of the table repeat the same exercise, but this time using data that were simulated to have the heteroskedasticity visible in our empirical series. The results are similar, with the following two exceptions: The sizes of the tests are slightly too large and the power against the alternative with fixed effects and $\rho = 0.99$ is actually slightly greater (note that this test is not size-adjusted). Both results are presumably due to the same fact: introducing some heterogeneity into the process reduces the probability of accepting the very restrictive null model if we impose homoskedasticity where it does not exist.

Table 19.2b reports the results of testing the hypothesis $\rho = 1$ using the CML estimator that allows for heteroskedasticity on data generated by the same homoskedastic and heteroskedastic processes as were used for Table 2a. The results are similar, except that the size of the test is now much too large and its corresponding power against large ρ alternatives much greater. Also, the t test on ρ now gives a result that is quite different from the likelihood ratio test in the large ρ case. It appears that estimating the individual variances leads to results that bias the estimated ρ downwards in samples of our size, in spite of the consistency result of Kruiniger (1999a, b).

The first panel of Table 19.3 shows the results of applying the HT test for a unit root to our simulated data. Not surprisingly, the results are very similar to those for the homoskedastic CMLE, with good power except when ρ is near unity, and too large a size when applied to heteroskedastic data. Thus, when N is large and T small, it makes little difference to the result whether we use the inconsistent LSDV estimator and bias-adjust the answer, or the consistent CMLE estimator, which does not require bias adjusting. The underlying model was the same in both cases, and both require homogeneity of the coefficients and variances under the null and the alternative.

The next test considered is the pooled OLS test, which relaxes the assumptions of constant variance across time and individuals. The results of this test conducted on our simulated data are shown in the final columns of Table 19.3. The size of the test is approximately correct for both homoskedastic and heteroskedastic data, and the power is considerably better than for the Harris–Tzavalis or CMLE tests when ρ is near one. In spite of this fact, but not surprisingly, the estimates of ρ are severely biased toward one when the data are generated under an alternative with a fixed firm effect. This test does almost as well on heteroskedastic data as on homoskedastic, reflecting the fact that both the estimator and the standard error estimates are consistent under the null in both cases.

The results of conducting the IPS test with and without individual-specific trends, but with a zero augmenting lag imposed are shown in Table 19.4. The statistic shown is the average of an augmented Dickey–Fuller statistic for the N unit root tests on the individual series, together with empirical size or power of the test, based on critical values given in the tables of the IPS paper. We present results for a model both with and without a firm-specific time trend; all results are for data with a single cross-sectional mean removed in each year (that is, a

Table 19.2b. *Testing for nonstationarity using CML–HS estimator simulated data* ($T = 12; N = 200$)

Estimation method: DGP:	Conditional ML with homoskedastic variance Homoskedastic variance (1000 draws)					Conditional ML with homoskedastic variance Heteroskedastic variance (100 draws)				
Time series process for DGP	Estimated ρ (s.d.)	Average t statistic on ρ (s.d.)	Empirical probability of rejection (# = 1.0)[a]	Average likelihood ratio test	Empirical probability of rejection (# = 1.0)[a]	Estimated ρ (s.d.)	Average t statistic on ρ (s.d.)	Empirical probability of rejection (# = 1.0)[a]	Average likelihood ratio test	Empirical probability of rejection (# = 1.0)[a]
Random walk	0.987 (.016)	−1.15 (0.73)	0.120	6.65 (5.28)	0.720	0.989 (.009)	−0.97 (0.55)	0.16	7.76 (3.93)	0.88
AR(1) with $\rho = 0.3$	0.299 (.025)	−26.4 (1.0)	1.000	515.4 (30.3)	1.000	0.290 (.023)	−26.8 (1.0)	1.00	525.8 (29.9)	1.00
AR(1) with $\rho = 0.9$	0.925 (.031)	−2.94 (1.05)	0.960	20.6 (9.5)	0.960	0.921 (.031)	−3.33 (1.24)	0.88	21.1 (8.0)	1.00
AR(1) with $\rho = 0.99$	0.982 (.016)	−1.33 (1.74)	0.320	6.33 (3.87)	0.720	0.986 (.011)	−1.03 (0.54)	0.12	5.21 (5.09)	0.52
Fixed effect	−0.006 (.025)	−39.3 (1.2)	1.000	954.1 (46.3)	1.000	−0.003 (.028)	−39.1 (1.4)	1.00	950.2 (49.8)	1.00
AR(1) FE, $\rho = 0.3$	0.307 (.032)	−26.2 (1.3)	1.000	508.2 (39.6)	1.000	0.399 (.027)	−26.5 (1.2)	1.00	517.3 (33.0)	1.00
AR(1) FE, $\rho = 0.9$	0.908 (.030)	−3.75 (1.25)	0.960	19.2 (8.9)	0.960	0.912 (.036)	−3.54 (1.39)	0.88	20.7 (8.0)	0.96
AR(1) FE, $\rho = 0.99$	0.984 (.013)	−1.07 (0.56)	0.200	4.59 (6.00)	0.560	0.985 (.018)	−1.12 (0.67)	0.16	7.62 (5.14)	0.84

Notes: In the first row, the column labeled size or power is the size of a one-tailed t test for $\rho < 1$ with nominal size 0.05.
In the other rows, it is the empirical probability of rejection by such a test.
The model estimated is $y(i, t) = a(i) + a(t) + \rho\, y(i, t-1) + e(i, t)$.
The method of estimation is conditional maximum likelihood (fixed effects conditioned out).
[a]The fraction that converged to exactly $\rho = 1.00$ is given in parentheses, when it is nonzero.

Table 19.3. *Testing for nonstationarity simulated data ($T = 12$, $N = 200$, 1,000 draws per simulation)*

DGP:	Harris–Tzavalis method[a] homoskedastic errors		Harris–Tzavalis method[a] heteroskedastic errors		Pooled OLS without fixed effects[b] homoskedastic errors			Pooled OLS w/o fixed effects[b] heteroskedastic errors		
Time series process for DGP	Average t statistic on ρ (s.d.)	Empirical probability of rejection	Average t statistic on ρ (s.d.)	Empirical probability of rejection	Estimate of ρ (s.d.)	Average t statistic on ρ (s.d.)	Empirical probability of rejection	Estimate of ρ (s.d.)	Average t statistic on ρ (s.d.)	Empirical probability of rejection
Random walk	−0.004 (1.03)	0.055	−0.16 (1.87)	0.210	1.000 (.003)	0.002 (1.09)	0.060	1.000 (.005)	−0.01 (1.04)	0.056
AR(1) with $\rho = 0.3$	−32.0 (1.3)	1.000	−31.98 (2.18)	1.000	0.298 (.022)	−35.9 (2.3)	1.000	0.298 (.022)	−35.8 (2.3)	1.000
AR(1) with $\rho = 0.9$	−4.00 (1.07)	0.987	−4.00 (1.04)	0.990	0.900 (.010)	−11.2 (1.2)	1.000	0.899 (.010)	−11.3 (1.3)	1.000
AR(1) with $\rho = 0.99$	−0.45 (1.02)	0.113	−0.43 (1.00)	0.111	0.990 (.003)	−3.41 (1.08)	0.963	0.990 (.003)	−3.49 (1.13)	0.953
Fixed effect	−47.0 (1.2)	1.000	−46.87 (2.21)	1.000	0.999 (.001)	1.82 (1.11)	0.558	0.982 (.006)	−6.63 (0.71)	1.000
AR(1) FE, $\rho = 0.3$	−31.9 (1.2)	1.000	−31.95 (2.29)	1.000	0.999 (.001)	−1.69 (1.11)	0.516	0.989 (.003)	−5.21 (0.90)	0.999
AR(1) FE, $\rho = 0.9$	−3.97 (1.07)	0.990	−4.12 (1.88)	0.909	0.995 (.002)	−2.41 (1.09)	0.771	0.997 (.002)	−1.94 (1.04)	0.610
AR(1) FE, $\rho = 0.99$	−0.40 (1.01)	0.106	−0.46 (1.79)	0.240	0.993 (.0003)	−2.93 (1.07)	0.891	1.000 (.001)	−0.77 (1.06)	0.207

Notes: In the first row, the column labeled size or power is the size of a one-tailed t test for $\rho < 1$ with nominal size 0.05.
In the other rows, it is the empirical probability of rejection by such a test.
The method of estimation is ordinary least squares (within or LSDV).
The method of estimation is seemingly unrelated regression, allowing for correlation across time.
[a]The model estimated is $y(i,t) = a(i) + a(t) + \rho y(i,t-1) + e(i,t)$.
[b]The model estimated is $y(i,t) = a(t) + \rho y(i,t-1) + e(i,t)$.

Table 19.4. *Testing for nonstationarity simulated data ($T = 12$, $N = 200$, 100 draws per simulation)*

	IPS Test (no trend, augmenting lags = 0)						IPS Test (trend, augmenting lags = 0)					
DGP disturbances:	Homoskedastic			Heteroskedastic			Homoskedastic			Heteroskedastic		
Data generating process	Average t statistic on ρ	Std. dev. of t statistic	Empirical probability of rejection	Average t statistic on ρ	Std. dev. of t statistic	Empirical probability of rejection	Average t statistic on ρ	Std. dev. of t statistic	Empirical probability of rejection	Average t statistic on ρ	Std. dev. of t statistic	Empirical probability of rejection
Random walk	−0.09	1.05	0.05	−0.22	1.06	0.07	−0.10	1.12	0.11	−0.12	1.15	0.09
AR(1) with $\rho = 0.3$	−41.15	1.13	1.00	−41.15	1.17	1.00	−23.97	1.21	1.00	−23.96	1.24	1.00
AR(1) with $\rho = 0.9$	−4.90	1.10	1.00	−4.86	1.22	0.99	−0.77	1.06	0.21	−0.92	1.11	0.23
AR(1) with $\rho = 0.99$	−0.68	1.14	0.19	−0.73	1.17	0.19	−0.39	1.30	0.18	−0.22	1.23	0.12
Fixed effect	−67.84	1.40	1.00	−67.74	1.26	1.00	−46.46	1.47	1.00	−46.35	−1.38	1.00
AR(1) FE, $\rho = 0.3$	−41.00	1.06	1.00	−41.03	1.16	1.00	−23.88	1.20	1.00	−23.77	1.19	1.00
AR(1) FE, $\rho = 0.9$	−4.74	1.02	1.00	−4.97	1.12	1.00	−1.04	1.20	0.27	−0.88	0.99	0.24
AR(1) FE, $\rho = 0.99$	−0.49	1.07	0.14	−0.62	1.05	0.19	−0.36	1.10	0.10	−0.31	1.13	0.10

Notes: In the first row, the column labeled size or power is the size of a one-tailed t test for $\rho < 1$ with nominal size 0.05. In the other rows, it is the empirical probability of rejection by such a test.

full set of time dummies), as suggested by IPS and as was done for the other tests considered in this paper. Because our simulated data have no time trend, we expect that removal of these means will make the two tests (with and without allowing for a time trend) equivalent. However, due to the small sample of time periods available, requiring estimation of another parameter (the trend) could be somewhat costly in terms of degrees of freedom and may reduce the power of the test for samples of our size.

The results using the simulated data confirm this: the test without a trend has more power to discriminate between a random walk and a fixed effect plus AR(1) model than that with a trend. In the latter case, the size is too large and the power against an alternative with $\rho = 0.9$ considerably weaker, whether or not there are also fixed effects in the model. Not surprisingly, the results are similar for the simulated heteroskedastic data. Because the IPS test is based on individual-level Dickey–Fuller tests, it allows for firm-level heterogeneity in variances, so adding this feature to the data generating process has only a limited effect on the results of the tests.

In Table 19.5 we present a summary of our results from these various tests. The first three columns contain results from the tests that are invalid when there is firm-level heteroskedasticity and last five columns results from those tests that remain valid in that case. We note first that the size of the former group of tests is larger than the theoretical value in the presence of the kind of heteroskedasticity displayed by our data, implying that these tests for a unit root will reject the null too often. In addition, all the tests have very low power against a near-unit root autoregressive model with fixed effects; recall that in this case, the fixed effect itself is multiplied by $(1 - \rho)$ and therefore very small, so this result is not that surprising.

Most of the other tests have good size properties, with the exception of the conditional maximum likelihood estimates that allow for firm-specific heteroskedasticity. The most likely reason for the problems with the t test based on the CML–HS estimates is that our standard error estimates are conventional and it is necessary to use a "sandwich" estimator here; see Kruiniger (1999b). The empirical standard error for the results in Table 19.2b was approximately 25–50 percent greater than the estimated standard error. However, we note also that our estimate of ρ does seem to be slightly downward biased in this case (see Table 19.2b), in spite of the fact that it is consistent, which implies that the rate of asymptotic convergence may be slow.

Restricting attention to the tests with the correct size that are robust to heteroskedasticity, we are left with the OLS and IPS tests without a trend. The results of these tests differ significantly, in that the OLS test has by far the greater power against near-unit root alternatives, whether or not there is a fixed effect. The difference in power is doubtless due to the difference in alternative hypotheses, in that the OLS test considers $\rho = 1$ versus a single value of $\rho < 1$ for all individuals, whereas the IPS test considers $\rho = 1$ for all individuals versus $\rho < 1$ for at least one individual. Our simulated alternatives were all closer to the former model than the latter, so it is not surprising that the test does better in this case.

Table 19.5. *Empirical probability of rejection panel data unit root tests*

Time series process for DGP	Invalid under Heteroskedasticity			Allows for Heteroskedasticity				
	CMLE t test	CMLE LR test	*HT* test	CML–HS t test	CML–HS LR test	Pooled OLS test	IPS Test (no trend)	IPS Test (trend)
				Homoskedastic data				
Random walk	0.06	0.04	0.06	**0.12**	**0.72**	0.06	0.05	**0.11**
AR(1) with $r = 0.3$	1.00	1.00	1.00	1.00	1.00	1.00	1.00	1.00
AR(1) with $r = 0.9$	0.99	1.00	0.99	0.96	0.96	1.00	1.00	**0.21**
AR(1) with $r = 0.99$	**0.15**	**0.09**	**0.11**	**0.32**	0.72	0.96	**0.19**	**0.18**
Fixed effect	1.00	1.00	1.00	1.00	1.00	0.56	1.00	1.00
AR(1) FE, $r = 0.3$	1.00	1.00	1.00	1.00	1.00	0.52	1.00	1.00
AR(1) FE, $r = 0.9$	1.00	1.00	0.99	0.96	0.96	0.77	1.00	**0.27**
AR(1) FE, $r = 0.99$	**0.12**	**0.07**	**0.11**	**0.32**	0.56	0.89	**0.14**	**0.10**
				Heteroskedastic data				
Random walk	**0.14**	**0.10**	**0.21**	**0.16**	**0.88**	0.06	0.07	**0.09**
AR(1) with $r = 0.3$	1.00	1.00	1.00	1.00	1.00	1.00	1.00	1.00
AR(1) with $r = 0.9$	1.00	1.00	0.99	0.88	1.00	1.00	0.99	**0.23**
AR(1) with $r = 0.99$	**0.16**	**0.10**	**0.11**	**0.12**	0.52	0.95	**0.19**	**0.12**
Fixed effect	1.00	1.00	1.00	1.00	1.00	1.00	1.00	1.00
AR(1) FE, $r = 0.3$	1.00	1.00	1.00	1.00	1.00	1.00	1.00	1.00
AR(1) FE, $r = 0.9$	0.96	0.96	0.91	0.88	0.96	0.61	1.00	**0.24**
AR(1) FE, $r = 0.99$	**0.28**	**0.23**	**0.24**	**0.16**	0.84	**0.21**	**0.19**	**0.10**

Notes: Figures in bold deviate from the correct size by 0.05 or more, or have power less than 0.50.

5. RESULTS OF UNIT ROOT TESTS FOR OBSERVED DATA

We now turn to our results for the observed data; details on the construction of these datasets and their characteristics are given in Hall et al. (1999).[25] Table 19.6 reports the results of the tests for unit roots on the real data, highlighting the tests which reject nonstationarity at the 5 percent level in bold. The HT test, which assumes homogenous time series processes that have no residual serial correlation beyond the first lag give essentially the same result as the IPS test without a trend: sales and employment are nonstationary and the remaining series are stationary, except for R&D in the United States. The IPS test with a trend is somewhat more likely to find a unit root, but as we have seen, the power of this test is low when the first order serial correlation is high.

The final two columns show one of our preferred tests for these data, the OLS test. Unlike the others, this test, which has more power against the alternative of stationarity with a very high autocorrelation coefficient, rejects nonstationarity in all cases except sales and employment in Japan. The estimated AR(1) coefficients are very high, so it is not surprising that we encountered difficulties with the tests that allow for the presence of fixed effects. Using the estimated values of $\rho - 1$, we conducted a small analysis of variance on these fifteen numbers which showed that the coefficients for US and Japan could not be distinguished, while those for France were slightly more negative (implying lower serial correlation). The most significant differences were between investment and cash flow on the one hand and sales, employment, and R&D on the other, with the latter having a differenced coefficient of almost zero, as we saw in Figures 19.1 and 19.2.

Table 19.7 shows the results for the tests based on the two different CML estimates. Those based on the homoskedastic estimator give results very similar to the HT test, as they should, since they rely on the same set of assumptions about the DGP. As in the earlier table, these results clearly reject nonstationarity for investment and cash flow, and for R&D in France and Japan. However, almost all of the real series reject the presence of a unit root when the heteroskedastic version of the CMLE is used. We suspect that some of the rejection may be due to the fact that both the coefficient and the standard error estimates seem to be systematically biased downward for samples of our size. Finally, we note that a likelihood ratio test for constancy of variances clearly rejects in all cases.[26]

[25] A description may also be found in an unpublished appendix to this paper, available at http://emlab.berkeley.edu/users/bhhall/index.html.

[26] Strictly speaking, this test is not valid asymptotically, since it is a test based on a number of parameters that grows at the same rate as the sample. Nevertheless, we report it as a heuristic indicator of the large difference allowing for heteroskedasticity makes to the likelihood.

Table 19.6. *Estimation and testing with normality and homoskedasticity (Scientific sector firms)*

	Harris–Tzavalis test		IPS tests		Pooled OLS estimates	
	AR (1) coeff.[a]	Normal test[b]	No trend[c] (*p*-value)	With trend[d] (*p*-value)	AR (1) Coeff[e]	*t* test[f] (*p*-value)
Sales						
US	0.819 (0.012)	0.069 (0.018)	1.31 (0.904)	2.73 (0.997)	**0.9925 (0.0020)**	**−3.69 (0.000)****
France	0.758 (0.017)	0.008 (0.020)	−0.10 (0.460)	2.10 (0.982)	**0.9923 (0.0024)**	**−3.19 (0.001)****
Japan	0.811 (0.013)	0.061 (0.012)	2.17 (0.985)	3.13 (0.999)	0.9956 (0.0025)	−1.76 (0.040)
R&D						
US	0.749 (0.014)	−0.001 (0.018)	5.27 (0.999)	6.68 (0.999)	**0.9916 (0.0028)**	**−2.98 (0.002)****
France	**0.648 (0.019)**	**−0.102 (0.020)****	**−1.93 (0.027)****	0.33 (0.629)	**0.9903 (0.0031)**	**−3.13 (0.001)****
Japan	**0.644 (0.015)**	**−0.106 (0.012)****	**−1.72 (0.043)****	2.25 (0.988)	**0.9869 (0.0029)**	**−4.49 (0.000)****
Investment						
US	**0.454 (0.020)**	**−0.296 (0.018)****	**−5.96 (0.000)****	**−2.81 (0.002)****	**0.9877 (0.0029)**	**−4.22 (0.000)****
France	**0.405 (0.023)**	**−0.245 (0.020)****	**−5.24 (0.000)****	**−3.99 (0.000)****	**0.9519 (0.0055)**	**−8.79 (0.000)****
Japan	**0.344 (0.020)**	**−0.406 (0.012)****	**−9.13 (0.000)****	**−4.49 (0.000)****	**0.9682 (0.0049)**	**−6.55 (0.000)****
Employment						
US	0.828 (0.012)	0.078 (0.018)	4.16 (0.999)	2.25 (0.988)	**0.9903 (0.0023)**	**−4.15 (0.000)****
France	0.890 (0.014)	0.140 (0.020)	6.89 (0.999)	1.81 (0.965)	**0.9849 (0.0024)**	**−6.32 (0.000)****
Japan	0.863 (0.010)	0.113 (0.012)	4.59 (0.999)	7.94 (0.999)	0.9983 (0.0015)	−1.09 (0.138)
Cash flow						
US	**0.576 (0.020)**	**−0.174 (0.018)****	−0.86 (0.194)	−0.18 (0.427)	**0.9874 (0.0028)**	**−4.39 (0.000)****
France	**0.235 (0.024)**	**−0.515 (0.020)****	**−9.92 (0.000)****	**−8.41 (0.000)****	**0.9480 (0.0088)**	**−5.89 (0.000)****
Japan	**0.468 (0.018)**	**−0.282 (0.012)****	**−2.57 (0.005)****	3.12 (0.999)	**0.9896 (0.0030)**	**−3.43 (0.000)****

[a] the estimated coefficient of the lag dependent variable in a regression with fixed effects. These estimates contain “Nickell” bias.
[b] the same coefficient corrected for bias and standardized by the SEE under the null (see Harris and Tzavalis, 1999, for details).
[c] Bold cells are those that reject a unit root at the 5 percent level of significance (conventional, not adjusted for true size).
[d] IPS tests are conducted with year means removed from the data, using a zero augmenting lag.
[e] the AR1 coefficient estimated using SUR; standard error robust to HS and serial correlation.
[f] the SUR t-statistic for $\rho = 0$, robust to heteroskedasticity and serial correlation.
** denotes lower tail significance at the 0.01 level.

Table 19.7. *CML estimation and testing with homoskedasticity and heteroskedasticity (Scientific sector firms)*

	CMLE estimates (Kruiniger 1999a,b)				CMLE estimates with heteroskedastic errors				Test for heteroskedasticity	
Variable (Country)	AR (1) coeff[a]	LR test[b] (*p*-value)	Variance[c] estimate	Log[d] likelihood	AR (1) coeff[e]	LR test[f] (*p*-value)	Mean of[g] variance est.	Log[h] likelihood	LR test[i]	*p*-value[j] (DF)
Sales										
US	>= 1.000	0.0 (1.000)	0.0272 (0.0008)	861.7	**0.9969 (0.0007)****	**50.4 (0.000)**	0.0316	1603.5	1483.5	0.000 (214)
France	0.998 (0.020)	0.01 (0.938)	0.0201 (0.0007)	917.8	**0.9700 (0.0114)****	–	0.0235	1414.8	994.1	0.000 (166)
Japan	>= 1.000	0.0 (1.000)	0.0152 (0.0005)	1481.0	**0.9984 (0.0006)****	**80.3 (0.000)**	0.0167	2199.8	1437.6	0.000 (231)
R&D										
US	>= 1.000	0.0 (1.000)	0.0668 (0.0020)	−148.3	**0.9951 (0.0023)****	**74.7 (0.000)**	0.0777	866.9	2030.3	0.000 (214)
France	**0.903 (0.025)****	**14.2 (0.000)**	0.0658 (0.0022)	−92.9	**0.9641 (0.0152)****	**9.9 (0.002)**	0.0697	498.2	1182.4	0.000 (166)
Japan	**0.901 (0.021)****	**21.5 (0.000)**	0.0152 (0.0034)	−720.7	**0.9611 (0.0081)****	**41.93 (0.000)**	0.1291	237.3	1916.0	0.000 (231)
Investment										
US	**0.643 (0.024)****	**173.7 (0.000)**	0.313 (0.009)	−1794.1	**0.720 (0.028)****	**94.2 (0.000)**	0.3239	−1294.9	998.6	0.000 (214)
France	**0.574 (0.027)****	**186.2 (0.000)**	0.362 (0.012)	−1470.1	**0.581 (0.031)****	**157.8 (0.000)**	0.3417	−1197.0	546.1	0.000 (166)
Japan	**0.516 (0.024)****	**279.2 (0.000)**	0.287 (0.009)	−1608.7	**0.506 (0.028)****	**251.0 (0.000)**	0.2549	−1224.4	768.6	0.000 (231)
Employment										
US	>= 1.000	0.0 (1.000)	0.0265 (0.0008)	888.6	0.9973 (0.0025)	**48.7 (0.000)**	0.0298	1696.3	1615.3	0.000 (214)
France	>= 1.000	0.0 (1.000)	0.0113 (0.0004)	1413.6	**0.9982 (0.0004)****	**107.0 (0.000)**	0.0075	2281.6	1736.0	0.000 (166)
Japan	>= 1.000	0.0 (1.000)	0.0031 (0.0001)	3227.2	**0.9990 (.0003)****	**210.6 (0.000)**	0.0034	4222.5	1990.6	0.000 (231)
Cash flow										
US	**0.863 (0.026)****	**25.9 (0.000)**	0.1178 (0.0038)	−656.1	0.997 (0.004)	**8.3 (0.004)**	0.1003	112.0	1536.2	0.000 (184)
France	**0.453 (0.034)****	**180.7 (0.000)**	0.3055 (0.0123)	−927.4	**0.517 (0.037)****	**104.5 (0.000)**	0.5441	−476.1	902.6	0.000 (114)
Japan	**0.784 (0.023)****	**73.2 (0.000)**	0.0769 (0.0023)	−262.6	0.995 (0.004)	**78.3 (0.000)**	0.0753	486.7	1498.5	0.000 (210)

Notes: Bold cells are tests that reject a unit root at the 5 percent level of significance (conventional, not adjusted for true size).
Note that the standard errors for the CML–HS estimates are conventional, and therefore incorrect.
[a] the AR1 coefficient estimated using ML conditioned on the effects (individual means removed).
[b] The likelihood ratio test corresponding to column (a) estimates.
[c] the estimated variance of the disturbance corresponding to the estimate in (2.1).
[d] The log likelihood corresponding to column (a) estimates.
[e] the AR1 coefficient estimated using ML conditioned on the effects and with $\mathrm{Var}(e) = \mathrm{sig}(I)\mathrm{sig}(t)$.
[f] The likelihood ratio test corresponding to column (e) estimates.
[g] the average of the estimated variances across the firms, with $\mathrm{sig}(t = 1)$ normalized at unity.
[h] The log likelihood corresponding to column (e) etimates.
[i] the likelihood ratio test for the heteroskedastic variances with degrees of freedom $= (N + T - 2)$.
[j] The *p*-value associated with the test in column (i)
** denotes lower tail significance at the 0.01 level.

6. CONCLUSIONS

We began this investigation with the question of whether it was possible to distinguish between a model with a unit root, or a model with a fixed effect and low order serial correlation when describing univariate time series data. Our principal conclusion is that the preferred model for our data is neither; rather it is a model with an extremely high serial correlation coefficient, but one that is less than one.

With respect to the menu of unit root tests for fixed T samples, we have learned several things. The first conclusion from our simulation study of unit root tests is that the pooled OLS test and the IPS test have good power against most alternatives, although results from these tests differ when the alternative includes a coefficient near unity, primarily because they consider two quite different alternatives. Second, CML estimation is surprisingly easy to perform, even in the presence of heteroskedasticity, and may be a useful addition to the panel data arsenal, even if it is not as robust as simple OLS for the very particular problem of unit root testing. Further investigation should explore the reasons for finite sample bias in the heteroskedastic version of the CML estimator.

Substantively, we concluded that a very simple autoregressive model with a coefficient on the lag dependent variable that is near unity is a more parsimonious description of our data than a model with fixed effects. In Table 19.5, we observed that the only test with power against the $\rho = 0.99$ alternative was the OLS test, and in Table 19.6, this is the only test that rejects nonstationarity in favor of stationarity with a very large auto-regressive coefficient for almost all the real series. An alternative interpretation of this result is possible: the OLS test may be inappropriate because the proper alternative is heterogeneous serial correlation across the firms, implying that the IPS test is more appropriate. We have favored the former conclusion, not because we do not believe in heterogeneity of this kind, but because the more parsimonious model seems to describe the data fairly well, and because when serial correlation is this high, whether homogeneous or heterogeneous, the presence or absence of fixed effects is of little import, since they are necessarily quite small.

This fact leads us to a somewhat more controversial view that short panels of firm data are better described as having highly varied and persistent initial conditions rather than permanent unobserved firm effects. This feature of the data has been described by some as "not-so-fixed" firm effects. We would prefer to shift the emphasis in our modeling toward the idea that firm level differences are better captured by the initial condition, with the apparent "permanence" of differences being ascribed to very high serial correlation rather than to some left-out unobserved and permanent difference. We believe that this view of the firm is closer to the reality of firm evolution.

With our results in mind, some future research questions suggest themselves. First is the possibility of testing for the presence of firm-specific drifts or trends. It is certainly feasible to construct a CMLE of the doubly-differenced model in order to test for these, although the data may not have enough power for estimation. Second, given the near unit root behavior of the series, it may be of interest to examine their cointegrating properties. Mairesse, Hall, and Mulkay (1999) have already shown that a well-behaved error-correcting version of an investment equation can be constructed using data to ours, which implies that sales and capital stock are cointegrated and move together in the "long run." The possible interpretive significance of such a result is to unify the commonly observed differences between cross-sectional and time series estimates based on panel data into a single model.

APPENDIX A: CML ESTIMATION WITH HETEROSKEDASTICITY

In this Appendix we describe the computational implementation of the conditional maximum likelihood estimation with heteroskedasticity.[27] The likelihood function we wish to maximize is the following:

$$\log L(\rho, \{\sigma_i^2\}, \{\sigma_t^2\}; \{y_{it}\}) = -\frac{(T-1)}{2}\log(2\pi) - \frac{(T-1)}{2}\sum_{i=1}^{N}\log(\sigma_i^2) - \frac{N}{2}\log|\Phi| - \sum_{i=1}^{N}\frac{1}{2\sigma_i^2}(Dy_i)'\Phi^{-1}Dy_i$$

where Φ is a $T-1$ by $T-1$ matrix that contains powers of ρ and the parameters given by $\sigma_t^2, t = 2, \ldots, T$:[28]

$$\Phi = DPV_\rho PD' \quad \text{and} \quad P = \text{diag}(\sigma_t)$$

Thus evaluating the likelihood involves manipulation of matrices of order of the number of time periods. To do this easily, we make use of the MLPROC procedure in TSP version 4.5. MLPROC takes a procedure that defines a log likelihood function as the output of a sequence of commands and maximizes the value returned by the procedure with respect to the chosen parameters, via repeated calling of the procedure to evaluate the function and its derivatives (numerically).

To simplify the computation of the likelihood as much as possible, we make use of the fact that estimators for $\sigma_i^2, i = 1, \ldots, N$ can be obtained from the first-order condition given values for ρ and the σ_t^2 and concentrate these parameters out of the likelihood function:

$$\sigma_i^2 = \frac{1}{N(T-1)}\sum_{i=1}^{N}(Dy_i)'\Phi^{-1}Dy_i = \frac{1}{N(T-1)}trace\left[\Phi^{-1}Z_i\right]$$

[27] The homoskedastic version is an obvious simplification of the algorithm described here.

[28] Note that the parametrization requires one normalization on the σ_i^2 or σ_t^2 in much the same way that including a second set of dummies in an equation requires an additional exclusion restriction. Our normalization is $\sigma_t^2 = 1$ for $t = 1$.

where

$$Z_i = (Dy_i)'Dy_i \quad \text{and} \quad Z = \sum_{i=1}^{N} Z_i = (Dy)'Dy$$

is the covariance matrix of the first differenced ys. As is well known, when it is possible to concentrate the likelihood, the standard error estimates for the remaining parameters (ρ and σ_t^2, $t = 2, \ldots, T$ in this case) are not affected by this procedure.

The algorithm is therefore the following:

1. Given values for ρ and σ_t^2, $t = 1, \ldots, T$, compute estimates of σ_i^2.
2. Use these estimates to compute the value of the likelihood using the following expression:

$$\begin{aligned}\log L\left(\rho, \left\{\sigma_t^2\right\}; \{y_{it}\}\right) = &-\frac{N(T-1)}{2}\log(2\pi + 1) \\ &-\frac{(T-1)}{2}\sum_{i=1}^{N}\log\left(\sigma_i^2\left[\rho, \left\{\sigma_t^2\right\}\right]\right) \\ &-\frac{N}{2}\log\left|\Phi\left[\rho, \left\{\sigma_t^2\right\}\right]\right|\end{aligned}$$

3. Iterate on 1 and 2 in the usual way, using a gradient method to maximize the likelihood with respect to ρ and σ_t^2.

APPENDIX B: AUTOCORRELOGRAMS OF THE DATA

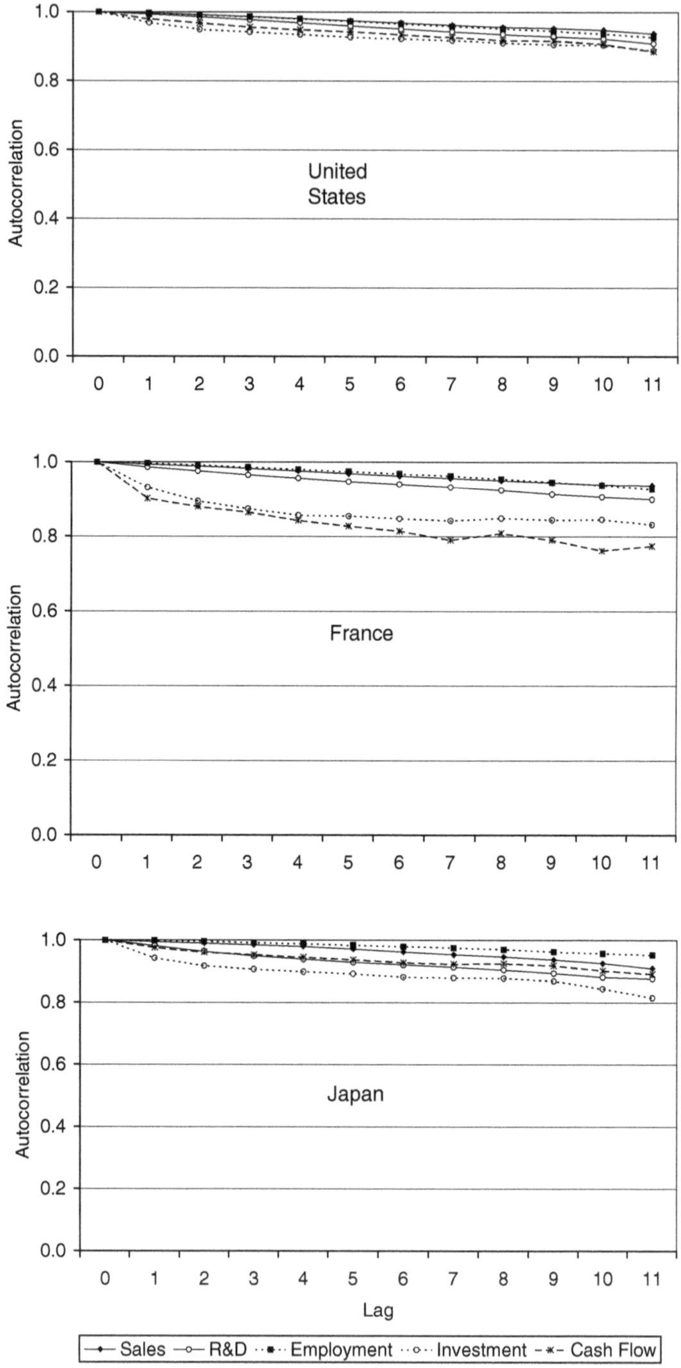

Figure B.1. Autocorrelation functions for logs of real variables.

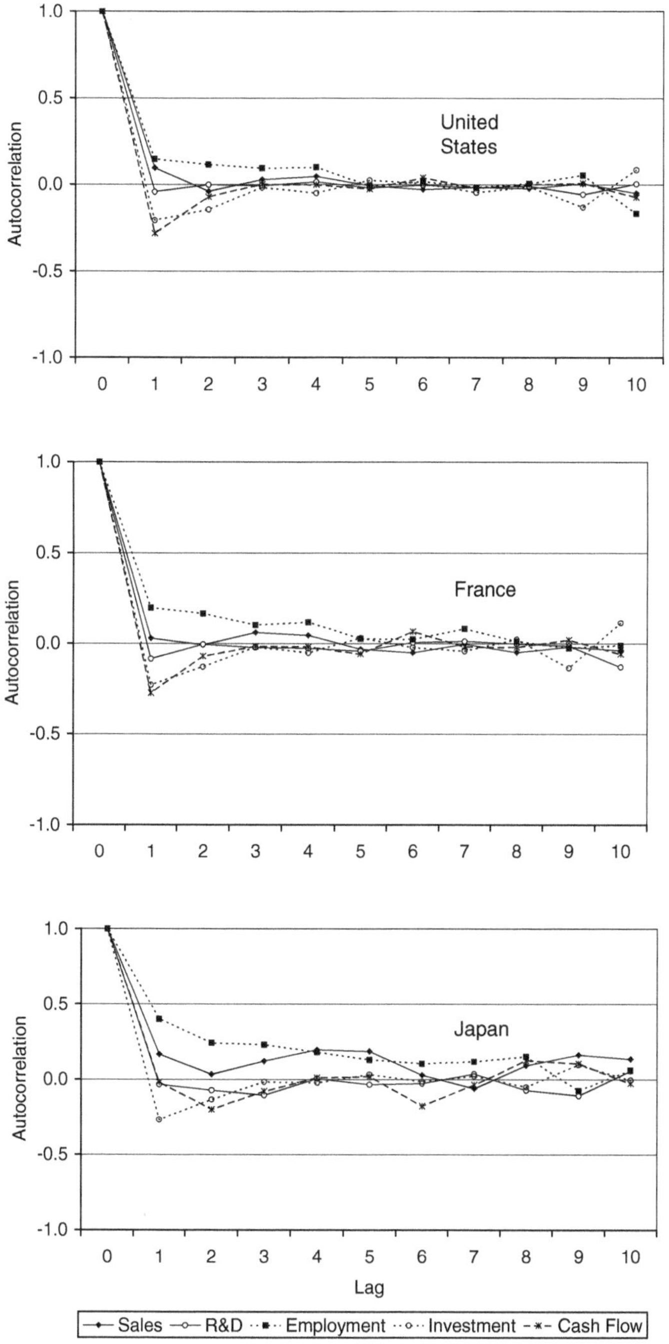

Figure B.2. Autocorrelation functions for differenced logs of real variables.

APPENDIX C: MODEL ESTIMATES USING SIMULATED DATA

Table C.1. *OLS and IV estimates for simulated data ($T = 12$, $N = 200$, 1,000 draws)*

Estimation method		Ordinary least-squares levels			Ordinary least-squares within			Ordinary least-squares differences			Instrumental variables differences		
Time series process for DGP	True value of ρ	Average estimate of ρ	Std. deviation of estimated ρ	Average estimated std. error on ρ	Average estimate of ρ	Std. deviation of estimated ρ	Average estimated std. error on ρ	Average estimate of ρ	Std. deviation of estimated ρ	Average estimated std. error on ρ	Average estimate of ρ	Std. deviation of estimated ρ	Average estimated std. error on ρ
Random walk	1	1.000	0.003	0.003	**0.749**	**0.018**	**0.015**	**−0.001**	**0.026**	**0.025**	0.318	0.718	0.991
AR(1) with $r = 0.3$	0.3	0.300	0.007	0.006	0.288	0.007	0.007	**−0.327**	**0.021**	**0.023**	0.294	0.052	0.058
AR(1) with $r = 0.9$	0.9	0.900	0.004	0.004	**0.822**	**0.012**	**0.010**	**0.125**	**0.029**	**0.024**	0.896	0.026	0.066
AR(1) with $r = 0.99$	0.99	0.990	0.003	0.003	**0.744**	**0.018**	**0.015**	**−0.006**	**0.024**	**0.025**	0.832	0.244	0.405
Fixed effect	0	**0.993**	**0.001**	**0.003**	−0.093	0.021	0.022	**−0.500**	**0.018**	**0.022**	−0.001	0.045	0.043
AR(1), FE, and $r = 0.3$	0.3	**0.993**	**0.001**	**0.003**	**0.182**	**0.021**	**0.022**	**−0.349**	**0.021**	**0.023**	0.300	0.070	0.068
AR(1), FE, and $r = 0.9$	0.9	**0.992**	**0.002**	**0.003**	**0.681**	**0.019**	**0.016**	**−0.046**	**0.024**	**0.025**	0.781	0.278	0.400
AR(1), FE,and $r = 0.99$	0.99	0.993	0.003	0.003	**0.742**	**0.018**	**0.015**	**−0.004**	**0.025**	**0.025**	0.746	0.374	0.562

Notes: The data are simulated using parameters derived from the first and second moments of log R&D in the United States, $E(y) = 2.5$; $V(y) = 4.59$; $E(dy) = 0.085$; $V(dy) = 0.0672$.
The model estimated in panel 1 is $y(i, t) = a0 + \text{delta}^* t + \rho^* y(i, t-1) + e(i, t)$.
The model estimated in panel 2 is $y(i, t) = a(i) + \text{delta}^* t + \rho^* y(i, t-1) + e(i, t)$.
The model estimated in panels 3 and 4 is $dy(i, t) = \text{delta} + \rho^* dy(i, t-1) + e(i, t)$.
The instruments in panel 4 are $dy(i, t-2)$, $dy(I, t-3)$ and $dy(I, t-4)$.

ACKNOWLEDGEMENTS

We are grateful to Karim Abadir, Stephen Bond, Andrew Chesher, Hugo Kruiniger and Neil Shephard for helpful comments on earlier versions of this paper. The paper has also benefited greatly from remarks and useful suggestions from James Stock and two referees.

References

Binder, M., C. Hsiao, and M. H. Pesaran (2000), "Estimation and Inference in Short Panel Vector Autoregressions with Unit Roots and Cointegration," Cambridge, UK: University of Cambridge DAE Working Paper No.0003.

Blundell, R. S., and S. Bond (1998), "Initial Conditions and Moment Restrictions in Dynamic Panel Data Models," *Journal of Econometrics*, 87: 115–43.

Bond, S., C. Nauges, and F. Windmeijer (2002), "Unit Roots and Identification in Autoregressive Panel Data Models: A Comparison of Alternative Tests," photocopy, Institute of Fiscal Studies, London.

Hall, B. H., and J. Mairesse (2001), "A Cautionary Note on Modeling the Univariate Behavior of Panel Data for Firms," paper presented to the German Classification Society Annual Meeting, Munich, Germany, March 14–15.

Hall, B. H., J. Mairesse, L. Branstetter, and B. Crepon (1999), "Does Cash Flow Cause Investment and R&D: An Exploration using Panel Data for French, Japanese, and United States Firms in the Scientific Sector," in *Innovation, Industry Evolution and Employment*, (ed. by D. Audretsch, and R. Thurik), Cambridge: Cambridge University Press.

Harris, R. D. F., and E. Tzavalis (1999), "Inference for Unit Roots in Dynamic Panels where the Time Dimension is Fixed," *Journal of Econometrics*, 91: 201–26.

Holtz-Eakin, D., W. Newey, and H. Rosen (1988), "Estimating Vector Autoregressions with Panel Data," *Econometrica*, 56: 1371–95.

Im, K. S., M. H. Pesaran, and Y. Shin (2003), "Testing for Unit Roots in Heterogeneous Panels," *Journal of Econometrics* 115: 53–74.

Kruiniger, H. (1999a), "GMM Estimation of Dynamic Panel Data Models with Persistent Data," London: Queen Mary and Westfield College Working Paper No. 428.

Kruiniger, H. (1999b), "Conditional Maximum Likelihood Estimation of Dynamic Panel Data Models," London: Queen Mary and Westfield College Working Paper No. 429.

Lancaster, T., and B. Lindenhovius (1996), "Biases in Dynamic Panel Data Models: A Reconsideration," Providence, RI: Brown University Department of Economics Working Paper No. 96-11.

Levin, A., C.-F. Lin, and C.-J. Chu (2002), "Unit Root Tests in Panel Data: Asymptotic and Finite Sample Properties," *Journal of Econometrics*, 108: 1–24.

Macurdy, T. E. (1985), "A Guide to Applying Time Series Models to Panel Data," photocopy, Stanford, CA: Stanford University.

Mairesse, J., B. H. Hall, and B. Mulkay (1999), "Firm-Level Investment in France and in the United States: An Exploration of What we Have Learned in Twenty Years," *Annales d'Economie et de Statistique*, 55–56, 27–69.

Nickell, S. (1981), "Biases in Dynamic Models with Fixed Effects," *Econometrica*, 49: 1399–416.

Quah, D. (1994), "Exploiting Cross-section Variations for Unit Root Inference in Dynamic Data," *Economics Letters*, 44, 9–19.

CHAPTER 20

Forecasting in the Presence of Structural Breaks and Policy Regime Shifts

David F. Hendry and Grayham E. Mizon

ABSTRACT

When no model coincides with a nonconstant data generation process, forecast failure occurs, and noncausal statistical devices may provide the best available forecasts: examples include intercept corrections and differenced-data VARs. However, such models are not a reliable basis for economic policy analyses and may even have no policy implications. Indeed, a "paradox" can result if their forecasts induce policy changes, which in turn alter the data outcome. This suggests correcting statistical forecasts by using the econometric model's estimate of the "scenario" change, and doing so is shown to yield reduced forecast-error biases.

1. INTRODUCTION

As the title of this volume indicates, the majority of Tom Rothenberg's contributions to econometrics and statistics were in the fields of identification and inference. However, we know that Tom has an interest in all areas of econometrics, even though his awareness of the numerous difficulties to be overcome in undertaking applied work has so far led him to concentrate on theoretical research topics. Therefore, we are delighted to offer our chapter on the use of econometric models in forecasting and economic policy analysis as an indication of some more problems – as well as an analysis of how several of these might be overcome.

A personal anecdote will explain our interest. When the first author reported in Hendry (1981) to the UK Parliamentary Select Committee on the Treasury and Civil Service Enquiry into Monetary Policy, he complained about the proliferation of theoretical models of money and the dearth of reliable empirical evidence; a decade later in Hendry (1991), he complained to the same committee (now on Official Economic Forecasting) about the abundance of empirical evidence on forecasting – and the absence of theoretical models thereof! We hope to fill a part of that second gap.

In Hendry and Mizon (2000), we investigated three aspects of the relationship between statistical forecasting devices and econometric models in the context of economic policy analysis. First, whether there were grounds for basing economic policy analysis on the "best" forecasting system. Second, whether forecast failure in an econometric model precluded its use for economic policy analysis. Finally, whether in the presence of policy change, improved forecasts could be obtained by using "scenario" changes derived from the econometric model, to modify an initial statistical forecast. To resolve these issues, we analyzed the problems arising when forecasting took place immediately after a structural break (i.e., a change in the parameters of the econometric system), but before a regime shift (i.e., a change in the behavior of nonmodeled, often policy, variables), perhaps in response to the break (Hendry and Mizon (1998) for discussion of this distinction). No forecasting system can be immune to unmodeled breaks that occur after forecasts are announced, whereas some devices are robust to breaks that occur prior to forecasting. Such robust devices are particularly relevant in real time when a structural break has occurred but, perhaps, is not yet known to have occurred. These three dichotomies, between econometric and statistical models, structural breaks and regime shifts, and pre- and post-forecasting events, remain central to our present results. Further particular concerns in the present chapter are working with open models and considering the effects of structural breaks in cointegrating vectors.

Statistical forecasting devices are taken to have no basis of economic theory (in contrast to econometric models for which this is central); so even when combined into a system, such devices will rarely have implications for economic policy analysis – and may not even entail links between target variables and policy instruments. This feature will be true of the forecasting devices we consider. Consequently, being the "best" available forecasting device is insufficient to ensure any value for policy analysis. Some "forecasting models," such as vector autoregressions (VARs), may also have policy implications, and we comment on such VARs later, but that does not vitiate the previous statement.[1]

The converse is more relevant: Does the existence of a dominating forecasting procedure invalidate the use of an econometric model for policy? In Hendry and Mizon (2000), our answer was almost the opposite of the Lucas (1976) critique: when forecast failure results from factors unrelated to policy changes – as Stock and Watson (1996) and Clements and Hendry (2001) show often occurs – an econometric model can continue to accurately characterize the responses of the economy to the policy, despite its forecast of those variables being inaccurate. However, forecast failure could also derive from incorrectly modeled policy reactions. Conversely, when forecast failure results from an in-sample structural break, forecasts from a statistical model that is robust to that structural break may be improved by combining them with the predicted response from an econometric model of a *known* out-of-sample policy change.

The structure of the chapter is as follows. In the next section, we summarize the relevant forecasting and economic policy concepts and issues to motivate the analysis, illustrated in Section 2.2 by an example of forecasting and policy in the presence of regime shifts. Section 3 formalizes the data generation

[1] Sims (1986) regards both classes of model distinguished here as "forecasting" models, but argues that nevertheless both can have policy implications.

process, namely a vector equilibrium-correction mechanism, and the forecasting model used as a comparator. Section 4 considers the impact of structural breaks in an open submodel. Then, Section 5 investigates the effects of these changes on forecasts from the statistical device, before Section 6 describes the policy-scenario changes. Section 7 presents the case for combining the forecasts from robust statistical devices with policy-scenario changes and contrasts these with forecast pooling and with intercept corrections. We present conclusions in Section 8.

2. BACKGROUND

The literature on economic policy is vast, even restricting attention to its implementation using econometric models: related analyses include Bryant, Hooper, and Mann (1993) on evaluating policy regimes; Budd (1998) on conducting economic policy with and without forecasts; Britton (1989) on the more general topic of policy making with macroeconomic models; Sims (1982), Turner, Wallis, and Whitley (1989), and Banerjee, Hendry, and Mizon (1996) on the econometric analysis of economic policy; and Burns (2001) on the costs of forecast errors in an economic policy context. However, the present focus on combining forecasts from models in the face of both structural breaks (specifically, ones which take the form of location shifts) and regime shifts is not prominent in that literature.

The specific rationale for our analysis is as follows. Using the taxonomy of forecast errors in Clements and Hendry (1995), Hendry and Doornik (1997) establish that shifts in the coefficients of deterministic variables (inducing location shifts) are the primary source of systematic forecast failure in econometric models. Deterministic variables include intercepts and linear trends – variables whose future values are known with certainty, but the parameters of which could change. Location shifts are viewed as any change in the unconditional expectation of the nonintegrated transformations of the variables. In the simplest location model of a variable y_t,

$$y_t = \alpha \times 1 + u_t, \tag{2.1}$$

with $\alpha \neq 0$ where $\{u_t\}$ is $\mathsf{I}(0)$, a location shift to α^* from T onwards induces:

$$y_{T+h} = \alpha^* \times 1 + u_{T+h} \equiv \alpha \times \mu + u_{T+h}, \tag{2.2}$$

where $\mu = \alpha^*/\alpha \neq 1$ is the shifted intercept for $h > 0$. Thus, shifts in parameters of deterministic terms are equivalent to location shifts, as are other factors that mimic deterministic shifts, such as misestimating or misspecifying deterministic components in models. The simulation evidence in Hendry (2000) confirms their pernicious effects on forecasts, as well as highlights the difficulty of detecting other forms of break (i.e., those associated with mean zero changes, namely those that have no effect on unconditional means). Moreover, Barrell (2001) illustrates the frequency of such breaks by considering six major episodes of change during the 1990s alone.

Despite location shifts being easier to detect than mean zero changes in general, they too may be overlooked if they occur at, or very near, the end of the sample period. However, there exist devices which can robustify forecasting models against breaks that have occurred prior to forecasting (see, e.g., Clements and Hendry 1996, and Hendry and Clements 2000): examples include imposing an additional unit root, or adding a specific form of intercept correction. Such "tricks" can help mitigate forecast failures, but they do not change a model's policy implications. This result nullifies the argument for using a forecast-based criterion to choose models in order to predict the effects of known policy changes: whether or not a given model forecasts well after a break may depend on its robustness to location shifts as much as on its "closeness" to the data generation process.

Importantly, no methods are robust to unanticipated breaks that occur after forecasts are announced, and Clements and Hendry (1999b) show that those same "robustifying" devices do not offset post-forecasting breaks. But location-shift policy changes that occur after forecasting will induce breaks in all models that do not embody the appropriate policy links: such models, even if unaffected by an earlier structural break, lose their robustness to post-forecasting regime shifts. Thus, the existence of a procedure that, in the presence of in-sample structural breaks, systematically produces better forecasts need not invalidate basing policy on another model. Indeed, despite possibly experiencing forecast failures from pre-forecasting breaks, econometric systems that do embody the relevant policy effects need not experience a post-forecasting break induced by an out-of-sample policy regime shift. Consequently, when both in-sample structural breaks and forecast-period regime shifts occur, neither class of model alone is adequate: this suggests investigating whether, and if so how, they should be combined.

Given the limited knowledge about the data generation process (DGP) that is available to empirical investigators, we adopt a framework in which the DGP is unknown and nonstationary (due to both unit roots and structural breaks), and the econometric model is misspecified for that DGP, if only by failing to correctly model breaks at the forecast origin. These features seem descriptive of operational economic forecasting and provide a rationale for using "intercept corrections" and differencing transformations. A key consequence of these results is that the best available forecasting model need not be based on the "causal determinants" of the actual economic process, and as the example in Section 2.2 shows, may be based on "noncausal" variables, that is, variables which do not enter the DGP.

The fact that a purely statistical device may provide the best available forecasts induces an apparent paradox when policy change is feasible. In a world characterized by the framework we adopt, when forecasting after a structural break, forecasts based on the currently best econometric model may be beaten by statistical devices. Assume for the moment that the statistical forecasting model does not depend on any policy variables and, hence, neither has policy implications nor produces any revisions to its forecasts following any policy changes. These "best" forecasts for some future period are presented to the finance minister of a given country, who thereupon decides that a major policy initiative is essential, and implements it. That the statistical forecasts are not then revised would be greeted with incredulity. More pertinently, providing the policy model did not fall foul of the critique in Granger and Deutsch (1992), so that changes to policy instruments in fact correctly altered target variables; then a better forecast seems likely by adding the policy change effects predicted by the econometric model to the previous forecasts. But this contradicts any claim to the effect that the statistical device produced the best forecasts in a world of structural change and policy regime shifts.

The resolution depends on distinguishing between unknown, or unanticipated, breaks that have occurred – where, for example, differenced models may deliver the best achievable forecast – and subsequent known changes, the consequences of which are partly measurable. An implication is that combining robustified statistical forecasts with the scenario changes from econometric systems subject to policy interventions may provide improved forecasts. This is the subject of Section 7. First, we establish our terminology and notation to clarify the analysis later.

2.1. Terminology

Consider the following illustrative static bivariate system:

$$\begin{aligned} y_t &= \alpha + \beta z_t + v_t \\ z_t &= \mu_z + \varepsilon_{z,t} \end{aligned} \quad \text{with} \quad \begin{pmatrix} v_t \\ \varepsilon_{z,t} \end{pmatrix} \sim \mathsf{IN}_2 \left[\begin{pmatrix} 0 \\ 0 \end{pmatrix}, \begin{pmatrix} \sigma_v^2 & 0 \\ 0 & \sigma_z^2 \end{pmatrix} \right], \tag{2.3}$$

where $(\alpha, \beta, \mu_z, \sigma_v^2, \sigma_z^2) \in \mathbb{R}^3 \times \mathbb{R}_+^2$. The first equation relating y_t to z_t is deemed to be causal here:

$$\frac{\partial y_t}{\partial z_t} = \beta,$$

with z_t strongly exogenous for $(\alpha, \beta, \sigma_v^2)$; whereas the second equation for z_t is a policy process. However, the specification in (2.3) does not directly entail how changes in any subset of parameters might affect the remainder, and so additional assumptions are required. Note that (2.3) can be solved to yield

$$\begin{aligned} y_t &= \mu_y + \varepsilon_{y,t} \\ z_t &= \mu_z + \varepsilon_{z,t} \end{aligned} \quad \text{with} \quad \begin{pmatrix} \varepsilon_{y,t} \\ \varepsilon_{z,t} \end{pmatrix} \sim \mathsf{IN}_2 \left[\begin{pmatrix} 0 \\ 0 \end{pmatrix}, \begin{pmatrix} \sigma_y^2 & \rho \\ \rho & \sigma_z^2 \end{pmatrix} \right], \tag{2.4}$$

where $\mu_y = \alpha + \beta\mu_z$, $\rho = \beta\sigma_z^2$, and $\sigma_y^2 = \sigma_v^2 + \beta\rho$.

A structural break occurs when the parameters of the causal model change (here either $\nabla\beta \neq 0$ or $\nabla\alpha \neq 0$, or both, using ∇ to denote a parameter change). A policy regime shift occurs when the parameters of the policy process change (here either $\nabla\mu_z \neq 0$ or $\nabla\sigma_z^2 \neq 0$, or both). Structural invariance occurs when

$\nabla\mu_z \neq 0$ or $\nabla\sigma_z^2 \neq 0$ does not result in changes to α, β, or σ_v^2, and so $\nabla\alpha = 0$, $\nabla\beta = 0$, and $\nabla\sigma_v^2 = 0$. A location shift is a change in an unconditional mean (e.g., $\nabla\mu_y \neq 0$ or $\nabla\mu_z \neq 0$), so that a regime shift with $\nabla\mu_z \neq 0$ is a special case of a location shift. A mean zero change is one that has no effect on unconditional means, such as a change in the coefficient of a variable that has a zero mean (e.g., $\nabla\beta \neq 0$ in $y_t = \mu_y + \beta(z_t - \mu_z) + v_t$ when μ_y is invariant to β). Contemporaneous mean co-breaking (Clements and Hendry 1999a; Hendry and Mizon 1998) occurs when α is invariant to changes in μ_z so[2]:

$$\nabla\mu_y = \beta\nabla\mu_z. \tag{2.5}$$

A change where $\nabla\mu_y \neq 0$ is called a target shift and is assumed to be the result of a regime shift as in (2.5). Finally, since

$$y_t - \mu_y = \beta\left(z_t - \mu_z\right) + v_t,$$

a zero mean change in β requires that $\mu_y = \alpha + \beta\mu_z$ stays constant, and so α must change in response to β: $\nabla\alpha = -\mu_z\nabla\beta$, partly offsetting the slope change by an intercept shift.

2.2. Forecasting and Policy Analysis across Regime Shifts

Hendry (1997) illustrates the potential role for statistical forecasting methods when an economy is subject to structural breaks and the econometric model is misspecified for the DGP. He considers an artificial economy where gross national product (GNP, denoted by y) is "caused" solely by the exchange rate (e_t) over a sample prior to forecasting, then the DGP changes to one in which y is only caused by the interest rate (r_t); but this switch is not known by the forecaster. The DGP is nondynamic, and, in particular, the lagged value of y does not affect its behavior (i.e., y_{t-1} is noncausal). Nevertheless, when forecasting after the regime change, on the criterion of forecast unbiasedness, a forecasting procedure that ignores the information on both causal variables and only uses y_{t-1} (namely predicting zero change in y by $\mathsf{E}[y_t|y_{t-1}] = y_{t-1}$) can have smaller bias than forecasts from models that include the previously correct causal variable. Here, neither the statistical model nor the econometric model based on *past* causal links is useful for policy.

Since policy analysis conducted on an incorrect model is rarely useful, we now consider what can be concluded in general settings. The paradigmatic example we have in mind is an econometric model of (say) the tax and benefits system that accurately portrays the relevant links and yields a good approximation to the changes in revenues and expenditures resulting from changes in the basic rates. Thus, its conditional predictions are accurate. However, it would not necessarily provide good time-series forecasts in an economy subject to

[2] In general, $\nabla\alpha = \nabla\mu_y - \beta\nabla\mu_z - \mu_z\nabla\beta$, so that if a regime shift is exactly offset by a structural break (i.e., $\beta\nabla\mu_z + \mu_z\nabla\beta = 0$), there need be no shift in the mean of y_t ($\nabla\mu_y = 0$).

structural breaks that affected macroeconomic variables such as total consumers' expenditure and inflation.

The policy implications of any given model in use may or may not change with a particular regime shift. For the situation just considered, if the exchange rate did not alter when the interest rate was changed in the first regime, so that r_t had no direct or indirect effect on y in that regime, then the policy implications of the first-regime model would be useless in the second regime. That seems unlikely here, but could happen in practice. If e_t is altered by changes in r_t, so will be y_t in both regimes. Policy analysis involves estimation of the target-instrument responses, which in this case means $\partial y_{t+h}/\partial r_t$ when y_t is the target variable and r_t the policy instrument changed at time t when the focus is the effect h periods later. For the particular statistical model $\Delta y_t = \varsigma_t$, this response is zero at all forecast horizons h, and so despite its robust forecasting abilities, such a model is uninformative for policy analysis. The first-regime econometric model, on the other hand, does provide an estimate of $\partial y_{t+h}/\partial r_t$ via, for example,

$$\widehat{\frac{\partial y_{t+h}}{\partial r_t}} = \sum_{i=0}^{h} \widehat{\frac{\partial y_{t+h}}{\partial e_{t+i}} \frac{\partial e_{t+i}}{\partial r_t}}. \tag{2.6}$$

In regime 2, the actual policy response is $\partial y_{t+h}/\partial r_t$, and so the regime 1 econometric model policy responses in (2.6) will be valuable when the model-based policy responses have the same sign and do not overestimate the actual response by more than double, whereas the statistical model is always uninformative in that it suggests a zero policy response.

The next section formalizes a more general DGP, before establishing results for forecasting in the face of both structural breaks and regime shifts, when the DGP is a cointegrated system dependent on policy-determined variables. In Section 7, we explore the possibility that some combination of statistical forecasts and estimated policy responses could dominate either alone.

3. THE DATA GENERATION PROCESS

The context for our analysis is an unknown in-sample DGP for the $n = n_1 + n_2$ $\mathsf{I}(1)$ variables $\mathbf{x}_t' = (\mathbf{y}_t', \mathbf{z}_t')$, where $\mathbf{y}_t$ includes target variables and $\mathbf{z}_t$ policy instruments. That DGP is subject to both structural breaks and regime shifts, as in Hendry and Mizon (2000). We concentrate on forecasting $\Delta \mathbf{y}_{T+h+1}$ from time $T + h$ when an unknown structural break occurred at time T, with a known policy regime shift effective at $T + h + 1$.

The class of DGP used in our analysis is an $\mathsf{I}(1)$ vector equilibrium–correction model (VEqCM):

$$\Delta \mathbf{x}_t = \boldsymbol{\tau} + \boldsymbol{\Gamma} \Delta \mathbf{x}_{t-1} + \boldsymbol{\alpha}\boldsymbol{\beta}' \mathbf{x}_{t-1} + \boldsymbol{\epsilon}_t \qquad \text{where } \boldsymbol{\epsilon}_t \sim \mathsf{IN}_n [\mathbf{0}, \boldsymbol{\Sigma}], \tag{3.1}$$

$\mathbf{x}_t$ is $n \times 1$, and $\boldsymbol{\alpha}$ and $\boldsymbol{\beta}$ are $n \times r$ of rank $r < n$, and all the eigenvalues of $\boldsymbol{\Gamma}$ lie inside the unit circle. For $t < T$, the $\mathsf{I}(0)$ variables $\Delta\mathbf{x}_t$ and $\boldsymbol{\beta}'\mathbf{x}_t$ are stationary in sample, so let

$$\mathsf{E}[\Delta\mathbf{x}_t] = \boldsymbol{\gamma} \quad \text{and} \quad \mathsf{E}\left[\boldsymbol{\beta}'\mathbf{x}_t\right] = \boldsymbol{\mu} \quad \forall t < T. \tag{3.2}$$

Taking expectations in (3.1) yields

$$\mathsf{E}[\Delta\mathbf{x}_t] = \boldsymbol{\tau} + \boldsymbol{\Gamma}\mathsf{E}[\Delta\mathbf{x}_t] + \boldsymbol{\alpha}\mathsf{E}\left[\boldsymbol{\beta}'\mathbf{x}_t\right],$$

so that

$$\boldsymbol{\tau} = (\mathbf{I}_n - \boldsymbol{\Gamma})\boldsymbol{\gamma} - \boldsymbol{\alpha}\boldsymbol{\mu}, \tag{3.3}$$

where $\mathsf{E}\left[\Delta\boldsymbol{\beta}'\mathbf{x}_t\right] = \boldsymbol{\beta}'\boldsymbol{\gamma} = \mathbf{0}$. Substituting from (3.3) into (3.1),

$$\Delta\mathbf{x}_t - \boldsymbol{\gamma} = \boldsymbol{\Gamma}(\Delta\mathbf{x}_{t-1} - \boldsymbol{\gamma}) + \boldsymbol{\alpha}\left(\boldsymbol{\beta}'\mathbf{x}_{t-1} - \boldsymbol{\mu}\right) + \boldsymbol{\epsilon}_t.$$

Factorizing (3.1) gives the in-sample open VEqCM for the $\mathsf{I}(1)$ variables $\mathbf{y}_t$, conditional on $\mathbf{z}_t$, representing the behavior of the private sector, which we take to be a causal relation:

$$\begin{aligned}\Delta\mathbf{y}_t - \boldsymbol{\gamma}_y &= \boldsymbol{\Pi}\left(\Delta\mathbf{z}_t - \boldsymbol{\gamma}_z\right) + \boldsymbol{\Lambda}(\Delta\mathbf{x}_{t-1} - \boldsymbol{\gamma}) \\ &\quad + \boldsymbol{\lambda}\left(\boldsymbol{\beta}'\mathbf{x}_{t-1} - \boldsymbol{\mu}\right) + \mathbf{u}_t,\end{aligned} \tag{3.4}$$

where $\boldsymbol{\Pi} = \boldsymbol{\Sigma}_{yz}\boldsymbol{\Sigma}_{zz}^{-1}$, $\boldsymbol{\Lambda} = \left(\boldsymbol{\Gamma}_y - \boldsymbol{\Pi}\boldsymbol{\Gamma}_z\right)$, $\boldsymbol{\lambda} = \left(\boldsymbol{\alpha}_y - \boldsymbol{\Pi}\boldsymbol{\alpha}_z\right)$, with

$$\begin{aligned}\boldsymbol{\Sigma} &= \begin{pmatrix}\boldsymbol{\Sigma}_{yy} & \boldsymbol{\Sigma}_{yz}\\ \boldsymbol{\Sigma}_{zy} & \boldsymbol{\Sigma}_{zz}\end{pmatrix}, \quad \boldsymbol{\Gamma} = \begin{pmatrix}\boldsymbol{\Gamma}_y\\ \boldsymbol{\Gamma}_z\end{pmatrix} = \begin{pmatrix}\boldsymbol{\Gamma}_{yy} & \boldsymbol{\Gamma}_{yz}\\ \boldsymbol{\Gamma}_{zy} & \boldsymbol{\Gamma}_{zz}\end{pmatrix}, \\ \boldsymbol{\alpha} &= \begin{pmatrix}\boldsymbol{\alpha}_y\\ \boldsymbol{\alpha}_z\end{pmatrix}, \quad \boldsymbol{\gamma} = \begin{pmatrix}\boldsymbol{\gamma}_y\\ \boldsymbol{\gamma}_z\end{pmatrix},\end{aligned} \tag{3.5}$$

and

$$\begin{pmatrix}\mathbf{u}_t\\ \boldsymbol{\epsilon}_{z,t}\end{pmatrix} \sim \mathsf{IN}_n\left[\begin{pmatrix}\mathbf{0}\\ \mathbf{0}\end{pmatrix}, \begin{pmatrix}\boldsymbol{\Omega} & \mathbf{0}\\ \mathbf{0} & \boldsymbol{\Sigma}_{zz}\end{pmatrix}\right], \tag{3.6}$$

in which $\boldsymbol{\Omega} = (\boldsymbol{\Sigma}_{yy} - \boldsymbol{\Pi}\boldsymbol{\Sigma}_{zz}\boldsymbol{\Pi}')$. The in-sample marginal model of the policy variables $\mathbf{z}_t$ is

$$\Delta\mathbf{z}_t - \boldsymbol{\gamma}_z = \boldsymbol{\Gamma}_z(\Delta\mathbf{x}_{t-1} - \boldsymbol{\gamma}) + \boldsymbol{\alpha}_z\left(\boldsymbol{\beta}'\mathbf{x}_{t-1} - \boldsymbol{\mu}\right) + \boldsymbol{\epsilon}_{z,t}. \tag{3.7}$$

The relevant policy instruments (e.g., interest rates and tax rates) are elements of $\mathbf{z}_t$ that are assumed to be under the control of the policy agency (e.g., a central bank, or Treasury). The fact that in modeling $\mathbf{z}_t$ it is treated as $\mathsf{I}(1)$ neither implies that it is intrinsically $\mathsf{I}(1)$ nor that it cannot be controlled by the policy agency. Further, although (3.7) is the representation in the econometric model of the evolution of $\mathbf{z}_t$, the marginal process may differ for particular policy rules in operation from time to time (i.e., because of regime shifts); see, for example, Johansen and Juselius (2000).

In a policy setting, $\mathbf{z}_t$ is unlikely to be weakly exogenous for the parameters of the conditional model, as policy reactions are often based on private sector disequilibria such as $\left(\boldsymbol{\beta}'\mathbf{x}_{t-1} - \boldsymbol{\mu}\right)$, so that $\boldsymbol{\alpha}_z$ is usually nonzero. Moreover, the growth rates are linked by the cointegration vectors as $\boldsymbol{\beta}'\boldsymbol{\gamma} = \mathbf{0}$, even when $\boldsymbol{\alpha}_z = \mathbf{0}$. The key to understanding the impact of policy changes in such formulations depends on the remaining (implicit) parameter links and invariances, particularly co-breaking relations: we deal with that case here and return briefly to the absence of appropriate co-breaking (a variant of the Lucas critique) in Section 7.3. As discussed by Hendry and Mizon (2000), if all the parameters in (3.4) and (3.7) were unconnected, the system would manifest "policy ineffectiveness," in that only deviations of $\Delta\mathbf{z}_t$ from $\boldsymbol{\gamma}_z$ would have an impact, so that only impulse responses would be of interest. However, shifts in $\boldsymbol{\gamma}_z$ must alter $\boldsymbol{\gamma}_y$ through the feedback relations (unless $r = 0$), and so the impact and long-run responses differ.

3.1. Forecasting Models

To establish the likely effects of structural breaks and policy regime shifts on alternative forecasting methods, a wide range of models could be considered. To illustrate the algebra, we first analyze the properties of the open VEqCM, which is also the in-sample DGP, and so correctly embodies policy responses over that period. Then we contrast those findings with the outcomes when using a diagonal VAR in second differences (denoted as DDV), where every forecasting equation has the form

$$\widehat{\Delta y}_{i,t} = \Delta y_{i,t-1},$$

which therefore does not have any policy implications. Clements and Hendry (1999b) show that these predictors have the same forecast biases for breaks that occur after forecasts are announced, but that the DDV is more robust to breaks in deterministic terms that have occurred before forecasting: importantly, that robustness does not require knowledge that breaks have occurred. Section 4 draws on their approach, extending it to open models and to forecasts of growth rates (rather than levels). In terms of the example in Section 7.4, forecasts are made after a regime shift resulting in a change in the appropriate measurement of the opportunity cost of holding money – which induces a structural break in models not incorporating that change – but before a further known policy regime shift. Since the open VEqCM has some response to the new policy, but the DDV does not, such comparisons yield insights into the effects of using robustified forecasting methods and then exploiting policy change information via an econometric system.

In the present context, a VAR is simply the unrestricted version of the econometric model and so is subject to the same drawbacks, namely, a lack of robustness to location shifts, exacerbated by the ill-determination of the estimated intercepts, which compound (small) growth rates with (potentially large) equilibrium means; see Equation (3.3). A VAR in first differences is misspecified by omitting the cointegration relations, often of central concern in policy, but thereby gains robustness to previous equilibrium mean shifts (see, e.g., Clements and Hendry 1999a). Although both these models are sometimes viewed as "statistical forecasting devices" with possible policy implications, they lie intermediate between the econometric system in (3.1) and the DDV, and so introducing them adds little to the understanding of the analysis; Clements and Hendry (1999a) analyze their susceptibility to location shifts before and after forecasting.

4. THE IMPACTS OF BREAKS ON THE VEqCM

Economic policy analysis, including forecasting after a structural break, is undertaken using the open model in (4.1), which is assumed to be congruent and encompassing for $t < T$ (see Hendry 1995, Mizon 1995, and Bontemps and Mizon 2003, for discussion of these concepts). Thus, we consider a structural break affecting the system at time T and for $t = T, T+1, T+2, \ldots$. The change alters γ to γ^* and β to β^*, with a new equilibrium mean $\mathsf{E}\left[\beta^{*\prime}\mathbf{x}_t^*\right] = \mu^*$, where $\beta^{*\prime}\gamma^* = \mathbf{0}$ for $t \geq T$. Other than possible concomitant changes in $\boldsymbol{\lambda}$ noted below, we leave the other parameters unchanged, since shifts in mean zero $\mathsf{I}(0)$ combinations of variables do not seem to be of primary importance for forecast failure. However, the precise timing of shifts in each type of parameter affects the results that eventuate; hence we consider a period $T + h$, where $h \geq 1$, so all parameters have then shifted: an equivalent effect is achieved by assuming that they all shifted at T.

In response to the structural break, we then consider a policy regime shift in Section 6 that alters the instruments $\mathbf{z}_t^*$ to $\mathbf{z}_t^p$, by shifting γ_z^* to γ_z^p. Such a policy regime shift in the DGP could also result in a structural break in (3.4) unless the parameters of the latter were invariant, an issue addressed in Section 7.3.

In this section, we consider the impacts of these parameter changes in the VEqCM DGP over the forecast period on the preexisting forecasting model, written as

$$\Delta\mathbf{y}_t = \gamma_0 + \boldsymbol{\Pi}\Delta\mathbf{z}_t + \boldsymbol{\Lambda}_z\Delta\mathbf{z}_{t-1} + \boldsymbol{\Lambda}_y\Delta\mathbf{y}_{t-1} + \boldsymbol{\lambda}\left(\beta'\mathbf{x}_{t-1} - \mu\right) + \mathbf{u}_t, \tag{4.1}$$

where

$$\gamma_0 = \left(\mathbf{I}_{n_1} - \boldsymbol{\Lambda}_y\right)\gamma_y - (\boldsymbol{\Pi} + \boldsymbol{\Lambda}_z)\gamma_z.$$

Following the parameter changes noted, (4.1) for $h \geq 1$ becomes

$$\begin{aligned}\Delta\mathbf{y}_{T+h}^* = {} & \gamma_y^* + \boldsymbol{\Pi}\left(\Delta\mathbf{z}_{T+h}^* - \gamma_z^*\right) + \boldsymbol{\Lambda}_z\left(\Delta\mathbf{z}_{T+h-1}^* - \gamma_z^*\right) \\ & + \boldsymbol{\Lambda}_y\left(\Delta\mathbf{y}_{T+h-1}^* - \gamma_y^*\right) + \boldsymbol{\lambda}^*\left(\beta^{*\prime}\mathbf{x}_{T+h-1}^* - \mu^*\right) + \mathbf{u}_{T+h}.\end{aligned} \tag{4.2}$$

It is assumed that the forecaster, though aware of the possibility of parameter changes, does not know that they have actually changed. As a result, the open VEqCM (4.1) estimated using data up to $t = T$, and indeed for $t = T + h$ for h/T small, will suffer forecast failure because of the shift in μ to μ^* and any additional nonzero components deriving from the unmodeled changes in the cointegration vectors.

4.1. Breaks in Cointegration Relations

The introduction of breaks in the cointegration relations raises a number of new considerations, depending on whether their impact induces I(0) or I(1) effects. We consider these in turn.

I(0) *Cases*

This case includes the change from $\boldsymbol{\beta}$ to $\boldsymbol{\beta}^*$ simply being a linear transformation (rotation), so that there exists an $r \times r$ matrix $\mathbf{D}$ of rank r, such that $\boldsymbol{\beta}^{*\prime} = \mathbf{D}\boldsymbol{\beta}'$ with a corresponding change in the equilibrium mean to $\boldsymbol{\mu}^* = \mathbf{D}\boldsymbol{\mu}$. Such a situation is essentially one of no change, merely a reparameterization as

$$\begin{aligned}\boldsymbol{\lambda}^* \left(\boldsymbol{\beta}^{*\prime}\mathbf{x}^*_{T+h-1} - \boldsymbol{\mu}^*\right) &= \boldsymbol{\lambda}^* \left(\mathbf{D}\boldsymbol{\beta}'\mathbf{x}^*_{T+h-1} - \mathbf{D}\boldsymbol{\mu}\right) \\ &= \boldsymbol{\lambda}\left(\boldsymbol{\beta}'\mathbf{x}^*_{T+h-1} - \boldsymbol{\mu}\right) \end{aligned} \tag{4.3}$$

as $\boldsymbol{\lambda}^*\mathbf{D} = \boldsymbol{\lambda}$.

A second class of changes in $\boldsymbol{\beta}$ that have only I(0) effects is when new cointegration relations are added. Here r changes to r^* (say), and so both $\boldsymbol{\lambda}$ and $\boldsymbol{\beta}$ are changed in dimension, and the outcome is the addition of a mean zero term, which has minimal effects on forecasts. Since $r^* > r$, let $\boldsymbol{\lambda}^* = \left(\boldsymbol{\lambda}, \boldsymbol{\lambda}^\dagger\right)$, $\boldsymbol{\beta}^* = \left(\boldsymbol{\beta}, \boldsymbol{\beta}^\dagger\right)$, and $\boldsymbol{\mu}^{*\prime} = \left(\boldsymbol{\mu}, \boldsymbol{\mu}^\dagger\right)$, so that the new and the old cointegration vectors are linked by

$$\boldsymbol{\lambda}^* \left(\boldsymbol{\beta}^{*\prime}\mathbf{x}^*_{T+h-1} - \boldsymbol{\mu}^*\right) = \boldsymbol{\lambda}\left(\boldsymbol{\beta}'\mathbf{x}^*_{T+h-1} - \boldsymbol{\mu}\right) + \boldsymbol{\lambda}^\dagger \left(\boldsymbol{\beta}^{\dagger\prime}\mathbf{x}^*_{T+h-1} - \boldsymbol{\mu}^\dagger\right),$$

and the model error over the forecast period becomes

$$\mathbf{u}^*_{T+h} = \mathbf{u}_{T+h} + \boldsymbol{\lambda}^\dagger \left(\boldsymbol{\beta}^{\dagger\prime}\mathbf{x}^*_{T+h-1} - \boldsymbol{\mu}^\dagger\right),$$

which remains I(0) with a zero mean, albeit perhaps autocorrelated. Potentially, however, there is an "initial conditions" problem, since the relevant variables that enter $\boldsymbol{\beta}^{\dagger\prime}\mathbf{x}^*_{T+h-1}$ were not previously cointegrated, and so could have drifted apart such that at $T+1$, $\left(\boldsymbol{\beta}^{\dagger\prime}\mathbf{x}^*_T - \boldsymbol{\mu}^\dagger\right)$ is sufficiently "large" to induce one-step forecast failure in models that exclude it (see, e.g., Hendry 2000).

In the third case, when fewer cointegration relations occur over the forecast period, the outcome is less clear, as some existing elements of $\boldsymbol{\beta}$ are eliminated. This is the case $r^* < r$, and so partitioning $\boldsymbol{\lambda}^*$, $\boldsymbol{\beta}$, and $\boldsymbol{\mu}$ into $(\boldsymbol{\lambda}^*_a, \boldsymbol{\lambda}^*_b) = (\boldsymbol{\lambda}_a, \mathbf{0})$, $\left(\boldsymbol{\beta}_a, \boldsymbol{\beta}_b\right)$, and $\left(\boldsymbol{\mu}_a, \boldsymbol{\mu}_b\right)$, respectively, the new and the old cointegration vectors are linked by

$$\begin{aligned}\boldsymbol{\lambda}^* \left(\boldsymbol{\beta}'\mathbf{x}^*_{T+h-1} - \boldsymbol{\mu}\right) &= \boldsymbol{\lambda}^*_a \left(\boldsymbol{\beta}'_a\mathbf{x}^*_{T+h-1} - \boldsymbol{\mu}_a\right) \\ &= \boldsymbol{\lambda}\left(\boldsymbol{\beta}'\mathbf{x}^*_{T+h-1} - \boldsymbol{\mu}\right) - \boldsymbol{\lambda}_b \left(\boldsymbol{\beta}'_b\mathbf{x}^*_{T+h-1} - \boldsymbol{\mu}_b\right),\end{aligned}$$

and so the model error over the forecast period becomes

$$\mathbf{u}^*_{T+h} = \mathbf{u}_{T+h} - \boldsymbol{\lambda}_b \left(\boldsymbol{\beta}'_b\mathbf{x}^*_{T+h-1} - \boldsymbol{\mu}_b\right).$$

This is only I(0) provided that $(\boldsymbol{\beta}_b'\mathbf{x}^*_{T+h-1} - \boldsymbol{\mu}_b)$ remains I(0), in which case, $\mathbf{u}^*_{T+h}$ is still an I(0) error with a zero mean. However, such an outcome seems unlikely: rather, although $\boldsymbol{\lambda}_b$ has become zero in the DGP, the forecasting model retains linear combinations of I(1) variables that are now I(1), and $\boldsymbol{\mu}_b$ has no meaning. Nevertheless, the simulation results in Hendry 2000 suggest that such changes are difficult to detect empirically from moderate sample sizes.

A final case is when there is a set of k additional I(1) variables, say $\mathbf{w}_t$, that are self-cointegrated within the DGP but have not been included in the forecasting model in any way, and so the I(0) combinations $\left(\boldsymbol{\beta}^{+\prime}\mathbf{w}_{T+h-1} - \boldsymbol{\delta}\right)$ have been omitted from the model when $\mathsf{E}[\boldsymbol{\beta}^{+\prime}\mathbf{w}_{T+h}] = \boldsymbol{\delta}$ for $h > 0$. None of these types of I(0) changes in $\boldsymbol{\beta}$ is liable to induce systematic forecast failure, and so they are not considered here.

I(1) *Cases*

An important type of break in the cointegration relations that induces I(1) effects arises in the last case when $\boldsymbol{\beta}'\mathbf{x}^*_{T+h}$ and $\boldsymbol{\beta}^{+\prime}\mathbf{w}_{T+h}$ cease to be I(0) individually. Now a system that excludes $\mathbf{w}_{T+h}$ will be seriously misspecified: both $\left(\boldsymbol{\beta}'\mathbf{x}_{T+h} - \boldsymbol{\mu}\right)$ and $\mathbf{u}^*_{T+h}$ will be I(1). As a result, $\left(\boldsymbol{\beta}'\mathbf{x}_{T+h} - \boldsymbol{\mu}\right)$ could become large, in which case forecast failure should manifest itself, forcing a revision to the model specification. This case comes close to the situation considered in the example in Section 7.4, in which the additional I(1) variable is R_o, the then newly legalized own interest rate on retail sight deposits.

The last case arises when the rank remains the same, but now cointegration becomes defined by new coefficients $\boldsymbol{\beta}^*$, so that the error in (4.3) becomes

$$\mathbf{u}^*_{T+h} = \mathbf{u}_{T+h} + \boldsymbol{\lambda}\left(\nabla\boldsymbol{\beta}^{*\prime}\mathbf{x}^*_{T+h-1} - \nabla\boldsymbol{\mu}^*\right),$$

with $\nabla\boldsymbol{\beta}^* = \left(\boldsymbol{\beta}^* - \boldsymbol{\beta}\right)$ and $\nabla\boldsymbol{\mu}^* = (\boldsymbol{\mu}^* - \boldsymbol{\mu})$. Although $(\boldsymbol{\beta}^{*\prime}\mathbf{x}^*_{T+h-1} - \boldsymbol{\mu}^*)$ is I(0), $\left(\boldsymbol{\beta}'\mathbf{x}^*_{T+h-1} - \boldsymbol{\mu}\right)$ will be I(1) after time T, and so the unmodified system will suffer consequences similar to the I(1) mistake case just noted. Even if the equilibrium mean did not change, so that $\nabla\boldsymbol{\mu}^* = \mathbf{0}$, the same problems would arise since $\mathbf{u}^*_{T+h}$ must be I(1) via the non-cointegrating combinations $\nabla\boldsymbol{\beta}^{*\prime}\mathbf{x}^*_{T+h-1}$. However, we note that even in the most favorable case for avoiding forecast failure (i.e., when $\boldsymbol{\mu} = \boldsymbol{\mu}^* = \mathbf{0}$), the simulation results in Hendry (2000) show quite high power in detecting changes in $\boldsymbol{\beta}$, at least in moderately large samples. Conversely, the situation where $\boldsymbol{\beta}^* = \boldsymbol{\beta}$ but $\boldsymbol{\mu}^* \neq \boldsymbol{\mu}$ is a pure location shift, adding $-\boldsymbol{\lambda}\nabla\boldsymbol{\mu}^*$ to the forecast error, and is readily detected when breaks exceed the equation error standard deviations.

4.2. Postbreak Forecasts

We consider forecasting $\Delta\mathbf{y}_{T+h+1}$ using information available at $T+h$ for $h \geq 0$, so that the structural break is an in-sample one – albeit unknown to the forecasters. Ignoring estimator variances, and assuming accurate data, an economist using the open VEqCM with $\mathbf{z}^*_{T+h+1}$ known would produce the following one-step-ahead forecast of $\Delta\mathbf{y}^*_{T+h+1}$:

$$\widehat{\Delta\mathbf{y}^*}_{T+h+1|T+h} = \gamma_0 + \boldsymbol{\Pi}\Delta\mathbf{z}^*_{T+h+1} + \boldsymbol{\Lambda}_y\Delta\mathbf{y}^*_{T+h} + \boldsymbol{\Lambda}_z\Delta\mathbf{z}^*_{T+h} + \boldsymbol{\lambda}\left(\boldsymbol{\beta}'\mathbf{x}^*_{T+h} - \boldsymbol{\mu}\right), \tag{4.4}$$

which has a forecast error (when $\boldsymbol{\lambda}^* = \boldsymbol{\lambda}$ and letting $\gamma_0^* = \left(\mathbf{I}_{n_1} - \boldsymbol{\Lambda}_y\right)\gamma_y^* - (\Pi + \boldsymbol{\Lambda}_z)\gamma_z^*$)

$$\begin{aligned}
&\widehat{\mathbf{u}}_{T+h+1|T+h} \\
&\quad = \Delta\mathbf{y}^*_{T+h+1} - \widehat{\Delta\mathbf{y}^*}_{T+h+1|T+h} \\
&\quad = \gamma_0^* + \Pi\Delta\mathbf{z}^*_{T+h+1} + \Lambda_y\Delta\mathbf{y}^*_{T+h} + \Lambda_z\Delta\mathbf{z}^*_{T+h} \\
&\qquad + \boldsymbol{\lambda}\left(\boldsymbol{\beta}^{*\prime}\mathbf{x}^*_{T+h} - \boldsymbol{\mu}^*\right) + \mathbf{u}_{T+h+1} - \gamma_0 - \boldsymbol{\Pi}\Delta\mathbf{z}^*_{T+h+1} \\
&\qquad - \boldsymbol{\Lambda}_y\Delta\mathbf{y}^*_{T+h} - \boldsymbol{\Lambda}_z\Delta\mathbf{z}^*_{T+h} - \boldsymbol{\lambda}\left(\boldsymbol{\beta}'\mathbf{x}^*_{T+h} - \boldsymbol{\mu}\right) \\
&\quad = \nabla\gamma_0^* + \boldsymbol{\lambda}\nabla\boldsymbol{\beta}^{*\prime}\mathbf{x}^*_{T+h} - \boldsymbol{\lambda}\nabla\boldsymbol{\mu}^* + \mathbf{u}_{T+h+1},
\end{aligned} \tag{4.5}$$

when $\nabla\gamma_0^* = (\gamma_0^* - \gamma_0)$. Hence, the conditional means and variances of the open VEqCM forecast errors are

$$\mathsf{E}\left[\widehat{\mathbf{u}}_{T+h+1|T+h} \mid \mathbf{x}^*_{T+h}, \mathbf{z}^*_{T+h+1}\right] = \nabla\gamma_0^* - \boldsymbol{\lambda}\nabla\boldsymbol{\mu}^* + \boldsymbol{\lambda}\nabla\boldsymbol{\beta}^{*\prime}\mathbf{x}^*_{T+h}, \tag{4.6}$$

and

$$\mathsf{V}\left[\widehat{\mathbf{u}}_{T+h+1|T+h} \mid \mathbf{x}^*_{T+h}, \mathbf{z}^*_{T+h+1}\right] = \mathsf{E}\left[\mathbf{u}_{T+h+1|T+h}\mathbf{u}'_{T+h+1|T+h}\right] = \Omega. \tag{4.7}$$

Note that the bias of the VEqCM forecast is primarily due to the changes in the parameters of the deterministic variables, but can also become large as a result of $\nabla\boldsymbol{\beta}^{*\prime}\mathbf{x}^*_{T+h}$ being I(1) after the structural break. However, in the absence of the structural breaks, the economist's forecast would be unbiased.

5. THE IMPACTS OF BREAKS ON THE FORECASTING MODEL

We now establish the likely effects of structural breaks and policy regime shifts on the restricted vector autoregression in second-differenced variables (denoted as DDV), our statistical forecasting device. It is shown that the DDV can have a smaller forecast bias than the open VEqCM, because it is robust to forecasting after the equilibrium-mean shift, though it will usually have a larger forecast error variance.

The one-step-ahead statistical model forecast from $T+h$ for $h \geq 0$ using the DDV is

$$\widetilde{\Delta\mathbf{y}^*}_{T+h+1|T+h} = \Delta\mathbf{y}^*_{T+h}, \tag{5.1}$$

which has a forecast error

$$\begin{aligned}
&\widetilde{\mathbf{u}}_{T+h+1|T+h} \\
&= \Delta \mathbf{y}^*_{T+h+1} - \Delta \mathbf{y}^*_{T+h} \\
&= \gamma^*_0 + \mathbf{\Pi} \Delta \mathbf{z}^*_{T+h+1} + \mathbf{\Lambda}_y \Delta \mathbf{y}^*_{T+h} + \mathbf{\Lambda}_z \Delta \mathbf{z}^*_{T+h} \\
&\quad + \boldsymbol{\lambda} \left(\boldsymbol{\beta}^{*\prime} \mathbf{x}^*_{T+h} - \boldsymbol{\mu}^*\right) + \mathbf{u}_{T+h+1} - \gamma^*_0 - \mathbf{\Pi} \Delta \mathbf{z}^*_{T+h} \\
&\quad - \mathbf{\Lambda}_y \Delta \mathbf{y}^*_{T+h-1} - \mathbf{\Lambda}_z \Delta \mathbf{z}^*_{T+h-1} - \boldsymbol{\lambda} \left(\boldsymbol{\beta}^{*\prime} \mathbf{x}^*_{T+h-1} - \boldsymbol{\mu}^*\right) - \mathbf{u}_{T+h} \\
&= \Delta \mathbf{u}_{T+h+1} + \mathbf{\Pi} \Delta^2 \mathbf{z}^*_{T+h+1} + \mathbf{\Lambda} \Delta^2 \mathbf{x}^*_{T+h} + \boldsymbol{\lambda} \boldsymbol{\beta}^{*\prime} \Delta \mathbf{x}^*_{T+h}. \qquad (5.2)
\end{aligned}$$

Thus, the conditional mean of the DDV forecast error is given by

$$\begin{aligned}
&\mathsf{E}\left[\widetilde{\mathbf{u}}_{T+h+1|T+h} \mid \mathbf{x}^*_{T+h}, \mathbf{z}^*_{T+h+1}\right] \\
&\quad = \mathbf{\Pi} \Delta^2 \mathbf{z}^*_{T+h+1} + \mathbf{\Lambda} \Delta^2 \mathbf{x}^*_{T+h} + \boldsymbol{\lambda} \boldsymbol{\beta}^{*\prime} \Delta \mathbf{x}^*_{T+h}, \qquad (5.3)
\end{aligned}$$

and the unconditional bias is

$$\begin{aligned}
&\mathsf{E}\left[\widetilde{\mathbf{u}}_{T+h+1|T+h}\right] \\
&\quad = \mathbf{\Pi} \mathsf{E}\left[\Delta^2 \mathbf{z}^*_{T+h+1}\right] + \mathbf{\Lambda} \mathsf{E}\left[\Delta^2 \mathbf{x}^*_{T+h}\right] + \boldsymbol{\lambda} \mathsf{E}\left[\boldsymbol{\beta}^{*\prime} \Delta \mathbf{x}^*_{T+h}\right] = \mathbf{0}. \qquad (5.4)
\end{aligned}$$

Thus the average bias of the DDV forecast is zero, whereas the conditional mean of the open VEqCM is (4.6), which may be large. However, as the elapsed time, h, between the structural break and making the forecast increases, it is more likely that the economist will become aware of the break. Nevertheless, it is possible for the DDV to have a much smaller forecast bias than the open VEqCM, though it will always have a higher variance, since (5.2) and (5.3) imply that the conditional variance of the DDV forecast error is[3]

$$\mathsf{V}\left[\widetilde{\mathbf{u}}_{T+h+1|T+h} \mid \mathbf{x}^*_{T+h}, \mathbf{z}^*_{T+h+1}\right] = 2\mathbf{\Omega}. \qquad (5.5)$$

Under the assumption that the DGP and the econometric model given in (3.4) and (3.7) coincide, it is possible to derive forecast error means and variances for a wider range of forecasting methods than the open VEqCM and the DDV considered here. This was done in Hendry and Mizon (2000) for a similar class of models, and so is not repeated here. However, their results emphasized the different susceptibilities of econometric models and robust statistical forecasting devices to the unknown structural breaks and known regime shifts, thereby indicating possibilities for using each to "correct" the other.

6. POLICY REGIME CHANGES

We next consider forecasting $\Delta \mathbf{y}_{T+h+1}$ in the presence of a policy change where an announced policy shift of γ^*_z to γ^p_z takes place at $T + h + 1$, which induces

[3] This assumes that the VEqCM is the DGP. If there are omitted variables from the former, then the error variance can actually decrease on differencing (Hendry 2004).

a further shift in the equilibrium mean from $\boldsymbol{\mu}^*$ to $\boldsymbol{\mu}^p$ and the growth rates to $\boldsymbol{\gamma}^p$, but does not affect the cointegration vectors, so that $\boldsymbol{\beta}^{*\prime}\boldsymbol{\gamma}^p = \mathbf{0}$. After the policy regime shift, the $\mathbf{z}_t$ process takes the form (considering the special case that $\boldsymbol{\alpha}_z = \mathbf{0}$ for simplicity)

$$\begin{aligned}\Delta\mathbf{z}^p_{T+h+1} &= \boldsymbol{\gamma}^p_z + \boldsymbol{\Gamma}_z\left(\Delta\mathbf{x}^*_{T+h} - \boldsymbol{\gamma}^*\right) + \boldsymbol{\epsilon}_{z,T+h+1}\\ \Delta\mathbf{z}^p_{T+h+j} &= \boldsymbol{\gamma}^p_z + \boldsymbol{\Gamma}_z\left(\Delta\mathbf{x}^p_{T+h+j-1} - \boldsymbol{\gamma}^p\right) + \boldsymbol{\epsilon}_{z,T+h+j} \quad \text{for } j > 1,\end{aligned} \tag{6.1}$$

and results in ($\boldsymbol{\gamma}^p_0 = \left(\mathbf{I}_{n_1} - \boldsymbol{\Lambda}_y\right)\boldsymbol{\gamma}^p_y - (\boldsymbol{\Pi} + \boldsymbol{\Lambda}_z)\boldsymbol{\gamma}^p_z$):

$$\begin{aligned}\Delta\mathbf{y}^p_{T+h+1} &= \left(\boldsymbol{\gamma}^p_y - \boldsymbol{\Lambda}_y\boldsymbol{\gamma}^*_y - \boldsymbol{\Pi}\boldsymbol{\gamma}^p_z - \boldsymbol{\Lambda}_z\boldsymbol{\gamma}^*_z\right) + \boldsymbol{\Pi}\Delta\mathbf{z}^p_{T+h+1}\\ &\quad + \boldsymbol{\Lambda}_y\Delta\mathbf{y}^*_{T+h} + \boldsymbol{\Lambda}_z\Delta\mathbf{z}^*_{T+h}\\ &\quad + \boldsymbol{\lambda}\left(\boldsymbol{\beta}^{*\prime}\mathbf{x}^*_{T+h} - \boldsymbol{\mu}^*\right) + \mathbf{u}_{T+h+1}\\ \Delta\mathbf{y}^p_{T+h+j} &= \boldsymbol{\gamma}^p_0 + \boldsymbol{\Pi}\Delta\mathbf{z}^p_{T+h+j} + \boldsymbol{\Lambda}_y\Delta\mathbf{y}^p_{T+h+j-1}\\ &\quad + \boldsymbol{\Lambda}_z\Delta\mathbf{z}^p_{T+h+j-1} + \boldsymbol{\lambda}\left(\boldsymbol{\beta}^{*\prime}\mathbf{x}^p_{T+h+j-1} - \boldsymbol{\mu}^p\right)\\ &\quad + \mathbf{u}_{T+h+j} \quad \text{for } j > 1.\end{aligned} \tag{6.2}$$

In our formulation, there is a one-period transition during which the lagged growth rates are unchanged: this represents the notion in (6.1) that the policy agency only changes the current value of $\boldsymbol{\gamma}^p_z$ carried over to (6.2) for consistency. An alternative would have been to shift the intercepts in both equations, replacing all values of $\boldsymbol{\gamma}^*$ by $\boldsymbol{\gamma}^p$, in which case the remaining bias in (7.7) would vanish.

The forecasting performance of the open VEqCM and the DDV are now compared with that of a "scenario-adjusted" DDV forecast that combines information from each.

7. POLICY CHANGE CORRECTIONS TO ROBUST FORECASTS

Any need to combine two disparate models on the same information set is evidence that both are incomplete (Clements and Hendry 1998). The encompassing principle argues for finding the congruent representation that can explain the failures of both models, but in the short run, doing so may prove infeasible. When the two models are differently susceptible to the causes of predictive failure, some combinations could be beneficial; however, the relevant combination must reflect the motivation for pooling (namely, to take account of the effects of known breaks), rather than the usual grounds as discussed in (say) Bates and Granger (1969).

The case of interest is when the robust forecast is made from the DDV, and that prompts a policy response to change the provisional setting $\mathbf{z}^*_{T+h+1}$ to the actual outcome $\mathbf{z}^p_{T+h+1}$ associated with $\boldsymbol{\gamma}^p_z$ (e.g., reducing the rate of income tax to increase total final expenditure in the example in Section 7.4). However, from (5.1) it follows that

$$\widetilde{\Delta \mathbf{y}^p}_{T+h+1|T+h} = \widetilde{\Delta \mathbf{y}}_{T+h+1|T+h} = \Delta \mathbf{y}^*_{T+h},$$

and so the DDV forecast is unaltered, implying that its forecast error changes one for one with the impact of the policy change. Thus, the forecast error is $\widetilde{\mathbf{u}}^p_{T+h+1|T+h} = \Delta \mathbf{y}^p_{T+h+1} - \Delta \mathbf{y}^*_{T+h}$, and so denoting by

$$\gamma^p_h = \gamma^p_y - \mathbf{\Lambda}_y \gamma^*_y - \mathbf{\Pi}\gamma^p_z - \mathbf{\Lambda}_z \gamma^*_z,$$

then

$$\begin{aligned}
&\widetilde{\mathbf{u}}^p_{T+h+1|T+h} \\
&\quad = \gamma^p_h + \mathbf{\Pi}\Delta \mathbf{z}^p_{T+h+1} + \mathbf{\Lambda}_y \Delta \mathbf{y}^*_{T+h} + \mathbf{\Lambda}_z \Delta \mathbf{z}^*_{T+h} \\
&\qquad + \boldsymbol{\lambda}\left(\boldsymbol{\beta}^{*\prime}\mathbf{x}^*_{T+h} - \boldsymbol{\mu}^*\right) + \mathbf{u}_{T+h+1} - \gamma^*_0 - \mathbf{\Pi}\Delta \mathbf{z}^*_{T+h} \\
&\qquad - \mathbf{\Lambda}_y \Delta \mathbf{y}^*_{T+h-1} - \mathbf{\Lambda}_z \Delta \mathbf{z}^*_{T+h-1} - \boldsymbol{\lambda}\left(\boldsymbol{\beta}^{*\prime}\mathbf{x}^*_{T+h-1} - \boldsymbol{\mu}^*\right) - \mathbf{u}_{T+h} \\
&\quad = \Delta \mathbf{u}_{T+h+1} + \left(\gamma^p_h - \gamma^*_0\right) + \mathbf{\Pi}\left(\Delta \mathbf{z}^p_{T+h+1} - \Delta \mathbf{z}^*_{T+h}\right) \\
&\qquad + \Lambda \Delta^2 \mathbf{x}^*_{T+h} + \boldsymbol{\lambda}\boldsymbol{\beta}^{*\prime}\Delta \mathbf{x}^*_{T+h}.
\end{aligned}$$

Consequently, the expected DDV unconditional forecast error is

$$\begin{aligned}
\mathsf{E}\left[\widetilde{\mathbf{u}}^p_{T+h+1|T+h}\right] &= \left(\gamma^p_h - \gamma^*_0\right) + \mathbf{\Pi}\left(\mathsf{E}\left[\Delta \mathbf{z}^p_{T+h+1}\right] - \mathsf{E}\left[\Delta \mathbf{z}^*_{T+h}\right]\right) \\
&= \left(\gamma^p_h - \gamma^*_0\right) + \mathbf{\Pi}\left(\gamma^p_z - \gamma^*_z\right) = \left(\gamma^p_y - \gamma^*_y\right). \quad (7.1)
\end{aligned}$$

As anticipated, a forecast bias results because the policy shift occurs after the DDV forecast is announced.

Forecasts from the open VEqCM, on the other hand, are now

$$\widehat{\Delta \mathbf{y}^p}_{T+h+1|T+h} = \gamma_0 + \mathbf{\Pi}\Delta \mathbf{z}^p_{T+h+1} + \mathbf{\Lambda}\Delta \mathbf{x}^*_{T+h} + \boldsymbol{\lambda}\left(\boldsymbol{\beta}'\mathbf{x}^*_{T+h} - \boldsymbol{\mu}\right). \quad (7.2)$$

Hence, the VEqCM has a forecast error of $\widehat{\mathbf{u}}^p_{T+h+1|T+h} = \Delta \mathbf{y}^p_{T+h+1} - \widehat{\Delta \mathbf{y}^p}_{T+h+1|T+h}$:

$$\begin{aligned}
&\widehat{\mathbf{u}}^p_{T+h+1|T+h} \\
&\quad = \gamma^p_h + \mathbf{\Pi}\Delta \mathbf{z}^p_{T+h+1} + \mathbf{\Lambda}_y \Delta \mathbf{y}^*_{T+h} + \mathbf{\Lambda}_z \Delta \mathbf{z}^*_{T+h} \\
&\qquad + \boldsymbol{\lambda}\left(\boldsymbol{\beta}^{*\prime}\mathbf{x}^*_{T+h} - \boldsymbol{\mu}^*\right) + \mathbf{u}_{T+h+1} \\
&\qquad - \left[\gamma_0 + \mathbf{\Pi}\Delta \mathbf{z}^p_{T+h+1} + \mathbf{\Lambda}\Delta \mathbf{x}^*_{T+h} + \boldsymbol{\lambda}\left(\boldsymbol{\beta}'\mathbf{x}^*_{T+h} - \boldsymbol{\mu}\right)\right] \\
&\quad = \left(\gamma^p_h - \gamma_0\right) + \boldsymbol{\lambda}\nabla\boldsymbol{\beta}^{*\prime}\mathbf{x}^*_{T+h} - \boldsymbol{\lambda}\nabla\boldsymbol{\mu}^* + \mathbf{u}_{T+h+1}, \quad (7.3)
\end{aligned}$$

with a conditional expectation of

$$\begin{aligned}
&\mathsf{E}\left[\Delta \mathbf{y}^p_{T+h+1} - \widehat{\Delta \mathbf{y}}^p_{T+h+1|T+h} \mid \mathbf{x}^*_{T+h}\right] \\
&\quad = \left(\gamma^p_h - \gamma_0\right) + \boldsymbol{\lambda}\nabla\boldsymbol{\beta}^{*\prime}\mathbf{x}^*_{T+h} - \boldsymbol{\lambda}\nabla\boldsymbol{\mu}^*. \quad (7.4)
\end{aligned}$$

It is easy to envisage conditions where (7.4) is much larger than (7.1).

Nevertheless, comparing (4.4) and (7.2), the VEqCM forecasts are revised from their pre–policy change values by the difference

$$\left[\widehat{\Delta \mathbf{y}}^{p}_{T+h+1|T+h} - \widehat{\Delta \mathbf{y}}^{*}_{T+h+1|T+h}\right] = \mathbf{\Pi}\left(\Delta \mathbf{z}^{p}_{T+h+1} - \Delta \mathbf{z}^{*}_{T+h+1}\right). \tag{7.5}$$

Consequently, if the policy regime shift at $t = T + h + 1$ does not lead to a structural break in $\mathbf{\Pi}$, the econometric model would correctly predict this aspect of the impact of the regime shift, despite the structural break at $t = T$ in deterministic terms. This opens up the possibility of a combined forecast improving over either the DDV or VEqCM alone. In particular, consider adding the scenario effect from (7.5) to the structural break–robust DDV forecast to give a combined forecast of the form

$$\overline{\Delta \mathbf{y}}_{T+h+1|T+h} = \widetilde{\Delta \mathbf{y}}^{p}_{T+h+1|T+h} + \left[\widehat{\Delta \mathbf{y}}^{p}_{T+h+1|T+h} - \widehat{\Delta \mathbf{y}}^{*}_{T+h+1|T+h}\right], \tag{7.6}$$

which might avoid much of the structural break, yet capture some, and possibly all, of the policy effect.

The unconditional bias of $\overline{\Delta \mathbf{y}}_{T+h+1|T+h}$ from (7.6) is

$$\begin{aligned}
&\mathsf{E}\left[\Delta \mathbf{y}^{p}_{T+h+1} - \overline{\Delta \mathbf{y}}_{T+h+1|T+h}\right] \\
&\quad = \mathsf{E}\left[\Delta \mathbf{y}^{p}_{T+h+1} - \widetilde{\Delta \mathbf{y}}^{p}_{T+h+1|T+h}\right] \\
&\quad\quad - \mathsf{E}\left[\widehat{\Delta \mathbf{y}}^{p}_{T+h+1|T+h} - \widehat{\Delta \mathbf{y}}^{*}_{T+h+1|T+h}\right] \\
&\quad = \left(\gamma^{p}_{y} - \gamma^{*}_{y}\right) - \mathbf{\Pi}\left(\gamma^{p}_{z} - \gamma^{*}_{z}\right).
\end{aligned} \tag{7.7}$$

Because the growth rates are linked by the cointegration relationships, cobreaking of the form $\gamma^{p}_{y} = \mathbf{\Pi}\gamma^{p}_{z}$ and $\gamma^{*}_{y} = \mathbf{\Pi}\gamma^{*}_{z}$ cannot hold, but there will nevertheless usually be considerable offset between the two components in (7.7). Thus, in the absence of additional model misspecifications (and abstracting from sampling variability), the scenario-corrected forecasts should be less biased than those from each model alone after the post-forecasting policy changes.

7.1. Pooling Forecasts

There is widespread evidence of benefits deriving from combining forecasts; see, inter alia, Makridakis and Hibon (2000) and Stock and Watson (1999). However, the outcome in Section 7 can differ considerably from what would happen in such "forecast pooling." We illustrate using the average of the two forecasts (based on the justification in Hendry and Clements 2004):

$$\overline{\overline{\Delta \mathbf{y}}}_{T+h+1|T+h} = \frac{1}{2}\left(\widehat{\Delta \mathbf{y}}^{p}_{T+h+1|T+h} + \widetilde{\Delta \mathbf{y}}^{p}_{T+h+1|T+h}\right), \tag{7.8}$$

while recognizing that other choices of weighting factors are also used. The unconditional bias (where it exists) in the post–policy VEqCM forecast is given by

$$\mathsf{E}\left[\widehat{\mathbf{u}}^{p}_{T+h+1|T+h}\right] = \left(\gamma^{p}_{h} - \gamma_{0}\right) + \boldsymbol{\lambda}\mathsf{E}\left[\nabla\boldsymbol{\beta}^{*\prime}\mathbf{x}^{*}_{T+h}\right] - \boldsymbol{\lambda}\nabla\boldsymbol{\mu}^{*} \tag{7.9}$$

so the unconditional bias of $\overline{\overline{\Delta\mathbf{y}}}_{T+h+1|T+h}$ from (7.8) is

$$\begin{aligned}
&\mathsf{E}\left[\Delta\mathbf{y}^{p}_{T+h+1} - \overline{\overline{\Delta\mathbf{y}}}_{T+h+1|T+h}\right] \\
&= \frac{1}{2}\mathsf{E}\left[\Delta\mathbf{y}^{p}_{T+h+1} - \widetilde{\Delta\mathbf{y}}^{p}_{T+h+1|T+h}\right] + \frac{1}{2}\mathsf{E}\left[\Delta\mathbf{y}^{p}_{T+h+1} - \widehat{\Delta\mathbf{y}}^{p}_{T+h+1|T+h}\right] \\
&= \frac{1}{2}\left[\left(\gamma^{p}_{y} - \gamma^{*}_{y}\right) + \left(\gamma^{p}_{h} - \gamma_{0}\right) + \boldsymbol{\lambda}\mathsf{E}\left[\nabla\boldsymbol{\beta}^{*\prime}\mathbf{x}^{*}_{T+h} - \nabla\boldsymbol{\mu}^{*}\right]\right].
\end{aligned}$$

Not only is this bias nonzero in general, it could be large as a result of $\boldsymbol{\beta}'\mathbf{x}^{*}_{T+h}$ being $\mathsf{I}(1)$ after the structural break in the cointegration relations. Moreover, both forecasting devices are likely to misforecast in the same direction after the policy change. Hence, there is little to be gained from pooling using positive weights here, since the requirement of offsetting both the structural break and the regime shift involves all three models, with the pre–regime change forecast entering negatively.

7.2. Intercept Corrections

The intercept correction we have in mind is simply "setting the model back on track" immediately prior to the forecast calculation and maintained as a permanent shift, corresponding to an indicator equal to unity from time $T+h$ on. This adds the last estimation sample error to the forecast, which at time $T+h$ is

$$\Delta\mathbf{y}^{*}_{T+h} - \widehat{\Delta\mathbf{y}^{*}}_{T+h|T+h} = \left(\gamma^{*}_{0} - \gamma_{0}\right) + \boldsymbol{\lambda}\left(\nabla\boldsymbol{\beta}^{*\prime}\mathbf{x}^{*}_{T+h-1} - \nabla\boldsymbol{\mu}^{*}\right) + \mathbf{u}_{T+h}.$$

Consequently, the forecast error of the intercept-corrected VEqCM forecast is given by

$$\begin{aligned}
\widehat{\mathbf{u}}^{p^{\mathrm{IC}}}_{T+h+1|T+h} &= \left(\Delta\mathbf{y}^{p}_{T+h+1} - \widehat{\Delta\mathbf{y}}^{p}_{T+h+1|T+h}\right) - \left(\Delta\mathbf{y}^{*}_{T+h} - \widehat{\Delta\mathbf{y}}^{*}_{T+h|T+h}\right) \\
&= \Delta\mathbf{u}_{T+h+1} + \left(\gamma^{p}_{h} - \gamma^{*}_{0}\right) + \boldsymbol{\lambda}\nabla\boldsymbol{\beta}^{*\prime}\Delta\mathbf{x}^{*}_{T+h} \\
&= \Delta\mathbf{u}_{T+h+1} + \left(\gamma^{p}_{y} - \gamma^{*}_{y}\right) - \Pi\left(\gamma^{p}_{z} - \gamma^{*}_{z}\right) \\
&\quad + \boldsymbol{\lambda}\nabla\boldsymbol{\beta}^{*\prime}\Delta\mathbf{x}^{*}_{T+h}.
\end{aligned} \tag{7.10}$$

Hence, most of the break will be corrected, just as with the scenario correction in (7.7). The only additional component unconditionally is $\boldsymbol{\lambda}\boldsymbol{\beta}^{*\prime}\gamma$, which will be small on average (e.g., if $\boldsymbol{\beta}^{*} = \boldsymbol{\beta}$, it would be precisely zero). Again, there are variance consequences (the forecast error variance is doubled for innovation errors), but these have been small relative to the sizes of structural breaks experienced historically – as manifest in the record of forecast failure – and seem likely to remain so. The greater practical difficulty is to correctly judge the need for an intercept correction, its form, and its timing.

7.3. Additional "Lucas Critique" Effects

If the parameters of the conditional model are not invariant to the policy changes, then additional departures from the above corrections will occur (Lucas 1976). In general, these will worsen the outcome of using scenario adjustments. In particular, changes in (say) $\mathbf{\Pi}$ entail that policy need not have the anticipated impact. The relevant extra errors would involve terms like $\left(\mathbf{\Pi}^* - \mathbf{\Pi}\right)$, whose main adverse impact would be from interacting with $\gamma_z^* - \gamma_z$. If all coefficients of deterministic terms were constant, only mean zero additional errors would occur, so that no forecast biases would be generated. However, policy changes would not have the anticipated effects.

7.4. Example

A potential example is one in which $\mathbf{y}_t$ includes real money holdings $(m - p)$ (M1), inflation Δp, and real total final expenditure f, whereas $\mathbf{z}_t$ includes the variables determining the opportunity cost of holding money. The effect of the UK Banking Act of 1984, which made the payment of interest on checking accounts legal, is represented in this framework by a change in the opportunity cost of holding money from R_a, the return from an alternative asset to money (e.g., the three-month local authority interest rate) to $R_n = R_a - R_o$, where R_o is the own interest rate paid on checking accounts (zero till 1984 3rd quarter). Money demand equations based on R_a experienced major forecast failure post 1985 as $(m - p)$ increased dramatically, although identical equations using R_n remained constant. Models of this aspect of the UK economy have been extensively analyzed by, inter alia, Hendry and Ericsson (1991), Boswijk (1992), Johansen (1992), Hendry and Mizon (1993), Harris (1995), Paruolo (1996), Rahbek, Kongsted, and Jørgensen (1999), and Doornik, Hendry, and Nielsen (1998).

Forecasting models of the DDV form, such as

$$\Delta\,(\widehat{m - p})_{T+1} = \Delta\,(m - p)_T,$$

did not suffer forecast failure from 1985 onwards; equally intercept corrections worked well from that date. A government that was concerned about the inflationary consequences of the resulting large increase in M1 might have responded by raising interest rates or income taxes, creating the combined event of interest in our analysis.

Some representative orders of magnitude may help to indicate when, and why, the DDV might dominate the VEqCM in forecasting when shifts occur in deterministic and related terms. In many estimated econometric equations, residual standard deviations lie between 0.5% and 1.5% of the levels of the dependent variables (albeit that some fall outside this region). Any deterministic shift in excess of 2% will, therefore, favor the DDV in short-term forecasts. The example of the 1984 Banking Act introducing interest-bearing sight deposits led to a more than 40% increase in holdings of M1 over a couple of years; the 1986 Building Societies Act (the UK analog of Savings and Loans Associations in the United States), which permitted borrowing on wholesale as well as retail money markets, induced a doubling in mortgage lending over four years. Such massive shifts swamp any uncertainty effects.

The UK M1 example also highlights the key practical problems confronting policy makers, namely, whether a structural break has occurred, and if so whether it necessitates a policy shift. With hindsight, the fact that the VEqCM is unaltered once the correct measure of opportunity cost is used shows that the increase in M1 was primarily a portfolio response (shifting into an asset with a greatly increased own yield). A policy response would have been counterproductive and, if based on raising interest rates, probably ineffective in changing M1 demands as these were based on the differential R_n. At the time, the Bank of England acted exactly that way and did not seek to intervene: inflation in fact fell considerably over the next few years, corroborating their judgement. In an important sense, however, there was a major policy change: instead of raising R_a as a policy response to M1 growing rapidly, the bank did not do so, in effect lowering their reaction parameter.

A similar situation more recently was the continued fall in inflation despite much lower unemployment rates, either occasioned by a structural shift in the NAIRU or a drop in the impact of any given departure from the NAIRU on inflation. Such settings correspond to those modeled above.

8. CONCLUSION

We consider the problem of forecasting when models are misspecified for a nonstationary data generation process, and policy may react to forecast changes. In such a setting, shifts in the coefficients of deterministic terms in the process relative to any models thereof (location shifts) induce forecast failure. Moreover, noncausal statistical devices that are robust to such location shifts – usually by imposing unnecessary additional unit roots – may provide the best available forecasts, but need have no policy implications. Since intercept corrections act like differencing and improve forecasts without altering policy conclusions, the best forecasting model is not necessarily a good basis for economic policy analysis.

Conversely, forecast failure in an econometric model need not preclude its use in policy analysis, since location shifts need not alter policy reactions. If so, such a model's implications from changes in policy regimes may be a useful guide to the outturn. Unfortunately, such "scenario changes" are not helpful in practice when the model is misforecasting badly.

Consequently, we analyze the impacts of a range of structural breaks and policy regime shifts on both econometric models and robustified forecasting devices. The results reveal that neither is immune to both changes: the econometric model fails for location shifts that occurred prior to forecasting, whereas the robust device does not; the robust device produces biased forecasts when the policy change then occurs, whereas the econometric model is no worse. Thus, we investigate correcting the statistical forecast using the econometric model's estimate of the "scenario" change resulting from the regime shift. The outcome is potentially an improvement over either forecast alone, and perhaps even over intercept correction, and dominates pooling the two forecasts by averaging.

The analysis also highlights the importance of the assumed links between the parameters of the policy equations and those of the private sector when the latter are subject to breaks, as well as the role of timing of breaks. Further, the assumptions that the econometric model coincides with the in-sample DGP and that the structural break is known are strong, and so practical applications will not attain the precise offsets found here. For example, an empirical policy model may be invalid because it embodies the wrong causal attributions; its target-instrument links are not autonomous; or its parameters are not invariant to the policy changes under analysis. While some of these problems may not be revealed in sample, the failure of a policy to produce the anticipated results would certainly do so – at a cost to society only partly mitigated by the benefits of improved knowledge of the economy. Nevertheless, even allowing for in-sample misspecification, the outcome seems likely to be worse than using either model alone only if the responses to policy are exceptionally poorly modeled.

Finally, although the timing and form of structural breaks are rarely known, and hence the appropriate policy reaction is unclear in real time, the components of our analysis indicate how to proceed, that is, combining econometric with robust forecasts and calculated scenario effects.

ACKNOWLEDGMENTS

Financial support from the UK Economic and Social Research Council under grant L138251009, and from the EUI Research Council, is gratefully acknowledged. We are indebted to Anindya Banerjee, Mike Clements, Jurgen Doornik, Neil Ericsson, John Muellbauer, Neil Shephard, Jim Stock, Ian Walker, and Ken Wallis for helpful comments.

References

Banerjee, A., D. F. Hendry, and G. E. Mizon (1996), "The Econometric Analysis of Economic Policy," *Oxford Bulletin of Economics and Statistics*, 58, 573–600.

Barrell, R. (2001), "Forecasting the World Economy," in *Understanding Economic Forecasts* (ed. by D. F. Hendry and N. R. Ericsson), Cambridge: MIT Press, 149–69.

Bates, J. M., and C. W. J. Granger (1969), "The Combination of Forecasts," *Operations Research Quarterly*, 20, 451–468. [Reprinted in T.C. Mills (Ed.) (1999), *Economic Forecasting*, Cheltenham, UK: Edward Elgar.

Bontemps, C., and G. E. Mizon (2003), "Congruence and Encompassing," in *Econometrics and the Philosophy of Economics* (ed. by B. P. Stigum), Princeton: Princeton University Press, 354–78.

Boswijk, H. P. (1992), *Cointegration, Identification and Exogeneity*, Vol. 37, Tinbergen Institute Research Series. Amsterdam: Thesis Publishers.

Britton, A. (Ed.) (1989), *Policy Making with Macroeconomic Models.* Aldershot, UK: Gower.

Bryant, R., P. Hooper, and C. L. Mann (Eds.) (1993), *Evaluating Policy Regimes: New Research in Empirical Macroeconomics.* Washington, DC: Brookings Institution.

Budd, A. (1998), "Economic Policy, with and without Forecasts," *Bank of England Quarterly Bulletin*, 38, 379–84.

Burns, T. (2001), "The Costs of Forecast Errors," in *Understanding Economic Forecasts* (ed. by D. F. Hendry and N. R. Ericsson), Cambridge: MIT Press, 170–84.

Clements, M. P., and D. F. Hendry (1995), "Forecasting in Macroeconomics," in *Time Series Models in Econometrics, Finance and Other Fields* (ed. by D. Cox, D. Hinkley, and O. Barndorff-Nielsen), London: Chapman & Hall, 99–138.

Clements, M. P., and D. F. Hendry (1996), "Intercept Corrections and Structural Change," *Journal of Applied Econometrics*, 11, 475–94.

Clements, M. P., and D. F. Hendry (1998), *Forecasting Economic Time Series.* Cambridge: Cambridge University Press.

Clements, M. P., and D. F. Hendry (1999a), *Forecasting Non-stationary Economic Time Series.* Cambridge: MIT Press.

Clements, M. P., and D. F. Hendry (1999b), "On Winning Forecasting Competitions in Economics," *Spanish Economic Review*, 1, 123–60.

Clements, M. P., and D. F. Hendry (2001), "An Historical Perspective on Forecast Errors," *National Institute Economic Review*, 177, 100–112.

Doornik, J. A., D. F. Hendry, and B. Nielsen (1998), "Inference in Cointegrated Models: UK M1 Revisited," *Journal of Economic Surveys*, 12, 533–72.

Granger, C. W. J., and M. Deutsch (1992), "Comments on the Evaluation of Policy Models," *Journal of Policy Modeling*, 14, 497–516.

Harris, R. I. D. (1995), *Using Cointegration Analysis in Econometric Modelling.* London: Prentice Hall.

Hendry, D. F. (1981), "Econometric Evidence in the Appraisal of UK Monetary Policy," in *The Third Report of the Select Committee of the House of Commons on the Treasury and Civil Service*, Vol. 3, HMSO, 1–21.

Hendry, D. F. (1991), "Economic Forecasting," in *Treasury and Civil Service Select Committee Memorandum*, HMSO.

Hendry, D. F. (1995), *Dynamic Econometrics.* Oxford: University Press.

Hendry, D. F. (1997), "The Econometrics of Macroeconomic Forecasting," *Economic Journal*, 107, 1330–57. [Reprinted in T.C. Mills (Ed.) (1999), *Economic Forecasting*, Cheltenham, UK: Edward Elgar.]

Hendry, D. F. (2000), "On Detectable and Non-detectable Structural Change," *Structural Change and Economic Dynamics*, 11, 45–65. [Reprinted in *The Economics of Structural Change*, H. Hagemann, M. Landesman, and R. Scazzieri (Eds.) (2002), Cheltenham, UK: Edward Elgar.

Hendry, D. F. (2004), "Robustifying Forecasts from Equilibrium-Correction Models," Unpublished paper, Economics Department, University of Oxford.

Hendry, D. F., and M. P. Clements (2000), "Economic Forecasting in the Face of Structural Breaks," in *Econometric Modelling: Techniques and Applications* (ed. by S. Holly and M. Weale), Cambridge: Cambridge University Press, 3–37.

Hendry, D. F., and M. P. Clements (2003), "Pooling of Forecasts," *Econometrics Journal*, 7, 1–31.
Hendry, D. F., and J. A. Doornik (1997), "The Implications for Econometric Modelling of Forecast Failure," Special issue, *Scottish Journal of Political Economy*, 44, 437–61.
Hendry, D. F., and N. R. Ericsson (1991), "Modeling the Demand for Narrow Money in the United Kingdom and the United States," *European Economic Review*, 35, 833–86.
Hendry, D. F., and G. E. Mizon (1993), "Evaluating Dynamic Econometric Models by Encompassing the VAR," in *Models, Methods and Applications of Econometrics* (ed. by P. C. B. Phillips), Oxford: Basil Blackwell, 272–300.
Hendry, D. F., and G. E. Mizon (1998), "Exogeneity, Causality, and Co-breaking in Economic Policy Analysis of a Small Econometric Model of Money in the UK," *Empirical Economics*, 23, 267–94.
Hendry, D. F., and G. E. Mizon (2000), "On Selecting Policy Analysis Models by Forecast Accuracy," in *Putting Economics to Work: Volume in Honour of Michio Morishima* (ed. by A. B. Atkinson, H. Glennester, and N. H. Stern), London: London School of Economics, 71–119.
Johansen, S. (1992), "Testing Weak Exogeneity and the Order of Cointegration in UK Money Demand," *Journal of Policy Modeling*, 14, 313–334.
Johansen, S., and K. Juselius (2000), "How to Control a Target Variable in the VAR Model," mimeo, European University Institute, Florence.
Lucas, R. E. (1976), "Econometric Policy Evaluation: A Critique," in *The Phillips Curve and Labor Markets* (ed. by K. Brunner and A. Meltzer), Vol. 1 of *Carnegie-Rochester Conferences on Public Policy*, Amsterdam: North-Holland, 19–46.
Makridakis, S., and M. Hibon (2000), "The M3-Competition: Results, Conclusions and Implications," *International Journal of Forecasting*, 16, 451–76.
Mizon, G. E. (1995), "Progressive Modelling of Macroeconomic Time Series: The LSE Methodology," in *Macroeconometrics: Developments, Tensions and Prospects* (ed. by K. D. Hoover), Dordrecht: Kluwer, 107–69.
Paruolo, P. (1996), "On the Determination of Integration Indices in I(2) Systems," *Journal of Econometrics*, 72, 313–356.
Rahbek, A., H. C. Kongsted, and C. Jørgensen (1999), "Trend-Stationarity in the I(2) Cointegration Model," *Journal of Econometrics*, 90, 265–89.
Sims, C. A. (1982), "Policy Analysis with Econometric Models," *Brookings Papers on Economic Activity*, 1, 107–64.
Sims, C. A. (1986), "Are Forecasting Models Useful for Policy Analysis?" *Federal Reserve Bank of Minneapolis Quarterly Review*, Winter, 2–16.
Stock, J. H., and M. W. Watson (1996), "Evidence on Structural Instability in Macroeconomic Time Series Relations," *Journal of Business and Economic Statistics*, 14, 11–30.
Stock, J. H., and M. W. Watson (1999), "A Comparison of Linear and Nonlinear Models for Forecasting Macroeconomic Time Series," in *Cointegration, Causality and Forecasting* (ed. by R. F. Engle, and H. White), Oxford: Oxford University Press, 1–44.
Turner, D. S., K. F. Wallis, and J. D. Whitley (1989), "Using Macroeconometric Models to Evaluate Policy Proposals," in *Policy Making with Macroeconomic Models* (ed. by A. Britton), Aldershot, UK: Gower.

PART IV

NONPARAMETRIC AND SEMIPARAMETRIC INFERENCE

CHAPTER 21

Nonparametric Testing of an Exclusion Restriction

Peter J. Bickel, Ya'acov Ritov, and Thomas M. Stoker

ABSTRACT

Following a framework proposed in Bickel, Ritov, and Stoker (2001) we propose and analyze the behavior of a broad family of tests for $H : E(Y \mid \mathbf{U}, \mathbf{V}) = E(Y \mid \mathbf{U})$ when we observe $(\mathbf{U}_i, \mathbf{V}_i, Y_i) \in R^{d_u+d_v+1}$ i.i.d., $i = 1, \ldots, n$.

1. INTRODUCTION

The practice of statistical testing plays several roles in empirical research. These roles range from the careful assessment of the evidence against specific scientific hypotheses to the judgment of whether an estimated model displays decent goodness of fit to the empirical data. The paradigmatic situation we consider is one where the investigator views some departures from the hypothesized model as being of primary importance with others of interest if sufficiently gross but otherwise secondary. For instance consider a signal hypothesized to be constant. Low frequency departures from a constant value might be considered of interest, even if of low amplitude, and high-frequency departures as less important, unless they are of high amplitude.

Bickel, Ritov, and Stoker (2001) follow this point of view by proposing a general approach to testing semiparametric hypotheses within a nonparametric model in the context of observing n i.i.d. observations. They proposed that tests should be tailored in such a way that on the $n^{-1/2}$ scale, power can be concentrated in a few selected directions with some power reserved at the same scale in all other directions. In that paper this methodology was applied to two classical problems: testing goodness-of-fit to a parametric model and testing independence. In this paper we show how this approach can be applied rigorously to generate tests for one of the simplest classical econometric hypotheses – that the conditional expectation of a response given a number of explanatory variables is in fact dependent only on a known subset of these. Such exclusion-model hypotheses have been widely discussed in the econometric literature. A recent review and a more standard type of test may be found in Ait Sahalia, Bickel, and Stoker (2001).

Formally we consider the following problem. We observe $\mathbf{Z}_i$, i.i.d. $i = 1, \ldots, n$ where $\mathbf{Z} = (\mathbf{X}, Y)$ where $\mathbf{X} = (\mathbf{U}, \mathbf{V})$, $\mathbf{U} \in \mathbf{R}^{d_u}$, $\mathbf{V} \in \mathbf{R}^{d_v}$ and $Y \in \mathbf{R}$. Assume that the joint probability density function (with respect to Lebesgue measure) of $\mathbf{X}$ and Y is given by $p(\mathbf{x}, y; f, \nu) = f(\mathbf{x}, y - \nu(\mathbf{x}))$. Let $\mathcal{P}$ be the collection of all distribution functions with such a density (i.e., for all possible f and ν satisfying the regularity assumption specified below). Finally, let H_0 be the hypothesis that $\nu(\mathbf{U}, \mathbf{V}) = \nu(\mathbf{U})$ almost surely, where the ν on the left-hand side maps $R^{d_u+d_v}$ to R while that on the right maps R^{d_u} to R. That is $E(Y \mid \mathbf{X}) = E(Y \mid \mathbf{U})$. These models contain the special case $E(Y \mid \mathbf{X}) = 0$. The extension of this last model where $E(Y \mid \mathbf{X})$ follows a parametric model was treated by Härdle and Mammen (1993).

In the general framework of Bickel et al. (2001), we test $\mathcal{P}_0$, a proper set of probability functions, against "everything," $\mathcal{P} = \mathcal{M} \equiv \{$All probabilities dominated by $\mu\}$ or at least $\mathcal{P}$ such that the tangent space is saturated,

$$\dot{\mathcal{P}}(P) = L_2^0(P) = \{h \in L_2(P) : P(h) = 0\}.$$

See Bickel et al. (1993) for a general discussion of semiparametric models and tangent spaces.

If $\dot{\mathcal{P}}_0(P)$ is the tangent space at $P_0 \in \mathcal{P}_0$, we can write the efficient score function at P_0 in a direction $a(\cdot) \in L_2^0(P)$, corresponding to a submodel of $\mathcal{P}$ containing P_0 as

$$\begin{aligned} Z_n(a, P_0) &= \frac{1}{\sqrt{n}} \sum_{i=1}^{n} (a - P_0(a) - \Pi(a, P_0))(\mathbf{Z}_i) \\ &= \frac{1}{\sqrt{n}} \sum_{i=1}^{n} \Pi^{\perp}(a, P_0)(\mathbf{Z}_i) \end{aligned} \tag{1.1}$$

for a in the tangent space, or at least in a subset $\mathcal{A}$ spanning the tangent space. Here, $\Pi(a, P_0)$ is the projection operator from $L_2(P_0)$ to the subspace $\dot{\mathcal{P}}_0(P_0)$ of $L_2^0(P_0)$, and $\Pi^{\perp}$ is the projection to the orthocomplement of $\dot{\mathcal{P}}_0(P_0)$ within $L_2^0(P_0)$. The identity uses $\Pi^{\perp}(h, P_0) = \Pi^{\perp}(h + c, P_0)$ for all c.

Call $Z_n(\cdot, P_0)$, the *score process*. In general, $Z_n(a, P_0)$ is not computable given the data, but if $\hat{P} \in \mathcal{P}_0$ is an estimate of P_0 we can consider

$$\hat{Z}_n(a) \equiv Z_n(a, \hat{P}) \tag{1.2}$$

defined on $\mathcal{A}$.

Typically we consider a parametric subfamily $\{a_\gamma, \gamma \in \Gamma\} \subset \mathcal{A}$. Having the score process, we can construct tailor-made tests by considering any functional $T(\hat{Z}_n)$. For example, two standard methods for constructing tests are

1. Cramér–von Mises type (or χ^2 goodness-of-fit) tests: $\int \omega(\gamma) \hat{Z}_n^2(a_\gamma)\, d\mu(\gamma)$ for some weight function ω and measure μ.
2. Kolmogorov–Smirnov type (or union-intersection) tests: $sup_{\gamma \in \Gamma} \omega(\gamma)|\hat{Z}_n(a_\gamma)|$.

This paper discusses the construction of $\hat{Z}_n(\cdot)$ in Section 2 and establishes the properties needed for its use, in Section 3. The definition of the actual test is left to the user although Section 4 discusses setting of critical values and gives the results of a small simulation on some natural candidate tests. A brief discussion in Section 5 and an Appendix complete the paper.

2. PRELIMINARIES

The tangent spaces are easy to characterize as shown in Bierens and Ploberger (1997) among others. The following lemma is proved for completeness.

Lemma 2.1. *We have*

$$\begin{aligned}
\dot{\mathcal{P}} &= \{a(\mathbf{X}, Y) : E_P[a^2(\mathbf{X}, Y)] < \infty,\ E_P[a(\mathbf{X}, Y)] = 0\} \\
\dot{\mathcal{P}}_0 &= \{a(\mathbf{X}, Y) = h(\mathbf{X}, Y - \nu(U)) + \ell'_{Y|\mathbf{X}}(Y - \nu(U))g(U) : \\
&\qquad a, h \in \dot{\mathcal{P}},\ \textstyle\int yh(\mathbf{X}, y)dy = 0,\ a.s.\} \\
\dot{\mathcal{P}}_0^{\perp} &= \{a(\mathbf{X}, Y) = [b(\mathbf{X}) - E(b(\mathbf{X}) \mid \mathbf{U})](Y - E(Y \mid \mathbf{U})) : a, b \in \dot{\mathcal{P}}\}.
\end{aligned}$$

where $\ell'_{Y|\mathbf{X}}(y \mid w)$ is the derivative of the conditional log-likelihood of Y given X at (y, w).

Proof. Since the "large" space is unrestricted, $\dot{\mathcal{P}}$ is "everything," but with the moment conditions. The structure of $\dot{\mathcal{P}}_0$ is obtained by considering the derivative of the general one-dimensional submodel $p_t(\mathbf{x}, y) = f_t(\mathbf{x}, y - \nu(\mathbf{u}) + tg(\mathbf{u}))$, where $h = f'_t/f_t|_{t=0}$. Finally, $\dot{\mathcal{P}}_0^{\perp}$ is the orthocomplement of $\dot{\mathcal{P}}_0$ in $\dot{\mathcal{P}}$. But $a\,(\mathbf{X}, Y)$ is orthonormal to

$$\left\{h\,(\mathbf{X}, Y - \nu\,(\mathbf{U}))\,,\ \int yh\,(\mathbf{X}, y)\,dy = 0\,a.s.\right\}$$

if and only if $a\,(\mathbf{X}, Y) = b\,(\mathbf{X})\,(Y - \nu\,(\mathbf{U}))$, a.s. This latter object is orthogonal to all functions in $\dot{\mathcal{P}}$ of the form $\ell'_y\,(\mathbf{X}, Y - \nu\,(\mathbf{U}))\,g\,(\mathbf{U})$ if and only if $E\,(b\,(\mathbf{X}) \mid \mathbf{U}) = 0\ a.s.$, which follows from the fact that for any p.d.f. q (with mean 0), we have $\int xq'\,(x)\,dx = -1$. ■

Therefore, our *score process* is defined by

$$\hat{Z}_n\,(a) \equiv \frac{1}{\sqrt{n}} \sum_{i=1}^{n} [a(\mathbf{X}_i) - E_{\hat{P}}(a(\mathbf{X}) \mid \mathbf{U}_i)]\left(Y_i - E_{\hat{P}}\,(Y \mid \mathbf{U}_i)\right) \tag{2.1}$$

where the estimator $\hat{P}$ is yet to be defined.

3. MAIN RESULT

We consider the case that $\mathcal{A}$ does not depend on P_0, the joint distribution of $(\mathbf{X}, Y - E(Y \mid \mathbf{X}) + E(Y \mid U))$. We will consider the standard Nadaraya–Watson estimates of $E_P(Y \mid U = u)$, $E_P(a(\mathbf{X}) \mid U = u)$. Let K be a symmetric kernel with bounded support on R and α vanishing moments, that is,

$$K : R \to R$$

(a) $K = 0$ outside $[-1, 1]$
(b) $\int K(u)du = 1$
(c) $\int u^j K(u)du = 0$, for $1 \leq j \leq \alpha$.

Let $\mathbb{K}_d : R^d \to R$ be the product kernel

$$\mathbb{K}_d(x_1, \ldots, x_d) = \prod_{j=1}^{d} K(x_j)$$

and $\mathbb{K}_d(\mathbf{x}; \sigma) \equiv \sigma^{-d}\mathbb{K}_d(\mathbf{x}/\sigma)$. We abuse notation writing $\hat{p}(\mathbf{x}, y)$ for the estimated joint density of $(\mathbf{X}, Y)$, $\hat{p}(\mathbf{u}, y)$ for the marginal estimated joint density of $(\mathbf{U}, Y)$ and dropping the subscript d in $\mathbb{K}_d$ when it is implicit. Then,

$$\hat{p}(\mathbf{x}, y) \equiv \int \mathbb{K}(\mathbf{x} - \mathbf{x}', y - y', \sigma) dP_n(\mathbf{x}', y')$$

$$\hat{p}(\mathbf{u}, y) = \int \mathbb{K}(\mathbf{u} - \mathbf{u}', y - y'; \sigma) dP_n(\mathbf{u}', y')$$

where we also use the convention that $P_n(\mathbf{x}, y)$ refers to the joint empirical distribution of $(\mathbf{X}, Y)$ etc. Finally,

$$\hat{E}(Y \mid \mathbf{U} = \mathbf{u}) \equiv \int y\hat{p}(\mathbf{u}, y)dy \bigg/ \int \hat{p}(\mathbf{u}, y)dy$$
$$= \int y\mathbb{K}(\mathbf{u} - \mathbf{u}'; \sigma) dP_n(\mathbf{u}', y)/\hat{p}(\mathbf{u})$$

where $\hat{p}(\mathbf{u}) \equiv \int \mathbb{K}(\mathbf{u} - \mathbf{u}'; \sigma) dP_n(\mathbf{u}')$. Here we use

$$\int y\hat{p}(\mathbf{u}, y)dy = \int y \int \mathbb{K}(\mathbf{u} - \mathbf{u}'; \sigma) K(y - y'; \sigma) dP_n(\mathbf{u}', y')dy \tag{3.1}$$

and

$$\int yK(y - y'; \sigma)dy = y'.$$

We define $\hat{E}(a(\mathbf{X}) \mid \mathbf{U} = \mathbf{u})$ similarly. We introduce the following assumptions.

I0: $\int yf(\mathbf{X}, y)\,dy = 0$ a.s., $\int (|\mathbf{x}|^2 + y^2) f(\mathbf{x}, y)\,dy\,d\mathbf{x} < \infty$, and $\int \nu^2(\mathbf{x}) f(\mathbf{x}, y)\,dy\,d\mathbf{x} < \infty$.
I1: The support of the distribution of $\mathbf{U}$ is a fixed compact, say $[-1, 1]^{d_{\mathbf{u}}}$, for all $P \in \mathcal{P}$.

I2: All $P \in \mathcal{P}$ are absolutely continuous with respect to Lebesgue measure and

(a) the density $p(\mathbf{u})$ has bounded derivatives of order greater than $\frac{3}{2}d_{\mathbf{u}}$.

(b) $Y \in L_2(P)$ and $\mathbf{u} \to E(Y \mid \mathbf{U} = \mathbf{u})$ is continuous.

Moreover

I3: There exists $\epsilon(P) > 0$ such that $\epsilon \leq p(\mathbf{u}) \leq 1/\epsilon$ for all $\mathbf{u} \in [-1, 1]^{d_{\mathbf{u}}}$.

I4: $\sup\{\|a\|_\infty : a \in \mathcal{A}\} < \infty$ and $\mathcal{A}^* \equiv \{a(\mathbf{u}) - Ea(\mathbf{X} \mid \mathbf{U} = \mathbf{u})\}$ is a VC class of functions in the sense of the definition on p. 141 of van der Vaart and Wellner (1996).

Discussion of I1–I4

1. Conditions (I1) and (I3) are very restrictive. Our argument suggests that compact support can be replaced by tail conditions on $p(\mathbf{u})$ but at the cost of a great deal of technical labor. What is essentially involved is a truncation argument – letting $\epsilon_n \to 0$ depending on n and showing that the probability of data leading to density estimates violating these restrictions is negligible. Alternatively test statistics that pay no attention to regions where $\mathbf{U}$ has low density, i.e., such that $a(\mathbf{X}) = 0$ for such $\mathbf{U}$ can be used.
2. Condition (I2) unfortunately seems necessary. It becomes more and more stringent as the dimension of $\mathbf{U}$ increases.
3. Condition (I4) is somewhat more restrictive than, say, universal Donsker. But all the usual classes, indicators of rectangles, etc., satisfy it given the smoothness conditions on $p(\mathbf{x}, \mathbf{u})$.

Then, defining $a = \Omega(b)$ iff both $\left|\frac{a}{b}\right|$ and $\left|\frac{b}{a}\right|$ are bounded, we state

Theorem 3.1. *Under I1–I4, if* $\sigma = \Omega(n^{-\frac{1}{2d+d_{\mathbf{u}}}})$ *and* K *has* α *vanishing moments where* $\alpha > \frac{3}{2}d_{\mathbf{u}}$ *then,*

$$\sup_{\mathcal{A}}\{|\hat{Z}_n(a) - Z_n(a, P_0)|\} = o_p(n^{-1/2}).$$

Proof. Write

$$\begin{aligned}
&\hat{Z}_n(a) - Z_n(a, P_0) \\
&= \int (\hat{E}(Y \mid \mathbf{U} = \mathbf{u}) - E(Y \mid \mathbf{U} = \mathbf{u})(a(\mathbf{x}) - E(a(\mathbf{X}) \mid \mathbf{U} = \mathbf{u})dP_n(\mathbf{x}) \\
&\quad + \int (\hat{E}(a(\mathbf{X}) \mid \mathbf{U} = \mathbf{u}) - E(a(\mathbf{X}) \mid \mathbf{U} = \mathbf{u}))(Y - E(Y \mid \mathbf{U} = \mathbf{u}))dP_n(\mathbf{x}) \\
&\quad + \int (\hat{E}(a(\mathbf{X}) \mid \mathbf{U} = \mathbf{u}) - E(a(\mathbf{X}) \mid \mathbf{U} = \mathbf{u}))(\hat{E}(Y \mid \mathbf{U} = \mathbf{u}) \\
&\quad - E(Y \mid \mathbf{U} = \mathbf{u}))dP_n(\mathbf{u}) \\
&= I + II + III, \quad \text{say.}
\end{aligned}$$

We argue now that under our conditions $\sup_{\mathcal{A}}|I|$, $\sup_{\mathcal{A}}|II|$, and $\sup_{\mathcal{A}}|III|$ are all $o_p(n^{-1/2})$.

To do so we require a lengthy argument some of which will be given in the appendix.

Let

$$\bar{p}(\mathbf{u}, y) = \int \mathbb{K}(\mathbf{u} - \mathbf{u}'; \sigma) p(\mathbf{u}', y) d\mathbf{u}'$$

and

$$a^*(\mathbf{x}) \equiv a(\mathbf{x}) - E(a(\mathbf{X}) \mid \mathbf{U} = \mathbf{u}).$$

Then define

$$\begin{aligned}\Delta_n^{(1)}(\mathbf{a}) &\equiv \int \left\{ \frac{\int y\hat{p}(\mathbf{u}, y)dy}{\bar{p}(\mathbf{u})} - \frac{\int y\bar{p}(\mathbf{u}, y)dy}{\bar{p}(\mathbf{u})} \right\} a^*(\mathbf{x}) dP_n(\mathbf{x}) \\ &= \int \bar{p}^{-1}(\mathbf{u}) \int y\mathbb{K}(\mathbf{u} - \mathbf{u}'; \sigma) d(P_n(\mathbf{u}', y) - P(\mathbf{u}', y)) a^*(\mathbf{x}) dP_n(\mathbf{x}).\end{aligned} \tag{3.2}$$

Similarly define

$$\Delta_n^{(2)}(\mathbf{a}) = -\int \frac{\int y\bar{p}(\mathbf{u}, y)dy}{\bar{p}^2(\mathbf{u})} (\hat{p}(\mathbf{u}) - \bar{p}(\mathbf{u})) a^*(\mathbf{x}) dP_n(\mathbf{x}) \tag{3.3}$$

$$\Delta_n^{(3)}(\mathbf{a}) = -\int \frac{\int y(p(\mathbf{u}, y) - \bar{p}(\mathbf{u}, y))dy}{\bar{p}(\mathbf{u})} a^*(\mathbf{x}) dP_n(\mathbf{x})$$

$$\Delta_n^{(4)}(\mathbf{a}) = -\int \frac{\int yp(\mathbf{u}, y)dy}{\bar{p}(\mathbf{u})p(\mathbf{u})} (\bar{p}(\mathbf{u}) - p(\mathbf{u})) a^*(\mathbf{x}) dP_n(\mathbf{x})$$

$$\Delta_n^{(5)}(\mathbf{a}) = -\int \frac{\int y(\hat{p}(\mathbf{u}, y) - \bar{p}(\mathbf{u}, y))}{\hat{p}\bar{p}(\mathbf{u})} (\hat{p}(\mathbf{u}) - \bar{p}(\mathbf{u})) a^*(\mathbf{x}) dP_n(\mathbf{x}) \tag{3.4}$$

$$\Delta_n^{(6)}(\mathbf{a}) = \int \frac{\left(\int y\bar{p}(\mathbf{u}, y)dy\right)}{\bar{p}^2(\mathbf{u})\hat{p}(\mathbf{u})} (\hat{p}(\mathbf{u}) - \bar{p}(\mathbf{u}))^2 a^*(\mathbf{x}) dP_n(\mathbf{x}). \tag{3.5}$$

Some algebra shows

$$I = \sum_{j=1}^{6} \Delta_n^{(j)}(\cdot).$$

For $g : \mathcal{A} \to R$ let $\|g\|_{\mathcal{A}} = \sup_{\mathcal{A}}|g(a)|$. We shall show that $\|\Delta_n^{(j)}\|_{\mathcal{A}} = o_p(n^{-1/2})$ for $j = 1, \ldots, 6$ and hence $\|I\|_{\mathcal{A}} = o_p(n^{-1/2})$. We can similarly establish $\|II\|_{\mathcal{A}} = o_p(n^{-1/2})$ and then argue in detail that $\|III\|_{\mathcal{A}} = o_p(n^{-1/2})$, establishing the theorem.

We proceed with $\Delta_n^{(1)}$ and note that

$$\Delta_n^{(1)}(\mathbf{a}) = \int \bar{p}^{-1}(\mathbf{u}) y \mathbb{K}(\mathbf{u} - \mathbf{u}'; \sigma) a^*(\mathbf{x}) d(P_n - P)(\mathbf{u}', y) d(P_n - P)(\mathbf{x}) \quad (3.6)$$

since for all $\mathbf{u}$

$$\int a^*(\mathbf{u}, \mathbf{v}) p(\mathbf{v} \mid \mathbf{u}) d\mathbf{v} = 0. \quad (3.7)$$

In the Appendix we show that

$$\|\Delta_n^{(1)}(\cdot) - \tilde{\Delta}_n^{(1)}(\cdot)\|_{\mathcal{A}} = o_p(n^{-1/2}) \quad (3.8)$$

where

$$\tilde{\Delta}_n^{(1)}(a) = \frac{2}{n^2} \sum_{i<j} C((\mathbf{X}_i, Y_i), (\mathbf{X}_j, Y_j), a^*; \sigma)$$

with

$$\begin{aligned} &C((\mathbf{x}, y), (\mathbf{x}', y'), a^*; \sigma) \\ &\equiv \frac{1}{2} \left\{ \frac{p(\mathbf{u})}{\bar{p}(\mathbf{u})} (y K(\mathbf{u} - \mathbf{u}'; \sigma) - E(Y K(\mathbf{u} - \mathbf{U}; \sigma))) a^*(\mathbf{x}) \right. \\ &\quad \left. + \frac{p(\mathbf{u}')}{\bar{p}(\mathbf{u})} (y' K(\mathbf{u} - \mathbf{u}'; \sigma) - E Y K(\mathbf{u}' - \mathbf{U}; \sigma)) a^*(\mathbf{x}') \right\} \end{aligned} \quad (3.9)$$

is a degenerate U statistic process and that by Theorem 2.5(b) of Arcones and Gine (1995), $\|\tilde{\Delta}_n^{(1)}\|_{\mathcal{A}} = o_p(n^{-1/2})$ under our conditions and hence $\|\Delta_n^{(1)}\|_{\mathcal{A}} = o_p(n^{-1/2})$. We now turn to $\Delta_n^{(2)}$. Again, by (3.7),

$$\begin{aligned} \Delta_n^{(2)}(\mathbf{a}) &= -\int \frac{\int y \bar{p}(\mathbf{u}, y) dy}{\bar{p}^2(\mathbf{u})} (\hat{p}(\mathbf{u}) - \bar{p}(\mathbf{u})) a^*(\mathbf{x}) d(P_n - P)(\mathbf{x}) \\ &= -\iint \left(\frac{\int y \bar{p}(u, y) dy}{\bar{p}^2(\mathbf{u})} \right) a^*(\mathbf{x}) \\ &\quad \times \mathbb{K}(\mathbf{u} - \mathbf{u}'; \sigma) \, d(P_n - P)(\mathbf{u}') d(P_n - P)(\mathbf{x}). \end{aligned} \quad (3.10)$$

This has the same structure as $\Delta_n^{(1)}$ and it can be similarly shown that $\|\Delta_n^{(2)}\|_{\mathcal{A}} = o_p(n^{-1/2})$. On the other hand, $\Delta_n^{(3)}$ and $\Delta_n^{(4)}$ can both be written in the form $\int Q(a^*; \sigma)(\mathbf{x}) d(P_n - P)(\mathbf{x})$, where $\{Q(a^*; \sigma) : a \in \mathcal{A},\ 0 \le \sigma \le 1\}$ (with $Q(a^*, 0) \equiv 0$) is a universal Donsker class in view of (I4). Since in both cases

$$\int Q^2(a^*; \sigma)(\mathbf{x}) p(\mathbf{x}) d\mathbf{x} \to 0$$

as $\sigma \to 0$ we can conclude from the theorem of van der Vaart and Wellner (1996) that $\|\Delta_n^{(j)}\|_{\mathcal{A}} = o_p(n^{-1/2})$ for $j = 3, 4$. Next,

$$\begin{aligned} |\Delta_n^{(5)}(\mathbf{a})| \le \left\| \frac{a^*}{2} \right\|_\infty &\left(\int \frac{\left(\int y (\hat{p}(\mathbf{u}, y) - \bar{p}(\mathbf{u}, y)) dy \right)^2}{\bar{p}^2(\mathbf{u})} d P_n(\mathbf{u}) \right. \\ &\quad \left. + \int \frac{(\hat{p}(\mathbf{u}) - \bar{p}(\mathbf{u}))^2}{\hat{p}^2(\mathbf{u})} d P_n(\mathbf{u}) \right). \end{aligned} \quad (3.11)$$

By (I2) and (3.13) below, $\|\hat{p}(\mathbf{u}) - \bar{p}(\mathbf{u})\|_\infty = o_p(1)$. Hence, by (I3) the denominators of both terms in (3.11) are bounded away from 0 with probability tending to 1. Write

$$\Delta_{n1}^{(5)} \equiv \int \left(\int y(\hat{p}(\mathbf{u}, y) - \bar{p}(\mathbf{u}, y))dy \right)^2 dP_n(\mathbf{u}) \qquad (3.12)$$
$$= \frac{1}{n^3} \sum_{i,j,k} A_{ij} A_{kj}$$

where

$$A_{ij} \equiv (Y_i \mathbb{K}(\mathbf{U}_j - \mathbf{U}_i; \sigma) - E(Y_i \mathbb{K}(\mathbf{U}_j - \mathbf{U}_i; \sigma) \mid \mathbf{U}_j)).$$

Note that $E A_{ij} A_{kj} = 0$ unless $i = k$. Thus

$$E\Delta_n^{(5)} \leq n^{-2} K^2(0; \sigma) E Y_1^2 + n^{-1} E Y_1^2 \mathbb{K}(\mathbf{U}_1 - \mathbf{U}_2; \sigma)$$
$$= O(n^{-2}\sigma^{-2d_\mathbf{u}}) + O(n^{-1}\sigma^{-d_\mathbf{u}}) = o\left(n^{-1/2}\right)$$

by the assumption $\sigma = \Omega(n^{-1/2\alpha + d_\mathbf{u}})$, $\int (\hat{p}(\mathbf{u}) - \bar{p}(\mathbf{u}))^2 dP_n(\mathbf{u})$ is bounded similarly and $\|\Delta_n^{(5)}\|_{\mathcal{A}} = o_p(n^{-1/2})$ follows. Similarly,

$$|\Delta_n^{(6)}(\mathbf{a})| \leq \|a^*\|_\infty \sup_\mathbf{u} (\hat{p}(\mathbf{u})$$
$$-\bar{p}(\mathbf{u}))^2 \sup_\mathbf{u} \bar{p}^{-2}(\mathbf{u}) \sup_\mathbf{u} \hat{p}^{-2}(\mathbf{u}) \frac{1}{n^2} \sum_{i,j} Y_i \mathbb{K}(\mathbf{u}_i - \mathbf{u}_j; \sigma).$$

Again by (I2) and (7.1) of Härdle and Mammen (1993),

$$\|\hat{p}(\mathbf{u}) - \bar{p}(\mathbf{u})\|_\infty = O_p\left(n^{-\frac{\alpha}{2\alpha + d_\mathbf{u}}} \log n\right). \qquad (3.13)$$

By (I3) the second two sups are $O_p(1)$, the first sup is $O_p(n^{-2\alpha(2\alpha + d_\mathbf{u})^{-1}} y^2 n)$. Finally, the last term is $O_p(1)$. Thus we conclude since $\alpha > \frac{3}{2} d_\mathbf{u}$ that $\|\Delta_n^{(6)}\|_{\mathcal{A}} = o_p(n^{-1/2})$ and $\sup_{\mathcal{A}} I = o_p(n^{-1/2})$.

For II we proceed similarly. Here

$$II(\mathbf{a}) = \sum_{j=1}^{6} \tilde{\Delta}_n^{(j)}(\mathbf{a}) \qquad (3.14)$$

$$\tilde{\Delta}_n^{(1)}(a) = \int \bar{p}^{-1}(\mathbf{u}) \int a(\mathbf{x}) \mathbb{K}(\mathbf{u} - \mathbf{u}'; \sigma) d(P_n - P)(\mathbf{u}', \mathbf{v}) e(y, \mathbf{u}) dP_n(y, \mathbf{u})$$

where $e(y, \mathbf{u}) \equiv y - E(Y \mid \mathbf{U} = \mathbf{u})$ and this is dealt with just as $\Delta_n^{(1)}$ was.

The same kind of argument applies to the terms corresponding to $\tilde{\Delta}_n^{(2)} - \tilde{\Delta}_n^{(6)}$. We finally turn to III.

$$|III(a)| \leq \frac{1}{2} \left(\int (\hat{E}(a(\mathbf{X}) \mid \mathbf{U} = \mathbf{u}) - E(a(\mathbf{X}) \mid \mathbf{U} = \mathbf{u}) \right)^2 dP_n(\mathbf{u})$$
$$+ \int (\hat{E}(Y \mid \mathbf{U} = \mathbf{u}) - E(Y \mid \mathbf{U} = \mathbf{u}))^2 dP_n(\mathbf{u}).$$

Decompose as for I and II. For instance,

$$\begin{aligned}
&\int (\hat{E}(a(\mathbf{X}) \mid \mathbf{U}=\mathbf{u}) - E(a(\mathbf{X}) \mid \mathbf{U}=\mathbf{u}))^2 dP_n(\mathbf{u}) \\
&\leq C\Bigg(\int \left(\int \frac{a(\mathbf{x})}{\bar{p}(\mathbf{u})}\mathbb{K}(\mathbf{u}-\mathbf{u}';\sigma)d(P_n - P)(\mathbf{u}',\mathbf{v})\right)^2 dP_n(\mathbf{u}) \\
&\quad + \int \left(\int a(\mathbf{x})(\hat{p}(\mathbf{u}) - \bar{p}(\mathbf{u}))\frac{\bar{p}(\mathbf{x})}{\bar{p}^2(\mathbf{u})}d\mathbf{v}\right)^2 dP_n(\mathbf{u}) \\
&\quad + \int \left(\int a(\mathbf{x})\frac{(p-\bar{p})}{\bar{p}(\mathbf{u})}(\mathbf{x})d\mathbf{v}\right)^2 dP_n(\mathbf{u}) \\
&\quad + \int \left(\int a(\mathbf{x})\frac{p(\mathbf{x})}{\bar{p}p(\mathbf{u})}(\bar{p}(\mathbf{u}) - p(\mathbf{u}))d\mathbf{v}\right)^2 dP_n(\mathbf{u}) \\
&\quad + \int \left(\int a(\mathbf{x})\frac{(\hat{p}(\mathbf{x}) - \bar{p}(\mathbf{x}))(\hat{p}(\mathbf{u}) - \bar{p}(\mathbf{u}))}{\hat{p}\bar{p}(\mathbf{u})}d\mathbf{v}\right)^2 dP_n(\mathbf{u}) \\
&\quad + \int \left(\int \frac{a(\mathbf{x})p(\mathbf{x})}{\hat{p}^2\bar{p}^2(\mathbf{u})}d\mathbf{v}(\hat{p}(\mathbf{u}) - p(\mathbf{u})^2 d\mathbf{v}\right)^2 dP_n(\mathbf{u})\Bigg) \qquad (3.15)
\end{aligned}$$

In the appendix we show that

$$\sup_{\mathcal{A},\mathbf{u}} \left(\int \frac{a(\mathbf{x})}{\bar{p}(\mathbf{u})}\mathbf{K}(\mathbf{u}-\mathbf{u}';\sigma)d(P_n - P)(\mathbf{u}',\mathbf{v})\right)^2 = o_p\left(n^{-1/2}\right) \qquad (3.16)$$

by using large deviation bounds on the empirical process applied to $\{a(\mathbf{u},\cdot)\mathbb{K}(\mathbf{u}-\cdot;\sigma) : a \in \mathcal{A}, \mathbf{u} \in K\}$.

The remaining terms are more straightforward. We can pull out the inf of $\hat{p}$ and $\bar{p}$ as well as the L_∞ norm of a and then argue as we did for $\Delta_n^{(5)}$. The argument for the term that involves $\hat{E}(Y \mid \cdot)$ is easy. The theorem follows. ■

A problem we have not yet tackled is how to set critical values for our tests. As the discussion in Bickel et al. (2001) indicates, two bootstraps are in principle possible. In the current model the "wild" bootstrap (see Härdle and Mammen, 1993) is also possible. We chose to implement the version proposed by Bickel and Ren (2001), i.e., simulate the distribution of $\sqrt{n}(\hat{Z}_n^*(\cdot) - \hat{Z}_n(\cdot))$ where $\hat{Z}_n^*$ is the $\hat{Z}_n$ process defined for the bootstrap sample $Z_1^*, \ldots, Z_n^*$ from the empirical of $Z_1, \ldots, Z_n$ where $Z_j = (\mathbf{V}_j, Y_j)$. Unfortunately the conditions of Theorems 1 and 2 of Bickel and Ren are not satisfied. We give a more special argument. Note that

$$\hat{Z}_n^*(a) = \int (y - \hat{E}^*(Y \mid \mathbf{U}=\mathbf{u}))(a(\mathbf{x}) - \hat{E}^*(a(\mathbf{X}) \mid \mathbf{U}=\mathbf{u}))dP_n^*(\mathbf{x}, y).$$

Let

$$\tilde{Z}_n(a) = \int (y - \hat{E}^*(Y \mid \mathbf{U} = \mathbf{u}))(a(\mathbf{x}) - E^*(a(\mathbf{x}) \mid \mathbf{U} = \mathbf{u}))dP_n(\mathbf{x}, y).$$

Showing that

$$\tilde{Z}_n(a) - Z_n(a, P_0) = o_p(n^{-1/2})$$

can be done by essentially the same argument as that used for Theorem 3.1. For instance, define $\tilde{\Delta}_n^{(1)}$ corresponding to $\Delta_n^{(1)}$ by simply replacing P_n by P_n^* in the inner differential. We are left with showing that

$$\int (E(Y \mid \mathbf{U} = \mathbf{u}) - \hat{E}^*(Y \mid \mathbf{U} = \mathbf{u}))(a(\mathbf{x}) - E(a(\mathbf{X}) \mid \mathbf{U} = \mathbf{u})) \times d(P_n^* - P_n)(\mathbf{x}) = o_p(n^{-1/2})$$

$$\int (y - E(Y \mid \mathbf{U} = \mathbf{u}))(Ea(\mathbf{X}) \mid \mathbf{U} = \mathbf{u}) - \hat{E}^*(a(\mathbf{X}) \mid \mathbf{U} = \mathbf{u})) \times d(P_n^* - P_n)(\mathbf{u}, y) = o_p(n^{-1/2})$$

and

$$\int (E(Y \mid \mathbf{U} = \mathbf{u}) - \hat{E}^*(Y \mid \mathbf{U} = \mathbf{u}))(E(a(\mathbf{X}) \mid \mathbf{U} = \mathbf{u}) - \hat{E}^*(a(\mathbf{X}) \mid \mathbf{U} = \mathbf{u}))d(P_n^* - P_n)(\mathbf{X}) = o_p(n^{-1/2}).$$

These terms can all be approximated by quantities of the form appearing on the right in $\Delta_n^{(1)} - \Delta_n^{(5)}$ and the validity of the bootstrap approximation established.

4. CRITICAL VALUES AND SIMULATIONS

We checked the behavior of different estimators using a small Monte Carlo experiment. We consider a sample of 500 independent observations from (U, V, Y) where $Y = \nu_\lambda(U, V) + \epsilon$, and where U, V, and ϵ are independent, $U, V \sim U(0, 1)$, $\epsilon \sim N(0, 1)$, and $\nu_\lambda(u, v) = 0.8 \sin(\lambda u) \sin(\lambda v)$, where $\lambda = 0, \pi/2, \pi, 6\pi$. Of course, $\lambda = 0$ is the null assumption. The three regression surfaces are shown in Figure 21.1.

The three test statistics we examined were all based on partition of the unit square to 10×5 blocks with the support of U divided into 10 blocks. The discretization of the range of U introduces a bias, since if it is not fine enough, a distribution in which Y and $\mathbf{X}$ are conditionally independent given U may not be conditionally independent given the blocks. Condition (I2) is necessary to ensure that the test will be asymptotically unbiased. On the other hand the wideness of the blocks on the V dimension is secondary and enters only through efficiency considerations and the behavior of the bootstrap.

With the division into blocks, one simple test is a standard ANOVA test for only the U effect (i.e., no V effect and no interaction). This is our first test statistic. The second is a Kolmogorov–Smirnov-like test with the quadrates

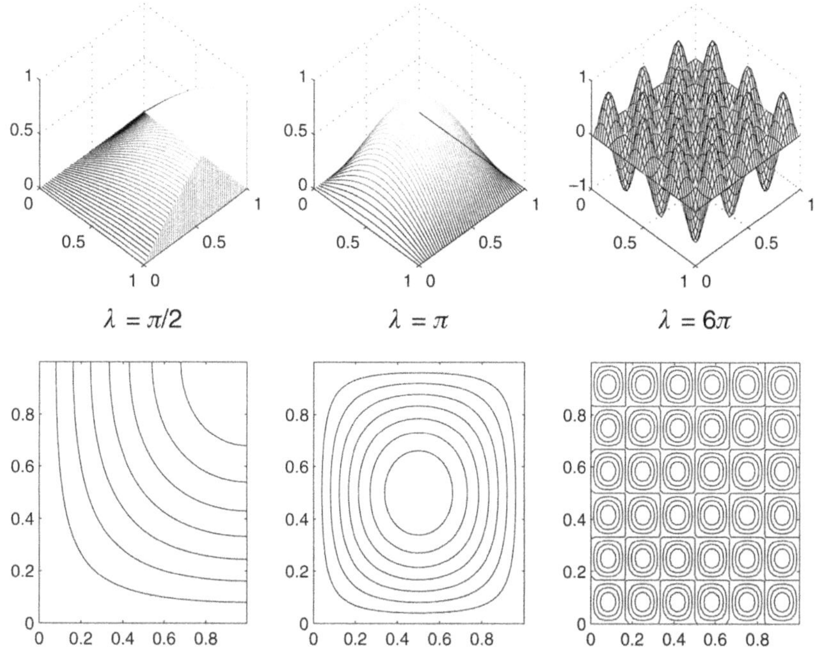

Figure 21.1. Different alternatives for the regression function.

$\{\mathbf{1}(u \geq \gamma_1,\ v \geq \gamma_2)\}$. The third is another Kolmogorov–Smirnov statistic with rectangles: $\{\mathbf{1}(\gamma < u \leq \gamma_2,\ \gamma_3 < v \leq \gamma_4)\}$.

The tests are defined formally as follows. With some abuse of notation let Y_{klm}, $k = 1, \ldots, K$, $l = 1, \ldots, L$, $m = 1, \ldots, n_{kl}$ be the the Y value of the mth observation in the kl block. Denote as usual $\bar{Y}_{kl\cdot} = n_{kl}^{-1} \sum_m Y_{klm}$ and $\bar{Y}_{k\cdot\cdot} = n_{k\cdot}^{-1} \sum_{lm} Y_{klm}$. Note that

$$\sum_{i=1}^{n} (a(\mathbf{X}_i) - E_{\hat{P}}(\mathbf{X} \mid U_i))(Y_i - E_{\hat{P}}(Y \mid U_i)) = \sum_{i=1}^{n} a(\mathbf{X}_i)(Y_i - E_{\hat{P}}(Y \mid U_i))$$

Then the three test statistics are

$$F = \frac{\sum_{kl} \bar{Y}_{kl\cdot}^2 n_{kl} - \sum_k \bar{Y}_{k\cdot\cdot}^2 n_{k\cdot}}{\sum_{klm} Y_{klm}^2 - \sum_k \bar{Y}_{k\cdot\cdot}^2 n_{k\cdot}}$$

$$KS_1 = \max_{kl} \left| \sum_{k'=k}^{K} \sum_{l'=l}^{L} \sum_{m=1}^{n_{k'l'}} (Y_{k'l'm} - \bar{Y}_{k\cdot\cdot}) \right|$$

$$KS_2 = \max_{k_1 l_1 k_2 l_2} \left| \sum_{k'=l_1}^{l_2} \sum_{l'=k_1}^{k_2} \sum_{m=1}^{n_{k'l'}} (Y_{k'l'm} - \bar{Y}_{k\cdot\cdot}) \right|$$

The three deviations were supposed to check the strengths and weaknesses of these tests. The first KS test was expected to be more powerful for deviations like the one with $\lambda = \pi/2$, in which the corners are different from the average.

Table 21.1.

Test statistic	λ = 0	$\pi/2$	π	6π
	$\alpha = 0.1$			
F	0.072	0.492	0.443	0.453
KS_1	0.115	0.970	0.565	0.122
KS_2	0.095	0.838	0.887	0.113
	$\alpha = .05$			
F	0.025	0.355	0.290	0.307
KS_1	0.052	0.922	0.395	0.072
KS_2	0.050	0.728	0.818	0.060

The second KS was expected to be more powerful against deviations that are concentrated in the center as in the case of $\lambda = \pi$. Finally, the F test disperses its strength among 40 degrees of freedom. Hence we expect it to be weak against particular deviations, but unlike the two KS tests, is relatively strong against more complicated deviations like the one with $\lambda = 6\pi$. (This paragraph was written before any simulation was done.)

The bootstrap was done essentially as described above. There were, however, two modifications. Theoretically the number of observations in a cell should increase to ∞, but in practice is finite, and may be quite small. (In our simulation there were, on the average, 10 observations in a cell.) Since we center the observations in a cell (so that we sample under H), this decreases the variance of the distribution from which the bootstrap samples are taken and, as a result, the spread of the test statistics is reduced. To correct that, we multiplied each observation in the kl cell by $\sqrt{n_{kl}/(n_{kl} - 1)}$. See Silverman (1981) for a similar correction. The KS-type tests were not conservative without the inflation. Of course the F test is invariant for this correction. The second modification was that the bootstrap was used only for the Y values (hence we conducted a conditional test on the $\mathbf{X}$s).

Rejection was defined if the test statistics was one of the $100(1 - \alpha)\%$ larger values among 200 observations where α is the declared level. The randomization (both the sampling and the bootstrapping) were common to the twenty-four combinations of test statistics and values of λ and α.

The powers at level $\alpha = .1$ and $.05$ of the various statistics are given in Table 21.1.

5. DISCUSSION

The simulation results show that it is possible to tailor tests against expected departures. The minimax F test does indeed perform far better than the other two for the $\lambda = 6\pi$ case but the relevance of this least favorable departure is unclear. This test also appears conservative for reasons not apparent to us. Unfortunately though, in these limited simulations not much power was conserved against alternatives quite different from the ones envisaged. For the cases we have considered one might be able to handle both types of situations by combining test statistics. But presumably then other directions would suffer. All we can hope for is good power in interesting directions when the signal-to-noise ratio is moderate and in uninteresting directions when the signal-to-noise ratio is really high. Much more extensive simulations would need to be done to go further.

Technical though our discussion is, it does not cover the more important case where the index is unknown, i.e., $\mathbf{U} = \mathbf{X}^T\boldsymbol{\theta}$ with $\boldsymbol{\theta}$ unknown. At the scale we are working with, the distribution of $\boldsymbol{\theta}$ will have an effect but again we expect to be able to tailor though formulating and checking regulatory conditions becomes even more tedious.

A new class of so-called adaptive tests for which minimax power is demanded over a range of scales (see Spokoiny 1996; Ingster 1992; and Horowitz and Spokoiny 2000) has recently gained popularity. We have not made explicit comparison with these procedures either theoretically or practically. We would expect that they have greater robustness of power but do not do as well in the directions we tailor (since our tests are essentially designed against parametric models while the minimax tests aim in all directions simultaneously). Of course, as e.g. Horowitz and Spokoiny (2000) point out, no tests such as ours can have behavior that is uniformly good – guarding against we believe unrealistic alternatives is the price of minimaxity.

APPENDIX

Proof of Theorem 6.1.

Proof of (3.8) and $\|\Delta_n^{(1)}\|_{\mathcal{A}} = o_p(n^{-1/2})$.

$$\begin{aligned}\Delta_n^{(1)}(a) &= n^{-2}\sum_{i,j}\frac{p(\mathbf{U}_i)}{\bar{p}(\mathbf{U}_i)}(Y_j\mathbb{K}(\mathbf{U}_i-\mathbf{U}_j;\sigma)\\ &\quad - E(Y_j\mathbb{K}(\mathbf{U}_i-\mathbf{U}_j;\sigma)\mid \mathbf{U}_i)a^*(\mathbf{X}_i)\\ &= \tilde{\Delta}_n^{(1)}(a) - n^{-2}\mathbb{K}(0;\sigma)\sum_{i=1}^{n}\frac{p(\mathbf{U}_i)}{\bar{p}(\mathbf{U}_i)}(Y_i - E(Y_i\mid \mathbf{U}_i))a^*(\mathbf{X}_i).\end{aligned} \tag{A.1}$$

The second term here is evidently $O_p(n^{-1}\sigma^{-d_{\mathbf{u}}}) = o_p(n^{-1/2})$ by (I3).

Note that

$$\begin{aligned}&\|C(\mathbf{x},\mathbf{x}',a^*;\sigma)\|_{\mathcal{A}}\\ &\le \frac{1}{2}\sup_{\mathcal{A}}\|a^*\|_\infty\left\|\frac{p(\mathbf{u})}{\bar{p}(\mathbf{u})}(y\mathbb{K}(\mathbf{u}-\mathbf{u}';\sigma) - E(YK(\mathbf{u}-\mathbf{U};\sigma))\right.\\ &\left.+\ \frac{p(\mathbf{u}')}{\bar{p}(\mathbf{u}')}(y'\mathbb{K}(\mathbf{u}-\mathbf{u}';\sigma - E(YK(\mathbf{u}-\mathbf{u}';\sigma))\right\|\\ &\le \sup_{\mathcal{A}}\|a^*\|_\infty\left(\frac{p(\mathbf{u})}{\bar{p}(\mathbf{u})}+\frac{p(\mathbf{u}')}{\bar{p}(\mathbf{u}')}\right)(|y|+E|Y|)\sigma^{-d_{\mathbf{u}}}.\end{aligned} \tag{A.2}$$

By Theorem 2.5(b) of Arcones and Gine (1995)

$$n(\log\log n)^2 E\|\tilde{\Delta}_n^{(1)}\|_{\mathcal{A}}^p \leq \sigma^{-pd_{\mathbf{u}}} 2E|Y|\epsilon^{-2}(P)\sup_{\mathcal{A}}\|a^*\|_\infty$$

for $0 < p < 2$ where $\epsilon(P)$ is the lower bound on $p(\mathbf{u})$. Hence,

$$\|\tilde{\Delta}_n^{(1)}\|_{\mathcal{A}} = O_p(n^{-1}\sigma^{-d_{\mathbf{u}}}(\log\log n)^2) = o_p(n^{-1/2}).$$

Proof of (3.16). Let $\mathcal{A}$ have metric entropy for Q given by

$$N(\mathcal{A}, L_2(Q)).$$

Let $\tilde{\mathcal{A}}_n = \left\{\frac{a(\mathbf{u},\cdot)}{\bar{p}(\mathbf{u})}\mathbb{K}(\mathbf{u} - \cdot;\sigma) : a \in \mathcal{A}, \mathbf{u} \in R^{d_{\mathbf{u}}}\right\}$. Given $\epsilon > 0$ by the smoothness of $\mathbb{K}$ we can find $\mathbf{u}_1^{(\epsilon)}, \ldots, \mathbf{u}_n^{(\epsilon)} \ni$ for some $j(\mathbf{u})$, $\|\mathbb{K}(\mathbf{u} - \cdot;\sigma) - \mathbb{K}(\mathbf{u}_j(\epsilon) - \cdot;\sigma)\|_\infty \leq \epsilon$ and $M = \Omega((\epsilon\sigma)^{-d_{\mathbf{u}}})$. Therefore

$$N(\tau, \tilde{\mathcal{A}}, L_2(Q)) = \Omega(N(\tau, \mathcal{A}, L_2(Q)) \cdot \Omega((\tau\sigma)^{-d_{\mathbf{u}}})$$

where $a_n = \Omega(b_n)$ iff $a_n = O(b_n)$, $b_n = O(a_n)$ and we can conclude from Theorem 2.14.9 of van der Vaart and Wellner (1996) that if $\mathbb{G}_n$ is the empirical process $\sqrt{n}(P_n - P)$ then,

$$\|\mathbb{G}_n\|_{\tilde{\mathcal{A}}} = O_p(\sigma^{-d_{\mathbf{u}}}). \quad \text{(A.3)}$$

Now (A.3) implies 3.16 since the left-hand side is $O_p(n^{-1}\sigma^{-2d_{\mathbf{u}}})$. ■

ACKNOWLEDGMENT

This research was partially supported by NSF grant FD01-04075.

References

Ait-Sahalia, Y., P. J. Bickel, and T. M. Stoker (2001), "Goodness-of-Fit Tests for Regression Using Kernel Methods," *Journal of Econometrics*, 105, 363–412.

Arcones, M., and E. Gine (1995), "On the Law of the Iterated Logarithm for Canonical *U* Processes," *Stochastic Proceses and Their Applications*, 58, 217–45.

Bickel, P. J., C. Klaassen, Y. Ritov, and J. A. Wellner (1993), *Efficient and Adaptive Estimation for Semiparametric Models*. London: Johns Hopkins University Press.

Bickel, P. J., and J. J. Ren (2001), "The Bootstrap in Hypothesis Testing," in de Gunsl, M., C. Klaasen, and A. van der Vaart, eds., *State of the Art in Probability and Statistics, IMS Lecture Notes*, vol. 36.

Bickel, P. J., Y. Ritov, and T. M. Stoker (2001), "Tailor-Made Tests for Goodness-of-Fit to Semi-Parametric Hypotheses," Technical report.

Bierens, H., and W. Ploberger (1997), "Asymptotic Theory of Integrated Conditional Moment Tests," *Econometrica*, 65, 1129–51.

Härdle, W., and E. Mammen (1993), "Comparing Nonparametric versus Parametric Regression Fits," *Annals of Statistics*, 21, 1926–47.

Horowitz, J. L., and V. G. Spokoiny (2000), "An Adaptive Rate Optimal Test of a Parametric Mean-Regression Model against a Nonparametric Alternative," *Econometrica*, 69, 599–631.

Ingster, Yu. I. (1993a,b,c), "Asymptotically Minimax Hypothesis Testing for Nonparametric Alternatives," *Mathematical Methods of Statistics*, 2, 85–114, 171–89, 249–68.

Silverman, B. (1981), "Using Bootstrap Kernel Density Estimates to Investigate Unimodality," *Journal of the Royal Statistical Society*, Series B, 43, 97–9.

Spokoiny, V. (1996), "Adaptive Hypothesis Testing Using Wavelets," *Annals of Statistics*, 24, 2477–98.

van der Vaart, A., and J. A. Wellner (1996), *Weak Convergence and Empirical Processes*. New York: Springer Verlag.

CHAPTER 22

Pairwise Difference Estimators for Nonlinear Models

Bo E. Honoré and James L. Powell

ABSTRACT

This paper uses insights from the literature on estimation of nonlinear panel data models to construct estimators of a number of semiparametric models with a partially linear index, including the partially linear logit model, the partially linear censored regression model, and the censored regression model with selection. We develop the relevant asymptotic theory for these estimators and we apply the theory to derive the asymptotic distribution of the estimator for the partially linear logit model. We evaluate the finite sample behavior of this estimator using a Monte Carlo study.

1. INTRODUCTION

For the linear panel data regression model with fixed effects,

$$y_{it} = \alpha_i + x_{it}\beta + \varepsilon_{it}, \tag{1.1}$$

in which the individual-specific intercept ("fixed effect") α_i can be arbitrarily related to the regressors x_{it}, a standard estimation approach is based upon "pairwise differencing" of the dependent variable y_{it} across time for a given individual to eliminate the fixed effect:

$$y_{it} - y_{is} = (x_{it} - x_{is})\beta + (\varepsilon_{it} - \varepsilon_{is}), \tag{1.2}$$

a form which eliminates the nuisance parameters $\{\alpha_i\}$ and is amenable to the usual estimation methods for linear regression models under suitable conditions on the error terms $\{\varepsilon_{it}\}$. For nonlinear models – that is, models which are not additively separable in the fixed effect α_i – this pairwise differencing approach is generally not applicable, and identification and consistent estimation of the β coefficients is problematic at best. Still, for certain nonlinear panel data models, variations of the "pairwise comparison" or "matching" approach can be used to construct estimators which circumvent the incidental-parameters problem caused by the presence of fixed effects; such models include the binary logit model (Rasch 1960, Chamberlain 1984), the censored regression model (Honoré 1992), and the Poisson regression model (Hausman, Hall, and Griliches 1984).

Powell (1987, 2001) and Ahn and Powell (1993) exploited an analogy between the linear panel data model (1.1) and semiparametric linear selection models for cross-section data to derive consistent estimators for the latter. These estimators treat the additive "selection correction term" as analogous to the fixed effect in the linear panel data model, and eliminate selectivity bias by differencing observations with approximately equal selection correction terms. The aim of this chapter is to extend this analogy between linear panel data models and linear selection models to those nonlinear panel data models, cited above, for which pairwise comparisons can be used to eliminate the fixed effects. This extension will yield consistent and asymptotically normal estimators for the linear regression coefficients in binary logit, censored regression, and Poisson regression models with additively separable nonparametric components – that is, nonlinear extensions of the "semiparametric regression model" proposed by Engle et al. (1986) – and also for the censored regression model with sample selection.

In the next section, more details of the analogy between linear panel data models and semiparametric regression and selection models are provided, and the resulting pairwise difference estimators for the various nonlinear models are precisely defined. These estimators are all defined as minimizers of "kernel-weighted U-statistics"; some general results for consistency and asymptotic normality of such estimators are provided in Section 3. One novel feature of the general asymptotic theory is a "generalized jackknife" method for direct bias reduction for the estimator, which is a computationally-convenient alternative to the usual requirement that the kernel weights be of "higher-order bias-reducing" form. The paper then specializes these general results to the pairwise-difference estimator for the partially linear logit model, and presents the results of a Monte Carlo study to evaluate the finite-sample performance of this estimator.

2. MOTIVATION FOR THE PROPOSED ESTIMATORS

In order to motivate the estimation approach proposed here, it is useful to first consider the partially linear model[1]

$$y_i = x_i\beta + g(w_i) + \varepsilon_i, \quad i = 1, \ldots, n, \tag{2.1}$$

where (y_i, x_i, w_i) are observed (and randomly sampled over i), β is the parameter of interest and $g(\cdot)$ is an unknown function which is assumed to be

[1] This model is also called the "semiparametric regression model" and the "semilinear regression model," and has been considered by Engle et al. (1986) and Robinson (1988), among others.

Estimation of both linear and nonlinear versions of this model, including the partially linear logit model discussed in the next section, is also considered by van de Geer (2000, Chapter 11, Section 1), who proposes penalized least-squares or maximum likelihood estimators, respectively, with smoothness penalty proportional to the Sobolev norm of g (i.e., integrated squared value of g and its derivatives), and derives root-n consistency, asymptotic normality, and semiparametric efficiency of the estimators of β_0 under somewhat different conditions than those imposed here.

"sufficiently smooth." The term $g(w_i)$ in (2.1) can represent "true nonlinearity" or may be the result of sample selection. For example, in the sample selection model (Type 2 Tobit model, in the terminology of Amemiya (1985)), the data is generated from

$$y_i^\star = x_i\beta + \varepsilon_i, \tag{2.2}$$

$$d_i = 1\{w_i\gamma + \eta_i > 0\}, \tag{2.3}$$

and the data consists of $y_i = d_i y_i^\star, d_i, x_i$, and w_i. If it is assumed that (ε_i, η_i) is independent of (x_i, w_i), then we can write

$$y_i = x_i\beta + g(w_i\gamma) + \nu_i, \quad E[\nu_i|x_i, w_i, d_i = 1] = 0,$$

where $g(w_i\gamma) = E[\varepsilon_i|w_i\gamma + \eta_i > 0]$ and $\nu_i = \varepsilon_i - g(w_i\gamma)$.

Powell (1987, 2001) proposed estimation of (2.2) (and implicitly also of (2.1)) using the idea that if $w_i\gamma$ equals $w_j\gamma$ then for observations i and j the terms $g(w_i\gamma)$ and $g(w_i\gamma)$ are analogous to the fixed effect α_i in (1.1), which can be differenced away as in (1.2). Since γ is typically unknown, and $w_i\gamma$ typically continuously distributed, a feasible version of this idea uses all pairs of observations and gives bigger weight to pairs for which $w_i\hat{\gamma}$ is close to $w_j\hat{\gamma}$, where $\hat{\gamma}$ is an estimator of γ. The weights are chosen in such a way that only pairs with $w_i\gamma - w_j\gamma$ in a shrinking neighborhood of zero will matter asymptotically.

The insight in this chapter is to observe that this pairwise difference idea can be applied to any model for which it is possible to "difference out" a fixed effect. We outline some examples of models in which the idea can be used.

2.1. Partially Linear Logit Model

The logit model with fixed effects is given by

$$y_{it} = 1\{\alpha_i + x_{it}\beta + \varepsilon_{it} \geq 0\} \quad t = 1, 2, i = 1, \ldots, n,$$

where $\{\varepsilon_{it} : t = 1, 2; i = 1, \ldots, n\}$ are i.i.d. logistically distributed random variables. In this model, Rasch (1960) observed that β can be estimated by maximizing the conditional log-likelihood (see also Chamberlain (1984), p. 1274)

$$\mathcal{L}_n(b) \equiv \sum_{i:y_{i1}\neq y_{i2}} -y_{i1}\ln(1 + \exp((x_{i2} - x_{i1})b)) - y_{i2}\ln(1 + \exp((x_{i1} - x_{i2})b)).$$

Now consider the partially linear logit model

$$y_i = \{x_i\beta + g(w_i) + \varepsilon_i \geq 0\} \quad i = 1, \ldots, n. \tag{2.4}$$

For observations with w_i close to w_j, the terms $g(w_i)$ and $g(w_j)$ are almost like fixed effects, provided that g is smooth. This suggests estimating β by maximizing

$$L_n(b) = \binom{n}{2}^{-1} \frac{1}{h_n^L} \sum_{\substack{i<j \\ y_i \neq y_j}} -K\left(\frac{w_i - w_j}{h_n}\right)(y_i \ln(1 + \exp((x_j - x_i)b)) + y_j \ln(1 + \exp((x_i - x_j)b))), \tag{2.5}$$

where $K(\cdot)$ is a kernel which gives the appropriate weight to the pair (i, j), and h_n is a bandwidth which shrinks as n increases. Here L denotes the dimensionality of w_i and the term $\binom{n}{2}^{-1}\frac{1}{h_n^L}$ will ensure that the objective function converges to a nondegenerate function under appropriate regularity conditions. The asymptotic theory will require that $K(\cdot)$ is chosen so that a number of regularity conditions, such as $K(u) \to 0$ as $|u| \to \infty$, are satisfied. The effect of the term $K\left(\frac{w_i - w_j}{h_n}\right)$ is to give more weight to comparisons of observations (i, j) for which z_i is close to z_j.

2.2. Partially Linear Tobit Models

The fixed-effect censored regression model is given by

$$y_{it} = \max\{0, \alpha_i + x_{it}\beta + \varepsilon_{it}\}.$$

Honoré (1992) showed that with two observations for each individual, and with the error terms being i.i.d. for a given individual,[2]

$$\beta = \arg\min_b E[q(y_{i1}, y_{i2}, (x_{i1} - x_{i2}b)], \tag{2.6}$$

where

$$q(y_1, y_2, \delta) = \begin{cases} \Xi(y_1) - (y_2 + \delta)\xi(y_1) & \text{if } \delta \leq -y_2; \\ \Xi(y_1 - y_2 - \delta) & \text{if } -y_2 < \delta < y_1; \\ \Xi(-y_2) - (\delta - y_1)\xi(-y_2) & \text{if } y_1 \leq \delta; \end{cases}$$

and $\Xi(d)$ is given by[3] either $\Xi(d) = |d|$ or $\Xi(d) = d^2$. The estimators for the fixed-effect censored regression model presented in Honoré (1992) are defined as minimizers of the sample analog of the minimand in (2.6),

$$S_n(b) \equiv \frac{1}{n} \sum_i q(y_{i1}, y_{i2}, (x_{i1} - x_{i2})b).$$

Applying the same logic, this suggests estimating β in the partially linear censored regression model

$$y_i = \max\{0, x_i\beta + g(w_i) + \varepsilon_i\},$$

[2] The assumption on the error terms made in Honoré (1992) allowed for very general serial correlation. However, for the discussion in this paper we will restrict ourselves to the i.i.d. assumption.

[3] Other convex loss functions, Ξ (), could be used as well.

by minimization of

$$S_n(b) = \binom{n}{2}^{-1} \frac{1}{h_n^L} \sum_{i<j} K\left(\frac{w_i - w_j}{h_n}\right) q(y_i, y_j, (x_i - x_j)b).$$

Honoré (1992) also proposed estimators of the truncated regression model with fixed effects. In the simplest version of the truncated regression model, (y, x) is observed only when $y > 0$, where $y = x\beta + \varepsilon$.

The idea in Honoré (1992) is that if $y_{it} = \alpha_i + x_{it}\beta + \varepsilon_{it}$ and if ε_{it} satisfies certain regularity conditions, then

$$E[r(y_{i1}, y_{i2}, (x_{i1} - x_{i2})b) | y_{i1} > 0, y_{i2} > 0] \tag{2.7}$$

is uniquely minimized at $b = \beta$, where

$$r(y_1, y_2, \delta) = \begin{cases} \Xi(y_1) & \text{if } \delta \leq -y_2; \\ \Xi(y_1 - y_2 - \delta) & \text{if } -y_2 < \delta < y_1; \\ \Xi(-y_2) & \text{if } y_1 \leq \delta; \end{cases}$$

and $\Xi\,()$ is as above.

This suggests that the partially linear truncated regression model, $y_i = x_i\beta + g(w_i) + \varepsilon_i$ with (y_i, x_i, w_i) observed only when $y_i > 0$, can be estimated by minimizing

$$T_n(b) = \binom{n}{2}^{-1} \frac{1}{h_n^L} \sum_{i<j} K\left(\frac{w_i - w_j}{h_n}\right) t(y_i, y_j, (x_i - x_j)b). \tag{2.8}$$

2.3. Partially Linear Poisson Regression Models

As a third example, consider the Poisson regression model with fixed effects:

$$y_{it} \sim \text{po}\,(\exp(\alpha_i + x_{it}\beta)) \quad t = 1, 2, i = 1, \ldots, n.$$

The coefficients β for this model can be estimated by maximizing (see, for example, Hausman et al., 1984):

$$\begin{aligned} \mathcal{L}_n(b) = \sum_i & -y_{i1} \ln\left(1 + \exp((x_{i2} - x_{i1})b)\right) \\ & -y_{i2} \ln\left(1 + \exp((x_{i1} - x_{i2})b)\right). \end{aligned}$$

Following the same logic as before, the coefficients for a partially linear Poisson regression model

$$y_i \sim \text{po}\,(\exp(x_i\beta + g(w_i))) \quad t = 1, 2, i = 1, \ldots, n,$$

can then be estimated by maximizing[4]

$$L_n(b) = \binom{n}{2}^{-1} \frac{1}{h_n^L} \sum_{i<j} K\left(\frac{w_i - w_j}{h_n}\right) \left(-y_i \ln\left(1 + \exp((x_j - x_i)b)\right)\right.$$
$$\left. - y_j \ln\left(1 + \exp((x_i - x_j)b)\right)\right).$$

2.4. Partially Linear Duration Models

Finally, Chamberlain (1985) has shown how to estimate a variety of duration models with fixed effects. Using the objective functions that he suggested, one can derive objective functions, the minimization of which will result in estimators of the linear part of partially linear versions of the same models.

2.5. Tobit Models with Selection

As mentioned earlier, the nonlinear term can sometimes result from sample selection. Consider for example a modification of the model defined by (2.2) and (2.3), in which $y_i^\star$ is both censored (as for the partially linear Tobit model) and subject to selectivity of the type described at the beginning of this section. One example of this would be a model of earnings, where the variable of interest is often censored from above by topcoding at some observable constant c_i, as well as subject to sample selection, because not everybody works. This model can be written as

$$y_i^\star = \min\{x_i\beta + \varepsilon_i, c_i\}, \qquad (2.9)$$
$$d_i = 1\{w_i\gamma + \eta_i > 0\}, \qquad (2.10)$$

where (ε_i, η_i) is independent of (x_i, w_i) and the data consists of $y_i = d_i y_i^\star$, d_i, x_i, and w_i. As usual, we can translate this model, which has right-censoring at c_i, to the Tobit framework with left-censoring at zero by taking $\tilde{y}_i \equiv d_i c_i - y_i$ as the dependent variable and $\tilde{x}_i \equiv -x_i$ as the regressor.

For the observations for which $d_i = 1$, the distribution of ε_i is conditional on $\eta_i > -w_i\gamma$. For two observations, i and j with $w_i\gamma = w_j\gamma$ and $d_i = d_j = 1$, ε_i and ε_j will be independent and identically distributed (conditionally on (x_i, x_j, w_i, w_j)). Therefore,

$$\beta = \arg\min_b E[q(\tilde{y}_i, \tilde{y}_j, (\tilde{x}_i - \tilde{x}_j)b) | d_i = d_j = 1, w_i\gamma = w_j\gamma].$$

[4] While this maximand is derived assuming a Poisson distribution for the dependent variable, the resulting estimator is likely to be robust to misspecification of the exact distribution of y_i, provided the conditional expectation is correctly specified. In the panel data context, Wooldridge (1999a) showed the consistency of the fixed-effect Poisson quasi-maximum likelihood estimator, and this argument should carry over to partially linear Poisson regression.

This suggests estimating β by minimization of

$$Q_n(b) = \binom{n}{2}^{-1} \frac{1}{h_n^L} \sum_{\substack{i<j \\ d_i=d_j=1}} K\left(\frac{w_i\hat{\gamma} - w_j\hat{\gamma}}{h_n}\right) q(\tilde{y}_i, \tilde{y}_j, (\tilde{x}_i - \tilde{x}_j)b), \tag{2.11}$$

where $\hat{\gamma}$ is a root-n-consistent preliminary estimator of γ in (2.10),[5] and L denotes the dimensionality of $w_i\gamma$. If there is no censoring, and if quadratic loss ($\Xi(d) = d^2$) is used, then the minimizer of (2.11) is the estimator suggested by Powell (1987, 2001).

Consistency of the estimator for the truncated regression model defined in (2.8) would require that the error, ε_i has a log-concave density. Whether it is possible to define an estimator for the truncated regression model with selection by

$$R_n(b) = \binom{n}{2}^{-1} \frac{1}{h_n^L} \sum_{\substack{i<j \\ d_i=d_j=1}} K\left(\frac{w_i\hat{\gamma} - w_j\hat{\gamma}}{h_n}\right) r(\tilde{y}_i, \tilde{y}_j, (\tilde{x}_i - \tilde{x}_j)b), \tag{2.12}$$

depends on one's willingness to assume that the conditional density of ε_i given $\eta_i > k$ is log-concave for all k. The estimators for the partially linear logit and partially linear Poisson regression models do not generalize in a straightforward manner to the case of selection, because the error-terms after selection will have non-logistic and non-Poisson distributions.

3. ASYMPTOTIC PROPERTIES OF ESTIMATORS DEFINED BY MINIMIZING KERNEL-WEIGHTED U-STATISTICS

The estimators defined in the previous section are all defined by minimizing objective functions of the form

$$Q_n(\widehat{\gamma}, b) = \binom{n}{2}^{-1} \sum_{i<j} q_n\left(z_i, z_j; \widehat{\gamma}, b\right), \tag{3.1}$$

with

$$q_n\left(z_i, z_j; \gamma, b\right) = \frac{1}{h_n^L} K\left(\frac{(w_i - w_j)\gamma}{h_n}\right) s\left(v_i, v_j; b\right), \tag{3.2}$$

$z_i = (y_i, x_i, w_i)$, and $v_i = (y_i, x_i)$. Note that, for the estimators of the partially linear models, $\gamma = I$ (the identity matrix). Let $\theta = (\gamma', \beta')'$ and $L = \dim(w\gamma)$. In the next two subsections we give conditions under which such estimators are consistent, and asymptotically normal around some pseudo–true value. The

[5] Numerous root-n-consistent semiparametric estimators for γ have been proposed, some of which are described in Powell (1994, Section 3.1).

third subsection will then show how to "jackknife" the estimator to recenter its asymptotically normal distribution around the true parameter value.

Throughout, we define $\Delta w_{ij} = w_i - w_j$.

3.1. Consistency

We will present two sets of assumptions under which the estimators defined by minimization of (3.1) are consistent. One set of assumptions will require a compact parameter space, whereas the other will assume a convex objective function. In both cases we will use the theorems found in Newey and McFadden (1994) to prove consistency.

Let m be a function of z_i, z_j, and b. It is useful to define two function k_m and ℓ_m by

$$k_m(a_1, a_2, b) = E\left[m\left(z_i, z_j; b\right)\middle| z_i = a_1, w_j\gamma_0 = a_2\right]$$

and

$$\ell_m(a_1, a_2, b) = E\left[m\left(z_i, z_j; b\right)\middle| z_i = a_1, w_j\gamma_0 = a_2\right] f_{w_i\gamma_0}(a_2),$$

where $f_{w_i\gamma_0}$ is the density function of $w_i\gamma_0$ (assumed continuously distributed). When m depends only on v_i, v_j, and b, we will write

$$k_m(a_1, a_2, b) = E\left[m\left(v_i, v_j; b\right)\middle| v_i = a_1, w_j\gamma_0 = a_2\right]$$

and

$$\ell_m(a_1, a_2, b) = E\left[m\left(v_i, v_j; b\right)\middle| v_i = a_1, w_j\gamma_0 = a_2\right] f_{w_i\gamma_0}(a_2).$$

Assumption 3.1. *All of the following assumptions are made on the distribution of the data*

1. $E[s(v_i, v_j; b)^2] < \infty$;
2. $E[\|\Delta w_{ij}\|^2] < \infty$;
3. $w_i\gamma_0$ *is continuously distributed with bounded density,* $f_{w_i\gamma_0}(\cdot)$, *and* $k_s(\cdot)$ *defined earlier exists and is a continuous function of each of its arguments;*
4. *for all* b, $|\ell_s(a_1, a_2, b)| \leq c_1(a_1, b)$ *with* $E[c_1(v_i, b)] < \infty$; *and*
5. $\{z_i, i = 1, \ldots, n\}$ *is an* i.i.d. *sample.*

Assumption 3.2. *One of the following assumptions is made on the nonrandom bandwidth sequence* h_n:

1. $h_n > 0$, $h_n = o(1)$ *and* $h_n^{-1} = o(n^{1/L})$; *or*
2. $h_n > 0$, $h_n = o(1)$ *and* $h_n^{-2} = o\left(n^{1/(L+1)}\right)$.

Assumption 3.3. K *is bounded, differentiable with bounded derivative* K', *and of bounded variation. Furthermore,* $\int K(u)\,du = 1$, $\int |K(u)|\,du < \infty$ *and* $\int |K(\eta)|\,\|\eta\|\,d\eta < \infty$.

The assumptions made on the kernel are satisfied for many commonly used kernels.

In some of the applications (to selection models) the argument γ of $Q_n(\cdot)$ will be replaced by a "first-stage" estimator $\hat{\gamma}$, which is assumed to converge at a parametric (root-n rate).

Assumption 3.4. *One of the following assumptions is made on* $\widehat{\gamma}$:

1. $\widehat{\gamma} = \gamma_0$; *or*
2. $\widehat{\gamma} = \gamma_0 + O_p\left(\frac{1}{\sqrt{n}}\right)$.

The following Lipschitz continuity assumption is imposed when the objective function Q_n is not convex in b.

Assumption 3.5. $\left|s\left(v_i, v_j; b_1\right) - s\left(v_i, v_j; b_2\right)\right| \le B_{ij} \left|b_1 - b_2\right|^{\alpha}$ *for some* $\alpha > 0$, *where* $E\left[B_{ij}^2\right] < \infty$.

3.1.1. *Limiting Objective Function*

Consistency of extremum estimators is usually proved by studying the limiting objective function and the exact manner in which the objective function approaches its limit. For this problem, the limiting objective function will be

$$Q(\gamma_0, b) = E\left[\ell_s\left(v_i, w_i\gamma_0, b\right)\right],$$

which is well-defined under Assumption 3.1.

3.1.2. *Pointwise Convergence to Limiting Objective Function*

In this section we will state conditions under which the objective function converges pointwise to its limit. It is useful to distinguish between the case with and without a preliminary estimator (i.e., between Assumptions 3.4(1) and 3.4(2)).

In the case of no preliminary estimator (i.e., $\hat{\gamma} = \gamma_0$ is known), we have

$$\begin{aligned}
&E\left[Q_n\left(\gamma_0, b\right)\right] \\
&= E\left[\frac{1}{h_n^L} K\left(\frac{w_i\gamma_0 - w_j\gamma_0}{h_n}\right) s\left(v_i, v_j; b\right)\right] \\
&= E\left[E\left[\frac{1}{h_n^L} K\left(\frac{w_i\gamma_0 - w_j\gamma_0}{h_n}\right) k_s\left(v_i, w_j\gamma_0, b\right) \middle| w_i, v_i\right]\right] \\
&= \int\int K(\eta)\, \ell_s\left(v_i, w_i\gamma_0 - h_n\eta, b\right) d\eta\, dF\left(w_i, u_i\right) \\
&\longrightarrow Q(\gamma_0, b)
\end{aligned} \tag{3.3}$$

by dominated convergence. Note that the first expectation exists because of Assumptions 3.1(1) and 3.3.

Imposing Assumptions 3.1, 3.2(1), and 3.3,

$$E\left[\left\{\frac{1}{h_n^L}K\left(\frac{\Delta w_{ij}\gamma_0}{h_n}\right)s\left(v_i, v_j; b\right)\right\}^2\right] = o(n),$$

and therefore (Powell, Stock, and Stoker, 1989, Lemma 3.1)

$$Q_n\left(\gamma_0, b\right) - E\left[Q_n\left(\gamma_0, b\right)\right] = o_p(1).$$

Combining these results,

$$Q_n\left(\gamma_0, b\right) \longrightarrow^p Q(\gamma_0, b)$$

when γ_0 is known.

In the case where $\widehat{\gamma} = \gamma_0 + O_p\left(\frac{1}{\sqrt{n}}\right)$ is estimated, we have

$$Q_n(\widehat{\gamma}, b) = \left(Q_n(\widehat{\gamma}, b) - Q_n\left(\gamma_0, b\right)\right) + Q_n\left(\gamma_0, b\right).$$

Pointwise convergence of $Q_n(\widehat{\gamma}, b)$ to $Q(\gamma_0, b)$ then follows from

$$\begin{aligned}
&Q_n(\widehat{\gamma}, b) - Q_n\left(\gamma_0, b\right) \\
&= \left|\binom{n}{2}^{-1}\sum_{i<j}\frac{1}{h_n^L}\left(K\left(\frac{\Delta w_{ij}\widehat{\gamma}}{h_n}\right) - K\left(\frac{\Delta w_{ij}\gamma_0}{h_n}\right)\right)s\left(v_i, v_j; b\right)\right| \\
&= \left|\binom{n}{2}^{-1}\sum_{i<j}\frac{1}{h_n^L}K'\left(c_{ij}^*\right)\frac{\Delta w_{ij}\left(\widehat{\gamma} - \gamma_0\right)}{h_n}s\left(v_i, v_j; b\right)\right| \\
&\le \binom{n}{2}^{-1}\sum_{i<j}\frac{1}{h_n^L}\left|K'\left(c_{ij}^*\right)\right|\frac{\left\|\Delta w_{ij}\right\|\left\|\widehat{\gamma} - \gamma_0\right\|}{h_n}\left|s\left(v_i, v_j; b\right)\right| \\
&\le \left\|\widehat{\gamma} - \gamma_0\right\|\frac{1}{h_n^{L+1}}C\binom{n}{2}^{-1}\sum_{i<j}\left\|\Delta w_{ij}\right\|\left|s\left(v_i, v_j; b\right)\right| \\
&= O_p\left(\frac{1}{n^{1/2}h_n^{L+1}}\right) \\
&= o_p(1),
\end{aligned}$$

where the last equality follows from imposing the stronger Assumption 3.2(2).

3.1.3. *Uniform Convergence to Limiting Objective Function*

With an objective function that is convex in b, the pointwise convergence suffices to establish consistency of $\hat{\beta}$, regardless of whether γ is estimated. Without a convex objective function, uniform convergence of the minimand is the key ingredient in the proof of consistency of extremum estimators. Invoking Assumption 3.1(1) and imposing compactness of the parameter space for β, uniform convergence will follow from Lemma 2.9 of Newey and McFadden (1994).

With no preliminary estimation of γ and the objective function is not convex, imposition of Assumption 3.5 yields

$$\begin{aligned}
&|Q_n(\widehat{\gamma}, b_1) - Q_n(\widehat{\gamma}, b_2)| \\
&\quad = \left|Q_n(\gamma_0, b_1) - Q_n(\gamma_0, b_2)\right| \\
&\quad = \left|\binom{n}{2}^{-1} \sum_{i<j} \frac{1}{h_n^L} K\left(\frac{\Delta w_{ij}\gamma_0}{h_n}\right) \left(s\left(v_i, v_j; b_1\right) - s\left(v_i, v_j; b_2\right)\right)\right| \\
&\quad \le \binom{n}{2}^{-1} \sum_{i<j} \frac{1}{h_n^L} \left|K\left(\frac{\Delta w_{ij}\gamma_0}{h_n}\right)\right| B_{ij} |b_1 - b_2|^{\alpha} \\
&\quad = O_p(1) |b_1 - b_2|^{\alpha}
\end{aligned}$$

When γ is estimated,

$$\begin{aligned}
&|Q_n(\widehat{\gamma}, b_1) - Q_n(\widehat{\gamma}, b_2)| \\
&\quad \le |Q_n(\gamma_0, b_1) - Q_n(\gamma_0, b_2)| + |(Q_n(\widehat{\gamma}, b_1) - Q_n(\widehat{\gamma}, b_2)) \\
&\qquad - (Q_n(\gamma_0, b_1) - Q_n(\gamma_0, b_2))|
\end{aligned}$$

and

$$\begin{aligned}
&\left|(Q_n(\widehat{\gamma}, b_1) - Q_n(\widehat{\gamma}, b_2)) - \left(Q_n(\gamma_0, b_1) - Q_n(\gamma_0, b_2)\right)\right| \\
&\quad = \left|\binom{n}{2}^{-1} \sum_{i<j} \frac{1}{h_n^L} \left(K\left(\frac{\Delta w_{ij}\widehat{\gamma}}{h_n}\right) - K\left(\frac{\Delta w_{ij}\gamma_0}{h_n}\right)\right) \left(s\left(v_i, v_j; b_1\right)\right.\right. \\
&\qquad \left.\left. - s\left(v_i, v_j; b_2\right)\right)\right| \\
&\quad = \binom{n}{2}^{-1} \sum_{i<j} \frac{1}{h_n^L} \left|K'\left(c_{ij}^*\right)\right| \frac{\left\|\Delta w_{ij}\right\| \left\|\widehat{\gamma} - \gamma_0\right\|}{h_n} \\
&\qquad \times \left(s\left(v_i, v_j; b_1\right) - s\left(v_i, v_j; b_2\right)\right) \\
&\quad \le \frac{1}{h_n^{L+1}} \left\|\widehat{\gamma} - \gamma_0\right\| \binom{n}{2}^{-1} \sum_{i<j} \left|K'\left(c_{ij}^*\right)\right| \left\|\Delta w_{ij}\right\| B_{ij} |b_1 - b_2|^{\alpha} \\
&\quad = O_p\left(\frac{1}{h_n^{L+1} n^{1/2}}\right) |b_1 - b_2|^{\alpha}.
\end{aligned}$$

3.1.4. *Identification*

The limiting objective function is uniquely minimized at β_0 provided that the following condition holds:

Assumption 3.6. $E\left[s\left(v_i, v_j; b\right) \mid \left(w_i - w_j\right)\gamma_0 = 0\right]$ *is uniquely minimized at* $b = \beta_0$.

3.1.5. *Consistency Theorem*

Combining the foregoing results, and referring to Newey and McFadden (1994) Theorem 2.7 and to Theorem 2.1 and Lemma 2.9, respectively, we have

Theorem 3.1. *If* $K\left(\frac{(w_i - w_j)\gamma}{h_n}\right) s\left(v_i, v_j; b\right)$ *is a continuous and convex function of b and the parameter space for* β *is a convex set with the true value,* β_0*, in its interior, then the minimizer* $\hat{\beta}$ *of* (3.1) *over the parameter space is (weakly) consistent under random sampling and Assumptions 3.1, 3.3, 3.6, and either 3.2(1) and 3.4(1) or 3.2(2) and 3.4(2).*

Theorem 3.2. *If* $K\left(\frac{(w_i - w_j)\gamma}{h_n}\right) s\left(v_i, v_j; b\right)$ *is a continuous function of b and the parameter space for* β *is compact and includes the true value,* β_0*, then the minimizer* $\hat{\beta}$ *of* (3.1) *over the parameter space is (weakly) consistent under random sampling and Assumptions 3.1, 3.3, 3.5, 3.6 and either 3.2(1) and 3.4(1) or 3.2(2) and 3.4(2).*

3.2. Asymptotic Normality

In this section we derive the asymptotic distribution of the estimator defined by minimizing (3.1). That is, we derive the limiting distribution of $\sqrt{n}(\widehat{\beta} - \beta_h)$ where β_h is the minimizer of $E[\frac{1}{h^L} K(\frac{(w_i - w_j)\gamma_0}{h}) s(v_i, v_j; \beta)]$. Note that the argument that leads to consistency of $\widehat{\beta}$ implies that $\beta_h \to \beta_0$; also note that β_h is nonstochastic. In Section 3.3 we discuss conditions under which

$$\beta_h = \beta_0 + \sum_{l=1}^{p} b_l h^l + o(h^p).$$

Here the estimator will have an asymptotic bias term, which we eliminate via a jackknife approach. The advantage of the this approach is that it is not necessary to employ a bias-reducing kernel, but instead can assume that the kernel K is nonnegative. This means that if s in equation (3.1) is convex, then the objective function Q_n in (3.2) will also be convex, simplifying both the conditions for consistency and the computation of the estimator $\hat{\beta}$. A disadvantage is that it may be necessary to calculate the estimator a number of times using several bandwidths; however, as we will see in Section 3.3, it is often possible to do the optimization only once, since estimators that are asymptotically equivalent to the remaining estimators can then be defined as the result of performing a finite number of Newton–Raphson steps from the original estimator.

The following assumption is standard.

Assumption 3.7. *The true parameter,* β_0*, is an interior point of the parameter space.*

In all the applications considered here, the objective function will be left and right differentiable. We therefore define

$$G_n(\widehat{\gamma}, \beta) = \binom{n}{2}^{-1} \sum_{i<j} p_n\left(z_i, z_j; \widehat{\gamma}, \beta\right),$$

where

$$p_n\left(z_i, z_j; \gamma, \beta\right) = \frac{1}{h_n^L} K\left(\frac{\left(w_i - w_j\right)\gamma}{h_n}\right) t\left(v_i, v_j; \beta\right)$$

and $t\left(v_i, v_j; \beta\right)$ is a convex combination of the left and right derivatives of $s\left(v_i, v_j; \beta\right)$ with respect to β.

It is useful to define the "projection functions"

$$\begin{aligned} p_{1n}(z_i; \gamma, \beta) &= E\left[p_n\left(z_i, z_j; \gamma, \beta\right) | z_i\right] - E\left[p_n\left(z_i, z_j; \gamma, \beta\right)\right], \\ p_{0n}(\gamma, \beta) &= E\left[p_n\left(z_i, z_j; \gamma, \beta\right)\right], \end{aligned}$$

where Assumption 3.8 guarantees that these expectations exist. We can then write

$$\begin{aligned} &\binom{n}{2}^{-1} \sum_{i<j} p_n\left(z_i, z_j; \gamma, \beta\right) \\ &\quad = p_{0n}(\gamma, \beta) + \frac{2}{n} \sum_{i=1}^{n} p_{1n}(z_i; \gamma, \beta) \\ &\qquad + \binom{n}{2}^{-1} \sum_{i<j} p_{2n}\left(z_i, z_j; \gamma, \beta\right), \end{aligned} \tag{3.4}$$

where p_{1n} and p_{2n} are P-degenerate (with P denoting the distribution of z_i). The function p_{2n} is defined implicitly by (3.4).

To justify these calculations, we assume

Assumption 3.8. *The derivative function $\{t(\cdot, \cdot; \beta) : \beta \in B\}$ is Euclidean for an envelope F, i.e.,*

$$\sup_{n,\beta} \left|t\left(z_i, z_j; \beta\right)\right| \leq F\left(z_i, z_j\right),$$

satisfying $E\left[F^2\right] < \infty$. The set B need not be the whole parameter space, but could be some other set with β_0 in its interior.

Assumption 3.8 is satisfied for all of the examples considered in Section 2. Assumptions 3 and 8 imply that $h_n^L p_n$ is Euclidean (for some envelope CF with $E[(CF)^2] < \infty$). This, in turn, implies that $h_n^L p_{2n}$ is Euclidean for an envelope with finite second moments (see Sherman, 1994b, Lemma 6). This will be important for the derivation here, because it allows us to ignore the "error" when we approximate the U-statistic, $\binom{n}{2}^{-1} \sum_{i<j} p_n\left(z_i, z_j; \gamma, \beta\right)$, by its projection, $p_{0n}(\gamma, \beta) + \frac{2}{n} \sum_{i=1}^{n} p_{1n}(z_i; \gamma, \beta)$.

We also define

$$\widetilde{p}_n(z_i, \gamma, \beta) = p_{0n}(\gamma, \beta) + 2p_{1n}(z_i; \gamma, \beta).$$

Note that this implies that $\widetilde{p}_n(z_i, \gamma_0, \beta_h) = 2p_{1n}(z_i, \gamma_0, \beta_h)$. It is convenient to impose:

Assumption 3.9.

1. *The function $\widetilde{p}_n(z_i, \gamma_0, \beta)$ is continuously differentiable in β with a derivative $\widetilde{p}_n^{\beta}(z_i, \gamma_0, \beta)$ with the property that for any sequence β^* that converges in probability to β_0, $\widetilde{p}_n^{\beta}(z_i, \gamma_0, \beta^*)$ converges to a matrix $\widetilde{p}_0^{\beta}(\gamma_0, \beta_0)$ which is nonsingular;*
2. *If γ is estimated (i.e., the distribution of $\hat{\gamma} - \gamma_0$ is nondegenerate), then $\widetilde{p}_n(z_i, \gamma, \beta)$ is continuously differentiable in (γ, β) with a derivative $\Delta\widetilde{p}_n(z_i, \gamma, \beta)$ with the property that for any sequence (γ^*, β^*) that converges in probability to (γ_0, β_0), $\Delta\widetilde{p}_n(z_i, \gamma^*, \beta^*)$ converges to a matrix $\Delta\widetilde{p}_0(\gamma_0, \beta_0)$, the lower part $\Delta\widetilde{p}_0^{\beta}(\gamma_0, \beta_0)$ (i.e., the part that corresponds to differentiation with respect to β) of which is nonsingular; and*
3. *for some function $p_1(z_i; \gamma_0, \beta_0)$ with $E[\|p_1(z_i; \gamma_0, \beta_0)\|^2] < \infty$,*

$$\frac{1}{\sqrt{n}}\sum_{i=1}^{n}\widetilde{p}_n(z_i; \gamma_0, \beta_h) - \frac{1}{\sqrt{n}}\sum_{i=1}^{n}p_1(z_i; \gamma_0, \beta_0) = o_p(1).$$

In the next subsection, we give results that are useful for verifying Assumption 3.9.

We can write

$$\begin{aligned}
G_n(\gamma, \beta) &= \binom{n}{2}^{-1}\sum_{i<j}p_n(z_i, z_j; \gamma, \beta) \\
&= p_{0n}(\gamma, \beta) + \frac{2}{n}\sum_i p_{1n}(z_i; \gamma, \beta) \\
&\quad + \binom{n}{2}^{-1}\sum_{i<j}p_{2n}(z_i, z_j; \gamma, \beta) \\
&= \frac{1}{n}\sum_i \widetilde{p}_n(z_i; \gamma, \beta) + \binom{n}{2}^{-1}\sum_{i<j}p_{2n}(z_i, z_j; \gamma, \beta) \\
&= \left(\frac{1}{n}\sum_i \Delta\widetilde{p}_n(z_i; \theta^*)\right)\begin{pmatrix}\gamma - \gamma_0 \\ \beta - \beta_h\end{pmatrix} \\
&\quad + \frac{1}{n}\sum_i \widetilde{p}_n(z_i; \gamma_0, \beta_h) \\
&\quad + \binom{n}{2}^{-1}\sum_{i<j}p_{2n}(z_i, z_j; \gamma, \beta),
\end{aligned}$$

where, as usual, $\Delta\widetilde{p}_n(z_i;\theta^*)$ should be interpreted as the derivative of $\widetilde{p}_n(z_i;\cdot)$ evaluated at a point (which may be different for different rows of $\Delta\widetilde{p}_n$) between (γ,β) and (γ_0,β_h).

Since $\{p_{2n}(z_i,z_j;\gamma,\beta)\}$ is Euclidean, Sherman's (1994a) Theorem 3 can be applied to the function $h^L p_{2n}(z_i,z_j;g,b)$ with $\Theta_n=\{\theta:\|\theta-\theta_0\|\le c\}$ for some constant c (with $\gamma_n=1$ and $k=2$ in Sherman's notation) to get

$$\sup_{\Theta_n}\binom{n}{2}^{-1}\sum_{i<j}h^L p_{2n}(z_i,z_j;g,b)=O_p\left(\frac{1}{n}\right)$$

or

$$\sup_{\Theta_n}\binom{n}{2}^{-1}\sum_{i<j}p_{2n}(z_i,z_j;g,b)=O_p\left(\frac{1}{h^L n}\right),$$

where the assumption on the envelope guarantee that $E[\sup_{\Theta_n}p_{2n}(z_i,z_j;\gamma,\beta)^2]<\infty$.[6]

This yields

$$\sqrt{n}\left(\widehat{\beta}-\beta_h\right)=\left(-\frac{1}{n}\sum_i\Delta\widetilde{p}_n^{\beta}(z_i;\theta^*)\right)^{-1}\left[\left(\frac{1}{n}\sum_i\Delta\widetilde{p}_n^{\gamma}(z_i;\theta^*)\right)\right.$$
$$\sqrt{n}\left(\widehat{\gamma}-\gamma_0\right)+\frac{2}{\sqrt{n}}\sum_i p_{1n}(z_i,\gamma_0,\beta_h)$$
$$\left.+\,O_p\left(\frac{1}{h^L\sqrt{n}}\right)-\sqrt{n}G_n(\gamma,\beta)\right].$$

We therefore have

Theorem 3.3. *If $\widehat{\beta}$ is a consistent estimator of β, $G_n(\widehat{\gamma},\widehat{\beta})=o_p(n^{-1/2})$, $1/h_n=o(n^{1/(2L)})$, $\sqrt{n}(\widehat{\gamma}-\gamma_0)=\frac{1}{\sqrt{n}}\sum_{i=1}^n\omega_i+o_p(1)$ and Assumptions 3.7, 3.8, and 3.9 are satisfied, then*

$$\sqrt{n}\left(\widehat{\beta}-\beta_h\right)=\frac{1}{\sqrt{n}}\sum_{i=1}^n\psi_i+o_p(1),$$

where

$$\psi_i=-\Delta\widetilde{p}_0^{\beta}(\gamma_0,\beta_0)^{-1}\Delta\widetilde{p}_0^{\gamma}(\gamma_0,\beta_0)\,\omega_i-2\Delta\widetilde{p}_0^{\beta}(\gamma_0,\beta_0)^{-1}p_1(z_i;\gamma_0,\beta_0).$$

Furthermore, assuming ω_i and $p_1(z_i;\gamma_0,\beta_0)$ are jointly i.i.d. with $E[\omega_i]=0$ and $E[\|\omega_i\|^2]<\infty$,

$$\sqrt{n}\left(\widehat{\beta}-\beta_h\right)\to^d\mathcal{N}(0,E[\psi_i\psi_i']).$$

[6] This is condition (ii) for Sherman's (1994a) Theorem 3.

3.2.1. Verifying some of the conditions

Theorem 3.3 makes some high-level assumptions. In this section, we will present some results which will be useful in verifying these assumptions.

The following lemma, which follows immediately from Lemma 3.1 in Honoré and Powell (1994), is useful for verifying that $G_n\left(\widehat{\gamma}, \widehat{\beta}\right) = o_p\left(\frac{1}{\sqrt{n}}\right)$.

Lemma 3.4. *If the true parameter value, β_0, is an interior point in the parameter space, and*

1. *$s\left(v_i, v_j; \beta\right)$ is left and right differentiable in each component of β in some open neighborhood of the true parameter β_0;*
2. *in an open neighborhood B_0 of β_0,*
$$\sup_{\beta \in B_0} \sum_{i<j} 1\left\{\frac{\partial^- s\left(v_i, v_j; \beta\right)}{\partial \beta_\ell} \neq \frac{\partial^+ s\left(v_i, v_j; \beta\right)}{\partial \beta_\ell}\right\} = O_p(1);$$
3. *in an open neighborhood of β_0,*
$$\left|\frac{\partial^- s\left(v_i, v_j; \beta\right)}{\partial \beta_\ell} - \frac{\partial^+ s\left(v_i, v_j; \beta\right)}{\partial \beta_\ell}\right| \leq h\left(v_i, v_j\right)$$
for some function h with $E\left[h\left(v_i, v_j\right)^{1+\delta}\right] < \infty$ for some δ, and
4. *K is bounded,*

then
$$G_n\left(\widehat{\gamma}, \widehat{\beta}\right) = o_p\left(n^{-2+2/(1+\delta)} h_n^{-L}\right).$$

We next turn to some assumptions under which the conditions of Assumption 3.9 are satisfied. Recall that by definition of k_m and ℓ_m,

$$k_t\left(z_i, a, b\right) = E\left[t\left(v_i, v_j, b\right) \middle| z_i, w_j \gamma_0 = a\right],$$
$$\ell_t\left(z_i, a, b\right) = E\left[t\left(v_i, v_j, b\right) \middle| z_i, w_j \gamma_0 = a\right] f_{w_j \gamma_0}(a).$$

In addition, define

$$t_1\left(z_i, z_j, \beta\right) = \left(w_i - w_j\right) t\left(v_i, v_j, \beta\right);$$

then k_{t_1} and ℓ_{t_1}, evaluated at $\beta = \beta_0$, become

$$k_{t_1}\left(z_i, a_2, \beta_0\right) = E\left[\left(w_i - w_j\right) t\left(v_i, v_j, \beta_0\right) \middle| z_i, w_j \gamma_0 = a_2\right],$$
$$\ell_{t_1}\left(z_i, a_2, \beta_0\right) = E\left[\left(w_i - w_j\right) t\left(v_i, v_j, \beta_0\right) \middle| z_i, w_j \gamma_0 = a_2\right] f_{w_i \gamma_0}(a_2).$$

Defining $\ell_t^{(j)}(\cdot)$ as the derivative of $\ell_t(\cdot)$ with respect to its jth argument, the following restrictions will be imposed on the derivatives of ℓ_t.

Assumption 3.10.

1. *The function ℓ_t is differentiable with respect to its third argument, and there is a function g with $E\left[g\left(z_i\right)\right] < \infty$, such that $\left|\ell_t^{(3)}\left(v_i, w_i \gamma_0 - h\eta, \beta_0\right)\right| \leq g\left(z_i\right)$.*

2. *The function* ℓ_{t_1} *is differentiable with respect to its second argument, and there is a function* g *with* $E\left[g(z_i)^2\right] < \infty$, *such that* $\left|\ell_{t_1}^{(2)}\left(z_i, w_i\gamma_0 - h\eta, \beta_0\right)\right| \le g(z_i)$. *Furthermore,*

$$K(\eta)\,\ell_{t_1}^{(2)}\left(z_i, w_i\gamma_0 - h\eta, \beta_0\right) \to 0 \quad \text{as } \eta \to \pm\infty.$$

Finally, $E\left[\left(w_i - w_j\right)t\left(v_i, v_j, \beta\right)\right] < \infty$.

3. *The function* ℓ_t *is differentiable with respect to its second argument, and there is a function* g *with* $E\left[g(z_i)\right] < \infty$, *such that* $\left|\ell_t^{(2)}\left(v_i, w_i\gamma_0 - h\eta, \beta_0\right)\right| \le g(z_i)$.

A number of results can be used to verify the convergence in Assumptions 3.9(1) and 3.9(2). For example, Amemiya's (1985) Theorem 4.1.4 gives conditions that can be used to verify that $\widetilde{p}_n'(z_i, \gamma^*, \beta^*)$ converges to lim $\widetilde{p}_n'\left(z_i, \gamma_0, \beta_0\right)$. The following two lemmata give the expressions for $\widetilde{p}_1'$ that appear in Assumptions 3.9(1) and 3.9(2) and in Theorem 3.3.

Lemma 3.5. *Let*

$$p_0^{\beta}\left(\gamma_0, \beta_0\right) = E\left[\ell_t^{(3)}\left(v_i, w_i\gamma_0, \beta_0\right)\right].$$

Then under Assumptions 3.3 and 3.10(1)

$$p_{0n}^{\beta}\left(\gamma_0, \beta_0\right) \to p_0^{\beta}\left(\gamma_0, \beta_0\right).$$

Lemma 3.6. *Let*

$$p_0^{\gamma}\left(\gamma_0, \beta_0\right) = -E\left[\ell_{t_1}^{(2)}\left(z_i, w_i\gamma_0, \beta_0\right)\right].$$

Then under Assumptions 3.3 and 3.10(2)

$$p_{0n}^{\gamma}\left(\gamma_0, \beta_0\right) \to p_0^{\gamma}\left(\gamma_0, \beta_0\right).$$

Combining, the next two lemmata will give conditions under which Assumption 3.9(3) is satisfied.

Lemma 3.7. *Suppose that* $p_{1n}\left(z_i; \gamma_0, \cdot\right)$ *is continuously differentiable in a neighborhood* $N\left(\beta_0\right)$ *of* β_0, *and that there is a function* $h(z_i)$ *with* $E\left[\|h(z_i)\|^2\right] < \infty$, *such that* $\left\|p_{1n}\left(z_i; \gamma_0, b\right)\right\| \le h(z_i)$ *for all* b *in* $N\left(\beta_0\right)$. *Then*

$$\frac{1}{\sqrt{n}}\sum\left[p_{1n}\left(z_i; \gamma_0, \beta_h\right) - p_{1n}\left(z_i; \gamma_0, \beta_0\right)\right] = o_p(1).$$

Lemma 3.8. *If*

$$\begin{aligned} p_1\left(z_i; \gamma_0, \beta_0\right) &= E\left[t\left(v_i, v_j; \beta\right)\middle| v_i, w_i, w_i\gamma_0 = w_j\gamma_0\right] f_{w_j\gamma_0}\left(w_i\gamma_0\right) \\ &= \ell_t\left(z_i, w_i\gamma_0, \beta_0\right), \end{aligned}$$

then under Assumptions 3.3 and 3.10(3)

$$\frac{1}{\sqrt{n}}\sum_{i=1}^{n} p_{1n}\left(z_i;\gamma_0,\beta_0\right) - \frac{1}{\sqrt{n}}\sum_{i=1}^{n} p_1\left(z_i;\gamma_0,\beta_0\right) = o_p(1).$$

3.3. Bias Reduction

The asymptotic normality result for $\widehat{\beta}$ in Theorem 3.3 centers the asymptotic distribution of $\widehat{\beta}$ at the pseudo–true value β_h; however, if the bandwidth sequence $h = h_n$ declines to zero slowly with n, as required by Assumption 3.2, the asymptotic bias term $\beta_h - \beta_0$ need not be $o(n^{-1/2})$, and $\widehat{\beta}$ will not be root-n-consistent. Although semiparametric methods typically ensure asymptotically negligible bias by assuming the relevant kernel function (here, $K(\cdot)$) is of "higher-order bias-reducing" form, such a requirement would be unattractive for many of the estimators proposed here, because the resulting negativity of the kernel function for some data points could compromise the convexity of the corresponding minimand, complicating both the asymptotic theory (through an additional compactness restriction) and computation of the estimator. As an alternative to use of higher-order kernels, we instead obtain a root-n-consistent estimator by using the familiar jackknife approach – that is, assuming the pseudo–true value β_h is a sufficiently smooth function of the bandwidth h, we construct a linear combination $\widehat{\widehat{\beta}}$ of different estimators of β_0 (involving different bandwidth choices) for which $\sqrt{n}(\widehat{\widehat{\beta}} - \beta_0)$ has the same asymptotic distribution as $\sqrt{n}(\widehat{\beta} - \beta_h)$ and will thus be root-n-consistent.[7]

For this jackknife approach to be applicable, we require existence of a Taylor series expansion of β_h around β_0 as a function of h (in a neighborhood of $h = 0$). That is, we assume that

$$\begin{aligned}\beta_h &= \beta_0 + \sum_{l=1}^{p} b_l h^l + o(h^p),\\ &= \beta_0 + \sum_{l=1}^{p} b_l h^l + o(n^{-1/2}),\end{aligned} \tag{3.5}$$

where the last line presumes p can be chosen large enough so that

$$h^p = O\left(n^{-1/2}\right),$$

while preserving the conditions of Theorem 3.3. Such a series approximation will exist if the differentiability conditions of Assumption 3.10 are strengthened to require $(p+2)$-order differentiability of the ℓ_t term, with similar dominance conditions as in Assumption 3.10(2). To see why this would suffice, note that

[7] Were the estimator $\hat{\beta}$ linear in the kernel weight $h^{-1}K(u/h)$ – as is the objective function Q_n and its derivatives, or the "weighted average derivative" estimator of Powell et al. (1989) – then applying the jackknife to the estimator would be identical to use of a high-order kernel. In general, though, the minimizer of $Q_n(b, \hat{\gamma})$ will be nonlinear in the kernel weight terms, and the two bias reduction approaches differ.

β_h is defined by the relationship

$$\begin{aligned} 0 &= E[Q_n(\gamma_0, \beta_h)] \equiv p_{0n}(\gamma_0, \beta_h), \\ &= E\left[\int K(\eta)\,\ell_t(v_i, w_i\gamma_0 - h\eta, \beta)\,d\eta\right], \\ &\equiv F(h, \beta_h), \end{aligned}$$

where the definition of F exploits the fact that p_{0n} depends on n only through h. Viewing the pseudo–true value β_h as an implicit function of the bandwidth h, it will have $(p+1)$ derivatives with respect to h in a neighborhood of zero if Assumption 3.9(1) holds and the function $F(h, \beta)$ has $(p+2)$ derivatives in both arguments in a neighborhood of $h = 0$ and $\beta = \beta_0$, by a higher-order version of the implicit function theorem (Magnus and Neudecker 1988, Chapter 7, Theorem A.3). This, in turn, would follow from $(p+2)$-order differentiability of ℓ_t in its second and third components, plus conditions permitting interchange of differentiation and integration (over η). In fact, if the kernel function $K(\eta)$ is chosen to be symmetric ($K(u) = K(-u)$), then it is straightforward to show that the coefficient b_1 of the first-order term in (3.5) is identically zero, so that we can derive the stronger condition

$$\beta_h = \beta_0 + \sum_{l=2}^{p} b_l h^l + o(n^{-1/2}). \tag{3.6}$$

Assuming this condition is satisfied, consider p estimators $\widehat{\beta}_{c_1 h}, \ldots, \widehat{\beta}_{c_p h}$ based on the bandwidths $c_1 \cdot h, \ldots, c_p \cdot h$, where $c_1, c_2, \ldots, c_p$ is any sequence of distinct positive numbers with $c_1 \equiv 1$. These estimators will have corresponding pseudo–true values $\beta_{c_1 h}, \beta_{c_2 h}, \ldots, \beta_{c_{p+1} h}$, each of which will satisfy the condition (3.6) for h sufficiently close to zero.Then, defining the jackknifed estimator $\widehat{\widehat{\beta}}$ as

$$\widehat{\widehat{\beta}} \equiv \sum_{k=1}^{p} a_k \widehat{\beta}_{c_k h}, \tag{3.7}$$

where the coefficients $a_1, \ldots, a_p$ are defined as the solution to the linear equations

$$\begin{pmatrix} 1 & 1 & \cdots & 1 \\ c_1^2 & c_2^2 & \cdots & c_p^2 \\ \vdots & \vdots & \ddots & \vdots \\ c_1^p & c_2^p & \cdots & c_p^p \end{pmatrix} \begin{pmatrix} a_1 \\ a_2 \\ \vdots \\ a_p \end{pmatrix} = \begin{pmatrix} 1 \\ 0 \\ \vdots \\ 0 \end{pmatrix},$$

the corresponding linear combination of pseudo–true values is easily shown to satisfy

$$\sum_{k=1}^{p} a_k \beta_{c_k h} = \beta_0 + o\left(n^{-1/2}\right) \tag{3.8}$$

when (3.6) applies. Since the coefficients $a_1, ..., a_p$ must sum to one, and the asymptotic linearity expression for $\sqrt{n}\left(\widehat{\beta} - \beta_h\right)$ in Theorem 3.3 does not depend explicitly on the bandwidth parameter h, the jackknifed estimator $\widehat{\widehat{\beta}}$ is asymptotically normal when centered at the true value β_0, as the following theorem states.

Theorem 3.9. *Under the conditions of Theorem 3.3, if condition (3.6) also holds, then*

$$\sqrt{n}\left(\widehat{\widehat{\beta}} - \beta_0\right) = \frac{1}{\sqrt{n}}\sum_{i=1}^{n}\psi_i + o_p(1),$$

where ψ_i is defined in the statement of that theorem, and

$$\sqrt{n}\left(\widehat{\widehat{\beta}} - \beta_0\right) \to^d \mathcal{N}(0, E[\psi_i\psi_i']).$$

3.3.1. *Estimation of the Asymptotic Variance*

In order to construct asymptotically valid test statistics and confidence regions using the results of Theorem 3.9, a consistent estimator of the asymptotic covariance matrix $C \equiv E[\psi_i\psi_i']$ of the jackknifed estimator $\widehat{\widehat{\beta}}$ is needed. Assuming the influence function ω_i of the preliminary estimator $\widehat{\gamma}$ of γ_0 has a consistent estimator $\widehat{\omega}_i$, which satisfies

$$\frac{1}{n}\sum_{i=1}^{n}\|\widehat{\omega}_i - \omega_i\|^2 = o_p(1), \tag{3.9}$$

a consistent estimator of C can be constructed if the remaining components of ψ_ι – namely, $\Delta\widetilde{p}_0^{\beta}(\gamma_0, \beta_0)$, $\Delta\widetilde{p}_0^{\gamma}(\gamma_0, \beta_0)$, and $p_1(z_i; \gamma_0, \beta_0) \equiv p_{1i}$ – can similarly be consistently estimated. Of these three terms, estimation of the latter two are most straightforward; defining

$$\widehat{p}_{1i} \equiv \frac{1}{(n-1)}\sum_{j\neq i}\frac{1}{h_n^L}K\left(\frac{(w_i - w_j)\widehat{\gamma}}{h_n}\right)t\left(v_i, v_j; \widehat{\widehat{\beta}}\right)$$

and

$$\widehat{\Gamma}^{\gamma} \equiv \frac{2}{n(n-1)h_n}\sum_{i<j}\frac{1}{h_n^{L+1}}t\left(v_i, v_j; \widehat{\widehat{\beta}}\right)\frac{\partial K\left(\frac{(w_i - w_j)\widehat{\gamma}}{h_n}\right)}{\partial u'}(w_i - w_j),$$

the same argument as for Lemma 6.2 of Powell (1987, 2001) yields

$$\frac{1}{n}\sum_{i=1}^{n}\|\widehat{p}_{1i} - p_{1i}\|^2 = o_p(1) \tag{3.10}$$

and

$$\widehat{\Gamma}^{\gamma} \to^p \Delta\widetilde{p}_0^{\gamma}(\gamma_0, \beta_0) \tag{3.11}$$

when the conditions of Theorem 3.3 are satisfied. Estimation of the derivative $\Delta\widetilde{p}_0^{\beta}(\gamma_0, \beta_0)$ is also straightforward if the function $t(v_i, v_j, \beta)$ is differentiable in β (as for the partially linear logit estimator). In this case

$$\widehat{\Gamma}^{\beta} \equiv \frac{2}{n(n-1)h_n} \sum_{i<j} \frac{1}{h_n^L} K\left(\frac{(w_i - w_j)\widehat{\gamma}}{h_n}\right) \frac{\partial t\left(v_i, v_j; \widehat{\beta}\right)}{\partial \beta'}$$

will have

$$\widehat{\Gamma}^{\beta} \rightarrow^p \Delta\widetilde{p}_0^{\beta}\left(\gamma_0, \beta_0\right), \tag{3.12}$$

as for $\widehat{\Gamma}^{\gamma}$. If the function $t\left(v_i, v_j, \beta\right)$ is not differentiable in β, the derivative matrix $\Delta\widetilde{p}_0^{\beta}$ must be estimated using some "smoothing" method, such as the numerical derivative approach described in Newey and McFadden (1994, Section 7.3). In either case, the resulting consistent estimator of the asymptotic covariance matrix C would be

$$\widehat{C} \equiv [\widehat{\Gamma}^{\beta}]^{-1}\widehat{V}[\widehat{\Gamma}^{\beta}]^{-1},$$

where $\widehat{V}$ is the joint sample covariance matrix of $\widehat{\Gamma}^{\gamma}\widehat{\omega}_i$ and $\widehat{p}_{1i}$. Consistency of this estimator follows directly from (3.9) through (3.12).

3.4. Asymptotic Properties of Partially Linear Logit Estimator

In this section we discuss how the general results of Section 3 might be used to derive the asymptotic properties of one of the estimators defined in Section 2, the partially linear logit model. For this model, the terms in the objective function (2.5) are convex if K is positive. We can therefore use Theorem 3.1 to prove consistency. With the notation in Section 3, and with $\Lambda(\eta) = \frac{\exp(\eta)}{1+\exp(\eta)}$, we have

$$\begin{aligned} s\left((y_i, x_i), (y_j, x_j); b\right) = -1\left\{y_i \neq y_j\right\}\big(&y_i \ln \Lambda\left((x_i - x_j)b\right) \\ &+ y_j \ln \Lambda\left(-(x_i - x_j)b\right)\big) \end{aligned}$$

and $\widehat{\gamma} = \gamma_0 = I$. Also

$$\begin{aligned} t\left((y_i, x_i), (y_j, x_j); b\right) = 1\left\{y_i \neq y_j\right\}\big(&y_i \Lambda\left(-(x_i - x_j)b\right) \\ &- y_j \Lambda\left((x_i - x_j)b\right)\big)(x_i - x_j)'. \end{aligned}$$

Theorem 3.10. *Assume a random sample $\{(y_i, x_i, w_i)\}_{i=1}^n$ from (2.4) ε_i logistically distributed. The estimator defined by minimizing (2.5) where h_n satisfies Assumption 3.2(2) and K satisfies Assumption 3.3, is consistent and asymptotically normal with*

$$\sqrt{n}\left(\widehat{\beta} - \beta_h\right) \longrightarrow^d N\left(0, 4\Gamma^{-1}V\Gamma^{-1}\right)$$

with

$$V = V\left[r\left(y_i, x_i, w_i; \beta_0\right)\right],$$

where

$$r(y_i, x_i, w_i; \beta) = E\left[1\{y_i \neq y_j\}\left(y_i - \frac{\exp((x_i - x_j)\beta)}{1 + \exp((x_i - x_j)\beta)}\right) \times (x_i - x_j)' \middle| y_i, x_i, w_i, w_j = w_i\right] f_w(w_i)$$

and

$$\Gamma = E\left[E\left[1\{y_i \neq y_j\} \frac{\exp((x_i - x_j)\beta)}{(1 + \exp((x_i - x_j)\beta))^2}(x_i - x_j)'(x_i - x_j) \middle| \times y_i, x_i, w_i, w_j = w_i\right] f_w(w_i)\right]$$

provided that

1. $E\left[\|x_i\|^2\right] < \infty$;
2. w_i *is continuously distributed with a bounded density,* f_{w_i}. *Also* $E\left[\|w_i\|^2\right] < \infty$;
3. $E\left[\|x_i\| \, |w_i = a\right] f_{w_i}(a)$ *is a bounded function of* a;
4. $(x_i - x_j)$ *has full rank conditional on* $w_i = w_j$; *and*
5. *the function* $r(y_i, x_i, w_i; \beta_0)$ *is differentiable in* w_i, *with derivative* $r^{(3)}$ *satisfying* $\|r^{(3)}(y_i, x_i, w_i; \beta_0)\| \leq g(y_i, x_i, w_i)$ *for some* $g(\cdot)$ *with* $E[g(y_i, x_i, w_i)] < \infty$.

Proof. First note that $|\log \Lambda(\eta)| \leq \log(2) + |\eta|$. Therefore, $|s((y_i, x_i), (y_j, x_j); b)| \leq \log(2) + |(x_i - x_j)'b| \leq \log(2) + (t\|x_i\| + \|x_j\|)\|b\|$. Assumptions 3.1(1), 3.1(2) and 3.1(3) are therefore satisfied. To verify Assumption 3.1(4), let $a_1 = (a_{y1}, a'_{x1}, a_{w1})'$, partitioned in the same way as $z_i \equiv (y_i, x'_i)'$. Then $|E[s(a_1, v_j, b)|w_j = a_2]| \leq E[|s(a_1, v_j, b)||w_j = a_2] \leq E[\log(2) + (\|a_{x1}\| + \|x_j\|)\|b\||w_j = a_2]$, from which Assumption 3.1(4) follows. Assumption 3.4 holds with $\hat{\gamma} = \gamma_0 = I$, and Assumption 3.6 follows from consistency of the maximizer of the conditional likelihood for logit models with fixed effects. Thus all the conditions in Theorem 3.1 hold, and $\widehat{\beta}$ is consistent.

To verify asymptotic normality, first note that Assumption 3.7 is automatically satisfied (with the parameter space for β_0 being Euclidean space), as are the conditions for Lemma 3.4 (by the convexity and differentiability of the conditional likelihood). Assumption 3.8 follows from condition 1 and the fact that $||t((y_i, x_i), (y_j, x_j); b)|| \leq 2[||x_i|| + ||x_j||]$, while Assumption 3.10(1) follows from conditions 1 through 3 and the fact that $t||r^{\beta}(y_i, x_i, w_i; \beta_0)|| \leq [||x_i|| + E[\|x_j\|||w_j = w_i]]f_w(w_i)$, which in turn implies Assumption 3.9(1) by Lemma 3.5 Finally, Assumption 3.10(3) follows directly from condition 5 on the joint distribution of x_i and w_i. ■

If condition 5 of Theorem 3.10 is strengthened to require $L+2$ derivatives of $r(y_i, x_i, w_i; \beta)$ with respect to β at $\beta = \beta_0$ with a corresponding moment dominance condition on the highest derivative, then condition (3.6) holds and the jackknifed estimator will be root-n-consistent as well as asymptotically normal.

Corollary 3.11. *Under the assumptions of Theorem 3.10, if condition (3.6) holds for $p = L+2$, the corresponding jackknifed estimator is root-n-consistent and asymptotically normal,*

$$\sqrt{n}\left(\widehat{\beta} - \beta_0\right) \longrightarrow^d N\left(0, 4\Gamma^{-1} V \Gamma^{-1}\right),$$

with V and Γ defined as in Theorem 3.10.

4. MONTE CARLO RESULTS

To get a sense of the small sample properties of the estimators of the partially linear models described earlier, we have performed a Monte Carlo investigation for the partially linear logit model for a particular design. The design is chosen to illustrate the method and is not meant to mimic a design that one would expect in a particular data set. The model is

$$y_i = 1\{x_{1i}\beta_1 + x_{2i}\beta_2 + g(z_i) + \varepsilon_i\}, \quad i = 1, 2, \ldots, n, \tag{4.1}$$

where $(\beta_1, \beta_2) = (1, 1)$, $g(z) = z^2 - 2$, x_{2i} has a discrete distribution with $P(x_{2i} = -1) = P(x_{2i} = 1) = \frac{1}{2}$, distributed independently of $z_i \sim N(0, 1)$, and $x_{i1} = v_i + z_i^2$ where $v_i \sim N(0, 1)$, independent of x_{2i} and z_i. With this design, $P(y_i = 1) \simeq 0.44$. For the design used here, ignoring the nonlinearity of $g(z)$ is expected to result in a bias in the estimators of both β_1 and β_2, although we expect the bias to be bigger for β_1, because $g(z_i)$ is independent of x_{2i}.

For each replication of the model, we calculate a number of estimators. First, we calculate the logit maximum likelihood estimator using a constant, x_{1i}, x_{2i}, and $g(z_i)$ as regressors. This estimator would be asymptotically efficient if one knew $g(\cdot)$; comparing the estimators proposed here to maximum likelihood will therefore give a measure of the cost of not knowing g (and using the estimators proposed here). Second, we calculate three estimators, $\widehat{\beta}_1$, $\widehat{\beta}_2$, and $\widehat{\beta}_3$, based on (2.5) with K being the biweight (quartic)[8] kernel and $h_n = c * std(z) * n^{-1/5}$ where c takes the values 0.3, 0.9, and 2.7, respectively. These bandwidths are somewhat arbitrary. The middle one is motivated to the rule of thumb suggested by Silverman (1986, p. 48) for estimation of densities (using normal kernel). That bandwidth is supposed to illustrate what happens if one uses a "reasonable" bandwidth. The two other bandwidths are supposed to be "small" and "big". We also calculate four jackknifed estimators. The first, $\widehat{\beta}_{123}$ combines the three estimators according to (3.7). This ignores the fact that $\int uK(u)\,du = 0$, and we therefore also consider the three jackknifed estimators based on combining two

[8] Throughout, the kernel was normalized to have mean 0 and variance 1.

Table 22.1. *Monte Carlo results, sample size = 100*

	Value	Bias	Standard deviation	RMSE	Median bias	MAD	MAE
	Logit MLE using constant, x_{1i}, x_{2i}, and $g(z_i)$ as regressors						
β_1	1.000	0.138	0.406	0.428	0.083	0.253	0.245
β_2	1.000	0.107	0.376	0.390	0.063	0.222	0.213
	Semiparmetric estimator $\hat{\beta}_1$ (small bandwidth)						
β_1	1.000	0.175	0.450	0.482	0.103	0.279	0.271
β_2	1.000	0.117	0.500	0.513	0.047	0.241	0.246
	Semiparmetric estimator $\hat{\beta}_2$ (medium bandwidth)						
β_1	1.000	0.249	0.402	0.473	0.198	0.248	0.251
β_2	1.000	0.065	0.372	0.377	0.026	0.228	0.223
	Semiparmetric estimator $\hat{\beta}_3$ (large bandwidth)						
β_1	1.000	0.427	0.370	0.565	0.373	0.233	0.373
β_2	1.000	0.010	0.333	0.333	−0.021	0.202	0.206
	Jackknife using $\widehat{\beta}_1$, $\widehat{\beta}_2$, and $\widehat{\beta}_2$						
β_1	1.000	0.136	0.504	0.521	0.057	0.309	0.307
β_2	1.000	0.150	0.621	0.638	0.071	0.265	0.271
	Jackknife using $\widehat{\beta}_1$ and $\widehat{\beta}_2$						
β_1	1.000	0.166	0.459	0.488	0.091	0.283	0.275
β_2	1.000	0.124	0.521	0.535	0.049	0.247	0.251
	Jackknife using $\widehat{\beta}_1$ and $\widehat{\beta}_3$						
β_1	1.000	0.172	0.451	0.483	0.099	0.281	0.272
β_2	1.000	0.119	0.503	0.516	0.049	0.243	0.246
	Jackknife using $\widehat{\beta}_2$ and $\widehat{\beta}_3$						
β_1	1.000	0.227	0.408	0.466	0.172	0.255	0.247
β_2	1.000	0.072	0.379	0.385	0.033	0.227	0.226

of the three estimators according to (3.7). These three estimators are denoted $\widehat{\beta}_{12}$, $\widehat{\beta}_{13}$, and $\widehat{\beta}_{23}$.

The results from 1000 replications with sample sizes 100, 400, and 1600 are given in Tables 22.1 through 22.3. In addition to the true parameter values, each table also reports bias, standard deviation, and root-mean-square error of the estimator, as well as the corresponding robust measures, the median bias, the median absolute deviation from the median, and the median absolute error. Since all the estimators discussed here are likely to have fat tails (they are not even finite with probability 1), the discussion here will focus on these robust measures. The sample sizes are not chosen because we think that they are realistic given the small number of explanatory variables, but rather because we want to confirm that for large samples the estimator behaves as predicted by the asymptotic theory. As expected, the (correctly specified) maximum likelihood estimator that uses x_{1i}, x_{2i}, and $g(z_i)$ as regressors outperforms the

Table 22.2. *Monte Carlo results, sample size = 400*

	Value	Bias	Standard deviation	RMSE	Median bias	MAD	MAE
	Logit MLE using constant, x_{1i}, x_{2i}, and $g(z_i)$ as regressors						
β_1	1.000	0.018	0.164	0.165	0.012	0.115	0.110
β_2	1.000	0.020	0.158	0.159	0.015	0.101	0.102
	Semiparametric estimator $\hat{\beta}_1$ (small bandwidth)						
β_1	1.000	0.030	0.181	0.184	0.024	0.123	0.122
β_2	1.000	0.017	0.170	0.170	0.005	0.109	0.110
	Semiparametric estimator $\hat{\beta}_2$ (small bandwidth)						
β_1	1.000	0.090	0.172	0.194	0.078	0.115	0.126
β_2	1.000	0.000	0.162	0.162	−0.008	0.106	0.107
	Semiparametric estimator $\hat{\beta}_3$ (large bandwidth)						
β_1	1.000	0.279	0.156	0.319	0.265	0.104	0.265
β_2	1.000	−0.041	0.151	0.157	−0.043	0.097	0.105
	Jackknife using $\widehat{\beta}_1$, $\widehat{\beta}_2$, and $\widehat{\beta}_2$						
β_1	1.000	0.001	0.190	0.189	−0.006	0.129	0.130
β_2	1.000	0.026	0.176	0.178	0.017	0.112	0.117
	Jackknife using $\widehat{\beta}_1$ and $\widehat{\beta}_2$						
β_1	1.000	0.023	0.183	0.184	0.016	0.125	0.124
β_2	1.000	0.019	0.171	0.172	0.006	0.110	0.111
	Jackknife using $\widehat{\beta}_1$ and $\widehat{\beta}_3$						
β_1	1.000	0.027	0.182	0.184	0.022	0.123	0.123
β_2	1.000	0.018	0.170	0.171	0.006	0.109	0.110
	Jackknife using $\widehat{\beta}_2$ and $\widehat{\beta}_3$						
β_1	1.000	0.066	0.175	0.187	0.058	0.118	0.120
β_2	1.000	0.006	0.164	0.164	−0.002	0.106	0.107

semiparametric estimators. However, the jackknifed estimators perform almost as well. For example, the median absolute error of the estimator based on jackknifing using $\widehat{\beta}_2$ and $\widehat{\beta}_3$ is within 10% of the median absolute error of the maximum likelihood estimator (and often closer).

The patterns of the bias and the dispersion of the three estimators based on (2.5) are expected – lower values of the bandwidth, h, give less bias but higher dispersion.

The proposed jackknife procedure generally succeeds in removing the bias of the proposed estimators. For example, focusing on the coefficient on x_{1i} (which has the bigger bias), the estimator that removes bias by comparing $\widehat{\beta}_2$ and $\widehat{\beta}_3$ has lower bias than either $\widehat{\beta}_2$ or $\widehat{\beta}_3$ for all sample sizes. Finally, for the largest sample sizes, there is almost no difference between the four bias-reduced estimators, which corresponds to the predictions of the asymptotic theory.

Table 22.3. *Monte Carlo results, sample size = 1600*

	Value	Bias	Standard deviation	RMSE	Median bias	MAD	MAE
	Logit MLE using constant, x_{1i}, x_{2i}, and $g(z_i)$ as regressors						
β_1	1.000	0.004	0.078	0.079	0.005	0.053	0.053
β_2	1.000	0.006	0.079	0.079	0.009	0.052	0.053
	Semiparmetric estimator $\hat{\beta}_1$ (small bandwidth)						
β_1	1.000	0.010	0.085	0.085	0.009	0.056	0.058
β_2	1.000	0.005	0.083	0.084	0.007	0.054	0.054
	Semiparmetric estimator $\hat{\beta}_2$ (medium bandwidth)						
β_1	1.000	0.048	0.082	0.095	0.047	0.055	0.067
β_2	1.000	−0.004	0.081	0.081	−0.003	0.053	0.053
	Semiparmetric estimator $\hat{\beta}_3$ (large bandwidth)						
β_1	1.000	0.213	0.076	0.226	0.214	0.051	0.214
β_2	1.000	−0.040	0.077	0.087	−0.038	0.051	0.057
	Jackknife using $\widehat{\beta}_1$, $\widehat{\beta}_2$, and $\widehat{\beta}_2$						
β_1	1.000	−0.005	0.086	0.086	−0.006	0.057	0.057
β_2	1.000	0.009	0.085	0.085	0.010	0.055	0.056
	Jackknife using $\widehat{\beta}_1$ and $\widehat{\beta}_2$						
β_1	1.000	0.006	0.085	0.085	0.005	0.056	0.057
β_2	1.000	0.006	0.084	0.084	0.008	0.053	0.054
	Jackknife using $\widehat{\beta}_1$ and $\widehat{\beta}_3$						
β_1	1.000	0.008	0.085	0.085	0.007	0.056	0.057
β_2	1.000	0.006	0.084	0.084	0.007	0.054	0.054
	Jackknife using $\widehat{\beta}_2$ and $\widehat{\beta}_3$						
β_1	1.000	0.027	0.084	0.088	0.027	0.056	0.060
β_2	1.000	0.001	0.082	0.082	0.001	0.053	0.053

Table 22.4 presents evidence for the effect of the bias term (as the bias reduction) on the performance of the test-statistics calculated on the basis of the estimators discussed here. For various sample sizes and for each of the semiparametric estimators, we calculated 90 and 95 percent confidence intervals. In order to do this, we estimated the (asymptotic variance) of the three non-bias-reduced estimators by $4\widehat{\Gamma}_k^{-1}\widehat{V}_k\widehat{\Gamma}_k^{-1}$ where $k = 1, 2, 3$ denotes the estimator and $\widehat{\Gamma}_k$ is the sample variance of r_i^k defined by

$$r_i^k = \frac{1}{(n-1)\,h_n}\sum_{j\neq i} 1\left\{y_i \neq y_j\right\}\cdot K\left(\frac{w_i - w_j}{h_h}\right)$$
$$\times\left(y_i - \frac{\exp\left((x_i - x_j)'\widehat{\beta}\right)}{1+\exp\left((x_i - x_j)'\widehat{\beta}\right)}\right)(x_i - x_j)'$$

Table 22.4. *Coverage probabilities for various sample sizes*

	$n = 100$	$n = 200$	$n = 400$	$n = 800$	$n = 1600$	$n = 3200$
			90% Confidence interval			
$\widehat{\beta}_1$	0.894	0.888	0.907	0.885	0.915	0.898
$\widehat{\beta}_2$	0.849	0.850	0.864	0.841	0.866	0.856
$\widehat{\beta}_3$	0.684	0.624	0.465	0.290	0.123	0.044
$\widehat{\beta}_{123}$	0.925	0.897	0.918	0.897	0.909	0.892
$\widehat{\beta}_{12}$	0.903	0.889	0.908	0.885	0.914	0.899
$\widehat{\beta}_{13}$	0.896	0.887	0.906	0.886	0.913	0.901
$\widehat{\beta}_{23}$	0.860	0.866	0.884	0.866	0.903	0.885
			95% Confidence interval			
$\widehat{\beta}_1$	0.948	0.938	0.962	0.933	0.958	0.940
$\widehat{\beta}_2$	0.905	0.927	0.927	0.917	0.931	0.912
$\widehat{\beta}_3$	0.801	0.726	0.573	0.391	0.202	0.080
$\widehat{\beta}_{123}$	0.968	0.943	0.957	0.931	0.960	0.940
$\widehat{\beta}_{12}$	0.950	0.937	0.965	0.934	0.961	0.940
$\widehat{\beta}_{13}$	0.948	0.938	0.963	0.933	0.961	0.941
$\widehat{\beta}_{23}$	0.910	0.932	0.945	0.929	0.948	0.940

and

$$\widehat{V}_k = \frac{2}{n(n-1)h_n} \sum_{i<j} 1\{y_i \neq y_j\} \cdot K\left(\frac{w_i - w_j}{h_h}\right)$$
$$\times \frac{\exp\left((x_i - x_j)\widehat{\beta}\right)}{\left(1 + \exp\left((x_i - x_j)\widehat{\beta}\right)\right)^2}(x_i - x_j)'(x_i - x_j).$$

The estimated variance of any of the three estimators could be used to estimate the asymptotic variance of the jackknifed estimators. However, in order to avoid arbitrarily choosing one variance estimator over an other, we estimated the joint asymptotic distribution of $\left(\widehat{\beta}_1', \widehat{\beta}_2', \widehat{\beta}_3'\right)'$ by $4\widehat{\Gamma}^{-1}\widehat{V}\widehat{\Gamma}^{-1}$ where $\widehat{\Gamma}$ is the sample variance of $\left(r_i^{1\prime}, r_i^{2\prime}, r_i^{3\prime}\right)'$ and

$$\widehat{\Gamma} = \begin{pmatrix} \widehat{\Gamma}_1 & 0 & 0 \\ 0 & \widehat{\Gamma}_2 & 0 \\ 0 & 0 & \widehat{\Gamma}_3 \end{pmatrix}.$$

Table 22.4 gives the fraction of the replications for which these confidence intervals covered the true parameter. Because the biases are more dramatic for β_1, we only present the results for that parameter. For all three sample sizes we see that the confidence interval that is based on the estimator, $\widehat{\beta}_1$, which is based on a very small bandwidth, has coverage probabilities that are close to 90 and 95 percent, whereas the coverage probabilities are smaller for the two other non-bias-reduced estimators, $\widehat{\beta}_2$ and $\widehat{\beta}_3$. Although the discrepancies are not enormous (except for $\widehat{\beta}_3$ in large samples), it is interesting to note that all the bias-corrected estimators perform better than $\widehat{\beta}_2$ and $\widehat{\beta}_3$ for all sample sizes.

The sample sizes discussed so far are unrealistically large relative to the number of parameters, and there is little reason to think that the design mimics designs that one might encounter in applications. In order to investigate whether the good performance of the proposed estimators is an artifact of the very simple Monte Carlo design, we performed an additional experiment using the labor force participation data given in Berndt (1991, from Mroz, 1987). Using a constant, log hourly earnings,[9] number of children below 6, number of children between 6 and 18, age, age-squared, age-cubed, education, local unemployment rate, a dummy variable for whether the person lived in a large city, and other family income as explanatory variables, we estimated a logit for whether a woman worked in 1975. The sample size was 753 (of whom 428 worked). Using the original 753 vectors of explanatory variables, we generated 1000 datasets from this model. We then estimated the parameters using the correctly specified logit maximum likelihood estimator and the semiparametric estimator that treats the functional form for the effect of age as unknown, and calculates the bandwidths as described for the original design.

The results for this empirically based simulation are presented in Table 22.5. Apart from the nonbias-reduced estimator with the largest bandwidth, $\widehat{\beta}_3$, the precision of the proposed estimators is quite close to that of correctly specified maximum likelihood, with median absolute errors typically around 5% larger than for the MLE. Similarly, coverage rates for the nominal 90% and 95% confidence intervals are quite close to the nominal levels (again with the exception of $\widehat{\beta}_3$). Perhaps even more than for the original Monte Carlo design, these results are reassuring that the proposed estimators are relatively precise for realistic sample sizes and data configurations, and that inference based upon the asymptotic normal theory can be reasonably accurate in finite samples.

5. POSSIBLE EXTENSIONS

Ahn and Powell (1993) extended the model given in (2.2) and (2.3) by allowing the nonparametric component to depend upon an unknown function $p(w_i)$, which itself must be estimated via nonparametric regression, rather than the parametric (linear) form $w_i'\gamma$, as assumed earlier. Making the same extension in (2.9) and (2.10) would lead to an estimator that minimizes a function of the form

$$Q_n(b) = \binom{n}{2}^{-1} \frac{1}{h_n} \sum_{\substack{i<j \\ d_i=d_j=1}} K\left(\frac{\hat{p}(w_i) - \hat{p}(w_j)}{h_n}\right) s(y_i, y_j, (x_i - x_j)b). \tag{5.1}$$

[9] This variable was imputed for the individuals who did not work.

Table 22.5. *Monte Carlo results for empirically based design*

	$\widehat{\beta}_1$	$\widehat{\beta}_2$	$\widehat{\beta}_3$	$\widehat{\beta}_{123}$	$\widehat{\beta}_{12}$	$\widehat{\beta}_{13}$	$\widehat{\beta}_{23}$
	Median absolute error relative to MLE						
Wage rate	1.0229	1.0161	0.9796	1.0531	1.0228	1.0260	1.0206
Children below 6	1.0342	0.9860	1.1623	1.0443	1.0273	1.0352	1.0065
Children between 6 and 18	1.0372	0.9928	1.7117	1.0560	1.0358	1.0416	1.0346
Education	1.0648	1.0303	1.0156	1.0711	1.0625	1.0640	1.0354
Local unemployment	1.0511	1.0439	1.0386	1.0876	1.0643	1.0518	1.0467
City	1.0454	1.0016	0.9609	1.0371	1.0336	1.0439	0.9909
Other income	1.0423	1.0181	1.0243	1.0207	1.0395	1.0432	1.0149
	Coverage rates for 90% confidence interval						
Wage rate	0.889	0.886	0.883	0.893	0.889	0.889	0.887
Children below 6	0.900	0.904	0.832	0.909	0.908	0.901	0.900
Children between 6 and 18	0.885	0.877	0.624	0.897	0.887	0.885	0.885
Education	0.889	0.890	0.883	0.890	0.891	0.890	0.890
Local unemployment	0.894	0.895	0.889	0.900	0.896	0.894	0.893
City	0.912	0.912	0.909	0.918	0.916	0.913	0.911
Other income	0.899	0.905	0.899	0.903	0.898	0.898	0.901
	Coverage rates for 95% confidence interval						
Wage rate	0.947	0.946	0.943	0.946	0.948	0.947	0.946
Children below 6	0.960	0.956	0.902	0.959	0.959	0.960	0.959
Children between 6 and 18	0.942	0.934	0.740	0.950	0.944	0.943	0.944
Education	0.944	0.936	0.935	0.945	0.943	0.944	0.942
Local unemployment	0.941	0.938	0.943	0.943	0.942	0.941	0.937
City	0.963	0.962	0.954	0.963	0.964	0.964	0.964
Other income	0.953	0.955	0.958	0.959	0.954	0.952	0.954

The estimator proposed by Ahn and Powell (1993) minimizes Q_n in (5.1), if there is no censoring and if quadratic loss ($\Xi(d) = d^2$) is used. Similar minimization problems arise in the estimation of semiparametric models with endogenous regressors (as discussed by, e.g., Blundell and Powell, 2003); in such applications $\widehat{p}(w_i)$ might represent residuals from a first-stage nonparametric regression, used as "control variates" to account for endogeneity of some components of x_i. Investigation of the properties of the estimator defined by (5.1) is an interesting avenue for further research.

It would also be useful to extend the estimation method to permit inverse probability weighting for stratified sampling, as considered by Wooldridge (1999b), and to extend the asymptotic theory to discontinuous (in β) objective functions, so that that rank-based estimators for binary response and single-index models proposed by Han (1987) and Cavanagh and Sherman (1998) might be extended to permit partially linear and selection models. Finally, it would be useful to combine the proposed coefficient estimators with nonparametric estimation techniques to more fully characterize the conditional distribution of the dependent variable y_i (or perhaps the latent dependent variable y_i^*) given x_i and/or w_i, which in turn could be used to average derivatives or treatment effects for target populations. At a minimum, such an extension would likely involve explicit nonparametric estimation of the partially linear component function $g(w_i)$ or $g(w_i'\gamma_0)$, and perhaps of the distribution of error terms for some of the nonlinear models, problems which have been sidestepped in our focus on estimation of the β coefficients.

ACKNOWLEDGMENTS

This study was supported by the National Science Foundation, the Gregory C. Chow Econometric Research Program at Princeton University, and the Danish National Research Foundation through CAM at The University of Copenhagen. We are grateful to Donald Andrews, Guido Imbens, Michael Jansson, Richard Juster, Ekaterini Kyriazidou, Thomas Rothenberg, Paul Ruud, and the referees for helpful comments on earlier versions. Part of this research was done while Honoré visited the Economics Department at the University of Copenhagen.

APPENDIX: THE MOST DULL DERIVATIONS

Proof of Lemma 5. By the definitions of $t(\cdot)$ and $\ell_t(\cdot)$,

$$\begin{aligned}
p_{0n}(\gamma_0, \beta) &= E\left[\frac{1}{h^L} K\left(\frac{w_i\gamma_0 - w_j\gamma_0}{h}\right) t(v_i, v_j, \beta)\right] \\
&= E\left[\frac{1}{h^L} K\left(\frac{w_i\gamma_0 - w_j\gamma_0}{h}\right) E\left[t(v_i, v_j, \beta) \middle| (v_i, w_i), w_j'\gamma_0\right]\right] \\
&= E\left[\frac{1}{h^L} K\left(\frac{w_i\gamma_0 - w_j\gamma_0}{h}\right) k_t(v_i, w_j'\gamma_0, \beta)\right] \\
&= E\left[\int \frac{1}{h^L} K\left(\frac{w_i\gamma_0 - \omega}{h}\right) k_t(v_i, \omega, \beta) f_{w_i\gamma_0}(\omega) d\omega\right] \\
&= E\left[\int K(\eta) \ell_t(v_i, w_i\gamma_0 - h\eta, \beta) d\eta\right].
\end{aligned}$$

By Assumption 3.10(1), we can differentiate under the expectation and integral:

$$\begin{aligned}
p_{0n}^{\beta}(\gamma_0, \beta_0) &= E\left[\int K(\eta) \ell_t^{(3)}(v_i, w_i\gamma_0 - h\eta, \beta_0) d\eta\right] \\
&\to E\left[\ell_t^{(3)}(v_i, w_i\gamma_0, \beta_0)\right],
\end{aligned}$$

where the limit follows from dominated convergence. ■

Proof of Lemma 6. Recall that

$$p_{0n}(\gamma,\beta)=E\left[\frac{1}{h^L}K\left(\frac{w_i\gamma-w_j\gamma}{h}\right)t\left(v_i,v_j,\beta\right)\right].$$

By Assumptions 3.3 and 3.10 (2), we can differentiate under the expectation:

$$p_{0n}^{\gamma}(\gamma,\beta)=E\left[\frac{1}{h^L}K'\left(\frac{w_i\gamma-w_j\gamma}{h}\right)\frac{w_i'-w_j'}{h}t\left(v_i,v_j,\beta\right)\right].$$

Evaluating this at (γ_0,β_0), we get

$$\begin{aligned}p_{0n}^{\gamma}\left(\gamma_0,\beta_0\right)&=E\left[\frac{1}{h^L}K'\left(\frac{w_i\gamma_0-w_j\gamma_0}{h}\right)\frac{w_i'-w_j'}{h}t\left(v_i,v_j,\beta_0\right)\right]\\&=E\left[E\left[E\left[\frac{1}{h^L}K'\left(\frac{w_i\gamma_0-w_j\gamma_0}{h}\right)\frac{w_i'-w_j'}{h}\right.\right.\right.\\&\qquad\left.\left.\left.\times\, t\left(v_i,v_j,\beta_0\right)\right| v_i,w_i,w_j\gamma_0\right]\right| v_i,w_i\Big]\Big]\\&=E\left[E\left[\frac{1}{h^{L+1}}K'\left(\frac{w_i\gamma_0-w_j\gamma_0}{h}\right)E\left[\left(w_i-w_j\right)\right.\right.\right.\\&\qquad\left.\left.\left.\times\, t\left(v_i,v_j,\beta_0\right)\right| v_i,w_i,w_j\gamma_0\right]\right| v_i,w_i\Big]\Big].\end{aligned}$$

With the definitions of k_{t_1} and ℓ_{t_1}, and using integration by parts, we have

$$\begin{aligned}&p_{0n}^{\gamma}\left(\gamma_0,\beta_0\right)\\&\quad=E\left[\int\frac{1}{h^{L+1}}K'\left(\frac{w_i\gamma_0-\omega}{h}\right)k_{t_1}\left(z_i,\omega,\beta_0\right)f_{w_i\gamma_0}(\omega)\,d\omega\right]\\&\quad=E\left[\int\frac{1}{h^{L+1}}K'\left(\frac{w_i\gamma_0-\omega}{h}\right)\ell_{t_1}\left(z_i,\omega,\beta_0\right)d\omega\right]\\&\quad=E\left[\int\frac{1}{h}K'(\eta)\,\ell_{t_1}\left(z_i,w_i\gamma_0-h\eta,\beta_0\right)d\eta\right]\\&\quad=-E\left[\int K(\eta)\,\ell_{t_1}^{(2)}\left(z_i,w_i\gamma_0-h\eta,\beta_0\right)d\eta\right]\\&\quad\to -E\left[\ell_{t_1}^{(2)}\left(z_i,w_i\gamma_0,\beta_0\right)\right],\end{aligned}$$

where the limit follows from dominated convergence. ∎

Proof of Lemma 8. Write

$$p_{1n}\left(z_i;\gamma_0,\beta_0\right)=r_n\left(z_i\right)-E\left[r_n\left(z_i\right)\right]$$

and

$$p_1\left(z_i\right)=\ell_t\left(z_i,w_i'\gamma_0,\beta_0\right)-E\left[\ell_t\left(z_i,w_i\gamma_0,\beta_0\right)\right],$$

where

$$\begin{aligned} r_n(z_i) &= E\left[p_n(z_i, z_j; \gamma_0, \beta_0) \middle| z_i \right] \\ &= \int \frac{1}{h^L} K\left(\frac{w_i \gamma_0 - \omega}{h} \right) \ell_t(v_i, \omega, \beta_0)\, d\omega \\ &= \int K(\eta)\, \ell_t(v_i, w_i \gamma_0 - h\eta, \beta_0)\, d\eta \end{aligned}$$

and $E\left[\ell_t(z_i, w_i \gamma_0, \beta_0)\right] = 0$. With $\delta_n(z_i) = r_n(z_i) - \ell_t(z_i, w_i \gamma_0, \beta_0)$, we then have

$$\begin{aligned} &\frac{1}{\sqrt{n}} \sum_{i=1}^{n} p_{1n}(z_i; \gamma_0, \beta_0) - \frac{1}{\sqrt{n}} \sum_{i=1}^{n} p_1(z_i; \gamma_0, \beta_0) \\ &\quad = \frac{1}{\sqrt{n}} \sum_{i=1}^{n} \delta_n(z_i) - E[\delta_n(z_i)]. \end{aligned}$$

The right-hand side has mean 0 and variance

$$\begin{aligned} &V\left[\frac{1}{\sqrt{n}} \sum_{i=1}^{n} \delta_n(z_i) - E[\delta_n(z_i)] \right] \\ &= V[\delta_n(z_i) - E[\delta_n(z_i)]] \\ &\le E\left[\delta_n(z_i)^2\right] \\ &= E\left[\left\{ r_n(z_i) - \ell_t(z_i, w_i \gamma_0, \beta_0) \right\}^2 \right] \\ &= E\left[\left\{ \int K(\eta)\, \ell_t(v_i, w_i \gamma_0 - h\eta, \beta_0)\, d\eta \right.\right. \\ &\quad \left.\left. - \ell_t(z_i, w_i \gamma_0, \beta_0) \right\}^2 \right] \\ &= E\left[\left\{ \int K(\eta) \left(\ell_t(v_i, w_i \gamma_0 - h\eta, \beta_0) \right.\right.\right. \\ &\quad \left.\left.\left. - \ell_t(z_i, w_i \gamma_0, \beta_0) \right) d\eta \right\}^2 \right] \\ &\le E\left[g(z_i)^2 h^2 \left\{ \int |K(\eta)|\, \|\eta\|\, d\eta \right\}^2 \right] \\ &= O\left(h^2\right) \to 0, \end{aligned}$$

where g is the function in Assumption 3.10 (3). ■

Proof of Lemma 7. For the duration of this proof, let p_{1n} denote one of the elements of p_{1n}. By definition of p_{1n} and by random sampling, the mean of the left-hand side is 0, while the variance is

$$\begin{aligned} &E\left[\left(p_{1n}(z_i; \gamma_0, \beta_h) - p_{1n}(z_i; \gamma_0, \beta_0) \right)^2 \right] \\ &\quad \le E\left[\left\| p_{1n}^{\beta}(z_i; \gamma_0, \beta_i^*) \right\|^2 \right] \left\| \beta_h - \beta_0 \right\|^2, \end{aligned}$$

where β_i^* is between β_h and β_0, but may depend on z_i (hence the subscript i). The result now follows from $\beta_h \to \beta_0$. ■

References

Ahn, H., and J. L. Powell (1993), "Semiparametric Estimation of Censored Selection Models with a Nonparametric Selection Mechanism," *Journal of Econometrics*, 58, 3–29.

Amemiya, T. (1985), *Advanced Econometrics*. Cambridge, MA: Harvard University Press.

Berndt, E. R. (1991), *The Practice of Econometrics: Classic and Contemporary.* Reading, MA: Addison-Wesley.

Blundell, R., and J. L. Powell (2003), "Endogeneity in Nonparametric and Semiparametric Regression Models", in *Advances in Economics and Econometrics: Theory and Applications, Eighth World Congress*, Volume II (ed. by L. P. Hansen and S. Turnovsky), Cambridge: Cambridge University Press.

Cavanagh, C., and R. Sherman (1998), "Rank Estimators for Monotonic Regression Models," *Journal of Econometrics*, 84, 351–81.

Chamberlain, G. (1984), "Panel Data," in *Handbook of Econometrics*, Vol. II (ed. by Z. Griliches and M. Intriligator), Amsterdam: North Holland.

Chamberlain, G. (1985), "Heterogeneity, Omitted Variable Bias, and Duration Dependence," in *Longitudinal Analysis of Labor Market Data* (ed. by J. J. Heckman and B. Singer). Cambridge: Cambridge University Press.

Engle, R. F, C. W. J. Granger, J. Rice, and A. Weiss (1986), "Semipaarametric Estimates of the Relation Between Weather and Electricity Sales," *Journal of the American Statistical Association,* 81, 310–20.

Han, A. K. (1987), "Non-parametric Analysis of a Generalized Regression Model: The Maximum Rank Correlation Estimator," *Journal of Econometrics*, 35(2–3), 303–16.

Hausman, J., B. Hall, and Z. Griliches (1984), "Econometric Models for Count Data with an Application to the Patents-R&D Relationship," *Econometrica*, 52(4), 909–38.

Honoré, B. E. (1992), "Trimmed LAD and Least Squares Estimation of Truncated and Censored Regression Models with Fixed Effects," *Econometrica*, 60(3), 533–65.

Honoré, B. E., and J. L. Powell (1994), "Pairwise Difference Estimators of Censored and Truncated Regression Models," *Journal of Econometrics*, 64(2), 241–78.

Magnus, J. R., and H. Neudecker (1988), *Matrix Differential Calculus with Applications in Statistics and Econometrics*. New York: Wiley.

Mroz, T. A. (1987), "The Sensitivity of an Empirical Model of Married Women's Hours of Work to Economic and Statistical Assumptions," *Econometrica*, 55(4), 765–99.

Newey, W. K. and D. McFadden (1994), "Large Sample Estimation and Hypothesis Testing," in *Handbook of Econometrics*, Vol. IV (ed. by R. F. Engle and D. L. McFadden), Amsterdam: North Holland.

Powell, J. L. (1987), "Semiparametric Estimation of Bivariate Latent Variable Models," Department of Economics, University of Wisconsin-Madison, SSRI Working Paper No. 8704.

Powell, J. L. (1994), "Estimation of Semiparametric Models," in *Handbook of Econometrics*, Vol. IV (ed. by R. F. Engle and D. L. McFadden). Amsterdam: North Holland.

Powell, J. L. (2001), "Semiparametric Estimation of Censored Selection Models" in *Nonlinear Statistical Modeling* (ed. by C. Hsiao, K. Morimune, and J.L. Powell), Cambridge: Cambridge University Press.

Powell, J. L., J. Stock, and T. Stoker (1989), "Semiparametric Estimation of Weighted Average Derivatives", *Econometrica*, 57, 1403-30.

Rasch, G. (1960), *Probabilistic Models for Some Intelligence and Attainment Tests*. Copenhagen: Denmarks Pædagogiske Institut.

Robinson, P. (1988), "Root-N-Consistent Semiparametric Regression," *Econometrica*, 56, 931–54.

Sherman, R. (1994a), "U–Processes in the Analysis of a Generalized Semiparametric Regression Estimator," *Econometric Theory*, 10, 372–95.

Sherman, R. (1994b), "Maximal Inequalities for Degenerate U–Processes with Applications to Optimization Estimators," *Annals of Statistics*, 22(1), 439–59.

Silverman, B. W. (1986), *Density Estimation for Statistics and Data Analysis*. London: Chapman and Hall.

van de Geer, S. (2000), *Empirical Processes in M-Estimation*. Cambridge: Cambridge University Press.

Wooldridge, J. M. (1999a), "Distribution-Free Estimation of Some Nonlinear Panel Data Models," *Journal of Econometrics*, 90, 77-97.

Wooldridge, J.M. (1999b), "Asymptotic Properties of Weighted M-Estimators for Variable Probability Samples," *Econometrtica*, 67, 1385–1406.

CHAPTER 23

Density Weighted Linear Least Squares

Whitney K. Newey and Paul A. Ruud

ABSTRACT

This paper considers inverse density weighted least-squares estimation for slope coefficients of index models. The estimator permits discontinuities in the index function while imposing smoothness in the density of the regressors. We show consistency and asymptotic normality of the estimator and give a consistent estimator of the asymptotic variance. We also consider asymptotic efficiency and report results from a Monte Carlo study of the performance of the estimators.

1. INTRODUCTION

Several semiparametric methods for index models have been developed. In a single index model, the conditional expectation of a dependent variable y given a $r \times 1$ vector of explanatory variables x is

$$E[y \mid x] = \tau(x'\beta_0) \tag{1.1}$$

for an unknown vector of parameters β_0 and an unknown univariate function $\tau(\cdot)$. This model is implied by many important limited dependent variable and regression models, as discussed in Ruud (1986) and Stoker (1986). Consistent estimators for β_0, up to an unknown scale factor, are given by Ruud (1986), Stoker (1986), Powell, Stock, and Stoker (1989), Ichimura (1993), and others.

In this paper, we return to a type of estimator developed by Ruud (1986). He proposed an inverse density weighted quasi–maximum likelihood estimator. We consider least-squares estimation that is weighted by the ratio of a density with a linear conditional expectation (LCE) property and compact support to a kernel estimator of the true density. The LCE is that the conditional expectation given any linear combination is a linear function of the linear combination. We give conditions for $\sqrt{n}$ consistency and asymptotic normality of the estimator, and derive a consistent estimator for the asymptotic variance. We also show that the first-order conditions for the scaled least-squares coefficients have a

This paper was presented at the 2001 Symposium on Identification and Inference in Econometrics, University of California, Berkeley. The NSF supported the research for this paper.

form analogous to the efficient score for an index model. This form is used to suggest ways to choose weights that have high efficiency.

Among the semiparametric index estimators, the inverse density weighted least-squares (DWLS) estimator is unique because it permits discontinuities in the transformation τ. Discontinuities in the conditional expectation of dependent variables arise in such economic problems as optimization over nonlinear budget sets and production frontiers. In labor supply, for example, nonconvexities in the budget frontier caused by welfare programs imply discontinuities in the desired hours of work. If there is no unobserved heterogeneity, these discontinuities translate into discontinuities in the conditional expectation of hours given socioeconomic covariates that control for observable heterogeneity. The estimators that we consider in this paper accommodate such breaks when the index model is linear. In contrast, the average derivative estimators of Stoker (1986) and Powell et al. (1989) and the kernel regression estimators of Ichimura (1993) all require that τ be differentiable. Thus, the results of this paper provide a way of estimating index parameters in nonsmooth cases that have previously been ruled out.

2. THE ESTIMATOR

Our estimator is based on the idea of Ruud (1986). Suppose that the density of x has LCE (that the conditional expectation of x given any linear combination of x is linear in that combination). Ruud (1986) shows that in this case quasi–maximum likelihood estimation (QMLE) is consistent for β_0, up to scale. He exploits this property by multiplying the quasi-likelihood function by the ratio of a LCE density to a nonparametric estimator of the true density of x. The resulting QMLE is consistent for slope coefficients, because the "reweighting" has the effect of making the limit the same as if the regressor density were the LCE density.

In this paper we focus on weighted least-squares estimators, because they are particularly simple to compute. To describe the estimator, let θ denote a parameter vector and $f(x,\theta)$ a density with LCE for all θ and with compact support (that can depend on θ). In particular, $f(x,\theta)$ could be an elliptically symmetric density, which is known to have the LCE. Let $\hat{\theta}$ denote an estimator of some value θ_0 of the parameter vector. For a kernel $K(u)$, satisyfing properties to be specified later, and a bandwidth parameter λ, let

$$\hat{h}(x) = \frac{1}{n}\sum_{i=1}^{n} K_\lambda(x - x_i), \qquad K_\lambda(u) = \lambda^{-r}K(u/\lambda),$$

where r is the dimension of x. This $\hat{h}(x)$ is a kernel density estimator. For $X = (1, x')'$, a DWLS estimator is obtained as

$$\hat{\gamma} = \left(\sum_{i=1}^{n} \hat{w}_i X_i X_i'\right)^{-1} \sum_{i=1}^{n} \hat{w}_i X_i y_i,\ \hat{w}_i = \hat{h}(x_i)^{-1} f(x_i, \hat{\theta}),$$

where the data observations are indexed by $i = 1, \ldots, n$.

The limit of this estimator behaves as if x had density $f(x, \theta_0)$. Thus, by Ruud (1986), we know that the coefficients of x in $\hat{\gamma}$ are consistent for β_0, up to a common scale factor. The density $f(x, \theta)$ is required to have compact support in order to deal with the technical problem that $\hat{h}(x)^{-1}$ could be large for outlying values of x. Also, the parameter estimates $\hat{\theta}$ are present in order to allow for centering the location and scale of the density. Furthermore, allowing for $\hat{\theta}$ can be important for efficiency, as discussed in Section 5.

The kernel $K(u)$ will be assumed to satisfy $\int K(u)du = 1$, have a compact support, and satisfy other regularity conditions given below. In practice the kernel should generally include a scale normalization, where $K(u) = \det(\hat{\Sigma})^{-1/2} p(\hat{\Sigma}^{-1/2}u)$ for a kernel $p(u)$ and $\hat{\Sigma}$ equal to the sample variance of x_i. For simplicity we restrict $K(u)$ to be nonrandom in the theory.

We explicitly allow for twicing kernels, which take the form

$$K(u) = 2k(u) - \int k(u - v)k(v)\, dv,$$

where $k(u)$ is a kernel with $\int k(u)du = 1$. Such a $K(u)$ has the small bias property (SBP) considered by Newey, Hsieh, and Robins (2000). The SBP means that the bias of DWLS is asymptotically smaller than the bias of a kernel estimator based on $k(u)$, without any additional smoothness conditions on the density $h(x)$.

To explain why twicing kernels have the SBP, we consider a dominating bias term in an asymptotic expansion of the estimator. As discussed in Newey and McFadden (1994) and Newey et al. (2000), after a linearization and centering at expectations, a dominating bias term is given by

$$\begin{aligned} B_\lambda &= E\left[\int v(x)\{\hat{h}(x) - h_0(x)\}\, dx\right] \\ &= \int v(x)\left\{\int K(u)[h_0(x - \lambda u) - h_0(x)\right\} du\, dx, \end{aligned}$$

where $v(x)$ is some function of x that is here given by $v(x) = -Xf(x, \theta_0)E[y|x]/h_0(x)$. Define $v_\lambda(x) = \int k(u)v(x - \lambda u)\, du$ and $h_\lambda(x) = \int k(u)h_0(x - \lambda u)\, du$. Assuming that the kernel $k(u)$ is symmetric, so that $k(u) = k(-u)$, changing variables gives

$$\begin{aligned} &\int\int\int v(x)k(u - t)k(t)h_0(x - \lambda u)\, dt\, du\, dx \\ &\quad = \int\int\int v(x)k(v)k(t)h_0(x - \lambda t - \lambda v)\, dt\, dv\, dx \\ &\quad = \int v_\lambda(x)h_\lambda(x)\, dx, \\ &\int\int v(x)h_\lambda(x)\, dx = \int\int v_\lambda(x)h_0(x)\, du\, dx. \end{aligned}$$

Then by the form of the twicing kernel,

$$\begin{aligned} B_\lambda &= -\int v(x)h_0(x)\,dx + \int v_\lambda(x)h_0(x)\,dx \\ &\quad + \int v(x)h_\lambda(x)\,dx - \int v_\lambda(x)h_\lambda(x)\,dx \\ &= -\int [v_\lambda(x) - v(x)][h_\lambda(x) - h_0(x)]\,dx. \end{aligned}$$

Now, each of $v_\lambda(x) - v(x)$ and $h_\lambda(x) - h_0(x)$ are pointwise biases from kernel estimation using $k(u)$. Thus we see that B_λ is minus the integral of the product of pointwise biases for $v(x)$ and $h_0(x)$ corresponding to $k(u)$. Since these pointwise biases will go to zero as λ shrinks to zero, for small λ we have B_λ smaller in magnitude than the pointwise density bias $h_\lambda(x) - h_0(x)$. This is the SBP mentioned earlier. The SBP even holds when $v(x)$ is not continuous, although the bias reduction is smaller in that case. These theoretical properties are consistent with our Monte Carlo results reported in Section 6.

The estimator that will be consistent for β_0 up to scale is the vector of coefficients of x that appear in $\hat{\gamma}$. A convenient way to normalize the scale is to suppose that the first coefficient in β_0 is 1 (which is just a normalization as long as it is nonzero). Partition $\gamma = (\gamma_1, \delta')$ and $\hat{\gamma} = (\hat{\gamma}_1, \hat{\delta}')'$ conformably, where γ_1 is a scalar (coefficient of the constant) and δ is an $r \times 1$ vector (the coefficients of x). Also, partition $\beta = (\beta_1, \beta_2')'$ and $\delta = (\delta_1, \delta_2')'$ conformably, where β_1 is a scalar, so that the dimension of β_2 is $r - 1$. The true value of β_1 is 1, by our scale normalization. An estimator of β_2 that includes this scale normalization is then

$$\hat{\beta}_2 = \hat{\delta}_2/\hat{\delta}_1.$$

That is, $\hat{\beta}_2$ is the ratio of the coefficients in $\hat{\gamma}$ of all the regressors except the first one to the first regressor coefficient.

An important practical problem is the choice of bandwidth λ. For standard kernels the regularity conditions for $\sqrt{n}$ consistency will require that λ be chosen to be smaller than the value that would minimize the asymptotic mean square error of $\hat{h}$, a feature that is often referred to as "undersmoothing." Thus, for standard kernels, choosing the bandwidth from cross-validation, or any other method that minimizes the asymptotic mean square error (MSE), will not lead to $\sqrt{n}$ consistency of $\hat{\gamma}$. For twicing kernels, undersmoothing is not needed, because of the SBP. Thus, a bandwidth that minimizes the MSE for a kernel estimator based on $k(u)$ can lead to $\sqrt{n}$ consistency. However, even with twicing kernels, such a bandwidth may not be optimal for the weighted least-squares estimator. One could derive a bandwidth that minimizes the MSE of DWLS, but it is beyond the scope of this paper to do so. A practical choice would be to use cross-validation and check the sensitivity of DWLS to bandwidth, focusing on smaller bandwidth values in the case of a standard kernel.

3. ASYMPTOTIC VARIANCE ESTIMATION

The estimator is a weighted least-squares estimator with an estimated weight. In our case, where the conditional expectation (1.1) is not linear, estimation of the weights will affect the limiting distribution, complicating asymptotic variance estimation. There are two sources of variability in the weights, the nonparametric density estimator in the denominator and the $\hat{\theta}$ estimator in the numerator. Both sources will affect the asymptotic variance of $\hat{\gamma}$, but the asymptotic variance of $\hat{\beta}_2$ will only be affected by estimation of the denominator (the true density). This simplification follows from Newey and McFadden (1993, Theorem 6.2), which says that the asymptotic variance of $\hat{\beta}_2$ is not affected by estimation of θ if the limit of $\hat{\theta}$ does not affect the limit of $\hat{\beta}_2$. Here, $\hat{\beta}_2$ will be consistent no matter what the limit of $\hat{\theta}$ is, because of LCE of $f(x, \theta)$ for *all* θ.

In most cases the parameters of interest are β_2, so that estimation of $\hat{\theta}$ can be ignored in the asymptotic variance. To avoid additional complication, we will focus on this case and derive an estimator of the asymptotic variance of $\hat{\beta}_2$. We prove its consistency below.

An estimator of the asymptotic variance of $\hat{\beta}_2$ can be constructed as follows. Let

$$\hat{g}(x) = \sum_{i=1}^{n} \frac{y_i K_\lambda(x - x_i)}{\hat{h}(x)}$$

be a kernel estimator of $E[y \mid x]$. Define

$$\hat{J} \equiv \hat{\delta}_1^{-1}[0_{r-1}, -\hat{\beta}_2, I_{r-1}]$$

$$\hat{Q} \equiv \frac{1}{n} \sum_{i=1}^{n} \hat{w}_i X_i X_i'$$

$$\hat{\Sigma} \equiv \frac{1}{n} \sum_{i=1}^{n} \hat{w}_i^2 X_i X_i' [y_i - \hat{g}(x_i)]^2,$$

where 0_{r-1} is an $(r-1)$-dimensional column vector of zeros and I_{r-1} is an $(r-1)$-dimensional identity matrix. Then a consistent estimator of the asymptotic variance of $\sqrt{n}(\hat{\beta}_2 - \beta_{20})$ will be

$$\hat{V} = \hat{J}' \hat{Q}^{-1} \hat{\Sigma} \hat{Q}^{-1} \hat{J}. \tag{3.1}$$

This estimator can be interpreted as being obtained by combining the delta method with an asymptotic variance estimator for $\hat{\gamma}$. Here $\hat{J}$ is the Jacobian of the transformation from $\hat{\gamma}$ to $\hat{\beta}_2$, while $\hat{Q}^{-1}\hat{\Sigma}\hat{Q}^{-1}$ is an estimator for the asymptotic variance of $\hat{\gamma}$ that ignores estimation of θ_0. Consistency of this estimator of the asymptotic variance will be shown in Section 4.

The form of this estimator can be motivated by deriving the asymptotic variance of $\hat{\gamma}$, assuming that $\hat{\theta} = \theta_0$. Let $h_0(x)$ denote the density of x, $w(x) = f(x, \theta_0)/h_0(x)$, and $\gamma_0 = Q^{-1} E[w(x) X y]$ be the limit of $\hat{\gamma}$, for

$Q = E[w(x)XX']$. Then, for $u = y - X'\gamma_0$,

$$\sqrt{n}(\hat{\gamma} - \gamma_0) = \frac{1}{\sqrt{n}}\hat{Q}^{-1}\sum_{i=1}^{n}\hat{w}_i X_i u_i. \tag{3.2}$$

Under appropriate regularity conditions, the first term will have limit Q^{-1}, and so the asymptotic variance of $\hat{\gamma}$ will be $Q^{-1}\Sigma Q^{-1}$, where Σ is the asymptotic variance of $\sum_{i=1}^{n}\hat{w}_i X_i u_i/\sqrt{n}$. To derive Σ we need to account for the presence of the nonparametric density $\hat{h}$. This can be done by using the general results of Newey (1994a, Proposition 5) on the effect of nonparametric density estimation. There it is shown that for a function $m(z, h)$ of a random variable z and a scalar h, any nonparametric density estimator $\hat{h}(x)$ satisfying certain regularity conditions, and the true density $h_0(x)$,

$$\sum_{i=1}^{n} m(z_i, \hat{h}(x_i))/\sqrt{n} = \sum_{i=1}^{n}\{m(z_i, h_0(x_i))$$
$$+ D(x_i)h_0(x_i) - E[D(x)h_0(x)]\}/\sqrt{n} + o_p(1),$$
$$D(x) = E[\partial m(z, h)/\partial h|_{h=h_0(x)}|x].$$

To apply this result let $m(z, h) = f(x, \theta_0)Xu/h$, so that

$$\begin{aligned}
D(x) &= E\left[f(x, \theta_0)Xu\partial h^{-1}/\partial h|_{h=h_0(x)}|x\right] \\
&= -E\left[f(x, \theta_0)Xu/h_0(x)^2|x\right] \\
&= -h_0(x)^{-1}w(x)XE[u|x] \\
&= -h_0(x)^{-1}w(x)X\{E[y|x] - X'\gamma_0\}.
\end{aligned}$$

Also, by the population least-squares first-order conditions, $E[D(x)h_0(x)] = -E[w(x)Xu] = 0$. Therefore,

$$\begin{aligned}
\sum_{i=1}^{n}\hat{w}_i X_i u_i/\sqrt{n} &= \sum_{i=1}^{n}\{w(x_i)X_i u_i + D(x_i)h_0(x_i)\}/\sqrt{n} + o_p(1) \\
&= \frac{1}{\sqrt{n}}\sum_{i=1}^{n} w(x_i)X_i\{y_i - E[y_i \mid x_i]\} + o_p(1). \qquad (3.3)
\end{aligned}$$

This equation is given precise justification in Lemma 4.1. From this equation and the central limit theorem, the asymptotic variance of the term $\sum_{i=1}^{n}\hat{w}_i X_i u_i/\sqrt{n}$ will be $\Sigma = E[w(x)^2XX'\{y - \tau(x'\beta_0)\}^2]$ when $\hat{\theta} = \theta_0$. The estimator $\hat{\Sigma}$ that appears in $\hat{V}$ is simply a sample analog of Σ, where $w(x)$ and $E[y \mid x]$ have been replaced by estimators.

It is interesting to note that estimation of the density has the effect of lowering the asymptotic variance of the estimator. If the estimated density in the denominator were replaced by the true density, then Σ in the asymptotic variance would be replaced by the variance of $w(x)Xu$. Because Σ is the variance of $w(x)Xu - E[w(x)Xu \mid x]$, it is smaller in the positive semidefinite sense than the variance of $w(x)Xu$. An analogous result is known to hold in other settings.

4. ASYMPTOTIC THEORY

This section presents regularity conditions for asymptotic normality and consistency of the asymptotic variance estimator. We first derive a useful intermediate result, on the asymptotic distribution of a sample average that is weighted by the inverse of a kernel density estimator. This result justifies the asymptotic variance calculation given in Section 3.

To obtain results it is useful to impose certain conditions on the kernel, the density, and the bandwidth.

Assumption 4.1. *$K(v)$ is Lipschitz, zero outside a bounded set, $\int K(v)\,dv = 1$, and there is a positive integer s such that for all r-tuples of nonnegative integers $(j_1, \ldots, j_r)$ with $\sum_{\ell=1}^{r} j_\ell < s$,*

$$\int \left(v_1^{j_1} v_2^{j_2} \cdots v_r^{j_r}\right) K(v)dv = 0.$$

The bounded support condition for the kernel is imposed here to keep the conditions relatively simple. The last condition requires that the kernel be a higher-order (bias-reducing) kernel of order s. It helps ensure that the bias of the kernel estimator is small relative to variance. We will give some conditions on s. These will require that $K(v)$ be a higher-order kernel (with $s \geq 2$). The next condition imposes smoothness on the density $h_0(x)$.

Assumption 4.2. *There is a nonnegative integer $d \geq s$ and a version of the density $h_0(x)$ of x that is continuously differentiable to order d with bounded derivatives on $\mathbf{R}^r$.*

This condition is used in conjunction with Assumption 4.1 to control the bias of the estimator. It rules out cases where the density of x and its derivatives are nonzero on the boundary of the support by requiring smoothness everywhere.

An important intermediate result concerns the effect of density estimation on the asymptotic variance. We will show that for any function $a(z)$ satisfying certain regularity conditions,

$$\frac{1}{\sqrt{n}} \sum_{i=1}^{n} \left[\hat{h}(x_i)^{-1} - h_0(x_i)^{-1}\right] a(z_i)$$
$$= -\frac{1}{\sqrt{n}} \sum_{i=1}^{n} \left\{ \frac{E[a(z)|x_i]}{h_0(x_i)} - E\left[\frac{a(z)}{h_0(x)}\right] \right\} + o_p(1). \tag{4.1}$$

The term following the equality is a "correction term" for the estimation of the density. Equation (3.3) is a special case with $a(z) = f(x, \theta_0)Xu$. The validity of this result depends on certain smoothness conditions being satisfied. With a twicing kernel some tradeoff between smoothness of $h_0(x)$ and smoothness of

$E[a(z)|x]$ is allowed, whereas with other kernels the density $h_0(x)$ must bear all the smoothness requirements. The next two assumptions correspond to these cases.

Assumption 4.3. *$E[a(z)|x]$ is bounded on X and continuous in x on a set of full Lebesgue measure. Also, $\lambda = \lambda(n)$ such that $\sqrt{n}\lambda^r / \ln(n) \to \infty$ and $\sqrt{n}\lambda^s \to 0$.*

This condition implies that $s > r$, so that the order of the kernel and the degree of differentiability of the density must be larger than the dimension of x. With a twicing kernel it is possible to weaken this smoothness requirement at the expense of imposing another smoothness condition.

Assumption 4.4. *$K(u) = 2k(u) - \int k(u - v)k(v)dv$ for $k(u)$ satisfying Assumption 4.1, $E[a(z)|x]$ is continuously differentiable of order $t \leq s$, and $\lambda = \lambda(n)$ such that $\sqrt{n}\lambda^r / \ln(n) \to \infty$ and $\sqrt{n}\lambda^{s+t} \to 0$.*

Here only the sum $s + t$ of the number of derivatives of $h_0(x)$ and $E[a(z)|x]$ that exist must be greater than the dimension. With either one of these assumptions, we obtain the expansion in Equation (4.1).

Lemma 4.1. *If Assumptions 4.1, 4.2, and either 4.3 or 4.4 are satisfied, $a(z) = 0$ except on a compact set $\mathcal{X}$, where $h_0(x)$ is bounded away from zero, and $E[\|a(z)\|^4] < \infty$, then equation (4.1) is satisfied.*

For $a(z) = f(x, \theta_0)Xu$, the conclusion of this result implies the limiting distribution result sketched in Section 3. Also, this result may be useful for other semiparametric estimators that depend on averages that are weighted by an inverse kernel density.

Some additional conditions are useful for showing asymptotic normality of the estimator from Section 2. The next condition imposes some requirements on the LCE density $f(x, \theta)$. Let $C(\theta)$ denote the closure of $\{f(x, \theta) \neq 0\}$ and θ_0 the probability limit of $\hat{\theta}$.

Assumption 4.5. *$C(\theta_0)$ is bounded, $h_0(x) > 0$ for $x \in C(\theta_0)$, $C(\theta)$ is a continuous correspondence for θ in a neighborhood Θ of θ_0, $f(x, \theta)$ is twice differentiable in θ with derivatives continuous in (x, θ), and $\sqrt{n}(\hat{\theta} - \theta_0) = O_p(1)$.*

This assumption, which restricts the density $h_0(x)$ to be bounded away from zero where $f(x, \theta_0)$ is positive (the set $C(\theta_0)$), is extremely useful. It negates the "denominator problem" that would be present if the density of x were allowed to approach zero. This is a type of fixed trimming that is theoretically more convenient than trimming that is relaxed as the sample size grows. Also, it may have the practical advantage of reducing outlier problems.

The final condition imposes conditions on y and X.

Assumption 4.6. *$E[y^4] < \infty$ and $Q = E[w(x)XX']$ is nonsingular.*

These conditions lead to the following asymptotic representation for $\hat{\gamma}$.

Theorem 4.1. *If Assumptions 4.1, 4.2, 4.5, 4.6, and either 4.3 or 4.4 are satisfied for $a(z) = f(x, \theta_0)Xu$, then*

$$\sqrt{n}(\hat{\gamma} - \gamma_0) = \frac{1}{\sqrt{n}} Q^{-1} \sum_{i=1}^{n} w(x_i)X_i\{y_i - E[y_i \mid x_i]\} + Q^{-1} E\left[\frac{Xu}{h_0(x)} \frac{\partial f(x, \theta_0)}{\partial \theta'}\right] \sqrt{n}(\hat{\theta} - \theta_0) + o_p(1).$$

The asymptotic distribution of $\hat{\beta}_2$ now follows in a straightforward way.

Theorem 4.2. *If Assumptions 4.1, 4.2, 4.5, 4.6, and either 4.3 or 4.4 are satisfied for $f(x, \theta_0)Xu$, $\delta_{10} \neq 0$, and $f(x, \theta)$ has the LCE for all θ in a neighborhood of θ_0, then*

$$\sqrt{n}(\hat{\beta}_2 - \beta_{20}) \xrightarrow{d} \mathcal{N}(0, J'Q^{-1}\Sigma Q^{-1}J).$$

The last result that remains to be proved is the consistency of the asymptotic variance estimator.

Theorem 4.3. *If Assumptions 4.1, 4.2, 4.5, 4.6, and either 4.3 or 4.4 with $a(z) = f(x, \theta_0)Xu$ are satisfied and $\delta_{10} \neq 0$, then*

$$\hat{J}'\hat{Q}^{-1}\hat{\Sigma}\hat{Q}^{-1}\hat{J} \xrightarrow{p} J'Q^{-1}\Sigma Q^{-1}J.$$

5. ASYMPTOTIC EFFICIENCY

The asymptotic efficiency of the estimator can be evaluated by comparing its asymptotic variance with the semiparametric variance bound for the index model of Equation (1.1). It follows from the analysis of Section 4 that the asymptotic variance of $\sqrt{n}(\hat{\beta}_2 - \beta_{20})$ is $V = J'Q^{-1}\Sigma Q^{-1}J$ for $J = \delta_{10}^{-1}[0, -\beta_{20}, I]$. It is straightforward to derive a more convenient expression, as in $V = E[\psi\psi']$, where $v = x'\beta_0$,

$$\psi = \delta_{10}^{-1}\{E_w[\mathrm{Var}_w(x_2 \mid v)]\}^{-1} w(x)\,[x_2 - E_w(x_2 \mid v)]\,[y - \tau(v)], \tag{5.1}$$

$$\delta_{10} = \mathrm{Cov}(\tau(v), v)/\mathrm{Var}(v). \tag{5.2}$$

and $E_w[\cdot] \equiv E[w(x)(\cdot)]$. Details of this derivation are given in Lemma A.2 in the Appendix. By way of comparison, the semiparametric variance bound for estimators of $\hat{\beta}_2$, as given by Newey and Stoker (1993), is $V^* = E[\psi^*\psi^{*\prime}]$, where

$$\psi^* = \{E_\sigma[\mathrm{Var}_\sigma(\tau_v x_2 \mid v)]\}^{-1}\,\sigma(x)^{-2}\tau_v(v)\,[x_2 - E_\sigma(x_2 \mid v)]\,[y - \tau(v)] \tag{5.3}$$

and $\sigma^2(x) = \text{Var}(y \mid x)$,

$$E_\sigma[\cdot] \equiv \frac{E\left[(\cdot)/\sigma^2(x)\right]}{E\left[1/\sigma^2(x)\right]},$$

and $\tau_v(v) = d\tau(v)/dv$ (assuming differentiability holds).

The formulas (5.1) and (5.3) are analogous but fundamentally different. First of all, the weight $w(x)$ in $E_w[\cdot]$ is replaced by $1/\sigma^2(x)$. The weighting by $1/\sigma^2(x)$ in the variance bound accounts for heteroskedasticity, while the weighting by $w(x)$ is necessary for consistency of the DWLS estimator. In addition, the efficiency bound contains the Jacobian term $\tau_v(x'\beta_0)$, which is not present in the DWLS case, effectively replacing x_2 with $\tau_v x_2$, while the DWLS estimator also depends on δ_{10}.

Some of the differences in the influence function can be accounted for by extending this analysis to nonlinear least squares. A nonlinear version of DWLS could be obtained as

$$\hat{\gamma} = \arg\min_{\gamma} \sum_{i=1}^{n} \hat{w}_i [y_i - t(X_i'\gamma)]^2,$$

for some known function $t(r)$. It will then follow, as in Ruud (1986), that $\hat{\gamma}$ converges in probability to $(\gamma_{10}, \delta_{10}(1, \beta_0'))'$, $(\gamma_{10}, \delta_{10}) = \arg\min_{\gamma,\delta} E[w(x)\{y - t(\gamma + \delta v)\}^2]$. If $t(\gamma_{10} + \delta_{10} v) = \tau(v)$, then ψ would be the same as ψ^* except that $w(x)$ replaces $\sigma(x)^{-2}$ in the influence function of DWLS.

Accounting for the differences between ψ and the efficient influence function due to the presence of $w(x)$ rather than $1/\sigma^2(x)$ is more problematic. For example, when $\sigma^2(x)$ is constant, then choosing $w(x) = 1$ would eliminate this difference between the influence functions, but this is not possible when $h_0(x)$ does not have the LCE. These comparisons do indicate that efficiency might be improved by choosing $f(x, \hat{\theta})$ so that $w(x)$ is close to $1/\sigma^2(x)$. In particular, if $\sigma^2(x)$ does not vary too much, it seems wise to choose $f(x, \hat{\theta})$ so that its location and scale match those of x_i, as can be done by including location and scale parameters in $\hat{\theta}$.

6. MONTE CARLO EXPERIMENTS

Ruud (1986) performed a simple Monte Carlo experiment to illustrate the use of density DWLS. We repeat that experiment here to consider the small sample properties of the estimators. The data were generated as follows. Two explanatory variables were drawn from a mixture of normal distributions:

$$h(x_1, x_2) = \phi(x_1 - 1/2)\phi(2x_2) + \phi(x_2 + 1/2)\phi(2x_1),$$

where ϕ is the standard normal pdf. In this way, positive x_1 tend to coincide with small x_2 and negative x_2 tend to coincide with small x_1. The dependent variable was generated by

$$y = \exp(x_1 + x_2 + u), \tag{6.1}$$

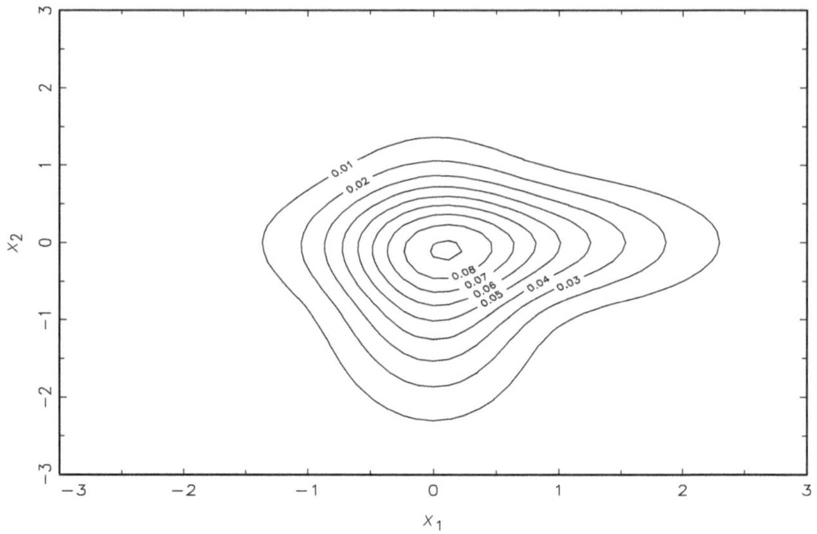

Figure 23.1. Contour plot of joint density of x_1 and x_2.

where u had a uniform distribution on $[-1/2, 1/2]$. Because the exponential function is convex, the OLS estimator for the linear regression of y on x_1, x_2, and a constant will overstate the relative effect of x_1 compared to the effect of x_2.

Level sets for the joint pdf for x_1 and x_2 are pictured in Figure 23.1. Despite the mixture of two normals, the joint density remains unimodal and does not appear to be strangely idiosyncratic. The conditional expectation of x_2 given $x_1 + x_2$ is pictured in Figure 23.2. This function has a slight convexity, but not a dramatic one. This convexity will cause the OLS estimator to be inconsistent for the ratio of the slope parameters. Figure 23.3 gives a plot of the pdf for $x'\beta = x_1 + x_2$ and the bounds on y conditional on $x'\beta$ from the data-generating process. There is substantial heteroskedasticity, with the variance increasing in the most informative region of the $x'\beta$ domain.

Table 23.1 holds the results of a Monte Carlo experiment for this data-generating process. The rows of this table contain the sample statistics of four different estimators: the ordinary least-squares fit (OLS) of y on a constant, x_1, and x_2; the weighted least-squares estimator (WLS) using infeasible weights containing the exact population density h; a feasible density weighted least-squares estimator (twicing) that uses a twicing kernel where $k(u)$ is the density of $N(0, 1)$ to estimate h; and a feasible density weighted least-squares estimator (kernel) that uses a standard kernel density estimator, with Gaussian kernel, for $\hat{h}$.

We used two pdf's for the elliptically symmetric pdf $f(x, \hat{\theta})$. In both cases, we centered and rescaled the x_i to have sample means equal to zero and a sample variance–covariance matrix equal to the identity matrix. Thus, $\hat{\theta}$ contains the sample mean vector $\bar{x}$ and variance–covariance matrix $\hat{\Sigma}$ of x. The first pdf was

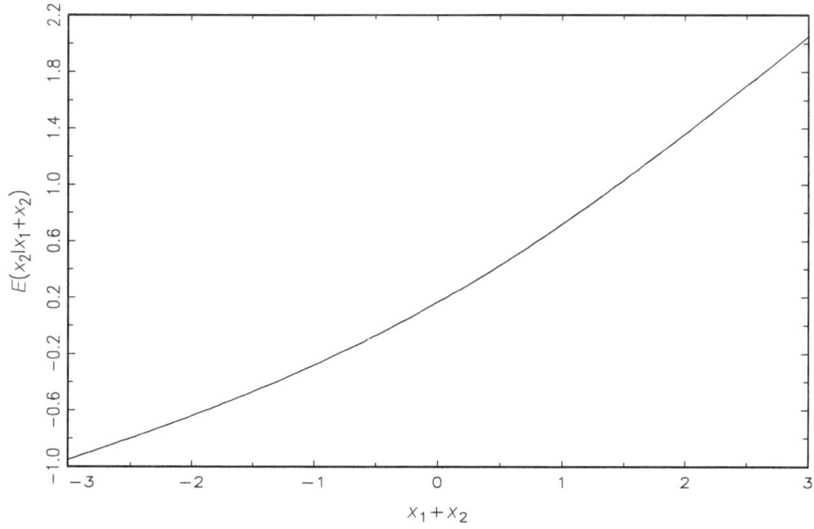

Figure 23.2. Conditional expectation of x_2 given $x_1 + x_2$.

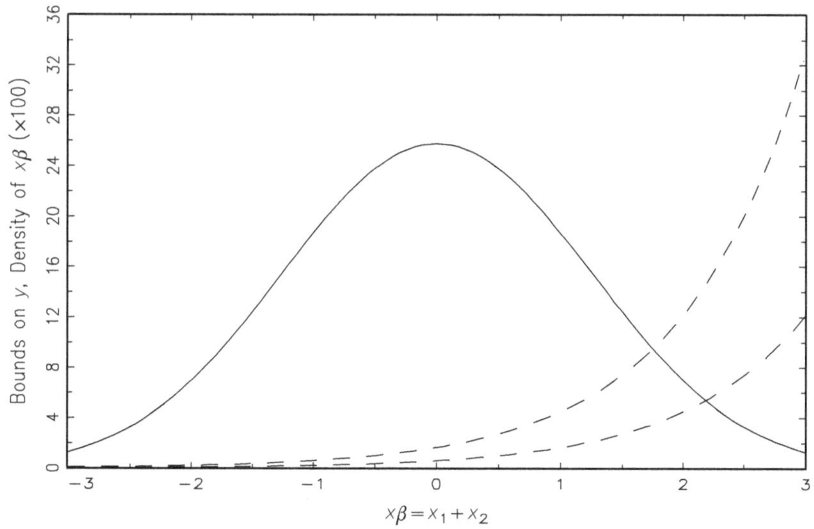

Figure 23.3. y versus $x'\beta = x_1 + x_2$.

a bivariate, standard normal, trimmed at a standard deviation from the mean of $\sqrt{6}$:

$$f(x, \hat{\theta}) = \frac{1}{2\pi} \exp\left(-\frac{(x - \bar{x})' \, \hat{\Sigma}^{-1} \, (x - \bar{x})}{2} \right) \cdot \mathbf{1}\{(x - \bar{x})' \, \hat{\Sigma}^{-1} \, (x - \bar{x}) \leq 6\}. \tag{6.2}$$

Table 23.1. *Monte Carlo experiment results (smooth case)*

Method	Mean	SD	10%	Median	90%
		Truncated Normal Density			
$n = 100, \lambda = 0.40$					
OLS	0.6113	0.1927	0.3953	0.5907	0.8409
WLS	0.9873	0.1597	0.7929	0.9744	1.1976
Twicing	0.8853	0.1190	0.7375	0.8809	1.0387
Kernel	0.8603	0.1170	0.7154	0.8564	1.0127
$n = 200, \lambda = 0.35$					
OLS	0.5874	0.1405	0.4251	0.5773	0.7585
WLS	0.9922	0.1140	0.8498	0.9872	1.1409
Twicing	0.9070	0.0845	0.8009	0.9045	1.0158
Kernel	0.8767	0.0815	0.7741	0.8751	0.9814
$n = 400, \lambda = 0.30$					
OLS	0.5767	0.1013	0.4552	0.5713	0.7001
WLS	0.9973	0.0818	0.8963	0.9922	1.1044
Twicing	0.9287	0.0610	0.8522	0.9267	1.0089
Kernel	0.8973	0.0585	0.8226	0.8960	0.9745
		Quartic Density			
$n = 100, \lambda = 0.40$					
OLS	0.6113	0.1927	0.3953	0.5907	0.8409
WLS	0.9940	0.1397	0.8219	0.9873	1.1741
Twicing	0.9123	0.1136	0.7712	0.9079	1.0579
Kernel	0.8861	0.1107	0.7483	0.8827	1.0288
$n = 200, \lambda = 0.35$					
OLS	0.5874	0.1405	0.4251	0.5773	0.7585
WLS	0.9963	0.0982	0.8713	0.9938	1.1236
Twicing	0.9334	0.0785	0.8348	0.9324	1.0351
Kernel	0.9011	0.0755	0.8060	0.9004	0.9979
$n = 400, \lambda = 0.30$					
OLS	0.5767	0.1013	0.4552	0.5713	0.7001
WLS	0.9991	0.0691	0.9136	0.9965	1.0902
Twicing	0.9532	0.0542	0.8850	0.9522	1.0233
Kernel	0.9193	0.0518	0.8534	0.9181	0.9858

The second pdf was proportional to a quartic function:

$$f(x, \hat{\theta}) \propto \left(1 - \frac{(x - \bar{x})' \, \hat{\Sigma}^{-1} \, (x - \bar{x})}{6}\right)^2 \cdot \mathbf{1}\{(x - \bar{x})' \, \hat{\Sigma}^{-1} \, (x - \bar{x}) \leq 6\}. \tag{6.3}$$

This pdf has the same support as the trimmed normal but approaches zero at the boundary of the support.

We report the results using various bandwidth parameters λ and sample sizes n. The bandwidth parameters were chosen as the approximate values that give the smallest bias in our estimators for each sample size. In these experiments, these bandwidth values are roughly the same for comparable estimators. For brevity we report only the outcomes for three bandwidth and sample size pairs. The columns of the table contain the sample mean, the sample standard deviation (SD), the first decile (10%), the median, and the last decile (90%) of the simulated estimators.

The extent of the inconsistency of OLS is shown in the first row of Table 23.1. For 100 observations, and 10,000 Monte Carlo replications, the average ratio of β_2/β_1 is 0.61. As expected, the relative importance of x_2 is diminished by its association with small values of $x'\beta$. The prediction of asymptotic approximation that a feasible DWLS estimator has smaller dispersion holds, but there is some bias in the feasible estimators. The kernel estimator exhibits more bias than the twicing estimator, showing that the anticipated bias-reduction holds in this example.

The first panel of results, corresponding to sample sizes of 100, 200, and 400, confirm that the bias in the feasible DWLS estimators falls as the sample size increases. The best bandwidth also falls as the sample grows. The second panel of results differs from the first in the numerator density employed. A comparison of the two panels shows that the quartic pdf (6.3) yields a smaller bias than the truncated normal pdf (6.2). This may be due to the smooth way in which the quartic pdf approaches zero on the boundary of its support.

The DWLS estimators apply to discontinuous τ functions, whereas most estimators do not. We ran a second experiment to investigate the success of DWLS with such functions. Using the same explanatory variables as in the first experiment, we changed (6.1) to

$$y = 1\{x_1 + x_2 > 1\} + u,$$

where u is normally distributed with a mean of zero and standard deviation of 0.2. In words, the data-generating process of y is a mixture of $\mathcal{N}(0, 0.04)$ and $\mathcal{N}(1, 0.04)$ distributions, with the mean determined discretely by $x_1 + x_2$. The Monte Carlo results from 10,000 replications of data sets appear in Table 23.2.

In this experiment, the OLS estimator (regressing y on a consant and the two xs) averaged 0.64 compared to the true ratio $\beta_2/\beta_1 = 1$, with a standard deviation of 0.20. The results for the DWLS estimators are qualitatively similar to the previous experiment: the infeasible DWLS estimator appears to be unbiased and its sampling variance is greater than its feasiable counterparts; the twicing estimator has less bias than the standard kernel estimator; the bias falls with sample size; and the quartic pdf yields a smaller bias than the truncated normal pdf. However, the bias in these estimators is larger than for the continuous case, and the sampling variances are larger.

Table 23.2. *Monte Carlo experiment results (discontinuous case)*

Method	Mean	SD	10%	Median	90%
		Truncated Normal Density			
$n = 100$, $\lambda = 0.40$					
OLS	0.6445	0.2022	0.4046	0.6277	0.9063
WLS	1.0268	0.4127	0.6288	0.9678	1.4698
Twicing	0.8719	0.2518	0.5820	0.8466	1.1873
Kernel	0.8273	0.2424	0.5472	0.8057	1.1254
$n = 200$, $\lambda = 0.35$					
OLS	0.6394	0.1353	0.4736	0.6325	0.8127
WLS	1.0120	0.2393	0.7330	0.9869	1.3188
Twicing	0.8984	0.1634	0.7018	0.8873	1.1090
Kernel	0.8470	0.1553	0.6588	0.8369	1.0465
$n = 400$, $\lambda = 0.30$					
OLS	0.6328	0.0941	0.5150	0.6301	0.7545
WLS	1.0030	0.1637	0.8068	0.9884	1.2145
Twicing	0.9230	0.1125	0.7846	0.9157	1.0698
Kernel	0.8705	0.1067	0.7390	0.8652	1.0090
		Quartic Density			
$n = 100$, $\lambda = 0.40$					
OLS	0.6490	0.1980	0.4143	0.6313	0.9027
WLS	1.0346	0.3755	0.6392	0.9812	1.4880
Twicing	0.8990	0.2750	0.5920	0.8706	1.2347
Kernel	0.8508	0.2633	0.5539	0.8230	1.1751
$n = 200$, $\lambda = 0.35$					
OLS	0.6380	0.1358	0.4716	0.6294	0.8155
WLS	1.0166	0.2390	0.7401	0.9906	1.3251
Twicing	0.9160	0.1737	0.7102	0.9023	1.1339
Kernel	0.8603	0.1659	0.6630	0.8481	1.0729
$n = 400$, $\lambda = 0.30$					
OLS	0.6344	0.0949	0.5157	0.6309	0.7571
WLS	1.0064	0.1626	0.8096	0.9939	1.2205
Twicing	0.9390	0.1171	0.7966	0.9319	1.0917
Kernel	0.8824	0.1121	0.7438	0.8762	1.0277

APPENDIX: PROOFS

We first give a result showing that the LCE holds for a spherically symmetric density.

Lemma A.1. *Let* $x \sim f[(x-\mu)'A^{-1}(x-\mu)]$ *be a random variable with an elliptically symmetric (about* μ*) pdf. If* $E[\|x\|]$ *exists, then* $E(x \mid \delta' x) = \alpha_0 + \alpha_1 \delta' x$.

Proof. Let $B = \delta(\delta' A\delta)^{-1}\delta'$ and $b = \delta' x$. According to the orthogonal decomposition,

$$A^{-1} = (I - BA)(A - ABA)^{-}(I - AB) + B,$$

where $(A - ABA)^{-}$ denotes a generalized inverse of $A - ABA$. We can write

$$(x-\mu)'A^{-1}(x-\mu) = (b - \delta'\mu)'(\delta' A\delta)^{-1}(b - \delta'\mu) \\ + (x-\gamma)'(A - ABA)^{-}(x-\gamma),$$

where

$$\gamma \equiv \mu + A\delta(\delta' A\delta)^{-1}(b - \delta'\mu).$$

Therefore the conditional distribution of x given $\delta' x = b$ is symmetric around the point $\mu + A\delta(\delta' A\delta)^{-1}(b - \delta'\mu)$. Under existence of $E[\|x\|]$, implying existence of the conditional expectation, the result follows with $\alpha_0 = \mu - AB\mu$ and $\alpha_1 = A\delta(\delta' A\delta)$. ■

Lemma A.2. *If Assumptions 4.1, 4.2, 4.5, 4.6, and either 4.3 or 4.4 are satisfied for* $a(z) = f(x, \theta_0)Xu$, *then the asymptotic variance of* $\hat{\beta}_2$ *is* $V = E[\psi\psi']$ *for* ψ *in Equation (5.1).*

Proof. Note that $X'\gamma = \gamma_1 + v\delta_1 + \delta_{10}x_2'\pi_2$, where $v = x'\beta_0$ and $\pi_2 = (\delta_2 - \beta_{20}\delta_1)/\delta_{10}$. Let $\hat{\pi}_2$ be the coefficient of $\delta_{10}x_2$ in the inverse density weighted least-squares regression of y on $(1, v, \delta_{10}x_2')$. By the usual least squares property, $\hat{\pi}_2 = (\hat{\delta}_2 - \beta_{20}\hat{\delta}_1)/\delta_{10}$. Noting that $\hat{\pi}_2$ is just a linearization of $\hat{\beta}_2$, the delta method implies that the asymptotic variance of $\hat{\beta}_2$ is the same as $\hat{v}_2$. Let $E_w[\cdot] = E[w(x)(\cdot)]$ denote the expectation when the pdf of x is $f(x, \theta_0)$. Then by elliptical symmetry of $f(x, \theta_0)$, the projection of $\delta_{10}x_2$ on $(1, v)$ equals $\delta_{10}E_w[x_2 \mid v]$. Then Equation (5.1) follows by the the usual partial least-squares formula. ■

Throughout the rest of the Appendix, C will denote a generic positive constant (not depending on N) that may be different in different uses, and $\sum_i = \sum_{i=1}^n$. The outline of the Appendix is that some useful lemmas will first be given, and then the results in the body of the paper proven.

Proof of Lemma 4.1. Under Assumption 4.3 the proof proceeds by verifying the conditions of Lemmas 5.2 and 5.4 of Newey (1994a). Let $\mathcal{X}$ denote a compact set where $h_0(x)$ is bounded away from zero and $a(z) = 0$ for x not in $\mathcal{X}$, and let $\|h\| = \sup_{x \notin \mathcal{X}} |h(x)|$. Also, let

$$m(z,h) = \frac{a(z)}{h(x)}, \quad D(z,h) = -\frac{a(z)h(x)}{h_0(x)^2}, \\ A(x) = E[a(z) \mid x], \quad m(h) = E[D(z,h)].$$

Note that $m(h) = \int \nu(x)h(x)\,dx$ for $\nu(x) = -E[a(z)\,|\,x]/h_0(x)$. Note that $\nu(x)$ is continuous almost everywhere (with respect to Lebesgue measure), zero outside the compact set $\mathcal{X}$, and bounded. Therefore, by Assumptions 4.1 and 4.2, the conditions of Lemma 5.2 of Newey (1994a) are satisfied, so that by its conclusion,

$$\sqrt{n}[m(\hat{h}) - m(h_0)] = \frac{1}{\sqrt{n}}\sum_i \{\nu(x_i) - E[\nu(x_i)]\} + o_p(1). \tag{A.1}$$

To show that this equation also holds under Assumption 4.4, we note that by the Fubini theorem, for $\upsilon_\lambda(x) = \int \upsilon(x+\lambda u)\,k(u)\,du$ and $h_\lambda(x) = \int h(x - \lambda u)\,k(u)\,du$,

$$\begin{aligned}
&E[m(\hat{h})] - m(h_0)\\
&= \int \upsilon(x) \int K_\lambda(x-w)\,h_0(w)\,dw\,dx - \int \upsilon(x)\,h_0(x)\,dx\\
&= \int \upsilon(x) \int K(u)\,h_0(x-\lambda u)\,du\,dx - \int \upsilon(x)\,h_0(x)\,dx\\
&= 2\int\int \upsilon(x)\,h_0(x-\lambda u)\,k(u)\,du\,dx\\
&\quad - \int\int\int \upsilon(x)\,h_0(x-\lambda u)\,k(v)\,k(u-v)\,du\,dx - \int \upsilon(x)\,h_0(x)\,dx\\
&= -\int [\upsilon_\lambda(x) - \upsilon(x)][h_\lambda(x) - h(x)]\,dx.
\end{aligned}$$

By standard arguments, there is a compact set $\tilde{\mathcal{X}}$ such that $\upsilon_\lambda(x) - \upsilon(x)$ and $h_\lambda(x) - h(x)$ are zero outside $\tilde{\mathcal{X}}$, and for all $x \in \tilde{\mathcal{X}}$, $|\upsilon_\lambda(x) - \upsilon(x)| \le C\lambda^t$ and $|h_\lambda(x) - h(x)| \le C\lambda^s$. It then follows that $|E[m(\hat{h})] - m(h_0)| \le C\lambda^{s+t}$. The rest of Equation (A.1) then follows precisely as in the proof of Lemma 5.2 of Newey (1994a).

To check the hypotheses of Lemma 5.4 of Newey (1994a), let $\Delta = \Delta_1 = \Delta_2 = 0$, so that the norm $\|h\|_\Delta$ of that result is $\|h\| = \sup_{x\in\mathcal{X}} |h(x)|$. Note that $D(z, h)$ is linear in h on the set where $\|h\| < \infty$; for $b(z) = \|a(z)\|$ and $\|h - h_0\| \le \epsilon$ for ϵ small enough,

$$\begin{aligned}
&\|m(z,h) - m(z,h_0) - D(z, h-h_0)\|\\
&\le \|a(z)\| \left|\frac{1}{h(x)} - \frac{1}{h_0(x)} + \frac{h(x)}{h_0(x)^2} - \frac{1}{h_0(x)}\right|\\
&= b(z)\left|\frac{1}{h_0(x)^2 h(x)}\right| \left|h_0(x)^2 - 2h(x)h_0(x) + h(x)^2\right|\\
&\le Cb(z)\ |h_0(x) - h(x)|^2\\
&\le Cb(z)\,\|h_0 - h\|^2;
\end{aligned}$$

$\|D(z,h)\| \le C\,\|a(z)\|\,\|h\|$ and $E[\|a(z)\|^4] < \infty$; for $\eta_n = [\ln(n)/(n\lambda^r)]^{1/2} + \lambda^s$, $\sqrt{n}\eta_n^2 \le C[\ln(n)/\sqrt{n}\,\lambda^r] + \sqrt{n}\lambda^{2s} \to 0$, and $\sqrt{n}\lambda^r \to 0$ by $r > s$. Then by the conclusion of Lemma 5.4 of Newey (1994a),

$$\frac{1}{\sqrt{n}}\sum_i [m(z_i,\hat{h}) - m(z_i,h_0)] = \sqrt{n}[m(\hat{h}) - m(h_0)] + o_p(1).$$

The conclusion then follows by the triangle inequality. ■

The following Lemma is useful for proving Theorem 4.1.

Lemma A.3. *If $h_0(x)$ is continuous and Assumption 4.5 is satisfied, then there is $\epsilon > 0$ and a compact set $\mathcal{X}$ such that $h_0(x) > 0$ for all $x \notin \mathcal{X}$ and $f(x,\theta) = 0$, $\partial f(x,\theta)/\partial\theta = 0$, and $\partial^2 f(x,\theta)/\partial\theta\partial\theta' = 0$ for all $x \notin \mathcal{X}$ and $\|\theta - \theta_0\| < \epsilon$.*

Proof. By continuity of $C(\theta)$ and $h_0(x)$, there is ϵ small enough that $h_0(x) > 0$ for all $x \notin \mathcal{X}$, where $\mathcal{X}$ is the closure of $\cup_{\|\theta-\theta_0\|<\epsilon} C(\theta)$. By continuity of $C(\theta)$, the set $\mathcal{X}$ is compact. Also, for any $x \notin \mathcal{X}$, $f(x,\theta) = 0$ for *all* θ with $\|\theta - \theta_0\| < \epsilon$, so differentiating this identity at any such θ implies $\partial f(x,\theta)/\partial\theta = 0$ and $\partial^2 f(x,\theta)/\partial\theta\partial\theta' = 0$. ■

Proof of Theorem 4.1. For the compact set $\mathcal{X}$ of Lemma A.3.

$$\sup_{x\in\mathcal{X}} \left|\hat{h}(x) - h_0(x)\right| \xrightarrow{p} 0$$

by Lemma B.3 of Newey (1994a). Then by $h_0(x)$ bounded away from zero on $\mathcal{X}$, $\hat{h}(x)$ is bounded away from zero on $\mathcal{X}$ with probability approaching 1. Also, for the ϵ of Lemma A.3, $\left\|\hat{\theta} - \theta_0\right\| < \epsilon$ with probability approaching 1, so that for all $x \notin \mathcal{X}$, $f(x,\bar{\theta}) = 0$, $\partial f(x,\bar{\theta})/\partial\theta = 0$, and $\partial^2 f(x,\bar{\theta})/\partial\theta\partial\theta'$, for any $\bar{\theta}$ on the line joining $\hat{\theta}$ and θ_0 (e.g., for $\bar{\theta} = \hat{\theta}$). It then follows that with probability approaching 1, by X bounded on $\mathcal{X}$ and $f(x,\theta)$ Lipschitz in θ,

$$\begin{aligned}\max_i |\hat{w}_i - w_i| &\le C \sup_{x\in\mathcal{X}}\left[\left|f(x,\hat{\theta})\right|\left|\frac{1}{\hat{h}(x)} - \frac{1}{h_0(x)}\right|\right. \\ &\qquad \left. + \frac{1}{h_0(x)}\left|f(x,\hat{\theta}) - f(x,\theta)\right|\right] \xrightarrow{p} 0.\end{aligned}$$

Then $\|\hat{Q} - \sum_i w_i X_i X_i'/n\| \le C\sum_i |\hat{w}_i - w_i|/n \xrightarrow{p} 0$. Also, by the law of large numbers, $\sum_i w_i X_i X_i'/n \xrightarrow{p} Q$, and so by the triangle inequality, $\hat{Q} \xrightarrow{p} Q$.

Next, by a mean value expansion, for $\tilde{w}_i = f(x_i,\theta_0)/\hat{h}(x_i)$,

$$\begin{aligned}&\frac{1}{\sqrt{n}}\sum_i \hat{w}_i X_i u_i \\ &= \frac{1}{\sqrt{n}}\sum_i \tilde{w}_i X_i u_i + \left[\frac{1}{n}\sum_i \frac{X_i u_i}{\hat{h}(x_i)}\frac{\partial f(x_i,\bar{\theta})}{\partial\theta'}\right]\sqrt{n}(\hat{\theta} - \theta_0).\end{aligned}$$

It follows similarly to the argument for $\hat{Q} \xrightarrow{p} Q$ that the matrix in the square brackets converges in probability to $E[X\,u/h_0(x)\,\partial f(x,\theta_0)/\partial\theta']$. It also follows by Lemma 4.1 that

$$\frac{1}{\sqrt{n}}\sum_i \tilde{w}_i X_i u_i = \frac{1}{\sqrt{n}}\sum_i w_i X_i u_i - \frac{1}{\sqrt{n}}\sum_i w_i X_i\{E[y_i \mid x_i] - X_i'\gamma_0\} + o_p(1).$$

The conclusion then follows by the triangle inequality. ■

Proof of Theorem 4.2. By Theorem 4.1, the delta method, and the central limit theorem, it sufficies to show that $J'Q^{-1}E[X\,u/h_0(x)\,\partial f(x,\theta_0)/\partial\theta'] = 0$. Let $Q(\theta) = \int XX'f(x,\theta)\,dx$ and $m(\theta) = \int X \cdot E[y\,|\,x]f(x,\theta)\,dx$. By boundedness of X, $E[y\,|\,x]$, and $f(x,\theta)$ on the set $\mathcal{X}$ of the proof of Theorem 4.1, both $Q(\theta)$ and $m(\theta)$ are differentiable, and $\partial m(\theta_0)/\partial\theta = E[Xu/h_0(x)\,\partial f(x,\theta_0)/\partial\theta']$. It follows by $Q(\theta_0) = Q$ nonsingular that $Q(\theta)$ is nonsingular for θ in a neighborhood of θ_0. On this neighborhood of $Q(\theta)$, let $\gamma(\theta) = (\gamma_1(\theta), \delta(\theta)')' = Q(\theta)^{-1}m(\theta)$. Note that $\delta(\theta)$ is a continuous function of θ and $\delta(\theta_0) = \delta_0$. Then by $\delta_{10} \neq 0$, there is an even smaller neighborhood where $\delta_1(\theta) \neq 0$. Let $\beta_2(\theta) = \delta_2(\theta)/\delta_1(\theta)$. By spherical symmetry of $f(x,\theta)$, it follows, as in Ruud (1986), that $\beta_2(\theta) = \beta_{20}$. Differentiating this identity gives $0 = J'\partial\gamma(\theta_0)/\partial\theta$. Furthermore, differentiating the identity $\int X\{E[y\,|\,x] - X'\gamma(\theta)\}f(x,\theta)\,dx = 0$ with respect to θ gives $\partial\gamma(\theta_0)/\partial\theta = Q^{-1}E[X\,u/h_0(x)\,\partial f(x,\theta_0)/\partial\theta']$. ■

Proof of Theorem 4.3. $\hat{J} \xrightarrow{p} J$ follows by $\hat{\gamma} \xrightarrow{p} \gamma_0$ and $\delta_{10} \neq 0$. Also $\hat{Q} \xrightarrow{p} Q$ follows as in the proof of Theorem 4.1. Therefore, by continuity of matrix inversion and multiplication, it only remains to show that $\hat{\Sigma} \xrightarrow{p} \Sigma$. Let $\hat{d}(x) = \sum_{i=1}^{n} K_\lambda(x - x_i)y_i$ and $d(x) = h_0(x)E[y\,|\,x]$. By a change of variables, $E[\hat{d}(x)] = \int K(u)\,d(x + u\lambda)\,du = \bar{d}(x)$, which is bounded on any bounded set by $K(u)$ having bounded support and $d(x)$ bounded on any bounded set. Furthermore, at each x where $d(x)$ is continuous, $d(x + u\lambda) \to d(x)$ as $\lambda \to 0$, and so by the dominated convergence theorem, $\bar{d}(x) \to d(x)$ at each such x. Since the set of such x values has full Lebesgue measure, the dominated convergence theorem implies that $\int_{\mathcal{X}}[\bar{d}(x) - d(x)]^2 h_0(x)\,dx \to 0$. By Lemma B.1 of Newey (1994a), $\sup_{x\in\mathcal{X}}|\hat{d}(x) - \bar{d}(x)| \xrightarrow{p} 0$. Let $1_i = 1(x_i \in \mathcal{X})$. Then $\sum_i 1_i \left|\bar{d}(x_i) - d(x_i)\right|^2/n \xrightarrow{p} 0$ by the Markov inequality. Also, by $\hat{h}(x)$ bounded away from zero uniformly on $\mathcal{X}$, with probability approaching 1,

$$\frac{1}{n}\sum_i 1_i\,|\hat{g}(x_i) - g(x_i)|^2 \le \frac{C}{n}\sum_i 1_i \left|\hat{d}(x_i) - \bar{d}(x_i)\right|^2 + \frac{1}{n}\sum_i 1_i \left|\bar{d}(x_i) - d(x_i)\right|^2$$

$$+\frac{1}{n}\sum_i 1_i\,|d(x_i)|^2\left|\frac{1}{\hat{h}(x_i)}-\frac{1}{h_0(x_i)}\right|^2$$
$$\leq C\sup_{x\in\mathcal{X}}\left|\hat{d}(x)-\bar{d}(x)\right|+o_p(1)$$
$$+\sup_{x\in\mathcal{X}}\left|\hat{h}(x)-h_0(x)\right|\xrightarrow{p}0.$$

Let $\tilde{\Sigma}=\sum_i \hat{w}_i^2 X_i X_i'[y_i-g(x_i)]/n$. Then arguing as in the proof of Theorem 4.1, using Lemma A.3, it follows by the Cauchy–Schwartz inequality that for $1_i = 1(x_i \in \mathcal{X})$,

$$\begin{aligned}\|\hat{\Sigma}-\tilde{\Sigma}\| &\leq \frac{C}{n}\sum_i 1_i\left[2\,|y_i|\,|\hat{g}(x_i)-g(x_i)|+\left|\hat{g}(x_i)^2-g(x_i)^2\right|\right]\\ &\leq \frac{C}{n}\sum_i 1_i\{[\hat{g}(x_i)-g(x_i)]^2+(|y_i|+|g(x_i)|)|\hat{g}(x_i)-g(x_i)|\}\\ &= o_p(1)+\ O_p(1)\left[\frac{1}{n}\sum_i 1_i\,|\hat{g}(x_i)-g(x_i)|^2\right]^{1/2}\xrightarrow{p}0.\end{aligned}$$

It also follows similarly to the proof that $\hat{Q}\xrightarrow{p}Q$ that $\tilde{\Sigma}\xrightarrow{p}\Sigma$. The conclusion that $\hat{\Sigma}\xrightarrow{p}\Sigma$ then follows by the triangle inequality. ■

References

Ichimura, H. (1993), "Semiparametric Least Squares (SLS) and Weighted SLS Estimation of Single-Index Models," *Journal of Econometrics*, 58(1–2), 71–120.

Newey, W. K. (1994a), "Kernel Estimation of Partial Means and a General Variance Estimator," *Econometric Theory,* 10, 233–53.

Newey, W. K. (1994b), "The Asymptotic Variance of Semiparametric Estimators," *Econometrica,* 62(6), 1349–82.

Newey, W. K., F. Hsieh, and J. Robins (July 2000), "Undersmoothing and Bias Corrected Functional Estimation," Working Paper, MIT.

Newey, W. K., and D. McFadden (1994), "Large Sample Estimation and Hypothesis Testing," in *Handbook of Econometrics*, Vol. 4 (ed. by R. Engle and D. McFadden), Amsterdam: North-Holland, 2111–245.

Newey, W. K., and T. M. Stoker (1993), "Efficiency of Weighted Average Derivative Estimators and Index Models," *Econometrica,* 61, 1199–223.

Powell, J. L., J. H. Stock, and T. M. Stoker (1989), "Semiparametric Estimation of Index Model Coefficients," *Econometrica*, 57, 1403–30.

Ruud, P. A. (1986), "Consistent Estimation of Limited Dependent Variable Models Despite Misspecification of Distribution," *Journal of Econometrics*, 32, 157–87.

Stoker, T. M. (1986), "Consistent Estimation of Scaled Coefficients," *Econometrica,* 54, 1461–81.

For EU product safety concerns, contact us at Calle de José Abascal, 56–1°,
28003 Madrid, Spain or eugpsr@cambridge.org.

www.ingramcontent.com/pod-product-compliance
Ingram Content Group UK Ltd.
Pitfield, Milton Keynes, MK11 3LW, UK
UKHW042316180425
457623UK00005B/13

* 9 7 8 0 5 2 1 8 4 4 4 1 3 *